www.wileyplus.com

ALL THE HELP, RESOURCES, AND PERSONAL SUPPORT YOU AND YOUR STUDENTS NEED!

www.wileyplus.com/resources

2-Minute Tutorials and all of the resources you & your students need to get started.

Student support from an experienced student user.

Collaborate with your colleagues, find a mentor, attend virtual and live events, and view resources.
www.WhereFacultyConnect.com

Pre-loaded, ready-to-use assignments and presentations. Created by subject matter experts.

Technical Support 24/7 FAQs, online chat, and phone support.
www.wileyplus.com/support

Your *WileyPLUS* Account Manager. Personal training and implementation support.

WILEY

John Wiley & Sons, Inc.

Louis E. Boone
University of South Alabama

David L. Kurtz
University of Arkansas

Contemporary
BUSINESS

INTERNATIONAL STUDENT VERSION
14TH EDITION

"The 14th edition of Contemporary Business is dedicated to Joseph S. Heider, who brought me to
John Wiley & Sons. Thank you, Joe."
—Dave

WileyPLUS for Students

WileyPLUS builds students' confidence because it takes the guesswork out of studying by providing a clear roadmap to academic success. *WileyPLUS* provides an online environment that integrates relevant resources, including the entire digital textbook, in an easy-to-navigate framework that helps you study more effectively.

With *WileyPLUS*, you receive 24/7 access to resources that promote positive learning outcomes.

Throughout each study session, you can assess your progress and gain immediate feedback on your strengths and weaknesses so you can be confident you are spending your time wisely.

Powered by proven technology and built on a foundation of cognitive research, *WileyPLUS* has enriched the education of millions of students, in over 20 countries around the world.

WileyPLUS is filled with student resources including:

Business Weekly Updates

Stay up to date on the very latest in business news stories. Each week you will find links to 5 new articles, video clips, business news stories, and so much more.

Audio Chapter Review Summaries

Available in English and Spanish, these reviews provide a quick overview of the main chapter concepts, so you can review them in the car, on foot, at the gym – anywhere!

iPhone Apps

You can now review chapter concepts and key terms on the go with our iPhone flashcard and self-study quiz apps.

Student Study Guide

Review key business concepts and test your knowledge so you're ready for the next quiz or exam.

The Wiley Business Video Series

Brand new end-of-chapter video cases include companies like Zipcar, Seventh Generation, New Harvest Coffee Roasters, and Comet Skateboards.

Acknowledgements

Contemporary Business has long benefited from the instructors who have offered their time as reviewers. Comprehensive reviews of the 14th edition and ancillary materials were provided by the following colleagues:

Nathaniel R. Calloway
University of Maryland University College

Gary Cohen
University of Maryland

Kellie Emrich
Cuyahoga Community College

Gil Feiertag
Columbus State Community College

Janice Feldbauer
Schoolcraft College

Chuck Foley
Columbus State Community College

Karen Halpern
South Puget Sound Community College

Tim Hatten
Mesa State College

Linda Hefferin
Elgin Community College

John Hilston
Brevard Community College

Martin Karamian
Pierce College

Cynthia Miree-Coppin
Oakland Unversity

David Oliver
Edison State College

Sally Proffitt
Tarrant County College

Jayre Reaves
Rutgers University

David Robinson
University of California, Berkeley

Patricia Setlik
Harper College

John Striebich
Monroe Community College

Rodney Thirion
Pikes Peak Community College

Sal Veas
Santa Monica College

Collette Wolfson
Ivy Tech Community College

Lisa Zingaro
Oakton Community College

Thanks also to all of our colleagues who have assisted us in previous editions in our continuing efforts to make the best business text even better. The new edition continues to reflect so many of their recommendations. Among the hundreds of reviewers and focus group participants who contributed to the book during previous editions, we acknowledge the special contributions of the following people:

Brenda Anthony
Tallahassee Community College

Lorraine P. Bassette
Prince George's Community College

Barbara Ching
Los Angeles City College

Rachna Condos
American River College

Susan J. Cremins
Westchester Community College

Tamara Davis
Davenport University

Colleen Dunn
Bucks County Community College

Joyce Ezrow
Anne Arundel Community College

Kathleen K. Ghahramani
Johnson County Community College

Connie Golden
Lakeland Community College

Susan Greer
Horry-Georgetown Technical College

James V. Isherwood
Community College of Rhode Island

Mary Beth Klinger
College of Southern Maryland

Claudia Levi
Edmonds Community College

Kathy Lorencz
Oakland Community College

Levi Richard
Citrus College

Jenny C. Rink
Community College of Philadelphia

Susan Roach
Georgia Southern University

Sandra Robertson
Thomas Nelson Community College

Barbara Rosenthal
Miami Dade College, Kendall Campus

JoDee Salisbury
Baker College

Rieann Spence-Gale
Northern Virginia Community College

Bob Urell
Irvine Valley College

Ed Becker
Housatonic Community College

Cathleen Behan
North Virginia Community College

Vicki Bjerke
Northeast Iowa Community College

Robert Brinkmeyer
University of Cincinnati

Ronald Cereola
James Madison University

Leo Chiantelli
Shasta College

John Cicero
Shasta College

Robert M. Clark
Horry-Georgetown Technical College

Douglas Crowe
Bradley University

Charles R. Fenner
State University of New York- Canton

Susan Greer
Horry-Georgetown Technical College

William Harvey
Henry Ford Community College

David Hollomon
Victor Valley College

Clark Lambert
Farmingdale State College

James R. Lashley
Bowie State University

Victor Lipe
Trident Technical College

Michael Mandel
Housatonic Community College

Gina McConoughey
Illinois Central College

Dennis R. Murphy
Horry-Georgetown Technical College

John Muzzo
Harold Washington University

Jack Partlow
Northern Virginia Community College

W.J. Patterson
Sullivan University

Michael Quinn
James Madison University

Rama Ramaswamy
Minneapolis Community and
Technical College

JoAnn Rawley
Reading Area Community College

Donna Scarlett
Iowa Western Community
College—Clarinda

Charles Smith
Horry-Georgetown Technical College

Michael Thomas
Henry Ford Community College

LaVena Wilkin
Sullivan University

Jamil Ahmad
Los Angeles Trade—Technical College

Sylvia Allen
Los Angeles Valley College

Kenneth F. Anderson
Borough of Manhattan Community
College

Andrea Bailey
Moraine Valley Community College

Norman E. Burns
Bergen Community College

Diana Carmel
Golden West College

Barbara Ching
Los Angeles City College

Ron Colley
South Suburban College

Scott Colvin
Naugatuck Community College

Peter Dawson
Collin County Community College

Dr. Richard L. Drury
Northern Virginia Community
College

John A. Fawcett
Norwalk Community College

Dr. Barry Freeman
Bergen Community College

Richard Ghidella
Fullerton College

Ross Gittell
University of New Hampshire

Clark Hallpike
Elgin Community College

Carnella Hardin
Glendale College—Arizona

Britt Hastey
Los Angeles City College

Dave Hickman
Frederick Community College

Nathan Himelstein
Essex County College

Scott Homan
Purdue—West Lafayette

Howard L. Irby, Jr.
Bronx Community College

Robert Ironside
North Lake College

Charlotte Jacobsen
Montgomery College

Bruce Johnson
College of the Desert

Judith Jones
Norwalk Community College

Marce Kelly
Santa Monica College

Gregory Kishel
Cypress College—Santa Ana College

Patricia Kishel
Cypress College

Andy Klein
DeVry University

Mary Beth Klinger
College of Southern Maryland

John S. Leahy
Palomar College

Delores Linton
Tarrant County College-Northwest
Campus

Stacy Martin
Southwestern Illinois College

Theresa Mastrianni
Kingsborough Community College

Bob Matthews
Oakton Community College

Hugh McCabe
Westchester Community College

Tricia McConville
Northeastern University

Rebecca Miles
Delaware Tech

Linda Morable
Richland College

Linda Mosley
Tarrant County College

Carol Murphy
Quinsigamond Community College

Andrew Nelson
Montgomery College

Greg Nesty
Humboldt College

Linda Newell
Saddleback College

Emmanuel Nkwenti
Pennsylvania College of Technology

Paul Okello
Tarrant County College

Lynn D. Pape
Northern Virginia Community
College—Alexandria Campus

Charles Pedersen
Quinsigamond Community College

John Pharr
Cedar Valley—Dallas County
Community College District

Jeff Podoshen
DeVry University

Jude A. Rathburn
University of Wisconsin—Milwaukee

Levi Richard
Citrus College

Joe Ryan
Valley College

Althea Seaborn
Norwalk Community College

John Seilo
Orange Coast Community College

Richard Sherer
Los Angeles Trade—Technical College

Gerald Silver
Purdue University—Calumet

Leon Singleton
Santa Monica College

Malcolm Skeeter
Norwalk Community College

Robert Smolin
Citrus College

Darrell Thompson
Mountain View College

Sandra Toy
Orange Coast College

Phil Vardiman
Abilene Christian University

Gina Vega
Merrimack College

Michelle Vybiral
Joliet Junior College

Rick Weidmann
Prince George's Community College

S. Martin Welc
Saddleback College

Steve Wong
Rock Valley College

Greg Akins
Lansing Community College

Ken Anderson
Borough of Manhattan Community College

Nancy Bailey
Middlesex Community College

Mary Barnum
Grand Rapids Community College

Sherry Bell
Ferris State University

Ellen Benowitz
Mercer Community College

Mike Bento
Owens Community College

Pat Bernson
County College of Morris

Trudy Borst
Ferris State University

David Braun
Pierce College

David England
John A. Logan College

Barry Freeman
Bergen Community College

Eric Glohr
Lansing Community College

Karen Hawkins
Miami Dade Community College

Nate Himelstein
Essex Community College

Kim Hurns
Washtenaw Community College

Dmitriy Kalyagin
Chabot College

Elias Konwufine
Keiser College

Carl Kovelowski
Mercer Community College

Pierre Laguerre
Bergen Community College

Stacy Martin
Southwestern Illinois College

Duane Miller
Utah Valley State College

Ed Mitchell
Hillsborough Community College

Frank Novakowski
Davenport University

Tom Passero
Owens Community College

Tom Perkins
Lansing Community College

Robert Reck
Western Michigan University

Paul Ricker
Broward Community College

Jenny Rink
Community College of Philadelphia

Susan Roach
Georgia Southern University

Edith Strickland
Tallahassee Community College

Keith Taylor
Lansing Community College

Joyce Thompson
Lehigh-Carbon Community College

Bob Urell
Irvine Valley College

Richard Warner
Lehigh-Carbon Community College

David Woolgar
Santa Ana College

Chuck Zellerbach
Orange Coast College

Alison Adderly-Pitman
Brevard Community College

David Alexander
Angelo State University

Kenneth Anderson
Mott Community College

Charles Armstrong
Kansas City Kansas Community College

Donald B. Armstrong
Mesa College

Nathaniel Barber
Winthrop University

Alan Bardwick
Community College of Aurora

Keith Batman
Cayuga Community College

Robb Bay
Community College of Southern Nevada

Charles Beem
Bucks County Community College

Carol Bibly
Triton College

Daniel Biddlecom
Erie Community College—North Campus

Joseph Billingere
Oxnard College

Larry Blenke
Sacramento City College

Paula E. Bobrowski
SUNY Oswego

Charlane Bomrad Held
Onandaga Community College

Brenda Bradford
Missouri Baptist College

Steven E. Bradley
Austin Community College

Willie Caldwell
Houston Community College

Barney Carlson
Yuba College

X   Acknowledgements

Bonnie Chavez
Santa Barbara City College

Felipe Chia
Harrisburg Area Community College

Rowland Chidomere
Winston-Salem State University

Marie Comstock
Allan Hancock College

Ronald C. Cooley
South Suburban College

Suzanne Counte
Jefferson College

Robert Cox
Salt Lake Community College

Pam Crader
Jefferson College

Norman B. Cregger
Central Michigan University

Dana D'Angelo
Drexel University

Dean Danielson
San Joaquin College

Kathy Daruty
Los Angeles Pierce College

David DeCook
Arapahoe Community College

Richard L. Drury
Northern Virginia Area Community College—Annandale

Linda Durkin
Delaware County Community College

Lance J. Edwards
Otero Junior College

William Ewald
Concordia University

Carol Fasso
Jamestown Community College

Jodson Faurer
Metropolitan State College at Denver

Jan Feldbauer
Austin Community College

Sandie Ferriter
Harford Community College

Steven H. Floyd
Manatee Community College

Nancy M. Fortunato
Bryant and Stratton

John G. Foster Jr.
Montgomery College—Rockville

William D. Foster
Fontbonne College

Blane Franckowiak
Tarrant County Community College

Edward Friese
Okaloosa-Walton Community College

Atlen Gastineau
Valencia Community College—West Campus

Milton Glisson
North Carolina A&T State University

Bob Googins
Shasta Community College

Robert Gora
Catawba Valley Community College

Don Gordon
Illinois Central College

Gary Greene
Manatee Community College

Blaine Greenfield
Bucks County Community College

Stephen W. Griffin
Tarrant County Community College

Maria Carmen Guerrero-Caldero
Oxnard College

Annette L. Halpin
Beaver College

Michael Hamberger
Northern Virginia Area Community College—Annandale

Neal Hannon
Bryant College

Douglas Heeter
Ferris State University

Paul Hegele
Elgin Community College

Chuck Henry
Coastline Community College

Thomas Herbek
Monroe Community College

Tom Heslin
Indiana University, Bloomington

Joseph Ho
College of Alameda

Alice J. Holt
Benedict College

Vince Howe
University of North Carolina, Wilmington

Eva M. Hyatt
Appalachian State University

Kathy Irwin
Catawba Valley Community College

Gloria M. Jackson
San Antonio College

Ralph Jagodka
Mount San Antonio College

Chris Jelepis
Drexel University

Steven R. Jennings
Highland Community College

Geraldine Jolly
Barton College

Dave Jones
LaSalle University

Don Kelley
Francis Marion University

Bill Kindsfather
Tarrant County Community College

Charles C. Kitzmiller
Indian River Community College

B. J. Kohlin
Pasadena City College

Carl Kovelowski
Mercer Community College

Ken Lafave
Mount San Jacinto College

Rex Lambrecht
Northeastern Junior College

Fay D. Lamphear
San Antonio College

Bruce Leppine
Delta College

Thomas Lloyd
Westmoreland County Community College

Jim Locke
Northern Virginia Area Community College—Annandale

Paul Londrigan
Mott Community College

Kathleen J. Lorencz
Oakland County Community College

John Mack
Salem State College

Paul Martin
Aims College

Lori Martynowicz
Bryant and Stratton

Michael Matukonis
SUNY Oneonta

Virginia Mayes
Montgomery College—Germantown

Joseph E. McAloon
Fitchburg State College

James McKee
Champlain College

Michael McLane
University of Texas, San Antonio

Ina Midkiff
Austin Community College

Rebecca Mihelcic
Howard Community College

Richard Miller
Harford Community College

Joseph Mislivec
Central Michigan University

Kimberly K. Montney
Kellogg Community College

Gail Moran
Harper College

Linda S. Munilla
Georgia Southern University

Kenneth R. Nail
Pasco-Hernando Community College

Joe Newton
Buffalo State College

Janet Nichols
Northeastern University

Frank Nickels
Pasco-Hernando Community College

Sharon Nickels
St. Petersburg Junior College

Nnamdi I. Osakwe
Livingstone College

Tibor Osatreicher
Baltimore City Community College

George Otto
Truman College

Thomas Paczkowski
Cayuga Community College

Alton Parish
Tarrant County Community College

Jack Partlow
Northern Virginia Area Community College—Annandale

Jeff Penley
Catawba Valley Community College

Robert Pollero
Anne Arundel Community College

Alton J. Purdy
Solano Community College

Surat P. Puri
Barber Scottia College

Angela Rabatin
Prince George's Community College

Linda Reynolds
Sacramento City College

Brenda Rhodes
Northeastern Junior College

Merle Rhodes
Morgan Community College

Pollis Robertson
Kellogg Community College

Robert Ross
Drexel University

Benjamin Sackmary
Buffalo State College

Catherina A. Sanders
San Antonio College

Lewis Schlossinger
Community College of Aurora

Gene Schneider
Austin Community College

Raymond Shea
Monroe Community College

Nora Jo Sherman
Houston Community College

Leon J. Singleton
Santa Monica College

Jeff Slater
North Shore Community College

Candy Smith
Folsom Lakes College

Solomon A. Solomon
Community College of Rhode Island

R. Southall
Laney College

Martin St. John
Westmoreland County Community College

E. George Stook
Anne Arundel Community College

James B. Stull
San Jose State University

Bill Syverstein
Fresno City College

Thomas Szezurek
Delaware County Community College

Daryl Taylor
Pasadena City College

John H. Teter
St. Petersburg Junior College

Gary Thomas
Anne Arundel Community College

Michael Thomas
Henry Ford Community College

Frank Titlow
St. Petersburg Junior College

Roland Tollefson
Anne Arundel Community College

Sheb True
Loyola Marymount University

Robert Ulbrich
Parkland College

Ariah Ullman
SUNY Binghamton

Sal Veas
Santa Monica College

Steven Wade
Santa Clara University

Dennis Wahler
San Jacinto Evergreen Community College District

W. J. Walters
Central Piedmont Community College

Timothy Weaver
Moorpark College

Richard Wertz
Concordia University

Darcelle D. White
Eastern Michigan University

Jean G. Wicks
Bornie State University

Tom Wiener
Iowa Central Community College

Dave Wiley
Anne Arundel Community College

Richard J. Williams
Santa Clara University

Joyce Wood
Northern Virginia Community College

Gregory Worosz
Schoolcraft College

Martha Zennis
Jamestown Community College

In Conclusion

I would like to thank Sue Nodine, Ingrid Benson, Heather Johnson, and the staff at Elm Street Publishing Services. Their unending efforts on behalf of *Contemporary Business* were truly extraordinary. I would also like to thank Tim Hatten at Mesa State College for his valuable feedback.

Let me conclude by noting that this new edition would never have become a reality without the outstanding efforts of the Wiley editorial, production, and marketing teams. Special thanks to George Hoffman, Lisé Johnson, Karolina Zarychta, Franny Kelly, and Maria Guarascio.

Dave Kurtz

| Brief Contents |

* Appendix A to E are online only - please go to www.wiley.com/go/global/boone or WileyPlus.

Contents

PART 2 How Firms Get Started and Survive in a Global Environment   143

[Chapter 5]

PART 3 Managers—A Key Ingredient in Contemporary Business   215

Opening Vignette
Indra Nooyi: PepsiCo's Top Executive

Solving an Ethical Controversy
Google Stands Alone: When Ethics and Business Don't Mix

Going Green
Johnson & Johnson: Caring for the World

Hit & Miss
Jeff Immelt Tries to Lead GE in a New Direction

Hit & Miss
Xerox Creates a New Image of Itself

BusinessEtiquette
Managing a Multigenerational Workforce

[Chapter 8]

Opening Vignette
NetApp Builds on Trust
and Simplicity

Hit & Miss
The Good, Bad, and Ugly of
Executive Pay

Solving an Ethical
Controversy
Should Paid Sick Leave Be
Required by Law?

BusinessEtiquette
How to Ask for a Raise

Hit & Miss
AOL Employees Don't Exit
Voluntarily

Going Green
Labor Unions and Green
Construction

PART 4 The Basic Tenets of Marketing   349

[Chapter 12]

Opening Vignette
The Buckle Shines Amid
Retail Gloom

Hit & Miss
Chattem Breathes Life into
Old Brands

Hit & Miss
SunChips Introduces Greener
Packaging

Going Green
Testa Produce Sells—and
Builds—Green

Solving an Ethical
Controversy
Teens at the Mall: Good or
Bad for Business?

BusinessEtiquette
Minding Your Social Media
Manners

PART 5 Using Technology, Information, and Accounting Tools   465

PART 6 Best Financial Practices   497

[Chapter 16]

Solving an Ethical
Controversy
Should Whistle-Blowers Be
Rewarded?

Hit & Miss
Accounting Is Booming in
Vietnam

Opening Vignette
Citigroup Closes Out the
Financial Supermarket

Going Green
TD Bank: "As Green as Our
Logo"

Hit & Miss
Citigroup Spins Off Primerica,
Inc.

Hit & Miss
How News Lifts—or Sinks—
World Stocks

BusinessEtiquette
What to Do When Your Credit
Gets Pulled

Solving an Ethical
Controversy
Can Wall Street Regulate
Itself?

* Appendix A to E are online only - please go to www.wiley.com/go/global/boone or WileyPlus.

Contemporary
BUSINESS

INTERNATIONAL STUDENT VERSION
14TH EDITION

PART

The Modern Business Environment

[Chapter 1]

Current Issues in
Contemporary
Business

[Chapter 2]

Today's Environment
for Business Ethics and
Related Social Issues

[Chapter 3]

The Most Challenging
Economy in Decades

[Chapter 4]

International
Business and
Marketing

Learning Objectives

[1] Distinguish between business and not-for-profit organizations.

[2] Identify and describe the factors of production.

[3] Describe the private enterprise system, including basic rights and entrepreneurship.

[4] Identify the six eras of business, and explain how the relationship era—including alliances, technology, and environmental concerns—influences contemporary business.

[5] Explain how today's business workforce and the nature of work itself is changing.

[6] Identify the skills and attributes managers need to lead businesses in the 21st century.

[7] Outline the characteristics that make a company admired by the business community.

Current Issues in Contemporary Business

iStockphoto

Snuggie: The Break-out Blanket Hit

If the first thing you do when preparing to curl up with a good textbook like this one is to reach for your Snuggie, you have plenty of company. Sales of the funky blanket with sleeves were expected to reach as high as 20 million units in just the second year the cozy accessory was available. Combined with the 5 million blankets sold in the first year, that volume will bring the value of total retail sales of the Snuggie to more than $300 million.

That's a respectable profit for an inexpensive product whose unique design and ungainly shape have made it the butt of YouTube parodies and late-night talk-show jokes. It means Allstar Marketing Group, which markets the Snuggie, is obviously doing something right, though Scott Boilen, president of the company, does admit to being surprised at his unlikely product's rapid rise to pop-culture success.

Despite being compared to a backwards coat, the fleecy Snuggie has ridden its growing popularity in two new directions: into much greater availability in a wider variety of stores and into a whole new range of styles and colors. Originally introduced in a now-famous television ad that encouraged viewers to respond with a phone call to place their order, the Snuggie was soon being distributed directly through a few store chains, including obvious choices like Bed Bath & Beyond and drug store chains like Walgreens. By its second year, however, it was also available at campus bookstores and such high-end retailers as Lord & Taylor.

The Snuggie has so far been the centerpiece of two annual New York City fashion runway shows, the second of which brought an avalanche of publicity from the more than 300 news reports that followed

the event. The blanket helped increase Internet sales from about 5 percent of Allstar's business to about half over the last few years. And it's become an official accessory of the rock band Weezer, which collaborated with Allstar to feature its own custom Snuggie (also available for sale) in a music video.

New Snuggie varieties include animal-print designs, Snuggies for kids, Snuggies for dogs (available in pet stores), and attention-getting Snuggies in a wide selection of official college colors complete with logos. More innovation is sure to come.

A recent spell of cold weather nearly exhausted stock of the Snuggie, and Allstar temporarily stopped its marketing effort while it replenished supplies. Being out of stock "is a nice problem to have," said the company's vice president of marketing, "but when people want their Snuggies, they want them now." Some detractors have complained about the product's quality, but its appeal has more to do with its status as a hot cultural icon than with its fit or even its durability. Meanwhile ardent Snuggie fan groups have organized Snuggie pub crawls, competitions, and get-togethers across the United States. Facebook boasts more than 300 Snuggie fan pages and twice as many groups.

Looking back on his surprise hit and the variety of ways in which consumers have become aware of it, Scott Boilen said, "You always need a combination of luck and a well-timed strategy. Snuggie took off with viral campaigns that were not part of us. Once we started seeing that, our whole marketing team got behind it." While the Snuggie may be an unusual product, its story is one that's becoming increasingly common in business today.[1]

Diane Bondareff/©AP/WideWorld Photos

Business is the nation's engine for growth. A growing economy—one that produces more goods and services with fewer resources over time—yields income for business owners, their employees, and stockholders. So a country depends on the wealth its businesses generate, from large enterprises like the Walt Disney Company to tiny online startups, and from venerable firms like 150-year-old jeans maker Levi Strauss & Company to powerhouses like Google. What all these companies and many others share is a creative approach to meeting society's needs and wants.

Businesses solve our transportation problems by marketing cars, tires, gasoline, and airline tickets. They bring food to our tables by growing, harvesting, processing, packaging, and shipping everything from spring water to cake mix and frozen shrimp. Restaurants buy, prepare, and serve food, and some even deliver. Construction companies build our schools, homes, and hospitals, while real estate firms bring property buyers and sellers together. Clothing manufacturers design, create, import, and deliver our jeans, sports shoes, work uniforms, and party wear. Entertainment for our leisure hours comes from hundreds of firms that create, produce, and distribute films, television shows, videogames, books, and music CDs and downloads.

To succeed, business firms must know what their customers want so that they can supply it quickly and efficiently. That means they often reflect changes in consumer tastes, such as the growing preference for sports drinks and vitamin-fortified water. But firms can also *lead* in advancing technology and other changes. They have the resources, the know-how, and the financial incentive to bring about real innovations, such as the iPad, new cancer treatments, and alternative energy sources like wind power. Thus, when businesses succeed, everybody wins.

You'll see throughout this book that businesses require physical inputs like auto parts, chemicals, sugar, thread, and electricity, as well as the accumulated knowledge and experience of their managers and employees. Yet they also rely heavily on their own ability to change with the times and with the marketplace. Flexibility is a key to long-term success—and to growth.

In short, business is at the forefront of our economy—and *Contemporary Business* is right there with it. This book explores the strategies that allow companies to grow and compete in today's interactive marketplace, along with the skills that you will need to turn ideas into action for your own success in business. This chapter sets the stage for the entire text by defining business and revealing its role in society. The chapter's discussion illustrates how the private enterprise system encourages competition and innovation while preserving business ethics.

What Is Business?

What comes to mind when you hear the word *business?* Do you think of big corporations like ExxonMobil or Target? Or does the local bakery or shoe store pop into your mind? Maybe you recall your first summer job. The term *business* is a broad, all-inclusive term that can be applied to many kinds of enterprises. Businesses provide the bulk of employment opportunities, as well as the products that people enjoy.

Business consists of all profit-seeking activities and enterprises that provide goods and services necessary to an economic system. Some businesses produce tangible goods, such as automobiles, breakfast cereals, and digital music players; others provide services such as insurance, hair styling, and entertainment ranging from Six Flags theme parks and sports events to concerts.

Business drives the economic pulse of a nation. It provides the means through which its citizens' standard of living improves. At the heart of every business endeavor is an exchange between a buyer and a seller. A buyer recognizes a need for a good or service and trades money with a seller to obtain that product. The seller participates in the process in hopes of gaining profits—a main ingredient in accomplishing the goals necessary for continuous improvement in the standard of living.

Profits represent rewards for businesspeople who take the risks involved in blending people, technology, and information to create and market want-satisfying goods and services. In contrast, accountants think of profits as the difference between a firm's revenues and the expenses it incurs in generating these revenues. More generally, however, profits serve as incentives for people to start companies, expand them, and provide consistently high-quality competitive goods and services.

The quest for profits is a central focus of business because without profits, a company could not survive. But businesspeople also recognize their social and ethical responsibilities. To succeed in the long run, companies must deal responsibly with employees, customers, suppliers, competitors, government, and the general public.

A business, such as this hair salon, survives through the exchange between buyer and seller. In this case, the customer and the stylist.

business all profit-seeking activities and enterprises that provide goods and services necessary to an economic system.

profits rewards for businesspeople who take the risks involved to offer goods and services to customers.

Not-for-Profit Organizations

What do Ohio State's athletic department, the U.S. Postal Service, the American Red Cross, and your local library have in common? They are all classified as **not-for-profit organizations**, businesslike establishments that have primary objectives other than returning profits to their owners. These organizations play important roles in society by placing public service above profits, although it is important to understand that these organizations need to raise money so that they can operate and achieve their social goals. Not-for-profit organizations operate in both the private and public sectors. Private-sector not-for-profits include museums, libraries, trade associations, and charitable and religious organizations.

not-for-profit organizations organization that has primary objectives such as public service rather than returning a profit to its owners.

Government agencies, political parties, and labor unions, all of which are part of the public sector, are also classified as not-for-profit organizations.

Not-for-profit organizations are a substantial part of the U.S. economy. Currently, more than 1.5 million nonprofit organizations are registered with the Internal Revenue Service in the United States, in categories ranging from arts and culture to science and technology.[2] These organizations control more than $2.6 trillion in assets and employ more people than the federal government and all 50 state governments combined.[3] In addition, millions of volunteers work for them in unpaid positions. Not-for-profits secure funding from both private sources, including donations, and government sources. They are commonly exempt from federal, state, and local taxes.

Although they focus on goals other than generating profits, managers of not-for-profit organizations face many of the same challenges as executives of profit-seeking businesses. Without funding, they cannot do research, obtain raw materials, or provide services. St. Jude Children's Research Hospital's pediatric treatment and research facility in Memphis treats nearly 5,000 children a year for catastrophic diseases, mainly cancer, immune system problems, and infectious and genetic disorders. Patients come from all 50 states and all over the world and are accepted without regard to the family's ability to pay. To provide top-quality care and to support its research in gene therapy, chemotherapy, bone marrow transplantation, and the psychological effects of illness, among many other critical areas, St. Jude relies on contributions, with some assistance from federal grants and investments.[4]

Other not-for-profits mobilize their resources to respond to emergencies, as the Red Cross and Doctors without Borders did following the devastating earthquake in Haiti that left hundreds of thousands of families homeless. Relief agencies around the world struggled to supply enough tents and tarpaulins for immediate shelter and turn their attention to more permanent construction as soon as it was feasible.[5]

■ The Red Cross mobilizes its efforts to respond to the earthquake disaster relief in Haiti.

Some not-for-profits sell merchandise or set up profit-generating arms to provide goods and services for which people are willing and able to pay. College bookstores sell everything from sweatshirts to coffee mugs with school logos imprinted on them, while the Sierra Club and the Appalachian Mountain Club both have full-fledged publishing programs. The Lance Armstrong Foundation has sold more than 40 million yellow LiveStrong wristbands as well as sports gear and accessories for men, women, and children in the United States and abroad, with the money earmarked to fight cancer and support patients and families.[6] Handling merchandising programs like these, as well as launching other fund-raising campaigns, requires managers of not-for-profit organizations to develop effective business skills and experience. Consequently, many of the concepts discussed in this book apply to not-for-profit organizations as well as to profit-oriented firms.

Factors of Production

An economic system requires certain inputs for successful operation. Economists use the term **factors of production** to refer to the four basic inputs: natural resources, capital, human resources, and entrepreneurship. Table 1.1 identifies each of these inputs and the type of payment received by firms and individuals who supply them.

Natural resources include all production inputs that are useful in their natural states, including agricultural land, building sites, forests, and mineral deposits. The largest wind farm in the world, the Roscoe Wind Complex near Roscoe, Texas, generates enough power to support almost a quarter million homes. Natural resources are the basic inputs required in any economic system.

Capital, another key resource, includes technology, tools, information, and physical facilities. *Technology* is a broad term that refers to such machinery and equipment as computers and software, telecommunications, and inventions designed to improve production. Information, frequently improved by technological innovations, is another critical factor because both managers and operating employees require accurate, timely information for effective performance of their assigned tasks. Technology plays an important role in the success of many businesses. Sometimes technology results in a new product, such as hybrid autos that run on a combination of gasoline and electricity. Most of the major car companies have introduced hybrid versions of their best-sellers in recent years.

Sometimes technology helps a company improve a product. Amazon.com's popular wireless reading device, the Kindle, uses Sprint's high-speed wireless network to free e-book readers from the need to download books via computer. Already in its second generation, it's

Assessment Check ✔

1. What activity lies at the heart of every business endeavor?
2. What are the primary objectives of a not-for-profit organization?

factors of production four basic inputs for effective operation: natural resources, capital, human resources, and entrepreneurship.

natural resources all production inputs that are useful in their natural states, including agricultural land, building sites, forests, and mineral deposits.

capital production inputs consisting of technology, tools, information, and physical facilities.

Table 1.1 **Factors of Production and Their Factor Payments**

FACTOR OF PRODUCTION	CORRESPONDING FACTOR PAYMENT
Natural resources	Rent
Capital	Interest
Human resources	Wages
Entrepreneurship	Profit

also small and comfortable enough to be held in your hands with improved battery life and storage capacity. Weighing in at considerably less than a pound, the Kindle reflects light for ease of reading and generates little heat.[7]

And sometimes technology helps a company operate more smoothly by tracking deliveries, providing more efficient communication, analyzing data, or training employees. The U.S. Postal Service, for example, is cutting costs by expanding the electronic side of its business. Although its attempts to provide electronic bill payment proved unsuccessful, the USPS lets customers order stamps and shipping supplies online and offers merchants like L.L. Bean and eBay the means to buy postage online and create merchandise shipping and return tickets. Automation, bar coding, and electronic kiosks are providing many services postal clerks used to perform.[8]

To remain competitive, a firm needs to continually acquire, maintain, and upgrade its capital, and businesses need money for that purpose. A company's funds may come from owner-investments, profits plowed back into the business, or loans extended by others. Money then goes to work building factories; purchasing raw materials and component parts; and hiring, training, and compensating workers. People and firms that supply capital receive factor payments in the form of interest.

human resources
production inputs consisting of anyone who works, including both the physical labor and the intellectual inputs contributed by workers.

Human resources represent another critical input in every economic system. Human resources include anyone who works, from the chief executive officer (CEO) of a huge corporation to a self-employed editor. This category encompasses both the physical labor and the intellectual inputs contributed by workers. Companies rely on their employees as a valued source of ideas and innovation, as well as physical effort. Some companies solicit employee ideas through traditional means, such as an online "suggestion box" or in staff meetings. Others encourage creative thinking during company-sponsored hiking or rafting trips or during social gatherings. Effective, well-trained human resources provide a significant competitive edge because competitors cannot easily match another company's talented,

iStockphoto

Competent, effective human resources can be a company's best asset. Providing perks to those employees to keep them is in a company's best interest, as software provider SAS has proven.

motivated employees in the way they can buy the same computer system or purchase the same grade of natural resources.

Hiring and keeping the right people matters, as we'll see later in the case at the end of this chapter. SAS continues to be a great place to work in part due to the attention the firm pays to retain their employees.[9]

Entrepreneurship is the willingness to take risks to create and operate a business. An entrepreneur is someone who sees a potentially profitable opportunity and then devises a plan to achieve success in the marketplace and earn those profits. Craig Rabin has big plans for his tech startup based in Seattle, but people keep telling him he is too young to make them succeed. "For me," he says, "with every form of 'no' I hear, I find myself getting stronger. . . . The real success comes when the once unthinkable becomes the now doable."[10]

U.S. businesses operate within an economic system called the *private enterprise system*. The next section looks at the private enterprise system, including competition, private property, and the entrepreneurship alternative.

entrepreneurship
willingness to take risks to create and operate a business.

Assessment Check ☑
1. Identify the four basic inputs to an economic system.
2. List four types of capital.

The Private Enterprise System

No business operates in a vacuum. All operate within a larger economic system that determines how goods and services are produced, distributed, and consumed in a society. The type of economic system employed in a society also determines patterns of resource use. Some economic systems, such as communism, feature strict controls on business ownership, profits, and resources to accomplish government goals.

In the United States, businesses function within the **private enterprise system**, an economic system that rewards firms for their ability to identify and serve the needs and demands of customers. The private enterprise system minimizes government interference in economic activity. Businesses that are adept at satisfying customers gain access to necessary factors of production and earn profits.

Another name for the private enterprise system is **capitalism**. Adam Smith, often identified as the father of capitalism, first described the concept in his book *The Wealth of Nations*, published in 1776. Smith believed that an economy is best regulated by the "invisible hand" of **competition**, the battle among businesses for consumer acceptance. Smith thought that competition among firms would lead to consumers' receiving the best possible products and prices because less efficient producers would gradually be driven from the marketplace.

The "invisible hand" concept is a basic premise of the private enterprise system. In the United States, competition regulates much of economic life. To compete successfully, each firm must find a basis for **competitive differentiation**, the unique combination of organizational abilities, products, and approaches that sets a company apart from competitors in the minds of customers. Businesses operating in a private enterprise system face a critical task of keeping up with changing marketplace conditions. Firms that fail to adjust to shifts in consumer preferences or ignore the actions of competitors leave themselves open to failure. Google, for instance, continues to challenge Microsoft's dominance in the market for business word-processing and spreadsheet software. It is expected to enable its Marketing Solutions Web site to sell third-party software to Google Apps customers. In the short time since it began its expansion into enterprise business applications, Google reports adding almost 2 million organizations for Gmail and Google Docs, an aggressive launch to which Microsoft must respond.[11]

private enterprise system economic system that rewards firms for their ability to identify and serve the needs and demands of customers.

capitalism economic system that rewards firms for their ability to perceive and serve the needs and demands of consumers; also called the private enterprise system.

competition battle among businesses for consumer acceptance.

competitive differentiation unique combination of organizational abilities, products, and approaches that sets a company apart from competitors in the minds of customers.

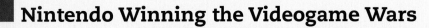
Nintendo Winning the Videogame Wars

A few years ago, irate customers were forced to wait for their Wii system because Nintendo didn't produce enough sets. But the firm bounced back with expanded inventory in time for holiday shopping the next year. The $250 system then sold more than 2 million units that November alone, selling twice as many as the same month the year before. Total sales rose to well over 15 million units. Nintendo leaped to the top spot in the videogame market, outselling Sony's PlayStation 3 and Microsoft's Xbox 360—and it hasn't looked back.

The $16 billion videogame market is on track to set a U.S. sales record in spite of the drop-off in consumer spending elsewhere. Still, the Wii's success "is mind-boggling," said one industry watcher.

Why the popularity? "Consumers ... are looking for the most value," says a Nintendo spokesperson. "With Nintendo products, they know they can get a system that is supported by hundreds of games and many, many hours of game play." The company's president agrees. "That the Wii and the DS [handheld device] represent the best entertainment value in the marketplace explains why these strong sales are happening," he says. The Wii is also easy to learn and relatively inexpensive, and its game applications tap directly into consumers' lifestyles.

With more than 40 million copies sold, *Wii* Sports ranks as "the most successful videogame of all time," according to VGChartz. Next is *Wii Play* with nearly 21 million copies. The innovative *Wii Fit* is third

with about 14 million; it has already attracted companion games like Electronic Arts' *EA Sports Active*, developed for the Wii with help from Oprah Winfrey's personal trainer. *Wii Music*, Nintendo's latest entry, is aimed at the fast-growing market dominated by Guitar Hero. *Wii Music* simulates performance on more than 60 different musical instruments. Nintendo hopes it will be at least as successful as *Wii Fit*, which is almost as popular with seniors and physical rehab patients as it is with game geeks and fitness enthusiasts.

Critical Thinking Questions

1. What do you think Nintendo has identified as its basis for competitive differentiation?
2. How would you expect Sony and Microsoft to react as the three companies fight for dominance in the game market?

Sources: Stephen Kamizuru, "Wii Sports Becomes Most Successful Videogame of All Time," *DailyTech*, February 2, 2009, http://www.dailytech.com; Mike Snider, "Nintendo Wii Sales Hint Video Games Still Play Well," *USA Today*, December 12, 2008, http://www.usatoday.com; Yi-Wyn Yen, "Nintendo Wii Officially Recession-Proof," *Fortune Techland*, December 11, 2008, http://techland.blogs.fortune.cnn.com; "Nintendo Profit Soars on Success of Its Wii Game Console," *International Herald Tribune*, July 30, 2008, http://www.iht.com; "EA Coming Out with Fitness Game for Wii," *Business Journal*, November 14, 2008, http://www.bizjournals.com; Mike Snider, " 'Sports Active' Takes Wii the Extra Mile," *USA Today*, November 13, 2008, http://www.usatoday.com.

Nintendo is challenging Microsoft on another front—the videogame industry. The Wii console and its interactive gameshave been best-sellers for consumers of all ages, as the "Hit & Miss" feature describes.

Throughout this book, our discussion focuses on the tools and methods that 21st-century businesses apply to compete and differentiate their goods and services. We also discuss many of the ways in which market changes will affect business and the private enterprise system in the years ahead.

Basic Rights in the Private Enterprise System

For capitalism to operate effectively, the citizens of a private enterprise economy must have certain rights. As shown in Figure 1.1, these include the rights to private property, profits, freedom of choice, and competition.

The right to **private property** is the most basic freedom under the private enterprise system. Every participant has the right to own, use, buy, sell, and bequeath most forms of property, including land, buildings, machinery, equipment, patents on inventions, individual possessions, and intangible properties.

The private enterprise system also guarantees business owners the right to all profits—after taxes—they earn through their activities. Although a business is not assured of earning a profit, its owner is legally and ethically entitled to any income it generates in excess of costs.

private property most basic freedom under the private enterprise system; the right to own, use, buy, sell, and bequeath land, buildings, machinery, equipment, patents, individual possessions, and various intangible kinds of property.

Freedom of choice means that a private enterprise system relies on the potential for citizens to choose their own employment, purchases, and investments. They can change jobs, negotiate wages, join labor unions, and choose among many different brands of goods and services. People living in the capitalist nations of North America, Europe, and other parts of the world are so accustomed to this freedom of choice that they sometimes forget its importance. A private enterprise economy maximizes individual prosperity by providing alternatives. Other economic systems sometimes limit freedom of choice to accomplish government goals, such as increasing industrial production of certain items or military strength.

The private enterprise system also permits fair competition by allowing the public to set rules for competitive activity. For this reason, the U.S. government has passed laws to prohibit "cutthroat" competition—excessively aggressive competitive practices designed to eliminate competition. It also has established ground rules that outlaw price discrimination, fraud in financial markets, and deceptive advertising and packaging. The Federal Communications Commission (FCC) recently closed a loophole in its rules that will help increase competition in the cable industry by forcing major companies to give up their exclusive rights to broadcast certain sports channels. "Consumers who want to switch video providers shouldn't have to give up their favorite team in the process," the FCC chairperson said. "Today the Commission levels the competitive playing field."[12]

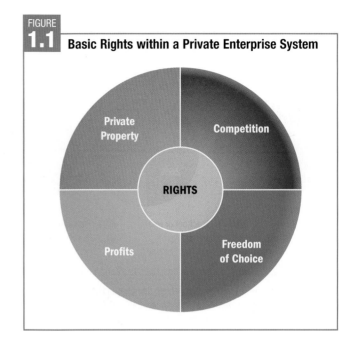

FIGURE 1.1 **Basic Rights within a Private Enterprise System**

The Entrepreneurship Alternative

The entrepreneurial spirit beats at the heart of private enterprise. An **entrepreneur** is a risk taker in the private enterprise system. You hear about entrepreneurs all the time—two college students starting a software business in their dorm room or a mom who invents a better baby carrier. Many times their success is modest, but once in a while, the risk pays off in huge profits. Individuals who recognize marketplace opportunities are free to use their capital, time, and talents to pursue those opportunities for profit. The willingness of individuals to start new ventures drives economic growth and keeps pressure on existing companies to continue to satisfy customers. If no one were willing to take economic risks, the private enterprise system wouldn't exist.

By almost any measure, the entrepreneurial spirit fuels growth in the U.S. economy. Of all the businesses operating in the United States, about one in seven firms started operations during the past year. These newly formed businesses are also the source of many of the nation's new jobs. Every year, they create more than one of every five new jobs in the economy. Most measures of entrepreneurship count the smallest or youngest businesses on the assumption that they are the enterprises in which entrepreneurship is most significant. These companies are a significant source of employment or self-employment. Of the nearly 27 million U.S. small businesses currently in operation, more than 20 million are self-employed people without any employees. More than 21 million U.S. employees currently work for a business with fewer than 20 employees.[13] Does starting a business require higher education? Not necessarily, although it can help. Figure 1.2 presents the results of a survey of small-business owners, which shows that about 24 percent of all respondents had graduated from college, and 19 percent had postgraduate degrees.

entrepreneur person who seeks a profitable opportunity and takes the necessary risks to set up and operate a business.

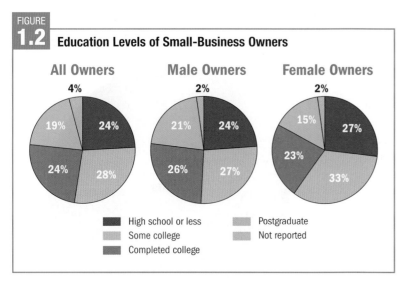

FIGURE 1.2 Education Levels of Small-Business Owners

All Owners

- 4%
- 19%
- 24%
- 24%
- 28%

Male Owners

- 2%
- 21%
- 24%
- 26%
- 27%

Female Owners

- 2%
- 15%
- 27%
- 23%
- 33%

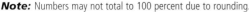

- High school or less
- Some college
- Completed college
- Postgraduate
- Not reported

Note: Numbers may not total to 100 percent due to rounding.

Source: Data from "Survey of Business Owners (SBO): Owner's Education Levels at Start-Up, Purchase, or Acquisition of the Business," U.S. Census Bureau, http://www.census.gov, accessed March 16, 2010.

Besides creating jobs and selling products, entrepreneurship provides the benefits of innovation. In contrast to more established firms, start-up companies tend to innovate most in fields of technology that are new and uncrowded with competitors, making new products available to businesses and consumers. Because small companies are more flexible, they can make changes to products and processes more quickly than larger corporations. Entrepreneurs often find new ways to use natural resources, technology, and other factors of production. Often, they do this because they have to—they may not have enough money to build an expensive prototype or launch a nationwide ad campaign. Sometimes an entrepreneur may innovate by simply tweaking an existing idea. Eric Hansen, owner of Competitive Lawn Care, a small lawn-care service in Illinois, wanted to prepare his business for a potential downturn during the 2009–2010 recession. He came up with the idea of running all the company's lawnmowers on propane, which would save money and reduce noise. A year-long journey to make his idea a reality took him from local government offices to obtain approval for opening the first private propane filling station in the country, to Kentucky to search for new equipment, and all the way to Europe to research technology from around the world. Says Hansen, "I am proud to say that after a year of hard work, Competitive Lawn Service Inc. will be the first company in the country to have a commercial lawn maintenance crew to operate 100 percent on propane as an alternative fuel, as well as a private propane fill station at our location. And our growing list of commercial and residential clients are listening and applauding. The future looks bright . . . and we are ready. Ready to branch out, expand, open new locations, and go where no company has gone before in the direction of alternative fuels, quality service, and a passion for making a difference in this world."[14]

Entrepreneurship is also important to existing companies in a private enterprise system. More and more, large firms are recognizing the value of entrepreneurial thinking among their employees, hoping to benefit from enhanced flexibility, improved innovation, and new market opportunities. Apple reaches out to its customers as well, inviting individual entrepreneurs of all kinds to develop applications for the iPhone and making it possible for them to profit from their efforts if the apps are successful. There are already more than 140,000 different applications for the device, including some developed by Apple itself, and all together they've been downloaded billions of times.[15]

As the next section explains, entrepreneurs have played a vital role in the history of U.S. business. They have helped create new

Dmitrijs Dmitrijevs/Shutterstock

Competitive Lawn Care's mowers all run on propane—the efforts to make this happen came from the entrepreneurial spirit of the company's owner, Eric Hansen.

industries, developed successful new business methods, and improved U.S. standing in global competition.

Six Eras in the History of Business

In the roughly 400 years since the first European settlements appeared on the North American continent, amazing changes have occurred in the size, focus, and goals of U.S. businesses. As Figure 1.3 indicates, U.S. business history is divided into six distinct time periods: (1) the Colonial period, (2) the Industrial Revolution, (3) the age of industrial entrepreneurs, (4) the production era, (5) the marketing era, and (6) the relationship era. The next sections describe how events in each of these time periods have influenced U.S. business practices.

The Colonial Period

Colonial society emphasized rural and agricultural production. Colonial towns were small compared with European cities, and they functioned as marketplaces for farmers and craftspeople. The economic focus of the nation centered on rural areas, because prosperity depended on the output of farms and plantations. The success or failure of crops influenced every aspect of the economy.

Colonists depended on England for manufactured items as well as financial backing for their infant industries. Even after the Revolutionary War (1776–1783), the United States maintained close economic ties with England. British investors continued to provide much of the financing for developing the U.S. business system, and this financial influence continued well into the 19th century.

The Industrial Revolution

The Industrial Revolution began in England around 1750. It moved business operations from an emphasis on independent, skilled workers who specialized in building products one by one to a factory system that mass-produced items by bringing together large numbers of semiskilled workers. The factories profited from the savings created by large-scale production, bolstered by increasing support from machines over time. As businesses grew, they could often purchase raw materials more cheaply in larger lots than

Assessment Check ☑

1. What is an alternative term for *private enterprise system?*
2. What is the most basic freedom under the private enterprise system?
3. What is an entrepreneur?

FIGURE 1.3 Six Eras in Business History

Era	Main Characteristics	Time Period
Clainolo	Primarily agricultural	Prior to 1776
Industrial Revolution	Mass production by semiskilled workers, aided by machines	1760–1850
Industrial entrepreneurs	Advances in technology and increased demand for manufactured goods, leading to enormous entrepreneurial opportunities	Late 1800s
Production	Emphasis on producing more goods faster, leading to production innovations such as assembly lines	Through the 1920s
Marketing	Consumer orientation, seeking to understand and satisfy needs and preferences of customer groups	Since 1950s
Relationship	Benefits derived from deep, ongoing links with individual customers, employees, suppliers, and other businesses	Began in 1990s

before. Specialization of labor, limiting each worker to a few specific tasks in the production process, also improved production efficiency.

Influenced by these events in England, business in the United States began a time of rapid industrialization. Agriculture became mechanized, and factories sprang up in cities. During the mid-1800s, the pace of the revolution was increased as newly built railroad systems provided fast, economical transportation. In California, for example, the combination of railroad construction and the gold rush fueled a tremendous demand for construction.

The Age of Industrial Entrepreneurs

Building on the opportunities created by the Industrial Revolution, entrepreneurship increased in the United States. In 1900, Arthur R. Wilson and several partners paid $10,000 in gold coins for a 27-acre parcel of granite-rich land in California. This natural resource was the basis for the Granite Rock Co., which provided the material for roads and buildings in California's booming economy. The company, now called Graniterock, evolved in response to technological, competitive, and marketplace demands and continues to survive in the 21st century. Today the firm, which has stores throughout California, offers consumer products such as granite countertops as well as many "green" products made from recycled materials.[16]

Inventors created a virtually endless array of commercially useful products and new production methods. Many of them are famous today:

- Eli Whitney introduced the concept of interchangeable parts, an idea that would later facilitate mass production on a previously impossible scale.

- Robert McCormick designed a horse-drawn reaper that reduced the labor involved in harvesting wheat. His son, Cyrus McCormick, saw the commercial potential of the reaper and launched a business to build and sell the machine. By 1902, the company was producing 35 percent of the nation's farm machinery.

- Cornelius Vanderbilt (railroads), J. P. Morgan (banking), and Andrew Carnegie (steel), among others, took advantage of the enormous opportunities waiting for anyone willing to take the risk of starting a new business.

Granite Rock Co., started in the Age of Industrial Entrepreneurs, has evolved in response to 21st-century demands.

The entrepreneurial spirit of this golden age in business did much to advance the U.S. business system and raise the overall standard of living of its citizens. That market transformation, in turn, created new demand for manufactured goods.

The Production Era

As demand for manufactured goods continued to increase through the 1920s, businesses focused even greater attention on the activities involved in producing those goods. Work became increasingly specialized, and huge, labor-intensive factories dominated U.S. business. Assembly lines, introduced by Henry Ford, became commonplace in major industries. Business owners turned over their responsibilities to a new class of managers trained in operating established companies. Their activities emphasized efforts to produce even more goods through quicker methods.

During the production era, business focused attention on internal processes rather than external influences. Marketing was almost an afterthought, designed solely to distribute items generated by production activities. Little attention was paid to consumer wants or needs. Instead, businesses tended to make decisions about what the market would get. If you wanted to buy a Ford Model T automobile, your color choice was black—the only color produced by the company.

The Marketing Era

The Great Depression of the early 1930s changed the shape of U.S. business yet again. As incomes nose-dived, businesses could no longer automatically count on selling everything they produced. Managers began to pay more attention to the markets for their goods and services, and sales and advertising took on new importance. During this period, selling was often synonymous with marketing.

Demand for all kinds of consumer goods exploded after World War II. After nearly five years of doing without new automobiles, appliances, and other items, consumers were buying again. At the same time, however, competition also heated up. Soon businesses began to think of marketing as more than just selling; they envisioned a process of determining what consumers wanted and needed and then designing products to satisfy those needs. In short, they developed a **consumer orientation**.

Businesses began to analyze consumer desires before beginning actual production. Consumer choices skyrocketed. Automobiles came in a wide variety of colors and styles, and car buyers could choose among them. Companies also discovered the need to distinguish their goods and services from those of competitors. **Branding**—the process of creating an identity in consumers' minds for a good, service, or company—is an important marketing tool. A **brand** can be a name, term, sign, symbol, design, or some combination that identifies the products of one firm and differentiates them from competitors' offerings.

The Home Depot, the world's largest home improvement specialty retailer, operates more than 2,200 retail stores in the United States, Canada, Mexico, and China and exports products around the world. Its carefully guarded brand name stands for excellent customer service, an entrepreneurial spirit, and the desire to give something back to the communities in which it operates. The company sells thousands of products, some under its own sub-brands including RIDGID® tools, BEHR® paint, LG® appliances, and Toro® lawn equipment.[17]

The marketing era has had a tremendous effect on the way business is conducted today. Even the smallest business owners recognize the importance of understanding what customers want and the reasons they buy.

The Relationship Era

As business continues in the 21st century, a significant change is taking place in the ways companies interact with customers. Since the Industrial Revolution, most businesses have concentrated on building and promoting products in the hope that enough customers will buy them to cover costs and earn acceptable profits, an approach called **transaction management**.

consumer orientation business philosophy that focuses first on determining unmet consumer wants and needs and then designing products to satisfy those needs.

branding process of creating an identity in consumers' minds for a good, service, or company; a major marketing tool in contemporary business.

brand name, term, sign, symbol, design, or some combination that identifies the products of one firm and differentiates them from competitors' offerings.

transaction management building and promoting products in the hope that enough customers will buy them to cover costs and earn profits.

relationship era the business era in which firms seek ways to actively nurture customer loyalty by carefully managing every interaction.

In contrast, in the **relationship era**, businesses are taking a different, longer-term approach to their interactions with customers. Firms now seek ways to actively nurture customer loyalty by carefully managing every interaction. They earn enormous paybacks for their efforts. A company that retains customers over the long haul reduces its advertising and sales costs. Because customer spending tends to accelerate over time, revenues also grow. Companies with long-term customers often can avoid costly reliance on price discounts to attract new business, and they find that many new buyers come from loyal customer referrals.

Business owners gain several advantages by developing ongoing relationships with customers. Because it is much less expensive to serve existing customers than to find new ones, businesses that develop long-term customer relationships can reduce their overall costs. Long-term relationships with customers enable businesses to improve their understanding of what customers want and prefer from the company. As a result, businesses enhance their chances of sustaining real advantages through competitive differentiation.

The relationship era is an age of connections—between businesses and customers, employers and employees, technology and manufacturing, and even separate companies. The world economy is increasingly interconnected, as businesses expand beyond their national boundaries. In this new environment, techniques for managing networks of people, businesses, information, and technology are critically important to contemporary business success. As you begin your own career, you will soon see how important relationships are, including your online presence; see the "Business Etiquette" feature for suggestions on presenting yourself in a positive way through social networking.

Managing Relationships through Technology

relationship management collection of activities that build and maintain ongoing, mutually beneficial ties with customers and other parties.

technology business application of knowledge based on scientific discoveries, inventions, and innovations.

Increasingly, businesses focus on **relationship management**, the collection of activities that build and maintain ongoing, mutually beneficial ties with customers and other parties. At its core, relationship management involves gathering knowledge of customer needs and preferences and applying that understanding to get as close to the customer as possible. Many of these activities are based on **technology**, or the business application of knowledge based on scientific discoveries, inventions, and innovations. In managing relationships with customers, technology most often takes the form of communication, via the Internet and cell phone.

Blogs are growing more influential as a link between companies and their customers, and more companies are beginning to take advantage of their directness. Some that are connecting with customers in a positive way through their company blogs are Kodak, Walmart, Patagonia, and LinkedIn.[18] Google recently used its corporate blog both to announce its new Buzz social networking product and to calm angry users with announcements about needed changes in the service.

Strategic Alliances

strategic alliance partnership formed to create a competitive advantage for the businesses involved; in international business, a business strategy in which a company finds a partner in the country where it wants to do business.

Businesses are also finding that they must form partnerships with other organizations to take full advantage of available opportunities. One form of partnership between organizations is a **strategic alliance**, a partnership formed to create a competitive advantage for the businesses involved.

E-business has created a whole new type of strategic alliance. A firm whose entire business is conducted online, such as Amazon or Overstock.com, may team up with traditional retailers that contribute their expertise in buying the right amount of the right merchandise, as well as their knowledge of distribution. Overstock.com, based in Salt Lake City, Utah, is an online-only retailer designed for bargain hunters looking for brand-name consumer goods including clothing, appliances, electronics, and sporting goods at discount prices. The manufacturers and distributors that Overstock.com partners with gain a new avenue for reducing their inventory and allow the firm to carry over 2 million different products on its Web site. Overstock.com earned revenues of more than $800 million in one recent year and received several top customer service awards.[19]

The Green Advantage

Another way of building relationships is to incorporate issues that your customers care about into your business. As environmental concerns continue to influence consumers' choices of everything from yogurt to clothing to cars and light bulbs, many observers say the question about "going green" is no longer whether, but how. The need to develop environmentally friendly products and processes is becoming a major new force in business today. Companies in every industry are researching ways to save energy, cut emissions and pollution, reduce waste, and, not incidentally, save money and increase profits as well. The family-owned Bigelow Tea Company is working with Connecticut's Clean Energy Fund to install solar panels on four different building levels at its headquarters in Fairfield. The panels are expected to supply almost 7 percent of the building's electrical energy needs, equivalent to the power used by 22 average homes.[20]

Energy is among the biggest costs for most firms, and carbon-based fuels such as coal are responsible for most of the additional carbon dioxide in the atmosphere. Ford Motor Company is upgrading lighting fixtures in its manufacturing

BusinessEtiquette

Social Networking

Most young people hear a lot of career advice, and one reliably good tip is to build a network of personal contacts in your chosen field. The social networks blossoming online make this especially easy—but the Internet's informality can also make it tricky to network in a professional way. Here are suggestions for presenting yourself in a positive light on sites like Facebook, LinkedIn, and others.

1 Know the purpose of the networking site you choose. Most people consider Facebook more social, while LinkedIn purposely maintains a more professional look and feel.

2 Remember that potential employers, mentors, and other professionals will check your Facebook page to learn about you, despite the site's mostly fun-oriented profile. Look objectively at what they'll see there.

3 Review and edit posted photos to be sure they present the image you're after.

4 Resist the impulse to share. Keep your posts brief and neither overly detailed nor overly personal. People you hope to tap for potential job leads don't need to know what you had for breakfast. Strictly limit information about family members, too.

5 Network with someone you haven't met, find someone you have in common and ask that person to make an online introduction.

6 Contribute to the community. "Help the people around you and you help yourself," advises one author. Posting interesting information about your area of professional expertise is one way of helping the community and building relationships.

7 Avoid posting anything about your current or past employers.

8 Always remember that everything you post is as public as the newspaper's front page. Edit yourself, and check your privacy settings.

Sources: G. Lynch "Facebook Etiquette: Five Dos and Don'ts," *PCWorld*, http://www.pcworld.com, accessed March 2010; Jimmy Wales and Andrea Weckerle, "Keep a Civil Cybertongue," *The Wall Street Journal*, December 29, 2009, p. A19; Laura M. Holson, "Short Outbursts? Big Problem," *The New York Times*, October 8, 2009, p. E1C.

Hit & Miss

Google Buzz a Bust?

As originally conceived, Google's Buzz must have sounded like a great idea: "a new way to start conversations about things you find interesting" that was "built right into Gmail, so you don't have to peck out an entirely new set of friends from scratch—it just works." Unfortunately, the features designed to make adopting Buzz effortless created an instant uproar over users' privacy.

Planned to compete with Facebook and Twitter, Buzz offered users a ready-made social network through an "auto-follow" function that automatically networked their most frequent Gmail contacts. It also automatically connected users with Picasa photo albums and links and videos shared on Google Reader. Tens of millions around the world reportedly sampled the new service in its first two days, posting more than 9 million messages and comments. Most, however, were angry and dismayed to discover how much personal information the auto-follow and other features made public within the network.

Within 48 hours Google announced steps to correct privacy concerns, including changing to an auto-suggest feature and making it easier for users to modify or disable the program. "We're very sorry for the concern we've caused and have been working hard ever since to improve things based on your feedback," Buzz's product manager told users. "We'll continue to do so."

Though some observers still worried that "Gmail users are being driven into a social networking service . . . they didn't sign up for," others conceded the high level of interest in Buzz suggested "Google might have a minor hit on its hands already."

Questions for Critical Thinking

1. Can a company carry its customer relationship-building efforts too far?
2. Do you think Google will recover customers' goodwill after introducing new privacy features into its Buzz network?

Sources: Miguel Helft, "Anger Leads to Apology from Google About Buzz," *The New York Times,* February 15, 2010, http://www.nytimes.com; David Coursey, "Google Apologizes for Buzz Privacy Issues," *PC World,* February 15, 2010, http://www.pcworld.com; "Millions of Buzz Users, and Improvements Based on Your Feedback," company Web site, February 11, 2010, http://gmailblog.blogspot.com; "Introducing Google Buzz," company Web site, February 9, 2010, http://googleblog.blogspot.com.

facilities, replacing old inefficient equipment with fluorescent lighting that saves energy and money and including motion detectors that reduce energy use during periods of low activity.[21] Clean solar energy is coming into its own and may soon be more viable and more widely available. SolarCity, a California installer of rooftop solar cells, is having trouble keeping up with growing demand. "It is hard to find installers," says the company's CEO. "We're at the stage where if we continue to grow at this pace, we won't be able to sustain the growth."[22]

Some "green" initiatives can themselves be costly for firms. General Electric, however, with its Ecomagination line of environmentally friendly products, is among those that have realized thinking "green" can satisfy not only consumers' environmental concerns but also those of shareholders by saving money and earning profits. "We've sold out in eco-certified products for [a year in advance]," says Bob Corcoran, the company's vice president for corporate citizenship, and energy-saving wind turbines are backordered for two years. Once criticized for its pollution of New York's Hudson River, the firm has helped form the U.S. Climate Action Partnership to push for a cap on carbon emissions in the United States. GE believes it is doing what its shareholders expect it to do. "No good business can call itself a good corporate citizen if it fritters away shareholder money," Corcoran says.[23]

Each new era in U.S. business history has forced managers to reexamine the tools and techniques they formerly used to compete. Tomorrow's managers will need creativity and vision to stay on top of rapidly changing technology and to manage complex relationships in

Going Green

Exelon Bets on Nuclear

"Time is not our friend with respect to global climate change. . . . the usual approach—doing too much, too late—will not work." So says John Rowe, CEO of the utility company Exelon, a recent winner of the National Safety Council's Green Cross for Safety. Exelon is betting on the world's growing demand for renewable energy sources to create a sound financial future for the company and its stakeholders while minimizing its environmental impact.

Created in 2000 from a merger between utility companies in Chicago and Philadelphia, Exelon sold most of its underperforming coal plants to focus on nuclear power generation. Its fleet of 17 reactors is the world's third-largest, topped only by utilities in France and Russia. Exelon earns $17 billion in sales and close to $3 billion in profits a year, returning more than twice as much to shareholders as other utilities. Its nuclear plants produce about 130 billion kilowatt-hours of electricity each year and have reduced greenhouse gas emissions more than 35 percent from earlier levels. That's equivalent to taking a million passenger cars off the road.

Legislation to cap or more heavily regulate carbon emissions will force Exelon's carbon-dependent competitors to raise prices. "I thought climate legislation would come sooner or later and that I'd rather have my money in the nuke fleet," says Rowe. The company plans to further shrink its carbon footprint by 2020 by eliminating more than 15 million metric tons of potential greenhouse gas emissions every year.

Questions for Critical Thinking

1. Exelon has tried and failed to acquire three smaller rival companies. What role, if any, do you think strategic partnerships might play in the company's future?

2. Exelon is the most valuable U.S. utility company in terms of market value and derives 92 percent of its power from nuclear plants. Do you think being environmentally aware and being profitable are compatible goals for a business? Why or why not?

Sources: Company Web site, www.exeloncorp.com, accessed February 12, 2010; Julie Schmit, "Exelon CEO: Deal with Emissions Now," *USA Today*, January 25, 2010, www.usatoday.com; Jonathan Fahey, "Exelon's Carbon Advantage," *Forbes*, January 18, 2010, http://www.forbes.com; "National Safety Council Names Exelon Nuclear as Recipient of 2010 Green Cross for Safety Medal," *PR Newswire*, January 5, 2010.

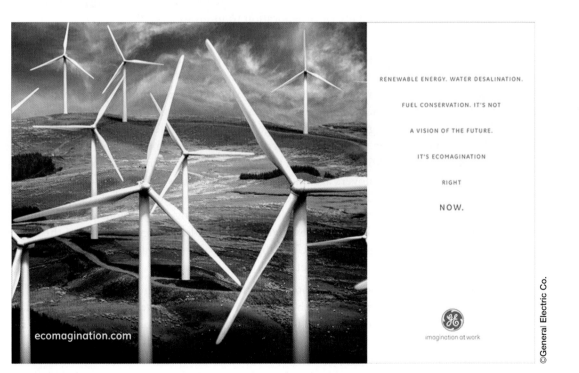

RENEWABLE ENERGY. WATER DESALINATION.

FUEL CONSERVATION. IT'S NOT

A VISION OF THE FUTURE.

IT'S ECOMAGINATION

RIGHT

NOW.

ecomagination.com

©General Electric Co.

Going green doesn't have to be expensive. General Electric's Ecomagination line has shown that green products can save money and earn profits as well as respond to consumers' environmental concerns.

Assessment Check ☑

1. What was the Industrial Revolution?
2. During which era was the idea of branding developed?
3. What is the difference between transaction management and relationship management?

the global business world of the fast-paced 21st century. As green operations become more cost-effective, and consumers and shareholders demand more responsive management, few firms will choose to be left behind. For a look at management issues in the energy industry, see the "Going Green" feature.

Today's Business Workforce

A skilled and knowledgeable workforce is an essential resource for keeping pace with the accelerating rate of change in today's business world. Employers need reliable workers who are dedicated to fostering strong ties with customers and partners. They must build workforces capable of efficient, high-quality production needed to compete in global markets. Savvy business leaders also realize that the brainpower of employees plays a vital role in a firm's ability to stay on top of new technologies and innovations. In short, a first-class workforce can be the foundation of a firm's competitive differentiation, providing important advantages over competing businesses.

Changes in the Workforce

Companies now face several trends that challenge their skills for managing and developing human resources. Those challenges include aging of the population and a shrinking labor pool, growing diversity of the workforce, the changing nature of work, the need for flexibility and mobility, and the use of collaboration to innovate.

Aging of the Population and Shrinking Labor Pool By 2030, the number of U.S. workers 65 or older will reach 72 million—double what it is today—and many of them will retire from the workforce, taking their experience and expertise with them. As Table 1.2 shows, the U.S. population as a whole is trending older. Yet today, many members of the Baby Boom generation, the huge number of people born between 1946 and 1964, are still hitting the peaks of their careers. At the same time, members of so-called Generation X (born from 1965 to 1981) and Generation Y (born from 1982 to 2005) are building their careers, so employers are finding more generations in the workforce simultaneously than ever before. This broad age diversity brings management challenges with it, such as accommodating a variety of work-life styles, changing expectations of work, and varying levels of technological expertise. Still, despite the widening age spectrum of the workforce, some economists predict the U.S. labor pool could soon fall short by as many as 10 million people as the Baby Boomers retire.

More sophisticated technology has intensified the hiring challenge by requiring workers to have ever more advanced skills. Although the number of college-educated workers has doubled in the past 20 years, the demand is still greater than the supply of these individuals. Because of these changes, companies are increasingly seeking—and finding—talent at the extreme ends of the working-age spectrum. Teenagers are entering the workforce sooner, and some seniors are staying longer—or seeking new careers after retiring from their primary careers. Many older workers work part-time or flexible hours. Dick Chevrette

1.2 Aging of the U.S. Population

AGE	2010	2020	2025
16–64	203 million	214 million	218 million
	66% of total	63% of total	61% of total
65 and older	40 million	55 million	64 million
	13% of total	16% of total	18% of total
Median	37 years	38 years	38.5 years

Source: U.S. Census Bureau, "Resident Population Projections by Sex and Age: 2010 to 2050," *Statistical Abstract of the United States*, http://www.census.gov, accessed March 2010.

worked for 38 years as a manager at Massachusetts General Hospital. When he hit 62, he wanted to still be mentally challenged and active so he scaled back his hours but didn't stop working. Meanwhile, for those older employees who do retire, employers must administer a variety of retirement planning and disability programs, retraining, and insurance benefits.

Increasingly Diverse Workforce The U.S. workforce is growing more diverse, in age and in every other way as well. The two fastest-growing ethnic populations in the U.S. are Hispanics and people of Asian origin. Currently, Hispanics represent about 16 percent of the U.S. population, a number expected to triple by 2050, and Asians represent about 5 percent and are expected to represent more than 9 percent by 2050.[24] Considering that minority groups now make up more than one-third of the U.S. population and will account for half within a generation, managers must learn to work effectively with diverse ethnic groups, cultures, and lifestyles to develop and retain a superior workforce for their company.

Diversity, blending individuals of different genders, ethnic backgrounds, cultures, religions, ages, and physical and mental abilities, can enhance a firm's chances of success. Some of the firms that made the top ten in a recent list of "Top 50 Companies for Diversity" were also leaders and innovators in their industries, including Johnson & Johnson (number one on the list), AT&T, the accounting firm Ernst & Young, Marriott International, and The Coca-Cola Company and IBM.[25] Several studies have shown that diverse employee teams and workforces tend to perform tasks more effectively and develop better solutions to business problems than homogeneous employee groups. This result is due in part to the varied perspectives and experiences that foster innovation and creativity in multicultural teams.

Practical managers also know that attention to diversity issues can help them avoid damaging legal battles. Losing a discrimination lawsuit can be very costly, yet in a recent survey, a majority of executives from racial and cultural minorities said they had seen discrimination in work assignments.[26]

diversity blending individuals of different genders, ethnic backgrounds, cultures, religions, ages, and physical and mental abilities to enhance a firm's chances of success.

Outsourcing and the Changing Nature of Work Not only is the U.S. workforce changing, but so is the very nature of work. Manufacturing used to account for most of U.S. annual output, but the balance has now shifted to services such as financial management and communications. This means firms must rely heavily on well-trained service workers with knowledge, technical skills, the ability to communicate and deal with people, and a talent for creative thinking. The Internet has made possible another business tool for staffing flexibility—**outsourcing**, using outside vendors to produce goods or fulfill services and functions that were previously handled in-house. In the best situation, outsourcing allows a firm to reduce costs and concentrate its resources on the things it does best while gaining access to expertise it may not have. But outsourcing also creates its own challenges, such as differences in language or culture.

Offshoring is the relocation of business processes to lower-cost locations overseas. This can include both production and services. In recent years, China has emerged as a dominant location for production offshoring for many firms, while India has become the key player in offshoring services. Some U.S. companies are now structured so that entire divisions or functions are developed and staffed overseas—the jobs were never in the United States to start with. Another trend in some industries is **nearshoring**, outsourcing production or services to nations near a firm's home base.

Flexibility and Mobility Younger workers in particular are looking for something other than the work-comes-first lifestyle exemplified by the Baby Boom generation. But workers of all ages are exploring different work arrangements, such as telecommuting from remote locations and sharing jobs with two or more employees. Employers are also hiring growing numbers of temporary and part-time employees, some of whom are less interested in advancing up the career ladder and more interested in using and developing their skills. While the cubicle-filled office will likely never become obsolete, technology makes productive networking and virtual team efforts possible by allowing people to work where they choose and easily share knowledge, a sense of purpose or mission, and a free flow of ideas across any geographical distance or time zone.

Managers of such far-flung workforces need to build and earn their trust, in order to retain valued employees and to ensure that all members are acting ethically and contributing their share without the day-to-day supervision of a more conventional work environment. These managers, and their employees, need to be flexible and responsive to change while work, technology, and the relationships between them continue to evolve.

Innovation through Collaboration Some observers also see a trend toward more collaborative work in the future, as opposed to individuals working alone. Businesses using teamwork hope to build a creative environment where all members contribute their knowledge and skills to solve problems or seize opportunities.

The old relationship between employers and employees was pretty simple: workers arrived at a certain hour, did their jobs, and went home every day at the same time. Companies rarely laid off workers, and employees rarely left for a job at another firm. But all that—and more—has changed. Employees are no longer likely to remain with a single company throughout their entire careers and do not necessarily expect lifetime loyalty from the companies they work for. They do not expect to give that loyalty either. Instead, they build their own careers however and wherever they can. These changes mean that many firms now recognize the value of a partnership with employees that encourages creative thinking and problem solving and that rewards risk taking and innovation.

---

outsourcing using outside vendors to produce goods or fulfill services and functions that were previously handled in-house or in-country.

offshoring relocation of business processes to lower-cost locations overseas.

nearshoring outsourcing production or services to locations near a firm's home base.

Assessment Check ☑

1. Define *outsourcing, offshoring,* and *nearshoring.*
2. Describe the importance of collaboration and employee partnership.

The 21st-Century Manager

Today's companies look for managers who are intelligent, highly motivated people with the ability to create and sustain a vision of how an organization can succeed. The 21st-century manager must also apply critical-thinking skills and creativity to business challenges and lead change.

The vision of a leader is crucial for an organization to succeed. David B. Snow Jr. has that vision for his firm, Medco Health Solutions.

Importance of Vision

To thrive in the 21st century, businesspeople need **vision**, the ability to perceive marketplace needs and what an organization must do to satisfy them. David B. Snow Jr., chair and CEO of Medco Health Solutions, has been recognized by several pharmaceutical industry groups for his dedication to improving patient health and to shaping a future in which medical prescriptions can be tailored to the individual's own genetic makeup. Medco serves more approximately 65 million workers, retirees, and seniors nationwide; employs more than 23,000 people globally (3,000 of them pharmacists and 600 nurses); and operates a chain of specialty pharmacies, a diabetes-care company, and several international operations. During Snow's tenure it has been named one of the most trustworthy U.S. companies (*Forbes* magazine) and one of the most admired in the world (*Fortune*) for its innovation and people management.[27]

> **vision** the ability to perceive marketplace needs and what an organization must do to satisfy them.

Importance of Critical Thinking and Creativity

Critical thinking and creativity are essential characteristics of the 21st-century workforce. Today's businesspeople need to look at a wide variety of situations, draw connections between disparate information, and develop future-oriented solutions. This need applies not only to top executives, but to midlevel managers and entry-level workers as well.

Critical thinking is the ability to analyze and assess information to pinpoint problems or opportunities. The critical-thinking process includes activities such as determining the authenticity, accuracy, and worth of information, knowledge, and arguments. It involves looking beneath the surface for deeper meaning and connections that can help identify critical issues and solutions. Without critical thinking, a firm may encounter serious problems.

> **critical thinking** ability to analyze and assess information to pinpoint problems or opportunities.

Creativity is the capacity to develop novel solutions to perceived organizational problems. Although most people think of it in relation to writers, artists, musicians, and inventors, that is a very limited definition. In business, creativity refers to the ability to see better and different ways of doing business. A computer engineer who solves a glitch in a software program is executing a creative act; so is a shipping clerk who finds a way to speed delivery of the company's overnight packages. Sometimes a crisis calls for creative leadership. Captain Chesley Sullenberger, who famously guided US Airways Flight 1549 to a safe landing in New York's Hudson River, had to make immediate and critical decisions when both his engines quit after hitting birds upon take-off. His passengers' and crew members'

> **creativity** capacity to develop novel solutions to perceived organizational problems.

lives—and lives on the ground—depended on his quick thinking and years of training. "Losing thrust on both engines, at low speed, at a low altitude, over one of the most densely populated areas on the planet. Yes, I knew it was a very challenging situation," he said. Losing altitude, Sullenberger ruled out returning to La Guardia Airport or attempting to land at a nearby New Jersey airport, opting instead to splash down in the river close to a ferry terminal. "I needed to touch down with the wings exactly level . . . the nose slightly up . . . [and] just above our minimum flying speed, but not below it." He accomplished those seemingly impossible feats and saved all 155 people on board.[28]

Some practice and mental exercise can cultivate your own ability to think creatively. Here are some exercises and guidelines:

- In a group, brainstorm by listing ideas as they come to mind. Build on other people's ideas, but don't criticize them. Wait until later to evaluate and organize the ideas.

- Think about how to make familiar concepts unfamiliar. A glue that doesn't stick very well? That's the basis for 3M's popular Post-it® notes.

- Plan ways to rearrange your thinking with simple questions such as, "What features can we leave out?" or by imagining what it feels like to be the customer.

- Cultivate curiosity, openness, risk, and energy as you meet people and encounter new situations. View these encounters as opportunities to learn.

- Treat failures as additional opportunities to learn.

- Get regular physical exercise. When you work out, your brain releases endorphins, and these chemicals stimulate creative thinking.

- Pay attention to your dreams and daydreams. You might find that you already know the answer to a problem.

Creativity and critical thinking must go beyond generating new ideas, however. They must lead to action. In addition to creating an environment in which employees can nurture ideas, managers must give them opportunities to take risks and try new solutions.

Ability to Lead Change

Today's business leaders must guide their employees and organizations through the changes brought about by technology, marketplace demands, and global competition. Managers must be skilled at recognizing employee strengths and motivating people to move toward common goals as members of a team. Throughout this book, real-world examples demonstrate how companies have initiated sweeping change initiatives. Most, if not all, have been led by managers comfortable with the tough decisions that today's fluctuating conditions require.

Factors that require organizational change can come from both external and internal sources; successful managers must be aware of both. External forces might include feedback from customers, developments in the international marketplace, economic trends, and new technologies. Internal factors might arise from new company goals, emerging employee needs, labor union demands, or production problems.

Assessment Check ☑

1. Why is vision an important managerial quality?
2. What is the difference between creativity and critical thinking?

What Makes a Company Admired?

Who is your hero? Is it someone who has achieved great feats in sports, government, entertainment, or business? Why do you admire the person—does he or she run a company, earn a lot of money, or give back to the community and society? Every year, business magazines and organizations publish lists of companies that they consider to be "most admired." Companies, like individuals, may be admired for many reasons. Most people would mention solid profits, stable growth, a safe and challenging work environment, high-quality goods and services, and business ethics and social responsibility. *Business ethics* refers to the standards of conduct and moral values involving decisions made in the work environment. *Social responsibility* is a management philosophy that includes contributing resources to the community, preserving the natural environment, and developing or participating in nonprofit programs designed to promote the well-being of the general public. You'll find business ethics and social responsibility examples throughout this book, as well as a deeper exploration of these topics in Chapter 2. For businesses to behave ethically and responsibly, their employees need to have strong moral compasses that guide them. The "Solving an Ethical Controversy" feature debates the responsibility that watchdogs have when they fail to perform their duties.

As you read this text, you'll be able to make up your mind about why companies should—or should not—be admired. *Fortune* publishes two lists of most-admired companies each year, one for U.S.-based firms and one for the world. The list is compiled from surveys and other research conducted by the Hay Group, a global human resources and organizational consulting firm. Criteria for making the list include innovation, people management, use of corporate assets, social responsibility, quality of management, and quality of products and services.[29] Table 1.3 lists the top ten "Most Admired Companies" for a recent year.

What's Ahead

As business speeds along in the 21st century, new technologies, population shifts, and shrinking global barriers are altering the world at a frantic pace. Businesspeople are catalysts for many of these changes, creating new opportunities for individuals who are prepared to take action. Studying contemporary business will help you prepare for the future.

Assessment Check ☑

1. Define *business ethics* and *social responsibility*.

2. Identify three criteria used to judge whether a company might be considered admirable.

Table

1.3 *Fortune's* Top Ten Most Admired Companies

1 Apple	4 Google	7 FedEx
2 Berkshire Hathaway	5 Johnson & Johnson	8 Southwest Airlines
3 Toyota Motor	6 Procter & Gamble	9 General Electric
		10 Microsoft

Source: "World's Most Admired Companies," from *Fortune*, http://money.cnn.com, accessed March 9, 2010. Copyright © 2009 by Time, Inc. All rights reserved. Used by permission and protected by the Copyright laws of the United States. The printing, copying, redistribution, or retransmission of the Material without express permission is prohibited.

Solving an Ethical Controversy

SEC Lax on Oversight?

The Securities and Exchange Commission (SEC) was created by Congress in 1934 to protect investors by monitoring the securities industry. According to the SEC's Web site, "The laws and rules that govern the securities industry in the United States derive from a simple and straightforward concept: all investors, whether large institutions or private individuals, should have access to certain basic facts about an investment prior to buying it, and so long as they hold it. To achieve this, the SEC requires public companies to disclose meaningful financial and other information to the public."

Recently, however, a whopping $65 billion securities fraud came to light when the investment company run by Bernard Madoff turned out to be the biggest Ponzi scheme of all time. Madoff used new investors' funds to pay off the older ones. All the investment profits Madoff claimed were an illusion. Independent investigator Harry Markopolos told Congress he had been warning the SEC about Madoff's activities for years. "I gift-wrapped and delivered the largest Ponzi scheme in history to them and somehow they couldn't be bothered to conduct a thorough and proper investigation because they were too busy on matters of higher priority," Markopolos testified. Thousands of individual and institutional investors faced financial ruin as Madoff's scheme evaporated.

Does the SEC bear part of the blame for investor losses if it is not doing its job?

PRO

1. A $65 billion fraud could flourish only under a flawed regulatory system. "Our current fragmented regulatory system can allow bad actors to engage in misconduct outside the view and reach of some regulators," said an officer of the securities industry's watchdog organization. "It is undeniable that . . . the system failed to protect investors."

2. "The SEC is . . . captive to the industry it regulates, and it is afraid of bringing big cases against the largest, most powerful firms," said Markopolos. "Clearly the SEC was afraid of Mr. Madoff."

CON

1. The SEC's director of enforcement told a Senate committee, "We don't turn a blind eye to fraud. If we see it and we suspect it, we pursue it. We don't want fraudsters out there."

2. The director also said the SEC doesn't have enough resources to pursue all the tip-offs of potential fraud that come before it: "If we had more resources we could clearly do more." Other regulators blamed lack of coordination among government agencies for the lapses in oversight that allowed Madoff to operate.

Summary

Madoff pled guilty to charges of felony securities fraud and was sentenced to 150 years in prison. The SEC is conducting an internal investigation to discover why it failed to act on information about him that Markopolos and others provided over the years.

Sources: Jenny Anderson and Zachery Kouwe, "SEC Enforcers Focus on Avoiding Madoff Repeat," *The New York Times*, www.nytimes.com, February 8, 2010; SEC Web site, http://www.sec.gov/about/whatwedo.shtml, accessed February 13, 2009; Linda Sandler, "Madoff Said Only Brother Could Do Audit, Witness Tells Congress," *Bloomberg News*, February 5, 2009, http://www.bloomberg.com; Allan Chernoff, "Madoff Whistleblower Blasts SEC," *CNNMoney*, February 4, 2009, http://www.cnnmoney.com; Dana B. Henriques, "Witness on Madoff Tells of Fear for Safety," The New York Times, February 4, 2009; http://www.nytimes.com; Julian Cummings, "Madoff: SEC Defends Its Role," *CNNMoney*, January 28, 2009; http://www.cnnmoney.com; Liz Moyer, "How Regulators Missed Madoff," *Forbes*, January 27, 2009, http://www.forbes.com.

Throughout this book, you'll be exposed to the real-life stories of many businesspeople. You'll learn about the range of business careers available and the daily decisions, tasks, and challenges that they face. By the end of the course, you'll understand how marketing, production, accounting, finance, and management work together to provide competitive advantages for firms. This knowledge can help you become a more capable employee and enhance your career potential.

Now that this chapter has introduced some basic terms and issues in the business world of the 21st century, Chapter 2 takes a detailed look at the ethical and social responsibility issues facing contemporary business. Chapter 3 deals with economic challenges, and Chapter 4 focuses on the difficulties and opportunities faced by firms competing in world markets.

Summary of Learning Objectives

[1] Distinguish between business and not-for-profit organizations.

Business consists of all profit-seeking activities that provide goods and services necessary to an economic system. Not-for-profit organizations are business-like establishments whose primary objectives involve social, political, governmental, educational, or similar functions—instead of profits.

Assessment Check Answers ☑

1.1 What activity lies at the heart of every business endeavor? At the heart of every business endeavor is an exchange between a buyer and a seller.

1.2 What are the primary objectives of a not-for-profit organization? Not-for-profit organizations place public service above profits, although they need to raise money in order to operate and achieve their social goals.

[2] Identify and describe the factors of production.

The factors of production consist of four basic inputs: natural resources, capital, human resources, and entrepreneurship. Natural resources include all productive inputs that are useful in their natural states. Capital includes technology, tools, information, and physical facilities. Human resources include anyone who works for the firm. Entrepreneurship is the willingness to take risks to create and operate a business.

Assessment Check Answers ☑

2.1 Identify the four basic inputs to an economic system. The four basic inputs are natural resources, capital, human resources, and entrepreneurship.

2.2 List four types of capital. Four types of capital are technology, tools, information, and physical facilities.

[3] Describe the private enterprise system, including basic rights and entrepreneurship.

The private enterprise system is an economic system that rewards firms for their ability to perceive and serve the needs and demands of consumers. Competition in the private enterprise system ensures success for firms that satisfy consumer demands. Citizens in a private enterprise economy enjoy the rights to private property, profits, freedom of choice, and competition. Entrepreneurship drives economic growth.

Assessment Check Answers ☑

3.1 What is an alternative term for private enterprise system? Capitalism is an alternative word for private enterprise system.

3.2 What is the most basic freedom under the private enterprise system? The most basic freedom is the right to private property.

3.3 What is an entrepreneur? An entrepreneur is a risk taker who is willing to start, own, and operate a business.

[4] Identify the six eras of business, and explain how the relationship era—including alliances, technology, and environmental concerns—influences contemporary business.

The six historical eras are the Colonial period, the Industrial Revolution, the age of industrial entrepreneurs, the production era, the marketing era, and the relationship era. In the Colonial period, businesses were small and rural, emphasizing agricultural production. The Industrial Revolution brought factories and mass production to business. The age of industrial entrepreneurs built on the Industrial Revolution through an expansion in the number and size of firms. The production era focused on the growth of factory operations through assembly lines and other efficient internal processes. During and following the Great Depression, businesses concentrated on finding markets for their products through advertising and selling, giving rise to the marketing era. In the relationship era, businesspeople focus on developing and sustaining long-term relationships with customers and other businesses. Technology promotes innovation and communication, while alliances create a competitive advantage through partnerships. Concern for the environment also helps build strong relationships with customers.

Assessment Check Answers ☑

4.1 What was the Industrial Revolution? The Industrial Revolution began around 1750 in England and moved business operations from an emphasis on independent, skilled workers to a factory system that mass-produced items.

4.2 During which era was the idea of branding developed? The idea of branding began in the marketing era.

4.3 What is the difference between transaction management and relationship management? Transaction management is an approach that focuses on building, promoting, and selling enough products to cover costs and earn profits. Relationship management is the collection of activities that build and maintain ongoing ties with customers and other parties.

[5] Explain how today's business workforce and the nature of work itself is changing.

The workforce is changing in several significant ways: (1) it is aging and the labor pool is shrinking, and (2) it is becoming increasingly diverse. The nature of work has shifted toward services and a focus on information. More firms now rely on outsourcing, offshoring, and nearshoring to produce goods or fulfill services and functions that were previously handled in-house or in-country. In addition, today's workplaces are becoming increasingly flexible, allowing employees to work from different locations and through different relationships. And companies are fostering innovation through teamwork and collaboration.

Assessment Check Answers ✅

5.1 Define *outsourcing,* *offshoring,* **and** *nearshoring.*
Outsourcing involves using outside vendors to produce goods or fulfill services and functions that were once handled in-house. Offshoring is the relocation of business processes to lower-cost locations overseas. Nearshoring is the outsourcing of production or services to nations near a firm's home base.

5.2 Describe the importance of collaboration and employee partnership. Businesses are increasingly focusing on collaboration, rather than on individuals working alone. No longer do employees just put in their time at a job they hold their entire career. The new employer–employee partnership encourages teamwork and creative thinking, problem solving, and innovation. Managers are trained to listen to and respect employees.

⌐6⌐ Identify the skills and attributes that managers need to lead businesses in the 21st century.

Today's managers need vision, the ability to perceive marketplace needs and the way their firm can satisfy them. Critical-thinking skills and creativity allow managers to pinpoint problems and opportunities and plan novel solutions. Finally, managers are dealing with rapid change, and they need skills to help lead their organizations through shifts in external and internal conditions.

Assessment Check Answers ✅

6.1 Why is vision an important managerial quality?
Managerial vision allows a firm to innovate and adapt to meet changes in the marketplace.

6.2 What is the difference between creativity and critical thinking? Critical thinking is the ability to analyze and assess information to pinpoint problems or opportunities. Creativity is the capacity to develop novel solutions to perceived organizational problems.

⌐7⌐ Outline the characteristics that make a company admired by the business community.

A company is usually admired for its solid profits, stable growth, a safe and challenging work environment, high-quality goods and services, and business ethics and social responsibility.

Assessment Check Answers ✅

7.1 Define *business ethics* **and** *social responsibility.*
Business ethics refers to the standards of conduct and moral values involving decisions made in the work environment. Social responsibility is a management philosophy that includes contributing resources to the community, preserving the natural environment, and developing or participating in nonprofit programs designed to promote the well-being of the general public.

7.2 Identify three criteria used to judge whether a company might be considered admirable. Criteria in judging whether companies are admirable include three of the following: solid profits, stable growth, a safe and challenging work environment, high-quality goods and services, and business ethics and social responsibility.

▮ Business Terms You Need to Know

business 5	entrepreneurship 9	branding 15	strategic alliance 16
profits 5	private enterprise system 9	brand 15	diversity 21
not-for-profit	capitalism 9	transaction	outsourcing 22
organizations 5	competition 9	management 15	offshoring 22
factors of production 7	competitive differentiation 9	relationship era 16	nearshoring 22
natural resources 7	private property 10	relationship	vision 23
capital 7	entrepreneur 11	management 16	critical thinking 23
human resources 8	consumer orientation 15	technology 16	creativity 23

▮ Review Questions

1. Why is business so important to a country's economy?

2. In what ways are not-for-profit organizations a substantial part of the U.S. economy? What challenges do not-for-profits face?

3. Identify and describe the four basic inputs that make up factors of production. Give an example of each factor of production that an auto manufacturer might use.

4. What is a private enterprise system? What four rights are critical to the operation of capitalism? Why would capitalism function poorly in a society that does not ensure these rights for its citizens?

5. In what ways is entrepreneurship vital to the private enterprise system?

6. Identify the six eras of business in the United States. How were businesses changed during each era?

7. Describe the focus of the most recent era of U.S. business. How is this different from previous eras?

8. Define *partnership* and *strategic alliance*. How might a motorcycle dealer and a local radio station benefit from an alliance?

9. Identify the major changes in the workforce that will affect the way managers build a world-class work-force in the 21st century. Why is brainpower so important?

10. Identify four qualities that the "new" managers of the 21st century must have. Why are these qualities important in a competitive business environment?

Projects and Teamwork Applications

1. The entrepreneurial spirit fuels growth in the U.S. economy. Choose a company that interests you—one you have worked for or dealt with as a customer—and read about the company in the library or visit its Web site. Learn what you can about the company's early history: Who founded it and why? Is the founder still with the organization? Do you think the founder's original vision is still embraced by the company? If not, how has the vision changed?

2. Brands distinguish one company's goods or services from its competitors. Each company you purchase from hopes that you will become loyal to its brand. Some well-known brands are Burger King, Coca-Cola, Hilton, and Old Navy. Choose a type of good or service you use regularly and identify the major brands associated with it. Are you loyal to a particular brand? Why or why not?

3. More and more businesses are forming strategic alliances to become more competitive. Sometimes, businesses pair up with not-for-profit organizations in a relationship that is beneficial to both. Choose a company whose goods or services interest you, such as Timberland, FedEx, General Mills, or Target. On your own or with a classmate, research the firm on the Internet to learn about its alliances with not-for-profit organizations. Then describe one of the alliances, including goals and benefits to both parties. Create a presentation for your class.

4. This chapter describes how the nature of the workforce is changing: the population is aging, the labor pool is shrinking, the workforce is becoming more diverse, the nature of work is changing, the workplace is becoming more flexible and mobile, and employers are fostering innovation and collaboration among their employees. Form teams of two to three students. Select a company and research how that company is responding to changes in the workforce. When you have completed your research, be prepared to present it to your class. Choose one of the following companies or select your own: State Farm Insurance, Archer Daniels Midland, 3M, Marriott, or Dell.

5. Many successful companies today use technology to help them improve their relationship management. Suppose a major supermarket chain's management team has asked you to assess its use of technology for this purpose. On your own or with a classmate, visit one or two local supermarkets and also explore their corporate Web sites. Note the ways in which firms in this industry already use technology to connect with their customers, and list at least three ideas for new ways or improvements to existing ones. Present your findings to the class as if they represented the management team.

Web Assignments

1. **Using search engines.** Gathering information is one of the most popular applications of the Web. Using two of the major search engines, such as Google and Bing, search the Web for information pertaining to brand and relationship management. Sort through your results—you're likely to gets thousands of "hits"—and identify the three most useful. What did you learn from this experience regarding the use of a search engine?

   http://www.google.com

   http://www.bing.com

2. **Companies and not-for-profits.** In addition to companies, virtually all not-for-profit organizations have Web sites. Four Web sites are listed below, two for companies (Alcoa and Sony) and two for not-for-profits (Cleveland Clinic and National Audubon Society). What is the purpose of each Web site? What type of information is available? How are the sites similar? How are they different?

   http://www.alcoa.com

   http://www.sony.com

   http://www.clevelandclinic.org

   http://www.audubon.org

3. **Characteristics of U.S. workforce.** Visit the Web site listed below. It is the home page for the *Statistical Abstract of the United States*. Published annually by the U.S. Census Bureau, the *Statistical Abstract* is a good source of basic demographic and economic data. Click on "Labor Force, Employment, and

Earnings." Use the relevant data tables to prepare a brief profile of the U.S. workforce (gender, age, educational level, and so forth). How is this profile expected to change over the next 10 to 20 years?

http://www.census.gov/compendia/statab/

Note: Internet Web addresses change frequently. If you don't find the exact sites listed, you may need to access the organization's home page and search from there or use a search engine such as Bing or Google.

Herman Miller Has Designs on the Future

Michigan-based Herman Miller is best known as the world's second-largest office furniture maker. But did you know it also focuses on "green" production and design? The company produces a programmable energy and data management system for office buildings, publishes a magazine about future trends, and supports environmental initiatives—like the U.S. Green Building Council. It is also involved in recycling its waste and using resources from renewable supply sources. The firm's broader focus is helping it establish new relationships with customers—and prosper.

Herman Miller's employees participate in the management and ownership of their firm. All full-time employees with one month of service are entitled to own stock in the company. With a real stake in the success of their firm, the staff focuses on quality and customer satisfaction.

Herman Miller sees its mission as solving people's problems. According to CEO Brian Walker, "We rarely start off saying, 'We just want a chair in this price point.' More often, we say, 'Here's a problem area that we see for folks. How do we solve it?' ... If you begin by trying to solve the problem, you get a different outcome than [by] saying, 'We need to go do a chair that's $200.' " This problem-solving approach applies to all the firm's activities.

The company also tries to think creatively by engaging it what it calls "global scenario planning." In that effort, staff members think beyond their day-to-day activities and try to imagine what changes may happen in the world a few years down the road. Then they try to devise strategies to meet that vision. Because of the looming presence of the Chinese market, Herman Miller executives and a team of designers visited the country to assess its challenges and opportunities. Of that trip, Walker says it "became clear that we were going to have to create some designs very specific to that marketplace and we would have to hire local people, both on the design and management side, to really understand the Chinese culture and be sensitive to it."

Design innovation comes easily to Herman Miller, but it doesn't necessarily come from within. The company outsources its creative work to a network of award-winning independent designers for what Walker calls "a fresh perspective on existing or emerging problems." He doesn't limit design to internal staff because that would limit the ideas considered. He wants instead to draw from fresh eyes and talent to create truly innovative designs. That strategy is working: more than 50 Herman Miller designs are in the permanent collections of major museums, such as New York's Museum of Modern Art, the Whitney Museum of American Art, the Smithsonian, and other institutions worldwide.

Here the company demonstrates its flexibility: "The central thing that we've learned," says Walker, "is a willingness to follow and give ourselves over to these designers ... following them to places that we may question in the beginning." The bottom line is that creative problem solving drives all the firm's efforts. The goal is to create great designs that solve real problems and creates commercial value. That combination is a winning formula for the company and its customers.

Questions for Critical Thinking

1. Explain how innovation, creativity, and flexibility have played a role in Herman Miller's success.

2. What kind of relationships does Herman Miller seem to have with its employees? With its customers? With its outside designers?

Sources: "Profits with Purpose: Herman Miller, Inc.," *Fast Company,* http://www.fastcompany.com, accessed February 20, 2009; "Herman Miller's Creative Network," *BusinessWeek,* February 15, 2008, http://www.businessweek.com; "Inside the Herman Miller Supply Chain: CEO Brian Walker Responds," *Harvard Business Review,* February 13, 2008, http://www.hbrgreen.org; Brad Kennedy, "Herman Miller: Business as Unusual," *IndustryWeek,* July 26, 2007, http://www.industryweek.com.

Among the many business projects launched by entrepreneur Paul English is a Web site called gethuman.com, designed to help frustrated consumers short-cut their way through large companies' automated phone systems. English's main job, however, is running a popular travel search engine he co-founded with Steve Hafner called Kayak.com, and in keeping with his fanatical focus on good customer service (just what those automated phone systems often don't provide), he and Kayak's engineers take regular turns personally responding to customers' e-mails and telephone calls. To those who say he could get the customer service job done for much less than an engineer's salary, English says, "If you make the engineers answer e-mails and phone calls from the customers, the second or third time they get the same question, they'll actually stop what they're doing and fix the code. Then we don't have those questions any more."

When English, who is also the company's chief technology officer, takes the calls himself, he's likely to give out his personal cell phone number and tell the caller, "If you have any follow-up questions, my name is Paul English; I'm the co-founder of the company." Only a handful of people will call him back, he says, "but they're blown away when I do that."

Kayak's staff of about 100 employees all talk, Twitter, or e-mail customers every day. Their work supports a Web site that lets millions of users compare prices for air travel, hotels, vacation deals, and rental cars. There are offices in Connecticut, where Hafner lives, Massachusetts, where English lives, and California, where the two bought a competing firm in 2007, as well as local sites across Europe. Hafner and English phone or instant-message each other every day. "We can practically read each other's minds," says English. "If an issue comes up, I know how he's going to weigh in and vice versa. We trust each other." They also trust their engineers and encourage them to chime in with solutions to problems.

English, who has founded three other firms and sold one of them to Intuit several years ago, is an early riser who describes himself as having "more ideas than I can get done in a day." After checking e-mail, practicing yoga, and taking his son to school, he arrives at work for a day that might start with meetings, including with nonprofits like Partners in Health or Village Health Works in which he plays an advisory role. "There are certain fundamental rights that I believe all people should have," he says. "Kids shouldn't be dying of drinking dirty water." English likes to leave half his day free of scheduled appointments and spend the time walking around the office's open-plan environment to "see what's going on and work on product issues and design strategy."

Acknowledging the company's growing success, and mindful that it needed more sophisticated marketing to keep it in the forefront of travel customers' minds, Kayak recently launched a national advertising campaign, which the cofounders took an active part in shaping. With a new logo and the tagline, "Search one and done," Kayak.com hopes to make more people aware that, as their ad agency's founder says, "it doesn't make sense to start their travel search anywhere else."

Questions for Critical Thinking

1. How does Paul English typify an entrepreneur? In what ways do you think his experience, background, or attitudes are unusual for an entrepreneur?

2. How well do you think Kayak.com manages its relationships with its users? If it grows considerably larger over the next few years, how do you think this may change that relationship?

Sources: "Kayak Launches National Advertising Campaign," *PR Newswire*, February 9, 2010; company Web site, http://www.kayak.com, accessed February 4, 2010; Paul English, "The Way I Work," *Inc.*, February 2, 2010, http://www.inc.com.

New Harvest Coffee Roasters Brews Up Fresh Business

If you're one of those people for whom the scent of freshly roasted coffee is irresistible, you have something in common with RikKleinfeldt. Kleinfeldt, the co-founder and president of New Harvest Coffee Roasters, is a self-pro-claimed coffee fanatic. He dwells on the aroma and flavor of coffee. He measures the freshness of roasted coffee in hours and days, instead of weeks and months. Kleinfeldt started New Harvest Coffee Roasters ten years ago as a way to pay homage to fresh coffee and build a business around it.

Kleinfeldt observes Starbucks' tremendous success at cre-ating gathering places for people to enjoy coffee and tea—as well as baked goods—in a relaxed social atmosphere. But he also notes with humor that, although cafes and coffee bars were thriving a decade ago, these popular hang-outs "weren't really about coffee. They were about smoothies and cookies. I thought, maybe it's time to get back to basics and roast some coffee." Kleinfeldt recalls that friends and col-leagues—fellow coffee fans—felt the same way. He believed that he had a basis to start a business. "We're coffee peo-ple," he explains. "There is a like-minded group of people."

Kleinfeldt also points out that the movement toward locally grown or produced foods has been a big help in establishing and building support for his business. "The idea of local coffee starts with the local roaster," he explains. Although the coffee beans themselves are grown else-where—mostly on farms in Costa Rica—they are roasted at New Harvest's facility in Rhode Island, where the company is based. "Freshness is a huge factor" in a good cup of cof-fee, says Kleinfeldt. "Once it's roasted, it's good for about two to twelve days, which is a good incentive to buy local."

Buying local is exactly what retailers and coffee shops like Blue State Coffee do, creating a collaborative relationship with New Harvest. Alex Payson, COO of Blue State Coffee—a thriving shop in Rhode Island—observes that most of his customers live within a five or ten-minute walk from his business. Blue State customers are educated about the coffee they drink. "They want to *know*," says Payson smiling. "We connect with our coffee farmers. Our customers ask about the story *behind* our coffee," includ-ing farming practices and working conditions. Payson and his colleagues from New Harvest have traveled together to some of the coffee farms in Costa Rica that grow the beans they purchase. In fact, loyal customers can view the progress of trips like this on New Harvest's Facebook page.

Relationships with companies like Blue State Coffee as well as with consumers are the basis for New Harvest's growth as a business. "We need strategic alliances," says RikKleinfeldt. "Blue State is a great example of that. "They buy into what we're doing and we support what they are doing. They collaborate with us—what's good for Blue State is also good for New Harvest." Blue State educates its customers and employees about the benefits of buying from a local firm like New Harvest, which in turn works with certified organic, free trade growers. When Blue State's workers are able to discuss their products knowledgeably with customers—including where and how they are grown, harvested and roasted—a relationship is developed.

Sharing activities, comments, news, and anecdotes with customers, retailers, and coffee shops through social media such as Facebook and Twitter allows New Harvest to broaden its base without spending more dollars on mar-keting and advertising. These connections also put a per-sonal face on the company and allow New Harvest to gain important knowledge about the views and preferences of its customers. In addition, they provide valuable opportuni-ties to showcase some of the company's work in the com-munity as well as its support for organizations such as the Rainforest Alliance and New England GreenStart.

"Our mission is to be the leader in our region in developing the palate and expectations of coffee drinkers, in order to create a permanent market for the coffee pro-duced by passionate and skilled growers," states the New Harvest Web site. For RikKleinfeldt's company and custom-ers, coffee is much more than a hot cup of joe in the morn-ing. Coffee—organically grown, freshly roasted, and served locally—represents a sustainable way to do business.

Questions for Critical Thinking

1. Give examples of each of the four factors of production that New Harvest must rely on to be a successful operation. How does each contribute to the firm's success?

2. Visit New Harvest's Facebook page. Note specific examples of the ways in which the firm is using social media to manage its relationships.

3. RikKleinfeldt notes the importance of strategic alliances with firms like Blue State Coffee. Describe how you think New Harvest benefits from alliances with not-for-profit organizations such as Rainforest Alliance, New England GreenStart, and Rhode Island PBS.

4. New Harvest builds much of its reputation on its efforts toward environmental sustainability. How does this reputation affect its relationship with consumers?

Sources: New Harvest Web site, http://www.newharvestcoffee.com, accessed August 18, 2010; Blue State Coffee Web site, http://www.bluestatecoffee.com, accessed August 18, 2010.

Learning Objectives

[1] Explain the concepts of business ethics and social responsibility.

[2] Describe the factors that influence business ethics.

[3] List the stages in the development of ethical standards, and discuss how organizations shape ethical behavior.

[4] Describe how businesses' social responsibility is measured, and summarize the responsibilities of business to the general public, customers, and employees.

[5] Explain why investors and the financial community are concerned with business ethics and social responsibility.

Today's Environment for Business Ethics and Related Social Issues

Entropy Surfboards Ride the Green Wave

Pioneers in many fields have changed our world. Creative businesspeople are a force for positive change, especially when it comes to protecting and preserving the natural environment. Santa Monica, California–based Entropy Surfboards was started by two surfing brothers—Desi and Rey Banatao—who had a different idea about how their products could be manufactured.

Despite their reputation for being free spirits, surfers tend to be traditionalists when it comes to performance. They want their boards to meet strict standards to carve the waves efficiently. Surfboards have long been made from toxic petroleum-based chemicals that also require large amounts of energy. Because of their light weight and durability, polyurethane and fiberglass are the most common construction materials. Yet both are environmental toxins. And when a surfer is ready to toss out an old board, it ends up in a landfill.

Entropy is trying to change that. Convinced that a surfboard can be as green as the ocean itself, Desi and Rey Banatao put their technology education to work on the sport they love. "Our dad gave us the idea to start the company, to make use of our tech degrees," recalls Rey. Their entry into the market was well timed because of the interest in environmentally friendly products. Also, a void occurred in the industry when the major supplier of low-cost surfboard cores was shut down. The Environmental Protection Agency had investigated the company because of the toxic gases that were emitted during production. The Banataos quickly went to work on their own alternative, researching the chemical and mechanical behavior of bio-composites and completing their first bio-boards just two years later. "For us, [the new board] means optimizing the balance between choice of materials, techniques, and performance," notes Rey.

The core, also called a *blank*, of an Entropy surfboard is made with a foam derived from sugar-beet oil instead of polyurethane. The beet polymer, developed by partner firm Ice-Nine, is nearly identical to polyurethane but is processed using fewer toxic chemicals. The blank is then wrapped in hemp and bamboo cloth and coated with a material derived from pine instead of a traditional epoxy resin. Where plastic is necessary, Entropy uses a bio-based material. The overall result, claims the company, is a 75 percent reduction in the use of petroleum-based materials. The Banataos refer to their construction process as an ecosystem. "Just like an actual ecosystem, all the different components work together and depend on each other to improve the whole thing," observes Rey.

Surfboards are generally produced by small workshops, and Entropy's are no exception. The surfboard shapers, as they are called, must outfit their shops and learn new manufacturing techniques. But these alternative processes benefit the shapers because the toxins and fumes are greatly reduced, creating fewer health hazards for workers.

Building boards with environmentally sustainable materials and processes is fine, but the boards have to perform. Surfers must be convinced that these boards can stand up to the stresses of monster waves. Entropy promises that its boards meet the highest standards. They are lightweight and durable, and each model matches features in its traditional counterparts. The Pocket Rocket is highly maneuverable, offering easy paddling and wave catching. The Kampachi has a raised deck for paddling power and narrow rails for quick turns. Finally comes the important issue of price. Of necessity, the new technologies are cost competitive; otherwise, the boards won't sell.

Now that the manufacture of their bio-boards is under way, Rey and Desi are looking further into the future. What happens to boards that have outlived their useful life? The brothers are researching ways to reuse worn out boards in their ecosystem of production so that the materials can be recycled into the next generation of boards. Although they have not quite solved that problem yet, the Banataos are confident that surfboard recycling represents the wave of the future. "At the end of the day, innovation is our only way to compete with the rest of the world," predicts Rey. "Whether it's innovation in shape, materials, or construction, we've got to keep progressing."[1]

Entropy Surfboards's efforts to create sustainable operations are not unique in the world of business—they just occur on a smaller scale than those of many other firms. Many companies are concerned about the environment and their societies. Sometimes that means growing more slowly than they might or reducing short-term profits for longer, sustained benefits. In Entropy's case, it means not only changing its own operations to help the environment but also persuading consumers that they should change their view of a sport they love.

Although most organizations strive to combine ethical behavior with profitable operation, some have struggled to overcome major ethical lapses in recent years. Ethical failures in a number of large or well-known firms led to lawsuits, indictments, and judgments against firms. The image of the CEO—and of business in general—suffered as the evening news carried reports of executives pocketing millions of dollars in compensation while their companies floundered.

But sometimes bad news is a prelude to good news. In the wake of such stories, both the government and companies have renewed their efforts to conduct themselves in an ethical manner and one that reflects a

responsibility to society, to consumers, and to the environment. In 2004 the Federal Sentencing Commission strengthened its guidelines for ethics compliance programs, and more and more firms began to pay attention to formulating more explicit standards and procedures for ethical behavior. Companies also began to recognize the enormous impact of setting a good example rather than a bad one. Today you are likely to hear about the goodwill that companies such as Target Corporation, Ford Motor Company, and Starbucks generate when they give back to their communities through youth reading programs, undertake recycling or energy-conservation programs, or seek to pay fair prices to suppliers.

As we discussed in Chapter 1, the underlying aim of business is to serve customers at a profit. But most companies today try to do more than that, looking for ways to give back to customers, society, and the environment. Sometimes they face difficult questions in the process. When does a company's self-interest conflict with society's and customers' well-being? And must the goal of seeking profits conflict with upholding high principles of right and wrong? In response to the second question, a growing number of businesses of all sizes are answering no.

Concern for Ethical and Societal Issues

An organization that wants to prosper over the long term is well advised to consider **business ethics**, the standards of conduct and moral values governing actions and decisions in the work environment. Businesses also must take into account a wide range of social issues, including how a decision will affect the environment, employees, and customers. These issues are at the heart of *social responsibility*, whose primary objective is the enhancement of society's welfare through philosophies, policies, procedures, and actions. In short, businesses must find the delicate balance between doing what is right and doing what is profitable. In 2010, General Motors announced that it would begin full-scale production of the fully electric plug-in hybrid Chevrolet Volt. The Volt will run for 40 miles after its battery pack is charged at an ordinary household outlet. After that, an internal-combustion engine takes over—to generate electricity to power the car farther. Planning to offer the car in limited markets at first, GM hopes to woo buyers with the prospect of owning a car that can achieve an astonishing 150 miles per gallon of liquid fuel.[2]

In business, as in life, deciding what is right or wrong in a given situation does not always involve a clear-cut choice. Firms have many responsibilities—to customers, to employees, to investors, and to society as a whole. Sometimes conflicts arise in trying to serve the different needs of these separate constituencies. The ethical values of executives and individual employees at all levels can influence the decisions and actions a business takes. Throughout your own career, you will encounter many situations in which you will need to weigh right and wrong before making a decision or taking action. So we begin our discussion of business ethics by focusing on individual ethics.

Business ethics are also shaped by the ethical climate within an organization. Codes of conduct and ethical standards play increasingly significant roles in businesses in which doing the right thing is both supported and applauded. This chapter demonstrates how a firm can create a framework to encourage—and even demand—high standards of ethical behavior and social responsibility from its employees. The chapter also considers the complex question of what business owes to society and how societal forces mold the actions of businesses. Finally, it examines the influence of business ethics and social responsibility on global business.

Assessment Check ✔

1. To whom do businesses have responsibilities?
2. If a firm is meeting all its responsibilities to others, why do ethical conflicts arise?

PhotoAlto / Frederic Cirou / Getty Images, Inc.

You will encounter many decisions in your career. How you choose to handle them will shape your ethical values.

The Contemporary Ethical Environment

Business ethics are now in the spotlight as never before. Companies realize that they have to work harder to earn the trust of the general public, and many have taken on the challenge as if their very survival depends on it. This movement toward *corporate social responsibility* should benefit all—consumers, the environment, and the companies themselves.

Most business owners and managers have built and maintained enduring companies without breaking the rules. One example of a firm with a longstanding commitment to ethical practice is Johnson & Johnson, the giant multinational manufacturer of healthcare products. The most admired pharmaceutical maker and the ninth-most-admired company in the world, according to *Fortune*, Johnson & Johnson has abided by the same basic code of ethics, its well-known Credo, for more than 50 years. The Credo, reproduced in Figure 2.1, remains the ethical standard against which the company's employees periodically evaluate how well their firm is performing. Management is pledged to address any lapses that are reported.[3]

Many companies are conscious of how ethical standards can translate into concern for the environment. In the fall of 2009, Walmart announced a plan to pursue three sustainability goals:

1. to use only renewable energy sources

2. to recycle all of its waste

3. to sell products that "sustain people and the environment," according to Matt Kistler, the company's senior vice president for sustainability.

That summer, the company conducted a survey of its suppliers on their sustainability practices as a first step in developing a "sustainability index" to help its customers assess the impact—on the environment and on society—of products in its stores. In addition, so far 40 Walmart stores make use of photovoltaic cells that generate electricity directly from sunlight.[4]

Although not all companies set and meet high ethical standards, the ethical climate seems to be improving despite the recent recession. The National Business Ethics Survey, conducted by the Ethics Resource Center, found that 49 percent of employees surveyed "witnessed misconduct on the job" in 2009, down from 56 percent in 2007. More employees said they reported misconduct when they saw it, up to 63 percent in 2009 from 58 percent in 2007. However, about one-quarter of employees said that the recession had had a negative impact on their

FIGURE 2.1 Johnson & Johnson Credo

Our Credo

We believe our first responsibility is to the doctors, nurses and patients, to mothers and fathers and all others who use our products and services. In meeting their needs everything we do must be of high quality. We must constantly strive to reduce our costs in order to maintain reasonable prices. Customers' orders must be serviced promptly and accurately. Our suppliers and distributors must have an opportunity to make a fair profit.

We are responsible to our employees, the men and women who work with us throughout the world. Everyone must be considered as an individual. We must respect their dignity and recognize their merit. They must have a sense of security in their jobs. Compensation must be fair and adequate, and working conditions clean, orderly and safe. We must be mindful of ways to help our employees fulfill their family responsibilities. Employees must feel free to make suggestions and complaints. There must be equal opportunity for employment, development and advancement for those qualified. We must provide competent management, and their actions must be just and ethical.

We are responsible to the communities in which we live and work and to the world community as well. We must be good citizens—support good works and charities and bear our fair share of taxes. We must encourage civic improvements and better health and education. We must maintain in good order the property we are privileged to use, protecting the environment and natural resources.

Our final responsibility is to our stockholders. Business must make a sound profit. We must experiment with new ideas. Research must be carried on, innovative programs developed and mistakes paid for. New equipment must be purchased, new facilities provided and new products launched. Reserves must be created to provide for adverse times. When we operate according to these principles, the stockholders should realize a fair return.

Source: "Our Company: Our Credo," Johnson & Johnson Web site, accessed February 4, 2010, http://www.jnj.com, © Johnson & Johnson.

company's ethics culture. In such cases, misconduct rose 16 points. About 10 percent said their company had lowered its ethical standards in order to survive the recession.[5]

The **Sarbanes-Oxley Act of 2002** established new rules and regulations for securities trading and accounting practices. Companies are now required to publish their code of ethics, if they have one, and inform the public of any changes made to it. The law may actually motivate even more firms to develop written codes and guidelines for ethical business behavior. The federal government also created the U.S. Sentencing Commission to institutionalize ethics compliance programs that would establish high ethical standards and end corporate misconduct. The requirements for such programs are shown in Table 2.1.

The current ethical environment of business also includes the appointment of new corporate officers specifically charged with deterring wrongdoing and ensuring that ethical standards are met. Ethics compliance officers, whose numbers are rapidly rising, are responsible for conducting employee training programs that help spot potential fraud and abuse within the firm, investigating sexual harassment and discrimination charges, and monitoring any potential conflicts of interest. But practicing corporate social responsibility is more than just monitoring behavior. Many companies now adopt a three-pronged approach to ethics and social responsibility:

1. engaging in traditional corporate philanthropy, which involves giving to worthy causes

2. anticipating and managing risks

3. identifying opportunities to create value by doing the right thing.[6]

Sarbanes-Oxley Act of 2002 Federal legislation designed to deter and punish corporate and accounting fraud and corruption and to protect the interests of workers and shareholders through enhanced financial disclosures, criminal penalties on CEOs and CFOs who defraud investors, safeguards for whistleblowers, and establishment of a new regulatory body for public accounting firms.

Table 2.1	Minimum Requirements for Ethics Compliance Programs

- Compliance standards and procedures. Establish standards and procedures, such as codes of ethics and identification of areas of risk, capable of reducing misconduct or criminal activities.

- High-level personnel responsibility. Assign high-level personnel, such as boards of directors and top executives, the overall responsibility to actively lead and oversee ethics compliance programs.

- Due care in assignments. Avoid delegating authority to individuals with a propensity for misconduct or illegal activities.

- Communication of standards and procedures. Communicate ethical requirements to high-level officials and other employees through ethics training programs or publications that explain in practical terms what is required.

- Establishment of monitoring and auditing systems and reporting system. Monitor and review ethical compliance systems, and establish a reporting system employees can use to notify the organization of misconduct without fear of retribution.

- Enforcement of standards through appropriate mechanisms. Consistently enforce ethical codes, including employee discipline.

- Appropriate responses to the offense. Take reasonable steps to respond to the offense and to prevent and detect further violations.

- Self-reporting. Report misconduct to the appropriate government agency.

- Applicable industry practice or standards. Follow government regulations and industry standards.

Sources: "An Overview of the United States Sentencing Commission and the Federal Sentencing Guidelines," U.S. Sentencing Commission, http://www.epic-online.net; "The Relationship between Law and Ethics, and the Significance of the Federal Sentencing Guidelines for Organizations," Ethics and Policy Integration Center, http://www.ethicaledge.com; U.S. Sentencing Commission, "Sentencing Commission Toughens Requirements for Corporate Compliance and Ethics Programs," USSC news release, http://www.ussc.gov.

Individuals Make a Difference

In today's business environment, individuals can make the difference in ethical expectations and behavior. As executives, managers, and employees demonstrate their personal ethical principles—or lack of ethical principles—the expectations and actions of those who work for and with them can change.

What is the current status of individual business ethics in the United States? Although ethical behavior can be difficult to track or define in all circumstances, evidence suggests that unfortunately some individuals act unethically or illegally on the job. The National Business Ethics Survey identifies such behaviors as putting one's own interests ahead of the organization, lying to employees, misreporting hours worked, Internet abuse, and safety violations, among others.[7]

Technology seems to have expanded the range and impact of unethical behavior. For example, anyone with computer access to data has the potential to steal or manipulate the data or to shut down the system, even from a remote location. Recently Radisson Hotels alerted customers that their credit-card security system had experienced a data breach in some U.S.-based and Canadian hotels. The cost of dealing with a data breach can total up to $6.6 million per incident.[8] While some might shrug these occurrences away, in fact they have an impact on how investors, customers, and the general public view a firm. It is difficult to rebuild a tarnished image, and long-term customers may be lost.

Nearly every employee, at every level, wrestles with ethical questions at some point or another. Some rationalize questionable behavior by saying, "Everybody's doing it." Others act unethically because they feel pressured in their jobs or have to meet performance quotas. Yet some avoid unethical acts that don't mesh with their personal values and morals. To help you understand the differences in the ways individuals arrive at ethical choices, the next section focuses on how personal ethics and morals develop.

FIGURE 2.2 Stages of Moral and Ethical Development

Stage 1: Preconventional
Individual is mainly looking out for his or her own interests. Rules are followed only out of fear of punishment or hope of reward.

↓

Stage 2: Conventional
Individual considers the interests and expectations of others in making decisions. Rules are followed because it is a part of belonging to the group.

↓

Stage 3: Postconventional
Individual follows personal principles for resolving ethical dilemmas. He or she considers personal, group, and societal interests.

Development of Individual Ethics

Individuals typically develop ethical standards in the three stages shown in Figure 2.2: the preconventional, conventional, and postconventional stages. In stage 1, the preconventional stage, individuals primarily consider their own needs and desires in making decisions. They obey external rules only because they are afraid of punishment or hope to receive rewards if they comply.

In stage 2, the conventional stage, individuals are aware of and act in response to their duty to others, including their obligations to their family members, coworkers, and organizations. The expectations of these groups influence how they choose between what is acceptable and unacceptable in certain situations. Self-interest, however, continues to play a role in decisions.

Stage 3, the postconventional stage, represents the highest level of ethical and moral behavior. The individual is able to move beyond mere self-interest and duty and take the larger needs of society into account as well. He or she has developed personal ethical principles for determining what is right and can apply those principles in a wide variety of situations. One issue that you may face at work is an ethically compromised or "sticky" situation; the "Business Etiquette" feature lists some tips to consider in deciding how to handle such a dilemma.

An individual's stage in moral and ethical development is determined by a huge number of factors. Experiences help shape responses to different situations.

A person's family, educational, cultural, and religious backgrounds can also play a role, as can the environment within the firm. Individuals can also have different styles of deciding ethical dilemmas, no matter what their stage of moral development.

To help you understand and prepare for the ethical dilemmas you may confront in your career, let's take a closer look at some of the factors involved in solving ethical questions on the job.

On-the-Job Ethical Dilemmas

In the fast-paced world of business, you will sometimes be called on to weigh the ethics of decisions that can affect not just your own future but possibly the futures of your fellow workers, your company, and its customers. As already noted, it's not always easy to distinguish between what is right and wrong in many business situations, especially when the needs and concerns of various parties conflict. In the recent past, some CEOs (or their companies) who were accused of wrongdoing simply claimed that they had no idea crimes were being committed, but today's top executives are making a greater effort to be informed of all activities taking place in their firms.

Many clothing retailers donate unworn, unsold garments to charities such as clothing banks. In January 2010, a graduate student discovered that the H&M store on New York's 34th Street was destroying unsold clothing instead. When she contacted store officials and then the company's headquarters in Sweden, her requests for information and offers of help to put H&M in contact with aid organizations went unanswered. She then contacted *The New York Times*, which published a story detailing how H&M—among other retailers—routinely mutilated unsold garments before discarding them to render them unsalable by street vendors or other black-market sellers. The New York City Clothing Bank, founded by the city's mayor during the 1980s, accepts unsold garments and slightly defaces them—not to destroy them but to protect retailers by negating the garments' street value. When

BusinessEtiquette

How to Handle Ethical Dilemmas at Work

How Can Business Support an Ethical Environment?

"Doing well begins with doing right," according to Sharon Allen, Deloitte LLP's chairman of the board. Her advice to companies in the current economy is to concentrate on ethics and by encouraging employees to work to high ethical standards, the organization will end up with strong performers.

Unethical behavior in the workplace can lead to lost earnings and damaged personal lives. In a recent survey the Association of Certified Fraud Examiners discovered that U.S. companies lose approximately 7 percent of their annual revenues to fraud. On the reverse side, companies that were deemed highly ethical on *Ethisphere*'s list saw increased growth.

Employees are eager to work for those companies that demonstrate good corporate social responsibility and high standards for ethical business conduct and customers put more trust into those organizations as well. To ensure the good ethical conduct for both employees and customers, companies should have ethical leaders, a code of ethics or similar policies, and ethics training for employees.

What Can You Do about an Ethical Dilemma?

The business journalist Suzy Welch claims that ethical dilemmas are difficult to resolve because we tend to jump to conclusions based on insufficient information. Welch suggests the following steps if you suspect unethical behavior in the office:

1 Get all the facts. Ask tactful questions of people you know are trustworthy—not sources of rumors or gossip. In return, beware of revealing anything told to you in confidence. Talk to your company's human resources department. Be investigative, not aggressive.

2 When you have the facts, ask yourself, Is this really a moral dilemma? Or is it a case of office politics? What may look like an ethical problem could be a power play in disguise.

3 If the situation really is an ethical dilemma, explain the issue to a trusted friend outside the company—and outside your family. That person may be able to take an unbiased view and advise you about what to do next.

Sources: Suzy Welch, "What to Do When Facing Ethical Problems at Work," *CNN*, www.cnn.com, August 3, 2009; Sharon Allen, "The New ROE: Return On Ethics," *Forbes.com*, www.forbes.com, July 21, 2009.

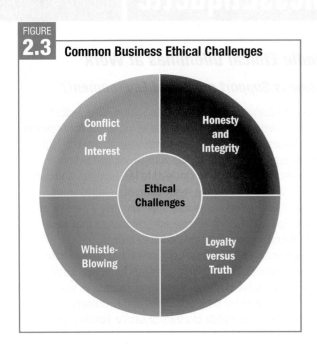

FIGURE 2.3 **Common Business Ethical Challenges**

Conflict of Interest

Honesty and Integrity

Ethical Challenges

Whistle-Blowing

Loyalty versus Truth

the story was published, H&M promised that it would stop destroying unsold clothing and instead donate the garments to charity. A company spokeswoman in New York declared, "It will not happen again. We are committed 100 percent to make sure this practice is not happening anywhere else, as it is not our standard practice."[9]

Businesses may sometimes refuse to purchase goods or services from a particular country because of civil rights abuses by the government of that country. Some of the world's largest and most prestigious jewelers, including Cartier and Tiffany & Co., announced that they would not purchase rubies and other gems from Myanmar (formerly Burma) because of the government's crackdown on protests by students and monks, as well as other civil rights violations. In addition, the United States and the European Union agreed to ban the import of gems from Myanmar.[10]

Solving ethical dilemmas is not easy. In many cases, each possible decision can have both unpleasant consequences and positive benefits that must be evaluated. The ethical issues that confront manufacturers with unsold merchandise are just one example of many different types of ethical questions encountered in the workplace. Figure 2.3 identifies four of the most common ethical challenges that businesspeople face: conflict of interest, honesty and integrity, loyalty versus truth, and whistle-blowing.

conflict of interest
Situation in which an employee must choose between a business's welfare and personal gain.

Conflict of Interest A **conflict of interest** occurs when a businessperson is faced with a situation in which an action benefiting one person or group has the potential to harm another. Conflicts of interest may pose ethical challenges when they involve the businessperson's own interests and those of someone to whom he or she has a duty or when they involve two parties to whom the businessperson has a duty. Lawyers, business consultants, or advertising agencies would face a conflict of interest if they represented two competing companies: a strategy that would most benefit one of the client companies might harm the other client. Similarly, a real estate agent would face an ethical conflict by representing both the buyer and seller in a transaction. Handling the situation responsibly would be possible, but it would also be difficult. A conflict may also exist between someone's personal interests and those of an organization or its customers. An offer of gifts or bribes for special treatment creates a situation in which the buyer, but not necessarily the company, may benefit personally.

A conflict of interest may also occur when one person holds two or more similar jobs in two different workplaces. Ethical ways to handle conflicts of interest include (1) avoiding them and (2) disclosing them. Some companies have policies against taking on clients who are competitors of existing clients. Most businesses and government agencies have written policies prohibiting employees from accepting gifts or specifying a maximum gift value. Or a member of a board of directors or committee might abstain from voting on a decision in which he or she has a personal interest. In other situations, people state their potential conflict of interest so that the people affected can decide whether to get information or help they need from another source instead.

integrity Adhering to deeply felt ethical principles in business situations.

Honesty and Integrity Employers highly value honesty and integrity. An employee who is honest can be counted on to tell the truth. An employee with **integrity** goes beyond truthfulness. Having integrity means adhering to deeply felt ethical principles in business situations. It includes doing what you say you will do and accepting responsibility for mistakes. Behaving with honesty and integrity inspires trust, and as a result, it can help build long-term relationships with customers, employers, suppliers, and the public. Employees, in turn, want their managers and the company as a whole to treat them honestly and with integrity.

Unfortunately, violations of honesty and integrity are all too common. Some people misrepresent their academic credentials and previous work experience on their résumés or job applications. Although it may seem tempting to embellish a résumé in a competitive job market, the act shows a lack of honesty and integrity—and eventually it will catch up with you. A recent news report details a city worker in Ohio, who after years of listing a bachelor's degree on her résumé had to admit that she only attended the school for six months and never graduated. She stepped down from her position.[11]

Employers and employees value honesty and integrity, but what should happen when employees misuse Internet privileges for personal purposes?

iStockphoto

Others steal from their employers by taking home supplies or products without permission or by carrying out personal business during the time they are being paid to work. For example, Internet misuse during the work day is increasing. Employees use the Internet during work hours for personal e-mail, shopping, gaming, and visiting bulletin boards and blogs or social networking sites such as Facebook and YouTube. The use of laptops, cell phones, and other wireless devices makes all of this misconduct easier to hide.[12] While the occurrence of such activity varies widely—and employers may feel more strongly about cracking down on some activities than others—most agree that Internet misuse is a problem. Some have resorted to electronic monitoring and surveillance. Compliance with laws regarding the privacy and security of client information is another major reason given for the continuing increase in such monitoring.

Loyalty versus Truth Businesspeople expect their employees to be loyal and to act in the best interests of the company. But when the truth about a company is not favorable, an ethical conflict can arise. Individuals may have to decide between loyalty to the company and truthfulness in business relationships. People resolve such dilemmas in various ways. Some place the highest value on loyalty, even at the expense of truth. Others avoid volunteering negative information but answer truthfully if someone asks them a specific question. People may emphasize truthfulness and actively disclose negative information, especially if the cost of silence is high, as in the case of operating a malfunctioning aircraft or selling tainted food items.

Whistle-Blowing When an individual encounters unethical or illegal actions at work, that person must decide what action to take. Sometimes it is possible to resolve the problem by working through channels within the organization. If that fails, the person should weigh the potential damages to the greater public good. If the damage is significant, a person may conclude that the only solution is to blow the whistle. **Whistle-blowing** is an employee's disclosure to company officials, government authorities, or the media of illegal, immoral, or unethical practices.

A whistle-blower must weigh a number of issues in deciding whether to come forward. Resolving an ethical problem within the organization can be more effective, assuming

whistle-blowing
Employee's disclosure to company officials, government authorities, or the media of illegal, immoral, or unethical practices committed by an organization.

higher-level managers cooperate. A company that values ethics will try to correct a problem, and staying at a company that does not value ethics may not be worthwhile. In some cases, however, people resort to whistle-blowing because they believe the unethical behavior is causing significant damage that outweighs the risk that the company will retaliate against the whistle-blower. Those risks have been real in some cases. State and federal laws protect whistle-blowers in certain situations, such as reports of discrimination, and the Sarbanes-Oxley Act of 2002 now requires that firms in the private sector provide procedures for anonymous reporting of accusations of fraud. Under the act, anyone who retaliates against an employee for taking concerns of unlawful conduct to a public official can be prosecuted. In addition, whistle-blowers can seek protection under the False Claims Act, a law that was passed in the 1800s, under which they can file a lawsuit on behalf of the government if they believe that a company has somehow defrauded the government. Charges against healthcare companies for fraudulent billing for Medicare or Medicaid are examples of this type of lawsuit. The American Recovery and Reinvestment Act of 2009—also known as the "stimulus package"—grants protection to other whistle-blowers. If an employee of a nonfederal organization (including state or local government) believes that organization has misused funds it received under the stimulus package, he or she will be protected against retaliation after reporting this information.[13]

Despite these protections, whistle-blowing still has its risks. For several years, George Green worked as an architect in Texas. He discovered activities of fraud on state construction projects including kickbacks and other gifts from contractors to supervisors in return for ignoring noncompliance issues. When Green reported the alleged illegal activities, he was instead investigated for abusing his sick days and making long-distance phone calls, and was subsequently fired. In order to clear his name, he filed a lawsuit under the Texas Whistleblower Act. Green won his lawsuit and was awarded $13.7 million in compensatory and punitive damages. Instead of collecting his judgment, the Texas Legislature refused to pay. Green lost everything—his job, his fiancée, and his home. "I lived all my life with what I thought was decency and courtesy, always respecting and deferring to authority," George Green says, ". . . I had truth on my side and lost. I lost everything but my self-respect."[14]

Obviously, whistle-blowing and other ethical issues arise relatively infrequently in firms with strong organizational climates of ethical behavior. The next section examines how a business can develop an environment that discourages unethical behavior among individuals.

How Organizations Shape Ethical Conduct

No individual makes decisions in a vacuum. Choices are strongly influenced by the standards of conduct established within the organizations where people work. Most ethical lapses in business reflect the values of the firms' corporate cultures.

As shown in Figure 2.4, development of a corporate culture to support business ethics happens on four levels:

1. ethical awareness
2. ethical reasoning

Assessment Check ✔

1. What role can an ethics compliance officer play in a firm?
2. What factors influence the ethical environment of a business?

3. ethical action

4. ethical leadership.

If any of these four factors is missing, the ethical climate in an organization will weaken.

Ethical Awareness

The foundation of an ethical climate is ethical awareness. As we have already seen, ethical dilemmas occur frequently in the workplace. So employees need help in identifying ethical problems when they occur. Workers also need guidance about how the firm expects them to respond.

One way for a firm to provide this support is to develop a **code of conduct**, a formal statement that defines how the organization expects employees to resolve ethical questions. Johnson & Johnson's Credo, presented earlier, is such a code. At the most basic level, a code of conduct may simply specify ground rules for acceptable behavior, such as identifying the laws and regulations that employees must obey. Other companies use their codes of conduct to identify key corporate values and provide frameworks that guide employees as they resolve moral and ethical dilemmas.

The aerospace giant Lockheed Martin, headquartered in Bethesda, Maryland, and with branch offices around the world, has issued a code of conduct to define its values and help employees put them into practice. The code of conduct emphasizes "maintaining a culture of integrity" and defines three basic core values: "do what's right; respect others; perform with excellence." The code applies to "all Lockheed Martin employees, members of the Board of Directors, agents, consultants, contract labor or others, when they are representing or acting for the corporation." All employees at every level are expected to treat fellow employees, suppliers, and customers with dignity and respect and to comply with environmental, health, and safety regulations. The code reminds leaders that their language and behavior must not put or even seem to put pressure on subordinates that might induce them to perform in a way that is contrary to the standards set forth in the code. The code also outlines procedures for reporting violations to a local company ethics officer, promising confidentiality and nonretaliation for problems reported in good faith. Lockheed Martin issues a copy of this code of conduct to each employee and also posts it (in more than 20 languages) on its Web site.[15]

Other firms incorporate similar codes in their policy manuals or mission statements; some issue a code of conduct or statement of values in the form of a small card that employees and managers can carry with them. Harley-Davidson has developed a brief code of ethics that employees can apply both at work and in their personal lives. It reads: "Tell the truth, keep your promises, be fair, respect the individual and encourage intellectual curiosity."

Ethical Education

Although a code of conduct can provide an overall framework, it cannot detail a solution for every ethical situation. Some ethical questions have black-and-white answers, but others

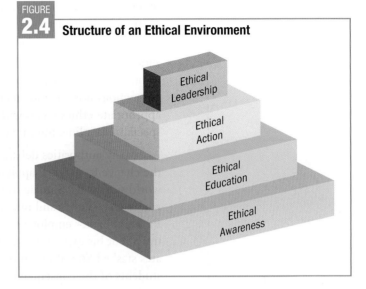

FIGURE 2.4 Structure of an Ethical Environment

Ethical Leadership

Ethical Action

Ethical Education

Ethical Awareness

code of conduct Formal statement that defines how an organization expects its employees to resolve ethical issues.

do not. Businesses must provide the tools employees need to evaluate the options and arrive at suitable decisions.

Many firms have either instituted their own ethics training programs or hired organizations such as Syrus Global, which provides outsourced ethics and compliance programs to businesses. Among other services, Syrus hosts employee reporting services with an anonymous hotline and an ethics case management system. It also helps companies develop appropriate ethics codes with ethics training customized to each company's needs, including specialized online, interactive training systems.[16]

Many authorities debate whether ethics can be taught, but training can give employees the chance to practice applying ethical values to hypothetical situations before they face real-world situations. Similar strategies are being used in many business school ethics programs, where case studies and practical scenarios work best. Convicted white-collar criminal Walter Pavlo, a former employee at telecommunications firm MCI, speaks at colleges and universities about his experiences in the firm and prison. Pavlo, who along with other MCI associates stashed $6 million in offshore accounts, speaks about his actions in an effort to warn students of the consequences of cheating.

Ethical Action

Codes of conduct and ethics training help employees recognize and reason through ethical problems. In addition, firms must provide structures and approaches that allow decisions to be turned into ethical actions. Texas Instruments gives its employees a reference card to help them make ethical decisions on the job. The size of a standard business card, it lists the following guidelines:

- Is the action legal?
- Does it comply with our values?
- If you do it, will you feel bad?
- How will it look in the newspaper?
- If you know it's wrong, don't do it!
- If you're not sure, ask.
- Keep asking until you get an answer.

Goals set for the business as a whole and for individual departments and employees can affect ethical behavior. A firm whose managers set unrealistic goals for employee performance may find an increase in cheating, lying, and other misdeeds, as employees attempt to protect themselves. In today's Internet economy, the high value placed on speed can create a climate in which ethical behavior is sometimes challenged. Ethical decisions often require careful and quiet thought, a challenging task in today's fast-paced business world.

Some companies encourage ethical action by providing support for employees faced with dilemmas. One common tool is an employee hotline, a telephone number that employees can call, often anonymously, for advice or to report unethical behavior they have witnessed. Ethics compliance officers at some firms, as mentioned previously, guide employees through ethical minefields.

Ethical Leadership

Executives must not only talk about ethical behavior but also demonstrate it in their actions. This requires employees to be personally committed to the company's core values and be willing to base their actions on them. The recent recession exposed executive-level misdeeds that damaged or even destroyed entire organizations and wiped out people's life savings. In the aftermath, two students at the Harvard Business School interviewed corporate leaders in their native India and Pakistan whom they regarded as highly moral. The students concluded that these "ethical mavericks" follow a moral code with three simple characteristics:

1. use clear, explicit language rather than euphemisms for corrupt behavior
2. encourage behavior that generates and fosters ethical values
3. practice moral absolutism, insisting on doing right, even if it proves financially costly.[17]

However, ethical leadership should also go one step further and charge each employee at every level with the responsibility to be an ethical leader. Everyone should be aware of problems and be willing to defend the organization's standards.

Unfortunately, not all organizations are able to build a solid framework of business ethics. Because the damage from ethical misconduct can powerfully affect a firm's __stakeholders__—customers, investors, employees, and the public—pressure is exerted on businesses to act in acceptable ways. But when businesses fail, the law must step in to enforce good business practices. Many of the laws that affect specific industries or individuals are described in other chapters in this book. For example, legislation affecting international business operations is discussed in Chapter 4. Laws designed to assist small businesses are examined in Chapter 5. Laws related to labor unions are described in Chapter 8. Legislation related to banking and the securities markets is discussed in Chapters 16 and 17. Finally, for an examination of the legal and governmental forces designed to safeguard society's interests when businesses fail at self-regulation, see Appendix A, "Business Law."

Acting Responsibly to Satisfy Society

A second major issue affecting business is the question of social responsibility. In a general sense, __social responsibility__ is management's acceptance of the obligation to consider profit, consumer satisfaction, and societal well-being of equal value in evaluating the firm's performance. It is the recognition that business must be concerned with the qualitative dimensions of consumer, employee, and societal benefits, as well as the quantitative measures of sales and profits, by which business performance is traditionally measured. Businesses may exercise social responsibility because such behavior is required by law, because it enhances the company's image, or because management believes it is the ethical course of action. The "Going Green" feature discusses the efforts of Starbucks to implement environmentally sound practices.

stakeholders Customers, investors, employees, and public affected by or with an interest in a company.

Assessment Check ✔

1. What is the preconventional stage in the development of ethical standards?

2. How can loyalty and truth come into conflict for an employee?

3. How does ethical leadership contribute to ethical standards throughout a company?

social responsibility Business's consideration of society's well-being and consumer satisfaction, in addition to profits.

Starbucks Introduces a New Store-Design Strategy

In June 2009, the coffee-selling giant Starbucks announced that as it builds new stores and renovates existing ones worldwide, the company plans to design them with two goals in mind: reflecting the character of the neighborhood and striving for a reduced environmental impact.

The project is part of Starbucks' efforts to reposition itself. Arthur Rubinfeld, the president of Starbucks Global Development, said, "We recognize the importance of continuously evolving with our customers' interests, lifestyles and values in order to stay relevant over the long term."

The company will employ local artisans and materials and use recycled and reclaimed materials to make each store unique. It has also commited itself to conserving water and energy, recycling where possible, and using "green" construction methods. Among its goals are:

- to use renewable resources for 50 percent of the energy used in its stores

- to make its stores 25 percent more energy efficient to reduce greenhouse gas emissions

- to meet U.S. Green Building Code LEED (Leadership in Energy and Environmental Design) certification standards for all its new stores

- to implement a 100 percent reusable or recyclable cup supply by 2015

- to have recycling in stores where it controls waste collection by 2015.

The company has already put some of these goals into practice. For instance, it reduces its prices by 10 cents for customers who bring their own travel cups. The company is also replacing incandescent light bulbs with LED bulbs to save energy and expense. Special signs will be installed in new and renovated stores to explain their "green" and sustainable features and construction methods.

Three stores now embody this new strategy: two in Starbucks' hometown of Seattle and one at the Paris Disney Village.

Questions for Critical Thinking

1. How do Starbucks' new plans for its stores reflect its sense of social responsibility?

2. How has Starbucks involved its customers in these efforts?

Sources: Company Web site, http://www.starbucks.com, accessed February 2010; Brian Clark Howard, "5 Major Companies Innovate by Going Green," *The Daily Green*, November 18, 2009, http://www.thedailygreen.com; Sharon van Schagen, "Starbucks Brews Global Green-Building Plan, Renovates Seattle Shop," *Grist*, June 30, 2009, http://www.thedailygreen.com; "Starbucks Reinvents the Store Experience to Speak to the Heart and Soul of Local Communities," June 25, 2009, http://news.starbucks.com.

Historically, a company's social performance has been measured by its contribution to the overall economy and the employment opportunities it provides. Variables such as total wages paid often indicate social performance. Although profits and employment remain important, today many factors contribute to an assessment of a firm's social performance, including providing equal employment opportunities; respecting the cultural diversity of employees; responding to environmental concerns; providing a safe, healthy workplace; and producing high-quality products that are safe to use.

A business is also judged by its interactions with the community. To demonstrate their social responsibility, many corporations highlight charitable contributions and community service in their annual reports and on their Web sites. The Mercadien Group, an accounting and business consulting firm based in Princeton, New Jersey, participates in the Toys for Tots program with the U.S. Marine Corps. The company's office is an official drop-off site for the program, and employees at all levels take part. Mercadien also invites its clients and other contacts to participate.[18]

Through its Box Tops for Education program, General Mills has helped more than 30,000 grade and middle schools across the nation to raise funds for everything from books to food service. According to the program's Web site, more than $200 million has been raised by consumers who cut out and submitted to participating schools "box top" coupons from General Mills's products such as Progresso soups, Green Giant vegetables, and cereals like Cheerios.[19]

Some firms measure social performance by conducting **social audits**, formal procedures that identify and evaluate all company activities that relate to social issues such as conservation,

social audits Formal procedure that identifies and evaluates all company activities that relate to social issues such as conservation, employment practices, environmental protection, and philanthropy.

employment practices, environmental protection, and philanthropy. The social audit informs management about how well the company is performing in these areas. Based on this information, management may revise current programs or develop new ones.

Outside groups may conduct their own evaluations of businesses. Various environmental, religious, and public-interest groups have created standards of corporate performance. Reports on many of these evaluations are available to the general public. The New York–based Council on Economic Priorities is one such group. Other groups publicize their evaluations and include critiques of the social responsibility performance of firms.

As Figure 2.5 shows, the social responsibilities of business can be classified according to its relationships to the general public, customers, employees, and investors and other members of the financial community. Many of these relationships extend beyond national borders.

Mercadien's participation in the Toys for Tots program highlights its commitment to the community in which they work and allows the firm to fulfill its social responsibility.

Responsibilities to the General Public

The responsibilities of business to the general public include dealing with public health issues, protecting the environment, and developing the quality of the workforce. Many would argue that businesses also have responsibilities to support charitable and social causes and organizations that work toward the greater public good. In other words, they should give back to the communities in which they earn profits. Such efforts are called *corporate philanthropy*.

Public-Health Issues One of the most complex issues facing business as it addresses its ethical and social responsibilities to the general public is public health. Central to the public-health debate is the question of what businesses should do about dangerous products such as tobacco and alcohol. Tobacco products represent a major health risk, contributing to heart disease, stroke, and cancer among smokers. Families and coworkers of smokers share this danger as well, as their exposure to secondhand smoke increases their risks for cancer, asthma, and respiratory infections. Many cities have not only banned smoking in public places, but also commercial businesses such as restaurants.

Heart disease, diabetes, and obesity have become major public health issues as the rates of these three conditions have been rising. A reported 5 million American children between the ages of 6 and 17 are

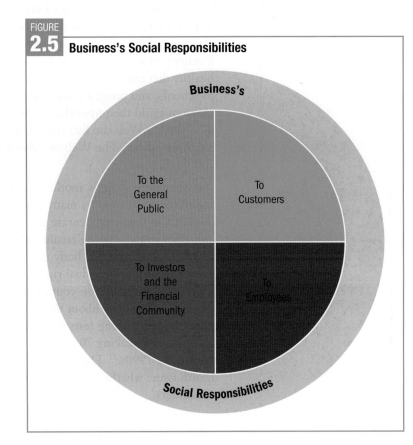

FIGURE
2.5 **Business's Social Responsibilities**

Business's

To the General Public

To Customers

To Investors and the Financial Community

To Employees

Social Responsibilities

To do their part to aid the general public, SUBWAY and the Jared Foundation focus on encouraging children to eat healthfully in the hopes of avoiding obesity problems later in life.

overweight. Three-quarters of obese teenagers will become obese adults at risk for these diseases. Jared Fogle became famous for losing 245 pounds over a two-year period through exercise and a diet that included SUBWAY sandwiches. He has since set up the Jared Foundation with the goal of fighting childhood obesity by encouraging children to develop healthy diet and exercise habits. Spreading his message through speaking tours, grants to schools, and programs for children and their families, Fogle says, "My goal is to help children avoid the physical and emotional hardships I went through living with obesity." SUBWAY's Web site lists the nutritional values of its menu items and sources of diet and nutrition advice. The Web site also features a linked page supporting the Jared Foundation and its mission.[20]

Substance abuse is another serious public health problem worldwide. Revelations of the use of illegal steroids by many athletes, particularly in professional baseball, highlights the difficulty of devising accurate tests for performance-enhancing and muscle-building drugs and fairly evaluating the results. Many of the drugs in question are so similar to compounds naturally present in the body that identification is extremely difficult. With regard to drug testing, athletes' individual rights to privacy have been questioned, particularly due to their widespread influence on youthful fans. Steroid use is on the rise among high school athletes, despite the publicity about the dangers of such drugs. Tougher penalties for professional players who fail drug tests are being formulated. In January 2010, Mark McGwire, who had hit a record-breaking 70 home runs in the 1998 season, admitted that he had used steroids during the 1990s.[21] The "Solving an Ethical Controversy" feature explores a related public health issue: whether advertisements for prescription drugs are informative or harmful to consumers.

Solving an Ethical Controversy

Are Prescription Drug Advertisements Helpful or Harmful to Consumers?

Since 1985 in the United States, drug manufacturers have used direct-to-consumer advertising (DTCA) to market name-brand prescription drugs. DTCA increased dramatically after 1997, when the Food and Drug Administration (FDA) no longer required detailed lists of possible side effects. In 2009, pharmaceutical companies spent $4.5 billion on advertising. New Zealand is the only other developed country where DTCA is legal.

Americans now spend more on prescription drugs than on any other area of health care. One reason is the sheer number of prescriptions. Another is that advertising costs have raised the prices of brand-name prescription drugs. Drug companies also market heavily to doctors. The medical community has voiced concern that DTCA may be harming both the public and the healthcare system.

Does direct-to-consumer advertising benefit the American public?

PRO

1. DTCA encourages people to ask their doctors about potentially harmful conditions that may be helped by nonsurgical treatment if caught early enough.

2. Drug companies use their profits to develop new drugs. This process involves considerable research and testing to win FDA approval of drugs that can improve or even save lives.

CON

1. Drug advertisements appeal to people's emotions while minimizing potential side effects. Advertisements may even persuade people to ask for unnecessary treatments.

2. Pharmaceutical companies usually advertise new drugs that have not been tested over time and are more expensive than slightly different, older drugs with well-known side effects. DTCA sometimes backfires.

Summary

Congress has repeatedly tried and failed to curb DTCA. Some proposals would end tax deductions for drug companies' advertising expenses or require a waiting period before advertising a new drug. Pharmaceutical companies have tried to introduce DTCA in Europe, but European Union countries voted overwhelmingly against even an "information to patients" section of a proposed regulation.

Sources: "U.S. Ad Spending Down Nine Percent . . ., Nielsen says," The Nielsen Company, February 24, 2010, http://en-us.nielsen.com; http://www.nytimes.com; "Should Prescription Drugs Be Advertised Directly to Consumers?" ProCon.org, http://prescriptiondrugs.procon.org, accessed February 12,2010. Dennis Thompson, "As TV Drug Ads Increase, So Do Concerns," *U.S. News & World Report,* October 4, 2009, http://www.usnews.com; World Health Organization, " Direct-to-Consumer Advertising Comes under Fire," *Bulletin of the World Health Organization* 87:8 (August 2009), http://www.who.int, accessed February 12, 2010; Natasha Singer, "Lawmakers Seek to Curb Drug Commercials, *The New York Times,* July 26, 2009.

Protecting the Environment Businesses consume huge amounts of energy, which increases the use of fossil fuels such as coal and oil for energy production. This activity introduces carbon dioxide and sulfur into the earth's atmosphere. Meanwhile, the sulfur from fossil fuels combines with water vapor in the air to form sulfuric acid. The acid rain that results can travel across continents, killing fish and trees and polluting groundwater. Although acid rain has been tracked for many decades now, companies are still being cited and punished for violations. Duke Energy was recently fined $1.75 million for violating provisions of the Clean Air Act and must spend roughly $85 million to reduce air pollution from a power plant in Indiana.[22]

Recycling can help companies do their part to protect the environment. Best Buy stores will take your old TVs, DVD players, computers, cell phones, and other electronic devices to avoid having them end up in landfills.

Nathan Gleave/iStockphoto

recycling Reprocessing of used materials for reuse.

Other production and manufacturing methods leave behind large quantities of waste materials that can further pollute the environment and fill already bulging landfills. Some products themselves, particularly electronics that contain toxins such as lead and mercury, are difficult to reuse or recycle. Few manufacturers are really equipped to deal with recycled materials; some refurbish junked products and sell them abroad—where later recycling is even less likely. Hewlett-Packard, however, is making its scanners with a combination of new and recycled plastics. Lead, mercury, and cadmium will soon be banned from new equipment manufactured in Europe. As stricter laws on electronic recycling come into effect, many manufacturers and retailers are offering take-back, mail-in, and trade-in programs for discarded electronic equipment. For example, all Best Buy stores now accept televisions, DVD players, computer monitors, cell phones, and other electronic devices. The stores charge a small fee for televisions 32 inches and under, CRTs (cathode ray tubes, now obsolete), monitors, and laptops, but will give customers a gift card in an equal amount.[23]

For many managers, finding ways to minimize pollution and other environmental damage caused by their products or operating processes has become an important economic, legal, and social issue. When General Motors unveiled the Chevrolet Volt, the new car instantly vaulted past conventional hybrids that run on a combination of electricity and gasoline. As we saw earlier, the Volt is entirely electric. After its battery runs down, a gasoline engine powers an on-board generator that recharges the battery. General Motors settled on a 40-mile range for the battery because Department of Transportation studies have shown that over three-quarters of commuters drive about that distance to and from work every day, and half of all American households drive even less per day. GM's Vehicle Line Director Tony Posawatz notes, "The beauty of the Volt is the size of the battery."[24]

Despite the difficulty, however, companies are finding that they can be environmentally friendly and profitable, too. Another solution to the problems of pollutants is **recycling**—reprocessing used materials for reuse. Recycling can sometimes provide much of the raw material that manufacturers need, thereby conserving the world's natural resources and reducing the need for landfills. The "Hit & Miss" feature describes a company with a creative twist on recycling, using shipping containers to construct economical, attractive new housing.

According to the Environmental Protection Agency, discarded electronic items now make up as much as 40 percent of the lead in landfills in the United States. The Institute of Scrap Recycling Industries estimates that about 2.8 billion pounds (1.4 million tons) of electronic equipment were recycled in a recent year. This amount comprised 65 million units of computer equipment such as CPUs, monitors, and printers. Electronics recycling processes resulted in 1.3 billion pounds of recyclable materials; more than half this amount consisted of metals. It is estimated that consumer electronics alone will soon amount to 3 million tons a year.[25] Manufacturers and federal agencies are struggling to devise a viable system for managing the problem; one possibility is a surcharge consumers would pay on each electronics purchase. In the meantime, as we have seen, Best Buy, Staples, and other retailers accept all gadgets for recycling no matter where they were purchased, and Hewlett-Packard and Dell have agreed not to send waste materials overseas. Cisco Systems has opened a green-technology center in a joint program with one of China's major universities as part of its long-term investment in that country. This will be a huge challenge because China's pollution problem exceeds that of the United States. But Cisco is committed to collaborating with China on its new technologies.[26]

Many consumers have favorable impressions of environmentally conscious businesses. To target these customers, companies often use **green marketing**, a marketing strategy that promotes environmentally safe products and production methods. A business cannot simply claim that its goods or services are environmentally friendly, however. The Federal Trade Commission (FTC) has issued guidelines for businesses to follow in making environmental claims. A firm must be able to prove that any environmental claim made about a product has been substantiated with reliable scientific evidence. In addition, as shown in Figure 2.6, the FTC has given specific directions about how various environmental terms may be used in advertising and marketing.

green marketing A marketing strategy that promotes environmentally safe products and production methods.

Other environmental issues—such as finding renewable sources of clean energy and developing **sustainable** agriculture—are the focus of many firms' efforts. Vinod Khosla, founder of Sun Microsystems, is now working with a group of high-powered entrepreneurs and investors in Silicon Valley to develop a new generation of energy.[27] Solar energy, geothermal energy, biodiesel, and wind power are just a few of the renewable sources of energy being developed by entrepreneurs, large energy firms, and small engineering companies.

sustainable the capacity to endure in ecology.

Mars Incorporated, the maker of Dove Chocolate and other candies, has committed to buying 100,000 tons of cocoa from Rainforest Alliance–certified farms. It is also working in conjunction with the market-oriented sustainability program UTZ Certified and intends to use sustainably grown cocoa in all of its chocolate products by 2020.[28]

FIGURE
2.6 **FTC Guidelines for Environmental Claims in Green Marketing**

If a business says a product is...	The product or package must . . .
Biodegradable	break down and return to nature in a reasonably short period of time.
Recyclable	be entirely reusable as new materials in the manufacture or assembly of a new product or package.
Refillable	be included in a system for the collection and return of the package for refill. If consumers have to find a way to refill it themselves, it is not **refillable**.
Ozone Safe/Ozone Friendly	must not contain any ozone-depleting ingredient.

Developing the Quality of the Workforce

In the past, a nation's wealth has often been based on its money, production equipment, and natural resources. A country's true wealth, however, lies in its people. An educated, skilled workforce provides the intellectual know-how required to develop new technology, improve productivity, and compete in the global marketplace. It is becoming increasingly clear that to remain competitive, U.S. business must assume more responsibility for enhancing the quality of its workforce, including encouraging diversity of all kinds.

In developed economies like that of the United States, many new jobs require college-educated workers. With demand high for workers with advanced skills, the difference between the highest-paid and lowest-paid workers has been increasing. Education plays an important role in earnings, despite success stories of those who dropped out of college or high school to start businesses. Workers with professional degrees earn an average of $2,749 a week, whereas those with some high school but no diploma earn about $449.[29] Businesses must encourage students to stay in school, continue their education, and sharpen their skills. Cheerios supports Spoonfuls of Stories, a national program to encourage young children and their parents to read together by distributing more than 40 million books in specially marked cereal boxes. It also contributes to First Book, a nonprofit that gives children from low-income households the chance to own their first new book.[30]

Organizations also face enormous responsibilities for helping women, members of various cultural groups, and those who are physically challenged to contribute fully to the economy. Failure to do so is not only a waste of more than half the nation's workforce but also devastating to a firm's public image. Some socially responsible firms also encourage diversity in their business suppliers. Retail giant JCPenney's Partnership Program is designed to foster relationships with minority- and women-owned businesses—an effort the company has worked at for more than 30 years.

Through a commitment to developing employee diversity, The Coca-Cola Company strives to create an inclusive atmosphere, offers diversity training for employees and managers, and encourages regular dialogue among colleagues, suppliers, customers, and stakeholders. "By building an inclusive workplace environment, The Coca-Cola Company seeks to leverage its worldwide team, which is rich in diverse people, talent, and ideas," says the company Web site.[31] For a global organization to function competitively, diversity is vital.

Corporate Philanthropy

As Chapter 1 pointed out, not-for-profit organizations play an important role in society by serving the public good. They provide the human resources that enhance the quality of life in communities around the world. To fulfill this mission, many not-for-profit organizations rely on financial contributions from the business community. Firms respond by donating billions of dollars each year to not-for-profit organizations. This **corporate philanthropy** includes cash contributions, donations of equipment and products, and supporting the volunteer efforts of company employees. Recipients

corporate philanthropy
Effort of an organization to make a contribution to the communities in which it earns profits.

include cultural organizations, adopt-a-school programs, community development agencies, and housing and job training programs.

Corporate philanthropy can have many positive benefits beyond the purely "feel-good" rewards of giving, such as higher employee morale, enhanced company image, and improved customer relationships. General Mills, for instance, is a major contributor to the Susan G. Komen Breast Cancer Foundation, through its line of yogurt products marketed under the Yoplait brand name. Yoplait's target market is health-conscious women, the same group most likely to know of or become involved with the Komen Foundation's fund-raising efforts. The firm also sponsors its My Hometown Helper program, a nationwide initiative that provides grants to communities, not-for-profit groups, and public schools for community improvement projects.[32]

Companies often seek to align their marketing efforts with their charitable giving. Many contribute to the Olympics and create advertising that features the company's sponsorship. This is known as *cause-related marketing.* In a recent survey, nearly nine out of ten young people said they believed companies had a duty to support social causes, and nearly seven in eight said they would switch brands in order to reward a company that did so. Consumers are often willing to pay even more for a product, such as Newman's Own salad dressings and salsa, because they know the proceeds are going to a good cause.

Another form of corporate philanthropy is volunteerism. In their roles as corporate citizens, thousands of businesses encourage their employees to contribute their efforts to projects as diverse as Habitat for Humanity, the Red Cross, and the Humane Society. In addition to making tangible contributions to the well-being of fellow citizens, such programs generate considerable public support and goodwill for the companies and their employees. In some cases, the volunteer efforts occur mostly during off-hours for employees. In other instances, firms permits their workforces to volunteer during regular working hours. Sometimes volunteers with special skills are indispensable. After the devastating earthquake in Haiti, the pilots' union at the shipping giant UPS volunteered to transport supplies and personnel in the relief effort.[33]

Corporate philanthropy can enhance a company's customer relationships. Through sales of its Yoplait yogurt line, General Mills contributes to the Susan G. Komen Breast Cancer Foundation, a charity that is important to the health-conscious consumers who buy Yoplait.

Responsibilities to Customers

Businesspeople share a social and ethical responsibility to treat their customers fairly and act in a manner that is not harmful to them. **Consumerism**—the public demand that a business consider the wants and needs of its customers in making decisions—has gained widespread acceptance. Consumerism is based on the belief that consumers have certain rights. A frequently quoted statement of consumer rights was made by President John F. Kennedy in 1962. Figure 2.7 summarizes these consumer rights. Numerous state and federal laws have been implemented since then to protect these rights.

consumerism Public demand that a business consider the wants and needs of its customers in making decisions.

The Right to Be Safe Contemporary businesspeople must recognize obligations, both moral and legal, to ensure the safe operation of their products. Consumers should feel assured that the products they purchase will not cause injuries in normal use. **Product liability** refers to the responsibility of manufacturers for injuries and damages caused by their products. Items that lead to injuries, either directly or indirectly, can have disastrous consequences for their makers.

Many companies put their products through rigorous testing to avoid safety problems. Still, testing alone cannot foresee every eventuality. Companies must try to consider all possibilities and provide adequate warning of potential dangers. When a product does pose a threat to customer safety, a responsible manufacturer responds quickly to either correct the

product liability The responsibility of manufacturers for injuries and damages caused by their products.

FIGURE
2.7

Consumer Rights as Proposed by President Kennedy

problem or recall the dangerous product. Although we take for granted that our food supply is safe, sometimes contamination leaks in, causing illness or even death among some consumers. Ippolito International once voluntarily recalled more than 1,700 cartons of bunched spinach after random testing found that some bunches were contaminated with salmonella, a microorganism that produces infections and sometimes death in young children, the elderly, and those with weakened immune systems. Fortunately, no illnesses were reported.[34]

The Right to Be Informed Consumers should have access to enough education and product information to make responsible buying decisions. In their efforts to promote and sell their goods and services, companies can easily neglect consumers' right to be fully informed. False or misleading advertising is a violation of the Wheeler-Lea Act, a federal law enacted in 1938. The FTC and other federal and state agencies have established rules and regulations that govern advertising truthfulness. These rules prohibit businesses from making unsubstantiated claims about the performance or superiority of their merchandise. They also require businesses to avoid misleading consumers. Businesses that fail to comply face scrutiny from the FTC and consumer protection organizations. For instance, Dannon Company settled a class-action lawsuit that charged the company with false advertising. Dannon claimed that two of its yogurt products, Activia, and DanActive, improved the immune system of the digestive tract. The company agreed to make changes in the labeling and advertising of those products, claiming instead that they merely interact with the immune system. Dannon also set up a Web site with information about the settlement and agreed to refund customers up to $100, depending on how much yogurt each customer bought.[35]

The Food and Drug Administration (FDA), which sets standards for advertising conducted by drug manufacturers, eased restrictions for prescription drug advertising on television. In print ads, drug makers are required to spell out potential side effects and the proper uses of prescription drugs. Because of the requirement to disclose this information, prescription drug television advertising was limited. Now, however, the FDA says drug ads on radio and television can directly promote a prescription drug's benefits if they provide a quick way for consumers to learn about side-effects, such as displaying a toll-free number or Internet address. As we have seen, the "Solving an Ethical Controversy" feature on page 51 discusses the pros and cons of such advertising.

The FDA also monitors "dietary supplements," including vitamins and herbs. This includes protecting consumers against fake and sometimes harmful versions of name-brand supplements. In 2010, the FDA issued a public alert to warn consumers about counterfeit versions of Alli, an over-the-counter weight-loss supplement. Instead of the correct active ingredient, the counterfeit Alli contained a controlled substance that should not be used without a doctor's supervision and that may actually harm certain patients. In addition, the packaging of the counterfeit was missing a "lot" code and differed in other, subtle ways from the genuine packaging. The fake capsules were different in size and shape from the real ones, too. Apparently all the fake Alli had been sold over the Internet rather than in stores, so customers could not inspect the packaging or the capsules before receiving the product.[36]

The responsibility of business to preserve consumers' right to be informed extends beyond avoiding misleading advertising. All communications with customers—from salespeople's comments to warranties and invoices—must be controlled to clearly and accurately inform customers. Most packaged-goods firms, personal-computer makers, and other makers of products bought for personal use by consumers include toll-free customer service numbers on their product labels so that consumers can get answers to questions about a product.

To protect their customers and avoid claims of insufficient disclosure, businesses often include warnings on products. As Figure 2.8 shows, sometimes these warnings go far beyond what a reasonable consumer would expect. Others are downright funny.

The Right to Choose Consumers should have the right to choose which goods and services they need and want to purchase. Socially responsible firms attempt to preserve this right, even if they reduce their own sales and profits in the process. Brand-name drug makers have recently gone on the defensive in a battle being waged by state governments, insurance companies, consumer groups, unions, and major employers such as General Motors and Verizon. These groups want to force down the rising price of prescription drugs by ensuring that consumers have the right and the opportunity to select cheaper generic brands.

The Right to Be Heard Consumers should be able to express legitimate complaints to appropriate parties. Many companies expend considerable effort to ensure full hearings for consumer complaints. The auction Web site eBay assists buyers and sellers who believe they were victimized in transactions conducted through the site. It deploys a 200-employee team to work with users and law enforcement agencies to combat fraud. The company has strict guidelines for buyers and sellers and rules for leaving feedback about a buyer or seller. For example, buyers must operate within a list of acceptable goods for sale and may not offer such items as alcohol, pornography, drugs, counterfeit currency, or artifacts from cave formations, graves, or Native American sites. The protection of copyrights is also an important part of eBay's policy.[37]

Responsibilities to Employees

Companies that can attract skilled and knowledgeable employees are better able to meet the challenges of competing globally. In return, businesses have wide-ranging responsibilities to their employees, both here and abroad. These include workplace safety, quality-of-life issues, ensuring equal opportunity on the job, avoiding age discrimination, and preventing sexual harassment and sexism.

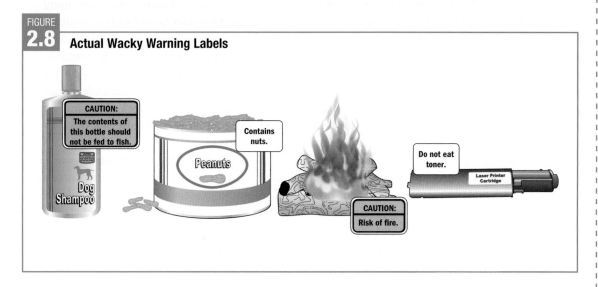

FIGURE 2.8 **Actual Wacky Warning Labels**

Workplace safety is an important business responsibility. In potentially dangerous areas workers are required to wear hard hats.

Vedran Vidovic/Shutterstock

Workplace Safety A century ago, few businesses paid much attention to the safety of their workers. In fact, most business owners viewed employees as mere cogs in the production process. Workers—many of whom were young children—toiled in frequently dangerous conditions. In 1911, a fire at the Triangle Shirtwaist Factory in New York City killed 146 people, mostly young girls. Contributing to the massive loss of life were the sweatshop working conditions at the factory, including overcrowding, blocked exits, and a lack of fire escapes. This horrifying tragedy forced businesses to begin to recognize their responsibility for their workers' safety.

The safety and health of workers on the job is now an important business responsibility. The Occupational Safety and Health Administration (OSHA) is the main federal regulatory force in setting workplace safety and health standards. These mandates range from broad guidelines on storing hazardous materials to specific standards for worker safety in industries such as construction, manufacturing, and mining. OSHA tracks and investigates workplace accidents and has the authority to fine employers who are found liable for injuries and deaths that occur on the job.

One unsettling fact is that about 70 teens die every year in the United States as a result of work injuries. Most of these fatalities occur because of unsafe equipment, inadequate safety training, and dangerous work that is illegal or inappropriate for youth. OSHA is taking steps to educate employers and teen workers about safety, health, and a positive work environment. The OSHA Web site has a special section for teens with the answers to most frequently asked questions about such issues as wages, labor standards, harassment issues, and safety at work. In addition, the U.S. Department of Labor has rolled out a new initiative called YouthRules!, a project designed to further educate and empower young workers. The YouthRules! Web page offers information and activities for teens, parents, educators, and employers.[38] Another issue that firms face is the rising cost of health care, as described in the "Hit & Miss" feature.

Quality-of-Life Issues Balancing work and family is becoming harder for many employees. They find themselves squeezed between working long hours and handling child-care problems, caring for elderly parents, and solving other family crises. A *sandwich generation* of households, those caring for two generations—their children and their aging parents—has arisen. As the population ages, the share of American households providing some type of care to a relative or friend age 50 or older has grown dramatically in the early years of the 21st century. At the same time, as married women spend more time working outside the home, they have fewer hours per week to spend on family. The employees juggling work with life's other demands aren't just working mothers. Childless couples, single people, and men all express frustration with the pressures of balancing work with family and personal needs. To help with the work–life balance, some employers are offering flexible work schedules so that parents can meet the needs of their children (or aging parents) as well as their jobs. *Working Mother* magazine offers up their list of 100 best companies to work for offering work–life balance. Of the 100 companies on the list, 100 percent offer telecommuting and flexible schedules, 98 percent offer job-sharing, 86 percent have backup child care, and 62 percent provide care for sick children.[39] Increasingly, women are starting their own businesses so they can set their own hours and goals.

Some companies have come up with truly innovative ways to deal with work schedules, including paid time off for vacation or illness. At some of its locations, IBM has done away with prescribed vacation time altogether—the focus is on results. Employees have an informal

Businesses Battle the High Cost of Health Care

Business owners often feel they are under siege, battling the costs of everything from supplies to wages. The rising cost of health care has forced companies to find new ways to pay for their employees' coverage without jeopardizing the health of their own bottom line.

Some firms now require employees to contribute more. During a recent year, nearly 60 percent of U.S. companies reported that they planned to increase employees' deductibles, co-pays, or out-of-pocket expenses. Health care costs have been increasing at about 6 percent a year. While that is less than in previous decades, the costs are now so high that even a small increase represents a big bite out of earnings.

Other firms are setting up onsite health clinics, which they claim can save thousands of dollars per employee. Hurst Boiler hired Worksite Rx to open and run a clinic for its 220 employees and their families. Within two years, the company's health care costs had decreased by 32 percent per employee. In addition, the number of sick days workers took decreased significantly. Of course, the firm had to make the initial investment in its health clinic, but the savings outweighed the costs.

Many firms—large and small—are paying much closer attention to the concept of wellness among employees. The idea is not only to prevent costly illnesses but to promote good health. Some firms have adopted incentive programs to entice employees to participate; others simply require participation as a condition of employment.

Firms have long offered health benefits that included gym memberships and healthful food offerings at the company cafeteria. Now they are getting more creative. Ottawa Dental Laboratory has a program called Vitality Bucks, through which employees earn redeemable "bucks" for reaching specific health goals. Those bucks translate to some impressive prizes, ranging from outdoor grills to big-screen TVs. Participating employees enroll in particular health programs and submit to regular testing to receive their bucks. The firm says that 98 percent of employees participate, and it reports an 8 percent reduction in overall health care costs.

Insurance companies have also jumped on the rewards bandwagon. Humana insurance now offers a program that awards points to its members for such activities as signing up for a weight-loss coach and logging daily steps taken. Employees can track their points online and redeem them for everything from movie tickets to golf clubs. Employers pay less for health care and experience a rise in productivity when their employees are healthy, report insurance industry experts.

Questions for Critical Thinking

1. Do you agree that employees should be required to contribute more to the cost of their health care? Why or why not?
2. Describe what you see as the benefits and drawbacks of health "rewards" programs. Brainstorm some creative ideas to help solve the health care crisis.

Sources: Jennifer Brown, "Insurance Plans Reward Good Health with Gifts," *The Atlanta-Journal Constitution*, January 26, 2009, http://www.ajc.com; Brian Klepper, "Work-site Clinics Control Health Care Costs," *Jacksonville Business Journal*, November 7, 2008, http://jacksonville.bizjournals.com; "U.S. Workers Face Higher Health Care Costs," *U.S. News & World Report*, September 4, 2008, http://health.usnews.com; Michael A. Fletcher, "Rising Health Costs Cut into Wages," *Washington Post*, March 24, 2008, http://www.washingtonpost.com; Adrienne Selko, "Prescription for Survival: How to Control Healthcare Costs," *Industry Week*, January 1, 2008, http://www.industryweek.com.

---

agreement with their supervisors about when they will be out of the office, based on their ability to complete their work on schedule. The number of days they take off is not tracked; instead vacation time is considered open ended. But the catch is, the work has to be done. Perhaps surprisingly, the firm found that employees put in just as many hours, if not more, under the new program. According to an IBM representative, ". . . there is no policing, and employees are empowered to take vacation when they want."[40]

Another solution has been to offer **family leave** to employees who need to deal with family matters. Under the Family and Medical Leave Act of 1993, businesses with 50 or more employees must provide unpaid leave annually for any employee who wants time off for the birth or adoption of a child; to become a foster parent; or to care for a seriously ill relative, spouse, or self if he or she has a serious health condition or injury. The law requires employers to grant up to 12 weeks of leave each year, and leave may be taken intermittently as medical conditions make necessary. This unpaid leave also applies to an employee who has a serious illness. Workers must meet certain eligibility requirements. Employers must continue to provide health benefits during the leave and guarantee that employees will return to equivalent jobs. The issue of who is entitled to health benefits can also create a dilemma as companies struggle to balance the needs of their employees against the staggering costs of health care.

family leave The Family and Medical Leave Act of 1993 states that businesses with 50 or more employees must provide unpaid leave up to 12 weeks annually for any employee who wants time off for the birth or adoption of a child, to become a foster parent, or to care for a seriously ill relative, spouse, or self if he or she has a serious health condition or injury.

Ensuring Equal Opportunity on the Job Businesspeople face many challenges managing an increasingly diverse workforce in the 21st century. Technological advances are expanding the ways people with physical disabilities can contribute in the workplace. Businesses also need to find ways to responsibly recruit and manage older workers and workers with varying lifestyles. In addition, beginning with Lotus Development in 1982, companies have begun to extend benefits equally to employees, regardless of sexual orientation. In particular, that means the company offers benefits such as health insurance to unmarried domestic partners if it offers them to spouses of married couples. Companies that now offer these gender-neutral benefits include Avon Products, Costco Wholesale, Disney, General Mills, and Mattel.

Table

2.2 Laws Designed to Ensure Equal Opportunity

LAW	KEY PROVISIONS
Title VII of the Civil Rights Act of 1964 (as amended by the Equal Employment Opportunity Act of 1972)	Prohibits discrimination in hiring, promotion, compensation, training, or dismissal on the basis of race, color, religion, sex, or national origin.
Age Discrimination in Employment Act of 1967 (as amended)	Prohibits discrimination in employment against anyone age 40 or older in hiring, promotion, compensation, training, or dismissal.
Equal Pay Act of 1963	Requires equal pay for men and women working for the same firm in jobs that require equal skill, effort, and responsibility.
Vocational Rehabilitation Act of 1973	Requires government contractors and subcontractors to take affirmative action to employ and promote qualified disabled workers. Coverage now extends to all federal employees. Coverage has been broadened by the passage of similar laws in more than 20 states and, through court rulings, to include people with communicable diseases, including AIDS.
Vietnam Era Veterans Readjustment Act of 1974	Requires government contractors and subcontractors to take affirmative action to employ and retain disabled veterans. Coverage now extends to all federal employees and has been broadened by the passage of similar laws in more than 20 states.
Pregnancy Discrimination Act of 1978	Requires employers to treat pregnant women and new mothers the same as other employees for all employment-related purposes, including receipt of benefits under company benefit programs.
Americans with Disabilities Act of 1990	Makes discrimination against the disabled illegal in public accommodations, transportation, and telecommunications; stiffens employer penalties for intentional discrimination on the basis of an employee's disability.
Civil Rights Act of 1991	Makes it easier for workers to sue their employers for alleged discrimination. Enables victims of sexual discrimination to collect punitive damages; includes employment decisions and on-the-job issues such as sexual harassment, unfair promotions, and unfair dismissal. The employer must prove that it did not engage in discrimination.
Family and Medical Leave Act of 1993	Requires all businesses with 50 or more employees to provide up to 12 weeks of unpaid leave annually to employees who have had a child or are adopting a child, are becoming foster parents, are caring for a seriously ill relative or spouse, or are themselves seriously ill. Workers must meet certain eligibility requirements.
Uniformed Services Employment and Reemployment Rights Act of 1994	Prohibits employers from denying employment benefits on the basis of employees' membership in or obligation to serve in the uniformed services and protects the rights of veterans, reservists, and National Guard members to reclaim their jobs after being absent due to military service or training.
Genetic Information Nondiscrimination Act of 2008	Prohibits employers from discriminating against employees or applicants on the basis of genetic information, including genetic tests of an individual or family member or an individual's personal or family medical history.

To a great extent, efforts at managing diversity are regulated by law. The Civil Rights Act (1964) outlawed many kinds of discriminatory practices, and Title VII of the act specifically prohibits **discrimination**—biased treatment of a job candidate or employee—in the workplace. As shown in Table 2.2, other nondiscrimination laws include the Equal Pay Act (1963), the Age Discrimination in Employment Act (1967), the Equal Employment Opportunity Act (1972), the Pregnancy Discrimination Act (1978), the Civil Rights Act of 1991, and numerous executive orders. The Americans with Disabilities Act (1990) protects the rights of physically challenged people. The Vietnam Era Veterans Readjustment Act (1974) protects the employment of veterans of the Vietnam War. The Genetic Information Nondiscrimination Act (2008) prohibits discrimination on the basis of genetic tests or the medical history of an individual or that individual's family.

The **Equal Employment Opportunity Commission (EEOC)** was created to increase job opportunities for women and minorities and to help end discrimination based on race, color, religion, disability, gender, or national origin in any personnel action. To enforce fair-employment laws, it investigates charges of discrimination and harassment and files suit against violators. The EEOC can also help employers set up programs to increase job opportunities for women, minorities, people with disabilities, and people in other protected categories.

Fair treatment of employees is more than a matter of complying with EEOC regulations, however. All employees want to be treated with respect. A minority employee who misses out on a plum assignment may miss out on the big raise that goes with it. As the employee's salary grows more slowly, managers may eventually begin to use the size of the salary as an indicator that the employee contributes less to the organization. While in the past the EEOC has focused on this type of individual situation, currently it is addressing what it terms "systemic discrimination," which it defines as "a pattern or practice, policy and/or class cases where the alleged discrimination has a broad impact on an industry, profession, company, or geographic location." A systemic discrimination charge usually becomes a class-action suit, which costs considerably more to defend than an individual lawsuit. So firms are examining their employment practices carefully to make sure they are not open to discrimination charges.[41] Chapter 9 takes a closer look at diversity and employment discrimination issues as part of a discussion of human resource management.

Age Discrimination With the average age of U.S. workers steadily rising, more than half the workforce is projected to be age 40 or older in a few years. Yet some employers find it less expensive to hire and retain younger workers, who generally have lower medical bills as well as lower salary and benefits packages. At the same time, many older workers have training and skills that younger workers have yet to acquire. The Age Discrimination in Employment Act of 1967 (ADEA) protects individuals who are age 40 or older, prohibiting discrimination on the basis of age and denial of benefits to older employees.

Ruling in a lawsuit brought under the ADEA, the Supreme Court determined that employers can be held liable for age discrimination against older workers even if they intended no harm. At the same time, the court allowed employers to use "reasonable" factors such as cost cutting to defend business practices that might have more severe impacts on older than on younger workers. However, in June 2009, a new Court ruling shifted the burden of proof onto employees seeking to prove that age discrimination was a factor in their demotion or dismissal.[42]

Legal issues aside, employers might do well to consider not only the experience that older workers bring to the workplace but also their enthusiasm. "Job satisfaction is especially high among those 65 and over because most people working at that age are not forced to still work, due to financial reasons, but choose to do so because they like their jobs," points out the leader of a study conducted by researchers at the University of Chicago. Nearly 75 percent of those over 65 who were interviewed said they were very happy with their jobs.[43]

discrimination Biased treatment of a job candidate or employee.

Equal Employment Opportunity Commission (EEOC) This commission was created to increase job opportunities for women and minorities and to help end discrimination based on race, color, religion, disability, gender, or national origin in any personnel action.

Employers are responsible for avoiding age discrimination in the workplace. As the average age of workers rises, employers will benefit from the older generation's knowledge.

In all cases, employers need to plan ahead for the aging of the workforce, finding ways to retain accumulated business wisdom, prepare for the demand for health services, and be ready for growth in the industries that serve seniors. The 55 to 64 age group will increase from just over 18 percent to almost 24 percent over the next few years, whereas the 35 to 44 age group will decrease by just over 4 percent. These numbers signify a coming shift in the workforce, as well as in the goods and services needed.[44]

Sexual Harassment and Sexism Every employer has a responsibility to ensure that all workers are treated fairly and are safe from sexual harassment. **Sexual harassment** refers to unwelcome and inappropriate actions of a sexual nature in the workplace. It is a form of sex discrimination that violates the Civil Rights Act of 1964, which gives both men and women the right to file lawsuits for intentional sexual harassment. Almost 14,000 sexual harassment complaints are filed with the EEOC each year, of which about 16 percent are filed by men.[45] Thousands of other cases are either handled internally by companies or never reported.

Two types of sexual harassment exist. The first type occurs when an employee is pressured to comply with unwelcome advances and requests for sexual favors in return for job security, promotions, and raises. The second type results from a hostile work environment in which an employee feels hassled or degraded because of unwelcome flirting, lewd comments, or obscene jokes. The courts have ruled that allowing sexually oriented materials in the workplace can create a hostile atmosphere that interferes with an employee's ability to do the job. Employers are also legally responsible to protect employees from sexual harassment by customers and clients. The EEOC's Web site informs employers and employees of criteria for identifying sexual harassment and how it should be handled in the workplace.

Preventing sexual harassment can be difficult because it involves regulating the conduct of individual employees. Sometimes victims, especially young employees, are intimidated or unaware of their rights, but the EEOC has set up a Youth@Work program

sexual harassment Unwelcome and inappropriate actions of a sexual nature in the workplace.

(http://www.eeoc.gov/youth) to ensure that young workers can learn about the various types of discrimination and ways to avoid them.

The cost in settlements or fines can be enormous. So in addition to ethical and legal reasons, it makes good business sense for firms to prevent this kind of behavior from happening. To avoid sexual harassment problems, many firms have established policies and employee education programs aimed at preventing such violations. An effective harassment prevention program should include the following measures:

- Issue a specific policy statement prohibiting sexual harassment.

- Develop a complaint procedure for employees to follow.

- Create a work atmosphere that encourages sexually harassed staffers to come forward.

- Investigate and resolve complaints quickly and take disciplinary action against harassers.

Unless all these components are supported by top management, sexual harassment is difficult to eliminate.

Sexual harassment is often part of the broader problem of **sexism**—discrimination against members of either sex, but primarily affecting women. One important sexism issue is equal pay for equal work.

Lilly Ledbetter was near retirement when she found out that for a considerable length of time, men at her management level had been getting paid more than she had been. But the Supreme Court threw out her case because she did not sue within the statute of limitations— that is, within 180 days of the first instance of a lower paycheck. In January 2009, President Barack Obama signed a law that extended the statute of limitations in such cases.[46]

On average, according to the American Association of University Women, a college-educated woman 25 years and older earns $50,600 per year working full time while her male counterpart earns $70,800. Education, occupation, work hours, and other factors don't seem to affect the gap, which remains unexplained other than the penalty of gender.[47] In some extreme cases, differences in pay and advancement can become the basis for sex discrimination suits, which, like sexual harassment suits, can be costly and time consuming to settle. As in all business practices, it is better to act legally and ethically in the first place.

Responsibilities to Investors and the Financial Community

Although a fundamental goal of any business is to make a profit for its shareholders, investors and the financial community demand that businesses behave ethically and legally. When firms fail in this responsibility, thousands of investors and consumers can suffer.

State and federal government agencies are responsible for protecting investors from financial misdeeds. At the federal level, the Securities and Exchange Commission (SEC) investigates suspicions of unethical or illegal behavior by publicly traded firms. It investigates accusations that a business is using faulty accounting practices to inaccurately portray its financial resources and profits to investors. Regulation FD ("Fair Disclosure") is an SEC rule that requires publicly traded companies to announce major information to the general public, rather than first disclosing the information to selected major investors. The agency also operates an Office of Internet Enforcement to target fraud in online trading and online sales of stock by unlicensed sellers. Recall that the Sarbanes-Oxley Act of 2002 also protects investors from unethical accounting practices. Chapter 17 discusses securities trading practices further.

sexism Discrimination against members of either sex, but primarily affecting women.

Assessment Check ☑

1. What is meant by social responsibility, and why do firms exercise it?

2. What is green marketing?

3. What are the four main consumer rights?

Assessment Check ☑

1. Why do firms need to do more than just earn a profit?

2. What is the role of the Securities and Exchange Commission?

What's Ahead

The decisions and actions of businesspeople are often influenced by outside forces such as the legal environment and society's expectations about business responsibility. Firms also are affected by the economic environments in which they operate. The next chapter discusses the broad economic issues that influence businesses around the world. Our discussion will focus on how factors such as supply and demand, unemployment, inflation, and government monetary policies pose both challenges and opportunities for firms seeking to compete in the global marketplace.

Summary of Learning Goals

1 Explain the concepts of business ethics and social responsibility.

Business ethics refers to the standards of conduct and moral values that businesspeople rely on to guide their actions and decisions in the workplace. Businesspeople must take a wide range of social issues into account when making decisions. Social responsibility refers to management's acceptance of the obligation to put an equal value on profit, consumer satisfaction, and societal well-being in evaluating the firm's performance.

Assessment Check Answers ✔️

1.1 To whom do businesses have responsibilities? Businesses are responsible to customers, employees, investors, and society.

1.2 If a firm is meeting all its responsibilities to others, why do ethical conflicts arise? Ethical conflicts arise because business must balance doing what is right and doing what is profitable.

2 Describe the factors that influence business ethics.

Among the many factors shaping individual ethics are personal experience, peer pressure, and organizational culture. Individual ethics are also influenced by family, cultural, and religious standards. Additionally, the culture of the organization where a person works can be a factor.

Assessment Check Answers ✔️

2.1 What role can an ethics compliance officer play in a firm? Ethics compliance officers are charged with deterring wrongdoing and ensuring that ethical standards are met.

2.2 What factors influence the ethical environment of a business? Individual ethics and technology influence the ethical environment of a business.

3 List the stages in the development of ethical standards, and discuss how organizations shape ethical behavior.

In the preconventional stage, individuals primarily consider their own needs and desires in making decisions. They obey external rules only from fear of punishment or hope of reward. In the conventional stage, individuals are aware of and respond to their duty to others. Expectations of groups, as well as self-interest, influence behavior. In the postconventional stage, the individual can move beyond self-interest and duty to include consideration of the needs of society. A person in this stage can apply personal ethical principles in a variety of situations. Conflicts of interest occur when a businessperson is faced with a situation in which an action benefiting one person has the potential to harm another, as when the person's own interests conflict with those of a customer. Honesty and integrity are valued qualities that engender trust, but a person's immediate self-interest may seem to require violating these principles. Loyalty to an employer sometimes conflicts with truthfulness. Whistle-blowing is a possible response to misconduct in the workplace, but the personal costs of doing so may be high. Employees are strongly influenced by the standards of conduct established and supported within the organizations where they work. Businesses can help shape ethical behavior by developing codes of conduct that define their expectations. Organizations can also use this training to develop employees' ethics awareness and reasoning. They can foster ethical action through decision-making tools, goals consistent with ethical behavior, and advice hotlines. Executives must also demonstrate ethical behavior in their decisions and actions to provide ethical leadership.

Assessment Check Answers ✔️

3.1 What is the preconventional stage in the development of ethical standards? In the preconventional stage, the individual looks out for his or her own interests and follows rules out of fear of punishment or hope of reward.

3.2 How can loyalty and truth come into conflict for an employee? Truth and loyalty can come into conflict when the truth about a company or situation is unfavorable.

3.3 How does ethical leadership contribute to ethical standards throughout a company? Employees more readily commit to the company's core values when they see that leaders and managers behave ethically.

⌈4⌉ Describe how businesses' social responsibility is measured, and summarize the responsibilities of business to the general public, customers, and employees.

Today's businesses are expected to weigh their qualitative impact on consumers and society, in addition to their quantitative economic contributions such as sales, employment levels, and profits. One measure is their compliance with labor and consumer protection laws and their charitable contributions. Another measure some businesses take is to conduct social audits. Public-interest groups also create standards and measure companies' performance relative to those standards. The responsibilities of business to the general public include protecting the public health and the environment and developing the quality of the workforce. Additionally, many would argue that businesses have a social responsibility to support charitable and social causes in the communities in which they earn profits. Business also must treat customers fairly and protect consumers, upholding their rights to be safe, to be informed, to choose, and to be heard. Businesses have wide-ranging responsibilities to their workers. They should make sure that the workplace is safe, address quality-of-life issues, ensure equal opportunity, and prevent sexual harassment and other forms of discrimination.

Assessment Check Answers ✔

4.1 What is meant by social responsibility, and why do firms exercise it? Social responsibility is management's acceptance of its obligation to consider profit, consumer satisfaction, and societal well-being to be of equal value when evaluating the firm's performance. Businesses exercise it because it is required by law, because it enhances the company's image, or because management believes it is the right thing to do.

4.2 What is green marketing? Green marketing is a marketing strategy that promotes environmentally safe products and production methods.

4.3 What are the four main consumer rights? The four main consumer rights are the right to be safe, to be informed, to choose, and to be heard.

⌈5⌉ Explain why investors and the financial community are concerned with business ethics and social responsibility.

Investors and the financial community demand that businesses behave ethically as well as legally in handling their financial transactions. Businesses must be honest in reporting their profits and financial performance to avoid misleading investors. The Securities and Exchange Commission is the federal agency responsible for investigating suspicions that publicly traded firms have engaged in unethical or illegal financial behavior.

Assessment Check Answers ✔

5.1 Why do firms need to do more than just earn a profit? Firms need to do more than just earn a profit because the law requires them to behave in a legal and ethical manner and because investors and shareholders demand such behavior.

5.2 What is the role of the Securities and Exchange Commission? Among other functions, the Securities and Exchange Commission investigates suspicions of unethical or illegal behavior by publicly traded firms.

▣ Business Terms You Need to Know

business ethics 36	code of conduct 45	sustainable 53	discrimination 60
Sarbanes-Oxley Act of 2002 39	stakeholders 47	corporate philanthropy 54	Equal Employment Opportunity Commission (EEOC) 61
conflict of interest 42	social responsibility 47	consumerism 55	
integrity 42	social audits 48	product liability 55	
whistle-blowing 43	recycling 52	fair trade 59	sexual harassment 62
	green marketing 53	family leave 59	sexism 63

▣ Review Questions

1. What do the terms *business ethics* and *social responsibility* mean? Why are they important components of a firm's overall philosophy in conducting business?

2. In what ways do individuals make a difference in a firm's commitment to ethics? Describe the three stages in which an individual develops ethical standards.

3. What type of ethical dilemma does each of the following illustrate? (A situation might involve more than one dilemma.)

   a. Due to the breakup with a client, an advertising agency suddenly finds itself representing rival companies.

   b. A newly hired employee learns that the office manager plays computer games on company time.

   c. A drug manufacturer offers a doctor an expensive gift as an inducement to prescribe a new brand-name drug.

   d. An employee is asked to destroy documents that implicate his or her firm in widespread pollution.

   e. A company spokesperson agrees to give a press conference that puts a positive spin on his or her firm's use of sweatshop labor.

4. Describe how ethical leadership contributes to the development of each of the other levels of ethical standards in a corporation.

5. In what ways do firms demonstrate their social responsibility?

6. What are the four major areas in which businesses have responsibilities to the general public? In what ways can meeting these responsibilities give a firm a competitive edge?

7. Identify and describe the four basic rights that consumerism tries to protect. How has consumerism improved the contemporary business environment? What challenges has it created for businesses?

8. What are the five major areas in which companies have responsibilities to their employees? What types of changes in society are now affecting these responsibilities?

9. Identify which Equal Opportunity law (or laws) protects workers in the following categories:

   a. an employee who must care for an elderly parent

   b. a National Guard member who is returning from deployment overseas

   c. a job applicant who is HIV positive

   d. a person who is over 40 years old

   e. a woman who has been sexually harassed on the job

   f. a woman with a family history of breast cancer

10. How does a company demonstrate its responsibility to investors and the financial community?

■ Projects and Teamwork Applications

1. Write your own personal code of ethics. Create standards for your behavior at school, in personal relationships, and on the job. Then assess how well you meet your own standards and revise them if necessary.

2. On your own or with a classmate, visit the Web site of one of the following firms, or choose another that interests you. On the basis of what you can learn about the company from the site, construct a chart or figure that illustrates examples of the firm's ethical awareness, ethical education, ethical actions, and ethical leadership. Present your findings to class.

   a. Sun Microsystems

   b. NFL, NHL, NBA, MLB, MLS (or any major professional sports league)

   c. Hewlett-Packard

   d. Foundation Health Systems

   e. Irving Oil

   f. Costco

   g. IKEA

3. Now take the company you studied for question 2 (or choose another one) and conduct a social audit on that firm. Do your findings match the firm's culture of ethics? If there are any differences, what are they and why might they occur?

4. On your own or with a classmate, go online, flip through a magazine, or surf television channels to identify a firm that is engaged in green marketing. If you see a commercial on television, go to the firm's Web site to learn more about the product or process advertised. Does the firm make claims that comply with the FTC guidelines? Present your findings in class.

5. As a consumer, you have come to expect a certain level of responsibility toward you on the part of companies with which you do business. Describe a situation in which you felt that a company did not recognize your rights as a consumer. How did you handle the situation? How did the company handle it? What was the final outcome?

■ Web Assignments

1. **Ethical standards.** Go to the Web site listed below. It summarizes the ethical standards for all employees and suppliers of John Deere and Company. Review the material and then write a brief report relating Deere's ethical standards to the material on corporate ethics discussed in the chapter. In addition, consider how Deere's ethical standards are integrated with the firm's overall global citizenship efforts.

   http://www.deere.com/en_US/globalcitizenship/values/ethics.html

2. **Starting a career.** Each year *BusinessWeek* magazine rates the best companies to begin a career. Visit the *BusinessWeek* Web site and review the most recent list. What criteria did *BusinessWeek* use when building this list? What role does ethics and social responsibility play?

   http://www.businessweek.com

3. **Social responsibility.** Athletic footwear manufacturer New Balance is one of the few companies in its industry that still manufactures products in the United States. Go to the Web site listed below and learn more about the firm's commitment to U.S. manufacturing. Prepare a report that relates this commitment to the firm's other core values.

   http://www.newbalance.com/company/

Note: Internet Web addresses change frequently. If you don't find the exact sites listed, you may need to access the organization's home page and search from there or use a search engine such as Bing or Google.

Pink ribbons for breast cancer research. Product Red merchandise for fighting HIV/AIDS and other diseases. Yellow LiveStrong bracelets for cancer research. These campaigns are examples of cause-related marketing. A typical cause-related marketing campaign teams one or more nonprofit organizations with for-profit ones. The for-profit organization announces publicly that it will donate some or all of the proceeds from a product or products to the nonprofit organization. For example, if you buy an iPod Nano Product [Red], a Starbucks [Red] card, or a Product [Red] T-shirt from the Gap, that corporation makes a contribution to the Global Fund to Fight AIDS, Tuberculosis, and Malaria. One hundred percent of the contribution goes to grants financed by the Global Fund for projects in Africa.

Cause-related marketing began in 1976 when the March of Dimes, which fights birth defects, wanted to raise funds in the West. It teamed with Marriott Corporation, which wanted to generate publicity for its new Great America theme park in California. The campaign was a huge success. Cause-related marketing has grown from almost nothing to roughly $1.57 billion. Social networking groups such as Facebook and Twitter have become official or unofficial resources for information and for spreading the word about causes such as education, fighting disease, clean water, and environmental issues.

After the recent recession, consumers spent less and turned to inexpensive, family-oriented activities. In this climate, a new type of cause-related partnership came into being.

Disney Parks announced its new "Give a Day, Get a Disney Day" program for 2010. In partnership with the HandsOn Network, a national volunteer network, Disney offered free one-day, one-park admission to the first million people who performed one day of certified volunteer work for a participating charity or other program. Habitat for Humanity and Ronald McDonald House Charities were just two of the nationwide programs, but volunteers could also clean up a local park; work at a homeless shelter, museum, or other institution; or walk or run for a cause such as diabetes or heart disease. Many of the activities were family oriented and were intended to help parents teach their children about volunteering. Families of up to

eight could volunteer together, and children as young as six could participate.

Jay Rasulo, the chairman of Walt Disney Parks and Resorts, said, ". . . we want to recognize . . . the contributions people make to their communities every day. We want to inspire 1 million volunteers—people who will invest time and energy to make their own communities and neighborhoods a better place."

Visitors can check the Disney Web site to find opportunities, arranged by location, for volunteering through the HandsOn network. So many people visited the sign-up page on that day that it crashed several times. Although Disney had no official social network pages, multiple unofficial ones were created. In addition, HandsOn publicized the program through its Facebook, Twitter, and YouTube accounts.

Tree Fresno's goal is to reforest areas near the San Joaquin Valley in California. More than 150 people, many in families, volunteered through the Disney program to spend a day planting seedlings. A thousand other people in family groups also signed up to volunteer. The program was closing in on its goal of 1 million volunteers. Although it is too soon to tell whether volunteer cause-related marketing will become more common, the success of "Give a Day, Get a Disney Day" has set a standard to which future projects can aspire.

Questions for Critical Thinking

1. How does Disney fulfill its responsibility to the general public?
2. Which organization benefits more from the "Give a Day, Get a Disney Day" program—Disney or HandsOn? Explain your answer.

Sources: Walt Disney Company and Affiliated Companies, "Give a Day of Volunteer Service in 2010, Get a Day of Disney Theme Park Fun—Free," September 29, 2009, http://corporate.disney.go.com, accessed February 2010; HandsOn Network, "Give a Day. Get a Disney Day," n.d., http://handsonnetwork.org; Carrie Urban Kapraun, "Disney and the HandsOn Network: Give a Day, Get a Disney Day," *IEG*, January 22, 2010, http://www.sponsorship.com; Nancy Osborne, "Give a Day, Get a Disney Day," *KFSN*, January 22, 2010; http://abclocal.go.com/kfsn; Rachael Chong, "Cause-Related Marketing: Just Plain Ol' Marketing?" *Huffington Post,* January 4, 2010; http://www.huffingtonpost.com; Product Red Web site, http://www.joinred.com; Joe Waters, "Why Social Media and Cause Marketing Belong Together," Selfish Giving, February 16, 2010, http://selfishgiving.com.

Greener Shipping—At Sea and in Port

For many years, environmentalists have advocated slower driving and slower flying as ways to save fuel and cut down on emissions of greenhouse gases. This equation applies at sea as well as on land and in the air. When the price of oil reached $145 a barrel, the container shipping giant Maersk Line decided to take action.

Based in Copenhagen, Maersk is the largest shipping line in the world, with more than 500 vessels. Instead of the standard speed of 24 or 25 knots (just under 29 miles per hour), the *Ebba Maersk* sails at 12 knots (just under 14 miles per hour), a speed known in the industry as "super slow steaming." Super slow steaming reduces fuel consumption from 350 tons per day to 100 to 150 tons and saves $5,000 an hour. Maersk has shifted hundreds of its ships to super slow steaming. Other shipping lines resisted slowing their vessels down at first, but now many of them have adopted "slow steaming" speed (20 knots, or 23 miles per hour) or super slow steaming.

The recent recession created a further incentive for container shipping lines to reduce costs and save energy. Among other measures, Maersk's ships have lowered their interior lighting and substituted rolls of paper towels for paper napkins in their dining salons. "The previous focus has been on 'What will it cost?' and 'Get it to me as fast as possible,' " said Søren Stig Nielsen, the director of environmental sustainability at Maersk. "But now there is a third dimension. What's the CO_2 footprint?"

Then there are the containers themselves. Whether empty or full, they occupy the same amount of space. Made of steel, they are still heavy even when empty. The Dutch company Cargoshell has devised a container that, when empty, collapses in less than half a minute to one-quarter the size of a full one. Thus Cargoshells can be stacked more compactly than steel containers. Steel containers usually have outward-opening doors that take up an entire side panel. The Cargoshell's door simply rolls up or down. Cargoshells are made of fiber-reinforced composite materials, so they weigh 25 percent less than steel containers. They need no paint because they do not corrode. The composites are good insulators, important for temperature control. Manufacturing Cargoshells generates less carbon dioxide than manufacturing steel containers. All these factors add up to reduced costs, energy savings, and lower carbon emissions.

The ports where cargo ships arrive and depart are crowded with cranes, trucks, trains, tugboats, and ferries—all of which emit diesel exhaust into the atmosphere. The U.S. Environmental Protection Agency (EPA) has declared diesel exhaust to be a possible carcinogen. To reduce exposure to it, the EPA has initiated Clean Ports USA, a voluntary, incentive-based program to encourage ports and truck fleet owners to reduce emissions. Strategies include changing to cleaner-burning diesel fuels; retrofitting or repairing existing diesel engines (which can last 20 or 30 years); replacing aging engines or vehicles with newer, less-polluting ones; and reducing time that engines are left idling. In an unlikely alliance, the Teamsters union and environmentalists have joined forces to persuade the Port of Los Angeles to ban older trucks from transporting goods away from port and have the trucking companies buy newer, cleaner-running rigs.

Taken separately, all these measures are worthy efforts to fight global warming. Taken together, they could add up to a "green" integration of almost all aspects of the shipping industry.

Questions for Critical Thinking

1. How do Maersk and Cargoshell carry out their responsibilities to society?
2. Many of the goods you buy and use are imported from overseas and sold more cheaply than if they were made in the United States. But do they have hidden, nonmonetary costs? Use the information in this case as a guide.

Sources: Steven Greenhouse, "Clearing the Air at American Ports," *The New York Times,* February 26, 2010, http://www.newyorktimes.com; Maersk Web site, http://www.maersk.com, accessed February 18, 2010; "Maersk Cuts Fuel Use, Emissions 30% by Slowing Down," *Environmental Leader,* February 18, 2020, http://www.environmentalleader.com; Elisabeth Rosenthal, "Slow and Steady Across the Sea Aids Profit and the Environment," *The New York Times,* February 17, 2010, http://www.newyorktimes.com; John W. Miller, "Maersk: Container Ship Cuts Costs to Stay Afloat," Polaris Institute, February 2010, http://www.polarisinstitute.org; Cargoshell Web site, http://www.cargoshell.com, accessed February 12, 2010; Clean Ports USA, U.S. Environmental Protection Agency, http://epa.gov, accessed February 12, 2010; Jace Shoemaker-Galloway, "Cargoshell Collapsible Shipping Containers: A Greener and Flatter Way to Transport Goods," *Triple Pundit,* February 5, 2010, http://www.triplepundit.com.

Seventh Generation was founded in Vermont twenty years ago on the premise that there's a better way to do business, one that protects both the planet and the people. The company's name is derived from the Great Law of the Iroquois, which mandates that "In every deliberation, we must consider the impact of our decision on the next seven generations." Co-founder and executive chairman Jeffrey Hollender takes this mandate literally.

Hollender refers to himself as "chief protagonist" of Seventh Generation. For two decades he has campaigned for environmentally responsible consumer products, manufacturing processes, and operations at Seventh Generation. In addition, he campaigns outside the company to raise awareness about the importance of consumerism in preservation of the environment.

Hollender admits to watershed moments in his own life that have led him to redirect his company. When his young son had a particularly severe asthma attack, the doctor told Hollender that the best way to controls his son's asthma was to control his environment—in particular, his household environment. Hollender recognized the enormity of this statement and took it on as a corporate challenge. EPA research had already revealed that the air in the average home is two to five times more polluted than outdoor air. "I realized then that Seventh Generation had a lot more to offer than protecting the outdoor environment, and it became the turning point for the company." If Seventh Generation could offer a broad spectrum of household products that did not contribute to indoor pollution—but performed cleaning and other tasks as effectively as products containing toxic chemicals—the company could achieve an entirely new level of corporate responsibility.

Senior chemist Cara Bondi describes the challenge she and her colleagues faced. "Prior to the last decade, companies would try to put out green products but they didn't really do the job," which resulted in these products failing in the marketplace. If they weren't effective at cleaning laundry or dishes, appealing to consumers' consciences wouldn't help. "If you expect someone to transition from a traditional cleaning product to green cleaning products, you need to have the performance that they expect," she explains. "It was a problem that needed to be addressed. We wanted to be able to give consumers a solution that was authentic and sustaining." In recent years, scientists have been able to isolate more naturally derived ingredients that are equal to chemically based ingredients. Now consumers must be re-educated about these products and convinced to give them another try. One such product has been developed by Seventh Generation in partnership with another firm, CleanWell. It is a disinfectant made from the garden herb thyme. The new product actually kills bacteria on surfaces without the use of toxic chemicals.

As chief executive, Hollender must consider his company as a whole organization—not just a chemistry lab. "When you think about sustainability and responsibility, you have to take a holistic approach," he notes. "You have to look at everything in your supply chain and the life cycle of the product." Hollender emphasizes that a socially responsible firm must consider every input and output, including raw materials, harvesting, manufacturing processes, warehousing, sales, and ultimate use—whether the consumer uses up the product, reuses or recycles it, or throws it away. Hollender describes how, in examining Seventh Generation's inputs and outputs, company researchers discovered that the single most energy-wasting feature of its soap products was the fact that they required hot water to perform effectively. So the firm's team reformulated them to function in cold water.

Seventh Generation continues to develop new and better products. The firm's Web site is filled with information on sustainability, including the blog "Ask the Science Man," where consumers can ask just about any question—such as how to find nontoxic nail polish. And though Hollender's involvement in day-to-day operations is reduced as he takes his message to a nationwide audience, he remains committed to his company's corporate responsibility. "Few businesses are willing to talk about their failures," he says. "But it's that level of transparency that will build deep loyalty with the consumer." Hollender is determined to build a loyalty that will last at least seven generations.

Questions for Critical Thinking

1. What might be some ethical issues faced by Seventh Generation managers, researchers, and employees?

2. What steps might Hollender take to ensure that ethical leadership continues as he spends more time away from Seventh Generation?

3. Give examples of ways in which Seventh Generation fulfills its social responsibilities in each of the four categories: to the general public; to customers; to investors; and to employees.

4. Visit the Seventh Generation Web site at http://www.seventhgeneration.com and read more about the firm's community involvement. Discuss the company's efforts. Do they match well with the Great Law of the Iroquois?

Sources: Seventh Generation Web site, http://www.seventhgeneration.com, accessed August 18, 2010; CleanWell Web site, http://www.cleanwelltoday.com, accessed August 18, 2010; "Seventh Generation and Walmart Announce Strategic Partnership," *Market Wire,* July 26, 2010, http://www.easyir.com; Danielle Sacks, "Jeffrey Hollender: Seventh Generation, Triple Bottom Line Entrepreneur," *Fast Company.com,* February 2, 2010, http://www.fastcompany.com.

Learning Objectives

[1] Distinguish between microeconomics and macroeconomics. Explain the factors that drive demand and supply.

[2] Describe each of the four different types of market structures in a private enterprise system, and compare the three major types of economic systems.

[3] Identify and describe the four stages of the business cycle. Explain how productivity, price level changes, and employment levels affect the stability of a nation's economy.

[4] Discuss how monetary policy and fiscal policy are used to manage an economy's performance.

[5] Describe the major global economic challenges of the 21st century.

The Most Challenging Economy in Decades

Steve Cole/iStockphoto

Obamanomics: Stimulus to Help the Economy

Chuck Kennedy/Bloomberg News/Getty Images, Inc.

As Barack Obama took his historic oath of office, the U.S. economy was faltering. Daily news headlined the worst downturn since the Great Depression. All eyes turned to Washington, D.C., for help getting cash and credit flowing into the financial system again. Opinions remained deeply divided about the new president's $787 billion economic stimulus plan, with some wanting less government spending and more tax cuts, but most people believed that the government had to do *something*. Reeling from a huge burden of bad debt left over from the bursting of the housing bubble, banks and other lending institutions had essentially withdrawn from the economic playing field, with too little cash or confidence to continue lending. Businesses that depended on short-term loans from these lenders were left without the funds they needed to conduct their everyday operations or expand for the future. As already debt-laden consumers grew wary of spending in an uncertain economy, sales slumped in industries across the board, inventories of unsold goods piled up, and companies like 3M, Home Depot, Starbucks, Microsoft, Nokia, and dozens more announced layoffs of thousands of workers in the wake of unprecedented financial losses. Unemployment was soaring, dampening consumer spending even further. Stock prices fell, sales of new homes—a major indicator of the economy's health—plunged, cars sat on dealers' lots, and retailers reported the worst holiday selling season in decades. The United States cut imports of foreign-made products like televisions and computers. Foreign manufacturers cut back production, and with less money to spend, overseas businesses trimmed demand for U.S. products as well, forcing the country's exports down. Bad news spread worldwide. In an ominous sign, the U.S. economy began to shrink. An economist at JPMorgan Chase noted, "The fact that you're not seeing any evidence that things are turning for the better has added quite a bit to the urgency to get things done and do something substantial."

After much debate, Congress adopted President Obama's plan to put government money into the economy, although it was certain to be only a partial solution. What was clear, however, was that only the government had both the funds to commit to such a huge economic rescue plan and the power to direct the money broadly to various projects that would create jobs across the nation. Jobs would generate income, increase confidence, and spur a recovery. In fact, President Obama hoped building projects in transportation and housing would quickly save or create at least 3.5 million jobs. The plan set aside almost $18 billion for investments in high-speed rail and mass transit projects and $48 billion for transportation improvements such as bridge and highway repair to kick-start that job creation. The rest of the $506 billion was divided among social programs that included roughly $87 billion for state Medicaid health insurance plans for lower- and middle-class families and over $82 billion for various education and job training programs. Cash payments to seniors and disabled veterans, financing to repair and modernize public housing, support for local law enforcement, and budgets to increase energy efficiency in government and military facilities, improve public parks, and modernize the nation's electric grid were among many other spending lines. The stimulus also provided tax relief to businesses that are trying to make payroll and create jobs and to individuals and families. Among the $281 billion in tax breaks were some that rewarded consumers for new home and car purchases and others for businesses to help improve their short-term finances. For instance, business tax incentives for renewable energy facilities added up to more than $14 billion, with millions more for hiring disadvantaged workers and expanding industrial development.

The government's goal was to inject money into the economy for both the short and long term so that businesses could continue to function, new jobs could put the unemployed back to work, and consumers could return money to the economy by picking up their spending on household goods, cars, and appliances, as well as on luxuries like restaurant meals and vacations. It will take time for parts of the plan to be implemented and for the nation to know how well it has worked. Adjustments will be needed along the way. But businesses and individuals were willing to work with the government to get the country back on its feet again. That will be a big step toward a global economic recovery.[1]

Overview

microeconomics study of small economic units, such as individual consumers, families, and businesses.

economics social science that analyzes the choices people and governments make in allocating scarce resources.

macroeconomics study of a nation's overall economic issues, such as how an economy maintains and allocates resources and how a government's policies affect the standards of living of its citizens.

When we examine the exchanges that companies and societies make as a whole, we are focusing on the *economic systems* operating in different nations. These systems reflect the combination of policies and choices a nation makes to allocate resources among its citizens. Countries vary in the ways they allocate scarce resources.

Economics, which analyzes the choices people and governments make in allocating scarce resources, affects each of us, because everyone is involved in producing, distributing, or simply consuming goods and services. In fact, your life is affected by economics every day. When you decide what goods to buy, what services to use, or what activities to fit into your schedule, you are making economic choices. Understanding how the activities of one industry affect those of other industries, and how they relate in the overall picture of a country, is an important part of understanding economics.

The choices you make actually may be international in scope. If you are in the market for a new car, you might visit several dealers in a row on the same street—Ford, Chrysler, Honda, Hyundai, and General Motors. You might decide on Hyundai—a Korean firm—but your car might very well be manufactured in the United States, using parts from all over the world. Although firms sometimes emphasize the American origin of their products in order to appeal to consumers' desire to support the U.S. economy, many items are made of components from a variety of nations.

Businesses and not-for-profit organizations also make economic decisions when they choose how to use human and natural resources; invest in equipment, machinery, and buildings; and form partnerships with

other firms. Economists refer to the study of small economic units, such as individual consumers, families, and businesses, as **microeconomics.**

The study of a country's overall economic issues is called **macroeconomics** (*macro* means "large"). Macroeconomics addresses such issues as how an economy uses its resources and how government policies affect people's standards of living. The substitution of ethanol for gasoline or biodiesel for diesel fuel has macroeconomic consequences—affecting many parts of the U.S. economy and suppliers around the world. Macroeconomics examines not just the economic policies of individual nations, but the ways in which those individual policies affect the overall world economy. Because so much business is conducted around the world, a law enacted in one country can easily affect a transaction that takes place in another country. Although macroeconomic issues have a broad scope, they help shape the decisions that individuals, families, and businesses make every day.

This chapter introduces economic theory and the economic challenges facing individuals, businesses, and governments in the global marketplace. We begin with the microeconomic concepts of supply and demand and their effect on the prices people pay for goods and services. Next we explain the various types of economic systems, along with tools for comparing and evaluating their performance. Then we examine the ways in which governments seek to manage economies to create stable business environments in their countries. The final section in the chapter looks at some of the driving economic forces currently affecting people's lives.

Microeconomics: The Forces of Demand and Supply

Think about your own economic activities. You shop for groceries, subscribe to a cell phone service, pay college tuition, fill your car's tank with gas. Now think about your family's economic activities. When you were growing up, your parents might have owned a home or rented an apartment. You might have taken a family vacation. Your parents may have shopped at discount clubs or at local stores. Each of these choices relates to the study of microeconomics. They also help determine both the prices of goods and services and the amounts sold. Information about these activities is vital to companies because their survival and ability to grow depends on selling enough products priced high enough to cover costs and earn profits. The same information is important to consumers who must make purchase decisions based on prices and the availability of the goods and services they need.

At the heart of every business endeavor is an exchange between a buyer and a seller. The buyer recognizes that he or she needs or wants a particular good or service—whether it's a hamburger or a haircut—and is willing to pay a seller for it. The seller requires the exchange in order to earn a profit and stay in business. So the exchange process involves both demand and supply. **Demand** refers to the willingness and ability of buyers to purchase goods and services at different prices. The other side of the exchange process is **supply**, the amount of goods and services for sale at different prices. Understanding the factors that determine demand and supply, as well as how the two interact, can help you understand many actions and decisions of individuals, businesses, and government. This section takes a closer look at these concepts.

Joshua Hodge Photography/iStockphoto

You shop for groceries, subscribe to a cell phone service, pay college tuition, fill your car's tank with gas. Each of these choices relates to the study of microeconomics. They also help determine the prices of goods and the amounts sold.

demand willingness and ability of buyers to purchase goods and services.

supply willingness and ability of sellers to provide goods and services.

Factors Driving Demand

For most of us, economics amounts to a balance between what we want and what we can afford. Because of this dilemma, each person must choose how much money to save and how much to spend. We must also decide among all the goods and services competing for our attention. Suppose you wanted to purchase a smart phone. You'd have to choose from a variety of brands and models. You'd also have to decide where you wanted to go to buy one. After shopping around, you might decide you didn't want a smart phone at all. Instead, you might purchase something else, or save your money.

Demand is driven by a number of factors that influence how people decide to spend their money, including price. It can be driven by consumer preferences. It may also be driven by outside circumstances or larger economic events. During the recent recession, the videogame industry—including portable players and consoles, software, and associated items—experienced an 8 percent decline in sales from a previous year. Nevertheless, the last several years were also the strongest for video game sales.[2]

Demand can also increase the availability of certain types of Web sites and services. Recognizing the enormous popularity of Google's YouTube, and believing the demand would grow, networks NBC and Fox teamed up to launch an advertising-supported online video site, which provides programming from different entertainment companies. The site, called Hulu.com, offers full-length movies and television shows. It also hosts programming from NBC and Fox and shows from Sony and Metro-Goldwyn-Mayer. (Disney joined later.)[3]

Eric Shelton/©AP/Wide World Photos

Demand is driven by consumer tastes and preferences as well as by economic conditions. Consumers tend to fill up their gas tanks more frequently when the per-gallon price is low.

demand curve graph of the amount of a product that buyers will purchase at different prices.

In general, as the price of a good or service goes up, people buy smaller amounts. In other words, as price rises, the quantity demanded declines. At lower prices, consumers are generally willing to buy more of a good. A **demand curve** is a graph of the amount of a product that buyers will purchase at different prices. Demand curves typically slope downward, meaning that lower and lower prices attract larger and larger purchases.

Gasoline provides a classic example of how demand curves work. The left side of Figure 3.1 shows a possible demand curve for the total amount of gasoline that people will purchase at different prices. The prices shown may not reflect the actual price in your location at this particular time, but they still demonstrate the concept. When gasoline is priced at $2.99 a gallon, drivers may fill up their tanks once or twice a week. At $3.39 a gallon, many of them start economizing. They may combine errands or carpool to work. So the quantity of gasoline demanded at $3.39 a gallon is lower than the amount demanded at $2.99 a gallon. The opposite happens at $2.59 a gallon. More gasoline is sold at $2.59 a gallon than at $2.99 a gallon, as people opt to run more errands or take a weekend trip. However, as mentioned earlier, other factors may cause consumers to accept higher prices anyway. They may have made vacation plans in advance and do not want to cancel them. Or they may be required to drive to work every day.

Economists make a clear distinction between changes in the quantity demanded at various prices and changes in overall demand. A change in quantity demanded, such as the change that occurs at different gasoline prices, is simply movement along the demand curve. A change in overall demand, on the other hand, results in an entirely new demand curve. Businesses are constantly trying to make predictions about both kinds of demand, and a miscalculation can cause problems. In the case of gasoline, which is derived from crude oil, many factors come into play. One factor that is beginning to make a major impact is the investment in and development of alternative fuels such as biodiesel, wind, and solar power. If alternatives are developed and readily available, then demand for oil may level off. Another issue is the U.S. economy. When a downturn occurs, so does the demand for oil and other goods. But disruptions in energy sources have the opposite effect; political unrest in oil-rich nations such as Nigeria or extreme weather that takes refineries offline increase the demand for the oil that is available.[4]

We can illustrate how the increased demand for gasoline worldwide has created a new demand curve, as shown in Figure 3.1. The new demand curve shifts to the right of the old demand curve, indicating that overall demand has increased at every price. A demand curve can also shift to the left when the demand for a good or service drops. However, the demand curve still has the same shape.

Although price is the underlying cause of movement along a demand curve, many factors can combine to determine the overall demand for a product—that is, the shape and position of the demand curve. These influences include customer preferences and incomes, the prices of substitute and complementary items, the number of buyers in a market, and the strength of their optimism regarding the future. Changes in any of these factors produce a new demand curve.

Changes in household income also change demand. As consumers have more money to spend, firms can sell more products at every price. This means the demand curve has

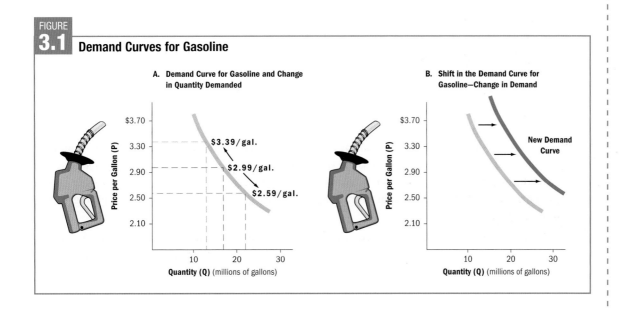

FIGURE 3.1 Demand Curves for Gasoline

A. Demand Curve for Gasoline and Change in Quantity Demanded

Price per Gallon (P)

$3.70
3.30 — $3.39/gal.
2.90 — $2.99/gal.
2.50 — $2.59/gal.
2.10

Quantity (Q) (millions of gallons)
10   20   30

B. Shift in the Demand Curve for Gasoline—Change in Demand

Price per Gallon (P)

$3.70
3.30   New Demand Curve
2.90
2.50
2.10

Quantity (Q) (millions of gallons)
10   20   30

shifted to the right. When income shrinks, nearly everyone suffers, and the demand curve shifts to the left. High-end retailers like Nordstrom, Saks, and Neiman Marcus experienced a decrease in demand for their luxury goods, as consumers thought twice about buying designer handbags, shoes, and clothing. Meanwhile, discount retailers such as Walmart experienced an increase in sales, so their demand curve shifted a bit to the right.[5] Table 3.1 describes how a demand curve is likely to respond to each of these changes.

For a business to succeed, management must carefully monitor the factors that may affect demand for the goods and services it hopes to sell. Costco has free sampling stations throughout its stores where customers can try small portions of various foods prepared on site. This practice encourages customers to buy something in the department where they are sampling.

Table 3.1 Expected Shifts in Demand Curves

	DEMAND CURVE SHIFTS	
FACTOR	**TO THE RIGHT _IF_:**	**TO THE LEFT _IF_:**
Customer preferences	Increase	Decrease
Number of buyers	Increase	Decrease
Buyers' incomes	Increase	Decrease
Prices of substitute goods	Increase	Decrease
Prices of complementary goods	Decrease	Increase
Future expectations become more	Optimistic	Pessimistic

Factors Driving Supply

Important economic factors also affect supply, the willingness and ability of firms to provide goods and services at different prices. Just as consumers must decide about how to spend their money, businesses must decide what products to sell, and how.

Sellers would prefer to charge higher prices for their products. A **supply curve** shows the relationship between different prices and the quantities that sellers will offer for sale, regardless of demand. Movement along the supply curve is the opposite of movement along the demand curve. So as price rises, the quantity that sellers are willing to supply also rises. At progressively lower prices, the quantity supplied decreases. In Figure 3.2, a possible supply curve for gasoline shows that increasing prices for gasoline should bring increasing supplies to market.

Businesses need certain inputs to operate effectively in producing their output. As discussed in Chapter 1, these *factors of production* include natural resources, capital, human resources, and entrepreneurship. Natural resources include land, building sites, forests, and mineral deposits. Capital refers to resources such as technology, tools, information, physical facilities, and financial capabilities. Human resources include the physical labor and intellectual inputs contributed by employees. Entrepreneurship is the willingness to take risks to create and operate a business. Factors of production play a central role in determining the overall supply of goods and services.

A change in the cost or availability of any of these inputs can shift the entire supply curve, either increasing or decreasing the amount available at every price. If the cost of land increases, a firm might not be able to purchase the site for a more efficient manufacturing plant, which would lower production levels, shifting the supply curve to the left. But if the company finds a way to speed up the production process, allowing it to turn out more products with less labor, the change reduces the overall cost of the finished products, which shifts the supply curve to the right.

Table 3.2 summarizes how changes in various factors can affect the supply curve. Sometimes forces of nature can affect the supply curve. During a record-breaking freeze

supply curve graph that shows the relationship between different prices and the quantities that sellers will offer for sale, regardless of demand.

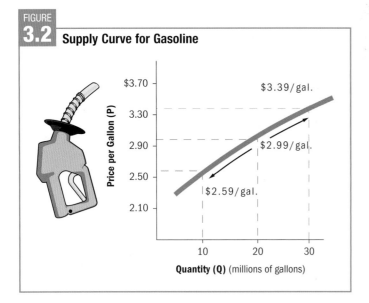

FIGURE 3.2 Supply Curve for Gasoline

Table 3.2 Expected Shifts in Supply Curves

FACTOR	SUPPLY CURVE SHIFTS	
	TO THE RIGHT *IF*:	TO THE LEFT *IF*:
Costs of inputs	Decrease	Increase
Costs of technologies	Decrease	Increase
Taxes	Decrease	Increase
Number of suppliers	Increase	Decrease

one recent January, a significant percentage of Florida's citrus crop, including oranges and lemons, was severely damaged. Because the fruit could not be harvested and shipped, supply dropped. The U.S. Department of Agriculture estimated that the next harvest could be the second lowest since 2000. The freeze could also affect the following year's crop if trees are not able to flower in the spring. However, growers said that even the frozen fruit could still be used for juice.[6]

The agriculture industry has often experienced such shifts in the supply curve. As consumers increase their demand for locally grown produce, more and more farmers in colder regions are extending the growing season by operating heated greenhouses to supply vegetables and fruits normally available only during the summer months. Winter farming—some of which is also organic—can boost rural economies by creating new jobs and bringing new income to a region. Paul Lorrain, a farmer in Lyman, Maine, operates greenhouses that yield about 300 pounds of produce per week between October and the beginning of May. He sells it to local restaurants, at a farmers market, and through a community food co-op. Lorrain says of the demand, "We have gone from not being able to give it away to not being able to grow enough."[7]

How Demand and Supply Interact

Separate shifts in demand and supply have obvious effects on prices and the availability of products. In the real world, changes do not alternatively affect demand and supply. Several factors often change at the same time—and they keep changing. Sometimes such changes in multiple factors cause contradictory pressures on prices and quantities. In other cases, the final direction of prices and quantities reflects the factor that has changed the most. The "Hit & Miss" feature discusses issues of demand and supply in the international oil market.

Figure 3.3 shows the interaction of both supply and demand curves for gasoline on a single graph. Notice that the two curves intersect at *P*. The law of supply and demand states that prices (*P*) are set by the intersection of the supply and demand curves. The point where the two curves meet identifies the **equilibrium price**, the prevailing market price at which you can buy an item.

equilibrium price
prevailing market price at which you can buy an item.

If the actual market price differs from the equilibrium price, buyers and sellers tend to make economic choices that restore the equilibrium level. The price of gold hit a record high in December 2009, but when the Federal Reserve Bank raised interest rates and the dollar gained strength against the euro, gold prices fell. Investors always seem to return to gold as a safe standard, according to economists, and consumers who are intent on buying jewelry most likely will do so, but they may buy more or fewer pieces as the price of gold changes over time.[8]

In other situations, suppliers react to market forces by reducing prices. For a number of years, fast-food chains such as McDonald's and Wendy's attracted customers by offering everyday value menus and coupons. However, the recent economic downturn has meant that people are more likely to eat at home and go out less, so the chains experienced a drop in profits. Competition among the chains, already strong, could grow even fiercer, depending on the length of the economic recovery.[9]

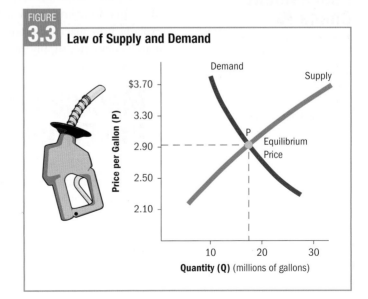

FIGURE
3.3 **Law of Supply and Demand**

Hit & Miss

Supply, Demand, and Swings in Oil Prices

Low crude oil prices are a boon for U.S. consumers, who depend on oil as an ingredient in everything from nonstick cookware to gasoline and home heating fuel. OPEC, the group of oil-producing nations that supplies the bulk of the world's crude oil, is usually able to control the price of crude, and ultimately of gasoline, by controlling the supply. If OPEC's members agree to reduce their output, for example, oil supplies in industrialized nations grow tight, and prices at the pump and factories generally rise. When OPEC starts producing again, supplies rise, and prices are forced down. But everything doesn't always go according to plan.

Following the global financial crisis, oil consumption fell as factories closed and consumer demand slowed, especially in the United States, the world's largest oil consumer. Rising unemployment and a weak economy drastically cut the number of vehicles on the road. Demand for oil fell almost 8 percent and was expected to continue dropping. The price of crude crashed after hitting a high of $145 only a few months before.

OPEC gradually slowed supply, hoping to prop the price up to its preferred level of at least $70 a barrel by reducing output by about 5 percent worldwide. But as much as oil producers want to keep prices up, in part to help meet rising production costs, many observers think any significant increase in the price of this critical factor of production will add more pain to the global economy.

Can the price be too low? From oil consumers' viewpoint, "politically it is better to say we need the lowest possible oil prices," says the director of a Swiss energy research firm. "But there are economic implications to low prices, and not just for OPEC producers." As long as oil is cheap, some fear that industrialized nations will continue to rely on it instead of investing in cheaper, cleaner, and ecologically renewable energy alternatives.

Meanwhile, the drastic swings in oil prices left oil producers shaken. "Our sector is no stranger to cycles," said the CEO of an Italian oil company. "But the turbulence we are currently experiencing— with oil doubling in … nine months … and then losing two-thirds of its value in the following six months—is unprecedented."

Further complicating the price picture are oil traders, who buy at low prices, wait for prices to rise, then sell at a profit. The International Monetary Fund reported that such speculation "has played a significant role in the run-up of oil prices" and contributed to a rapid glut of what one observer calls "historic proportions."

While producers are cutting back production to keep prices from falling further, one thing is certain. As an economic recovery gets under way in earnest, global demand will rise again, and so will the price.

Questions for Critical Thinking

1. What roles do supply and demand play in the economics of oil production?
2. What have you observed at your local gas station that suggests the fluctuation of oil supply and oil demand?

Sources: "Crude Oil Falls as Recession Batters U.S.," *MSNBC*, February 6, 2009, http://www.msnbc.com; Jad Mouawad, "OPEC Achieves Cut in Output, Halting Price Slide," *The New York Times*, January 26, 2009, http://www.nytimes.com; Donna Abu-Nasr, "CEO of Eni Says Oil Price Bumps Unprecedented," Associated Press, January 26, 2009, http://www.google.com/hostednews/ap/; Greg Flakus, "Oil Storage at Record Levels as Speculators Await Higher Prices," *VOA News*, January 23, 2009, http://www.voanews.com.

Assessment Check ✔

1. Define microeconomics and macroeconomics.
2. Explain demand and supply curves.
3. How do factors of production influence the overall supply of goods and services?

As pointed out earlier, the forces of demand and supply can be affected by a variety of factors. One important variable is the larger economic environment. The next section explains how macroeconomics and economic systems influence market forces and, ultimately, demand, supply, and prices.

Macroeconomics: Issues for the Entire Economy

Every country faces decisions about how to best use the four basic factors of production. Each nation's policies and choices help determine its economic system. But the political, social, and legal environments differ in every country. So no two countries have exactly the same economic system. In general, however, these systems can be classified into three categories: private enterprise systems; planned economies; or combinations of the two, referred to as mixed economies. As business becomes an increasingly global undertaking, it is important to understand the primary features of the various economic systems operating around the world.

Capitalism: The Private Enterprise System and Competition

Most industrialized nations operate economies based on the *private enterprise system*, also known as *capitalism* or a *market economy*. A private enterprise system rewards businesses for meeting the needs and demands of consumers. Government tends to favor a hands-off attitude toward controlling business ownership, profits, and resource allocations. Instead, competition regulates economic life, creating opportunities and challenges that businesspeople must handle to succeed.

The relative competitiveness of a particular industry is an important consideration for every firm because it determines the ease and cost of doing business within that industry. Four basic types of competition take shape in a private enterprise system: pure competition, monopolistic competition, oligopoly, and monopoly. Table 3.3 highlights the main differences among these types of competition.

<u>Pure competition</u> is a market structure, like that of small-scale agriculture or fishing, in which large numbers of buyers and sellers exchange homogeneous products and no single participant has a significant influence on price. Instead, prices are set by the market as the forces of supply and demand interact. Firms can easily enter or leave a purely competitive market because no single company dominates. Also, in pure competition, buyers see little difference between the goods and services offered by competitors.

Fishing and agriculture are good examples of pure competition. The wheat grown and sold by one farmer in the Midwest is virtually identical to that sold by others. As rainfall and

pure competition
market structure in which large numbers of buyers and sellers exchange homogeneous products and no single participant has a significant influence on price.

Table
3.3 **Types of Competition**

CHARACTERISTICS	TYPES OF COMPETITION			
	PURE COMPETITION	MONOPOLISTIC COMPETITION	OLIGOPOLY	MONOPOLY
Number of competitors	Many	Few to many	Few	No direct competition
Ease of entry into industry by new firms	Easy	Somewhat difficult	Difficult	Regulated by government
Similarity of goods or services offered by competing firms	Similar	Different	Similar or different	No directly competing products
Control over price by individual firms	None	Some	Some	Considerable in a pure monopoly; little in a regulated monopoly
Examples	Small-scale farmer in Indiana	Local fitness center	Boeing Aircraft	Rawlings Sporting Goods, exclusive supplier of major-league baseballs

Paul Poplis/Food Pix/Getty Images, Inc.

Fishing is a good example of pure competition. Because clams gathered by one individual are virtually identical to those gathered by others, the price rises and falls with changes in supply and demand. Whenever a poisonous "red tide" of algae infests the clam beds off the coast of New England, the supply of fresh clams plummets and the price skyrockets.

temperatures affect the crop growth, the price for this commodity rises or falls according to the law of supply and demand. The same concept applies to the fishing industry gathering clams and mussels off the coast of New England. The region's notorious "red tide" of algae sometimes contaminates part of the season's supply of shellfish just when summer tourists want them the most—and prices skyrocket.

Monopolistic competition is a market structure, like that for retailing, in which large numbers of buyers and sellers exchange differentiated (heterogeneous) products, so each participant has some control over price. Sellers can differentiate their products from competing offerings on the basis of price, quality, or other features. In an industry that features monopolistic competition, it is relatively easy for a firm to begin or stop selling a good or service. The success of one seller often attracts new competitors to such a market. Individual firms also have some control over how their goods and services are priced.

One example of monopolistic competition is the market for pet food. Consumers can choose from private-label (store brands such as Walmart's Ol'Roy) and brand-name products like Purina in bags, boxes, and cans. Producers of pet food and the stores that sell it have wide latitude in setting prices. Consumers can choose the store or brand with the lowest prices, or sellers can convince them that a more expensive offering, for example the Fromm brand, is worth more because it offers better nutrition, more convenience, or other benefits.

An **oligopoly** is a market situation in which relatively few sellers compete and high start-up costs form barriers to keep out new competitors. In some oligopolistic industries, such as paper and steel, competitors offer similar products. In others, such as aircraft and automobiles, they sell different models and features. The huge investment required to enter an oligopoly market tends to discourage new competitors. The limited number of sellers also enhances the control these firms exercise over price. Competing products in an oligopoly usually sell for very similar prices because substantial price competition would reduce profits for all firms in the industry. So a price cut by one firm in an oligopoly will typically be met by its competitors. However, prices can vary from one market to another, as from one country to another.

The final type of market structure is a **monopoly**, in which a single seller dominates trade in a good or service for which buyers can find no close substitutes. A pure monopoly occurs when a firm possesses unique characteristics so important to competition in its industry that they serve as barriers to prevent entry by would-be competitors. After presiding over what many called monopolies in their respective areas, Microsoft and Google are expanding into each other's territory. Google launched Google Apps, an online suite of business applications, to compete with Microsoft's Exchange Server. Meanwhile, Microsoft launched its own search engine, Bing. Later, Microsoft and Yahoo Inc. announced plans to team up to challenge Google's domination of the Internet search market. The competition between Microsoft and Google may ultimately benefit consumers.[10]

Many firms create short-term monopolies when research breakthroughs permit them to receive exclusive patents on new products. In the pharmaceuticals industry, drug giants such as Merck and Pfizer invest billions in research and development programs. When the research leads to successful new drugs, the companies can enjoy the benefits of their

monopolistic competition market structure in which large numbers of buyers and sellers exchange heterogeneous products so each participant has some control over price.

oligopoly market situation in which relatively few sellers compete and high start-up costs form barriers to keep out new competitors.

monopoly market situation in which a single seller dominates trade in a good or service for which buyers can find no close substitutes.

Microsoft and Google are expanding into each other's territory. Microsoft launched its own search engine, Bing, and announced plans to team up with Yahoo! to challenge Google's domination of the Internet search market.

patents: the ability to set prices without fear of competitors undercutting them. Once the patent expires, generic substitutes enter the market, driving down prices.

Because a monopoly market lacks the benefits of competition, many governments regulate monopolies. Besides issuing patents and limiting their life, the government prohibits most pure monopolies through antitrust legislation such as the Sherman Act and the Clayton Act. The U.S. government has applied these laws against monopoly behavior by Microsoft and by disallowing proposed mergers of large companies in some industries. In other cases, the government permits certain monopolies in exchange for regulating their activities.

With **regulated monopolies**, a local, state, or federal government grants exclusive rights in a certain market to a single firm. Pricing decisions—particularly rate-increase requests—are subject to control by regulatory authorities such as state public service commissions. An example is the delivery of first-class mail, a monopoly held by the U.S. Postal Service. The USPS is a self-supporting corporation wholly owned by the federal government. Although it is no longer run by Congress, postal rates are set by a Postal Commission and approved by a Board of Governors.

During the 1980s and 1990s, the U.S. government trended away from regulated monopolies and toward deregulation. Regulated monopolies that have been deregulated include long-distance and local telephone service, cable television, cell phones, and electric utilities. The idea is to improve customer service and reduce prices for customers through increased competition. The Federal Communications Commission recently adopted a rule that bans cable operators from entering into exclusive agreements with owners of apartment buildings. This change will have an impact on the 30 percent of Americans who live in multiple-unit dwellings such as apartments, duplexes, and condominiums. Instead of being forced into a contract with one cable provider, residents of each apartment will have competitive choices. Phone companies such as AT&T and Verizon, which also offer cable service, are included in the rule.[11]

regulated monopolies local, state, or federal government grants exclusive rights in a certain market to a single firm.

Planned Economies: Socialism and Communism

planned economy government controls determine business ownership, profits, and resource allocation to accomplish government goals rather than those set by individual firms.

socialism economic system characterized by government ownership and operation of major industries such as communications.

communism economic system in which all property would be shared equally by the people of a community under the direction of a strong central government.

In a **planned economy**, government controls determine business ownership, profits, and resource allocation to accomplish government goals rather than those set by individual firms. Two forms of planned economies are communism and socialism.

Socialism is characterized by government ownership and operation of major industries such as communications. Socialists assert that major industries are too important to a society to be left in private hands and that government-owned businesses can serve the public's interest better than private firms. However, socialism allows private ownership in industries considered less crucial to social welfare, such as retail shops, restaurants, and certain types of manufacturing facilities. Scandinavian countries such as Denmark, Sweden, and Finland have many socialist features in their societies, as do some African nations and India.

The writings of Karl Marx in the mid-1800s formed the basis of communist theory. Marx believed that private enterprise economies created unfair conditions and led to worker exploitation because business owners controlled most of society's resources and reaped most of the economy's rewards. Instead, he suggested an economic system called **communism**, in which all property would be shared equally by the people of a community under the direction of a strong central government. Marx believed that elimination of private ownership of property and businesses would ensure the emergence of a classless society that would benefit all. Each individual would contribute to the nation's overall economic success, and resources would be distributed according to each person's needs. Under communism, the central government owns the means of production, and the people work for state-owned enterprises. The government determines what people can buy because it dictates what is produced in the nation's factories and farms.

Several nations adopted communist-like economic systems during the early 20th century in an effort to correct abuses they believed existed in their previous systems. In practice, however, these new governments typically gave less freedom of choice in regard to jobs and purchases. These governments might be best described as totalitarian socialism. These nations often made mistakes in allocating resources to compete in the growing global marketplace. Government-owned monopolies often suffer from inefficiency.

Consider the former Soviet Union, where large government bureaucracies controlled nearly every aspect of daily life. Shortages became chronic because producers had little or no incentive to satisfy customers. The quality of goods and services also suffered for the same reason. When Mikhail Gorbachev became the last president of the dying Soviet Union, he tried to improve the quality of Soviet-made products. Effectively shut out of trading in the global marketplace and caught up in a treasury-depleting arms race with the United States, the Soviet Union faced severe financial problems. Eventually, these events led to the collapse of Soviet communism and the breakup of the Soviet Union itself.

Today, communist-like systems exist in just a few countries, such as North Korea. By contrast, the People's Republic of China has shifted toward a more market-oriented economy. The national government has given local government and individual plant managers more say in business decisions and has permitted some private businesses. Households now have more control over agriculture, in contrast to the collectivized farms introduced during an earlier era. In addition, Western products such as McDonald's restaurants and Coca-Cola soft drinks are now part of Chinese consumers' lives, and Chinese workers manufacture products for export to other countries.

Mixed Market Economies

Private enterprise systems and planned economies adopt basically opposite approaches to operating economies. In reality, though, many countries operate **mixed market economies**, economic systems that draw from both types of economies, to different degrees. In nations generally considered to have a private enterprise economy, government-owned firms frequently operate alongside private enterprises. In the United States, programs like Medicare are government run.

France has blended socialist and free enterprise policies for hundreds of years. The nation's energy production, public transportation, and defense industries are run as nationalized industries, controlled by the government. Meanwhile, a market economy operates in other industries. Over the past two decades, the French government has loosened its reins on state-owned companies, inviting both competition and private investment into industries previously operated as government monopolies.

The proportions of private and public enterprise can vary widely in mixed economies, and the mix frequently changes. Dozens of countries have converted government-owned and operated companies into privately held businesses in a trend known as **privatization**. Even the United States has seen proposals to privatize everything from the postal service to Social Security.

Governments may privatize state-owned enterprises in an effort to raise funds and improve their economies. The objective is to cut costs and run the operation more efficiently. For most of its existence, Air Canada was a state-owned airline. But in 1989 the airline became fully privatized, and in 2000 the firm acquired Canadian Airlines International, becoming the world's tenth-largest international air carrier. Air Canada now maintains an extensive global network, with destinations in the United States, Europe, the Middle East, Asia, Australia, the Caribbean, Mexico, and South America. It offers such amenities as à la carte pricing, personal entertainment systems in seat backs, and fold-flat beds for transatlantic flights.[12]

Table 3.4 compares the alternative economic systems on the basis of ownership and management of enterprises, rights to profits, employee rights, and worker incentives.

Evaluating Economic Performance

Ideally, an economic system should provide two important benefits for its citizens: a stable business environment and sustained growth. In a stable business environment, the overall supply of needed goods and services is aligned with the overall demand for these items. No wild fluctuations in price or availability to complicate economic decisions. Consumers and businesses not only have access to ample supplies of desired products at affordable prices but also have money to buy the items they demand.

Growth is another important economic goal. An ideal economy incorporates steady change directed toward continually expanding the amount of goods and services produced from the nation's resources. Growth leads to expanded job opportunities, improved wages, and a rising standard of living.

mixed market economy economic system that draws from both types of economies, to different degrees.

privatization conversion of government-owned and operated companies into privately held businesses.

Assessment Check ☑

1. What is the difference between pure competition and monopolistic competition?
2. On which economic system is the U.S. economy based?
3. What is privatization?

3.4 Comparison of Alternative Economic Systems

SYSTEM FEATURES	CAPITALISM (PRIVATE ENTERPRISE)	PLANNED ECONOMIES		
		COMMUNISM	SOCIALISM	MIXED ECONOMY
Ownership of enterprises	Businesses are owned privately, often by large numbers of people. Minimal government ownership leaves production in private hands.	Government owns the means of production with few exceptions, such as small plots of land.	Government owns basic industries, but private owners operate some small enterprises.	A strong private sector blends with public enterprises.
Management of enterprises	Enterprises are managed by owners or their representatives, with minimal government interference.	Centralized management controls all state enterprises in line with three- to five-year plans. Planning now is being decentralized.	Significant government planning pervades socialist nations. State enterprises are managed directly by government bureaucrats.	Management of the private sector resembles that under capitalism. Professionals may also manage state enterprises.
Rights to profits	Entrepreneurs and investors are entitled to all profits (minus taxes) that their firms earn.	Profits are not allowed under communism.	Only the private sector of a socialist economy generates profits.	Entrepreneurs and investors are entitled to private-sector profits, although they often must pay high taxes. State enterprises are also expected to produce returns.
Rights of employees	The rights to choose one's occupation and to join a labor union have long been recognized.	Employee rights are limited in exchange for promised protection against unemployment.	Workers may choose their occupations and join labor unions, but the government influences career decisions for many people.	Workers may choose jobs and labor union membership. Unions often become quite strong.
Worker incentives	Considerable incentives motivate people to perform at their highest levels.	Incentives are emerging in communist countries.	Incentives usually are limited in state enterprises but do motivate workers in the private sector.	Capitalist-style incentives operate in the private sector. More limited incentives influence public-sector activities.

Flattening the Business Cycle

A nation's economy tends to flow through various stages of a business cycle: prosperity, recession, depression, and recovery. No true economic depressions have occurred in the United States since the 1930s, and most economists believe that society is capable of preventing future depressions through effective economic policies. Consequently, they

Solving an Ethical Controversy

Should Alternative Energy Development Be Relied on to Create New Jobs?

Eventually, we will run out of fossil fuels such as oil and coal. The development of alternative energy sources—solar, wind, ethanol, biodiesel, geothermal, and nuclear—could create thousands of new jobs, help revive the economy, and slow down global warming.

A study sponsored by American renewable-energy corporations urges Congress to enact a federal standard of 25 percent reliance on alternative energy by 2025. Supporters claim that a national Renewable Electricity Standard (RES) of 25 percent would create hundreds of thousands of jobs in renewable energy fields. China has now surpassed Denmark, Germany, Spain, and the United States to become the leading manufacturer of wind turbines. Don Furman of Iberdrola Renewables says, "Without a strong RES, the U.S. wind industry will see no net job growth, and will likely lose jobs to overseas competitors."

Should we develop alternative energy sources to aid economic recovery and create jobs?

PRO

1. Investing in clean, alternative sources of energy could create new "green" jobs for Americans. Some energy sources—wind and solar power, for example—are renewable and sustainable.

2. Clean, renewable energy will help end America's unsustainable dependence on foreign oil. Fossil fuels cause environmental destruction and their prices fluctuate.

CON

1. Fossil fuels will last for many more years. Continual advances could keep them the more energy-efficient, economical choice.

2. Alternative energy sources are still in early development. It will take more time—and costly research—before they become economical and viable on a national scale.

Summary

The United States is not alone in developing "green" energy sources. Several European countries along the North Sea have joined to create an environmentally clean "supergrid" that will get its energy from green sources in Scotland, Germany, and Norway, connected by a network of energy-efficient undersea cables.

Sources: "Stronger National Renewable Electricity Standard Needed for Significant Clean Energy Job Stability and Growth, Study Finds," American Wind Energy Association, February 4, 2010, http://www.awea.org; "Can Alternative Energy Effectively Replace Fossil Fuels?" ProCon, http://alternativeenergy.procon.org, accessed February 4, 2010; Keith Bradsher, "China Leading Global Race to Make Clean Energy," *The New York Times*, January 30, 2010, http://www.newyorktimes.com; "Renewable Energy 'Supergrid' Coming to Europe," Energy Economy, December 31, 2009, http://www.alternative-energy-news.info.

expect recessions to give way to periods of economic recovery. The "Solving an Ethical Controversy" feature explores whether developing alternative sources of energy will create new jobs to stimulate the economy.

Both business decisions and consumer buying patterns differ at each stage of the business cycle. In periods of economic prosperity, unemployment remains low, consumer confidence about the future leads to more purchases, and businesses expand—by hiring more employees, investing in new technology, and making similar purchases—to take advantage of new opportunities.

As recent events show, during a **recession**—a cyclical economic contraction that lasts for six months or longer—consumers frequently postpone major purchases and shift buying patterns toward basic, functional products carrying low prices. Businesses mirror these changes in the marketplace by slowing production, postponing expansion plans, reducing inventories, and often cutting the size of their workforces. During recessions, people facing layoffs and

recession cyclical economic contraction that lasts for six months or longer.

During a recession, consumers may shift buying patterns toward basic, functional products carrying low prices. People facing layoffs and depletions of household savings become much more conservative in their spending and often sell cars, jewelry, and stocks to make ends meet.

depletions of household savings become much more conservative in their spending, postponing luxury purchases and vacations. They often turn to lower-priced retailers like Target, Kohl's, and JC Penney for the goods they need. And they have sold cars, jewelry, and stocks to make ends meet. They also sold everything from old books to artwork to kitchenware on eBay.

If an economic slowdown continues in a downward spiral over an extended period of time, the economy falls into depression. Many Americans have grown up hearing stories about their great-grandparents who lived through the Great Depression of the 1930s, when food and other basic necessities were scarce and jobs were rare.

In the recovery stage of the business cycle, the economy emerges from recession and consumer spending picks up steam. Even though businesses often continue to rely on part-time and other temporary workers during the early stages of a recovery, unemployment begins to decline as business activity accelerates and firms seek additional workers to meet growing production demands. Gradually, the concerns of recession begin to disappear, and consumers start eating out at restaurants, booking vacations, and purchasing new cars again.

Productivity and the Nation's Gross Domestic Product

productivity relationship between the number of units produced and the number of human and other production inputs necessary to produce them.

An important concern for every economy is **productivity**, the relationship between the goods and services produced in a nation each year and the inputs needed to produce them. In general, as productivity rises, so does an economy's growth and the wealth of its citizens. In a recession, productivity stalls or even declines.

Productivity describes the relationship between the number of units produced and the number of human and other production inputs necessary to produce them. Productivity is a ratio of output to input. When a constant amount of inputs generates increased outputs, an increase in productivity occurs.

Total productivity considers all inputs necessary to produce a specific amount of outputs. Stated in equation form, it can be written as follows:

$$\text{Total Productivity} = \frac{\text{Output (goods or services produced)}}{\text{Input (human / natural resources, capital)}}$$

Many productivity ratios focus on only one of the inputs in the equation: labor productivity or output per labor-hour. An increase in labor productivity means that the same amount of work produces more goods and services than before. Many of the gains in U.S. productivity are attributed to technology, and in recent years the United States appears to be enjoying the fruits of technology and productivity.

Productivity is a widely recognized measure of a company's efficiency. In turn, the total productivity of a nation's businesses has become a measure of its economic strength and standard of living. Economists refer to this measure as a country's **gross domestic product (GDP)**—the sum of all goods and services produced within its boundaries. The GDP is based on the per-capita output of a country—in other words, total national output divided by the number of citizens. As Figure 3.4 shows, only the European Union's GDP exceeds that of the United States. China comes in a distant third.[13]

In the United States, GDP is tracked by the Bureau of Economic Analysis (BEA), a division of the U.S. Department of Commerce. Current updates and historical data on the GDP are available at the BEA's Web site (http://www.bea.gov).

gross domestic product (GDP) sum of all goods and services produced within a country's boundaries during a specific time period, such as a year.

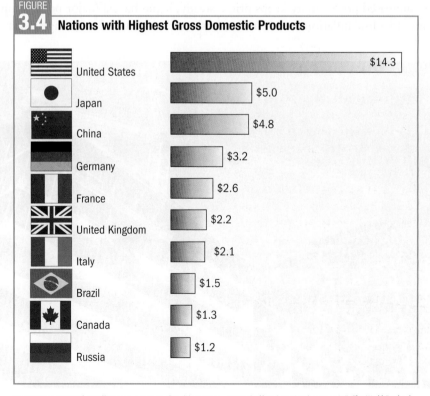

FIGURE 3.4 **Nations with Highest Gross Domestic Products**

Country	GDP
United States	$14.3
Japan	$5.0
China	$4.8
Germany	$3.2
France	$2.6
United Kingdom	$2.2
Italy	$2.1
Brazil	$1.5
Canada	$1.3
Russia	$1.2

Source: Central Intelligence Agency, "Field Listing—GDP (Official Exchange Rate)," *The World Factbook,* accessed February 4, 2010, https://www.cia.gov.

Price-Level Changes

inflation rising prices caused by a combination of excess consumer demand and increases in the costs of raw materials, component parts, human resources, and other factors of production.

core inflation rate inflation rate of an economy after energy and food prices are removed.

hyperinflation economic situation characterized by soaring prices.

Another important indicator of an economy's stability is the general level of prices. For the last 100 years, economic decision makers concerned themselves with **inflation**, rising prices caused by a combination of excess consumer demand and increases in the costs of raw materials, component parts, human resources, and other factors of production. The **core inflation rate** is the inflation rate of an economy after energy and food prices are removed. This measure is often an accurate prediction of the inflation rate that consumers, businesses, and other organizations can expect to experience during the near future.

Excess consumer demand generates what is known as demand-pull inflation while increases in the costs of factors of production generates cost-push inflation. America's most severe inflationary period during the last half of the 20th century peaked in 1980, when general price levels jumped almost 14 percent in a single year. In extreme cases, an economy may experience **hyperinflation**—an economic situation characterized by soaring prices. This situation has occurred in South America, as well as in countries that once formed the Soviet Union.

Inflation devalues money as persistent price increases reduce the amount of goods and services people can purchase with a given amount of money. This is bad news for people whose earnings do not keep up with inflation, who live on fixed incomes, or who have most of their wealth in investments paying a fixed rate of interest. Inflation can be good news to people whose income is rising or those with debts at a fixed rate of interest. A homeowner with a fixed-rate mortgage during inflationary times is paying off that debt with money that is worth less and less each year. Over the past decade, inflation helped a strong stock market drive up the number of millionaires to more than 7.8 million.[14] And because of inflation, being a millionaire does not make a person as rich as it once did. To live like a 1960s millionaire, you would need almost $7 million today.

When increased productivity keeps prices steady, it can have a major positive impact on an economy. In a low-inflation environment, businesses can make long-range plans

Lya Cattel/iStockphoto

When increased productivity keeps prices steady, it can have a major positive impact on an economy. Low interest rates encourage firms to invest in capital improvements—such as building a new company headquarters or expanding its existing space—which are likely to produce productivity gains.

without the constant worry of sudden inflationary shocks. Low interest rates encourage firms to invest in research and development and capital improvements, both of which are likely to produce productivity gains. Consumers can purchase growing stocks of goods and services with the same amount of money, and low interest rates encourage major acquisitions such as new homes and autos. But there are concerns. The fluctuating cost of oil—which is used to produce many goods—is a continuing issue. Businesses need to raise prices to cover their costs. Also, smaller firms have gone out of business or have been merged with larger companies, reducing the amount of competition and increasing the purchasing power of the larger corporations. Business owners continue to keep a watchful eye on signs of inflation.

The opposite situation—**deflation**—occurs when prices continue to fall. In Japan, where deflation has been a reality for several years, shoppers pay less for a variety of products ranging from groceries to homes. While this situation may sound ideal to consumers, it can weaken the economy. For instance, industries such as housing and auto manufacturing need to maintain strong prices in order to support all the related businesses that depend on them.

deflation opposite of inflation, occurs when prices continue to fall.

Measuring Price Level Changes In the United States, the government tracks changes in price levels with the **Consumer Price Index (CPI)**, which measures the monthly average change in prices of goods and services. The federal Bureau of Labor Statistics (BLS) calculates the CPI monthly based on prices of a "market basket," a compilation of the goods and services most commonly purchased by urban consumers. Figure 3.5 shows the categories included in the CPI market basket. Each month, BLS representatives

Consumer Price Index (CPI) measurement of the monthly average change in prices of goods and services.

FIGURE
3.5 **Contents of the CPI Market Basket**

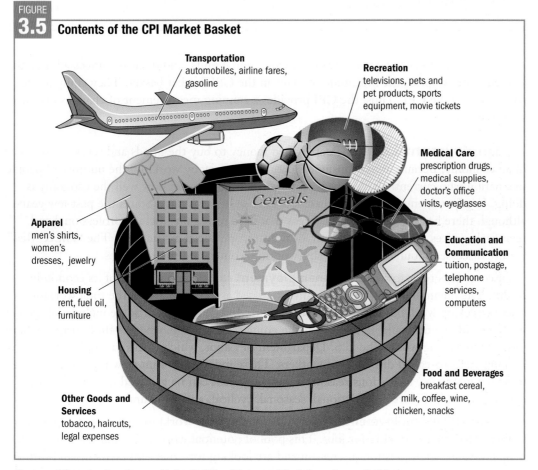

Transportation
automobiles, airline fares, gasoline

Recreation
televisions, pets and pet products, sports equipment, movie tickets

Medical Care
prescription drugs, medical supplies, doctor's office visits, eyeglasses

Apparel
men's shirts, women's dresses, jewelry

Education and Communication
tuition, postage, telephone services, computers

Housing
rent, fuel oil, furniture

Food and Beverages
breakfast cereal, milk, coffee, wine, chicken, snacks

Other Goods and Services
tobacco, haircuts, legal expenses

Source: Information from Bureau of Labor Statistics, "Consumer Price Indexes: Frequently Asked Questions," accessed February 4, 2010, http://www.bls.gov/cpi.

Hit & Miss

Microloans Aid Women's Businesses

Almost half of American workers are women, including working mothers. Regardless of income, all saw their economic status deteriorate during the recession. In a recent survey, although most women thought conditions would improve eventually, more than half of working mothers say they are working more hours just to meet basic needs.

In response to the demands of childcare and earning a living, many women have started their own businesses. After a career in the fashion industry, Tory Burch launched a successful design company. Learning from her own experience as a working mother, she later established the Tory Burch Foundation. Her research revealed some grim statistics: the majority of poor people in the United States are women. Having a child is one of the leading factors when a woman's income falls below the cost of living. Single mothers are most likely to be self-employed—but are also in the greatest danger of poverty.

Inspired by microloan organizations in the developing world, Burch formed a partnership with ACCION USA, a microlender in the United States. At $500 to $50,000, ACCION USA's loans are somewhat larger than those in developing nations, but many have the same purpose: "to economically empower women." Their clients have low to moderate incomes and are more likely to be rejected by traditional banks, so these microloans are essential to their success. Forty percent are

women, and more than 80 percent are members of minority groups. ACCION USA reports that more than 90 percent of these microloans have been repaid.

Burch says, "I like microfinance . . . because it isn't charity in the traditional sense. . . . It gives entrepreneurs the opportunities many of us take for granted, and it is sustainable. . . . It's also incredibly important to the economic recovery of our country."

Questions for Critical Thinking

1. Why might having a baby cause a single mother's income to fall?
2. Why do you think that the payback rate on microloans is so high?

Sources: Tory Burch Foundation Web site, http://www.toryburchfoundation.org, accessed February 4, 2010; ACCION USA Web site, http://www.accionusa.org, accessed February 4, 2010; "Female Power," *The Economist*, December 30, 2009, http://www.economist.com; "National Citi Survey Finds Women Across All Income Levels Are Experiencing Pain of the Recession," *Business Wire*, October 14, 2009, http://www.businesswire.com; "GuestPost: Tory Burch on Helping Small Businesses," CNNMoney.com—Fortune, September 17, 2009, http://postcards.blogs.fortune.conn.com.

---

visit thousands of stores, service establishments, rental units, and doctors' offices all over the United States to price the multitude of items in the CPI market basket. They compile the data to create the CPI. Thus, the CPI provides a running measurement of changes in consumer prices.

Employment Levels People need money to buy the goods and services produced in an economy. Because most consumers earn that money by working, the number of people in a nation who currently have jobs is an important indicator of how well the economy is doing. In general, employment has been on the rise in the United States the past few years, although there have been some dips. Areas that have seen gains include professional and technical services, as well as education, healthcare, and social assistance.[15] The "Hit & Miss" feature discusses a foundation that helps working women and their families.

Economists refer to a nation's **unemployment rate** as an indicator of its economic health. The unemployment rate is usually expressed as a percentage of the total workforce actively seeking work but are currently unemployed. The total labor force includes all people who are willing and available to work at the going market wage, whether they currently have jobs or are seeking work. The U.S. Department of Labor, which tracks unemployment rates, also measures so-called discouraged workers. These individuals want to work but have given up looking for jobs, for various reasons. Unemployment can be grouped into the four categories shown in Figure 3.6: frictional, seasonal, cyclical, and structural.

Frictional unemployment applies to members of the workforce who are temporarily not working but are looking for jobs. This pool of potential workers includes new graduates, people who have left jobs for any reason and are looking for other employment, and former workers who have decided to return to the labor force. **Seasonal unemployment**

unemployment rate percentage of the total workforce actively seeking work but are currently unemployed.

frictional unemployment applies to members of the workforce who are temporarily not working but are looking for jobs.

seasonal unemployment joblessness of workers in a seasonal industry.

is the joblessness of people in a seasonal industry. Construction workers, farm laborers, fishing boat operators, and landscape employees may contend with bouts of seasonal unemployment when wintry conditions make work unavailable.

Cyclical unemployment includes people who are out of work because of a cyclical contraction in the economy. During periods of economic expansion, overall employment is likely to rise, but as growth slows and a recession begins, unemployment levels commonly rise. At such times, even workers with good job skills may face temporary unemployment. Workers in high-tech industries, air travel, and manufacturing have all faced unemployment during economic contraction.

Structural unemployment applies to people who remain unemployed for long periods of time, often with little hope of finding new jobs like their old ones. This situation may arise because these workers lack the necessary skills for available jobs or because the skills they have are no longer in demand. For instance, technological developments have increased the demand for people with computer-related skills but have created structural unemployment among many types of manual laborers or workers who may have been injured and unable to return to work.

FIGURE
3.6 Four Types of Unemployment

Frictional Unemployment
· Temporarily not working
· Looking for a job
Example: New graduates entering the workforce

Seasonal Unemployment
· Not working during some months
· Not looking for a job
Example: Farm workers needed only when a crop is in season

Structural Unemployment
· Not working due to no demand for skills
· May be retraining for a new job
Example: Assembly line employees whose jobs are now done by robots

Cyclical Unemployment
· Not working due to economic slowdown
· Looking for a job
Example: Executives laid off during corporate downsizing or recessionary periods

Managing the Economy's Performance

Government can use both monetary policy and fiscal policy in its efforts to fight unemployment, increase business and consumer spending, and reduce the length and severity of economic recessions. For instance, the Federal Reserve System can increase or reduce interest rates, and the federal government can enact tax cuts and rebates, or propose other reforms.

Monetary Policy

A common method of influencing economic activity is **monetary policy**, government actions to increase or decrease the money supply and change banking requirements and interest rates to influence spending by altering bankers' willingness to make loans.

cyclical unemployment people who are out of work because of a cyclical contraction in the economy.

structural unemployment people who remain unemployed for long periods of time, often with little hope of finding new jobs like their old ones.

Assessment Check ✓

1. Describe the four stages of the business cycle.

2. What are some measures that economists use to determine the health of an economy?

monetary policy government actions to increase or decrease the money supply and change banking requirements and interest rates to influence bankers' willingness to make loans.

The Federal Reserve uses a number of tools to regulate the economy. The Fed lends money to member banks, which in turn make loans to business and individual borrowers.

An **expansionary monetary policy** increases the money supply in an effort to cut the cost of borrowing, which encourages business decision makers to make new investments, in turn stimulating employment and economic growth. By contrast, a **restrictive monetary policy** reduces the money supply to curb rising prices, overexpansion, and concerns about overly rapid economic growth.

In the United States, the Federal Reserve System ("the Fed") is responsible for formulating and implementing the nation's monetary policy. It is headed by a chairman and board of governors, all of whom are nominated by the president. The current chairman is Ben Bernanke, who also serves as chairman of the Federal Open Market Committee, the Fed's main agency for monetary policymaking. All national banks must be members of this system and keep some percentage of their checking and savings funds on deposit at the Fed.

The Fed's board of governors uses a number of tools to regulate the economy. By changing the required percentage of checking and savings accounts that banks must deposit with the Fed, the governors can expand or shrink funds available to lend. The Fed also lends money to member banks, which in turn make loans at higher interest rates to business and individual borrowers. By changing the interest rates charged to commercial banks, the Fed affects the interest rates charged to borrowers and, consequently, their willingness to borrow.

Fiscal Policy

Governments also influence economic activities by making decisions about taxes and spending. Through revenues and expenses, the government implements **fiscal policy**. This is the second technique that officials use to control inflation, reduce unemployment, improve the general standard of living, and encourage economic growth. Increased taxes may restrict economic activities, while lower taxes and increased government spending usually boost spending and profits, cut unemployment rates, and fuel economic expansion. On some occasions, the U.S. federal government has issued tax rebates to its citizens and businesses in an effort to stimulate investment and spending. The "Going Green" feature discusses federal tax credits for energy-efficient products.

International Fiscal Policy Nations in the industrial world, including the United States, are currently struggling to find ways to help developing nations modernize their economies. One proposal is to forgive the debts of some of these countries, particularly

expansionary monetary policy increases the money supply in an effort to cut the cost of borrowing, which encourages business decision makers to make new investments, in turn stimulating employment and economic growth.

restrictive monetary policy reducing the money supply to curb rising prices, overexpansion, and concerns about overly rapid economic growth.

fiscal policy government spending and taxation decisions designed to control inflation, reduce unemployment, improve the general welfare of citizens, and encourage economic growth.

Going Green

Tax Credits for an Energy Star

To encourage Americans to save energy and reduce pollution, the Environmental Protection Administration (EPA) launched the "ENERGY STAR" program in 1992. Later, the Energy Department and the EPA began granting makers of appliances and building materials the familiar ENERGY STAR seal if their products met federal standards for energy efficiency. The American Recovery and Reinvestment Act of 2009 revised a program begun earlier that awards federal income-tax credits to consumers who buy these products. The stimulus package also contains funds for rebates to consumers who buy new, ENERGY STAR–qualified appliances. Each U.S. state and territory has developed its own rebate plan.

Hybrid gas-electric vehicles and those using alternative fuels are eligible for tax credits, as are plug-in electric vehicles. You can also get a tax credit equivalent to 10 percent of the cost if you convert a conventional vehicle to a plug-in, electric-drive motor.

In the state-administered rebate program, replacing certain appliances with qualified ones will not only get you a rebate but will also lower your utility bills. Depending on climate, geography, and other factors, your state may choose from among boilers, central or room air conditioners, washing machines, dishwashers, freezers, oil and gas furnaces, heat pumps (air source and geothermal), refrigerators, and water heaters.

Certain kinds of home improvements are eligible for tax credits. You might invest in a new, qualified central air-conditioning system, heat pump, or furnace. If you live in a cold climate, you might choose to insulate or seal your windows. You might install a biomass stove that burns agricultural and wood waste, plants and residues, or wood pellets. Not only will you get a tax credit, you will also see long-run savings on your fuel bill and help protect the environment.

Questions for Critical Thinking

1. How will paying out rebates and granting tax credits stimulate the economy?
2. Which would you prefer to receive—an income-tax credit or a rebate? Why?

Sources: U.S. Department of Energy, "Consumer Energy Tax Incentives: What the American Recovery and Reinvestment Act Means to You," http://www.energy.gov, accessed February 4, 2010; Alliance to Save Energy, "Energy-Efficient Home and Vehicle Tax Credits," http://ase.org, accessed February 4, 2010; "Federal Tax Credits for Consumer Energy Efficiency," http://www.energystar.gov, accessed February 4, 2010; Environmental Protection Administration, "Environmental Progress," http://www.epa.gov, accessed February 4, 2010; U.S. Department of Energy, "Rebates for ENERGY STAR Appliances," http://www.energysavers.gov, accessed February 4, 2010.

---

those in Africa, to stimulate their economies to grow. But not all fiscal experts agree with this idea. They suggest that any debt forgiveness should come with certain conditions so that these countries can build their own fiscal policies. Countries should encourage and allow citizens to own property, lower their tax rates, avoid devaluing their currencies, lay a path for new businesses to start, and reduce trade barriers. In addition, they must improve agriculture, education, and health care so their citizens can begin to set and reach financial goals. The World Bank is an organization that offers such programs as low-interest loans and interest-free credit and grants to developing countries. The World Bank has been involved in helping Haiti recover from the catastrophic earthquake of 2010.[16]

The Federal Budget Each year, the president proposes a **budget** for the federal government, a plan for how it will raise and spend money during the coming year, and presents it to Congress for approval. A typical federal budget proposal undergoes months of deliberation and many modifications before receiving approval. The federal budget includes a number of different spending categories, ranging from defense and Social Security to interest payments on the national debt. The decisions about what to include in the budget have a direct effect on various sectors of the economy. During a recession, the federal government may approve increased spending on interstate highway repairs to improve transportation and increase employment in the construction industry. During prosperity, the government may allocate more money for scientific research toward medical breakthroughs or alternative fuels.

budget organization's plan for how it will raise and spend money during a given period of time.

budget deficit situation in which the government spends more than the amount of money it raises through taxes.

national debt money owed by government to individuals, businesses, and government agencies who purchase Treasury bills, Treasury notes, and Treasury bonds sold to cover expenditures.

budget surplus excess funding that occurs when government spends less than the amount of funds raised through taxes and fees.

balanced budget situation in which total revenues raised by taxes and fees equal total proposed government spending for the year.

Assessment Check ☑

1. What is the difference between an expansionary monetary policy and a restrictive monetary policy?

2. What are the three primary sources of government funds?

3. Does a balanced budget erase the federal debt?

The primary sources of government funds to cover the costs of the annual budget are taxes, fees, and borrowing. Both the overall amount of these funds and their specific combination have major effects on the economic well-being of the nation. One way governments raise money is to impose taxes on sales, income, and other sources. But increasing taxes leaves people and businesses with less money to spend. This might reduce inflation, but overly high taxes can also slow economic growth. Governments then try to balance taxes to give people necessary services without slowing economic growth.

Taxes don't always generate enough funds to cover every spending project the government hopes to undertake. When the government spends more than the amount of money it raises through taxes, it creates a **budget deficit**. To cover the deficit, the U.S. government borrows money by selling Treasury bills, Treasury notes, and Treasury bonds to investors. All of this borrowing makes up the **national debt**. If the government takes in more money than it spends, it is said to have a **budget surplus**. A **balanced budget** means total revenues raised by taxes equal the total proposed spending for the year.

Achieving a balanced budget—or even a budget surplus—does not erase the national debt. U.S. legislators continually debate how fast the nation should use revenues to reduce its debt. Most families want to wipe out debt—from credit cards, automobile purchases, and college, to name a few sources. To put the national debt into personal perspective, with roughly 308 million U.S. citizens, each one owes about $40,260 as his or her share.

But for the federal government, the decision is more complex. When the government raises money by selling Treasury bills, it makes safe investments available to investors worldwide. If foreign investors cannot buy Treasury notes, they might turn to other countries, reducing the amount of money flowing into the United States. U.S. government debt has also been used as a basis for pricing riskier investments. If the government issues less debt, the interest rates it commands are higher, raising the overall cost of debt to private borrowers. In addition, the government uses the funds from borrowing, at least in part, to invest in such public services as education and scientific research.

Global Economic Challenges of the 21st Century

Businesses face a number of important economic challenges in the 21st century. As the economies of countries around the globe become increasingly interconnected, governments and businesses must compete throughout the world. Although no one can predict the future, both governments and businesses will likely need to meet several challenges to maintain their global competitiveness. Table 3.5 identifies five key challenges: (1) the economic impact of the continuing threat of international terrorism, (2) the shift to a global information economy, (3) the aging of the world's population, (4) the growth of China and India, and (5) efforts to enhance the competitiveness of every country's workforce.

No country is an economic island in today's global economy. Not only is an ever-increasing stream of goods and services crossing national borders, but a growing number of businesses have become true multinational firms, operating manufacturing plants and other facilities around the world. As global trade and investments grow, events in one nation can reverberate around the globe. The "Business Etiquette" feature offers some tips for international travel.

Despite the risks of world trade, global expansion can offer huge opportunities to U.S. firms. With U.S. residents accounting for just over 1 in every 22 of the world's nearly 7 billion people, growth-oriented American companies cannot afford to ignore the world market.[17] U.S. businesses also benefit from the lower labor costs in other parts of the world, and some are finding successful niches importing goods and services provided by foreign firms. Still, it is extremely important for U.S. firms to keep track of the foreign firms that supply their products. When it became apparent that some plastic toys supplied to U.S. toymakers by Chinese manufacturers contained lead paint that could be harmful to children, the U.S. firms issued massive recalls of these toys. A subsequent investigation by the Associated Press revealed that some Chinese manufacturers had substituted cadmium, another soft metal, for lead in children's jewelry sold in the United States. Cadmium is known to cause cancer. Like lead, it impairs brain development in young children. Federal and state agencies warned Asian firms not to use other toxic substances in place of lead and began investigating products sold in America that might contain cadmium or other toxic heavy metals. Inez Tenenbaum, the chairwoman of the U.S. Consumer Product Safety Commission, said, "All of us should be committed to keeping hazardous or toxic levels of heavy metals out of . . . toys and children's products. . . . Voluntary efforts will only take us so far."[18]

U.S. firms must also develop strategies for competing with each other overseas. In the huge but fragmented beverage industry, Coca-Cola still edges out Pepsi as the top-selling cola worldwide. Industry experts predict that China will be the next great battleground for the two soda giants. Coca-Cola still maintains better name recognition, but Pepsi is closing in.[19]

BusinessEtiquette

Tips for International Travel

Good manners and good communication have always been important in business and are becoming even more crucial as global business increases. If your work takes you to a foreign country—or even to an international videoconference—it is essential for you to understand the manners and etiquette of the place you are visiting, either actually or virtually. Here are some useful tips for international business travel, based on suggestions by Dana Persia of DP Image Consulting.

Before Leaving

1 Do as much research as you can on the business etiquette and customs of the country you will visit. Travel guides—and, of course, the Internet, especially the U.S. State Department Web site—can be very helpful.

2 If the native language is not English, learn a few important phrases. Your hosts will appreciate the effort, even if your pronunciation is less than perfect.

3 Compare American business and casual dress with what is appropriate in the country you are visiting. Standards of modesty for women are stricter in many countries. In general, try to fit in as best you can.

Getting There

1 If possible, arrive enough in advance to adapt to time-zone changes, especially before an important conference or meeting.

2 Be sure to get enough sleep before you travel to help mitigate the effects of jet lag.

3 Drinking water before, during, and after your flight will also help with jet lag. Avoid alcohol and caffeine, which are dehydrating.

When You Arrive

Your pretravel research should include gender roles, especially for women; when and where talking about business is permissible; and the etiquette surrounding business cards, alcohol, and gifts. What is appropriate in one country may be unacceptable somewhere else!

Sources: DP Image Consulting Web site, http://www.dpimageconsulting.com, accessed February 4, 2010; International Business Etiquette and Manners, http://www.cyborlink.com, accessed February 4, 2010; U.S. Department of State Web site, http://www.state.gov, accessed February 4, 2010; Phillip Khan-Panni, "20 Tips on International Business Etiquette," *Eacademy*, June 12, 2009, http:www.eacademy.com.

3.5 Global Economic Challenges

CHALLENGE	FACTS AND EXAMPLES
International terrorism	• Assistance in locating and detaining known terrorists by dozens of nations • Cooperation in modifying banking laws in most nations in an effort to cut off funds to terrorist organizations. • Concerns over the safety of mass-transit systems following bombings in Moscow and elsewhere.
Shift to a global information economy	• Half of all American workers hold jobs in information technology or in industries that intensively use information technology, goods, and services. • Software industry in India expects to employ more than 2.3 million people. • Internet users in Asia and western Europe have more than doubled in five years.
Aging of the world's population	• Median age of the U.S. population is 36 plus, and by 2025, more than 64 million Americans will be age 65 or older—nearly double today's number. This will increase demands for health care, retirement benefits, and other support services, putting budgetary pressure on governments. • As Baby Boomers, now reaching their early 60s, begin to retire, businesses around the globe will need to find ways to replace their workplace skills.
Growth of India and China straining commodity prices	• China and India now make up more than one-third of the world's population. China's economic growth has been in the industrial sector, and India's focused more in services. Both countries are now consumers of oil and other commodities, affecting prices.
Enhancing competitiveness of every country's workforce	• Leaner organizations (with fewer supervisors) require employees with the skills to control, combine, and supervise work operations.

Assessment Check ✔

1. Why is virtually no country an economic island these days?

2. Describe two ways in which global expansion can benefit a U.S. firm.

What's Ahead

Global competition is a key factor in today's economy. In Chapter 4, we focus on the global dimensions of business. We cover basic concepts of doing business internationally and examine how nations can position themselves to benefit from the global economy. Then we describe the specific methods used by individual businesses to expand beyond their national borders and compete successfully in the global marketplace.

Summary of Learning Objectives

1 Distinguish between microeconomics and macroeconomics. Explain the factors that drive demand and supply.

Microeconomics is the study of economic behavior among individual consumers, families, and businesses whose collective behavior in the marketplace determines the quantity of goods and services demanded and supplied at different prices. Macroeconomics is the study of the broader economic picture and how an economic system maintains and

allocates its resources; it focuses on how a government's monetary and fiscal policies affect the overall operation of an economic system.

Demand is the willingness and ability of buyers to purchase goods and services at different prices. Factors that drive demand for a good or service include customer preferences, the number of buyers and their incomes, the prices of substitute goods, the prices of complementary goods, and consumer expectations about the future. Supply is the willingness and ability of businesses to offer products for sale at different prices. Supply is determined by the cost of inputs and technology resources, taxes, and the number of suppliers operating in the market.

Assessment Check Answers ☑

1.1 Define *microeconomics* and *macroeconomics*. *Microeconomics* is the study of economic behavior among individual consumers, families, and businesses whose collective behavior in the marketplace determines the quantity of goods and services demanded and supplied at different prices. *Macroeconomics* is the study of the broader economic picture and how an economic system maintains and allocates its resources.

1.2 Explain demand and supply curves. A demand curve is a graph of the amount of a product that buyers will purchase at different prices. A supply curve shows the relationship between different prices and the quantities that sellers will offer for sale, regardless of demand.

1.3 How do factors of production influence the overall supply of goods and services? A change in the cost or availability of any of the inputs considered to be factors of production can shift the entire supply curve, either increasing or decreasing the amount available at every price.

┌─┐
│2│ Describe each of the four different types of market struc-
└─┘ tures in a private enterprise system, and compare the
three major types of economic systems.

Four basic models characterize competition in a private enterprise system: pure competition, monopolistic competition, oligopoly, and monopoly. Pure competition is a market structure, like that in small-scale agriculture, in which large numbers of buyers and sellers exchange homogeneous products and no single participant has a significant influence on price. Monopolistic competition is a market structure, like that of retailing, in which large numbers of buyers and sellers exchange differentiated products, so each participant has some control over price. Oligopolies are market situations, like those in the steel and airline industries, in which relatively few sellers compete and high start-up costs form barriers to keep out new competitors. In a monopoly, one seller dominates trade in a good or service, for which buyers can find no close substitutes.

The major economic systems are private enterprise economy, planned economy (such as communism or socialism), and mixed market economy. In a private enterprise system, individuals and private businesses pursue their own interests—including investment decisions and profits—without undue governmental restriction. In a planned economy, the government exerts stronger control over business ownership, profits, and resources to accomplish governmental and societal—rather than individual—goals. Socialism, one type of planned

economic system, is characterized by government ownership and operation of all major industries. Communism is an economic system without private property; goods are owned in common, and factors of production and production decisions are controlled by the state. A mixed market economy blends government ownership and private enterprise, combining characteristics of both planned and private enterprise economies.

Assessment Check Answers ☑

2.1 What is the difference between pure competition and monopolistic competition? Pure competition is a market structure in which large numbers of buyers and sellers exchange homogeneous products. Monopolistic competition is a market structure in which large numbers of buyers and sellers exchange differentiated products.

2.2 On which economic system is the U.S. economy based? The U.S. economy is based on the private enterprise system.

2.3 What is privatization? Privatization is the conversion of government-owned and operated agencies into privately held businesses.

┌─┐
│3│ Identify and describe the four stages of the business cycle.
└─┘ Explain how productivity, price level changes, and employment levels affect the stability of a nation's economy.

The four stages are prosperity, recession, depression, and recovery. Prosperity is characterized by low unemployment and strong consumer confidence. In a recession, consumers often postpone major purchases, layoffs occur, and household savings may be depleted. A depression occurs when an economic slowdown continues in a downward spiral over a long period of time. During recovery, consumer spending begins to increase and business activity accelerates, leading to an increased number of jobs.

As productivity rises, so do an economy's growth and the wealth of its citizens. In a recession, productivity stalls or possibly declines. Changes in general price levels—inflation or deflation—are important indicators of an economy's general stability. The U.S. government measures price-level changes by the Consumer Price Index. A nation's unemployment rate is an indicator of both overall stability and growth. The unemployment rate shows, as a percentage of the total labor force, the number of people actively seeking employment who are unable to find jobs.

Assessment Check Answers ☑

3.1 Describe the four stages of the business cycle. The four stages are prosperity, recession, depression, and recovery. Prosperity is characterized by low unemployment and strong consumer confidence. Recession may include consumers postponing major purchases, layoffs, and decreased household savings. A depression occurs when an economic slowdown continues in a downward spiral over a long period of time. In recovery, consumer spending increases and business activity accelerates.

3.2 What are some measures that economists use to determine the health of an economy? Gross domestic product (GDP), general level of prices, core inflation rate, the Consumer Price Index, and the unemployment rate are all measures used to determine the health of an economy.

```
[4]
```
Discuss how monetary policy and fiscal policy are used to manage an economy's performance.

Monetary policy encompasses a government's efforts to control the size of the nation's money supply. Various methods of increasing or decreasing the overall money supply affect interest rates and therefore affect borrowing and investment decisions. By changing the size of the money supply, government can encourage growth or control inflation. Fiscal policy involves decisions regarding government revenues and expenditures. Changes in government spending affect economic growth and employment levels in the private sector. However, a government must also raise money, through taxes or borrowing, to finance its expenditures. Because tax payments represent funds that might otherwise have been spent by individuals and businesses, any taxation changes also affect the overall economy.

Assessment Check Answers ✔

4.1 What is the difference between an expansionary monetary policy and a restrictive monetary policy? An expansionary monetary policy increases the money supply in an effort to cut the cost of borrowing. A restrictive monetary policy reduces the money supply to curb rising prices, overexpansion, and concerns about overly rapid economic growth.

4.2 What are the three primary sources of government funds? The U.S. government acquires funds through taxes, fees, and borrowing.

4.3 Does a balanced budget erase the federal debt? No, a balanced budget does not erase the national debt; it just doesn't increase it.

```
[5]
```
Describe the major global economic challenges of the 21st century.

Businesses face five key challenges in the 21st century: (1) the threat of international terrorism; (2) the shift to a global information economy; (3) the aging of the world's population; (4) the growth of India and China, which compete for resources; and (5) efforts to enhance the competitiveness of every country's workforce.

Assessment Check Answers ✔

5.1 Why is virtually no country an economic island these days? No business or country is an economic island because many goods and services travel across national borders. Companies now are becoming multinational firms.

5.2 Describe two ways in which global expansion can benefit a U.S. firm. A firm can benefit from global expansion by attracting more customers and using less expensive labor and production to produce goods and services.

▉ Business Terms You Need to Know

economics 72	monopoly 80	inflation 88	monetary policy 91
microeconomics 72	regulated monopolies 81	core inflation rate 88	expansionary monetary
macroeconomics 72	planned economy 82	hyperinflation 88	policy 92
demand 73	socialism 82	deflation 89	restrictive monetary
supply 73	communism 82	Consumer Price Index	policy 92
demand curve 74	mixed market economy 83	(CPI) 89	fiscal policy 92
supply curve 76	privatization 83	unemployment rate 90	budget 93
equilibrium price 77	recession 85	frictional unemployment 90	budget deficit 94
pure competition 79	productivity 86	seasonal unemployment 90	national debt 94
monopolistic competition 80	gross domestic product	cyclical unemployment 91	budget surplus 94
oligopoly 80	(GDP) 87	structural unemployment 91	balanced budget 94

▉ Review Questions

1. How does microeconomics impact business? How does macroeconomics affect business? Why is it important for businesspeople to understand the fundamentals of each?

2. Draw supply and demand graphs that estimate what will happen to demand, supply, and the equilibrium price of coffee if these events occur:

a. Widely reported medical studies suggest that coffee drinkers are less likely to develop certain diseases.

b. The cost of manufacturing paper cups increases.

c. The state imposes a new tax on takeout beverages.

d. The biggest coffee chain leaves the area.

3. Describe the four different types of competition in the private enterprise system. In which type of competition would each of the following businesses be likely to engage?

a. large drug stores chain

b. small yoga studio

c. steel mill

d. large farm whose major crop is corn

e. Microsoft

4. Distinguish between the two types of planned economies. What factors do you think keep them from flourishing in today's environment?

5. What are the four stages of the business cycle? In which stage do you believe the U.S. economy is now? Why?

6. What is the gross domestic product? What is its relationship to productivity?

7. What are the effects of inflation on an economy? What are the effects of deflation? How does the Consumer Price Index work?

8. What does a nation's unemployment rate indicate? Describe what type of unemployment you think each of the following illustrates:

a. discharged armed forces veteran

b. bus driver who has been laid off due to cuts in his or her city's transit budget

c. worker who was injured on the job and must start a new career

d. lifeguard

e. dental hygienist who has quit one job and is looking for another

9. Explain the difference between monetary policy and fiscal policy. How does the government raise funds to cover the costs of its annual budget?

10. What is the difference between the budget deficit and the national debt? What are the benefits of paying down the national debt? What might be the negative effects?

▪ Projects and Teamwork Applications

1. Describe a situation in which you have had to make an economic choice in an attempt to balance your wants with limited means. What factors influenced your decision?

2. Choose one of the following products and describe the different factors that you think might affect its supply and demand.

a. UGG boots

b. Kindle

c. Miles by Discover credit card

d. newly created name-brand drug

e. bicycling tour in Europe

3. Go online to research one of the following government agencies—its responsibilities, its budget, and the like. Then make the case for privatizing it:

a. Veterans Administration

b. Bureau of the Census

c. Smithsonian Institution

d. Transportation and Security Administration

e. Social Security

4. Some businesses automatically experience seasonal unemployment. Increasingly however, owners of these businesses are making efforts to increase demand—and employment—during the off-season. Choose a classmate

to be your business partner, and together select one of the following businesses. Create a plan for developing business and keeping employees for a season during which your business does not customarily operate:

a. children's summer camp

b. ski lodge

c. inn located near a beach resort

d. house painting service

e. greenhouse

5. On your own or with a classmate, go online to research the economy of one of the following countries. Learn what you can about the type of economy the country has, its major industries, and its competitive issues. (Note which industries or services are privatized and which are government owned.) Take notes on unemployment rates, monetary policies, and fiscal policies. Present your findings to the class.

a. China

b. New Zealand

c. India

d. Sweden

e. Mexico

f. Canada

g. Brazil

Web Assignments

1. **Credit card regulations.** Several new federal regulations governing credit cards went into effect recently. Visit the Web site listed here and click on "New Credit Card Rules." After reviewing these rules, prepare a brief report highlighting the most significant changes.

   http://federalreserve.gov/creditcard/

2. **Unemployment.** In the United States, the Bureau of Labor Statistics (BLS) compiles and publishes data on unemployment. Go to the BLS Web site (http://www.bls.gov) and click on "Unemployment." Read through the most recent report and answer the following questions:

   a. What is the current unemployment rate in the United States? How does it compare to other developed countries?

   b. Which state has the highest unemployment rate? Which state has the lowest unemployment rate?

   c. What is the so-called underemployment rate?

3. **Gross domestic product.** Visit the Web site of the Bureau of Economic Analysis (http://www.bea.gov) and access the most recent statistics on the U.S. GDP. Prepare a brief report. What is the current GDP? What is the difference between real and nominal GDP? What are the individual components that make up GDP?

Note: Internet Web addresses change frequently. If you don't find the exact sites listed, you may need to access the organization's home page and search from there or use a search engine such as Bing or Google.

CASE 3.1   An Economic Windfall: The Rise of Wind Energy

Texas is well known for big things—its size, its houses, its ranches, its dreams. So it's no surprise that the state is going big for wind energy, as the search for clean, renewable energy sources becomes urgent. Currently, Texas is leading the nation in harnessing wind power, partly because its location and topography create the perfect conditions for wind. West Texas, in particular, experiences a near-constant wind speed of 17 miles per hour over wide-open terrain. It also has landowners who are ready and willing to invest in a new business. In addition, state lawmakers passed legislation requiring utilities to buy renewable power, and federal tax credits await those who invest in wind power. Finally, Texas is on its own power grid, separate from the rest of the country. All of this points toward economic opportunity for small towns that have seen a downturn.

Roscoe is one of these towns. The train doesn't stop there anymore, and the Dairy Queen closed. Stores don't have a lot to sell, and the 1,300 people who live there aren't shopping anyway—at least they weren't until recently. Together with Airtricity, an energy firm based in the United Kingdom, the town of Roscoe has built one of the biggest wind farms in the world. The Roscoe Wind Farm generates 209 megawatts of electricity—enough to power about 60,000 homes and save about 375,000 tons per year in greenhouse gas emissions. The wind power is sold through TXU Wholesale under a five-year contract. In addition, the landowners, on whose property the farm is built, will eventually receive royalties on the electricity sales. "We used to cuss the wind," recalls Cliff Etheredge, a local cotton farmer who helped originate the project with Airtricity. "Now, we love the wind." Etheredge also proudly cites the economic rejuvenation of Roscoe: two new restaurants and other businesses that are opening or expanding. "Hopefully, we'll see Roscoe reborn here."

The wind energy industry in Texas has much broader implications than for a single small town, as companies bid for the rights to develop wind farms off the state's coast in the Gulf of Mexico. "The future of the nation's offshore wind industry is off the coast of Texas," asserts the state's Land Office commissioner. The Land Office has jurisdiction over the waters up to 10 miles offshore. "There's international interest in these tracts, and this will be the first time the market will be able to place a value on what I think is a very valuable asset."

Across the nation in upstate New York, an environmental engineering firm named Tetra Tech is working on the Maple Ridge Wind Energy Program as part of the state's initiative to reduce its traditional energy use by the year 2015. The firm is working toward the goal of helping to ensure that one-fourth of New York's energy is produced by renewable sources by 2013. New York officials believe that wind is the most economical resource compared with traditional sources, but wind turbines must be built to certain specifications in order to maximize their output and minimize their impact. Still, wind power is showing great promise.

Questions for Critical Thinking

1. What factors do you think will affect the supply and demand curve for wind energy?
2. Describe what type of competition you predict will arise in the wind energy industry.

Sources: Tetra Tech Web site, http://www.tetratech.com, accessed February 24, 2009; Airtricity Web site, www.aitricity.com, accessed October 2008; John Burnett, "Winds of Change Blow into Roscoe, Texas," *National Public Radio,* November 30, 2007, http://www.npr.org; John A. Sullivan and Bobette Riner, "Texas Holds Nation's First Lease Sale for Wind Tract," *Natural Gas Week,* October 8, 2007, http://www.lexisnexic.com.library.uark.edu; Liz Moucka, "Harvesting the Wind," *Texas Contractor,* September 3, 2007, http://www.acppubs.com.

Music and Money: Breaking Record-Labels' Stranglehold on Artists

CASE 3.2

You probably have access to digital downloads of your favorite tunes—whether it's for an iPod, MP3 player, laptop or desktop computer, or other device. You might have discovered the next big hit by watching YouTube or MySpace. The music industry has finally recognized the influence of new technologies on their business. The big record labels have acknowledged that they no longer have as much control over music creation or its distribution as they once did. Whereas a decade ago musicians earned 60 percent of their income through record labels from prerecorded music and the rest from concerts, endorsements, and merchandise, today those percentages are reversed. Concert ticket sales have nearly tripled, and the record labels don't profit from them. As these companies are trying to stop the flood of music and dollars out their own doors, they are also rethinking their business models in an attempt to find new ways of attracting talent and distributing their music.

Some labels such as EMI are revising their contracts with artists. Called multiple-rights or all-rights contracts, these new agreements encompass live music, merchandise, and endorsements, instead of a simple cut of CD sales. Although artists are not enthusiastic about the new agreements, record executives insist that they are necessary. "It's a discussion you have with every new artist now," says Jeanne Meyer of EMI.

Some musicians have said no to the new arrangement, preferring to launch on their own or teaming up with smaller, start-up firms like Musicane, Indie911, Fuzz, Snocap, and TuneCore. Nine Inch Nails, Radiohead, Oasis, and Madonna are just a few of the increasing number

of such groups. Trent Reznor of Nine Inch Nails left EMI and went to Musicane, where he dictated his own requirements for Web design, pricing, and other aspects of his music. He also helped the company's programmers, administrators, and designers produce albums for other artists. Reznor is an example of the new musician who is savvy about both technology and business. "Trent is well-informed, articulate and is very knowledgeable about technology," notes Musicane CEO Dushin Shahani.

But the big labels aren't through yet. One of the new business models being adopted by larger firms involves bundling music subscriptions with the price of Internet access so that the music downloads appear to be free. Nokia Corp. is launching a service called Comes With Music, which allows users of certain cell phones a year of unlimited access to music without extra charges. In addition, the music labels are planning to license songs for ad-supported Web sites, where users watch videos or listen to full-length tracks posted by other users for free. Finally, four of the world's largest recording companies—Sony BMG, Vivendi SA's Universal Music Group, Warner Music Group, and EMI—agreed to license music for sale online as unprotected MP3 files, which mean they can be played on multiple devices. "It seems clear there's an accelerated pace of change that comes hand in glove with accelerated decline in traditional business," observes Eric Garland, CEO of a firm that tracks online entertainment.

The big companies are a bit grudging about the changes, acknowledging their necessity if somewhat unenthusiastically. "There's no denying that Warner Music Group and the industry as a whole have been struggling for almost a decade now with the challenges and opportunities that the digital space presents," admits Edgar Bronfman, chairman and CEO. "The recent trend of dramatic changes in the recorded music market will continue … And, though it's a cliché, it's a cliché because it's true: technology will also provide us with new opportunities."

Questions for Critical Thinking

1. How has the rapid development of technology affected competition in the music industry?

2. How does this technology affect supply and demand in the music industry?

Sources: "Music Industry Changes Coming," *The Business Journal,* January 12, 2008, http://www.biz-journal.com; David Byrne, "David Byrne's Survival Strategies for Emerging Artists—and Megastars," *Wired,* December 18, 2007, http://www.wired.com; James Montgomery, "Madonna Ditches Label, Radiohead Go Renegade: The Year the Music Industry Broke," *MTV News,* December 17, 2007, http://www.mtv.com; Greg Sandoval, "When Rockers Cut Ties from Labels," *CNET News,* November 2, 2007, http://news.cnet.com; Anders Bylund, "Record Label Defections by Major Acts a Troubling Sign for Recording Industry," *Ars Technica,* October 9, 2007, http://arstechnica.com; "A Change of Tune," *The Economist,* July 5, 2007, http://www.economist.com.

CASE 3.3

Secret Acres: Selling Comics Is Serious Business

Just about everyone remembers a favorite comic book from childhood—whether it was *Spiderman, Tin Tin,* or even *Garfield.* Leon Avelino and Barry Matthews readily acknowledge that they are kids in grown-up bodies with real day jobs (Avelino works for *Sports Illustrated* and Matthews is an accountant for an e-commerce firm) who happen to love comic books and their latest incarnation, graphic novels. Their love for comics in all forms—along with the desire to start their own business—led them to found Secret Acres, a comic book and graphic novel publisher based in New York City. In addition to publishing several works from up-and-coming authors (they have eight books on their list so far), the Secret Acres duo sells books from independent distributors. Often asked whether they think Secret Acres will succeed or fail in the next few years, Avelino quips, "People think we're too small to fail anyway." He laughs but then adds, "That pisses me off. I think we can totally fail."

But Avelino and Matthews have no intention of failing. Acknowledging that Secret Acres faces many economic challenges if it's going to hang on and eventually succeed, Matthews observes, "Every decision we make, we know what the outcome is going to be because it's all small and it's very close to us." Right now, Secret Acres can use its small size to build relationships with its customers. "We are able, because we're small, to produce a very specific kind of comic book, a specific kind of graphic novel, that appeals to a specific audience," explains Matthews. "I love that. We have a lot of control over what we do and we're not doing anything specifically to turn a buck." That said, the accountant in Matthews knows that in order to stay in business, Secret Acres must sell enough

books to push unit costs down, keeping production expenses and prices as low as possible.

Matthews also refers to relationships with book stores, which are personal because he and Avelino do all the communicating themselves. "When you have a small group of stores you are selling from, you have to collect from them on a one-to-one basis," says Matthews. Sometimes the relationship becomes awkward when Matthews or Avelino has to remind a book store owner personally of an unpaid balance.

Another challenge facing the duo is the uncertain future of the print publishing market. The introduction of e-readers such as Amazon's Kindle and Barnes & Noble's Nook creates a new delivery system for printed work. While the e-reader hasn't created the sensation among consumers that its manufacturers had hoped (some competing models have already disappeared from the marketplace), online delivery of printed matter is alive and well—and it's likely that some form of e-reader will eventually catch on. "Publishers are nervous because no one knows how popular e-readers will be in the long run," says Matthews.

Another phenomenon that has taken hold over the last decade is the graphic novel, the fiction genre that combines comic book techniques with the longer, more complex structure of a novel. Graphic novels are particularly popular among teens and college students, but they have received serious attention from the literary world. College courses are now taught around the graphic novel, and the American Library Association publishes a list of recommended graphic novels for teens each year. A firm like Secret Acres could capitalize on a literary trend that continues to gain ground.

Matthews and Avelino haven't quit their day jobs yet. They know it will be awhile before they can call themselves full-time publishers. But they love the comic book business and they are willing to wait for the good times they believe are ahead. "We have faith in the fact that if these books find the right audience, they'll do fine," says Avelino. "I'm OK with being patient. We need to keep going long enough to build a back list that is self-supporting." And Secret Acres already has a following among comic fans—their secret is out.

Questions for Critical Thinking

1. What steps might Matthews and Avelino take to create demand for their books? How must a small business like Secret Acres balance supply with demand?

2. How might Secret Acres make the most of an economy that is recovering slowly? What advantages and disadvantages might the firm have over a large publishing company?

3. How would you categorize the competition that Secret Acres faces?

4. Do you think Secret Acres should pursue online distribution through e-readers and other delivery systems? Why or why not?

Sources: Secret Acres Web site, http://www.secretacres.com, accessed August 19, 2010; "Great Graphic Novels for Teens," *Young Adult Library Services Association,* http://www.ala.org/yalsa, accessed August 19, 2010; Harry McCracken, "E-Readers May Be Dead, But They're Not Going Away Yet," *PC World,* August 17, 2010, http://www.pcworld.com.

Chapter 4

Learning Objectives

[1] Explain the importance of international business and the primary reasons nations trade, and discuss the concepts of absolute and comparative advantage in international trade.

[2] Describe how nations measure international trade and the significance of exchange rates.

[3] Identify the major barriers that confront global businesses.

[4] Explain how international trade organizations and economic communities reduce barriers to international trade.

[5] Compare the different levels of involvement used by businesses when entering global markets.

[6] Distinguish between a global business strategy and a multidomestic business strategy.

International Business and Marketing

Lululemon Athletica Stretches Its Global Reach

©Masterfile

Yoga has been around for centuries but has not always been well understood in Western cultures. Today, yoga is gaining ground in the United States. More and more people are trying a variety of styles and levels of yoga and discovering its physical and mental benefits. As its popularity has increased, so has the business of yoga—from classes to related gear and specially designed apparel.

Gone are bulky cotton sweatpants, nylon running shorts, and old gym mats. Instead, you'll see gently form-fitting, stretchy pants and tops made from high-tech fabrics and soft, dense mats that pad the joints and hug the floor. Many of these articles are made by Canada-based Lululemon Athletica, which is dedicated to offering the highest quality yoga apparel and gear to students and their instructors. Founder Chip Wilson created the company after taking a yoga class in Vancouver, where he was living. He loved the class but hated the clothes. So he started a design studio to make innovative yoga clothes and gave them to local instructors in return for their honest feedback.

The clothes were a hit, and the first Lululemon retail store opened in the beach area of Vancouver two years later. Wilson's vision was to make the store more than just a retail outlet for clothing and gear. He wanted it to be a hub for people interested in learning more about yoga, healthy eating, and positive thinking. Salespeople were trained as educators so that "they could in fact positively influence their families, communities, and the people walking into our stores." Each Lululemon store contains a community bulletin board where shoppers can get information about what classes are scheduled, including yoga, Pilates, children's classes, and organized runs; where to find a local nutritionist; or how to recycle an old yoga mat. Because of this local approach, Lululemon quickly developed a devoted following. Wilson and his team realized that one store wasn't enough and began expanding. Currently, the firm operates 43 stores in Canada, 44 in the United States, and 7 in Australia. The company is planning to add about 35 more stores in North America. Although the firm attempted to enter the Japanese market, it decided to close

those stores because they contributed less than 1.5 percent in sales and required intensive management. Lululemon manufactures its products around the world—in Canada, China, India, Indonesia, Israel, Taiwan, and the United States. The firm chooses factories worldwide based on their commitment to quality and ethical work practices. Lululemon evaluates the conditions at each overseas factory before entering into a working relationship and follows the health and safety standards of the International Labour Organization, a United Nations agency. The company's own Workplace Code of Conduct sets labor standards related to wages and overtime, health and safety, nondiscrimination, prohibition of child or forced labor, and environmental practices. Teams make regular visits to the overseas facilities to evaluate working conditions and product quality. But Lululemon also retains a significant manufacturing base in Vancouver so that new designs can be brought to market quickly and help dodge the threat of cheap knock-offs.

Lululemon recently appointed a new CEO, Christine Day, a former executive at Starbucks Asia-Pacific division. Chip Wilson continues as chairman of the board and chief product designer. Day plans to find ways to grow the company while remaining true to its core values of education and health. "Lululemon has an extraordinary brand with a loyal and growing following around the globe who have embraced our yoga inspired apparel and unique store experience," notes Day.

One new area the firm is exploring is an expanded online presence. The company has an informational Web site containing descriptions of products ranging from tank tops to yoga mats, store locators, and general information about yoga. But Lululemon resisted selling its clothing online, instead relying on the personal experience its in-store educators offered. The firm is now changing course and developing an e-business Web site. The firm is retaining control of key product decisions and customer service functions while using partners for technical support and product distribution. The goal? Allowing yoga aficionados who don't happen to live close to a Lululemon store to enjoy its products while expanding Lululemon's reach.[1]

Consider for a moment how many products you used today that came from outside the United States. Maybe you drank Brazilian coffee with your breakfast, wore clothes manufactured in Honduras or Malaysia, drove to class in a German or Japanese car fueled by gasoline refined from Venezuelan crude oil, and watched a movie on a television set assembled in Mexico for a Japanese company such as Sony. A fellow student in Germany may be wearing Zara jeans, using a Samsung cell phone, and drinking Pepsi.

U.S. and foreign companies alike recognize the importance of international trade to their future success. Economic interdependence is increasing throughout the world as companies seek additional markets for their goods and services and the most cost-effective locations for production facilities. No longer can businesses rely only on domestic sales. Today, foreign sales are essential to U.S. manufacturing, agricultural, and service firms as sources of new markets and profit opportunities. Foreign companies also frequently look to the United States when they seek new markets.

Thousands of products cross national borders every day. The computers that U.S. manufacturers sell in Canada are **exports**, domestically produced goods and services sold in markets in other countries. **Imports** are foreign-made products purchased by

domestic consumers. Together, U.S. exports and imports make up about a quarter of the U.S. gross domestic product (GDP). The United States is fourth in the world among exporting nations, with exports near $1 trillion, and annual imports of about $1.5 trillion. That total amount is more than double the nation's imports and exports of just a decade ago.[2]

Transactions that cross national boundaries may expose a company to an additional set of environmental factors such as new social and cultural practices, economic and political environments, and legal restrictions. Before venturing into world markets, companies must adapt their domestic business strategies and plans to accommodate these differences.

This chapter travels through the world of international business to see how both large and small companies approach globalization. First, we consider the reasons nations trade, the importance and characteristics of the global marketplace, and the ways nations measure international trade. Then we examine barriers to international trade that arise from cultural and environmental differences. To reduce these barriers, countries turn to organizations that promote global business. Finally, we look at the strategies firms implement for entering foreign markets and the way they develop international business strategies.

exports domestically produced goods and services sold in other countries.

imports foreign goods and services purchased by domestic customers.

Why Nations Trade

As domestic markets mature and sales growth slows, companies in every industry recognize the increasing importance of efforts to develop business in other countries. Walmart operates stores in Mexico, Boeing sells jetliners in Asia, and soccer fans in Britain watch their teams being bought by U.S. billionaires. These are only a few of the thousands of U.S. companies taking advantage of large populations, substantial resources, and rising standards of living abroad that boost foreign interest in their goods and services. Likewise, the U.S. market, with the world's highest purchasing power, attracts thousands of foreign companies to its shores.

International trade is vital to a nation and its businesses because it boosts economic growth by providing a market for its products and access to needed resources. Companies can expand their markets, seek growth opportunities in other nations, and make their production and distribution systems more efficient. They also reduce their dependence on the economies of their home nations.

International Sources of Factors of Production

Business decisions to operate abroad depend on the availability, price, and quality of labor, natural resources, capital, and entrepreneurship—the basic factors of production—in the foreign country. Indian colleges and universities produce thousands of highly qualified computer scientists and engineers each year. To take advantage of this talent, many U.S. computer software and hardware firms have set up operations in India, and many others are outsourcing information technology and customer service jobs there.

Trading with other countries also allows a company to spread risk because different nations may be at different stages of the business cycle or in different phases of development. If demand falls off in one country, the company may still enjoy strong demand in other nations. Companies such as Kellogg's and IKEA have long used international sales to offset lower domestic demand.

Size of the International Marketplace

In addition to human and natural resources, entrepreneurship, and capital, companies are attracted to international business by the sheer size of the global marketplace. Only one in six of the world's nearly 6 billion people live in a relatively well-developed country. The share of the world's population in the less developed countries will increase over the coming years because more developed nations have lower birthrates. But the U.S. Census Bureau says the global birthrate is slowing overall, and the average woman in today's world bears half as many children as her counterpart did 35 years ago.[3]

As developing nations expand their involvement in global business, the potential for reaching new groups of customers dramatically increases. Firms looking for new revenue are inevitably attracted to giant markets such as China and India, with respective populations of about 1.3 billion and 1.2 billion. However, people alone are not enough to create a market. Consumer demand also requires purchasing power. As Table 4.1 shows, population size is no guarantee of economic prosperity. Of the ten most populous countries, only the United States appears on the list of those with the highest per-capita GDPs.

Although people in the developing nations have lower per-capita incomes than those in the highly developed economies of North America and western Europe, their huge

Table
4.1
The World's Top Ten Nations Based on Population and Wealth

COUNTRY	POPULATION (IN MILLIONS)	COUNTRY	PER-CAPITA GDP (IN U.S. DOLLARS)
China	1,323	Qatar	$87,717
India	1,156	Luxembourg	$78,723
United States	308	Norway	$53,269
Indonesia	240	Brunei	$50,103
Brazil	199	Singapore	$49,433
Pakistan	175	United States	$46,443
Bangladesh	156	Switzerland	$42,948
Nigeria	150	Hong Kong	$42,574
Russia	140	Ireland	$39,441
Japan	127	Netherlands	$39,278

Sources: U.S. Census Bureau, International Data Base, "Countries and Areas Ranked by Population" www.census.gov, accessed March 8, 2010; International Monetary Fund, "World Economic Outlook Database—October 2009," www.imf.org, accessed January 28, 2010.

populations do represent lucrative markets. Even when the higher-income segments are only a small percentage of the entire country's population, their sheer numbers may still represent significant and growing markets.

Also, many developing countries have typically posted high growth rates of annual GDP. Until the recent economic slowdown, U.S. GDP grew at an annual rate of about 4.4 percent. By contrast, GDP growth in less developed countries was much greater—China's GDP growth rate averaged 10.1 percent over a recent three-year period, and India's averaged 7.5 percent.[4] These markets represent opportunities for global businesses, even though their per-capita incomes lag behind those in more developed countries. Many firms are establishing operations in these and other developing countries to position themselves to benefit from local sales driven by expanding economies and rising standards of living. Walmart is one of those companies. The retail giant has opened dozens of new stores in developing countries from China to Brazil. It now has nearly 4,000 stores in 15 different countries worldwide and considers itself to be "progressing from being a domestic company with an international division to being a global company."[5]

The United States trades with many other nations. As Figure 4.1 shows, the top five are Canada, China, Mexico, Japan, and the Federal Republic of Germany. With the United Kingdom, South Korea, France, Taiwan, and Brazil, they represent nearly two-thirds of U.S. imports and exports every year.[6] Foreign trade is such an important part of the U.S. economy that it makes up a large portion of the business activity in many of the country's individual states as well. Texas exports more than $163 billion of goods annually, and California exports more than $120 billion. Other big exporting states include Florida, Illinois, New York, and Pennsylvania.[7]

Absolute and Comparative Advantage

Few countries can produce all the goods and services their people need. For centuries, trading has been the way that countries can meet the demand. If a country focuses on producing what it does best, it can export surplus domestic output and buy foreign products that it lacks or cannot efficiently produce. The potential for foreign sales of a particular item depends largely on whether the country has an absolute advantage or a comparative advantage.

A country has an *absolute advantage* in making a product for which it can maintain a monopoly or that it can produce at a lower cost than any competitor. For centuries, China enjoyed an absolute advantage in silk production. The fabric was woven from fibers recovered from silkworm cocoons, making it a prized raw material in high-quality clothing. Demand among Europeans for silk led to establishment of the famous Silk Road, a 5,000-mile link between Rome and the ancient Chinese capital city of Xian.

FIGURE 4.1 Top Ten Trading Partners with the United States

Country	Total U.S. Imports and Exports per Month
Canada	$40 billion
China	$35
Mexico	$29
Japan	$14
Germany	$11
United Kingdom	$8
South Korea	$6
France	$5
Taiwan	$4.6
Brazil	$4.3

Source: Data from U.S. Census Bureau, "Top Ten Countries with which the U.S. Trades," http://www.census.gov/ foreign-trade/top/dst/current/balance.html, accessed March 8, 2010.

Absolute advantages are rare these days. But some countries manage to approximate absolute advantages in some products. Climate differences can give some nations or regions an advantage in growing certain plants. Saffron, perhaps the world's most expensive spice at around $130 per ounce, is the stigma of a flowering plant in the crocus family. It is native to the Mediterranean, Asia Minor, and India. Today, however, saffron is cultivated primarily in Spain, where the plant thrives in its soil and climate. Attempts to grow saffron in other parts of the world have generally been unsuccessful.[8]

A nation can develop a *comparative advantage* if it can supply its products more efficiently and at a lower price than it can supply other goods, compared with the outputs of other countries. China is profiting from its comparative advantage in producing textiles. On the other hand, ensuring that its people are well educated is another way a nation can develop a comparative advantage in skilled human resources. India, for example, has acquired a comparative advantage in software development with its highly educated workforce and low wage scale. As a result, several companies have moved part or all of their software development to India.

To boost its longstanding advantage in research and innovation as global competition increases, IBM recently took the unusual step of forming six global research collaborations with companies, universities, and governments in Saudi Arabia, China, Switzerland, Ireland, Taiwan, and India. The company hopes to sign at least four more such international partnerships, breaking with decades of tradition that dictate doing research in secret. "The world is our lab now," says IBM's director of research.[9]

Assessment Check ✔

1. Why do nations trade?

2. Cite some measures of the size of the international marketplace.

3. How does a nation acquire a comparative advantage?

Saffron, possibly the world's most expensive spice, is extracted from crocus flowers. Because the plants grow well in very few places outside Spain, that country enjoys a near absolute advantage in saffron production.

Measuring Trade between Nations

Clearly, engaging in international trade provides tremendous competitive advantages to both the countries and individual companies involved. But how do we measure global business activity? To understand what the trade inflows and outflows mean for a country, we need to examine the concepts of balance of trade and balance of payments. Another important factor is currency exchange rates for each country.

A nation's **balance of trade** is the difference between its exports and imports. If a country exports more than it imports, it achieves a positive balance of trade, called a *trade surplus*. If it imports more than it exports, it produces a negative balance of trade, called a *trade deficit*. The United States has run a trade deficit every year since 1976. Despite being one of the world's top exporters, the United States has an even greater appetite for foreign-made goods, which creates a trade deficit.

balance of trade difference between a nation's exports and imports.

A nation's balance of trade plays a central role in determining its **balance of payments**—the overall flow of money into or out of a country. Other factors also affect the balance of payments, including overseas loans and borrowing, international investments, profits from such investments, and foreign aid payments. To calculate a nation's balance of payments, subtract the monetary outflows from the monetary inflows. A positive balance of payments, or a *balance-of-payments surplus*, means more money has moved into a country than out of it. A negative balance of payments, or *balance-of-payments deficit*, means more money has gone out of the country than entered it.

balance of payments overall money flows into and out of a country.

Major U.S. Exports and Imports

The United States, with combined exports and imports of about $2.5 trillion, leads the world in the international trade of goods and services. As listed in Table 4.2, the leading categories of goods exchanged by U.S. exporters and importers range from machinery and vehicles to crude oil and chemicals. Strong U.S. demand for imported goods is partly a reflection of the nation's prosperity and diversity.

Although the United States imports more goods than it exports, the opposite is true for services. U.S. exporters sell more than $507 billion in services annually. Much of that money comes from travel and tourism—money spent by foreign nationals visiting the United States.[10] The increase in that figure is especially significant because the dollar has declined and continues to fluctuate in terms of foreign currencies in recent years. U.S. service exports also include business and technical services such as engineering, financial services, computing, legal services, and entertainment, as well as royalties and licensing fees. Major service exporters include Citibank, Walt Disney, Allstate Insurance, and Federal Express, as well as retailers such as McDonald's and Starbucks.

Businesses in many foreign countries want the expertise of U.S. financial and business professionals. Accountants are in high demand in Russia, China, the Netherlands, and Australia—Sydney has become one of Asia's biggest financial centers. Entertainment is

4.2 Top Ten U.S. Merchandise Exports and Imports

EXPORTS	AMOUNT (IN BILLIONS)	IMPORTS	AMOUNT (IN BILLIONS)
Agricultural commodities	$11.52	Crude oil	$353.5
Motor vehicles	98.9	Motor vehicles	190.8
Electrical machinery	82.0	Television, VCR	133.2
Alcoholic beverages	80.2	Electrical machinery	112.6
Mineral fuel	76.0	Automated data processing equipment	96.5
General industrial machinery	55.2	Petroleum preparations	87.1
Specialized industrial machinery	51.9	Agricultural commodities	80.7
Petroleum preparations	51.4	Clothing	78.9
Scientific instruments	42.5	General industrial machinery	66.9
Chemicals—plastics	34.3	Chemicals—medicinal	59.2

Source: U.S. Census Bureau, "U.S. Exports and General Imports by Selected SITC Commodity Groups," *Statistical Abstract of the United States: 2010,* http://www.census.gov, accessed March 17, 2010.

another major growth area for U.S. service exports. The Walt Disney Company has long had theme parks in Europe and Asia and will begin a new one in Shanghai with the approval of China's central government.[11]

With annual imports reaching nearly $2 trillion, the United States is by far the world's leading importer. American tastes for foreign-made goods for everything from clothing to consumer electronics show up as huge trade deficits with the consumer-goods-exporting nations of China and Japan.

Exchange Rates

A nation's **exchange rate** is the rate at which its currency can be exchanged for the currencies of other nations. It is important to learn how foreign exchange works because we live in a global community and the value of currency is an important economic thermometer for every country. Each currency's exchange rate is usually quoted in terms of another currency, such as the number of Mexican pesos needed to purchase one U.S. dollar. Roughly 12 pesos are needed to exchange for a dollar. A Canadian dollar can be exchanged for approximately $1 in the United States. The euro, the currency used in most of the European Union (EU) member-countries, has made considerable moves in exchange value during its few years in circulation. European consumers and businesses now use the euro to pay bills by check, credit card, or bank transfer. Euro coins and notes are also used in many EU member-countries.

Foreign exchange rates are influenced by a number of factors, including domestic economic and political conditions, central bank intervention, balance-of-payments position, and speculation over future currency values. Currency values fluctuate, or "float," depending on the supply and demand for each currency in the international market. In this system of

exchange rate value of one nation's currency relative to the currencies of other countries.

🇺🇸 USA	USD	0.9103
🇬🇧 UNITED KINGDOM	GBP	27
🇨🇦 CANADA	CAD	0.9978
CHINA	CNY	31
EURO	EUR	0.6263
🇯🇵 JAPAN	JPY	71
SINGAPORE	SGD	1.3355
🇭🇰 HONG KONG	HKD	56
NEW ZEALAND	NZD	1.3247
MALAYSIA	MYR	37
THAILAND	THB	32.6 10
INDONESIA	IDR	2.6

David Franklin/iStockphoto

Because we live in a global community it is important to understand how currency exchange rates work. Those rates can be influenced by a variety of factors.

devaluation reduction in a currency's value relative to other currencies or to a fixed standard.

Assessment Check ☑

1. Compare balance of trade and balance of payments.
2. Explain the function of an exchange rate.
3. What happens when a currency is devalued?

floating exchange rates, currency traders create a market for the world's currencies based on each country's relative trade and investment prospects. In theory, this market permits exchange rates to vary freely according to supply and demand. In practice, exchange rates do not float in total freedom. National governments often intervene in currency markets to adjust their exchange rates.

Nations influence exchange rates in other ways as well. They may form currency blocs by linking their exchange rates to each other. Many governments practice protectionist policies that seek to guard their economies against trade imbalances. For instance, nations sometimes take deliberate action to devalue their currencies as a way to increase exports and stimulate foreign investment. **Devaluation** describes a drop in a currency's value relative to other currencies or to a fixed standard. In Brazil, a currency devaluation made investing in that country relatively cheap, so the devaluation was followed by a flood of foreign investment. Pillsbury bought Brazil's Brisco, which makes a local staple, *pao de queijo*, a cheese bread formed into rolls and served with morning coffee. Other foreign companies invested in Brazil's construction, tourism, banking, communications, and other industries.

For an individual business, the impact of currency devaluation depends on where that business buys its materials and where it sells its products. Business transactions are usually conducted in the currency of the particular region in which they take place. When business is conducted in Japan, transactions are likely to be in yen. In the United Kingdom, transactions are in pounds. With the adoption of the euro in the EU, the number of currencies in that region has been reduced. At present, the EU member-countries using the euro include Austria, Belgium, Finland, France, Germany, Greece, Ireland, Italy, Luxembourg, the Netherlands, Portugal, Slovenia, and Spain. Other countries' currencies include the British pound, Australian dollar, the Indian rupee, the Brazilian real, the Mexican peso, the Taiwanese dollar, and the South African rand.

Exchange rate changes can quickly create—or wipe out—a competitive advantage, so they are important factors in decisions about whether to invest abroad. In Europe, a declining dollar means that a price of ten euros is worth more, so companies are pressured to lower prices. At the same time, if the dollar falls it makes European vacations less affordable for U.S. tourists because their dollars are worth less relative to the euro.

On the Internet you can find currency converters such as those located at http://beginnersinvest.about.com/od/currencycalc/Currency_Calculator.htm, which can help in your monetary conversions. It also helps you understand how much spending power a U.S. dollar has in other countries.

Currencies that owners can easily convert into other currencies are called *hard currencies*. Examples include the euro, the U.S. dollar, and the Japanese yen. The Russian ruble and many central European currencies are considered soft currencies because they cannot be readily converted. Exporters trading with these countries sometimes prefer to barter, accepting payment in oil, timber, or other commodities that they can resell for hard-currency payments.

The foreign currency market is the largest financial market in the world, with a daily volume in excess of 3 trillion U.S. dollars.[12] This is about ten times the size of all the world's stock markets combined, so the foreign exchange market is the most liquid and efficient financial market in the world.

Barriers to International Trade

All businesses encounter barriers in their operations, whether they sell only to local customers or trade in international markets. Countries such as Australia and New Zealand regulate the hours and days retailers may be open. Besides complying with a variety of laws and exchanging currencies, international companies may also have to reformulate their products to accommodate different tastes in new locations. After many years of disappointing results in China, Kraft recently won nearly a quarter of China's $1.6 billion cookie market by making its Oreo cookies less sweet to suit local tastes and launching new products including Oreo Wafer Sticks, Wafer Rolls, Soft Cakes, and Strawberry Cremes.[13]

In addition to social and cultural differences, companies engaged in international business face economic barriers as well as legal and political ones. Some of the hurdles shown in Figure 4.2 are easily breached, but others require major changes in a company's business strategy. To successfully compete in global markets, companies and their managers must understand not only how these barriers affect international trade but also how to overcome them.

Social and Cultural Differences

The social and cultural differences among nations range from language and customs to educational background and religious holidays. Understanding and respecting these differences are critical to pave the way for international business success. Businesspeople with knowledge of host countries' cultures, languages, social values, and religious attitudes and practices are well equipped for the marketplace and the negotiating table. Sensitivity to such elements as local attitudes, forms of address, and expectations regarding dress, body language, and timeliness also helps them win customers and achieve their business objectives. It is not only U.S. executives who are adapting to the global business environment. Considering the number of transactions that are sealed on the golf links, Chinese students at Xiamen University must learn golf, as well as business and law, and Peking University is building a practice green. The "Business Etiquette" feature offers suggestions for understanding the Japanese culture.

Language English is the second most widely spoken language in the world, followed by Hindustani, Spanish, Russian, and Arabic. Only Mandarin Chinese is more commonly used. It is not uncommon for students abroad for whom English is not their first language to spend eight years of elementary and high school in English language classes. Understanding a business colleague's primary language may prove to be the difference between closing an

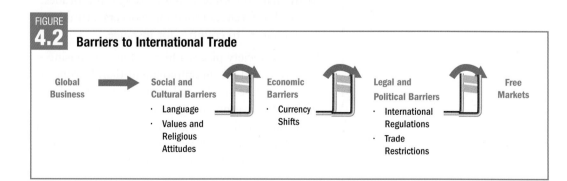

FIGURE
4.2 **Barriers to International Trade**

Global Business → Social and Cultural Barriers
· Language
· Values and Religious Attitudes

Economic Barriers
· Currency Shifts

Legal and Political Barriers
· International Regulations
· Trade Restrictions

Free Markets

BusinessEtiquette

Tips for Understanding Japanese Culture

Japan's 125 million people live in a fairly small area and tend to be reserved and introverted; their culture emphasizes conformity more than in the United States. Their literacy rate is nearly 100 percent; 95 percent of the population has completed high school. Buddhism and Shintoism are the dominant religions. Here are some tips for respecting Japanese culture that can help you in your global business dealings.

- Dress to impress. Casual wear is not appropriate in work situations.

- Because you will often remove your shoes indoors in Japan, choose slip-on styles that are easy to get on and off.

- Avoid large hand gestures and pointing; the Japanese do not talk with their hands and may find it distracting.

- Respect others' personal space. While handshakes are becoming more common, bowing is still the traditional greeting.

- Remember that in Japan a smile can legitimately mean many things, including anger, sorrow, or embarrassment.

- Keep in mind that the Japanese don't make frequent eye contact and are very comfortable with silence. Don't feel you need to fill conversational gaps.

- Business entertaining most often occurs in bars and restaurants after the end of the workday. Tipping is not required.

- If you are invited to a Japanese home, consider yourself honored.

- Remember to give and receive business cards with both hands. Show respect for a business card you are given by examining it carefully.

- Always wrap gifts. In Japan it's safest to have the store wrap your gifts to ensure the paper and other details are appropriate. White, for instance, symbolizes death.

- Keep in mind that the Japanese dislike criticism. They also prefer not saying no and may say yes when they mean otherwise.

Sources: "Japanese Etiquette," *Cultural Savvy.com*, www.culturalsavvy.com, accessed March 17, 2010; "Japan," *Cyborlink.com*, www.cyborlink.com, accessed March 9, 2010; Emily Maltby, "Expanding Abroad? Avoid Cultural Gaffes," *The Wall Street Journal*, January 19, 2010, p. B5.

---

international business transaction and losing the sale to someone else. Company representatives operating in foreign markets must not only choose correct and appropriate words but also translate words correctly to convey the intended meanings. Firms may also need to rename products or rewrite slogans for foreign markets.

Potential communication barriers include more than mistranslation. Companies may present messages through inappropriate media, overlook local customs and regulations, or ignore differences in taste. One U.S. executive recently lost a deal in China by giving the prospective client a set of four antique clocks wrapped in white paper. Unfortunately, the number four and the Chinese word for clock are similar to the word "death," while white is the traditional color for funerals.[14] Cultural sensitivity is especially critical in cyberspace. Web site developers must be aware that visitors to a site may come from anywhere in the world. Some icons that seem friendly to U.S. Internet users may shock people from other countries. A person making a high-five hand gesture would be insulting people in Greece; the same is true of making a circle with the thumb and index finger in Brazil, a thumbs-up sign in Egypt, and a two-fingered peace sign with the back of the hand facing out in Great Britain.

Gift-giving traditions employ the language of symbolism. For example, in Latin America, knives and scissors should not be given as gifts because they represent the severing of friendship. Flowers are generally acceptable, but Mexicans use yellow flowers in their Day of the Dead festivities, so they are associated with death.

Values and Religious Attitudes

Even though today's world is shrinking in many ways, people in different countries do not necessarily share the same values or religious attitudes. Marked differences remain in workers' attitudes from country to country, for instance.

U.S. society places a higher value on business efficiency and low unemployment than European society, where employee benefits are more valued. The U.S. government does not regulate vacation time, and employees typically receive no paid vacation during their first year of employment, then two weeks' vacation, and eventually up to three or four weeks if they stay with the same employer for many years. In contrast, the EU mandates a minimum paid vacation of four weeks per year, and most Europeans get five or six weeks. In these countries, a U.S. company that opens a manufacturing plant would not be able to hire any local employees without offering vacations in line with a nation's business practices.

U.S. culture values national unity, with tolerance of regional differences. The United States is viewed as a national market with a single economy. European countries that are part of the 27-member EU are trying to create a similar marketplace. However, many resist the idea of being European citizens first and British, Danish, or Dutch citizens second. British consumers differ from Italians in important ways, and U.S. companies that fail to recognize this variation will run into problems with brand acceptance.

Religion plays an important role in every society, so businesspeople must also cultivate sensitivity to the dominant religions in countries where they operate. Understanding religious cycles and the timing of major holidays can help prevent embarrassing moments when scheduling meetings, trade shows, conferences, or events such as the opening of a new manufacturing plant. People doing business in Saudi Arabia must take into account Islam's month-long observance of Ramadan, when work ends at noon. Friday is the Muslim Sabbath, so the Saudi workweek runs from Saturday through Thursday. Also, Muslims abstain from alcohol and consider pork unclean, so gifts of pigskin or liquor would be offensive.

Economic Differences

Business opportunities are flourishing in densely populated countries such as China and India, as local consumers eagerly buy Western products. Although such prospects might tempt American firms, managers must first consider the economic factors involved in doing business in these markets. A country's size, per-capita income, and stage of economic development are among the economic factors to consider when evaluating it as a candidate for an international business venture. Making a wrong move—or moving too late—can spell disaster for a firm, as the "Hit & Miss" feature describes.

Infrastructure Along with other economic measures, businesses should consider a country's **infrastructure**. Infrastructure refers to basic systems of communication (telecommunications, television, radio, and print media), transportation (roads and highways, railroads, and airports), and energy facilities (power plants and gas and electric utilities). The Internet and technology use can also be considered part of infrastructure.

infrastructure basic systems of communication, transportation, and energy facilities in a country.

India's growing industrialization and its latest projections of 30 million air passengers a year mean the country will soon need at least 400 new airports, according to the country's civil aviation minister. With the Indian aviation industry growing at nearly 20 percent a year, 3,000 new planes will also be needed. Bidding for contractors to work on construction of a new airport in the capital city of Mumbai will take about a year to complete. "Our job is not over by creating infrastructure for aviation industry to grow," said the minister. "We need safe and secure aviation. Indian aviation will not grow at the cost of safety and security." Part of India's new air travel security is a CT scanner to inspect luggage at the country's biggest new airport, built in a record three years in New Delhi.[15]

Financial systems also provide a type of infrastructure for businesses. In the United States, buyers have widespread access to checks, credit cards, and debit cards, as well as electronic systems for processing these forms of payment. In many African countries, such as Ethiopia, local businesses do not accept credit cards, so travelers to the capital city, Addis Ababa, are warned to bring plenty of cash and traveler's checks.

Waterford Wedgwood Cracks under Economic Pressure

When the giant crystal ball descended into New York City's Times Square at midnight one recent New Year's Eve, it forecast the end of an era. The ball is made of Waterford crystal, whose company—Waterford Wedgwood—went into the British equivalent of bankruptcy shortly afterward. To many in Ireland and England, where the company has its roots, it was like the death of an old friend. Waterford was founded in Ireland in 1783, and Wedgwood was established in England in 1759. For more than 200 years, Waterford crystal and Wedgwood china have graced the tables of royalty and celebrities. Families treasured their pieces, handing them down from generation to generation. About 20 years ago, the two companies were joined, becoming Waterford Wedgwood.

The rich history of Waterford Wedgwood may provide a clue to its downfall. Although pieces of crystal or china might be given to world leaders or to couples as wedding gifts, fewer and fewer families sit down for formal dinners. They don't need or use entire settings of fine china to the extent that families did a few generations ago. "Young people are so happy to have TV dinners," observes an older owner of a china shop that itself is struggling. "They're far more practical than my age group, where I always had a best set." Even if younger families do not consume TV dinners, they still may not need or want the expensive, formal styles offered by Waterford Wedgwood. The company tried to respond to changing tastes by offering more casual and simpler designs but was not successful enough to sustain the business.

Even under normal economic circumstances, plunking down $85 or more for a single wine goblet that needs to be washed by hand can be hard to justify. But in tough times, consumers concentrate on basics and forgo luxuries. A crystal goblet or fine china seems out of reach for many consumers as they worry about their job security and homes.

Some experts also point to Waterford Wedgwood's delay in moving some of its manufacturing operations overseas, where labor is cheaper. The firm does in fact employ several thousand workers at foreign facilities, including 1,500 people at a plant in Jakarta, Indonesia, which produces many Wedgwood ceramics. However, the move seems to have come too late to make a difference. And Waterford crystal is still made at the same Irish factory where it has been produced for generations. The mayor of Waterford announced that it would be a "national disaster" if production were halted.

Questions for Critical Thinking

1. What steps do you think Waterford Wedgwood might have taken to prevent bankruptcy?

2. Do you think it is worth trying to save a firm like Waterford Wedgwood? Why or why not?

Sources: Company Web site, http://www.waterfordwedgwood.com, accessed February 18, 2009; "Waterford Gets Takeover Bids," *CNNMoney*, February 1, 2009, http://money.cnn.com; "Famous Crystal Company Goes Bust," *CBS News*, January 6, 2009, http://www.cbsnews.com; Julia Werdigier, "Waterford Wedgwood Is in Receivership," *The New York Times*, January 6, 2009, http://www.nytimes.com; "Waterford Wedgwood in Bankruptcy," *Chicago Tribune*, January 6, 2009, http://archives.chicagotribune.com; Graeme Wearden and Henry McDonald, "After 250 Years, Waterford Wedgwood Falls into Administration," *The Guardian*, January 5, 2009, http://www.guardian.co.uk; Jane Wardell, "Crystal, China Maker Waterford Wedgwood Collapses," Associated Press, January 5, 2009, http://news.yahoo.com.

Currency Conversion and Shifts Despite growing similarities in infrastructure, businesses crossing national borders encounter basic economic differences: national currencies. Foreign currency fluctuations may present added problems for global businesses. As explained earlier in the chapter, the values of the world's major currencies fluctuate—sometimes drastically—in relation to each other. Rapid and unexpected currency shifts can make pricing in local currencies difficult. Shifts in exchange rates can also influence the attractiveness of various business decisions. A devalued currency may make a nation less desirable as an export destination because of reduced demand in that market. However, devaluation can make the nation desirable as an investment opportunity because investments there will be a bargain in terms of the investor's currency.

Political and Legal Differences

Like social, cultural, and economic differences, legal and political differences in host countries can pose barriers to international trade. Government oversight of Internet use in China is so strict that many Chinese Web sites are now registering overseas to try to avoid censorship.[16] Such actions pose threats to those considering doing business there.

To compete in today's world marketplace, managers involved in international business must be well versed in legislation that affects their industries. Some countries impose general

Solving an Ethical Controversy

How Fair Is Fair Trade?

While demand for candy remains high, the price of cocoa is near a 30-year-high. One reason is that to win the coveted "fair trade" designation for their products, chocolate makers must pay small cocoa farmers an extra $150 per ton for the raw ingredient and accept a price of at least $1,600 a ton overall. Nestlé recently announced its popular Kit Kat chocolate bars, which represent about a quarter of the company's U.K. candy sales, will now include only fair trade chocolate from West Africa. Still, the company has come under criticism for allegedly lagging on other possible problems such as child labor.

Is "fair trade" fair enough?

PRO

1. As one of the world's largest buyers of cocoa beans for Kit Kat, Nestlé is taking a strong lead in social responsibility, even though high fair-trade cocoa prices are "going to put pressure on our business," according to the firm's U.K. head.

2. Nestlé's efforts will provide poor cocoa farmers with cash, trees, and training, and help them keep children in school.

CON

1. If a company allows the use of child labor on its behalf abroad, its fair trade claims are mere window-dressing.

2. Firms can and should ensure that all their actions are socially responsible at every level, at home and abroad.

Summary

The share of fair trade chocolate sold in the U.K. was expected to soon rise to about 10 percent, a ten-fold increase, in part because of Nestlé's efforts. Nestlé has promised to plant millions of disease-resistant cocoa trees in Africa over the next few years and to spend at least $445 million on sustainable farming projects in the same period. It has also agreed to a global initiative to improve cocoa farmers' access to health care and to combat child labor.

Sources: Roberta Cruger, "Is Fair Trade Chocolate Fair Enough?" The *Independent/RelaxNews,* www.treehugger.com, February 14, 2010; Thomas Muller, "Nestle Sees Stagnant U.K. Chocolate Market as Cocoa Prices Soar," *Bloomberg.com,* www.bloomberg.com, December 12, 2009; "Organizations Question Nestlé's Commitment to Fair Trade Cocoa," Laborrights.org, www.laborrights.org, December 7, 2009; Deborah Ball, "Nestle Moves to Fair-Trade Chocolate for KitKat Candy in U.K.," *The Wall Street Journal,* www.online.wsj.com, December 7, 2009.

---

trade restrictions. Others have established detailed rules that regulate how foreign companies can operate.

Political Climate An important factor in any international business investment is the stability of the political climate. The political structures of many nations promote stability similar to that in the United States. Other nations, such as Indonesia, Congo, and Bosnia, feature quite different—and frequently changing—structures. Host nations often pass laws designed to protect their own interests, sometimes at the expense of foreign businesses. See the "Ethical Controversy" feature for a look at how fair trade laws work.

The political structures of Russia, Turkey, the former Yugoslavia, Hong Kong, and several central European countries, including the Czech Republic and Poland, have seen dramatic changes. Such political changes almost always bring changes in the legal environment. Hong Kong's status as part of China makes it an economy where political developments produced changes in the legal and cultural environments. Since the collapse of the Soviet Union, Russia has struggled to develop a new market structure and political processes.

Legal Environment When conducting business internationally, managers must be familiar with three dimensions of the legal environment: U.S. law, international regulations, and the laws of the countries in which they plan to trade. Some laws protect the rights of foreign companies to compete in the United States. Others dictate actions allowed for U.S. companies doing business in foreign countries.

The *Foreign Corrupt Practices Act* forbids U.S. companies from bribing foreign officials, political candidates, or government representatives. This act prescribes fines and jail time for U.S. managers who are aware of illegal payoffs. Until recently, many countries, including France and Germany, not only accepted the practice of bribing foreign officials in countries where such practices were customary but allowed tax deductions for these expenses. The United States, United Kingdom, France, Germany, and 36 other countries have signed the Organization for Economic Cooperation and Development Anti-Bribery Convention. Though active enforcement has been slight, this agreement makes offering or paying bribes a criminal offense and ends the deductibility of bribes.[17]

Still, corruption continues to be an international problem. Its pervasiveness, combined with U.S. prohibitions, creates a difficult obstacle for U.S. businesspeople whom want to do business in many foreign countries. Chinese pay *huilu*, and Russians rely on *vzyatka*. In the Middle East, palms are greased with *baksheesh*. Figure 4.3 compares 179 countries based on surveys of perceived corruption. This Corruption Perceptions Index is computed by Transparency International, a Berlin-based organization that rates the degree of corruption observed by businesspeople and the general public.

The growth of online business has introduced new elements to the legal climate of international business. Patents, brand names, trademarks, copyrights, and other intellectual property are difficult to police, given the availability of information on the Internet. However, some countries are adopting laws to protect information obtained by electronic contacts.

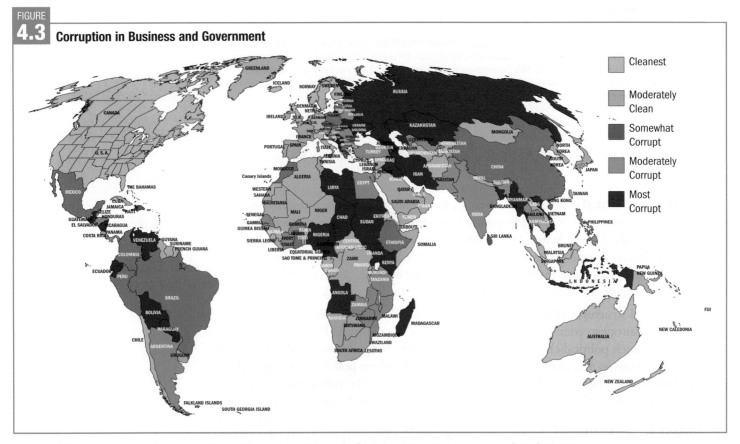

FIGURE 4.3 Corruption in Business and Government

Legend:
- Cleanest
- Moderately Clean
- Somewhat Corrupt
- Moderately Corrupt
- Most Corrupt

Source: Data from Transparency International, "Annual Corruption Perceptions Index," http://www.transparency.org, accessed March 17, 2010.

IBM Helps Keep Water Flowing

Did you know it takes 11 gallons of water to manufacture one slice of bread, and 35 gallons to make a single cup of coffee? Water, one of our most abundant resources, is under ever-greater stress. One in five people worldwide lack access to safe drinking water.

IBM is taking major steps to protect the Earth's finite supply of water. Though this essential resource exists worldwide, there is no global market for it and little international or even national exchange of information about how to conserve it. "Water is about quantity, quality, space, and time," says IBM's Global Innovation Outlook report on the world's water management problems. "Whether you have a big problem or not depends entirely on where you live."

IBM is addressing the future of water management in several ways. It is setting up networks of meters and sensors with special IBM software to monitor the capacity and quality of water systems that serve nations, communities, organizations, and individual homes. The company is working to ensure that treated drinking water is subject to less waste from thousands of miles of aging underground pipes and IBM's acoustic technology helps locate the worst leaks for priority repairs. IBM is also collecting data on pollution, marine life, and waves for commercial fishermen, and improving filters to inex-

pensively eliminate arsenic and salt from drinking water in developing countries.

"We're not going to create water where there is none," says the vice president of IBM's Big Green Innovations. "But where we know water is under stress, we need to monitor what's going on and better manage it."

Questions for Critical Thinking

1. For its water-management efforts, *Fast Company* magazine recently voted IBM 18th in the world in innovation. What do you think makes IBM particularly suited for this award?

2. IBM is an information services company. What do you think other socially responsible firms could learn from its water-management efforts?

Sources: "Advanced Water Management," www-935.ibm.com, accessed March 23, 2010; "Smarter Water Management," www.ibm.com, accessed March 23, 2010; "Chuck Salter, #18. IBM," *Fast Company,* www.fastcompany.com, February 17, 2010; Mary Tripsas, "Everybody in the Pool of Green Innovation," *The New York Times,* www .nytimes.com, November 1, 2009.

Malaysia imposes stiff fines and long jail terms on those convicted of illegally accessing computers and using information that passes through them.

International Regulations To regulate international commerce, the United States and many other countries have ratified treaties and signed agreements that dictate the conduct of international business and protect some of its activities. The United States has entered into many *friendship, commerce, and navigation treaties* with other nations. Such treaties address many aspects of international business relations, including the right to conduct business in the treaty partner's domestic market. Other international business agreements involve product standards, patents, trademarks, reciprocal tax policies, export controls, international air travel, and international communications. One area in which there are no international regulations involves the use/protection of water supplies. IBM is stepping in to help provide the international community with water-management methods and tools as we see in the "Going Green" feature.

When Congress granted China full trade relations with the United States, China agreed to lower trade barriers, including subsidies that held down the prices of food exports, restrictions on where foreign law firms can open offices, and taxes charged on imported goods. In exchange for China's promise to halve these taxes, called *tariffs,* the United States granted Chinese businesses equal access to U.S. markets enjoyed by most other countries.

Many types of regulations affect the actions of managers doing business in international markets. Not only must worldwide producers and marketers maintain required minimum quality levels for all the countries in which they operate, but they must comply with numerous specific local regulations. Britain prevents advertisers from encouraging children to engage in such unhealthy behavior as overeating or replacing regular meals with candy and snack foods. Malaysia's Censorship Board prohibits nudity and profanity on TV. Germany and France allow publishers to set prices that retailers charge for their books.

The British government, as part of an initiative to fight violence against women, recently commissioned a report showing that children and teens are being increasingly exposed to unhealthy pressures by images of "hyper-sexualised images" of an adult nature in the media. "They are facing pressures that children in the past simply did not have to face," the report said, including the idea that it is necessary to look "hot" and "sexy." The report proposed that parental controls in new videogame consoles and mobile phones be switched on before sale, that men's magazines carry age warnings, and that sexually oriented music videos be broadcast only late in the evening.[18]

Types of Trade Restrictions

Trade restrictions such as taxes on imports and complicated administrative procedures create additional barriers to international business. They may limit consumer choices while increasing the costs of foreign-made products. Trade restrictions are also imposed to protect citizens' security, health, and jobs. A government may limit exports of strategic and defense-related goods to unfriendly countries to protect its security, ban imports of insecticide-contaminated farm products to protect health, and restrict imports to protect domestic jobs in the importing country.

Other restrictions are imposed to promote trade with certain countries. Still others protect countries from unfair competition. Regardless of the political reasons for trade restrictions, most take the form of tariffs. In addition to tariffs, governments impose a number of nontariff—or administrative—barriers. These include quotas, embargoes, and exchange controls.

tariffs tax imposed on imported goods.

Tariffs Taxes, surcharges, or duties on foreign products are referred to as **tariffs**. Governments assess two types of tariffs—revenue and protective tariffs—both of which make imports more expensive for domestic buyers. Revenue tariffs generate income for the government. Upon returning home, U.S. leisure travelers who are out of the country more than 48 hours and who bring back goods purchased abroad must pay import taxes on their value in excess of $200 to $1,600, depending on the country of origin. This duty goes directly to the U.S. Treasury. The sole purpose of a protective tariff is to raise the retail price of imported products to match or exceed the prices of similar products manufactured in the home country. In other words, protective tariffs seek to limit imports and level the playing field for local competitors.

Of course, tariffs create a disadvantage to companies that want to export to the countries imposing the tariffs. In addition, governments do not always agree on the reasons behind protective tariffs. So they do not always have the desired effect. The United States imposes a tariff on foreign competitors accused of selling products at lower prices in the United States than U.S. manufacturers charge. The government passed a bill giving the money from these tariffs directly to U.S. plaintiff companies, instead of to the Treasury as in the past. The European Union imposes tariffs on some electronics products, which the United States says violates the 1997 Information Technology Agreement (ITA) calling for the elimination of tariffs on such items as computers and computer parts.[19]

Nontariff Barriers Nontariff, or administrative, trade barriers restrict imports in more subtle ways than tariffs. These measures may take such forms as quotas on imports, restrictive standards for imports, and export subsidies. Because many countries have recently substantially reduced tariffs or eliminated them entirely, they increasingly use nontariff barriers to control flows of imported products.

Quotas limit the amounts of particular products that countries can import during specified time periods. Limits may be set as quantities, such as number of cars or bushels of wheat, or as values, such as dollars' worth of cigarettes. Governments regularly set quotas for agricultural products and sometimes for imported automobiles. The United States, for example, sets a quota on imports of sugar. Imports under the quota amount are subject to a lower tariff than shipments above the quota. Sugar and related products imported at the higher rate may enter the country in unlimited quantities, however.[20]

International trade restrictions include *quotas,* or limits, on the amount of a product that can be imported into a country. In the United States, sugar is subject to import quotas.

Richardo Azoury/iStockphoto

Quotas help prevent **dumping**. In one form of dumping, a company sells products abroad at prices below its cost of production. In another, a company exports a large quantity of a product at a lower price than the same product in the home market and drives down the price of the domestic product. Dumping benefits domestic consumers in the importing market, but it hurts domestic producers. It also allows companies to gain quick entry to foreign markets.

More severe than a quota, an **embargo** imposes a total ban on importing a specified product or even a total halt to trading with a particular country. The United States has a longstanding trade embargo with Cuba. Embargo durations can vary to accommodate changes in foreign policy.

Another form of administrative trade restriction is **exchange control**. Imposed through a central bank or government agency, exchange controls affect both exporters and importers. Firms that gain foreign currencies through exporting are required to sell them to the central bank or another agency. Importers must buy foreign currencies to pay for their purchases from the same agency. The exchange control authority can then allocate, expand, or restrict foreign exchange in accordance with national policy.

Reducing Barriers to International Trade

Although tariffs and administrative barriers still restrict trade, overall the world is moving toward free trade. Several types of organizations ease barriers to international trade, including groups that monitor trade policies and practices and institutions that offer monetary assistance. Another type of federation designed to ease trade barriers is the multinational economic community, such as the European Union. This section looks at the roles these organizations play.

quota limit set on the amounts of particular products that can be imported.

dumping selling products abroad at prices below production costs or below typical prices in the home market to capture market share from domestic competitors.

embargo total ban on importing specific products or a total halt to trading with a particular country.

exchange control restriction on importation of certain products or against certain companies to reduce trade and expenditures of foreign currency.

Assessment Check ☑

1. How might values and attitudes form a barrier to trade, and how can they be overcome?

2. What is a tariff? What is its purpose?

3. Why is dumping a problem for companies marketing goods internationally?

Organizations Promoting International Trade

General Agreement on Tariffs and Trade (GATT) international trade accord that substantially reduced worldwide tariffs and other trade barriers.

For the 60-plus years of its existence, the **General Agreement on Tariffs and Trade (GATT)**, an international trade accord, sponsored a series of negotiations, called rounds, which substantially reduced worldwide tariffs and other barriers. Major industrialized nations founded the multinational organization in 1947 to work toward reducing tariffs and relaxing import quotas. The last set of completed negotiations—the Uruguay Round—cut average tariffs by one-third, in excess of $700 billion; reduced farm subsidies; and improved protection for copyright and patent holders. In addition, international trading rules now apply to various service industries. Finally, the new agreement established the **World Trade Organization (WTO)** to succeed GATT. This organization includes representatives from 153 countries.

World Trade Organization (WTO) 153-member international institution that monitors GATT agreements and mediates international trade disputes.

World Trade Organization Since 1995, the WTO has monitored GATT agreements among the member-nations, mediated disputes, and continued the effort to reduce trade barriers throughout the world. Unlike provisions in GATT, the WTO's decisions are binding on parties involved in disputes.

The WTO has grown more controversial in recent years as it issues decisions that have implications for working conditions and the environment in member nations. Concerns have been expressed that the WTO's focus on lowering trade barriers encourages businesses to keep costs down through practices that may increase pollution and human rights abuses. Particularly worrisome is the fact that the organization's member-countries must agree on policies, and developing countries tend not to be eager to lose their low-cost advantage by enacting stricter labor and environmental laws. Other critics claim that if well-funded U.S. firms such as fast-food chains, entertainment companies, and Internet retailers can freely enter foreign markets, they will wipe out smaller foreign businesses serving the distinct tastes and practices of other countries' cultures.

Trade unions in developed nations complain that the WTO's support of free trade makes it easier to export manufacturing jobs to low-wage countries. U.S. glassmaking is undergoing a long decline that began in the 1990s, aided by increased imports and bigger profits to be made overseas.[21]

But many small and midsize firms have benefited from the WTO's reduction of trade barriers and lowering of the cost of trade. They currently make up 97 percent of all firms that export goods and services, according to the Department of Commerce.

The most recent round of WTO talks was called the *Doha Round* after the city in Qatar where it began. After several years of heated disputes and collapsed negotiations, the eight leading industrial nations recommitted themselves to successful conclusion of the talks. Under discussion were ways to improve global agricultural trade and trade among developing countries. The leaders worked to reduce domestic price supports, eliminate export subsidies, and improve market access for goods. Such changes could help farmers in developing countries compete in the global marketplace.[22]

World Bank organization established by industrialized nations to lend money to less developed countries.

World Bank Shortly after the end of World War II, industrialized nations formed an organization to lend money to less developed and developing countries. The **World Bank** primarily funds projects that build or expand nations' infrastructure such as transportation, education, and medical systems and facilities. The World Bank and other development banks provide the largest source of advice and assistance to developing nations. Often, in exchange for granting loans, the World Bank imposes requirements intended to build the economies of borrower nations.

The World Bank has been criticized for making loans with conditions that ultimately hurt the borrower nations. When developing nations are required to balance government budgets, they are sometimes forced to cut vital social programs. Critics also say that the World Bank should consider the impact of its loans on the environment and working conditions.

International Monetary Fund Established a year after the World Bank, the **International Monetary Fund (IMF)** was created to promote trade through financial cooperation and, in the process, eliminate barriers. The IMF makes short-term loans to member nations that are unable to meet their expenses. It operates as a lender of last resort for troubled nations. In exchange for these emergency loans, IMF lenders frequently require significant commitments from the borrowing nations to address the problems that led to the crises. These steps may include curtailing imports or even devaluing currencies. Throughout its existence, the IMF has worked to prevent financial crises by warning the international business community when countries encounter problems meeting their financial obligations. Often, the IMF lends to countries to keep them from defaulting on prior debts and to prevent economic crises in particular countries from spreading to other nations.

International Monetary Fund (IMF) organization created to promote trade, eliminate barriers, and make short-term loans to member nations that are unable to meet their budgets.

However, some countries owe far more money than they can ever hope to repay, and the debt payments make it impossible for their governments to deliver desperately needed services to their citizens. Following a devastating earthquake in Haiti, the G7 countries (the world's most industrialized nations including the United States, Canada, France, and Brazil) promised to cancel any remaining debt owed them by Haiti. The World Bank not only pledged financial support as Haiti struggled to get back on its feet but also waived payment on Haiti's debt for five years while it sought a way to cancel the remaining debt.[23]

International Economic Communities

International economic communities reduce trade barriers and promote regional economic integration. In the simplest approach, countries may establish a *free-trade area* in which they trade freely among themselves without tariffs or trade restrictions. Each maintains its own tariffs for trade outside this area. A *customs union* sets up a free-trade area and specifies a uniform tariff structure for members' trade with nonmember nations. In a *common market*, or economic union, members go beyond a customs union and try to bring all of their trade rules into agreement.

One example of a free-trade area is the **North American Free Trade Agreement (NAFTA)** enacted by the United States, Canada, and Mexico. Other examples of regional trading blocs include the MERCOSUR customs union (joining Brazil, Argentina, Paraguay, Uruguay, Chile, and Bolivia) and the ten-country Association of South East Asian Nations (ASEAN).

North American Free Trade Agreement (NAFTA) agreement among the United States, Canada, and Mexico to break down tariffs and trade restrictions.

NAFTA

NAFTA became effective in 1994, creating the world's largest free-trade zone with the United States, Canada, and Mexico. With a combined population of more than 450 million and a total GDP of more than $15 trillion, North America represents one of the world's most attractive markets. The United States—the single largest market—dominates North America's business environment. Although fewer than 1 person in 20 lives in the United States, the nation's more than $14 trillion GDP represents about one-fifth of total world output.[24]

With NAFTA allowing free trade for the United States, Canada, and Mexico, the amount of goods and services traded is healthy for Canada's economy as well as the United States.

Canada is far less densely populated but has achieved a similar level of economic development. In fact, Canada's economy has been growing at a faster rate than the U.S. economy in recent years. More than two-thirds of Canada's GDP is generated in the services sector, and three of every four Canadian workers are engaged in service occupations. The country's per-capita GDP places Canada among the top nations in terms of its people's spending power. Canada's economy is fueled by trade with the United States, and its home markets are strong as well. The United States and Canada are each other's biggest trading partners. About 78 percent of Canada's exports and about 53 percent of its imports are to or from the United States.[25] U.S. business is also attracted by Canada's human resources. For instance, all major U.S. automakers have large production facilities in Canada.

Mexico is moving from developing nation to industrial nation status, thanks largely to NAFTA. Mexico's trade with the United States and Canada has tripled since the signing of NAFTA, although 18 percent of the country's 111 million people live below the poverty line and per-capita income is about a quarter that of the United States. But Mexico's border with the United States is busy with a nearly endless stream of traffic transporting goods from Mexican factories into the United States. The United States is Mexico's largest trading partner by far, accounting for about 80 percent of total exports and almost 50 percent of all Mexico's imports.[26]

By eliminating all trade barriers and investment restrictions among the United States, Canada, and Mexico over a 15-year period, NAFTA opened more doors for free trade. The agreement also eased regulations governing services, such as banking, and established uniform legal requirements for protection of intellectual property. The three nations can now trade with one another without tariffs or other trade barriers, simplifying shipments of goods across the partners' borders. Standardized customs and uniform labeling regulations create economic efficiencies and smooth import and export procedures. Trade among the partners has increased steadily, more than doubling since NAFTA took effect.

CAFTA-DR

Central America–Dominican Republic Free Trade Agreement (CAFTA-DR) agreement among the United States, Costa Rica, the Dominican Republic, El Salvador, Guatemala, Honduras, and Nicaragua to reduce tariffs and trade restrictions.

The **Central America–Dominican Republic Free Trade Agreement (CAFTA-DR)** created a free-trade area among the United States, Costa Rica, the Dominican Republic (the DR of the title), El Salvador, Guatemala, Honduras, and Nicaragua. The agreement ends most tariffs on nearly $33 billion in products traded between the United States and its Latin American neighbors. Agricultural producers such as corn, soybean, and dairy farmers stand to gain under the relaxed trade rules. U.S. sugar producers, which were supported by subsidies keeping their prices higher than the rest of the world, fought against CAFTA-DR's passage. And labor unions complained that the agreement would lower labor standards and export millions more jobs to lower-wage countries. But overall, CAFTA-DR's effects should be positive, increasing both exports and imports substantially, much as NAFTA did.

European Union

Perhaps the best-known example of a common market is the **European Union (EU)**. The EU combines 27 countries, nearly 500 million people, and a total GDP of roughly $12.28 trillion to form a huge common market.[27] As Figure 4.4 shows, 12 countries—Cyprus, Malta, Estonia, Latvia, Lithuania, Hungary, Poland, the Czech Republic, Slovakia, Slovenia, Bulgaria, and Romania—are the latest EU members. The Treaty of Lisbon took effect in 2009, with its goal to be making the union governance more efficient.

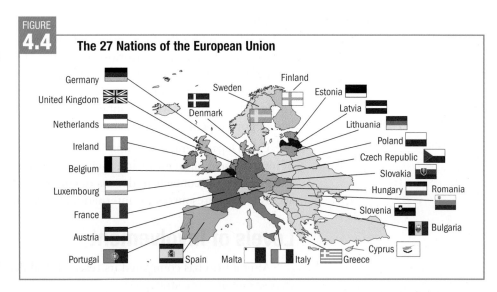

FIGURE 4.4

The 27 Nations of the European Union

Germany, United Kingdom, Netherlands, Ireland, Belgium, Luxembourg, France, Austria, Portugal, Sweden, Denmark, Spain, Malta, Italy, Finland, Estonia, Latvia, Lithuania, Poland, Czech Republic, Slovakia, Hungary, Romania, Slovenia, Bulgaria, Cyprus, Greece

The EU's goals include promoting economic and social progress, introducing European citizenship as a complement to national citizenship, and giving the EU a significant role in international affairs. To achieve its goal of a borderless Europe, the EU is removing barriers to free trade among its members. This highly complex process involves standardizing business regulations and requirements, standardizing import duties and taxes, and eliminating customs checks so that companies can transport goods from England to Italy or Poland as easily as from New York to Boston.

Unifying standards and laws can contribute to economic growth. But just as NAFTA sparked fears in the United States about free trade with Mexico, some people in western Europe worried that opening trade with such countries as Poland, Hungary, and the Czech Republic would cause jobs to flow eastward to lower-wage economies.

The EU also introduced the euro to replace currencies such as the French franc and Italian lira. For the 13 member-states that have adopted the euro, potential benefits include eliminating the economic costs of currency exchange and simplifying price comparisons. Businesses and their customers now make check and credit card transactions in euros and use euro notes and coins in making cash purchases.

Going Global

While expanding into overseas markets can increase profits and marketing opportunities, it also introduces new complexities to a firm's business operations. Before deciding to go global, a company faces a number of key decisions, beginning with the following:

- determining which foreign market(s) to enter

- analyzing the expenditures required to enter a new market

- deciding the best way to organize the overseas operations.

These issues vary in importance depending on the level of involvement a company chooses. Education and employee training in the host country would be much more important for an electronics manufacturer building an Asian factory than for a firm that is simply planning to export American-made products.

European Union (EU) 27-nation European economic alliance.

Assessment Check ✔

1. What international trade organization succeeded GATT, and what is its goal?

2. Compare and contrast the goals of the World Bank and the International Monetary Fund.

3. What are the goals of the European Union, and how do they promote international trade?

The choice of which markets to enter usually follows extensive research focusing on local demand for the firm's products, availability of needed resources, and ability of the local workforce to produce world-class quality. Other factors include existing and potential competition, tariff rates, currency stability, and investment barriers. A variety of government and other sources are available to facilitate this research process. A good starting place is the CIA's *World Factbook*, which contains country-by-country information on geography, population, government, economy, and infrastructure.

U.S. Department of Commerce counselors working at district offices offer a full range of international business advice, including computerized market data and names of business and government contacts in dozens of countries. As Table 4.3 shows, the Internet provides access to many resources for international trade information.

Levels of Involvement

After a firm has completed its research and decided to do business overseas, it can choose one or more strategies:

- exporting or importing
- entering into contractual agreements such as franchising, licensing, and subcontracting deals
- direct investment in the foreign market through acquisitions, joint ventures, or establishment of an overseas division.

Although the company's risk increases with the level of its involvement, so does its overall control of all aspects of producing and selling its goods or services.

Table 4.3 **International Trade Research Resources on the Internet**

WEB SITE AND ADDRESS	GENERAL DESCRIPTION
Asia Inc. http://www.asia-inc.com	Business news in Asia, featuring articles on Asian countries from India to Japan
Europages http://www.europages.com	Directory of and links to Europe's top 500,000 companies in 33 European countries
World Trade Organization http://www.wto.int	Details on the trade policies of various governments
CIA *World Factbook* https://www.cia.gov/cia/library/publications/the-world-factbook	Basic facts about the world's nations, from geography to economic conditions
STAT-USA http://www.stat-usa.gov	Extensive trade and economic data, information about trends, daily intelligence reports, and background data (access requires paid subscription to the service)
U.S. Commercial Service http://trade.gov/cs	Information about Commerce Department counseling services, trade events, and U.S. export regulations
U.S. Business Advisor http://www.business.gov	One-stop access to a range of federal government information, services, and transactions
U.S. State Department http://www.travel.state.gov/travel/cis_pa_tw/tw/tw_1764.html	Listing of the State Department's latest travel warnings about conditions that may affect safety abroad, supplemented by the list of consulate addresses and country information

Hycrete Inc., a U.S. firm that makes waterproof and corrosion-resistant building materials, is both green and global. Its environmentally friendly products, which reduce reliance on petroleum-based products for waterproofing, are manufactured overseas for use in structures in India and eastern Europe. Folbot Inc., based in Charleston, South Carolina, has been making kayaks and folding boats for more than 75 years. Recently faced with flat U.S. sales, it signed exclusive distribution deals in Sweden and Norway that helped double its percentage of international sales. Folbot has also worked with UPS to reduce shipping costs, which its overseas dealers pay. "We have to do the best we can," said Folbot's owner. "The more expensive it is for [our customers], the less attractive the purchase is." And eDressMe Inc., a tiny dress retailer with a Manhattan store and a Web site, recently reached overseas with its affiliate marketing program (which rewards other Web site owners for referring traffic to eDressMe's site), connecting with more than 3,000 affiliates and drawing customers from as far away as Belarus, Bulgaria, and the United Kingdom. The move boosted eDressMe's sales to nearly $7 million.[28]

Folbot's exclusive distribution deals in Sweden and Norway opened up new sales opportunities for the company.

Importers and Exporters When a firm brings in goods produced abroad to sell domestically, it is an importer. Conversely, companies are exporters when they produce—or purchase—goods at home and sell them in overseas markets. An importing or exporting strategy provides the most basic level of international involvement, with the least risk and control.

Fuel Systems Solutions Inc. is a U.S. firm headquartered in New York that provides propane and natural gas fuel systems and components for use in industry and transportation. It has sales facilities on five continents and distributors and dealers in more than 70 countries.[29]

Exports are frequently handled by special intermediaries called export trading companies. These firms search out competitively priced local merchandise and then resell it abroad at prices high enough to cover expenses and earn profits. When a retail chain such as Dallas-based Pier 1 Imports wants to purchase West African products for its store shelves, it may contact an export trading company operating in a country such as Ghana. The local firm is responsible for monitoring quality, packaging the order for transatlantic shipment, arranging transportation, and arranging for completion of customs paperwork and other steps required to move the product from Ghana to the United States.

Firms engage in exporting of two types: indirect and direct. A company engages in *indirect exporting* when it manufactures a product, such as an electronic component, that becomes part of another product sold in foreign markets. The second method, *direct exporting*, occurs when a company seeks to sell its products in markets outside its own country. Often the first step for companies entering foreign markets, direct exporting is the most common form of international business. Firms that succeed at this may then move to other strategies. Crops are imported and exported globally.

In addition to reaching foreign markets by dealing with export trading companies, exporters may choose two other alternatives: export management companies and offset agreements. Rather than simply relying on an export trading company to assist in foreign markets, an exporting firm may turn to an *export management company* for advice and expertise. These international specialists help the exporter complete paperwork, make contacts with local buyers, and comply with local laws governing labeling, product safety, and performance testing. At the same time, the exporting firm retains much more control than would be possible with an export trading company.

An *offset agreement* matches a small business with a major international firm. It basically makes the small firm a subcontractor to the larger one. Such an entry strategy helps a new exporter by allowing it to share in the larger company's international expertise. The small firm also benefits in such important areas as international transaction documents and financing, while the larger company benefits from the local expertise and capabilities of its smaller partner.

Countertrade A sizable share of international trade involves payments made in the form of local products, not currency. This system of international bartering agreements is called **countertrade**.

A common reason for resorting to international barter is inadequate access to needed foreign currency. To complete an international sales agreement, the seller may agree to accept part or all of the purchase cost in merchandise rather than currency. Because the seller may decide to locate a buyer for the bartered goods before completing the transaction, a number of international buyers and sellers frequently join together in a single agreement.

countertrade barter agreement whereby trade between two or more nations involves payment made in the form of local products instead of currency.

Countertrade may often be a firm's only opportunity to enter a particular market. Many developing countries simply cannot obtain enough credit or financial assistance to afford the imports that their people want. Countries with heavy debt burdens also resort to countertrade. Russian buyers, whose currency is often less acceptable to foreign traders than the stronger currencies of countries such as the United States, Great Britain, Japan, and EU countries, may resort to trading local products ranging from crude oil to diamonds to vodka as payments for purchases from foreign companies unwilling to accept Russian rubles. Still, other countries such as China may restrict imports. Under such circumstances, countertrade may be the only practical way to win government approval to import needed products.

Contractual Agreements Once a company, large or small, gains some experience in international sales, it may decide to enter into contractual agreements with local parties. These arrangements can include franchising, foreign licensing, and subcontracting.

Franchising Common among U.S. companies, franchising can work well for companies seeking to expand into international markets, too. A **franchise**, as described in detail in Chapter 5, is a contractual agreement in which a wholesaler or retailer (the franchisee) gains the right to sell the franchisor's products under that company's brand name if it agrees to the related operating requirements. The franchisee can also receive marketing, management, and business services from the franchisor. While these arrangements are common among leading fast-food brands such as McDonald's and KFC, other kinds of service providers also often look to franchising as an international marketplace option.

Domino's Pizza has expanded to more than 8,000 stores in more than 60 international markets around the world. Its largest international market is in Mexico, but wherever it operates, the company fine-tunes its menus to meet local tastes with such specialties as barbecued chicken in the Bahamas, black bean sauce in Guatemala, squid in Japan, and chorizo in Mexico.[30]

Foreign Licensing In a **foreign licensing agreement**, one firm allows another to produce or sell its product, or use its trademark, patent, or manufacturing processes, in a specific geographical area. In return, the firm gets a royalty or other compensation.

Licensing can be advantageous for a small manufacturer eager to launch a well-known product overseas. Not only does it get a proven product from another market, but little or no investment is required to begin operating. The arrangement can also allow entry into a market otherwise closed to imports due to government restrictions. Sometimes a licensing agreement can ensure product freshness by allowing manufacturing to take place in the local market. Morinaga, a Japanese food manufacturer, holds licenses to produce Lipton teas, Kraft cheeses, and Sunkist fruit drinks and desserts in Japan.[31]

Subcontracting The third type of contractual agreement, **subcontracting**, involves hiring local companies to produce, distribute, or sell goods or services. This move allows a foreign firm to take advantage of the subcontractor's expertise in local culture, contacts, and regulations. Subcontracting works equally well for mail-order companies, which can farm out order fulfillment and customer service functions to local businesses. Manufacturers practice subcontracting to save money on import duties and labor costs, and businesses go this route to market products best sold by locals in a given country. Some firms, such as Maryland-based Pacific Bridge Medical, help medical manufacturers find reliable subcontractors and parts suppliers in Asia.

franchise contractual agreement in which a franchisee gains the right to produce and/or sell the franchisor's products under that company's brand name if they agree to certain operating requirements.

foreign licensing agreement international agreement in which one firm allows another to produce or sell its product, or use its trademark, patent, or manufacturing processes, in a specific geographical area in return for royalties or other compensation.

subcontracting international agreement that involves hiring local companies to produce, distribute, or sell goods or services in a specific country or geographical region.

A key disadvantage of subcontracting is that companies cannot always control their subcontractors' business practices. Several major U.S. companies have been embarrassed by reports that their subcontractors used child labor to manufacture clothing.

Offshoring While it is not generally considered a way of initiating business internationally, *offshoring*, or the relocation of business processes to a lower-cost location overseas, has become a widespread practice. China has emerged as the preferred destination for production offshoring and India for services offshoring. Many business leaders argue, in favor of offshoring, that global firms must keep their costs as low as possible to remain competitive. But the apparent link between jobs sent overseas and jobs lost at home has made the practice controversial. Legislatures of various states have tried to slow the tide of offshoring through new laws, but many observers believe the real goal should be to improve corporate research and development efforts in the United States.

Offshoring shows no signs of slowing down, but it is changing, particularly for manufacturers. Mexico, India, and Vietnam are now the countries with the lowest manufacturing costs. "There was huge momentum and almost herd behavior around going to China back in 2005 or 2006," says one consultant. "China was more competitive than other low-cost countries and had more infrastructure. Now, some of that has changed. Rising transportation costs and material costs, which hurt China in 2007 and 2008, applied to a much lesser degree in Mexico." If companies are manufacturing abroad to sell to foreign markets, offshoring may make more sense than making heavy or bulky products abroad and transporting them to North American markets for sale. Time in transport is also a factor. Not surprisingly, maintaining flexibility by offshoring to a few different low-cost locations may be U.S. firms' lowest-risk strategy for the future. "If the rupee strengthens," says the consultant, "you can shift some work to Vietnam. If transportation costs go crazy, you can move some more work to Mexico."[32]

International Direct Investment Investing directly in production and marketing operations in a foreign country is the ultimate level of global involvement. Over time, a firm may become successful at conducting business in other countries through exporting and contractual agreements. Its managers may then decide to establish manufacturing facilities in those countries, open branch offices, or buy ownership interests in local companies. Toyota is a good example, with car manufacturing plants in countries outside Japan, including the United States. See the "Hit & Miss" feature for a description of Toyota's recent public relations problems when it recalled millions of cars.

In an *acquisition*, a company purchases another existing firm in the host country. An acquisition permits a largely domestic business operation to gain an international presence very quickly. Polaris Industries Inc., a U.S. firm, recently acquired Swissauto Powersports, a Swiss designer of high-performance engines for recreational and racing vehicles founded in 1987. The two companies had a long history of partnering together, but the acquisition will brighten Polaris's international profile. It "directly supports our stated objectives to be the best in powersports and a global market leader," said Polaris's CEO.[33]

joint venture partnership between companies formed for a specific undertaking.

Joint ventures allow companies to share risks, costs, profits, and management responsibilities with one or more host country nationals. By setting up an *overseas division*, a company can conduct a significant amount of its business overseas. This strategy differs from that of a multinational company in that a firm with overseas divisions remains primarily a domestic organization with international operations. Matsushita established Panasonic Automotive Systems Asia Pacific to develop and sell new technology products in India, Thailand, Indonesia, Malaysia, the Philippines, and Vietnam.

Hit & Miss

Toyota's Recall Woes

Toyota Motor Company grew dramatically in the last decade, doubling production capacity in its drive to become the world's top automaker. While rapid growth doesn't excuse the recent recall of millions of Toyotas worldwide due to faulty accelerator pedals, it could help explain why the public relations aspect of the recall made the revered company stumble so badly.

"What they did this week, they should've done last. . . . You want to rip off that Band-Aid all at once," said one public relations expert. Instead, Toyota first denied the accelerator pedals were mechanically flawed and insisted customers had incorrectly installed their floor mats, interfering with the pedals' operation. But even when the problem became clear, Toyota was slow to react. Customers were left confused and angry as they waited for information and repairs.

Finally CEO Akio Toyoda told the world, "I apologize from the bottom of my heart for all the concern that we have given to so many of our customers." Writing in the *Washington Post,* he also said, "We have not lived up to the high standards you have come to expect from us. I am deeply disappointed by that and apologize. As the president of Toyota, I take personal responsibility."

Time will tell whether the world's number-one automaker can recover from what one observer called "the worst-handled auto recall in history," a debacle that will cost Toyota more than $2 billion in repairs and lost sales.

Questions for Critical Thinking

1. Do you think Toyota could or should have used social media like Twitter and Facebook in alerting customers about the problem and solution? Why or why not?
2. Why do you think Toyota's CEO felt he had to apologize? What effect do you think his actions had on Toyota owners?

Sources: Bill Saporito, "Behind the Troubles at Toyota," *Time,* www.time.com, February 11, 2010; "Toyota's Recall Woes," editorial, *The New York Times,* www.nytimes.com, February 9, 2010; Matthew Phillips, "Toyota's Digital Disaster," *Newsweek,* www.newsweek.com, February 3, 2010.

From Multinational Corporation to Global Business

A **multinational corporation (MNC)** is an organization with significant foreign operations. As Table 4.4 shows, firms headquartered in the United States make up half the list of the world's largest multinationals. The Netherlands and the United Kingdom each have two companies on the list, and Japan rounds out the top ten, with one company on the list.

Many U.S. multinationals, including Nike and Walmart, have expanded their overseas operations because they believe that domestic markets are peaking and foreign markets offer greater sales and profit potential. Other MNCs are making substantial investments in developing countries in part because these countries provide low-cost labor compared with the United States and western Europe. In addition, many MNCs are locating high-tech facilities in countries with large numbers of technical school graduates.

multinational corporation (MNC) firm with significant operations and marketing activities outside its home country.

Assessment Check ✅

1. Name three possible strategies for beginning overseas operations.
2. What is countertrade?
3. Compare and contrast licensing and subcontracting.
4. Describe joint ventures.

Developing a Strategy for International Business

In developing a framework in which to conduct international business, managers must first evaluate their corporate objectives, organizational strengths and weaknesses, and strategies for product development and marketing. They can choose to combine these elements in either a global strategy or a multidomestic strategy.

Table
4.4

The World's Top Ten Leading Companies (Based on a Combined Ranking for Sales, Profits, Assets, and Market Value)

RANK	COMPANY	BUSINESS	COUNTRY OF ORIGIN
1	General Electric	Conglomerate	United States
2	Royal Dutch Shell	Oil and gas operations	Netherlands
3	Toyota Motor	Consumer durables	Japan
4	ExxonMobil	Oil and gas operations	United States
5	BP	Oil and gas operations	United Kingdom
6	HSBC Holdings	Banking	United Kingdom
7	AT&T	Telecommunications	United States
8	Walmart Stores	Retailing	United States
9	Banco Santander	Banking	Spain
10	Chevron	Oil and gas operations	United States

Source: "The Global 2000," *Forbes,* http://www.forbes.com, accessed March 17, 2010.

Global Business Strategies

global business strategy offering a standardized, worldwide product and selling it in essentially the same manner throughout a firm's domestic and foreign markets.

In a **global business** (or *standardization*) **strategy**, a firm sells the same product in essentially the same manner throughout the world. Many companies simply modify their domestic business strategies by translating promotional brochures and product-use instructions into the languages of the host nations.

A global marketing perspective can be appropriate for some goods and services and certain market segments that are common to many nations. The approach works for products with nearly universal appeal, for luxury items such as jewelry and for commodities like chemicals and metals. Alcoa, for instance, is the world's biggest producers of aluminum for markets that include aerospace, automotive, building and construction, consumer electronics, packaging, and commercial transportation. Because in many applications aluminum's strength and light weight mean there are no good substitutes for it, the company forecasts a long-term increase in global demand, especially in China, India, Russia, the Middle East, and Latin America. It also sees itself as committed to a global strategy that incorporates sustainability, meaning it will "build financial success, environmental excellence, and social responsibility through partnerships in order to deliver net long-term benefits to our shareowners, employees, customers, suppliers, and the communities in which we operate."[34]

multidomestic business strategy developing and marketing products to serve different needs and tastes of separate national markets.

Multidomestic Business Strategies

Under a **multidomestic business** (or *adaptation*) **strategy**, the firm treats each national market in a different way. It develops products and marketing strategies that appeal to the customs, tastes, and buying habits of particular national markets. Companies that

Assessment Check

1. What is a global business strategy? What are its advantages?

2. What is a multidomestic business strategy? What are its advantages?

neglect the global nature of the Internet can unwittingly cause problems for potential customers by failing to adapt their strategy. European consumers, for instance, were at first hesitant to adopt online ordering of products ranging from books to railroad tickets. But in recent years, Internet use in western Europe has grown dramatically. Companies as diverse as the European divisions of Amazon.com; Egg PLC of London, an online financial services company; and the French national railroad have seen the numbers of visitors to their Web sites climbing, along with Internet revenues.

What's Ahead

Internet users in western Europe are no longer as concerned making purchases for such items as railroad tickets online. As this businessman enjoys the ability to work on the train, he may be purchasing his return ticket through his online connection.

Examples in this chapter indicate that both large and small businesses are relying on world trade, not just major corporations. Chapter 5 examines the special advantages and challenges that small-business owners encounter. In addition, a critical decision facing any new business is the choice of the most appropriate form of business ownership. Chapter 5 also examines the major ownership structures—sole proprietorship, partnership, and corporation—and assesses the pros and cons of each. The chapter closes with a discussion of recent trends affecting business ownership, such as the growing impact of franchising and business consolidations through mergers and acquisitions.

Summary of Learning Objectives

⌐1⌐ Explain the importance of international business and the primary reasons nations trade, and discuss the concepts of absolute and comparative advantage in international trade.

The United States is both the world's largest importer and the largest exporter, although less than 5 percent of the world's population lives within its borders. With the increasing globalization of the world's economies, the international marketplace offers tremendous opportunities for U.S. and foreign businesses to expand into new markets for their goods and services. Doing business globally provides new sources of materials and labor. Trading with other countries also reduces a company's dependence on economic conditions in its home market. Countries that encourage international trade enjoy higher levels of economic activity, employment, and wages than those that restrict it.

Nations usually benefit if they specialize in producing certain goods or services. A country has an absolute advantage if it holds a monopoly or produces a good or service at a lower cost than other nations. It has a comparative advantage if it can supply a particular product more efficiently or at a lower cost than it can produce other items.

Assessment Check Answers ✓

1.1 Why do nations trade? Nations trade because trading boosts economic growth by providing a market for products and access to needed resources. This makes production and distribution systems more efficient and reduces dependence on the economy of the domestic market.

1.2 Cite some measures of the size of the international marketplace. Although developing countries have lower per-capita incomes than developed nations in North America and western Europe, their populations are large and growing. China's population is about 1.3 billion and India's is roughly 1.1 billion.

1.3 How does a nation acquire a comparative advantage? Comparative advantage exists when a nation can supply a product more efficiently and at a lower price than it can supply other goods, compared with the outputs of other countries.

Countries measure the level of international trade by comparing exports and imports and then calculating whether a trade surplus or a deficit exists. This is the balance of trade, which represents the difference between exports and imports. The term *balance of payments* refers to the overall flow of money into or out of a country, including overseas loans and borrowing, international investments, and profits from such investments. An exchange rate is the value of a nation's currency relative to the currency of another nation. Currency values typically fluctuate, or "float," relative to the supply and demand for specific currencies in the world market. When the value of the dollar falls compared with other currencies, the cost paid by foreign businesses and households for U.S. products declines, and demand for exports may rise. An increase in the value of the dollar raises the prices of U.S. products sold abroad, but it reduces the prices of foreign products sold in the United States.

Assessment Check Answers ✔

2.1 Compare balance of trade and balance of payments. Balance of trade is the difference between exports and imports; balance of payments is the overall flow of money into or out of a country.

2.2 Explain the function of an exchange rate. A nation's exchange rate is the rate at which its currency can be exchanged for the currencies of other nations to make it easier for them to trade with one another.

2.3 What happens when a currency is devalued? Devaluation describes a fall in a currency's value relative to other currencies or to a fixed standard.

┌3┐ Identify the major barriers that confront global businesses.
└ ┘

Businesses face several obstacles in the global marketplace. Companies must be sensitive to social and cultural differences, such as languages, values, and religions, when operating in other countries. Economic differences include standard-of-living variations and levels of infrastructure development. Legal and political barriers are among the most difficult to judge. Each country sets its own laws regulating business practices. Trade restrictions such as tariffs and administrative barriers also present obstacles to international business.

Assessment Check Answers ✔

3.1 How might values and attitudes form a barrier to trade, and how can they be overcome? Marked differences in values and attitudes, such as religious attitudes, can form barriers between traditionally capitalist countries and those adapting new capitalist systems. Many of these can be overcome by learning about and respecting such differences.

3.2 What is a tariff? What is its purpose? A tariff is a surcharge or duty charged on foreign products. Its purpose is to protect domestic producers of those items.

3.3 Why is dumping a problem for companies marketing goods internationally? Dumping is selling products abroad at prices below the cost of production or exporting products at a lower price than charged in the home market. It drives the cost of products sharply down in the market where they are dumped, thus hurting the domestic producers of those products.

┌4┐ Explain how international trade organizations and economic communities reduce barriers to international trade.
└ ┘

Many international organizations seek to promote international trade by reducing barriers among nations. Examples include the World Trade Organization, the World Bank, and the International Monetary Fund. Multinational economic communities create partnerships to remove barriers to the flow of goods, capital, and people across the borders of members. Three such economic agreements are the North American Free Trade Agreement, CAFTA-DR, and the European Union.

Assessment Check Answers ✔

4.1 What international trade organization succeeded GATT, and what is its goal? The World Trade Organization (WTO) succeeded GATT with the goal of monitoring GATT agreements, mediating disputes, and continuing the effort to reduce trade barriers throughout the world.

4.2 Compare and contrast the goals of the World Bank and the International Monetary Fund. The World Bank funds projects that build or expand nations' infrastructure such as transportation, education, and health systems and facilities. The International Monetary Fund makes short-term loans to member nations that are unable to meet their budgets. The fund operates as a lender of last resort.

4.3 What are the goals of the European Union, and how do they promote international trade? The European Union's goals include promoting economic and social progress, introducing European citizenship as a complement to national citizenship, and giving the EU a significant role in international affairs. Unifying standards and laws is expected to contribute to international trade and economic growth.

┌5┐ Compare the different levels of involvement used by businesses when entering global markets.
└ ┘

Exporting and importing, the first level of involvement in international business, involves the lowest degree of both risk and control. Companies may rely on export trading or management companies to help distribute their products. Contractual agreements such as franchising, foreign licensing, and subcontracting offer additional options. Franchising and licensing are especially appropriate for services. Companies may also choose local subcontractors to produce goods for local sales. International direct investment in production and marketing facilities provides the highest degree of control but also the greatest risk. Firms make direct investments by acquiring foreign companies or facilities, forming joint ventures with local firms and setting up their own overseas divisions.

Assessment Check Answers ✅

5.1 Name three possible strategies for beginning overseas business operations. Strategies are exporting or importing; contractual agreements such as franchising, licensing, or subcontracting; and making direct investments in foreign markets through acquisition, joint venture, or establishment of an overseas division.

5.2 What is countertrade? Countertrade consists of payments made in the form of local products, not currency.

5.3 Compare and contrast licensing and subcontracting. In a foreign licensing agreement, one firm allows another to produce or sell its product or use its trademark, patent, or manufacturing process in a specific geographical area in return for royalty payments or other compensations. In subcontracting a firm hires local companies abroad to produce, distribute, or sell its goods and services.

5.4 Describe joint ventures. Joint ventures allow companies to share risks, costs, profits, and management responsibilities with one or more host-country nationals.

⌐6⌐ Distinguish between a global business strategy and a multidomestic business strategy.

A company that adopts a global (or standardization) strategy develops a single, standardized product and marketing strategy for implementation throughout the world. The firm sells the same product in essentially the same manner in all countries in which it operates. Under a multidomestic (or adaptation) strategy, the firm develops a different treatment for each foreign market. It develops products and marketing strategies that appeal to the customs, tastes, and buying habits of particular nations.

Assessment Check Answers ✅

6.1 What is a global business strategy? What are its advantages? A global business strategy specifies a standardized competitive strategy in which the firm sells the same product in essentially the same manner throughout the world. It works well for goods and services that are common to many nations and allows the firm to market them without making significant changes.

6.2 What is a multidomestic business strategy? What are its advantages? A multidomestic business strategy allows the firm to treat each foreign market in a different way to appeal to the customs, tastes, and buying habits of particular national markets. It allows the firm to customize its marketing appeals for individual cultures or areas.

▧ Business Terms You Need to Know

exports 106	embargo 121	North American Free	foreign licensing
imports 106	exchange control 121	Trade Agreement	agreement 129
balance of trade 110	General Agreement on	(NAFTA) 123	subcontracting 129
balance of payments 110	Tariffs and Trade	Central America–Dominican	joint ventures 130
exchange rate 111	(GATT) 122	Republic Free Trade	multinational corporation
devaluation 112	World Trade Organization	Agreement	(MNC) 131
infrastructure 115	(WTO) 122	(CAFTA-DR) 124	global business
tariffs 120	World Bank 122	European Union (EU) 125	strategy 132
quotas 121	International Monetary	countertrade 128	multidomestic business
dumping 121	Fund (IMF) 123	franchise 129	strategy 132

▧ Review Questions

1. How does a business decide whether to trade with a foreign country? What are the key factors for participating in the information economy on a global basis?

2. Why are developing countries such as China and India becoming important international markets?

3. What is the difference between absolute advantage and comparative advantage? Give an example of each.

4. Can a nation have a favorable balance of trade and an unfavorable balance of payments? Why or why not?

5. Identify several potential barriers to communication when a company attempts to conduct business in another country. How might these be overcome?

6. Identify and describe briefly the three dimensions of the legal environment for global business.

7. What are the major nontariff restrictions affecting international business? Describe the difference between tariff and nontariff restrictions.

8. What is NAFTA? How does it work?

9. How has the EU helped trade among European businesses?

10. What are the key choices a company must make before reaching the final decision to go global?

Projects and Teamwork Applications

1. When Britain transferred Hong Kong to China in 1997, China agreed to grant Hong Kong a high degree of autonomy as a capitalist economy for 50 years. Do you think this agreement is holding up? Why or why not? Consider China's economy, population, infrastructure, and other factors in your answer.

2. The tremendous growth of online business has introduced new elements to the legal climate of international business. Patents, brand names, copyrights, and trademarks are difficult to monitor because of the boundaryless nature of the Internet. What steps could businesses take to protect their trademarks and brands in this environment? Come up with at least five suggestions, and compare your list with your classmates'.

3. The WTO monitors GATT agreements, mediates disputes, and continues the effort to reduce trade barriers throughout the world. However, widespread concerns have been expressed that the WTO's focus on lowering trade barriers may encourage businesses to keep costs down through practices that may lead to pollution and human rights abuses. Others argue that human rights should not be linked to

international business. Do you think environmental and human rights issues should be linked to trade? Why or why not?

4. Describe briefly the EU and its goals. What are the pros and cons of the EU? Do you predict that the European alliance will hold up over the next 20 years? Why or why not?

5. Use the most recent edition of "The *Fortune* Global 500," which is published in *Fortune* magazine normally in late July or early August, or go to *Fortune*'s online version at http://money.cnn.com/magazines/fortune/global500, to answer the following questions.

   a. On what is the Global 500 ranking based (e.g., profits, number of employees, revenues)?

   b. Among the world's ten largest corporations, list the countries in which they are based.

   c. Identify the top-ranked company, along with its Global 500 ranking and country, for the following industry classifications: Food and Drug Stores; Industrial and Farm Equipment; Petroleum Refining; Utilities: Gas and Electric; Telecommunications; Pharmaceuticals.

Web Assignments

1. **WTO.** Visit the Web site of the World Trade Organization (http://www.wto.org). Research two current trade disputes. Which countries and products are involved? What, if anything, do the two disputes have in common? What procedures does the WTO follow in resolving trade disputes between member-countries?

2. **EU.** Europa.eu is the Web portal for the European Union. Go to the following Web site (http://europa.eu/index_en.htm) and answer the following questions:

   a. What are the steps a country must take to become a member of the EU?

   b. How many EU members have adopted the euro? Which countries will be adopting the euro over the next few years?

   c. What is the combined GDP of EU members? Which EU member has the largest GDP? Which has the smallest GDP?

3. **Nestlé.** Nestlé is one of the world's largest global corporations. Visit the firm's Web site (http://www.nestle.com). Where is the company headquartered? What are some of its best-known brands? Are these brands sold in specific countries or are they sold worldwide? Make a list of three of four issues Nestle faces as a global corporation.

Note: Internet Web addresses change frequently. If you do not find the exact sites listed, you may need to access the organization's or company's home page and search from there or use a search engine such as Bing or Google.

Google and Facebook Face Off in India's Social Networking Wars

India is the world's largest democracy and, with 1.2 billion people, the second-most populous country (after China). It is considered a major growth Internet market, with a tradition of free speech, a growing middle class that is still discovering the Internet (only about 5 percent of the Indian population is online so far), and huge market opportunities for providers of Web search and advertising.

Orkut, owned by Google, has long been India's most popular social networking site, growing 35 percent a year and averaging 15 to 16 million unique visitors a month. Facebook, its closest rival, was launched around the same time in 2004. Despite steady growth, Facebook has since been running a fairly distant second to Orkut, recently reaching 7.5 to 8.2 million visitors a month. But Facebook has been turning up the heat in the social networking wars, and in one recent month it gained 700,000 visitors. Orkut's numbers dropped by 800,00 for the same month, the largest dip in a year. Many observers of India's Internet scene believe these two statistics signal a leap forward for Facebook that may put it on track to soon surpass Google's Orkut as India's premier online social network.

In fact, Facebook grew its audience about 230 percent in one recent year. What accounts for its success? One factor is a special software tool the site is promoting to let new users easily import their friends from Orkut and other sites. The tool speeds the process of establishing a Facebook presence and was created especially for Orkut. Facebook is also available in a number of widely used Indian languages, including Hindi, Punjabi, Bengali, Telugu, Tamil, and Malayalam. And Facebook hired away a top Google advertising executive and has been buying ads on Google's India portal. Finally, a "lite" version of Facebook, designed for users in developing countries that have limited access to high-speed Internet connections, was also added recently.

Meanwhile, Google faces some potential problems in India that are common to many multinational and Internet companies. Fearing a backlash in the midst of emotional public mourning for an Indian official killed in a helicopter crash, it recently removed offensive comments posted about him on Orkut, along with the entire user group to which they were posted. Says one leading India civil liberties lawyer, "Communal tensions become largely an excuse for denial of civil liberties and denial of freedom of speech. It's a very thin line that's being tread."

"In those gray areas it is really hard," agrees Google's deputy general counsel. Company policy is to review posted material that Orkut users have flagged. Anything that violates its global bans on child pornography and hate speech, or the laws of the country in which it is operating, is removed.

Questions for Critical Thinking

1. Do you think Facebook can become India's leading social networking site? Why or why not? What else can Facebook do to ensure success?

2. How well do you think Google is handling the problem of censoring content on its international sites such as Orkut? How do you think its solutions of these problems affect its plans to keep ahead of Facebook?

Sources: Robin Wauters, "In India Facebook Uses Google AdWords to Leapfrog Orkut," *Tech Crunch*, http://techcrunch.com, January 22, 2010; Amol Sharma and Jessica E. Vascellaro, "Google and India Test the Limits of Liberty," *The Wall Street Journal*, www.online.wsj.com, January 2, 2010; Leena Rao, "Facebook's Plan to Trounce Orkut in India May Be Working," *Tech Crunch*, http://techcrunch.com, November 30, 2009; "Orkut Vs. Facebook: What the Indians Are Looking For," *Social Media News*, http://socialmedia.globalthoughtz.com, November 19, 2009.

McDonald's Delivers for Foreign Markets

To stimulate profit growth in a slowing market, McDonald's now encourages owners of its tightly run franchises around the world to do something a little different—experiment. Some owners in China serve corn instead of fries, and some French and Australian stores have coffee lounges. But the most profitable and most widely adopted idea so far originated in Egypt, where the owner suggested offering a delivery service to compete with other chains and restaurants in the area. Today nearly all McDonald's in the Cairo area deliver.

Delivery proved so profitable that McDonald's now brings food to customers in 25 cities worldwide; most are congested hubs like Manila, Taipei, Beirut, Riyadh, São Paolo, Montevideo, New Delhi, and Mumbai. They charge a small fee, between 50 cents and $1, which more than pays for processing the orders and operating fleets of speedy scooters and motorbikes. As the company's president of operations outside the Americas and Europe notes, "We don't even have to clean up a table. It's incremental profit for us."

Deliveries make up 27 percent of McDonald's revenue in Egypt and were expected to pass $110 million, growing 20 to 30 percent each year, or more than three times the company's overall rate of growth. McDonald's is investing heavily to promote its delivery business in India, adopting another idea that made the Egyptian launch so successful—one toll-free number for all neighborhoods.

Observers approve of the innovations. "Management is looking beyond Oak Brook [headquarters] for inspiration," said one industry expert. "They're becoming better at sharing the best ideas around the globe." Meanwhile, in the United Kingdom, McDonald's plans to collect and recycle the cooking oil from all its stores to supply 85 percent of the fuel mix needed by its delivery fleet of 155 vehicles. Could this be the next idea heard round the world?

Questions for Critical Thinking

1. How do you think "sharing the best ideas around the globe" can benefit McDonald's?
2. Fast-food chains like McDonald's cultivate customer loyalty by offering similar experiences at all their stores. How much do you think McDonald's can let franchise owners in international locations experiment before it risks losing the consistency it relies on for its competitive advantage?

Sources: Company Web site, http://www.mcdonalds.com, accessed February 2009; Michael Arndt, "Knock Knock, It's Your Big Mac," *BusinessWeek,* July 23, 2007, p. 36; Clare Watson, "McDonald's to Run UK Delivery Fleet on Its Own Cooking Oil," *Food Business Review,* July 2, 2007, http://www.food-business-review.com; "McDonald's to Strengthen Home Delivery Services," *Business Line,* March 18, 2007, http://thehindubusinessline.com.

CASE 4.3 — Smart Design: Life Is In the Details

When you peel a potato or run your pizza cutter through to cut a slice, it's likely that you only notice the tool you are using if it doesn't work—if it sticks or snags, gouges the potato or tears the pizza crust. The team at Smart Design doesn't mind not being noticed. They operate quietly behind the scenes, developing a wide range of designs for products made and sold by companies around the world. They come up with designs that make everything from toothbrushes to automobiles function better in human hands. Smart Design engineers developed the popular OXO Good Grips line of kitchen utensils as well as the SmartGauge instrument cluster for the Ford Fusion Hybrid.

"Smart Design is about designing products for people in their everyday life," explains Richard Whitehall, vice president of industrial design for Smart Design. "There are little things you might see in a product that you'd think, 'I wish I'd thought of that—it's a great idea.'" Sometimes it's the simplest or smallest detail in the engineering of a product that makes a difference in whether consumers will continue to use the product or purchase it again. Smart Design tries to make products that work well universally for a wide range of people in different situations. This is where the global challenge comes in—differences in cultural preferences, product use, language, and other factors can make universal product development difficult. But Smart Design has offices in both the U.S. and abroad, with testing locations in Europe and Asia, and employees representing more than 20 different countries.

Ted Booth, director of interactive design says, "Interactive design is anything with a 'chip' in it. I can't imagine approaching interactive design without a global perspective." Booth explains how Smart Design develops the design for a mobile phone. "The way people use it varies from country to country," he notes. "So what might look like a new feature in one country is really old hat in another." Booth observes that it is very common for consumers in Finland and South Korea to pay for most goods and services from their mobile phones, whereas this is not a common practice among U.S. consumers. Some of this practice is driven by industry standards, but much of it has to do with cultural expectations. "It's important to have a global perspective [in design] so you know the trends in other countries. You need to design and shape the experience to hit the market and bring something new to the market, but also adapt to individual markets," concludes Booth.

Booth describes his company's work on the "Q" control for HP—a single navigation controller that can be used across all HP products, ranging from TV remotes to printers to cameras. Smart Design tested the Q control in the U.S., Germany, Spain, and South Korea. Researchers discovered that, while a few local adaptations were necessary, there was one universal preference among all consumers: everyone needed a "back" button in order to go forward. Booth explains that there is a universal need for people to know that there is an escape, undo—or back—for every function in order for users to feel comfortable completing an interactive task.

Smart Design has an impressive list of worldwide clients, including Ford, Bell Canada, ESPN, World Kitchen, Microsoft, Samsung, and Kellogg's among many others. The firm has won many accolades, including nationally recognized design awards. But Smart Design remains focused on the details. The firm recently developed the Reach Wondergrip children's toothbrush for Johnson & Johnson when it became apparent that traditional children's toothbrushes were just scaled down from the adult models. Kids couldn't hold them easily and were less likely to brush their teeth. The new Wondergrip children's model changed the industry standard for children's toothbrushes—and brushing habits. Smart Design also developed a women's sports watch for Nike—based on needs and preferences of women runners. And there's that line of kitchen tools that make food preparation and cooking just a little bit easier and more fun.

Richard Whitehall, who actually began his career working for a firm that manufactured mountaineering gear, describes the importance of design in every product used by consumers. "We were trying to think of a situation people were in and trying to design a product in a way that people from different countries—whether they were stuck in the Alps or on a boat—could use in all these different situations." Whether you are climbing a mountain in Switzerland or cutting your pizza in Boston, you want your gear to work flawlessly—and that is the goal of Smart Design.

Questions for Critical Thinking

1. Ted Booth and Richard Whitehall mention some of the cultural barriers that Smart Design faces in developing products for worldwide use. Give examples of other barriers the firm might face in international trade.

2. Describe what you believe would be the best level of involvement for Smart Design to have when doing business in Europe. Remember to take into consideration the European Union.

3. Smart Design already has a presence in South Korea. How might the firm best approach developing products for the market in India? In China?

4. Do you believe it is possible to develop truly universal products? Why or why not?

Sources: Smart Design Web site, http://www.smartdesignworldwide.com, accessed August 19, 2010; "National Design Awards," *Cooper-Hewitt, National Design Museum,* http://www.nationaldesignawards.org, accessed August 19, 2010; Alissa Walker, "Biomimicry Challenge: For IBM, Smart Design Draws Water Inspiration from Ecosystems," *Fast Company.com,* May 17, 2010, http://www.fastcompany.com.

PART 1

GREENSBURG, KS
New Ways to Be a Better Town

Greensburg, Kansas, had been struggling for years. Located along Highway 54, a major trucking route, the town was merely a pit stop for people on their way somewhere else. It did have a few tourist attractions: the Big Well, the world's largest hand-dug well, and a 1,000-pound meteorite that fell from the sky in 2006.

Lonnie McCollum, the town's mayor, had been looking into ways to breathe new life into the town. McCollum wanted to add a little vintage charm to its quaint Main Street, but could not raise the money. And he had launched a campaign to put the "green" back in Greensburg by promoting green building technology. But the idea, which many residents associated with hippies and tree-huggers, did not go over well.

Then everything changed. "My town is gone," announced Town Administrator Steve Hewitt on May 5, 2007, after surveying the damage caused by a devastating tornado. "I believe 95 percent of the homes are gone. Downtown buildings are gone, my home is gone." With a clean slate and 700 homes to replace, Hewitt vowed to rebuild Greensburg using sustainable materials. He believed the town had a unique opportunity to control its environmental impact and reduce operating costs through increased energy efficiency.

"What if we turned this tragedy into something beautiful?" asked resident Dan Wallach in a new business plan he wrote shortly after the disaster. Wallach and his wife had long been interested in sustainable Green living. Using their experience in developing nonprofits, the two launched

Greensburg GreenTown, an organization designed to support Greensburg's green building efforts through education, fund-raising, and public relations management.

One of Wallach's favorite new projects was BTI Greensburg, the local John Deere dealership. Owners Kelly and Mike Estes had decided to replace their ruined building with an energy-efficient, technologically state-of-the-art showroom featuring radiant heat, solar energy, passive cooling, and wind power. With corporate support from John Deere, BTI Greensburg would become a flagship green dealership.

Long-term plans for Greensburg include a business incubator, to help displaced businesses get back on their feet and bring new businesses to town; a green industrial park, green museum, and green school system; green building codes and zoning restrictions; and a community of green homes and businesses.

Questions

After viewing the video, answer the following questions:

1. In what ways is the town of Greensburg like any other business?
2. In what ways is the town of Greensburg a socially responsible organization?
3. What might be the effects of the town's new green building guidelines on residents and businesses? On the regional economy?
4. What kind of business is Greensburg GreenTown? How does its structure differ from John Deere's?

LAUNCHING YOUR
[Global Business and Economics Career]

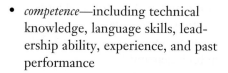

In Part 1, "Business in a Global Environment," you learned about the background and current issues driving contemporary business. The part includes four chapters covering such issues as the changing face of business, business ethics and social responsibility, economic challenges facing contemporary business, and competing in world markets. Business has always been an exciting career field, whether you choose to start your own company, work at a local business, or set your sights on a position with a multinational corporation. But today's environment is especially attractive because businesses are expanding their horizons to compete in a global economy—and they need dedicated and talented people to help them accomplish their goals. In fact, professional and business service jobs are found in some of the fastest-growing industries in the U.S. economy and are projected to grow by more than 23 percent over a decade.[1] So now is the time to explore several different career options that can lead you to your dream job. Each part in this text profiles the many opportunities available in business. Here are a few related to Chapters 1 through 4.

If you're good at number crunching and are interested in how societies and companies function, then maybe a career as an *economist* is in your future. Economists study how resources are allocated, conduct research by collecting and analyzing data, monitor economic trends, and develop forecasts.

They look into such vital areas as the cost of energy, foreign trade and exchange between countries, the effect of taxes, and employment levels—both from a big-picture national or global viewpoint and from the perspective of individual businesses. Economists work for corporations to help them run more efficiently, for consulting firms to offer special expertise, or for government agencies to oversee economic decision making. Typically, advanced degrees are needed to climb to top-level positions. Economists usually earn about $83,590 per year.[2]

Or perhaps you are interested in global business. Companies increasingly search the world for the best employees, supplies, and markets. So you could work in the United States for a foreign-based firm such as Nokia or Toyota; abroad in Australia, Asia, Europe, or Latin America for a U.S.-based firm such as Microsoft; or with overseas coworkers via computer networks to develop new products for a firm such as General Electric. With technology and telecommunications, distance is no longer a barrier to conducting business. Global business careers exist in all the areas you'll be reading about in this text—business ownership, management, marketing, technology, and finance.

Global business leaders are not born but made—so how can you start on that career path? Here are the three areas that businesses consider when selecting employees for overseas assignment:

- *competence*—including technical knowledge, language skills, leadership ability, experience, and past performance

- *adaptability*—including interest in overseas work, communication and other personal skills, empathy for other cultures, and appreciation for varied management styles and work environments

- *personal characteristics*—level of education, experience, and social compatibility with the host country.[3]

Solid experience in your field or company ranks at the top of the list of needed skills. Firms want to send employees who have expertise in their business and loyalty to the firm to represent them overseas. Those who obtain their master's of business administration (MBA) degree are reaping rewards financially: in a recent year, the average salary for MBA graduates a few years out of school reached $126,000.[4] Companies are reluctant to send new graduates abroad immediately. Instead, they invest in training to orient employees to the new assignment.

Knowledge of and interest in other languages and cultures is the second-highest priority. Businesspeople need to function smoothly in another society, so they are selected based on their familiarity with other languages and cultures. Because China is a business hotspot, some people have become fluent in Mandarin Chinese to boost their career prospects. Also, some school systems are offering Chinese language classes in addition to their standard offerings of Spanish, French, German, and Russian.

Finally, employees are evaluated on their personal characteristics to be certain that they will fit well in their new country. A person's talent is still foremost in making assignments, but executives with cross-cultural skills are in high demand.[5]

Career Assessment Exercises in Economics and Global Business

1. With the ups and downs in the U.S. economy, economists have been highlighted in the news. The head of the Federal Reserve, Benjamin Bernanke, has been managing the country's general financial condition. To get an idea of the role economists play in a federal government agency, research Bernanke's background and qualifications. Assess how he is performing at the Fed. Now make a list of your own skills. Where is there a match of your skills to his? What do you need to change?

2. To see the effect of the global economy in your community, go to a major retailer. Look at the number of different countries represented in the products on the shelves. Compare your list with those of your classmates to see who found the most countries and what goods those countries provided. Go online to research the career opportunities at the retailer's Web site.

3. To learn more about other countries, do research online for a country in which you are interested. Here are some sources that may be useful:

   - *The World Factbook*, published by the Central Intelligence Agency, https://www.cia.gov/library/publications/the-world-factbook/. This publication, updated yearly, contains a wealth of information about countries—geography and climate, population statistics, cultural and political information, transportation and communications methods, and economic data.

   - *BusinessWeek* magazine, http://www.businessweek.com. The Web site has links to Asia and Europe, where you can explore breaking news or information on global companies.

   - Online news sites Yahoo! News and Google News, http://news.yahoo.com and http://news.google.com. Both of these online news sites have links to global business news. The Yahoo! site has a link for "Business" and then "Global Economy." The Google site has a "Business" link and then lists sites for many countries and many languages.

   Write a one-page summary of what you found. Make a list of abilities you would need to function well as a businessperson in that country. Concentrate on the areas of competence, adaptability, and personal characteristics. Now formulate a plan to gain those skills.

PART 2

How Firms Get Started and Survive in a Global Environment

[**Chapter 5**]

Structuring
Contemporary
Business

[**Chapter 6**]

The Role of
Entrepreneurs in a
Competitive Economy

Chapter

5

Learning Objectives

1. Distinguish between small and large businesses.
2. Discuss the contributions of small businesses to the economy.
3. Discuss the survival rate of small businesses.
4. Describe the features of an effective business plan.
5. Describe funding opportunities for small businesses, including the role of the Small Business Administration (SBA).
6. Explain how franchising can provide opportunities for both franchisors and franchisees.
7. Outline the three main legal forms of business ownership and summarize the features of businesses owned by employees and families, as well as not-for-profit organizations.
8. Describe public and collective (cooperative) business ownership.
9. Identify types of corporations and the levels of corporate management.
10. Describe mergers, acquisitions, and joint ventures.

Structuring Contemporary Business

Mark LaMoyne/iStockphoto

Nokia: From Trees to Telecommunications

©Nokia Corporation/NewsCom

Success brings staying power in business. Many of today's well-run companies have been in existence for a long time, some for generations. Over the years, most have undergone many changes in organization, size, and direction, branching into new areas to take advantage of opportunities and abandoning old ones to cut losses. Probably very few, however, can rival the dramatic transformations of a small Finnish paper mill as it became one of the world's top cell phone makers. Almost 150 years ago, Nokia was a wood-pulp mill on the banks of the Nokia River in southern Finland. With several mergers and a move to become a corporation along the way, Nokia is now an international communications technology giant, with over 68,000 employees in 15 manufacturing facilities around the globe and operating profits in excess of 5 billion euros. Nokia is a public company incorporated in Finland and listed on the stock exchanges of Helsinki, Frankfurt, and New York. Its history is one of slow but steady growth and change. Some years after the Nokia paper mill's founding back in the mid-19th century, another prosperous Finnish firm began to grow—this one specializing in rubber products. Then early in the 20th century a third company, called Finnish Cable Works, was founded; by the 1960s this firm had established an electronics department to operate and sell computers and other devices. In 1967, all three companies formally merged to create Nokia Incorporated, which was by then ideally positioned to take a leading role in the evolution of mobile communications in Europe. Its first joint venture was a radio telephone company launched with a Finnish television manufacturer. By 1984, Nokia had produced its first portable phone, the Mobira Talkman, with more innovations in handheld technologies to follow.

Then came the most influential strategic decision in the company's history, when Jorma Ollila became president and CEO in 1992. Ollila set Nokia on a promising new course, focusing on global telecommunications. Only two years later, the world's first satellite call was placed using a Nokia handset. A phone-based videogame was the next big first for the firm, and soon Nokia had become the world leader in the design and manufacture of mobile phones. The firm sold its milestone one billionth cell phone in Nigeria in 2005. For at least the last decade, Nokia has been the top firm in the highly competitive cell phone market and is considered one of the most valuable brands in the world. Nokia continues to innovate under new president and CEO Olli-Pekka Kallasvuo, who came on staff in 2006, with Ollila serving as chairman of the board. In 2007, the company became the first phone manufacturer to build into its cell phones an energy-saving alert to unplug the charger when it is finished.

Meanwhile, Nokia was not done transforming itself. In 2008 it completely revamped its corporate structure, which formerly had three business groups working on mobile devices with a set of shared support groups. Now the firm consists of three major areas: Services & Software, which specializes in Internet services and software; Devices, which develops new products and their components; and Markets, which manages the company's supply chains, sales channels, and brand and marketing functions. NAVTEQ is a smaller division that provides digital data for mapping and satellite GPS systems for business and government; its focus is on making maps and voice-guided navigation systems available for portable devices. Finally, Nokia Siemens Networks is a separate joint venture with German electronics and engineering powerhouse Siemens that manages the company's technology infrastructure and related services. All these business units are supported by a corporate headquarters and overseen by the executive board of directors.

Nokia hopes its new structure will help it fend off attacks by Korean mobile phone makers Samsung and LG, which have passed U.S. firm Motorola in sales and are mounting a challenge to the market leader. LG's Chocolate cell phone was a smash hit, and Samsung plans to market no fewer than 20 smart phones to follow its success in Great Britain and the United States. Nokia recently released a compact new camera phone and a smart phone that receives Web-based e-mail. It is also partnering with Facebook and MySpace to open an online software and media store, following the shift to software development started by Apple's applications-rich iPhone.

With a global economic recession, cell phone makers face a contracting market. But the past has taught a valuable lesson: The future will be won by companies that are structured for quick and nimble responses to market changes. When it comes to transformation, Nokia has more experience than most.[1]

Do you hope to work for a big company or a small one? Do you plan to start your own business? If you're thinking about striking out on your own, you're not alone. On any given day in the United States, more people are in the process of starting a new business than getting married or having a baby. But before you enter the business world—as an employee or an owner—you need to understand the industry in which a company operates, as well as the size and framework of the firm's organization. Nokia started as a small paper mill but underwent several transformations to become a leader in telecommunications. The firm recently reorganized to compete more effectively and began an online service for software downloads. It's important to remember that most larger businesses—like Ford and Apple—began as small businesses.

Several variables affect the way a business is organized, including how easily it can be set up, access to financing, tolerance of financial risk, strengths and weaknesses that exist in competing firms, as well as the strengths and weaknesses of your firm.

This chapter begins by focusing on small-business ownership, including the advantages and disadvantages of small-business ventures, the contributions of small business to the economy, and the reasons small businesses fail. The chapter examines the services provided by the U.S. government's Small Business Administration, the role of women and minorities in small business, as well as alternatives for small businesses such as franchising.

The chapter then moves on to an overview of the forms of private business ownership—sole proprietorships, partnerships, and corporations. In addition, the features of businesses owned by employees and families, as well as not-for-profit organizations, are discussed. Public and collective ownership are examined. The chapter concludes with an explanation of structures and operations typical of larger companies, and a review of the major types of business alliances.

Most Businesses Are Small Businesses

Although many people associate the term *business* with corporate giants such as Kraft, Target, Disney, and ExxonMobil, 98 percent of all U.S. companies are considered small businesses. These firms have generated 64 percent of new jobs during the past 15 years and employ more than half of all private-sector (nongovernment) workers.[2] Small business is also the launching pad for new ideas and products. They hire 40 percent of high-tech workers such as scientists, engineers, and computer programmers, who devote their time to developing new goods and services.[3]

What Is a Small Business?

How can you tell a small business from a large one? The Small Business Administration (SBA), the federal agency most directly involved with this sector of the economy, defines a **small business** as an "independent business having fewer than 500 employees." However, those bidding for government contracts or applying for government assistance may vary in size according to industry. For example, small manufacturers fall in the 500-worker range, whereas wholesalers must employ fewer than 100. Retailers may generate up to $6 million in annual sales and still be considered small businesses, while farms or other agricultural businesses are designated small if they generate less than $750,000 annually.[4]

Logan Green and John Zimmer started Zimride, a California-based service that would let carpoolers connect with each other online. At the beginning, Zimride's customers, who pay about $10,000 a year to use the platform, were mostly colleges and universities, but its 35 clients now include Cigna and Walmart. Zimride employs six people and reports that its annual revenues are around $400,000—and making a profit.[5] By SBA standards, Zimride is a small business.

Because government agencies offer benefits designed to help small businesses compete with larger firms, small-business owners want to determine whether their companies meet the standards for small-business designation. If it qualifies, a company may be eligible for government loans or for government purchasing programs that encourage proposals from smaller suppliers. With assistance like this, Zimride might eventually expand to other areas of the country, and eventually become a larger business.

small business independent business with fewer than 500 employees, not dominant in its market

Typical Small-Business Ventures

Small businesses have always competed against each other as well as against some of the world's largest organizations. ModCloth, an online clothing retailer founded by husband-and-wife team Eric and Susan Koger, does both. Launched while the owners were still in college, the business offers trendy fashions by independent designers. The Kogers say they compete successfully against other clothing e-tailers because they develop a close relationship with designers and sell their inventory well before they have to pay for it. Their 104 employees are mostly young women who buy the types of clothes ModCloth sells. Because of these relationships, ModCloth can compete against other clothing e-tailers of any size.[6]

The past 15 years have seen a steady erosion of small businesses in some industries as larger firms have bought out small independent businesses and replaced them with larger operations. The number of independent bookstores and hardware stores has fallen dramatically as Barnes & Noble and Lowe's have increased the size and number of their stores. But as Table 5.1 reveals, the businesses least likely to be gobbled up are those that sell personalized services, rely on certain locations, and keep their overhead costs low.

Nonfarming-related small firms create more than half the nation's gross domestic product (GDP). In the past, many of these businesses focused on retailing or

In California, Logan Green and John Zimmer started Zimride, a service that lets carpoolers connect with each other online. This small business creates a social network for sharing rides.

Courtesy John Zimmer, Zimride, Inc.

Table 5.1

Business Sectors Most Dominated and Least Dominated by Small Firms

MOST LIKELY TO BE A SMALL FIRM	FEWER THAN 20 WORKERS
Home builders	97%
Florists	97%
Hair salons	96%
Auto repair	96%
Funeral homes	94%
LEAST LIKELY TO BE A SMALL FIRM	**FEWER THAN 20 WORKERS**
Hospitals	14%
Nursing homes	23%
Paper mills	33%
Electric utilities	38%
Oil pipelines	38%

Source: U.S. Census Bureau, "Number of Firms, Number of Establishments, Employment, and Annual Payroll by Employment Size of the Enterprise for the United States, All Industries," accessed June 23, 2010, http://www.census.gov.

a service industry such as insurance. More recently, however, small firms have carved out an important niche for themselves: providing busy consumers with customized services that range from pet-sitting to personal shopping. These businesses cater to the needs of individual customers in a way that big firms can't.

As Figure 5.1 shows, small businesses provide most jobs in the construction, agricultural services, wholesale trade, services, and retail trade industries. Retailing to the consumer is another important industry for small firms. Retailing giants such as Amazon and Macy's may be the best-known firms, but smaller stores and Web sites outnumber them. And these small firms can be very successful, as the owners of ModCloth illustrate, often because they can keep their overhead expenses low.

Small business also plays a significant role in agriculture. Although most farm acreage is in the hands of large corporate farms, most U.S. farms are owned by individual farmers or families, not partners or shareholders.[7] The family farm is a classic example of a small-business operation. It is independently owned and operated, with a limited number of employees, including family members. Cider Hill Farm in Massachusetts is one such farm. Three generations of the Cook family operate the farm together—it produces fruit and vegetables, including a wide variety of cooking and eating apples from its orchards, and honey from its on-site beehives. In addition, Cider Hill makes its own fresh cider and cider doughnuts every day and operates a well-stocked country store on the property. During growing season, the farm hosts field trips for schools, offers hay rides, and creates a corn maze in its fields. All of these activities contribute to the income of the farm. The Cooks are also dedicated to environmentally friendly farming technologies. Cider Hill operates three wind turbines and uses solar cells to help power its buildings.[8]

Fifty-two percent of small businesses in the United States are **home-based businesses**—firms operated from the residence of the business owner. There are about 16 million such businesses in the United States.[9] People who operate home-based firms often do so because this type of work allows them more control over their business as well as their personal time. Whether you're a morning person or a night owl, in many cases you can structure your business hours accordingly. Access to the Internet and availability of communications devices such as the BlackBerry and other smart phone technology makes it convenient to run a home-based business. Freedom from overhead costs such as leasing office or warehouse space is another major attraction of home-based businesses. Drawbacks include isolation and less visibility to customers—except, of course, if your customers visit you online. In that case, they don't care where your office is located.

Many small-business start-ups are more competitive because of the Internet. The Internet doesn't guarantee success—there are so many Web sites that a small firm needs to find ways to make its online presence effective. But establishing a Web site is generally less expensive than opening a retail store and reaches a broader spectrum of potential customers. Connecticut-based eBeanstalk.com is an online toy store. How does this small business compete with the likes of online giants such as Amazon and Toys 'R' Us? The company specializes in learning toys that "help plant the seeds that help children grow." Two teams of experts (including 700 moms) hired by eBeanstalk evaluate more than 10,000 toys from manufacturers, to narrow the selection down to around 600 of what they consider to be the best learning toys. That group may shrink even further. Only the selected toys are included on the site. Consumers appreciate this screening process, knowing they can go straight to eBeanstalk for the toys they want.[10]

American business history is filled with inspirational stories of great inventors who launched companies in barns, garages, warehouses, and attics. For young visionaries such as Apple Computer founders Steve Jobs and Steve Wozniak, the logical option for transforming their technical idea into a commercial reality was to begin work in a family garage. The impact of today's entrepreneurs, including home-based businesses, is discussed in more depth in Chapter 6.

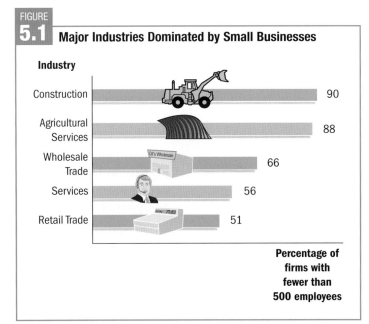

Source: Office of Advocacy, U.S. Small Business Administration, "Small Business Profile: United States," accessed June 23, 2010, http://www.sba.gov/advo.

home-based business firm operated from the residence of the business owner

Assessment Check ✓

1. How does the Small Business Administration (SBA) define *small business?*

2. In what industries do small businesses play a significant role?

Contributions of Small Business to the Economy

Small businesses form the core of the U.S. economy. Businesses with fewer than 500 employees generate more than half the nation's gross domestic product (GDP). These companies account for more than 97 percent of known U.S. exporters, shipping more than 30 percent of all exported goods overseas each year.[11] Small firms are credited with U.S. competitiveness in a number of world markets.[12]

Creating New Jobs

Small businesses make tremendous contributions to the U.S. economy and to society as a whole. One impressive contribution is the number of new jobs created each year by small businesses. While it varies from year to year, on average three of every four new jobs are created by companies with fewer than 500 employees.[13] A significant share of these jobs are created by the smallest companies, those with four or fewer employees. Small businesses that provide services have experienced a greater increase in new jobs than those that produce goods.[14]

Small businesses also contribute to the economy by hiring workers who traditionally have had difficulty finding jobs at larger firms, such as women returning to the workforce, former welfare recipients, and workers with various challenges. The Small Business Administration provides incentives for companies to hire these types of workers.

Even if you never plan to start your own company, you will probably work for a small business at some point in your career, particularly at the beginning. Small firms often hire the youngest workers. Table 5.2 illustrates some of the newest jobs within both traditional and new industries, many of which can be found in small businesses.

Creating New Industries

Small firms give businesspeople the opportunity and outlet for developing new ideas. Sometimes these new ideas become entirely new industries. Many of today's largest and most successful firms, such as Whole Foods, Google, and Amazon, began as small businesses. Facebook co-founders Mark Zuckerberg, Dustin Moskovitz, Chris Hughes, and Eduardo Saverin launched their new business from their college dorm room. Within five years, Facebook had logged more than 300 million users and positioned itself as a leader in the new industry of social networking.[15]

New industries are sometimes created when small businesses adapt to provide needed services to a larger corporate community. Corporate downsizing has created a demand for other businesses to perform activities previously handled by in-house employees. These support businesses may become an industry themselves. The need for wireless communication

Table

5.2 New Job Opportunities for Small Businesses

INDUSTRY	JOBS
Green energy	Wind-farm engineers; solar installers and technicians; green-collar specialists and consultants
Health care	Informatics specialists (workers cross-trained in healthcare and information technology)
Management	Business continuity planners (help businesses plan for cyberattacks and other security breaches or natural disasters); spa managers
Education	Distance-learning coordinators (prepare and help run online courses for colleges, trade schools, charter schools, and companies)
Media	User-experience designers (focus on improving user experience with interactive media

Sources: Larry Buhl, "Newest Professions, Growing Salaries," *Yahoo! Hot Jobs,* accessed June 23, 2010, http://hotjobs.yahoo.com/jobseeker; Mary Nemko and Liz Wolgemuth, "Choosing the Career Path Less Traveled," *U.S. News & World Report,* May 2009, pp. 22–24.

New industries can be created when small businesses adapt to shifts in consumer interests and preferences. Joanna Van Vleck's online Trunk Club uses Web cams to interview men who are too busy to shop for clothes, then she selects and ships them their new wardrobe.

devices and services to support businesses has resulted in a proliferation of small businesses to fill this niche.

New industries can be created when small businesses adapt to shifts in consumer interests and preferences. For example, the idea of offering customized services to busy consumers has taken root in the U.S. economy. Joanna Van Vleck offers one such service through her online Trunk Club. Using Web cams to meet with men who are too busy to shop for clothes, Van Vleck interviews her customers and assesses their clothing needs, then selects and ships a new wardrobe directly to them.[16]

Finally, new industries may be created when both the business world and consumers recognize a need for change. The recent emphasis on environmental responsibility—ranging from recycling and reuse of goods to reducing the amount of energy consumed—has fostered a whole new industry of green goods and services, many produced by small companies. One such firm is Boston-based Emergent Energy Group, a renewable energy consulting business founded by Jesse Gossett and Jayson Uppal. The two created their firm to "spread and enhance the discussion surrounding all aspects of the transforming global energy industry." Emergent helps cities and private companies evaluate their energy use and create sustainable practices.[17] The "Going Green" feature describes one small-business owner who is pouring her passion and talent into environmentally responsible services.

Innovation

Small businesses are adept at developing new and improved goods and services. Innovation is often the entire reason for the founding of a new business. In a typical year, small firms develop twice as many product innovations per employee as larger firms. They also produce 13 times more patents per employee than larger firms.[18]

Green Mama: Small Business with a Big Message

The Green Mama isn't a mythical figure. She's a consultant, writer, and environmentalist who believes the world can be made a more sustainable place one mom at a time. Manda Aufochs Gillespie had been living and promoting an environmentally conscious lifestyle for several years when she was featured in a *Chicago Tribune* article. Suddenly, Gillespie became a guru for like-minded parents who simply wanted to improve the health and lives of their families while reducing their impact on the planet. Since then she has launched a Web site, www.thegreenmama.com; hosts a weekly playgroup/seminar for parents called the Green Mama Café; writes a regular blog; consults for daycare businesses and educational institutions; gives workshops; appears on television; and provides everyday advice to consumers. She's also a mom.

The Web site is the center of Gillespie's green universe. "The site is for people who are trying to be green parents in any major city," she explains. "It's a tool for living." Visitors to the site can get shopping tips for the best cloth diapers, learn how to clean their floors with white vinegar (instead of commercial cleaners), become informed about buying local produce, and get the real scoop on everything from the effectiveness of hand sanitizers to the cost of organic produce. No question is too elementary for Gillespie. In addition, she offers suggestions for saving money—as well as reducing waste—such as re-gifting a gently used child's garment to another child instead of buying a new piece of clothing for a birthday gift.

How does all of this philosophy translate to business? It's not just the $5 that each mom pays to attend one of Gillespie's workshops in person at the Green Mama Café, or any consulting fees she may charge. It's the fact that, according to marketing experts, these moms represent a group of about 20 million consumers who are beginning to demand green goods and services. It's not just cloth diapers and natural floor cleaners. These consumers are now scrutinizing every item they put in their reusable shopping bags. If they have to pay a bit more for those products, they will—because in many cases they are saving money elsewhere. "It turns out that what saves money also saves resources and what is better for the environment can also make parenting easier, if you have the right mindset," says one mom who attends Gillespie's Green Mama seminars. It is estimated that these green moms wield nearly $210 billion in purchasing power—something that manufacturers, media, and service providers have begun to notice.

Questions for Critical Thinking

1. Manda Gillespie is part of a movement of small businesses that are creating a whole new industry: green goods and services for parents. What factors do you believe will contribute to the success of this movement? What pitfalls might they face?

2. As a consumer, have you embraced any green goods or services? Why or why not? Have they been offered by small or large companies?

Sources: Green Mama Web site, http://www.thegreenmama.com, accessed April 2, 2010; Jessica Levco, "The Green Mama Speaks," *Chicago Magazine,* May 2009, http://www.chicagomag.com; Robyn Monaghan, "Green Mamas Unite," *Chicago Parent,* March 20, 2009, http://www.chicagoparent.com.

Assessment Check ☑

1. What are the three key ways in which small businesses contribute to the economy?

2. How are new industries formed?

Key 20th-century innovations developed by small businesses include the airplane, the personal computer, soft contact lenses, and the zipper. Innovations that already drive small businesses in the 21st century include those that fall into social networking, security, and green energy industries. The "Business Etiquette" feature offers tips for using online social networking successfully.

Why Small Businesses Fail

Small businesses play a huge role in the U.S. economy. But one of the reasons they are so successful is also the reason they may fail—their founders are willing to take a risk. Some of the most common shortcomings that plague a small firm include management inexperience, inadequate financing, and the challenge of meeting government regulations.

As Figure 5.2 shows, 7 out of every 10 new businesses survive at least two years. About 50 percent make it to the five-year mark. But by the tenth year, 82 percent will have closed.[19] Let's look a little more closely at why this happens.

Management Shortcomings

One of the most common causes of small-business failure is the shortcomings of management. These may include lack of people skills, inadequate knowledge of finance, inability to track inventory or sales, poor assessment of the competition, or simply the lack of time to do everything required. Whereas large firms often have the resources to recruit specialists in areas such as marketing and finance, the owner of a small business often winds up wearing too many hats at once.

This could result in bad decision making that could end in the firm's failure. Krispy Kreme was once a small business that expanded too fast as a result of poor decisions made by management. The company's near failure had nothing to do with the quality of its doughnuts. Instead, as the company grew bigger, so did its debt. Allegations of management misconduct were made. Meanwhile, consumers began to turn their attention away from doughnuts and toward more healthful snacks and breakfast foods produced by competitors. Now under new management and operating at a leaner size, the firm is recovering.[20]

Owners of small businesses can increase their chances of success if they become educated in the principles of business; know the industry in which they intend to operate; develop good interpersonal skills; understand their own limitations; hire motivated employees; and seek professional advice on issues like finance, regulations, and other legal matters.[21]

Inadequate Financing

Money is the foundation of any business. Every business—large or small—needs a certain amount of financing in order to operate, thrive, and grow. Another leading problem of small businesses is inadequate financing. First-time business owners often assume that their firms will generate enough funds from their initial sales to finance continuing operations. But building a business takes time. Products need to be developed, employees have to be hired, a Web site must be constructed, distribution has to be determined, office or retail space might have to be secured,

BusinessEtiquette

How to Use Social Networking in Your Job Search

Online social networking is likely part of your every day life. But you can put this technology to powerful use when you are looking for a job. During one recent year, networking sites such as LinkedIn registered about 1 million new users per month. Worried about getting lost in the social-networking shuffle? Use a few simple tips from the pros to help you stand out from the millions of other job-seekers who have discovered the benefits of social networking.

- *Research a network before jumping in.* Some networks, such as Facebook, exist mostly to connect friends with each other. Others, such as LinkedIn, have a stronger employment focus. Twitter, on the other hand, attracts both types of users. To adopt the right approach—and make the most of a site—learn something about it before you log on to search for an employer.

- *Complete your online profile.* Help prospective employers by filling out your online profile. Update your bio as frequently as possible. Provide a link to your own blog or Web page if you have one. Don't try to be perfect—if you know your shortcomings or have made a mistake in a previous job, describe how you've improved or made the most of your decision.

- *Share information.* Be willing to share information about companies or career opportunities with like-minded job-seekers. You can help an online recruiter find the right person—even if it's not you.

- *Search for people.* Look for companies that interest you, then try to make connections with friends, family members, classmates, alumni—anyone who might be able to help you establish contact within those companies. A specific job might not be available at the moment, but a personal connection could help you when that job does open up.

- *Respect privacy.* Just as you only want to present certain information about yourself online, respect the privacy of potential employers and colleagues. Familiarize yourself with the privacy settings of a social networking site and abide by them.

Sources: DeLynn Senna, "Recruiters Reveal Pet Peeves About Job Seekers," *Yahoo! Hot Jobs,* http://hotjobs.yahoo.com, accessed April 2, 2010; Alex Williams, "Mind Your BlackBerry or Mind Your Manners," *The New York Times,* June 21, 2009; David LaGesse, "Turning Social Networking into a Job Offer," *U.S. News & World Report,* May 2009, pp. 44–45.

FIGURE
5.2 **Rate of Business Failures**

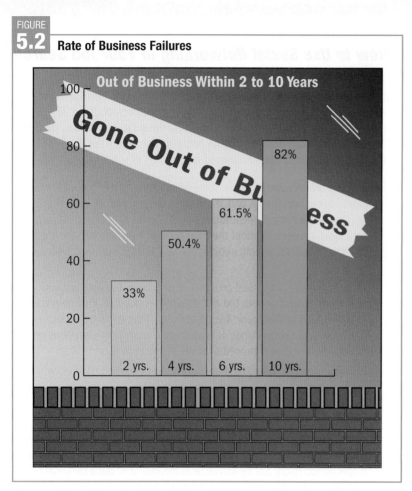

Out of Business Within 2 to 10 Years

Gone Out of Business

			82%
		61.5%	
	50.4%		
33%			
2 yrs.	4 yrs.	6 yrs.	10 yrs.

Source: Office of Advocacy, U.S. Small Business Administration, "Frequently Asked Questions: Advocacy Small Business Statistics and Research," accessed June 23, 2010, http://app1.sba.gov/faqs.

Asafumi Yamashita started his business with $500 to buy specialty vegetable seeds from Japan. Within a year, Yamashita was supplying several top restaurants around Paris. Yamashita has deliberately limited his number of customers and has no employees, so he needs less financing and maintains control over every basket of vegetables he grows.

Brittney McChristy/iStockphoto

and so forth. Most small businesses—even those with minimal start-up costs—sometimes don't turn a profit for months or even years.[22]

Although there are stories about business founders starting firms with just a few hundred dollars loaned by a friend or with a cash advance from a credit card, commercial banks and other financial institutions are the largest lenders to small businesses, accounting for 65 percent of total traditional credit to small firms. This type of financing includes credit lines and loans for nonresidential mortgages, vehicles, specialized equipment, and leases.[23]

Figure 5.3 shows that despite their relatively high interest rates, credit cards do remain an important source of financing for small businesses. The heaviest users of credit cards for business financing are firms with fewer than ten employees. Inadequate financing can compound management shortcomings by making it more difficult for small businesses to attract and keep talented people. Typically, a big company can offer a better benefits package and a higher salary.

With less money to spend on employees, marketing, inventory, and other business costs, successful small companies need to be creative. Asafumi Yamashita started his business with $500, with which he bought specialty vegetable seeds from Japan. In his own greenhouse, he planted Japanese spinach, radishes, and other delicacies. Yamashita had become friends with the head chef at a Japanese restaurant in Paris, who told Yamashita that these vegetables were nearly impossible to obtain locally. Within a year of planting those first seeds, Yamashita was supplying several top restaurants around Paris. Word of Yamashita's high-quality vegetables spread, and he now supplies his crop only to the most exclusive establishments in the area. Yamashita has deliberately limited his number of customers and has no employees, so he needs less financing and maintains control over every basket of vegetables that leaves his garden.[24]

Government Regulation

Small-business owners cite their struggle to comply with government regulations as one of the biggest challenges they face. Some firms fold because of this burden alone. Paperwork costs account for billions of small-business dollars each year. A large company can better cope with requirements for forms and reports.

Larger firms often find that it makes economic sense to hire or contract with specialists in specific types of regulation, such as employment law and workplace safety regulations. By contrast, small businesses often struggle to absorb the costs of government paperwork because of their more limited staff and budgets. The smallest firms—those with fewer than 20 employees—spend 45 percent more per employee than larger firms just to comply with federal regulations.[25]

Recognizing the burden of regulation on small businesses, Congress sometimes exempts the smallest companies from certain regulations. For example, small businesses with 49 or fewer employees are exempt from the Family and Medical Leave Act, which gives employees up to 12 weeks of unpaid leave each year to take care of a newborn child, adopt a child, or care for a family member who has serious health problems.[26] Most small-business owners comply with employment and other laws, believing that such compliance is ethically correct and fosters better employee relations than trying to determine which regulations don't apply to a small business.

Taxes are another burdensome expense for a small business. In addition to local, state, and federal income taxes, employers must pay taxes covering workers' compensation insurance, Social Security payments, and unemployment benefits. Although large companies have similar expenses, they generally have more resources to cover them. But there are also tax incentives designed to help small businesses. These incentives cover a broad range including tax credits for use of biodiesel and renewable fuels, increased research activities, pension plan start-up, and access for individuals with disabilities.[27]

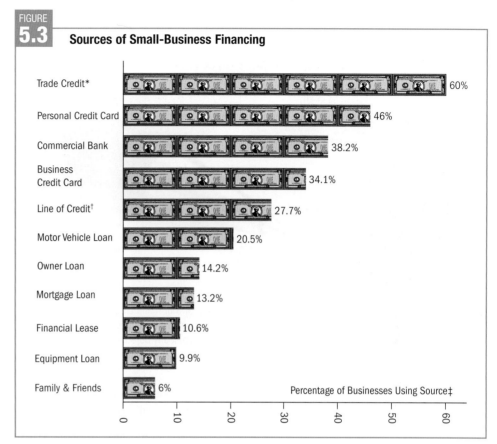

FIGURE 5.3

Sources of Small-Business Financing

Source	Percentage
Trade Credit*	60%
Personal Credit Card	46%
Commercial Bank	38.2%
Business Credit Card	34.1%
Line of Credit†	27.7%
Motor Vehicle Loan	20.5%
Owner Loan	14.2%
Mortgage Loan	13.2%
Financial Lease	10.6%
Equipment Loan	9.9%
Family & Friends	6%

Percentage of Businesses Using Source‡

*Trade credit is purchasing goods or equipment from a supplier who finances the purchase by delaying the date of payment for those goods.

†A line of credit is an agreement between a bank and a borrower, indicating the maximum amount of credit the bank will extend to the borrower.

Note: Total exceeds 100 percent because businesses typically use more than one source of financing.

Source: Small Business Administration, Office of Advocacy, "Financing Patterns of Small Firms," accessed June 23, 2010, http://www.sba.gov/advo; Susan Coleman, "Free and Costly Trade Credit: A Comparison of Small Firms," Academy of Entrepreneurial Finance, February 2008, www.google.com, accessed June 23, 2010.

The Business Plan: A Foundation for Success

Large or small, every business needs a plan in order to succeed. While there are tales of firms launched from an idea scribbled on a napkin at a restaurant or sketched out on graph paper in a dorm room, the idea must be backed by a solid plan in order to become reality. A **business plan** is a written document that provides an orderly statement of a company's

Assessment Check ☑

1. What percentage of small businesses remain in operation five years after starting? Ten years?

2. What are the three main causes of small-business failure?

business plan written document that provides an orderly statement of a company's goals, methods, and standards

The business plan is often the document that secures financing for a firm and creates a framework for the organization. Business plans identify the firm's mission and goals. They create measurable standards and outline a strategy for reaching company objectives.

goals, the methods by which it intends to achieve these goals, and the standards by which it will measure its achievements. The business plan is often the document that secures financing for a firm and creates a framework for the organization.

Business plans give the organization a sense of purpose. They identify the firm's mission and goals. They create measurable standards and outline a strategy for reaching company objectives. A typical business plan includes the following sections:

- an *executive summary* that briefly answers the who, what, where, when, why, and how questions for the business

- an *introduction* that includes a general statement of the concept, purpose, and objectives of the proposed business

- separate *financial* and *marketing sections* that describe the firm's target market and marketing plan as well as detailed financial forecasts of the need for funds and when the firm is expected to break even—the level of sales at which revenues equal costs

- *résumés of principals*—especially in plans written to obtain financing.

Within this structure, an effective business plan contains the written soul of a firm. A good plan addresses the following issues:

- *The company's mission and the vision of its founders.* Look at the home page of any firm's Web site and you will find its mission. At the Web site for TOMs Shoes, visitors learn that "TOMs shoes was founded on a simple premise: With every pair you purchase, TOMs will give a pair of new shoes to a child in need. One for one. Using the purchasing power of individuals to benefit the greater good is what we're all about."[28] This simple declaration states why the company was founded and what it intends to accomplish.

- *An outline of what makes the company unique.* Why start a business that's just like hundreds of others? An effective business plan describes what distinguishes the firm and its products from the rest of the pack. TOMs Shoes illustrates a unique business model with its "one-for-one" donation program.

- *The customers.* A business plan identifies who the firm's customers will be and how it will serve their needs.

- *The competition.* A business plan addresses its existing and potential competitors as legitimate entities, with a strategy for creating superior or unique offerings. Studying the competition can provide valuable information about what works and what doesn't in the marketplace.

- *Financial evaluation of the industry and market conditions.* This knowledge helps develop a credible financial forecast and budget.

- *Assessment of the risks.* Every business undertaking involves risks. A solid business plan acknowledges these and outlines a strategy for dealing with them.[29]

Assessment Check ✔

1. What are the five main sections of a business plan?

2. Why is an effective business plan important to the success of a firm?

Whether a firm's intention is to revolutionize an entire industry on a global scale or improve the lives of children by providing them with shoes, the business plan is a major factor in its success. For more detailed information on how to write a business plan, see Appendix D, "Developing a Business Plan," on page A-43.

Assistance for Small Businesses

An important part of organizing a small business is financing its activities. Once a business plan has been created, various sources can be tapped for loans and other types of financing. These include government agencies as well as private investors. In the scramble for dollars, sometimes government allocation of funds to certain firms is subject to criticism, as discussed in the "Solving an Ethical Controversy" feature.

Small Business Administration

Small businesses can benefit from using the resources provided by the **Small Business Administration (SBA)**. The SBA is the principal government agency concerned with helping small U.S. firms, and it is the advocate for small businesses within the federal government. More than 2,100 employees staff the SBA's Washington headquarters and its regional and field offices.[30] The SBA is "committed to helping small businesses, which are the backbone of the nation's economy, thrive. Working closely with a wide range of lending partners across the country, SBA has developed a number of financial programs that address the various needs of small businesses."[31]

Small Business Administration (SBA) principal government agency concerned with helping small U.S. firms

Phil McCarton/Reuters/Landov LLC

Fisker Automotive received government loans to build a plug-in hybrid sports car called the Karma. That sounds like a win–win situation—investment in alternative energy vehicles, creation of new jobs, rejuvenation of the auto industry—but the new car will be built in Finland and priced around $89,000, out of reach for the average car buyer.

Solving an Ethical Controversy

Good Karma or Bad Karma?

During the recent economic downturn, many businesses—large and small—received funds from the federal government to survive and ultimately grow. One such business was Fisker Automotive, a California start-up automaker that received $528 million in government loans to build a plug–in hybrid sports car called the Karma. That sounds like a win-win situation for everyone—investment in vehicles powered by alternative energy, the creation of new jobs, rejuvenation of the auto industry. But the allocation has its critics, largely because the new car will be built in Finland—and will be priced at about $89,000, out of reach for the average car buyer.

Should federal funds be allocated to support firms that manufacture luxury goods overseas?

PRO

1. According to Fisker Automotive, no federal funds will be used for operations overseas. Instead, much of the loan money will be used for the purchase of components from U.S. suppliers, as well as engineering and design, which will be done in the U.S. The Department of Energy estimates that the loans will save or create about 5,000 jobs.

2. Although the Karma carries a hefty sticker price, the design of the car should attract buyers who might otherwise purchase traditional sports cars whose fuel consumption and emissions are high. Fisker claims that with projected tax credits, the Karma will ultimately cost around $39,000.

CON

1. Investing in a product that can only be purchased by the wealthiest car buyers is not an equitable distribution of government funds. "This is not for average Americans," argues a spokesperson for Citizens Against Government Waste. "It's a status symbol thing."

2. Other firms, including those that applied for much smaller loans to develop alternatively powered vehicles at a lower price point, were rejected by the government. More companies could have been supported, with more jobs created, and more hybrid cars could have been sold to average car buyers if the funds had been distributed more equitably.

Summary

Fisker has pledged to repay the government loans with interest and to offer a superior product to luxury car buyers. The firm claims that the launch of the Karma, the world's first production plug-in hybrid car, will "put the American auto industry ahead of foreign competition." But detractors say that federal funds should be reserved for firms that produce goods and services to benefit a wider range of consumers.

Sources: Company Web site, http://karma.fiskerautomotive.com, accessed April 2, 2010; Josh Mitchell and Stephen Power, "Gore-Backed Car Firm Gets Large U.S. Loan," *The Wall Street Journal,* September 25, 2009, http://online.wsj.com; Ken Thomas, "California Automaker Receives $528.7 Million Government Loan," *Associated Press,* September 23, 2009, http://autos.yahoo.com.

Financial Assistance from the SBA Contrary to popular belief, the SBA seldom provides direct business loans. Nor does it provide outright grants to start or expand small businesses.[32] Instead, the SBA *guarantees* small-business loans made by private lenders, including banks and other institutions. To qualify for an SBA-backed loan, borrowers must be "unable to secure conventional commercial financing on reasonable terms and be a 'small business' as defined by SBA size standards."[33] Direct SBA loans are available in only a few special situations, such as natural disaster recovery and energy conservation or development programs. Under the 2009 Recovery Act, the SBA temporarily eliminated specific loan fees and raised the guarantee level on some of its loans.[34]

microloans small-business loans often used to buy equipment or operate a business

The SBA also guarantees **microloans** of up to $35,000 to start-ups and other very small firms. The average loan is $13,000 with a maximum term of six years.[35] Microloans may be used to buy equipment or operate a business but not to buy real estate or pay off other loans. These loans are available from nonprofit organizations located in most states. Other sources of microloans include the federal Economic Development Administration, some state governments, and certain private lenders, such as credit unions and community development groups. The most frequent suppliers of credit to small firms are banks.

Small-business loans are also available through SBA-licensed organizations called *Small Business Investment Companies (SBICs)*, which are run by experienced venture capitalists. SBICs use their own capital, supplemented with government loans, to invest in small businesses. Like banks, SBICs are profit-making enterprises, but they are likely to be more flexible than banks in their lending decisions. Large companies that used SBIC financing when they were small start-ups include Apple, Federal Express, and Staples.

Other Specialized Assistance Although government purchases represent a huge market, small companies have difficulty competing for this business with giant firms, which employ specialists to handle the volumes of paperwork involved in preparing proposals and completing bid applications. Today, many government procurement programs set aside portions of government spending for small companies; an additional SBA role is to help small firms secure these contracts. With set-aside programs for small businesses, up to 23 percent of certain government contracts are designated for small businesses.

Every federal agency with buying authority must maintain an Office of Small and Disadvantaged Business Utilization to ensure that small businesses receive a reasonable portion of government procurement contracts. To help connect small businesses with government agencies, the SBA's Web site offers Central Contractor Registration, which includes a search engine for finding business opportunities as well as a chance for small businesses to provide information about themselves. Set-aside programs are also common in the private sector, particularly among major corporations.

In addition to help with financing and government procurement, the SBA delivers a variety of other services to small businesses. It provides information and advice through toll-free telephone numbers and its Web site, http://www.sba.gov. Through its Small Business Training Network, the SBA offers free online courses; sponsors inexpensive training courses on topics such as taxes, networking, and start-ups in cities and small towns throughout the nation; and provides a free online library of more than 200 SBA publications and additional business resources. Business owners can find local resources by logging on to the SBA Web site and searching for SBA partners in their region. Local resource partners include small-business development centers, women's business centers, U.S. export assistance centers, and veterans business outreach centers.[36]

Local Assistance for Small Businesses

In conjunction with the federal government or on their own, state and local governments often have programs in place to help small businesses get established and grow. One such region is Washington state's Thurston County. The Thurston County Economic Development Council was founded more than 25 years ago with the mission of "creating a vital and sustainable economy throughout our County that supports the livelihood and values of our residents."[37] The Thurston County EDC provides information and assistance in business planning, licenses and registrations, taxes, and employment considerations. In addition, the council works to connect local businesses with each other and with industry experts, create marketing messages that attract new businesses and customers, and ensure that Thurston County plays an important role in the region's economy.[38] Organizations like the Thurston County EDC offer important resources and links for small businesses around the country.

Business Incubators Some community agencies interested in encouraging business development have implemented a concept called a **business incubator** to provide low-cost shared business facilities to small start-up ventures. See the "Hit and Miss" feature to read about Turning Technologies' incubator experience. A typical incubator might section off space in an abandoned plant and rent it to various small firms. Tenants often share clerical staff, computers, and other business services. The objective is that, after a few months or years, the fledgling business will be ready to move out and operate on its own.

More than 1,000 business incubator programs operate nationwide. Ninety-four percent of them are run by not-for-profit organizations focused on economic development. More than half of these programs are operated in urban areas, while about 20 percent of them are sponsored by academic institutions.[39]

Private Investors

A small business may start with cash from a personal savings account or a loan from a family member. But small-business owners soon begin to look for greater sums of money in order to continue operating and eventually grow. They may want to continue with assistance from private investors. **Venture capital**—money invested in the small business by another business firm or group of individuals in exchange for an ownership share—can give the small business a boost. Even when the economy is sluggish, venture capitalists are looking for companies in which to invest. Recently the National Venture Capital Association reported that venture capitalists had invested more than $7 billion in small start-up firms despite a sluggish economy. These investors showed preference for small-business owners with a proven track record and for those proposing innovative ways to commercialize products like solar energy, low-emission cars, and new medications. They're tough in their requirements for a solid business plan and expect small-businesses owners to run lean operations.[40]

Small-Business Opportunities for Women and Minorities

In the United States today, more than 10 million firms are owned by women, employing more than 13 million workers and generating nearly $2 trillion in sales. In fact, 40 percent of all privately held companies are owned by women. Further, nearly 2 million businesses are owned by women of color, employing 1.2 million people and generating $165 billion in annual revenues.[41]

Shama Kabani researched the power of social networking suggesting that businesses could use these tools to market their goods and services. When she couldn't convince larger corporations of this powerful tool, she started her own full-time online consulting firm.

Women, like men, have a variety of reasons for starting their own companies. Some have a unique business idea that they want to bring to life. Others decide to strike out on their own when they lose their jobs or become frustrated with the bureaucracies in large companies. When Shama Kabani wrote her master's thesis on the power of social networking, her research suggested that businesses could use these tools to market their goods and services. But when she pitched her idea to a large consulting firm, the company rejected it as a fad. So Kabani set out on her own. She founded her own full-time online consulting firm called Click to Client (now called The Marketing Zen Group), to build Web sites and create and manage social media campaigns for clients. Kabani now has six employees and expects to hit $1 million in annual revenues soon.[42]

Hit & Miss

Turning Technologies Creates High-Tech Jobs

Young companies that grow and add jobs to boost their local economies make a lot of people happy about their success. That's why so many people are smiling in Youngstown, Ohio, since a new technology company came to town.

Helped along by a business organization that provides start-up tech firms with free rent and utilities, Turning Technologies was founded in Youngstown. Its breathtaking growth brought dozens of new jobs to a city with 18 percent unemployment that is haunted by the decline of its old steel mills. Turning pays corporate income taxes on more than $30 million annual revenue, and it has already been called the fastest growing privately held software company in the United States—ranked at 18th overall. The firm boasts more than 6,500 clients, and more than a million people use its audience-response products.

Audience-response systems are the wireless keypads you've probably seen spectators using on TV game shows to register their opinions or answers to questions. Thanks to Turning's affordable hardware and the availability of both its free and licensed software programs, teachers from kindergarten through college are now enjoying the benefits of audience-response technology. Instructors can ask questions in class using other programs like PowerPoint, Blackboard, and WebCT; have students key in answers—anonymously or not—using their remotes; and instantly collate the responses to see how many students answered correctly.

Government agencies and not-for-profit organizations also use the systems for their training programs. "Audience involvement boosts focus and comprehension levels," says Turning's CEO Mike Broderick, and instructors agree. "It gives you the opportunity to reteach if you need to and then move on if you don't," says one middle school teacher. Adds a school principal about applications of the Turning program, "We have some teachers that are working hard to find the many avenues they can go beyond. You're really only limited by your creativity."

And it gets better. "Not only can we identify how each student is responding," says Turning's vice president for education sales, but "we can compile that data by classroom, by building, and by district and tag the data to specific standards." Among the impressive results already confirmed is "an increase of 15 points in test scores when our technology is used frequently and effectively."

Most of Turning's 120 employees are young Ohioans who enjoy some of the same benefits as their Silicon Valley counterparts, such as in-house foosball and air hockey for work breaks. The firm takes pride in being the kind of success story people have long thought "doesn't happen here." It has had double- or triple-digit growth since its launch. "I would not be surprised to see Turning Technologies at 2,000 workers in three to four years," says the CEO of the organization that helped the company get its start.

That's music to Youngstown's ears. The bottom line? Good products that are affordable, easy to use, and well marketed can help small companies become engines of growth and job creators.

Questions for Critical Thinking

1. Why might a company such as Turning Technologies locate outside the high-tech hotspots where most firms are? List some possible advantages and disadvantages to that strategy.

2. What should a company like Turning Technologies do if, as it grows, it needs to hire people with technical experience or skills that are hard to find in a depressed area?

Sources: Company Web site, http://www.turningtechnologies.com, accessed April 2, 2010; "In Ohio, You Can Maintain Your Balance No Matter How Fast You Grow," *Ohio Means Business,* http://www.ohiomeansbusiness.com, accessed April 2, 2010; "Upside/Downside: Youngstown Business Incubator a Bright Spot in Region," WCPN Ideastream transcript, February 12, 2009, http://www.wcpn.org; Matt Sanctis, "Champaign Students Learning by Remote Control," *Springfield News-Sun,* February 8, 2009, http://www.springfieldnewssun.com; Angie Schmitt, "Turning Technologies Unveils New K–12 Programs and Services," *TMCNet,* January 23, 2009, http://www.tmcnet.com.

In other cases, women leave large corporations when they feel blocked from opportunities for advancement. Sometimes this occurs because they hit the so-called glass ceiling. Because women are more likely than men to be the primary caregivers in their families, some may seek self-employment as a way to achieve flexible working hours so they can spend more time with their families.

Many nationwide business assistance programs are geared toward women-owned firms. Among the programs offered by the Small Business Administration are the Contract Assistance for Women Business Owners program, which teaches women how to market to the federal government, and the Women's Network for Entrepreneurial Training, which matches experienced businesswomen with women trying to get started. Organizations like the Center for Women's Business Research provide information, contacts, and other resources as well.

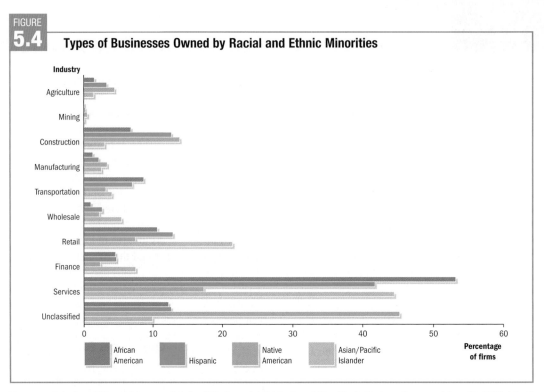

FIGURE 5.4 Types of Businesses Owned by Racial and Ethnic Minorities

Industry

Agriculture
Mining
Construction
Manufacturing
Transportation
Wholesale
Retail
Finance
Services
Unclassified

0   10   20   30   40   50   60

African American   Hispanic   Native American   Asian/Pacific Islander

Percentage of firms

Source: Data from Office of Advocacy, U.S. Small Business Administration, "Minorities in Business," accessed June 23, 2010, http://www.sba.gov/advo.

Business ownership is also an important opportunity for America's racial and ethnic minorities. In recent years, the growth in the number of businesses owned by African Americans, Hispanics, and Asian Americans has far outpaced the growth in the number of U.S. businesses overall. Figure 5.4 shows the percentages of minority ownership in major industries. The relatively strong presence of minorities in the services and retail industries is especially significant because these industries contain the greatest number of businesses.

The Small Business Administration has programs targeted to minority-owned small businesses. One is the Mentor-Protégé Program, which pairs an established, financially healthy business with a small minority-owned business. Through the program, the protégé firm gains technical and financial assistance as well as subcontract support.[43]

Franchising

Franchising combines large and small businesses into a single entity, and is a major factor in the growth of small businesses. **Franchising** is a contractual business arrangement between a manufacturer or another supplier and a dealer such as a restaurant operator or a retailer. The contract specifies the methods by which the dealer markets the product of the supplier. Franchises can involve both goods and services, such as food and wait staff. The top ten franchises are shown in Table 5.3.

Starting a small, independent company can be a risky, time-consuming endeavor, but franchising can reduce the amount of time and effort needed to expand. The parent company has already developed and tested the concept, and the brand is often familiar to prospective customers.

Assessment Check ✓

1. What are the various ways the SBA helps small businesses?

2. What are business incubators?

3. Why are small businesses good opportunities for women and minorities?

franchising contractual business arrangement between a manufacturer or other supplier, and a dealer such as a restaurant operator or retailer

Table 5.3	Top Ten Franchises	
1 SUBWAY	**4** Hampton Inn/Hampton Inn & Suites	**7** Dunkin' Donuts
2 McDonald's	**5** Supercuts	**8** Jani-King
3 7-Eleven Inc.	**6** H & R Block	**9** Servpro
		10 ampm Mini Market

Source: "2010 Franchise 500 Top 10: Everything From Footlongs to Fill-ups," *Entrepreneur*, http://www.entrepreneur.com, accessed April 2, 2010.

The Franchising Sector

Franchised businesses are a huge part of the U.S. economy, accounting for nearly 50 percent of all retail sales. The International Franchise Association reported that franchising is responsible for 760,000 businesses, 18 million jobs, and more than $500 billion in payroll. Total sales by franchises continue to grow and approach $2 trillion. A new franchise is opened every eight minutes every business day.[44]

Franchising overseas is also a growing trend for businesses whose goal is to expand into foreign markets. It seems that anywhere you go in the world, you can get a McDonald's burger. But other international franchises are becoming more common. Baskin-Robbins, now owned by Dunkin' Brands, has more than 6,000 stores in more than 35 countries including Australia, Canada, China, Japan, Malaysia, and Russia. In Japan alone, there are more than 850 Baskin-Robbins ice cream stores. Baskin-Robbins holds the 13th rank of top U.S.-based franchises.[45]

International franchises are becoming more common. Baskin-Robbins has more than 6,000 stores in more than 35 countries including Australia, Canada, China, Japan, Vietnam, and Russia.

Jim Gensheimer/San Jose Mercury News/Krt/NewsCom

Franchising Agreements

The two principals in a franchising agreement are the franchisee and the franchisor. The individual or business firm purchasing the franchise is called the **franchisee.** This business owner agrees to sell the goods or services of the franchisor under certain terms. The **franchisor** is the firm whose products are sold by the franchisee. For example, McDonald's Corp. is a franchisor. Your local McDonald's restaurant owner is a franchisee.

Franchise agreements can be complex. They involve an initial purchase fee plus agreed-upon start-up costs. Because the franchisee is representing the franchisor's brand, the franchisor usually stipulates the purchase of certain ingredients or equipment, pricing, and marketing efforts. McDonald's is one of the more expensive franchises—total start-up costs

franchisee individual or business firm purchasing a franchise

franchisor firm whose products are sold to customers by the franchisee

can run more than $1 million. In contrast, the total start-up cost for a SUBWAY franchise may reach $228,000.[46] For this reason, businesspeople interested in purchasing a more expensive franchise often group together.

Benefits and Problems of Franchising

As with any other type of business arrangement, franchising has its benefits and drawbacks. Benefits for the franchisor include opportunities for expansion that might not otherwise be available. A franchised business can move into new geographic locations, including those overseas, at less expense and with the advantages of employing local workers and businesspeople who have intimate knowledge of consumer preferences. A good franchisor can manage a much larger and more complex business—with fewer direct employees—than could be handled without the franchise option. In most cases, franchisees will be highly attentive to the management of their franchises because of their stake as business owners. If the business is run efficiently, the franchisor will probably experience a greater return on investment than if the firm were run entirely as a company-owned chain of retail shops, restaurants, or service establishments.

Finally, a successful franchisor can usually negotiate better deals on ingredients, supplies, even real estate, because of its financial strength. This clout also benefits the franchisees if the savings are passed along to them.[47]

Franchising can be the quickest way to become a business owner. Some people contend that it's also the least risky. Franchisees have the benefit of name recognition—McDonald's, SUBWAY, Pizza Hut, and Super 8—that usually includes a loyal following of customers. The management system of the franchisor has already been established and a performance record is readily available. In addition, franchisors provide a wide range of support to franchisees, including financing, assistance in obtaining a location, business training, supplies, and marketing tools.[48]

Franchisees themselves say they are drawn to the idea of franchising because it combines the freedom of business ownership with the support of a large company. Like other small-business owners, franchisees want to make their own business decisions and determine their own work hours. And they want to have more control over the amount of wealth they can possibly accumulate, as opposed to what they might earn in a salaried job. In an economic slowdown, franchisees might very well be executives who have been laid off during a downsizing or reorganization effort by previous employers. These are highly trained and motivated businesspeople looking for a way to restart their careers.[49] Sometimes the ideas or successes of individual franchisees can benefit the entire company, as was the case with SUBWAY, described in the "Hit & Miss" feature.

Franchising can have its downside—for both franchisors and franchisees. For the franchisor, if its franchisees fail in any way, that failure reflects on the brand as well as the bottom line. The same holds true for the franchisee: a firm that is mismanaged at the top level can spell doom for the smaller business owners who are actually running the individual units. Krispy Kreme, mentioned earlier, is an example of a franchised company that stumbled due to overexpansion. When a firm initially decides to offer franchise opportunities, the company overall may lose money for several years. Of course, in offering franchise opportunities, the franchisor—often the founder of what was once a small business—loses absolute control over every aspect of the business. This uncertainty can make the process of selecting the right franchisees to carry out the company's mission a difficult one.[50]

Hit & Miss

One Small Franchise Produces One Big Idea

SUBWAY has enjoyed top franchise rankings consistently for more than a decade. With 30,000 sandwich restaurants in nearly 80 countries, the firm is poised to become the single largest fast-food chain in the world. But SUBWAY is made up of many small businesses—franchises—and sometimes what seems to be an insignificant idea on the part of one franchisee can change the shape of the entire organization.

Stuart Frankel is one such franchisee, and his idea was simple: on weekends, charge a special price of $5 for a footlong SUBWAY sandwich. Since this was a price decrease of about $1 per sandwich, it took awhile for Frankel and two other local Florida SUBWAY franchisees to convince corporate leadership that the idea was a good one. The economy was sluggish, food costs had crept upward, and SUBWAY shops were virtually empty because consumers were eating at home instead of dining out. Frankel's employees stood idle at their stations as sandwich sales declined. But after pressing hard, Frankel got the OK from corporate headquarters. From there, a chain reaction began.

"I like round numbers," quipped Frankel about the $5 price. SUBWAY customers liked the number too. As soon as the special pricing was announced, they returned in droves. Sales increased by double digits. Employees made sandwiches as fast as their fingers could fly. Meanwhile, SUBWAY's corporate marketing team pushed the $5 promotion nationwide—franchises from New York to New Orleans began offering $5 footlongs. When the initial four-week time span for the promotion was up, marketing executives extended it to seven weeks. When that time lapsed, they decided to extend it indefinitely but with a limited number of sandwich variations.

Something else happened. Demand for the $5 footlongs was so great that franchise owners began to experience shortages of certain ingredients. They couldn't get enough bread, turkey, ham, or tuna. One franchisee recalls being in a panic. "The whole thing took on a life of its own," notes Jeff Moody, CEO of SUBWAY's advertising arm.

With one motion, Stuart Frankel struck a chord with consumers who were looking for ways to enjoy themselves and stretch each dollar at the same time. "There are only a few times when a chain has been able to scramble up the whole industry, and this is one of them," notes restaurant consultant Jeffrey T. Davis. "It's huge." Sometimes a small idea is really big.

Questions for Critical Thinking

1. Why do you think Stuart Frankel's idea was so successful with consumers? Would it have been as successful during different economic circumstances? Why or why not?

2. A franchise company is only as good as its franchisees. And a franchisee's success is based in part on the decisions and support of corporate leadership. If the $5 footlong promotion had failed, how do you think the outcome would have affected Frankel's franchise business? How might it have affected SUBWAY?

Sources: "Subway Brand Ranked Number One Provider of Healthy Options in Zagat Survey," http://www.subway.com, accessed April 2, 2010; "Subway Restaurants Again Named #1 Worldwide Franchise Opportunity for 2009," http://www.subway.com, accessed April 2, 2010; Matthew Boyle, "The Accidental Hero," *BusinessWeek*, November 10, 2009, http://www.businessweek.com.

The franchisee faces an outlay of cash in the form of an initial investment, franchise fees, supplies, maintenance, leases, and the like. The most expensive franchises generally are those that involve hotels and resorts, which can run in the millions.[51] Start-up costs for McDonald's restaurants can also top several million, depending on the location. For this reason, it is not unusual for groups of businesspeople to purchase a franchise (or several franchise locations).[52] Payments to the franchisor can add to the burden of keeping the business afloat until the owner begins to earn a profit. Choosing a low-cost start up such as Guard-a-Kid may be a good alternative option. Guard-a-Kid is the largest child-identity franchise in the nation. It offers franchisees a complete start-up kit, including two days of training and supplies ranging from a laptop computer and digital camera to logo T-shirts and personalized business cards for a fee of $10,000 to $20,000 depending on territory size.[53] But it's important for potential franchisees to evaluate carefully how much profit they can make once their cost obligations are met.

Because franchises are so closely linked to their brand, franchisors and franchisees must work well together to maintain standards of quality in their goods and services. If customers are unhappy with their experience at one franchise location, they might avoid stopping at another one several miles away, even if the second one is owned and operated by someone else. This is especially true where food is involved. The discovery of tainted meat or produce at one franchise restaurant can cause panic to spread throughout the entire chain. A potential franchisee would be wise to thoroughly research the financial performance and reputation of the franchisor, using resources such as other franchisees, the Better Business Bureau, and the Federal Trade Commission.

Some franchisees have found the franchising agreement to be too confining. As the saying goes, you can't add a tuna salad sandwich to the menu at McDonald's no matter how many stores you own. The agreements are usually fairly strict, and that generally helps to maintain the integrity of the brand. Toward this end, some franchise companies control promotional activities, select the site location, or even become involved in hiring decisions. But these activities may seem overly restrictive to some franchisees, especially those seeking independence and autonomy.

Restrictions can also cost franchisees more than they feel is fair. Recently, the National Franchise Association, a group that represents more than 80 percent of Burger King's U.S. franchisees, sued the hamburger company for forcing its members to offer consumers a $1 double cheeseburger on its menu, complying with the company's promotional efforts. While the $1 burger offering may seem like a great way to attract and serve hungry consumers, BK franchisees claim that the promotion has cost them a loss of at least 10 cents per burger. In other words, it costs most franchises $1.10 to make and serve a cheeseburger for which they must charge $1.[54]

Assessment Check ✔

1. What is the difference between a franchisor and a franchisee?
2. What are the benefits to both parties of franchising?
3. What are the potential drawbacks of franchising for both parties?

Forms of Private Business Ownership

Regardless of its size, every business is organized according to one of three categories of legal structure: sole proprietorship, partnership, or corporation. As Figure 5.5 shows, sole proprietorships are the most common form of business ownership, accounting for more than 70 percent of all firms in the United States. Although far fewer firms are organized as corporations, the revenues earned by these companies are 19 times greater than those earned by sole proprietorships.

Each legal structure offers unique advantages and disadvantages. But because there is no universal formula for every situation, some business owners prefer to organize their companies further as S corporations, limited-liability partnerships, and limited-liability companies. In some cases, corporations are owned by their employees.

In addition to the three main legal structures, several other options for ownership exist. These include employee-owned businesses, family-owned businesses and not-for-profit organizations.

Sole Proprietorships

sole proprietorship business ownership in which there is no legal distinction between the sole proprietor's status as an individual and his or her status as a business owner

The most common form of business ownership, the **sole proprietorship** is also the oldest and the simplest. In a sole proprietorship, no legal distinction separates the sole proprietor's status as an individual from his or her status as a business owner. Although sole proprietorships are common in a variety of industries, they are concentrated primarily among small businesses such as repair shops, small retail stores, and service providers such as plumbers, hair stylists, and photographers.

Sole proprietorships offer some unique advantages. Because such businesses involve a single owner, they are easy to form *and* dissolve. A sole proprietorship gives the owner maximum management flexibility, along with the right to all profits after payment of business-related bills and taxes. A highly motivated owner of a sole proprietorship directly reaps the benefits of his or her hard work.

Minimal legal requirements simplify entering and exiting a sole proprietorship. The owner registers the business or trade name—to guarantee that two firms do not use the same name—and takes out any necessary licenses. Local governments require certain licenses for businesses such as restaurants, motels or hotels, and retail stores. In addition, some occupational licenses require business owners to obtain specific insurance such as liability coverage.

Sole proprietorships are also easy to dissolve. This advantage is particularly important to temporary or seasonal businesses that set up for a limited period of time. It's also helpful if the owner needs or wants to close the business for any reason—say, to relocate or to accept a full-time position with a larger firm.

Management flexibility is another advantage of a sole proprietorship. The owner can make decisions without reporting to a manager, take quick action, and keep trade secrets. A sole proprietorship always bears the individual "stamp" or flair of its owner, whether it's a certain way of styling hair or the way a store window is decorated.

The greatest disadvantage of the sole proprietorship is the owner's personal financial liability for all debts of the business. Also, the business must operate with financial resources limited to the owner's personal funds and money that he or she can borrow. Such financing limitations can keep the business from expanding.

Another disadvantage is that the owner must wear many hats, handling a wide range of management and operational responsibilities. He or she may not have expertise in every area, which may inhibit the firm's growth or even cause the firm damage. In addition, sole proprietors may face a higher chance of being audited by the Internal Revenue Service than other types of business owners. Finally, a sole proprietorship usually lacks long-term continuity, because a change in personal circumstances or finances can terminate the business on short notice.

FIGURE 5.5 Forms of Business Ownership

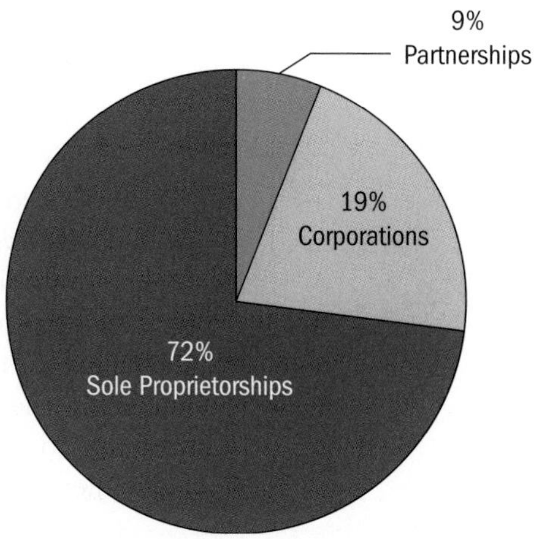

- 9% Partnerships
- 19% Corporations
- 72% Sole Proprietorships

Source: Data from U.S. Census Bureau, "Statistical Abstract," accessed June 23, 2010, http://www.census.gov.

Partnerships

Another option for organizing a business is to form a partnership. The Uniform Partnership Act, which regulates this ownership form in most states, defines a **partnership** as an association of two or more persons who operate a business as co-owners by voluntary legal agreement. Many small businesses begin as partnerships between co-founders.

Partnerships are easy to form. All the partners need to do is register the business name and obtain any necessary licenses. Having a partner generally means greater financial capability and someone to share in the tasks and decision making of a business. It's even better if one partner has a particular skill such as design, while the other has a knack for financials.

Most partnerships have the disadvantage of being exposed to unlimited financial liability. Each partner bears full responsibility for the debts of the firm, and each is legally liable

partnership association of two or more persons who operate a business as co-owners by voluntary legal agreement

for the actions of the other partners. If the firm fails and is left with debt—no matter who is at fault—every partner is responsible for those debts. If one partner defaults, the others are responsible for the firm's debts, even if it means dipping into personal funds. To avoid these problems, many firms establish a limited-liability partnership, which limits the liability of partners to the value of their interests in the company.

Breaking up a partnership is more complicated than dissolving a sole proprietorship. Rather than simply withdrawing funds from the bank, the partner who wants out may need to find someone to buy his or her interest in the firm. The death of a partner also threatens the survival of a partnership. A new partnership must be formed, and the estate of the deceased is entitled to a share of the firm's value. To ease the financial strains of such events, business planners recommend life insurance coverage for each partner, combined with a buy-sell agreement. The insurance proceeds can be used to repay the deceased partner's heirs and allow the surviving partner to retain control of the business. Because partnerships are vulnerable to personal conflicts that can quickly escalate, it's important for partners to choose each other carefully—not just because they are best friends—and try to plan for the future.

Corporations

A **corporation** is a legal organization with assets and liabilities separate from those of its owner(s). A corporation can be a large or small business. It can be Ford Motor Corp. or a local auto repair shop.

Corporate ownership offers considerable advantages. Because a corporation is a separate legal entity, its stockholders have only limited financial risk. If the firm fails, they lose only the money they have invested. This applies to the firm's managers and executives as well. Because they are not the sole proprietors or partners in the business, their personal savings are not at risk if the company folds or goes bankrupt. This protection also extends to legal risk. Class-action suits involving automakers, drug manufacturers, and food producers are filed against the companies, not the owners of those companies. Though companies such as T-Mobile and GE recently experienced class-action suits, their employees and stockholders were not required to pay the settlements from their own bank accounts.[55]

Corporations offer other advantages. They gain access to expanded financial capabilities based on the opportunity to offer direct outside investments such as stock sales. A large corporation can legally generate internal financing for many projects by transferring money from one part of the corporation to another.

One major disadvantage for a corporation is the double taxation of corporate earnings. After a corporation pays federal, state, and local income taxes on its profits, its owners (stockholders) also pay personal taxes on any distributions of those profits they receive from the corporation in the form of dividends.

S Corporations and Limited Liability Corporations

To avoid double taxation of business income while minimizing financial liability for their owners, many smaller firms (those with fewer than 100 stockholders) organize as **S corporations.** These companies can elect to pay federal income taxes as partnerships while retaining the liability limitations typical of corporations. S corporations are only taxed once. Unlike regular corporations, S corporations do not pay corporate taxes on their profits. Instead, the untaxed profits of S corporations are paid directly as dividends to shareholders, who then pay the individual tax rate. This tax advantage has resulted in a tremendous increase in the number of S corporations. Consequently, the IRS is closely auditing S corporations because some businesses don't meet the legal requirements to form S corporations.[56]

corporation legal organization with assets and liabilities separate from those of its owner(s)

S corporations corporations that do not pay corporate taxes on profits; instead, profits are distributed to shareholders, who pay individual income taxes

Business owners may also form **limited-liability companies (LLCs)** to secure the corporate advantage of limited liability while avoiding the double taxation characteristic of corporations. An LLC combines the pass-through taxation of a partnership or sole proprietorship with the limited liability of a corporation.

An LLC is governed by an operating agreement that resembles a partnership agreement, except that it reduces each partner's liability for the actions of the other owners. Corporations of professionals, such as lawyers, accountants, and physicians, use a similar approach, with the letters *PC* attached to the business name. LLCs appear to be the wave of the future. Immediately after the first LLC law was passed, most major CPA (certified public accountant) firms in the U.S. converted to LLC status. Today you'll see the LLC or PC designation attached to small businesses ranging from bowling alleys to veterinary hospitals. On a much larger scale, Amazon.com is also an LLC.

limited-liability corporation (LLC) corporation that secures the corporate advantage of limited liability while avoiding the double taxation characteristic of a traditional corporation

Employee-Owned Corporations

Another alternative for creating a corporation is **employee ownership**, in which workers buy shares of stock in the company that employs them. The corporate organization stays the same, but most stockholders are also employees.

employee ownership business ownership in which workers buy shares of stock in the company that employs them

The popularity of this form of corporation is growing. The number of employee ownership plans has increased dramatically. Today about 20 percent of all employees of for-profit companies report owning stock in their companies; approximately 25 million Americans own employer stock through *employee stock ownership plans (ESOPs)*, options, stock purchase plans, 401(k) plans, and other plans.

Several trends underlie the rise in employee ownership. One is that employees want to share in whatever profit their company earns. Another is that company executives want employees to care deeply about their firm's success and contribute their best effort. These firms remain committed to this kind of involvement and compensation for their workers. Because human resources are so essential to the success of a modern business, employers want to build their employees' commitment to the organization. However, managers also admit that often employees below the executive level are not as informed about the programs as they should be, and their companies could do a better job of educating employees at all levels.[57] Some of the country's most successful public corporations, including Procter & Gamble, Lowe's, and Southwest Airlines, have embraced employee ownership and watched their stock values hold up better than other companies.

Family-Owned Businesses

Family-owned firms are considered by many to be the backbone of American business. The Waltons and the Fords are viewed as pioneers because each of these firms—Walmart and Ford Motor Corp.—was once a small, family-owned company. Family-owned firms come in a variety of sizes and legal structures. But because of the complex nature of family relationships, family-owned firms experience some unique challenges.

Whether a family-owned business is structured as a partnership, limited liability corporation, or traditional corporation, its members must make decisions regarding succession, marriages and divorces, compensation, hierarchy and authority, shareholder control, and the like. Whereas some family members may prefer a loose structure—perhaps not even putting certain agreements in writing—experienced businesspeople caution that failing to choose the right legal structure for a family-owned firm can doom the business from the start.

Family-owned companies are considered by many to be the backbone of American business. Walmart's Walton family started with Walton's Five and Dime store.

"For family-owned businesses, especially those with multi-generational owners, lack of a formal structure is a frequent cause of turmoil and legal disputes which often result in very contentious litigation and, ultimately, the dissolution of the business," asserts one expert in family businesses.[58]

Succession is a major benefit—and drawback—to family-owned firms. On the one hand, a clearly documented plan for succession from one generation to the next is a huge source of security for the firm's continuity. But lack of legal planning, or situations in which succession is challenged, can cause chaos. In fact, only a small percentage of family-owned businesses survive into the second or even third generation.

A small family firm that has managed to thrive for five generations is Squamscott Beverages. Originally called Connermade, the company was founded in 1883 when William H. Conner began producing his own "tonic" beverage—a spruce beer that came in glass bottles with porcelain and wire stoppers. Conner ran the company until his son Alfred took over in 1911. Alfred remained in charge until 1948, when he handed the reins to his own son, Alfred Jr. Today, Tom Conner and his son Dan manage most aspects of running the firm, which is still headquartered on the family's rural property. Squamscott Beverages produces soda drinks in a variety of flavors, including birch beer, cola, cream, orange, grape, and ginger ale. Bottles are distributed to small grocery outlets, or customers can visit the bottling plant to select whatever flavors they want. Recently the company sent its first shipment of soda to California and is considering further expanding its distribution. "We have made it through the Great Depression," notes Dan Conner. "We made it through the early '80s housing crunch. We're always going to be here."[59] The Conners are not as famous or as wealthy as the Waltons or Fords, but the chance of their business surviving through future generations is strong.

Not-for-Profit Corporations

not-for-profit corporation organization whose goals do not include pursuing a profit

The same business concepts that apply to commercial companies also apply to **not-for-profit corporations**—organizations whose goals do not include pursuing a profit. About 1.5 million not-for-profits operate in the United States, including charitable groups, social-welfare organizations, government agencies, and religious congregations. This sector also includes museums, libraries, hospitals, conservation groups, private schools, and the like.

Most states set out separate legal provisions for organizational structures and operations of not-for-profit corporations. These organizations do not issue stock certificates, because they pay no dividends to owners, and ownership rarely changes. They are also exempt from paying income taxes. However, they must meet very strict regulations in order to maintain their not-for-profit status.

City Year Inc. is a not-for-profit organization that supports community service efforts by young people in their late teens and early twenties. City Year has a number of programs in which volunteers can participate. Its signature program, the City Year Youth Corps, invites 1,500 volunteers between the ages of 17 and 24 to commit to a year of full-time community service in activities such as mentoring and tutoring inner-city school children, helping to restore and reclaim public spaces, and staffing youth summer camps. The organization also partners with for-profit corporations such as Timberland, Comcast, and Pepsi to fund and implement its efforts.[60]

Public and Collective Ownership of Business

Assessment Check ✔

1. What are the key differences between sole proprietorships and partnerships?
2. What is a corporation?
3. What is the main distinction of a not-for-profit corporation?

Though most businesses in the U.S. are owned by the private sector, some firms are actually owned by local, state, or the federal government. Alaskan Railroad Corp., East Alabama Medical Center, and the Iowa Lottery are all government-owned businesses.[61]

In another type of ownership structure, groups of customers may collectively own a company. Recreational Equipment Inc. (REI) is a collectively owned retailer that sells outdoor gear and apparel. Finally, groups of smaller firms may collectively own a larger organization. Both of these collective ownership structures are also referred to as cooperatives.

Public (Government) Ownership

One alternative to private ownership is some form of *public ownership*, in which a unit or agency of government owns and operates an organization. In the United States, local governments often own parking structures and water systems. The Pennsylvania Turnpike Authority operates a vital highway link across the Keystone State. The federal government operates Hoover Dam in Nevada to provide electricity over a large region.

Sometimes public ownership results when private investors are unwilling to invest in a high-risk project—or find that operating an important service is simply unprofitable. The National Railroad Passenger Corporation—better known as Amtrak—is a for-profit corporation that operates inter-city passenger rail service in 46 states and the District of Columbia. Congress created Amtrak in the Rail Passenger Service Act of 1970, thereby removing from private railroads the obligation of transporting passengers, because passenger rail travel was generally unprofitable. In exchange, the private railroads granted Amtrak access to their existing tracks at a low cost. The Amtrak board of directors is made up of seven voting members appointed for five-year terms by the President of the United States.[62]

Collective (Cooperative) Ownership

Collective ownership establishes an organization referred to as a *cooperative* (or *co-op*), whose owners join forces to operate all or part of the activities in their firm or industry. Currently, there are about 100 million people worldwide employed by cooperatives.[63] Cooperatives allow small businesses to pool their resources on purchases, marketing, equipment, distribution, and the like. Discount savings can be split among members. Cooperatives can share equipment and expertise. During difficult economic times, members find a variety of ways to support each other.

Cooperatives are frequently found among agricultural businesses. Cabot Creamery is a cooperative of 1,500 small dairy farms spread throughout New England and upstate New York. Cabot is owned and operated by its members—farmers and their families. In addition, Cabot works with other cooperatives around the country to produce and distribute high-quality cheese, butter, and other dairy products.[64]

Assessment Check ✔

1. What is public ownership?
2. What is collective ownership? Where are cooperatives typically found, and what benefits do they provide small businesses?

Organizing a Corporation

A corporation is a legal structure, but it also requires a certain organizational structure that is more complex than the structure of a sole proprietorship or a partnership. This is why people often think of a corporation as a large entity, even though it does not have to be a specific size.

Types of Corporations

Corporations fall into three categories: domestic, foreign, and alien. A firm is considered a *domestic corporation* in the state where it is incorporated. When a company does business in states other than the one where it has filed incorporation papers, it is registered as a *foreign corporation* in each of those states. A firm incorporated in one nation that operates in another is known as an *alien corporation* where it operates. Some firms—particularly large corporations with operations scattered around the world—may operate under all three of these designations.

Where and How Businesses Incorporate

Businesses owners who want to incorporate must decide where to locate their headquarters and follow the correct procedure for submitting the legal document that establishes the corporation.

Where to Incorporate Deciding where to incorporate—and establish headquarters—may be based on a number of factors. Most businesses want to be near their customers. Real estate prices as well as services such as public transportation and communications networks are other variables. Access to a good labor pool is another reason for choosing a location. Online businesses such as Amazon.com and eBay don't need to worry about positioning themselves near their customers, but they should consider the local labor pool.

Although most small- and medium-sized businesses are incorporated in the states in which they operate, a U.S. firm can actually incorporate in any state it chooses. The founders of large corporations, or of those that will do business nationwide, often compare the benefits—such as tax incentives—provided by each state. Some states are considered to be more "business friendly" than others. Delaware is one of the easiest states in which to incorporate.

The Corporate Charter Each state has a specific procedure for incorporating a business. Most states require at least three *incorporators*—the individuals who create the corporation. In addition, the new corporation must select a name that is different from names used by other businesses. Figure 5.6 lists the ten elements that most states require for chartering a corporation.

The information provided in the articles of incorporation forms the basis on which a state grants a *corporate charter*, which is the legal document that formally establishes a corporation. After

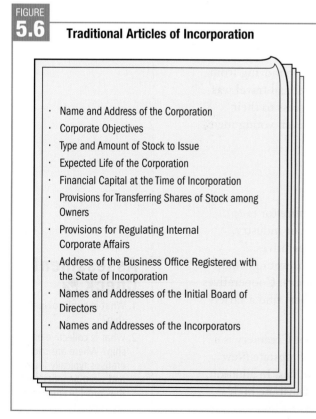

FIGURE 5.6

Traditional Articles of Incorporation

- Name and Address of the Corporation
- Corporate Objectives
- Type and Amount of Stock to Issue
- Expected Life of the Corporation
- Financial Capital at the Time of Incorporation
- Provisions for Transferring Shares of Stock among Owners
- Provisions for Regulating Internal Corporate Affairs
- Address of the Business Office Registered with the State of Incorporation
- Names and Addresses of the Initial Board of Directors
- Names and Addresses of the Incorporators

securing the charter, the owners prepare the company's bylaws, which describe the rules and procedures for its operation.

Corporate Management

Regardless of its size, every corporation has levels of management and ownership. Figure 5.7 illustrates those that are typical—although a smaller firm might not contain all five of these. These levels range from stockholders down to supervisory management.

Stock Ownership and Stockholder Rights At the top of Figure 5.7 are **stockholders**. They buy shares of stock in the corporation, becoming part owners of it. Some companies, such as family businesses, are owned by relatively few stockholders, and the stock is generally unavailable to outsiders. In such a firm, known as a *closed* or *closely held corporation*, the stockholders also control and manage all of the company's activities. S.C. Johnson & Son is one such firm.

In contrast, an open corporation, also called a *publicly held corporation*, sells stock to the general public, establishing diversified ownership and often leading to a broader scope of operations than those of a closed corporation. Publicly held corporations usually hold annual stockholders' meetings. During these meetings, managers report on corporate activities, and stockholders vote on any decisions that require their approval, including elections of officers. Walmart holds the nation's largest stockholder meeting at the University of Arkansas Bud Walton Arena. Approximately 16,000 people attend. In addition to standard shareholder business, the Walmart meeting has featured celebrities and entertainers such as Tim McGraw, Mary J. Blige, and Jamie Foxx.

Stockholders' role in the corporation depends on the class of stock they own. Shares are usually classified as common or preferred stock. Although owners of **preferred stock** have limited voting rights, they are entitled to receive dividends before holders of common stock. If the corporation is dissolved, they have first claims on assets, once debtors are repaid. Owners of **common stock** have voting rights but only residual claims on the firm's assets, which means they are last to receive any income distributions. Because one share is typically worth only one vote, small stockholders generally have little influence on corporate management actions.

Board of Directors Stockholders elect a **board of directors**—the governing body of a corporation. The board sets overall policy, authorizes major transactions involving the corporation, and hires the chief executive officer (CEO). Most boards include both inside directors (corporate executives) and outside directors—people who are not otherwise employed by the organization. Sometimes the corporation's top executive also chairs the board. Generally, outside directors are also stockholders, so they have a financial stake in the company's performance.

Corporate Officers and Managers The CEO and other members of top management, such as the chief operating officer (COO), chief financial officer (CFO), and the chief information officer (CIO) make most major corporate decisions. Managers at the next level down the hierarchy, middle management, handle the ongoing operational

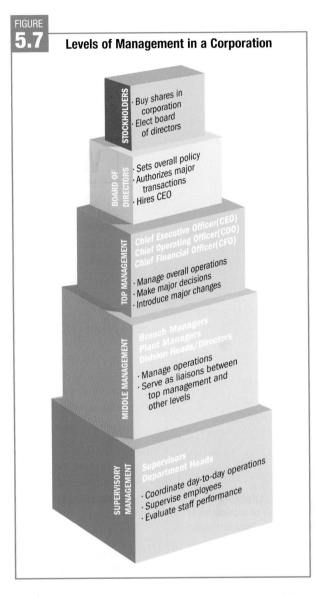

FIGURE
5.7 **Levels of Management in a Corporation**

STOCKHOLDERS
· Buy shares in corporation
· Elect board of directors

BOARD OF DIRECTORS
· Sets overall policy
· Authorizes major transactions
· Hires CEO

TOP MANAGEMENT
Chief Executive Officer (CEO)
Chief Operating Officer (COO)
Chief Financial Officer (CFO)
· Manage overall operations
· Make major decisions
· Introduce major changes

MIDDLE MANAGEMENT
Branch Managers
Plant Managers
Division Heads/Directors
· Manage operations
· Serve as liaisons between top management and other levels

SUPERVISORY MANAGEMENT
Supervisors
Department Heads
· Coordinate day-to-day operations
· Supervise employees
· Evaluate staff performance

stockholders owners of a corporation due to their purchase of stock in the corporation

preferred stock shares that give owners limited voting rights, and the right to receive dividends or assets before owners of common stock

common stock shares that give owners voting rights but only residual claims to the firm's assets and income distributions

board of directors governing body of a corporation

1. What are the two key
elements of the incorpo-
ration process?

2. Identify the five main
levels of corporate own-
ership and management.

functions of the company. At the first tier of management, supervisory personnel coordinate day-to-day operations, assign specific tasks to employees, and evaluate job performance.

Today's CEOs and CFOs are bound by stricter regulations than in the past. They must verify in writing the accuracy of their firm's financial statements, and the process for nominating candidates for the board has become more complex. In short, more checks and balances are in place for the governance of corporations.

When Businesses Join Forces

Today's business environment contains many complex relationships among businesses as well as not-for-profit organizations. Two firms may team up to develop a product or co-market products. One company may buy out another. Large corporations may split into smaller units. The list of alliances is a varied as the organizations themselves, but the major trends in corporate ownership include mergers and acquisitions and joint ventures.

Mergers and Acquisitions (M&A)

In recent years, mergers and acquisitions among U.S. corporations have hit an all-time high. Airlines, financial institutions, telecommunications companies, and media corporations are just a few of the types of businesses that have merged into giants. Recently, Comcast announced its intention to buy a majority stake in NBC Universal from General Electric for $13.75 billion, which would give the nation's largest cable company 51 percent control of the TV network as well as lucrative cable channels and a major movie studio.[65]

merger agreement in which two or more firms combine to form one company

acquisition agreement in which one firm purchases another

vertical merger merger that combines firms operating at different levels in the production and marketing process

The terms *merger* and *acquisition* are often used interchangeably, but their meanings are different. In a **merger**, two or more firms combine to form one company. In an **acquisition**, one firm purchases the other. This means that not only does the buyer acquire the firm's property and assets, it also takes on any debt obligations. Acquisitions also occur when one firm buys a division or subsidiary from another firm. HP acquired Compaq a number of years ago, letting the brand languish except in Asia, where it was always popular. But as U.S. consumers have recently become more focused on price, HP has made a move to revitalize its Compaq unit—offering a full-size Compaq laptop with all the bells and whistles, at a low price of $399. HP is now betting that its original investment in Compaq will pay off.[66]

Mergers can be classified as vertical, horizontal, or conglomerate. A **vertical merger** combines firms operating at different levels in the production and marketing process—the combination of a manufacturer and a large retailer, for instance. A vertical merger pursues one of two primary goals: (1) to ensure adequate flows of raw materials and supplies needed for a firm's products or (2) to increase distribution. Software giant Microsoft is well known for acquiring small firms that have developed products with strong market potential, such as Teleo, a provider of voice over Internet protocol (VoIP) software and services that can be used to make phone calls via the Internet.

horizontal merger merger that joins firms in the same industry for the purpose of diversification, increasing customer bases, cutting costs, or expanding product lines.

A **horizontal merger** joins firms in the same industry. This is done for the purpose of diversification, increasing customer bases, cutting costs, or expanding product lines. This type of merger is particularly popular in the auto industry. India-base Tata Motors bought the Jaguar and Land Rover brands from Ford Motor Corp. Volkswagen owns Audi and Porsche.

A <u>conglomerate merger</u> combines unrelated firms. The most common reasons for a conglomerate merger are to diversify, spur sales growth, or spend a cash surplus that might otherwise make the firm a tempting target for a takeover effort. Conglomerate mergers may join firms in totally unrelated industries. General Electric is, in fact, well known for its conglomerate mergers—including its ownership of healthcare services and household appliances. Experts debate whether conglomerate mergers are beneficial. The usual argument in favor of such mergers is that a company can use its management expertise to succeed in a variety of industries. But the obvious drawback is that a huge conglomerate can spread its resources too thin to be dominant in any one market.

Joint Ventures: Specialized Partnerships

A <u>joint venture</u> is a partnership between companies formed for a specific undertaking. Sometimes a company enters into a joint venture with a local firm, sharing the operation's costs, risks, management, and profits with its local partner. This is particularly common when a firm wants to enter into business in a foreign market. A joint venture also may enable companies to solve a mutual problem.

Joint ventures between for-profit firms and not-for-profit organizations are becoming more and more common. These partnerships provide great benefits for both parties. Not-for-profit organizations receive the funding, marketing exposure, and sometimes manpower they might not otherwise generate. City Year, mentioned earlier, enjoys these benefits from partnerships with Timberland, Pepsi, and Comcast along with other firms such as Starbucks and MSNBC. Recently, Starbucks partnered with MSNBC to publicize a program of community involvement called Brewing Together a Day of Service, in which Starbucks employees participated in shorter-term City Year projects.[67]

Joint ventures between not-for profits and for-profit firms often benefit the businesses as well. This is particularly true in the area of environmental conservation and sustainability, where costs can be cut, energy saved, and waste reduced. In a partnership with the Environmental Defense Fund, McDonald's has succeeded in phasing out toxic packaging; converting much of its cooking oil to biodiesel; eliminating more than 300 million pounds of packaging; and reducing restaurant waste by more than 30 percent.[68]

What's Ahead

The next chapter focuses on the driving forces behind the formation of new businesses: entrepreneurs. It examines the differences between a small-business owner and an entrepreneur and identifies certain personality traits typical of entrepreneurs. The chapter also details the process of launching a new venture, including identifying opportunities, locating needed financing, and turning good ideas into successful businesses. Finally, the chapter explores a method for infusing the entrepreneurial spirit into established businesses—intrapreneurship.

conglomerate merger merger that combines unrelated firms, usually with the goal of diversification, spurring sales growth, or spending a cash surplus in order to avoid a takeover attempt

joint venture partnership between companies formed for a specific undertaking

Assessment Check ☑

1. Distinguish between a merger and an acquisition.
2. What are the different kinds of mergers?
3. What is a joint venture?

Cheryl Gerber/MSNBC/NBCUPB/ ©AP/Wide World Photos

Joint ventures between for-profit firms and not-for-profit organizations provide great benefits for both parties. Starbucks partnered with MSNBC to publicize a program of community involvement called Brewing Together Day of Service, in which Starbucks employees participated in shorter-term City Year (a not-for-profit organization) projects.

Summary of Learning Objectives

[1] **Distinguish between small and large businesses.**

A small business is an independently owned business having fewer than 500 employees. Generally it is not dominant in its field and meets industry-specific size standards for income or number of employees. A business is classified as large when it exceeds these specifications.

Assessment Check Answers ✓

1.1 How does the Small Business Administration (SBA) define *small business?* A small business is defined as an independent business having fewer than 500 employees. However, those bidding for government contracts or applying for government assistance may vary in size according to industry.

1.2 In what industries do small businesses play a significant role? Small businesses provide most jobs in construction, agriculture, wholesale trade, services, and retail trade. In addition, home-based businesses make up 52 percent of small businesses in the U.S.

[2] **Discuss the contributions of small businesses to the economy.**

Small businesses create new jobs and new industries. They often hire workers who traditionally have had difficulty finding employment at larger firms. Small firms give people the opportunity and outlet for developing new ideas, which can turn into entirely new industries. Small businesses also develop new and improved goods and services.

Assessment Check Answers ✓

2.1 What are the three key ways in which small businesses contribute to the economy? Small businesses create new jobs, new industries, and provide innovation.

2.2 How are new industries formed? New industries are formed when small businesses adapt to shifts in consumer interests and preferences. Innovation and new technology can play a significant role. In addition, new industries may be created when both the business world and consumers recognize a need for change.

[3] **Discuss the survival rate of small businesses.**

About seven of every ten new (small) businesses survive at least two years. But by the tenth year, 82 percent have closed. Failure is often attributed to management shortcomings, inadequate financing, and difficulty meeting government regulations.

Assessment Check Answers ✓

3.1 What percentage of small businesses remain in operation five years after starting? Ten years? About 50 percent are in business after five years; about 82 percent have folded by the ten year mark.

3.2 What are the three main causes of small-business failure? The three main causes of small-business failure are management shortcomings, inadequate financing, and difficulty complying with government regulations.

[4] **Describe the features of an effective business plan.**

A complete business plan contains an executive summary, an introduction, financial and marketing sections, and resumes of the business principals. Within this structure, an effective business plan includes the company's mission, an outline of what makes the company unique, identification of customers and competitors, financial evaluation of the industry and market, and an assessment of the risks.

Assessment Check Answers ✓

4.1 What are the five main sections of a business plan? The five sections are the executive summary, introduction, financial section, marketing section, and resumes of principals.

4.2 Why is an effective business plan important to the success of a firm? The business plan puts in writing all the reasons the firm can be successful. It contains the written soul of the firm. It is the document that secures financing and creates a framework for the organization.

[5] **Describe funding opportunities for small businesses, including the role of the Small Business Administration (SBA).**

The SBA guarantees loans made by private lenders, including microloans and those funded by Small Business Investment Companies. It offers training and information resources, so business owners can improve their odds of success. The SBA also advocates small-business interests within the federal government and provides specific support for businesses owned by women and minorities. State and local governments also have programs designed to help small businesses get established and grow. Venture capitalists are firms that invest in small businesses in return for an ownership stake.

Assessment Check Answers ✓

5.1 What are the various ways the SBA helps small businesses? The SBA guarantees business loans; helps small businesses compete for government set-aside programs; and provides business information, advice, and training to owners of small businesses.

5.2 What are business incubators? Business incubators are programs organized by community agencies that provide such services as rental space, clerical staff, and office equipment in an effort to help small businesses get started.

5.3 Why are small businesses good opportunities for women and minorities? Women feel they can achieve more as small-business owners and can balance family and work more easily if they own their own firms. Minority business owners can receive special assistance from programs like the Mentor-Protégé program provided by the SBA.

⌐6⌐ **Explain how franchising can provide opportunities for both franchisors and franchisees.**

A franchisor is a large firm that permits a small-business owner (franchisee) to market and sell its products under its brand name, in return for a fee. Benefits to the franchisor include opportunities for expansion and greater profits. Benefits to the franchisee include name recognition, quick start-up, support from the franchisor, and the freedom of small-business ownership.

Assessment Check Answers ✅

6.1 What is the difference between a franchisor and a franchisee? A franchisor permits a small-business owner (franchisee) to market and sell its products under its brand name, in return for a fee.

6.2 What are the benefits to both parties of franchising? Benefits to the franchisor include opportunities for expansion and greater profits. Benefits to the franchisee include name recognition, quick start-up, support from the franchisor, and the freedom of small-business ownership.

6.3 What are the potential drawbacks of franchising for both parties? The drawbacks for the franchisor include mismanagement and failure on the part of any of its franchisees, overexpansion, and loss of absolute control over the business. Drawbacks for the franchisee include an initial outlay of expenses, problems due to failure on the part of the franchisor or other franchisees; and restrictive franchise agreements.

⌐7⌐ **Outline the three legal forms of business ownership, and summarize the features of businesses owned by employees and families, as well as not-for-profit organizations.**

A sole proprietorship is owned and operated by one person. While sole proprietorships are easy to set up and offer great operating flexibility, the owner remains personally liable for all of the firm's debts and legal settlements. In a partnership, two or more individuals share responsibility for owning and running the business. Partnerships are relatively easy to set up, but they do not offer protection from liability. When a business is set up as a corporation, it becomes a separate legal entity. Investors receive shares of stock in the firm. Owners have no legal and financial liability beyond their individual investments. In an employee-owned business, most stockholders are also employees. Family-owned businesses may be structured legally in any of these three ways but face unique challenges, including succession and complex relationships. The legal structure of a not-for-profit corporation stipulates that its goals do not include earning a profit.

Assessment Check Answers ✅

7.1 What are the key differences among sole proprietorships and partnerships? Sole proprietorships and partnerships expose their owners to unlimited financial liability from their businesses. Sole proprietorships are more flexible and easier to dissolve than partnerships. Partnerships involve shared work load and decision making, whereas sole proprietorships are entirely the responsibility of one business owner.

7.2 What is a corporation? A corporation is a legal organization with assets and liabilities separate from those of its owners. A corporation can be a large or small business.

7.3 What is the main distinction of a not-for-profit corporation? A not-for-profit organization is set up legally so that its goals do not include pursuing a profit. Most states set out specific legal provisions for organizational structures and operations of not-for-profit corporations. They are exempt from paying income taxes.

⌐8⌐ **Describe public and collective (cooperative) business ownership.**

Public ownership occurs when a unit or agency of government owns and operates an organization. Collective ownership establishes an organization referred to as a cooperative, whose owners join forces to operate all or part of the functions in their firm or industry.

Assessment Check Answers ✅

8.1 What is public ownership? Public ownership occurs when a unit or agency of government owns and operates an organization.

8.2 What is collective ownership? Where are cooperatives typically found, and what benefits do they provide small businesses? Collective ownership establishes an organization referred to as a cooperative (co-op), whose owners join forces to operate all or part of the functions in their firm or industry. Cooperatives are frequently found among agricultural businesses. They can also occur in retail. Cooperatives allow small firms to pool their resources, share equipment and expertise, and help each other through difficult times.

⌐9⌐ **Identify types of corporations and the levels of corporate management.**

There are three types of corporations: domestic, foreign, and alien. Stockholders, or shareholders, own a corporation. In return for their financial investments, they receive shares of stock in the company. Stockholders elect a board of directors, who set overall policy. The board hires the chief executive officer (CEO), who then hires managers.

Assessment Check Answers ✅

9.1 What are the two key elements of the incorporation process? The two key elements are where to incorporate and the corporate charter.

9.2 Identify the five main levels of corporate ownership and management. The five levels are: stockholders, board of directors, top management, middle management, and supervisory management.

[10] Describe mergers, acquisitions, and joint ventures.

In a merger, two or more firms combine to form one company. A vertical merger combines firms operating at different levels in the production and marketing process. A horizontal merger joins firms in the same industry. A conglomerate merger combines unrelated firms. An acquisition occurs when one firm purchases another. A joint venture is a partnership between companies formed for a specific undertaking.

■ Key Terms

small business 147	franchising 162
home-based business 149	franchisee 163
business plan 155	franchisor 163
Small Business Administration (SBA) 157	sole proprietorship 166
	partnership 167
microloans 158	corporation 168
business incubator 160	S corporation 168
venture capital 160	

limited-liability company (LLC) 169	board of directors 173
	merger 174
employee ownership 169	acquisition 174
not-for-profit corporation 170	vertical merger 174
stockholder 173	horizontal merger 174
preferred stock 173	conglomerate merger 175
common stock 173	joint venture 175

■ Review Questions

1. Describe how a small business might use innovation to create new jobs.

2. Why do so many small businesses fail before they reach their tenth year?

3. What are the benefits of developing and writing an effective business plan?

4. What is the Small Business Administration? How does it assist small companies, financially and in other specialized ways?

5. Describe how local governments and business incubators help small firms get established and grow.

6. Why are so many small-business owners attracted to franchising? Under what circumstances might it be better

■ Projects and Teamwork Applications

1. Research a large firm to find out more about its beginnings as a small business. Who founded the company? Does the firm still produce its original offerings, or has it moved entirely away from them?

2. Go to the Web site Entrepreneur.com and research information on franchises. Choose one that interests you and evaluate the information about its start-up requirements. Would you consider a partnership in your franchise with someone you know? Why or why not? Present your findings in class.

3. Brainstorm a small business idea. Research the industry and major competition online. Draft a business plan. Include

Assessment Check Answers ✓

10.1 Distinguish between a merger and an acquisition. In a merger, two or more firms combine to form one company. In an acquisition, one firm purchases the property and assumes the obligations of another. Acquisitions also occur when one firm buys a division or subsidiary from another firm.

10.2 What are the different kinds of mergers? Mergers can be classified as vertical, horizontal, or conglomerate.

10.3 What is a joint venture? A joint venture is a partnership between organizations formed for a specific undertaking.

to start an entirely new business instead of purchasing a franchise?

7. What are the benefits and drawbacks to traditional corporate structure? How do S corporations and limited liability corporations enhance the corporate legal structure?

8. Cooperatives appear frequently in agriculture. Describe another industry in which you think collective ownership would be beneficial, and explain why.

9. In a proprietorship and in partnerships the owners and the managers of the business are the same people. How are ownership and management separated in corporations?

10. How might a joint venture between a commercial firm and a not-for-profit organization help both achieve their goals?

your decision on whether your firm will be a sole proprietorship or a partnership.

4. Identify an organization—such as Americorps or the United States Postal Service—that is owned by a unit or agency of government. Imagine that you have been hired by that agency as a consultant to decide whether the organization should remain publicly owned. Research its successes and failures, and write a memo explaining your conclusion.

5. Identify a business and a not-for-profit organization that could form a joint venture beneficial to both. Either draft a written proposal or create an advertisement for the event that would result.

Web Assignments

1. **Small-business successes.** Visit the Web site at http://www.businessweek.com/smallbiz/successstories/. Scroll through the titles of success stories and choose one that interests you. Read the feature and prepare a brief report answering these questions:

   a. What does the firm do?

   b. Where did the idea originate?

   c. What expertise does the owner have?

   d. How did the business begin?

   e. Who are its competitors?

2. **Great small workplaces.** Winning Workplaces is a not-for-profit organization that is "committed to helping small and midsize organizations create high-performance workplaces." Visit the organization's Web site at http://www.winningworkplaces.com and read at least two postings or articles there that interest you. Summarize the articles and explain how they help fulfill the Winning Workplaces' mission of helping small businesses succeed.

3. **Family-business tips for success.** Go to the Web site for *Family Business Magazine* at http://www.familybusinessmagazine.com and click on the feature article. Read the piece to learn about a particular family-owned business. Alternatively, choose a family-owned business such as S.C. Johnson (large) or Cider Hill Farm (small) and visit the firm's Web site to learn how the company has grown over the years and achieved success.

Note: Internet Web addresses change frequently. If you do not find the exact sites listed, you may need to access the organization's or company's home page and search from there.

Military Veteran Robbie Doughty Finds a Second Life as a Business Owner

CASE 5.1

For Robbie Doughty, running a Little Caesars pizza store seems easy—at least compared with other challenges he's had in his life. A former Army staff sergeant, Doughty joined the military for adventure and a career. He served on a peacekeeping mission in Haiti in 1994, worked as an Army recruiter, then went to Iraq in May 2004 as a special operations intelligence soldier. On July 8, 2004, Doughty's convoy was ambushed, and his Humvee hit by a mortar round. Doughty lost both legs.

At Walter Reed Army Medical Center, Doughty was determined to recover as soon as possible. He stood again only two months after the ambush and left the center after a six-month stay, much quicker than the typical two years needed for rehabilitation. Fitted with high-tech prosthetic legs, Doughty headed home to Paducah, Kentucky, to figure out what his new life would be.

The Little Caesars connection began when Michael Ilitch, the chain's owner who also owns the Detroit Tigers and the Detroit Red Wings, read a *USA Today* article about Doughty as he recuperated at Walter Reed. Ilitch was so moved that he called Doughty to thank him for serving his country. But he wanted to do more than offer appreciation. After several conversations, Ilitch was impressed by Doughty's courage and determination and offered him a Little Caesars franchise—free, complete with building, equipment, and a special chair for Doughty behind the counter. The veteran accepted the offer and followed Ilitch's suggestion to partner with someone he could trust. The natural choice was Lloyd Allard, his friend and former colleague in Iraq who had just retired from the service.

Working with Doughty and Allard inspired Little Caesars to launch a veterans' program that gives qualified, honorably discharged veterans a $5,000 reduction on the franchise fee, financing benefits, and a $5,000 credit on their store's first equipment order. The company waives the entire $20,000 franchise fee for service-disabled veterans like Doughty and provides them more financing benefits, a $10,000 credit for equipment, and help with grand-opening marketing.

A year after they opened their first Little Caesars in Paducah, the team opened a second in Allard's hometown of Clarksville, Tennessee. Allard planned to run it with help from his family. Doughty says the company's ongoing support helped them expand. The pizza chain provides six weeks of training—required for franchisees—and in-store instruction on the operating system. Little Caesars also helps with real estate and site selection.

Little Caesars is one of the largest pizza brands, with more than 1,000 outlets on five continents. The chain's recent strategy has been to expand in markets like St. Louis, Minneapolis, Denver, Atlanta, and the East Coast, while competitors have been increasing the number of units abroad. New franchisees are helping the long-established company reemerge as a force in the restaurant industry.

Franchisors like Little Caesars consider military veterans excellent franchise candidates because they are disciplined team players who show dedication and leadership skills. "They were trained by one of the greatest systems in the world—the U.S. military," says Terry Hill, a spokesman for the International Franchise Association. "The franchise community is looking for people who know how to fit into a system, how to follow processes, and how to make things happen on schedule." The association's veteran transition program, called VetFran, encourages franchisors to offer financial incentives to veterans wishing to become business owners. Hundreds of companies in many industries—The UPS Store, Handyman Connection, Learning Express, Fantastic Sam's, and Little Caesars, to name a few—have joined VetFran. Nearly 700 veterans in 48 states have acquired franchises through the program. The Web site, http://www.franchise.org, provides details about the program and participating companies.

Veterans agree that they fit well with franchising. Patricia Evans, owner of a Little Caesars in Valdosta, Georgia, expects the skills she learned in the military, including a focus on teamwork, dedication, and a familiarity with processes, to help her become an effective franchisee.

Questions for Critical Thinking

1. What motivates franchisors to give initiatives to military veterans to become business owners in their communities?
2. What personal qualities are important for success as a franchisee? Why are such qualities so important?

Sources: "Veteran Who Inspired Little Caesars Veterans Program Opens Second Location," *PRNewswire,* accessed March 3, 2009, http://www.prnewswire.com; "Robbie Doughty and Lloyd Allard, Paducah, Kentucky," accessed October 2008, http://franchise.littlecaesars.com; Gregg Cebrzynski, "Emerging CiCi, Revitalized Little Caesars Intensify Competition in Pizza Segment with Expansion Pushes," *Nation's Restaurant News,* June 25, 2007, pp. 102–105; Dina Berta, "Chains Aim to Attract Military Vets as Franchisees," *Nation's Restaurant News,* May 21, 2007, pp. 12–14; "Little Caesars Pizza Reaches Milestone with Innovative Veterans Program," April 30, 2007, news release, http://www.littlecaesars.com; "Franchises Creating Opportunities for Veterans," *Franchising World,* January 2007, p. 104.

CASE 5.2

Cooperative Helps Furniture Stores Compete

Small furniture stores are struggling as online shopping, competition from large chains, and international product sourcing change the industry. One route to survival is through a purchasing cooperative like Furniture First, which enables members to make volume purchases like large chain stores while remaining independent, local stores with their own brand identity.

About 130 members/stockholders representing 300 stores with $1.3 million in buying power make up Furniture First, which was begun in 1994 in Harrisburg, Pennsylvania. The co-op provides benefits that few independent dealers could afford on their own. It negotiates volume discounts on merchandise, including specialty product packages, and offers financing options. A co-op consultant trains managers and salespeople at member stores to increase their average sales. With products coming increasingly from countries like Canada, China, or Vietnam, Furniture First does whatever it can—from teaching global business practices to sharing shipping containers—to help members compete.

Members also receive the advantage of networking in person and online. At a recent Furniture First trade show, for example, members discussed the advertising that works best for them. The co-op's password-protected Web site contains information on the group's suppliers, including best-selling products, prices, and the best sales representatives. The online bulletin board lets members talk with other dealers. The co-op's public Web site features consumer education—furniture buying tips and interior design—and is available for individual members to put on

their own sites, a good move, because most furniture buyers do research online before they buy.

Furniture First, with 16 employees, is governed by elected officers and board members and financed by members' dues and supplier discounts. Members invest in its stock and must buy 30 percent of their inventory through the co-op within their first two years. Furniture First works best for dealers with at least $2 million in yearly revenues in a full-line furniture store, according to president Bill Hartman. "Our average member store has been in business for over 40 years and is family-owned and operated," Hartman says. With Furniture First, stores with names like Riley's Furniture in Monroe, Ohio, and Mike's Furniture in Joliet, Illinois, may increase the chance of being in business 40 years from now.

Questions for Critical Thinking

1. Which of Furniture First's service would be most valuable to an independent furniture-store owner? Which other services could Furniture First offer to increase its membership value?
2. How might co-op membership affect the independence prized by most small business owners?

Sources: "About Us," accessed March 2009, http://www.furniturefirst.com; Karen E. Klein, "Small Retailers Band Together," *BusinessWeek SmallBiz,* October 24, 2007, http://www.businessweek.com/smallbiz; Clint Engel, "Furniture First Adds Stores, Elects New Officers, Board," *Furniture Today,* April 23, 2007, http://www.furnituretoday.com.

Seventh Generation isn't as old as its company name suggests. In fact, the firm has been in business for a bit more than two decades, merely allowing time for a second generation of employees to move the company's mission forward. But the firm is focused clearly on the future—seven generations in the future, to be precise. Seventh Generation's mission is based on the Great Law of the Iroquois, which states: "In every deliberation, we must consider the impact of our decision on the next seven generations." With that in mind, the company manufactures and sells household products carefully designed and produced to leave as little impact on the natural environment as possible.

Jeffrey Hollender, Seventh Generation's cofounder and executive chairman, is passionate about the planet. "This is a moment in time that we may not have again," he says of his company's efforts to educate consumers about the impact of the products they buy and use—and its alternative offerings. It's true that Seventh Generation is now a large enough company that Hollender can speak with a voice heard by media, legislators, and the general public. But it wasn't always this way. "We started in 1988 selling energy products like compact fluorescent lightbulbs (CFLs) that cost about $28 a piece," recalls Hollender. His company operated out of a single room in Vermont with half a dozen employees. At first, most consumers were reluctant to pay the high price for CFLs or the firm's organic bedding and cleaning products. But Hollender and his staff remained committed. "We basically sold products we needed to live a more responsible, natural lifestyle," explains Hollender.

Despite the company's small size, word about its fresh ideas in household cleaning and energy use spread quickly. "We grew a lot the first three years," says Hollender. "We went from $100,000 to $1 million to $8 million in sales—then we crashed, we hit a wall." Seventh Generation experienced the growing pains that nearly every small business goes through. Hollender admits that the most difficult aspect of growth was realizing it had happened too fast. He cut his own salary, but the decision that caused Hollender the most pain was the layoffs necessary to keep the firm running. "Letting someone go because we had failed to be financially viable enough to employ them, that's my failing," he asserts. "Letting people go has to be the absolute last resort."

But the firm regained its balance and began to grow again with a new sense of purpose. Today, Seventh Generation is nearing $200 million in sales, a figure that allows the company to hire experts in research and development, build stronger relationships with suppliers

and customers, engage in business practices that promote sustainability, and market products that fulfill its promise to reduce human impact on the natural environment. "Growth brings credibility," observes Dave Rappaport, Seventh Generation's director of corporate consciousness.

Hollender agrees. "Our size allows a platform to influence the way business is done in America," he comments. Hollender, who recently turned the job of CEO over to Chuck Maniscalco, now uses his clout to spend more time on not-for-profit environmental initiatives such as the Sustainability Institute.

In addition, Seventh Generation has entered into a strategic partnership with retail giant Walmart to offer environmentally friendly products at more than 1,500 of its stores nationwide as well as on Walmart.com. As part of the alliance, Walmart stores will now carry a range of Seventh Generation's cleaning products, including its best-selling laundry detergent, dish soap, and cleaning spray. An expanded array of products, including baby diapers and wipes, are offered on Walmart.com. CEO Maniscalco is enthusiastic about the partnership. "Seventh Generation and Walmart are committed to helping people learn about natural alternatives and ways to protect themselves and their families," he remarked recently.

Jeffrey Hollender notes that Seventh Generation's work is far from finished. "We need to become a business that is all good rather than less bad," he states. When his company reaches that point, he predicts, its growth could have no limits.

Questions for Critical Thinking

1. Describe specific contributions that you believe Seventh Generation makes to the economy.
2. Given the high failure rate of small businesses, why do you think Seventh Generation has survived?
3. Seventh Generation is a privately held company. Create a chart showing possible benefits and pitfalls for the company if its management decided to sell stock to the general public.
4. Seventh Generation has entered into a strategic partnership with Walmart. Do you think this partnership will be a successful match for both parties? Why or why not?

Sources: Seventh Generation Web site, http://www.seventhgeneration.com, accessed August 17, 2010; "Seventh Generation and Walmart Announce Strategic Partnership," *Market Wire*, July 26, 2010, http://www.easyir.com; Danielle Sacks, "Jeffrey Hollender: Seventh Generation, Triple Bottom Line Entrepreneur," *Fast Company.com*, February 2, 2010, http://fastcompany.com.

Chapter 6

Learning Objectives

1. Define the term *entrepreneur,* and distinguish among entrepreneurs, small-business owners, and managers.

2. Identify the different types of entrepreneurs.

3. Explain why people choose to become entrepreneurs.

4. Discuss factors that support and expand opportunities for entrepreneurs.

5. Identify personality traits that typically characterize successful entrepreneurs.

6. Summarize the process of starting a new venture.

7. Explain how organizations promote intrapreneurship.

The Role of Entrepreneurs in a Competitive Economy

Aldo Murillo/iStockphoto

Revolution Foods Serves Kids a Tasty Lunch

School lunches—who can forget them? Cafeteria lines offered deep-fried chicken, French fries, mystery meatloaf, cakes, and cookies. Most of these foods contained fats, preservatives, and a lot of sugar. Recently, some schools have tried to serve more healthful choices to students, offering salads and carrot sticks, apples and honey. But given the choice, many kids opt for the bad stuff—soft drinks instead of water, a bag of chips instead of a handful of almonds. But two California entrepreneurs are trying to change that by rewriting the menu. Kirsten Tobey and Kristin Groos Richmond founded Revolution Foods in an effort to produce fresh, nutritious, great-tasting lunches for schoolchildren. Both women have backgrounds in education, so they understood the type of food that children were served at school. And they wanted to start their own business. To gain greater knowledge about the needs of their local school communities, Tobey and Richmond interviewed teachers, students, families, and administrators. Then they searched for financing. They drummed up $4.5 million in capital from angel investors—wealthy individuals who wanted to be involved—and socially responsible investment firms. Tobey and Richmond set up shop in an abandoned McDonald's restaurant. They removed the flash fryers and replaced the cast-iron sewer pipes that were corroded from thrown-out soft drinks. They outfitted the restaurant with new equipment and stocked the refrigerator with fresh produce, lean meats, and hormone-free milk.

In addition to their initial financing, Tobey and Richmond secured a vital partnership with Whole Foods, which gave them a $75,000 low-interest loan and the opportunity to purchase a variety of goods at wholesale prices. In turn, Whole Foods would make some of Revolution's organic branded food items—such as peanut butter and applesauce—available in its stores. With chef Amy Klein, who is also a business partner, Tobey and Richmond hired production workers to cook, pack, and ship the lunches. The team signed agreements with several California school districts and began serving a whole new style of school lunch.

Today, Revolution Foods employs 70 workers and produces roughly 20,000 nutritious breakfasts, lunches, and snacks each day for students in 150 California schools and after-school programs. Most students come from low-income families, so the meals are critical for their nutrition and learning. A typical breakfast might include cereal, yogurt, organic cheese, and fresh fruit. Lunch often includes Revolution's own organic peanut butter and concord grape jelly sandwiches or the more exotic chicken teriyaki with fresh vegetables and organic brown rice. A favorite among students is fresh quesadillas and tamales. Snacks include yogurt, whole-grain crackers and chips, and fruit and nut snack bars. The kids often come back for more.

Although Revolution expects to see revenues of $10 million in the coming year, it may be a bit longer before the company turns profitable. New start-ups take time, and investors know they are betting on two savvy businesswomen who are fulfilling a growing need. Currently, Revolution charges $3 to $3.25 for student meals and $5 for the meals it sells to teachers. Public schools are reimbursed for a portion of the cost through the National School Lunch Program. Revolution plans to expand into more school districts to grow revenues.

The firm also offers its branded lunchbox foods to parents who pack their children's meals at home. Kids can enjoy Pop Alongs organic whole-grain chips or Jammy Sammy snack bars. A box of five Jammy Sammy peanut-butter-and-jelly snack bars sells for $4 at Whole Foods, and a bag of the chips is about $3. The prices aren't cheap, but parents know that the food is good. In addition to expanding its product line, Revolution keeps its costs down by buying ingredients in bulk from local companies and through its wholesale purchases from Whole Foods. As their business grows, Tobey and Richmond are determined to remain true to their original vision. "We believe that all children deserve healthy, fresh food every day. Our goal is to serve as many students as we possibly can," says Tobey. Richmond echoes her partner's view. "A well-balanced diet can be challenging for kids. We believe that healthy food choices are key drivers of wellness, education, and the future productivity of our youth."[1]

You think you want to start and run your own company. Perhaps, like Revolution Foods founders, you've spent time trying to devise a concept for a business you could launch. If you've been bitten by the entrepreneurial bug, you're not alone. More than ever, people like you, your classmates, and your friends are choosing the path of entrepreneurship.

How do you become an entrepreneur? Experts advise aspiring entrepreneurs to learn as much as possible about business by completing academic programs such as the one in which you are currently enrolled and by gaining practical experience by working part- or full-time for businesses. In addition, you can obtain valuable insights about the pleasures and pitfalls of entrepreneurship by reading newspaper and magazine articles and biographies of successful entrepreneurs. These sources will help you learn how entrepreneurs handle the challenges of starting their businesses. For advice on how to launch and grow a new venture, turn to magazines such as *Entrepreneur, Forbes, Fast Company, Success, Black Enterprise, Hispanic,* and *Inc.* Entrepreneurship associations such as the Association of African-American Women Business Owners and the Entrepreneurs'

Organization also provide valuable assistance. Finally, any aspiring entrepreneur should visit these Web sites:

- U.S. Chamber of Commerce (http://www.uschamber.com)
- Entrepreneur.com (http://www.entrepreneur.com)
- Kauffman Foundation (http://www.kauffman.org)
- The Small Business Administration (http://www.sba.gov)
- *The Wall Street Journal* Small Business (http://online.wsj.com/small-business)

In this chapter, we focus on pathways for entering the world of entrepreneurship, describing the activities of entrepreneurs, the different kinds of entrepreneurs, and the reason a growing number of people choose to be entrepreneurs. It discusses the business environment in which entrepreneurs work, the characteristics that help entrepreneurs succeed, and the ways they start new ventures. The chapter ends with a discussion of methods by which large companies try to incorporate the entrepreneurial spirit.

What Is an Entrepreneur?

entrepreneur person who seeks a profitable opportunity and takes the necessary risks to set up and operate a business.

An **entrepreneur** is a risk taker in the private enterprise system, a person who seeks a profitable opportunity and takes the necessary risks to set up and operate a business. Consider Sam Walton, Walmart's founder, who started by franchising a few small Ben Franklin variety stores, and then opened his own Walton Five and Dime stores. Forty-five years later, this small venture has grown into a multibillion-dollar global business that is the largest company on earth.

Entrepreneurs differ from many small-business owners. Although many small-business owners possess the same drive, creative energy, and desire to succeed, what makes entrepreneurs different is that one of their major goals is expansion and growth. (Many small-business owners prefer to keep their businesses small.) Sam Walton wasn't satisfied with just one successful Ben Franklin franchise, so he purchased others. And when that wasn't enough, he started and grew his own stores. Entrepreneurs combine their ideas and drive with money, employees, and other resources to create a business that fills a market need. That entrepreneurial role can make something significant out of a small beginning. Walmart, the company that Sam Walton started, reported net sales in excess of $405 billion for one recent year.[2]

Entrepreneurs also differ from managers. Managers are employees who direct the efforts of others to achieve an organization's goals. Owners of some small start-up firms serve as owner-managers to implement their plans for their businesses and to offset human resource limitations at their fledgling companies. Entrepreneurs may also perform a managerial role, but their overriding responsibility is to use the resources of their organizations—employees, money, equipment, and facilities—to accomplish their goals. When Hollywood socialite Bobbie Weiner found herself struggling for cash, she signed up for a special-effects makeup course, hoping that she could earn just a few dollars working for the movie industry. But the result has been a huge success. She realized that specialized makeup is needed by many categories of people—actors, the military, Halloween revelers, sports fans, and funeral directors. After doing a few makeup jobs on horror films, Weiner was recruited to work on the blockbuster *Titanic*. That led to a rush of other movies, a contract with the military for camouflage paint, worldwide requests from funeral homes, and her own product line. Although Weiner is now worth millions and employs 250 people at her company—called Bloody Mary—she is still very much in charge of the firm's mission, goals, and image.[3]

Studies have identified certain personality traits and behaviors common to entrepreneurs that differ from those required for managerial success. One of these traits is the willingness to assume the risks involved in starting a new venture. Some, like Bobbie Weiner, take that risk out of necessity—they've left or lost previous jobs or simply need a way to generate cash. Others want a challenge or a different quality of life. Entrepreneurial characteristics are examined in detail in a later section of this chapter.

Categories of Entrepreneurs

Entrepreneurs apply their talents in different situations. These differences can be classified into distinct categories: classic entrepreneurs, serial entrepreneurs, and social entrepreneurs.

__Classic entrepreneurs__ identify business opportunities and allocate available resources to tap those markets. Dana Hood is a classic entrepreneur. She recognized that dog owners want special attention for their pets when they leave those animals in the care of others. She also knew that pet owners spent $3.4 billion for boarding and daycare centers during one recent year. So, when she founded her daycare center for dogs in Denver, she made certain that her services stood out from the average kennel. At For the Love of Dog, Hood and her staff offer customized services such as grooming and anesthesia-free teeth-cleaning, a treadmill, swimming pools, and water misters to cool off her customers' pets during hot weather. In addition, pet owners can purchase high-end organic foods and treats, beds and toys, as well as other retail goods. "It's a great way to take advantage of a captive audience," notes Hood.[4]

Assessment Check ☑

1. What tools do entrepreneurs use to create a new business?

2. How do entrepreneurs differ from managers?

classic entrepreneur person who identifies a business opportunity and allocates available resources to tap that market.

Dana Hood recognized that dog owners were willing to pay for special attention to be paid to their pets. When she founded her daycare center for dogs, she included custom services. Hood is a classic entrepreneur, who identified a business opportunity and then marshalled the resources to pursue it.

serial entrepreneur
person who starts one business, runs it, and then starts and runs additional businesses in succession.

social entrepreneur
person who recognizes societal problems and uses business principles to develop innovative solutions.

Assessment Check ✔

1. What do classic entrepreneurs and social entrepreneurs have in common?

2. Is a social entrepreneur simply a philanthropist?

While a classic entrepreneur starts a new company by identifying a business opportunity and allocating resources to tap a new market, **serial entrepreneurs** start one business, run it, and then start and run additional businesses in succession. Juha Christensen is a serial entrepreneur. He never earned a college degree but gained experience working in his family's small aviation company outside Copenhagen. At age 17 he started a computer-reselling business. For more than two decades he has been a big player in the wireless sector: he helped pioneer personal digital assistants before there was a Palm Pilot; he persuaded some of the world's top cell phone manufacturers to adopt a common operating system called Symbian; he headed Microsoft's move into smart phones; a few years later he moved on to Web start-up Macromedia and made millions when the company was sold to Adobe Systems. Then he created Sonopia, which leases part of the radio communications spectrum owned by Verizon Wireless and resells it to other companies who sign up their own customers. Using customized handsets and customer support provided by Sonopia, small, diverse organizations can become phone companies with their own networks. More recently, Christensen became a venture partner at Sunstone Capital, a leading European venture capital firm that provides funding for start-ups.[5]

Some entrepreneurs focus on solving society's challenges through their businesses. **Social entrepreneurs** recognize a societal problem and use business principles to develop innovative solutions. Social entrepreneurs are pioneers of innovations that benefit humanity. When a group of seven Indian women gathered one afternoon more than 50 years ago to roll out dough for traditional crackers, they recognized a potential opportunity to produce and market this popular food for a wider audience. They established a women's cooperative based on this idea called Lijjat Papad, with the intent to empower Indian women entrepreneurs. Since then, the cooperative's president, Jyoti Naik, has led the cooperative to become one of India's most successful business ventures. The company now produces a wide variety of bakery products, spices, and flour, with 62 branches around the country. The cooperative brand is one of the most popular and trusted in India, and viewed as the best-run small-village cooperative in the nation.[6]

Reasons to Choose Entrepreneurship as a Career Path

If you want to run your own business someday, you'll have plenty of company. During one recent year, about 530,000 new businesses were created each month in the United States, with services and the construction industry experiencing the highest rates of activity.[7]

The past few decades have witnessed a heightened interest in entrepreneurial careers, spurred in part by publicity celebrating the successes of entrepreneurs such as Michael Dell, who launched what would become computer giant Dell following his freshman year at the University of Texas; Oprah Winfrey, who parlayed her career as a reporter into the media-production empire Harpo; and Bill Gates, who left Harvard to start Microsoft with friend Paul Allen.

People choose to become entrepreneurs for many different reasons. Some are motivated by dissatisfaction with the traditional work world—they want a more flexible schedule or freedom to make all the decisions. Others launch businesses to fill a gap in goods or services that they could use themselves. Still others start their own firms out of financial necessity, like Bobbie Weiner did with her makeup business. Carol Craig is another such entrepreneur. Craig was a flight officer and computer engineer, specializing in anti-submarine and subsurface warfare for the U.S. Navy. When unsuccessful knee surgery left her with a disabled veteran discharge, she didn't know what to do. She followed her husband, also a naval officer, around to military posts and discovered that the military needed her after all—as a civilian consultant. So she founded Craig Technologies head-quartered in Florida, which provides avionic software development, project management, software systems engineering, Web design, and data ware-housing services to the military. In one decade, the firm has grown from one employee—Carol Craig—to more than 170 employees and $20 million in income. Although Craig didn't plan this to be her career, she says "I was never afraid of trying new things. I'm an accidental entrepreneur."[8]

As pointed out in Figure 6.1, people become entrepreneurs for one or more of four major reasons: a desire to be their own boss, succeed financially, attain job security, and improve their quality of life. Each of these reasons is described in more detail in the following sections.

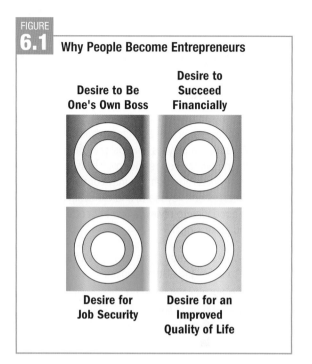

FIGURE 6.1 Why People Become Entrepreneurs

Desire to Be One's Own Boss

Desire to Succeed Financially

Desire for Job Security

Desire for an Improved Quality of Life

Being Your Own Boss

The freedom to make all the decisions—being your own boss—is one of the biggest lures of entrepreneurship. After 20 years of working in the fitness industry, Peter Taunton wanted out of the big-box health club scene. But he wasn't finished with fitness. He decided to create a different kind of gym, one for average people who prefer to work out without wearing Spandex shorts or being bombarded by loud music and big-screen TVs. Taunton founded Taunton's Snap Fitness—small, neighborhood-oriented fitness clubs based on affordability, convenience, and cleanliness. Snap Fitness clubs—there are now nearly 2,000 fran-chised locations—are smaller than the average gym but are open 24 hours a day. They feature up-to-date cardio and training equipment, but that's about all. There are no childcare facilities or smoothie bars, no pools or racquetball courts. This means that the cost of membership falls way below the national average. Taunton likes the fact that he had the authority to put his dreams into action. And his customers seem to agree with his decisions. "People see us, I think, as a breath of fresh air," Taunton observes.[9]

Being your own boss generally means getting to make all the important decisions. It also means engaging in much—if not all—of the communication related to your business, including

Frank Couch/Birmingham News/Landov LLC

After 20 years in the fitness industry, Peter Taunton wanted a change, but he wasn't finished with fitness. He created small, neighborhood-oriented fitness clubs based on affordability, convenience, and cleanliness. For many entrepreneurs, controlling when, where, and how they work is a major motivator.

Communicating by E-mail, Text Message, or Social Networking Updates: You Don't Have to Be All Thumbs

Most entrepreneurs rely heavily on e-mail, texting, social networking updates, and other modes of electronic communication to reach their customers, suppliers, distributors, employees, and others. Often that communication takes place on the run; when you're your own boss, you are busy taking care of many tasks at once. Although you may consider yourself adept with the cell phone or smart phone keyboard, and can whip off an e-mail in no time, it might be a good idea to review a few etiquette tips to make sure your messages sound professional.

- Don't write in all caps. It makes the message sound frenetic, or as if you meant to be yelling at the recipient.
- On the subject line, don't write "Important—Please Read." Your message is likely to end up in someone's "delete" box, unread. Likewise, try to avoid sending any kind of "forwarded" messages—for the same reason. Instead, use a short but descriptive subject line so the recipient knows what the message is about. An example might be "Review of Tuesday's Meeting."
- Avoid slang expressions and shorthand such as "LOL," "ru," and "L8." Also avoid smiley or sad-face icons.
- Be friendly but not overly familiar. Never include jokes in a business e-mail or text message.
- Be brief. A short message is much more helpful than a long one. If more discussion is necessary, conclude with a note that you will follow up with a phone call.
- Remember that your computer or your phone is like a tape recorder. Messages can be saved and stored. For that reason, you don't want to make an unprofessional comment that could come back to haunt you. Never include personal messages within professional ones, and refrain from insults or criticisms that could damage your company's image or the reputation of others.

Sources: Mark Grossman, "Email Etiquette Is Important," *Grossman Law Group*, http://www.ecomputerlaw.com, accessed March 16, 2010; "Business Email Etiquette: What You Should Know BEFORE You Hit Send," http://www.evancarmichael.com/Women-Entrepreneurs, accessed March 16, 2010; Karl Stolley and Allen Brizee, "Email Etiquette," *Purdue Owl*, http://owl.english.purdue.edu, accessed March 16, 2010; Nina Kaufman, "Making it Legal," *Entrepreneur.com*, http://legal.entrepreneur.com, accessed March 16, 2010.

customers, suppliers, distributors, retailers, and the like. The "Business Etiquette" feature offers tips for professional-style communication—even if you're on the run and using your thumbs.

Financial Success

Entrepreneurs are wealth creators. Many start their ventures with the specific goal of becoming rich—or at least financially successful. Often they believe they have an idea for a superior product and they want to be the first to bring it to market, reaping the financial rewards as a result. Entrepreneurs believe they won't achieve their greatest success by working for someone else, and they're generally right. Of course, the downside is that when they fail, they don't have the cushion of employment.

Kara Goldin was diagnosed with gestational diabetes while she was pregnant. One of the first things she cut from her diet was beverages made with sugar. Her blood-sugar levels improved, but Goldin still craved the flavor of sugared drinks. She couldn't find a beverage that was sugar-free but tasted good, so she created one. Goldin developed Hint—a line of sugar-free, zero-calorie water drinks that are flavored naturally with fruit such as lime and blueberry. Priced at $1.79 each, Hint drinks are less expensive than other high-end beverages. Goldin and her husband Theo, who is also her business partner, focused on selling the drinks through health-food stores and yoga studios, where careful consumers want healthful products at a reasonable price. As a result, Hint has been successful from the beginning. "Consumers want to feel as though they've discovered something new," observes Goldin. "They want to stumble upon emerging products." With revenues of more than $12 million, the Goldins plan to expand their marketing efforts by advertising in online newspapers and magazines such as *InStyle*.[10]

Job Security

Although the demand for skilled employees remains high in many industries, working for a company, even a *Fortune* 500 firm, is no guarantee of job security. In fact, over the past ten years, large companies sought efficiency by downsizing and actually eliminated more jobs than they created.

As a result, a growing number of American workers—both first-time job seekers and laid-off long-term employees—are deciding to create their own job security by starting their own businesses. While running your own business doesn't guarantee job security, the U.S. Small Business Administration has found that most newly created jobs come from small businesses, with a significant share of those jobs coming from new companies.[11]

Overseas, as economies are changing, workers are discovering the benefits of entrepreneurship compared to employment by big firms. In China, where entire industries such as banking, steel, and telecommunications, are government-owned, young businesspeople are starting their own small firms. There are nearly 500 million people under the age of 30 in China, and their role models are Bill Gates and Michael Dell, reports an entrepreneurship professor at the Europe International Business School in Shanghai.[12]

Quality of Life

Entrepreneurship is an attractive career option for people seeking to improve their quality of life. Starting a business gives the founder independence and some freedom to decide when, where, and how to work. A **lifestyle entrepreneur** is a person who starts a business to gain flexibility in work hours and control over his or her life. But this does *not* mean working fewer hours or with less intensity. Generally it is the opposite—people who start their own businesses often work longer and harder than ever before, at least in the beginning. But they enjoy the satisfaction of success, both materially and in the way they live their lives.

Zhena Muzyka, a single mom in California, needed a job that gave her flexibility and earning power. Her young son, "needed operations [for kidney disease], and the insurance wasn't going to cover them. I had to come up with a job where I could have him with me because he had special needs," Muzyka explains. So she combined her interest in herbal medicine with knowledge gained from travels in which she discovered the importance of fair-trade practices, to establish her firm Gypsy Tea. Today, Muzyka's son is healthy, and Gypsy Tea is a multimillion-dollar firm that produces flavored teas grown on fair-trade farms in Peru, India, and other countries. Workers at these farms are guaranteed health care, clean water, maternity leave, child care, and other benefits. New products have been added to the Gypsy Tea line, including candles and beads. "It's the most 'worth-it' thing I've ever done," says Muzyka of Gypsy Tea.[13] Marc Ecko is another entrepreneur who has followed his interest. Ecko has built an empire based on urban-style clothing, as the "Hit & Miss" feature describes.

> **lifestyle entrepreneur** person who starts a business to reduce work hours and create a more relaxed lifestyle.

Assessment Check ☑
1. What are the four main reasons people choose to become entrepeneurs?
2. What factors affect the entrepreneur's job security?

The Environment for Entrepreneurs

Are you ready to start your own company? Do some research about the environment in which you will be conducting business. There are several important overall factors to consider. There's the economy—whether it is lagging or booming, you may find opportunities. Consider where you want to locate your business. Currently, the states with the highest rate of entrepreneurial activity are Georgia, New Mexico, Montana, Arizona, Alaska, and California. And the metropolitan area with the highest rate of activity is Atlanta.[14]

Overall, the general attitude toward entrepreneurs in the United States is positive. In addition to favorable public attitudes toward entrepreneurs and the growing number of financing options, several other factors—identified in Figure 6.2—also support and expand opportunities for entrepreneurs: globalization, education, information technology, and demographic and

Marc Ecko's Edgy Designs

You know Marc Ecko is unconventional when you watch his video of graffiti artists writing the words "Still Free" on Air Force One, then listen to him explain why he posted it on the Web—to support art, creativity, and free speech. You might guess that he's a former graffiti artist, but you may not surmise that he's the creator of a billion-dollar business.

Ecko (born Marc Milecofsky) is chairman and chief creative officer of Marc Ecko Enterprises, co-founded and owned with his twin sister, Marci Tapper, and friend Seth Gerszberg. Started in 1993, the company produces urban-edgy clothing, accessories, videogames, and a magazine and has annual sales of more than $1.5 billion.

Marc Ecko started in business at 14, painting T-shirts in the family garage. While a Rutgers University pharmacology student, he used his knowledge of graffiti art and skateboard and hip-hop culture to start a men's clothing line. The Ecko⁻ Unlimited brand (ecko⁻ unltd) with its urban style and rhinoceros mascot, was the first of the company's many brands. The company now has a lineup including Zoo York action sports, Avirex sportswear, the Red women's line, Cut 'N' Sew, and G-Unit Clothing, a joint venture with rapper Curtis "50 Cent" Jackson. Ecko clothing, watches, and other accessories are sold in specialty stores and large retailers like Macy's and Lord & Taylor and in 38 Ecko⁻ Unlimited outlets.

Quick expansion threatened the cash-strapped company in its early years. The partners looked for someone to buy them out, but no one wanted a company with sales of $16 million and debt of $7 million. An investor linked to a clothing company—with a warehouse, production shops, and computer systems—came to the rescue. Focused on marketing and production, the three founders took sales to $96 million in 18 months and repaid their creditor. The missteps weren't over, however.

Ecko designed a new clothing line that bombed in retail stores. He then turned his focus from hands-on design to leading his team of artists.

The company has begun an ambitious expansion in the fiercely competitive retail industry. It plans to open 150 stores, including one in New York City's Times Square. "Retail expansion is a great cultural shift for our company, controlling our own destiny," Ecko says. He wants his destiny to include large-scale social projects in public school reform and public art. He and his partners founded and fully support a Ukrainian orphanage, to keep a pledge that they would donate a big portion of their profits to a children's charity if the company was able to pay back its large debts.

Meanwhile, Ecko publishes *Complex*, a bimonthly men's magazine and develops more videogames "just to have fun—that's the most important thing," he says. His first, *Getting Up: Contents Under Pressure*, features graffiti artists in a future universe. By the way, Ecko's Air Force One graffiti video (http://www.stillfree.com) looked realistic enough to prompt government officials to make sure the plane shown wasn't the real Air Force One.

Questions for Critical Thinking

1. What entrepreneurial characteristics describe Marc Ecko? Explain.

2. When the company needed cash in its early years, why do you think Ecko and his partners used debt financing rather than other funding methods?

Sources: Jake Chessum, "It's Going to Be Big," *Inc.*, March 2009, pp. 52–57; Andrea Cooper, "Who Wants to Be a Billionaire?" *Entrepreneur*, February 2008, http://www.entrepreneur.com; Lee Hawkins, "Marc Ecko's Urbanwear Line to Expand," *The Wall Street Journal*, March 9, 2007, p. B3.

FIGURE 6.2

Factors Supporting and Expanding Opportunities for Entrepreneurs

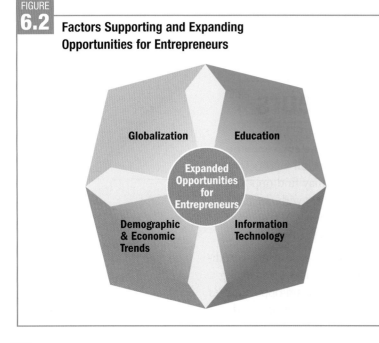

economic trends. Each of these factors is discussed in the following sections.

Globalization

The rapid globalization of business has created many opportunities for entrepreneurs. Entrepreneurs market their products abroad and hire international talent. Among the fastest-growing small U.S. companies, almost two of every five have international sales. Despite her location in Wisconsin, Margaret Maggard sells her yoga-inspired, handmade jewelry—called Bhati Beads—all over the world, including to celebrities. The jewelry, which often features hand-carved beads strung on a soft leather cord, has been showcased on models in magazines ranging from *Lucky* and *Sports Illustrated* to the European fashion magazine *Grazia*.[15]

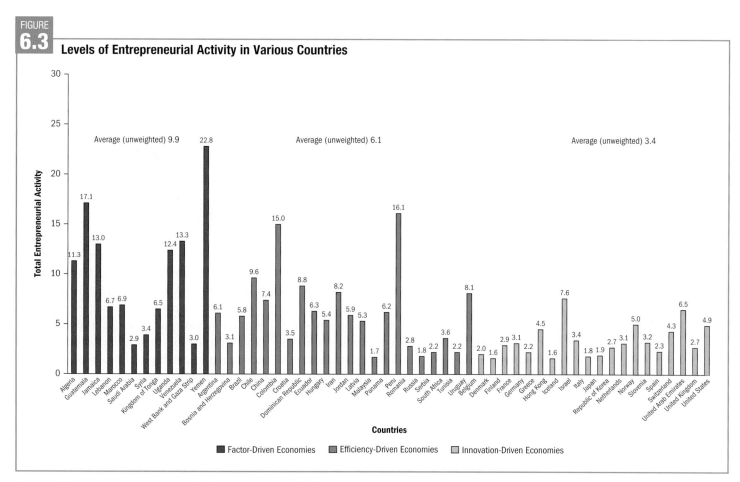

FIGURE 6.3

Levels of Entrepreneurial Activity in Various Countries

Source: Neils Bosma and Jonathan Levie, "2009 Executive Report," *Global Entrepreneurship Monitor*, 2010, p. 21

Growth in entrepreneurship is a worldwide phenomenon. The role of entrepreneurs is growing in most industrialized and newly industrialized nations, as well as in the emerging free-market countries in central and eastern Europe. However, as shown in Figure 6.3, the level of entrepreneurship varies considerably. Worldwide, more than 9 percent of adults are starting or managing a new business. Thailand leads in the number of adults engaged in entrepreneurial activity (27 percent), followed by Peru (26 percent), Colombia (23 percent), Venezuela (20 percent), Dominican Republic (17 percent), and China (16 percent). The United States, with more than 9 percent of adults qualifying as entrepreneurs, is currently in 13th place.[16]

India has experienced a significant increase in the number of female entrepreneurs engaged in a wide range of business activities. Recognizing the effects that chemical-based beauty care products can have on consumers as well as the environment, Shahnaz Husain opened India's first professional herbal salon on the balcony of her house in Delhi in 1971. She now runs a highly respected beauty care empire called Ayurvedic. Husain's Ayurvedic products contain natural ingredients ranging from vegetables to diamond dust. "The ancient Indian system of Ayurveda is the oldest and most organized system of herbal healing in the world. I was convinced that it could offer ideal answers to cosmetic care," explains Husain. "I entered highly competitive international markets, without commercial advertising or fancy packaging." Ayurvedic supplies its products to high-end stores in London, Paris, and Milan as well as to shops located in Spain and Japan.[17]

Education

The past two decades have brought tremendous growth in the number of educational opportunities for would-be entrepreneurs. Today, more than 100 U.S. universities offer full-fledged majors in entrepreneurship, dozens of others offer an emphasis in entrepreneurship, and hundreds more offer one or two courses in how to start a business.

In addition to traditional classroom experience, a number of schools offer opportunities to intern with a start-up or actually work toward launching a company. The Entrepreneurship and Innovation Group at Northeastern University in Boston, which is staffed by professors who are entrepreneurs themselves, provides students with the chance to work in entrepreneurial settings in a variety of industries including retail, commercial real estate development, financial services, health care, and high-growth technology.[18]

Besides schools, many organizations have sprouted up in recent years to teach entrepreneurship to young people. The Kauffman Center for Entrepreneurial Leadership offers training programs for learners from kindergarten through community college. The center's Entreprep summer program, which is taught in conjunction with local colleges and universities, teaches high school juniors how to start and manage a company. Students in Free Enterprise (SIFE) is a worldwide not-for-profit organization in which college students, working with faculty advisors, teach grade school and high school students and other community members the value of private enterprise and entrepreneurship.[19] The Association of Collegiate Entrepreneurs has chapters on many college campuses in the United States and Canada.

You don't have to major in business to become an entrepreneur, but students who do major in entrepreneurship or take entrepreneurship courses are three times more likely to start their own business or help someone else start a business.[20] In fact, you don't have to wait for graduation to launch your first startup, and your business idea doesn't have to change the world. College students are launching their own ventures—while still in school—in record numbers. While a junior in a cramped dorm at Syracuse University, Ryan Dickerson figured out how to turn his bed into a couch during the day—optimizing his furniture and space. He designed a special bolster pillow the length of his bed that served as the "back" of the bed-turned-couch during the day. Called the Rylaxer, the pillows were first made locally and sold on campus, but Dickerson immediately drew up a business plan for selling them nationwide.[21]

Information Technology

The explosion in information technology (IT) has provided one of the biggest boosts for entrepreneurs. As computer and communications technologies have merged and dropped dramatically in cost, entrepreneurs have gained tools that help them compete with large companies. Information technology helps entrepreneurs work quickly and efficiently, provide immediate and attentive customer service, increase sales, and project professional images. In fact, technology has leveled the playing field to the point that, with the use of smartphones and other wireless devices, along with instant Web distribution, a dorm-room innovator can compete with a much larger firm. Technology has also assisted in the tremendous increase of homepreneurs—entrepreneurs who run home-based businesses. These successful ventures are described in the "Hit & Miss" feature.

Social networking has further transformed the business environment for entrepreneurs. According to a recent study, more than 90 percent of successful companies now use at least

Businesses Based at Home Are Booming

The idea itself makes perfect sense: you're laid off from your full-time job, or you've recently moved to a new area, or you just had a baby. Working from home seems like the ideal solution. But until a few years ago, home-based businesses were not really considered legitimate by the business community in general. Most people viewed home-based work as no more challenging—or lucrative—than stuffing envelopes. All that has changed. Today, more than 6.6 million home-based businesses contribute at least half of their owners' household income. It is estimated that homepreneurs employ about one in every ten private-sector workers—and their businesses are as competitive as any other. Technology has made all this possible.

Some homepreneurs run businesses entirely based on technology, such as Web development. Stephen Labuda, president of Agency3, is a former programmer for Deutsche Bank, a large international banking firm. He built Web sites on the side for several years before he quit his job and made Agency3 his full-time, home-based career in Boston. The firm's revenues are now in the millions and Labuda has about half a dozen employees. Labuda loves working from home. "I'm not intending to go rent office space," he notes.

Other homepreneurs rely on technology to reach customers, fulfill orders, ship goods, or provide other services. When Michael and Mary Ferrari retired, they realized they needed to supplement their savings—and they didn't necessarily want to stop working. So they formed UnusualThreads.com based in California, which sells fashions worn by celebrities. The couple still only works the site part time, but they earn enough money to augment their savings and can take time off to travel. Another such homepreneur is Marco Barberini, who launched OvernightPetTags.com in Michigan several years ago and now grosses more than $8,000 a month. Barberini discovered a way to manufacture and ship pet-identification tags cheaper than his competition. His goal is to tag every pet in the United States Barberini echoes the advice of every successful homepreneur. "Most people give up too quickly," he says. "Just make sure that [your product] is going to be something that's in demand, and do it."

Questions for Critical Thinking

1. Could any of these home-based businesses succeed without the heavy use of information technology? Why or why not?

2. Outline your own idea for a home-based business that would rely on technology.

Sources: Steven Berglas, "Wake-up Call for Newly Hatched Entrepreneurs," *Forbes.com*, February 6, 2010, http://www.forbes.com; Carol Tice, "Homepreneur Winners Keep Growing Despite Downturn," *Entrepreneur.com*, February 1, 2010, http://blog.entrpreneur.com; John Tozzi, "The Rise of the Homepreneur," *BusinessWeek*, accessed January 8, 2010, http://www.businessweek.com.

one social media tool. Many entrepreneurs have fully embraced the use of sites such as Twitter, LinkedIn, and Facebook as part of their business strategy. They believe that social media will help them reach more customers and grow faster, giving them a competitive edge. Eric Mattson, a researcher for *Inc.* magazine, believes that social networking is more useful to small firms run by entrepreneurs than to larger firms because "in smaller organizations, there is more room for innovation because it requires [fewer] processes to adopt."[22]

Demographic and Economic Trends

Who might be starting a business alongside you? Immigrants to the United States are the most likely to start their own businesses, as well as those between the ages of 55 and 64.[23] As Baby Boomers continue to age and control a large share of wealth in this country, the trend can only be expected to continue. Older entrepreneurs will also have access to their retirement funds and home equity for financing. Many Boomers also plan to work after retirement from traditional jobs or careers, either because they want to or in order to boost income and savings.

As mentioned earlier, college students are jumping on the entrepreneurial wagon in greater numbers too. Alfonso Olvera started RailTronix while a student at the University of Houston. RailTronix is a Web-based software system that helps rail shippers in the oil industry track their shipments in real time. RailTronix produced $250,000 in revenues in its first year. Now Olvera is developing a similar system for the grain industry.[24] Chrissie Harsh launched Chrissie's Cookies while at the University of Texas at Austin, simply because word of her exceptional baking traveled around campus. Harsh's classmates could order Finger-Lickin Peanut Butter or Cranberry White Chocolate Chip cookies online or request special ingredients. Harsh uses Facebook to market her business and keep in touch with customers. Her Facebook page cites a bold mission statement: "Changing the world one cookie at a time." Every year, Harsh bakes cookies for a local benefit that raises funds to dig drinking wells in Africa.[25]

Demographic trends—including the aging of the U.S. population, the growth of ethnic groups, and the predominance of two-income families—create opportunities for entrepreneurs. Convenience products for busy parents, foods that cater to ethnic preferences, and services designed specifically for older consumers all enjoy an opportunity for success. And as the economy fluctuates, entrepreneurs who are flexible enough to adapt quickly stand the best chance for success. During times when consumers are less willing to spend money, a shoe-repair shop is likely to have an increase in business, as would a clothing consignment shop. Trendsetter's Boutique in Massachusetts makes a profit by selling used designer clothing to eager customers—teens and women—at a fraction of the original cost. One of the bargains includes a big bin of shoes that sell for $2 a pair. "These are a big hit," says one of the owners. "Teenagers love it and they are consigning some of their clothing which is making parents happy."[26]

Characteristics of Entrepreneurs

People who strike out on their own are pioneers in their own right. They aren't satisfied with the status quo and want to achieve certain goals on their own terms. Successful entrepreneurs are often likely to have had parents who were entrepreneurs—or dreams of starting their own business. They also tend to possess specific personality traits. Researchers who study successful entrepreneurs report that they are more likely to be curious, passionate, self-motivated, honest, courageous, and flexible. The eight traits summarized in Figure 6.4 are especially important for people who want to succeed as entrepreneurs.

Assessment Check

1. To what extent is entrepreneurship possible in different countries, and what opportunities does globalization create for today's entrepreneurs?

2. Identify the educational factors that help expand current opportunities for entrepreneurs.

3. Describe current demographic trends that suggest new goods and services for entrepreneurial businesses.

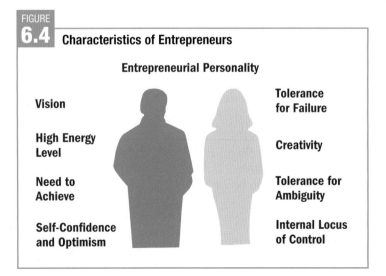

FIGURE 6.4 Characteristics of Entrepreneurs

Entrepreneurial Personality

Vision

High Energy Level

Need to Achieve

Self-Confidence and Optimism

Tolerance for Failure

Creativity

Tolerance for Ambiguity

Internal Locus of Control

Vision

Entrepreneurs generally begin with a *vision*—an overall idea for how to make their business idea a success. Then they pursue this vision with relentless passion. Bill Gates and Paul Allen launched Microsoft with the vision of a computer on every desk and in every home, all running Microsoft software. Their vision helped Microsoft become the world's largest marketer of computer software. It guided the company and provided clear direction for employees as Microsoft grew, adapted, and prospered in an industry characterized by tremendous technological change.

Arguably, every invention from the light bulb to the cell phone originated from a person with vision—someone who viewed the world in a slightly different way. Sometimes inventions have occurred out of necessity or even a mistake. True entrepreneurs know how to turn these situations into opportunities. In the healthcare field, it is well known that penicillin was created by accident. Products with narrower niches have found their way to market this way, too. Jodi Pliszka has an autoimmune disorder that causes baldness. She's an athlete who spent years searching for a product that would keep her head cool and dry under helmets and during exercise. There was nothing on the market to serve her need, but instead of giving up, she invented one. The result is called HeadlineIt, a thin, lightweight disposable liner worn beneath helmets, wigs, and hats. Within a few years Pliszka obtained a design patent for her product, and sales hit the $1 million mark. Pliszka, who was first a clinical therapist and author, is now a successful entrepreneur as well.[27]

High Energy Level

Entrepreneurs work long and hard to realize their visions. Many entrepreneurs work full-time at their regular day jobs and spend weeknights and weekends launching their start-ups. Many entrepreneurs work alone or with a very small staff, which means that they often wear most—if not all—of the hats required to get the business going, filling design, marketing, sales, and financial roles. Most entrepreneurs spend at least 70 hours a week on their new business, which can affect their other job (if they have one) and the quality of their personal life—at least in the beginning.[28] Thus, they need a high level of energy in order to succeed.

Need to Achieve

Entrepreneurs work hard because they want to excel. Their strong competitive drive helps them enjoy the challenge of reaching difficult goals and promotes dedication to personal success. A poll conducted by About.com showed Oprah Winfrey as the most admired entrepreneur among adults. The first African American woman billionaire, Winfrey has built an empire stretching from television to magazines to radio. Her own words best illustrate her strong drive: "I don't think of myself as a poor, deprived ghetto girl who made good. I think of myself as somebody who from an early age knew I was responsible for myself, and had to make good."[29] But when teens were polled by the organization Junior Achievement, Apple founder Steven Jobs emerged as the top pick. Teens said this was because Jobs "made a difference in/improved people's lives or made the world a better place."[30] Both of these entrepreneurs have, in fact, achieved very lofty goals.

Self-Confidence and Optimism

Entrepreneurs believe in their ability to succeed, and they instill their optimism in others. Often their optimism resembles fearlessness in the face of difficult odds. They see opportunities where others see danger lurking. Ishita Khanna founded her not-for-profit organization, Ecosphere, in one of the harshest living environments on the planet, the Spiti valley in Tibet. Ironically, it is also one of the most beautiful—and sought after—locations for eco-travelers. Khanna believed that if small entrepreneurial ventures in Tibet—particularly those run by women—could be linked, they would have more power. She knew it wouldn't be easy. "Spiti's geographical isolation and poor communication infrastructure

Entrepreneurs often succeed simply because they won't give up. When sales of Bobbi Brown's cosmetics line stalled, she moved the company to a new location and revamped its advertising. In the process, she successfully differentiated her company from the competition.

has been one of the major hurdles," Khanna now admits. But Khanna didn't give up, and Ecosphere recently received the Green Livelihoods Achievement Award from The Sierra Club. "There are numerous doubts that plague one before one takes the plunge," Khanna says. "But if you are passionate about what you want to do, that is half the battle won already."[31]

Tolerance for Failure

Entrepreneurs often succeed by sheer will and the ability to try and try again when others would give up. They also view setbacks and failures as learning experiences and are not easily discouraged or disappointed when things don't go as planned. Bobbi Brown has built a big name in the cosmetics industry. Estée Lauder bought her company, and Brown stayed on in an active role. The brand faced some setbacks after its acquisition and sales went flat, but Brown never gave up. She met with the CEO, who said the problem was that the cosmetics were not setting themselves apart from the competition. Brown took the criticism in stride, learned from the setback, and decided to change the culture of the company. She moved out of the GM building to a loft in the SoHo section of Manhattan, made advertising photographs more editorial, and approached the cosmetics business as if it were a magazine. The company's numbers vastly improved and eventually hit half a billion dollars.[32]

When things go well, it's easy to take personal credit. But when poor business decisions result in failure, it's a bit more difficult. Truly successful entrepreneurs are willing to take responsibility for their mistakes. That is why an important part of launching any new business is establishing a code of ethics, as discussed in the "Solving an Ethical Controversy" feature.

Creativity

Entrepreneurs typically conceive new ideas for goods and services, and they devise innovative ways to overcome difficult problems and situations. If we look at the top entrepreneurs in the world, we can see that creativity is the common denominator. *Inc.* magazine presents an annual list of the 500 top small businesses, most of which were started by entrepreneurs. The word *solution* is one of the most common to appear in the names of these companies.

Some entrepreneurs find creative solutions to problems; others find creative ways to accomplish a task or provide a service. Still others create entirely new products. The Lubbers family in Vermont started a 120-acre sustainable farm—instead of buying groceries with unknown or potentially toxic ingredients—in order to address the health issues suffered by their daughter. Today the farm earns about $100,000 a year.[33]

©Richard Drew/AP/Wide World Photos

Solving an Ethical Controversy

Entrepreneurs and Ethics: It's Good Business

When you're starting a new business, it's easy to get caught up in the excitement of it: a fresh start, a new idea, visions of fame and fortune. It might seem harmless to present an overly optimistic sales picture or be a bit vague about where and how your product will be produced—after all, once your invention hits the stores, sales will skyrocket and all will be forgiven. But experts in every industry warn against such fuzzy communication and decision making. Not only might your venture fall flat as a result, but failure may come in the form of a damaged reputation or legal ramifications. And while you might be someone who can tolerate some failures, a wise entrepreneur knows how to prevent others—such as a failure of ethics.

Should every new business have a formal code of ethics?

PRO

1. A code of ethics "embodies the ethical commitments of your organization," writes business author Chris MacDonald. "It tells the world who you are, what you stand for, and what to expect when conducting business with you." It also demonstrates leadership.

2. A code of ethics is a necessity in today's business environment. Without it, if there is a difficult incident or event, a small firm may be exposed to "greater risk from regulatory and prosecutorial authorities," observes Michael Connor, publisher of *Business Ethics.*

CON

1. Not every entrepreneurial enterprise, particularly those run by one person, needs a formal code of ethics. A person's word or a handshake is just as effective. The important thing is to convey integrity about the way your firm will do business.

2. There are too many stories in the media about businesspeople who have failed to make ethical decisions—and not enough accounts of the many entrepreneurs who conduct business every day in an ethical manner. A code of ethics will not make a bad person good; nor will lack of a code turn a good person bad.

Summary

Some people argue that writing a formal code of ethics takes too much time; others recommend outsourcing it to a consultant or another third party. However, the overwhelming majority of business experts advise taking the time and effort to develop these formal guidelines. If a company has more than one employee, then all employees should be required to become familiar with the code. As an entrepreneur, you will face many challenges and probably a few failures; but none should be a failure of ethics.

Sources: "Business Ethics," Small Business Administration, http://www.sba.gov, accessed March 16, 2010; Carter McNamara, "Complete Guide to Ethics Management," *Management Help,* http://www.managementhelp.org, accessed March 16, 2010; Chris MacDonald, "Considerations for Writing a Code of Ethics," *Streetwise Small Business Book of Lists,* accessed March 16, 2010; Josh Spiro, "How To Write a Code of Ethics for Business," *Inc.com,* February 24, 2010, http://www.inc.com; Don Knauss, "The Role of Business Ethics in Relationships with Customers," *Forbes.com,* January 19, 2010, http://www.forbes.com.

Aaron Patzer started Mint.com in California because he and his friends and family were frustrated with Intuit's Quicken products. He insisted that he could develop more user-friendly personal-finance software, and he did. Two years later, Patzer sold his Web site to Intuit for $170 million.[34]

When his grandmother died, college student Curtis Funk got the idea to record the proceedings and memories of funerals onto CDs and sell them to families through funeral homes. Families of deceased loved ones appreciated the CDs so much that Funk's company, FuneralRecording.com located in Utah now has several employees and coordinates with more than 200 funeral homes around the United States to provide live streaming audio and video, transcripts, CDs, and other services.[35] Each of these ventures reflects creativity on the part of their founders.

Tolerance for Ambiguity

Entrepreneurs take in stride the uncertainties associated with launching a venture. Dealing with unexpected events is the norm for most entrepreneurs. Tolerance for ambiguity is different from the love of risk taking that many people associate with entrepreneurship. Successful entrepreneurship is a far cry from gambling because entrepreneurs look for strategies that they believe have a good chance of success, and they quickly make adjustments when a strategy isn't working. An important way entrepreneurs manage ambiguity is by staying close to customers so that they can adjust their offerings in keeping with customer desires. One such entrepreneur is Kevin Mitnick. In the mid-1990s, Mitnick was arrested by the FBI for computer hacking, after which he served five years in prison. When he was released, Mitnick could have hidden his identity and started a new life—or gone on to further crimes. Instead, Mitnick went legitimate, opening his own computer security consulting company. He maintains a solid relationship with the businesses whose systems he once might have compromised. "The lifestyle of an entrepreneur is not so different from that of a hacker," quips Mitnick. "The only thing lacking is the sneakiness, the seduction of adventure." His Nevada-based firm, Mitnick Security Company, is earning more than $750,000 a year.[36]

Internal Locus of Control

Entrepreneurs have an internal locus of control, which means they believe that they control their own destinies. You won't find entrepreneurs blaming others or outside events for their successes or failures—they own it all.

Ralph Braun was diagnosed with a degenerative illness when he was 6 years old. By the time he was 14, he was confined to a wheelchair. Braun attended college for one year but had to drop out because he just couldn't navigate the large campus in his traditional wheelchair. So he decided to design his own transportation. Within about four months, he had built his first scooter. Then he got a job at a local automotive supply factory, where he was able to get around quite easily on his scooter. People noticed, told him about friends or family members who needed such a scooter, and he built them to order. Braun began to focus on the cumbersome van he was driving—and redesigned the interior of that as well, including a lift that is now standard on buses and mass transit. Again, he received requests to convert the vans of other wheelchair-bound drivers. Eventually Braun quit his factory job so he could focus on his business full-time. BraunAbility, located in Indiana, is now a $200 million empire. As he began building scooters, Braun recalls "everyone told me it wasn't going to work. But when it comes to commonsense engineering, I'm very blessed. I think it is a [natural] ability." Braun is clearly in charge of his fate.[37]

After reading this summary of typical personality traits, maybe you're wondering if you have what it takes to become an entrepreneur. Take the test in Figure 6.5 to find out. Your results may help you determine whether you would succeed in starting your own company.

Assessment Check ☑

1. What is meant by an entrepreneur's vision?
2. Why is it important for an entrepreneur to have a high energy level and a strong need for achievement?
3. How do entrepreneurs generally feel about the possibility of failure?

FIGURE
6.5
Quiz for Small Business Success

Choose the answer you think is best for each question. There are no "wrong" answers.

1. What is the key to business success:
   a. business knowledge
   b. market awareness
   c. hands on management
   d. sufficient capital
   e. hard work

2. If a relative ever asks me for advice about starting a business I will tell them to:
   a. work for someone else in the field first
   b. write a business plan
   c. study marketing
   d. give up the idea
   e. learn about budgeting

3. Which is the largest potential trouble spot:
   a. too much growth
   b. too little growth
   c. too fast growth
   d. too slow growth
   e. sporadic growth

4. I trust: (select as many as apply)
   a. nobody
   b. myself
   c. my partner
   d. a few key employees
   e. my customers

5. I am unhappy when my employees are:
   a. late
   b. unhappy
   c. abrupt with customers
   d. resigning
   e. less dedicated than me

6. My customers are: (select as many as apply)
   a. always right
   b. too fussy
   c. demanding
   d. worth listening to
   e. dumb

7. Rank these in order of importance for small-business marketing success:
   a. word-of-mouth
   b. advertising
   c. signs
   d. location
   e. community events

8. When it comes to money I am:
   a. careful
   b. too carefree
   c. emotional
   d. shrewd
   e. hardnosed

9. Financially my firm:
   a. has trouble with cash-flow
   b. has a good line of credit
   c. is financed totally by receipt—no credit
   d. is making better profits this year than last
   e. knows exactly where it is all the time

10. In hiring people:
    a. I take far too long
    b. I look for the cheapest person
    c. personality is more Important than experience
    d. I look for the best person, and am willing to pay
    e. I only hire at the trainee level

11. With my employees:
    a. I treat everybody the same
    b. I try to talk privately to everybody once a week
    c. To whatever extent possible I tailor assignments to personalities
    d. I encourage them to talk to me about the business
    e. I try to work alongside them whenever possible

12. The real key to business success is:
    a. hard work and perseverance
    b. fine products and service
    c. advertising
    d. knowing the fundamentals of business
    e. employees

13. Competition is:
    a. dumb
    b. smart
    c. cunning
    d. everywhere
    e. a constant threat

14. The best competitive advantage is:
    a. experience
    b. understanding what the market wants
    c. confidence
    d. conducting a business ethically
    e. a detailed plan

15. I keep:
    a. careful financial records
    b. in touch with my customers
    c. in touch with my employees
    d. trying new techniques
    e. wanting to retire

16. My dream is:
    a. to grow the business until someone else can run it
    b. to work until I drop
    c. to give up these headaches and have more fun at work
    d. to try another business
    e. to take a vacation

17. I think business plans are:
    a. for the birds
    b. nice but not necessary
    c. something I can do with my accountant
    d. useful and informative
    e. essential—wouldn't do business without them

18. What makes a terrific entrepreneur?
    a. creativity
    b. discipline
    c. consumer orientation
    d. technical proficiency
    e. flexibility

19. What does a business need most?
    a. money
    b. market research
    c. help
    d. time
    e. a solid business plan

20 What is essential to marketing?
    a. "a sixth sense"
    b. market research
    c. customer awareness
    d. experience
    e. testing

Source: U.S. Small Business Administration, http://www.sba.gov/small/businessplanner/manage/makedecisions/serv_manage_q4.html, accessed March 22, 2010.

Starting a New Venture

The examples of entrepreneurs presented so far have introduced many ways to start a business. This section discusses the process of choosing an idea for a new venture and transforming the idea into a working business.

Selecting a Business Idea

In choosing an idea for your business, the two most important considerations are (1) finding something you love to do and are good at doing and (2) determining whether your idea can satisfy a need in the marketplace. People willingly work hard doing something they love, and the experience will bring personal fulfillment. The old adages "Do what makes you happy" and "Be true to yourself" are the best guidelines for deciding on a business idea.

Success also depends on customers, so would-be entrepreneurs must also be sure that the idea they choose has interest in the marketplace. The most successful entrepreneurs tend to operate in industries in which a great deal of change is taking place and in which customers have difficulty pinpointing their precise needs. These industries allow entrepreneurs to capitalize on their strengths, such as creativity, hard work, and tolerance of ambiguity, to build customer relationships. Nevertheless, examples of outstanding entrepreneurial success occur in every industry. Whether you want to build a business based on your grandmother's cookie recipes or know that you have a better idea for tax-preparation software, you are more likely to succeed if you ask yourself the right questions from the beginning.

Consider the following guidelines as you think about your business ideas:

- List your interests and abilities. Include your values and beliefs, your goals and dreams, things you like and dislike doing, and your job experiences.
- Make another list of the types of businesses that match your interests and abilities.
- Read newspapers and business and consumer magazines to learn about demographic and economic trends that identify future needs for products that no one yet offers.
- Carefully evaluate existing goods and services, looking for ways you can improve them.
- Decide on a business that matches what you want and offers profit potential.
- Conduct marketing research to determine whether your business idea will attract enough customers to earn a profit.
- Learn as much as you can about the industry in which your new venture will operate, your merchandise or service, and your competitors. Read surveys that project growth in various industries.

Eric Casaburi already knew that he loved the fitness industry—he had owned two licensed fitness centers and liked the energy of the business. But he thought he could do a better job. "I felt there was a niche for a low-cost provider that gave a high-end experience," Casaburi explains. And he wanted to do it with a twist. "Nostalgia for the 1980s has never disappeared," he observes. So Casaburi developed the idea for Retrofitness—a chain of gyms along the East Coast with a 1980s theme. The gyms, which feature Retro Cardio Movie Theaters, RetroBlends, juice bars, bright red-and-yellow weight machines, and Rubik's Cubes at the front desk. Retrofitness is a hit. While traditional gyms are struggling to hang onto customers, Retrofitness is swelling with new members. Why? "If you keep people entertained," says Casaburi, "they don't mind the sweat." Casaburi doesn't mind the sweat either—he plans to expand the number of Retrofitness locations to 300 over the next few years.[38]

Many entrepreneurs who start new businesses invent new products or processes. When that happens, the inventor–entrepreneur needs to protect the rights to his or her invention by securing a patent. The U.S. Patent and Trademark Office's Web site (http://www.uspto.gov) provides information about this process, along with forms to apply for a patent. Inventors can also apply for a patent online.

Adam Lowry and Eric Ryan started their firm, Method, because they believed they could make better household cleaning supplies than the larger firms. Today, they are credited with reinventing an industry, as described in the "Going Green" feature.

Adam Lowry and Eric Ryan: There's a Method to Their Madness

To most people, the household cleaning industry would seem to be as dull as dishwater—but not childhood buddies Adam Lowry and Eric Ryan. Where others saw dreariness, the two entrepreneurs saw green—in both senses of the word. They believed they could create more eco-friendly soaps, dishwashing liquids, and laundry detergents than the big companies; package them more attractively; and make huge profits. With their Califonia-based company Method, they have achieved these goals.

More than a decade ago, the budding entrepreneurs brainstormed about products they could reinvent that would challenge industry giants. What could evoke more drudgery than cleaning? Even the products were boring. They were made with harsh chemicals and packaged in dull plastic bottles. But they pulled in the profits for their manufacturers. So Lowry and Ryan's solution was simple: come up with nontoxic products and package them in cool-looking bottles and jars.

Method wasn't an overnight success. The partners' economic timing was off—their first cleaning product hit the market just as the economy stumbled, and they ran through the $100,000 in savings they had put up as seed capital. They found themselves mixing batches of the cleaning brew in a bathtub and delivering orders in a pick-up truck. Then they maxed out their credit cards and couldn't pay their vendors. "We had to appeal to the inner entrepreneur in each of our vendors," recalls Lowry. "We had to sell them on the fact that Eric and I could do something that had never been done before."

Slowly the cleaning tide began to turn, and a year later Method products were beginning to appear in about 800 stores—including Target. But this wasn't enough for Lowry and Ryan; they wanted to make a bold statement about nontoxic cleaners. To build visibility for their brand, they went to well-known product designer Karim Rashid, who liked the idea and came aboard Method as the company's chief creative officer. From there, the business took off. Because the company was so small, its innovations in product and design could reach the marketplace in weeks instead of months or years. Method now markets about 150 products ranging from hand soap to bathroom cleaners, and is always looking for the next new thing—as long as it is green. The firm's marketing slogan, "People against dirty," has caught on with consumers around the country. "Our challenge is getting consumers to rethink how they do laundry," says Ryan. As for a business idea, they have found their Method.

Questions for Critical Thinking

1. Adam Lowry and Eric Ryan set challenging goals when they selected their business idea. They could have failed. Why do you think they have succeeded?

2. You often hear the advice to "do what makes you happy." No one loves washing dishes or doing laundry. Why do you think Lowry and Ryan chose household cleaners as their business—what is there about the business that could make them happy?

Sources: Company Web site, http://www.methodhome.com, accessed March 23, 2010; "How Two Friends Built a $100 Million Company," *Inc.com,* http://www.inc.com, accessed March 16, 2010; Stuart Elliott, "A Clean Break With Staid Detergent Ads," *The New York Times,* February 3, 2010, http://www.nytimes.com; Julie Scelfo, "Begone, Carbon Footprint!," *The New York Times,* January 27, 2010, http://www.nytimes.com.

Buying an Existing Business Some entrepreneurs prefer to buy established businesses rather than assume the risks of starting new ones. Buying an existing business brings many advantages: employees are already in place to serve established customers and deal with familiar suppliers, the good or service is known in the marketplace, and the necessary permits and licenses have already been secured. Getting financing for an existing business also is easier than it is for most start-ups. Some sellers may even help the buyers by providing financing and offering to serve as consultants. Most people want to buy a healthy business so that they can build on its success, but an experienced entrepreneur might purchase a struggling business with the intent of turning it around. There are many resources for entrepreneurs who are considering the purchase of a business, ranging from information provided by government agencies such as the Small Business Administration to Web sites listing actual companies for sale.

Buying a Franchise Like buying an established business, buying a franchise offers a less risky way to begin a business than starting an entirely new firm. But franchising, which was discussed in detail in Chapter 5, still involves risks, and it is wise to do thorough research before taking the plunge. While there are a multitude of franchises from which to

Preparing a business plan is advisable and necessary, particularly if an entrepreneur is seeking funds from outside sources. When Shez Zamrudeen felt she was ready to open her Jersey City boutique in New Jersey, called Deen, she developed a plan for her new business.

Courtesy Shez Zamrudeen

choose, one area that is experiencing tremendous growth is firms whose goods and services are targeted for children and their parents. These businesses offer everything from photography to tutoring to security. "They are pretty much recession resistant," says Jeff Elgin, CEO of FranChoice, "since people are going to scrimp in a lot of areas before they start cutting stuff for their children."[39]

Creating a Business Plan

In the past, many entrepreneurs launched their ventures without creating formal business plans. Although planning is an integral part of managing in contemporary business, entrepreneurs typically seize opportunities as they arise and change course as necessary. Flexibility seems to be the key to business start-ups, especially in rapidly changing markets. But because of the risks inherent in starting a business, it has become apparent that at least some planning is not only advisable but necessary, particularly if an entrepreneur is seeking funds from outside sources.

When Shez Zamrudeen felt she was ready to put her passion for fashion to work in the form of her own boutique called Deen, she developed a plan for her new business. A major part of Zamrudeen's plan involved finding a way to distinguish her shop from many others in her New Jersey area. She decided to place her flagship store in New Jersey's Powerhouse Arts District in Jersey City—complete with original art work decorating the walls. "There is no other boutique in the area that has an art gallery and clothing store in one," claims Zamrudeen. When the recession hit, Zamrudeen was undaunted. "I had to adjust my current business plan and long-term goals," she admits. "I had to be smarter and more careful with my inventory." But Zamrudeen says she still plans to achieve all her business goals within the next five to ten years.[40]

Chapter 5 and Appendix D discuss business plans in more detail. The Internet also offers a variety of resources for creating business plans. Table 6.1 lists some of these online resources.

Table 6.1 Online Resources for Preparing a Business Plan

AllBusiness.com http://www.allbusiness.com	The "Business Advice" page provides links to examples, templates, and tips for writing a plan.
Inc. http://www.inc.com	Under "Departments," click "How-To-Guides" and then "Writing a Business Plan," which links to 150+ articles about how to write a business plan.
Kauffman eVenturing http://www.kauffman.org/eventuring	The "Explore Topics" section has links to information and resources for researching and writing a plan, as well as presenting it to lenders or investors.
MoreBusiness.com http://www.morebusiness.com	To see a sample plan, select "Business & Marketing Plans" from the list of templates.

Finding Financing

A key issue in any business plan is financing. Requirements for **seed capital**, funds used to launch a company, depend on the nature of the business. They can range as high as several million—say, for the purchase of a McDonald's franchise in a lucrative area—or as low as $1,000 for Web site design. Many entrepreneurs rely on personal savings or loans from business associates, family members, or even friends for start-up funds. Table 6.2 lists the common sources of start-up capital.

Debt Financing When entrepreneurs use **debt financing**, they borrow money that they must repay. Loans from banks, finance companies, credit-card companies, and family or friends are all sources of debt financing. Although some entrepreneurs charge business expenses to personal credit cards because they are relatively easy to obtain, high interest rates make this source of funding expensive, and the Small Business Administration (SBA) recommends finding alternative methods of funding.

Many banks turn down requests for loans to fund start-ups, fearful of the high risk such ventures entail. This has been particularly true over the last several years. Only a small percentage of start-ups raise seed capital through bank loans, although some new firms can get SBA-backed loans, as discussed in Chapter 5. Applying for a bank loan requires careful preparation. Bank loan officers want to see a business plan and will evaluate the entrepreneur's credit history. Because a start-up has not yet established a business credit history, banks often base lending decisions on evaluations of entrepreneurs' personal credit histories. Banks are more willing to make loans to entrepreneurs who have been in business for a while, show a profit on rising revenues, and need funds to finance expansion. Some entrepreneurs have found that local community banks are more interested in their loan applications than are the major national banks.

seed capital initial funding needed to launch a new venture.

debt financing borrowed funds that entrepreneurs must repay.

Table
6.2 Funding Used by Entrepreneurs for Start-ups

SOURCE	PERCENTAGE OF ENTREPRENEURS*
Self-financing	82%
Loans from family, friends, or business associates	22%
Bank loans	18%
Lines of credit	18%
Venture capital	8%
SBA or other government funds	4%

*Percentages do not total 100 because entrepreneurs often use multiple sources to finance start-ups.

Source: "Entrepreneurial America: A Comprehensive Look at Today's Fastest-Growing Private Companies," *Inc. The Handbook of the American Entrepreneur*, http://www.inc.com, accessed April 9, 2010.

Even entrepreneurs who have previously received funding from banks—and have maintained a good relationship with their lenders—have experienced a credit crunch in recent years. After several years in business, Kevin Semcken got a call from his loan officer informing him that the bank would no longer fund his $2.5 million line of credit. A line of credit is an approved loan that a business can borrow from when funds are needed. Without that money, Colorado-based Able Planet could no longer pay for the raw materials and manufacturing of audio equipment already ordered by customers like Costco and Walmart. Quickly, Semcken reevaluated his business plan, changed its focus, and found alternative funding.[41]

equity financing funds invested in new ventures in exchange for part ownership.

Equity Financing To secure <u>equity financing</u>, entrepreneurs exchange a share of ownership in their company for money supplied by one or more investors. Entrepreneurs invest their own money along with funds supplied by other people and firms that become co-owners of the start-ups. An entrepreneur does not have to repay equity funds. Rather, the investors share in the success of the business. Sources of equity financing include family and friends, business partners, venture capital firms, and private investors. Kevin Semcken, owner of Able Planet, was able to secure some equity funding.[42]

Teaming up with a partner who has funds to invest may benefit an entrepreneur with a good idea and skills but little or no money. Investors may also have business experience, which they will be eager to share because the company's prosperity will benefit them. Like borrowing, however, equity financing has its drawbacks. One is that investment partners may not agree on the future direction of the business, and in the case of partnerships, if they cannot resolve disputes, one partner may have to buy out the other to keep operating.

venture capitalists business firms or groups of individuals that invest in new and growing firms in exchange for an ownership share.

Some entrepreneurs find creative ways to obtain equity financing. Gavin McClurg did that when he came up with a timeshare business model for his start-up. His venture, called Offshore Odysseys, is actually a five-year sailing expedition aboard a $1.2 million catamaran named *Discovery* that will cover the world. Investors buy timeshare segments for between $20,000 and $30,000 on the journey, during which they might swim across the equator or paraglide above Tahiti. Shareholders may purchase more than one segment—a prominent Australian anesthesiologist has eight, and a former Wall Street executive owns six. Shareholders also pay annual fees to cover operating expenses as well as food and beverages on the trip. Shares and fees cover McClurg's salary and living expenses—so at the end of the journey, he will likely have pocketed about $500,000 after taxes. He hopes to turn the *Discovery* into a fleet of several boats.[43]

Jody MacDonald Photography

Some entrepreneurs find creative ways to obtain equity financing. Gavin McClurg's venture, Offshore Odysseys, is a sailing expedition aboard a catamaran named *Discovery*. Investors buy timeshare segments for between $20,000 and $30,000 on the journey, during which they might swim across the equator or paraglide above Tahiti.

<u>**Venture capitalists**</u> are business organizations or groups of private individuals that invest in early-stage, high-potential, growth companies. Venture capitalists typically back companies in high technology industries such as biotechnology. In exchange for taking a risk with their own funds, these investors expect high rates of return, along with a stake in the company. Typical terms for accepting venture capital include agreement on how much the company is worth, how much stock both the investors and the founders will retain, control of the company's board, payment of dividends, and the period of time during which the founders are prohibited from "shopping" for further investments.[44] Venture capitalists require a combination of extremely rare qualities, like

innovative technology, potential for rapid growth, a well-developed business model, and an impressive management team.

Angel investors, wealthy individuals who invest money directly in new ventures in exchange for equity, are a larger source of investment capital for start-up firms. In contrast to venture capitalists, angels focus primarily on new ventures. Many angel investors are successful entrepreneurs who want to help aspiring business owners through the familiar difficulties of launching their businesses. Angel investors back a wide variety of new ventures. Because most entrepreneurs have trouble finding wealthy private investors, angel networks form to match business angels with start-ups in need of capital.

The Small Business Administration's Active Capital provides online listings to connect would-be angels with small businesses seeking financing. Venture capitalists that focus on women include Isabella Capital (http://www.fundisabella.com) and Springboard Enterprises (http://springboardenterprises.org). Those interested in minority-owned business include the U.S. Hispanic Chamber of Commerce (http://www.ushcc.com).

angel investors wealthy individuals who invest directly in a new venture in exchange for an equity stake.

Government Support for New Ventures

Federal, state, and local governments support new ventures in a number of ways, as discussed in Chapter 5. The Small Business Administration (SBA), state and local agencies, as well as business incubators all offer information, resources, and sometimes even access to financing for entrepreneurs.

Another way to encourage entrepreneurship is through *enterprise zones*, specific geographic areas designated for economic revitalization. Enterprise zones encourage investment, often in distressed areas, by offering tax advantages and incentives to businesses locating within the boundaries of the zone. The state of Florida has 56 enterprise zones and allows a business located within urban zones to take tax credits for 20 or 30 percent of wages paid to new employees who reside within the urban enterprise zone. Colorado has 16 zones, while Ohio has designated 19 zones.

Government legislation can also encourage investment in the U.S. economy. The Immigration Act of 1990 (IMMACT 90) recognizes the growing globalization of business. It contains a provision that sets aside visas for immigrants wishing to invest money in a new venture in a *targeted employment area*—a rural area or an area that has experienced an unemployment rate of at least 150 percent of the national average. In addition, IMMACT 90 enables more experts in the fields such as science, engineering, and computer programming to be hired by U.S. firms.[45]

Assessment Check ✓

1. What are the two most important considerations in choosing an idea for a new business?
2. What is the difference between debt financing and equity financing?
3. What is seed capital?

Intrapreneurship

Established companies try to retain the entrepreneurial spirit by encouraging **intrapreneurship**, the process of promoting innovation within their organizational structures. Today's fast-changing business climate compels established firms to innovate continually to maintain their competitive advantages.

Many companies encourage intrapreneurship—30 percent of large firms now allocate funds toward intrapreneurship.[46] Perhaps none has benefited more from the practice than 3M. To foster creativity, 3M encourages engineers to "bootleg," or borrow up to 15 percent

intrapreneurship process of promoting innovation within the structure of an existing organization.

of their time from other assignments to explore new product ideas of their choosing. Bootlegging has led to some of 3M's most successful products including Scotch tape and Post-It notes.[47]

Established companies such as 3M support intrapreneurial activity in varied ways. In addition to allowing bootlegging time for traditional product development, 3M implements two intrapreneurial approaches: skunkworks and pacing programs. A *skunkworks* project is initiated by an employee who conceives an idea and then recruits resources from within 3M to turn it into a commercial product. *Pacing programs* are company-initiated projects that focus on a few products and technologies in which 3M sees potential for rapid marketplace winners. The company provides financing, equipment, and people to support such pacing projects.[48]

What's Ahead

In upcoming chapters, we look at other trends that are reshaping the business world of the 21st century. For example, in the next part of *Managers-A Key Ingredient in Contemporary Business* we explore the critical issues of how companies organize, lead, and manage their work processes; manage and motivate their employees; empower their employees through teamwork and enhanced communication; handle labor and workplace disputes; and create and produce world-class goods and services.

Assessment Check ☑

1. Why would large companies support intrapreneurship?
2. What is a skunkworks?

Summary of Learning Objectives

⌐1⌐ **Define the term *entrepreneur*, and distinguish among entrepreneurs, small-business owners, and managers.**

Unlike many small-business owners, entrepreneurs typically own and run their businesses with the goal of building significant firms that create wealth and add jobs. Entrepreneurs are visionaries. They identify opportunities and take the initiative to gather the resources they need to start their businesses quickly. Both managers and entrepreneurs use the resources of their companies to achieve the goals of those organizations.

Assessment Check Answers ☑

1.1 What tools do entrepreneurs use to create a new business? Entrepreneurs combine their ideas and drive with money, employees, and other resources to create a business that fills a market need.

1.2 How do entrepreneurs differ from managers? Managers direct the efforts of others to achieve an organization's goals. The drive and impatience that entrepreneurs have to make their companies successful may hurt their ability to manage.

⌐2⌐ **Identify the different types of entrepreneurs.**

A classic entrepreneur identifies a business opportunity and allocates available resources to tap that market. A serial entrepreneur starts one business, runs it, and then starts and runs additional businesses in succession. A social entrepreneur uses business principles to solve social problems.

Assessment Check Answers ☑

2.1 What do classic entrepreneurs and social entrepreneurs have in common? They both identify opportunities and allocate resources to pioneer new innovations.

2.2 Is a social entrepreneur simply a philanthropist? A philanthropist generally promotes human welfare through charitable donations, while a social entrepreneur pioneers new ways to advance social causes and thus enhance social welfare.

⌐3⌐ **Explain why people choose to become entrepreneurs.**

There are many reasons people choose to become entrepreneurs. Some reasons are: desire to be one's own boss; desire to achieve financial success, desire for job security; desire to improve one's quality of life.

Assessment Check Answers ✔

3.1 What are the four main reasons people choose to become entrepreneurs? People generally choose to become entrepreneurs because they want to be their own boss, they believe they will achieve greater financial success, they believe they have more control over job security, and they want to enhance their quality of life.

3.2 What factors affect the entrepreneur's job security? An entrepreneur's job security depends on the decisions of customers and investors and on the cooperation and commitment of the entrepreneur's own employees.

⌐4⌐ Discuss factors that support and expand opportunities for entrepreneurs.

A favorable public perception, availability of financing, the falling cost and widespread availability of information technology, globalization, entrepreneurship education, and changing demographic and economic trends all contribute to a fertile environment for people to start new ventures.

Assessment Check Answers ✔

4.1 To what extent is entrepreneurship possible in different countries, and what opportunities does globalization create for today's entrepreneurs? More than 9 percent of adults worldwide are starting or managing a new business. As for globalization opportunities, entrepreneurs market their products abroad and hire international talent. Among the fastest-growing small U.S. companies, almost two of every five have international sales.

4.2 Identify the educational factors that help expand current opportunities for entrepreneurs. More than 100 U.S. universities offer majors in entrepreneurship, dozens of others offer an entrepreneurship emphasis, and hundreds more offer courses in how to start a business. Also, organizations such as the Kauffman Center for Entrepreneurial Leadership, Entreprep, and Students in Free Enterprise encourage and teach entrepreneurship.

4.3 Describe current demographic trends that suggest new goods and services for entrepreneurial businesses. The aging of the U.S. population, the emergence of Hispanics as the nation's largest ethnic group, and the growth of two-income families are creating opportunities for entrepreneurs to market new goods and services.

⌐5⌐ Identify personality traits that typically characterize successful entrepreneurs.

Successful entrepreneurs share several typical traits, including vision, high energy levels, the need to achieve, self-confidence and optimism, tolerance for failure, creativity, tolerance for ambiguity, and an internal locus of control.

Assessment Check Answers ✔

5.1 What is meant by an entrepreneur's vision? Entrepreneurs begin with a vision, an overall idea for how to make their business idea a success, and then passionately pursue it.

5.2 Why is it important for an entrepreneur to have a high energy level and a strong need for achievement? Because start-up companies typically have a small staff and struggle to raise enough capital, the entrepreneur has to make up the difference by working long hours. A strong need for achievement helps entrepreneurs enjoy the challenge of reaching difficult goals and promotes dedication to personal success.

5.3 How do entrepreneurs generally feel about the possibility of failure? They view failure as a learning experience and are not easily discouraged or disappointed when things don't go as planned.

⌐6⌐ Summarize the process of starting a new venture.

Entrepreneurs must select an idea for their business, develop a business plan, obtain financing, and organize the resources they need to operate their start-ups.

Assessment Check Answers ✔

6.1 What are the two most important considerations in choosing an idea for a new business? Two important considerations are finding something you love to do and are good at doing and determining whether your idea can satisfy a need in the marketplace.

6.2 What is the difference between debt financing and equity financing? Debt financing is money borrowed that must be repaid. Equity financing is an exchange of ownership shares in their company for money supplied by one or more investors.

6.3 What is seed capital? Seed capital is the money that is used to start a company.

⌐7⌐ Explain how organizations promote intrapreneurship.

Organizations encourage intrapreneurial activity within the company in a variety of ways, including hiring practices, dedicated programs such as skunkworks, access to resources, and wide latitude to innovate within established firms.

Assessment Check Answers ✔

7.1 Why would large companies support intrapreneurship? Large firms support intrapreneurship to retain an entrepreneurial spirit and to promote innovation and change.

7.2 What is a skunkworks? A skunkworks project is initiated by an employee who conceives an idea and then recruits resources from within the company to turn that idea into a commercial product.

Business Terms You Need to Know

entrepreneur 184	social entrepreneur 186	debt financing 203	angel investors 205
classic entrepreneur 185	lifestyle entrepreneur 189	equity financing 204	intrapreneurship 205
serial entrepreneur 186	seed capital 203	venture capitalists 204	

Review Questions

1. Identify the three categories of entrepreneurs. How are they different from each other? How might an entrepreneur fall into more than one category?

2. People often become entrepreneurs because they want to be their own boss, and be in control of most or all of the major decisions related to their business. How might this relate to potential financial success? If there are downsides, what might they be?

3. How have globalization and information technology created new opportunities for entrepreneurs? Describe current demographic trends that suggest new goods and services for entrepreneurial businesses.

4. Identify the eight characteristics that are attributed to successful entrepreneurs. Which trait or traits do you believe are the most important for success? Why? Are there any traits that you think might actually contribute to potential failure? If so, which ones—and why?

5. When selecting a business idea, why is the advice to "do what makes you happy" and "be true to yourself" so important?

6. Suppose an entrepreneur is considering buying an existing business or franchise. Which of the eight entrepreneurial traits do you think would most apply to this person, and why?

7. Imagine that you and a partner are planning to launch a business that sells backpacks, briefcases, and soft luggage made out of recycled materials. You'll need seed capital for your venture. Outline how you would use that seed capital.

8. Describe the two main types of financing that entrepreneurs may seek for their businesses. What are the risks and benefits involved with each?

9. What is an enterprise zone? Describe what types of businesses might benefit from opening in such a zone—and how their success might be interconnected.

10. What is intrapreneurship? How does it differ from entrepreneurship?

Projects and Teamwork Applications

1. Interview an entrepreneur—you can do this in person, by e-mail, or on the phone. The person can be a local shop or restaurant owner, a hair salon owner, a pet groomer, a consultant—any field is fine. Find out why that person decided to become an entrepreneur. Ask whether his or her viewpoint has changed since starting a business. Decide whether the person is a classic, serial, or social entrepreneur. Present your findings to the class.

2. Certain demographic trends can represent opportunities for entrepreneurs—the aging of the U.S. population, the increasing diversity of the U.S. population, the growth in population of some states, and the predominance of two-income families to name a few. On your own or with a classmate, choose a demographic trend and brainstorm for business ideas that could capitalize on the trend. Create a poster or PowerPoint presentation to present your idea—and its relationship to the trend—to your class.

3. Review the eight characteristics of successful entrepreneurs. Which characteristics do you possess? Do you think you would be a good entrepreneur? Why or why not? Create an outline of the traits you believe are your strengths—and those that might be your weaknesses.

4. Many entrepreneurs turn a hobby or area of interest into a business idea. Others get their ideas from situations or daily problems for which they believe they have a solution—or a better solution than those already offered. Think about an area of personal interest—or a problem you think you could solve with a new good or service—and create the first part of a potential business plan, the introduction to your new company and its offerings. Then outline briefly what kind of financing you think would work best for your business, and what steps you would take to secure the funds.

5. Enterprise zones are designed to revitalize economically distressed areas. Choose an area with which you are familiar—it may be as close as a local neighborhood, or as far away as a city in which you might like to live someday. Do some online research about the area. Then outline your own plan for an enterprise zone—including businesses that you think would do well in the area, jobs that might be created, housing creation, and other factors.

Web Assignments

1. **Tools for entrepreneurs.** American Express has established something it calls "Open Forum" to allow entrepreneurs and small business owners to communicate with one another and share ideas. Visit the Open Forum Web site and review the available material. Prepare a short report on how Open Forum could help an entrepreneur start and grow a business. http://www.openforum.com/

2. **Venture capitalists.** Venture capital firms are an important source of financing for entrepreneurs. Most actively solicit funding proposals. Go to the Web site shown here to learn more about venture capital. What are some of the famous businesses that were originally financed by venture capitalists?

   http://www.nvca.org/

3. **Getting started.** Visit the Web site of *Entrepreneur* magazine and click on "Starting a Business." How should you go about researching a business idea? What are the steps involved in getting a product to market?

   http://www.entrepreneur.com

Note: Internet Web addresses change frequently. If you don't find the exact sites listed, you may need to access the organization's home page and search from there or use a search engine such as Bing or Google.

Entrepreneurs Help Revitalize New Orleans

CASE 6.1

An online trading company, a digital design firm, an online marketing business, a modular home company, restaurants and cafés, and a hip nightclub are vital part of the "new" New Orleans. The young entrepreneurs who have launched these and other ventures are helping the city's future while building their own.

Despite continuing problems—high crime rate, less-than-adequate infrastructure, still-abandoned areas, and high insurance costs—New Orleans is a "new entrepreneurial frontier," as a local development agency official describes it. Lifelong residents committed to the city's economic and civic development have been joined by an estimated 3,000 young professionals who have arrived since Hurricane Katrina to work in government and not-for-profit organizations or start their own firms.

Ambitious entrepreneurs are attracted by the city's rebuilding buzz and its low rents, relatively low salaries, and supply of qualified graduates from the local universities—Tulane, Loyola, the University of New Orleans, and Louisiana State in Baton Rouge. Business start-ups often are eligible for tax breaks and research and development grants, such as those offered by The Idea Village, a not-for-profit group that supports entrepreneurship. Of more than 1,000 applications Idea Village has received for grants, loans, or other assistance, nearly 40 percent have been for new ventures. "If you're into innovation and entrepreneurship, New Orleans is a laboratory for that," says Idea Village founder Tim Williamson. He calls the city an environment for social change and a magnet for fresh talent.

Many new businesses are in media and Internet technology, rather than the city's traditional industries of tourism, oil, and shipping. Internet-based businesses bring educated young workers, innovation, and the advantage of mobility and continued operations in the event of future storms. "New Orleans has extremely great long-term potential in the sense that we're crafting a new city," says Chris Brown, who has turned his digital design firm, Plaine Studios, into a full-time business. Other entrepreneurs and their start-ups, both techno and other types, include the following:

- Blake Killian started Killian Interactive, an online marketing firm.
- Neel Sus quit his job at Northrup Grumman to focus on his two companies, a business process improvement firm and a venture that provides a way to send patient information to doctors' smart phones, an innovation he hopes will help the city's hospitals improve care.
- Justin Brownhill, a former Citibank managing director, and Nicholas Perkin, a former videogame advertising executive, chose New Orleans over New York and San Francisco as a base for their online trading company, the New Orleans Exchange, which buys and sells accounts receivable, invoices, and other assets used as collateral for business loans. With plans to expand into global markets, they think New Orleans's widely recognized name is a good choice.
- Shawn Burst started a modular building materials company in his native city even though his target market is northern California. He licensed the innovative system from a German firm, invested $2 million, and built a prototype on New Orleans's Canal Boulevard.
- Robert LeBlanc opened Republic New Orleans, a nightclub and center frequented by natives and newcomers alike.
- Tony Osorio operates four *loncheras*, "taco trucks," and a Mexican restaurant, purchased for $120,000 cash.

For some, staying in New Orleans boosted their entrepreneurial spirit. Josh Besh, who fed red beans and rice and fried chicken to emergency workers free of charge after Katrina, kept his restaurant business afloat by reducing prices at his upscale Restaurant August and catering meals for workers brought in to clean up oil spills. Besh has since developed the catering side business and opened two new restaurants, La Provence and Luke, financed with cash flow from his original venues, Restaurant August and August Steak House. PJ's Coffee, a local tradition for 30 years, suffered damage at its roasting facility and in all 25 shops in the city. PJ's faced the challenge of getting supplies in and shipping coffee out to franchisees throughout the Gulf Region and to out-of-state markets. While two locations never recovered, PJ's rebuilt and expanded from 42 regional stores to 60 and plans to franchise more. Renaming the brand PJ's Coffee of New Orleans emphasizes its proud heritage and commitment.

Questions for Critical Thinking

1. Do you think the entrepreneurs featured in the case are lifestyle entrepreneurs? Explain.

2. How will entrepreneurship help revitalize New Orleans? What will be the effects of new information technology companies?

Sources: Carolyn Walkup, "Revived and Thriving," *Nation's Restaurant News,* January 28, 2008, pp. 122–123; Mario Villarreal and Daniel M. Rothschild, "The New Latin Quarter," *The Wall Street Journal,* August 28, 2007, p. A12; John Tozzi, "New Orleans: A Startup Laboratory," *BusinessWeek SmallBiz,* August 27, 2007, http://www.businessweek.com; Molly Reid, "Two Years after Katrina," Reports from the *Birmingham News,* August 26, 2007, http://blog.al.com/bn; "Rebirth of a New Orleans Coffee Tradition," *BusinessWeek SmallBiz,* August 24, 2007, http://www.businessweek.com; Rick Jervis, "New Online Trading Biz Helps Put Big Easy in 'Start-up Mode,'" *USA Today,* August 20, 2007, http://www.usatoday.com.

CASE 6.2

Social Entrepreneurs Run Business for the Common Good

Social entrepreneurs start ventures to do well in business and do good in the world, and they often end up changing "business as usual." When actor Paul Newman and his friend A. E. Hotchner launched Newman's Own, the two had Newman's favorite salad dressing recipe, $40,000, and no business plan. The actor balked at having his picture on the bottle but then decided he could engage in "shameless exploitation" if the proceeds went to charity. Now Newman's Own is known for its all-natural products and its practice of donating 100 percent of its after-tax profits to worthy causes. The company has given more than $200 million to charities worldwide and founded Hole in the Wall Camps for children with cancer and other life-threatening illnesses to attend summer camp free.

Michael J. Fox is another of the rich and famous driven by a social mission. Diagnosed with Parkinson's disease, Fox started an organization to find new treatments for the disorder and got big-name investors to join the cause. While spending more than $100 million on research, the Michael J. Fox Foundation has tried to change how scientific funding works by reducing bureaucracy and staying involved with researchers to get more accountability and faster results.

Not only the well known and well connected are social entrepreneurs. Record producer Louis Posen has given more than $1 million to charity through his small punk rock label. After a degenerative eye disease left him virtually blind and ended his plan of a film career, Posen started Hopeless Records, which employs nine workers and grosses about $5 million a year, a feat in the small punk rock segment. Artists can choose to release their records on either Hopeless or Posen's second label, Sub City—a name derived from subsidy and subculture—that donates 5 percent of the gross profits to charity. Half the money from the Sub City label comes from artists' royalties and half from Posen's profits. According to an executive at Warner Music Group, which helps distribute Posen's albums, "Louis has the spirit of an entrepreneur and a heart of gold."

Questions for Critical Thinking

1. What characteristics do you think are common among social entrepreneurs?

2. What should be a social entrepreneur's primary goal? Why?

Sources: "The Common Good," accessed March 2009, http://www.newmansown.com; Christopher Tkaczyk, "The Business of Giving: The Star," *Fortune,* January 21, 2008, p. 62; Christopher Palmeri, "The Paul Newman of Punk Rock," *BusinessWeek SmallBiz,* September 21, 2007, http://www.businessweek.com.

CASE 6.3

Comet Skateboards: It's a Smooth Ride

Jason Salfi loves skateboarding. This is how many small businesses begin. The founder has a passion for something—whether it's cooking or surfing or creating video games—and wants to turn it into a business. In Salfi's case, it's skateboarding. The company, now in business for more than a decade, is Comet Skateboards. When Salfi graduated from Cornell University, he did what a lot of recent graduates do: he headed west. He lived on a boat off the coast of California for awhile and partnered with a friend tinkering around with skateboards, which the pair sold to other skateboard fans among their circle of friends. Salfi desired something more. He wanted to find a better way to manufacture skateboards as well as the means to support his newly started family. "Back then, skateboards were made with 7 layers of maple and sprayed with a lacquer based coating," he recalls. "Skateboards were accounting for 35 to 40 percent of the natural maple being harvested each year." Salfi loved skateboarding, but he didn't like the way boards were made. He believed that a skateboard could be built with more environmentally sustainable processes and materials. "I wanted to start a company that would make an impression on people and build an awareness around the use of natural resources," Salfi says.

Not long after he established Comet Skateboards, Salfi moved his company and his family back east to Ithaca, New York where he partnered with e2e Materials, a small start-up out of Cornell. The firm specializes in regionally sourced bio-composite materials; they manufacture their own soy-based resin and bio-composites that Salfi describes as "incredibly strong *and* biodegradable." The formula was exactly what Salfi was looking for. He set up shop and hired several employees, including Bob Rossi, who is head of Web development for Comet as well as president of the Green Resource Hub, an organization that focuses on finding ways for businesses to practice sustainability.

Rossi is impressed with Salfi's total commitment to finding the best way to manufacture his products, even if it means moving cross country. "To move your business into the opportunity, to create a greener product, that is pretty impressive to me," observes Rossi. "There's a lot of green-washing out there," says Rossi. He knows the difference. Comet goes much farther than simply purchasing e2e's materials; the firm has adopted a closed-loop manufacturing process, which means that it reduces or eliminates waste by examining the life cycle of all the materials used in its manufacturing process.

It might seem like Salfi and Rossi aren't cut from the same cloth as the previous generation of skateboarders—they're busy doing good things for the environment and for their community instead of rolling along the fringes of society like the bad boys of original skateboarding. But Salfi remains true to his skateboarding heritage (Rossi admits to being new to the sport). Comet boards have names like The Voodoo Doll and Shred City, and are built for specialists who prefer downhill or freeriding. Riders are invited to contribute ideas for the shapes, graphics, and names of new boards. Comet, which has found a way to actually increase profit potential by using green materials,

receives kudos from business bloggers as well as diehard boarding bloggers. It appears that Salfi has found a way to blend doing good with doing good business—in a sport that was once considered far out of the mainstream.

Salfi hopes that Comet Skateboards will ultimately serve as an example of a small business that can make a big difference—while making products that provide fun. "We look at everything we do through the lens of how we can create a model that people can replicate in the future," he says. Salfi observes proudly that although Comet has only been in Ithaca for a few years, so far the company has a 100-percent retention rate of employees. He wants Comet to be a company that is known for its positive working environment, a place where people can develop long-term careers.

"We know that in the grand scheme of things, we're a small company, but through the many means of getting the message out—the Internet, video, music, and photography—we can actually have a broad footprint and make the idea of sustainability and social justice appealing to a broader market," predicts Salfi. While the bottom line—turning a profit—is vital to Comet's survival and growth, Salfi believes that this new way of doing business is more important in the long run. "We like to think we're creating a blueprint for the kind of company that will be around for 100 or 200 years," he muses. Then the skateboarder emerges. With a grin Salfi adds, "At the end of the day we're making skateboards, and we don't want to bum anybody out."

Questions for Critical Thinking

1. In which category (or categories) would you place Jason Salfi as an entrepreneur? Why? Give examples.

2. Salfi notes that the use of information technology—part of the environment for entrepreneurs—can help Comet Skateboards reach a broader audience. Can you identify any demographic and economic trends that might provide opportunities for Comet Skateboard's growth as a business?

3. Which of the traditional characteristics of entrepreneurs do you believe best describe Jason Salfi? Why?

4. As Comet Skateboards reaches the next level of growth, where might the firm have the best chance of obtaining further financing? Why?

Sources: Comet Skateboards Web site, http://www.cometskateboards .com, accessed August 20, 2010; "GOOD Products," Halogen TV, http://www.halogentv.com, accessed August 20, 2010; Nadia Hosni, "Triple Bottom Line: Comet Skateboards," *Tonic,* April 27, 2010, http://www.tonic.com.

GREENSBURG, KS

Greensburg: A Great Place to Start

Ashley Petty started taking massage therapy classes while studying for her business degree. After graduating, she worked for several years as a massage therapist, until the spa where she worked closed. Ashley was job hunting when the tornado hit her hometown of Greensburg, Kansas. Watching volunteers, residents, and relief workers exhaust themselves cleaning up the devastated town, she saw an opportunity. She would return home to start her own spa in Greensburg.

It was definitely a risky venture—the last thing she would have expected to find in Greensburg before the storm. Armed with a business plan she had written in college, Ashley drove to Town Hall and applied for one of the temporary trailers that were brought in to house displaced businesses. She got her trailer—a 1970s singlewide, complete with imitation wood paneling, stinky carpet, and a leaky roof. Not exactly the luxe spa she had envisioned in her business plan, but a good enough start. With a fresh coat of paint, some scented candles, and new drapes, she opened Elements Therapeutic Massage and Day Spa.

Ashley had expected that her spa would be a hard sell. The storm had destroyed the town's communications, so traditional advertising was out. To build a client base, Ashley turned to word of mouth. She went to town meetings, talked to old friends, met with volunteers from all over the country. Still, months went by and she still had barely enough clients to pay her expenses.

Winter hit. It was cold, the ancient furnace ran constantly, drafts blew in the new curtains, and rain soaked the freshly steamed carpet. Elements was the last place anyone would want to go to escape the stress of rebuilding—even Ashley couldn't stand to be there. Under normal circumstances, she would have considered more extensive capital improvements, but the trailer was only temporary and she was out of money.

At one town meeting, green architecture firm BNIM presented a plan for the new Downtown Greensburg, including a business incubator to sustain old businesses and promote new ones. Traditionally, a business incubator is reserved for start-ups, but in Greensburg, once-successful businesses needed help getting back on their feet. The incubator would be housed in a totally energy-efficient retail/office building with space for approximately ten new businesses. The rent would be reasonable, and the utility costs next to nothing. Ashley jumped at the chance to apply for a place in the building.

Questions

After viewing the video, answer the following questions:

1. What major challenges does Ashley Petty face in starting her business?
2. How will Greensburg's business incubator stimulate economic development?
3. What are some of the challenges Greensburg faces in recruiting new businesses? What incentives would you offer to encourage new business development there?
4. Would you start a new business in Greensburg? Why or why not?

LAUNCHING YOUR
[Entrepreneurial Career]

In Part 2, "Starting and Growing Your Business," you learned about the many ways that business owners have achieved their dreams of owning their own company and being their own boss. The part's two chapters introduced you to the wide variety of entrepreneurial or small businesses; the forms they can take—sole proprietorship, partnership, or corporation—and the reasons that some new ventures succeed and others fail. You learned that entrepreneurs are visionaries who build firms that create wealth and that they share traits such as vision and creativity, high energy, optimism, a strong need to achieve, and a tolerance for failure. By now you might be wondering how you can make all this information work for you. Here are some career ideas and opportunities in the small-business and e-business areas.

First, whatever field attracts you as a future business owner, try to acquire experience by working for someone else in the industry initially. The information and skills you pick up will be invaluable when you start out on your own. Lack of experience is often cited as a leading reason for small-business failure.[1]

Next, look for a good fit between your own skills, abilities, and characteristics and a market need or niche. For instance, the U.S. Department of Labor reports that opportunities in many healthcare fields are rising with the nation's increased demand for health services.[2] As the population of older people rises, and as young families find themselves increas-

ingly pressed for time, the need for child care and elder services will also increase—and so will the opportunities for new businesses in those areas. So keep your eyes on trends to find ideas that you can use or adapt.

Another way to look for market needs is to talk to current customers or business associates. When the owner of Michigan-based Moon Valley Rustic Furniture wanted to retire, he went to see Rick Detkowski, who was in the real estate business. The owner intended to offer the buildings to Detkowski and close the business down. But the real estate agent, who owned several pieces of Moon Valley furniture himself, instead decided to buy, not just the buildings, but the furniture business, too. Before the sale was completed—and to determine whether he could run Moon Valley profitably—Detkowski talked with existing customers and furniture dealers, who had been hoping for years that the company would expand its line of sturdy cedar and pine items from the traditional summer lawn furniture into more innovative designs. Further research showed that the general environmental trend among consumers was boosting demand for rustic furniture, in contrast with the overall housing slump. So Detkowski took the plunge and is now in the furniture manufacturing business. He has expanded the company's product lines and reorganized the factory floor for more efficiency—and cost savings.[3]

Are you intrigued by the idea of being your own boss but worried

about risking your savings to get a completely new and untried business off the ground? Then owning a franchise, such as Quiznos or Dunkin' Donuts, might be for you. The Small Business Administration advises aspiring entrepreneurs that while franchising can be less risky than starting a new business from scratch, it still requires hard work and sacrifice. In addition, you need to completely understand both the resources to which you'll be entitled and the responsibilities you'll assume under the franchise agreement. Again, filling a market need is important for success. To find more information about franchising, access the Federal Trade Commission's consumer guide to buying a franchise at http://www.ftc.gov/bcp/edu/pubs/consumer/invest/inv05.shtm.

Are you skilled in a particular area of business, technology, or science? The consulting industry will be a rapidly growing area for several years, according to the Bureau of Labor Statistics.[4] Consulting firms offer their expertise to clients in private, government, not-for-profit, and even foreign business operations. Business consultants influence clients' decisions in marketing, finance, manufacturing, information systems, e-business, human resources, and many other areas including corporate strategy and organization. Technology consultants support businesses in all fields, with services ranging from setting up a secure Web site or training employees in the use of new software to managing an off-site help desk or planning for disaster recovery. Science consulting firms find plenty of work in the field of environmental consulting, helping businesses deal with pollution cleanup and control, habitat protection, and compliance with government's environmental regulations and standards.

But perhaps none of these areas appeal to you quite so much as tinkering with gears and machinery or with computer graphics and code. If you think you have the insight and creativity to invent something completely new, you need to make sure you're informed about patents, trademarks, and copyright laws to protect your ideas.[5] Each area offers different protections for your work, and none will guarantee success. Here again, hard work, persistence, and a little bit of luck will help you succeed.

Career Assessment Exercises in Entrepreneurship and Business Ownership

1. Find out whether you have what it takes to be an entrepreneur. Review the material on the SBA's Web site http://www.sba.gov/smallbusinessplanner/index.html. or take the Brigham Young University's Entrepreneurial Test at http://marriottschool.byu.edu/cfe/startingout/test.cfm. Answer the questions there. After you've finished, use the scoring guides to determine how ready you are to strike out on your own. What weak areas did your results disclose? What can you do to strengthen them?

2. Find an independent business or franchise in your area, and make an appointment to talk to the owner about his or her start-up experience. Prepare a list of questions for a 10- to 15-minute interview, and remember to ask about details such as the number of hours worked per week, approximate start-up costs, goals of the business, available resources, lessons learned since opening, and rewards of owning the business. How different are the owner's answers from what you expected?

3. Search online for information about how to file for a patent, trademark, or copyright. A good starting point is http://www.uspto.gov. Assume you have an invention you wish to protect. Find out what forms are required; what fees are necessary; how much time is typically needed to complete the legal steps; and what rights and protections you will gain.

PART 3

Managers—A Key Ingredient in Contemporary Business

ColorBlind Images/Getty Images, Inc.

Chapter 7

Learning Objectives

[1] Define *management* and the three types of skills necessary for managerial success.

[2] Explain the role of vision and ethical standards in business success.

[3] Summarize the major benefits of planning, and distinguish among strategic planning, tactical planning, and operational planning.

[4] Describe the strategic planning process.

[5] Contrast the two major types of business decisions, and list the steps in the decision-making process.

[6] Define *leadership,* and compare different leadership styles.

[7] Discuss the meaning and importance of corporate culture.

[8] Identify the five major forms of departmentalization and the four main types of organization structures.

How the Managerial Hierarchy Operates within a Business Organization

David Selman/©Corbis

Indra Nooyi: PepsiCo's Top Executive

What's it like to be one of the most powerful businesswomen in the United States? Indra Nooyi is CEO of PepsiCo—one of the largest consumer companies in the world with corporate headquarters in New York. She'd probably answer that her job represents a huge challenge as well as a great opportunity. Nooyi, who grew up in India, spent each evening at dinner engaged in competition with her sister to solve a world problem presented by their mother. Today, Nooyi travels the world in search of opportunities and challenges for her company.

As CEO of a global firm, Nooyi is engaged in planning her company's strategy for the long term. She also likes to see for herself what is happening in the marketplace. Recently she has devoted a lot of time and attention to China, where Pepsi—which makes Lay's potato chips and other snacks—operates vast potato farms. Nooyi doesn't just stay in conference rooms chatting with other executives; she also gets out to the farms. This is because China is not only a supplier of raw materials for Pepsi's products, it is also a huge potential consumer market of more than 1 billion people. "China represents our single largest opportunity today outside the U.S.," Nooyi notes. "It's going to remain that way and will extend that lead." Pepsi already has a third of the market in China for carbonated beverages—and lays claim to the most popular cola there. "The opportunity is enormous," says Nooyi, observing that young Chinese consumers prefer foreign brands. So China is a big part of PepsiCo's long-range planning.

As for product-related planning, Nooyi has backed the effort to offer more healthful Pepsi products as consumers demand them. The firm recently announced its goal to cut the sodium in each serving of its top products by 25 percent over the next five years. Over the next ten years, Pepsi's objective is to cut the average added sugar per serving by 25 percent and saturated fat by 15 percent. Pepsi adopted guidelines to stop selling sugared drinks in U.S. schools several years ago.

Nooyi is known for her assertive leadership style, evident in a recent move by Pepsi to acquire its two largest bottlers—Pepsi Bottling Group and Pepsi Americas. She's outspoken in her views about everything from the creation of jobs to emerging markets. And she views PepsiCo as an important player in the global economy, including emerging markets. "The one thing about PepsiCo is that we are a global company, a great global company, headquartered in the United States, but we are local in every company in which we operate because you cannot export soft drinks and chips. You have to be local." Which markets does Nooyi view as important to Pepsi's planning? South America is particularly vibrant. "Especially in markets like Brazil, there is a lot of optimism; people are feeling great about that market," she comments. Nooyi also has her eye on her native country of India. "In markets like India we are seeing a level of excitement that is unbelievable." Under the direction of Indra Nooyi, PepsiCo plans to be part of that excitement.[1]

Chapter

7 Overview

A management career brings challenges that appeal to many students in introductory business courses. When asked about their professional objectives, many students say, "I want to be a manager." You may think that the role of a manager is basically being the boss. But in today's business world, companies are looking for much more than bosses. They want managers who understand technology, can adapt quickly to change, can skillfully motivate employees, and realize the importance of satisfying customers. Managers who can master those skills will continue to be in great demand because their commitment strongly affects their firms' performance.

This chapter begins by examining how successful organizations use management to turn visions into reality. It describes the levels of management, the skills that managers need, and the functions that managers perform. The chapter explains how the first of these functions, planning, helps managers meet the challenges of a rapidly changing business environment and develop strategies that guide a company's future. Other sections of the chapter explore the types of decisions that managers make, the role of managers as leaders, and the importance of corporate culture. The chapter concludes by examining the second function of management—organizing.

What Is Management?

management process of achieving organizational objectives through people and other resources.

Management is the process of achieving organizational objectives through people and other resources. The manager's job is to combine human and technical resources in the best way possible to achieve the company's goals.

Management principles and concepts apply to not-for-profit organizations as well as profit-seeking firms. A city mayor, the president of the Appalachian Mountain Club, and a superintendent of schools all perform the managerial functions described later in this chapter. Management happens at many levels, from that of a family-owned restaurant manager to a national sales manager for a major manufacturer.

The Management Hierarchy

Your local supermarket works through a fairly simple organization that consists of a store manager, several assistant or department managers, and employees who may range from baggers to cashiers to stock clerks. However, if your supermarket is part of a regional or national chain, there will be corporate managers above the store manager. The Stop & Shop Supermarket Company has more than 350 supermarkets located from New Hampshire to New Jersey, as well as headquarters located in Massachusetts. Within each store there are managers for everything from the meat department to human resources. But at

Stop & Shop headquarters, you'll find top-level managers for such functions as finance, consumer affairs, real estate, information technology, sales and operations, and pharmacy among others.[2]

All of these people are managers because they combine human and other resources to achieve company objectives. Their jobs differ, however, because they work at different levels of the organization.

A firm's management usually has three levels: top, middle, and supervisory. These levels of management form a management hierarchy, as shown in Figure 7.1. The hierarchy is the traditional structure found in most organizations. Managers at each level perform different activities.

The highest level of management is *top management*. Top managers include such positions as chief executive officer (CEO), chief financial officer (CFO), and executive vice president. Top managers devote most of their time to developing long-range plans for their organizations. They make decisions such as whether to introduce new products, purchase other companies, or enter new geographical markets. Top managers set a direction for their organization and inspire the company's executives and employees to achieve their vision for the company's future.

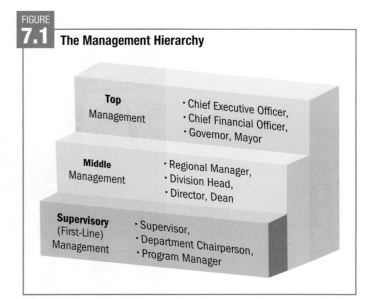

FIGURE 7.1 **The Management Hierarchy**

Top Management
- Chief Executive Officer,
- Chief Financial Officer,
- Governor, Mayor

Middle Management
- Regional Manager,
- Division Head,
- Director, Dean

Supervisory (First-Line) Management
- Supervisor,
- Department Chairperson,
- Program Manager

The job isn't easy. Many top managers must steer their firms through the storms of an economic downturn, a slump in sales, a quality crisis, and the like. Taleo's chief executive, Michael Gregoire, is one such manager. Despite a recession and a major accounting review of the firm, Gregoire kept California-based Taleo—which makes software that tracks job applicant and employee data—afloat. While Gregoire dealt with financial, legal, and technological issues, he also found a way to keep his employees motivated and focused on their own jobs. "My job was to keep the company moving forward," Gregoire notes. He recalls that every day he walked into the office and reassured his employees that doing their own jobs was the most important thing. "What we can do is take care of our customers," he told his workers. "We can build great software. We can sell software." Today, Taleo's customers are happy with Taleo's software products and the firm's earnings are up significantly.[3]

Middle management, the second tier in the management hierarchy, includes positions such as general managers, plant managers, division managers, and branch managers. Middle managers' attention focuses on specific operations, products, or customer groups within an organization. They are responsible for developing detailed plans and procedures to implement the firm's strategic plans. If top management decided to broaden the distribution of a product, a sales manager would be responsible for determining the number of sales personnel required. Middle managers are responsible for targeting the products and customers who are the source of the sales and profit growth expected by their CEOs. To achieve these goals, middle managers might budget money for product development, identify new uses for existing products, and improve the ways they train and motivate salespeople. Because they are more familiar with day-to-day operations than CEOs, middle managers often come up with new ways to increase sales or solve company problems.

Supervisory management, or first-line management, includes positions such as supervisor, section chief, and team leader. These managers are directly responsible for assigning

L.L. Bean ranks in the top tier of *BusinessWeek*'s annual top customer-service providing companies. The first-line managers make sure that customer service is a priority for all employees.

nonmanagerial employees to specific jobs and evaluating their performance. Managers at this first level of the hierarchy work directly with the employees who produce and sell the firm's goods and services. They are responsible for implementing middle managers' plans by motivating workers to accomplish daily, weekly, and monthly goals. In *BusinessWeek*'s most recent annual ranking of customer service champs, all of the top-ranked firms have first-line managers who implement the firms' strategies to provide superior customer service. L.L. Bean, Nordstrom, the Ritz-Carlton, and Ace Hardware all have in common first-line managers who see that customer service is a top priority among its employees.[4]

Skills Needed for Managerial Success

Managers at every level in the management hierarchy must exercise three basic types of skills: technical, human, and conceptual. All managers must acquire these skills in varying proportions, although the importance of each skill changes at different management levels.

Technical skills are the manager's ability to understand and use the techniques, knowledge, and tools and equipment of a specific discipline or department. Technical skills are especially important for first-line managers and become less important at higher levels of the management hierarchy. But most top executives started out as technical experts. The résumé of a vice president for information systems probably lists experience as a computer analyst and that of a vice president for marketing usually shows a background in sales. Many firms, including Home Depot and Dell have increased training programs for first-line managers to boost technical skills and worker productivity. Cold Stone Creamery, which operates franchises for its premium ice-cream stores nationwide, carefully trains managers and crew members in the art of preparing its specialty ice cream for hungry customers. "We set high standards and provide world-class training," says the company.[5]

Human skills are interpersonal skills that enable managers to work effectively with and through people. Human skills include the ability to communicate with, motivate, and lead employees to complete assigned activities. Managers need human skills to interact with people both inside and outside the organization. It would be tough for a manager to succeed without such skills, even though they must be adapted to different forms—for instance, mastering and communicating effectively with staff through e-mail, cell phones, pagers, faxes, and text messaging, all of which are widely used in today's offices. As you can imagine, it is important for managers of Cold Stone Creamery ice cream stores to have excellent human skills not only with customers but also with employees.

Conceptual skills determine a manager's ability to see the organization as a unified whole and to understand how each part of the overall organization interacts with other parts. These skills involve an ability to see the big picture by acquiring, analyzing, and interpreting information. Conceptual skills are especially important for top-level managers, who must develop long-range plans for the future direction of their organization. After selling his own company, LinkExchange, to Microsoft for $265 million, Tony Hsieh joined Zappos as an advisor and eventually became its CEO. Hsieh's conceptual skills helped Zappos to grow sales to more than $1 billion annually while at the same time winning accolades for being an excellent place to work. Recently, Hsieh helped engineer the sale of Zappos to Amazon in a deal worth $1.2 billion.[6]

Managerial Functions

In the course of a typical day, managers spend time meeting and talking with people, reading, thinking, and sending text or e-mail messages. As they perform all these activities, managers are carrying out four basic functions: planning, organizing, directing, and controlling. Planning activities lay the groundwork, and the other functions are aimed at carrying out the plans.

Planning Planning is the process of anticipating future events and conditions and determining courses of actions for achieving organizational objectives. Effective planning helps a business focus its vision, avoid costly mistakes, and seize opportunities. Planning should be flexible and responsive to changes in the business environment, and should involve managers from all levels of the organization. As global competition intensifies, technology expands, and the speed at which firms bring new innovations to market increases, planning for the future becomes even more critical. For example, a CEO and other top-level managers need to plan for succession—those who will follow in their footsteps. Some CEOs resist this kind of planning, fearing that doing so might shorten their time at the helm of a company. But management experts encourage planning ahead for the next generation of management, in order to keep the company's position in the marketplace strong.[7]

After 32 years of leadership at St. Joseph's Hospital in Chippewa Falls, Wisconsin, David Fish will retire from his position as president and CEO and transition to a new senior advisor role. Former St. Joseph's chief operating officer (COO), Joan Coffman, was named the incoming president and CEO for the hospital. Because Coffman was in a senior leadership position and Fish will still be involved with St. Joseph's as an advisor, the transition of leadership was well thought-out through careful planning.[8]

Organizing Once plans have been developed, the next step in the management process typically is organizing—the process of blending human and material resources through a formal structure of tasks and authority; arranging work, dividing tasks among employees,

planning process of anticipating future events and conditions and determining courses of action for achieving organizational objectives.

organizing process of blending human and material resources through a formal structure of tasks and authority; arranging work, dividing tasks among employees, and coordinating them to ensure implementation of plans and accomplishment of objectives.

and coordinating them to ensure implementation of plans and accomplishment of objectives. Organizing involves classifying and dividing work into manageable units with a logical structure. Managers staff the organization with the best possible employees for each job. Sometimes the organizing function requires studying a company's existing structure and determining whether to restructure it in order to operate more efficiently, cost effectively, or sustainably.

Directing Once an organization has been established, managers focus on **directing**, or guiding and motivating employees to accomplish organizational objectives. Directing might include training (or retraining), setting up schedules, delegating certain tasks, and monitoring progress. To fulfill the objective of reducing the office electricity bill, an office manager might have incandescent light bulbs replaced by compact fluorescents, ask employees to turn off the lights when they leave a room and direct the IT staff to program all the office computer screens to turn off after 15 minutes of inactivity.[9]

Often when managers take time to listen to their employees, the manager gains insight and the employee gets a motivational boost. Christopher Mills, co-owner of Prime Debt Services in Dallas, meets with employees each week. "I found the more I listened, the better they pepped up," he says.[10]

Controlling The **controlling** function evaluates an organization's performance against its objectives. Controlling assesses the success of the planning function and provides feedback for future rounds of planning.

The four basic steps in controlling are to establish performance standards, monitor actual performance, compare actual performance with established standards, and make corrections if necessary. Under the provisions of the Sarbanes-Oxley Act, for example, CEOs and CFOs must monitor the performance of the firm's accounting staff more closely than has been done in the past. They must personally attest to the truth of financial reports filed with the Securities and Exchange Commission.

Assessment Check ☑

1. What is management?
2. How do the jobs of top managers, middle managers, and supervisory managers differ?
3. What is the relationship between the manager's planning and controlling functions?

Setting a Vision and Ethical Standards for the Firm

A business begins with a **vision**, its founder's perception of marketplace needs and the ways a firm can satisfy them. Vision serves as the target for a firm's actions, helping direct the company toward opportunities and differentiating it from its competitors. "My whole vision is to build an online empire," says Troy Rhodes Jr., founder of Missouri-based MyBookBorrow.com. Rhodes, who started his business while a student at the University of Missouri, isn't daunted by giant competitors like Amazon or eBay.[11]

Another Missouri-based company, Garmin, which manufactures popular GPS (global positioning system) navigation devices, was founded on the "principles of innovation, convenience, performance, value, and service." Co-founders Gary Burrell and Dr. Min Kao state that the firm's mission is "to create navigational and communication devices that can enrich our customers' lives."[12]

A company's vision must be focused and yet flexible enough to adapt to changes in the business environment. Also critical to a firm's long-term relationship with its customers, suppliers, and the general public are the ethical standards that top management sets. Sometimes

Solving an Ethical Controversy

Google Stands Alone: When Ethics and Business Don't Mix

When Google first entered the Chinese market, the firm was battered by criticism for its agreement to a compromise on censorship with the Chinese government, which controls the distribution of information to its public. Google did so in the hope that the Chinese government would eventually relax its stand and allow its citizens the same access to Internet information as others have around the world. But that didn't happen—in fact, censorship seemed to grow tighter, along with evidence that someone was using Google to identify Chinese dissidents. So, Google announced that it was shutting down operations in China and rerouting users to a safe site in Hong Kong. While Google received praise from the Internet community for its move, the firm got only lackluster support from the business world.

Should the ethical standards set by a U.S. business override repressive laws and regulations established by any of the countries in which it operates?

PRO

1. Many multinational firms now have global ethics policies that apply to each country in which they do business, regardless of national law. This helps managers make consistent decisions, even if it means losing some profits.

2. Ethical standards must always take precedence over practices that compromise human rights. "If any corporate executive finds that he or she is actually considering putting profit ahead of humanity," argues Mickey Edwards, vice president of the international nonprofit Aspen Institute, "it is time for that person to reflect seriously on how and when the moral compass, and one's own claim to humanity, got lost."

CON

1. Ethical standards are not always the same from one country to the next. Google's move may, in fact, have a negative impact on Chinese consumers who at least had access to some information while Google was there. "Leaving may look and feel great to those of us in the West, but exiting a market may not always have the desired impact," writes one expert.

2. Companies willing to compromise with such governments could actually use their influence with consumers to drive change. One way to do this is to create demand for their goods and services. Another is to become active in the community through service projects such as building schools.

Summary

Google's exit from China was a clear-cut decision to some people; to others, it was not. "China is a very important market," noted one analyst. "What's the incentive for a government or another company to join with Google? There is none and that's why you haven't seen it happen." Others point out that while China represents a market of more than 1 billion consumers, it is hard to predict how open that market will be in the next five or ten years. Complicating things further, "there is a barrage of new rules and regulations for foreign companies operating in China," notes a businessperson with experience in China. "And everybody is trying to figure out what it means."

Sources: Alexei Oreskovic and Paul Eckert, "Google Finds Few Allies in China Battle," *Reuters*, March 25, 2010, http://www.reuters.com; Steve Pearlstein and Raju Narisetti, "Doing Right at What Cost?" *The Washington Post*, March 25, 2010, http://views.washingtonpost.com; Aron Cramer and Dunstan Allison Hope, "Google and China: When Should Business Leave On Human Rights Grounds?" *Huffington Post*, March 22, 2010, http://www.huffingtonpost.com.

ethical standards are set in compliance with industry or federal regulations, such as safety or quality standards. Sometimes new standards are set in response to unethical actions by managers, such as the financial accounting activities that resulted in the Sarbanes-Oxley Act. Currently, firms are taking a closer look at large compensation packages received by their CEOs and other top executives. Due to public outcry, compensation committees are reevaluating their criteria for salaries, bonuses, and other benefits.[13]

The ethical tone that a top management team establishes can reap monetary as well as nonmonetary rewards. Setting a high ethical standard does not merely restrain employees

A firm's vision serves as the target for its actions, helping direct the company toward opportunities and differentiating it from its competitors. Troy Rhodes Jr. of MyBookBorrow.com states his vision is "to build an online empire."

Courtesy Troy Rhodes

from doing wrong, but it encourages, motivates, and inspires them to achieve goals they never thought possible. Such satisfaction creates a more productive, stable workforce—one that can create a long-term competitive advantage for the organization. In practice, ethical decisions are not always clear-cut, and managers must make difficult decisions. Sometimes a firm operates in a country where standards differ from those in the United States. In other situations, a manager might have to make an ethical decision that undermines profits or even causes people to lose their jobs. And while it's tempting to think that a large firm—by virtue of its size—will have a harder time adopting ethical practices than a small firm, consider toymaker giant Mattel, which has repeatedly earned recognition for its ethical standards. Named one of the "World's Most Ethical Companies" by the Ethisphere Institute, California-based Mattel consistently demonstrates high standards in a number of areas. "Our commitment to 'play fair' is at the core of our organization's culture and is the cornerstone of our ethical compliance program," notes chairman and CEO Robert A. Eckert.

Alex Brigham, executive director of the New York–based Ethisphere Institute, observes the connection between ethics and good business. "Mattel's promotion of a sound ethical environment shines within its industry and shows a clear understanding that operating under the highest standards for business behavior goes beyond goodwill and is intimately linked to performance and profitability," he says.[14]

Sometimes taking an ethical stand can actually cost a firm in lost revenues and other support. When Google announced a reversal of its original stance on censorship in China—essentially shutting down operations there and rerouting traffic to an uncensored site in Hong Kong—not only did the company lose business, it found itself standing eerily alone on the issue. Google's decision and the consequences are discussed in the "Solving an Ethical Controversy" feature.

Assessment Check ✔

1. What is meant by a vision for the firm?
2. Why is it important for a top executive to set high ethical standards?

Importance of Planning

Turning a vision into reality takes planning. When Reid Hoffman first got the idea for the professional social network LinkedIn headquartered in Mountain View, California, he recalls that he was "very interested in this whole notion of each of us as individual professionals who are on the Internet and how that changes the way we do business, our careers, our brand identity. I realized that the world was transforming every individual into a small business." As Hoffman developed the idea, he considered how a professional social network could be used, asking himself and other businesspeople questions that helped develop his initial plan. "How do you positively influence your brand on the Net? How do you assemble a team fast? Who has the expertise to guide you?" Answers to these questions and many more became the plan for LinkedIn.[15]

Types of Planning

Planning can be categorized by scope and breadth. Some plans are very broad and long range, while others are short range and very narrow, affecting selected parts of the organization rather than the whole thing. Planning can be divided into the following categories: strategic, tactical, operational, and contingency, with each step including more specific information than the last. From the mission statement (described in the next section) to objectives to specific plans, each phase must fit into a comprehensive planning framework. The framework also must include narrow, functional plans aimed at individual employees and work areas relevant to individual tasks. These plans must fit within the firm's overall planning framework and help it reach objectives and achieve its mission.

Strategic Planning The most far-reaching level of planning is *strategic planning*—the process of determining the primary objectives of an organization and then acting and allocating resources to achieve those objectives. Generally, strategic planning is undertaken by top executives in a company. As part of its strategy of using company resources to raise environmental awareness—and develop or improve products—Staples sponsors its annual Staples Global EcoEasy Challenge, a competition in which college students develop new products or redesign existing ones in a way that represents an innovative approach to sustainability.[16]

Tactical Planning *Tactical planning* involves implementing the activities specified by strategic plans. Tactical plans guide the current and near-term activities required to implement overall strategies. The Staples Global EcoEasy Challenge is a tactic that reflects strategic planning around environmentally responsible products. Another tactic for the same strategy is Staples' development of its EcoEasy and Sustainable Earth product lines. "Staples' commitment to designing more environmentally responsible products as compared to conventional products is evident by our own EcoEasy and Sustainable Earth brands," notes Staples' vice president of environmental affairs Mark Buckley.[17]

Operational Planning

Operational planning creates the detailed standards that guide implementation of tactical plans. This activity involves choosing specific work targets and assigning employees and teams to carry out plans. Unlike strategic planning, which focuses on the organization as a whole, operational planning deals with developing and implementing tactics in specific functional areas. Operational planning related to the Staples EcoEasy Challenge might include identifying competition categories such as creating a product using eco-innovative materials; selecting judges; setting deadlines; reviewing contestant applications; and the like.

As an example of strategic planning, Staples is using its company resources to raise environmental awareness, and develop and improve products through its annual Staples Global EcoEasy Challenge competition for college students.

©Brian Ach Photography 2010

Contingency Planning Planning cannot foresee every possibility. Major accidents, natural disasters, and rapid economic downturns can throw even the best-laid plans into chaos. To handle the possibility of business disruption from events of this nature, many firms use *contingency planning*, which allows them to resume operations as quickly and as smoothly as possible after a crisis while openly communicating with the public about what happened. This planning activity involves two components: business continuation and public communication. Many firms have developed management strategies to speed recovery from accidents such as loss of data, breaches of security, product failures, and natural disasters such as floods or fire. If a major disaster or business disruption occurs, a company's contingency plan usually designates a chain of command for crisis management, assigning specific functions to particular managers and employees in an emergency. But crisis more often occurs on a less global scale. For example, a product delivery might go astray, a key person might be sick and unable to attend an important customer meeting, or the power might go out for a day. These instances require contingency planning as well. When British Airways cabin crews walked off their jobs, the airline was forced to cancel or delay hundreds of flights. This left many travelers stranded, rerouted, or struggling to find flights on different airlines. But by the second day of the strike, the airline claimed that due to successful contingency planning, many of its flights were reinstated. Anticipating the strike, BA had retrained some on-ground staffers to serve as cabin crew, and leased planes and crew from some of its competitors. "Our contingency plans are continuing to work well . . . around the world," stated an airline spokesperson.[18]

Assessment Check ✔

1. Outline the planning process.

2. Describe the purpose of tactical planning.

3. Compare the kinds of plans made by top managers and middle managers. How does their focus differ?

Planning at Different Organizational Levels

Although managers spend some time on planning virtually every day, the total time spent and the type of planning done differ according to the level of management. As Table 7.1 points out, top managers, including a firm's board of directors and CEO, spend a great deal of time on long-range planning, while middle-level managers and supervisors focus on short-term, tactical and operational planning. Employees at all levels can benefit themselves and their company by making plans to meet their own specific goals.

Table

⌐7.1⌐ Planning at Different Management Levels

PRIMARY TYPE OF PLANNING	MANAGERIAL LEVEL	EXAMPLES
Strategic	Top management	Organizational objectives, fundamental strategies, long-term plans
Tactical	Middle management	Quarterly and semiannual plans, departmental policies and procedures
Operational	Supervisory management	Daily and weekly plans, rules, and procedures for each department
Contingency	Primarily top management, but all levels contribute	Ongoing plans for actions and communications in an emergency

The Strategic Planning Process

Strategic planning often makes the difference between an organization's success and failure. Strategic planning has formed the basis of many fundamental management decisions. Successful strategic planners typically follow the six steps shown in Figure 7.2: defining a mission, assessing the organization's competitive position, setting organizational objectives, creating strategies for competitive differentiation, implementing the strategy, and evaluating the results and refining the plan.

Defining the Organization's Mission

The first step in strategic planning is to translate the firm's vision into a **mission statement**. A mission statement is a written explanation of an organization's business intentions and aims. It is an enduring statement of a firm's purpose, possibly highlighting the scope of operations, the market it seeks to serve, and the ways it will attempt to set itself apart from competitors. A mission statement guides the actions of employees, and publicizes the company's reasons for existence.

Mission statements can be short or long:

- Starbucks: "To inspire and nurture the human spirit—one person, one cup and one neighborhood at a time."

- Disney: "We create happiness by providing the finest in entertainment for people of all ages, everywhere."

- Nike: "To bring inspiration and innovation to every athlete in the world."

- Sony: "To experience the joy of advancing and applying technology for the benefit of the public."

mission statement
written explanation of an organization's business intentions and aims.

FIGURE 7.2 Steps in the Strategic Planning Process

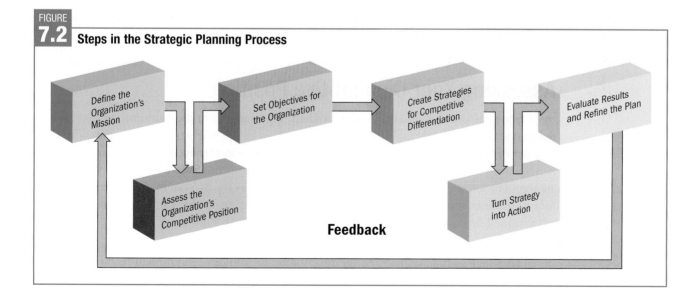

Define the Organization's Mission → Set Objectives for the Organization → Create Strategies for Competitive Differentiation → Evaluate Results and Refine the Plan

Assess the Organization's Competitive Position

Turn Strategy into Action

Feedback

Johnson & Johnson: Caring for the World

In its company statement of values, Johnson & Johnson promises that "We must maintain in good order the property we are privileged to use, protecting the environment and natural resources." That's a simple statement, but a complex pledge to fulfill. Johnson & Johnson makes a wide range of consumer products such as Band-Aids, Listerine, and Johnson's Baby Lotion. It also produces medical devices and prescription drugs. Doing so can result in a giant carbon footprint made by manufacturing emissions, chemicals in products and processes, and a tremendous use of energy. Yet Johnson & Johnson is committed to reaching its environmental goals and has put the management in place to do so.

The firm sets new long-term goals every five years, under its "Healthy Planet" program. Some of these have included using direct purchase of low-impact hydro and wind power, on-site solar power and landfill gas, and purchasing renewable energy certificates from wind power and biomass facilities. Johnson & Johnson believes these practices not only benefit the environment, but also the company because it provides the firm with reliable, affordable sources of energy. In addition, Johnson & Johnson operates the largest fleet of hybrid vehicles owned by a corporation in the world.

Part of the "Healthy Planet" program also involves being truthful about green advertising—avoiding so-called greenwashing. Company management believes in transparency—informing employees, suppliers, consumers, and shareholders of what's green and what's not. This also means being specific about sustainability measures. "Provide your consumers with real numbers that inform and empower them," says the Web site. And while Johnson & Johnson refuses to overstate its accomplishments, the firm is beginning to publicize its efforts so that consumers can share in them. For example, the company is the second-largest producer of solar panels in the United States, and was recently ranked number three on *Newsweek*'s Green Ranking List.

None of these goals could be achieved without support from Johnson & Johnson's leadership. Chairman and CEO William Weldon is committed to his company's sustainability initiatives as they relate to people and the planet. He writes, "More than ever, we know that caring for the health and well-being of people is not only an outstanding business but a mission that truly touches lives."

Questions for Critical Thinking

1. What role does the CEO's leadership play in accomplishing Johnson & Johnson's green goals?
2. How does the company's mission relate to sustainability?

Sources: Company Web site, http://www.jnj.com accessed April 12, 2010; "To Our Shareholders," *Annual Report*, http://www.investor.jnj.com, accessed April 12, 2010; "Partner Profile," *Green Power Partnership*, March 22, 2010, http://www.epa.gov.

A good mission statement states the firm's purpose for being in business and its overall goal. The most effective mission statements are memorable as well. The "Going Green" feature describes the mission of Johnson & Johnson, a global manufacturer of pharmaceuticals and healthcare products.

Assessing Your Competitive Position

Once a mission statement has been created, the next step in the planning process is to determine the firm's current—or potential—position in the marketplace. The company's founder or top managers evaluate the factors that may help it grow or could cause it to fail. A frequently used tool in this phase of strategic planning is the **SWOT analysis**. SWOT is an acronym for *strengths, weaknesses, opportunities*, and *threats*. By systematically evaluating all four of these factors, a firm can then develop the best strategies for gaining a competitive advantage. The framework for a SWOT analysis appears in Figure 7.3.

To evaluate a firm's strengths and weaknesses, its managers may examine each functional area such as finance, marketing, information technology, and human resources. Or they might evaluate strengths and weaknesses of each office, plant, or store. Entrepreneurs may focus on the individual skills and experience they bring to a new business.

SWOT analysis SWOT is an acronym for *strengths, weaknesses, opportunities*, and *threats*. By systematically evaluating all four of these factors, a firm can then develop the best strategies for gaining a competitive advantage.

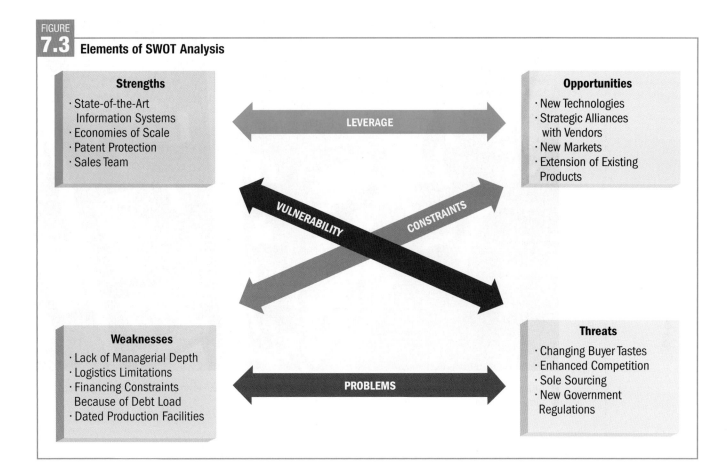

FIGURE 7.3 Elements of SWOT Analysis

Strengths
· State-of-the-Art Information Systems
· Economies of Scale
· Patent Protection
· Sales Team

LEVERAGE

Opportunities
· New Technologies
· Strategic Alliances with Vendors
· New Markets
· Extension of Existing Products

VULNERABILITY

CONSTRAINTS

Weaknesses
· Lack of Managerial Depth
· Logistics Limitations
· Financing Constraints Because of Debt Load
· Dated Production Facilities

PROBLEMS

Threats
· Changing Buyer Tastes
· Enhanced Competition
· Sole Sourcing
· New Government Regulations

For Starbucks, a key strength is consumers' positive image of the company's brand, which gets them to stand in line to pay premium prices for coffee. That positive image comes from Starbucks's being one of the best 100 companies to work for in the United States, according to *Fortune*, and from its socially responsible corporate policies. The company's strategic plans have included various ways to build on Starbucks's strong brand loyalty by attaching it to new products and expanding into new markets. The expansion efforts have included creating a Music WiFi Community on its Web site; offering bottled Frappuccino drinks in grocery stores; and opening thousands of Starbucks outlets in Europe, Asia, and the Middle East. Weaknesses include saturating some markets with too many stores and not paying attention to store design. Starbucks eventually addressed these weaknesses by closing some stores and redesigning others.[19]

SWOT analysis continues with an attempt to define the major opportunities and threats the firm is likely to face. Threats might include an economic recession—during which consumers are not willing to pay a premium for products—or a change in federal regulations. Starbucks addressed the threat of an economic downturn by beginning to offer less-expensive, instant coffee in stores like Costco and Target. Opportunities include such phenomena as the growth of social media. So Starbucks added links to Facebook and Twitter from its Web site.[20]

A SWOT analysis isn't carved in stone. Strengths and weaknesses, like opportunities and threats, may shift over time. A strength may eventually become a weakness and a threat may turn into an opportunity. But the analysis gives managers a place to start.

Extending Starbucks' strong brand loyalty to new products and markets is one example of the company's strategic turnaround plan.

Kevork Djansezian/©AP/WideWorld Photos

Setting Objectives for the Organization

The next step in planning is to develop objectives for the firm. **Objectives** set guideposts by which managers define the organization's desired performance in such areas as new-product development, sales, customer service, growth, environmental and social responsibility, and employee satisfaction. While the mission statement identifies a company's overall goals, objectives are more concrete.

One of Ford Motor Company's objectives is to update the styling of its Taurus model. New Taurus features include a T-handle shifter and a built-in navigation system.[21] One of Quiznos' objectives is to reduce the eco-footprint of its packaging. Quiznos now serves its drinks in 100-percent compostable wax-coated paper cups, and its salad bowls are made from renewable sugarcane.[22]

Creating Strategies for Competitive Differentiation

Developing a mission statement and setting objectives point a business in a specific direction. But the firm needs to identify the strategies it will use to reach its destination ahead of the competition. The underlying goal of strategy development is *competitive differentiation*—the unique combination of a company's abilities and resources that set it apart from its competitors. A firm might differentiate itself by being the first to introduce a product such as the iPad to a widespread market; or by offering exceptional customer service such as Nordstrom; or by offering bargains such as Costco. Pittsburgh-based PurBlu founder and CEO Ben Lewis differentiates his brand of bottled water, called Give Water, by marketing the fact that a portion of each bottle sold is donated to local charities. The firm's line of energy drinks, Give Energy, generates funds for grassroots sustainability initiatives.[23]

Implementing the Strategy

Once the first four phases of the strategic planning process are complete, managers are ready to put those plans into action. Often, it's the middle managers or supervisors who actually implement a strategy. But studies show that top company officials are still reluctant to empower these managers with the authority to make decisions that could benefit the company. Companies that are willing to empower employees generally reap the benefits.[24]

In an effort to accomplish the strategy of cutting costs, avoiding layoffs, and maintaining a high level of customer service, insurance and financial services giant USAA started cross-training its call-center representatives. As a result, when customers place calls about certain issues, they don't automatically have to be transferred to someone else. A call rep who answers investment queries can also answer questions about insurance. While this may seem an obvious solution—without much tangible effect—in fact, the cross-training has reduced the cost of running the call center, saved jobs, and increased customer satisfaction. Call reps are now more empowered to help customers directly, which also boosts employee morale.[25]

Monitoring and Adapting Strategic Plans

The final step in the strategic planning process is to monitor and adapt plans when the actual performance fails to meet goals. Monitoring involves securing feedback about performance. Managers might compare actual sales against forecasts; compile information from surveys; listen to complaints from the customer hot line; interview employees who are involved; and review reports prepared by production, finance, marketing, or other company units. If an Internet advertisement doesn't result in enough response or sales, managers might evaluate whether to continue the advertisement, change it, or discontinue it. If a retailer observes customers buying more jeans when they are displayed near the front door, likely the display area will stay near the door—and perhaps be enlarged. Ongoing use of such tools as SWOT analysis and forecasting can help managers adapt their objectives and functional plans as changes occur.

Assessment Check ☑

1. What is the purpose of a mission statement?
2. Which of the firm's characteristics does a SWOT analysis compare?
3. How do managers use objectives?

Managers as Decision Makers

Managers make decisions every day, whether it involves shutting down a manufacturing plant or adding grilled cheese sandwiches to a lunch menu. **Decision making** is the process of recognizing a problem or opportunity, evaluating alternative solutions, selecting and implementing an alternative, and assessing the results. Managers make two basic kinds of decisions: programmed decisions and nonprogrammed decisions.

Programmed and Nonprogrammed Decisions

A *programmed decision* involves simple, common, and frequently occurring problems for which solutions have already been determined. Examples of programmed decisions include reordering office supplies, renewing a lease, and referring to an established discount for bulk orders. Programmed decisions are made in advance—the firm sets rules, policies, and procedures for managers and employees to follow on a routine basis. Programmed decisions actually save managers time and companies money because new decisions don't have to be made each time the situation arises.

decision making process of recognizing a problem or opportunity, evaluating alternative solutions, selecting and implementing an alternative, and assessing the results.

| The release of the iPad was a nonprogrammed decision made by Apple involving a complex and unique opportunity with important consequences for the company.

A *nonprogrammed decision* involves a complex and unique problem or opportunity with important consequences for the organization. Examples of nonprogrammed decisions include entering a new market, deleting a product from the line, or developing a new product. Apple's decision to develop and launch its new product the iPad was a nonprogrammed decision that involved research and development, finances, technology, production, and marketing. Decisions were made about everything from what kinds of apps and accessories the iPad would offer to how much the new device would cost consumers.[26]

How Managers Make Decisions

In a narrow sense, decision making involves choosing among two or more alternatives, with the chosen alternative becoming the decision. In a broader sense, decision making involves a systematic, step-by-step process that helps managers make effective choices. This process begins when someone recognizes a problem or opportunity, develops possible courses of action, evaluates the alternatives, selects and implements one of them, and assesses the outcome. It's important to keep in mind that managers are *human* decision makers, and while they can follow the decision-making process as shown in Figure 7.4 step-by-step, the outcome of their decisions depends on many factors, including the accuracy of their information and the experience, creativity, and wisdom of the person.

Making good decisions is never easy. A decision might hurt or help the sales of a product; it might offend or disappoint a customer or coworker; it might affect the manager's own career or reputation. Managers' decisions can have complex legal and ethical dimensions. *CRO Magazine* publishes an annual list of "The 100 Best Corporate Citizens." These companies make decisions that are ethical, environmentally responsible, fair toward employees,

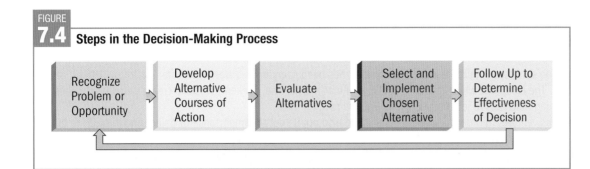

FIGURE
7.4 **Steps in the Decision-Making Process**

Recognize Problem or Opportunity → Develop Alternative Courses of Action → Evaluate Alternatives → Select and Implement Chosen Alternative → Follow Up to Determine Effectiveness of Decision

and accountable to local communities and that provide responsible goods and services to customers and a healthy return to investors. These organizations prove that good corporate citizenship is good behavior. The top ten corporate citizens named one recent year were: Hewlett-Packard, Intel, General Mills, IBM, Kimberly-Clark, Abbott Laboratories, Bristol-Myers Squibb, The Coca-Cola Company, Gap Inc., and Hess Corporation.[27]

Managers as Leaders

A manager must demonstrate **leadership**, directing or inspiring people to attain certain goals. Great leaders do not all share the same qualities, but three traits are often mentioned: empathy (the ability to imagine yourself in someone else's position), self-awareness, and objectivity. While it might seem as though empathy and objectivity are opposite traits, they do balance each other. Many leaders share other traits—courage, passion, commitment, innovation, and flexibility to name a few.

Leadership involves the use of influence or power. This influence may come from one or more sources. One source of power is the leader's position in the company. A national sales manager has the authority to direct the activities of the sales force. Another source of power is a leader's expertise and experience. A first-line supervisor with expert machinist skills will most likely be respected by employees in the machining department. Some leaders derive power from their personalities. Employees may admire a leader because they recognize an exceptionally kind and fair, humorous, energetic, or enthusiastic person. Admiration, inspiration, and motivation are especially important during difficult economic times or when a leader has to make tough decisions for the company. This has been true of Jeffrey Immelt, chairman and CEO of General Electric (GE), as described in the "Hit & Miss" feature.

When Doug Conant took over the CEO job at Campbell's Soup nearly a decade ago, the company headquartered in Camden, New Jersey, was decidedly ho-hum. Instead of boiling with innovation, the firm had left new ideas simmering on the back burner. Conant looked around his company, which produces one of the best-known brands in the world, with frustration. "The

Assessment Check ✓

1. Distinguish between programmed and non-programmed decisions.
2. What are the steps in the decision-making process?

leadership ability to direct or inspire people to attain certain goals.

Doug Conant, Campbell's Soup CEO, believes that action is the best demonstration of leadership.

Mel Evans/©AP/Wide World Photos

Jeff Immelt Tries to Lead GE in a New Direction

GE, once considered one of the nation's most recognizable and respected firms, has fallen on hard times. The company, which manufactures everything from toasters to washing machines to jet engines, has been forced to pull the plug on various ventures in order to save itself. The man in charge of the power at GE is its CEO, Jeffrey Immelt.

Over the years, GE has grown into a conglomerate, straying far from its roots as a manufacturer of electrical appliances. Its GE Capital unit, which accounted for more than half of the company's overall profits, is now burdened with a huge number of bad loans. GE's stake in NBC Universal and the NBC network will likely be sold to cable operator Comcast. But shareholders and others are asking, "Why was GE involved in these businesses in the first place?"

Jeffrey Immelt has vowed to change the direction of the company. "GE must be an industrial company first," he notes. "We need a new strategy for this economy. We should clear away any arrogance, false assumptions, or a sense that things will be OK just because we are [in] America."

Financially, GE can't just walk away from its GE Capital commitments. But Immelt has promised to reduce its size and renew the firm's focus on its industrial roots, including a significant investment in clean energy projects. He takes his leadership role, as well as the leadership role of GE itself, very seriously. "We need to invest more in innovation. We need to target this innovation toward fulfilling big needs like clean energy," he says. "Nothing of consequence is accomplished without leadership."

Immelt observes that today's leaders must adopt a democratic style that encourages input from employees. "Twenty-first century leaders listen. They use external inputs as a catalyst. They put their ego in check. They ask more questions than they answer. They welcome dissent and debate, and are constantly seeking more intelligence."

Immelt has been spending his weekends listening to the 185 officers of GE—one at a time. The weekend sessions create personal connections with his team.

He also points out the importance of delegating in order to innovate more easily and regain a competitive standing in the marketplace. "GE is a big organization. The problem with size is that it can be too slow. At GE, we must push decision-making down in the organization and we must delegate more."

Immelt has demonstrated his commitment to GE, his employees, and the firm's shareholders by declining his bonus two years in a row. This doesn't mean he isn't paid well—he still earns more than $5.5 million per year. Immelt is determined to regain the respect for his firm that it once enjoyed. As a leader, he understands this cannot be accomplished without inspired employees. "Leaders must motivate with vision," he observes. His vision includes a much brighter light for GE.

Questions for Critical Thinking

1. How would you characterize Immelt's leadership style? Is it appropriate for a big organization like GE? Why or why not?

2. Do you think Immelt is an effective motivator? Would you want to work for him? Why or why not?

Sources: Diane Brady, "Can GE Still Manage?" *Bloomberg BusinessWeek*, April 25, 2010, 26–32; GE Web site, http://www.ge.com, accessed April 9, 2010; "Renewing American Leadership: Immelt at West Point," *GE Reports*, http://www.gereports.com, accessed April 9, 2010; Stephen Manning, "GE's CEO Declines Bonus for 2nd Year," *BusinessWeek*, March 5, 2010, http://www.businessweek.com.

---

microwave was invented in 1947, but it took us until 2002 to put together a microwave-able soup pack," he pointed out to his researchers, marketers, and managers. So Conant got to work on updating the world's largest soup company. He cut all products that were not number one or number two in their categories. He poured resources into developing products that shrieked value, nutrition, and convenience to consumers. And he engineered a new focus on two of the world's largest soup-eating nations: China and Russia. Conant believes that action is the best demonstration of leadership. "You can't talk your way out of something you behaved your way into," he says.[28]

Leadership Styles

The way a person uses power to lead others determines his or her leadership style. Leadership styles range along a continuum with autocratic leadership at one extreme end and free-rein leadership at the other. *Autocratic leadership* is centered on the boss. Autocratic leaders make decisions on their own without consulting employees. They reach decisions, communicate them to subordinates, and expect automatic implementation.

Democratic leadership includes subordinates in the decision-making process. This leadership style centers on employees' contributions. Democratic leaders delegate assignments, ask employees for suggestions, and encourage participation. An important outgrowth of democratic leadership in business is the concept of **empowerment**, in which employees share authority, responsibility, and decision making with their managers.

At the other end of the continuum from autocratic leadership is *free-rein leadership*. Free-rein leaders believe in minimal supervision. They allow subordinates to make most of their own decisions. Free-rein leaders communicate with employees frequently, as the situation warrants. For the first decade of its existence, Google was proud of its free-rein leadership style. Engineers were encouraged to pursue any and all ideas; teams formed or disbanded on their own; employees spent as much or as little time as they wanted to on any given project. But as the firm entered its second decade, it became apparent that not every innovation was worth pursuing—

When US Airways flight 1549 was forced to ditch into the Hudson River, the quick thinking and decision-making leadership style of Chesley Sullenberger saved the lives of everyone on that flight.

Charlotte Observer/MCT/Landov LLC

and some valuable ideas were getting lost in the chaos. CEO Eric Schmidt noted, "We were concerned that some of the biggest ideas were getting squashed." So the firm established a process for reviewing new project ideas in order to identify those most likely to succeed.[29]

Which Leadership Style Is Best?

No single leadership style is best for every firm in every situation. Sometimes leadership styles require change in order for a company to grow, as has been the case for Google. In a crisis, an autocratic leadership style might save the company—and sometimes the lives of customers and employees. This was the case when US Airways flight 1549 was forced to ditch into the Hudson River after hitting a wayward flock of Canada geese. Quick, autocratic decisions made by pilot Chesley Sullenberger resulted in the survival of everyone on board the flight. But US Airways management on the ground activated a democratic style of leadership in which managers at many levels were empowered to take actions to help the passengers and their families. For example, one executive arrived on the scene with a bag of emergency cash for passengers and credit cards for employees so they could purchase medicines, food, or anything else they needed.[30] A company that recognizes which leadership style works best for its employees, customers, and business conditions is most likely to choose the best leaders for its particular needs.

Corporate Culture

An organization's **corporate culture** is its system of principles, beliefs, and values. The leadership style of its managers, the way it communicates, and the overall work environment influence a firm's corporate culture. A corporate culture is typically shaped by the leaders who founded and developed the company and by those who have succeeded them. Although

empowerment giving employees shared authority, responsibility, and decision making with their managers.

Assessment Check ✔

1. How is *leadership* defined?
2. Identify the styles of leadership as they appear along a continuum of greater or lesser employee participation.

corporate culture organization's system of principles, beliefs, and values.

Google has grown by leaps and bounds since its launch, the firm still tries to maintain the culture of innovation, creativity, and flexibility that its co-founders Larry Page and Sergey Brin promoted from the beginning. Google now has offices around the world, staffed by thousands of workers who speak a multitude of languages. "We are aggressively inclusive in our hiring, and we favor ability over experience," states the Web site. "The result is a team that reflects the global audience Google serves. When not at work, Googlers pursue interests from cross-country cycling to wine tasting, from flying to Frisbee."[31]

Managers use symbols, rituals, ceremonies, and stories to reinforce corporate culture. The corporate culture at the Walt Disney Company is almost as famous as the original Disney characters themselves. In fact, every Disney employee is known as a cast member. All new employees attend training seminars in which they learn the language, customs, traditions, stories, product lines—everything there is to know about the Disney culture and its original founder, Walt Disney.[32]

Corporate cultures can be very strong and enduring, but sometimes they are forced to change to meet new demands in the business environment. A firm that is steeped in tradition and bureaucracy might have to shift to a leaner, more flexible culture in order to respond to shifts in technology or customer preferences. A firm that grows quickly—like Google—generally has to make some adjustments in its culture to accommodate more customers and employees.

In an organization with a strong culture, everyone knows and supports the same principles, beliefs, and values. To achieve its goals, a business must also provide structure, which results from the management function of organizing.

Assessment Check ✓

1. What is the relationship between leadership style and corporate culture?

2. What is a strong corporate culture?

organization structured group of people working together to achieve common goals.

Organizational Structures

An **organization** is a structured group of people working together to achieve common goals. An organization features three key elements: human interaction, goal-directed activities, and structure. The organizing process, much of which is led by managers, should result in an overall structure that permits interactions among individuals and departments needed to achieve company goals. The "Hit & Miss" feature describes how chairwoman and former CEO Anne Mulcahy changed the structure of Xerox when its profits were falling.

FIGURE 7.5 Steps in the Organizing Process

1. Determine Specific Work Activities Necessary to Implement Plans and Achieve Objectives	2. Group Work Activities into a Logical Pattern or Structure	3. Assign Activities to Specific Positions and People and Allocate Necessary Resources	4. Coordinate Activities of Different Groups and Individuals	5. Evaluate Results of the Organizing Process

Hit & Miss

Xerox Creates a New Image of Itself

Anne Mulcahy took the CEO position at Xerox when the company was facing possible bankruptcy. Shareholders wanted quick solutions to the company's complicated problems. Some dumped their stock, causing the price to drop 26 percent in one day. Mulcahy is a tough executive who is loyal to her company—she has been with Xerox for more than 25 years. She resisted the urge to declare bankruptcy, which would have cleared the firm's $18 billion in debt.

Despite advice that she should cut research and development or field sales, Mulcahy instead hacked away at Xerox's bloated organization. She authorized the sale of pieces of Fuji Xerox and outsourced portions of manufacturing. Entire divisions were shut down, and more than 30 percent of the company's workforce—roughly 30,000 jobs—were eliminated. Billions of dollars in expenses were cut. In the process, Xerox was transformed from a black-and-white copier manufacturer to an up-to-date supplier of office network services and color printing systems.

The firm is on the comeback. Shareholders are happy with Mulcahy's restructuring; the stock price has tripled from where it was just a few years ago. The firm's focus has shifted dramatically. As the printing market continues to shift with the expansion of wireless communications systems, Xerox has launched 100 new printing technologies in three years. It is a leader in the specialized color printing market; its digital systems make it easy for customers to produce their own brochures, posters, and books.

Unlike other executives who turn around companies and then depart for new challenges, Mulcahy has no intention of leaving Xerox. Although she stepped down as CEO in May 2009, she is staying on as the company's chairwoman.

Questions for Critical Thinking

1. What type of organization do you think best represents the new direction of Xerox? Why?
2. Anne Mulcahy made some very bold moves. Do you agree with her approach? Why or why not?

Sources: Franklin Paul, "Xerox Profit Falls on Restructuring Costs," *Reuters*, January 23, 2009, http://www.reuters.com; Bill George, "The Courage to Say No to Wall Street," *U.S. News & World Report*, December 8, 2008, pp. 50–51; "Xerox Cutting 5 Percent of Workforce," *The Business Review*, October 24, 2008, http://albany.bizjournals.com; Jacquie McNish, "Xerox's Success Is a Reflection of Her Dedication," *The Globe and Mail*, September 11, 2008, http://www.theglobeandmail.com; "Anne Mulcahy—The 100 Most Powerful Women," *Forbes*, August 27, 2008, http://www.forbes.com.

The steps involved in the organizing process are shown in Figure 7.5. Managers first determine the specific activities needed to implement plans and achieve goals. Next, they group these work activities into a logical structure. Then they assign work to specific employees and give the people the resources they need to complete it. Managers coordinate the work of different groups and employees within the firm. Finally, they evaluate the results of the organizing process to ensure effective and efficient progress toward planned goals. Evaluation sometimes results in changes to the way work is organized.

Many factors influence the results of organizing. The list includes a firm's goals and competitive strategy, the type of product it offers, the way it uses technology to accomplish work, and its size. Small firms typically create very simple structures. The owner of a dry-cleaning business generally is the top manager, who hires several employees to process orders, clean the clothing, and make deliveries. The owner handles the functions of purchasing supplies such as detergents and hangers, hiring and training employees and coordinating their work, preparing advertisements for the local newspaper, and keeping accounting records.

As a company grows, its structure increases in complexity. With increased size comes specialization and growing numbers of employees. A larger firm may employ many

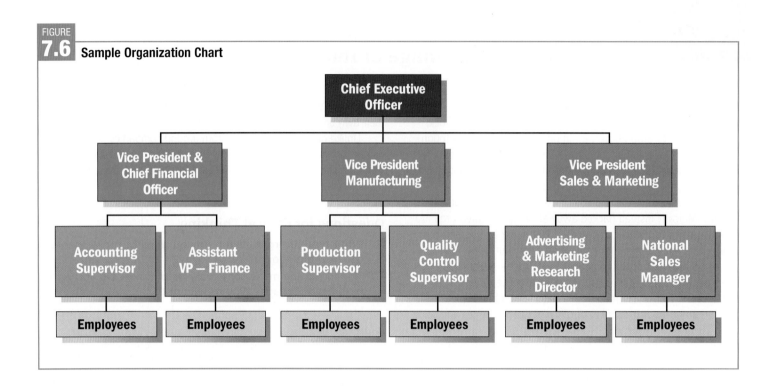

FIGURE 7.6 Sample Organization Chart

salespeople, along with a sales manager to direct and coordinate their work, or organize an accounting department.

An effective structure is one that is clear and easy to understand: employees know what is expected of them and to whom they report. They also know how their jobs contribute to the company's mission and overall strategic plan. An *organization chart* can help clarify the structure of a firm. Figure 7.6 illustrates a sample organization chart.

Not-for-profit organizations also organize through formal structures so they can function efficiently and carry out their goals. These organizations, such as the Salvation Army and the American Society for Prevention of Cruelty to Animals (ASPCA), sometimes have a blend of paid staff and volunteers in their organizational structure.

Departmentalization

departmentalization process of dividing work activities into units within the organization.

Departmentalization is the process of dividing work activities into units within the organization. In this arrangement, employees specialize in certain jobs—such as marketing, finance, or design. Depending on the size of the firm, usually an executive runs the department, followed by middle-level managers and supervisors. The five major forms of departmentalization subdivide work by product, geographical area, customer, function, and process.

- *Product departmentalization.* This approach organizes work units based on the goods and services a company offers. California's Activision Blizzard Inc. recently restructured its organization by product. The videogame publisher is now divided into four divisions: "Call of Duty," a military game; internally owned games such as

These familiar office products represent only one of 3M Corporation's many product lines. Because 3M serves such a broad spectrum of customers, it is organized on the basis of customer departmentalization.

©R. Alcorn, Photographed for John Wiley & Sons

"Guitar Hero" and "Tony Hawk"; licensed properties; and Blizzard Entertainment, maker of the online game "World of Warcraft."[33]

- *Geographical departmentalization.* This form organizes units by geographical regions within a country or, for a multinational firm, by region throughout the world. Enterprise Rent-A-Car, based in St. Louis, is organized by geography, staffing 7,000 rental locations in the United States, Canada, Germany, Ireland, and England.[34]

- *Customer departmentalization.* A firm that offers a variety of goods and services targeted at different types of customers might structure itself based on customer departmentalization. Management of Minnesota-based 3M's wide array of products is divided among six business units: consumer and office; display and graphics; electro and communications; healthcare; industrial and transportation; and safety, security, and protection services.[35]

- *Functional departmentalization.* Some firms organize work units according to business functions such as finance, marketing, human resources, and production. An advertising agency may create departments for creative personnel (say, copywriters), media buyers, and account executives.

- *Process departmentalization.* Some goods and services require multiple work processes to complete their production. A manufacturer may set up separate departments for cutting material, heat-treating it, forming it into its final shape, and painting it.

As Figure 7.7 illustrates, a single company may implement several different departmentalization schemes. In deciding on a form of departmentalization, managers take into account the type of product they produce, the size of their company, their customer base, and the locations of their customers.

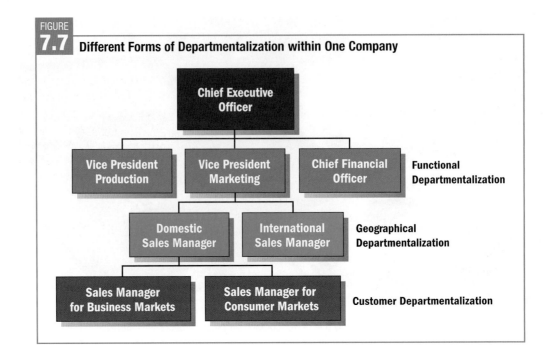

FIGURE 7.7 **Different Forms of Departmentalization within One Company**

Delegating Work Assignments

delegation managerial process of assigning work to employees.

Managers assign work to employees, a process called **delegation**. Employees might be responsible for answering customer calls, scooping ice cream, processing returns, making deliveries, opening or closing a store, cooking or serving food, contributing to new-product design, calculating a return on investment, or any of thousands of other tasks. Just as important, employees are given a certain amount of authority to make decisions.

Companies like Zappos, the online shoe retailer, that empower their workers to make decisions that could better serve their customers generally have happier employees and more satisfied customers.[36] As employees receive greater authority, they also must be accountable for their actions and decisions—they receive credit when things go well, and must accept responsibility when they don't. Managers also must figure out the best way to delegate responsibilities to employees who belong to different age groups, as discussed in the "Business Etiquette" feature.

Span of Management The *span of management*, or span of control, is the number of employees a manager supervises. These employees are often referred to as direct reports. First-line managers have wider spans of management, monitoring the work of many employees. The span of management varies depending on many factors, including the type of work performed and employees' training. In recent years, a growing trend has brought wider spans of control, as companies have reduced their layers of management to flatten their organizational structures, in the process increasing the decision-making responsibility they give employees.

Centralization and Decentralization How widely should managers disperse decision-making authority throughout an organization? A company that emphasizes *centralization* retains decision making at the top of the management hierarchy. A company that emphasizes *decentralization* locates decision making at lower levels. A trend toward decentralization has pushed decision making down to operating employees in many cases. Firms that have decentralized believe that the change can improve their ability to serve customers. For example, the front desk clerk at a hotel is much better equipped to fulfill a guest's request for a crib or a wake-up call than the hotel's general manager.

Types of Organization Structures

The four basic types of organization structures are line, line-and-staff, committee, and matrix. While some companies do follow one type of structure, most use a combination.

Line Organizations A *line organization*, the oldest and simplest organization structure, establishes a direct flow of authority from the chief executive to employees. The line organization defines a simple, clear *chain of command*—a hierarchy of managers and workers. With a clear chain of command, everyone knows who is in charge and decisions can be made quickly. This structure is particularly effective in a crisis situation. But a line organization has its drawbacks. Each manager has complete responsibility for a range of activities; in a medium-sized or large organization, however, this person can't possibly be expert in all of them. In a small organization such as a local hair salon, or dentist's office, a line organization is probably the most efficient way to run the business.

Line-and-Staff Organizations A *line-and-staff organization* combines the direct flow of authority of a line organization with staff departments that support the line departments. Line departments participate directly in decisions that affect the core operations of the organization. Staff departments lend specialized technical support. Figure 7.8 illustrates a line-and-staff organization. Accounting, engineering, and human resources are staff departments that support the line authority extending from the plant manager to the production manager and supervisors.

BusinessEtiquette

Managing a Multigenerational Workforce

Today's firms comprised of employees spanning a wide range of ages. Though management experts warn against stereotyping, they do suggest making an effort to understand each group and taking steps to open communication so that the workforce functions well together. Baby Boomers, those workers born between 1946 and 1964, tend to be competitive and believe younger employees should work their way up the company ladder. Gen Xers, born between 1965 and 1977, are more skeptical, independent thinkers. Gen Ys—also called the Millenials—were born in 1978 or later and prefer teamwork, feedback, and technology.

Managers can more effectively delegate work to employees in these groups by doing the following:

- Offering—and nurturing—mentoring between younger and older employees. Cross-generational communication and support facilitates understanding.
- Recognizing and accommodating different learning—and work—styles.
- Engaging employees through training, education, and career development opportunities.
- Discarding rigid routines for those who work best without them.
- Using different forms of communication. Older employees may prefer chatting on the phone or in person. Millenials might do best with e-mails, text messages, or via social networking.
- Giving everyone an equal voice. Everyone wants to be heard and understood. Offer opportunities for all employees to voice their opinions.

Sources: Sally Kane, "The Multigenerational Workforce," *About.com*, http://legalcareers.about.com, accessed March 29, 2010; "How to Manage Different Generations," *The Wall Street Journal*, http://guides.wsj.com, accessed March 29, 2010; Tammy Erickson, "Finally, Gen X Takes Over," *BusinessWeek*, January 13, 2009, http://www.businessweek.com.

FIGURE
7.8 Line-and-Staff Organization

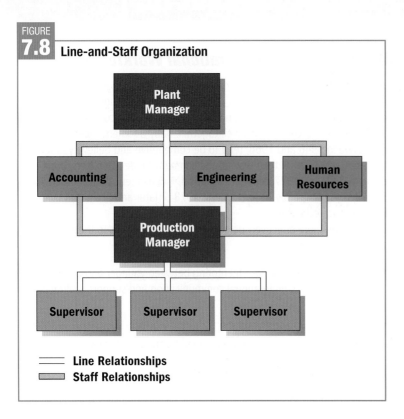

Plant Manager

Accounting   **Engineering**   **Human Resources**

Production Manager

Supervisor   **Supervisor**   **Supervisor**

─── Line Relationships
▭ Staff Relationships

A line manager and a staff manager differ significantly in their authority relationships. A line manager forms part of the primary line of authority that flows throughout the organization. Line managers interact directly with the functions of production, financing, or marketing—the functions needed to produce and sell goods and services. A staff manager provides information, advice, or technical assistance to aid line managers. Staff managers do not have authority to give orders outside their own departments or to compel line managers to take action.

The line-and-staff organization is common in midsize and large organizations. It is an effective structure because it combines the line organization's capabilities for rapid decision making and direct communication with the expert knowledge of staff specialists.

Committee Organizations

A *committee organization* is a structure that places authority and responsibility jointly in the hands of a group of individuals rather than a single manager. This model typically appears as part of a regular line-and-staff structure.

Committees also work in areas such as new-product development. A new-product committee may include managers from such areas as accounting, engineering, finance, manufacturing, marketing, and technical research. By including representatives from all areas involved in creating and marketing products, such a committee generally improves planning and employee morale because decisions reflect diverse perspectives.

Committees tend to act slowly and conservatively, however, and may make decisions by compromising conflicting interests rather than by choosing the best alternative. The definition of a camel as "a racehorse designed by committee" provides an apt description of some limitations of committee decisions. At Nordstrom, the six-person office of the co-presidency was eventually abandoned for a more traditional structure.

Matrix Organizations

Some organizations use a matrix or product management design to customize their structures. The *matrix structure* links employees from different parts of the organization to work together on specific projects. Figure 7.9 diagrams a matrix structure. A project manager assembles a group of employees from different functional areas. The employees keep their ties to the line-and-staff structure, as shown in the vertical white lines. As the horizontal gold lines show, employees are also members of project teams. When the project is completed, employees return to their "regular" jobs.

In the matrix structure, each employee reports to two managers: one line manager and one project manager. Employees who are chosen to work on a special project receive instructions from the project manager (horizontal authority), but they continue as employees in their permanent functional departments (vertical authority). The term *matrix* comes from the intersecting grid of horizontal and vertical lines of authority.

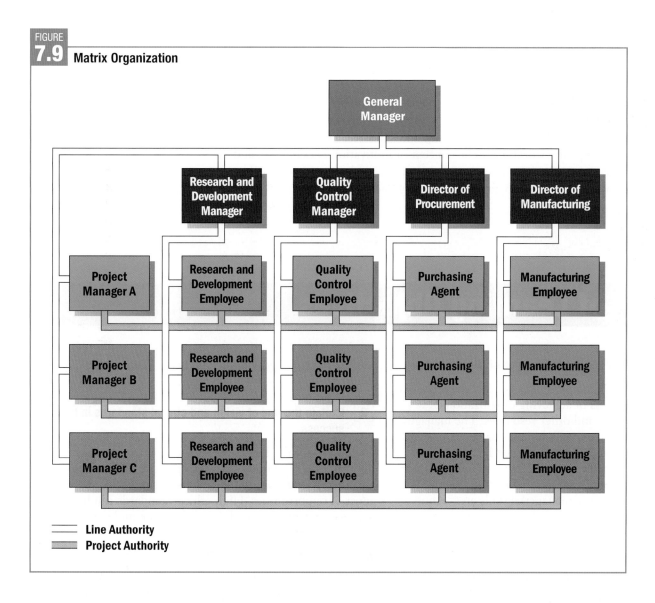

FIGURE 7.9 Matrix Organization

General Manager

Research and Development Manager | Quality Control Manager | Director of Procurement | Director of Manufacturing

Project Manager A | Research and Development Employee | Quality Control Employee | Purchasing Agent | Manufacturing Employee

Project Manager B | Research and Development Employee | Quality Control Employee | Purchasing Agent | Manufacturing Employee

Project Manager C | Research and Development Employee | Quality Control Employee | Purchasing Agent | Manufacturing Employee

— Line Authority
▬ Project Authority

The matrix structure is popular at high-technology and multinational corporations, as well as hospitals and consulting firms. Dow Chemical and Procter & Gamble have both used matrix structures. The major benefits of the matrix structure come from its flexibility in adapting quickly to rapid changes in the environment and its capability of focusing resources on major problems or products. It also provides an outlet for employees' creativity and initiative. However, it challenges project managers to integrate the skills of specialists from many departments into a coordinated team. It also means that team members' permanent functional managers must adjust their employees' regular workloads.

The matrix structure is most effective when company leaders empower project managers to use whatever resources are available to achieve the project's objectives. Good project managers know how to make the project goals clear and keep team members focused. A firm that truly embraces the matrix structure also nurtures a project culture by making sure staffing is adequate, the workload is reasonable, and other company resources are available to project managers.[37]

Assessment Check ☑

1. What is the purpose of an organization chart?

2. What are the five major forms of departmentalization?

3. What does *span of management* mean?

What's Ahead

In the next chapter, we sharpen our focus on the importance of people—the human resource—in shaping the growth and profitability of the organization. We examine how firms recruit, select, train, evaluate, and compensate employees in their attempts to attract, retain, and motivate a high-quality workforce. The concept of motivation is examined, and we will discuss how managers apply theories of motivation in the modern workplace. The next chapter also looks at the important topic of labor–management relations.

Summary of Learning Objectives

⌐1⌐ Define *management* and the three types of skills necessary for managerial success.

Management is the process of achieving organizational objectives through people and other resources. The management hierarchy is generally as follows: top managers provide overall direction for company activities, middle managers implement the strategies of top managers and direct the activities of supervisors, and supervisors interact directly with workers. The three basic managerial skills are: technical, human or interpersonal, and conceptual.

Assessment Check Answers ✔

1.1 What is management? Management is the process of achieving organizational objectives through people and other resources. The manager's job is to combine human and technical resources in the best way possible to achieve the company's goals.

1.2 How do the jobs of top managers, middle managers, and supervisory managers differ? Top managers develop long-range plans, set a direction for their organization, and inspire all employees to achieve the company's vision. Middle managers focus on specific operations, products, or customers. They develop procedures to implement the firm's strategic plans. Supervisory managers interact directly with nonmanagerial employees who produce and sell the firm's goods and services. They are responsible for implementing the plans developed by middle managers and motivating workers to accomplish immediate goals.

1.3 What is the relationship between the manager's planning and controlling functions? Controlling is evaluating an organization's performance to determine whether it is accomplishing its objectives. The basic purpose of controlling is to assess the success of the planning function.

Controlling also provides feedback for future rounds of planning.

⌐2⌐ Explain the role of vision and ethical standards in business success.

Vision is the founder's perception of the marketplace needs and the firm's methods for meeting them. Vision helps clarify a firm's purpose and the actions it can take to make the most of opportunities. High ethical standards can help build success for a firm through job satisfaction and customer loyalty.

Assessment Check Answers ✔

2.1 What is meant by a vision for the firm? A vision serves as the target for a firm's actions, helping direct the company toward opportunities and differentiating it from its competitors.

2.2 Why is it important for a top executive to set high ethical standards? High ethical standards often result in a stable workforce, job satisfaction, and customer loyalty.

⌐3⌐ Summarize the major benefits of planning, and distinguish among strategic planning, tactical planning, and operational planning.

The planning process identifies organizational goals and develops the actions necessary to reach them. Planning helps a company turn vision into action, take advantage of opportunities, and avoid costly mistakes. Strategic planning is a far-reaching process. It views the world through a wide-angle lens to determine the long-range focus and activities of the organization. Tactical planning focuses on the current and short-range activities required to implement the organization's strategies. Operational planning sets standards and work targets for functional areas such as production, human resources, and marketing.

Assessment Check Answers ✅

3.1 Outline the planning process. Some plans are very broad and long range, focusing on key organizational objectives; others are more detailed and specify how particular objectives will be achieved. From the mission statement to objectives to specific plans, each phase must fit into a comprehensive planning framework.

3.2 Describe the purpose of tactical planning. The purpose of tactical planning is to determine which short-term activities should be implemented to accomplish the firm's overall strategy.

3.3 Compare the kinds of plans made by top managers and middle managers. How does their focus differ? Top managers focus on long-range, strategic plans. In contrast, middle-level managers and supervisors focus on short-term, tactical planning.

[4] Describe the strategic planning process.

The first step of strategic planning is to translate the firm's vision into a mission statement that explains its overall intentions and aims. Next, planners must assess the firm's current competitive position using tools such as SWOT analysis. Managers then set specific objectives. The next step is to develop strategies for reaching objectives that will differentiate the firm from its competitors. Managers then develop an action plan that outlines the specific methods for implementing the strategy. Finally, the results achieved by the plan are evaluated, and the plan is adjusted as needed.

Assessment Check Answers ✅

4.1 What is the purpose of a mission statement? A mission statement is a public declaration of a firm's purpose, the reason it exists, the customers it will serve, and the way it is different from competitors. A mission statement guides the actions of company managers and employees.

4.2 Which of the firm's characteristics does a SWOT analysis compare? A SWOT analysis determines a firm's strengths, weaknesses, opportunities, and threats relative to its competitors. A SWOT analysis helps determine a firm's competitive position in the marketplace.

4.3 How do managers use objectives? Objectives, which are derived from the firm's mission statement, are used to define desired performance levels in areas such as profitability, customer service, and employee satisfaction.

[5] Contrast the two major types of business decisions, and list the steps in the decision-making process.

A programmed decision applies a company rule or policy to solve a frequently occurring problem. A nonprogrammed decision forms a response to a complex and unique problem with important consequences for the organization. The five-step approach to decision making includes recognizing a problem or opportunity, developing alternative courses of action, evaluating the alternatives, selecting and implementing an alternative, and following up the decision to determine its effectiveness.

Assessment Check Answers ✅

5.1 Distinguish between programmed and nonprogrammed decisions. Programmed decisions, such as reordering office supplies, are simple and happen frequently, so procedures for these can streamline the process. Nonprogrammed decisions, such as the purchase of real estate or equipment, require more individual evaluation.

5.2 What are the steps in the decision-making process? The decision-making steps are recognition of a problem or opportunity, development of alternatives, evaluation of alternatives, selection and implementation of the chosen alternative, and follow-up to determine effectiveness of the decision.

[6] Define *leadership,* and compare different leadership styles.

Leadership is the act of motivating others to achieve certain goals. The basic leadership styles are autocratic, democratic, and free-rein leadership. The best leadership style depends on three elements: the leader, the followers, and the situation.

Assessment Check Answers ✅

6.1 How is *leadership* defined? Leadership means directing or inspiring people to attain organizational goals. Effective leaders share several traits, such as empathy, self-awareness, and objectivity in dealing with others. Leaders also use the power of their jobs, expertise, and experience to influence others.

6.2 Identify the styles of leadership as they appear along a continuum of greater or lesser employee participation. At one end of the continuum, autocratic leaders make decisions without consulting employees. In the middle of the continuum, democratic leaders ask employees for suggestions and encourage participation. At the other end of the continuum, free-rein leaders leave most decisions to their employees.

[7] Discuss the meaning and importance of corporate culture.

Corporate culture refers to an organization's principles, beliefs, and values. It is typically shaped by a firm's founder and perpetuated through formal programs such as training, rituals, and ceremonies, as well as through informal discussions among employees. Corporate culture can influence a firm's success by giving it a competitive advantage.

Assessment Check Answers ✓

7.1 What is the relationship between leadership style and corporate culture? The best leadership style to adopt often depends on the organization's corporate culture and its system of principles, beliefs, and values. Managerial philosophies, communications networks, and workplace environments and practices all influence corporate culture.

7.2 What is a strong corporate culture? A corporate culture is an organization's system of principles, beliefs, and values. In an organization with a strong culture, everyone knows and supports the same principles, beliefs, and values.

┌ 8 ┐ **Identify the five major forms of departmentalization and the four main types of organization structures.**

The subdivision of work activities into units within the organization is called *departmentalization*. It may be based on products, geographical locations, customers, functions, or processes. Most firms implement one or more of four structures: line, line-and-staff, committee, and matrix structures.

Assessment Check Answers ✓

8.1 What is the purpose of an organization chart? An organization chart is a visual representation of a firm's structure that illustrates job positions and functions.

8.2 What are the five major forms of departmentalization? Product departmentalization organizes units by the different goods and services a company offers. Geographical departmentalization organizes units by geographical regions. Customer departmentalization organizes units by different types of customers. Functional departmentalization organizes units by business functions such as finance, marketing, human resources, and production. Process departmentalization organizes units by the steps or work processes it takes to complete production or provide a service.

8.3 What does *span of management* mean? The span of management, or span of control, is the number of employees a manager supervises.

■ Business Terms You Need to Know

management 218	controlling 222	objectives 230	corporate culture 235
planning 221	vision 222	decision making 231	organization 236
organizing 221	mission statement 227	leadership 233	departmentalization 238
directing 222	SWOT analysis 228	empowerment 235	delegation 240

■ Review Questions

1. What are the three levels of management hierarchy? For each level, which management skills might be considered most important, and why?

2. Identify the four basic managerial functions. Suppose you were hired to be the manager of a local restaurant. Which managerial functions would likely be the biggest part of your job? In what ways?

3. Describe the link between a company's vision and its ethical standards. Why is it important for top management to put forth a clear vision and ethical standards for a company?

4. Identify the four types of planning, then think about the following scenario. Suppose you planned a large cookout with your friends, but when you woke up on the morning of the party, it was pouring rain. What type of planning would you use prior to the storm? What type of planning would allow you to cope with the rain? Specifically, what could you do?

5. What is the link between a firm's vision and its mission statement? Think about your own career as a start-up venture. What is your vision? What might be your mission statement?

6. Define *objectives*. Outline objectives you might have for your own college education and career. How might this outline help you implement your own career strategy?

7. Identify each of the following as a programmed or nonprogrammed decision:
   a. reordering printer cartridges
   b. selecting a cell phone provider
   c. buying your favorite toothpaste or shampoo at the supermarket
   d. selecting a college to attend
   e. filling your car with gasoline

8. From what sources might a leader derive power? Which leadership style might work best for a manager whose firm is forced to make cost-cutting decisions? Why?

9. Why is a strong corporate culture important to a company's success? How might the corporate culture be linked to leadership style?

10. Which type of organization structure provides a firm with the most flexibility to respond to changes in the marketplace and engage in innovation? What might be the drawbacks of this structure?

Projects and Teamwork Applications

1. Imagine that you've been hired as a supervisor by a bakery shop called Claire's Cakes that is beginning to grow. The founder, whose name is Claire, is looking for ways to increase production capacity, expand its deliveries, and eventually open several more shops in the area. Create a job description for yourself, including the managerial functions you think you'll need and skills you believe you'll need for success.

2. On your own or with a classmate, create a mission statement for Claire's Cakes. Think about the type of company it is, the products it offers customers (cakes for special occasions or milestones), and the type of growth it is planning.

3. Contingency planning requires a combination of foresight and adaptability. Josh James, founder of Omniture, the Web analytics firm he recently sold to Adobe, recalls the importance of being able to adapt when his company seemed on the brink of disaster. "There were times when I lay down on the floor at night, close to crying. Then my wife would come over and kick me and say, 'Get up and figure it out.' "[38] Research the news headlines for situations that could (or did) require contingency planning. Report to the class what the challenge was, and how the managers involved handled it. Remark on whether the planning was effective or successful.

4. Identify someone who you think is a good leader—it can be someone you know personally or a public figure. Describe the traits that you think are most important in making this person an effective leader. Would this person's leadership style work in situations other than his or her current position? Why or why not?

5. Research a firm whose goods or services you purchase or admire. Learn what you can about the organization's culture. Do you think you would be an effective manager in this culture? Why or why not? Share your findings with the class.

Web Assignments

1. **Strategic planning.** Visit the Web site listed below. It summarizes Johnson & Johnson's strategic planning philosophy. Review several recent acquisitions by Johnson & Johnson and prepare a brief report discussing how the acquisitions resulted from the company's strategic planning process.

   http://www.investor.jnj.com/strategic.cfm

2. **Mission statements.** Go to the Web sites of two organizations, a for-profit firm and a not-for-profit organization. Print out both organization's mission statements. Take the material with you to class to participate in a discussion on mission statements.

3. **Management structure.** Visit the Web site listed below. Click on "corporate governance" and answer the following questions:

   a. How would you characterize Target's organizational structure?

   b. What is the composition of Target's board of directors?

   http://investors.target.com/phoenix.zhtml?c=65828&p=irol-IRHome

Note: Internet Web addresses change frequently. If you don't find the exact sites listed, you may need to access the organization's home page and search from there or use a search engine such as Bing or Google.

Ford Drives Out of the Financial Mud

Recently, when the other major U.S. automakers accepted federal funds in order to stay in business, Ford Motor Company—in the voice of CEO Alan R. Mulally—said no. The federal funds were to come in the form of short-term loans, which Ford determined that it didn't need at the time to survive. Several years earlier, the firm had faced financial decisions and restructured its debt in such a way that, when the economy slowed down, Ford didn't.

Mulally observes that this timing was a bit of luck and a bit of strategic planning. "I go back to the fundamental point of view that the Ford Motor Company has taken about the future going forward, and the actions that we have taken to create that future," he observes. "[Several years] ago we decided that fuel efficiency was going to be very, very important going forward, along with quality and safety and good value. We also decided that we wanted to provide customers with an absolutely clear vision of Ford and focus on the Ford brand." As part of this overall strategy, Ford sold off its luxury brands Aston Martin, Jaguar, and Land Rover. Meanwhile, it invested in the development of moderately priced, fuel-efficient cars and trucks. Ford took on some extra debt at the time as a hedge against a recession—and had the cash on hand when the other two automakers didn't.

Decisions like this are typical of the responsibilities that are faced by top managers like Mulally. They require strong leadership qualities that include a willingness to persist during tough times. But Mulally wasn't always CEO of Ford. His first management position was as an engineering supervisor at Boeing. He overmanaged his employees so closely that one engineer finally quit. Mulally says that this was an important experience early in his management career. He realized that his job as a manager was "to help connect people to a bigger goal, a bigger program and help them move forward to even bigger contributions. That experience stayed with me forever on what it really means to manage and lead."

Mulally believes that every employee has something to offer an organization and that each worker must be clear about the firm's mission. "I think the most important thing is coming to a shared view about what we're trying to accomplish," he says. "What are we? What is our real purpose? And then, how do you include everybody so you know where you are on that plan?"

As the company's leader, Mulally says that his job is to focus on four things: (1) the process of connecting his firm to the outside world, (2) keeping track of the firm's identity in the marketplace, (3) balancing short-term objectives with long-term goals, and (4) the values and standards of the organization. Mulally notes that keeping his eye on these four variables keeps Ford on the road. "I'm the one who needs to focus on those four things, because if I do that, the entire team will have a collective point of view and an understanding of all four of these areas." When asked what career advice he would give to young recruits to the business world, Mulally answers without hesitation: "Don't manage your career. Follow your dream and contribute."

Questions for Critical Thinking

1. How does Alan Mulally's "focus on four things" help him with strategic planning for Ford? Do you believe it made a difference in the firm's decision to decline the federal loan?

2. Mulally emphasizes the importance of having every employee understand the firm's mission. How might this understanding help employees contribute to the company's performance?

Sources: Paul Ingrassia, "Ford's Renaissance Man," *The Wall Street Journal,* http://www.online.wsj.com; accessed March 29, 2010; Keith Naughton and Ian King, "Mulally: Ford Marking Tremendous Progress," *BusinessWeek,* January 7, 2010, http://www.businessweek.com; Adam Bryant, "Planes, Cars, and Cathedrals," *The New York Times,* September 9, 2009, http://www.nytimes.com; John Hockenberry, "Interview with Ford CEO Alan Mulally," *PRI/WNYC,* April 3, 2009, http://www.pri.org; Excerpt from "Interview with Ford CEO Alan Mulally," from The Takeaway, a co-production of Public Radio International and WNYC. Reprinted with permission.

While the music business remains in turmoil, Live Nation keeps rocking on. The two-year-old company, a spin-off of Clear Channel, generated more than $4 billion in revenue in a recent year. Michael Rapino produces more concert tours than any other company in the world, and he owns both large and small venues such as the House of Blues chain and a string of smaller clubs named after the famous Fillmore halls. As CEO of Live Nation, the 42-year-old Rapino is one of the few people in the music industry who has managed to grow revenue in recent years. Genesis, Roger Waters of Pink Floyd fame, and the newly reunited Police are some of the bands he has taken on the road.

The music business has changed dramatically, in large part due to file sharing and the iPod. Artists once made the bulk of their money selling CDs and toured to promote their albums. Today artists make most of their money touring, and Live Nation, the world's largest live-music company, is leading the way. But Rapino isn't stopping with concerts. Because he operates the tours of many musicians, he wants to turn Live Nation into a company that can handle all their musical needs. Rapino thinks he can offer one-stop service to musical artists creating their albums, selling their merchandise, and handling their Web sites. Live Nation also recently broke from Ticketmaster to form its own ticketing business.

In short, Rapino is mounting an all-out assault on record labels and believes he is in a great position to pull it off. Madonna has already left Warner Bros. to sign a ten-year contract with Live Music, who will handle every aspect of her business except publishing. According to her manager, Guy Oseary, companies have to be involved in all aspects of the music business today to do well. Rapino's strategy is fairly simple—to connect with the millions of people who attend a Live Nation show each year. According to Rapino, "I should be e-mailing you the morning after the Jay-Z concert, saying 'Want a CD? A download? Want a video of the show? Want a set list? Want a signed shirt with Jay-Z? We printed a limited edition.' The possibilities are endless."

Rapino's strategy is not without its critics. Some argue that he will need the resources of a major label to produce and market CDs; this job will eventually have to be licensed to a label. In addition, some record companies are following Rapino's lead and signing bands to similar comprehensive deals. Rapino's response to the critics is that he knows how to market and ultimately will sign many superstars in the years ahead. Investors appear skeptical, as Live Nation's stock fell 30 percent after the Madonna deal. But Rapino has complete confidence in his approach—while the CD business languished, live music is where the action is.

Questions for Critical Thinking

1. What are some of Live Nation's strengths, weaknesses, opportunities, and threats?
2. What is Live Nation's strategy for competitive differentiation?

Sources: Ellen Smith, "Ticketmaster and Cablevision May Acquire 49% of AEG Live," *The Wall Street Journal,* February 29, 2008, p. C3; Paul Sloan, "Keep on Rocking in the Free World," *Fortune,* December 10, 2007, pp. 156–160; Devin Leonard, "Question Authority," *Fortune,* May 14, 2007, p. 26.

Dan Formosa: At the Forefront of Smart Design

Like many new businesses, Smart Design was founded by a collection of college classmates who wanted to change something. Dan Formosa, along with several college friends, had a background in design and ergonomics. The group believed that design should be about people, not things—and Smart Design was born. In the beginning, it was a hard sell—not the designs themselves, but the idea that the needs of individual *people* should be involved in the development of design. Formosa was interested in "how design can affect our quality of life, improve performance, and affect behavior." The original Smart Design team "pulled together techniques in biomechanics and cognitive psychology," recalls Formosa. "This was a type of an approach that no other design group was undertaking in the U.S. at the time, so it was an early test of our beliefs about what and where design should be." Smart Design was successful throughout the 1980s, but Formosa admits that it was an uphill battle to convince clients that design was, indeed, for everyone.

Then came OXO. Around 1990, Smart Design acquired the manufacturing firm OXO as a client, giving Formosa's team a chance to re-invent the design of common household products ranging from can openers to scissors, resulting in the OXO Good Grips line of kitchen utensils. Because of the mundane nature of these products—consumers weren't accustomed to shopping for a potato peeler that actually felt comfortable in the hand—once they caught on, the idea that everyday design matters began to take hold in the marketplace. Smart Design's client base grew significantly, as did the company. Firms such as Ford, ESPN, Samsung, Nike, and Microsoft began to request Smart Design's services, and the number of employees increased.

No matter how much talent lies in the firm, though, managing a company of designers can be like trying to herd cats. Everyone has an idea, and everyone is running headlong in a different direction. So leadership is critical to the firm's success. Paulette Bluhm-Sauriol, director of brand communication, observes that while most designers are detail oriented, "Someone has to make sure that the team is keeping the big picture in mind, not just the details." That's part of her job as well as Formosa's:

maintaining the overall vision. She also notes that, as a leader, Formosa has the natural gift of connecting and empathizing with people, whether it is employees or potential end-users of Smart Design's products. "Dan has the ability to make going into people's lives and becoming part of their lives comfortable," she observes.

This was particularly true during the development of a new type of pre-filled medical syringe that Smart Design undertook for UCB/OXO Cimzia. The medication Cimzia is a solution that alleviates chronic pain in patients with certain conditions. If patients could administer the solution themselves in a comfortable way, it would enhance their lives. When the pharmaceutical maker UCB and OXO partnered to develop the new product, they went to Smart Design for the design. Formosa asked his team to go straight to the patients themselves to ask them what they needed. Designers met and observed patients in their own environment, giving them a chance to express their wishes. "It can be uncomfortable, but it's amazing how you can get to the big ideas by approaching the project his way," says Paulette Bluhm-Sauriol.

The syringe has met with marketplace success, and has even won an International Design Excellence Award. Most important, patients are getting what they need, which is exactly what Formosa strives for in each product his firm designs. "If someone buys a product or signs up for a service, they expect it to work. If you actually encounter a product or service that exceeds expectations, that is the sign of a great design," he says. Formosa also contends that the same principles can be applied to the design of a delicate hospital instrument as are applied to a pizza cutter. "Since our focus is designing for people, then that is the common ground," he asserts.

At Smart Design, the corporate culture supports the notion that the ideas of every employee are important. Regardless of job title, each person is considered a designer, with something valuable to contribute to the process. Formosa doesn't mind the potential chaos of this kind of organization—it's how he operates. "When we have everybody thinking everything, it's a positive sign," he says. It's a formula that works.

Questions for Critical Thinking

1. Describe Dan Formosa's vision for Smart Design. Why do you think it took so long to gain popularity in the marketplace?

2. Identify Smart Design's strategy for competitive differentiation.

3. How would you describe Dan Formosa's leadership style? Do you think it is the best style for Smart Design? Why or why not?

4. Discuss Smart Design's corporate culture. Do you think it is effective for the kind of business the company engages in? Why or why not?

Sources: Smart Design Web site, http://www.smartdesignworldwide.com, accessed August 24, 2010; "Smart Design," National Design Awards, http://www.nationaldesignawards.org/2010, accessed August 19, 2010; Ralph Goldsworthy, "Dan Formosa of Smart Design, Designer Q&A," *Design Droplets.com,* April 28, 2010, http://designdroplets.com.

Chapter

8

Learning Objectives

[1] Explain the role and responsibilities of human resource management.

[2] Describe how recruitment and selection contribute to placing the right person in a job.

[3] Discuss how orientation, training programs, and performance appraisals help companies develop their employees.

[4] Describe how firms compensate employees through pay systems and benefit programs.

[5] Discuss employee separation and the impact of downsizing and outsourcing.

[6] Explain the different methods and theories of motivation.

[7] Discuss the role of labor unions, the collective bargaining process, and methods for settling labor–management disputes.

Motivating People and Labor Relations

Fancy/Alamy

NetApp Builds on Trust and Simplicity

©Robyn Twomey

NetApp may not be the flashiest young company in the high-tech industry. The Sunnyvale, California–based firm makes data storage equipment. With about 5,400 U.S. employees and another 3,000 abroad, it's not the biggest either. And despite experiencing tremendous growth since its founding, the company struggled recently with revenue shortfalls as recession forced its customers to cut their spending. But it is still getting attention. NetApp rose to the top of two prestigious lists of the best companies to work for in the United States. Both Fortune and Great Places to Work Institute recognized the value of its down-to-earth, team-oriented corporate culture in attracting and retaining employees who simply love working there. When James Lau and David Hitz founded the company in 1992, they hired Dan Warmenhoven as CEO. Warmenhoven's top priorities were to build revenue and create an effective management team. Among the results: worldwide revenues topping $3 billion and more than 45,000 applicants for fewer than 600 job openings in a recent year.

NetApp's commitment to its employees shows up in large ways and small. Simplicity is a key value, and it is based largely on trust between employees and managers. A 12-page employee travel policy, for instance, was simplified to three straightforward sentences: "We are a frugal company. But don't show up dog-tired to save a few bucks. Use your common sense." Employees also are free to ask questions, share ideas, and make decisions. Says one, "I have been given lots of freedom to implement my ideas to make things better and also am able to make decisions in order to get the job done.... I can look back and see what I have been able to accomplish with a great feeling of satisfaction." Says another, "It is expected that you get your work done, and if you do that late at night or early in the morning, that is your choice... the atmosphere is positive, creative, and the bar is higher, [but] no one is watching your movements; it is about performance." Performance is rewarded through three separate programs that recognize and encourage knowledge sharing, sales success, and patent filings for new ideas. In a recent year, the company awarded over $1 million to 543 employees for creating patent-worthy innovations. But recognition goes beyond these one-time awards; it happens every day at NetApp. An employee explains, "I have never been at a company where the top executives actually *call* me to thank me for a job well done and great attitude. Even the 'little' people get noticed by... our vice chairman.... Makes me much more committed to my career and job here."

Ongoing training gives employees the opportunities they need to learn new skills, develop their careers, and remain challenged to take risks. NetApp's U.S. employees recently completed more than 26,000 hours of annual training, and the company encourages self-assessment and the use of coaches. NetApp University promotes professional development. One assistant attended a week-long out-of-state training program to learn new Web site software. "To me, that is exciting and a great chance to learn a new skill! I will be spreading my wings a little and learning to lead a team."

At some firms, rapid growth builds layers between employees and managers, but NetApp strives to keep communication open. "I've personally experienced Dan, our CEO, choose to share difficult information in the spirit of candor rather than pushing it under the rug," says an employee. The company holds a Vice President's Forum every two weeks so that its leaders can share information about the industry and the economy and also asks employees about what is on their minds. After the meetings, the vice presidents share what they've learned with everyone on their teams. Recognizing that bad news is harder to share, the company even developed a communication kit for managers, called "Communicating with Employees during Tough Times."

Unlike some other firms, NetApp doesn't clean employees' clothes or change the oil in their cars. It does, however, serve fruit, bagels, and yogurt; offer five paid days off for volunteer work; provide same-sex couples with domestic partner benefits; offer child adoption benefits; sponsor community activities; donate equipment to needy organizations; and offer telecommuting, flexible schedules, and job sharing on the principle of "whatever works to get the job done." A unique NetApp medical benefit has paid 43 employees to cover treatment of autism for family members. All in all, it's little wonder that, in the words of a NetApp employee, "Everyone loves working here."[1]

The importance of employees to the success of any organization is the very basis of management. In this chapter, we explore the important issues of human resource management and motivation. We begin with a discussion of the ways organizations attract, develop, and retain employees. Then we describe the concepts behind motivation and the way human resource managers apply them to increase employee satisfaction and organizational effectiveness.

We also discuss the reasons why labor unions exist, and focus on legislation that affects labor–management relations. The process of collective bargaining is then discussed, along with tools used by unions and management in seeking their objectives.

human resource management function of attracting, developing, and retaining employees who can perform the activities necessary to accomplish organizational objectives.

Human Resources: The People Behind the People

A company is only as good as its workers. If people come to work each day eager to see each other, to do their very best on the job, to serve their customers, and to help their firm compete, then it's very likely that company will be a success. The best companies value their employees just as much as their customers—without workers, there would be no goods or services to offer customers. Firms like Children's Creative Learning Centers (CCLC) understand this, and do their best to hire top-quality employees and support them while they provide top-quality child care to customers. Achieving this level of job satisfaction and dedication among employees is the goal of **human resource management**, which attracts, develops, and retains the employees who can perform the activities necessary to accomplish organizational objectives.

Not every firm is large enough to have an entire human resources department. But whoever performs this function generally does the following: plan for staffing needs, recruit and hire workers, provide for training and evaluate performance, determine compensation and benefits, and oversee employee separation. In accomplishing these five tasks, shown in Figure 8.1, human resource managers achieve their objectives of

Blend/Getty Images, Inc.

The best companies value their employees just as much as their customers. Firms like Children's Creative Learning Centers (CCLC) understand this, and do their best to hire top-quality employees and support them while they provide top-quality child care to customers.

1. providing qualified, well-trained employees for the organization;

2. maximizing employee effectiveness in the organization; and

3. satisfying individual employee needs through monetary compensation, benefits, opportunities to advance, and job satisfaction.

Human resource plans must be based on an organization's overall competitive strategies. In conjunction with other managers, human resource managers predict how many employees a firm or department will need, and what skills those workers should bring to the job—along with what skills they might learn on the job. Human resource managers are often consulted when a firm is considering reducing costs by laying off workers, or increasing costs by hiring new ones. They may be involved in both long-term and short-term planning.

FIGURE 8.1 **Human Resource Management Responsibilities**

Employee Recruitment and Selection

Employee Training and Performance Evaluation

Planning for Staffing Needs

Core Responsibilities of Human Resource Management

Employee Separation

Employee Compensation and Benefits

Recruitment and Selection

Human resource managers recruit and help select the right workers for a company. To ensure that job candidates bring the necessary skills to the job or have the desire and ability to learn them, most firms implement the recruitment and selection process shown in Figure 8.2.

Finding Qualified Candidates

When the economy dips and jobs are lost, many people compete for a limited number of positions. When a company develops a great reputation for benefits or working conditions, it might be inundated with applications. But even with a large number of job candidates competing for a small number of openings, companies often have trouble finding the right person for each position. According to a recent survey, more than half the responding firms reported that while they had plenty of applicants, the "quality of candidates" was lacking. "We get tons of résumés from people," laments one director of human resources. "We are just not getting highly qualified candidates."[2]

In addition to traditional methods of recruiting, such as college job fairs, personal referrals, and want ads, most companies now rely on their Web sites. A firm's Web site might contain a career section with general employment information and a listing of open positions. Applicants are often able to submit a résumé and apply for an open position online. Appendix E, Careers in Contemporary Business, points out that some firms also post job openings on sites such as Monster.com.

Internet recruiting is such a quick, efficient, and inexpensive way to reach a large pool of job seekers that the vast majority of companies currently use the Internet, including social networking sites, to fill job openings. This is also the best way for firms to reach new college graduates and workers in their 20s and even 30s. Instead of focusing on handing out pamphlets at college job fairs, aerospace giant Boeing began posting job ads on Facebook.

Assessment Check ☑

1. What are the five main tasks of a human resource manager?

2. What are the three overall objectives of a human resource manager?

FIGURE
8.2

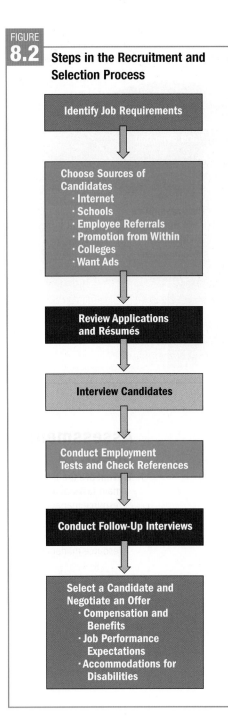

Steps in the Recruitment and Selection Process

Identify Job Requirements

Choose Sources of Candidates
- Internet
- Schools
- Employee Referrals
- Promotion from Within
- Colleges
- Want Ads

Review Applications and Résumés

Interview Candidates

Conduct Employment Tests and Check References

Conduct Follow-Up Interviews

Select a Candidate and Negotiate an Offer
- Compensation and Benefits
- Job Performance Expectations
- Accommodations for Disabilities

Recruits were impressed. "My first impression was that Boeing is getting with the times," said one college senior. "It shows the company is making an effort to talk to us on our level." Boeing also uses Facebook to communicate with workers, including interns, who have been hired through more traditional channels. "We've got to go to their turf," observes Rob Papandrea, who works in Boeing's human resources department.[3]

Recruiting techniques continue to evolve as technology advances. JobsinPods.com is an online library of podcast interviews with hiring managers and employees at a variety of U.S. companies, including AT&T, Intel, and IBM. New podcasts, also called jobcasts, are posted in a blog format, and older podcasts are archived. Some describe employers' hiring needs, while others talk about what it's like to work at a particular company. Job seekers can also download the podcasts to an iPod and listen to them at their leisure.[4]

Selecting and Hiring Employees

It's the human resource manager's job to select and hire employees, often in conjunction with department managers or supervisors. Every firm must follow state and federal employment laws. Title VII of the Civil Rights Act of 1964 prohibits employers from discriminating against applicants based on their race, religion, color, sex, or national origin. The Americans with Disabilities Act of 1990 prohibits employers from discriminating against disabled applicants. The Civil Rights Act created the *Equal Employment Opportunity Commission (EEOC)* to investigate discrimination complaints. The Uniform Employee Selection Guidelines were adopted by the EEOC in 1978 to further clarify ways in which employers must ensure that their employees will be hired and managed without discrimination.[5] The EEOC also helps employers set up *affirmative action programs* to increase job opportunities for women, minorities, people with disabilities, and other protected groups. The Civil Rights Act of 1991 expanded the alternatives available to victims of employment discrimination by including the right to a jury trial, punitive damages, and damages for emotional distress. At the same time, opponents to such laws have launched initiatives to restrict affirmative action standards and protect employers against unnecessary litigation.

These laws, which are designed to level the playing field for all job seekers, have been the basis for thousands of legal cases over the years. Recently, UPS Freight agreed to pay a $46,000 settlement to a former employee because of religious discrimination. The employee, who is a Rastafarian, was told to shave his beard and cut his hair to comply with company grooming policy. Because long hair and a beard are part of Rastafarian worship, the employee requested accommodation. UPS fired him, which was a violation of his civil rights.[6] Failure to comply with equal employment opportunity legislation can result in costly legal fees, expensive fines, bad publicity, and poor employee morale.

Because of the high cost of such lawsuits and settlements, human resource managers must understand the laws in order to prevent unintended violations. Even the process of interviewing a job candidate is covered by law. An interviewer may not ask any questions about marital status, children, race or nationality, religion, age, criminal records, mental illness, medical history, or alcohol and substance abuse problems. For more information about employment law, visit the Web sites of the Society for Human Resource Management (http://www.shrm.org) and the EEOC (http://www.eeoc.gov).

Navigating the maze of hiring restrictions is a challenge. Some firms try to screen out high-risk employees by requiring drug testing for job applicants, particularly in industries that deal with public safety—such as air travel or truck driving. But drug testing is controversial because of privacy issues. Also, positive test results may not be accurate. Another issue is whether employees can be required to speak a particular language—usually English—in the workplace. Although the EEOC views this as discrimination, a bill was recently introduced in the Tennessee legislature that would allow businesses to make this requirement as "an allowable employment practice."[7] Employers may legally establish requirements for specific jobs—a bona fide occupational qualification (BFOQ)—that may cut across EEOC protected classes. For example, a designer of women's clothes by necessity is permitted to hire only female models to show off new designs.

Internet recruiting is such a quick, efficient, and inexpensive way to reach a large pool of job seekers that the vast majority of companies currently use the Internet, including social-networking sites, to fill job openings. Instead of focusing on handing out pamphlets at college job fairs, aerospace giant Boeing began posting job ads on Facebook.

Daniel Acker/Bloomberg/Getty Images, Inc.

Recruitment and selection are expensive. There are costs for advertising, interviewing, administering employment tests and even medical exams. Once an applicant is hired, there are costs for training and perhaps equipment such as a computer. But a bad hiring decision is even more expensive, because the firm has to go through the whole process again to find the right person. One formula estimates that the total cost of a hiring mistake amounts to 24 times the applicant's annual pay.[8] So it's especially important for human resource managers to make the best choices when it comes to recruitment and selection.

To avoid these mistakes—and to get the right person for the job—many employers require applicants to complete employment tests. These tests may verify certain skills, including mechanical, technical, language, and computer skills. One example is the Wonderlic Basic Skills Test, which measures basic math and verbal skills. The Wonderlic is a cognitive ability test, which measures a person's abilities in understanding words, numbers, and logic. Cognitive ability tests accurately predict job performance on many types of jobs.

Assessment Check ✓

1. Describe several recruiting techniques used by human resource managers.

2. What is the function of the Equal Employment Opportunity Commission (EEOC)?

Orientation, Training, and Evaluation

Once hired, employees need to know what is expected of them and how well they are performing. Companies provide this information through orientation, training, and evaluation. A new hire may complete an orientation program administered jointly by the human resource personnel and the department in which the employee will work. During orientation, employees learn about company policies regarding their rights and benefits. They might receive an employee manual that includes the company's code of ethics and code of conduct. And they'll usually receive some form of training.

Training Programs

Training is a good investment for both employers and employees. Training provides workers with an opportunity to build their skills and knowledge, preparing them for new job opportunities within the company. It also provides employers with a better chance at retaining long-term, loyal, high-performing workers. Verizon's training program is ranked among the top in the United States. Verizon, which spends more than $450 million per year in employee development, education, and training, believes it's the best investment any company could make. "We depend on a highly skilled workforce to deliver the best networks and customer solutions," explains Marc Reed, executive vice president for human resources.[9]

On-the-Job Training One popular teaching method is *on-the-job training*, which prepares employees for job duties by allowing them to perform tasks under the guidance of experienced employees. A variation of on-the-job training is apprenticeship training, in which an employee learns a job by serving for a time as an assistant to a trained worker. While American apprenticeships usually focus on blue-collar trades—such as plumbing and heating services—in Europe, many new entrants to white-collar professions complete apprenticeships. McDonald's now has apprenticeship-training programs in its U.K. restaurants as part of an economic stimulus plan launched by the British government. McDonald's offered 6,000 apprenticeships in the first year of its program, increasing the number to 10,000 the following year. "We're letting people know that we're as serious about education as we are about burgers and fries," notes the company's Web site.[10]

Classroom and Computer-Based Training Many firms offer some form of classroom instruction such as lectures, conferences, and workshops or seminars. Ernst & Young, a large tax-service firm, offers a training program called Ernst & Young and You (EYU), focusing on classroom learning, experiential learning, and coaching.[11]

Many firms are replacing classroom training with computer-based training programs, which can significantly reduce the cost of training. Computer-based training offers consistent presentations, along with videos that can simulate the work environment. Employees can learn at their own pace without having to sign up for a class. Through online training programs, employees can engage in interactive learning—they might conference with a mentor or instructor who is located elsewhere; or they might participate in a simulation requiring them to make decisions related to their work. In general, human resources managers agree on the value of training. In a study conducted about training, Accenture discovered that for every hour its competitors spent on training, Accenture spent two hours. Accenture invests heavily in its employees because it believes these workers will be capable of providing their company with a competitive edge in the marketplace.[12]

Management Development A *management development program* provides training designed to improve the skills and broaden the knowledge of current or future managers and executives. Training may be aimed at increasing specific technical knowledge or more general knowledge in areas such as leadership and interpersonal skills. Glimmerglass Consulting Group, based in New Hampshire, provides management training in leadership, team development, and strategic implementation. After assessing a client's work environment as well as the strengths and weaknesses of its management team, Glimmerglass coaches design a program intended to strengthen management's leadership and team skills. The program may involve an outdoor learning experience such as rock climbing. Glimmerglass's client list includes such firms as Wyeth Pharmaceuticals, Shell International, Eastern Mountain Sports, and Big Brothers/Big Sisters.[13]

Despite the importance of training talented employees for managerial jobs, many companies are searching for new hires to fill gaps in their executive ranks because they failed to develop future managers. In a move that surprised the international banking world, David de

Rothschild appointed a successor from outside his family—the first in 200 years—to take over running the group of financial advisory and wealth management companies that make up the Rothschild banking empire. Nigel Higgins is no stranger to the firm; he has worked there for 27 years. But Rothschild chose Higgins because there was no family member ready to handle the job. "If you're not totally self-centered, which I hope I am not, one thinks about how to increase the stability of the firm internally and externally," explains Rothschild, who is only semi-retiring.[14]

Employees value face-to-face feedback on their performance. Evaluations that are fair and consistent can improve an organization's productivity and profitability.

Performance Appraisals

Feedback about performance is the best way for a company—and its employees to improve. Most firms use annual **performance appraisals** to evaluate an employee's job performance and provide feedback about it. A performance appraisal can include assessments of everything from attendance to goals met. Based on this evaluation, a manager will make decisions about compensation, promotion, additional training needs, transfers, or even termination. While performance appraisals are common, not everyone agrees about their usefulness. Some management experts argue that a performance review is skewed in favor of a single manager's subjective opinion—whether it's positive or negative—and that most employees are afraid to speak honestly to their managers during a performance review.[15] If a performance review is to be at all effective, it should meet the following criteria:

- take place several times a year;
- be linked to organizational goals;
- be based on objective criteria;
- take place in the form of a two-way conversation.[16]

Some firms conduct peer reviews, in which employees assess the performance of their coworkers, while other firms ask employees to review their supervisors and managers. One such performance appraisal is the *360-degree performance review*, a process that gathers feedback from a review panel of 8 to 12 people, including coworkers, supervisors, team members, subordinates, and sometimes even customers. The idea is to get as much frank feedback from as many perspectives as possible. By its very nature, this kind of review involves a lot of work, but employees benefit from it because they are more involved with the process and ultimately better understand their own strengths, weaknesses, and roles in the company. Managers benefit because they get much more in-depth feedback from all parts of the organization. Firms such as Halogen Software, with headquarters in Canada, offer computer programs to help firms gather and sift through this type of performance review data.[17]A potential weakness of 360-degree performance reviews is their anonymous nature—workers with personal likes and dislikes might try to influence the outcome.

performance appraisal evaluation of and feedback on an employee's job performance

Assessment Check ☑

1. What are the benefits of computer-based training?

2. What is a management development program?

3. What are the four criteria of an effective performance appraisal?

Tetra Images/Getty Images, Inc.

Compensation

compensation amount employees are paid in money and benefits.

Compensation—how much employees are paid in money and benefits—is one of the most highly charged issues faced by human resource managers. The amount employees are paid, along with whatever benefits they receive, has a tremendous influence on where they live, what they eat, and how they spend their leisure time. It also has an effect on job satisfaction. Balancing compensation for employees at all job levels can be a challenge for human resource managers.

Everyone likes to read about the companies—or the jobs—that pay their employees the most in cash and benefits. *Fortune* magazine lists an annual "100 Best Companies to Work For," which includes information on compensation. Among the current compensation leaders are the Memphis-based law firm of Baker Donelson, whose partners receive an average of $320,000 (legal secretaries at the firm earn about $50,000 a year), and Salesforce.com, whose senior account executives bring home an average of $250,000 annually.[18] Of course, top executives at large companies earn a lot more than this—which has been brought up as an issue among employees and shareholders. The "Hit & Miss" feature discusses this topic.

The terms *wages* and *salary* are often used interchangeably, but actually are different. **Wages** are based on an hourly pay rate or the amount of work accomplished. Typical wage earners are factory workers, construction workers, auto mechanics, retail salespeople, and restaurant wait staff. **Salaries** are calculated periodically, such as weekly or monthly. Salaried employees receive a set amount of pay that does not fluctuate with the number of hours worked. Whereas wage earners receive overtime pay, salaried workers do not. Office personnel, executives, and professional employees usually receive salaries.

An effective compensation system should attract well-qualified workers, keep them satisfied in their jobs, and inspire them to succeed. It's also important to note that certain laws, including minimum wage, must be taken into account. The Lilly Ledbetter Fair Pay Act of 2009 is one such law, which now gives workers more time to file a complaint for pay discrimination.[19]

Most firms base their compensation policies on the following factors: (1) what competing companies are paying, (2) government regulation, (3) cost of living, (4) company profits, and (5) an employee's productivity. Many firms try to balance rewarding workers with maintaining profits by linking more of their pay to superior performance. Firms try to motivate employees to excel by offering some type of incentive compensation in addition to salaries or wages. These programs include the following:

- profit sharing, which awards bonuses based on company profits;
- gain sharing, when companies share the financial value of productivity gains, cost savings, or quality improvements with their workers;
- lump-sum bonuses and stock options, which reward one-time cash payments and the right to purchase stock in the company based on performance;
- pay for knowledge, which distributes wage or salary increases as employees learn new job tasks.

Figure 8.3 summarizes the four types of incentive compensation programs.

compensation amount employees are paid in money and benefits.

wage pay based on an hourly rate or the amount of work accomplished.

salary pay calculated on a periodic basis, such as weekly or monthly.

The Good, Bad, and Ugly of Executive Pay

Executives at large institutions—particularly those on Wall Street—are accustomed to receiving huge compensation packages and multimillion-dollar bonuses each year. That may be fine when their firms are raking in profits. The problem is that they have continued to receive large paychecks despite steep financial losses. Making matters worse is the fact that some of the financial institutions for which they work accepted government assistance from the economic stimulus package.

Congress reacted to taxpayer outrage by enacting new rules, in which top executives at the firms receiving assistance must accept limits on their cash bonuses. Lavish severance packages are now banned, and shareholders must approve executive pay. Despite these new regulations, some firms continue to run amok when it comes to executive compensation. One such CEO took home a pay increase despite the fact that the company did so poorly it had to lay off employees. But others have voluntarily risen to the occasion. Aflac CEO Daniel Amos declined his bonus of nearly $3 million, and top executives at Ford Motor Company cut their own pay by 30 percent.

At the federal level, Kenneth Feinberg—a.k.a. the pay czar—has proposed new ground rules for executive compensation for companies everywhere. According to Feinberg, executives should be limited to $500,000 annually in cash compensation—anything additional should come in the form of stock or other benefits. Executives should pay for their own entertainment perks—like golf club memberships.

Overall, it appears that some true reforms may be on the horizon. Some executives might not like the new practices, but engaging in them voluntarily might be preferable. Companies and their boards will have to "adopt a set of core principles like accountability, alignment, fairness, and transparency," predicts compensation expert Donald Delves.

Questions for Critical Thinking

1. Some critics of the proposed changes in executive compensation argue that reducing performance rewards will encourage talented managers to go elsewhere. Do you think this is a valid objection to pay limits? Why or why not?

2. Do you think shareholders and boards should have input on the size of compensation packages for CEOs? Why or why not?

Sources: Devin Leonard, "Bargain Rates for a CEO?" *The New York Times,* April 2, 2010, http://nytimes.com; "Stricter Pay Limits for Bailed Out Execs," *CBS News,* March 23, 2010, http://www.cbsnews.com; "Executive Pay Trends for 2010," *BusinessWeek,* accessed January 8, 2010, http://www.businessweek.com.

Employee Benefits

In addition to wages and salaries, firms provide benefits to employees and their families as part of their compensation. **Employee benefits**—such as vacation, retirement plans, profit-sharing, health insurance, gym memberships, child and elder care, and tuition reimbursement—are paid entirely or in part by the company. Benefits represent a large component of an employee's total compensation. Although wages and salaries account for around 70 percent of the typical employee's earnings, the other 30 percent takes the form of employee benefits.[20] Table 8.1 shows the breakdown of an average worker's benefits as compared to wages or salary.

Some benefits are required by law. U.S. firms are required to make Social Security and Medicare contributions, as well as payments to state unemployment insurance and workers' compensation programs, which protect workers in case of job-related injuries or illnesses. The Family and Medical Leave Act of 1993 requires covered employers to offer up to 12 weeks of unpaid, job-protected leave to eligible employees. Firms voluntarily provide other employee benefits, such as child care and health insurance, to help them attract and retain employees. California is the first state to make paid family leave into law.[21] As the "Solving an Ethical Controversy" feature discusses, some advocates are pressing state and federal lawmakers to require businesses to provide paid sick leave.

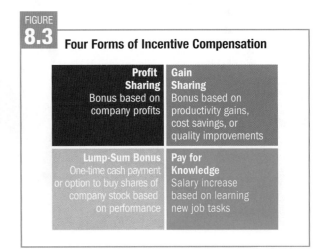

FIGURE 8.3

Four Forms of Incentive Compensation

| **Profit Sharing** Bonus based on company profits | **Gain Sharing** Bonus based on productivity gains, cost savings, or quality improvements |
| **Lump-Sum Bonus** One-time cash payment or option to buy shares of company stock based on performance | **Pay for Knowledge** Salary increase based on learning new job tasks |

employee benefits additional compensation such as vacation, retirement plans, profit-sharing, health insurance, gym memberships, child and elder care, and tuition reimbursement, paid entirely or in part by the company.

8.1 Costs for Employee Compensation

TYPE OF COMPENSATION	PERCENTAGE OF TOTAL COMPENSATION
Wages and salaries	70. 8
Benefits	29.2
Paid leave	6.8
Supplemental pay	3.0
Insurance	7.8
Health benefits	7.3
Retirement and savings	3.4
Legally required benefits	8.2

Source: "Legally Required Benefits Costs in Private Industry," Bureau of Labor Statistics, March 10, 2010, http://www.bls.gov.

Benefits like on-site fitness facilities improve both the company's health and that of employees.

In the past, companies have picked up most of the tab for healthcare benefits, with employees paying little of the cost. However, with costs soaring nearly 15 percent each year, employers are passing along premium increases to employees. Many companies now offer incentives for workers to live healthier lives. Gym memberships, nutrition programs, wellness visits to the doctor, and smoking-cessation classes are all examples of these incentives. SAS has its own medical center, along with a free on-site gym. The firm provides an abundance of other employee benefits as well, including on-site daycare, unlimited sick days, and a summer camp for kids. In addition to all of that, SAS still pays 90 percent of its employees' monthly insurance premiums.[22]

Pensions and other retirement plans make up a chunk of employee benefits. Recently, some companies have shrunk the matching contributions they will make to workers' *401(k) plans*—retirement savings plans to which employees can make pretax contributions. Some firms have cut back on cash contributions to their employees' plans and now contribute company stock instead. However, others have managed to continue with a higher rate of funding. Raytheon Solipsys offers a 401(k) with a 200 percent match on employee contributions.[23]

Comstock/Getty Images, Inc.

Solving an Ethical Controversy

Should Paid Sick Leave Be Required by Law?

The United States is the only one of the world's major economic powers that does not require employers to provide paid sick days. Advocates say the country should follow the lead of other developed nations and make paid sick days a basic labor standard.

U.S. businesses voluntarily provide paid sick days for about 86 percent of full-time workers. The Family and medical Leave Act (FMLA) requires that all businesses with more than 50 employees provide their workers with up to 12 weeks of unpaid leave for illness, childbirth or adoption, or care of a family member who is sick. The proposed Healthy Families Act (HFA) is an attempt to close the gap between these two situations. The HFA would require employers to provide their workers with a specified number of paid sick days each year.

Should businesses be required to provide paid sick leave for their employees?

PRO

1. A healthy workforce is vital to the competitiveness of any firm. When an employee is unable to seek time off for medical treatment for an illness, it puts the company at risk. "Not only is this situation bad for sick workers and their families, but it puts other workers and the public at risk of contracting infectious illnesses," points out one public official.

2. No worker should be penalized for being ill. "The purpose of this bill [HFA] is that you cannot be fired because you're sick," notes Maine Senate President Elizabeth Mitchell.

CON

1. Requiring firms to pay for sick leave adds to the cost of doing business, and employers may be forced to cut other benefits, institute a hiring freeze, or lay people off because they can't afford the added expense.

2. Workers may be encouraged to misuse their sick leave, and when one takes unplanned time off, an employer may be forced to pay a temporary worker in addition to the permanent employee who is out sick.

Summary

Those in favor of paid sick leave argue that it is a matter of basic workers' rights, and would benefit mostly low-income employees who are already struggling to make ends meet. Opponents say that the burden is too great for most businesses and would result in lost productivity, a reduction in wages to offset the cost, and perhaps a loss in the number of jobs altogether.

Sources: "Editorial: Reject Mandate for Paid Sick Leave," *The New Haven Register,* April 1, 2010, http://www.nhregister.com; A. J. Higgins, "Paid Sick Leave Bill Significantly Weakened," *Maine Public Broadcasting Network,* March 29, 2010, http://www.mpbn.net; Laura Fishman, "Paid Sick Leave Strikes Debate," *The Houston Employment Law Blog,* February 12, 2010, http://houstonemployment-lawsblog.com; Christine Stuart, "Lamont Not Sold on Paid Sick Days for Small Businesses," *CTNewsjunkie.com,* February 9, 2010, http://www.ctnewsjunkie.com; James Sherk, "Mandatory Paid Sick Leave: The Heritage Foundation 2010 Labor Boot Camp," *The Heritage Foundation,* January 14, 2010, http://www.heritage.org.

Flexible Benefits

In response to increasing diversity in the workplace, firms are developing creative ways to tailor their benefit plans to the needs of employees. One approach sets up *flexible benefit plans*, also called cafeteria plans. This system offers employees a choice of benefits, including different types of medical insurance, dental and vision plans, and life and disability insurance. This flexibility allows one working spouse to choose medical coverage for the entire family, while the other spouse uses benefit dollars to buy other types of coverage. Typically, each employee receives a set allowance (called flex dollars or credits) to pay for benefits depending on his or her needs. Contributions to cafeteria accounts can be made by both the employee and employer. Cafeteria plans also offer tax benefits to both employees and employers.

Another way of increasing the flexibility of employee benefits involves time off from work. Instead of establishing set numbers of holidays, vacation days, and sick days, some

A two-career couple heads for the daycare center and work. Many employees use flextime to mesh their work schedules with opening and closing times at schools and daycare programs.

Rayn McVay/Photodisc/Alamy

employers give each employee a bank of *paid time off (PTO)*. Employees use days from their PTO accounts without having to explain why they need the time. The greatest advantage of PTO is the freedom it gives workers to make their own choices; the greatest disadvantage is that it is an expensive benefit for employers.[24]

Flexible Work

Some firms are moving toward the option of *flexible work plans*, which are benefits that allow employees to adjust their working hours or places of work according to their needs. Flexible work plan options include flextime, compressed workweeks, job sharing, and home-based work (telecommuting). These benefit programs have reduced employee turnover and absenteeism, and boosted productivity and job satisfaction. Flexible work has become critical in attracting and keeping talented human resources.

Flextime allows employees to set their own work hours within certain constraints. Rather than scheduling everyone to work between 8:00 a.m. and 5:00 p.m., a manager might stipulate that all employees be at work between the core hours of 10:00 a.m. and 3:00 p.m. Outside the core hours, employees can choose to start and end early, or start and end late. Flextime works well in jobs that are independent, but not so well when teams or direct customer service are involved. Flextime is popular in Europe, where 56 percent of all companies offer some kind of flextime arrangement.[25]

With the help of programs from BidShift, a San Diego company that specializes in Internet-based scheduling software, the logistic problems of flexible scheduling are solved for users such as the San Angelo Community Medical Center. BidShift's programs allow managers to post schedules online, where employees log in and request certain shifts or schedule changes.[26]

Some companies offer a *compressed workweek*, which allows employees to work longer hours on fewer days. Employees might work four 10-hour days and then have three days off each week. Such arrangements not only reduce the number of hours employees spend commuting each week, but can stretch out the company's overall workday, providing more availability to customers in other time zones. Hospitals, police and fire departments, and airlines often offer work schedules that allow several long days matched by several days off. About 40 percent of Macy's employees opt for a compressed workweek. According to the retailer's human resource department, this benefit is valued second only to pay and medical insurance. "We've invested a lot in our people," notes Ed Cooney, senior vice president of human resources. "When we offer work options, it's not totally unselfish. We know it results in more loyalty and less absenteeism."[27]

A *job sharing program* allows two or more employees to divide the tasks of one job. This plan appeals to a growing number of people who prefer to work part-time rather than full-time—such as older workers, students, working parents, and people of all ages who want to devote time to personal interests or leisure. Job sharing requires a lot cooperation and communication between the partners, but a company can benefit from the talents of both people. Some economists believe that a federal job-sharing program, which would give workers access to emergency unemployment insurance, would help prevent layoffs during times when unemployment is high. Seventeen states have already adopted such legislation. However, opponents disagree because of the cost.[28]

Home-based work programs allow employees to perform their jobs from home instead of at the workplace. These *telecommuters* are connected to their employers via the Internet, voice and video conferencing, and mobile devices. Working from home generally appeals to employees who want freedom, but also to persons with disabilities, older workers, and parents. Companies benefit from telework arrangements because they can expand their pool of talent and increase productivity without increasing costs.[29] Telecommuters need to be self-disciplined and reliable employees. They also need managers who are comfortable with setting goals and managing from afar. Forrester Research predicts that telecommuting will grow from its current 34 million workers to 63 million by the year 2016.[30]

More than 70 percent of Generation Y professionals—those just entering the workforce—are concerned with balancing career with personal life. Most simply reject the idea of sitting in an office cubicle for 8 to 10 hours a day. They want the flexibility to do their jobs anywhere, any time.[31] This is placing increasing pressure on companies to offer options like job sharing, compressed workweeks, and telecommuting.

Employee Separation

Employee separation is a broad term covering the loss of an employee for any reason, voluntary or involuntary. Voluntary separation includes workers who resign to take a job at another firm or start a business. Involuntary separation includes downsizing and outsourcing.

Voluntary and Involuntary Turnover

Turnover occurs when an employee leaves his or her job. Voluntary turnover occurs when the employee decides to resign—perhaps to take another job, start a new business, or retire. The human resource manager might ask the employee for an exit interview to find out why he or she is leaving; this conversation can provide valuable information to a firm. An employee might decide to resign because of lack of career opportunities. Learning this, the human resource manager might offer ongoing training.[32] Another might resign because of low pay. In that case, the human resource manager might offer a raise. The "Business Etiquette" feature offers some advice on how to ask for a raise. Sometimes employees choose to resign and accept jobs at other firms because they fear upcoming layoffs. In this case, the human resource manager might be able to allay fears about job security.

Involuntary turnover occurs when employees are terminated because of poor job performance or unethical behavior in business practices or in the workplace. No matter how necessary a termination may be, it is never easy for either the human resource manager or the employee. The employee may react with anger or tears; coworkers may take sides. Human resource managers should remain calm and professional, and must be educated in employment laws. Protests against wrongful dismissal are often involved in complaints filed by the EEOC or by lawsuits brought by fired employees. Involuntary turnover also occurs when firms are forced to eliminate jobs as a cost-cutting measure, as in the case of downsizing or outsourcing.

Downsizing

As the economy tightens, companies are often faced with the hard choice of terminating employees in order to cut costs or streamline the organization. **Downsizing** is the process of reducing the number of employees within a firm by eliminating jobs. Downsizing can be

Assessment Check ✓

1. Explain the difference between *wage* and *salary*.

2. What are flexible benefit plans? How do they work?

employee separation broad term covering the loss of an employee for any reason, voluntary or involuntary.

downsizing process of reducing the number of employees within a firm by eliminating jobs.

BusinessEtiquette

How to Ask for a Raise

Just thinking about asking your boss for a raise might cause your hands to sweat. You fear rejection or worse, retaliation. But if you know that you are doing a superior job—including taking the initiative when it's not required—or it's been more than a year since your last increase, then perhaps it's time to make a case for yourself. You should be able to at least open the conversation with your boss. Here are a few tips for making your effort successful:

- *Be prepared.* Find out whether there is a policy for raises at your company, including a range or sliding scale for each position. Learn where your current pay lies along the scale.

- *Gather important data about yourself.* Consistently document your work accomplishments, including extra projects or tasks you've undertaken and done well. Keep a log of positive feedback from coworkers, other supervisors, and customers. If the praise is already in writing, that's even better.

- *Think through exactly what you want.* Is it a percentage increase? A dollar amount? Or perhaps expanded vacation time or time off for career education? Make sure your request is reasonable. When you meet with your supervisor, be as specific as possible.

- *Don't be pushy or hasty in your conversation.* At the same time, put forth your argument with confidence. Your goal is to get your supervisor to open up to thinking about the possibility of meeting your request.

- If your supervisor turns down your request, *ask for specifics about what you need to do in order to qualify for the raise*—and when. If possible, ask for a follow-up meeting within a certain period of time, such as two months.

- When you return to your desk or office, *send your supervisor an e-mail thanking him or her for meeting with you,* and politely recap the results of the conversation. If your request has been granted, make sure your performance lives up to it. If your supervisor has deferred a decision, don't give up. Get back to work, document everything, and earn that raise.

Sources: Smantha Maziarz Christmann, "Asking For More: Don't Be Afraid to Ask for a Raise," *Buffalo News,* March 15, 2010, http://www.buffalonews.com; "How to Negotiate for a Raise—Even in a Bad Economy," *EmploymentDigest.net,* March 4, 2010, http://www.employment digest.net; Mary Sevinsky, "Is a Raise in Your Future for 2010?," *CareerRealism.com,* January 15, 2010, http://www.careerealism.com.

accomplished through early retirement plans or voluntary severance programs. But these options don't always accomplish the goal, as was the case for AOL in the recent downsizing effort described in the "Hit & Miss" feature.

While some firms report improvements in profits, market share, employee productivity, quality, and customer service after downsizing, research is beginning to show that downsizing doesn't guarantee those improvements. "Much of the conventional wisdom about downsizing—like the fact that it automatically drives a company's stock price higher, or increases profitability—turns out to be wrong," notes Jeffrey Pfeffer of Stanford University.[33] Downsizing can have the following negative effects:

- Anxiety, health problems, and lost productivity among remaining workers.

- Expensive severance packages paid to laid-off workers.

- A domino effect on the local economy—unemployed workers have less money to spend, creating less demand for consumer goods and services, increasing the likelihood of more layoffs and other failing businesses.[34]

If downsizing is ultimately the only alternative for company survival, then there are steps that managers can take to make sure it is done the best way possible. If a firm is committed to its workforce as part of its mission, then it will do everything it can to support both the workers who must leave and those who will stay. When Xilinx Inc., a California semiconductor manufacturer, was forced to shrink its operations or close altogether, the company took several steps to avoid outright layoffs. Xilinx temporarily shut down plants and offered voluntary retirement plans and sabbatical leaves. Human resource managers discussed the situation with employees before making pay cuts. By taking these measures—in which all employees made some sacrifice—the company survived its downturn without making any involuntary terminations.[35]

AOL Employees Don't Exit Voluntarily

People don't want to leave their jobs, especially when the economy is tighter than usual and unemployment numbers are already high. But that's what AOL asked its workers to do in a recent effort to downsize the company and control costs. AOL asked for 2,500 volunteer separations and only received 1,100. That left a gap of 1,400 workers. The goal was to reduce the firm's workforce by more than 30 percent, from 6,900 to about 4,400.

AOL, which had been struggling for several years under the merger with Time Warner, finally spun off as an independent company—but a damaged one. AOL management decided that the only way to turn the company around was to trim as much expense as possible, from every limb of the organization. The turnaround initiative, dubbed Project Everest, was led by new CEO Tim Armstrong, a former sales executive for Google. After downsizing the workforce, Armstrong planned to refocus AOL's business in a few select areas, including content, online advertising, and communications. "Project Everest is the completion of phase one of AOL's turnaround," noted a company spokesperson.

If all of this sounds a bit cold-hearted and short-sighted to you, it does to others as well. One of the greatest blows to a company in the wake of layoffs is to the remaining workers' morale. Layoffs are devastating to those who are let go and just as traumatic to those who remain. Productivity often slides, as does the image of the company. "There's substantial research into the physical and health effects of downsizing on employees—research that reinforces the notion that

layoffs are literally killing people," warns Jeffrey Pfeffer of Stanford University. In the case of AOL, the firm actually hired new salespeople to ensure continued advertising client coverage. In addition, AOL managers held meetings with advertisers to inform them of the actions being taken, and sent notes to certain clients containing private contact information for top executives. Despite these measures, some advertising clients have decided to take their business elsewhere. In an effort to rebuild its business, AOL may have lost one of its most valuable assets—its best people.

Questions for Critical Thinking

1. Do you think it was a good decision for AOL to ask for volunteers to resign before making layoffs? Why or why not?

2. Could AOL managers have better prepared their clients for the downsizing?

Sources: Dustin Ensinger, "Why Layoffs Are Not Beneficial to Companies," *Economy in Crisis*, February 8, 2010, http://www.economyincrisis.org; Nicholas Carlson, "AOL Is Hiring Sales People to Make Sure Layoffs Don't Interrupt Coverage," *Business Insider*, January 13, 2010, http://www.businessinsider.com; "AOL Layoffs Begin: 1,400 Jobs to be Slashed," *Mashable.com*, January 11, 2010, http://www.mashable.com; Miguel Helft, "AOL Begins 1,200 Layoffs," *The New York Times*, January 11, 2010, http://bits.blogs.nytimes.com; Juan Carlos Perez, "AOL Voluntary Layoff Program Falls Short," *ComputerWorld*, January 5, 2010, http://www.computerworld.com.

Outsourcing

Another way that firms shrink themselves into leaner organizations is by **outsourcing**. Outsourcing involves transferring jobs from inside a firm to outside the firm. Jobs that are typically outsourced include office maintenance, deliveries, food service, and security. However, other job functions can be outsourced as well, including manufacturing, design, information technology (IT), and accounting. In general, in order to save expenses and remain flexible, companies will try to outsource functions that are not part of their core business.

Although outsourcing might work on paper, the reality might be different. When United Airlines announced plans to outsource some of its engineering work from its San Francisco maintenance hub to India, employees, government officials, safety experts, and the general public questioned the move. Fifty employees were scheduled to be laid off, but that wasn't the main issue. Instead, the airline was questioned for potentially compromising the safety of its aircraft and those on board. "I am particularly concerned by the idea of engineering drawings being done overseas and then being handed off to personnel in the U.S.," noted one official, "perhaps without an opportunity for the overseas and domestic personnel to address fundamental flaws in proposed repairs." The airline responded to say that safety would remain their top concern.[36]

outsourcing transferring jobs from inside a firm to outside the firm

Assessment Check ✔

1. What is the difference between voluntary and involuntary turnover?

2. What is downsizing? How is it different from outsourcing?

Motivating Employees

Motivating employees to commit to their company and perform their best on the job is one of the main goals of a manager. Motivation starts with good employee morale. Morale is the mental attitude of employees toward their employer and jobs, involving a common sense of purpose.

High employee morale occurs in organizations where workers feel valued, heard, and empowered to contribute what they do best. High morale generally results from good management, including an understanding of human needs and an effort to satisfy those needs in ways that move the company forward. Low employee morale, on the other hand, usually signals a poor relationship between managers and employees and often results in absenteeism, voluntary turnover, and a lack of motivation.

Generally speaking, managers use rewards and punishments to motivate employees. Extrinsic rewards are external to the work itself, such as pay, fringe benefits, and praise. Intrinsic rewards are feelings related to performing the job, such as feeling proud about meeting a deadline or achieving a sales goal. Punishment involves a negative consequence for such behavior as being late, skipping staff meetings, or treating a customer poorly.

There are several theories of motivation, all of which relate back to the basic process of motivation itself, which involves the recognition of a need, the move toward meeting that need, and the satisfaction of that need. For instance, if you are hungry you might be motivated to make yourself a peanut butter sandwich. Once you have eaten the sandwich, the need is satisfied and you are no longer hungry. Figure 8.4 illustrates the process of motivation.

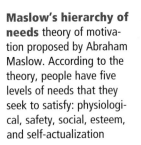

Maslow's hierarchy of needs theory of motivation proposed by Abraham Maslow. According to the theory, people have five levels of needs that they seek to satisfy: physiological, safety, social, esteem, and self-actualization

Maslow's Hierarchy of Needs Theory

The studies of psychologist Abraham H. Maslow suggest how managers can motivate employees. **Maslow's hierarchy of needs** has become a widely accepted list of human needs based on these important assumptions:

- People's needs depend on what they already possess.

- A satisfied need is not a motivator; only needs that remain unsatisfied can influence behavior.

- People's needs are arranged in a hierarchy of importance; once they satisfy one need, at least partially, another emerges and demands satisfaction.

In his theory, Maslow proposed that all people have basic needs such as hunger and protection that they must satisfy before they can consider higher-order needs such as social relationships or self-worth. He identified five types of needs:

Everyone, including employees, has a need to belong. Occasional office parties allow workers to relax and socialize, lifting their morale and motivating them to do a good job.

John Giustina/Iconica/Getty Images, Inc.

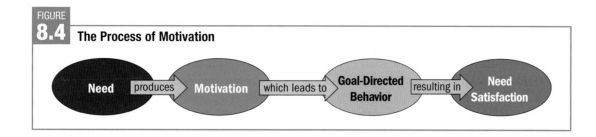

FIGURE 8.4 The Process of Motivation

Need → produces → Motivation → which leads to → Goal-Directed Behavior → resulting in → Need Satisfaction

1. *Physiological needs.* These basic human needs include food, shelter, and clothing. On the job, employers satisfy these needs by paying salaries and wages and providing a heated or cooled workspace.

2. *Safety needs.* These needs refer to desires for physical and economic protection. Companies satisfy these needs with benefits like health insurance and meeting safety standards in the workplace.

3. *Social (belongingness) needs.* People want to be accepted by family, friends and coworkers. Managers might satisfy these needs through teamwork and group lunches.

4. *Esteem needs.* People like to feel valued and recognized by others. Managers can meet these needs through special awards or privileges.

5. *Self-actualization needs.* These needs drive people to seek fulfillment of their dreams and capabilities. Employers can satisfy these needs by offering challenging or creative projects, along with opportunities for education and advancement.[37]

According to Maslow, people must satisfy the lower-order needs in the hierarchy (physiological and safety needs) before they are motivated to satisfy higher-order needs (social, esteem, and self-actualization needs).

Herzberg's Two-Factor Model of Motivation

More than 50 years ago, Frederick Herzberg—a social psychologist and consultant—came up with a theory of motivation and work that is still popular today. Herzberg surveyed workers to find out when they felt good or bad about their jobs. He learned that certain factors were important to job satisfaction though they might not contribute directly to motivation. These *hygiene factors* (or maintenance factors) refer to aspects of work that are not directly related to a task itself but related to the job environment, including pay, job security, working conditions, status, interpersonal relations, technical supervision, and company policies.

Motivator factors, on the other hand, can produce high levels of motivation when they are present. These relate directly to the specific aspects of a job, including job responsibilities, achievement and recognition, and opportunities for growth. Hygiene factors are extrinsic, while motivators are intrinsic. Managers should remember that hygiene factors, though not motivational, can result in satisfaction. But if managers wish to motivate employees, they should emphasize recognition, achievement, and growth. Companies that make the various lists of "best places to work" always have managers who understand what it takes to motivate employees, regardless of how large or small the firms are. *Madison Magazine* ranks its top companies based on criteria such as trust, rewards, and work–life balance. Wisconsin-based HospiceCare, which has 348 workers, recently earned the top spot on the list because, "Just as HospiceCare considers its patients and their families a mission and a calling, it realizes that it cannot care for patients without employees who are cared for as well."[38]

Expectancy Theory and Equity Theory

expectancy theory the process people use to evaluate the likelihood that their efforts will yield the results they want, along with the degree to which they want those results.

Victor Vroom's **expectancy theory** of motivation describes the process people use to evaluate the likelihood that their efforts will yield the results they want, along with the degree to which they want those results. Expectancy theory suggests that people use three factors to determine how much effort to put forth. First is a person's subjective prediction that a certain effort will lead to the desired result. This is the "can do" component of an employee's approach to work. Second is the value of the outcome (reward) to the person. Third is the person's assessment of how likely a successful performance will lead to a desirable reward. Vroom's expectancy theory is summarized in Figure 8.5. In short, an employee is motivated if he or she thinks he or she can complete a task. Next, the employee assesses the reward for accomplishing the task and is motivated if the reward is worth the effort.

equity theory an individual's perception of fair and equitable treatment.

Equity theory is concerned with an individual's perception of fair and equitable treatment. In their work, employees first consider their effort and then their rewards. Next, employees compare their results against those of their coworkers. As shown in Figure 8.6, if employees feel they are under-rewarded for their effort in comparison with others doing similar work, equity theory suggests they will decrease their effort to restore the balance. Conversely, if employees feel they are over-rewarded, they will feel guilty and put more effort into their job to restore equity and reduce guilt.

Many workers are willing to work hard as long as the burden is shared. Income inequality is higher in the United States than in any other developed society in the world. The top 10 percent of U.S. employees now earn 50 percent of all income. Many employees who, arguably, work just as hard as top managers, believe this is unfair. A bill called the Income Equity Act has been introduced several times in Congress, but has been defeated.[39]

goal-setting theory says that people will be motivated to the extent to which they accept specific, challenging goals and receive feedback that indicates their progress toward goal achievement.

Goal-Setting Theory and Management by Objectives

Needs motivate people to direct their behavior toward something that will satisfy their needs. That something is a goal. A goal is a target, objective, or result that someone tries to accomplish. **Goal-setting theory** says that people will be motivated to the extent to which

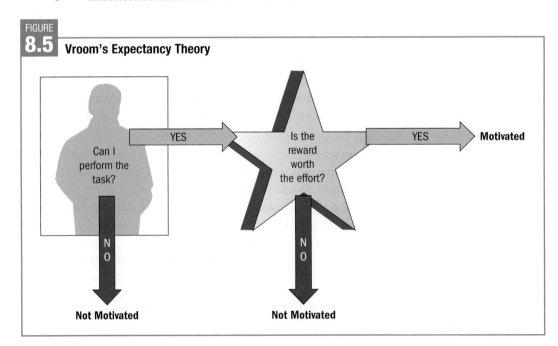

FIGURE 8.5 Vroom's Expectancy Theory

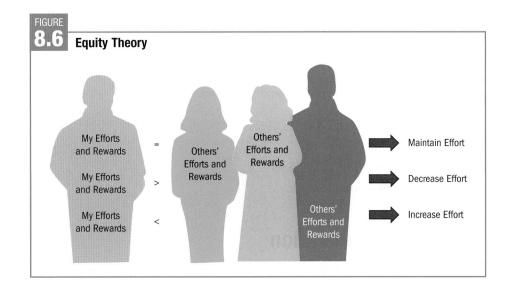

FIGURE
8.6 Equity Theory

My Efforts and Rewards = Others' Efforts and Rewards → Maintain Effort

My Efforts and Rewards > Others' Efforts and Rewards → Decrease Effort

My Efforts and Rewards < Others' Efforts and Rewards → Increase Effort

they accept specific, challenging goals and receive feedback that indicates their progress toward goal achievement. As shown in Figure 8.7, the basic components of goal-setting theory are goal specificity, goal difficulty, goal acceptance, and performance feedback.

Goal specificity is the extent to which goals are clear and concrete. A goal such as "we want to reduce our carbon footprint" is vague and hard to pin down. But, "we want to reduce our carbon footprint by 2 percent" gives employees a clear target. Goal difficulty outlines how hard the goal is to reach. A more difficult goal, such as "we want to reduce our carbon footprint by 5 percent in three years" is actually more motivating than the easier goal.

Goal acceptance is the extent to which people understand and agree to the goal. If a goal is too challenging—such as reducing the firm's carbon footprint by 20 percent in two years—people are likely to reject it. Finally, performance feedback is information about performance and how well the goal has been met. Goal setting typically won't work unless performance feedback is provided.

Goals help focus workers' attention on the important parts of their jobs. Goals also energize and motivate people. They create a positive tension between the current state of affairs and the desired state. This tension is satisfied by meeting the goal or abandoning it.

Fifty years ago, Peter Drucker introduced a goal-setting technique called **management by objectives (MBO)** in his book, *The Practice of Management*. MBO is a systematic approach that allows managers to focus on attainable goals and to achieve the best results based on the organization's resources. MBO helps motivate individuals by aligning their objectives with the goals of the organization, increasing overall organizational performance.

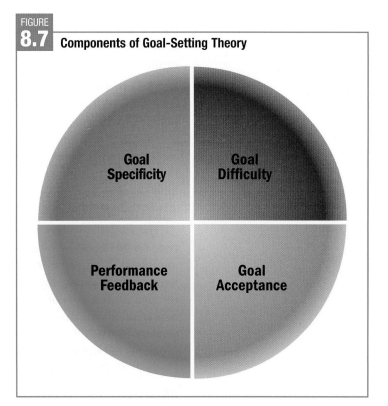

FIGURE
8.7 Components of Goal-Setting Theory

Goal Specificity

Goal Difficulty

Performance Feedback

Goal Acceptance

management by objectives systematic approach that allows managers to focus on attainable goals and to achieve the best results based on the organization's resources.

MBO clearly outlines people's tasks, goals, and contributions to the company. MBO is a collaborative process between managers and employees. MBO principles include the following:

- a series of related organizational goals and objectives;
- specific objectives for each person;
- participative decision making;
- a set time period to accomplish goals; and
- performance evaluation and feedback.

Job Design and Motivation

Today's human resource managers constantly search for ways to motivate employees through their jobs. Three ways that jobs can be restructured to be more motivating are through job enlargement, job enrichment, and job rotation.

Job enlargement is a job design that expands an employee's responsibilities by increasing the number and variety of tasks. Redesigning the production process is one way to accomplish this. Instead of having an assembly line on which each worker repeatedly completes the same task, modular work areas allow employees to complete a variety of tasks, which may result in the construction of an entire product.

Job enrichment involves an expansion of job duties that empowers an employee to make decisions and learn new skills leading toward career growth. The Pampered Chef is a direct seller of kitchen tools and housewares that gives its managers and sales consultants the power to make decisions about many aspects of their work. Kitchen consultants, who organize home sales parties, can decide how much or how little they want to work and receive various incentive rewards for performance. The company's mission is to provide "opportunities for individuals to develop their talents and skills to their fullest potential for the benefit of themselves, their families, our customers, and the company."[40]

Job rotation involves systematically moving employees from one job to another. Job rotation increases the range of activities by introducing workers to more jobs and therefore more tasks. The goal is to increase employees' interest in their jobs and allow them to learn more about the company. Nurses might rotate from oncology to the ICU in a hospital. Job rotation is often part of a training program, as is the case at EMC, a global provider of business solutions for data backup, information security, risk and compliance, and many other products. EMC offers motivated employees the chance to participate in rotational training programs in business, leadership, finance, and other areas.[41]

Managers' Attitudes and Motivation

A manager's attitude toward his or her employees greatly influences their motivation. Maslow's theory, described earlier, has helped managers understand that employees have a range of needs beyond their paychecks. Psychologist Douglas McGregor, a student of Maslow, studied motivation from the perspective of how managers view employees. After observing managers' interactions with employees, McGregor created two basic labels for the assumptions that different managers make about their workers' behavior, and how these assumptions affect management styles.

- *Theory X* assumes that employees dislike work and try to avoid it whenever possible, so management must coerce them to do their jobs. Theory X managers believe that the average worker prefers to receive instructions, avoid responsibility, take little initiative, and views money and job security as the only valid motivators—Maslow's lower order of needs.

- *Theory Y* assumes that the typical person actually likes work and will seek and accept greater responsibility. Theory Y managers assume that most people can think of creative ways to solve work-related problems, and should be given the opportunity to participate in decision making. Unlike the traditional management philosophy that relies on external control and constant supervision, Theory Y emphasizes self-control and self-direction—Maslow's higher order of needs.

Another perspective on management, proposed by management professor William Ouchi, has been labeled *Theory Z*. Organizations structured on Theory Z concepts attempt to blend the best of American and Japanese management practices. This approach views worker involvement as the key to increased productivity for the company and improved quality of work life for employees. Many U.S. firms have adopted the participative management style used in Japanese firms by asking workers for suggestions to improve their jobs and then giving them the authority to implement proposed changes.

Labor–Management Relations

The U.S. workplace is far different from what it was a century ago, when child labor, unsafe working conditions, and a 72-hour workweek were common. The development of labor unions, labor legislation, and the collective bargaining process have contributed to the changed environment. Today's human resource managers must be educated in labor-management relations, the settling of disputes, and the competitive tactics of unions and management.

Development of Labor Unions

A **labor union** is a group of workers who have banded together to achieve common goals in the areas of wages, hours, and working conditions. The organized efforts of Philadelphia printers in 1786 resulted in the first U.S. minimum wage—$1 a day. One hundred years later, New York City streetcar conductors were able to negotiate a reduction in their workday from 17 to 12 hours.

Labor unions can be found at the local, national, and international levels. A *local union* represents union members in a specific area, such as a single community, while a *national union* is a labor organization consisting of numerous local chapters. An *international union* is a national union with membership outside the United States, usually in Canada. More than 15 million U.S. workers—about 12 percent of the nation's full-time workforce—belong to labor unions.[42] Although only about 8 percent of workers in the private sector are unionized, more than one-third of government workers belong to unions. The largest union in the United States is the 3.2 million-member National Education Association (NEA), representing public school teachers and other support personnel. Other large unions include the 2.2 million

Assessment Check ✓

1. What are the four steps in the process of motivation?
2. Explain how goal setting works.
3. Describe the three ways that managers structure jobs for increased motivation.

labor union group of workers who have banded together to achieve common goals in the areas of wages, hours, and working conditions.

members of the Service Employees International Union (SEIU), the 1.4 million members of the International Brotherhood of Teamsters, the 1.3 million members of the United Food and Commercial Workers, and the 640,000 members of the United Auto Workers.

Labor Legislation

Over the past century, some major pieces of labor legislation have been enacted, including the following:

- *National Labor Relations Act of 1935 (Wagner Act).* Legalized collective bargaining and required employers to negotiate with elected representatives of their employees. Established the National Labor Relations Board (NLRB) to supervise union elections and prohibit unfair labor practices such as firing workers for joining unions, refusing to hire union sympathizers, threatening to close if workers unionize, interfering with or dominating the administration of a union, and refusing to bargain with a union.

- *Fair Labor Standards Act of 1938.* Set the first federal minimum wage (25 cents an hour), and maximum basic workweek for certain industries. Also outlawed child labor.

- *Taft-Hartley Act of 1947 (Labor–Management Relations Act).* Limited unions' power by banning such practices as coercing employees to join unions, coercing employers to discriminate against employees who are not union members, discrimination against non-union employees, picketing or conducting secondary boycotts or strikes for illegal purposes, and excessive initiation fees.

- *Landrum-Griffin Act of 1959 (Labor–Management Reporting and Disclosure Act).* Amended the Taft-Hartley Act to promote honesty and democracy in running unions' internal affairs. Required unions to set up a constitution and bylaws and to hold regularly scheduled elections of union officers by secret ballot. Set forth a bill of rights for members. Required unions to submit certain financial reports to the U.S. Secretary of Labor.

The Collective Bargaining Process

Labor unions work to increase job security for their members and to improve wages, hours, and working conditions. These goals are achieved primarily through **collective bargaining**, the process of negotiation between management and union representatives.

Union contracts, which typically cover a two- or three-year period, are often the result of weeks or months of discussion, disagreement, compromise, and eventual agreement. Once agreement is reached, union members must vote to accept or reject the contract. If the contract is rejected, union representatives may resume the bargaining process with management representatives, or union members may strike to obtain their demands.

Settling Labor–Management Disputes

Strikes make the headlines, but most labor–management negotiations result in a signed contract. If a dispute arises, it is usually settled through a mechanism such as a grievance

collective bargaining
process of negotiation between management and union representatives.

procedure, mediation, or arbitration. Any of these alternatives is quicker and less expensive than a strike.

The union contract serves as a guide to relations between the firm's management and its employees. The rights of each party are stated in the agreement. But no contract, regardless of how detailed, will eliminate the possibility of disagreement. Such differences can be the beginning of a *grievance*, a complaint—by a single employee or by the entire union—that management is violating some portion of the contract. Almost all union contracts require these complaints to be submitted through a formal grievance procedure similar to the one shown in Figure 8.8. A grievance might involve a dispute about pay, working hours, or the workplace itself. The grievance procedure usually begins with an employee's supervisor and then moves up the company's hierarchy. If the highest level of management can't settle the grievance, it is submitted to an outside party for mediation or arbitration.

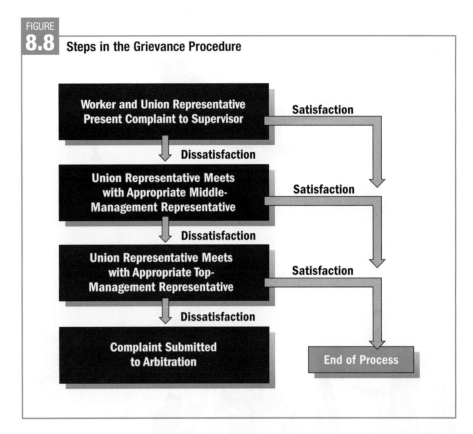

FIGURE **8.8** **Steps in the Grievance Procedure**

Mediation is the process of settling labor–management disputes through an impartial third party. Although the mediator does not make the final decision, he or she can hear the whole story and make objective recommendations. If the dispute remains unresolved, the two parties can turn to *arbitration*—bringing in an outside arbitrator, who renders a legally binding decision. The arbitrator must be acceptable both to the union and to management, and his or her decision is final. Most union negotiations go to arbitration if union and management representatives fail to reach a contract agreement.

Competitive Tactics of Unions and Management

Both unions and management use tactics to make their views known and to win support.

Union Tactics The chief tactics of unions are strikes, picketing, and boycotts. The *strike*, or walkout, is one of the most effective tools of the labor union. It involves a temporary work stoppage by workers until a dispute has been settled or a contract signed. A strike generally seeks to disrupt business as usual, calling attention to workers' needs and union demands. Strikes can last for days or weeks and can be costly to both sides. One recent strike between Bell Helicopter Textron and the United Auto Workers involved 2,500 workers and lasted 27 days, amounting to 67,500 lost work days.[43] Although a strike is powerful, it can also be damaging to the very people it is trying to help. Surrounding businesses may suffer too. If striking workers aren't eating at their usual lunch haunts, those businesses will lose profits.

Picketing, which involves workers marching in a public protest against their employer, is another effective form of union pressure. As long as picketing does not involve violence

STEVE PARSONS/PA Photos/Landov LLC.

Picket lines went up at British Airways as members of the cabin crews went on strike. Strikes are a last-ditch tactic that can empty union coffers, injure an entire industry, and even damage the economy.

or intimidation, it is protected under the U.S. Constitution as freedom of speech. Picketing may accompany a strike, or it may be a protest against alleged unfair labor practices. Hundreds of striking British Airways workers picketed a soccer field near Heathrow airport during a particularly tense standoff during a strike over a holiday weekend. Although planes continued to take off and land over the field, passengers could see the angry workers below.[44]

A *boycott* is an organized attempt to keep the public from purchasing the goods or services of a firm. Some unions have been quite successful in organizing boycotts, and some unions even fine members who defy a boycott.

Management Tactics

Management also has tactics for competing with organized labor when negotiations break down. In the past, it has used the lockout—a management "strike" to put pressure on union members by closing the firm. However, companies more commonly try to recruit strikebreakers in highly visible fields such as professional sports, or transfer supervisors and other nonunion employees to continue operations during strikes. In the British Airways strike described earlier, management leased aircraft from other airlines and used volunteer pilots and managers to take the place of the striking cabin crews.[45]

The Future of Labor Unions

Union membership and influence grew through most of the 20th century by giving industrial workers a voice in decisions about their wages, benefits, and working conditions. However, as the United States, western Europe, and Japan have shifted from manufacturing economies to information and service economies, union membership and influence has declined. Today, 52 percent of all union members are government employees; three times more union members now work for the U.S. Postal Service than work in the auto industry.[46]

How can labor unions change to maintain their relevance? They can be more flexible and adapt to a global economy and diverse workforce. They can respond to the growing

Assessment Check ✓

1. What is a labor union? What is collective bargaining?

2. What are the three main tactics used by unions to win support for their demands?

Labor Unions and Green Construction

The construction industry has nearly unlimited opportunities to change the look of the world—or at least, make it greener. One labor union, the Operative Plasterers and Cement Masons International Association (OPCMIA) has already recognized this and is training its members in the use of new green technologies and processes that will ultimately improve the energy efficiency and reduce the carbon footprint of the nation's infrastructure. As the construction industry begins implementing these new technologies, particularly to achieve LEED status, workers need to know how to use them.

The OPCMIA training program is called Green Five. It is now being incorporated into existing training curricula in order to reach about 5,400 participants in 70 programs spread across local chapters, community colleges, vocational/technical schools, and OPCMIA Joint Apprenticeship and Training Centers. The Green Five program is training plasterers and cement masons in the sustainable use and application of the following materials: polished concrete, pervious concrete, exterior insulation finish systems, and American Clay. American Clay is a color mineral coating that is toxin free, VOC (volatile organic compound) free, and mold resistant. Training in the use of this product involves the preparation, mixing the material, hand application, primers, additives and sealers, and maintaining and repairing walls.

The Green Five program includes Green Awareness Training, which deals with energy-efficient building construction in general, addresses the process of energy assessment and retrofitting existing buildings, and provides an overview of environmentally sustainable products and manufacturing processes. Leadership training and "train-the-trainer" courses are offered as well. "Program participants include construction workers, building engineers, and energy auditors as part of our outreach toward making green construction knowledge accessible to the whole of the industry," says Gerry Ryan, director of training, health and safety for OPCMIA.

Questions for Critical Thinking

1. In what ways does adopting a progressive stance toward "green" training help secure an important industry role for OPCMIA going forward?

2. In addition to construction, what other industries might benefit from unions taking a leadership role in sustainability training? How might these steps benefit workers, unions, and management?

Sources: David Bradley, "TR10: Green Concrete," *Technology Review,* May/June 2010, http://www.technologyreview.com; "About OPCMIA," OPCMIA Web site, http://www.opcmia.org, accessed April 29, 2010; Gerry Ryan, "The Green Five Program," *Green Labor Journal,* April 29, 2010, http://greenlaborjournal.com.

---

need for environmentally responsible business and manufacturing processes, as the Operative Plasterers and Cement Masons International Association (OPCMIA) is doing, described in the "Going Green" feature. Unions can establish collaborative relationships with human resource managers and other management officials. And they can recognize the potential for prosperity for all—management and union workers included.

What's Ahead

Treating employees well by enriching the work environment will continue to gain importance as a way to recruit and retain a highly motivated workforce. In addition, managers can tap the full potential of their employees by empowering them to make decisions, leading them to work effectively as teams, and fostering clear, positive communication. The next chapter covers these three means of improving performance. By involving employees more fully through empowerment, teamwork, and communication, companies can benefit from their knowledge while employees enjoy a more meaningful role in the company.

Summary of Learning Objectives

[1] **Explain the role and responsibilities of human resource management.**

Human resource managers are responsible for attracting, developing, and retaining the employees who can perform the activities necessary to accomplish organizational objectives. They plan for staffing needs, recruit and hire workers, provide for training, evaluate performance, determine compensation and benefits, and oversee employee separation.

Assessment Check Answers

1.1 What are the five main tasks of a human resource manager? The five main tasks are planning for staffing needs, recruiting and hiring workers, providing for training, and evaluating performance, determining compensation and benefits, and overseeing employee separation.

1.2 What are the three overall objectives of a human resource manager? The three overall objectives are providing qualified, well-trained employees for the organization; maximizing employee effectiveness; and satisfying individual employee needs through monetary compensation.

[2] **Describe how recruitment and selection contribute to placing the right person in a job.**

Human resource managers use internal and external methods to recruit qualified employees. They may use college job fairs, personal referrals, want ads, and other resources. Internet recruiting is now the fastest, most efficient, and inexpensive way to reach a large pool of job seekers. Firms must abide by employment laws during selection in order to avoid lawsuits. Before hiring candidates, human resource managers may require employment tests that evaluate certain skills or aptitudes. When all of this is complete, there is a better chance that the right person will be hired for the job.

Assessment Check Answers

2.1 Describe several recruiting techniques used by human resource managers. Techniques include college job fairs, personal referrals, want ads, company Web sites, online job sites, and online interviews such as jobcasts.

2.2 What is the function of the Equal Employment Opportunity Commission (EEOC)? The EEOC investigates discrimination complaints and helps employers set up affirmative action programs.

[3] **Discuss how orientation, training programs, and performance appraisals help companies develop their employees.**

New employees often participate in an orientation where they learn about company policies and practices. Training programs provide opportunities for employees to build their skills and knowledge and prepare them for new job opportunities within the company. They also give employers a better chance of retaining employees. Performance appraisals give employees feedback about their strengths and weaknesses and how they can improve.

Assessment Check Answers

3.1 What are the benefits of computer-based training? Computer-based training offers consistent presentations, interactive learning, and employees can learn at their own pace. It is also less expensive than other types of training.

3.2 What is a management development program? A management development program provides training designed to improve the skills and broaden the knowledge of current and potential executives.

3.3 What are the four criteria of an effective performance appraisal? A performance appraisal should take place several times a year, be linked to organizational goals, be based on objective criteria, and be a two-way conversation.

[4] **Describe how firms compensate employees through pay systems and benefit programs.**

Firms compensate employees with wages, salaries, incentive pay systems, and benefits. Benefit programs vary among firms, but most companies offer healthcare programs, insurance, retirement plans, paid time off, and sick leave. A growing number of companies are offering flexible benefit plans and flexible work plans, such as flextime, compressed workweeks, job sharing, and home-based work.

Assessment Check Answers

4.1 Explain the difference between *wage* and *salary*. Wages are based on an hourly pay rate or the amount of work accomplished. Salaries are paid periodically, such as weekly or monthly. Salaries do not fluctuate with hours worked.

4.2 What are flexible benefit plans? How do they work? Flexible benefit plans offer a choice of benefits, including different types of medical insurance, dental and vision, and life and disability insurance. Typically, each employee receives a set allowance to pay for these benefits depending on his or her needs.

[5] **Discuss employee separation and the impact of downsizing and outsourcing.**

Employee separation occurs when a worker leaves his or her job, voluntarily or involuntarily. Sometimes an employee is terminated because of poor job performance or unethical behavior. Downsizing is the process of reducing the number of employees within a firm in order to cut costs and achieve a leaner organization. However, some negative effects include anxiety and lost productivity among remaining workers; expensive severance packages; and a domino effect in the local economy. Outsourcing involves transferring jobs from inside a firm to outside the firm. While some expenses may be cut, a firm may experience a backlash in performance and public image.

Assessment Check Answers ✓

5.1 What is the difference between voluntary and involuntary turnover? Voluntary turnover occurs when employees leave firms to start their own businesses, take jobs with other firms, move to another community, or retire. Involuntary turnover occurs because of poor job performance or unethical behavior in business practices or the workplace. It can also occur when a company is forced to eliminate jobs.

5.2 What is downsizing? How is it different from outsourcing? Downsizing is the process of reducing the number of employees within a firm by eliminating jobs. Downsizing is done to cut overhead costs and streamline the organizational structure. With outsourcing, companies contract with other firms to perform noncore jobs or business functions, such as housekeeping, maintenance, or relocation services. This allows companies to focus on what they do best, and can result in a downsized workforce.

⌐6⌐ **Explain the different methods and theories of motivation.**

Employee motivation starts with high employee morale. According to Maslow's hierarchy of needs, people satisfy lower-order needs (such as food and safety) before moving to higher-order needs (such as esteem and fulfillment). Herzberg's two-factor model of motivation is based on the fulfillment of hygiene factors and motivation factors. Expectancy theory suggests that people use these factors to determine whether to put forth the effort to complete a task. Equity theory refers to a person's perception of fair and equitable treatment. Goal-setting theory says that people will be motivated to the extent to which they accept specific, challenging goals. Job design is also used by managers for motivation.

Assessment Check Answers ✓

6.1 What are the four steps in the process of motivation? The four steps are need, motivation, goal-directed behavior, and need satisfaction.

6.2 Explain how goal setting works. People will be motivated to the extent to which they accept specific, challenging goals and receive feedback that indicates their progress toward goal achievement.

6.3 Describe the three ways that managers structure jobs for increased motivation. Three ways that employers apply motivational theories to restructure jobs are job enlargement, job enrichment, and job rotation. Job enlargement is a job design that expands an employee's responsibilities by increasing the number and variety of tasks they entail. Job enrichment is a change in job duties to increase employees' authority in planning their work, deciding how it should be done, and learning new skills that help them grow. Job rotation involves systematically moving employees from one job to another.

⌐7⌐ **Discuss the role of labor unions, the collective bargaining process, and methods for settling labor–management disputes.**

Labor unions have resulted in the improvement of wages and working conditions for many workers over the past century, along with the passage of significant labor laws. Unions achieve these improvements through the collective bargaining process, resulting in an agreement. Most labor–management disputes are settled through the grievance process, in which sometimes mediation or arbitration is necessary.

Assessment Check Answers ✓

7.1 What is a labor union? What is collective bargaining? A labor union is a group of workers who have banded together to achieve common goals in the areas of wages, hours, and working conditions. Collective bargaining is the process of negotiation between management and union representatives.

7.2 What are the three main tactics used by unions to win support for their demands? Unions use strikes (walkouts), picketing, and boycotts.

▪ Business Terms You Need to Know

human resource management 254	salary 260	Maslow's hierarchy of needs 268	management by objectives (MBO) 271
performance appraisal 259	employee benefits 261	expectancy theory 270	labor union 273
compensation 260	employee separation 265	equity theory 270	collective bargaining 274
wage 260	downsizing 265	goal-setting theory 270	
	outsourcing 267		

Review Questions

1. Why has Internet recruiting become such an important tool for human resource managers?

2. Recruitment and selection are expensive. So, what precautions do human resource managers take to make sure they are hiring the right person for each job?

3. Give an example of a type of job that would be appropriate for on-the-job training. Then describe specifically how you think this type of training would work for your selected job, including types of tasks a new hire might learn this way.

4. On what five factors are compensation policies usually based? Name at least three employee benefits that are required by law and three more that are provided voluntarily by many firms.

5. Describe four types of flexible work plans. Identify an industry that would be well suited to each type of plan, and explain why.

6. Why do companies downsize? What are some of the drawbacks to downsizing? Why do companies outsource? What are some of the drawbacks to outsourcing?

7. Select three different theories of motivation, and explain how each can be used by managers to motivate employees.

8. Suppose a manager of a popular sandwich shop maintains a Theory X assumption about employees. At the beginning of each workweek, what types of things might the manager tell his or her employees? Now suppose the manager has a Theory Y assumption; then Theory Z. Describe what he or she might say to employees.

9. In what major ways has labor legislation changed the workplace over the past century? How might the workplace be different today without this legislation?

10. What are mediation and arbitration? Describe a situation that you think might result in arbitration.

Projects and Teamwork Applications

1. On your own or with a classmate, research consulting firms that provide management training programs—like Glimmerglass Consulting Group, described in the chapter. Prepare a presentation about one of these firms, describing the approach it takes as well as some of the specific elements of the program.

2. Choose one of the following companies, or one that you think you might like to work for sometime in the future. Using the firm's Web site and one of the job Web sites such as Monster.com (if applicable), research the company's benefits. Outline the firm's benefits and then determine if you still want to work for that company, and why. Suggested firms:
   a. Timberland
   b. SAS
   c. NextEra Energy Resources
   d. Kraft Foods
   e. FedEx

3. With a classmate, choose an on-campus job and outline how you would share that job. Create a schedule and division of tasks.

4. Choose what you think would be your dream job five years from now. Then create a chart according to Maslow's hierarchy of needs, and identify the ways in which you envision this job fulfilling each level of need.

5. Research one of the major labor laws outlined in the text to learn more about the circumstances that led to its proposal and passage. In what ways do you believe this law has (or has not) affected the working world that you expect to enter when you graduate?

Web Assignments

1. **Human resources (HR) as a profession.** Go to the Web site listed here and review the material. Answer the following questions:
   a. How many people are employed in HR?
   b. What are the educational requirements to become an HR manager?
   c. How rapidly is the occupation expected to grow over the next decade?

   http://www.bls.gov/oco/ocos021.htm

2. **Performance reviews.** Visit the Web sites listed here. Each lists some tips for conducting employee performance reviews. Print out the material and bring it to class to participate in a class discussion on performance reviews.

   http://www.squidoo.com/employeeperformancereview

   http://articles.techrepublic.com.com/5100-10878_11-1049853.html

   http://smallbusiness.dnb.com/human-resources/workforce-management/1385-1.html

3. **Teamsters.** The Teamsters is one of the nation's largest and oldest labor unions. Go to the union's Web site (http://www.teamster.org) and review the material. When was the union founded? Originally, the union represented workers in what industry? How many members do the Teamsters currently have? Other than the United States, in what other country does the union represent workers?

Note: Internet Web addresses change frequently. If you don't find the exact sites listed, you may need to access the organization's home page and search from there or use a search engine such as Bing or Google.

Google Transforms Human Resource Management

CASE 8.1

Looking for a great company to work for? Your search might take you to Google. It was named the best company to work for in *Fortune* magazine's annual rankings for two years in a row. Now recognized as the fastest-growing media company in history, Google is run by managers who believe happy people are more productive.

Co-founder Larry Page notes that labor has come a long way since his grandfather worked on the auto assembly line in Flint, Michigan. During sit-down strikes, he carried a lead pipe to protect himself from company strongmen. That was two generations ago. Google employees don't need to carry weapons to work, says Page with extreme understatement.

Google's strategy is to "hire great people and encourage them to make their dreams a reality." The company has transformed human resource management like no other. Google grew from a handful of employees to more than 12,000 worldwide through a creative approach to recruiting, motivating, and retaining top talent. The results have been spectacular. The average employee generates more than $1 million in annual revenue, compared with $564,000 for Yahoo! and $647,000 for Microsoft.

With no advertising, Google receives more than 760,000 job applications a year. The process begins when individuals search the Web site and apply for a job. If their skills fit a job, the applicants are interviewed by phone for 30 to 40 minutes to assess their technical skills and determine whether an in-person interview is warranted. During on-site interviews, candidates meet engineers from different teams to get a firsthand view of work life at Google. Interviewers question applicants about their areas of interest, present them with a typical problem, and expect immediate solutions. Right or wrong answers are not as important as showing a thoughtful process and creativity, and applicants may even go to the whiteboard to demonstrate some computer-coding skills. Every prospective Google employee completes at least four interviews, and all the interviewers' opinions count. The company's philosophy is that great people hire more great people.

Once you're hired at Google, the fun literally begins. Co-founders Larry Page and Sergey Brin never believed work and fun were mutually exclusive. From its innovative training program to generous benefits, Google does everything possible to make sure employees enjoy their jobs and have fun. Instead of traditional training programs, Google's employee development is decentralized, with courses playing only a small part. The work changes quickly, so most employees don't end up in positions they were hired for anyway. Because Google hires self-starters with a thirst for learning, most training is shifted to employees, with 30 percent of their time allocated to their own development

and innovation. Development also takes place through on-the-job learning by continual rotation to new projects, use of new-hire mentors, department "tech-talks," and on-site speakers like former TV news anchor Tom Brokaw.

Google's approach to motivation and performance management is also innovative. Motivation is spurred by constant change, rapid decision making, and a culture that expects ambitious ideas. Limited bureaucracy lets employees be free to make decisions and take risks without fearing the consequences of failure. Ideas are approved in days, not months. Google managers believe all employees are high performers and accept the blame should someone fall short. The company supports its culture with a generous benefit package that is as highly publicized as Google's search tools.

The company knows employees have diverse needs and celebrates this diversity through flexible and individually directed benefits. The basics include the choice among three medical insurance carriers, comprehensive dental insurance, vision insurance, and a flexible spending account. An employee assistance program provides employees and dependents free short-term counseling, legal consultations, child care referrals, and financial counseling. Life and accidental death insurance is offered at two times annual salary, employees may select additional voluntary life insurance, they receive short-term and long-term disability, and the company provides business travel accident insurance. Employees also receive stock options along with a generous 401(k) retirement plan. Vacation policies are generous, with 15 vacation days for new employees, 20 days after four years, and 26 after six. Other paid time off includes 12 paid holidays, a variety of leaves and sabbaticals, and unlimited sick leave.

Beyond the basics, Google gives tuition reimbursement of up to $8,000 per year, a $2,000 bonus for referring a new hire, back-up child care, a child care center, and up to $5,000 reimbursement for the costs of adopting a child. Going way beyond the basics, Google also provides free lunch and dinner at 17 cafés at the Mountain Valley, California, campus and between-meal snacks. There's also an on-site doctor, shuttle service to several East Bay and South Bay locations, financial planning classes, oil changes and car washes for employees' cars, dry cleaning, gym facilities, and massage therapy. Google employees, the thinking goes, are too valuable to spend time running to a dry cleaner. Other fabulous benefits include ski trips, picnics, movies, and an outdoor volleyball court.

Google's founders like to say they are only serious about search. Google puts users first when it comes to its online search engine, and it puts employees first when it comes to daily life at work. Says CEO Eric Schmidt: "The goal is to strip away everything that gets in our employees way … Let's face it: programmers want to program, they don't want to do their laundry. So we make it easy for them to do both."

Questions for Critical Thinking

1. How does Google's training program differ from more traditional programs?

2. Which motivation theories can be used to explain how human resource managers motivate employees at Google?

Sources: "Google Jobs," Google Web site, accessed March 2009, http://www.google.com; Adam Lashinsky, "Back2Back Champs," *Fortune,* February 4, 2008, p. 70; John Sullivan, "The Last Word," *Workforce Management,* November 19, 2007, p. 42.

CASE 8.2 — Strikes: Who Wins, Who Loses?

As a consumer, there are many strikes you'll probably never notice. They won't affect your daily life, what you eat, how you get to work or to school, or your access to communication and information. But a strike that stops a major form of transportation generally has the effect that its union wants: people notice. That was the case in Britain recently when union railworkers threatened to strike over a major holiday weekend during which thousands of people were scheduled to travel by train.

The major issue leading to the strike vote was Network Rail's announcement that it would be eliminating 1,500 jobs in an effort to cut costs. Network Rail, which is state owned, maintains the track and signaling system over which private train operating companies run their train services. It also hires out track engineering and replacement contracts to private contractors. The workers involved in the dispute belong to the Rail Maritime Transport Workers Union (RMT). When RMT maintenance workers voted a 77 percent majority in favor of the strikes, Network Rail threatened to fire all 13,000 of them and reemploy a smaller number of them based on new terms and conditions. Because of budget cuts, a private subcontractor had already filed for bankruptcy—representing another 1,100 lost jobs.

Had the strike gone ahead as planned it would have been Britain's first in more than 16 years.

It would have disrupted travel throughout the nation, including passenger travel and the shipping of goods. But the strike was blocked by a British judge who cited irregularities in the union's strike ballot—a technicality. Union representatives were outraged by the decision. "This judgment is an attack on the whole trade union movement and twists the anti-union laws even further in favor of the bosses," argued Bob Crow, general secretary for RMT. Network Rail's head of operations, Robin Gisby, played to the general public. "This is good news for the millions of passengers who rely on us every day, and for our freight users and for the country as a whole," he said. "We have a responsibility to our people to continue talking to the unions to find a settlement."

Questions for Critical Thinking

1. If the RMT strike had gone ahead, what do you think might have been the result? How would the general public view RMT? How would Network Rail be viewed?

2. Do you think the union was a help or a hindrance to negotiations between workers and Network Rail? Why?

Sources: "UK Judge Blocks National Rail Strike," *The Star,* April 1, 2010, http://thestar.com.my; Adam Gabbatt, "Rail Strike Dates Announcement Likely Today," *Guardian,* March 25, 2010, http;//www.guardian.co.uk.

CASE 8.3 — Seventh Generation Promotes Company Ownership

Common sense dictates that companies who treat their employees well—from fair compensation to dignity in the workplace—will attract and retain the best workers.

But from there, the picture becomes a bit murky. Traditional models of human resource management are being reevaluated and sometimes tossed out by firms whose goals and values these models do not fit. Seventh Generation is one such company. "When we win an award for being one of the best places to work in America, that to me is the most important award we can win because it's the hardest thing we do," says co-founder Jeffrey Hollender. Seventh Generation was founded on the premise of sustainability—that every product it manufactures, whether it is laundry detergent or paper towels, must be designed and produced in such a way that it leaves little or no impact on the environment. Sustainability includes its recruitment and development of human resources over the long term.

Most of the 100-plus employees at Seventh Generation have had at least some experience with another employer. Hollender points out that these employees arrive at Seventh Generation with all of the relationship patterns, values, and attitudes toward work they have learned elsewhere. "Most businesses teach us not to have a voice, not to speak up, not to challenge authority, not to unleash the maximum potential we have as individuals," he says. Because Seventh Generation incorporates a different set of values into its organizational culture, "the responsibility at Seventh Generation is to *unteach* people all of those habits and patterns, and unleash the potential that all of those other businesses have stifled," Hollender asserts.

Stephanie Lowe works in human resources at Seventh Generation. She notes that when she was hired, the company had only 30 employees—now there are more than 100. The increase in the number of employees has presented a challenge. Not only have people arrived from other firms with a variety of experience and expectations, the logistics of managing 100 employees are different from those of managing 30. "We can't do things as casually," says Lowe with some regret. "Things just wouldn't get done. It's a hard line to walk, and it's a challenge." In addition, the core value of sustainability is built into every decision the firm makes. "How do you do compensation in a socially responsible company?" asks Lowe. "How do you do that in a company that values different things, where people are asked to value themselves and bring more of themselves to work?"

Seventh Generation's answer to the compensation/social responsibility/sustainability question is ownership. Every person who works at Seventh Generation has a financial stake in the company. "The most significant way Seventh Generation's philosophy translates into HR is ownership," remarks Hollender. He points out that a firm can give employees health insurance, time off, grants for the purchase of hybrid vehicles, on-site fitness centers, and the like; but none of these benefits translates to ownership. "The most important thing is to let the people who are creating value by building the business participate in the value they create," Hollender asserts.

Stephanie Lowe echoes this philosophy. "We aren't trying to distinguish between the employees and the corporation," she explains. At Seventh Generation, the people are the company. Employees not only participate in company ownership, they are viewed as contributors in ways that reach outside their job descriptions. "We are shifting away from traditional performance management to personal development plans," says Lowe. "We do look at what employees need to work on to hit company goals, but also what each person needs to grow personally—and we let them define that." Employees write personal initiatives that help the company recognize talents and potential that may not be readily evident during the performance of a particular job. "It's based on the concept that you measure what you value," explains Lowe. "We value volunteer time, making a difference in the world, raising more responsible global citizens." To that end, Seventh Generation encourages employees at every level to speak out with ideas for more sustainable products and processes.

When speaking about the Seventh Generation workforce, Hollender sounds more like a tribal elder than a business manager. Perhaps that's no coincidence, as Seventh Generation's mission is based on the Great Law of the Iroquois, which counsels each tribe member to consider the impact of all decisions on the next seven generations. "The thing I'm most proud of is the success of our employees at Seventh Generation," boasts Hollender, "their growth, the things they have thought of that I would never have dreamed of, the tough questions that they ask me that I wouldn't ask myself. Unleashing that potential—that is the mostmagical thing about running a business."

Questions for Critical Thinking

1. Visit the Seventh Generation Web site at http://www.seventhgeneration.com and view the current job listings there. What kinds of qualities in job candidates does the firm look for that might be different from those at other companies?

2. What might be the potential benefits and pitfalls of Seventh Generation's view of performance and compensation?

3. Choose one of the motivational theories described in the chapter and discuss how the theory would pertain to Seventh Generation's approach to motivating employees.

4. Do you predict that employees at Seventh Generation will attempt to unionize? Why or why not? If they did, how do you think the firm would respond?

Sources: Seventh Generation Web site, http://www.seventhgeneration .com, accessed August 21, 2010; "Sustainability Study," *Accenture,* http://microsite.accenture.com, accessed August 21, 2010; "Study Says Companies Should Train Managers in Sustainability," *7GenBlog,* July 2, 2010, http://www.seventhgeneration.com; Danielle Sacks, "Jeffrey Hollender: Seventh Generation, Triple Bottom Line Entrepreneur," *Fast Company.com,* February 2, 2010, http://www.fastcompany.com.

Chapter 9

Learning Objectives

1. Describe why and how organizations empower employees.

2. Distinguish among the five types of teams in the workplace.

3. Identify the characteristics of an effective team, and summarize the stages of team development.

4. Relate team cohesiveness and norms to effective team performance.

5. Describe the factors that can cause conflict in teams and ways to manage conflict.

6. Explain the importance and process of effective communication.

7. Compare the different types of communication.

8. Explain external communication and methods of managing a public crisis.

Empowering Associates Through Teamwork and Communications

Dean Mitchell/iStockphoto

IDEO's Innovative Design Teams

P alo Alto, California–based IDEO uses teams to create breakthroughs in products that people really use—everything from Apple's first computer mouse to new train interiors for Amtrak to baby strollers for Evenflo. IDEO's clients include a variety of organizations, such as Procter & Gamble, Intel, the Mayo Clinic, and the American Red Cross. IDEO uses cross-functional design teams—groups of professionals with different areas of expertise, such as industrial design, mechanical engineering, architecture, psychology, and anthropology. Considering the human factor is central to IDEO's philosophy—that empathy is vital to the successful design of every product. So IDEO teams are dispatched all over the world to observe consumers using goods and services in their daily lives. Team members watch how consumers use items and note ways in which they could be improved. Whenever possible, they put themselves in the place of the consumer. One IDEO team member had himself strapped to a hospital gurney and wheeled through the emergency room admission process so that he could learn how a hospital could improve its services. IDEO also believes that teamwork is the foundation of creativity and innovation. IDEO executives and staff use teams to share and improve ideas, build problem-solving skills, and spark a multitude of new ideas. A single team meeting can generate ideas for a variety of tasks or projects, not just the one at hand. At IDEO, team brainstorming and discussion sessions aren't secret. Members are encouraged to test ideas with family, friends, and colleagues. This way, simultaneous innovation occurs—an idea that may not work for one product may work beautifully for another. But the design process itself is careful and thorough. IDEO teams take a five-step approach for every project:

- They start by researching existing goods and services.
- They observe consumers using these products.
- They visualize improvements or solutions.
- They evaluate their initial ideas.
- Finally, they refine and implement their solutions to their clients' problems—perhaps in the form of an improvement or a new product altogether.

The human factor lies at the core of everything IDEO does. Tim Brown, IDEO's president and CEO, notes that design and innovation "encourage us to take a human-centered, empathic approach to business problems as well as social problems," and by viewing problems or ideas that way, IDEO is able to make connections between seemingly unrelated areas. From the human-centered focus came the idea of strapping a team member to a hospital gurney. They discovered that patients often become confused and disoriented when lying on a gurney simply because they can't see signs on the hospital walls. They don't necessarily know which room they've been in or where they are going—particularly if they are handed off from one staff member to another. So the IDEO team came up with a Patient Journey Punch Card that would show each person where he or she had been, what had taken place, and what would be happening next. They figured they might also be able to learn something from smooth-functioning, precise NASCAR pit crews that could be applied to hospital emergency room (ER) procedures. So the team took their clients to watch the pit crews during a race. They discovered that those teams work under similarly stressful, time-constrained conditions. They realized that ER staff and pit crews ultimately want to make everyone comfortable and happy—as quickly as possible. "Seeing something that is analogous can be inspirational," notes Chris Flink, a partner at IDEO. "The pit crew's behavior was something the ER team could consider. The sense of wanting to help people, for example in the health care professions, can get lost over time." But viewing the race teams helped the ER employees reconnect and rethink how they approached their business from the patient's point of view.

When given the task of developing a better baby stroller for Evenflo, the four members of the IDEO stroller team immediately dismantled just about every stroller on the market to see how they worked. Evenflo wanted a stroller that would be compatible with any infant car seat. It also wanted a stroller that would grab people's attention, maneuver easily, and be comfortable. Armed with this objective and knowledge about existing strollers, the team hit the street. They watched how parents and nannies pivoted, pushed, and pulled their strollers. They observed how strollers handled bumps and curbs. The IDEO team generated literally hundreds of possible solutions to the problems raised by Evenflo, and in the end delivered several models for Evenflo's approval. IDEO's team approach to every project works because its members collaborate to find solutions. "IDEO likes to hire people whose mindset allows them to see opportunities rather than problems," says Chris Flink.[1]

Overview

Top managers at most firms at Fandango recognize that teamwork and communication are essential for empowering employees to perform their best. This chapter focuses on how organizations involve employees by sharing information and empowering them to make critical decisions, allowing them to work in teams, and fostering communication. We begin by discussing the ways managers can empower their employees' decision-making authority and responsibility. Then we explain why and how a growing number of firms rely on teams of workers rather than individuals to make decisions and carry out assignments. Finally, we discuss how effective communication allows workers to share information that improves the quality of decision making.

Empowering Employees

empowerment giving employees authority and responsibility to make decisions about their work.

An important component of effective management is the **empowerment** of employees. Managers promote this goal by giving employees the authority and responsibility to make decisions about their work. Empowerment seeks to tap the brainpower of all workers to find improved ways of doing their jobs, better serving customers, and achieving organizational goals. Empowerment frees managers from hands-on control of workers. It also motivates workers by adding challenges to their jobs and giving them a feeling of ownership. Managers empower employees by sharing company information and decision-making authority and by rewarding them for their performance—as well as the company's. The topic of employee empowerment is discussed in the "Solving an Ethical Controversy" feature.

Sharing Information and Decision-Making Authority

One of the most effective methods of empowering employees is to keep them informed about the company's financial performance. Companies such as Virginia-based engineering firm Anderson & Associates (A&A) provide regular reports to their employees on key financial information, such as profit-and-loss statements. A&A, which designs roads, water and sewer lines, and water-treatment facilities, posts financial statements, training schedules, policy documents, and other information on the company's internal Web site. A&A practices open-book management—any employee can visit the site and look up the company's cash flow, design standards, and photos of coworkers in other cities, as well as basic measures of financial performance. Like other companies that practice this strategy, A&A also trains its employees to interpret financial statements so that they can understand how their work contributes to company profits. Using information technology to empower employees does carry some risks. One is that information may reach competitors. Although A&A considered this problem, management decided that sharing information was essential to the company's strategy.[2]

Solving an Ethical Controversy

Employee Empowerment: Yes or No?

Many firms today recognize the benefits of empowering employees—entrusting them with decision-making authority that may improve sales outcomes, relationships with customers, and the ultimate success of a firm. But not all managers are convinced that handing over the reins to their employees is the best way to run a company. They worry about the consequences of allowing employees to make decisions that could cost the company dearly if those choices turn out to be wrong.

Should firms empower employees to make decisions that could improve company relationships and overall performance?

PRO

1. Employees who are empowered to make decisions within their job descriptions and realm of expertise can help build relationships as well as sales. For example, an employee who has direct contact with customers can market products and solve customer problems more effectively if given the authority to do so. A salesperson who can authorize a return or a discount on the spot could cement a relationship with a customer and ensure repeat business.

2. Empowered employees are motivated to increase their own performance as well as that of the firm. Workers who are entrusted with making decisions about their own jobs are more invested in their company's overall performance. Employees who are motivated to display the commitment, initiative, and creativity that decision-making requires help propel their company to success.

CON

1. When things go wrong at a firm—such as a major product recall or the discovery of poor working conditions at an outsourced facility—customers, investors, and the public turn their attention immediately to the company's leadership. If the company's top management appears unaware of the decision making that led to these mistakes, then customers, investors, and the public quickly lose faith in the firm's credibility. Employee decision making can result in this type of communication breakdown within an organization.

2. When employees are empowered without proper training, customers or suppliers might receive insufficient or inaccurate information that could lead to failed solutions, damaged relationships, and lost sales.

Summary

While most firms are now practicing at least some degree of empowerment among employees, some managers are reluctant to delegate this kind of decision-making authority. However, even those managers who support empowerment agree that employees must be trained in decision-making skills and educated about the goods and services marketed by their firm. The company must create a cohesive message so all customers are treated equally and fairly by different employees. When it is implemented effectively, empowerment can be an important force in moving an organization forward.

Sources: George N. Root, "Challenges of Employee Empowerment," *Small Business-Chron.com,* http://smallbusiness.chron.com, accessed August 16, 2010; Cameron Kauffman, "Employee Involvement: A New Blueprint for Success," *Journal of Accountancy,* May 2010, http://www.journalofaccountancy.com; Bob Reynolds, "Thoughts from the shower—Pros and Cons to Empowering Your Employees," *Snoitulos Ten,* April 30, 2010, http://www.snoitulosten.com; Stacy Blackman, "How to Empower Employees with the Illusionof Control," *Blogs Bnet.com,* April 16, 2010, http://blogs.bnet.com.

The second way in which companies empower employees is to give them broad authority to make workplace decisions that implement a firm's vision and its competitive strategy. Even among non-management staff, empowerment extends to decisions and activities traditionally handled by managers. Employees might be responsible for such tasks as purchasing supplies, making hiring decisions, scheduling production or work hours, overseeing the safety program, and granting pay increases.

This can be an especially powerful tool in many healthcare environments. At Lebanon Valley Brethren Homes, a long-term care facility in Pennsylvania, workers at all levels

are empowered to do whatever it takes to improve the quality of their elderly residents' lives. Each care worker attends to the same residents every day, so caregivers and residents form a strong personal bond. Caregivers are responsible for the overall management of their household including meals and housekeeping. They make decisions for individual residents ranging from sleep schedules to room lighting. As a result, each Green House—or household within the larger community—feels like a home.[3]

Empowerment can take other forms as well. The "Hit & Miss" feature describes how Nugget Market empowers employees to deliver excellent service.

A way in which companies empower employees is to give them broad authority to make workplace decisions that implement a firm's vision and its competitive strategy. At Lebanon Valley Brethren Homes, a long-term care facility in Pennsylvania, workers at all levels are empowered to do whatever it takes to improve the quality of their elderly residents' lives.

Jacob Wackerhausen/iStockphoto

Linking Rewards to Company Performance

Perhaps the ultimate step in convincing employees of their stake in the prosperity of their firm is worker ownership. Two widely used ways that companies provide worker ownership are employee stock ownership plans and stock options. Table 9.1 compares these two methods of employee ownership.

Employee Stock Ownership Plans Almost 13 million workers participate in 10,500 *employee stock ownership plans (ESOPs)* worth more than $900 billion.[4] These plans benefit employees by giving them ownership stakes in their companies, leading to potential profits as the value of their firm increases. Under ESOPs, the employer buys shares

Table
9.1 Employee Stock Ownership Plans and Stock Options

ESOP	STOCK OPTIONS
Company-sponsored trust fund holds shares of stock for employees	Company gives employees the option to buy shares of its stock
Usually covers all full-time employees	Can be granted to one, a few, or all employees
Employer pays for the shares of stock	Employees pay a set price to exercise the option
Employees receive stock shares (or value of stock) upon retiring or leaving the company	Employees receive shares of stock when (and if) they exercise the option, usually during a set period

Sources: "Employee Stock Options and Ownership (ESOP)," *Reference for Business,* http://www.referenceforbusiness.com, accessed April 19, 2010; "Employee Stock Options Fact Sheet," The National Center for Employee Ownership, http://www.nceo.org, accessed April 19, 2010.

Nugget Market Employees: The Power of Gold

Nugget Market is more than a supermarket; it's a shopping destination. The California chain features elegant merchandise displays, a vast selection—600 varieties of produce and 400 types of cheese—fresh meat and fish, restaurant-quality ready-to-cook entrees baked-from-scratch treats, a deli, tea and espresso bar, sushi bar, olive bar, soup and hot pizza counters, a café with wine by the glass, and more.

But the chain is known for more than that. Nugget prices its goods competitively and delivers first-rate service. Employees are called "associates," and customers are "guests." When choosing associates, managers look for "can-do people that want to enjoy what they do for a living." CEO Eric Stille says Nugget's success comes from the family feeling in the stores. His goal is to make Nugget "a great place to be every day" for both associates and guests. The company, which has made the Fortune 100 Best Companies to Work For list several times, gives employees generous benefits, training and opportunities for personal development and promotion, and the responsibility to serve customers well.

As Nugget is committed to associates, so are the associates committed to guests. When a guest asked about the availability of a specific green chili pepper, a produce director whipped out his cell phone, found out that the pepper is available only from August to October, and told the customer, "Come back in August. We'll take care of you."

Nugget associates are also trusted to develop their own departments. Wine steward Larry Otterness stocks the wine, beer, and spirits in Nugget's Roseville, California, store with a huge selection of domestic and imported beers and wines, including those from California vintners. At Friday night wine tastings, he interacts with guests and teaches them about wine. He says he loves his job. In the same way that I'm able to take chances in ordering, I can also takes chances in other areas, because I know everyone will rise to the occasion. We are empowered to think big."

Questions for Critical Thinking

1. What do you think is the first step in empowering employees at Nugget Market?

2. How does calling employees "associates" contribute to empowerment at Nugget stores?

Sources: Mike Roberts, "Employees Treated Like Gold at Nugget Market," *Village Life*, February 4, 2009, http://www.villagelife.com; Tim Menicutch, "A Shiny, New Nugget Opens Today," El Dorado Hills, California, *Telegraph*, January 30, 2008, http://www.edhtelegraph.com, accessed October 21, 2008; Meg Major, "Striking Gold," *Progressive Grocer*, September 1, 2007, pp. 40–48.

of the company stock on behalf of the employee as a retirement benefit. The accounts continue to grow in value tax-free, and when employees leave the company, they can cash in their stock shares. Employees are motivated to work harder and smarter than they would without ESOPs because, as part owners, they share in their firm's financial success. About 60 percent of companies surveyed that offer ESOPs report an increase in employee productivity.[5]

As retirement plans, ESOPs must comply with government regulations designed to protect pension benefits. Because ESOPs can be expensive to set up, they are more common in larger firms than in smaller ones. Public companies with ESOPs average around 14,000 employees, while private companies average about 1,500 employees.[6] One danger with ESOPs is that if the majority of an employee's retirement funds are in company stock and the value falls dramatically, the employee may be financially harmed.[7]

Stock Options Another popular way for companies to share ownership with their employees is through the use of *stock options*, or rights to buy a specified amount of company stock at a given price within a given time period. In contrast to an ESOP, in which the company holds stock for the benefit of employees, stock options give employees a chance to own the stock themselves if they exercise their options by completing the stock purchase. If an employee receives an option on 100 shares at $10 per share and the stock price goes up to $20, the employee can exercise the option to buy those 100 at $10 each, sell them at the market price of $20, and keep the difference. If the stock price never goes above the option price, the employee isn't required to exercise the option.[8]

1. What is empowerment?
2. What kinds of information can companies provide employees to help them share decision-making responsibility?
3. How do employee stock ownership plans and stock options reward employees and encourage empowerment?

team group of people with certain skills who are committed to a common purpose, approach, and set of performance goals.

work teams relatively permanent group of employees with complementary skills who perform the day-to-day work of organizations.

Although options were once limited to senior executives and members of the board of directors, some companies now grant stock options to employees at all levels. Federal labor laws allow stock options to be granted to both hourly and salaried employees. It is estimated that 9 million employees in thousands of companies hold stock options.[9] About one-third of all stock options issued by U.S. corporations go to the top five executives at each firm. Much of the remainder goes to other executives and managers, who make up only about 2 percent of the U.S. workforce. Yet there is solid evidence that stock options motivate regular employees to perform better. Some argue that to be most effective as motivators, stock options need to be granted to a much broader base of employees.

Stock options have turned hundreds of employees at firms such as Home Depot, Microsoft, and Google into millionaires. But such success stories are no guarantee, especially when stock prices drop during economic downturns. As with ESOPs, employees face risks when they rely on a single company's stock to provide for them. In addition to stock options and ESOPs, many firms offer their executives other perks, or special privileges.

Teams

A **team** is a group of people with certain skills who are committed to a common purpose, approach, and set of performance goals. All team members hold themselves mutually responsible and accountable for accomplishing their objectives. Teams are widely used in business and in many not-for-profit organizations such as hospitals and government agencies. Teams are one of the most frequently discussed topics in employee training programs, because teams require that people learn how to work effectively together. Many firms emphasize the importance of teams during their hiring processes, asking job applicants about their previous experiences as team members. Why? Because companies want to hire people who can work well with other people and pool their talents and ideas to achieve more together than they could achieve working alone. Figure 9.1 outlines five basic types of teams: work teams, problem-solving teams, self-managed teams, cross-functional teams, and virtual teams.

About two-thirds of U.S. firms currently use **work teams**, which are relatively permanent groups of employees. In this approach, people with complementary skills perform the day-to-day work of the organization. A work team might include all the workers involved in assembling and packaging a product—it could be anything from cupcakes to cars. Most of Walmart's major vendors maintain offices near its headquarters in Bentonville, Arkansas. Typically, the vendor offices operate as work teams, and the head of these vendor offices often has the title of "team leader."

FIGURE
9.1 **Five Types of Teams**

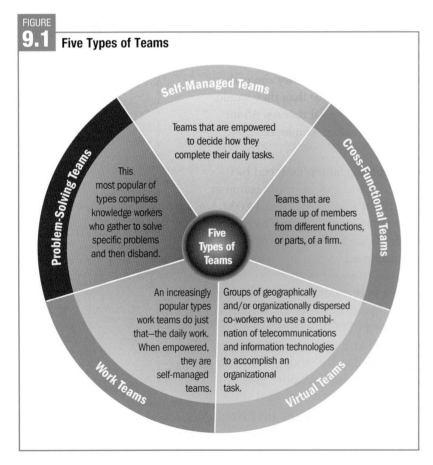

Self-Managed Teams
Teams that are empowered to decide how they complete their daily tasks.

Problem-Solving Teams
This most popular of types comprises knowledge workers who gather to solve specific problems and then disband.

Cross-Functional Teams
Teams that are made up of members from different functions, or parts, of a firm.

Five Types of Teams

Work Teams
An increasingly popular types work teams do just that—the daily work. When empowered, they are self-managed teams.

Virtual Teams
Groups of geographically and/or organizationally dispersed co-workers who use a combination of telecommunications and information technologies to accomplish an organizational task.

In contrast to work teams, a **problem-solving team** is a temporary combination of workers who gather to solve a specific problem and then disband. They differ from work teams in important ways, though. Work teams are permanent units designed to handle any business problem that arises, but problem-solving teams pursue specific missions. When Toyota was faced with serious quality problems—unintended acceleration, faulty brakes, and then questions about tires—and was forced to recall thousands of vehicles, the company formed Rapid Response Swift Market Analysis Response Teams (SMART) to deal with the technical problems. SMART were made up of field technology specialists, engineers from manufacturing and design, and product engineers from the United States with specialists from Japan on call. Together team members worked with dealers across the country to contact customers and arrange for on-site analyses of each problem vehicle to determine what went wrong and why. Teams were encouraged to "listen and react" to customers' descriptions of their experiences as part of their investigation.[10] Typically when a problem is solved, the team disbands—but in some cases, the team may develop a more permanent role within the firm.

A work team empowered with the authority to decide how its members complete their daily tasks is called a **self-managed team**. A self-managed team works most effectively when it combines employees with a range of skills and functions. Members are cross-trained to perform each other's jobs as needed. Distributing decision-making authority in this way can free members to concentrate on satisfying customers. Whole Foods Market has a structure based on self-managed work teams. Company managers decided that Whole Foods could be most innovative if employees made decisions themselves. Every employee is part of a team, and each store has about ten teams handling separate functions, such as groceries, bakery, and customer service. Each team handles responsibilities related to setting goals, hiring and training employees, scheduling team members, and purchasing goods to stock. Teams meet at least monthly to review goals and performance, solve problems, and explore new ideas. Whole Foods awards bonuses based on the teams' performance relative to their goals.[11]

A team made up of members from different functions, such as production, marketing, and finance, is called a **cross-functional team**. Most often, cross-functional teams work on specific problems or projects, but they can also serve as permanent work team arrangements. The value of cross-functional teams comes from their ability to bring different perspectives—as well as different types of expertise—to a work effort. At Harley-Davidson, cross-functional teams are working to find new ways to enhance the unique sound of its motorcycles while reducing unwanted noise. "We're aggressively moving from a tribal way of working to a cross-functional approach," notes Alex Bozmoski, manager of the cross-functional teams.[12]

Virtual teams are groups of geographically or organizationally dispersed coworkers who use a combination of telecommunications and information technologies to accomplish an organizational task. Because of the availability of e-mail, videoconferencing, and group communication software, members of virtual teams rarely meet face-to-face. The principal advantage of virtual

problem-solving team temporary combination of workers who gather to solve a specific problem and then disband.

self-managed team work team that has the authority to decide how its members complete their daily tasks.

cross-functional team a team made up of members from different functions, such as production, marketing, and finance.

virtual teams group of geographically or organizationally dispersed coworkers who use a combination of telecommunications and information technologies to accomplish an organizational task.

Image Source/Getty Images

Although members of a virtual team rarely meet in person, they stay in touch through new technologies, like videoconferencing. In today's global marketplace, the flexibility of virtual teams is a distinct advantage.

Assessment Check ✔

1. What is a team?
2. What are the five types of teams, and how are they different?

teams is that they are very flexible. Employees can work with each other regardless of physical location, time zone, or organizational affiliation. Because of their very nature, virtual teams that are scattered across the globe can be difficult to manage. But firms that are committed to them believe that the benefits outweigh the drawbacks.

Team Characteristics

Effective teams share a number of characteristics. They must be an appropriate size to accomplish their work. In addition to size, teams also can be categorized according to the similarities and differences among team members, called *level* and *diversity*. We discuss these three characteristics next.

Team Size

Teams can range in size from as small as 2 people to as large as 150 people. In practice, however, most teams have fewer than 12 members. Although no ideal size limit applies to every team, research on team effectiveness indicates that they achieve their best results with about 6 or 7 members. A group of this size is big enough to benefit from a variety of diverse skills, yet small enough to allow members to communicate easily and feel part of a close-knit group.

Certainly, groups smaller or larger than this can be effective, but they also create added challenges for team leaders. Participants in small teams of two to four members often show a desire to get along with each other. They tend to favor informal interactions marked by discussions of personal topics, and they make only limited demands on team leaders. A large team with more than 12 members poses a different challenge for team leaders because decision making may work slowly and participants may feel less committed to team goals. Larger teams also tend to foster disagreements, absenteeism, and membership turnover. Subgroups may form, leading to possible conflicts among various functions. As a general rule, a team of more than 20 people should be divided into sub-teams, each with its own members and goals.

team level average level of ability, experience, personality, or any other factor on a team.

team diversity variances or differences in ability, experience, personality, or any other factor on a team.

Joe Gough/iStockphoto

Strong teams not only have talented members, but also members who are different in terms of ability, experience, or personality. Team diversity is an important consideration for teams that must complete a wide range of different tasks or particularly complex tasks. For instance, the British Broadcasting Corporation (BBC) routinely creates teams for a variety of events such as the FIFA World Cup or the Olympic Games.

Team Level and Team Diversity

Team level is the average level of ability, experience, personality, or any other factor on a team. Businesses consider team level when they need teams with a particular set of skills or capabilities to do their jobs well. For example, an environmental engineering firm might put together a team with a high level of experience to write a proposal for a large contract.

While team level represents the average level or capability on a team, **team diversity** represents the differences in ability, experience, personality, or any other factor on a

United's Clean Teams Send Customer Satisfaction Soaring

In the wake of soaring fuel costs and fewer passengers willing to pay full fare, airlines pruned their cleaning staff and materials to cut expenses. United Airlines admits that its aircraft would go from 6 to 18 months between thorough cleanings, which entails heavy scrubbing of the cabin from top to bottom. But leaving crumbs on the cabin floor and wadded up paper towels in the bathroom isn't the same as reducing food service to pretzels and nuts. To many consumers, an unclean plane represents a new low. In fact, airlines discovered that dirty planes affect travelers' perceptions of all services.

So airlines—United in particular—have begun reversing this trend. Recognizing the need to attract more passengers to stay in business, they now dispatch teams to scour their aircraft from top to bottom more frequently. Paul Sanders, United's general manager for cabin appearance—dubbed Mr. Clean by his team—operates with military precision and thoroughness. He makes sure that intensive cleanings are accomplished on United jets every 15 to 30 days—carpets are shampooed, seat cushions removed and checked for stains, every nook and cranny of the planes searched for dirt.

Moments after a United flight taxis to the gate, a cleaning team swarms onto the empty plane, plucking coffee cups, tissues, and other trash from the seats and floor. Reading materials are placed in their seat-back pockets, trays are wiped, bathrooms and galleys are scrubbed to gleaming. Overhead bins are checked for belongings, and blankets are folded. If a team leader notices a suspicious odor or smudge of grime, he or she points it out to the cleaning crew.

Clean has struck a chord with United's passengers. The airline's passenger ratings for cabin cleanliness increased dramatically just a few months after the new cleaning program was put in place. Satisfied travelers are likely to pass the good word to friends, family, and colleagues. Something as simple as a clean passenger cabin may actually give United a competitive advantage.

Questions for Critical Thinking

1. How would you classify the type of cleaning teams that work for United? Do you think any other type of team would be as effective? Why or why not?

2. How does United's focus on teamwork positively differentiate it from its competitors?

Sources: Carl Unger, "American, United Aim for Cleaner Planes," *Smarter Travel*, January 30, 2009, http://www.smatertravel.com; "Airlines Clean Up Planes to Bring Back Flyers," AHN, January 30, 2009, http://www.allheadlinenews.com; Julie Johnson, "United, Others Get Serious about Clean Planes," *Chicago Tribune*, January 29, 2009, http://www.chicago-tribune.com; Matt Bartosik, "Airlines Clean Up Their Act," *NBC Chicago*, January 29, 2009, http://www.nbcchicago.com.

---

team. Strong teams not only have talented members—as demonstrated by their team level— but also members who are different in terms of ability, experience, or personality. Team diversity is an important consideration for teams that must complete a wide range of different tasks or particularly complex tasks. For instance, the British Broadcasting Corporation (BBC) routinely creates teams for a variety of events such as the FIFA World Cup or the Olympic Games. These teams involve production and broadcast groups larger than 100 people, many of whom are part-time employees. Team members typically come from more than 15 different countries, with skills ranging from electrician to statistician, or from scheduling to producing. And because an event at any of the sports venues only takes place once, the BBC teams have one chance to get it right.[13]

Stages of Team Development

Teams typically progress through five stages of development: forming, storming, norming, performing, and adjourning. Although not every team passes through each of these stages, those teams that do are usually better performers. These stages are summarized in Figure 9.2.

FIGURE
9.2 Stages of Team Development

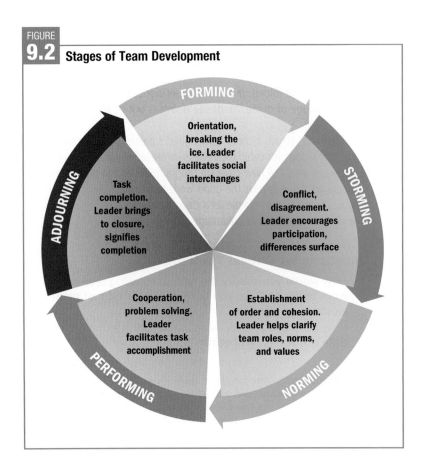

Stage 1: Forming The forming is an orientation period during which team members get to know each other and find out what behaviors are acceptable to the group. Team members begin with curiosity about expectations of them and whether they will fit in with the group. An effective team leader provides time for members to become acquainted.

Stage 2: Storming The personalities of team members begin to emerge at the storming stage, as members clarify their roles and expectations. Conflicts may arise, as people disagree over the team's mission and jockey for position and control of the group. Subgroups may form based on common interests or concerns. At this stage, the team leader must encourage everyone to participate, allowing members to work through their uncertainties and conflicts. Teams must move beyond this stage to achieve real productivity.

Stage 3: Norming During the norming stage, members resolve differences, accept each other, and reach broad agreement about the roles of the team leader and other participants. This stage is usually brief, and the team leader should use it to emphasize the team's unity and the importance of its objectives.

Stage 4: Performing While performing, members focus on solving problems and accomplishing tasks. They interact frequently and handle conflicts in constructive ways. The team leader encourages contributions from all members. He or she should attempt to get any non-participating team members involved.

Stage 5: Adjourning The team adjourns after members have completed their assigned task or solved the problem. During this phase, the focus is on wrapping up and summarizing the team's experiences and accomplishments. The team leader may recognize the team's accomplishments with a celebration, perhaps handing out plaques or awards.

Team Cohesiveness and Norms

Teams tend to maximize productivity when they form into highly cohesive units. **Team cohesiveness** is the extent to which members feel attracted to the team and motivated to remain part of it. This cohesiveness typically increases when members interact frequently, share common attitudes and goals, and enjoy being together. Cohesive groups have a better chance of retaining their members than those that do not achieve cohesiveness. As a result, cohesive groups typically experience lower turnover. In addition, team cohesiveness promotes cooperative behavior, generosity, and a willingness on the part of team members to help each other. When team cohesiveness is high, team members are more motivated to contribute to the team, because they want the approval of other team members.

Assessment Check ✔

1. Explain team level and team diversity.
2. Explain how teams progress through the stages of team development.

team cohesiveness
extent to which team members feel attracted to the team and motivated to remain part of it.

Part 3 *Managers—A Key Ingredient in Contemporary Business*

Not surprisingly, studies have clearly established that cohesive teams quickly achieve high levels of performance and consistently perform better.

Team-building retreats are one way to encourage cohesiveness and improve satisfaction and retention. Gulf Coast Community Foundation of Venice, Florida, uses team retreats, where members participate in team-building exercises and games. "We are getting away from the office and having people get to know each other on a human level," says CEO Teri Hansen. She notes that the bonds created on these retreats return with team members to the workplace.[14] Many approaches to training teams also emphasize building cohesion through techniques like cross-training team members in each others' roles or training team members to develop the skills needed to support the team task.[15]

A **team norm** is a standard of conduct shared by team members that guides their behavior. Norms are not formal written guidelines; they are informal standards that identify key values and clarify team members' expectations. In highly productive teams, norms contribute to constructive work and the accomplishment of team goals. In Illinois, the Rockford Public Schools and Rock Valley College recently formed an alliance to create work teams of high school teachers and college faculty members to draft recommendations for the alignment of coursework so high school students would be better prepared to attend college.[16] In this case, team norms would include standards of conduct during meetings as well as a shared vision for the preparation of students.

Team Conflict

Conflict occurs when one person or group's needs do not match those of another, and attempts may be made to block the opposing side's intentions or goals. Conflict and disagreement are inevitable in most teams. But this shouldn't surprise anyone. People who work together are naturally going to disagree about what and how things are done. What causes conflict in teams? Although almost anything can lead to conflict—casual remarks that unintentionally offend a team member or fighting over scarce resources—the primary cause of team conflict is disagreement over goals and priorities. Other common causes of team conflict include disagreements over task-related issues, interpersonal incompatibilities, simple fatigue, and team diversity.

Earlier in this chapter we noted how teams can experience diversity among members. While diversity brings stimulation, challenge, and energy, it can also lead to conflict. The job of the manager is to create an environment in which differences are appreciated and in which a team of diverse individuals works productively together. Diversity awareness training programs can reduce conflict by bringing these differences out in the open and identifying the unique talents of diverse individuals.

Although most people think conflict should be avoided, management experts note that conflict can actually enhance team performance. The key to dealing with conflict is making sure that the team experiences the right kind of conflict. **Cognitive conflict** focuses on problem-related differences of opinion, and reconciling these differences strongly improves team performance. With cognitive conflict, team members disagree because their different experiences and expertise lead them to different views of the problem and its solutions. Cognitive conflict is also characterized by a willingness to examine, compare, and reconcile differences to produce the best possible solution. By contrast, **affective conflict** refers to the emotional reactions that can occur when disagreements become personal rather than professional, and these differences strongly decrease team performance. Because affective conflict often results in hostility, anger, resentment, distrust, cynicism, and apathy, it can make people uncomfortable, cause them to withdraw, decrease their commitment to a team, lower the satisfaction of team members, and decrease team cohesiveness. So, unlike cognitive conflict, affective conflict undermines team performance by preventing teams from engaging in activities that are critical to team effectiveness.

What can managers do to manage team conflict—and even make it work for them? Perhaps the team leader's most important contribution to conflict resolution can be facilitating good communication so that teammates respect each other and are free to disagree with each other. Ongoing, effective communication ensures that team members perceive each other accurately, understand what is expected of them, and obtain the information they need. Taking this a step further, organizations should evaluate situations or conditions in the workplace that might be causing conflict. Solving a single conflict isn't helpful if there are problems systemic to the team or to the company. Team-building exercises, listening exercises, and role-playing can help employees learn to become better team members.[17]

Assessment Check ✓

1. What is cognitive conflict, and how does it affect teams?
2. Explain affective conflict and its impact on teams.

The Importance of Effective Communication

Countries like China, India, and Mexico are home to businesses that provide goods and services to companies or consumers in the United States. But the more parties involved in the production process, the harder it is to coordinate communication. Japanese Toyota found itself in a whirlpool of miscommunication as it tried to document a consistent timeline for the discovery and reporting of unintended acceleration in a number of its vehicles worldwide. While speculation about the cause—loose floor mats, stuck gas pedals, and electronics— raged, U.S. officials learned that European dealers had received information and repair kits from Toyota months earlier.[18]

communication meaningful exchange of information through messages.

Communication can be defined as a meaningful exchange of information through messages. Few businesses can succeed without effective communication. In fact, as illustrated by the Toyota example, miscommunication can result in damage to the company. Toyota was ordered to pay a record-breaking $16.4 million in fines for its failure to communicate.[19]

Managers spend about 80 percent of their time—6 hours and 24 minutes of every eight-hour day—in direct communication with others, whether on the telephone, in meetings, via e-mail, or in individual conversations. Company recruiters consistently rate effective communication, such as listening, conversing, and giving feedback, as the most important skill they look for when hiring new employees. In this last half of the chapter, you'll learn about the communication process, the basic forms of communication, and ways to improve communication within organizations.

The Process of Communication

Every communication follows a step-by-step process that involves interactions among six elements: sender, message, channel, audience, feedback, and context. This process is illustrated in Figure 9.3.

In the first step, the *sender* composes the message and sends it through a communication carrier, or channel. Encoding a message means that the sender translates its meaning into understandable terms and a form that allows transmission through a chosen channel. The sender can communicate a particular message through many different channels, including face-to-face conversations, phone calls, and e-mail or texting. A promotional message to the firm's customers may be communicated through such forms as radio and television ads, billboards, magazines and newspapers, sales presentations, and social media such as Facebook and Twitter. The audience consists of the people who receive the message. In decoding, the receiver of the message interprets its meaning. Feedback from the audience—in response to the sender's communication—helps the sender determine whether the audience has correctly interpreted the intended meaning of the message.

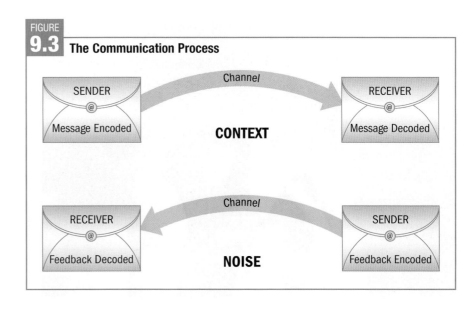

FIGURE 9.3 The Communication Process

Every communication takes place in some sort of situational or cultural context. The *context* can exert a powerful influence on how well the process works. A conversation between two people in a quiet office, for example, may be a very different experience from the same conversation held at a noisy party. An American who orders chips in an English tavern will receive French fries.

Anthropologists classify cultures as low context and high context. Communication in *low-context cultures* tends to rely on explicit written and verbal messages. Examples include Switzerland, Austria, Germany, and the United States. In contrast, communication in *high-context cultures*—such as those of Japan, Latin America, and India—depends not only on the message itself but also on the conditions that surround it, including nonverbal cues, past and present experiences, and personal relationships between the parties. Westerners must carefully temper their low-context style to the expectations of colleagues and clients from high-context countries. Although Americans tend to favor direct interactions and want to "get down to business" soon after shaking hands or sitting down to a business dinner, businesspeople in Mexico and Asian countries prefer to become acquainted before discussing details. When conducting business in these cultures, wise visitors allow time for relaxed meals during which business-related topics are avoided.

Senders must pay attention to audience feedback, even requesting it if none is forthcoming, because this response clarifies whether the communication has conveyed the intended message. Feedback can indicate whether the receiver heard the message and was able to decode it accurately. Even when the receiver tries to understand, the communication may fail if the message contained jargon or ambiguous words.

Noise during the communication process is some type of interference that influences the transmission of messages and feedback. Noise can result from simple physical factors such as poor reception of a cell phone message or static that drowns out a radio commercial. It can also be caused by more complex differences in people's attitudes and perceptions. Consequently, even when people are exposed to the same communications, they can end up with very different perceptions and understandings because of communication noise.

Noise during the communication process can result from simple physical factors such as poor reception of a cell phone message or static that drowns out a radio commercial. Consequently, even when people are exposed to the same communications, they may end up with very different perceptions and understandings because of communication noise.

Noise can be present at any point in the communication process. This is why managers must learn how to cut through noise when communicating with employees. Managers at i-level, a digital communications agency, found a creative way to cut through noise to communicate its plans to transition from a paper-based benefits process to an online system. First they distributed "i" character mugs to office staff. Then they sent messages to employees' mobile phones. Those with iPhones received animated messages. New hires and prospective employees without company phones received a USB stick with the messages. "The communications felt really innovative and it was good using digital media because at the end of the day, that's what we're about as a company," says James Miller, the company's human resource director. "People have found it really good fun and I'm really, really pleased with the concept we have come up with."[20]

Basic Forms of Communication

Managers and coworkers communicate in many different ways—by making a phone call, sending an e-mail, holding a staff meeting, or chatting in the hallway. They also communicate with facial expressions, gestures, and other body language. Subtle variations can significantly influence the reception of a message. As Table 9.2 points out, communication takes various forms: oral and written, formal and informal, and nonverbal.

Oral Communication

Managers spend a lot of time engaged in oral communication, both in person and on the phone. Some people prefer to communicate this way, believing that oral channels more accurately convey messages. Face-to-face oral communication allows people to combine words with such cues as facial expressions and tone of voice. Oral communication over the telephone lacks visual cues, but it does allow people to hear the tone of voice and provide immediate feedback by asking questions or restating the message. Because of its immediacy, oral communication has drawbacks. If one person is agitated or nervous during a conversation, noise enters the communication process. A hurried manager might brush off an employee who has an important message to deliver. A frustrated employee might feel compelled to fire a harsh retort at an unsupportive supervisor instead of thinking before responding.

In any medium, a vital component of oral communication is **listening**—receiving a message and interpreting its genuine meaning by accurately grasping the facts and feeling conveyed. Although listening may be the most important communication skill, most of us don't use it enough—or as well as we should.

listening receiving a message and interpreting its intended meaning by grasping the facts and feelings it conveys.

9.2 Forms of Communication

FORM	DESCRIPTION	EXAMPLES
Oral communication	Communication transmitted through speech	Personal conversations, speeches, meetings, voice mail, telephone conversations, videoconferences
Written communication	Communication transmitted through writing	Letters, memos, formal reports, news releases, e-mail, faxes, online discussion groups, Internet messaging
Formal communication	Communication transmitted through the chain of command within an organization to other members or to people outside the organization	Internal—memos, reports, meetings, written proposals, oral presentations, meeting minutes; external—letters, written proposals, oral presentations, speeches, news releases, press conferences
Informal communication	Communication transmitted outside formal channels without regard for the organization's hierarchy of authority	Rumors spread informally among employees via the grapevine
Nonverbal communication	Communication transmitted through actions and behaviors rather than through words	Gestures, facial expressions, posture, body language, dress, makeup

Listening may seem easy, because the listener appears to make no effort. But the average person talks at a rate of roughly 150 words per minute, while the brain can handle up to 400 words per minute. This gap can lead to boredom, inattention, and misinterpretation. In fact, immediately after listening to a message, the average person can recall only half of it. After several days, the proportion of a message that a listener can recall falls to 25 percent or less.

Certain types of listening behaviors are common in both business and personal interactions:

- *Cynical or defensive listening.* This type of listening occurs when the receiver of a message feels that the sender is trying to gain some advantage from the communication.

- *Offensive listening.* In this type of listening, the receiver tries to catch the speaker in a mistake or contradiction.

- *Polite listening.* In this mechanical type of listening, the receiver listens to be polite rather than to contribute to communication. Polite listeners are usually inattentive and spend their time rehearsing what they want to say when the speaker finishes.

- *Active listening.* This form of listening requires involvement with the information and empathy with the speaker's situation. In both business and personal life, active listening is the basis for effective communication.

Learning how to be an active listener is an especially important goal for business leaders because effective communication is essential to their role. Listening is hard work, but it pays off with increased learning, better interpersonal relationships, and greater influence.[21] Both managers and employees can develop skills to make them better listeners, as described in the "Business Etiquette" feature.

Listening may seem easy, because the listener appears to make no effort. But the average person talks at a rate of roughly 150 words per minute, while the brain can handle up to 400 words per minute. This gap can lead to boredom, inattention, and misinterpretation.

Written Communication

Channels for written communication include reports, letters, memos, online discussion boards and social media, e-mails, and text messages. Many of these channels permit only delayed feedback and create a record of the message. So it is important for the sender of a written communication to prepare the message carefully and review it to avoid misunderstandings—particularly before pressing that "send" button.

Effective written communication reflects its audience, the channel carrying the message, and the appropriate degree of formality. When writing a formal business document such as a complex marketing research report, a manager must plan in advance and carefully construct the document. The process of writing a formal document involves planning, research, organization, composition and design, and revision. Written communication via e-mail may call for a less-formal writing style, including short sentences, phrases, and lists.

E-mail is a very effective communication channel, especially for delivering straightforward messages and information. But e-mail's effectiveness also leads to its biggest problem: too much e-mail! Many workers find their valuable time being consumed with e-mail. To relieve this burden and leave more time for performing the most important aspects of the job, some companies are looking into ways to reduce the time employees spend sending and reading e-mail. To fulfill this need, there are now firms that provide e-mail management services. One such company is DakotaPro.biz, which provides customized e-mail solutions for firms that have been struggling to keep up with the volume of e-mail they receive and the time it takes to operate an in-house server.[22]

Other e-mail issues are security and retention. Because e-mail messages are often informal, senders occasionally forget that they are creating a written record. Even if the recipient deletes an e-mail message, other copies exist on company e-mail servers. E-mails on company servers can be used as evidence in a legal case or disciplinary action.

Formal Communication

A *formal communication channel* carries messages that flow within the chain of command structure defined by an organization. The most familiar channel, downward communication, carries messages from someone who holds a senior position in the organization to subordinates. Managers may communicate downward by sending employees e-mail messages, presiding at department meetings, giving employees policy manuals, posting notices on bulletin boards, and reporting news in company newsletters. The most important factor in formal communication is to be open and honest. "Spinning" bad news to make it look better almost always backfires. In a work environment characterized by open communication, employees feel free to express opinions, offer suggestions, and even voice complaints. Research has shown that open communication has the following seven characteristics:

1. *Employees are valued.* Employees are happier and more motivated when they feel they are valued and their opinions are heard.

2. *A high level of trust exists.* Telling the truth maintains a high level of trust; this forms the foundation for open communication and employee motivation and retention.

3. *Conflict is invited and resolved positively.* Without conflict, innovation and creativity are stifled.

4. *Creative dissent is welcomed.* By expressing unique ideas, employees feel they have contributed to the company and improved performance.

5. *Employee input is solicited.* The key to any company's success is input from employees, which establishes a sense of involvement and improves working relations.

6. *Employees are well informed.* Employees are kept informed about what is happening within the organization.

7. *Feedback is ongoing.* Both positive and negative feedback must be ongoing and provided in a manner that builds relationships rather than assigns blame.[23]

Many firms also define formal channels for upward communications. These channels encourage communication from employees to supervisors and upward to top management levels. Some examples of upward communication channels are employee surveys, suggestion boxes, and systems that allow employees to propose ideas for new products or voice complaints. Upward communication is also necessary for managers to evaluate the effectiveness of downward communication. Figure 9.4 illustrates the forms of organizational communication, both formal and informal.

BusinessEtiquette

Tune Up Your Listening Skills

Smart managers know that good listening is an important key to business success. Tuning in to employees, customers, and competitors can provide a wealth of valuable insight and information. Listening means paying attention to verbal and nonverbal cues. It means turning off your cell phone during a face-to-face conversation or meeting. It involves strategies for understanding the message that is conveyed. Here are a few tips for enhancing your listening skills:

- *Be attentive.* If culturally appropriate, maintain eye contact with the speaker—without staring. Nod your head to convey that you are hearing the person. Screen out distractions like background noise and irrelevant thoughts.

- *Keep an open mind.* Hear the other person all the way through, even if you are certain you will disagree. This not only shows respect for the speaker, it will result in your own informed reply.

- *Don't interrupt.* Even if you are absolutely certain of what the person is going to say—or convinced you have a solution or answer—wait until the speaker is finished. Then you can ask a question or make your point.

- *Ask questions.* Ask at least one question or paraphrase portions of the speaker's discussion to ensure that you understand the other person's point.

- *Be empathetic.* Laugh or be consoling where appropriate. You don't have to agree with the speaker, but even in the heat of disagreement, you can show empathy.

Sources: Norma Chew, "Are You a Good Listener?" *Associated Content,* http://www.associatedcontent.com, accessed April 19, 2010; Dianne Schilling, "Listening Skills: 10 Steps to Effective Learning," *WomensMedia.com,* March 20, 2010, http://www.womensmedia.com; "Are You an Active Listener?" *New Horizons,* February 16, 2010, http://www.newhorizons123.com.

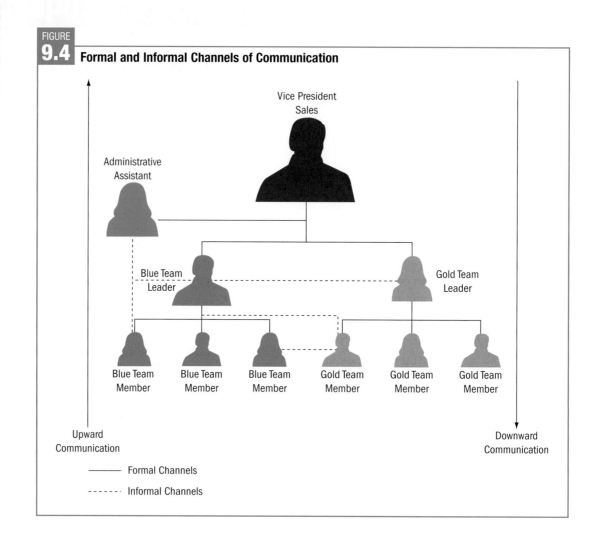

FIGURE
9.4 **Formal and Informal Channels of Communication**

Vice President
Sales

Administrative
Assistant

Blue Team
Leader

Gold Team
Leader

Blue Team
Member

Blue Team
Member

Blue Team
Member

Gold Team
Member

Gold Team
Member

Gold Team
Member

Upward
Communication

Downward
Communication

———— Formal Channels

- - - - - Informal Channels

Informal Communication

Informal communication channels carry messages outside formally authorized channels within an organization's hierarchy. A familiar example of an informal channel is the **grapevine**, an internal channel that passes information from unofficial sources. All organizations, large or small, have grapevines. Grapevines disseminate information with speed and economy and are surprisingly reliable. But company communications must be managed effectively so that the grapevine is not the main source of information. When properly nurtured, the grapevine can help managers get a feel for the morale of companies, understand the anxieties of the workforce, and evaluate the effectiveness of formal communications. Managers can improve the quality of information circulating through the company grapevine by sharing what they know, even if it is preliminary or partial information. By feeding information to selected people, smart leaders can harness the power of the grapevine.

Gossip—which usually travels along the grapevine—is the main drawback of this communication channel. Chronic gossipers often spread misinformation and undermine morale. A manager should deal directly with the gossiper, taking appropriate action depending on the severity of the situation. The manager can then use the grapevine and other communication channels to spread accurate information about the company.[24]

grapevine internal
information channel that
transmits information from
unofficial sources.

As organizations become more decentralized and more globally dispersed, informal communication—more than ever before—provides an important source of information, through e-mail, texting, and social media.

Nonverbal Communication

So far, this section has considered different forms of verbal communication, or communication that conveys meaning through words. Equally important is *nonverbal communication*, which transmits messages through actions and behaviors. Gestures, posture, eye contact, tone and volume of voice, and even clothing choices are all nonverbal actions that become communication cues. Nonverbal cues can have a far greater impact on communications than many people realize. In fact, it is estimated that 70 percent of interpersonal communication is conveyed through nonverbal cues. Top salespeople are particularly adept at reading and using these cues. For example, they practice "mirroring" a customer's gestures and body language in order to indicate agreement.[25]

Even personal space—the physical distance between people who are engaging in communication—can convey powerful messages. Figure 9.5 shows a continuum of personal space and social interaction with four zones: intimate, personal, social, and public. In the United States, most business conversations occur within the social zone, roughly between 4 and 12 feet apart. If one person tries to approach closer than that, the other will likely feel uncomfortable or even threatened.

Interpreting nonverbal cues can be especially challenging for people with different cultural backgrounds. Concepts of appropriate personal space differ dramatically throughout most of the world. Latin Americans conduct business discussions in positions that most Americans and northern Europeans would find uncomfortably close. Americans often back away to preserve their personal space, a gesture that Latin Americans perceive as a sign of

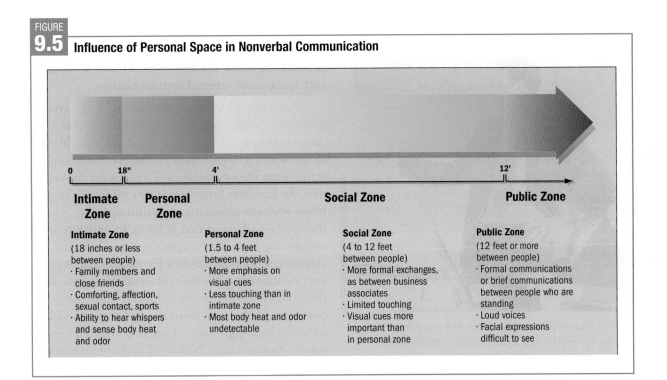

FIGURE 9.5 Influence of Personal Space in Nonverbal Communication

| Intimate Zone | Personal Zone | Social Zone | Public Zone |

Intimate Zone
(18 inches or less between people)
· Family members and close friends
· Comforting, affection, sexual contact, sports
· Ability to hear whispers and sense body heat and odor

Personal Zone
(1.5 to 4 feet between people)
· More emphasis on visual cues
· Less touching than in intimate zone
· Most body heat and odor undetectable

Social Zone
(4 to 12 feet between people)
· More formal exchanges, as between business associates
· Limited touching
· Visual cues more important than in personal zone

Public Zone
(12 feet or more between people)
· Formal communications or brief communications between people who are standing
· Loud voices
· Facial expressions difficult to see

cold and unfriendly relations. To protect their personal space, some Americans separate themselves across desks or tables from their Latin American counterparts—at the risk of challenging their colleagues to maneuver around those obstacles to reduce the uncomfortable distance.

People send nonverbal messages even when they consciously try to avoid doing so. Sometimes nonverbal cues convey a person's true attitudes and thoughts, which may differ from spoken meanings. Generally, when verbal and nonverbal cues conflict, receivers of the communication tend to believe the nonverbal content. This is why firms seeking to hire people with good attitudes and a team orientation closely watch nonverbal behavior during job interviews in which job applicants participate in group sessions with other job candidates applying for the same job. If in those group interviews an applicant frowns or looks discouraged when a competing candidate gives a good answer, that nonverbal behavior suggests that this person may not be strongly team oriented.

Assessment Check ✔

1. Define the four common listening behaviors.
2. What are the differences between formal and informal communication?

external communication meaningful exchange of information through messages transmitted between an organization and its major audiences.

External Communication and Crisis Management

External communication is a meaningful exchange of information through messages transmitted between an organization and its major audiences, such as customers, suppliers, other firms, the general public, and government officials. Businesses use external communication to keep their operations functioning, to maintain their positions in the marketplace, and to build customer relationships by supplying information about topics such as product modifications and price changes. Every communication with customers—including sales presentations and advertisements—should create goodwill and contribute to customer satisfaction. Firms like Clorox use their Web sites to publish good news about the company, as described in the "Going Green" feature. Letting the public know about new initiatives for environmentally friendly processes as well as community projects and other socially responsible activities in which the firm is involved is an important function of external communication.

However, all of this is threatened when companies experience a public relations crisis that threatens their reputation or goodwill. Nestlé, one of the world's largest food producers, faced such a crisis when the organization Greenpeace reported that the firm was importing palm oil from suppliers who are damaging the rainforests in Indonesia—a habitat that is home to endangered orangutans and other fragile species. Outraged consumers flooded Nestlé's Facebook page with angry comments. Nestlé's lukewarm response to the problem turned more definitive after these postings—including admonishing Facebook visitors for their aggression. This step angered consumers further, until Nestlé's Facebook moderator apologized "for being rude."[26]

Jacob Wackerhausen/iStockphoto

Businesses use external communication to keep their operations functioning, to maintain their positions in the marketplace, and to build customer relationships. Every communication with customers—including sales presentations and advertisements—should create goodwill and contribute to customer satisfaction.

Going Green

Clorox Comes Clean—Naturally

You've probably seen the Green Works brand of household and commercial cleaning solutions at your local supermarket—but you might not know that this line of natural, environmentally responsible cleaners is manufactured by the same people who make bleach. Clorox has committed itself wholeheartedly to ambitious initiatives aimed at reducing its impact on the environment through its manufacturing processes and the ingredients in its products. To accomplish this, the firm has established a department of Environmental Sustainability Strategy and an Eco Office. Its line of Green Works products meets strict environmental standards for ingredients, fragrances, packaging, and manufacturing processes. In addition, Clorox is working on similar efforts toward improving its traditional products.

One of the first bits of external communication about its new focus on product ingredients was literally a list of ingredients, so consumers would have more information about the products they were buying. The list has grown in detail—Clorox now provides more detailed information about its safety processes, guidelines used to screen ingredients, and data on fragrances (a major component of cleaning solutions). Clorox asks all of its fragrance suppliers to adhere to increasingly strict fragrance standards in the development of new products. In fact, Clorox is the first major consumer packaged goods company to go to such lengths to communicate to consumers exactly what its products contain and how they are made.

In order to spread the word farther, Clorox recently launched its own Corporate Social Responsibility (CSR) Web site that contains a wealth of information about its processes and products. The site is easy to navigate, offers access to a complete listing of product ingredients, and provides a comprehensive glossary of terms so consumers fully understand the function of each ingredient used in a product. Though the Web site is currently entirely in English, Clorox has plans for French and Spanish versions of the product ingredient section of the site.

Reaching even skeptical audiences, Clorox has gained the trust of the Sierra Club, with whom it has begun to partner on some of its programs. Together, Clorox and the Sierra Club trumpet the benefits of green cleaning. "Clorox is continuing to demonstrate the kind of progress we need companies to make," notes Sierra Club Chairman Carl Pope. "Since we began working with them on the Green Works brand, we've seen their commitment to important areas such as product innovation, ingredient communication, environmental stewardship and the transition to eliminate chlorine transportation from their U.S. supply chain. We applaud their approach to becoming even more open in communicating about their business practices and CSR commitments."

Questions for Critical Thinking

1. Clorox uses its CSR Web site to publish information and news about its green processes and products. How might the company use a social network such as Facebook to broaden its online external communication?

2. Do you think there is a downside to using the Internet for this type of communication? Why or why not?

Sources: Clorox Web site, http://www.cloroxcsr.com, accessed April 29, 2010; "2010 Best Companies for America's Children," *Working Mother*, http://www.workingmother.com, accessed April 29, 1010; "Clorox's New CSR Web Site Features Upgraded 'Ingredients Inside' Product Information," *CSRwire*, February 1, 2010, http://www.csrwire.com.

How a company like Nestlé handles such an event can determine whether its reputation can be restored. Putting together a plan of action and dealing with facts and rumors immediately could be the difference between regaining trust and disaster. The following communication steps can help calm a public relations crisis:

1. When a crisis occurs, a firm should respond quickly. Executives should prepare a written statement—and stick to it. The statement should mention the time, place, initial description of what occurred (not the cause), and the number and status of the people involved.

2. As soon as possible, top company management should appear in public—if possible, to the press. Because the public will hold top management accountable, it's best to have top managers responding to reporters' questions.

3. When answering questions at an initial press conference or in an interview, the management representative must stick to the facts. It's likely that details about the event, the cause, and people's roles will not yet be known; the spokesperson shouldn't speculate. As information becomes available, the firm can provide accurate updates.

4. If a question is currently unanswerable, the executive can offer to find out the answer, which should be delivered in a timely manner. It's not advisable to answer a question by saying, "No comment." It's much better to say, "I don't know."

5. The firm should acknowledge problems, explain solutions, and welcome feedback. If a question or factual statement puts the organization in a negative light, the manager should acknowledge the problem, and then explain how the firm is correcting it.

6. The press conference or interview will be most effective if the executive speaks briefly, clearly and provides visual images. If available, a video with positive images—such as thriving rainforests—can be useful.[27]

The crisis faced by Nestlé—the allegation that it was purchasing palm oil from a supplier that was contributing to the destruction of rainforest—was exacerbated by the criticism it received on social media sites. Despite the fact that Nestle announced it would immediately stop purchasing the oil from this supplier, pointing out that this was only 1.25 percent of its total palm oil use, debate over the company's environmental practices continued to rage online. Nestlé spokeswoman Nina Backes notes that it is in these instances it is difficult "to show that we are listening, which we obviously are, while not getting into a shouting match." Daniel Kessler, press officer at Greenpeace, acknowledges that social media present a new challenge for companies as they try to manage external communication. "This is the place where major corporations are very vulnerable," he remarks.[28]

What's Ahead

Today's consumers expect the products they buy to be of the highest value for the price. Firms ensure this value by developing efficient systems for producing goods and services, as well as maintaining high quality. The next chapter examines the ways in which businesses produce world-class goods and services, efficiently organize their production facilities, purchase what they need to produce their goods and services, and manage large inventories to maximize efficiency and reduce costs.

Assessment Check ✔

1. What is external communication?
2. What is the first thing a company should do when a public crisis occurs?

Summary of Learning Objectives

⌐1⌐ Describe why and how organizations empower employees.

Managers empower employees by giving them the authority and responsibility to make decisions about their work. Empowerment seeks to tap the brainpower of all workers to find improved ways of doing their jobs, better serving customers, and achieving organizational goals. Empowerment often includes linking rewards to company performance through employee stock ownership plans (ESOPs) and stock options.

Assessment Check Answers ✔

1.1 What is empowerment? Empowerment is giving employees authority and responsibility to make decisions about their work without traditional managerial approval and control.

1.2 What kinds of information can companies provide employees to help them share decision-making responsibility? Sharing information about company performance, particularly financial performance, is one of the best ways to share decision-making responsibility.

1.3 How do employee stock ownership plans and stock options reward employees and encourage empowerment? Employee stock ownership plans (ESOPs) benefit employees by giving them ownership stakes in their companies. Employees are motivated to work harder and smarter than they would without ESOPS because they share in their firm's financial success. In contrast to an ESOP, in which the company holds stock for the benefit of employees (when employees leave the company, they cash in their stock), stock options give employees a chance to own the stock themselves if they exercise their options by completing the stock purchase.

2. Distinguish among the five types of teams in the workplace.

The five basic types of teams are work teams, problem-solving teams, self-managed teams, cross-functional teams, and virtual teams. Work teams are permanent groups of coworkers who perform the day-to-day tasks necessary to operate the organization. Problem-solving teams are temporary groups of employees who gather to solve specific problems and then disband. Self-managed teams have the authority to make decisions about how their members complete their daily tasks. Cross-functional teams are made up of members from different units, such as production, marketing, and finance. Virtual teams are groups of geographically or organizationally dispersed coworkers who use a combination of telecommunications and information technologies to accomplish an organizational task.

Assessment Check Answers ✔

2.1 What is a team? A team is a group of employees who are committed to a common purpose, approach, and set of performance goals.

2.2 What are the five types of teams, and how are they different? Work teams are permanent, while problem-solving teams are temporary. Unlike work teams, self-managed teams have the authority to change how they get their work done. Cross-functional teams are composed of people from different backgrounds, while virtual teams are composed of people from different locations.

3. Identify the characteristics of an effective team, and summarize the stages of team development.

Three important characteristics of a team are its size, team level, and team diversity. The ideal team size is about six or seven members. Team level is the average level of ability, experience, personality, or any other factor on a team. Team diversity represents the variances or differences in ability, experience, personality, or any other factor on a team. Team diversity is an important consideration for teams that must complete a wide range of different tasks of particularly complex tasks. Teams pass through five stages of development: (1) Forming is an orientation period during which members get to know each other and find out what behaviors are acceptable to the group. (2) Storming is the stage during which individual personalities emerge as members clarify their roles and expectations. (3) Norming is the stage at which differences are resolved, members accept each other, and consensus emerges about the roles of the team leader and other participants. (4) Performing is characterized by problem solving and a focus on task accomplishment. (5) Adjourning is the final stage, with a focus on wrapping up and summarizing the team's experiences and accomplishments.

Assessment Check Answers ✔

3.1 Explain team level and team diversity. While team level represents the average level or capability on a team, team diversity represents the variances or differences in ability, experience, personality, or any other factor on a team.

3.2 Explain how teams progress through the stages of team development. Teams pass through five stages of development: forming, storming, norming, performing, and adjourning.

4. Relate team cohesiveness and norms to effective team performance.

Team cohesiveness is the extent to which team members feel attracted to the team and motivated to remain on it. Team norms are standards of conduct shared by team members that guide their behavior. Highly cohesive teams whose members share certain standards of conduct tend to be more productive and effective.

Assessment Check Answers ✔

4.1 How does cohesiveness affect teams? Members of cohesive teams interact more often, share common attitudes and goals, have higher morale, and are more likely to help each other. Cohesive teams also perform better.

4.2 Explain how team norms positively and negatively affect teams. Norms are informal standards that identify key values and clarify team members' expectations. But those norms can be positive or negative. Positive norms contribute to constructive work and the accomplishment of team goals. Negative norms can, for example, contribute to reduced work effort, reduced quality, and poor job attendance.

5. Describe the factors that can cause conflict in teams and ways to manage conflict.

Conflict and disagreement are inevitable in most teams. Conflict can stem from many sources: disagreements about goals and priorities, task-related issues, interpersonal incompatibilities, scarce resources, and simple fatigue. The key to dealing with team conflict is not avoiding it, but making sure that the team experiences the right kind of conflict. Cognitive conflict focuses on problem-related differences of opinion and, when reconciled, strongly improves team performance. By contrast, affective conflict refers to the emotional reactions that can occur when disagreements become personal rather than professional, and these differences strongly decrease team performance. A team leader can manage team conflict by fostering good communication so team members perceive each other accurately, understand what is expected of them, and obtain the information they need.

Assessment Check Answers ✔

5.1 What is cognitive conflict, and how does it affect teams? With cognitive conflict, team members disagree because their different experiences and expertise lead them to different views of the problem and its solutions. Cognitive conflict is characterized by a willingness to examine, compare, and reconcile differences to produce the best possible solution.

5.2 Explain affective conflict and its impact on teams. Because affective conflict often results in hostility, anger, resentment, distrust, cynicism, and apathy, it can make people uncomfortable, cause them to withdraw, decrease their commitment to a team, lower the satisfaction of team members, and decrease team cohesiveness.

⌈6⌉ **Explain the importance and process of effective communication.**

Managers spend about 80 percent of their time in direct communication with others. Company recruiters consistently rate effective communication—such as listening, conversing, and giving feedback—as the most important skill they look for when hiring new employees. The communication process follows a step-by-step process that involves interactions among six elements: sender, message, channel, audience, feedback, and context. The sender composes the message and sends it through the channel. The audience receives the message and interprets its meaning. The receiver gives feedback to the sender. The communication takes place in a situational or cultural context.

Assessment Check Answers ✔

6.1 What is the difference between communication in low-context and high-context cultures? Communication in low-context cultures tends to rely on explicit written and verbal messages. By contrast, communication in high-context cultures depends not only on the message itself but also on the conditions that surround it, including nonverbal cues, past and present experiences, and personal relationships between the parties.

6.2 In the context of the communication process, what is noise? Noise interferes with the transmission of messages and feedback. Noise can result from physical factors such as poor reception of a cell phone message or differences in people's attitudes and perceptions.

⌈7⌉ **Compare the different types of communication.**

People exchange messages in many ways: oral and written, formal and informal, verbal and nonverbal communication. Effective written communication reflects its audience, its channel, and the appropriate degree of formality. Formal communication channels carry messages within the chain of command. Informal communication channels, such as the grapevine, carry messages outside the formal chain of command. Nonverbal communication plays a larger role than most people realize. Generally, when verbal and nonverbal cues conflict, the receiver of a message tends to believe the meaning conveyed by nonverbal cues.

Assessment Check Answers ✔

7.1 Define the four common listening behaviors. Cynical listening occurs when the receiver of a message feels that the sender is trying to gain some advantage from the communication. Offensive listening occurs when the receiver tries to catch the speaker in a mistake or contradiction. Polite listening occurs when the receiver is rehearsing what he or she wants to say when the speaker finishes. Active listening requires involvement with the information and empathy with the speaker's situation.

7.2 What are the differences between formal and informal communication? Formal communication occurs within the formal chain of command defined by an organization. Informal communication occurs outside the organization's hierarchy.

⌈8⌉ **Explain external communication and methods of managing a public crisis.**

External communication is a meaningful exchange of information through messages transmitted between an organization and its major audiences, such as customers, suppliers, other firms, the general public, and government officials. Every communication with customers should create goodwill and contribute to customer satisfaction. However, all of this is threatened when companies experience a public crisis that threatens their reputations or goodwill. To manage a public crisis, businesses should respond quickly and honestly, with a member of top management present.

Assessment Check Answers ✔

8.1 What is external communication? External communication is a meaningful exchange of information through messages transmitted between an organization and its major audiences.

8.2 What is the first thing a company should do when a public crisis occurs? The firm should respond quickly by preparing a written statement that includes the time, place, description of the event, and the number and status of people involved.

▮ Business Terms You Need to Know

empowerment 286	cross-functional team 291	team cohesiveness 294	communication 296
team 290	virtual teams 291	team norm 295	listening 298
work teams 290	team level 292	conflict 295	grapevine 302
problem-solving team 291	team diversity 292	cognitive conflict 295	external communication 304
self-managed team 291		affective conflict 295	

Review Questions

1. How do companies benefit from empowering their employees? How do employees benefit from empowerment?

2. How might a firm that manufactures shoes use teams to determine ways to improve its environmental standards in terms of products and processes? What type (or types) of teams would be best for this initiative? Why?

3. How do team level and team diversity affect team performance?

4. What are the characteristics of an effective team? Why are these features so significant?

5. At what stages of development might a team not be able to move forward? How might a team leader or manager resolve the situation?

6. Describe the norms associated with your business class. How do these norms influence the way you behave?

7. What steps can managers take to manage team conflict?

8. In what ways is context a powerful influence on the effectiveness of communication? Describe an instance in which situational or cultural context influenced one of your communication processes.

9. What are the benefits and drawbacks of oral and written communication?

10. What is the role of external communication? Why is it so important to companies?

Projects and Teamwork Applications

1. Having the power and authority to make decisions about work is the essence of empowerment. For this project, the teacher steps back and gives the class free rein to plan and implement a day of classwork. The class might appoint a leader, divide into teams (to plan a lecture, come up with an assignment, plan a field trip, and the like). It's completely up to the students how to organize and conduct the one-day class. After the class, discuss the experience—including the upside and downside (if any) of empowerment.

2. Divide the class into teams of relatively equal size. Each team may select one of the following problems it intends to solve, or decide on one of its own: arranging for a certain speaker or expanding the vegetarian menu in the cafeteria. While it is not necessary to complete the entire problem-solving process, each team should go through the forming stage of team development and establish norms during which it outlines a plan for accomplishing the group's task. Is each team cohesive? Why or why not?

3. Try this listening exercise with a partner. First, spend a few minutes writing a paragraph or two about the most

important thing that happened to you this week. Second, read your paragraph out loud to your partner. Next, have your partner read his or her paragraph. Finally, each take turns summarizing the most important points in each other's stories. See how well you listened to each other.

4. On your own or with a classmate, visit the college library, mall, or anywhere else people gather. For about 10 or 15 minutes, observe the nonverbal cues that people give each other: Does the librarian smile at students? What is the body language of students gathered in groups? When you leave the venue, jot down as many of your observations as you can. Notice things like changes in nonverbal communication when someone joins a group or leaves it.

5. Choose a company with which you are familiar, or whose products you use. Research the company's offerings as well as some of its socially responsible and sustainability initiatives (e.g., if the firm has set a goal to reduce its energy consumption by 20 percent). Create an advertisement that focuses on one of these initiatives as an example of positive external communication from the company.

Web Assignments

1. **Team-building exercises.** The Web site Teampedia is "a collaborative encyclopedia of free team building activities, free icebreakers, teamwork resources, and tools for teams that anyone can edit!" You want to select a team-building exercise to help break down stereotypes. What are some of the suggested activities?

   http://www.teampedia.net/wiki/index.php?title=Main_Page

2. **Writing better business letters.** Assume you'd like to improve your business letter writing ability. Using a search engine, such as Google or Bing, search the Web for sites with tips and suggestions to improve letter writing skills.

(An example is shown here.) Select two of these sites and review the material. Prepare a brief summary.

http://www.askoxford.com/betterwriting/letterwriting/?view=uk

3. **Employee stock ownership plans.** Visit the Web site of the ESOP Association (http://www.esopassociation.org). Click on "use of ESOP." Print out the material and bring it to class to participate in a class discussion on employee stock ownership plans.

Note: Internet Web addresses change frequently. If you don't find the exact sites listed, you may need to access the organization's home page and search from there or use a search engine such as Bing or Google.

Over the years, thousands of Orlando's SeaWorld visitors have been enthralled by the skilled antics of resident whales and their trainers. Most people recognize that at least some risk to the whales' trainers is involved, partly because of the gigantic size and strength of these mammals. But no one expected the tragedy that unfolded when a veteran trainer was yanked into the water by her pony tail by one of her favorite partners, Tilikum the Orca whale. Within moments, the trainer lost her life.

SeaWorld faced a huge public crisis in which communication would prove to be crucial. The company was immediately bombarded with demands for answers. Were consumers in danger? Should all of SeaWorld be shut down? The fate of Tilikum ("Tilly") was called into question—should he be safely quarantined or put down? Were there other, equally dangerous animals performing at the theme park? All of these questions were overshadowed by the fact that SeaWorld, including its managers and employees, had lost a beloved colleague.

SeaWorld immediately halted all Orca whale shows at its Orlando location as well as its sister parks in San Antonio and San Diego while details of the tragedy were reviewed. Although Orlando SeaWorld President Dan Brown held a press conference shortly after the event, crisis experts pointed out that he faltered when he didn't correct the local sheriff's spokesman, who stated that the trainer had accidentally fallen into the water alongside the whale. Brown only said, "She drowned in an incident with one of our killer whales." When it was later revealed that Tilly had actually pulled the trainer into the water, Brown's credibility was tainted. Once the discrepancy was cleared up, SeaWorld made its head trainer available to answer further questions posed by the press and explain more thoroughly SeaWorld's training methods.

SeaWorld fielded accusations and attacks from all sides—from frightened families to animal rights advocates. As rumors began to swirl about Tilly's rambunctious history and his ultimate fate, it became apparent that there would be no easy solution. "If [SeaWorld] were to make even the slightest hint or suggestion that [Tilly] should be put down, I can only imagine the backlash that would come from animal rights groups from around the world on that one," observed Steve Huxter, the former head trainer at Sealand of the Pacific, where Tilly lived before being transferred to SeaWorld.

Meanwhile, another wave was gathering to sweep across SeaWorld's shore—this time in the form of Facebook and Twitter. SeaWorld was one of the early big companies to recognize the value of direct interaction with its customers by establishing a Facebook site and Twitter account. Both accounts were now deluged with comments from worried fans and barbs from critics. Eventually SeaWorld was forced to shut down its Facebook wall temporarily because of reportedly inappropriate photos relating to the tragedy. And @Shamu, the popular Twitter blog "ghostwritten" by Shamu the whale, was silenced.

But the Facebook site was reactivated shortly thereafter, and SeaWorld spokesman Fred Jacobs encouraged people to revisit it. He said that SeaWorld only censors postings that contain profanity or harassment, or would be insensitive to the trainer's family and friends. "If you were to get on Facebook right now and ask a question about the morality of keeping whales in captivity, we'll get back to you," Jacobs promised. "Now is not the time to circle the wagons. There's a value proposition between a company and the people who follow it on social media." While some people were skeptical about the wisdom of opening itself up to so much direct interaction with the public, SeaWorld officials were firm in their stance: this was their cue to listen.

Questions for Critical Thinking

1. How might SeaWorld's Dan Brown have better handled his initial press conference after the accident?

2. Going forward, how might SeaWorld use social media to heal and strengthen its relationship with the public?

Sources: "New Details About Whale Attack Responsible for SeaWorld Trainer's Death," *Radar,* March 1, 2010, http://www.radaronline.com; Laura Wides-Munoz, "SeaWorld Faces Major Public Relations Challenge," *The Examiner,* February 26, 2010, http://www.washingtonexaminer.com; Larry Rice, "Trainer: Orca Whale's Instinct Was to Play," *MyNorthwest.com,* February 26, 2010, http://www.mynorthwest.com; Beth Kassab, "Shamu Attack Exposes Social Media Risks," *OrlandoSentinel.com,* February 25, 2010, http://www.orlandosentinel.com.

Interaction Associates is a consulting firm with offices in San Francisco and Cambridge, Massachusetts. The company specializes in developing collaborative approaches to coaching, leadership, managing change, and team building. Co-founders David Straus and Michael Doyle wrote the book How to Make Meetings Work, and Straus wrote How to Make Collaboration Work. Their firm has helped hundreds of firms around the world improve performance by building collaborative workplaces. How do you suppose the firm would put its expertise to work on itself? By using teams to find a new office.

When the lease on its San Francisco office was about to expire, Interaction Associates set up employee teams to decide where to move. "You need to give people a voice in what they're doing and how they're going to experience their work every day," says president and CEO Linda Dunkel, named one of America's best bosses by workplace assessment organization Winning Workplaces. She chose a five-member team to find a location closer to the city's center and to save at least $100,000 a year on the lease. While staying in the present building was an option, Dunkel wanted to be closer to downtown where employees were involved in volunteer work and where mass transit was available.

The diverse team members came from marketing, consulting, operations, information technology, and fulfillment and logistics. Team leader Beth O'Neill was chosen for her frankness and wide range of experience with the company. The team met for about an hour a week in the beginning and involvement increased as time went on. The task took eight months before the final move. During that period, team members met with brokers, selected a location, developed a floor plan, and even picked office colors.

Occasionally, team members checked in with the president for guidance, but they generally managed themselves.

The road to the new office contained a few bumps along the way. For instance, while the relocation team debated the pros and cons of one desirable office space, another tenant snapped it up. But the team eventually selected an office with lots of windows near Union Station. It wasn't Dunkel's first choice of the final three buildings the team considered, but she realized the importance of letting team members complete the task and did not want to override their decision. In the end, she came around to the team's way of thinking. Says Dunkel, "Now that I see the final result, it's a better decision than if I'd made it on my own, and that's a powerful message. It speaks to the power of a group to pull out a variety of interests and thrash things through and ultimately come up with a better decision."

Questions for Critical Thinking

1. What were the benefits of selecting a diverse team to find the new office location? Why did Beth O'Neill make a good team leader?

2. Why was it important for the president to let the team select the final location even though it wasn't her first choice? What could have been some negative consequences of overriding the team?

Sources: "Interactive Associates Partners with Leading Responsibility Expert to Help Clients Execute Profitable CSR Strategies," *CSRwire*, accessed March 2009, http://www.csrwire.com; "About Interaction Associates," accessed March 2009, http://www.interactionassociates.com; Laura Lorber, "Giving Employees a Say in Where They'll Work," *The Wall Street Journal*, January 9, 2008, http://online.wsj.com.

The hotel and restaurant industry caters to its guests, but it has always had a reputation for being somewhat inhospitable to its employees. Traditionally, hotel and restaurant workers put in long hours for low pay and little or no recognition; they're the invisible hosts who fluff the pillows and sweep away crumbs. But Kimpton Hotels is setting a new example by treating its employees as something better than family: they are, in many ways, business partners.

Kimpton Hotels was founded in 1981 by Bill Kimpton, an investment banker with a vision for boutique hotels: small, luxurious hotels with impeccably intimate service and gourmet restaurants. Today, Kimpton operates 50 hotels and restaurants around the country, each beautifully designed and furnished. "But more than that," notes COO Niki Leondakis, "the people really separate us" from other hotels. As COO, Leondakis knows first-hand the difference at Kimpton. Leondakis talks about her company's full-blown commitment to empowering employees to make decisions, to take part in running the business, to grow as professionals. "The employee of today wants more and expects more, and is not willing just to be a servant, loyal worker, or soldier," she says. Leondakis is proud of that fact and of the army of top-flight employees and managers who work at Kimpton's various locations.

One of those managers is Peggy Trott, the general manager of the Kimpton Hotel Palomar in Philadelphia. Trott explains how Kimpton empowers its employees. "Kimpton wants each general manager to be an entrepreneur," she says. "They want you to operate your hotel as if it is your own business. So there's a lot of leeway." While some managers might argue that this puts undue pressure on them to perform as business owners, Trott views the challenge as an opportunity. She notes that the attitude toward empowerment travels from the top down in the organization. She says that each of her employees is charged with being a hero every day, especially when it comes to guest service. If an employee is acting on behalf of a guest, then he or she is free to make the decision on the spot.

"I have high expectations, but I think that when you give people high expectations, they rise to the occasion," says Trott. For example, if a housekeeper sees that one of her guest rooms is housing a family of two parents and two children, the housekeeper is expected to stock the room with extra towels instead of waiting for the guests to call the front desk requesting more towels. No matter how large or small the task might seem, "We expect people to be self-leaders," notes Niki Leondakis. "We expect employees to use their heads."

Because each of the 50 Kimpton hotel and restaurant properties is unique to its location and local population, Kimpton actively recruits employees with diverse backgrounds and qualifications, then gives them the authority to serve their guests as they see best. Individuality is nurtured rather than squelched. Niki Leondakis observes that, because her employees come with a wide range of experience at different locations in the hospitality industry, sometimes it is difficult to get them to leave behind their previous assumptions about their role as hotel workers. "The biggest challenge with employee empowerment and communication is that we're all products of our past," Leondakis says. New employees often have to be retrained to think outside the box, make decisions, and "rock the boat," as Leondakis puts it.

The results of this retraining toward empowerment have not gone unnoticed. Kimpton Hotels consistently win awards for service, and the group has received many accolades for its approach to human resource management, including a recent award from the Human Rights Campaign for "Workplace Equality Innovation." In addition, Kimpton is regularly named to *Fortune's* list of "100 Best Companies to Work For."

Recent praise from the industry publication *Hospitality Design* included a statement from Kimpton CEO, Michael Depatie, crediting Niki Leondakis with much of the company's HR success. "Niki has an extraordinary ability to connect with people, from guests she meets on the road to each and every one of our employees," said Depatie. Leondakis, managers like Peggy Trott, and the entire staff, embody their company's assertion that "Our employees are our brand."

Questions for Critical Thinking

1. Give three specific reasons why empowerment is key to the success of a firm like Kimpton Hotels. How might this distinguish it from other hotel companies?

2. Select the concept of either a problem-solving team or a self-managed team. How might this team function at a Kimpton hotel? Who might be on the team, and what role might it play in the running of the hotel?

3. Give an example of a situation in which informal communication would function well among empowered employees at a Kimpton hotel.

4. Currently all Kimpton hotels are located in the U.S., which is a low-context culture. If the firm decided to open a hotel in a high-context culture such as Japan, how might communication between staff and guests differ?

Sources: Kimpton Hotels & Restaurants Web site, http://www.kimptonhotels.com, accessed August 22, 2010; "Why Work for Kimpton?, "http://www.imkimpton.com, accessed August 22, 2010; Sam Guidino, Mike Desimone, Jeff Jenssen, Lynn Alley, "Kimpton Takes Philly," *Wine Spectator,* July 31, 2010; http://www.winespectator.com; "Kimpton Hotels Aim for 100 Percent Green Seal Certification," *GreenerBuildings,* March 31, 2010, http://www.greenbiz.com.

Learning Objectives

[1] Explain the strategic importance of the production function.

[2] Identify and describe the four main categories of production processes.

[3] Explain the role of technology in the production process.

[4] Identify the factors involved in a plant location decision.

[5] Explain the major tasks of production and operations managers, and outline the three activities involved in implementing the production plan.

[6] Identify the steps in the production control process.

[7] Discuss the importance of quality control.

Operational and Production Aspects of Contemporary Business

The World Cup Gets a Kick Out of Jabulani

NewsCom

A soccer ball seems like a simple thing to make—some panels stitched together in a globe and inflated with air. But ask anyone involved in World Cup soccer (called "football" around most of the world), or in production at Adidas, and they'll tell you different. Manufacturing a soccer ball, particularly the official model for the FIFA World Cup soccer championships, is a complex process. Adidas has been the lucky winner of the contract to produce the official championship soccer ball numerous times since 1970. Despite its consistent performance, the firm never rests on its laurels. Instead, its design and production teams strive to come up with a better product every time.

So when the latest model was unveiled, soccer fans had reason to celebrate. Called the Jabulani, which means "to celebrate" in isiZulu, the soccer ball's name paid homage to the year's host nation of the World Cup—the Republic of South Africa. The ball was produced in 11 colors—representing the 11 players on every team, the 11 official languages of South Africa, the 11 South African tribes that make up the nation, and the 11th Adidas World Cup ball. Each ball contained four triangle-shaped figures on a white background, emulating traditional African designs.

But there was much more to the new match ball than bright colors. The ball featured innovative technology, including eight 3-D globe-shaped panels that were molded in the interior of the ball for perfect roundness. Reducing the number of outer panels and seams gave the ball a 70 percent larger striking surface. A feature from the previous model, the goose-bump surface, was improved to give players more control over the ball no matter what the weather on the field. From the first practice kick, the players loved the new ball. "Fantastic, the ball does exactly what I wanted it to," praised one player. Another player agreed: "A very strong ball, true to hit."

Before the Jabulani ever reached the toes of World Cup soccer players, it went through rigorous testing at Adidas's labs in England and Germany, where robots kicked at prototypes and simulated wind gusts attempted to blow them off course. By the time the final product was ready, it was as near to perfection as Adidas's designers, engineers, production staff, and testers could make it. Of course, the Jabulani had to meet all the required specifications for a match ball, including weight, circumference, diameter, air pressure, and even water absorption.

Adidas also had to meet production demand for the World Cup (for official teams as well as consumers). The company contracted with the Pakistani manufacturing plant, Forward Group, to produce the entire supply of hand-stitched replica Jabulani models to be sold to the mass market. Forward Group expected to ship 6 million replica balls in one year, despite chronic power outages and other production problems. In fact, the economy of Sialkot, the town where the balls were produced, depends on soccer ball manufacturing. The official Jabulani match balls were produced by a factory in China, which had the capacity for the thermally bonded balls used in World Cup play. The balls were then shipped from both countries to the shelves of sporting goods stores around the world, and to the bright green fields of the World Cup in South Africa.[1]

production use of resources, such as workers and machinery, to convert materials into finished goods and services.

production and operations management oversee the production process by managing people and machinery in converting materials and resources into finished goods and services.

By producing and marketing the goods and services that people want, businesses satisfy their commitment to society as a whole. They create what economists call *utility*—the want-satisfying power of a good or service. Businesses can create or enhance four basic kinds of utility: time, place, ownership, and form. A firm's marketing operation generates time, place, and ownership utility by offering products to customers at a time and place that is convenient for purchase.

Production creates form utility by converting raw materials and other inputs into finished products, such as Adidas' Jabulani soccer ball. **Production** uses resources, including workers and machinery, to convert materials into finished goods and services. This conversion process may make major changes in raw materials or simply combine already finished parts into new products. The task of **production and operations management** in a firm is to oversee the production process by managing people and machinery in converting materials and resources into finished goods and services, which is illustrated by Figure 10.1.

People sometimes use the terms *production* and *manufacturing* interchangeably, but

the two are actually different. Production spans both manufacturing and nonmanufacturing industries. For instance, companies that engage in fishing or mining engage in production, as do firms that provide package deliveries or lodging. Figure 10.2 lists five examples of production systems for a variety of goods and services.

But whether the production process results in a tangible good such as a car or an intangible service such as cable television, it always converts inputs into outputs. A cabinetmaker combines wood, tools, and skill to create finished kitchen cabinets for a new home. A transit system combines buses, trains, and employees to create its output: passenger transportation. Both of these production processes create utility.

This chapter describes the process of producing goods and services. It looks at the importance of production and operations management and discusses the new technologies that are transforming the production function. It then discusses the tasks of the production and operations manager, the importance of quality, and the methods businesses use to ensure high quality.

FIGURE

10.1 The Production Process: Converting Inputs to Outputs

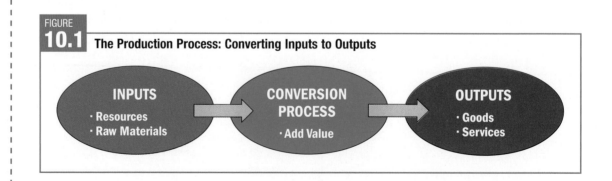

FIGURE
10.2 Typical Production Systems

Example	Primary Inputs	Transformation	Outputs
Computer Factory	Hard drives, computer memory, computer chips, keyboards, cases, power supply, DVD drives, central circuit board, boards for network and Internet access and graphics, monitors, and software	Assembles components to meet customer orders, including specialized orders for hardware and software	Desktop or laptop computers
Trucking Firm	Trucks, personnel, buildings, fuel, goods to be shipped, packaging supplies, truck parts, utilities	Packages and transports goods from sources to destinations	Delivered goods
Retail Store	Buildings, displays, scanners, merchandise, personnel, supplies, utilities	Attracts customers, stores goods, sells products	Merchandise sold
Automobile Body Shop	Damaged autos, paints, supplies, machines, tools, buildings, personnel, utilities	Transforms damaged auto bodies into facsimiles of the originals	Repaired automobile bodies
County Sheriff's Department	Personnel, police equipment, automobiles, office furniture, buildings, utilities	Detects crimes and brings criminals to justice	Lower crime rates and peaceful communities

The Strategic Importance of Production

Along with marketing and finance, production is a vital business activity. Without products to sell, companies cannot generate money to pay their employees, lenders, and stockholders. And without the profits from products, firms quickly fail. The production process is just as crucial in nonprofit organizations, such as the St. Jude Children's Research Hospital and Goodwill Industries, because the goods or services they offer justify their existence. Effective production and operations management can lower a firm's costs of production, boost the quality of its goods and services, allow it to respond dependably to customer demands, and enable it to renew itself by providing new products. Let's look at the differences among mass, flexible, and customer-driven production.

Mass Production

mass production a
system for manufacturing
products in large quantities
through effective combinations of employees, with
specialized skills, mechanization, and standardization.

From its beginnings as a colonial supplier of raw materials to Europe, the United States has evolved into an industrial giant. Much of this change has resulted from **mass production**, a system for manufacturing products in large quantities through effective combinations of employees with specialized skills, mechanization, and standardization. Mass production makes outputs (goods and services) available in large quantities at lower prices than individually crafted items would cost. It is mass production that brought cars, computers, televisions, books, and even homes to the majority of the population—that's right, even homes. William Levitt made homes affordable to the average American from the 1940s to the 1960s, by removing the most expensive items—the basements—and mass-producing them at the rate of one every 16 minutes. Levitt's first planned community, Levittown, brought his company a profit of about $5 million more than 60 years ago. Levitt, often called the Pioneer of Suburbs, followed a simple strategy. "Any fool can build homes," he quipped. "What counts is how many you can sell for how little."[2]

Mass production begins with the specialization of labor, dividing work into its simplest components so that each worker can concentrate on performing one task. By separating jobs into small tasks, managers create conditions for high productivity through mechanization, in which machines perform much of the work previously done by people. Standardization, the third element of mass production, involves producing uniform, interchangeable goods and parts. Standardized parts simplify the replacement of defective or worn-out components. For instance, if your car's windshield wiper blades wear out, you can easily buy replacements at a local auto parts store such as AutoZone.

A logical extension of these principles of specialization, mechanization, and standardization led to development of the *assembly line*. This manufacturing method moves the product along a conveyor belt past a number of workstations, where workers perform specialized tasks such as welding, painting, installing individual parts, and tightening bolts. Henry Ford's application of this concept revolutionized auto assembly. Before the assembly line, it took Ford's workers 12 hours to assemble a Model T car. But with an assembly line, it took just 1.5 hours to make the same car. Not surprisingly, dozens of other industries soon adopted the assembly-line process.

Although mass production has important advantages, it has limitations, too. While mass production is highly efficient for producing large numbers of similar products, it is highly inefficient when producing small batches of different items. This trade-off might tempt some companies to focus on efficient production methods rather than on making what customers really want. In addition, the labor specialization associated with mass production can lead to boring jobs, because workers keep repeating the same task. To improve their competitive capabilities, many firms adopt flexible production and customer-driven production systems. These methods won't replace mass production in every case, but in many instances might lead to improved product quality and greater job satisfaction. It might also enhance the use of mass production.

Flexible Production

While mass production is effective for creating large quantities of one item, *flexible production* is usually more cost-effective for producing smaller runs. Flexible production can take many forms, but it generally involves using information technology to share the details of customer orders, programmable equipment to fulfill the orders, and skilled people to carry out whatever tasks are needed to fill a particular order. This system is even more beneficial when combined with lean production methods that use automation and information technology to reduce requirements for workers and inventory. Flexible production requires a lot of communication among everyone in the organization.

Flexible production is now widely used in the auto industry; whereas Henry Ford revolutionized auto production in the early 20th century, automakers such as Toyota and Honda are innovating with new methods of production. Changing from mass production to flexible production has enabled these companies to produce different kinds of cars at the same plant. Honda now builds 15 different models spread across four plants in North America. "Using our flexible manufacturing capacity, we plan to continue to maintain our local production levels at approximately 80 percent of our annual sales," states a company spokesperson.[3] This is good news for U.S. workers and consumers.

© Paul Vernon/AP/Wide World Photos

This Honda auto plant uses flexible production techniques to turn out several different models. The auto industry, which developed mass production methods, now finds flexible production to be more efficient.

Customer-Driven Production

A *customer-driven production* system evaluates customer demands in order to make the connection between products manufactured and products bought. Many firms use this approach with great success. One method is to establish computer links between factories and retailers' scanners, using data about sales as the basis for creating short-term forecasts and designing production schedules to meet those forecasts. Another approach to customer-driven production systems is simply not to make the product until a customer orders it—whether it's a taco or a computer. Massachusetts-based Shibui Designs creates custom-made dresses in high-end fabrics for female executives and other women over 40. Each item of clothing is custom cut and fit to a single customer's measurements. Founder Elizabeth Nill, who is over 60, started the business because she couldn't find clothing that fit well. "I don't have the body of a model, and the bulges are real. Truly made classic clothing that is custom made-to-measure helps camouflage these inevitable imperfections and makes me feel more elegant." Nill's customers agree.[4]

Production Processes

Not surprisingly, the production processes and time required to make an Apple iPad and a gallon of gasoline are different. Production processes use either an analytic or synthetic system; time requirements call for either a continuous or an intermittent process.

An analytic production system reduces a raw material to its component parts in order to extract one or more marketable products. Petroleum refining breaks down crude oil into several marketable products, including gasoline, heating oil, and aviation fuel. When corn is processed, the resulting marketable food products include animal feed and corn sweetener.

A synthetic production system is the reverse of an analytic system. It combines a number of raw materials or parts or transforms raw materials to produce finished products. Canon's assembly line produces a camera by assembling various parts such as a shutter or a lens cap. Other synthetic production systems make drugs, chemicals, computer chips, and canned soup.

Assessment Check ✔

1. What is mass production?
2. What is the difference between flexible production and customer-driven production?

A continuous production process generates finished products over a lengthy period of time. The steel industry provides a classic example. Its blast furnaces never completely shut down except for malfunctions. Petroleum refineries, chemical plants, and nuclear power facilities also practice continuous production. A shutdown can damage sensitive equipment, with extremely costly results.

An intermittent production process generates products in short production runs, shutting down machines frequently or changing their configurations to produce different products. Most services result from intermittent production systems. For instance, accountants, plumbers, and dentists traditionally have not attempted to standardize their services because each service provider confronts different problems that require individual approaches. However, some companies such as Jiffy Lube (auto service), H&R Block (tax preparation service), and Lawn Dawg (lawn-care service), offer standardized services as part of a strategy to operate more efficiently and compete with lower prices. McDonald's, well-known for its nearly continuous production of food, has moved toward a more intermittent production model. The fast-food chain invested millions in new cooking equipment to set up kitchens for preparing sandwiches quickly to order, rather than producing large batches ahead of time and then keeping them warm under heat lamps.

Assessment Check ✔

1. What are the two main production systems?
2. What are the two time-related production processes?

Technology and the Production Process

Production continues to change rapidly as computer technologies develop. Many manufacturing plants are now "lights out" facilities that are completely automated—meaning no workers are required to build or make the products. While this signals a change in the types of jobs available in manufacturing, it also means that companies can design, produce, and adapt products more quickly to meet customers' changing needs.

Green Manufacturing Processes

More and more firms are pouring resources into the development of manufacturing processes that result in a reduction of waste, energy use, and pollution. Companies ranging in size from Walmart to the local café are finding ways to operate in a more sustainable manner—whether it is using biofuel to power a fleet of delivery trucks or eliminating unnecessary packaging, firms have begun to view the steps they take with pride. Vermont-based Seventh Generation, which makes household goods and cleaning products, has implemented sustainable manufacturing processes from the very outset. The firm uses a systemic approach to its operations, considering the entire impact of its processes and products on the environment. Seventh Generation consistently audits and makes changes in its processes, whether it is cutting emissions from its distribution system or redesigning its packages. "It's the best insurance any company can have for long-term success," notes co-founder and top executive Jeffrey Hollender.[5] The "Going Green" feature describes how energy firms are developing new methods for drilling for natural gas that are much less damaging to the environment than traditional methods.

Firms that are involved in construction—or are thinking of building new offices or manufacturing plants—are turning their attention to **LEED (Leadership in Energy and Environmental Design)** certification for their facilities. LEED is a voluntary certification

LEED (Leadership in Energy and Environmental Design) voluntary certification program administered by the U.S. Green Building Council, aimed at promoting the most sustainable construction processes available.

Drilling for Natural Gas—Clean Alternatives

Drilling for natural gas doesn't usually conjure up images of an undisturbed landscape. In fact, studies by the EPA as well as private environmental groups reveal that the major method for extracting natural gas from the earth—hydraulic fracturing—can result in contaminated water supplies. Hydraulic fracturing involves injecting millions of gallons of water, sand, and chemicals deep into the ground to crack open the beds of shale containing natural gas, allowing the gas to rise to the surface. Environmental scientists as well as residents of communities near where the drilling takes place are concerned about the amount of water being used as well as potential contamination of surrounding water supplies by the chemicals used in the process.

A number of the energy companies—including those that drill for oil and natural gas—are paying attention to these concerns. Environmental Technologies Ltd. is making a nontoxic alternative to the toxic chemicals, stating that their product kills bacteria just as effectively. Ecosphere Technologies Inc., with headquarters in Florida, claims it can eliminate the need for anti-bacterial chemicals completely by killing the bacteria at the surface before water is injected into the gas wells. Ecosphere also helps energy producers reuse the water from hydraulic fracturing in order to reduce water use and waste. Traditionally, companies have paid to have millions of gallons of waste water shipped to treatment plants or disposal sites.

None of these firms is advocating the cessation of drilling. Drew Bledsoe, former NFL player who is now an investor in Ecosphere

Technologies, explains why. "We've got so much gas under the ground here domestically that we can really take a bite out of our dependence on foreign energy," he says. Instead, the firms are researching and developing greener technologies. In fact, new companies—and divisions or subsidiaries of the larger energy firms—are forming rapidly to take advantage of this business opportunity. "There's a lot of companies trying to get into the business," observes Jack Stabenau, a former Halliburton manager who has been hired by Water Tectonics to run its new division Blu Energy Solutions. "I've literally had people send me stuff that they've been working on in their garage."

Questions for Critical Thinking

1. How would you classify the natural gas drilling production system? Explain why.
2. Do you predict that the firms that are investing in greener processes will ultimately be successful? Why or why not?

Sources: "Hydraulic Fracturing," EPA Web site, http://www.epa.gov, accessed April 29, 2010; "Sustainable Technology," Baker Hughes Web site, http://www.bakerhughes.com, accessed April 29, 2010; Ben Casselman, "Firms See Green in Natural-Gas Production," *The Wall Street Journal*, March 30, 2010, http://www.wsj.com; "EPA Launches Hydraulic Fracturing Study," *Environmental Leader*, March 19, 2010, http://www.environmentalleader.com.

---

program administered by the U.S. Green Building Council, aimed at promoting the most sustainable construction processes available. The LEED certification process is rigorous and involves meeting standards in energy savings, water efficiency, CO^2 emissions reduction, improved indoor environmental quality (including air and natural light), and other categories.[6]

Robots

A growing number of manufacturers have freed workers from boring, sometimes dangerous jobs by replacing them with robots. A *robot* is a reprogrammable machine capable of performing a variety of tasks that require the repeated manipulation of materials and tools. Robots can repeat the same tasks many times without varying their movements. Many factories use robots today to stack their products on pallets and shrink-wrap them for shipping. Boston Scientific, a firm that makes medical devices, uses robots made by Kiva in two of its distribution centers. Saks Fifth Avenue recently purchased a Kiva robot system for its Maryland distribution center as the initial move in an effort to convert its fulfillment center from manual to automated operations.[7]

Historically, robots were most common in automotive and electronics manufacturing, but growing numbers of industries are adding robots to production lines as improvements in technology make them less expensive and more useful. Firms operate many different types of robots. The simplest kind, a pick-and-place robot, moves in only two or three directions

Remote-controlled robots are especially well suited for work in dangerous environments. This field robot, developed for use by bomb squads, can photograph suspicious-looking devices, move them to a safer location, and blow them up.

as it picks up something from one spot and places it in another. So-called field robots assist people in nonmanufacturing, often hazardous, environments such as nuclear power plants, the international space station, and even battlefields. Police use robots to remotely dispose of suspected bombs. However, the same technology can be used in factories. Using vision systems, infrared sensors, and bumpers on mobile platforms, robots can automatically move parts or finished goods from one place to another, while either following or avoiding people, whichever is necessary to do the job. For instance, machine vision systems are being used more frequently for complex applications such as quality assurance in the manufacturing of medical devices. The advancements in machine vision components like cameras, illumination systems, and processors have greatly improved their capabilities. Companies like Minnesota-based PPT Vision help firms such as B. Braun Penang (Malaysia) boost productivity, manage risk, and improve quality across all of its product lines including syringe needles, pharmaceutical vials, and intravenous (IV) infusion bottles.[8]

Computer-Aided Design and Manufacturing

computer-aided design (CAD) process that allows engineers to design components as well as entire products on computer screens faster and with fewer mistakes than they could achieve working with traditional drafting systems.

A process called **computer-aided design (CAD)** allows engineers to design components as well as entire products on computer screens faster and with fewer mistakes than they could achieve working with traditional drafting systems. Using an electronic pen, an engineer can sketch three-dimensional (3-D) designs on an electronic drafting board or directly on the screen. The computer then provides tools to make major and minor design changes and to analyze the results for particular characteristics or problems. Engineers can put a new car design through a simulated road test to project its real-world performance. If they find a problem with weight distribution, for example, they can make the necessary changes virtually—without actually test-driving the car. With advanced CAD software, prototyping is as much "virtual" as it is "hands-on." Actual prototypes or parts aren't built until the engineers are satisfied that the required structural characteristics in their virtual designs have been met. Dentistry has benefited from CAD, which can design and create on-site such products as caps and crowns that fit a patient's mouth or jaw perfectly.[9]

computer-aided manufacturing (CAM) computer tools to analyze CAD output and enable a manufacturer to analyze the steps that a machine must take to produce a needed product or part.

The process of **computer-aided manufacturing (CAM)** picks up where the CAD system leaves off. Computer tools enable a manufacturer to analyze the steps that a machine must take to produce a needed product or part. Electronic signals transmitted to processing equipment provide instructions for performing the appropriate production steps in the correct order. Both CAD and CAM technologies are now used together at most modern production facilities. These so-called CAD/CAM systems are linked electronically to automatically transfer computerized designs into the production facilities, saving both time and effort. They also allow more precise manufacturing of parts.

Flexible Manufacturing Systems

flexible manufacturing system (FMS) production facility that workers can quickly modify to manufacture different products.

A **flexible manufacturing system (FMS)** is a production facility that workers can quickly modify to manufacture different products. The typical system consists of computer-controlled machining centers to produce metal parts, robots to handle the parts, and remote-controlled carts to deliver materials. All components are linked by electronic controls that dictate activities at each stage of the manufacturing sequence, even automatically replacing broken or worn-out drill bits and other implements.

Flexible manufacturing systems have been enhanced by powerful new software that allows machine tools to be reprogrammed while they are running. This capability allows the same machine to make hundreds of different parts without the operator having to shut the machine down each time to load new programs. The software also connects to the Internet to receive updates or to control machine tools at other sites. And because the software resides on a company's computer network, engineers can use it to diagnose production problems any time, from anywhere they can access the network. Nissan Motor Co. recently expanded its flexible manufacturing system to join venture plants in emerging markets that include China, Thailand, and India. In general, this allows the firm to cut its lead time and investment in half when launching new models. However, the move is not without kinks that will take time to smooth out.[10]

Computer-Integrated Manufacturing

Companies integrate robots, CAD/CAM, FMS, computers, and other technologies to implement **computer-integrated manufacturing (CIM)**, a production system in which computers help workers design products, control machines, handle materials, and control the production function in an integrated fashion. This type of manufacturing does not necessarily imply more automation and fewer people than other alternatives. It does, however, involve a new type of automation organized around the computer. The key to CIM is a centralized computer system running software that integrates and controls separate processes and functions. The advantages of CIM include increased productivity, decreased design costs, increased equipment utilization, and improved quality.

CIM is widely used in the printing industry to coordinate thousands of printing jobs, some very small. CIM saves money by combining many small jobs into one larger one and by automating the printing process from design to delivery. Global printing company MAN Roland uses CIM to provide printing solutions for its business customers. One of its products, PRINTVALUE, offers a complete line of solutions for every aspect of a customer's pressroom.[11]

The Location Decision

The decision of where to locate a production facility hinges on transportation, human, and physical factors, as shown in Table 10.1. Transportation factors include proximity to markets and raw materials, along with availability of alternative modes for transporting both inputs and outputs. Automobile assembly plants are located near major rail lines. Inputs—such as engines, plastics, and metal parts—arrive by rail, and the finished vehicles are shipped out by rail. Shopping malls are often located next to major streets and freeways in suburban areas, because most customers arrive by car.

Physical variables involve such issues as weather, water supplies, available energy, and options for disposing of hazardous waste. Theme parks, such as Walt Disney World, are often located in warm climates so they can be open, and attract visitors, year-round. A manufacturing business that wants to locate near a community must prepare an *environmental*

computer-integrated manufacturing (CIM) production system in which computers help workers design products, control machines, handle materials, and control the production function in an integrated fashion.

Assessment Check ☑

1. List some of the reasons businesses invest in robots.

2. What is a flexible manufacturing system (FMS)?

3. What are the major benefits of computer-integrated manufacturing (CIM)?

Table 10.1 Factors in the Location Decision

LOCATION FACTOR	EXAMPLES OF AFFECTED BUSINESSES
Transportation	
Proximity to markets	Baking companies and manufacturers of other perishable products, dry cleaners, hotels, other services
Proximity to raw materials	Paper mills
Availability of transportation alternatives	Brick manufacturers, retail stores
Physical Factors	
Water supply	Computer chip fabrication plants
Energy	Aluminum, chemical, and fertilizer manufacturers
Hazardous wastes	All businesses
Human Factors	
Labor supply	Auto manufacturers, software developers
Local zoning regulations	Manufacturing and distribution companies
Community living conditions	All businesses
Taxes	All businesses

Ian Dagnall/Alamy

Deciding where to locate a production facility can often depend on the weather. Some theme parks, such as Walt Disney World, are located in warm climates so they can be open, and attract visitors, year-round.

impact study that analyzes how a proposed plant would affect the quality of life in the surrounding area. Regulatory agencies typically require these studies to cover topics such as the impact on transportation facilities; energy requirements; water and sewage treatment needs; natural plant life and wildlife; and water, air, and noise pollution. The "Hit & Miss" feature explains how a small company uses renewable energy resources to power its production facility.

Human factors in the location decision include an area's labor supply, local regulations, taxes, and living conditions. Management considers local labor costs, as well as the availability of workers with needed qualifications. Software makers and other computer-related firms concentrate in areas with the technical talent they need, including California's Silicon Valley, Boston, and Austin, Texas. By contrast, some labor-intensive industries have located plants in rural areas with readily available labor pools and limited high-wage alternatives. And some firms with headquarters in the United States and other industrialized countries have moved production off-shore in search of low wages. But no matter what type of industry a firm is in, a production and operations manager's facility location decision must consider the following factors:

- proximity to suppliers, warehouses, and service operations

- insurance and taxes

- availability of such employee needs as housing, schools, mass transportation, day care, shopping, and recreational facilities

- size, skills, and costs of the labor force

- ample space for current and future needs of the firm

- distance to market for goods

- receptiveness of the community

- economical transportation for materials and supplies, as well as for finished goods

- climate and environment that matches the industry's needs and employees' lifestyle

- amount and cost of energy services

- government incentives.

A recent trend in location strategy is bringing production facilities closer to the final markets where the goods will be sold. One reason for this is reduced time and cost for shipping. Another reason is a closer cultural affinity between the parent company and supplier (in cases where production remains overseas). This has led some business developers to label Central America "the new Asia."[12] German automaker Volkswagen decided to build a $1 billion manufacturing plant in Chattanooga, Tennessee, for the construction of its new midsize sedan. Volkswagen expects to roll 150,000 vehicles out of the plant each year, with possibilities for a major expansion that would increase production capacity even more. CEO Stefan Jacoby notes that the plant is part of Volkswagen's overall strategy for capturing more of the U.S. auto market. "With Chattanooga, we're laying the groundwork to be profitable in the U.S. and have a durable business in the U.S.," he explains.[13]

State and local governments may offer incentives to businesses that are willing to locate in their region. These incentives may take the form of tax breaks, agreements to improve infrastructure, and the like.

Assessment Check ☑

1. How does an environmental impact study influence the location decision?

2. What human factors are relevant to the location decision?

NRG Models Energy Efficiency

When Vermont-based NRG Systems needed more space, the decision for the wind-energy company was not whether to go green but how. The answer: a new 46,000-square-foot building featuring energy-efficient technology and powered mostly by renewable energy. The facility provides much more than just space for the company's growth. "We also wanted to create a workplace that was healthy, functional, and beautiful for our employees, while supporting our company's mission of furthering the use of renewable energy," says president and CEO Jan Blittersdorf. She owns the company with her husband, David, NRG's founder.

NRG makes wind assessment systems, towers, instruments, and sensors that measure and analyze wind speed, direction, and other data to locate and operate wind-energy projects. NRG's products can be found in 110 countries, with about half of its sales in the United States. Customers include electric utilities, wind-farm developers, research facilities, universities, government agencies, and homeowners.

NRG chose the latest in green design and technology for its new facility, which includes a café, kitchen, swimming pool, and fitness center in addition to space for offices, manufacturing, tower production and assembly, and shipping. The facility consumes about a third of the energy that conventional buildings of the same size do. Solar panels and a wind turbine behind the facility supply two-thirds of the company's electricity, which also avoids the emission of 105,000 pounds of carbon dioxide a year. Wood pellets from lumber milling waste are used for its heating needs. Water-saving devices such as dual-flushing toilets and faucet aerators save more than 100,000 gallons of water per year. Motion sensors that detect when spaces are occupied turn lights off when they aren't needed. Rows of skylights and windows take advantage of natural light, provide natural ventilation, and give workers views of the outdoors. Employees use laptop computers and Energy Star–rated office equipment, which were selected to reduce electricity use and heat gain. NRG also uses "smart" production technology that automates processes. For example, machinery runs only during the manufacturing process and is in a no-power mode at other times.

Making the building energy efficient increased costs about 8 percent. "We spent more money to build our facility green," says David Blittersdorf, "but we see it as a long-term investment that will more than pay for itself in terms of productivity gains and energy and operating savings costs." The green, energy-lean building has brought NRG some gold. It is one of a small number of industrial buildings to be LEED Gold certified. The designation—LEED stands for Leadership in Energy and Environmental Design—recognizes a high level of performance in building design, construction, and operation based on national standards developed by the U.S. Green Building Council.

Questions for Critical Thinking

1. What environmental impact do you suppose NRG's green facility will have on the community in which it is located?
2. In the future, do you think many businesses will pay more to make their facilities energy efficient? Why or why not?

Sources: "NRG Holds Grand Opening for New Building," http://www.nrgsystems.com, accessed March 12, 2009; "Walking the Talk in a Global Market," http://www.wiinning-workplaces.org; accessed March 12, 2009; Lisa Sutor, "Green Manufacturing Comes of Age," *Control Engineering*, November 2007, p. 69.

The Job of Production Managers

Production and operations managers oversee the work of people and machinery to convert inputs (materials and resources) into finished goods and services. As Figure 10.3 shows, these managers perform four major tasks.

1. Plan the overall production process.
2. Determine the best layout for the firm's facilities.
3. Implement the production plan.
4. Control the manufacturing process to maintain the highest possible quality.

Part of the control process involves continuous evaluation of results. If problems occur, managers return to the first step and make adjustments.

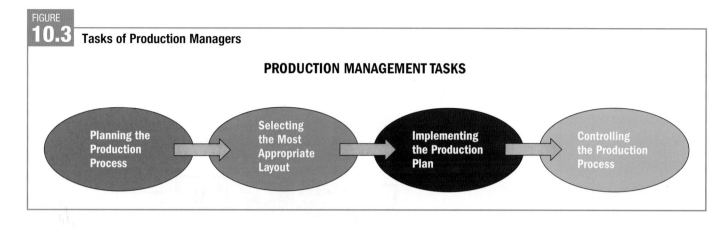

FIGURE 10.3 Tasks of Production Managers

PRODUCTION MANAGEMENT TASKS

Planning the Production Process → Selecting the Most Appropriate Layout → Implementing the Production Plan → Controlling the Production Process

Planning the Production Process

Production planning begins by choosing what goods or services to offer to customers. This decision is the essence of every company's reason for operating. Other decisions such as machinery purchases, pricing decisions, and selection of retail outlets all grow out of product planning. But with product planning, it's not enough to plan products that satisfy customers. Products must satisfy customers *and* be produced as efficiently and inexpensively as possible. So while marketing research studies determine consumer reactions to proposed products and estimate potential sales and profitability levels, production departments focus on planning the production process when they (1) convert original product ideas into final specifications and (2) design the most efficient facilities to produce those products.

It is important for production managers to understand how a project fits into the company's structure because this will affect the success of the project. In a traditional manufacturing organization, each production manager is given a specific area of authority and responsibility such as purchasing or inventory control. One drawback to this structure is that it may actually pit the purchasing manager against the inventory control manager. As more organizations have moved toward team-oriented structures, some organizations assign team members to specific projects reporting to the production manager. Each team is responsible for the quality of its products and has the authority to make changes to improve performance and quality. The major difference between the two approaches is that all workers on teams are responsible for their output, and teamwork avoids the competitiveness between managers often found in traditional structures.

Determining the Facility Layout

The next production management task is determining the best layout for the facility. An efficient facility layout can reduce material handling, decrease costs, and improve product flow through the facility. This decision requires managers to consider all phases of production and the necessary inputs at each step. Figure 10.4 shows three common layout designs: process, product, and fixed-position layouts. It also shows a customer-oriented layout typical of service providers' production systems.

A *process layout* groups machinery and equipment according to their functions. The work in process moves around the plant to reach different workstations. A process layout often facilitates production of a variety of nonstandard items in relatively small batches.

FIGURE

10.4 Basic Facility Layouts

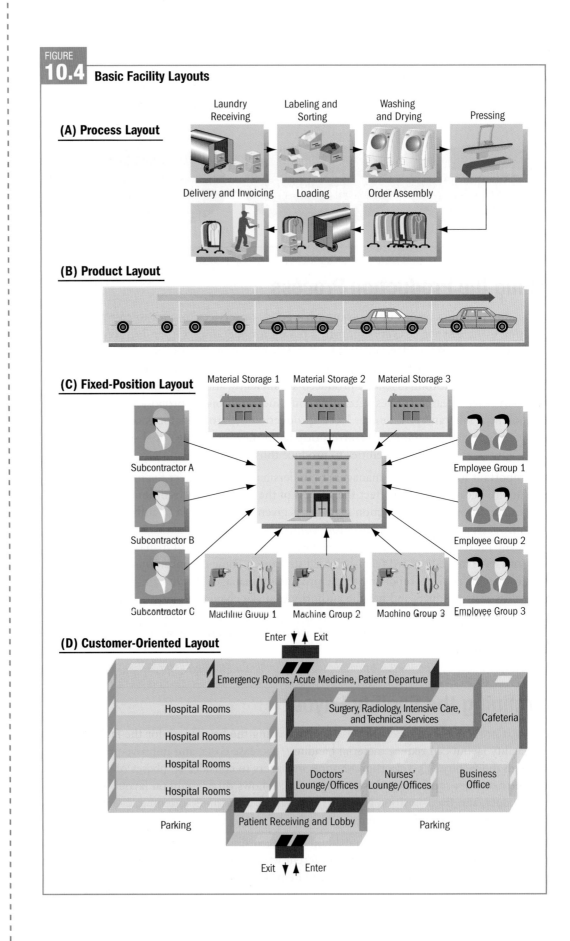

(A) Process Layout

Laundry Receiving · Labeling and Sorting · Washing and Drying · Pressing

Delivery and Invoicing · Loading · Order Assembly

(B) Product Layout

(C) Fixed-Position Layout

Material Storage 1 · Material Storage 2 · Material Storage 3

Subcontractor A · Subcontractor B · Subcontractor C

Employee Group 1 · Employee Group 2 · Employee Group 3

Machine Group 1 · Machine Group 2 · Machine Group 3

(D) Customer-Oriented Layout

Enter ▼ ▲ Exit

Emergency Rooms, Acute Medicine, Patient Departure

Hospital Rooms

Surgery, Radiology, Intensive Care, and Technical Services

Cafeteria

Hospital Rooms

Hospital Rooms

Doctors' Lounge/Offices · Nurses' Lounge/Offices · Business Office

Hospital Rooms

Parking

Patient Receiving and Lobby

Parking

Exit ▼ ▲ Enter

business functions or tasks. In other words, benchmarking is the process of determining other firms' standards and best practices. Automobile companies routinely purchase each other's cars and then take them completely apart to examine and compare the design, components, and materials used to make even the smallest part. They then make improvements to match or exceed the quality found in their competitors' cars. Companies may use many different benchmarks, depending on their objectives. For instance, some organizations that want to make more money may compare their operating profits or expenses to those of other firms. Retailers concerned with productivity may want to benchmark sales per square foot.

It's important when benchmarking for a firm to establish what it wants to accomplish, what it wants to measure, and which company can provide the most useful benchmarking information. A firm might choose a direct competitor for benchmarking, or it might select a company in an entirely different industry—but one that has processes the firm wants to study and emulate.[27]

Quality Control

Quality control involves measuring output against established quality standards. Firms need such checks to spot defective products and to avoid delivering inferior shipments to customers. Standards should be set high enough to meet customer expectations. A 90 or 95 percent success rate might seem to be a good number, but consider what your phone service or ATM network would be like if it worked only 90 percent of the time. You would feel frustrated and inconvenienced, and would probably switch your account to another bank or service provider.

Manufacturing firms can monitor quality levels through visual inspections, electronic sensors, robots, and X-rays. Surveys can provide quality-control information to services. Negative feedback from customers or a high rejection rate on a product or component sends a signal that production is not achieving quality standards. Firms that outsource operations may face a greater challenge in monitoring quality and assuring customers of the quality of their goods or services, especially if they are highly visible companies such as airlines. The "Solving an Ethical Controversy" feature discusses recent concerns over the quality of multivitamins manufactured for U.S. companies by facilities in China.

Because the typical factory can spend up to half its operating budget identifying and fixing mistakes, a company cannot rely solely on inspections to achieve its quality goals. Instead, quality-driven production managers identify all processes involved in producing goods and services and work to maximize their efficiency. The causes of problems in the processes must be found and eliminated. If a company concentrates its efforts on better designs of products and processes with clear quality targets, it can ensure virtually defect-free production.

General Electric, Heinz, 3M, Sears, and the U.S. military are just a few of the growing number of major organizations using the Six Sigma concept to achieve quality goals. *Six Sigma* means a company tries to make error-free products 99.9997 percent of the time—a tiny 3.4 errors per million opportunities. The goal of Six Sigma programs is for companies to eliminate virtually all defects in output, processes, and transactions. Motorola—also a Six Sigma firm—recently completed an initiative to redesign and simplify much of its software architecture in order to improve operational efficiencies and cut costs by reducing redundant IT applications.[28]

quality control measuring output against established quality standards.

Solving an Ethical Controversy

Multivitamins Produced in China: Are Stricter Quality Controls Necessary?

Chinese manufacturing seems to be plagued by quality control issues, ranging from contamination of pet food and baby food to the paint on children's toys. Now it's multivitamins, which reportedly contain dangerous levels of lead and toxic bacteria—and are showing up in U.S. stores. In response, some legislators have called for stricter quality standards. Some vitamin firms have decided to seize the oppor-tunity and source their ingredients elsewhere. One firm has begun offering Opurity, a new premium multivitamin whose ingredients come from other countries, labeling the bottle "China Free."

Should tighter quality controls be placed on Chinese manufacturing of U.S. goods?

PRO

1. According to the Chinese Ministry of Commerce, 85 percent of Chinese citizens rank quality concerns high for food and drugs made in their own country. Tighter controls would not only benefit U.S. and European consumers, they would benefit Chinese consumers as well.

2. Vitamins that are stamped "Made in Germany" or "Made in the USA" might still contain ingredients from China. Because it has already been demonstrated that these products contain high levels of toxic sub-stances, tighter quality controls must be put into place.

CON

1. Many vitamins contain ingredients from multiple sources, so it is impossible to target China as the sole source of contamination.

2. Chinese production offers companies good value—labor and other services are far less expensive than in other countries, savings that can be passed along to the consumer.

Summary

A former senior official at the Food & Drug Administration (FDA) points out that the FDA doesn't have enough inspectors to identify all the quality violations—so the incidence of contamination may be much higher than is already known. At the very least, the origin of ingredients in multivitamins should be made known to consumers so they can make their own choice about which vitamins to buy. For those who want assurance that the vitamins they purchase are free of ingredients sourced from China, products like Opurity are available.

Sources: "New Multivitamins Target Concern Over China's Quality Problems," *EIN,* April 27, 2010, http://www.einpresswire.com; "China Outsourcing: A Benefit to Companies Worldwide," *New Articles,* April 27, 2010, http://newarticles.co.tv; Kimberly Palmer, "Explaining China's Quality Control Problems," *U.S. News & World Report,* April 23, 2009, http://www.usnews.com.

International Organization for Standardization, (ISO) organization whose mission is to develop and promote International Standards for business, government and society to facilitate global trade and cooperation.

ISO Standards

For many goods and services, an important measure of quality is to meet the standards of the **International Organization for Standardization**, known as **ISO** for short—not an acronym but a shorter name derived from the Greek word *isos,* meaning "equal." Operating since 1947, ISO is a network of national standards bodies from 163 countries . Its mission is to develop and promote International Standards for business, government and society to facilitate global trade and cooperation. ISO has developed voluntary standards for everything from the format of banking and telephone cards to freight containers to paper sizes to metric screw threads. The U.S. member body of ISO is the American National Standards Institute.

The ISO 9000 family of standards give requirements and guidance for quality management to help organizations ensure that their products and services achieve customer satisfaction and also provide a framework for continual improvement. The ISO 14000 family of standards for environmental management helps organizations to ensure that their operations cause minimal harm to the environment and to achieve continual improvement of their environmental performance.

ISO 9001:2008 and ISO 14001:2004 respectively give the requirements for a quality management system and an environmental management system. Both can be used for certification, which means that the organization's management system (the way it manages its processes) is independently audited by a certification body (also known in North American as a registration body, or registrar) and confirmed as conforming to the requirements of the standard. The organization is then issued with an ISO 9001:2008 or an ISO 14001:2004 certificate.

Courtesy ISO

Many consumers prefer to buy from companies that are ISO 9000-certified.

It should be noted that certification is not a requirement of either standard, which can be implemented solely for the benefits it provides the organization and its customers. However, many organizations opt to seek certification because of the perception that an independent audit adds confidence in its abilities. Business partners, customers, suppliers and consumers may prefer to deal with or buy products and services from a certified organization. Certifications have to be periodically renewed through accompanying audits.

A second point is that ISO itself develops standards but does not itself carry out auditing and certification. This is done independently of ISO by hundreds of certification bodies around the world. The certificates they issue carry their own logo, but not ISO's because the latter does not approve or control their activities.

Whether or not an organization decides to seek certification of its management system, many have reported significant benefits from implementing ISO's mananagement system standards, such as increased efficiency, better teamwork, improved customer satisfaction and reduced consumption of resources.[29]

Assessment Check ✓

1. What are some ways in which a company can monitor the quality level of its output?
2. List some of the benefits of acquiring ISO 9000 certification.

What's Ahead

Maintaining high quality is an important part of satisfying customers. Product quality and customer satisfaction are also objectives of the business function of marketing. The next part consists of three chapters that explore the many activities involved in customer-driven marketing. These activities include product development, distribution, promotion, and pricing.

Summary of Learning Objectives

⌐1⌐ **Explain the strategic importance of the production function.**

Production and operations management is a vital business function. Without a quality good or service, a company cannot create profits, and it soon fails. The production process is also crucial in a not-for-profit organization, because the good or service it produces justifies the organization's existence. Production and operations management plays an important strategic role by lowering the costs of production, boosting output quality, and allowing the firm to respond flexibly and dependably to customers' demands.

Assessment Check Answers ✔

1.1 What is mass production? Mass production is a system for manufacturing products in large quantities through effective combinations of employees with specialized skills, mechanization, and standardization.

1.2 What is the difference between flexible production and customer-driven production? Flexible production generally involves using technology to receive and fulfill orders and skilled people to carry out tasks needed to fill a particular order. Customer-driven production evaluates customer demands in order to make the connection between products manufactured and products bought.

⌐2⌐ **Identify and describe the four main categories of production processes.**

The four main categories of production processes are the analytic production system, which reduces a raw material to its component parts in order to extract one or more marketable products; the synthetic production system, which combines a number of raw materials or parts to produce finished products; the continuous production process, which generates finished products over a lengthy period of time; and the intermittent production process, which generates products in short production runs.

Assessment Check Answers ✔

2.1 What are the two main production systems? The two systems are analytic production and synthetic production.

2.2 What are the two time-related production processes? The two time-related production processes are the continuous production process and the intermittent production process.

⌐3⌐ **Explain the role of technology in the production process.**

Computer-driven automation allows companies to design, create, and modify products rapidly and produce them in ways that effectively meet customers' changing needs. Important design and production technologies include robots, computer-aided design (CAD), computer-aided manufacturing (CAM), and computer-integrated manufacturing (CIM). Many firms are pouring resources into the development of manufacturing processes that result in a reduction of waste, energy use, and pollution.

Assessment Check Answers ✔

3.1 List some of the reasons businesses invest in robots. Businesses use robots to free people from sometimes dangerous assignments and to move heavy items from one place to another in a factory.

3.2 What is a flexible manufacturing system (FMS)? An FMS is a production facility that workers can quickly modify to manufacture different products.

3.3 What are the major benefits of computer-integrated manufacturing (CIM)? The main benefits are increased productivity, decreased design costs, increased equipment utilization, and improved quality.

⌐4⌐ **Identify the factors involved in a plant location decision.**

Criteria for choosing the best site for a production facility fall into three categories: transportation, human, and physical factors. Transportation factors include proximity to markets and raw materials, along with availability of transportation alternatives. Physical variables involve such issues as water supply, available energy, and options for disposing of hazardous wastes. Human factors include the area's labor supply, local regulations, taxes, and living conditions.

Assessment Check Answers ✔

4.1 How does an environmental impact study influence the location decision? An environmental impact study influences the location decision because it studies how transportation, energy use, water and sewer treatment needs, and other factors will affect plants, wildlife, water, air, and other features of the natural environment.

4.2 What human factors are relevant to the location decision? Human factors include an area's labor supply, labor costs, local regulations, taxes, and living conditions.

⌐5⌐ **Explain the major tasks of production and operations managers, and outline the three activities involved in implementing the production plan.**

Production and operations managers use people and machinery to convert inputs (materials and resources) into finished goods and services. Four major tasks are involved. First, the managers must plan the overall production process. Next, they must pick the best layout for their facilities. Then they implement their production plans. Finally, they control the production process and evaluate results to maintain the highest possible quality.

Implementation involves deciding whether to make, buy, or lease components; selecting the best suppliers for materials; and controlling inventory to keep enough, but not too much, on hand.

Assessment Check Answers ✔

5.1 List the four major tasks of production and operations managers. The four tasks are planning overall production, laying out the firm's facilities, implementing the production plan, and controlling manufacturing to achieve high quality.

5.2 What is the difference between a traditional manufacturing structure and a team-based structure? In the traditional structure, each manager is given a specific area of authority. In a team-based structure, all workers are responsible for their output.

5.3 What factors affect the make, buy, or lease decision? The costs of leasing or purchasing parts from vendors, versus producing them in house, the availability of dependable outside suppliers, and the need for confidentiality affect this decision.

⌐6⌐ Identify the steps in the production control process.

The production control process consists of five steps: planning, routing, scheduling, dispatching, and follow-up. Quality control is an important consideration throughout this process. Coordination of each of these phases should result in high production efficiency and low production costs.

Assessment Check Answers ✔

6.1 What five steps are involved in controlling the production process? The five steps are planning, routing, scheduling, dispatching, and follow-up.

6.2 What is the difference between a PERT chart and a Gantt chart? PERT charts, which seek to minimize delays by coordinating all aspects of the production process, are used for more complex projects; Gantt charts, which track projected and actual work progress over time, are used for scheduling relatively simple projects.

⌐7⌐ Discuss the importance of quality control.

Quality control involves evaluating goods and services against established quality standards. Such checks are necessary to spot defective products and to see that they are not shipped to customers. Devices for monitoring quality levels of the firm's output include visual inspection, electronic sensors, robots, and X-rays. Companies are increasing the quality of their goods and services by using Six Sigma techniques and by becoming ISO 9000 and 14000 certified.

Assessment Check Answers ✔

7.1 What are some ways in which a company can monitor the quality level of its output? Benchmarking, quality control, Six Sigma, and ISO standards are ways of monitoring quality.

7.2 List some of the benefits of acquiring ISO 9000 certification. These standards define how a company should ensure that its products meet customers' requirements. Studies show that customers prefer to buy from companies that are ISO 9000 certified.

▉ Business Terms You Need to Know

production 316
production and operations
  management 316
mass production 318
LEED (Leadership in Energy
  and Environmental
  Design) 320
computer-aided design
  (CAD) 322

computer-aided
  manufacturing
  (CAM) 322
flexible manufacturing
  system (FMS) 322
computer-integrated
  manufacturing (CIM) 323
make, buy, or lease
  decision 329

inventory
  control 332
just-in-time (JIT)
  system 332
materials requirement
  planning (MRP) 333
production
  control 333
quality 336

benchmarking 336
quality control 337
International
  Organization for
  Standardization
  (ISO) 338

▉ Review Questions

1. What is utility? How does production create utility?

2. Why is production such an important business activity? In what ways does it create value for the company and its customers?

3. Why are firms now moving more toward flexible production and customer-driven production instead of mass production? Describe a product that you think would be better suited to flexible production or customer-driven production than mass production. Explain your choice.

4. Identify which production system—analytic or synthetic—applies to each of the following products:

   a. logging

   b. medical care

   c. cotton farming

   d. fishing

   e. construction

5. Industries such as home construction and dentistry benefit from the use of CAD. In both of these, CAM could be used as well—in the manufacture of home components as well as dental implants, crowns, and the like. Choose another industry that seems like a candidate for the use of both CAD and CAM systems. Explain how the industry could use both.

6. SeaWorld has facilities in Florida, Texas, and California. What specific factors might have contributed to these choices?

7. What would be the best facility layout for each of the following?

   a. movie rental shop

   b. nail salon

   c. car wash

   d. sandwich shop

8. What might be the factors involved in the selection of suppliers for a steakhouse restaurant?

9. What is inventory control? Why is the management of inventory crucial to a company's success?

10. What is benchmarking? How can it help a firm improve the quality of its goods and services?

Projects and Teamwork Applications

1. Imagine that you recently became the owner of a popular ice cream shop. You want to attract more customers and ultimately expand the business. Choose the type of production process—continuous or intermittent—you think would best fit your business. Then create a plan outlining specifically how you would use this process and why it would help you achieve your goal as a business owner.

2. On your own or with a classmate, imagine that you've been hired to help a business group design a shopping mall. Taking into account the factors listed in the chapter, come up with recommendations for where the mall should be located—and why. Present your plan to the class.

3. On your own or with a classmate, select one of the following businesses and sketch or describe the layout that you think would be best for attracting and serving customers:

   a. Mexican restaurant

   b. home furnishings store

   c. pet store

   d. motorcycle dealership

   e. dentist office

4. Suppose you and your best friend decided to operate a house-painting service. Draft a production plan for your business, including the following decisions: (a) make, buy, or lease; (b) suppliers; and (c) inventory control.

5. Choose two firms for comparison (one firm should provide a good benchmarking opportunity for its production processes). Keep in mind that the benchmarking firm doesn't necessarily have to be in the same industry as the other selected firm. Present your decisions to the class and explain why you made both choices.

Web Assignments

1. Just-in-time inventory management systems. Go to the Web sites listed here to learn more about just-in-time inventory management systems. Make some notes on what you learned and bring them to class to participate in a class discussion.

http://www.wisegeek.com/what-is-a-just-in-time-inventory.htm

http://smallbusiness.dnb.com/manage/finances/12375503-1.html

http://www.smcdata.com/software-choices/just-in-time-inventory-control-systems-1.html

2. Plant location decision. Using an Internet news service, such as Google news (http://news.google.com) or Yahoo! news (http://news.yahoo.com), search for information on a recent plant location decision. An example is VW's recent decision to build a new production facility in Chattanooga, Tennessee. Research the decision and then prepare a brief report outlining the factors that went into the firm's decision to locate the plant where it did.

http://www.vw.com/vwbuzz/browse/en/us/detail/Volkswagen_Group_of_America_announces_it_will_produce_cars_in_Chattanooga/219.

3. ISO certification. Visit the Web site of the International Organization for Standardization (http://www.iso.org). Click on "standards development" and then "processes and procedures." What are some of the products for which ISO standards are currently being developed?

Note: Internet Web addresses change frequently. If you don't find the exact sites listed, you may need to access the organization's home page and search from there or use a search engine such as Bing or Google.

At Zara, fashion paradise awaits shoppers constantly on the lookout for chic new clothing. New designs appear twice a week, and the items showcased in the windows are in stock. Regular Zara shoppers know they should scan the clothes on the black plastic hangers for the latest looks.

Zara leads the industry in making and shipping "fast fashion"—inexpensive trendy clothing. Its parent company is Spain-based Inditex, whose seven brands include Massimo Dutti and Bershka. With 3,700 stores in 68 countries and annual sales of $12 billion, Inditex is the world's second-largest clothing retailer by sales after Gap. Inditex is famous for opening a new store every day of the year in some part of the world and for getting products to the stores at lightning speed. Zara makes up 60 percent of Inditex's business.

When it opened the first store in a Spanish port town, Zara capitalized on two strengths: a keen sense for customer tastes and a production process that began with the final price and worked back to the most efficient operations. Later Zara brought a local business-school professor on board to refine shipping and distribution and consulted with professors from the MIT Sloan School of Management to develop the best system of replenishing stores rapidly. Zara collections are small and often sell out, and the company prefers to move a clothing group out of a store if some pieces or sizes are out of stock. The MIT group designed a mathematical model to handle the enormous number of decisions involved in determining every garment and every size needed at every store.

At Inditex company headquarters outside La Coruña, Spain, sales managers at computers monitor sales at every store around the world. When apparel sells well—or doesn't—they tell nearby designers to come up with new designs. Downstairs other designers decide on window displays and store layouts. They set up displays in mock store windows lining a simulated street full of shops. The designers take pictures to show how different storefronts should look, from London's Regent Street to New York's Fifth Avenue. Every two weeks, new displays are photographed and e-mailed to stores to replicate.

Zara store managers use hand-held computers that show how garments rank by sales, so clerks can reorder fast-moving merchandise in less than an hour. These orders arrive, with new items, two days later. Alarm tags are attached at the factory, to save sales staff's time and allow them to spend more time serving customers. Clothes are shipped directly from the factory to stores. Unlike competitors that manufacture most of their clothing in Asia, Inditex produces only a third of its goods there. Factories in Spain, Portugal, Morocco, and Turkey make two-thirds of the merchandise. While labor costs are higher in these countries than in Asia, Inditex wants the flexibility of having most of its production near its warehouses, which are all in Spain. The company combines merchandise for its various store brands and ships the large volume of goods twice a week via Air France Cargo or Emirates Airline. Planes from Spain fly to Bahrain with merchandise for Inditex stores in the Middle East, proceed to Asia, and return to Spain with raw materials and partially finished clothing.

Some retail specialists question whether Zara's local production can continue to be successful. Producing the majority of its merchandise so close to home may lose some benefit as more stores open farther away. Zara has been able to make up some of its production and distribution costs by charging more for its clothing sold overseas. In the United States, for example, Zara pieces cost as much as 40 percent more than in Spain. That inconsistency, critics say, could be risky in a global business. Meanwhile, Zara's quick production and distribution has prompted other retailers to increase the number of new styles they offer each year and to get the new looks into stores faster.

Questions for Critical Thinking

1. Do you think the advantages of locating most of Zara's production in Spain and other nearby countries outweigh the disadvantages?

2. Describe Zara's inventory control system. How does it affect production?

Sources: Leslie Crawford, "Can Zara Style Out the Downturn?" *Financial Times*, March 31, 2008, p. 32; Cecilie Rohwedder and Keith Johnson, "Pace-Setting Zara Seeks More Speed to Fight Its Rising Cheap-Chic Rivals," *The Wall Street Journal*, February 20, 2008, p. B1; Connie Robbins Gentry, "European Fashion Stores Edge Past US Counterparts," *Chain Store Age*, December 2007, p. 100.

CASE 10.2 Zappos: How Not to Get Zapped by Customer Service

If you like shoes, you've heard of Zappos. Perhaps you've ordered a pair (or two or three) from the popular Web site, taking advantage of the free shipping and free returns. Tony Hsieh, CEO of Zappos, wants you to be happy. He wants to you be happy with your shoes, and if you're not, he wants to make returns easy for you. This is because he wants you to come back and order more shoes—which you probably will. Hsieh believes that the best way to attract and keep customers is to "wow" them with customer service. It's a formula that works—Zappos reports that nearly 75 percent of its business comes from repeat customers.

Although Zappos is now owned by Amazon, and has also grown to offer apparel, accessories, and other products, the company's commitment to customer service has not changed. Delivering top service, which includes fulfilling and shipping orders as quickly as possible, is a significant part of Zappos' production function. While Internet and other computer technology helps speed delivery and turnaround time, it also sets the bar higher than ever before. One survey recently revealed that consumers would be willing to pay nearly 11 percent more for superior customer service at online shopping sites. "Due to the seemingly distant and remote nature of online shopping, it makes sense that consumers would pay a higher premium to have the comfort and peace of mind that they will be taken care of in the case of a serious question, concern or problem," concluded the survey.

Customer service is also an investment in quality. Zappos currently has a Customer Loyalty department staffed by 380 employees whose job it is to communicate among the different departments of the company and with customers. The customer loyalty team interfaces with the resource desk, order verification (anti-fraud team), quality assurance, kaizen (continuous training), and e-mail/ live chat, along with other departments as necessary. Customer loyalty team members have the authority to send individual customers personal notes or request flowers for a wedding or anniversary celebration. They don't need to ask permission to issue refunds or coupons or to give out their contact information. At Zappos, the outlook is that everyone is a customer and should be treated with respect.

Constant improvement is also part of the company culture. "Let's take our learnings and improve, constantly," says marketing chief Aaron Magness. "If we rest, we'll be passed by the next more hungry business." Tony Hsieh agrees, adding that it is necessary to embrace change, recognizing opportunities in the industry and the marketplace. The formula must work—Zappos rakes in more than $1 billion each year selling shoes online to customers who haven't even tried them on to see if they can wiggle their toes.

Questions for Critical Thinking

1. Explain how customer service fulfills a significant portion of Zappos' production function.
2. What kind of firm might Zappos use for benchmarking? Why?

Sources: Sean Smith, "What Can Zappos CEO Tony Hsieh Teach You About Online Business Success?" *Power of More,* April 19, 2010, http://powerofmore.net; "Zappos' Customer Service Draws Raves in a New Report," *Internet Retailer,* March 22, 2010, http://www.internetretailer.com; Brandon Gutman, "Zappos' Marketing Chief: Customer Service is the New Marketing!" *Fast Company,* March 15, 2010, http://www.fastcompany.com; Eric Friedman, "Zappos and the Continued Power of Customer Service," *Marketing,* March 12, 2010, http://www.marketing.fm; Graham Charlton, "Q&A: Zappos' Jane Judd on Customer Loyalty," *Ecoconsultancy,* November 4, 2009, http://ecoconsultancy.com.

CASE 10.3 Kimpton Hotels Puts Green Initiatives to Work

It's one thing for a company to talk about green initiatives; it's quite another for the firm to put those initiatives into practice. Kimpton Hotels & Restaurants began putting green initiatives to work in its hotels and restaurants nearly thirty years ago, long before these practices became popular. Of course, it's the operations function of the business that implements this type of plan; it's the hotel manager, the dishwasher in the restaurant, the housekeeping staff, the front desk clerk. "*How* we do what we do defines us," observes NikiLeondakis, COO of

Kimpton Hotels & Restaurants, which runs 50 boutique-style luxury hotels and restaurants across the U.S.

Although Kimpton began its green practices long ago, in 2005 the company launched a company-wide program called EarthCare in order to standardize these practices across all of its hotels and restaurants. Frank Kawecki, director of operations for Kimpton Restaurants in the Northeast, recalls that Kimpton's green efforts started first in the restaurants with the chefs, then spread. When the EarthCare program began, the company asked for volunteers from each property who were devoted to the green effort because they were already committed to the idea and could communicate best between management and staff. Volunteers ranged from bartenders to general managers who were willing to meet once a month. One of the first initiatives—which came from restaurant servers—was to eliminate imported bottled water, shifting instead to locally bottled water and the use of recycled water bottles.

As EarthCare has expanded throughout the company, standard guidelines have been set for nearly every facet of the firm's operation. Home office materials and procedures include shifting to online publication of many documents; using post-consumer recycled paper and eco-friendly inks for those documents that are printed; making hotel keycards from recycled plastic; offering continuous education in green initiatives for staff, and more. At the hotels themselves, all hotel in-room materials and bills are printed on recycled paper; phone books are offered by request only; all plumbing is water-efficient; lighting is LED or CFL, and subject to motion sensors; rooms are stocked with green-certified linens and towels; guest room soaps are made of natural ingredients, and carpet cleaning is done with non-toxic products. If the list seems endless, it nearly is—and the complexity of the operations management required to implement standards such as these is daunting.

Waste management is a category unto itself, with hotel and restaurant-wide recycling and reuse of everything from cardboard and paper to batteries and computers. Restaurants in particular present a huge challenge. "There's an enormous amount of waste from a lot of restaurants," observes Frank Kawecki. "A lot of it can be composted, recycled, or reused. There can be a 40-percent savings in waste removal. Waste removal was traditionally a fixed expense that we have manipulated," through EarthCare. In addition to reducing waste and energy use, Kimpton restaurants purchase and serve as many certified organic products as possible, ranging from local produce and seafood to coffee, tea, and wine.

Saving the planet can be expensive. Running a business incurs costs as well. One of the challenges of implementing the EarthCare program is monitoring costs. "Green efforts can't compromise the experience for our guests and it can't cost our shareholders more money. If we go out of business, saving the planet as hoteliers goes away," notes Niki Leondakis. "So that premise was very good in helping us decide what we would tackle first—water savings, energy savings." Whatever is good for the planet has to be good for the bottom line. One way that Kimpton Hotels meets this goal is by looking at ways for certain costs to off-set each other. If purchasing recycled paper costs more, there might be a way to find savings in another area. "We put measurements on all of our efforts to see what impact they have on the bottom line," says Leondakis. "We've still been able to say that it saves us money."

Recently Kimpton Hotels announced its plan to seek third-party Green Seal certification on all 50 of its properties; ten properties have already been certified. Green Seal certification involves an application process and evaluation similar to LEED certification, which the company is also seeking for its new or renovated properties. "It will be an ongoing work in progress forever," predicts Leondakis. But Kimpton Hotels has a head start.

Questions for Critical Thinking

1. Location is certainly a production factor for Kimpton Hotels & Restaurants, which are located in cities such as New York, Los Angeles, Boston, Chicago, and Seattle. What location factors might Kimpton managers consider when thinking about whether to acquire or build a new Kimpton hotel and restaurant?

2. According to the EarthCare program, what factors might a Kimpton restaurant chef or manager consider when selecting suppliers?

3. A daily staff meeting at a Kimpton hotel can be considered part of production control, contributing to the smooth running of the hotel. Who might attend such a meeting? What kinds of topics might they discuss?

4. Quality is top priority at Kimpton Hotels & Restaurants. What steps can a Kimpton hotel manager take to balance quality and the initiatives of the EarthCare program?

Sources: Kimpton Hotels Web site, http://www.kimptonhotels.com, accessed August 22, 2010; Matt Courtland, "Environmental Mission Statements: A List of Hotel Sustainability Policies," *Environmental Leader,* March 18, 2010, http://www.environmentalleader.com; "Kimpton Hotels Aim for 100 Percent Green Seal Certification," *GreenerBuildings,* March 31, 2010, http://www.greenbiz.com.

GREENSBURG, KS

No Time to Micromanage

"This is a stepping stone for me," thought Greensburg's town administrator, Steve Hewitt. Hewitt, who had grown up in Greensburg, had moved back home and taken a position in the tiny rural town of 1,500. Standing in what was left of his kitchen on the night of Friday, May 4, 2007, he realized he had gotten more than he bargained for.

Across town, Mayor Lonnie McCollum and his wife had survived by clinging to a mattress as the storm ravaged their home. A write-in candidate in the past election, McCollum had accepted the job and set out to revive the dying town. Among his many ideas, the most innovative had been green building. McCollum was no tree-hugger; he was simply looking for a way to save money on fuel and utilities, to conserve the town's resources.

Like many people in town, Hewitt and McCollum had no idea of the extent of the damage. They would later learn that the two-mile-wide F5 tornado drove right through the two-mile-wide town. By the end of the weekend, though, they knew that Greensburg was gone. At a press conference, McCollum announced that the town would rebuild, and would do it using green technology.

By May 2008, the town was on its third mayor since the disaster, but Steve Hewitt was still the town administrator. He had expanded his staff from 20 to 35 people, establishing a full-time fire department, a planning department, and a community development department. Each week Hewitt spent hours giving interviews to reporters from all over the world. "He's very open as far as information," said Recovery Coordinator and Assistant Town Administrator Kim Alderfer. "He's very good about delegating authority. He gives you the authority to do your job. He doesn't have time to micromanage."

Meanwhile, residents Janice and John Haney had rebuilt their family farm on the outskirts of town. Although their new home, an earth berm structure, was full of energy-efficient features, Janice wasn't convinced that the plan to rebuild Greensburg using green technology was the right one. "I do worry that it will be a T-shirt slogan," said Haney. "I personally don't think the persons that are living in Greensburg right now are really committed to it. We didn't have a choice. You MUST go green. That's really not everybody's option." She added that many people feared higher taxes would force some families out of town.

Questions

After viewing the video, answer the following questions:

1. What kind of leader is Steve Hewitt?
2. How would you describe Greensburg's culture?
3. Do you believe that as town administrator, Hewitt had the right to impose green building codes on residents and businesses?
4. Perform a SWOT analysis of Greensburg's green initiative.

LAUNCHING YOUR
[Management Career]

Part 3, "Management: Empowering People to Achieve Business Objectives," covers Chapters 7 through 10, which discuss management, leadership, and the internal organization; human resource management, motivation, and labor–management relations; improving performance through empowerment, teamwork, and communication; and production and operations management. In those chapters, you read about top executives and company founders who not only direct their companies' strategy but lead others in their day-to-day tasks to keep them on track, middle managers who devise plans to turn the strategies into realities, and supervisors who work directly with employees to create strong teams that satisfy customers. An incredible variety of jobs is available to those choosing management careers. And the demand for managers will continue to grow. The U.S. Department of Labor estimates that managerial jobs will grow by nearly 15 percent over the next decade.[1]

So what kinds of jobs might you be able to choose from if you launch a management career? As you learned in Chapter 7, three types of management jobs exist: supervisory managers, middle managers, and top managers. Supervisory management, or first-line management, includes positions such as supervisor, office manager, department manager, section chief, and team leader. Managers at this level

work directly with the employees who produce and sell a firm's goods and services.

Middle management includes positions such as general managers, plant managers, division managers, and regional or branch managers. They are responsible for setting objectives consistent with top management's goals and planning and implementing strategies for achieving those objectives.

Top managers include such positions as chief executive officer (CEO), chief operating officer (COO), chief financial officer (CFO), chief information officer (CIO), and executive vice president. Top managers devote most of their time to developing long-range plans, setting a direction for their organization, and inspiring a company's executives and employees to achieve their vision for the company's future. Top managers travel frequently between local, national, and global offices as they meet and work with customers, suppliers, and company managers and employees.

Most managers start their careers in areas such as sales, production, or finance, so you likely will start in a similar entry-level job. If you do that job and other jobs well, you may be considered for a supervisory position. Then, if you are interested and have the technical, human, and conceptual skills to succeed, you'll begin your management career path. But what

kinds of supervisory management jobs are typically available? Let's review the exciting possibilities.

Administrative services managers manage basic services—such as clerical work, payroll, travel, printing and copying, data records, telecommunications, security, parking, and supplies—without which no organization could operate. On average, administrative service managers earn $75,000 a year.[2]

Construction managers plan, schedule, and coordinate the building of homes, commercial buildings such as offices and stores, and industrial facilities such as manufacturing plants and distribution centers. Unlike administrative service managers, who work in offices, construction managers typically work on building sites with architects, engineers, construction workers, and suppliers. On average, construction managers earn almost $78,000 a year.[3]

Food service managers run restaurants and services that prepare and offer meals to customers. They coordinate workers and suppliers in kitchens, dining areas, and banquet operations; are responsible for those who order and purchase food inventories; maintain kitchen equipment; and recruit, hire, and train new workers. Food service managers can work for chains such as Ruby Tuesday or Olive Garden, for local restaurants, and for corporate food service departments in organizations. On average, food service managers earn more than $49,500 a year.[4]

Human resource managers help organizations follow federal and local labor laws; effectively recruit, hire, train, and retain talented workers; administer corporate pay and benefits plans; develop and administer organizational human resource policies; and, when necessary, participate in contract negotiations or handle disputes. Human resource management jobs vary widely, depending on how specialized the requirements are. On average, human resource managers earn from $45,000 to $96,000 a year, depending on the area in which they specialize.[5]

Lodging managers work in hotels and motels but also help run camps, ranches, and recreational resorts. They may oversee guest services, front desk, kitchen, restaurant, banquet, house cleaning, and maintenance workers. Because they are expected to help satisfy customers around the clock, they often work long hours and may be on call when not at work. On average, lodging managers earn about $45,000 a year.[6]

Medical and health services managers work in hospitals, nursing homes, doctors' offices, and corporate and university settings. They run departments that offer clinical services; ensure that state and federal laws are followed; and handle decisions related to the management of patient care, nursing, surgery, therapy, medical records, and

financial payments. On average, medical and health service managers earn $75,000 a year.[7]

Purchasing managers lead and control organizational supply chains that ensure that companies have needed materials to produce the goods and services they sell, purchase materials at reasonable prices, and oversee deliveries when and where they are needed. Purchasing managers work with wholesale and retail buyers, buying goods that are then resold to others; purchasing agents, who buy supplies and raw materials for their organizations; and contract specialists, who negotiate and supervise purchasing contracts with key suppliers and vendors. On average, purchasing managers earn nearly $89,000 a year.[8]

Production managers direct and coordinate operations that manufacture goods. They work with employees who produce parts and assemble products, help determine which new machines should be purchased and when existing machines need maintenance, and are responsible for achieving production goals that specify the quality, cost, schedule, and quantity of units to be produced. On average, production managers earn almost $83,000 a year.[9]

Career Assessment Exercises in Management

1. The American Management Association is a global, not-for-profit

professional organization that provides a range of management development and educational services to individuals, companies, and government agencies. Access the AMA's Web site at http://www.amanet.org. Explore the "Free Resources" link there (you will have to register). Pick an article or research area that interests you. Provide a one-page summary of the management issues discussed in the feature.

2. Go online to a business news service, such as Yahoo! News or Google News, or look at the business section of your local newspaper. Find a story relating to a first-line supervisor, middle manager, or top executive. Summarize that person's duties. What decisions does that person make and how do those decisions affect his or her organization?

3. Pick a supervisory management position from the descriptions provided here that interests you. Research the career field. What skills do you possess that would make you a good candidate for a management position in that field? What work and other experience do you need to help you get started? Create a list of both your strengths and weaknesses and formulate a plan to add to your strengths.

PART

4

The Basic Tenets of Marketing

[**Chapter 11**]

Introduction to
Marketing Strategies

[**Chapter 12**]

Producing and
Distributing Goods
and Services

[**Chapter 13**]

Promotion and
Pricing of Goods and
Services

Tim Mantoani/Masterfile

Chapter 11

Learning Objectives

[1] Summarize the ways in which marketing creates utility.

[2] Discuss the marketing concept.

[3] Describe not-for-profit marketing, and identify the five major categories of nontraditional marketing.

[4] Outline the basic steps in developing a marketing strategy.

[5] Describe the marketing research function.

[6] Identify and explain each of the methods available for segmenting consumer and business markets.

[7] Outline the determinants of consumer behavior.

[8] Discuss the benefits of and tools for relationship marketing.

Introduction to Marketing Strategies

PetSmart Pampers Pooches

Purebred poodle or Pomeranian, hybrid of hound and husky, everyone loves the family dog. But some people's attachment goes deeper, and PetSmart, the largest U.S. pet-store chain, aims to meet the needs of the finickiest owner. The company has pinpointed a group of consumers whose passion for their pets is so great that the animals are considered full-fledged family members. PetSmart calls these customers "pet parents" and offers services geared directly to them.

Pet owners can pick up a dog leash, toy, or food in one of nearly 1,000 PetSmart retail stores. But several hundred stores now also offer upscale lodging in their PetSmart PetsHotels. The PetsHotel provides personalized day and overnight care for dogs and cats. At a PetsHotel, family pooches enjoy extended play time, salon services, and healthful snacks including lactose-free soft-serve ice cream. The facilities are sparkling clean, resembling a luxury hotel, and the staff is knowledgeable and well trained. A PetsHotel suite, which goes for about $31 per night, includes a room with a window, dog beds with lambskin blankets, and a TV that plays videos such as Disney's *101 Dalmations*. Pet owners often say they wouldn't mind staying at the hotel themselves. Doggie Day Camp, the day-care option located inside the PetsHotel, is a program that provides hours of supervised play with other dogs in climate-controlled playrooms. Doggie Day Camp is open seven days a week—except for Thanksgiving and Christmas—and has flexible drop-off and pick-up times.

Pet owners use both of these programs for a number of reasons. Some are traveling. Others use the day care as an alternative to leaving a dog home alone. Some drop their dogs off for a few hours of exercise and interaction with other dogs to prevent mischievous behavior from occurring at home.

PetSmart markets its services to pet parents who want specialized care for their dogs, pointing out on its Web site the benefits of its own programs over those of competitors. Each dog is carefully screened to identify those that are best suited to the programs and to make certain that the programs can meet customers' needs. The pet parent is interviewed, then the health and temperament of the dog is assessed, including confirmation of specific vaccinations. Finally, the dog is introduced to the group with which it will play for the duration of its stay. If all three stages go well, the dog becomes a member of the PetSmart family. PetSmart Pet Care Specialists are safety certified and trained in behavior assessment—not just part-time pet sitters. The indoor facilities provide a safe, clean environment for all the dogs that stay either for the day program or overnight.

PetSmart offers a frequent-user program to pet parents who plan to use Doggie Day Camp regularly. For every 10 sessions purchased during select months with a PetPerks Savings Card, customers receive 1 session free. Coupons for the free sessions are mailed to customers, but program users can also check their rewards status online.

How successful is PetSmart at recognizing the needs of passionate pet owners? Its revenues from its PetsHotel and Doggie Day Camp services have increased more than 25 percent each year since their start. The services are twice as profitable as the sale of pet toys, accessories, and food.

But success should come as no surprise when more than 80 percent of dog owners refer to their pooches as family members. "We are benefiting from the trend toward the humanization of pets," says PetSmart spokesperson David Lenhardt. "It's that passion for pets that makes the pet hotel work."[1]

Overview

Business success in the 21st century is directly tied to a company's ability to identify and serve its target markets. In fact, all organizations—profit-oriented and not-for-profit, manufacturing and retailing—*must* serve customer needs to succeed, just as PetSmart does by offering pet parents day care and overnight stays for their canine family members. Marketing is the link between the organization and the people who buy and use its goods and services. It is the way organizations determine buyer needs and inform potential customers that their firms can meet those needs by supplying a quality product at a reasonable price. And it is the path to developing loyal, long-term customers.

Although consumers who purchase goods for their own use and enjoyment, or business purchasers seeking products to use in their firm's operation, may seem to be a large number of undifferentiated masses, marketers see distinct wants and needs for each group. To understand buyers, from manufacturers to Web surfers to shoppers in the grocery aisles, companies gather mountains of data on every aspect of consumer lifestyles and buying behaviors. Marketers use the data to understand the needs and wants of both final customers and business buyers. Satisfying customers goes a long way toward building relationships with them. It's not always easy. To establish links with the buying public, Whole Foods CEO John Mackey invites e-mails from consumers who may—or may not—be customers. After several weeks of electronic debate with an animal welfare activist over Whole Foods's practice of selling duck meat from a particular source, Mackey asked the activist to help rewrite his firm's policies on farm animal treatment. This relationship, which developed through direct communication between the CEO and a consumer, has helped Whole Foods cement its relationship with customers who have certain food-source concerns.

This chapter begins with an examination of the marketing concept and the way businesspeople develop a marketing strategy. We then turn to marketing research techniques, leading to an explanation of how businesses apply data to market segmentation and understanding customer behavior. The chapter closes with a detailed look at the important role customer relationships play in today's highly competitive business world.

What Is Marketing?

Every organization—from profit-seeking firms such as McDonald's and Drugstore.com to such not-for-profits as the Make-a-Wish Foundation and the American Cancer Society—must serve customer needs to succeed. Perhaps retail pioneer J. C. Penney best expressed this priority when he told his store managers, "Either you or your replacement will greet the customer within the first 60 seconds."

According to the American Marketing Association, **marketing** is "an organizational function and a set of processes for creating, communicating, and delivering value to customers and for managing customer relationships in ways that benefit the organization and its stakeholders."[2] In addition to selling goods and services, marketing techniques help people advocate ideas or viewpoints and educate others. The American Diabetes Association mails out questionnaires that ask, "Are you at risk for diabetes?" The documents help educate the general public about this widespread disease by listing its risk factors and common symptoms and describing the work of the association.

Department store founder Marshall Field explained marketing quite clearly when he advised one employee to "give the lady what she wants." The phrase

The best marketers give consumers what they want and anticipate their needs. NetJets offers fractional jet ownership to executives who want the luxury and flexibility of private ownership without the cost of owning their own plane.

became the company motto, and it remains a business truism today. The best marketers not only give consumers what they want but even anticipate consumers' needs before those needs surface. Ideally, they can get a jump on the competition by creating a link in consumers' minds between the new need and the fulfillment of that need by the marketers' products. Principal Financial Group, with headquarters in Iowa, markets employee retirement plans to other firms that then custom tailor those plans to retain key employees. NetJets offers fractional jet ownership to executives who want the luxury and flexibility of private ownership without the cost of owning their own plane. Samsung offers its next generation of high-definition TV with its trademarked Internet@TV. Owners can connect their televisions to their home Internet connection, then add widgets to track the weather, check eBay, view Flickr albums, and check for Twitter updates—all in real time. In addition, they can get Video-on-Demand service through Blockbuster and Amazon. "Get the best of the Web right on your TV!" their promotion says.

As these examples illustrate, marketing is more than just selling. It is a process that begins with discovering unmet customer needs and continues with researching the potential market; producing a good or service capable of satisfying the targeted customers; and promoting, pricing, and distributing that good or service. Throughout the entire marketing process, a successful organization focuses on building customer relationships.

When two or more parties benefit from trading things of value, they have entered into an **exchange process**. When you purchase a cup of coffee, the other party may be a convenience store clerk, a vending machine, or a Dunkin' Donuts server. The exchange seems simple—some money changes hands, and you receive your cup of coffee. But the exchange process is more complex than that. It could not occur if you didn't feel the need for a cup of coffee or if the convenience store or vending machine were not available. You wouldn't choose Dunkin' Donuts unless you were aware of the brand. Because of marketing, your desire for a flavored blend, decaf, or plain black coffee is identified, and the coffee manufacturer's business is successful.

marketing organizational function and set of processes for creating, communicating, and delivering value to customers and for managing customer relationships in ways that benefit the organization and its stakeholders.

exchange process activity in which two or more parties give something of value to each other to satisfy perceived needs.

Hit & Miss

Moosejaw Mountaineering Markets a Little Mobile Madness

Moosejaw Mountaineering may sound like a tongue twister. Yet, the outdoor gear and apparel retailer's marketing efforts are anything but twisted. Founder Robert Wolfe and his crew, including his brother and sister, believe that the key to a successful exchange with consumers is interactivity and creating utility—time, place, and ownership. "Moosejaw's goal is to sell the finest outdoor, surf, skate, and snowboard products in the world and have as much fun as possible while doing it," says Wolfe. "The customer experience, which we call Moosejaw Madness, is the core of our entire strategy." Some of the fun activities offered at Moosejaw's retail stores include in-store whiffle-ball games or a concert of dueling xylophones. Go online to the firm's Web site and you can enter a contest to win an invisible coffee mug.

Fun involves interactions with customers, which is the foundation of Moosejaw's marketing strategy. Recently the company launched a text-messaging campaign in which customers could sign up to receive biweekly messages from Moosejaw. It was a huge success. Instead of sending out coupons or sales alerts, Moosejaw texted games and trivia questions designed to spark consumers' interest. One text read: "Text me back with rock, paper, or scissors. I already know what I'm throwing and if you beat me, I'll add 100 Moosejaw Points to your [frequent buyer] account now." The text generated a 66-percent response and helped build a closer bond with customers.

Another wireless initiative is a bit more practical—providing customers the option to receive their order numbers and UPS tracking information via text message. This offer creates both time and place utility—quick information conveniently sent to a cell phone and a confirmation of a product order and shipment. People love it. "Twenty percent of our customers have signed up," notes Wolfe with a little surprise. "I would've expected less than 1 percent." But after launching the initiative, he realized why it was popular. Is it important to have your tracking information sent to your phone rather than waiting a couple of hours to check your e-mail? Certainly not. "But it is cool, and will you tell three friends about the service? Absolutely."

Questions for Critical Thinking

1. Describe another way that Moosejaw could use text messaging to create marketing utility.

2. Why is interactivity such a vital component to Moosejaw's marketing efforts?

Sources: Tiffany Meyers, "Innovate in a Recession," *Entrepreneur*, February 2009, p. 110; "Moosejaw Mountaineering Embarks on New Online Effort to Engage the Socially Connected Customer," *Yahoo! Finance*, September 30, 2008, http://biz.yahoo.com; "Moosejaw Spreading the Madness across Channels," *PRWeb*, September 4, 2008, http://www.prweb.com; Tom Dellner, "A Method to Their Madness," *Electronic Retailer Magazine*, January 2008, http://www.eletronicretailermag.com.

How Marketing Creates Utility

utility power of a good or service to satisfy a want or need.

Marketing affects many aspects of an organization and its dealings with customers. The ability of a good or service to satisfy the wants and needs of customers is called **utility**. A company's production function creates *form utility* by converting raw materials, component parts, and other inputs into finished goods and services. But the marketing function creates time, place, and ownership utility. *Time utility* is created by making a good or service available when customers want to purchase it. *Place utility* is created by making a product available in a location convenient for customers. *Ownership utility* refers to an orderly transfer of goods and services from the seller to the buyer. Firms may be able to create all three forms of utility. Target is the first nationwide retailer to offer bar-coded, scannable mobile coupons direct to cell phones. Guests can sign on to the program either on their personal computers or on their cell phones. Each month, they receive a text message with a link to a mobile Web site page where they will find offers for various products. They can use the mobile coupons at any Target store nationwide because Target is the first retailer to have point-of-sale scanning technology for the coupons in all of its stores. Steve Eastman, the president of Target.com, says, "At Target, we know that mobile phones are an integral part of our guests' lives, and mobile coupons are just another way we're providing convenient, on-the-go shopping solutions."[3] Retailer Moosejaw Mountaineering has also created several forms of utility for its customers through wireless technology, as described in the "Hit & Miss" feature.

Assessment Check ☑

1. What is utility?

2. Identify ways in which marketing creates utility.

Evolution of the Marketing Concept

Marketing has always been a part of business, from the earliest village traders to large 21st-century organizations producing and selling complex goods and services. Over time, however, marketing activities evolved through the four eras shown in Figure 11.1: the production, sales, and marketing eras, and now the relationship era. Note that these eras parallel some of the time periods discussed in Chapter 1.

For centuries, organizations of the *production era* stressed efficiency in producing quality products. Their philosophy could be summed up by the remark, "A good product will sell itself." Although this production orientation continued into the 20th century, it gradually gave way to the *sales era*, in which businesses assumed that consumers would buy as a result of energetic sales efforts. Organizations didn't fully recognize the importance of their customers until the *marketing era* of the 1950s, when they began to adopt a consumer orientation. This focus has intensified in recent years, leading to the emergence of the *relationship era* in the 1990s, which continues to this day. In the relationship era, companies emphasize customer satisfaction and building long-term business relationships.

Emergence of the Marketing Concept

The term **marketing concept** refers to a companywide customer orientation with the objective of achieving long-run success. The basic idea of the marketing concept is that marketplace success begins with the customer. A firm should analyze each customer's needs and then work backward to offer products that fulfill them. The emergence of the marketing concept can be explained best by the shift from a *seller's market*, one with a shortage of goods and services, to a *buyer's market*, one with an abundance of goods and services. During the

marketing concept companywide consumer orientation to promote long-run success.

FIGURE
11.1 **Four Eras in the History of Marketing**

DEGREE OF EMPHASIS

High | Low

RELATIONSHIP
"Long-term relationships lead to success."

MARKETING
"The consumer is king! Find a need and fill it."

SALES
"Creative advertising and selling will overcome consumers' resistance and convince them to buy."

PRODUCTION
"A good product will sell itself."

1900 | 1950 | 2009

1950s, the United States became a strong buyer's market, forcing companies to satisfy customers rather than just producing and selling goods and services.

Today, much competition among firms centers on the effort to satisfy customers. Apple's iPhone followed on the heels of its wildly successful iPod, with the combined features of a cell phone, widescreen iPod with touch controls, and Internet link. Like its predecessors, the 3G iPhone operates completely by touch screen, has a 3.5-inch display, contains a full Safari Web browser, and even takes pictures with a 3-megapixel camera. The more recent iPod Touch borrowed some of the iPhone's revolutionary features, and Apple then introduced the iPad, a touchscreen tablet computer and reader with WiFi or WiFi plus 3G. Some observers wonder whether the iPad will be as big a success as the iPod or the iPhone, but Apple is well known for anticipating and responding quickly to consumers' needs. "Apple clearly wants potential buyers to think of the iPad as a casual entertainment device," says one industry watcher.[4]

Assessment Check ☑

1. What is the marketing concept?

2. How is the marketing concept tied to the relationship era of marketing?

Not-for-Profit and Nontraditional Marketing

The marketing concept has traditionally been associated with products of profit-seeking organizations. Today, however, it is also being applied to not-for-profit sectors and other nontraditional areas ranging from religious organizations to political campaigns.

Not-for-Profit Marketing

Residents of every continent benefit in various ways from the approximately 20 million not-for-profit organizations currently operating around the globe. Some 1.9 million of them are located in the United States, where they employ some 12.9 million workers and benefit from volunteers representing the equivalent of 9 million full-time employees.[5] By counting the value of those equivalent volunteers, Canada leads the world in contributions to its gross domestic product by not-for-profit organizations, with the United States a close second.[6] The largest not-for-profit organization in the world is the Red Cross/Red Crescent. Other not-for-profits range from Habitat for Humanity to the Boys & Girls Clubs of America to the National Multiple Sclerosis Society. These organizations all benefit by applying many of the strategies and business concepts used by profit-seeking firms. They apply marketing tools to reach audiences, secure funding, and accomplish their overall missions. Marketing strategies are important for not-for-profit organizations because they are all competing for dollars—from individuals, foundations, and corporations—just as commercial businesses are.

Not-for-profit organizations operate in both public and private sectors. Public groups include federal, state, and local government units as well as agencies that receive tax funding. A state's department of natural resources, for instance, regulates land conservation and environmental programs; the local animal control officer enforces ordinances protecting people and animals; a city's public health board ensures safe drinking water for its citizens. The private not-for-profit sector comprises many different types of organizations, including the Houston Zoo, the United States Olympic Committee, and the American Academy of Pediatrics. Although some private not-for-profits generate surplus revenue, their primary

Sometimes, not-for-profit organizations form a partnership with a profit-seeking company to promote the firm's message or distribute its goods and services. This partnership usually benefits both organizations. The National Football League and the United Way formed the "Hometown Huddle."

goals are not earning profits. If they earn funds beyond their expenses, they invest the excess in their organizational missions.

In some cases, not-for-profit organizations form a partnership with a profit-seeking company to promote the firm's message or distribute its goods and services. This partnership usually benefits both organizations. The National Football League and the United Way joined to form one of the longest-running public-service partnerships in the United States. NFL athletes and other personalities appear in public-service advertisements and in person to promote community service and fundraising. Since 1999, the "Hometown Huddle" has been an NFL-wide day of service when team members, their families, coaches, and staff members participate in local community service activities.[7]

Celebrities are particularly visible campaigning for not-for-profit organizations—their own as well as others. The actress Reese Witherspoon is the Avon Global Ambassador and Honorary Chairperson of the Avon Foundation for Women. Witherspoon helped present a $500,000 grant to the Fund for Global Women's Leadership. The grant was intended to help the worldwide movement to end violence toward women.[8]

Nontraditional Marketing

Not-for-profit organizations often engage in one or more of five major categories of nontraditional marketing: person marketing, place marketing, event marketing, cause marketing, and organization marketing. Figure 11.2 provides examples of these types of marketing. As described in the "Going Green" feature, through each of these types of marketing,

Going Green

The Tap Project

Recently, *Esquire* magazine challenged David Droga, the founder of the Droga5 advertising firm, to prove that his creative thinking deserved the magazine's "Best and Brightest" award. After seeing a documentary about New Orleans after Hurricane Katrina, Droga started thinking about how many people don't have access to clean, safe drinking water—which most Americans take for granted. When he was served the typical free glass of tap water at a New York City restaurant, he got the inspiration for his next advertising campaign. Droga remembers thinking, "We have to make people aware of the luxury we have and help others who don't have it." He presented his idea to UNICEF, and the Tap Project was born.

Approximately 900 million people around the world—about half of them children—lack safe, accessible drinking water. UNICEF and the Tap Project hope to cut that number in half by 2015. Every day, 4,100 children under age 5 die of water-borne diseases.

During the UN's World Water Week, top restaurants in New York City asked their patrons to donate one dollar or more for a glass of tap water. Since then, the Tap Project has raised almost $1.5 million in the United States. All donations go to UNICEF's water, sanitation, and hygiene programs. One dollar allows UNICEF to provide safe drinking water to one child for 40 days. Funds raised in 2010 went primarily to Haiti, the Central African Republic, Guatemala, Togo, and Vietnam. Caryl Stein, the president and CEO of the U.S. Fund for UNICEF, noted, "In Haiti alone, less than 60 percent of people had access to safe water even before the earthquake."

Leading advertising agencies in the United States have participated in the Tap Project. Casanova Pendrill Publicidad, which aims at the Hispanic market, won the top prize in *Advertising Age's* Non-Traditional/Guerrilla Marketing category. In its "Agua Sucia" ("dirty water") campaign, the firm bottled dirty water as if it were mineral water and sold the bottles for $1 from vending machines on New York City streets. "Customers" could choose from such "flavors" as cholera, typhoid, hepatitis, and dysentery. The agency's slogan was, "You'd never drink dirty water, the rest of the world shouldn't have to, either."

In succeeding years, the Tap Project spread to other U.S. cities and advertising agencies. In a recent year, 21 agencies produced advertisements that ran in 19 cities, in addition to efforts nationwide and on the Internet. For the most recent World Water Week, the Tap Project changed its focus. More than 1,000 restaurants participated, but volunteers also hosted 250 other fund-raising events around the country. The campaign established a presence on Facebook and Twitter as well as an online radio station. However, only five cities—Chicago, Los Angeles, New York, Seattle, and Washington, DC—and eight advertising agencies were involved. Ryu Mizuno, the director of marketing at the U.S. Fund for UNICEF, said the Tap Project was "maturing as a brand" and that the fund preferred "doing a few things in a great way instead of being all over the map."

Some observers claim that such changes are typical of nontraditional marketing campaigns, especially those where ad agencies have volunteered their services. Another difference from the first years is that the Tap Project's very success has spawned other water charities, all vying for donations and volunteers. The earthquake in Haiti also had an impact. However, UNICEF planned to grow the campaign again in 2011. Mr. Mizuno said, "Agencies that participated in the past and didn't participate this year are staying in touch with us."

Questions for Critical Thinking

1. What types of nontraditional marketing does the Tap Project engage in?
2. As this feature mentions, fewer cities and advertisers participated in World Water Week. What steps would you suggest to improve participation in future years?

Sources: Tap Project Web site, http://www.tapproject.org, accessed April 14, 2010; Tap Project online radio station, http://www.tapprojectradio.org, accessed April 14, 2010; Droga5 Web site, http://www.droga5.com, accessed April 14, 2010; Karyn McCormack, "UNICEF: Tapping the Power of Water," *BusinessWeek*, http://www.businessweek.com, accessed April 14, 2010; Alessandra Bulow, "UNICEF Tap Project," *Food & Wine*, March 22, 2010, http://www.foodandwine.com; Helena Bottemiller, "Restaurants Join in Clean Water Project," *Food Safety News*, March 20, 2010, http://www.foodsafetynews.com; United States Fund for UNICEF, "2010 UNICEF Tap Project Launches to Help Provide Safe Water to Children Worldwide," March 11, 2010, http://www.unicefusa.org.

---

an organization seeks to connect with the audience that is most likely to offer time, money, or other resources. In some cases, the effort may reach the market the organization intends to serve.

person marketing use of efforts designed to attract the attention, interest, and preference of a target market toward a person.

Person Marketing Efforts designed to attract the attention, interest, and preference of a target market toward a person are called **person marketing**. Campaign managers for a political candidate conduct marketing research; identify groups of voters and financial supporters; and then design advertising campaigns, fund-raising events, and political rallies to reach them. In another example of person marketing, T-Mobile brought back its former spokeswoman, Catherine Zeta-Jones, for a new advertising campaign that was launched during an *American Idol* season finale.[9]

Many successful job seekers apply the tools of person marketing. They research the wants and needs of prospective employers, and they identify ways they can meet them. They seek employers through a variety of channels, sending messages that emphasize how they can benefit the employer.

Place Marketing As the term suggests, place marketing attempts to attract people to a particular area, such as a city, state, or nation. It may involve appealing to consumers as a tourist destination or to businesses as a desirable business location. A strategy for place marketing often includes advertising.

Place marketing may be combined with event marketing, such as the Olympics. The city of Vancouver used three mythical cartoon critters, named Quatchi, Miga, and Sumi, to promote the Olympic and Paralympic Winter Games. Merchandise featuring the mascots was available for sale to the public more than two years before the actual games took place.[10]

FIGURE 11.2 Categories of Nontraditional Marketing

Cause Marketing

American Cancer Society — "No one deserves to get cancer but everyone deserves the right to fight it."

Bowing Green State University — "Changing the world by degrees."

Place Marketing

Chicago — "Come play all day, stay all night."

Organization Marketing

Alison Krauss and Union Station

Major League Baseball World Series

Person Marketing

Event Marketing

Event Marketing Marketing or sponsoring short-term events such as athletic competitions and cultural and charitable performances is known as event marketing. Target recently sponsored the first women's junior professional surfing competition. The American Diabetes Association sponsored the "Tour de Cure," a series of fund-raising cycling events held across the United States to raise funds to support its mission to prevent and cure diabetes.[11]

Event marketing often forges partnerships between not-for-profit and profit-seeking organizations. Many businesses sponsor events such as 10K runs to raise funds for health-related charities. These occasions require a marketing effort to plan the event and attract participants and sponsors. Events may be intended to raise money or awareness, or both.

Cause Marketing Marketing that promotes awareness of, or raises money for, a cause or social issue, such as drug abuse prevention or childhood hunger is cause marketing. Cause marketing seeks to educate the public and may or may not attempt to directly raise funds. An advertisement often contains a phone number or Web site address through which people can obtain more information about the organization or issue. Then they can either donate money or take other actions of support. The international accounting firm Deloitte sponsors the United Way's Alternative Spring Break program. Instead of heading for the beach, young adults and student volunteers participated in community activities such as the continuing rebuilding of communities devastated by Hurricanes Katrina, Rita, and Ike, or conducting their own local programs.[12]

place marketing attempt to attract people to a particular area, such as a city, state, or nation.

event marketing marketing or sponsoring short-term events such as athletic competitions and cultural and charitable performances.

cause marketing marketing that promotes a cause or social issue, such as preventing child abuse, anti-littering efforts, and stop-smoking campaigns.

The sightseeing guide, an example of *place marketing,* is published by the state of Minnesota to encourage tourism.

Profit-seeking companies look for ways to contribute to their communities by joining forces with charities and causes, providing financial, marketing, and human resources. Timberland is well known for participating in the City Year program, through which young adults contract to perform a year of volunteer service in their communities. For-profit firms can also combine their goods and services with a cause. Seventh Generation, which makes household cleaning and paper products, is committed to educating consumers about how "green" products can make their homes healthier and safer.[13]

Organization Marketing The final category of nontraditional marketing, <u>organization marketing</u>, influences consumers to accept the goals of, receive the services of, or contribute in some way to an organization. The U.S. Postal Service, the American Cancer Society, and Oprah Winfrey's Angel Network are all examples of organizations that engage in marketing. They use their own Web sites, advertise in magazines, and send mail directly to consumers in their efforts to market their organizations. The Angel Network was established by Oprah Winfrey more than a decade ago in an order to "encourage people around the world to make a difference in the lives of others." The organization initiates its own charitable projects as well as supporting the projects of other not-for-profits such as Habitat for Humanity and The Boys & Girls Clubs of America.[14]

organization marketing marketing strategy that influences consumers to accept the goals of, receive the services of, or contribute in some way to an organization.

Assessment Check ✔

1. Why do not-for-profit organizations engage in marketing?

2. What are the five types of nontraditional marketing used by not-for-profit organizations?

Developing a Marketing Strategy

Decision makers in any successful organization, for-profit or not-for-profit, follow a two-step process to develop a *marketing strategy.* First, they study and analyze potential target markets and choose among them. Second, they create a marketing mix to satisfy the chosen market. Figure 11.3 shows the relationships among the target market, the marketing mix variables, and the marketing environment. Later discussions refer back to this figure as they cover each topic. This section describes the development of a marketing strategy designed to attract and build relationships with customers. Sometimes, in an effort to do this, marketers use questionable methods, as described in the "Solving an Ethical Controversy" feature.

Earlier chapters of this book introduced many of the environmental factors that affect the success or failure of a firm's business strategy, including today's rapidly changing and highly competitive world of business, a vast array of social and cultural factors, economic challenges, political and legal factors, and technological innovations. Although these external forces frequently operate outside managers' control, marketers must still consider the impact of environmental factors on their decisions.

A marketing plan is a key component of a firm's overall business plan. The marketing plan outlines its marketing strategy and includes information about the target market, sales and revenue goals, the marketing budget, and the timing for implementing the elements of the marketing mix.

Solving an Ethical Controversy

When Free Credit Reports Aren't Free

When times are tough and credit is tight, consumers are more likely to search for and monitor their credit scores. The Fair Credit Reporting Act (FCRA) requires the three major consumer reporting companies—Equifax, Experian, and TransUnion—to provide consumers a free copy of their credit report once a year. Consumers must request the report through the official Annual Credit Report Request Service by phone or mail, or online at AnnualCreditReport.com. Credit report companies claim to offer free credit reports—but many offers contain hidden charges. Also, Experian has profited because consumers confuse its FreeCreditReport.com division with the federal government's AnnualCreditReport.com, the only truly free Web site.

Should firms be allowed to use the word "free" in advertising for credit reports if the service contains hidden charges?

PRO

1. If the credit score itself is free, but related services are not, then the advertising is truthful. Ty Taylor, the president of Experian's Consumer Direct Division, says, "You get a free credit report and free score for test-driving our services."

2. Some promotional offers contain free credit scores, with a tie-in to additional services for a fee. Other industries make similar offers for a free month of phone, cable, or Internet service.

CON

1. The word "free" is a powerful enticement in advertising. Some companies provide "free" reports, then bill consumers for services they have to cancel.

2. Consumer advocates say firms exploit people's fears. Edgar Dworsky, the founder of ConsumerWorld.org and formerly on Experian's consumer advisory panel, says, "Does the average person really need to see their credit reports more than once every four months? Do you need to look at it daily? That's paranoia."

Summary

The Federal Trade Commission's Free Credit Reports Rule requires credit report Web sites to carry the following across the top of each page: "THIS NOTICE IS REQUIRED BY LAW. Read more at FTC.GOV. You have the right to a free credit report from AnnualCreditReport.com or 877-322-8228, the ONLY authorized source under federal law." Very recently, rather than including this disclosure, Experian began charging $1 for a credit report and donating the fee to charity.

Sources: Ron Lieber, "Free Credit on Credit? No Longer," *The New York Times,* April 7, 2010, http://www.nytimes.com; "FREE Annual Credit Reports," Federal Trade Commission, http://www.ftc.gov/freereports, accessed April 2, 2010; Joe Taylor, "New Laws Crack Down on Free Credit Report Marketing," *CardRatings,* March 30, 2010, http://www.cardratings.com; Michelle Singletary, "Free Credit Reports Get Easier to Find," *The Washington Post,* March 4, 2010, http://www.boston.com.

Selecting a Target Market

The expression "find a need and fill it" is perhaps the simplest explanation of the two elements of a marketing strategy. A firm's marketers find a need through careful and continuing study of the individuals and business decision makers in its potential market. A market consists of people with purchasing power, willingness to buy, and authority to make purchase decisions.

Markets can be classified by type of product. **Consumer products**—often known as business-to-consumer **(B2C)** products—are goods and services, such as GPS systems, tomato sauce, and a haircut, that are purchased by end users. **Business products**—or business-to-business **(B2B)** products—are goods and services purchased to be used, either directly or indirectly, in the production of other goods for resale. Some products can fit either classification depending on who buys them and why. A computer or credit card can be used by a business or a consumer.

An organization's **target market** is the group of potential customers toward whom it directs its marketing efforts. Customer needs and wants vary considerably, and no single organization

consumer (B2C) product good or service that is purchased by end users.

business (B2B) product good or service purchased to be used, either directly or indirectly, in the production of other goods for resale.

target market group of people toward whom an organization markets its goods, services, or ideas with a strategy designed to satisfy their specific needs and preferences.

FIGURE
11.3

Target Market and Marketing Mix within the Marketing Environment

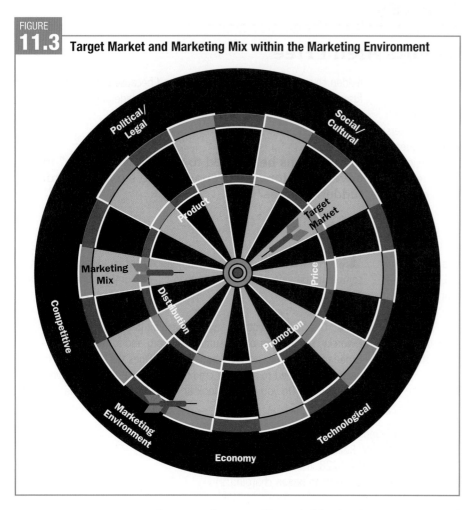

has the resources to satisfy everyone. *Popular Science* is geared toward readers who are interested in science and technology, whereas *Bon Appétit* is aimed at readers who are interested in fine food and cooking.

Decisions about marketing involve strategies for four areas of marketing activity: product, distribution, promotion, and pricing. A firm's **marketing mix** blends the four strategies to fit the needs and preferences of a specific target market. Marketing success depends not on the four individual strategies but on their unique combination.

Product strategy involves more than just designing a good or service with needed attributes. It also includes decisions about package design, brand names, trademarks, warranties, product image, new-product development, and customer service. Think about your favorite pair of jeans. Do you like them because they fit the best, or do other attributes—such as styling and overall image—also contribute to your brand preference? *Distribution strategy*, the second marketing mix variable, ensures that customers receive their purchases in the proper quantities at the right times and locations. *Promotional strategy*, another marketing mix element, effectively blends advertising, personal selling, sales promotion, and public relations to achieve its goals of informing, persuading, and influencing purchase decisions.

Pricing strategy, the final mix element, is also one of the most difficult areas of marketing decision making in setting profitable and justifiable prices for the firm's product offerings. Such actions are sometimes subject to government regulation and considerable public scrutiny. They also represent a powerful competitive weapon and frequently produce responses by the other firms in the industry, who match price changes to avoid losing customers. Think about your jeans again. Would you continue to purchase them if they were priced either much higher or much lower?

marketing mix blending of the four elements of marketing strategy—product, distribution, promotion, and pricing—to satisfy chosen customer segments.

Retail clinics are low-cost, walk-in medical facilities usually found in supermarkets, chain drugstores, and big-box stores. Patients typically see nurse practitioners or physician assistants, who can diagnose and treat minor medical conditions and prescribe some medications. The clinics are open late in the evenings and on weekends and also offer appropriate vaccinations and inexpensive sports and summer-camp physicals for children. They proved to be a popular alternative to primary care in areas where primary care physicians are scarce and because of their low cost, usually from $55 to $65 per visit. Retail clinics increased dramatically from just 200 to about 1,200 over the past few years. But after that, growth stalled, and both CVS and Walgreens closed some clinics. Some problems are the seasonality of such offerings as flu shots and the summer-camp physicals, oversaturation of the market in some areas, and difficulty in reaching potential patients who don't shop at the particular parent store. Retail clinics are evolving with the changing economic landscape, and how the operators of the clinics will solve these marketing problems remains to be seen.[15]

Developing a Marketing Mix for International Markets

Marketing a good or service in foreign markets means deciding whether to offer the same marketing mix in every market *(standardization)* or to develop a unique mix to fit each market *(adaptation)*. The advantages of standardizing the marketing mix include reliable marketing performance and low costs. This approach works best with B2B goods, such as steel, chemicals, and aircraft, which require little sensitivity to a nation's culture.

Adaptation, on the other hand, lets marketers vary their marketing mix to suit local competitive conditions, consumer preferences, and government regulations. Consumer tastes are often shaped by local cultures. Because consumer products generally tend to be more culture dependent than business products, they more often require adaptation. Subway, which already has 144 stores in China, plans to open 500 new stores in the next five years and hopes to match the Chinese presence of McDonald's in 10 years. As Subway opens stores in different regions, it plans to adapt its menu to local tastes with such offerings as Beijing roast duck sandwiches and "hot spicy Szechuan sauce." Why do these firms go out of their way to adapt to Chinese preferences? China is a market with 1.3 billion potential consumers.[16]

Marketers also try to build adaptability into the designs of standardized goods and services for international and domestic markets. *Mass customization* allows a firm to mass produce goods and services while adding unique features to individual or small groups of orders. For example, online firm Blank Label specializes in custom men's dress shirts and allows customers to choose their own fabric, style, individual features, and size. Spreadshirt, with U.S. headquarters in Boston, specializes in customized casual wear, accessories, and even personalized underwear.[17]

Assessment Check ✓

1. Distinguish between consumer products and business products.

2. What are the steps in developing a marketing strategy?

Karen Cowled/Alamy

Adaptation allows marketers to vary their marketing mix to suit local competitive conditions, consumer preferences, and government regulations. Because consumer products generally tend to be more culture dependent than business products, they more often require adaptation. Subway, which already has 144 stores in China, plans to open 500 new stores there.

Marketing Research

Marketing research involves more than just collecting data. Researchers must decide how to collect data, interpret the results, convert the data into decision-oriented information, and communicate those results to managers for use in decision making. **Marketing research** is the process of collecting and evaluating information to help marketers make effective decisions. It links business decision makers to the marketplace by providing data about potential target markets that help them design effective marketing mixes.

marketing research collecting and evaluating information to support marketing decision making.

Obtaining Marketing Research Data

Marketing researchers need both internal and external data. Firms generate *internal data* within their organizations. Financial records provide a tremendous amount of useful information, such as changes in unpaid bills; inventory levels; sales generated by different categories of customers or product lines; profitability of particular divisions; or comparisons of sales by territories, salespeople, customers, or product lines.

Researchers gather *external data* from outside sources, including previously published data. Trade associations publish reports on activities in particular industries. Advertising agencies collect information on the audiences reached by various media. National marketing research firms offer information through subscription services. Some of these professional research firms specialize in specific markets, such as teens or ethnic groups. This information helps companies make decisions about developing or modifying products. A recent report by the marketing research firm comScore on smart phone purchases indicates that Research in Motion's BlackBerry was still the best seller, with 43 percent of the market. Apple's iPhone was second, with 25 percent. In a surprising development, Palm's Pre, formerly in third place, was overtaken by Google's Android-based devices. Microsoft devices also showed a decline. Such data can give indirect but very clear indications of what consumers are looking for in a product.[18]

The largest consumer-goods manufacturer in the world, Procter & Gamble, has excelled in marketing research for a long time; it created its own marketing research department in 1923 and began conducting its research online in 2001. To help the company recover from the global recession, Bob McDonald, the company's chief executive officer, has set the goal of reaching 1 billion new customers by 2015. This expansion involves reaching customers in developing regions. As part of this strategy, he traveled undercover to 30 countries, posing as a marketing researcher.[19]

Secondary data, or previously published data, are low cost and easy to obtain. Federal, state, and local government publications are excellent data sources, and most are available online. The most frequently used government statistics include census data, which contain the population's age, gender, education level, household size and composition, occupation, employment status, and income. Even private research firms such as TRU (formerly Teenage Research Unlimited), which studies the purchasing habits of teens, provide some free information on their Web sites. This information helps firms evaluate consumers' buying behavior, anticipate possible changes in the marketplace, and identify new markets.

Even though secondary data are a quick and inexpensive resource, marketing researchers sometimes discover that this information isn't specific or current enough for their needs. If so, researchers may conclude that they must collect *primary data*—data collected firsthand through such methods as observation and surveys.

Observational studies view the actions of consumers either directly or through mechanical devices. As more retailers watch their customers via video cameras, they can solve problems such as widening a too-narrow aisle to allow shoppers easier access, but such close monitoring has also raised privacy concerns.[20] Procter & Gamble spends about $200 million on consumer observation each year, citing it as the firm's most important type of marketing research. CEO McDonald says, "If we can continue to innovate and continue to mind consumer needs and delight consumers, that ability outweighs any macroeconomic force."[21]

Simply observing customers cannot provide some types of information. A researcher might observe a customer buying a red sweater, but have no idea why the purchase was made—or for whom. When researchers need information about consumers' attitudes, opinions, and motives, they need to ask the consumers themselves. They may conduct surveys by telephone, in person, online, or in focus groups.

A *focus group* gathers 8 to 12 people in a room or over the Internet to discuss a particular topic. A focus group can generate new ideas, address consumers' needs, and even point out flaws in existing products. Pottery Barn Kids, a division of Pottery Barn, developed its Learning Toys Collection through observation, reading, and focus groups. Focus groups that included both parents and children were gathered and observed as they played with and talked about the new toys. Marketing researchers have also begun to take advantage of social media outlets such as Facebook, Twitter, and blogs as well as mobile marketing.[22]

Applying Marketing Research Data

As the accuracy of information collected by researchers increases, so does the effectiveness of resulting marketing strategies. One field of research is known as **business intelligence**, which uses various activities and technologies to gather, store, and analyze data to make better competitive decisions. Dell established its IdeaStorm Web site to gather information, criticism, compliments, and ideas for developing new computer products and improving existing ones. New users must register at the site and follow guidelines in order to post their ideas and reactions. Submitted ideas receive scores for their popularity, which helps Dell sort through material and decide which ideas to pursue. Recently, Dell added "Storm Sessions," where the company posts a topic and asks visitors to contribute their ideas. To make the discussions specific and relevant to the topic, each session is open only for a limited time. "Our commitment is to listen to your input and ideas to improve our products and services, and the way we do business," reads a welcoming note to the site. "We will do our best to keep you posted on how Dell brings customer ideas to life."[23]

business intelligence activities and technologies for gathering, storing, and analyzing data to make better competitive decisions.

Data Mining

Once a company has built a database, marketers must be able to analyze the data and use the information it provides. **Data mining**, part of the broader field of business intelligence, is the task of using computer-based technology to evaluate data in a database and identify useful trends. These trends or patterns may suggest predictive models of real-world business activities. Accurate data mining can help researchers forecast recessions and pinpoint sales prospects.

Data mining uses **data warehouses**, which are sophisticated customer databases that allow managers to combine data from several different organizational functions. Companies such as San Franciso's Rapleaf Inc. collect publicly available personal information from social-networking sites such as Facebook, Twitter, and other forums. They then sell this

data mining computer searches of customer data to detect patterns and relationships.

data warehouse customer database that allows managers to combine data from several different organizational functions.

information to entities such as airlines and credit card companies that regard those individuals as potential customers. Such information can include everything from your blogging or posting habits to your credit rating. Among the issues arising from data mining are ownership of Web user data, the targeting capabilities of the Web, government supervision—and, of course, privacy.

A few days after Google launched its social network Google Buzz, it had to make some changes to protect users' privacy. More reprogramming may be needed, pending a petition to the Federal Trade Commission and a class-action lawsuit. However, Google Buzz does give users the choice of whether to state publicly who is following them and whom they are following. Some observers feel that privacy norms are changing, with confidentiality giving way to increasing openness.[24] Turiya Media's product Leafnode mines and analyzes the behavior of online game players by tracking the number of hours they spend on which games, then creating behavioral profiles. Game publishers pay a monthly fee for the resulting data, which enable them to "proactively identify and retain their best customers, and target them with personalized recommendations."[25]

Assessment Check ✔

1. What is the difference between primary data and secondary data?

2. What is data mining?

market segmentation process of dividing a total market into several relatively homogeneous groups.

Market Segmentation

Market segmentation is the process of dividing a market into several relatively homogeneous groups. Both profit-seeking and not-for-profit organizations use segmentation to help them reach desirable target markets. Market segmentation is often based on the results of research, which attempts to identify trends among certain groups of people. For instance, one survey of online teens revealed that the number of online teenagers and young adults who blog dropped from 28 percent in one recent year to 14 or 15 percent just a few years later. Social networking seems to have taken over communications functions among these two groups, with use growing to 73 percent and 72 percent, respectively. Only 8 percent of teenagers polled use Twitter.[26] This kind of information can help marketers decide what types of products to develop and to whom they should be marketed.

Market segmentation attempts to isolate the traits that distinguish a certain group of customers from the overall market. However, segmentation doesn't automatically produce marketing success. Table 11.1 lists several criteria that marketers should consider. The effectiveness of a segmentation strategy depends on how well the market meets these criteria. Once marketers identify a market segment to target, they can create an appropriate marketing strategy.

Table
11.1 Criteria for Market Segmentation

CRITERION	EXAMPLE
A segment must be a measurable group.	Data can be collected on the dollar amount and number of purchases by college students.
A segment must be accessible for communication.	A growing number of seniors are going online, so they can be reached through Internet channels.
A segment must be large enough to offer profit potential.	In a small community, a store carrying only large-size shoes might not be profitable. Similarly, a specialty retail chain may not locate in a small market.

Knowing that the holiday season can make or break their entire business year, retailers need to predict accurately—months ahead of time—trends and customer spending patterns, especially during or after difficult economic times. The toy retailing giant Toys "R" Us identified a hot toy trend among children during one recent holiday season, so the firm kicked into high gear to stock the toy. Zhu Zhu Pets, plush mechanical hamsters, did indeed prove to be a huge hit, with parents camped out in parking lots, waiting to buy them. Gerald Storch, the company's CEO, said, "history has shown that the future rewards companies which are aggressive during economic downturns."[27]

How Market Segmentation Works

An immediate segmentation distinction involves whether the firm is offering goods and services to customers for their own use or to purchasers who will use them directly or indirectly in providing other products for resale (the so-called B2B market). Depending on whether their firms offer consumer or business products, marketers segment their target markets differently. Four common bases for segmenting consumer markets are geographical segmentation, demographic segmentation, psychographic segmentation, and product-related segmentation. By contrast, business markets can segment on three criteria: customer-based segmentation, end-use segmentation, and geographical segmentation. Figure 11.4 illustrates the segmentation methods for these two types of markets.

Segmenting Consumer Markets

Market segmentation has been practiced since people first began selling products. Tailors made some clothing items for men and others for women. Tea was imported from India for tea drinkers in England and other European countries. In addition to demographic

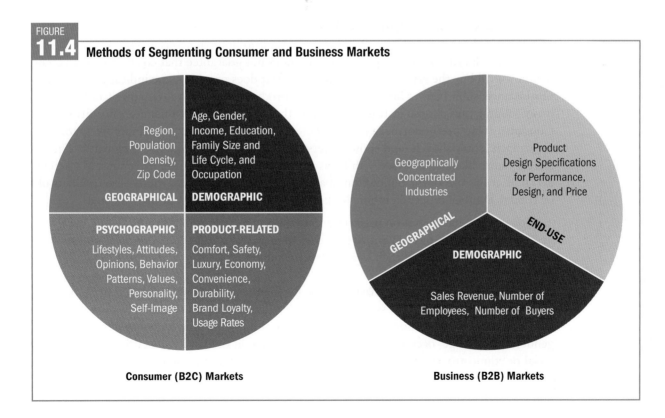

FIGURE 11.4 Methods of Segmenting Consumer and Business Markets

Consumer (B2C) Markets

GEOGRAPHICAL: Region, Population Density, Zip Code

DEMOGRAPHIC: Age, Gender, Income, Education, Family Size and Life Cycle, and Occupation

PSYCHOGRAPHIC: Lifestyles, Attitudes, Opinions, Behavior Patterns, Values, Personality, Self-Image

PRODUCT-RELATED: Comfort, Safety, Luxury, Economy, Convenience, Durability, Brand Loyalty, Usage Rates

Business (B2B) Markets

GEOGRAPHICAL: Geographically Concentrated Industries

END-USE: Product Design Specifications for Performance, Design, and Price

DEMOGRAPHIC: Sales Revenue, Number of Employees, Number of Buyers

A kids catalog, such as the one shown on the top of this pile, with this image on the cover would illustrate demographic segmentation by stage of the family life cycle.

and geographical segmentation, today's marketers also define customer groups based on psychographic—lifestyle and values—criteria as well as product-related distinctions.

Geographical Segmentation

geographical segmentation dividing an overall market into homogeneous groups on the basis of their locations.

Geographical Segmentation The oldest segmentation method is **geographical segmentation**—dividing a market into homogeneous groups on the basis of their locations. Geographical location does not guarantee that consumers in a certain region will all buy the same kinds of products, but it does provide some indication of needs. For instance, suburbanites buy more lawn-care products than central-city dwellers. However, many suburbanites choose instead to purchase the services of a lawn maintenance firm. Consumers who live in northern states, where winter is more severe, are more likely to buy ice scrapers, snow shovels, and snowblowers than those who live in warmer climates. They are also more likely to contract with firms who remove the snow from driveways. Marketers also look at the size of the population of an area, as well as who lives there—are residents old or young? Do they reflect an ethnic background? What is the level of their income?

Job growth and migration patterns are important considerations as well. Some businesses combine areas or even entire countries that share similar population and product-use patterns instead of treating each as an independent segment.

demographic segmentation dividing markets on the basis of various demographic or socioeconomic characteristics such as gender, age, income, occupation, household size, stage in family life cycle, education, or ethnic group.

Demographic Segmentation By far the most common method of market segmentation, **demographic segmentation** distinguishes markets on the basis of various demographic or socioeconomic characteristics. Common demographic measures include gender, income, age, occupation, household size, stage in the family life cycle, education, and racial or ethnic group. The U.S. Census Bureau is one of the best sources of demographic information for the domestic market. Figure 11.5 lists some of the measures used in demographic segmentation.

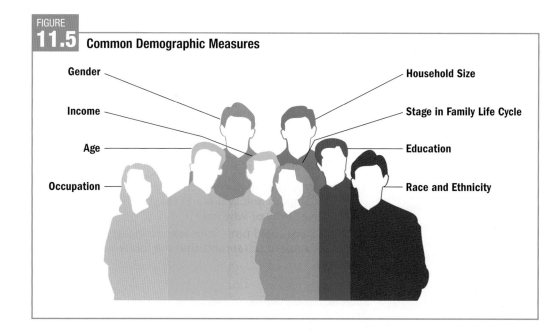

FIGURE
11.5 **Common Demographic Measures**

Gender

Income

Age

Occupation

Household Size

Stage in Family Life Cycle

Education

Race and Ethnicity

Police departments around the United States constitute a highly specialized occupational demographic group. Popular for its durability, the Ford Crown Victoria has long held 75 percent of the patrol-car market share. Ford plans to phase out the "Crown Vic," replacing it with the Police Interceptor, modeled on the Taurus sedan but modified for the extreme circumstances of police work. The Interceptor's fuel efficiency is 25 percent better than the Crown Vic's. Its 365-horsepower engine outguns the Crown Vic's by 115 horsepower. Ford's police advisory board helped develop the Interceptor, but it may face competition from General Motors, Chrysler, and Carbon Motors (based in Indiana), which produce or are planning police vehicles of their own.[28]

Gender used to be a simple way to define markets for certain products—jewelry and skin care products for women; tools and motorcycles for men. Much of that has changed— dramatically. Men now buy jewelry and skin care products, and women buy tools and motorcycles. But marketers have also found that even though these shifts have blurred the lines between products, there are still differences in the *way* that women and men shop. These differences may go as far back as humanity's earliest days, when males generally hunted for food and females generally gathered it. One study revealed that many male shoppers behave similarly to early hunters, who once they found a prey animal, tracked it, killed it, and brought it back home as fast as possible. Many female shoppers behave more like early gatherers, who spent time carefully inspecting a variety of plants, choosing only those that were ripe.[29]

Another shift involves purchasing power. Women now control an estimated 85 percent of the $7 trillion spent each year on personal consumption items.[30] One study predicts that women will soon control 60 percent of all wealth in the United States, in part because they live longer than men.[31]

Age is perhaps the most volatile factor in demographic segmentation in the United States, with our rapidly aging population. Of the 308-plus million people who live in the United States, more than 97 million will be age 55 or older by the year 2020.[32] Based on these statistics, marketers for travel and leisure products, as well as retirement and business investments, are working hard to attract the attention of this age group, the aging Baby Boomers—those born between 1946 and 1964. Active-adult housing communities are one

Pollo Campero and Wal-Mart Cater to Hispanic Tastes

Guatemala-based Pollo Campero, which means country chicken in Spanish, was founded by the Gutierrez family 30 years ago. Its food began to cross the border when passengers traveling to the United States brought the takeout chicken aboard their flights. The firm opened its first U.S. restaurant in 2002, which was an immediate hit. Known mostly for its fried chicken and authentic side dishes such as yucca fries and sweet plantains, Pollo Campero is a family friendly restaurant where diners can eat in or take out.

Wal-Mart serves a large segment of Hispanic customers, so the pairing between the retail giant and Pollo Campero seems natural. Wal-Mart is installing about 20 Pollo Campero restaurants in its stores and intends to increase the number over time. Pollo Campero remains a small portion of Wal-Mart's overall restaurant offerings—currently about 1,000 McDonald's and 1,400 Subway sandwich outlets operate in Wal-Mart stores. But marketers at both Pollo Campero and Wal-Mart are confident the partnership will grow.

Because Wal-Mart's total customer base is diverse, Pollo Campero isn't limiting its offerings to traditional Latin cuisine. The restaurant is expanding its menu to other products. The new offerings include such items as bone-in grilled chicken seasoned with a blend of lime and orange juice, red bell peppers, and herbs. Other choices include grilled chicken Caesar salads and grilled chicken wraps. However, Pollo's famous fried chicken remains the most popular.

Questions for Critical Thinking

1. What type(s) of segmentation strategy is being used by Pollo Campero and Wal-Mart? Do you think it will be effective? Why or why not?
2. What steps could both firms take to increase traffic in the Pollo Campero restaurants that are located in Wal-Mart stores?

Sources: Company Web site, http://www.pollocampero.com, accessed March 11, 2009; Amanda Jones Hoyle, "Guatemalan Eatery Pollo Campero Makes Raleigh a Regional HQ," May 30, 2008, http://triangle.bizjournals.com; "Pollo Campero Franchise Expanding to Wal-Mart," New York Daily News, May 12, 2008, http://www.nydailynews.com; "Pollo Campero Beats Competition to Market with Choice of Grilled and Fried Bone-In Chicken," company press release, March 14, 2008.

---

result of these efforts. Some developers built communities with a resort-style atmosphere in desirable locations such as Colorado ski country or the outskirts of a large city such as Chicago or San Francisco. However, because of the recession, many such communities have actually seen their populations decrease. According to Mark Mather, associate vice president of the Population Reference Bureau, "Baby boomers helped fuel housing and population growth in retirement areas earlier in the decade, and now they are playing an important role in the decline."[33]

Teens are another rapidly growing market. The entire scope of Generation Y—those born between 1976 and 1997—encompasses about 113 million young Americans, or a little more than one-third of the total population. Often called the Millennials, these consumers are tech-savvy shoppers who influence not only their own purchases but also those of their families and friends. They are educated consumers who comparison shop and usually avoid impulse purchases, partly because of the recession and partly because they are spending their own money. According to a Nielsen survey, compared with older generations, such as the Greatest Generation (those who lived through World War II) and the Baby Boomers, Generation Y consumers shop less often but buy more when they do, preferring megastores and big box-retailers.[34]

Statistics can be helpful, but they don't tell the whole story. Marketers must also learn where people live, how old they are, what language or languages they speak, and how much income they have in order to serve them well. Sometimes, marketers must do intensive research in order to reach a particular age or gender group, or both, as described in the "Hit & Miss" feature. Finally, they must learn cultural tastes and preferences.

Above all, companies must avoid stereotyping if they are going to market successfully to a diverse group of consumers. One way to do this is to break a large group into smaller segments. For instance, the Hispanic market is made up of many smaller segments, based on country of origin, language, lifestyle, and cultural values. In an attempt to target a younger Hispanic audience, three television networks have begun to offer bilingual, Spanish, and English-language programming with Hispanic themes. Because many Hispanic American teens and young adults are bilingual, the networks are trying to capture their attention while their parents and grandparents continue to watch Spanish-only programming. The mun2 (pronounced "moon-dos," for Telemundo 2) network targets young, bicultural Hispanics between 18 and 34. It recently launched a half-hour show, *The mun2 Look*, which explores the influence of American Hispanics on today's fashions. Gloria Medel, the executive producer of the network says that "mun2 understands that the young contemporary U.S. Latino experience is about standing out and embracing a personal style. 'The mun2 Look' celebrates our viewers' uniquely American fashion and reflects the cultural creativity unique to the U.S. Latino lifestyle."[35]

PR NewsFoto/©AP Wide World Photos

This television ad combined an English caption with a Spanish voiceover to appeal to both English- and Spanish-speaking viewers. Such advertisements recognize the purchasing power of Hispanics, the fastest growing demographic group in the United States.

Entrepreneurs who are members of minority groups may start their own businesses out of frustration at not being able to find food, clothing, entertainment, or other goods and services that fit their tastes and needs. In fact, 12.5 percent of all businesses in the United States are owned by immigrants. Mexicans are the largest group, with 2.22 percent of immigrant-owned businesses. Motivated by the American dream that hard work will bring success and the good life, extended families often work in these businesses, which also support their ethnic communities. This localization makes them particularly vulnerable during hard times, but many immigrant entrepreneurs remain optimistic. Christos Koskiniotis and his mother emigrated from Greece during the 1970s and run a dry cleaning business in Chicago. He says, "For the long term, this is the best place to be. You're going to hit rough spots no matter where you're at. . . . I don't think the American dream is ever going to die. To think that would be like giving up on hope."[36]

Psychographic Segmentation Lifestyle is the sum of a person's needs, preferences, motives, attitudes, social habits, and cultural background. In recent years, marketing researchers have tried to formulate lifestyle portraits of consumers. This effort has led to another strategy for segmenting target markets, **psychographic segmentation**, which divides consumer markets into groups with similar psychological characteristics, values, and lifestyles.

Psychographic studies have evaluated motivations for purchases of hundreds of goods and services, ranging from soft drinks to healthcare services. Using the resulting data, firms tailor their marketing strategies to carefully chosen market segments. A frequently used

psychographic segmentation dividing consumer markets into groups with similar attitudes, values, and lifestyles.

method of developing psychographic profiles involves the use of *AIO statements*—people's verbal descriptions of various attitudes, interests, and opinions. Researchers survey a sample of consumers, asking them whether they agree or disagree with each statement. The answers are then tabulated and analyzed for use in identifying various lifestyle categories.

Another way to get current information from consumers about their lifestyles is to create *blogs* to which consumers may respond. Companies including Stonyfield Farm, Verizon, and Microsoft have hired bloggers to run online Web journals as a way to connect with and receive information from consumers. Other firms encourage employees at all levels to use blogs to communicate with consumers. General Motors has several blogs at its GMblogs.com site, each tailored to a specific brand or consumer interest. The FastLane blog discusses GM cars and trucks, inviting consumers to offer their thoughts and ideas. Chevrolet Voltage is aimed at fans of the Volt and other electric vehicles. The Lab is where GM's advanced design team talks about its work and invites feedback from community members.[37]

Although demographic classifications such as age, gender, and income are relatively easy to identify and measure, researchers also need to define psychographic categories. Often marketing research firms conduct extensive studies of consumers and then share their psychographic data with clients. In addition, businesses look to studies done by sociologists and psychologists to help them understand their customers. For instance, while children may fall into one age group and their parents in another, they also live certain lifestyles together. Recent marketing research reveals that today's parents are willing and able to spend more on goods and services for their children than parents were a generation or two ago. Spending on toys and videogames for children topped $41 billion for a recent year in the United States.[38] These are just a few trends identified by the researchers, but they provide valuable information to firms that may be considering developing games, designing the interiors of family vehicles, or implementing new wireless plans.

Product-Related Segmentation Using **product-related segmentation**, sellers can divide a consumer market into groups based on buyers' relationships to the good or service. The three most popular approaches to product-related segmentation are based on benefits sought, usage rates, and brand loyalty levels.

Segmenting by *benefits sought* focuses on the attributes that people seek in a good or service and the benefits they expect to receive from it. As more firms shift toward consumer demand for products that are eco-friendly, marketers find ways to emphasize the benefits of these products. Home goods retailer Crate & Barrel has begun to offer tables and chairs made of mango wood, which is harvested only after the trees' fruit-bearing capabilities have passed. Consumers can also select a sofa whose cushions are made of recycled fibers that are filled with a natural, soy-based foam. According to the company's Web site, "While our collection has featured renewable woods and sustainable materials for a number of years, we are now introducing important initiatives that will help make our homes more thoughtful environments."[39]

Consumer markets can also be segmented according to the amounts of a product that people buy and use. Segmentation by *product usage rate* usually defines such categories as heavy users, medium users, and light users. The 80/20 principle states that roughly 80 percent of a product's revenues come from only 20 percent of its buyers. Companies can now pinpoint which of their customers are the heaviest users—and even the most profitable customers—and direct their heaviest marketing efforts to those customers.

The third technique for product-related segmentation divides customers by *brand loyalty*—the degree to which consumers recognize, prefer, and insist on a particular brand.

product-related segmentation dividing consumer markets into groups based on benefits sought by buyers, usage rates, and loyalty levels.

Marketers define groups of consumers with similar degrees of brand loyalty. They then attempt to tie loyal customers to a good or service by giving away premiums, which can be anything from a logo-emblazoned T-shirt to a pair of free tickets to a concert or sports event.

Segmenting Business Markets

In many ways, the segmentation process for business markets resembles that for consumer markets. However, some specific methods differ. Business markets can be divided through geographical segmentation; demographic, or customer-based, segmentation; and end-use segmentation.

Geographical segmentation methods for business markets resemble those for consumer markets. Many B2B marketers target geographically concentrated industries, such as aircraft manufacturing, automobiles, and oil field equipment. Especially on an international scale, customer needs, languages, and other variables may require differences in the marketing mix from one location to another.

Demographic, or *customer-based, segmentation* begins with a good or service design intended to suit a specific organizational market. Sodexho Marriott Services is the largest provider of food services in North America. Its customers include healthcare institutions, business and government offices, schools, and colleges and universities. Within these broad business segments, Sodexho identifies more specific segments, which might include colleges in the South or universities with culturally diverse populations—and differing food preferences or dining styles. Sodexho uses data obtained from surveys that cover students' lifestyles, attitudes, preferences for consumer products in general, services, and media categories. In addition, it uses targeted surveys that identify preferences for restaurant brands or certain foods, meal habits, amount of spending, and the like. Marketers evaluate the data, which sometime reveal surprising trends. At one university in the rural Northeast, students indicated that they liked foods with an international flavor. So Sodexho adapted its offerings accordingly.[40]

To simplify the process of focusing on a particular type of business customer, the federal government has developed a system for subdividing the business marketplace into detailed segments. The six-digit *North American Industry Classification System (NAICS)* provides a common classification system used by the member nations of NAFTA (the United States, Canada, and Mexico). It divides industries into broad categories such as agriculture, forestry, and fishing; manufacturing; transportation; and retail and wholesale trade. Each major category is further subdivided into smaller segments—such as gas stations with convenience food and warehouse clubs—for more detailed information and to facilitate comparison among the member-nations.

Another way to group firms by their demographics is to segment them by size based on their sales revenues or numbers of employees. Some firms collect data from visitors to its Web site and use the data to segment customers by size. Modern information processing also enables companies to segment business markets based on how much they buy, not just how big they are.

End-use segmentation focuses on the precise way a B2B purchaser will use a product. Resembling benefits-sought segmentation for consumer markets, this method helps small and mid-size companies target specific end-user markets rather than competing directly with large firms for wider customer groups. A company might also design a marketing mix based on certain criteria for making a purchase.

end-use segmentation marketing strategy that focuses on the precise way a B2B purchaser will use a product.

Assessment Check ☑

1. What is the most common form of segmentation for consumer markets?

2. What are the three approaches to product-related segmentation?

3. What is end-use segmentation in the B2B market?

Consumer Behavior

A fundamental marketing task is to find out why people buy one product and not another. The answer requires an understanding of consumer behavior, the actions of ultimate consumers directly involved in obtaining, consuming, and disposing of products and the decision processes that precede and follow these actions.

Determinants of Consumer Behavior

By studying people's purchasing behavior, businesses can identify consumers' attitudes toward and uses of their products. This information also helps marketers reach their targeted customers. Both personal and interpersonal factors influence the way buyers behave. Personal influences on **consumer behavior** include individual needs and motives, perceptions, attitudes, learned experiences, and self-concept. For instance, today people are constantly looking for ways to save time, so firms do everything they can to provide goods and services designed for convenience. However, when it comes to products such as dinner foods, consumers want convenience, but they also want to enjoy the flavor of a home-cooked meal and spend quality time with their families. So companies such as Stouffer's offer frozen lasagna or manicotti in family sizes, and supermarkets have entire sections devoted to freshly prepared take-out meals that range from roast turkey to filet mignon.

McDonald's is betting that consumers who drink premium coffee beverages also like to buy them at bargain prices. In many U.S. locations, McDonald's has placed McCafé coffee bars—serving cappuccinos, lattes, and mochas—near the cash register. Almost 70 percent of McDonald's stores now serve these beverages, putting the company in direct competition with Starbucks.[41]

The interpersonal determinants of consumer behavior include cultural, social, and family influences. In the area of convenience foods, cultural, social, and family influences come into play as much as an individual's need to save time. Understanding that many consumers value the time they spend with their families and want to care for them by providing good nutrition, marketers often emphasize these values in advertisements for convenience food products.

Sometimes external events influence consumer behavior. One study suggests that as a result of the recession, consumers may have permanently altered their buying and spending behavior. The survey found that 72 percent of consumers said that they had significantly or somewhat changed their shopping habits; only 7 percent said they had made no change. Manufacturers and retailers—and especially small businesses—will need to create new marketing strategies in response to these challenges.[42]

Determinants of Business Buying Behavior

Because a number of people can influence purchases of B2B products, business buyers face a variety of organizational influences in addition to their own preferences. A design engineer may help set the specifications that potential vendors must satisfy. A procurement manager may invite selected companies to bid on a purchase. A production supervisor may evaluate the operational aspects of the proposals that the firm receives, and the vice president of manufacturing may head a committee making the final decision.

consumer behavior actions of ultimate consumers directly involved in obtaining, consuming, and disposing of products and the decision processes that precede and follow these actions.

Steps in the Consumer Behavior Process

Consumer decision making follows the sequential process outlined in Figure 11.6, with interpersonal and personal influences affecting every step. The process begins when the consumer recognizes a problem or opportunity. If someone needs a new pair of shoes, that need becomes a problem to solve. If you receive a promotion at work and a 20 percent salary increase, that change may also become a purchase opportunity.

To solve the problem or take advantage of the opportunity, the consumer seeks information about his or her intended purchase and evaluates alternatives, such as available brands. The goal is to find the best response to the problem or opportunity.

Eventually, the consumer reaches a decision and completes the transaction. Later, he or she evaluates the experience by making a postpurchase evaluation. Feelings about the experience serve as feedback that will influence future purchase decisions. The various steps in the sequence are affected by both interpersonal and personal factors.

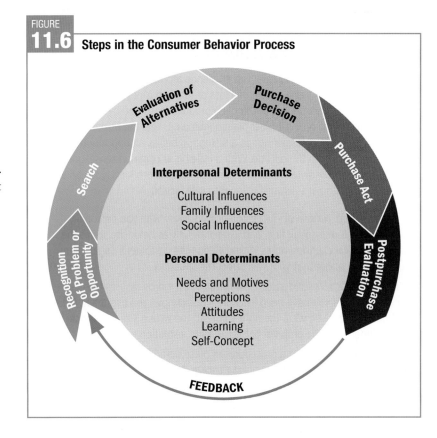

FIGURE 11.6 Steps in the Consumer Behavior Process

Evaluation of Alternatives

Purchase Decision

Search

Purchase Act

Interpersonal Determinants

Cultural Influences
Family Influences
Social Influences

Recognition of Problem or Opportunity

Postpurchase Evaluation

Personal Determinants

Needs and Motives
Perceptions
Attitudes
Learning
Self-Concept

FEEDBACK

Relationship Marketing

The past decade has brought rapid change to most industries, as customers have become better-informed and more-demanding purchasers through closely comparing competing goods and services. They expect, even demand, new benefits from the companies that supply them, making it harder for firms to gain a competitive advantage based on product features alone.

In today's hypercompetitive era, businesses need to find new ways of relating to customers if they hope to maintain long-term success. Businesses are developing strategies and tactics that draw them into tighter connections with their customers, suppliers, and even employees. As a result, many firms are turning their attention to the issues of relationship marketing. **Relationship marketing** goes beyond an effort toward making the sale. Instead, it develops and maintains long-term, cost-effective exchange relationships with partners. These partners include individual customers, suppliers, and employees. As its ultimate goal, relationship marketing seeks to achieve customer satisfaction.

Managing relationships instead of simply completing transactions often leads to creative partnerships. However, customers enter into relationships with firms only if they are assured that the relationship will somehow benefit them. As the intensity of commitment increases, so does the likelihood of a business continuing a long-term relationship with its customers.

Assessment Check ☑

1. Define *consumer behavior*.

2. What are some determinants of consumer behavior?

relationship marketing developing and maintaining long-term, cost-effective exchange relationships with partners.

Calming the Angry Customer

In any business, an angry customer is a challenge representing not only an immediate problem but also a potential loss of future business. The customer may be upset over poor service or a broken product, frustrated by lack of attention from the company, or just plain demanding. You, the businessperson, should view this customer not as a disruption but as an opportunity to see your company from the outside. With a little bit of common sense, good personal skills, and knowledge of your company and its products, you can very likely turn the customer's dissatisfaction into satisfaction.

- *Remain calm and professional.* The customer isn't angry with you personally. Let the customer speak first, and listen carefully as he or she states the problem. Make written notes. Acknowledge the customer's anger, then assure him or her that you will correct the situation.

- *Repeat the customer's stated problem.* Using your own words assures the customer that you have been listening. For example, you might say, "The shoes you received were the right color but the wrong size." Make sure you understand the problem before offering a solution.

- *Focus on the solution.* Having procedures in place beforehand can help you resolve a problem quickly. If you can't solve the problem yourself, immediately refer it to someone who can. Fast action will let the customer know that you are on his or her side.

- *Thank the customer for his or her patience.* By bringing the problem to your attention, the customer is actually giving you an opportunity to improve service to all your clients.

- *Follow up.* If appropriate, send an e-mail or make a phone call to make sure the correct pair of shoes arrived. Your professionalism will strengthen the customer's relationship with your firm—and positive word of mouth may even bring you new customers.

Sources: Lynne McClure, "Handling Angry Customers," Impact Publications, http://impactpublications.com, accessed April 4, 2010; Katy Tynan, "Conflict Management Part 2—Calming an Irate Customer," *Ezinearticles.com,* http://ezinearticles.com, accessed April 4, 2010; "How to Calm an Angry Customer," *BusinessKnowledgeSource.com,* http://www.businessknowledgesource.com, accessed April 4, 2010.

Businesses are building relationships by partnering with customers, suppliers, and other businesses. Timberland, maker of footwear and clothing, creates many partnerships that foster long-term relationships. The firm partners with not-for-profit organizations such as CARE, City Year, and Clean Air–Cool Planet to complete service projects for communities and the environment. Through its Serv-a-Palooza, hundreds of Timberland employees engage in volunteer tasks in their communities. Those opportunities even extend to customers who have expressed an interest in participating in programs in their own regions. If you want to volunteer for a food drive or to help restore a marsh, just log on to the Timberland Web site to see what's available. All of these activities help build relationships with customers, communities, and other organizations.[43]

Benefits of Relationship Marketing

Relationship marketing helps all parties involved. In addition to providing mutual protection against competitors, businesses that forge solid links with vendors and customers are often rewarded with lower costs and higher profits than they would generate on their own. Long-term agreements with a few high-quality suppliers frequently reduce a firm's production costs. Unlike one-time sales, these ongoing relationships encourage suppliers to offer customers preferential treatment, quickly adjusting shipments to accommodate changes in orders and correcting any quality problems that might arise.

Good relationships with customers can be vital strategic weapons for a firm. By identifying current purchasers and maintaining positive relationships with them, organizations can efficiently target their best customers. Studying current customers' buying habits and preferences can help marketers identify potential new customers and establish ongoing contact with them. Attracting a new customer can cost five times as much as keeping an existing one. Not only do marketing costs go down, but long-term customers usually buy more, require less service, refer other customers, and provide valuable feedback. Together, these elements contribute to a higher **lifetime value of a customer**—the revenues and intangible benefits (referrals and customer feedback) from the customer over the life of the relationship, minus the amount the company must spend to acquire and serve that customer. Keeping that customer may occasionally require some extra effort, especially if the customer has become upset or dissatisfied with a good or service. But good marketers can overcome this particular challenge, as described in the "Business Etiquette" feature.

Businesses also benefit from strong relationships with other companies. Purchasers who repeatedly buy from one business may find that they save time and gain service quality as the business learns their specific needs. Some relationship-oriented companies also customize items based on customer preferences. Because many businesses reward loyal customers with discounts or bonuses, some buyers may even find that they save money by developing long-term relationships. Alliances with other firms to serve the same customers also can be rewarding. The partners combine their capabilities and resources to accomplish goals that they could not reach on their own. In addition, alliances with other firms may help businesses develop the skills and experience they need to successfully enter new markets or improve service to current customers.

Tools for Nurturing Customer Relationships

Although relationship marketing has important benefits for both customers and businesses, most relationship-oriented businesses quickly discover that some customers generate more profitable business than others. If 20 percent of a firm's customers account for 80 percent of its sales and profits—the 80/20 principle mentioned earlier in the chapter—a customer in that category undoubtedly has a higher lifetime value than a customer who buys only once or twice or who makes small purchases.

While businesses shouldn't ignore any customer, they need to allocate their marketing resources wisely. A firm may choose to customize goods or services for high-value customers while working to increase repeat sales of stock products to less-valuable customers. Differentiating between these two groups also helps marketers focus on each in an effort to increase their commitment.

Frequency Marketing and Affinity Marketing Programs Popular techniques through which firms try to build and protect customer relationships include frequent-buyer or -user programs. These so-called **frequency marketing** programs reward purchasers with cash, rebates, merchandise, or other premiums. Frequency programs have grown more sophisticated over the years. They offer more personalization and customization than in the past. Airlines, hotel groups, restaurants, and many retailers including supermarkets offer frequency programs. Customers who join the Marriott Rewards program have the option to spend their earned points at nearly 3,000 hotels, resorts, spas, and golf locations in 67 countries and territories worldwide.[44]

Affinity programs are another tool for building emotional links with customers. An affinity program is a marketing effort sponsored by an organization that solicits involvement by individuals who share common interests and activities. Affinity programs are common in the credit card industry. For instance, a person can sign up for a credit card emblazoned with

lifetime value of a customer revenues and intangible benefits (referrals and customer feedback) from a customer over the life of the relationship, minus the amount the company must spend to acquire and serve that customer.

frequency marketing marketing initiative that rewards frequent purchases with cash, rebates, merchandise, or other premiums.

affinity program marketing effort sponsored by an organization that solicits involvement by individuals who share common interests and activities.

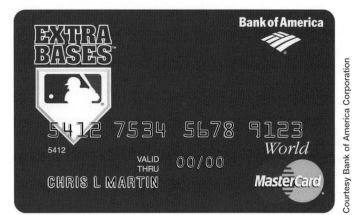

Affinity programs are another tool for building emotional links with customers and common in the credit card industry. For instance, Bank of America offers credit cards featuring baseball-themed logos, like the one pictured here, as well as the logos of all the Major League Baseball teams.

the logo of a favorite charity, a sports or entertainment celebrity, or a photograph of his or her college. Bank of America offers credit cards featuring the logos of all the Major League Baseball teams.

Many businesses also use comarketing and cobranding. In a **comarketing** deal, two businesses jointly market each other's products. When two or more businesses link their names to a single product, **cobranding** occurs. When two seemingly unlikely businesses team up, the marketing sparks fly—and two very different groups of consumers may come together to buy the same product. Nike and iPod have marketed the Nike + iPod Sport kit, which allows a runner to insert a special sensor into a built-in pocket in a Nike+ shoe, which synchronizes the runner's activity with workout data and music that plays through the iPod. Enthusiasts can also purchase specially designed Nike workout apparel that has pockets designed to hold an iPod nano itself.[45]

comarketing cooperative arrangement in which two businesses jointly market each other's products.

cobranding cooperative arrangement in which two or more businesses team up to closely link their names on a single product.

One-on-One Marketing The ability to customize products and rapidly deliver goods and services has become increasingly dependent on technology such as computer-aided design and manufacturing (CAD/CAM). The Internet offers a way for businesses to connect with customers in a direct and intimate manner. Companies can take orders for customized products, gather data about buyers, and predict what items a customer might want in the future. Computer databases provide strong support for effective relationship marketing. Marketers can maintain databases on customer tastes, price-range preferences, and lifestyles, and they can quickly obtain names and other information about promising prospects. Amazon.com greets each online customer with a list of suggested books he or she might like to purchase. Many online retailers send their customers e-mails about upcoming sales, new products, and special events.

Assessment Check ✓

1. What is the lifetime value of a customer?
2. Discuss the increasing importance of one-on-one marketing efforts.

Small and large companies often rely on *customer relationship management (CRM)* software technology that helps them gather, sort, and interpret data about customers. Software firms develop this software in order to help businesses build and manage their relationships with customers. QueueBuster is one such product. The software offers callers the choice of receiving an automated return call instead of waiting on hold for the next available representative. After implementing the software, travel agency STA reported that its customer satisfaction ratings had improved to 98 percent. This simple solution to customers' frustration probably not only helped build customer loyalty but also helped save STA from lost business as well.[46]

What's Ahead

The next two chapters examine each of the four elements of the marketing mix that marketers use to satisfy their selected target markets. Chapter 12 focuses on products and their distribution through various channels to different outlets. Chapter 13 covers promotion and the various methods marketers use to communicate with their target customers, along with strategies for setting prices for different products.

Summary of Learning Goals

1 Summarize the ways in which marketing creates utility.

Utility is the ability of a good or service to satisfy the wants and needs of customers. The production function creates form utility by converting inputs to finished goods and services. Marketing creates time, place, and ownership utility by making the product available when and where consumers want to buy and by arranging for orderly transfers of ownership.

Assessment Check Answers ✓

1.1 What is utility? Utility is the ability of a good or service to satisfy the wants and needs of customers.

1.2 Identify ways in which marketing creates utility. Marketing creates time utility by making a good or service available when customers want to purchase it, place utility by making the product available in a convenient location, and ownership utility by transferring the product from the buyer to the seller.

2 Discuss the marketing concept.

The marketing concept refers to a companywide customer orientation with the objective of achieving long-run success. This concept is essential in today's marketplace, which is primarily a buyer's market, meaning buyers can choose from an abundance of goods and services. Marketing now centers on the satisfaction of customers and building long-term relationships with those customers.

Assessment Check Answers ✓

2.1 What is the marketing concept? The marketing concept is a companywide customer orientation with the objective of achieving long-run success. According to the marketing concept, success begins with the customer.

2.2 How is the marketing concept tied to the relationship era of marketing? Most marketing now centers on the satisfaction of customers and building long-term relationships with them, rather than simply producing and selling goods and services.

3 Describe not-for-profit marketing, and identify the five major categories of nontraditional marketing.

Not-for-profit organizations must engage in marketing just as for-profit firms do. Not-for-profit organizations operate in both the public and private sectors, and use marketing to obtain volunteers and donations, make people aware of their existence, achieve certain goals for society, and so on. Not-for-profit organizations may engage in several types of nontraditional marketing—person, place, event, cause, or organization marketing. They may rely on one type or a combination.

Assessment Check Answers ✓

3.1 Why do not-for-profit organizations engage in marketing? Not-for-profit organizations use marketing to attract volunteers and donors, communicate their message, and achieve their societal goals.

3.2 What are the five types of nontraditional marketing used by not-for-profit organizations? The five types of nontraditional marketing are person, place, event, cause, and organization marketing.

4 Outline the basic steps in developing a marketing strategy.

All organizations develop marketing strategies to reach customers. This process involves analyzing the overall market, selecting a target market, and developing a marketing mix that blends elements related to product, distribution, promotion, and pricing decisions.

Assessment Check Answers ✓

4.1 Distinguish between consumer products and business products. Business products are goods and services purchased to be used, either directly or indirectly, in the production of other goods for resale. Consumer products are purchased by end users.

4.2 What are the steps in developing a marketing strategy? The steps in developing a marketing strategy are to analyze the overall market, select a target market, and develop a marketing mix.

5 Describe the marketing research function.

Marketing research is the information-gathering function that links marketers to the marketplace. It provides valuable information about potential target markets. Firms may generate internal data or gather external data. They may use secondary data or conduct research to obtain primary data. Data mining, which involves computer searches through customer data to detect patterns or relationships, is one helpful tool in forecasting various trends such as sales revenues and consumer behavior.

Assessment Check Answers ✓

5.1 What is the difference between primary data and secondary data? Secondary data are previously published facts that are inexpensive to retrieve and easy to obtain. Primary data are collected firsthand through observation or surveys.

5.2 What is data mining? Data mining involves computer searches through customer data in order to evaluate the data and identify useful trends.

6 Identify and explain each of the methods available for segmenting consumer and business markets.

Consumer markets can be divided according to four criteria: geographical factors; demographic characteristics, such as age and family size; psychographic variables, which involve behavioral and lifestyle profiles; and product-related variables, such as the benefits consumers seek when buying a product or the degree of brand loyalty they feel toward it. Business markets are segmented according to three criteria: geographical characteristics, customer-based specifications for products, and end-user applications.

Assessment Check Answers ✔

6.1 What is the most common form of segmentation for consumer markets? Demographics is the most commonly used consumer market segmentation method.

6.2 What are the three approaches to product-related segmentation? The three approaches to product-related segmentation are by benefits sought, product usage rate, and brand loyalty.

6.3 What is end-use segmentation in the B2B market? End-use segmentation focuses on the precise way a B2B purchaser will use a product.

7 Outline the determinants of consumer behavior.

Consumer behavior refers to the actions of ultimate consumers with direct effects on obtaining, consuming, and disposing of products, as well as the decision processes that precede and follow these actions. Personal influences on consumer behavior include an individual's needs and motives, perceptions, attitudes, learned experiences, and self-concept. The interpersonal determinants include cultural influences, social influences, and family influences. A number of people within a firm may participate in business purchase decisions, so business buyers must consider a variety of organizational influences in addition to their own preferences.

Assessment Check Answers ✔

7.1 Define *consumer behavior*. Consumer behavior refers to the actions of ultimate consumers directly involved in obtaining, consuming, and disposing of products, along with the decision processes surrounding these actions.

7.2 What are some determinants of consumer behavior? Determinants of consumer behavior include both personal influences and interpersonal influences. Personal influences include an individual's needs and motives; perceptions, attitudes, and experiences; and self-concept. Interpersonal influences include cultural, social and family influences.

8 Discuss the benefits of and tools for relationship marketing.

Relationship marketing is an organization's attempt to develop long-term, cost-effective links with individual customers for mutual benefit. Good relationships with customers can be a vital strategic weapon for a firm. By identifying current purchasers and maintaining a positive relationship with them, an organization can efficiently target its best customers, fulfill their needs, and create loyalty. Information technologies, frequency and affinity programs, and one-on-one efforts all help build relationships with customers.

Assessment Check Answers ✔

8.1 What is the lifetime value of a customer? The lifetime value of a customer incorporates the revenues and intangible benefits from the customer over the life of the relationship with a firm, minus the amount the company must spend to acquire and serve the customer.

8.2 Discuss the increasing importance of one-on-one marketing efforts. One-on-one marketing is increasing in importance as consumers demand more customization in goods and services. It is also increasingly dependent on technology such as computer-aided design and manufacturing (CAD/CAM). The Internet also offers a way for businesses to connect with customers in a direct and personal manner.

■ Key Terms

marketing 353	consumer (B2C) product 361	market segmentation 366	consumer behavior 374
exchange process 353	business (B2B) product 361	geographical segmentation 368	relationship marketing 375
utility 354		demographic segmentation 368	lifetime value of a customer 377
marketing concept 355	target market 361	psychographic segmentation 371	frequency marketing 377
person marketing 358	marketing mix 362		affinity program 377
place marketing 359	marketing research 364	product-related segmentation 372	comarketing 378
event marketing 359	business intelligence 365	end-use segmentation 373	cobranding 378
cause marketing 359	data mining 365		
organization marketing 360	data warehouse 365		

Review Questions

1. Define the four different types of utility and explain how marketing contributes to the creation of utility. Then choose one of the following companies and describe how it creates each type of utility with its goods or services:

   a. Burger King

   b. Polo Ralph Lauren

   c. Borders bookstore

   d. Supercuts hair salons

   e. Adobe Systems

2. Describe the shift from a seller's market to a buyer's market. Why was this move important to marketers?

3. Describe how an organization might combine person marketing and event marketing. Give an example.

4. Describe how an organization might combine cause marketing and organization marketing. Give an example.

5. Identify each of the following as a consumer product or a business product, or classify it as both:

   a. cup of coffee

   b. iPad

   c. gasoline

   d. boat trailer

   e. hand sanitizer

   f. hair gel

6. Identify and describe the four strategies that blend to create a marketing mix.

7. What is a target market? Why is target market selection usually the first step in the development of a marketing strategy?

8. Identify the two strategies that a firm could use to develop a marketing mix for international markets. What are the advantages and disadvantages of each?

9. Describe the types of data that someone who is thinking of starting an accounting service might choose to gather. How might this businessperson use the data in making the startup decision?

10. Explain each of the methods used to segment consumer and business markets. Which methods do you think would be most effective for each of the following and why? (Note that a combination of methods might be applicable.)

    a. supermarket featuring organic foods

    b. hair-care products

    c. tour bus company

    d. line of baby food

    e. dental insurance

    f. dry cleaner

11. What are the three major determinants of consumer behavior? Give an example of how each one might influence a person's purchasing decision.

12. What are the benefits of relationship marketing? Describe how frequency and affinity programs work toward building relationships.

Projects and Teamwork Applications

1. On your own or with a classmate, choose one of the following products and create an advertisement that illustrates how your firm creates time, place, and form utility in its delivery of the product to the customer.

   a. auto repair service

   b. hiking tours

   c. craft supply store

   d. pet-sitting service

2. Choose one of the following nonprofit organizations or find one on your own. Research the organization online to learn more about it. Outline your proposed contents for a fundraising event based on the chapter discussion of nontraditional marketing, such as cause marketing or organization marketing.

   a. ASPCA

   b. Prostate Cancer Foundation

   c. Red Cross

   d. Salvation Army

3. As a marketer, if you can find ways to classify your firm's goods and services as both business and consumer products, most likely your company's sales will increase as you build relationships with a new category of customers. On your own or with a classmate, choose one of the following products, and outline a marketing strategy for attracting the classification of customer that is *opposite* from the one listed in parentheses.

   a. hybrid car (consumer)

   b. LCD TV (consumer)

   c. limousine service (business)

   d. office furniture (business)

4. Think of two situations in which you have been a customer: one in which you were satisfied with the merchandise you received and one in which you were not. Make a list of the reasons you were satisfied in the first case and another list of the reasons you were not satisfied in the second case. Would you say that the failure was the result of the seller not understanding your needs?

5. Comarketing and cobranding are techniques that organizations often use to market their own and each other's products, such as Nike running shoes and the Apple iPod. On your own or with a classmate, choose two firms with goods and/or services you think would work well together for comarketing separate products or cobranding a single product. Then create an advertisement for your comarketing or cobranding effort.

Web Assignments

1. **Demographic trends.** The *Statistical Abstract of the United States* is an excellent source of demographic and economic data about the United States. Visit the Web site listed here and click on "population." In terms of age and race, what does the U.S. population currently look like? What will the U.S. population look like in the decades to come?

   http://www.census.gov/compendia/statab/

2. **Market segmentation.** Go to the Web site of Canon USA and review the company's array of product offerings. Prepare a brief report on how Canon segments its markets.

   http://www.usa.canon.com/home

3. **Customer loyalty programs.** Airlines and hotel chains have extensive customer loyalty programs. Pick an airline and hotel chain and print out information on the firm's customer loyalty program. (Two examples are listed here.) Bring the material to class to participate in a discussion on this topic.

   http://www.southwest.com/rapid_rewards/

   http://www.marriott.com/rewards/rewards-program.mi

   Note: Internet Web addresses change frequently. If you don't find the exact sites listed, you may need to access the organization's home page and search from there or use a search engine such as Bing or Google.

CASE 11.1

Green Marketing: Good for Customers, Businesses, and the Earth

Green marketing has finally grown up. Once considered a quirky trend that appealed to a certain niche of environmentally concerned consumers, it has now become part of the overall business and marketing strategy of both small companies and major global corporations. As awareness of the importance of protecting and maintaining the resources of the planet has seeped into the mainstream, the idea of sustainability—meeting the needs of humans without damaging the environment—has become the basis of a new direction for many firms. Global consumer products manufacturer Unilever, which produces everything from Dove soap and Sunsilk shampoo to Lipton tea and Wishbone dressing, keeps the environment in mind in all of its processes. As part of its overall mission, the firm strives to improve people's health through nutrition and hygiene, minimize its environmental footprint, obtain renewable supplies of raw materials, and add wealth and other benefits to developing communities.

As it researches, develops, produces, and markets its products, Unilever undertakes projects designed to improve the lives of people and their environment. In Brazil, the firm funds a farming program that is helping tomato growers convert to environmentally friendly drip irrigation and recycles 17 tons of waste each year at its toothpaste factory. In Ghana, the firm is teaching palm oil producers to reuse plant waste. Unilever also reports publicly the amount of carbon dioxide and hazardous waste its factories discharge each year—all while taking steps to reduce those emissions.

These efforts are not only good for consumers, producers, and the environment but also necessary for the survival of companies like Unilever. Environmental regulations are tightening in the United States, Europe, and many other places around the world. If companies do not invest in technologies that preserve the environment in which they operate, eventually they will go out of business. "You can't ignore the impact your company has on the community and environment," warns Unilever CEO Patrick Cescau. "It's also about growth and innovation. In the future, it will be the only way to do business."

Unilever is just one of many companies moving in this direction. Toyota, the leading manufacturer of hybrid vehicles, is also now one of the largest auto manufacturers in the world. Toyota's reputation as a green corporation has propelled its sales past the competition. Marketing firm Interbrand reports that since the launch of the Prius and subsequent roll-outs of hybrid models of the Highlander, Camry, and others, Toyota's brand value has accelerated by nearly 50 percent. Meanwhile, automakers that were late to the game missed out not only on sales but on the opportunity to create a positive image in the minds of consumers. "We didn't appreciate the image value of hybrids," admits Larry Burns, chief of research and development at GM. "We missed that."

Meanwhile, not-for-profit organizations are working on new forms of green marketing as well. Instead of emphasizing individual endangered species such as the aardvark or the dugong, they are beginning to see the value of focusing on "flagship" or "heartland" areas around the world, chunks of land that contain intense concentrations of wildlife. Land conservation is not new, but this approach includes hotspots with a huge variety of plant and animal species. Marketed properly—for instance, allowing consumers to "adopt" a square of landscape—organizations like the African Wildlife Foundation and Conservation International are discovering that they can raise the money needed to implement important conservation projects.

Organizations have come to realize that consumers want to participate in environmental sustainability and that marketing messages informing shoppers of a company's green practices are helpful both to its image and its bottom line. As Dow Chemical increases its research on products such as roof tiles that deliver solar power, CEO Andrew N. Liveris explains why. "There is 100 percent overlap between our business drivers and social environmental interests." Going forward, a company can't have one without the other.

Questions for Critical Thinking

1. Go online and research any of the companies mentioned—or another one that interests you— to find out more about the firm's green marketing. Then create a new slogan reflecting the company's green marketing practices.

2. How might green marketing affect consumer behavior and help build customer relationships?

Sources: Company Web site, http://www.unilever.com, "Environment & Society," accessed March 2009; "Branding Land," *The Economist*, January 7, 2008, http://www.economist.com; Eric Newman, "Study: Retailers Push Charity, Ecology to Boost Sales," *Brandweek*, November 28, 2007, http://www.brandweek.com; Pete Engardio, "Beyond the Green Corporation," *BusinessWeek*, January 29, 2007, pp. 50–64.

Marketing Gone Wrong: Johnson & Johnson and Risperdal

CASE 11.2

Several years ago, the Food and Drug Administration (FDA) approved Johnson & Johnson's drug Risperdal to treat psychotic disorders, such as schizophrenia, in adults. However, the National Institute of Mental Health found that schizophrenia affects only about 1.1 percent of adults in the United States. According to a lawsuit by the state of Louisiana, Johnson & Johnson therefore decided to seek a wider market for the drug by indirectly promoting it for other purposes.

Under U.S. law, if the FDA has approved a drug for treating at least one disorder, doctors are permitted to prescribe it "off label," for any other disorder they think the drug will help—even if the FDA has not approved it for that disorder. (The condition the drug is intended to treat must be stated on the labeling.) However, drug manufacturers are forbidden to promote a drug for any other use than the FDA-approved one.

Recently, the U.S. Department of Justice charged Johnson & Johnson with paying hundreds of millions of dollars in kickbacks to Omnicare Inc. to buy and promote Risperdal, among other drugs, for off-label uses. Omnicare, the largest pharmacy for U.S. nursing-home patients, allegedly advocated prescribing Risperdal for elderly patients with Alzheimer's disease—even though the FDA never approved Risperdal for treating Alzheimer's. Johnson & Johnson stated, "We believe airing the facts will confirm that our conduct, including rebating programs like those the government now challenges, was lawful and appropriate. We look forward to the opportunity to present our evidence in court."

As far back as 1994—just one year after it approved Risperdal for psychotic disorders—the FDA ordered Johnson & Johnson to stop its claims that Risperdal was more effective than competing drugs. In 1999, the FDA warned the company that its marketing literature exaggerated Risperdal's benefits for elderly patients with Alzheimer's disease and understated the risks. Nonetheless, a Johnson & Johnson business plan revealed the company's intention to increase Risperdal's sales to these vulnerable patients well into the 21st century (as Baby Boomers age). Sales of Risperdal peaked at $4.5 billion in 2007, before the patent expired and other companies could legally manufacture cheaper, generic versions of the drug.

In 2005, the FDA issued a public health advisory, warning that Risperdal and similar drugs actually increased the chances of death among elderly Alzheimer's patients, usually from heart failure or pneumonia. The FDA has also required Risperdal to carry a "black box" warning, the most stringent in the FDA's arsenal.

Ten states have filed lawsuits against Johnson & Johnson for promoting Risperdal off label. Louisiana sued to force the company to pay millions of dollars in fines and to regain public money spent on Risperdal. Johnson & Johnson's lawyers argued that Louisiana did not cite any evidence of misrepresentation or off-label promotion. The company also claimed that there was no connection between its marketing and Louisiana doctors' decision to prescribe Risperdal. The judge rejected this argument, and the trial date was set. A spokesman for Johnson & Johnson said that the case "should be decided on the body of evidence, including testimony, not on the basis of excerpts from documents." The company has not put any money aside toward a settlement.

Omnicare paid $98 million to settle charges of running kickback plans with nursing homes and other drug manufacturers. Neither Omnicare nor Johnson & Johnson acknowledged doing anything wrong.

Questions for Critical Thinking

1. Do you think that recommending nonapproved uses of a drug is an appropriate marketing strategy? Why or why not?
2. Which market segmentation strategy do you think Johnson & Johnson was using when it decided to promote Risperdal for Alzheimer's patients? What did the company fail to take into account when developing this strategy?

Sources: Margaret Cronin Fisk, Jef Feeley, and David Voreacos, "Did J&J Plan to Break Rules?" *BusinessWeek*, March 11, 2010, http://www.businessweek.com; Margaret Cronin Fisk, Jeff Feeley, and David Voreacos, "J&J Pushed Risperdal for Elderly after U.S. Warning, Files Show," *Bloomberg.com,* March 10, 2010, http://www.bloomberg.com; Natasha Singer, "Johnson & Johnson Accused of Drug Kickbacks," *The New York Times,* January 16, 2010, http://www.nytimes.com; Michael Winter, "Johnson and Johnson Accused of Drug Kickbacks," *USA Today,* January 15, 2010, http://content.usatoday.com; Jim Edwards, "J&J Nursing Home Kickback Scheme Tripled Sales, DOJ Alleges," *BNET,* January 15, 2010, http://industry.bnet.com.

CASE 11.3

Zipcar and UNH: Customer-Driven Marketing

When you're a college student, getting around campus (or off-campus) can sometimes be a challenge. You can walk. You can ride your bike or your skateboard. But when rain is pummeling your backpack or when you have to carry that heavy box of marketing flyers across campus, you wish you had a car—not to mention if you want to head off-campus for a weekend road trip. So you decide to bring a car to campus, but discover that you're forking over several hundred dollars for a parking permit and you can't find a place to park anyway. Then there's the expense of gas and insurance, and the nattering of friends who want a ride or who want to borrow your car—just for an hour or an evening. Depending on where you go to school, Zipcar has got you covered. If you happen to attend the University of New Hampshire, you're in luck.

Zipcar is a car-sharing network based in Cambridge, Massachusetts that operates in metropolitan areas and on university campuses around the U.S., Canada, and the United Kingdom. Car-sharing was already popular in Europe ten years ago when Zipcar founders decided to see if the idea would fly in the U.S. Shortly after its introduction to urban dwellers and U.S. students, Zipcar's message had wheels.

At the University of New Hampshire (UNH), students and faculty already had several transportation options, including an Amtrak station nearby and several bus services. But Brett Pasinella, who works for the University Office of Sustainability, wanted to find a way to link the different transportation options and expand them in a sustainable fashion. His research told him that Zipcar fit UNH's existing options. "We went through a bidding process to get the right company," Pasinella says. The firm had to meet UNH's requirement that membership include insurance and fuel. "Zipcar really stood out because of their technology and understanding of the services and what we were looking for," explains Pasinella. But UNH still had to sell the idea to budget-conscious students in order to make it work.

The Zipcar system is simple: for a $35 annual fee, UNH students or faculty get round-the-clock access to

Zipcars that are parked in designated parking spots around campus. When they join, members receive their own Zipcard (like a key card) that unlocks any Zipcar. Members reserve a car online, then use their Zipcard to access it. Gas and insurance are included with membership, as well as an average of 180 miles per day.

To sell the concept to UNH students, Brett Pasinella engaged a senior class of marketing students to develop a marketing plan for all the transportation systems available on campus. The class split into teams, one of which chose the Zipcar project. The marketing students created presentations designed to answer questions and help classmates overcome the hurdle of a $35 fee. Once they realized that an annual parking permit at UNH is $400—and that gas and insurance are included with Zipcar membership—they began to recognize the benefits. In addition, they saw Zipcars parked around the campus so they became familiar with the brand.

Brett Pasinella notes that UNH is also a sustainable campus, and that most of his job is focused on finding ways to reduce waste and energy use—including throughout the university's transportation system. Zipcar's entire fleet is EPA Smart Way certified and includes hybrids as well as other zero-emission vehicles. But Pasinella and UNH marketing student Erin Badger point out the realities of college life. "A lot of students will focus on the fact that Zipcar is easier for them and saves them money," concedes Erin Badger. "We have to promote Zipcar toward what students are looking for, and those are the two biggest factors."

After the first year in operation at UNH, Zipcar membership is growing. Pasinella plans to market the service proactively in coming years—sending Zipcar information to incoming students and faculty before they arrive on campus with their own vehicles. UNH conducted a survey of members and discovered that users like the convenience and visibility of the cars as well as the low cost. Erin Badger might be the Zipcar's best spokesperson at UNH. "I wish I'd figured it out a lot sooner," she admits. She accrued a lot of parking tickets around campus before she joined Zipcar. "I'd have saved myself a lot of money if I'd joined sooner," she says.

Questions for Critical Thinking

1. Who is Zipcar's target market? How might Zipcar's market be further segmented?

2. Describe how Zipcar might create a marketing mix for colleges and universities.

3. Just as Zipcar must market to UNH, UNH in turn must market the Zipcar concept to its customers—students and faculty. Describe how studying consumer behavior could help select a strategy for UNH's marketing effort.

4. What steps can Zipcar take to manage its relationship with UNH?

Sources: Zipcar Web site, http://www.zipcar.com, accessed August 24, 2010; University of New Hampshire Transportation Services, http://www.unh.edu/transportation, accessed August 24, 2010; "Zipcar, Inc.," *Bloomberg Businessweek,* http://investingbusinessweek.com, accessed August 24, 2010.

Chapter

12

Learning Objectives

1. Explain marketing's definition of a product; differentiate among convenience, shopping, and specialty products; and distinguish between a product mix and a product line.

2. Briefly describe each of the four stages of the product life cycle with their marketing implications.

3. Explain how firms identify their products.

4. Outline and briefly describe each of the major components of an effective distribution strategy.

5. Distinguish between the different types of wholesaling intermediaries.

6. Describe the various types of retailers, and identify retail strategies.

7. Identify the various categories of distribution channels, and discuss the factors that influence channel selection.

Producing and Distributing Goods and Services

David H. Lewis/iStockphoto

The Buckle Shines Amid Retail Gloom

©R. Alcorn, Photographed for John Wiley & Sons

Retailers are smarting from the pinch of consumers' tightened wallets. Many reported slow sales even during the usually busy holiday season. But one clothing retailer has actually seen its sales grow by double digits. At youth-oriented retail chain The Buckle, sales climbed more than 13 percent recently—and more than 20 percent during a holiday season when other stores saw declines. The Buckle's 388 mall stores are keeping up the momentum, too. Annual sales are expected to soon reach $780 million, a stellar performance in a generally dismal shopping year.

What accounts for the chain's continued growth and popularity? One key is the racks of fresh merchandise arriving at stores every day. Another factor is the stores' 15- to 25-year-old customers, who are keen shoppers with money to spend. "This is their first recession," notes one retail expert. "They're not as scared as everyone else. Their home equity is not at stake, and their 401(k) [retirement plan] is just getting started." But like any other retailer, The Buckle ultimately rises and falls on the quality of its merchandise. And that's where The Buckle is shining with its inventory of high-fashion shirts, jeans, shoes, and accessories for men and women.

The chain stocks the hottest high-quality brands, like Fossil and Guess, which make up about 70 percent of its sales. The rest comes from the store's own BKE brand of mostly denim pieces. But whatever the manufacturer, The Buckle usually carries each style in only a few sizes. It restocks in different colors or different designs than the ones that have already sold. This strategy ensures that the chain's most loyal customers won't see their friends wearing the same outfits they've just chosen, a benefit Buckle fans prize. One teen in a customer focus group said, "I shop The Buckle because it seems to offer more opportunity to look different from everyone else. I buy classic pieces and edgy accessories and create my own look."

Another young shopper agreed. "I feel I can create a distinctive style with their clothes," he said. The wide product assortment and constantly changing choices that keep fashion-conscious customers coming back might present a logistical challenge to a chain with stores in 38 states. But the Nebraska-based firm runs a highly efficient distribution system that keeps items flowing. That's important considering that despite its narrow range for each item, the store carries some unusual sizes, such as extra extra extra long jeans. One happy shopper reported, "I was always stretching my jeans to make them as long as possible, but then a friend recommended I try out The Buckle."

The store also trains its young and energetic salespeople carefully to help promote its merchandise. One important strategy is to get the customer into a dressing room. Once there, the shopper is fed a stream of suggestions for coordinating a look. A salesperson whose customer is trying on jeans, for instance, will deliver, unasked, a couple of T-shirts and a belt to go with them. "I end up trying on clothes faster and faster, finding more stuff I like, then never even taking the time to look at the prices," said one young shopper. "I know I buy more because of it."

The Buckle is careful about where its clothing comes from, too. It has a corporate goal of providing the most enjoyable shopping experience possible—with high-quality products at the best value in the most equitable manner. That requires "sound business and human rights ethics from our suppliers" as set out in the company's Code of Conduct and Standards of Engagement. The code includes health, safety, employment, and environmental practices. The Buckle gives a copy to all its suppliers to sign.

Top-quality products in the right assortment with attentive service—it all adds up to a store full of products that customers love.[1]

In this chapter we examine ways in which organizations design and implement marketing strategies that address customers' needs and wants. Two of the most powerful such tools are strategies that relate to products, which include both goods and services, and those that relate to the distribution of those products.

As the story of The Buckle illustrates, successful companies cater to the tastes of their customers. The retail chain continues to perfect its recipe for success with customers by offering the clothes and styles they want to wear in limited quantities to avoid duplication with other teen wardrobes. In addition, the creation of new products is the lifeblood of an organization. Because products do not remain economically viable forever, companies must constantly develop new ones to ensure their survival and long-term growth. Providing new styles continually to meet fashion's changing tastes keeps The Buckle on the upswing in a depressed retail market.

This chapter focuses on the first two elements of the marketing mix: product and distribution. Our discussion of product strategy begins by describing the classifications of goods and services, customer service, product lines and the product mix, and the product life cycle. Companies often shape their marketing strategies differently when they are introducing a new product, when the product has established itself in the marketplace, and when it is declining in popularity. We also discuss product identification through brand name and distinctive packaging, and the ways in which companies foster loyalty to their brands to keep customers coming back for more.

Distribution, the second mix variable discussed, focuses on moving goods and services from producer to wholesaler to retailer to buyers. Managing the distribution process includes making decisions such as what kind of wholesaler to use and where to offer products for sale. Retailers can range from specialty stores to factory outlets and everything in between, and they must choose appropriate customer service, pricing, and location strategies in order to succeed. The chapter concludes with a look at logistics, the process of coordinating the flow of information, goods, and services among suppliers and on to final consumers.

Product Strategy

product bundle of physical, service, and symbolic characteristics designed to satisfy consumer wants.

Most people respond to the question "What is a product?" by listing its physical features. By contrast, marketers take a broader view. To them, a **product** is a bundle of physical, service, and symbolic characteristics designed to satisfy consumer wants. The chief executive officer of a major tool manufacturer once startled his stockholders with this statement: "Last year our customers bought over 1 million quarter-inch drill bits, and none of them wanted to buy the product. They all wanted quarter-inch holes." Product strategy involves considerably more than just producing a good or service; instead, it focuses on benefits. The marketing conception of a product includes decisions about package design, brand name, trademarks, warranties, product image, new-product development, and customer service. Think, for instance, about your favorite soft drink. Do you like it for its taste alone? Or do other attributes, such as clever ads, attractive packaging, ease of purchase from vending machines and other convenient locations, and overall image, also attract you? These other attributes may influence your choice more than you realize.

Classifying Goods and Services

Marketers have found it useful to classify goods and services as either B2C or B2B, depending on whether the purchasers of the particular item are consumers or businesses. These classifications can be subdivided further, and each type requires a different competitive strategy.

Classifying Consumer Goods and Services

The classification typically used for ultimate consumers who purchase products for their own use and enjoyment and not for resale is based on consumer buying habits. *Convenience products* are items the consumer seeks to purchase frequently, immediately, and with little effort. Items stocked in gas-station markets, vending machines, and local newsstands are usually convenience products—for example, newspapers, snacks, candy, coffee, and bread.

Shopping products are those typically purchased only after the buyer has compared competing products in competing stores. A person intent on buying a new sofa or dining room table may visit many stores, examine perhaps dozens of pieces of furniture, and spend days making the final decision. *Specialty products*, the third category of consumer products, are those that a purchaser is willing to make a special effort to obtain. The purchaser is already familiar with the item and considers it to have no reasonable substitute. The nearest MINI dealer may be 75 miles away, but if you have decided you want one, you will make the trip.

Note that a shopping product for one person may be a convenience item for someone else. Each item's product classification is based on buying patterns of the majority of people who purchase it.

The interrelationship of the marketing mix factors is shown in Figure 12.1. By knowing the appropriate classification for a specific product, the marketing decision maker knows quite a bit about how the other mix variables will adapt to create a profitable, customer-driven marketing strategy.

Buying a *specialty product* takes extra effort. The MINI is sold in a limited number of places.

FIGURE
12.1 Marketing Impacts of Consumer Product Classification

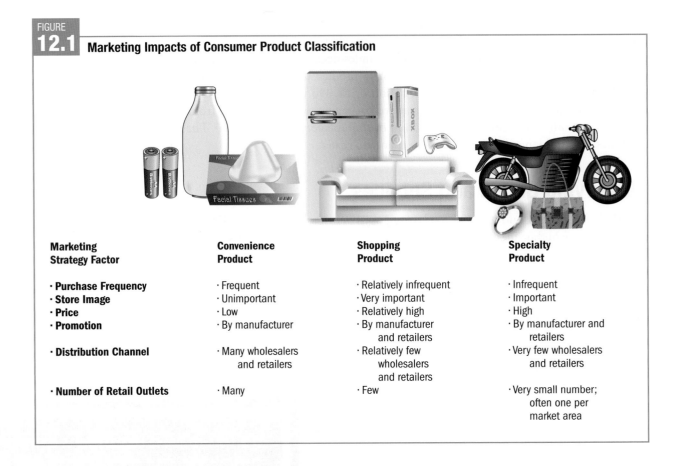

Marketing Strategy Factor	Convenience Product	Shopping Product	Specialty Product
· Purchase Frequency	· Frequent	· Relatively infrequent	· Infrequent
· Store Image	· Unimportant	· Very important	· Important
· Price	· Low	· Relatively high	· High
· Promotion	· By manufacturer	· By manufacturer and retailers	· By manufacturer and retailers
· Distribution Channel	· Many wholesalers and retailers	· Relatively few wholesalers and retailers	· Very few wholesalers and retailers
· Number of Retail Outlets	· Many	· Few	· Very small number; often one per market area

Classifying Business Goods *Business products* are goods and services such as paycheck services and huge multifunction copying machines used in operating an organization; they also include machinery, tools, raw materials, components, and buildings used to produce other items for resale. While consumer products are classified by buying habits, business products are classified based on how they are used and by their basic characteristics. Products that are long-lived and relatively expensive are called *capital items*. Less costly products that are consumed within a year are referred to as *expense items*.

Five basic categories of B2B products exist: installations, accessory equipment, component parts and materials, raw materials, and supplies. *Installations* are major capital items, such as new factories, heavy equipment and machinery, and custom-made equipment. Installations are expensive and often involve buyer and seller negotiations that may last for more than a year before a purchase actually is made. Purchase approval frequently involves a number of different people—production specialists, representatives from the purchasing department, and members of top management—who must agree on the final choice.

Although *accessory equipment* also includes capital items, they are usually less expensive and shorter lived than installations and involve fewer decision makers. Examples include hand tools and fax machines. *Component parts and materials* are finished business goods that become part of a final product, such as disk drives that are sold to computer manufacturers or batteries purchased by automakers. *Raw materials* are farm and natural products used in producing other final products. Examples include milk, wood, leather, and soybeans. *Supplies* are expense items used in a firm's daily operation that do not become part of the final product. Often referred to as MRO (maintenance, repair, and operating supplies), they include paper clips, light bulbs, and copy paper.

Classifying Services Services can be classified as either B2C or B2B. Child and elder care centers and auto detail shops provide services for consumers, while the Pinkerton security patrol at a local factory and Kelly Services' temporary office workers are examples of business services. In some cases, a service can accommodate both consumer and business markets. For example, when ServiceMaster cleans the upholstery in a home, it is a B2C service, but when it spruces up the painting system and robots in a manufacturing plant, it is a B2B service.

Like tangible goods, services can also be convenience, shopping, or specialty products depending on the buying patterns of customers. However, they are distinguished from goods in several ways. First, services, unlike goods, are intangible. In addition, they are perishable because firms cannot stockpile them in inventory. They are also difficult to standardize, because they must meet individual customers' needs. Finally, from a buyer's perspective, the service provider is the service; the two are inseparable in the buyer's mind.

Marketing Strategy Implications

The consumer product classification system is a useful tool in marketing strategy. As described in Figure 12.1, because a new refrigerator is classified as a shopping good, its marketers have a better idea of its promotion, pricing, and distribution needs.

Each group of business products, however, requires a different marketing strategy. Because most installations and many component parts are frequently marketed directly from manufacturer to business buyer, the promotional emphasis is on personal selling rather than on advertising. By contrast, marketers of supplies and accessory equipment rely more on advertising, because their products are often sold through an intermediary, such as a wholesaler. Producers of installations and component parts may involve their customers in new-product development, especially when the business product is custom made. Finally, firms selling supplies and accessory equipment place greater emphasis on competitive pricing strategies than do other B2B marketers, who tend to concentrate more on product quality and customer service.

Product Lines and Product Mix

Few firms operate with a single product. If their initial entry is successful, they tend to increase their profit and growth chances by adding new offerings. The iPhone and iPad, with their touchscreen technology and App Stores, may be harbingers of things to come. Although most "mainstream knowledge workers" will probably continue to use conventional computers for some time, one IT research company predicts that by 2015, more than half of personal computers bought for users aged 15 and under will have touchscreens. The firm also predicts that touchscreen devices have a huge potential in education—which would mean that an entire generation will grow up with touchscreen technology.[2]

A company's **product line** is a group of related products marked by physical similarities or intended for a similar market. A **product mix** is the assortment of product lines and individual goods and services that a firm offers to consumers and business users. The Coca-Cola Company and PepsiCo both have product lines that include old standards—Coke Classic and Diet Coke, Pepsi and Diet Pepsi. But recently, PepsiCo announced it would start distributing Tampico Plus in selected states. Unlike other products from Tampico Beverages, Tampico Plus drinks contain vitamins A, C, and E. They also have half as much sugar as regular Tampico drinks. Thus, they meet the guidelines for beverages that can be sold in U.S. high schools, which want to limit the amount of sugar in drinks available to students.[3]

product line group of related products marked by physical similarities or intended for a similar market.

product mix the assortment of product lines and individual goods and services that a firm offers to consumers and business users.

A *product line* includes several related products designed to have the same appearance, like these PepsiCo products.

Marketers must assess their product mix continually to ensure company growth, to satisfy changing consumer needs and wants, and to adjust to competitors' offerings. To remain competitive, marketers look for gaps in their product lines and fill them with new offerings or modified versions of existing ones. A helpful tool that is frequently used in making product decisions is the product life cycle.

Product Life Cycle

Once a product is on the market, it usually goes through four stages known as the **product life cycle**: introduction, growth, maturity, and decline. As Figure 12.2 shows, industry sales and profits vary depending on the life-cycle stage of an item.

Product life cycles are not set in stone; not all products follow this pattern precisely, and different products may spend different periods of time in each stage, as the "Hit & Miss" feature describes. The concept, however, helps the marketing planner anticipate developments throughout the various stages of a product's life. Profits assume a predictable pattern through the stages, and promotional emphasis shifts from dispensing product information in the early stages to heavy brand promotion in the later ones.

Stages of the Product Life Cycle

In the *introduction stage*, the firm tries to promote demand for its new offering; inform the market about it; give free samples to entice consumers to make a trial purchase; and explain its features, uses, and benefits. Sometimes companies partner at this stage to promote new products, as did General Mills and Warner Bros. Pictures and Legendary Pictures to

Assessment Check ✔

1. How do consumer products differ from business products?

2. Differentiate among convenience, shopping, and specialty products.

product life cycle four basic stages—introduction, growth, maturity, and decline—through which a successful product progresses.

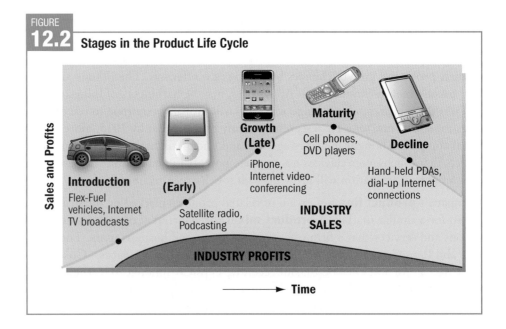

FIGURE 12.2 Stages in the Product Life Cycle

launch Yoplait Greek Yogurt. General Mills invited women to "discover their inner goddess" in connection with the film companies' *Clash of the Titans*. Izabella Miko, who played the goddess Athena in the film, was the spokesperson for the new yogurt.[4] The developers of Crocs sandals spent the introduction stage selling their product from booths at boat shows. That product moved to the next stage very quickly.

New-product development costs and extensive introductory promotional campaigns to acquaint prospective buyers with the merits of the innovation, though essential to later success, are expensive and commonly lead to losses in the introductory stage. Some firms are seeking to lower these costs through ultra-low-cost product development, which involves meeting customer needs with the lowest-cost innovations possible, designing from scratch with a stripped-down budget, and the simplest engineering possible.[5] But all these expenditures are necessary if the firm is to profit later.

During the *growth stage*, sales climb quickly as new customers join early users who now are repurchasing the item. Word-of-mouth referrals and continued advertising and other special promotions by the firm induce others to make trial purchases. At this point, the company begins to earn profits on the new product. This success encourages competitors to enter the field with similar offerings, and price competition develops. After its initial success with the Kindle digital reader, Amazon faced competition from the Barnes & Noble Nook and the Sony Reader. Amazon rushed to get its Kindle iPad app to the App Store in time for the debut of Apple's iPad.[6]

In the *maturity stage*, industry sales at first increase, but they eventually reach a saturation level at which further expansion is difficult. Competition also intensifies, increasing the availability of the product. Firms concentrate on capturing competitors' customers, often dropping prices to further the appeal. Cell phones are in the maturity stage: competitors compete not only on price but also on features such as calendars, e-mail and attachments, messaging capability, full-color screens, keyboards, and fax and word-processing functions. Flat-screen TVs are also in the maturity stage, so companies are trying to entice consumers to buy new ones by offering even bigger TVs than they have before, topping the 50-inch mark. As worldwide production of high-definition TVs increases dramatically, some observers predict that makers of LED backlight displays will lower their prices dramatically to stay competitive with other, less expensive display options.[7]

Sales volume fades late in the maturity stage, and some of the weaker competitors leave the market. During this stage, firms promote mature products aggressively to protect their market share and to distinguish their products from those of competitors. Alberto Culver is changing the old tub of Noxzema—the tub itself will remain, but with a new look. Through a new online and print campaign, the promotion of the product is changing into a fresh, tingling face cleansing experience for women.[8]

Sales continue to fall in the *decline stage*, the fourth phase of the product life cycle. Profits decline and may become losses as further price-cutting occurs in the reduced overall market for the item. Competitors gradually exit, making some profits possible for the remaining firms in the shrinking market. The decline stage usually is caused by a product innovation or a shift in consumer preferences. Sometimes technology change can hasten the decline stage for a product. Eighty percent of U.S. residences contain at least one DVD player. High-definition DVDs, once touted as the ultimate in DVD technology, have been superseded by Blu-ray. Online sites where consumers can simply download movies or television shows are becoming another major competitor for entertainment as the link between computer and television is becoming faster and more reliable.[9]

Hit & Miss

Chattem Breathes Life into Old Brands

Where do brands go to die? If they're lucky, they don't die at all. They are bought by Chattem instead. The 130-year-old company succeeds these days, not by creating new products, but by pouring new life into old brand-name health products, toiletries, and pain relievers.

Chattem carries about 26 brands from such parent firms as Procter & Gamble and Johnson & Johnson. The company recently purchased Selsun Blue dandruff shampoo, Kaopectate stomach soother, and Balmex diaper rash cream. It spent $410 million for five brands it purchased from Johnson & Johnson in a recent year.

The company adds new touches to products that need them. When it purchased over-the-counter sleep aid Unisom, it reformulated it as a meltable tablet that can be swallowed without water. Occasionally, Chattem's efforts to save a product are in vain. After it spent almost $100 million to purchase diet drug Dexatrim, the FDA recalled it and other remedies that contained an ingredient believed to increase the risk of stroke. Chattem withdrew all its Dexatrim brand products but was still on the hook for nearly 400 consumer claims that cost it over $56 million to settle.

Chattem usually spends about $120 million a year on advertising and promotion, including 15-second TV spots, catchy jingles and slogans, and sometimes even a celebrity spokesperson. Model Christie Brinkley is endorsing ACT mouthwash, now available in seven versions. Chattem has already promoted the product's ability to restore tooth enamel and doubled ACT's sales to $60 million.

And with sales of $450 million and a growth rate around 12 percent a year, it seems to have found a winning strategy.

Questions for Critical Thinking

1. How does Chattem determine whether an aging product is still viable in the marketplace? What other measures do you think it might use to tell good products from bad, and why?

2. Why would a company sell a viable brand-name product to a firm like Chattem?

Sources: Company Web site, http://www.chattem.com, accessed March 4, 2009; "Chattem Unbottles Potent Profits, Defying Economy," *iStockAnalyst*, January 30, 2009, http://www.istockanalyst.com; Jonathan Heller, "Chattem Creates Value in Consumer Products," *Real Money*, January 27, 2009, http://biz.yahoo.com; Helen Coster, "Old Brands in New Bottles," *Forbes*, October 27, 2008, pp. 134–137.

Marketing Strategy Implications of the Product Life Cycle

Like the product classification system, the product life cycle is a useful concept for designing a marketing strategy that will be flexible enough to accommodate changing marketplace characteristics. These competitive moves may involve developing new products, lowering prices, increasing distribution coverage, creating new promotional campaigns, or any combination of these approaches. In general, the marketer's objective is to extend the product life cycle as long as the item is profitable. Some products can be highly profitable during the later stages of their life cycle, because all the initial development costs have already been recovered.

A commonly used strategy for extending the life cycle is to increase customers' frequency of use. Walmart and Meijer offer grocery sections in their stores in order to increase the frequency of shopper visits. Another strategy is to add new users. Marketers for Old Spice grooming products decided that Old Spice didn't have to be old hat. So they came up with a campaign to freshen up the product line's image and attract younger men. Called "The Man Your Man Could Smell Like," it cleverly poked fun at the idea that merely using Old Spice would make younger men irresistible to women—while promising, with a wink, that it would.[10]

Arm & Hammer used a third approach: finding new uses for its products. The original use of the firm's baking soda in baking has been augmented by its newer uses as a toothpaste, refrigerator freshener, and flame extinguisher. A fourth product life cycle extension strategy is changing package sizes, labels, and product designs. Many times, changing the product design means finding a way to give it an online application. To bolster its doll sales, which had declined almost 20 percent, the toymaker Mattel did this by teaming its iconic Barbie doll with the White House Project and the Take Our Daughters And Sons To Work Foundation. Consumers were invited to celebrate Barbie's 125th career by voting online to choose from among architect, computer engineer, environmentalist, news anchor, and surgeon. The winners, announced at the recent New York Toy Fair, were Computer Engineer Barbie (by popular vote) and News Anchor Barbie (by girls' vote). Both were part of Barbie's "I Can Be" series.[11]

Stages in New-Product Development

New-product development is expensive, time consuming, and risky, because only about one-third of new products become success stories. Products can fail for many reasons. Some are not properly developed and tested, some are poorly packaged, and others lack adequate promotional support or distribution or do not satisfy a consumer need or want. Even successful products eventually reach the end of the decline stage and must be replaced with new-product offerings.

Most of today's newly developed items are aimed at satisfying specific consumer demands. New-product development is becoming increasingly efficient and cost-effective because marketers use a systematic approach in developing new products. As Figure 12.3 shows, the new-product development process has six stages. Each stage requires a "go/no-go" decision by management before moving on to subsequent stages. Because items that go through each development stage only to be rejected at one of the final stages involve significant investments in both time and money, the sooner decision makers can identify a marginal product and drop it from further consideration, the less time and money will be wasted.

The starting point in the new-product development process is generating ideas for new offerings. Ideas come from many sources, including customer suggestions, suppliers, employees, research scientists, marketing research, inventors outside the firm, and competitive products. The most successful ideas are directly related to satisfying customer needs. Procter & Gamble recently expanded its Febreze home collection with the Flameless Luminary In-Home Scent Delivery System. Instead of a potentially dangerous candle, a battery-operated, flameless light diffuses fragrance from a decorative, scented shade. The light automatically turns off after four hours. The design was a finalist in the Consumer Packaged Goods—Household Segment category of the Edison Best New Product Awards.[12]

In the second stage, screening eliminates ideas that do not mesh with overall company objectives or that cannot be developed given the company's resources. Some firms

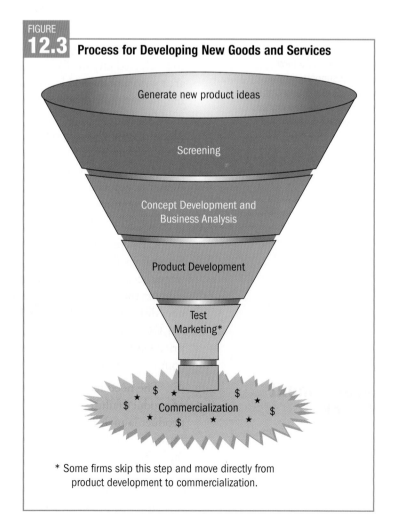

FIGURE
12.3 **Process for Developing New Goods and Services**

Generate new product ideas

Screening

Concept Development and Business Analysis

Product Development

Test Marketing*

Commercialization

* Some firms skip this step and move directly from product development to commercialization.

hold open discussions of new-product ideas with specialists who work in different functional areas in the organization.

During the concept development and business analysis phase, further screening occurs. The analysis involves assessing the new product's potential sales, profits, growth rate, and competitive strengths and determining whether it fits with the company's product, distribution, and promotional resources. *Concept testing*—marketing research designed to solicit initial consumer reaction to new-product ideas—may be used at this stage. For example, potential consumers might be asked about proposed brand names and other methods of product identification. *Focus groups* are formal sessions in which consumers meet with marketers to discuss what they like or dislike about current products and perhaps test or sample a new offering to provide some immediate feedback.

Next, an actual product is developed, subjected to a series of tests, and revised. Functioning prototypes or detailed descriptions of the product may be created. These designs are the joint responsibility of the firm's development staff and its marketers, who provide feedback on consumer reactions to the proposed product design, color, and other physical features. Sometimes prototypes do not meet the stated requirements. The U.S. Marine Corps' infantry combat equipment program recently asked four companies to develop a new plastic helmet that would be lighter and more durable than the current Kevlar headgear. The Marine Corps and the Army both required the new helmets to be 35 percent more effective against fragmentation as well as handgun and small-arms bullets. However, all four prototypes failed either to stop bullets or to stand up against blunt force, or both, so more work was necessary to meet the government's requirements.[13]

test marketing
introduction of a new product supported by a complete marketing campaign to a selected city or TV coverage area.

Test marketing introduces a new product supported by a complete marketing campaign to a selected city or TV coverage area. Marketers look for a location or television coverage area with a manageable size, where residents match their target market's demographic profile, to test their product. During the test marketing stage, the item is sold in a limited area while the company examines both consumer responses to the new offering and the marketing effort used to support it. Test market results can help managers determine the product's likely performance in a full-scale introduction. Some firms skip test marketing, however, because of concerns that the test could reveal their product strategies to the competition. Also, the expense of doing limited production runs of complex products such as a new auto or refrigerator is sometimes so high that the test marketing stage is skipped and the development process moves directly to the next stage.

In the final stage, commercialization, the product is made available in the marketplace. Sometimes this stage is referred to as a product launch. Considerable planning goes into this stage, because the firm's distribution, promotion, and pricing strategies must all be geared to support the new product offering. The videogame maker Electronic Arts (EA) announced a new distribution strategy for future games. EA will release premium downloadable content (PLDC) for a game before releasing the complete, packaged version. The PLDC will be priced at $15 and will include three to four hours of playing time. The company will invite comments from reviewers and players and make changes to the final version prior to release.[14]

Assessment Check ☑

1. What are the stages of the product life cycle?

2. What are the marketing implications of each stage?

The need for a steady stream of new products to offer the firm's customers, the chances of product failure, and the tens of millions of dollars needed to complete a successful new-product launch make new-product development a vital process for 21st-century firms. However, as Table 12.1 illustrates, success is not guaranteed until the new-product offering achieves customer acceptance. Microsoft introduced a new operating system, Windows Vista, but it just never caught on. The next version of Windows, Windows 7, has fared better. A computer device was supposed to bring the sense of smell to online shopping or browsing. But the company, DigiScent, didn't think through its plan carefully. Aside from

12.1 The Worst-Made Cars on the Road

RANK	AUTO	TYPICAL OWNER COMMENT
1	Yugo	"I once test drove a Yugo, during which the radio fell out, the gear shift knob came off in my hand, and I saw daylight through the strip around the windshield."
2	Chevy Vega	"As near as I could tell, the car was built from compressed rust."
3	Ford Pinto	"The barbecue that seats four."
4	AMC Gremlin	"It was entirely possible to read a Russian novel during the pause between stepping on the gas and feeling any semblance of forward motion."
5	Chevy Chevette	"The ad didn't show the car going anywhere fast . . . because it couldn't."

Source: Reported in "Car Talk," http://www.cartalk.com, accessed April 30, 2010; Claire Martin, "The Worst Cars Ever," *MSN Autos,* April 22, 2010, http://editorial.autos.msn.com.

rejecting the idea of being assaulted with unwanted aromas in addition to pop-up ads, consumers turned a thumbs-down on the product's name—iSmell.[15]

Product Identification

A major aspect of developing a successful new product involves methods used for identifying a product and distinguishing it from competing offerings. Both tangible goods and intangible services are identified by brands, brand names, and trademarks. A **brand** is a name, term, sign, symbol, design, or some combination that identifies the products of one firm and differentiates them from competitors' offerings. Tropicana, Pepsi, and Gatorade are all made by PepsiCo, but a unique combination of name, symbol, and package design distinguishes each brand from the others.

A **brand name** is that part of the brand consisting of words or letters included in a name used to identify and distinguish the firm's offerings from those of competitors. The brand name is the part of the brand that can be vocalized. Many brand names, such as Coca-Cola, McDonald's, American Express, Google, and Nike, are famous around the world. Likewise, the "golden arches" brand mark of McDonald's also is widely recognized.

A **trademark** is a brand that has been given legal protection. The protection is granted solely to the brand's owner. Trademark protection includes not only the brand name but also design logos, slogans, packaging elements, and product features such as color and shape. A well-designed trademark, such as the Nike "swoosh," can make a difference in how positively consumers perceive a brand.

Selecting an Effective Brand Name

Good brands are easy to pronounce, recognize, and remember: Crest, Visa, and Dell are examples. Global firms face a real problem in selecting brand names, because an excellent brand name in one country may prove disastrous in another. Most languages have a short *a*, so Coca-Cola is pronounceable almost anywhere. But an advertising campaign for E-Z

brand name, term, sign, symbol, design, or some combination that identifies the products of one firm and differentiates them from competitors' offerings.

brand name part of the brand consisting of words or letters included in a name used to identify and distinguish the firm's offerings from those of competitors.

trademark brand that has been given legal protection

To be effective, such *brand names* must be easy for consumers to pronounce, recognize, and remember.

Daniel Acker/Bloomberg/Getty Images, Inc.

washing machines failed in the United Kingdom because the British pronounce *z* as "zed."

Brand names should also convey the right image to the buyer. One effective technique is to create a name that links the product with its positioning strategy. The name Dial reinforces the concept of 24-hour protection; Dove soap and beauty products give an impression of mildness, and Taster's Choice instant coffee supports the promotional claim "Tastes and smells like ground roast coffee."

Brand names also must be legally protectable. Trademark law specifies that brand names cannot contain words in general use, such as *television* or *automobile*. Generic words—words that describe a type of product—cannot be used exclusively by any organization. On the other hand, if a brand name becomes so popular that it passes into common language and turns into a generic word, the company can no longer use it as a brand name. Once upon a time, aspirin, linoleum, and zipper were exclusive brand names, but today they have become generic terms and are no longer legally protectable.

Brand Categories

A brand offered and promoted by a manufacturer is known as a *manufacturer's* (or *national*) *brand*. Examples are Tide, Cheerios, Windex, Fossil, and Nike. But not all brand names belong to manufacturers; some are the property of retailers or distributors. A *private* (or *store*) *brand* identifies a product that is not linked to the manufacturer but instead carries a wholesaler's or retailer's label. Sears's Craftsman tools and Walmart's Ol' Roy dog food are examples.

Another branding decision marketers must make is whether to use a family branding strategy or an individual branding strategy. A *family brand* is a single brand name used for several related products. KitchenAid, Johnson & Johnson, Hewlett-Packard, and Arm & Hammer use a family name for their entire line of products. When a firm using family branding introduces a new product, both customers and retailers recognize the familiar brand name. The promotion of individual products within a line benefits all the products because the family brand is well known.

Other firms use an *individual branding* strategy by giving each product within a line a different name. For example, Procter & Gamble has individual brand names for its different laundry detergents, including Tide, Cheer, and Dash. Each brand targets a unique market segment. Consumers who want a cold-water detergent can choose Cheer over Tide or Dash, instead of purchasing a competitor's brand. Individual branding also builds competition within a firm and enables the company to increase overall sales.

Brand Loyalty and Brand Equity

Brands achieve varying consumer familiarity and acceptance. While a homeowner may insist on Anderson windows when renovating, the consumer buying a loaf of bread may not prefer any brand. Consumer loyalty increases a brand's value, so marketers try to strengthen brand loyalty. When a brand image suffers, marketers try to recreate a positive image.

Brand Loyalty Marketers measure brand loyalty in three stages: brand recognition, brand preference, and brand insistence. *Brand recognition* is brand acceptance strong enough that the consumer is aware of the brand, but not strong enough to cause a preference over other brands. A consumer might have heard of L'Oréal hair care products, for instance, without necessarily preferring them to Redken. Advertising, free samples, and discount coupons are among the most common ways to increase brand recognition.

Brand preference occurs when a consumer chooses one firm's brand over a competitor's. At this stage, the consumer usually relies on previous experience in selecting the product. Furniture and other home furnishings fall into this category. A shopper who purchased an IKEA dining room table and chairs and was satisfied with them is likely to return to purchase a bedroom set. While there, this shopper might pick up a set of mixing bowls for the kitchen or a lamp for the family room—because he or she knows and likes the IKEA brand.

Brand insistence is the ultimate degree of brand loyalty, in which the consumer will look for it at another outlet, special-order it from a dealer, order by mail, or search the Internet. Shoppers who insist on IKEA products for their homes may drive an hour or two—making a day excursion of the venture—to visit an IKEA store. The combination of value for the money and the concept of IKEA as a shopping destination have given the brand a unique allure for shoppers.[16]

Brand-building strategies were once limited to the consumer realm, but now they are becoming more important for B2B brands as well. Intel, Xerox, IBM, and service providers such as Krystal Klean and Cisco are among the suppliers who have built brand names among business customers.

Brand Equity Brand loyalty is at the heart of **brand equity**, the added value that a respected and successful name gives to a product. This value results from a combination of factors, including awareness, loyalty, and perceived quality, as well as any feelings or images the customer associates with the brand. High brand equity offers financial advantages to a firm, because the product commands a relatively large market share and sometimes reduces price sensitivity, generating higher profits. Figure 12.4 shows the world's ten most valuable brands and their estimated worth.

Brand awareness means the product is the first one that comes to mind when a product category is mentioned. If someone says "coffee," do you think of Starbucks, Dunkin' Donuts, or Folgers? Brand association is the link between a brand and other favorable images. A recent survey of small- and midsize-business owners and executives by American City

IKEA installed this clever showpiece, meant to look like a bus stop, in New York City during Design Week. The retailer of affordable, well-designed contemporary furniture enjoys *brand insistence*—the ultimate expression of brand loyalty. For devoted IKEA fans, no other brand will do.

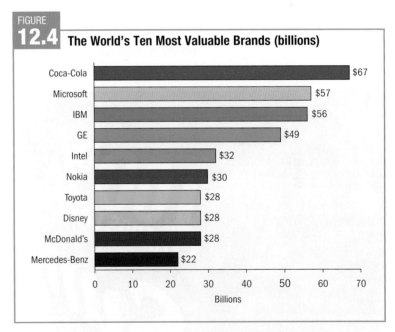

FIGURE 12.4 The World's Ten Most Valuable Brands (billions)

Brand	Billions
Coca-Cola	$67
Microsoft	$57
IBM	$56
GE	$49
Intel	$32
Nokia	$30
Toyota	$28
Disney	$28
McDonald's	$28
Mercedes-Benz	$22

Source: Data from "100 Best Global Brands," *Bloomberg BusinessWeek*, February 25, 2010, http://bwnt.businessweek.com, accessed April 22, 2010.

brand equity added value that a respected and successful name gives to a product.

Business Journals revealed that Southwest Airlines, Apple, UPS, Intuit, and the iPhone were the most recognizable brands in a field of 25.[17]

Large companies have typically assigned the task of managing a brand's marketing strategies to a *brand manager*, who may also be called a *product manager* at some firms. This marketing professional plans and implements the balance of promotional, pricing, distribution, and product arrangements that leads to strong brand equity. A *category manager*, a newer type of professional, oversees an entire group of products. Unlike traditional brand or product managers, category managers have profit responsibility for their product group. These managers are assisted by associates, usually called *analysts*. Part of the shift to category management was initiated by large retailers, when they realized there could be a benefit from the marketing muscle of large grocery and household goods producers such as Kraft and Procter & Gamble. As a result, producers began to focus their attention on in-store merchandising instead of mass-market advertising. A few years ago, Kraft reorganized its sales force so that each representative was responsible for a retailer's needs instead of pushing a single brand.

A **category advisor** functions in the B2B context. This vendor is the major supplier designated by a business customer to assume responsibility for dealing with all the other vendors for a project and presenting the entire package to the business buyer.

category advisor vendor that is designated by the business customer as the major supplier to assume responsibility for dealing with all the other vendors for a project and presenting the entire package to the business buyer.

Packages and Labels

Packaging and labels are important in product identification. They also play an important role in a firm's overall product strategy. Packaging affects the durability, image, and convenience of an item and is responsible for one of the biggest costs in many consumer products. Due to a growing demand to produce smaller, more environmentally friendly packages, box manufacturers and chemical companies are now working harder to create more compact packaging that is made from renewable sources and is recyclable. Frito-Lay recently introduced compostable packaging for its SunChips multigrain snacks, as the "Hit & Miss" feature explains. One-third of America's waste consists of containers and packaging, much of it from fast-food chains. Quiznos recently launched its "Eat Toasty, Be Green" campaign, which introduced new, environmentally friendly packaging. Among the changes to reduce the chain's environmental impact are 100 percent compostable, wax-coated paper cups; salad containers made of renewable sugarcane; napkins made from 100 percent recycled materials; and plastic lids made from 30 percent recycled PET bottles. Even the employees' uniforms are being changed, with hats and aprons made from 100 percent recycled soda bottles.[18]

Choosing the right package is especially crucial in international marketing because marketers must be aware of such factors as language variations and cultural preferences. Consumers in African nations often prefer bold colors, but use of the country's flag colors may be problematic. Some countries

Teri Stratford

Due to a growing demand to produce more environmentally friendly packages, box manufacturers and chemical companies are now working harder to create more compact packaging that is made from renewable sources and is recyclable. Frito-Lay recently introduced compostable packaging for its SunChips multigrain snacks.

SunChips Introduces Greener Packaging

Everybody loves to snack on chips, but surely nobody can love what happens to the empty bag, which eventually ends up in a landfill—and may never decompose. Frito-Lay's brand SunChips aimed to change that when it introduced what it called "the world's first compostable chip bag" on Earth Day.

In a recent survey, 75 percent of those questioned thought that recyclable packaging was "somewhat important"; 51 percent felt that compostable packaging was "somewhat important." A recyclable item can be used repeatedly, whereas a compostable item breaks down in the presence of water and oxygen.

The company had to meet the challenge of developing packaging that was ecologically sound while preserving the contents. After four years of research and testing, the company had a bag made of more than 90 percent plant-based, and therefore renewable, materials. The outer layer is made of corn-based polylactic acid (PLA). Although the bag is 100 percent compostable, researchers are currently developing an environmentally friendly inner layer that will keep the contents crisp and edible. Frito-Lay makes it clear that the bag decomposes most quickly— in about 14 weeks—in a hot, active composting bin. If the bag is simply left on the ground, it will still break down, but less efficiently.

While assuring its customers that SunChips will still taste the same, Frito-Lay is marketing the fact that because of the different material, the new bag sounds somewhat different from conventional packaging. It is promoting the difference as the "new sound of green" and even has a clip of the sound on its Web site, along with a link to Facebook.

The Biodegradable Products Institute has certified the new packaging, but getting Americans to recognize the importance of composting is another matter. A Frito-Lay executive acknowledged the challenge—and the opportunity to educate consumers.

Questions for Critical Thinking

1. What role does the new, compostable packaging play in the overall marketing strategy for SunChips?
2. How do you think SunChips can most effectively educate Americans about the importance of composting?

Sources: Company Web site, http://www.sunchips.com, accessed May 4, 2010; Kate Galbraith, "A Compostable Chips Bag Hits the Shelves," *The New York Times*, March 16, 2010, http://greeninc.blogs.nytimes.com; Kathryn Siranosian, "New SunChips Bag: 90% Plant-Based, 100% Compostable," *Triple Pundit,* February 22, 2010, http://www.triplepundit.com.

---

frown on other uses of their flag. Also, in Africa red is often associated with death or witchcraft. Package size can vary according to the purchasing patterns and market conditions of a country. In countries with small refrigerators, people may want to buy their beverages one at a time rather than in six-packs. Package weight is another important issue, because shipping costs are often based on weight.

Labeling is an integral part of the packaging process as well. In the United States, labeling must meet federal laws requiring companies to provide enough information to allow consumers to make value comparisons among competitive products and, in the case of food packaging, provide nutrition information on the label. Marketers who ship products to other countries have to comply with labeling requirements in those nations. This means knowing the answers to such questions as the following:

- Should the labels be in more than one language?

- Should ingredients be specified?

- Do the labels give enough information about the product to meet government standards?

Recently, the Food and Drug Administration (FDA) issued a statement by its commissioner, Dr. Margaret Hamburg, that encouraged food companies to ensure that their labeling complied with FDA regulations, and that the labeling was accurate and did not mislead the public. In the following year, the FDA informed 17 food companies that the labeling of almost two dozen of their products violated the Food, Drug, and Cosmetic Act. Among the violations were unauthorized health claims, unauthorized nutrient content claims, and unauthorized use of such terms as "healthy" and others that have strict regulatory definitions. In an open letter to the food industry, Dr. Hamburg stated, "Today, ready access to reliable information about the calorie and nutrient content of food is even more important, given the prevalence of obesity and diet-related diseases in the United States."[19]

Another important aspect of packaging and labeling is the *universal product code (UPC)*, the bar code read by optical scanners that print the name of the item and the price on a receipt. For many stores, these identifiers are useful not just for packaging and labeling but also for simplifying and speeding retail transactions and for evaluating customer purchases and controlling inventory. Radio-frequency identification (RFID) technology—embedded chips that can broadcast their product information to receivers—may replace UPC bar codes, however, as we'll discuss later in this chapter.

Distribution Strategy

The next element of the marketing mix, **distribution strategy**, deals with the marketing activities and institutions involved in getting the right good or service to the firm's customers. Distribution decisions involve modes of transportation, warehousing, inventory control, order processing, and selection of marketing channels. Marketing channels typically are made up of intermediaries such as retailers and wholesalers that move a product from producer to final purchaser.

The two major components of an organization's distribution strategy are distribution channels and physical distribution. **Distribution channels** are the paths that products—and legal ownership of them—follow from producer to consumer or business user. They are the means by which all organizations distribute their goods and services. **Physical distribution** is the actual movement of products from producer to consumers or business users. Physical distribution covers a broad range of activities, including customer service, transportation, inventory control, materials handling, order processing, and warehousing. As explained in the "Going Green" feature, Testa Produce, a food distributor, is building a new "green" facility to house its headquarters and its produce-distribution facility.

Distribution Channels

In their first decision for distribution channel selection, marketers choose which type of channel will best meet both their firm's marketing objectives and the needs of their customers. As shown in Figure 12.5, marketers can choose either a *direct distribution channel*, which carries goods directly from producer to consumer or business user, or distribution channels that involve several different marketing intermediaries. A *marketing intermediary* (also called a *middleman*) is a business firm that moves goods between producers and consumers or business users. Marketing intermediaries perform various functions that help the distribution channel operate smoothly, such as buying, selling, storing, and transporting products; sorting and grading bulky items; and providing information to other channel members. The two main categories of marketing intermediaries are wholesalers and retailers.

No one channel suits every product. The best choice depends on the circumstances of the market and on customer needs. The most appropriate channel choice may also change over time as new opportunities arise and marketers strive to maintain their competitiveness.

Assessment Check ✔

1. Differentiate among a brand, a brand name, and a trademark.
2. Define *brand equity*.

distribution strategy deals with the marketing activities and institutions involved in getting the right good or service to the firm's customers.

distribution channels path that products—and legal ownership of them—follow from producer to consumers or business user.

physical distribution actual movement of products from producer to consumers or business users.

Testa Produce Sells—and Builds—Green

Since 1912, when Dominick Testa began selling fruits and vegetables door to door, Testa Produce Inc. has grown to become the Chicago area's premier independent produce distributor. The current generation is making changes that Dominick could not have imagined. Ground was broken for a new company headquarters and warehouse. Testa Produce anticipated having the first food-distribution facility with the Leadership for Energy and Environmental Development (LEED) Platinum certification—the highest granted to a "green" building by the U.S. Green Building Council.

At $20 million, the new space cost 20 percent more and will have a longer return on investment than a conventional design. But Peter Testa, the company president, said, "[W]e . . . committed from the start to raising the bar on sustainability in our industry, which has a fairly large carbon footprint."

Testa Produce's new headquarters is equipped with the most advanced sustainable technological features, with room for future expansion and further advances in green technology.

A 245-foot-tall wind turbine and solar panels generate half of the building's power. Solar collectors heat water for all sinks, showers, and sanitary facilities. Skylights provide natural, ambient lighting, and a solar tracking system adjusts the ambient light over the course of the day.

The roof is about 50 percent vegetated to prevent rain runoff and slopes down to form a dramatic green wall at the building's entrance.

An internal filtered cistern and a retention pond outside capture rainwater and recycle it for nondrinking purposes. Permeable paving materials on walkways and in parking areas allow rainwater to drain into live wetlands. The landscaping features native plants that don't need constant irrigation. Watering should be necessary only during severe droughts.

Five thousand sites around the world are now LEED certified, but only 5 percent of those have won the coveted Platinum certification.

Questions for Critical Thinking

1. As a distributor, Testa Produce doesn't have direct contact with the public. How might the company go about alerting consumers to its "green" initiatives?

2. What are some ways that Testa Produce might encourage its employees to follow "green" practices?

Sources: Company Web site, http://www.testaproduce.com, accessed May 3, 2010; "Testa Produce Turns a Brighter Shade of Green with Its New HQ," *Refrigerated Transport,* April 12, 2010, http://refrigeratedtrans.com; Sam Carlson, "Construction Under Way on Testa's Green Distribution Center," *Packer,* April 9, 2010, http://thepacker.com; Testa Produce, Inc., "Testa Produce Turns a Brighter Shade of Green," press release, April 7, 2010, https://ssl117.alentus.com; Betsy Kraat, "Epstein Designs 'Green' Headquarters/ Produce Distribution Facility for Testa Produce, Inc.," *metroGREEN+BUSINESS,* March 4, 2010, http://www.metrogreenbusiness.com.

Currently, most smart phones sold in the United States are tied to a single wireless carrier that controls all distribution of its particular phone. Consumers can choose a smart phone but can't choose a carrier. Recently, Google announced the release of its Nexus One smart phone, for sale at a new, Google-hosted Web store. The Nexus One offers some new features, but Google's long-range goal is to change the distribution channels for smart phones. Buyers have the option of buying a conventional version of the Nexus One that is locked to T-Mobile's service plan and therefore controlled by T-Mobile, or an unlocked version—that is, one that can be used with any wireless service plan. By offering an unlocked smart phone, Google is gambling that consumers will choose a distribution channel that isn't tied to a wireless carrier and that Google itself will be able to create software that can compete with that available for the iPhone. In this type of business model, buyers would be able to select a phone first and then sign up with a carrier, much as they can now buy any brand of computer regardless of their Internet service provider.[20]

Direct Distribution The shortest and simplest means of connecting producers and customers is direct contact between the two parties. This approach is most common in the B2B market. Consumers who buy fresh fruits and vegetables at rural roadside stands or farmers markets use direct distribution, as do services ranging from banking and ten-minute oil changes to ear piercing and Mary Kay Cosmetics.

Direct distribution is commonly found in the marketing of relatively expensive, complex products that may require demonstrations. Most major B2B products such as installations,

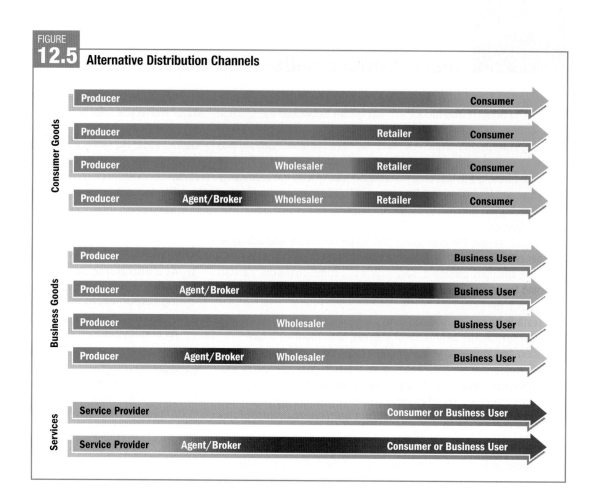

FIGURE 12.5 Alternative Distribution Channels

Consumer Goods

Producer → Consumer

Producer → Retailer → Consumer

Producer → Wholesaler → Retailer → Consumer

Producer → Agent/Broker → Wholesaler → Retailer → Consumer

Business Goods

Producer → Business User

Producer → Agent/Broker → Business User

Producer → Wholesaler → Business User

Producer → Agent/Broker → Wholesaler → Business User

Services

Service Provider → Consumer or Business User

Service Provider → Agent/Broker → Consumer or Business User

accessory equipment, component parts, business services, and even raw materials are typically marketed through direct contacts between producers and business buyers. The Internet has also made direct distribution an attractive option for many retail companies and service providers. FedEx customers have long used online tools to track conventional shipments. Fedex's new International Priority Direct Distribution service allows users to ship more than one package from a single country of origin to a different recipients in single destination country. The packages are cleared through customs as a single shipment. In addition, multiple shipments to multiple recipients in multiple European Union countries can be cleared through customs as a single shipment through Charles de Gaulle Airport near Paris.[21]

Distribution Channels Using Marketing Intermediaries Although direct channels allow simple and straightforward connections between producers and their customers, the list of channel alternatives in Figure 12.5 suggests that direct distribution is not the best choice in every instance. Some products sell in small quantities for relatively low prices to thousands of widely scattered consumers. Makers of such products cannot cost effectively contact each of their customers, so they distribute products through specialized intermediaries called *wholesalers* and *retailers*.

Although you might think that adding intermediaries to the distribution process would increase the final cost of products, more often than not this choice actually lowers consumer prices. Intermediaries such as wholesalers and retailers often add significant value to a product as it moves through the distribution channel. They do so by creating utility, providing additional services, and reducing costs.

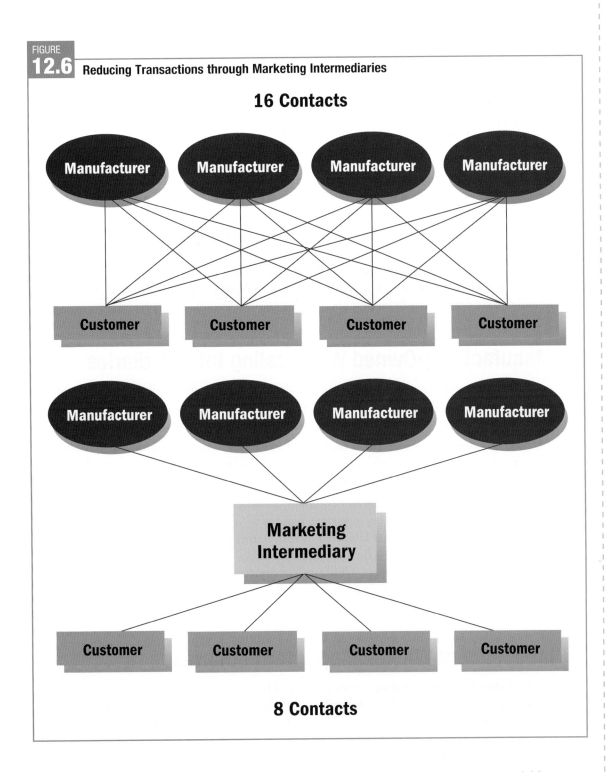

FIGURE 12.6 Reducing Transactions through Marketing Intermediaries

16 Contacts

Manufacturer Manufacturer Manufacturer Manufacturer

Customer Customer Customer Customer

Manufacturer Manufacturer Manufacturer Manufacturer

Marketing Intermediary

Customer Customer Customer Customer

8 Contacts

Marketing utility is created when intermediaries help ensure that products are available for sale when and where customers want to purchase them. If you want something warm to eat on a cold winter night, you don't call up Campbell's Soup and ask them to ship a can of chicken noodle soup. Instead, you go to the nearest grocery store, where you find utility in the form of product availability. In addition, intermediaries perform such important services as transporting merchandise to convenient locations. Finally, by representing numerous producers, a marketing intermediary can cut the costs of buying and selling. As Figure 12.6 shows, if four manufacturers each sold directly to four consumers, this would require 16

Assessment Check ✓

1. Define *distribution channels*.

2. What is a marketing intermediary?

separate transactions. Adding a marketing intermediary, such as a retailer, to the exchange cuts the number of necessary transactions to 8.

Wholesaling

A <u>wholesaler</u> is a distribution channel member that sells primarily to retailers, other wholesalers, or business users. For instance, Sysco is a wholesaler that buys food products from producers and then resells them to restaurants, hotels, and other institutions in the United States and Canada.

Wholesaling is a crucial part of the distribution channel for many products, particularly consumer goods and business supplies. Wholesaling intermediaries can be classified on the basis of ownership; some are owned by manufacturers, some are owned by retailers, and others are independently owned. The United States has about 430,000 wholesalers, 85 percent of which have fewer than 20 employees.[22]

Manufacturer-Owned Wholesaling Intermediaries

A manufacturer's marketing manager may decide to distribute goods directly through company-owned facilities to control distribution or customer service. Firms operate two main types of manufacturer-owned wholesaling intermediaries: sales branches and sales offices.

Sales branches stock the products they distribute and fill orders from their inventories. They also provide offices for sales representatives. Sales branches are common in the chemical, petroleum products, motor vehicle, and machine and equipment industries.

A *sales office* is exactly what its name implies: an office for a producer's salespeople. Manufacturers set up sales offices in various regions to support local selling efforts and improve customer service. Some kitchen and bath fixture manufacturers maintain showrooms to display their products. Builders and decorators can visit these showrooms to see how the items would look in place. Unlike sales branches, however, sales offices do not store any inventory. When a customer orders from a showroom or other sales office, the merchandise is delivered from a separate warehouse.

Independent Wholesaling Intermediaries

An independent wholesaling intermediary is a business that represents a number of different manufacturers and makes sales calls on retailers, manufacturers, and other business accounts. Independent wholesalers are classified as either merchant wholesalers or agents and brokers, depending on whether they take title to the products they handle.

Merchant wholesalers, like apparel wholesaler WholesaleSarong.com, are independently owned wholesaling intermediaries that take title to the goods they handle. Within this category, a *full-function merchant wholesaler* provides a complete assortment of services for retailers or industrial buyers, such as warehousing, shipping, and even financing. A subtype of full-function merchant is a *rack jobber*, such as Ohio-based Arrow Distributing, which handles distribution of CDs and DVDs to retail stores. This type of firm stocks, displays, and services particular retail products, such as paperback books or greeting cards in a drugstore or supermarket. Usually, the retailer receives a commission based on actual sales as payment for providing merchandise space to a rack jobber.

A *limited-function merchant wholesaler* also takes legal title to the products it handles, but it provides fewer services to the retailers to which it sells. Some limited-function merchant wholesalers only warehouse products but do not offer delivery service. Others warehouse and deliver products but provide no financing. One type of limited-function merchant wholesaler is a *drop shipper* such as Kate Aspen, an Atlanta-based wholesaler of wedding favors. Drop shippers also operate in such industries as coal and lumber, characterized by bulky products for which no single producer can provide a complete assortment. They give access to many related goods by contacting numerous producers and negotiating the best possible prices. Cost considerations call for producers to ship such products directly to the drop shipper's customers.

Another category of independent wholesaling intermediaries consists of *agents* and *brokers*. They may or may not take possession of the goods they handle, but they never take title, working mainly to bring buyers and sellers together. Stockbrokers such as Charles Schwab and real estate agents such as RE/MAX perform functions similar to those of agents and brokers, but at the retail level. They do not take title to the sellers' property; instead, they create time and ownership utility for both buyer and seller by helping carry out transactions.

Manufacturers' reps act as independent sales forces by representing the manufacturers of related but noncompeting products. These agent intermediaries, sometimes referred to as *manufacturers' agents*, receive commissions based on a percentage of the sales they make.

Retailer-Owned Cooperatives and Buying Offices

Retailers sometimes band together to form their own wholesaling organizations. Such organizations can take the form of either a buying group or a cooperative. The participating retailers set up the new operation to reduce costs or to provide some special service that is not readily available in the marketplace. To achieve cost savings through quantity purchases, independent retailers may form a buying group that negotiates bulk sales with manufacturers. One such buying group is Florida-based Retail Advantage Group, which buys products for its member hospital gift shops and gift shop chains. Members join for a year at a time and can receive up to 10 percent discounts on orders they place, while remaining free to buy from any other vendors.[23] In a cooperative, an independent group of retailers may decide to band together to share functions such as shipping or warehousing.

Retailing

Retailers, in contrast to wholesalers, are distribution channel members that sell goods and services to individuals for their own use rather than for resale. Consumers usually buy their food, clothing, shampoo, furniture, and appliances from some type of retailer. The supermarket where you buy your groceries may have bought some of its items from a wholesaler such as Unified Grocers and then resold them to you.

Retailers are the final link—the so-called last three feet—of the distribution channel. Because they are often the only channel members that deal directly with consumers, it is essential that retailers remain alert to changing shopper needs. For instance, soaring gas prices affect consumers' budgets, so they may make fewer trips to the mall or cut back on nonessential purchases. As a result, retailers may need to offer special sales or events to lure customers to their shops. It is also important for retailers to keep pace with developments in the fast-changing business environment, such as the disruption in delivery of supplies from widespread wildfires or storms.

FIGURE
12.7

Types of Nonstore Retailing

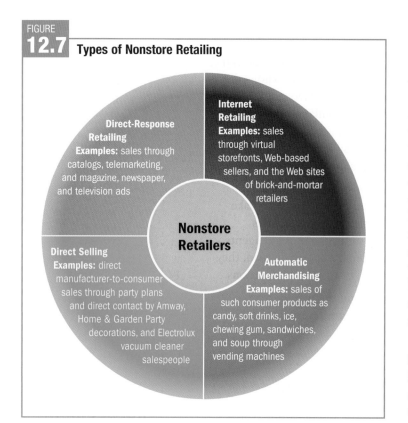

Nonstore Retailers

Direct-Response Retailing
Examples: sales through catalogs, telemarketing, and magazine, newspaper, and television ads

Internet Retailing
Examples: sales through virtual storefronts, Web-based sellers, and the Web sites of brick-and-mortar retailers

Direct Selling
Examples: direct manufacturer-to-consumer sales through party plans and direct contact by Amway, Home & Garden Party decorations, and Electrolux vacuum cleaner salespeople

Automatic Merchandising
Examples: sales of such consumer products as candy, soft drinks, ice, chewing gum, sandwiches, and soup through vending machines

PRNewsFoto/Zoom Systems/NewsCom

This Proactiv Solution kiosk dispenses skin care products automatically, just as an ATM dispenses cash. *Automatic merchandising* is a form of nonstore retailing.

Nonstore Retailers

Two categories of retailers exist: store and nonstore. As Figure 12.7 shows, nonstore retailing includes four forms: direct-response retailing, Internet retailing, automatic merchandising, and direct selling. *Direct-response retailing* reaches prospective customers through catalogs; telemarketing; and even magazine, newspaper, and television ads. Shoppers order merchandise by mail, telephone, computer, and fax machine and then receive home delivery or pick the merchandise up at a local store. Lands' End has long stood out as a highly successful direct-response retailer; its well-known clothing catalog and stellar customer service have set the standard for this type of distribution channel. With the retailer's purchase by Sears, however, customers can now see, feel, and try on its clothing at Lands' End Shops in Sears locations around the country.

Internet retailing, the second form of nonstore retailing, has grown rapidly. Tens of thousands of retailers have set up shop online, with sales growing at a rate of about 5 percent a year (as compared with declines in total retail sales). Today, online sales account for about 3.8 percent of total retail sales.[24] A severe shakeout saw hundreds of Internet enterprises shut down during the first few years of the 21st century, but firms that survived have stronger business models than those that failed. Two examples of successful pure dot-coms are Amazon and eBay. A major shift in retailing has seen traditional brick-and-mortar retailers competing with pure dot-com start-ups by setting up their own Web sites as an option for shoppers. Nordstrom, JCPenney, and Walmart report strong online sales. Shopping sites are among the most popular Internet destinations, and sales of clothing and DVDs in particular have risen.

The last two forms of nonstore retailing are automatic merchandising and direct selling. *Automatic merchandising* provides convenience through the use of vending machines. ATMs may soon join the ranks of vending machines as banks find new ways to compete for customers. Some ATMs offer extra services such as check cashing and stamps, as well as concert tickets and road maps. Future ATMs will be able to connect wirelessly to cell phones to allow customers to download and pay for games and music. *Direct selling* includes direct-to-consumer sales by Pampered Chef kitchen representatives and salespeople for Silpada sterling silver jewelry through party-plan selling methods. Both are forms of direct selling.

Companies that previously relied heavily on telemarketing in generating new customers have encountered consumer resistance to intrusive phone calls. Among the growing barriers are caller ID, call-blocking devices such as the TeleZapper, and the National Do Not Call list, which made it illegal for most companies to call people who are registered. As a result, dozens of companies, including telecommunications and regional utilities, have sent direct-mail pieces to promote such services as phones, cable television, and natural gas distributors.

Store Retailers

In-store sales still outpace nonstore retailing methods like direct-response retailing and Internet selling. Store retailers range in size from tiny newsstands to multistory department stores and multiacre warehouselike retailers such as Sam's Club. Table 12.2 lists the different types of store retailers, with examples of each type. Clearly, there are many approaches to retailing and a variety of services, prices, and product lines offered by each retail outlet.

The Wheel of Retailing Retailers are subject to constant change as new stores replace older establishments. In a process called the *wheel of retailing*, new retailers enter the market by offering lower prices made possible through reductions in service. Supermarkets and discount houses, for example, gained their initial market footholds through low-price,

Table

12.2 Types of Retail Stores

STORE TYPE	DESCRIPTION	EXAMPLE
Specialty store	Offers complete selection in a narrow line of merchandise	Bass Pro Shops, Dick's Sporting Goods, Williams-Sonoma
Convenience store	Offers staple convenience goods, easily accessible locations, extended store hours, and rapid checkouts	7-Eleven, Mobil Mart, QuikTrip
Discount store	Offers wide selection of merchandise at low prices; off-price discounters offer designer or brand-name merchandise	Target, Walmart, Nordstrom Rack, Marshalls
Warehouse club	Large, warehouse-style store selling food and general merchandise at discount prices to membership card-holders	Costco, Sam's Club, BJ's
Factory outlet	Manufacturer-owned store selling seconds, production overruns, or discontinued lines	Adidas, Coach, Pottery Barn, Ralph Lauren
Supermarket	Large, self-service retailer offering a wide selection of food and nonfood merchandise	Safeway, Whole Foods Market, Kroger
Supercenter	Giant store offering food and general merchandise at discount prices	Walmart Supercenter, Super Target
Department store	Offers a wide variety of merchandise selections (furniture, cosmetics, housewares, clothing) and many customer services	Nordstrom, Macy's, Neiman Marcus

FIGURE
12.8 The Wheel of Retailing

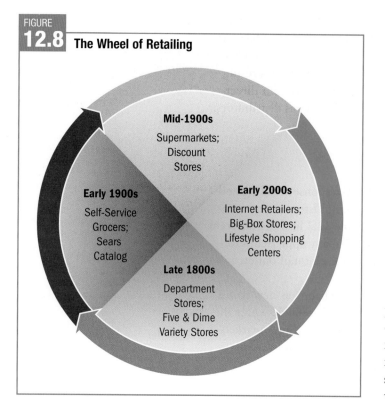

limited-service appeals. These new entries gradually add services as they grow and ultimately become targets for new retailers.

As Figure 12.8 shows, most major developments in retailing appear to fit the wheel pattern. The low-price, limited-service strategy characterized supermarkets, catalog retailers, discount stores, and, most recently, Internet retailers and giant "big-box" stores, such as PetSmart, Borders, and Office Depot. Corner grocery stores gave way to supermarkets and then to warehouse clubs such as Costco or BJ's. Department stores lost market share to discount clothing retailers such as Target and Marshalls. Independent bookstores have lost business to giant chains like Barnes & Noble, Borders, and such online-only sellers as Amazon.com and Buy.com.

Even though the wheel of retailing does not fit every pattern of retail evolution—for example, automatic merchandising has always been a relatively high-priced method of retailing—it does give retail managers a general idea of what is likely to occur during the evolution of retailing. It also shows that business success involves the "survival of the fittest." Retailers that fail to change fail to survive.

How Retailers Compete

Retailers compete with each other in many ways. Nonstore retailers focus on making the shopping experience as convenient as possible. Shoppers at stores such as Saks Fifth Avenue enjoy a luxurious atmosphere and personal service. In fact, those who visit the new shoe department at the flagship store in New York have the run of the entire eighth floor, which is entirely devoted to shoes—with its own Zip code. Saks recently began a new campaign called "Special Delivery to 10022-SHOE" to introduce shoes by new designers. Some of the shoes are exclusive to Saks. According to Cody Kondo, Saks senior vice president and general merchandising manager, "With Special Delivery, the team [of buyers] selected those styles that were unlike anything else being shown . . . those shoes that the merchants fell in love with."[25]

Like manufacturers, retailers must develop marketing strategies based on goals and strategic plans. Successful retailers convey images that alert consumers to the stores' identities and the shopping experiences they provide. To create that image, all components of a retailer's strategy must complement each other. After identifying their target markets, retailers must choose merchandising, customer service, pricing, and location strategies that will attract customers in those market segments.

Identifying a Target Market The first step in developing a competitive retailing strategy is to select a target market. This choice requires careful evaluation of the size and profit potential of the chosen market segment and the current level of competition for the segment's business. Bargain stores such as Family Dollar target consumers who are extremely price conscious, for example, while convenience stores like 7-Eleven target consumers who want an easy way to purchase items they buy frequently. Seventh Generation, which makes "green" home- and personal-care items, began as a mail-order company, then started selling at natural-food stores, then grew into a major business whose products are featured at supermarkets nationwide as well as at Target and at Amazon.com. Seventh Generation, which is committed to increasing consumer awareness of environmentally safe cleaning and household products, recently began its "Protecting Planet Home" campaign. The company plans to build on its 45 percent profits by launching its first national marketing campaign online, in print, and in TV commercials. The company's goal is to get 45 percent of American households to try at least one Seventh Generation product.[26]

Seventh Generation determined its *target market* were the people committed to of environmentally safe cleaning and household products.

Selecting a Product Strategy Next, the retailer must develop a product strategy to determine the best mix of merchandise to carry to satisfy that market. Retail strategists must decide on the general product categories, product lines, and variety to offer. Sometimes that involves expanding the product mix and sometime it involves contracting it. Polaroid's parent company signed a five-year licensing agreement with Starlight, a leading consumer electronics manufacturer and distributer. Under the agreement, Starlight will develop a range of Polaroid-brand consumer electronics equipment, including Blu-ray players, stand-alone and portable DVD players, e-readers, iPod docking stations, and home theater systems.[27]

Shaping a Customer Service Strategy A retailer's customer service strategy focuses on attracting and retaining target customers to maximize sales and profits. Some stores offer a wide variety of services, such as gift wrapping, alterations, returns, interior design services, and delivery. Other stores offer bare-bones customer service, stressing low price instead. Some grocery shoppers, for instance, can find convenience online through a service like Peapod, which handles product selection, packing, and delivery. They can visit a supermarket and make their own selections. Or they can go to a discount supermarket like Minnesota-based Cub Foods, a division of SuperValu, where they not only assemble their orders but also bag their purchases.

Selecting a Pricing Strategy Retailers base their pricing decisions on the costs of purchasing products from other channel members and offering services to customers. Pricing can play a major role in consumers' perceptions of a retailer, and not just because they appreciate low prices. The grocery retailer Trader Joe's offers organic and gourmet foods under its own private labels at rock-bottom prices. Customers enjoy shopping for Trader Jose's Mexican specialties and Trader Darwin's nutritional supplements at prices lower than other gourmet or organic markets.[28] Pricing strategy is covered in more detail in Chapter 13.

Choosing a Location A good location often marks the difference between success and failure in retailing. The location decision depends on the retailer's size, financial resources, product offerings, competition, and, of course, its target market. Traffic patterns, the visibility of the store's signage, parking, and the location of complementary stores also influence the choice of a retail location. Consider the rivalry between PetSmart and Petco. Petco tends to have smaller stores in greater numbers, located in strip malls, than PetSmart,

Solving an Ethical Controversy

Teens at the Mall: Good or Bad for Business?

Some shopping malls have banned unsupervised minors on weekend evenings. Others are considering a total ban on teens who are not accompanied by adults. Teenagers go to malls not only to hang out with their friends but also to spend money. Mall merchants who used to complain about groups of unsupervised teenagers have now pinned their hopes on these young spenders to increase sales. Although they are more cautious shoppers than before the recession, teenagers are once again snacking at the food court and shopping at stores such as American Eagle and Abercrombie & Fitch.

Should malls that have essentially imposed curfews on teenagers consider lifting those bans to help boost business?

PRO

1. According to Thompson Reuters, spending by teenagers has increased, contrary to expectations after almost a year and a half of declining figures. Malls should encourage teens to shop.

2. Most teenagers are well behaved and should not be banned as a group because of the bad behavior of a few.

CON

1. Some merchants are still wary. One said, "Parents drop their kids off, and they don't know what their kids do while they are away."

2. The attractiveness of teenage free spending has to be considered in the light of crowd behavior. At one mall, more than a dozen teenagers were arrested after a fight broke out.

Summary

Just as adults spent much less during the recent recession, so did their children. "Bank of Mom and Dad—on pretty much all levels—basically shut down," said one retail analyst. Teenagers have now returned in some measure to their impulsive shopping habits. Mall owners and civic leaders will need to find a balance between maintaining order and encouraging these consumers of tomorrow.

Sources: Andrea Chang, "Free-Spending Teens Return to Malls," *Los Angeles Times,* March 28, 2010, http://articles.latimes.com; Erica Shaffer, "City Leaders Recommend Total Ban of Unsupervised Teens at Mall," WTOL, February 18, 2010, http://www.wtol.com; Fran Daniel, "Mall May Limit Teens: Policy Expected to Require Parental Supervision on Friday, Saturday Evenings," *Winston-Salem Journal,* February 9, 2010, http://www2.journalnow.com.

---

whose strategy is to build bigger "power centers" right beside other large discount chains. PetSmart has added pet services—adoption, grooming, day care, and boarding—in some of its stores. Petco uses its stores to promote a broader selection of goods for offbeat pets, such as tarantulas and unusual reptiles. Both companies have implemented "green" initiatives.[29]

A *planned shopping center* is a group of retail stores planned, coordinated, and marketed as a unit to shoppers in a geographical trade area. By providing single convenient locations with free parking, shopping centers have largely replaced downtown shopping in many urban areas. But time-pressed consumers are increasingly looking for more efficient ways to shop, including catalogs, Internet retailers, and one-stop shopping at large free-standing stores such as Walmart Supercenters. To lure more customers, shopping centers are recasting themselves as entertainment destinations, with movie theaters, art displays, carousel rides, and musical entertainment. The giant Mall of America in Bloomington, Minnesota, features a seven-acre amusement park and an aquarium.

Shopping malls are well-known magnets for teens, who often meet there to socialize with friends. Businesses want to welcome their teen customers, but sometimes the cluster of teens hanging around the mall causes difficulties for other customers and some retailers, as described in the "Solving an Ethical Controversy" feature.

To varying degrees in recent years, large regional malls have also witnessed a growing shift in shopping center traffic to smaller strip centers, name-brand outlet centers, and *lifestyle centers*, open-air complexes containing retailers that often focus on specific shopper segments and product interests. Victoria Gardens, a lifestyle center in California, recently formed partnerships with local businesses that sponsor its family-loyalty program, VG Kidz. VG Kidz promotes healthy food choices and an active lifestyle for children and their families. According to Masa Liles, the director of marketing for Victoria Gardens, "The current economy has forced all of us to be creative about our marketing initiatives and VG is no exception. These paid sponsorships will not only help our bottom line, but give depth to our programming and another way shoppers can interact with our property."[30]

Building a Promotional Strategy A retailer designs advertisements and develops other promotions to stimulate demand and to provide information such as the store's location, merchandise offerings, prices, and hours. When a recent year proved to be difficult, Starbucks turned to social media for a new promotional strategy. The chain launched MyStarbucksIdea.com, a forum where customers could ask questions, offer suggestions, and even voice their dislikes. The site's 180,000 registered users have offered 80,000 ideas, of which 50 have been implemented. The Starbucks Facebook page has some 5.7 million fans; the chain also has 775,000 Twitter followers. Charles Bruzzo, the chain's vice president for brand, content, and online, says the company is seeing the beginning of an "interesection between digital and physical."[31]

Nonstore retailers provide their phone numbers and Web site addresses. More recently, online retailers have scaled back their big advertising campaigns and worked to build traffic through word of mouth and clever promotions. Promotional strategy is also discussed in depth in Chapter 13.

Creating a Store Atmosphere A successful retailer closely aligns its merchandising, pricing, and promotion strategies with *store atmospherics*, the physical characteristics of a store and its amenities, to influence consumers' perceptions of the shopping experience. Atmospherics begin with the store's exterior, which may use eye-catching architectural elements and signage to attract customer attention and interest. Interior atmospheric elements include store layout, merchandise presentation, lighting, color, sound, and cleanliness. A high-end store such as Nordstrom, for instance, features high-ceilings in selling areas that spotlight tasteful and meticulously cared-for displays of carefully chosen items of obvious quality. Dick's Sporting Goods, on the other hand, carries an ever-changing array of moderately priced clothing and gear in its warehouselike settings furnished with industrial-style display hardware.

Distribution Channel Decisions and Logistics

Every firm faces two major decisions when choosing how to distribute its goods or services: selecting a specific distribution channel and deciding on the level of distribution intensity. In deciding which distribution channel is most efficient, business managers need to consider four factors: the market, the product, the producer, and the competition. These factors are often interrelated and may change over time. In today's global business environment, strong relationships with customers and suppliers are important for survival. One way

Assessment Check ☑

1. Define *retailer*.

2. What are the elements of a retailer's marketing strategy?

Minding Your Social Media Manners

More and more entrepreneurs are using social networking media to promote their small or medium-size businesses. Facebook, Twitter, LinkedIn, and myriad blogs and forums offer endless marketing opportunities. A recent survey found that 70 percent of small businesses planned to increase their use of social media. Seventy-nine percent did not plan to run TV commercials, and 70 percent didn't use radio.

Just as in the real business world, good manners, common courtesy, and common sense will take you far in the virtual business world. Here are a few tips on good manners for social media:

1 *Even though you join social networks to promote your business, don't make it too obvious.* Instead of promoting yourself or your business nonstop, use selected posts to indicate that you have something of value to offer to interested people. Otherwise, you run the risk of being considered a spammer.

2 *Be aware that you are in social networks for the long haul.* Group or forum members are real people with real interests and ideas. Get to know the members of your forums, find out what those interests are, and learn how the community as a whole works. Virtual networks of "friends" have unwritten rules, just as real networks do.

3 *It's not the numbers that count.* Getting your brand known or achieving other marketing goals doesn't necessarily depend on how many Twitter followers you have but on how you engage with them.

4 *Be careful of what you say.* Avoid vulgar language, off-color jokes, or any hint of racial or gender bias. Don't bring up religion, politics, or other delicate subjects. Leave any strong opinions out of your marketing profile.

5 *Remember that your customers will be discussing you on their own networks.* Your reputation may travel farther than you know!

Sources: Mickie Kennedy, "Do You Have Good Social Media Manners?" *eReleases,* March 23, 2010, http://www.ereleases.com; Michelle Bowles, "5 Social Media Tips for ecommerce Marketing," *Online Marketing Blog,* March 12, 2010, http://www.toprankblog.com; Kim States, "Five Social Media Tips to Connect Small Businesses," *AzBiz.com,* January 2, 2010, http://www.azbiz.com; Sean Rasmussen.

to help cement such relationships online is to practice proper social media manners, as the "Business Etiquette" feature explains.

Selecting Distribution Channels

Market factors may be the most important consideration in choosing a distribution channel. To reach a target market with a small number of buyers or buyers concentrated in a geographical area, the most feasible alternative may be a direct channel. In contrast, if the firm must reach customers who are dispersed or who make frequent small purchases, then the channel may need to incorporate marketing intermediaries to make goods available when and where customers want them.

In general, standardized products or items with low unit values usually pass through relatively long distribution channels. On the other hand, products that are complex, expensive, custom made, or perishable move through shorter distribution channels involving few—or no—intermediaries. The increasing prevalence of e-commerce is resulting in changes in traditional distribution practices. The European Commission recently issued a set of rules, effective until 2022, that permit makers of goods with less than a 30 percent market share—usually high-end manufacturers—to block Internet-only retailers from carrying their products. The commission declared that "suppliers should normally be free to decide on the number and type of distributors they want to have in their distribution systems. . . . More generally, suppliers may only want to sell to distributors that have one or more physical points of present [actual "bricks-and-mortar" stores] where the suppliers' goods can be touched, smelled, tried, etc." The European Alliance—which represents luxury goods manufacturers such as LVMH Louis Vuitton Moët Hennessey, Gucci, and Burberry—lobbied for and welcomed the new rules as a way to protect the quality image of their products. Online-only retailers, such as Amazon, eBay, and their European counterparts, called for repeal of the "bricks-and-mortar" requirement and warned that some manufacturers would use the new rules to "restrict the availability" of their products online and thus keep prices high.[32]

The Greek entrepreneur Stelios Haji-Ioannou, however, finds the Internet the perfect channel for easyGroup, the private investment group for his "easy" brand. The company represents a variety of businesses with the "easy" tag—including easyJet.com, easyCar.com, easyJobs.com, easyPizza.com, and even an easyBus route between Gatwick Airport and London. Each business offers a no-frills, low-cost approach to services that consumers can order online. EasyJet is one of Europe's biggest Internet retailers, selling 95 percent of its seats online.[33]

Producers that offer a broad product line, with the financial and marketing resources to distribute and promote it, are more likely to choose a shorter channel. Instead of depending on marketing intermediaries, financially strong manufacturers with broad product lines typically use their own sales representatives, warehouses, and credit departments to serve both retailers and consumers.

In many cases, start-up manufacturers turn to direct channels because they can't persuade intermediaries to carry their products or because they want to extend their sales reach. Some companies employ direct channels to carry intangible goods as well. Based in New York City, Art Meets Commerce uses the Internet and social networking to promote small Broadway and off-Broadway shows with tight marketing budgets. The company posts short videos of its client shows on YouTube and takes advantage of Facebook and Twitter to amplify traditional word-of-mouth publicity. When celebrities see the shows and post favorable tweets, their followers may feel encouraged to see the shows too.[34]

Competitive performance is the fourth key consideration when choosing a distribution channel. A producer loses customers when an intermediary fails to achieve promotion or product delivery. Channels used by established competitors as well as new market entries also can influence decisions. Sometimes a joint venture between competitors can work well. Best Buy and Apple have teamed up to sell their products under the same roof. Under the agreement, Apple controls its own retail space within Best Buy stores. Although Apple has a well-established retail business, it can't match the size of electronics giant Best Buy. Best Buy benefits by generating more traffic from customers who want to see and buy Apple's innovative products in convenient locations. The strategy has worked well, as the sales of Macs in particular have increased. Best Buy was the only non-Apple retailer in the United States to carry the iPad. All of Best Buy's 673 stores with Apple shops sold out their stock of iPads in four days.[35]

Selecting Distribution Intensity

A second key distribution decision involves *distribution intensity*—the number of intermediaries or outlets through which a manufacturer distributes its goods. Only one BMW dealership may be operating in your immediate area, but you can find Coca-Cola everywhere—in supermarkets, convenience stores, gas stations, vending machines, and restaurants. BMW has chosen a different level of distribution intensity than that used for Coca-Cola. In general, market coverage varies along a continuum with three different intensity levels:

1. *Intensive distribution* involves placing a firm's products in nearly every available outlet. Generally, intensive distribution suits low-priced convenience goods such as milk, newspapers, and soft drinks. This kind of market saturation requires cooperation by many intermediaries, including wholesalers and retailers, to achieve maximum coverage.

2. *Selective distribution* is a market-coverage strategy in which a manufacturer selects only a limited number of retailers to distribute its product lines. Selective distribution can reduce total marketing costs and establish strong working relationships within the channel.

Daniel Acker/Bloomberg/Getty Images, Inc.

Exclusive distribution limits market coverage in a specific geographical region. The approach suits relatively expensive specialty products such as Rolex watches. Retailers are carefully selected to enhance the product's image to the market.

3. *Exclusive distribution*, at the other end of the continuum from intensive distribution, limits market coverage in a specific geographical region. The approach suits relatively expensive specialty products such as Rolex watches. Retailers are carefully selected to enhance the product's image to the market and to ensure that well-trained personnel will contribute to customer satisfaction. Although producers may sacrifice some market coverage by granting an exclusive territory to a single intermediary, the decision usually pays off in developing and maintaining an image of quality and prestige.

When companies are offloading excess inventory, even high-priced retailers may look to discounters to help them clear the merchandise from their warehouses. To satisfy consumers' taste for luxury goods, designer outlet malls offer shoppers a chance to buy status items at lower prices. Philadelphia Premium Outlets shopping center contains more than 100 stores carrying such brands as Calphalon kitchenware, Coach handbags, and Neiman Marcus Last Call. Other similar outlet malls are Woodbury Common Premium Outlets, north of New York City, and Desert Hills Premium Outlets in Cabazon, California.[36]

Logistics and Physical Distribution

supply chain complete sequence of suppliers that contribute to creating a good or service and delivering it to business users and final consumers.

A firm's choice of distribution channels creates the final link in the **supply chain**, the complete sequence of suppliers that contribute to creating a good or service and delivering it to business users and final consumers. The supply chain begins when the raw materials used in production are delivered to the producer and continues with the actual production activities that create finished goods. Finally, the finished goods move through the producer's distribution channels to end customers.

logistics process of coordinating the flow of goods, services, and information among members of the supply chain.

The process of coordinating the flow of goods, services, and information among members of the supply chain is called **logistics**. The term originally referred to strategic movements of military troops and supplies. Today, however, it describes all of the business activities involved in the supply chain with the ultimate goal of getting finished goods to customers.

Physical Distribution A major focus of logistics management—identified earlier in the chapter as one of the two basic dimensions of distribution strategy—is *physical distribution*, the activities aimed at efficiently moving finished goods from the production line to the consumer or business buyer. As Figure 12.9 shows, physical distribution is a broad concept that includes transportation and numerous other elements that help link buyers and sellers. An effectively managed physical distribution system can increase customer satisfaction by ensuring reliable movements of products through the supply chain. For instance, Walmart

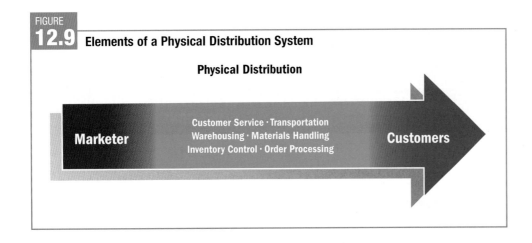

FIGURE 12.9 Elements of a Physical Distribution System

Physical Distribution

Marketer

Customer Service · Transportation
Warehousing · Materials Handling
Inventory Control · Order Processing

Customers

studies the speed with which goods can be shelved once they arrive at the store because strategies that look efficient at the warehouse, such as completely filling pallets with goods, can actually be time-consuming or costly in the aisles.

Radio-frequency identification (RFID) technology relies on a computer chip implanted somewhere on a product or its packaging that emits a low-frequency radio signal identifying the item. The radio signal doesn't require a line of sight to register on the store's computers the way a bar code does, so a hand-held RFID reader can scan crates and cartons before they are unloaded. Because the chip can store information about the product's progress through the distribution channel, retailers can efficiently manage inventories, maintain stock levels, reduce loss, track stolen goods, and cut costs. The technology is similar to that already used to identify lost pets and speed vehicles through toll booths. Walmart, Target, the U.S. Department of Defense, and the German retailer Metro Group already require their suppliers to use RFID technology. The U.S. Army is now using solar power to activate battery-powered RFIDs, which are particularly useful in remote areas. Automakers are also using RFID technology to improve their production processes by tracking parts and other supplies. A new version of the RFID chip can be printed on paper or plastic. RFID technology brings with it privacy and counterfeiting concerns. Recently one company developed a process that uses unique silicon "fingerprints" to generate unclonable RFID chips.[37]

Warehousing is the physical distribution activity that involves the storage of products. *Materials handling* is moving items within factories, warehouses, transportation terminals, and stores. Inventory control involves managing inventory costs, such as storage facilities, insurance, taxes, and handling. The physical distribution activity of *order processing* includes preparing orders for shipment and receiving orders when shipments arrive.

The wide use of electronic data interchange (EDI) and the constant pressure on suppliers to improve their response time have led to **vendor-managed inventory**, in which the producer and the retailer agree that the producer (or the wholesaler) will determine how much of a product a buyer needs and automatically ship new supplies when needed.

The form of transportation used to ship products depends primarily on the kind of product, the distance involved, and the cost. The logistics manager can choose from a number of companies and modes of transportation. As Table 12.3 shows, the five major transport modes are—in order of total expenditures—trucks (with about 75 percent of total expenditures), railroads (approximately 12 percent), water carriers (6 percent), air freight

vendor-managed inventory process in which the producer and the retailer agree that the producer (or the wholesaler) will determine how much of a product a buyer needs and automatically ship new supplies when needed.

12.3 Comparison of Transportation Modes

MODE	SPEED	DEPENDABILITY IN MEETING SCHEDULES	FREQUENCY OF SHIPMENTS	AVAILABILITY IN DIFFERENT LOCATIONS	FLEXIBILITY IN HANDLING	COST
Truck	Fast	High	High	Very extensive	Average	High
Rail	Average	Average	Low	Low	High	Average
Water	Very slow	Average	Very low	Limited	Very high	Very low
Air	Very fast	High	Average	Average	Low	Very high
Pipeline	Slow	High	High	Very limited	Very Low	Low

(4 percent), and pipelines (3 percent). The faster methods typically cost more than the slower ones. Speed, reliable delivery, shipment frequency, location availability, handling flexibility, and cost are all important considerations when choosing the most appropriate mode of transportation.

About 15.5 million trucks operate in the United States, carrying most finished goods all or part of the way to the consumer. Nearly 2 million of these are tractor trailers.[38] But railroads, which compete with many truck routes despite their recent loss of market share, are a major mode of transportation. The 565 freight railroads in the United States, Canada, and Mexico operate across more than 202,000 miles of track and earn almost $75 billion in revenues. Seventy percent of all autos manufactured in the United States travel to their destinations by train, as does 70 percent of the country's coal. A freight train needs only 1 gallon of diesel fuel to transport 1 ton of cargo almost 425 miles.[39]

Customer Service Customer service is a vital component of both product and distribution strategies. *Customer service standards* measure the quality of service a firm provides for its customers. Managers frequently set quantitative guidelines—for example, that all orders be processed within 24 hours after they are received or that salespeople approach shoppers within two minutes after they enter the store. Sometimes customers set their own service standards and choose suppliers that meet or exceed them.

The customer service components of product strategy include warranty and repair service programs. *Warranties* are firms' promises to repair a defective product, refund money paid, or replace a product if it proves unsatisfactory. Repair services are also important. Consumers want to know that help is available if something goes wrong. Those who shop for home computers, for example, often choose retailers that not only feature low prices but also offer repair services and tech support centers. Products with inadequate service backing quickly disappear from the market as a result of word-of-mouth criticism.

Consumers' complaints of the impersonal service they received at Web sites led dot-coms to take a number of steps to "humanize" their customer interactions and deal with complaints. Many Web sites contain button help icons that link the visitor to a representative.

Assessment Check ✓

1. What is distribution intensity?

2. Define *supply chain.*

3. What do customer service standards measure?

What's Ahead

This chapter covered two of the elements of the marketing mix: product and distribution. It introduced the key marketing tasks of developing, marketing, and packaging want-satisfying goods and services. It also focused on the three major components of an organization's distribution strategy: the design of efficient distribution channels; wholesalers and retailers who make up many distribution channels; and logistics and physical distribution. We now turn to the remaining two—promotion and pricing—in Chapter 13.

Summary of Learning Goals

⌐1⌐ **Explain marketing's definition of a product; differentiate among convenience, shopping, and specialty products; and distinguish between a product mix and a product line.**

A product is a bundle of physical, service, and symbolic attributes designed to satisfy consumer wants. The marketing conception of a product includes the brand, product image, warranty, service attributes, packaging, and labeling, in addition to the physical or functional characteristics of the good or service.

Goods and services can be classified as consumer (B2C) or business (B2B) products. Consumer products are those purchased by ultimate consumers for their own use. They can be convenience products, shopping products, or specialty products, depending on consumer habits in buying them. Business products are those purchased for use either directly or indirectly in the production of other goods and services for resale. They can be classified as installations, accessory equipment, component parts and materials, raw materials, and supplies. This classification is based on how the items are used and product characteristics. Services can be classified as either consumer or business services.

A product mix is the assortment of goods and services a firm offers to individual consumers and B2B users. A product line is a series of related products.

Assessment Check Answers ✔

1.1 How do consumer products differ from business products? Business products, such as drill presses, are sold to firms or organizations. Consumer products, such as personal-care items, are sold to final users.

1.2 Differentiate among convenience, shopping, and specialty products. Convenience products are items the consumer seeks to purchase frequently, immediately, and with little effort. Shopping products are typically purchased after the buyer has compared competing products in

competing stores. Specialty products are those a purchaser is willing to make a special effort to obtain.

⌐2⌐ **Briefly describe each of the four stages of the product life cycle with their marketing implications.**

Every successful new product passes through four stages in its product life cycle: introduction, growth, maturity, and decline. In the introduction stage, the firm attempts to elicit demand for the new product. In the product's growth stage, sales climb, and the company earns its initial profits. In the maturity stage, sales reach a saturation level. In the decline stage, both sales and profits decline. Marketers sometimes employ strategies to extend the product life cycle, including increasing the frequency of use, adding new users, finding new uses for the product, and changing package size, labeling, or product quality.

The new-product development process for most products has six stages: idea generation, screening, concept development and business analysis, product development, test marketing, and commercialization. At each stage, marketers must decide whether to continue to the next stage, modify the new product, or discontinue the development process. Some new products skip the test marketing stage due to the desire to quickly introduce a new product with excellent potential, a desire not to reveal new-product strategies to competitors, and the high costs involved in limited production runs.

Assessment Check Answers ✔

2.1 What are the stages of the product life cycle? In the introduction stage, the firm attempts to elicit demand for the new product. In the product's growth stage, sales climb, and the company earns its initial profits. In the maturity stage, sales reach a saturation level. In the decline stage, both sales and profits decline.

2.2 What are the marketing implications of each stage? Marketers sometimes employ strategies to extend the product life cycle, including increasing frequency of use, adding new users, finding new uses for the product, and changing package size, labeling, or product quality.

⌐3⌐ Explain how firms identify their products.

Products are identified by brands, brand names, and trademarks, which are important elements of product images. Effective brand names are easy to pronounce, recognize, and remember, and they project the right images to buyers. Brand names cannot contain generic words. Under certain circumstances, companies lose exclusive rights to their brand names if common use makes them generic terms for product categories. Some brand names belong to retailers or distributors rather than to manufacturers. Brand loyalty is measured in three degrees: brand recognition, brand preference, and brand insistence. Some marketers use family brands to identify several related items in a product line. Others employ individual branding strategies by giving each product within a line a different brand name.

Assessment Check Answers ☑

3.1 Differentiate among a brand, a brand name, and a trademark. A brand is a name, term, sign, symbol, design, or some combination thereof used to identify the products of one firm and differentiate them from competitive offerings. A brand name is that part of the brand consisting of words or letters used to identify and distinguish the firm's offerings from those of competitors. A trademark is a brand that has been given legal protection.

3.2 Define *brand equity*. Brand equity is the added value that a respected and successful brand name gives to a product.

⌐4⌐ Outline and briefly describe each of the major components of an effective distribution strategy.

A firm must consider whether to move products through direct or indirect distribution. Once the decision is made, the company needs to identify the types of marketing intermediaries, if any, through which it will distribute its goods and services. The Internet has made direct distribution an attractive option for many retail companies. Another component is distribution intensity. The business must decide on the amount of market coverage—intensive, selective, or exclusive—needed to achieve its marketing strategies. Finally, attention must be paid to managing the distribution channel. It is vital to minimize conflict between channel members.

Assessment Check Answers ☑

4.1 Define *distribution channels*. Distribution channels are the paths that products, and title to them, follow from producer to consumer or business user.

4.2 What is a marketing intermediary? A marketing intermediary (also called a middleman) is a business firm that moves goods between producers and consumers or business users.

⌐5⌐ Distinguish between different types of wholesaling intermediaries.

Wholesaling is a crucial part of the distribution channel for many products, particularly consumer goods and business supplies. Wholesaling intermediaries can be classified on the basis of ownership; some are owned by manufacturers, some are owned by retailers, and others are independently owned. Firms operate two main types of manufacturer-owned wholesaling intermediaries: sales branches and sales offices.

An independent wholesaling intermediary is a business that represents a number of different manufacturers and makes sales calls on retailers, manufacturers, and other business accounts. Independent wholesalers are classified as either merchant wholesalers or agents and brokers, depending on whether they take title to the products they handle.

Retailers sometimes band together to form their own wholesaling organizations. Such organizations can take the form of either a buying group or a cooperative.

Assessment Check Answers ☑

5.1 Define *wholesaling*. Wholesaling is a crucial part of the distribution channel for many products, particularly consumer goods and business supplies.

5.2 Differentiate between a merchant wholesaler and an agent or broker in terms of title to the goods. Merchant wholesalers are independently owned wholesaling intermediaries that take title to the goods they handle. Agents and brokers may or may not take possession of the goods they handle, but they never take title, working mainly to bring buyers and sellers together.

⌐6⌐ Describe the various types of retailers, and identify retail strategies.

Retailers, in contrast to wholesalers, are distribution channel members that sell goods and services to individuals for their own use rather than for resale. Nonstore retailing includes four forms: direct-response retailing, Internet retailing, automatic merchandising, and direct selling. Store retailers range in size from tiny newsstands to multistory department stores and warehouselike retailers such as Sam's Club.

The first step in developing a competitive retailing strategy is to select a target market. Next, the retailer must develop a product strategy to determine the best mix of merchandise to carry to satisfy that market. A retailer's customer service strategy focuses on attracting and retaining target customers to maximize sales and profits. Retailers base their pricing decisions on the costs of purchasing products from other channel members and offering services to customers. A good location often marks the difference between success and failure in retailing. A retailer designs advertisements and develops other promotions to stimulate demand and to provide information such as the store's location, merchandise offerings, prices, and hours. A successful retailer closely aligns its merchandising, pricing, and promotion strategies with store atmospherics, the physical characteristics of a store and its amenities, to influence consumers' perceptions of the shopping experience.

Assessment Check Answers ✓

6.1 Define *retailer.* Retailers are distribution channel members that sell goods and services to individuals for their own use rather than for resale.

6.2 What are the elements of a retailer's marketing strategy? After identifying their target markets, retailers must choose merchandising, customer service, pricing, and location strategies that will attract customers in those market segments.

⌐7⌐ **Identify the various categories of distribution channels, and discuss the factors that influence channel selection.**

Marketers can choose either a direct distribution channel, which moves goods directly from the producer to the consumer, or indirect distribution channels, which involve marketing intermediaries in the paths through which products—and legal ownership of them—flow from producer to the final customer. Ideally, the choice of a distribution channel should support a firm's overall marketing strategy. Before selecting distribution channels, firms must consider their target markets, the types of goods being distributed, their own internal systems and concerns, and competitive factors.

Assessment Check Answers ✓

7.1 What is distribution intensity? Distribution intensity is the number of intermediaries or outlets through which a manufacturer distributes its goods.

7.2 Define *supply chain.* A supply chain is the sequence of suppliers that contribute to creating a good or service and delivering it to business users and final consumers.

7.3 What do customer service standards measure? Customer service standards measure the quality of service a firm provides for its customers.

▮ Business Terms You Need to Know

product 388	brand 397	distribution	retailer 407
product line 391	brand name 397	strategy 402	supply chain 416
product mix 391	trademark 397	distribution channels 402	logistics 416
product life cycle 392	brand equity 399	physical distribution 402	vendor-managed
test marketing 396	category advisor 400	wholesaler 406	inventory 417

▮ Review Questions

1. Classify each of the following business-to-consumer (B2C) and business-to-business (B2B) goods and services. Then choose one and describe how it could be classified as both.

   a. *Runner's World* or *Esquire* magazine

   b. six-pack of apple juice

   c. limousine service

   d. tech support for a communications system

   e. golf course

   f. Thai restaurant

2. What is the relationship between a product line and a product mix? Give an example of each.

3. Identify and briefly describe the six stages of new-product development.

4. What is the difference between a manufacturer's brand and a private brand? What is the difference between a family brand and an individual brand?

5. What are the three stages of brand loyalty? Why is the progression to the last stage so important to marketers?

6. What are the advantages of direct distribution? When is a producer most likely to use direct distribution?

7. What is the wheel of retailing? How has the Internet affected the wheel of retailing?

8. Identify and briefly describe the four different types of nonstore retailers. Give an example of at least one type of good or service that would be suited to each type of nonstore retailer.

9. What are the three intensity levels of distribution? Give an example of two products for each level.

10. Define *logistics*. How does it relate to physical distribution?

◼ Projects and Teamwork Applications

1. On your own or with a classmate, choose one of the following goods or services. Decide whether you want to market it as a consumer product or a business product. Now create a brand name and marketing strategy for your product.

    a. lawnmower repair service

    b. hardware store

    c. soft drink

    d. English-language class

    e. accounting firm

2. Choose one of the following products that is either in the maturity or decline stage of its life cycle (or select one of your own), and develop a marketing strategy for extending its life cycle.

    a. popcorn

    b. fast-food restaurant chain

    c. newspaper

    d. music CDs

    e. paper stationery or notecards

3. Where do you do most of your shopping—in stores or online? Choose your favorite retailer and analyze why you like it. Outline your reasons for shopping there, then add two or three suggestions for improvement.

4. Choose one of the following products and select a distribution intensity for the product. Describe specifically where and how your product would be sold. Then describe the reasons for your strategy.

    a. line of furniture manufactured from recycled or reclaimed materials

    b. custom-designed jewelry

    c. house-painting service

    d. handicraft supplies

    e. talk radio show

◼ Web Assignments

1. **Product classification.** Visit the Web site of Johnson & Johnson (http://www.jnj.com) and click on "Our Products." Review the material in the chapter on product classification and then classify Johnson & Johnson's vast array of products.

2. **Shopping centers.** The Mall of America in Minnesota is the nation's largest shopping center. Go to the Mall's Web site (http://www.mallofamerica.com) to learn more about it. Make a list of five interesting facts you learned about the Mall of America.

3. **Railroad statistics.** Visit the Web site of the American Association of Railroads (http://www.aar.org). Click on

"Statistics and Publication" and then "Railroad Statistics." Review the material and answer the following questions:

    a. What is a so-called Class I railroad? How many are there?

    b. How many workers do these railroads employ?

    c. How much freight did Class I railroads carry during the most recent year for which data are available?

Note: Internet Web addresses change frequently. If you don't find the exact sites listed, you may need to access the organization's home page and search from there or use a search engine such as Bing or Google.

Chanel. Armani. BMW. Cartier. These long-established, high-end brands are very interested in Generation Y, also known as the Millennials—those born during the 1980s and who are now between 18 and 28 years old. The newest challenge these once-exclusive brands face is marketing to this age group.

According to a recent marketing survey, Millennials are the "largest consumer group in U.S. history," even bigger than the baby-boom generation, the previous record holders. At 70 to 85 million, Millennials make up 25 percent of the American population. They are the most ethnically diverse group ever, as well as the least bound by gender stereotypes. They spend over $200 billion a year on purchases. As they enter the workforce and set up their own households, they will overtake the soon-to-retire baby boomers in spending power.

Even more important is how Millennials get information and communicate. Unlike any previous generation, they have grown up with digital technology and take cell phones, video games, and other high-speed electronic devices and media for granted. They are used to instantly available information and communication. A recent survey by the Pew Research Center notes that 75 percent of Generation Y uses social networking, in contrast to 50 percent of Generation X (30 to 45 years old) and 30 percent of baby boomers (46 to 64 years old).

Millennials are very aware of the value of what they buy. The marketing survey found that 65 percent of female Millennials and 61 percent of males describe themselves as brand conscious. But heritage and exclusivity, formerly effective marketing tools for prestige brands, mean little to Millennials, who instead value quality, authenticity, and image. They shun anything that resembles self-promotion in either brands or people, including prominently displayed corporate logos.

Burberry, a maker of high-end clothing and accessories established in 1836, recently began an ambitious multimedia effort to reach Millennials in the digital universe. One of the company's first moves was to hire the actress Emma Watson, world famous for playing Hermione Granger in the Harry Potter movies. A Millennial born in 1990, she was the new face of Burberry's spring–summer campaign. In addition to traditional print advertising and, of course, its home Web site, Burberry has employed live streaming and 3D filming of its fashion shows. With the photo blogger Scott Schuman, known as the Sartorialist, the company also launched a special Web site, Art of the Trench, to promote its classic trench coat. Burberry's Facebook page calls Art of the Trench "a living celebration of the trench coat and the people who wear it." The Web site, essentially a social networking blog, invites owners to submit photos of themselves wearing their trench coats—or to submit videos to its YouTube channel. Links allow visitors to "view details," "like," "share," and "leave comments" on the photos. They can also sort the photos by popularity, gender, styling, trench color, and weather. The site features music by the Maccabees, White Lies, and other groups, with links to their Web sites. Burberry's CEO, Angela Ahrendts, said, "Attracting the Millennial customer to luxury started two years ago—I said that we can either get crushed or ride the greatest wave of our life."

Scott Galloway of New York University's School of Business says, "Gen Y goodwill is arguably the closest thing to a crystal ball for predicting a brand's long-term prospects. Just as Boomers drove the luxury sector for the last 20 years, brands that resonate with Gen Y, whose purchasing power will surpass that of Boomers by 2017, will be the new icons of prestige."

Questions for Critical Thinking

1. Millennials are brand conscious but generally dislike conspicuous, flashy brand logos. How might this affect a company's brand equity?

2. Burberry is basing its product strategy on how Millennials use the Internet and social media, as opposed to how their elders do. Do you think this difference in use will continue as the Millennials mature? If so, how might Burberry change its product strategy?

Sources: Company Web site, http://us.burberry.com, accessed August 3, 2010; Art of the Trench, http://artofthetrench.com, accessed August 3, 2010; Sharalyn Hartwell, "Millennials Love Brands, Not Branding," Generation Y Examiner, May 6, 2010, http://www.examiner.com; Scott Galloway, "Gen Y Prestige Brand Ranking," May 3, 2010, http://l2thinktank.com/Gen_Y_Report.pdf; Pew Research Center, "The Millennials: Confident. Connected. Open to Change," February 24, 2010, http://pewresearch.org/pubs/1501/millennials-new-survey-generational-personality-upbeat-open-new-ideas-technology-bound; Jessica Bumpus, "Millennial Burberry," Vogue.com, March 3, 2010, http://www.vogue.co.uk; Suzy Menkes, "Marketing to the Millennials," *New York Times,* March 2, 2010, http://www.nytimes.com.

Nearly all observers are sure that someday soon, consumers will watch televisions anywhere, on any device—television, computer, or smartphone. Today, once major shows are aired, broadcast TV networks upload them onto their Web sites or to sites such as Hulu and YouTube. One survey reported that in one month alone, more than 178 million Americans watched 33 billion TV shows online.

Across the Atlantic, Britons use BBC's iPlayer to catch up with missed TV episodes online. The BBC and other British networks plan to unite broadcast television with online media in a new, hybrid configuration.

In the United States, viewers have enjoyed watching TV shows on their computers for free. Those days may be over soon—or then again, it may take a little longer.

Advertising fees bring a total of $70 billion to broadcast and cable television networks. Cable and satellite providers pay broadcast networks billions more in retransmission fees and make billions in fees from subscribers.

But when broadcast television networks upload their shows to the Internet, viewers don't have to pay cable and satellite providers, and the networks lose the revenue from cable and satellite licensing fees. Advertisers pay the networks for the right to embed their ads within the video content. But many advertisers shy away from online television because there is still no clear way to measure how effective their commercials will be. One observer says, "Advertisers aren't going to pay for the right to sponsor content [TV shows] unless they know how many people are watching it. The technology is available, but it is still in the process of being implemented."

Online television still has one major drawback: most of it is not live. CBS had live, online coverage of the recent NCAA basketball tournament, but that was an exception. Live broadcasts of shows such as *American Idol* and the Super Bowl charge the highest advertising fees. But online licensing problems and technical issues have made TV networks wary of live online broadcasting.

As viewers exercise their increasing options to watch what they want when they want it, some analysts predict that the only programs that large numbers of people will view at the same time will be sports events and news programs. Some viewers have even stopped their cable subscriptions and watch TV exclusively online via downloads from Netflix, iTunes, and Amazon.

Another difficulty is that no one has yet developed a way to make the potentially infinite array of Internet programming available on television in a user-friendly manner. But as in Europe, Internet-ready televisions will be available in the United States. Best Buy has announced that soon all the Internet-ready televisions it sells will give buyers the option of subscribing to a Best Buy trove of downloadable broadcast materials. Other TV manufacturers will likely make similar offers.

Subscription television services may be the way of the future, although some generic shows, such as news, cooking shows, and how-to programs will remain free just because they are not unique. Recently, Microsoft unveiled its Mediaroom 2.0, which combines client software with cloud-based services to allow consumers to watch shows either on a flat-screen TV, a personal computer, or, in the future, on compatible smart phones. Enrique Rodriguez, Microsoft's corporate vice president for TV, Video and Music Business, says, "We want to make it easier for consumers to find and discover great content, to watch, listen and engage in new ways, and to do so anywhere and on any screen."

Questions for Critical Thinking

1. At what stage would you say broadcast television is in the product life cycle? What steps have the broadcast networks taken to prolong the life cycle of their product?

2. At this time, broadcast and cable television, Internet programming, and advertisers all have different distribution strategies. How might they bring these strategies closer together?

Sources: David Goldman, "Get Ready to Pay for Online TV," *CNN Money*, February 24, 2010, http://money.cnn.com; Steve Plunkett, "Why 2010 Will Be the Year TV and the Web Really Converge," *Guardian*, February 16, 2010, http://guardian.co.uk; "Microsoft Mediaroom 2.0 Delivers the Future of TV," press release, January 6, 2010, http://www.microsoft.com; Holman W. Jenkins, Jr., "The Future on TV," *The Wall Street Journal*, January 5, 2010, http://online.wsj.com.

No matter how powerful they are, comic book heroes can't get themselves into bookstores—and readers' hands—without a little help. Leon Avelino and Barry Matthews, co-founders of Secret Acres, know that one of the greatest challenges of publishing is getting books onto the shelves and into readers' shopping carts. The task is even more difficult for small publishers—in this case, small publishers of comic books and graphic novels—because they don't have the wide distribution network of major publishers. But Avelino and Matthews, whose authors consider them the superheroes of comicbook publishing, are undaunted. They know what they are trying to achieve and work doggedly to make it happen.

"Distribution is a difficult thing right now," admits Matthews. "The publishing industry is changing and comic books themselves have a different distribution methodology and wholesale methodology than traditional books do." Unlike conventional book shops, comic book shops do not operate on a return basis. Conventional bookstores receive a small discount when they purchase books from a publisher, but then have the option to return any unsold books to the publisher. Comic book shops take a deeper discount but make no returns. Matthews also notes that currently there is only one major distributor of comic books—Diamond Distributors—which has the leverage to dictate much of what happens in the business of comic book distribution. In addition, Matthews observes that Secret Acres' graphic novels could easily be sold to the general book market, but many general book distributors prefer not to deal with smaller publishers because they simply don't produce enough books to be profitable.

All of that said, Matthews explains that they are learning alternative ways to distribute their books. "Amazon is great," he says. "They make it very easy for smaller publishers. They treat your books as if they are Amazon books, giving them the sheen of being part of a larger retail channel." Amazon does take a significant cut of sales, but Matthews says it's worth it to broaden the distribution of Secret Acres products. Of course, Secret Acres also sells its entire line directly through its Web site at http://www.secretacres.com, along with some books from other independent authors and publishers. This sales method is the most profitable for Secret Acres. More importantly, it allows Matthews and Avelino to keep closer tabs on their readers. Matthews explains that because orders are filled on an individual basis, he can slip promotional materials, notices of upcoming events or new books, and tie-ins right into the package of a customer whose preferences he knows. This one-on-one interaction helps in the management of customer relationships.

Matthews and Avelino also enjoy one other form of distribution—attending comic book conventions around the country, such as the Stumptown Comics Fest in Portland, Oregon. There, they have the opportunity to interact with readers, other publishers, comic book authors and artists, and even some smaller distributors who have begun to attend these events. They note that readers in particular love to meet the authors and artists. "It feeds the interest in what we're doing," says Matthews. While at an event, Matthews and Avelino try to carve out some time to meet with other small publishers. "A lot of small publishers are in the same position" with regard to distribution, Matthews explains. "So we have been talking with them to see if we can band together to share resources."

For the future, Matthews admits that he and Avelino have no idea how some of the new technologies, including e-readers, will ultimately affect distribution, but they plan to research the possibility of digitizing some of Secret Acres' titles for online distribution.

Despite its small size, Secret Acres' authors consider the firm a mighty one. Theo Ellsworth, author of such titles as *Capacity* and *Sleeper Car*, praises Secret Acres for its personal attention and efforts to market and distribute his books. "It feels good to have the distribution part in someone else's hands," says Ellsworth. He explains that having someone else take care of that aspect of publishing frees him up to concentrate on his art, producing more posters and books—which is, after all, the author's job.

Questions for Critical Thinking

1. Visit Secret Acres' web site at http://www.secretacres.com to learn more about the firm's product line. Write a marketing blurb describing the line to a potential distributor.

2. What steps can Secret Acres take to develop brand loyalty and ultimately brand equity for its products?

3. How might Secret Acres expand its Internet retailing presence?

4. Secret Acres is a tiny firm with limited distribution. How can the company use customer service to create a competitive advantage, increase distribution, and help it grow?

Sources: Secret Acres Web site, http://www.secretacres.com, accessed August 25, 2010; Stumptown Comics Fest, http://www.stumptowncomics.com, accessed August 25, 2010; "Great Graphic Novels for Teens," *Young Adult Library Services Association,* http://www.ala.org/yalsa, accessed August 19, 2010; Harry McCracken, "E-Readers May Be Dead, But They're Not Going Away Yet," *PC World,* August 17, 2010, http://www.pcworld.com.

Learning Objectives

1. Discuss how integrated marketing communications relates to a firm's overall promotional strategy, and explain the concept of a promotional mix along with outlining the objectives of promotion.

2. Summarize the different types of advertising and advertising media.

3. Outline the roles of sales promotion, personal selling, and public relations in a promotional strategy.

4. Describe pushing and pulling promotional strategies.

5. Outline the different types of pricing objectives.

6. Discuss how firms set prices in the marketplace, and describe the four alternative pricing strategies.

7. Discuss consumer perceptions of price.

Promotion and Pricing of Goods and Services

The E*Trade Baby Talks Value

Babies and young children often utter funny, surprising, and insightful comments on the world around them. Online stock trading, investing, and banking firm E*Trade has bet its advertising budget on cuteness, creating a series of television commercials featuring a talking baby who knows more about investing than the average adult. He's adorable, funny, and smart. He text messages friends and even hires a clown with his profits, commenting that he underestimated the clown's creepiness. But at the conclusion of the most talked-about of the ads, he spits up on his computer keyboard—reminding viewers that, after all, he is just a baby. E*Trade debuted new installments of the Talking Baby series during Super Bowl broadcasts over a period of three years. The third commercial was so popular that it was rated higher than ads for Pepsi starring Justin Timberlake, Doritos, Coca-Cola, and even Bud Light.

Making stock trading funny or even memorable is not easy, especially during difficult economic times. But E*Trade succeeded—viewers remembered the cute wisecracking baby. Despite the daunting task of trying to understand online stock trading, they came away with the impression that E*Trade makes it so easy that even a smart child can do it. By advertising during such a visible program as the Super Bowl, and in such a challenging economy, E*Trade was taking a risk. But it was a calculated one that has been part of E*Trade's promotional strategy all along. "History repeatedly has shown that those who continue to make smart marketing investments when economic times are uncertain are best positioned for success when the economy rebounds," explains Nicholas Utton, chief marketing officer for E*Trade. "That's why, in this uncertain economic climate, reinforcing the strength of our brand and value proposition is critical."

The talking toddler fits squarely with E*Trade's image as a firm that thumbs its nose at large, traditional brokerages. E*Trade encourages investors to take control of their own portfolios instead of leaving all the decisions in the hands of professionals. By doing so, investors can take advantage of the better deals that E*Trade can offer because it doesn't have the overhead costs associated with traditional brokerage firms. The company's Web site promises that its "pricing is clear, competitive, and fair." Trades can be made for $9.99 or less, and the firm provides special deals that go even lower for qualified customers. "E*Trade has always flown in the face of traditional brokerages," notes Tor Myhren of Grey New York, the advertising agency that created the talking baby ads. "And this little, financially savvy, street-wise baby has seemed to really tap a nerve with more independent investors. He shows that anyone can do it. Seeing how easy it is for him helps people overcome their fears of what they perceive as complicated technology."

The talking baby spots didn't just appear on TV. To generate interest in the commercial, particularly among young adults, E*Trade launched the talking baby on the Web prior to the Super Bowl. Several days before the game, E*Trade posted selected outtakes of the commercial—footage that didn't make it to the final version—on its branded YouTube channel. The company even created a Facebook page for the famous baby. By the time the actual commercial aired on game night, people were already talking about it. "We succeeded in creating something memorable that engages retail investors in a meaningful way through multiple channels, and more importantly, has produced significant return on investment," notes Myhren. The baby actually got nervous adult investors to give online investing with E*Trade a try. And that's not child's play.[1]

promotion function of informing, persuading, and influencing a purchase decision.

This chapter focuses on the different types of promotional activities and the way prices are established for goods and services. **Promotion** is the function of informing, persuading, and influencing a purchase decision. This activity is as important to not-for-profit organizations as it is to profit-seeking companies.

Some promotional strategies try to develop *primary demand*, or consumer desire for a general product category. The objective of such a campaign is to stimulate sales for an entire industry so that individual firms benefit from this market growth. A popular example is the dairy industry's "Got Milk?" campaign. Print and television messages about the nutritional benefits of milk show various celebrities. Other promotional campaigns aimed at increasing

per-capita consumption have been commissioned by the California Strawberry Commission and the National Cattlemen's Beef Association.

Most promotional strategies, in contrast, seek to stimulate *selective demand*—desire for a specific brand. Every driver needs some type of car insurance, and the Geico gecko wants consumers to pick its firm for low rates. Country-Western star Toby Keith promotes Ford F-150 trucks, which encourages his fans to choose that brand over competitors. Sales promotions that offered teens a free iTunes song download for trying on a pair of Gap jeans also encouraged shoppers to purchase a specific brand.

Marketers choose from among many promotional options to communicate with potential customers. Each marketing

Most promotional strategies seek to stimulate *selective demand*—desire for a specific brand. Country-Western star Toby Keith wants to encourage his fans to choose Ford F-150 trucks over competitors.

message a buyer receives—through a television or radio commercial, newspaper or magazine ad, Web site, direct-mail flyer, or sales call—reflects the product, place, person, cause, or organization promoted in the content. Through **integrated marketing communications (IMC)**, marketers coordinate all promotional activities—media advertising, direct mail, personal selling, sales promotion, and public relations—to produce a unified, customer-focused promotional strategy. This coordination is designed to avoid confusing the consumer and to focus positive attention on the promotional message.

This chapter begins by explaining the role of IMC and then discusses the objectives of promotion and the importance of promotional planning. Next, it examines the components of the promotional mix: advertising, sales promotion, personal selling, and public relations. Finally, the chapter addresses pricing strategies for goods and services.

integrated marketing communications (IMC) coordination of all promotional activities—media advertising, direct mail, personal selling, sales promotion, and public relations—to produce a unified, customer-focused promotional strategy.

Integrated Marketing Communications

An integrated marketing communications strategy focuses on customer needs to create a unified promotional message in the firm's ads, in-store displays, product samples, and presentations by company sales representatives. To gain a competitive advantage, marketers that implement IMC need a broad view of promotion. Media options continue to multiply, and marketers cannot simply rely on traditional broadcast and print media and direct mail. Plans must include all forms of customer contact. Packaging, store displays, sales promotions, sales presentations, and online and interactive media also communicate information about a brand or organization. With IMC, marketers create a unified personality and message for the good, brand, or service they promote. Coordinated activities also enhance the effectiveness of reaching and serving target markets.

Marketing managers set the goals and objectives for the firm's promotional strategy with overall organizational objectives and marketing goals in mind. Based on these objectives, marketers weave the various elements of the strategy—personal selling, advertising, sales promotion, publicity, and public relations—into an integrated communications plan. This document becomes a central part of the firm's total marketing strategy to reach its selected target market. Feedback, including marketing research and sales reports, completes the system by identifying any deviations from the plan and suggesting improvements.

In its stepped-up IMC campaign "Get a Monster Advantage," the job search engine Monster.com combined a number of marketing promotions. The campaign's first TV commercial, featuring a down-on-his-luck Boogeyman who goes to Monster.com to find the perfect new job, aired during the AFC Championship Game. A second commercial, featuring another character, aired during a recent Super Bowl game. Other spots were aired on national cable networks and included social media extensions. Humorous interactive links on sites such as Facebook and advertising on other sites further engaged the online audience. Print ads appeared in *The Wall Street Journal* and more than a hundred regional dailies as well as in monthly business publications and human resource publications such as *HR Executive*, *Wired*, and *Fast Company*.[2]

The Promotional Mix

Just as every organization creates a marketing mix combining product, distribution, promotion, and pricing strategies, each also requires a similar mix to blend the many facets of promotion into a cohesive plan. The **promotional mix** consists of two components—personal and nonpersonal selling—that marketers combine to meet the needs of their firm's target customers and effectively and efficiently communicate its message to them. **Personal selling** is the most basic form of promotion: a direct person-to-person promotional presentation to a potential buyer. The buyer–seller communication can occur during a face-to-face meeting or via telephone, videoconference, or interactive computer link.

Nonpersonal selling consists of advertising, sales promotion, direct marketing, and public relations. Advertising is the best-known form of nonpersonal selling, but sales promotion accounts for about half of these marketing expenditures. Spending for sponsorships, which involves marketing messages delivered in association with another activity such as a golf tournament or a benefit concert, is on the rise as well. Marketers need to be careful about the types of promotion they choose or risk alienating the very people they are trying to reach.

Each component in the promotional mix offers its own advantages and disadvantages, as Table 13.1 demonstrates. By selecting the most effective combination of promotional mix elements, a firm may reach its promotional objectives. Spending within the promotional mix varies by industry. Manufacturers of many business-to-business (B2B) products typically spend more on personal selling than on advertising because those products—such as a new telecommunications system—may require a significant investment. Consumer-goods marketers may focus more on advertising and sponsorships. Later sections of this chapter discuss how the parts of the mix contribute to effective promotion.

promotional mix combination of personal and nonpersonal selling components designed to meet the needs of their firm's target customers and effectively and efficiently communicate its message to them.

personal selling the most basic form of promotion: a direct person-to-person promotional presentation to a potential buyer.

nonpersonal selling consists of advertising, sales promotion, direct marketing, and public relations.

Table 13.1 Comparing the Components of the Promotional Mix

COMPONENT	ADVANTAGES	DISADVANTAGES
Advertising	Reaches large consumer audience at low cost per contact Allows strong control of the message Message can be modified to match different audiences	Difficult to measure effectiveness Limited value for closing sales
Personal selling	Message can be tailored for each customer Produces immediate buyer response Effectiveness is easily measured	High cost per contact High expense and difficulty of attracting and retaining effective salespeople
Sales promotion	Attracts attention and creates awareness Effectiveness is easily measured Produces short-term sales increases	Difficult to differentiate from similar programs of competitors Nonpersonal appeal
Public relations	Enhances product or firm credibility Creates a positive attitude about the product or company	Difficult to measure effectiveness Often devoted to nonmarketing activities
Sponsorships	Viewed positively by consumers Enhances brand awareness	Difficult to control message

Objectives of Promotional Strategy

Promotional strategy objectives vary among organizations. Some use promotion to expand their markets, and others use it to defend their current positions. As Figure 13.1 illustrates, common objectives include providing information, differentiating a product, increasing sales, stabilizing sales, and accentuating a product's value.

Marketers often pursue multiple promotional objectives at the same time. To promote its Microsoft Office software, Microsoft has to convince business owners, who buy the software, and their employees, who use the software, that the product is a worthwhile investment.

Marketers need to keep their firm's promotional objectives in mind at all times. Sometimes the objectives are obscured by a fast-paced, creative ad campaign. In this case, the message—or worse, the brand name or image—is lost. The series of comic Geico ads that featured grumpy Neanderthals and the tag line "So easy a caveman could do it" were an instant hit. They were widely viewed on YouTube and even inspired a short-lived TV sitcom. But despite their quirky originality, the ads allowed humor to overtake the message; few viewers remembered the product—car insurance.

FIGURE 13.1 Five Major Promotional Objectives

DIFFERENTIATE PRODUCT
Example: Television ad comparing performance of two leading laundry detergents

ACCENTUATE PRODUCT VALUE
Example: Warranty programs and guarantees that make a product more attractive than its major competitors

PROVIDE INFORMATION
Example: Print ad describing features and availability of a new breakfast cereal

INCREASE SALES
Example: End-of-aisle grocery displays, or "end caps," to encourage impulse purchases

STABILIZE SALES
Example: Even out sales patterns by promoting low weekend rates for hotels, holding contests during slow sales periods, or advertising cold fruit soups during summer months

Providing Information A major portion of U.S. advertising is information oriented. Credit card ads provide information about benefits and rates. Ads for hair-care products include information about benefits such as shine and volume. Ads for breakfast cereals often contain nutritional information. Television ads for prescription drugs, a nearly $2 billion industry, are sometimes criticized for relying on emotional appeals rather than providing information about the causes, risk factors, and especially the prevention of disease.[3] But print advertisements for drugs often contain an entire page of warnings, side-effects, and usage guidelines.

Differentiating a Product Promotion can also be used to differentiate a firm's offerings from the competition. Applying a concept called **positioning**, marketers attempt to establish their products in the minds of customers. The idea is to communicate to buyers meaningful distinctions about the attributes, price, quality, or use of a good or service.

When you set out to purchase a car, you have hundreds of brands from which to choose. How do you decide which one to buy? Carmakers do their best to differentiate their vehicles by style, performance, safety features, and price. They must make their vehicles stand out to individual consumers. General Motors intends its new Cheverolet Cruze compact car to replace the discontinued Cobalt model. Traditionally, compact cars have been less expensive than midsize cars but also have reputations for mediocrity. The Cruze costs more than the Cobalt, but GM is promoting its higher quality and—especially—its high-quality safety engineering and safety features. A version of the Cruze has been on sale in other countries

positioning concept in which marketers attempt to establish their products in the minds of customers by communicating to buyers meaningful distinctions about the attributes, price, quality, or use of a good or service.

for a few years and received the highest crash-safety score ever in the European New Car Assessment Program.[4]

Increasing Sales Increasing sales volume is the most common objective of a promotional strategy. Naturalizer became the third-largest seller of women's dress shoes by appealing to Baby Boomers. But as these women have grown older, they have bought fewer pairs of shoes each year. Naturalizer wants to keep these customers but also attract the younger generation. So the firm developed a new line of trendy shoes. The promotional strategy included ads in magazines read by younger women—such as *Elle* and *Marie Claire*—featuring young women in beach attire and Naturalizer shoes. The response to this strategy was a substantial increase in Naturalizer's sales through department stores.

Stabilizing Sales Sales stabilization is another goal of promotional strategy. Firms often use sales contests during slack periods, motivating salespeople by offering prizes such as vacations, TVs, smart phones, and cash to those who meet certain goals. Companies distribute sales promotion materials—such as calendars, pens, and notepads—to customers to stimulate sales during the off-season. Jiffy Lube puts that little sticker on your windshield to remind you when to have your car's next oil change—the regular visits help stabilize sales. A stable sales pattern brings several advantages. It evens out the production cycle, reduces some management and production costs, and simplifies financial, purchasing, and marketing planning. An effective promotional strategy can contribute to these goals.

McDonald's came up with the new mocha- and caramel-flavor McFrappés iced drinks in its campaign to boost coffee sales in the summer. The marketing campaign in San Diego features multilayered advertising. Seventy taxis got new "extension tops" for greater product visibility. They show a two-dimensional image of a McFrappé—with the foamy topping actually emerging from the taxi top. On the back of each taxi receipt is a printed coupon inviting taxi passengers to "Buy one McFrappé, get one free." Almost 400 taxi drivers will have the coupons to hand out to their customers; the 118 local individual McDonald's owners are hoping the coupons will help boost their sales.[5]

Accentuating the Product's Value Some promotional strategies enhance product values by explaining hidden benefits of ownership. Carmakers offer long-term warranty programs; life insurance companies promote certain policies as investments. The creation of brand awareness and brand loyalty also enhances a product's image and increases its desirability. Advertising with luxurious images supports the reputation of premium brands like Jaguar, Tiffany, and Rolex.

Promotional Planning

Today's marketers can promote their products in many ways, and the lines between the different elements of the promotional mix are blurring. Consider the practice of **product placement**. A growing number of marketers pay placement fees to have their products showcased in various media, ranging from newspapers and magazines to television and movies. Coca-Cola gets prominent placement on *American Idol*, for instance, and *The Tonight Show with Jay Leno* and *Extreme Makeover: Home Edition* are other popular shows with high product-placement appeal.[6] Product and brand placements have skyrocketed with the increasing number of reality TV shows and with improving technology that allows viewers to fast forward through conventional, stand-alone commercials. NBC's reality show *The Biggest Loser* had the highest number of product placements—more than 6,200—in one recent season. *American Idol* was second, with more than 4,600. The industry report *Product Placement Spending in Media*

product placement
form of promotion in which marketers pay placement fees to have their products showcased in various media, ranging from newspapers and magazines to television and movies.

Michael Becker/FOX/PictureGroup/©AP/wide World Photos

Coca-Cola gets prominent placement on *American Idol.* Product and brand placements have skyrocketed with the increasing number of reality TV shows and with improving technology that allows viewers to fast forward through conventional, stand-alone commercials.

estimates that product placement spending—also known as brand entertainment spending—came to more than $3.5 billion in one year.[7]

Another type of promotional planning must be considered by firms with small budgets. **Guerrilla marketing** is innovative, low-cost marketing efforts designed to get consumers' attention in unusual ways. Guerrilla marketing is an increasingly popular tactic for marketers, especially those with limited promotional budgets. The Coca-Cola Company recently maximized a humorous guerrilla marketing effort by combining it with social media marketing. How many times have you tried to get a snack or a drink from a vending machine, only to have the machine keep your change, or worse, not give you your requested item? A vending machine at St. John's University in Queens, New York, was apparently broken. It gave the student customer a Coke—and then another, and another, and another. The pleased student handed out the unexpected bonus drinks, getting huge smiles from other students. The whole incident was filmed, guerrilla style, and posted on YouTube. It quickly went viral as viewers tweeted and blogged about it and sent the link to their friends.[8]

Marketers for larger companies have caught on and are using guerrilla approaches as well, with mixed success. The computer-game maker Electronic Arts (EA) faced an unusual challenge in marketing its videogame "Dante's Inferno," based on the first part of Dante Alighieri's medieval epic poem *The Divine Comedy*. In a survey EA conducted before starting its campaign, it found that fewer than 20 percent of those questioned knew anything about the "Inferno" besides the name. Not only did EA have to generate excitement about the game, it also had to educate prospective buyers about the poem. Dante assigned sinners to one of nine regions, or circles, of hell according to their sins. The circles descended from lust, gluttony, greed, and so on, down to treachery, the worst sin, in the lowest circle. The company's campaign, Nine Months of Hell, took as its theme Dante's imagined structure as adapted to EA's gaming needs. The campaign got off to a rocky start in the form of

guerrilla marketing
innovative, low-cost marketing efforts designed to get consumers' attention in unusual ways.

Assessment Check ✅

1. What is the objective of an integrated marketing communications program?

2. Why do firms pursue multiple promotional objectives at the same time?

3. What are product placement and guerrilla marketing?

staged, phony protests against the game by phony religious groups. Although the protests were quickly unmasked as a hoax, they set up negative expectations about the rest of the campaign. Things went from bad to worse with the next circle, lust. The blatantly sexist "Sin to Win" contest at ComicCon, the biggest comic-book and gaming convention in the country, outraged female gamers—a large portion of the market—who already felt alienated and ignored by the gaming industry. The marketers apologized, learned from their mistakes, and tried for a somewhat more intellectual—though still edgy—approach. Phil Marineau, the senior product manager for the game, said, " 'Sin to Win' was a great eye-opener for us, and we're glad it happened early on, so we could learn from it." In the end, the campaign was both praised and criticized within the marketing industry.[9]

From this overview of the promotional mix, we now turn to discussions of each of its elements. The following sections detail the major components of advertising, sales promotion, personal selling, and public relations.

Advertising

Consumers receive from 4,000 to 5,000 marketing messages each day, many of them in the form of advertising.[10] Advertising is the most visible form of nonpersonal promotion—and the most effective for many firms. **Advertising** refers to paid nonpersonal communication usually targeted at large numbers of potential buyers. Although U.S. citizens often think of advertising as a typically American function, it is a global activity. Procter & Gamble leads the list of global advertisers, with measured media spending of $9.73 billion. The firm devotes 65 percent of that amount to advertising in international markets. The other members of the top ten are Unilever, L'Oréal, General Motors, Toyota, The Coca-Cola Company, Johnson & Johnson, Ford, Reckitt Benckiser, and Nestlé. Of the six non-U.S.-based companies that spend more than half of their advertising budgets in the United States, four are European-based pharmaceutical firms. Pharmaceutical firms are forbidden to engage in direct-to-consumer prescription-drug advertising in Europe but are free to do so in the United States.[11]

Advertising expenditures vary among industries, companies, and media. Automotive, retail, and telecommunications take top honors for spending in the United States—carmakers spend a whopping $20 billion per year. Top car advertiser General Motors spent $3.6 billion in one recent year.[12] Because advertising expenditures are so great, and because consumers are bombarded with so many messages, firms need to be more and more creative and efficient at getting consumers' attention.

Types of Advertising

The two basic types of ads are product and institutional advertisements. **Product advertising** consists of messages designed to sell a particular good or service. Advertisements for Nantucket Nectars juices, iPods, and Capital One credit cards are examples of product advertising. **Institutional advertising** involves messages that promote concepts, ideas, philosophies, or goodwill for industries, companies, organizations, or government entities. Each year, the Juvenile Diabetes Research Foundation promotes its "Walk for the Cure" fund-raising event, and your college may place advertisements in local papers or news shows to promote its activities. As the "Hit & Miss" feature describes, Heritage Oaks Bank's "Expect Success" campaign is an example of institutional advertising.

A form of institutional advertising that is growing in importance, **cause advertising**, promotes a specific viewpoint on a public issue as a way to influence public opinion and the

advertising paid nonpersonal communication usually targeted at large numbers of potential buyers.

product advertising consists of messages designed to sell a particular good or service.

institutional advertising involves messages that promote concepts, ideas, philosophies, or goodwill for industries, companies, organizations, or government entities.

cause advertising form of institutional advertising that promotes a specific viewpoint on a public issue as a way to influence public opinion and the legislative process.

Heritage Oaks: "Expect Success"

Heritage Oaks Bank is a community bank serving San Luís Obispo County on California's Central Coast. The bank recently launched a new and different advertising campaign. Called "Expect Success," the campaign highlights clients of the bank who have established personal and professional presences in the community.

The campaign takes the form of testimonials, giving the clients the opportunity to speak in their own words about their role models, the goals they have set for themselves, their favorite community moments, a saying they live by, and why Heritage Oaks Bank is their bank of choice. The bank advertises "Expect Success" in print and on television, with one-on-one interview testimonials available on its Web site. The campaign highlights a law firm partner, a furniture store owner, two winery owners, and a high-school sports coach, among others.

One example is Alex Posada. For 30 years he has been the director of parks and recreation for the city of Santa Maria. His role models were his parents. The goals he set for himself "include working to make the community a better place to live by taking an active part in community endeavors." He lives by the saying, "Learn from your mistakes. Just don't learn too much." Posada is also a volunteer with the Special Olympics. His favorite community moment occurred when the Special Olympics Torch was carried through the area on its way to the Summer Games. He banks at Heritage Oaks because of the "convenience, excellent customer service, and community relations." Mitch Massey, the bank's senior vice president for marketing, says, "I have always felt that the best way to tell our company's story is to have those who have grown their businesses, with our bank's involvement, share their success story."

Questions for Critical Thinking

1. What message does Heritage Oaks Bank's "Expect Success" campaign promote?

2. Imagine you are the marketing director for an institution such as a bank or a hospital. What message do you want to get across? How and where would you communicate it?

Sources: Company Web site, http://www.heritageoaksbank.com, accessed May 11, 2010; "Heritage Oaks Bank Kicks Off 'Expect Success' Ad Campaign," *slo-business. com*, January 19, 2010, http://www.slo-business.com; "Heritage Oaks Bank," *Bloomberg Businessweek*, n.d., http://investing.businessweek.com.

---

legislative process about issues such as literacy, hunger and poverty, and alternative energy sources. Both not-for-profit organizations and businesses use cause advertising, sometimes called *advocacy advertising*. As part of Avon's corporate responsibility, the Avon Foundation promotes its Speak Out Against Domestic Violence program with celebrity endorsements from Reese Witherspoon in its advertising.[13]

The Bill and Melinda Gates Foundation is a not-for-profit organization dedicated to raising public awareness and generating legislation and other efforts in the fight against poverty, lack of education, and disease. Funded through grants from the Gates fund and investment guru Warren Buffett, the foundation operates in all 50 states, the District of Columbia, and more than 100 countries. Through well-publicized grants of $1.37 billion to the United Negro College fund for its Millennium Scholars Program and tours abroad to personally oversee vaccination programs, the Gates fund generates interest in their causes. For their efforts they received a recent *Time* Person of the Year award.[14]

Advertising and the Product Life Cycle

Both product and institutional advertising fall into one of three categories based on whether the ads are intended to inform, persuade, or remind. A firm uses *informative advertising* to build initial demand for a product in the introductory phase of the product life cycle. Highly publicized new-product entries attract the interest of potential buyers who seek information about the advantages of the new products over existing ones, warranties provided, prices, and places that offer the new products. Ads for new cell phones boast of new features, colors, designs, and pricing options to attract new customers.

Product advertising consists of messages designed to sell a particular good or service.

Persuasive advertising attempts to improve the competitive status of a product, institution, or concept, usually in the growth and maturity stages of the product life cycle. One of the most popular types of persuasive product advertising, *comparative advertising*, compares products directly with their competitors—either by name or by inference. Tylenol advertisements mention the possible stomach problems that the generic drug aspirin could cause, stating that its pain reliever does not irritate the stomach. But advertisers need to be careful when they name competing brands in comparison ads because they might leave themselves open to controversy or even legal action by competitors. Notice that Tylenol does not mention a specific aspirin brand in its promotions.

Reminder-oriented advertising often appears in the late maturity or decline stages of the product life cycle to maintain awareness of the importance and usefulness of a product, concept, or institution. Triscuits have been around for a long time, but Nabisco attempts to mobilize sales with up-to-date advertising that appeals to health and fitness–conscious consumers. The advertising mentions its new no-trans-fat formulations.

Advertising Media

Marketers must choose how to allocate their advertising budgets among various media. All media offer advantages and disadvantages. Cost is an important consideration in media selection, but marketers must also choose the media best suited for communicating their message. As Figure 13.2 indicates, the three leading media outlets for advertising are television, newspapers, and magazines. However, Internet advertising is growing fast. Consumers now receive ads when they download news and other information to their hand-held wireless devices.

Advertising executives agree that firms need to rethink traditional ad campaigns to incorporate new media as well as updated uses of traditional media. Google is looking for ways to combine the targeting capabilities of Internet advertising and the richness of the television medium. Google and Intel are working with the television manufacturer Sony to develop TVs and set-top boxes that allow viewers to navigate the Web, including social-networking sites such as Twitter. The software is based on Google's Android operating system for its smart phones. Logitech is developing a remote control for the system, including a miniature keyboard.[15] The project has advanced to the point where Google is testing a TV Web-search service with Dish Network Corp. Google is far from alone in the effort to bring television and the Web closer together. It faces stiff competition from Microsoft and Apple, among others.[16]

Television   Television is still one of America's leading national advertising media. Television advertising can be classified as network, national, local, and cable ads. The four major national networks—ABC, CBS, NBC, and Fox—along with the CW, broadcast almost one-fifth of all television ads. Despite a decline in audience share and growing competition from cable, network television remains the easiest way for advertisers to reach large numbers of viewers—10 million to 20 million with a single commercial. Automakers, fast-food restaurants, and food manufacturers are heavy users of network TV advertising.

About 58 percent of U.S. households with TVs now subscribe to cable, drawn to the more than 800 channels available through cable

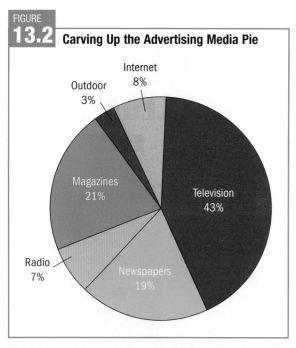

FIGURE
13.2 **Carving Up the Advertising Media Pie**

Internet 8%
Outdoor 3%
Magazines 21%
Radio 7%
Newspapers 19%
Television 43%

Note: Percentages do not total to 100% due to rounding. Direct mail was not measured in these data.

Source: Data from "100 Leading National Advertisers Index," *Advertising Age,* accessed January 8, 2010, http://adage.com/datacenter.

or satellite services. But the cable and satellite networks are facing new competition. One survey indicates that 60 percent of American homes have one or more videogame consoles. People are using the consoles to download apps and video-on-demand offerings. And a small but growing number of viewers are discontinuing their cable service and opting for online services such as Netflix, Hulu, Apple's iTunes, and the networks' own Web sites. Recently, 1.3 million people watched at least part of the Masters golf tournament online, double the number who did so the previous year. People still prefer free, advertising-supported downloads, although online network advertising made up only 2.5 percent of the yearly $62 billion in advertising revenues. However, the number of homes with digital video recorders (DVRs) and high-definition (HD) televisions is increasing steadily. Recent research suggests that even people who can use their DVRs to skip TV ads don't always do so. According to the Nielsen Company, many DVR users still watch shows at their scheduled times, when they must watch the ads, and even those who record shows for later viewing watch almost half the ads they could skip. With more people watching playbacks of their favorite shows, the networks' ratings—and commercial watching—increase too.[17]

Although—or perhaps because—television reaches the greatest number of consumers at once, it is the most expensive advertising medium. NBC's *Sunday Night Football* has long been the most expensive regularly broadcast program of the fall season. A 30-second ad costs an average of almost $340,000. Super Bowl ads have been known to command prices of nearly $3 million for 30 seconds, but more recently, those spots sold for between $2.5 million and $2.8 million.[18] Marketers want to be certain that their commercials reach the greatest number of viewers. Because of the high cost, advertisers may demand guarantees of audience size and receive compensation if a show fails to deliver the promised number of viewers.

Newspapers Daily and weekly newspapers continue to dominate local advertising. Marketers can easily tailor newspaper advertising for local tastes and preferences. Advertisers can also coordinate advertisements with other promotional efforts such as discount coupons from supermarkets and one-day sales at department stores. A disadvantage comes from the relatively short life span; people usually discard their newspapers soon after reading. Retailers and automobile dealers rank first among newspaper advertisers. Most newspapers now maintain Web sites, some of which offer separate material and features, to complement their print editions.

Radio Despite the proliferation of other media, the average U.S. household owns five radios—including those in cars—a market penetration that makes radio an important advertising medium. Advertisers like the captive audience of listeners as they commute to and from work. As a result, morning and evening drive-time shows command top ad rates. In major markets, many stations serve different demographic groups with targeted programming. Internet radio programming also offers opportunities for yet more focused targeting.

Satellite stations offer great potential for advertisers. Sirius and XM both offer commercial-free music, with advertising on news and talk shows. A recent study predicts that Internet radio will have 185 million listeners by 2020, although 250 million will still listen to AM/FM (sometimes referred to as terrestrial) radio. Internet advertising revenues reached $260 million in a year, with an additional $28 million from podcasting.[19] Google recently updated its AdWords application to include ads that can be broadcast by traditional radio stations. An advertiser fills out a questionnaire indicating the target audience and where and how often the ad should be run. The advertiser pays a fee each time the ad is aired and can have the ad tracked to find the best possible time to reach the desired audience.[20]

Magazines Magazines include consumer publications and business trade journals. *Time*, *Reader's Digest*, and *Sports Illustrated* are consumer magazines, whereas *Advertising Age* and *Oil & Gas Journal* fall into the trade category.

Magazines may customize their publications and target advertising messages to different regions of the country. One method places local advertising in regional editions of the magazines. Other magazines attach wraparounds—half-size covers on top of full-size covers—to highlight articles inside that relate to particular areas; different wraparounds appear in different parts of the country.

Magazines are a natural choice for targeted advertising. Media buyers study demographics of subscribers and select magazines that attract the desired readers. American Express advertises in *Fortune* and *Forbes* to reach businesspeople, while PacSun clothes and Clearasil skin medications are advertised in *teenVogue*.

Direct Mail The average U.S. household receives about 550 pieces of direct mail each year, including 100 catalogs. The huge growth in the variety of direct-mail offerings combined with the convenience they offer today's busy, time-pressed shoppers has made direct-mail advertising a multibillion-dollar business. Even consumers who like to shop online often page through a catalog before placing an online order. Although direct mail is expensive per person, a small business can afford a limited direct-mail campaign but not a television or radio ad. For businesses with a small advertising budget, a carefully targeted direct-mail effort can be highly effective. E-mail is a low-cost form of direct marketing. Marketers can target the most interested Internet users by offering Web site visitors an option to register to receive e-mail. Companies like Amazon.com, Spring Hill Nurseries, and Abercrombie & Fitch routinely send e-mails to regular customers.

Address lists are at the heart of direct-mail advertising. Using data-mining techniques to segment markets, direct-mail marketers create profiles that show the traits of consumers who are likely to buy their products or donate to their organizations. Catalog retailers sometimes experiment by sending direct-mail pieces randomly to people who subscribe to particular magazines. Next, they analyze the orders received from the mailings and develop profiles of purchasers. Finally, they rent lists of additional subscriber names that match the profiles they have developed.

Studies have shown that most U.S. consumers are annoyed by the amount of so-called "junk mail" they receive every day, including catalogs, advertising postcards, and flyers. Among Internet users, a major pet peeve is *spam*, or junk e-mail. Many states have outlawed such practices as sending e-mail promotions without legitimate return addresses, although it is difficult to track down and catch offenders.

The Direct Marketing Association (DMA; www.the-dma.org) helps marketers combat negative attitudes by offering its members guidelines on ethical business practices. The DMA also provides consumer information at its Web site, as well as services that enable consumers to opt out of receiving unsolicited offers. In addition, Federal Trade Commission regulations have taken effect for direct mail in certain industries. Now when you receive that unsolicited, preapproved credit card application in the mail, it must be accompanied by a prominent notice telling you how to get off the bank's mailing list. This law will affect millions of consumers. In the period from 2004 to 2007, more than 7 billion credit card offers were mailed. That rate plummeted during the recession, falling to about 2 billion overall, but increased during the fourth quarter of that year. Consumers can also opt out of receiving such offers for five years.[21]

Outdoor Advertising In one year, outdoor advertising accounted for $5.9 billion in advertising expenditures.[22] The majority of spending on outdoor advertising is for billboards, but spending for other types of outdoor advertising, such as signs in transit stations, stores, airports, and sports stadiums, is growing fast. Advertisers are exploring new forms of outdoor media, many of which involve technology: computerized paintings, video billboards, "trivision" that displays three revolving images on a single billboard, and moving billboards mounted on trucks. Other innovations include ads displayed on the Goodyear blimp, using an electronic system that offers animation and video.

Chicago's North Park University launched an outdoor advertising campaign featuring current students. The advertising invited viewers to a Web site where those students discussed how their education at North Park affected their lives. Digital advertising will soon be available on taxi tops. With almost 13,000 yellow medallion taxis in New York City alone, the potential visibility is enormous. Clear Channel Outdoor Advertising offers its Digital Outdoor Networks, a complete line of electronic advertising.[23] CBS Outdoor recently unveiled the first-ever high-definition, 3D projection display in New York City's Grand Central Station. And The Coca-Cola Company inaugurated its Digital Network, 28 electronic billboards that it owns in 27 locations. (The company leases the space from outdoor advertising firms such as Clear Channel Outdoor and Boardworks but owns the boards themselves.) Its first advertising on the billboards was a promotion of its special-edition Daytona 500 Coke cans. The Outdoor Advertising Association of America predicts that several hundred digital billboards will be introduced each year, with a total of 1,800 so far.[24] Outdoor advertising suffers from several disadvantages, however. The medium requires brief messages, and billboards are often attacked by preservation and conservation groups.

Advertisers are exploring new forms of outdoor media, many of which involve technology: computerized paintings, video billboards, "trivision" that displays three revolving images on a single billboard, and moving billboards mounted on trucks.

Internet Advertising

Sales from online advertising and marketing now surpass sales from print media. Companies spend almost $120 billion on advertising in online and digital media and almost $112 billion on advertising in newspapers and magazines.[25] Search engine marketing, display ads, and even classified ads are surging.

Online and interactive media have already changed the nature of advertising. Starting with simple banner ads, Internet advertising has become much more complex and sophisticated. Miniature television screen images, called *widgets* or *gadgets*, can carry marketing messages only a few inches high on a Web site, blog, or desktop display. And they contain embedded links to their home sites. Online advertising can take other forms as well. Ford Motor Company's Fiesta subcompact was available in Europe but not in the United States. To educate the American public about the Fiesta, soon to become available, the company launched its Fiesta Movement by giving 100 consumers European Fiestas for six months and having them use the cars to complete various missions each month. (Ford paid for the gas.) Some people used the cars for charitable work, such as delivering Meals On Wheels. Others used them for real adventures or even for actually eloping. As part of the project, the consumers documented their missions and posted the results on YouTube, Flickr, Facebook, and Twitter. In the next phase of the Fiesta Movement, consumers will compete for cash prizes and the chance to win a Fiesta of their own. Google, which owns YouTube, predicts that the Web site will soon be in the black for the first time. Advertising on YouTube was nearly sold out. Eric Schmidt, Google's CEO, predicted that more advertisers would use YouTube in their ad campaigns. He said that YouTube "has gone from being a nice to have to an essential part of the media mix of any display campaign."[26]

Another example is *viral advertising*, which creates a message that is novel or entertaining enough for consumers to forward it to others, spreading it like a virus. The great advantage is that spreading the word online, which often relies on social networking on sites like MySpace and Facebook, costs the advertiser nothing. While viral marketing can be risky, the best campaigns are edgy and often funny. Among the most effective viral video ads of late were "Will It Blend?" which depicts what happens when an iPhone meets a blender; T-Mobile Dance, a film of a dancing flash mob in London's Liverpool Street Railway Station; and "United Breaks Guitars," about a member of the band Sons of Maxwell, his guitar, and United Airlines.[27]

Some viral campaigns rely on personal word-of-mouth promotions, and when ordinary consumers are recruited as "brand ambassadors" or "buzz agents" for pay, questions can arise about ethics. One company, BzzAgent, gives its members products instead of money. But these ambassadors are not required to tell others that they're being paid or receiving free gifts to discuss products, which some view as problematic.[28]

Sponsorship   One of the hottest trends in promotion offers marketers the ability to integrate several elements of the promotional mix. **Sponsorship** involves providing funds for a sporting or cultural event in exchange for a direct association with the event. Sports sponsorships attract two-thirds of total sponsorship dollars in the United States alone. Entertainment, festivals, causes, and the arts divide up the remaining third of sponsorship dollars.

NASCAR, the biggest spectator sport in the United States, thrives on sponsorships. Because it can cost as much as $20 to $25 million a year to run a top NASCAR team, drivers depend on sponsorships from companies to keep the wheels turning. Some companies were unwilling or unable to continue their sponsorships.[29] Firms may also sponsor charitable or other not-for-profit awards or events. In conjunction with sports network ESPN, Gatorade sponsors its High School Athlete of the Year award, presented to the top male and female high school athletes who "strive for their best on and off the field."

Sponsors benefit in two major ways: exposure to the event's audience and association with the image of the activity. If a celebrity is involved, sponsors usually earn the right to use his or her name along with the name of the event in advertisements. They can set up signs at the event, offer sales promotions, and the like. Sponsorships play an important role in relationship marketing, bringing together the event, its participants, and the sponsoring firms.

Other Media Options   As consumers filter out familiar advertising messages, marketers look for novel ways to catch their attention. In addition to the major media, firms promote through many other vehicles such as infomercials and specialized media. **Infomercials** are a form of broadcast direct marketing, also called *direct-response television (DRTV)*. These 30-minute programs resemble regular television programs but are devoted to selling goods or services such as exercise equipment, skin-care products, or kitchenware. The long format allows an advertiser to thoroughly present product benefits, increase awareness, and make an impact on consumers. Advertisers also receive immediate responses in the form of sales or inquiries because most infomercials feature toll-free phone numbers. Infomercial stars may become celebrities in their own right, attracting more customers wherever they go. The most effective infomercials tend to be for auto-care products, beauty and personal-care items, investing and business opportunities, collectibles, fitness and self-improvement products, and housewares and electronics.[30]

Advertisers use just about any medium they can find. They place messages on New York City MetroCard transit cards and toll receipts on the Massachusetts Turnpike. A more recent development is the use of ATMs for advertising. Some ATMs can play 15-second commercials on their screens, and many can print advertising messages on receipts. An ATM screen has a captive audience because the user must watch the screen to complete a transaction. Directory advertising includes the familiar Yellow Pages listings in telephone books and thousands of other types of directories, most presenting business-related promotions. Besides local and regional directories, publishers also have produced special printed and online versions of the Yellow Pages that target ethnic groups.

Sales Promotion

Traditionally viewed as a supplement to a firm's sales or advertising efforts, sales promotion has emerged as an integral part of the promotional mix. Promotion now accounts for more than half as many marketing dollars as are spent on advertising, and promotion spending is rising faster than ad spending. **Sales promotion** consists of forms of promotion such as coupons, product samples, and rebates that support advertising and personal selling.

Both retailers and manufacturers use sales promotions to offer consumers extra incentives to buy. Beyond the short-term advantage of increased sales, sales promotions can also help marketers build brand equity and enhance customer relationships. Examples include samples, coupons, contests, displays, trade shows, and dealer incentives.

Consumer-Oriented Promotions

The goal of a consumer-oriented sales promotion is to get new and existing customers to try or buy products. In addition, marketers want to encourage repeat purchases by rewarding current users, increase sales of complimentary products, and boost impulse purchases. Figure 13.3 shows how marketers allocate their consumer-oriented spending among the categories of promotions.

Promotions can also popularize an idea, such as the growing awareness of how much pollution plastic shopping bags contribute to the environment. The "Going Green" feature discusses the growing trend of banning plastic shopping bags.

Premiums, Coupons, Rebates, and Samples Nearly six of every ten sales promotion dollars are spent on *premiums*—items given free or at a reduced price with the purchase of another product. Cosmetics companies such as Clinique offer sample kits with purchases of their products. Fast-food restaurants are also big users of premiums. McDonald's and Burger King include a toy with every children's meal—the toys often tie in with new movies or popular cartoon shows. In general, marketers choose premiums that are likely to get consumers thinking about and caring about the brand and the product. People who purchase health foods at a grocery store may find an offer for a free personal training session at a local health club printed on the back of their sales receipt.

Customers redeem *coupons* for small price discounts when they purchase the promoted products. Such offers may persuade a customer to try a new or different product. Some large supermarket

Assessment Check ✔

1. What are the two basic types of advertising? Into what three categories do they fall?
2. What is the leading advertising medium in the United States?
3. In what two major ways do firms benefit from sponsorship?

sales promotion consists of forms of promotion such as coupons, product samples, and rebates that support advertising and personal selling.

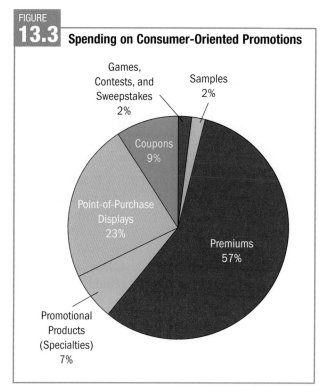

FIGURE **13.3** Spending on Consumer-Oriented Promotions

- Games, Contests, and Sweepstakes 2%
- Samples 2%
- Coupons 9%
- Point-of-Purchase Displays 23%
- Premiums 57%
- Promotional Products (Specialties) 7%

Source: Data from Kathleen M. Joyce, "Higher Gear," Promo Magazine, http://promomagazine.com, accessed April 26, 2010.

How Much Would You Pay for a Plastic Shopping Bag?

The U.S. Environmental Protection Agency estimates that almost 4 billion tons of plastics waste—in the form of bags, sacks, and wrapping—were generated in one year. Made from foreign oil, the plastic can take 1,000 years to degrade. Only about 1 percent is ever recycled.

A growing number of people want to reduce these statistics. For instance, San Francisco enacted an outright ban on plastic bags. New York City started requiring certain retailers to accept plastic bags for recycling. Los Angeles also banned plastic bags. In a first, Washington, D.C., imposed a tax of 5 cents on every plastic bag for supermarket customers. The city plans to use the revenue to restore a polluted local river.

But such laws have not always met with approval. In eco-friendly Seattle, voters overturned a law charging 20 cents per plastic bag, perhaps because they were already recycling and reusing the bags. The mayor of Washington, D.C., hopes that the tax on plastic bags will encourage shoppers to change their habits so they won't have to pay the tax at all.

The retailing giant Walmart already sells reusable bags for 50 cents. In three of its California stores, it is introducing the option of a 15 cent reusable bag that is expected to survive 75 shopping trips. The bag can then be recycled in existing bins in the stores.

Questions for Critical Thinking

1. Can stores that provide eco-friendly shopping bags or other ways to reduce the polluting effects of plastic reap promotional benefits from their efforts? How can cities that ban or tax plastic bags promote their actions?

2. What other ways can you think of to promote the idea of recycling plastic bags or reducing their use?

Sources: "NYCWasteLe$$," Plastic Bag Recycling, http://www.nyc.gov, accessed May 11, 2010; Dave Gram, "Vt. Plastic Bag Tax Proposal Seen Coming Too Late," *Rutland Herald,* April 16, 2010, http:// http://www.rutlandherald.com; Melissa Eddy, "Plastic Bag Ban: Would You Pay 5 Cents for a Bag?" *Huffington Post,* February 22, 2010, http:// www.huffingtonpost.com; Steve Painter, "3 Wal-Marts Testing Purge of Plastic Bags," *Arkansas Democrat-Gazette,* January 24, 2010, http://ww6.lexisnexis.com; Stephen Messenger, "Washington D.C.'s Plastic Bag Tax Takes Effect This Week," *TreeHugger.com,* January 3, 2010, http://www.treehugger.com.

chains double the face value of manufacturers' coupons. Coupons have the disadvantage of focusing customers on price rather than brand loyalty. While some consumers complain that clipping or printing out coupons is too time consuming, others relish the savings, particularly when money is tight and prices seem to be high.

American consumers' use of coupons increased 27 percent in a year, using 3.3 billion coupons to redeem $3.5 billion. Internet coupon use skyrocketed a whopping 360 percent. Marketers issued 367 billion coupons with a face value averaging $1.44, but shortened the expiration periods by some 10 percent. Some analysts predict that the growing use of paperless mobile coupons, which consumers can access on their Web-enabled cellphones while shopping and pioneered by such retailers as Target, could soon make clippable or even printed-out coupons obsolete.[31]

Rebates offer cash back to consumers who mail in required proofs of purchase. Rebates help packaged-goods manufacturers increase purchase rates, promote multiple purchases, and reward product users. Other types of companies also offer rebates, especially for electronics, computers and their accessories, and automobiles. Processing rebates gives marketers a way to collect data about their customers, but many shoppers find it inconvenient to collect the required receipts, forms, and UPC codes and then wait several weeks for their refund. Services such as RebateRemedy can cut the waiting time to days instead of weeks but take a 20 to 30 percent cut of the rebate, plus a processing fee. Some stores and manufacturers are phasing out mail-in rebates. After a brief period of testing mail-in rebates on some cell phones, Verizon found that customers preferred and expected instant online discounts, so the company has ended its mail-in rebate program on the Palm Pre and the Pixi Plus.[32]

A *sample* is a gift of a product distributed by mail, door to door, in a demonstration, or inside packages of another product. On any given day you might receive a sample moisturizer, a bar of soap, or a packet of laundry detergent. Three of every four consumers who receive samples will try them.

Games, Contests, and Sweepstakes Contests, sweepstakes, and games offer cash, merchandise, or travel as prizes to participating winners. Firms often sponsor these activities to introduce new goods and services and to attract additional customers. Games and contests require entrants to solve problems or write essays and sometimes provide proof of purchase. Sweepstakes choose winners by chance and require no product purchase. Consumers typically prefer them because games and contests require more effort. Companies like sweepstakes, too, because they are inexpensive to run and determine the number of winners from the beginning. With games and contests, the company cannot predict the number of people who will correctly complete a puzzle or gather the right number of symbols from scratch-off cards. Sweepstakes, games, and contests can reinforce a company's image and advertising message, but consumer attention may focus on the promotion rather than the product.

In recent years, court rulings and legal restrictions have limited the use of games and contests. Companies must proceed carefully in advertising their contests and games and the prizes they award. Marketers must indicate the chances of winning and avoid false promises such as implying that a person has already won.

Specialty Advertising Do you have any pens, T-shirts, or refrigerator magnets imprinted with a business name that you received for free? These offers are examples of **specialty advertising** or *advertising specialties*. This type of sales promotion involves the gift of useful merchandise carrying the name, logo, or slogan of a profit-seeking business or a not-for-profit organization. Because those products are useful and sometimes personalized with recipients' names, people tend to keep and use them, giving advertisers repeated exposure. Originally designed to identify and create goodwill for advertisers, advertising specialties now generate sales leads and develop traffic for stores and trade show exhibitors. Like premiums, these promotions should reinforce the brand's image and its relationship with the recipient.

specialty advertising promotional items that prominently display a firm's name, logo, or business slogan.

Trade-Oriented Promotions

Sales promotion techniques can also contribute to campaigns directed to retailers and wholesalers. **Trade promotion** is sales promotion geared to marketing intermediaries rather than to consumers. Marketers use trade promotion to encourage retailers to stock new products, continue carrying existing ones, and promote both new and existing products effectively to consumers. Successful trade promotions offer financial incentives. They require careful timing, attention to costs, and easy implementation for intermediaries. These promotions should bring quick results and improve retail sales. Major trade promotions include point-of-purchase advertising and trade shows.

trade promotion sales promotion geared to marketing intermediaries rather than to final consumers.

Point-of-purchase (POP) advertising consists of displays or demonstrations that promote products when and where consumers buy them, such as in retail stores. When the Swiffer floor cleaner was being introduced, Procter & Gamble used in-store demonstrations to show consumers how it worked. Marketing research has shown that consumers are more likely to purchase certain products when such displays are present. Sunscreen, painting supplies, and snacks are typically displayed this way. A high-tech version of POP advertising is digital advertising consoles mounted on grocery carts. With impulse purchases making up 53 percent of total buying, POP has already begun to evolve into what is being called "mobile advertising." Although privacy is still an issue, more and more Web sites and other

point-of-purchase (POP) advertising displays or demonstrations that promote products when and where consumers buy them, such as in retail stores.

How to Negotiate in a Difficult Economy

Despite the arrival of electronic media, many businesses still rely on personal selling. Even when the economy is weak, you can still find ways to negotiate effectively. Here are five tips for successful negotiation in good and difficult economic times:

1 *Be a good listener.* This is always a good idea. Like good detectives, good negotiators ask questions—and then listen as the other negotiator or prospect speaks. You'll establish trust—and learn whether your proposal will meet your prospect's needs.

2 *Be prepared.* Before you negotiate, do as much research as possible on your prospect, the prospect's business, what effect the economy has on his or her industry, and so on. Preparation is the only part of negotiation that is completely within your control.

3 *Be patient.* Americans seem always to be in a hurry, whereas in Asia, South America, or the Middle East, people realize that if you rush, you may make mistakes. Taking your time may also give you a psychological advantage over the other negotiator.

4 *Decide what is important to you.* What can you absolutely not do without? What would you be willing to give up, if you must compromise?

5 *Keep your options open.* If you feel you can't make a satisfactory agreement even with the best of intentions, leave yourself the option of walking away.

Sources: Ed Brodow, "Ten Tips for Negotiating in 2010," Ed Brodow Seminars, http://www.brodow.com, accessed May 11, 2010; Ken Dooley, "6 Tips for Negotiating in a Tough Economy," *BusinessBrief,* March 9, 2010, http://www.businessbrief.com; Ken Dooley, "The Keys to Successful Negotiation," *BusinessBrief,* February 16, 2010, http://www.businessbrief.com.

services are now able to locate Internet users, and location-based mobile spending is expected to increase from a current $34 million to $4 billion in 2015. About 25 percent of the 500 million Facebook members open the site via mobile electronic devices. Location-based advertising will not be directed primarily to stationary computers but to smart phones, iPads, Kindles, game consoles, and automobiles.[33]

Manufacturers and other sellers often exhibit at *trade shows* to promote goods or services to members of their distribution channels. These shows are often organized by industry trade associations. Each year, thousands of trade shows attract millions of exhibitors and hundreds of millions of attendees. Such shows are particularly important in fast-changing industries like those for computers, toys, furniture, and fashions. The annual Consumer Electronics Show, which is held in Las Vegas and attracts more than 100,000 visitors, is the nation's largest. But shows in the medical and healthcare, RV and camping, and even woodworking machinery fields remain strong. These shows are especially effective for introducing new products and generating sales leads.

Personal Selling

Many companies consider personal selling—a person-to-person promotional presentation to a potential buyer—the key to marketing effectiveness. Unless a seller matches a firm's goods or services to the needs of a particular client or customer, none of the firm's other activities produces any benefits. Today, sales and sales-related jobs employ about 16 million U.S. workers.[34] Businesses often spend five to ten times as much on personal selling as on advertising. Given the significant cost of hiring, training, benefits, and salaries, businesses are very concerned with the effectiveness of their sales personnel. One of their continuing concerns is with the way representatives communicate with others. The "Business Etiquette" feature discusses how to negotiate during difficult economic times.

How do marketers decide whether to make personal selling the primary component of their firm's marketing mix? In general, firms are likely to emphasize personal selling rather than advertising or sales promotion under four conditions:

1. Customers are relatively few in number and geographically concentrated.

2. The product is technically complex, involves trade-ins, or requires special handling.

3. The product carries a relatively high price.

4. It moves through direct-distribution channels.

Selling Piper Cub airplanes is a good example. Customers tend to be wealthy people who value their freedom and privacy, not to mention the luxury of having their own plane. "It is a way of life I am selling," says veteran sales rep Bruce Keller, "not just aluminum. I want the customer to share that with me. If you look at my airplane and you sit in it, you are going flying."[35]

The sales functions of most companies are experiencing rapid change. Today's sales-people are more concerned with establishing long-term buyer–seller relationships and acting as consultants to their customers than in the past. In the aftermath of the recession, sales-people face a new challenge—consumers who haggle over prices, even on retail items. One survey found that 88 percent of those questioned had haggled over at least one price in the preceding six months. Unlike in the Great Depression of the 1930s, the last time Americans engaged in serious amounts of haggling, today's consumers have advantages that would astound their predecessors. Anyone with a Web-enabled cell phone can Google competing prices of merchandise while standing in front of it in a retail store. Many have learned to bargain via Web sites such as eBay or have used Priceline to negotiate deals on travel. The survey found that hagglers had better than a 75 percent success rate in making deals on clothing, appliances, and jewelry. Consumers who negotiated medical bills were successful 58 percent of the time.[36]

Personal selling can occur in several environments, each of which can involve business-to-business or business-to-consumer selling. Sales representatives who make sales calls on prospective customers at their businesses are involved in *field selling*. Companies that sell major industrial equipment typically rely heavily on field selling. *Over-the-counter selling* describes sales activities in retailing and some wholesale locations, where customers visit the seller's facility to purchase items. *Telemarketing* sales representatives make their presentations over the phone. A later section reviews telemarketing in more detail.

Sales Tasks   All sales activities involve assisting customers in some manner. Although a salesperson's work can vary significantly from one company or situation to another, it usually includes a mix of three basic tasks: order processing, creative selling, and missionary selling.

Order Processing   Although both field selling and telemarketing involve this activity, **order processing** is most often related to retail and wholesale firms. The sales-person identifies customer needs, points out merchandise to meet them, and processes the order. Route sales personnel process orders for such consumer goods as bread, milk, soft drinks, and snack foods. They check each store's stock, report inventory needs to the store manager, and complete the sale. Most of these jobs include at least minor order-processing functions.

order processing form of selling, mostly at the wholesale and retail levels, that involves identifying customer needs, pointing them out to customers, and completing orders.

Creative Selling   Sales representatives for most business products and some consumer items perform **creative selling**, a persuasive type of promotional presentation. Creative selling promotes a good or service whose benefits are not readily apparent or whose purchase decision requires a close analysis of alternatives. Sales of intangible products such as insurance rely heavily on creative selling, but sales of tangible goods benefit as well.

creative selling persuasive type of promotional presentation.

Many retail salespeople just process orders, but many consumers are looking for more in the form of customer service, which is where creative selling comes in. Trained sales staff at Talbots women's clothing stores hold seasonal wardrobe-building workshops at the stores, helping customers select and purchase coordinating clothing, accessories, and shoes from the Talbots line—which they might not have purchased without such advice.

Missionary Selling Sales work also includes an indirect form of selling in which the representative promotes goodwill for a company or provides technical or operational assistance to the customer; this practice is called **missionary selling**. Many businesses that sell technical equipment, such as Oracle and Fujitsu, provide systems specialists who act as consultants to customers. These salespeople work to solve problems and sometimes help their clients with questions not directly related to their employers' products. Other industries also use missionary selling techniques. Pharmaceutical company representatives—called *detailers*—visit physicians to describe the firm's latest offerings, although some firms are finding success with more subtle methods, including Web-based sales calls outside office hours. The pharmaceutical giant Pfizer recently cut back its sales force and has increasingly turned to electronic marketing. The company has found electronic detailing especially advantageous. With it, doctors can get the latest information on drugs when and where they choose. It also can be strictly controlled, and the company runs much less risk of its salespeople's being accused of marketing drugs for off-label uses—that is, for treating conditions other than those they were originally intended to help.[37] The actual sales, in any case, are handled through pharmacies, which fill the prescriptions.

Telemarketing **Telemarketing**, personal selling conducted by telephone, provides a firm's marketers with a high return on their expenditures, an immediate response, and an opportunity for personalized two-way conversation. Many firms use telemarketing because expense or other obstacles prevent salespeople from meeting many potential customers in person. Telemarketers can use databases to target prospects based on demographic data. Telemarketing takes two forms. A sales representative who calls you is practicing *outbound telemarketing*. On the other hand, *inbound telemarketing* occurs when you call a toll-free phone number to get product information or place an order.

Outbound telemarketers must abide by the Federal Trade Commission's 1996 Telemarketing Sales Rule. Telemarketers must disclose that they are selling something and on whose behalf they are calling before they make their presentations. The rule also limits calls to between 8 a.m. and 9 p.m., requires sellers to disclose details on exchange policies, and requires them to keep lists of people who do not want to receive calls. In some states, it is also against the law for telemarketers to leave messages on consumers' answering machines. Congress enacted another law in 2003 creating the National Do Not Call registry intended to help consumers block unwanted telemarketing calls. Consumers who want to be on the list must call a special number or visit a Web site to register. Telemarketers must stop calling registered numbers within 31 days or face stiff fines of up to $11,000 for each violation.[38] Charities, surveys, and political campaign calls are exempt from these restrictions. Businesses with which consumers already have a relationship, such as the bank where they have accounts or the dealership where they buy their cars, may conduct telemarketing calls under the guidelines of the Telemarketing Sales Rule.

The Sales Process The sales process typically follows the seven-step sequence shown in Figure 13.4: prospecting and qualifying, the approach, presentation, the demonstration, handling objections, closing, and the follow-up. Remember the importance of flexibility, though; a good salesperson is not afraid to vary the sales process based on a customer's responses and needs. The process of selling to a potential customer who is unfamiliar with a

missionary selling indirect form of selling in which the representative promotes goodwill for a company or provides technical or operational assistance to the customer.

telemarketing personal selling conducted entirely by telephone, which provides a firm's marketers with a high return on their expenditures, an immediate response, and an opportunity for personalized two-way conversation.

company's products differs from the process of serving a long-time customer.

Prospecting, Qualifying, and Approaching

At the prospecting stage, salespeople identify potential customers. They may seek leads for prospective sales from such sources as existing customers, friends and family, and business associates. The qualifying process identifies potential customers who have the financial ability and authority to buy.

Companies use different tactics to identify and qualify prospects. Some companies rely on business development teams to do this legwork. They use the responses from direct mail to provide leads to sales reps. Other companies believe in personal visits from sales representatives; others use e-mail, which is inexpensive and boasts a good response rate. Many B2B firms are taking advantage of electronic social media such as electronic newsletters, Web events, virtual trade shows, podcasts, videos, online demonstrations, blogs, and many others.[39]

Successful salespeople make careful preparations, analyzing available data about a prospective customer's product lines and other pertinent information before making the initial contact. They realize the importance of a first impression in influencing a customer's future attitudes toward the selling company and its products.

Presentation and Demonstration

At the presentation stage, salespeople communicate promotional messages. They may describe the major features of their products, highlight the advantages, and cite examples of satisfied consumers. A demonstration helps reinforce the message that the salesperson has been communicating—a critical step in the sales process. Department-store shoppers can get a free makeover at the cosmetics counter. Anyone looking to buy a car will take it for a test drive before deciding whether to purchase it.

Some products are too large to transport to prospective buyers or require special installation to demonstrate. Using laptop computers, multimedia presentations, graphic programs like SmartDraw, Web conferences, and even podcasts, sales representatives can demonstrate these products for customers.[40] Others, such as services, are intangible. So a presentation including testimonials from satisfied customers or graphs illustrating results may be helpful.

Handling Objections

Some salespeople fear potential customers' objections because they view the questions as criticism. But a good salesperson can use objections as an opportunity to answer questions and explain how the product will benefit the customer. As a general rule, the key is to sell benefits, not features: How will this product help the customer?

Closing

The critical point in the sales process—the time at which the salesperson actually asks the prospect to buy—is the closing. If the presentation effectively matches

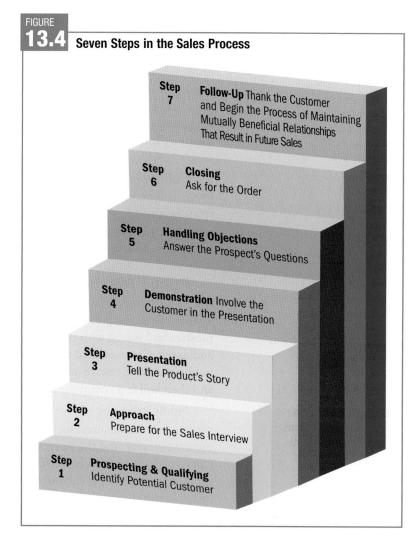

FIGURE 13.4 Seven Steps in the Sales Process

Step 7   **Follow-Up** Thank the Customer and Begin the Process of Maintaining Mutually Beneficial Relationships That Result in Future Sales

Step 6   **Closing** Ask for the Order

Step 5   **Handling Objections** Answer the Prospect's Questions

Step 4   **Demonstration** Involve the Customer in the Presentation

Step 3   **Presentation** Tell the Product's Story

Step 2   **Approach** Prepare for the Sales Interview

Step 1   **Prospecting & Qualifying** Identify Potential Customer

product benefits to customer needs, the closing should be a natural conclusion. If there are more bumps in the process, the salesperson can try some different techniques, such as offering alternative products, offering a special incentive for purchase, or restating the product benefits. Closing the sale—and beginning a relationship in which the customer builds loyalty to the brand or product—is the ideal outcome of this interaction. But even if the sale is not made at this time, the salesperson should regard the interaction as the beginning of a potential relationship anyway. The prospect might very well become a customer in the future.

Follow-Up A salesperson's actions after the sale may determine whether the customer will make another purchase. Follow-up is an important part of building a long-lasting relationship. After closing, the salesperson should process the order efficiently. By calling soon after a purchase, the salesperson provides reassurance about the customer's decision to buy and creates an opportunity to correct any problems.

Public Relations A final element of the promotional mix, public relations (PR)—including publicity—supports advertising, personal selling, and sales promotion, usually by pursuing broader objectives. Through PR, companies attempt to improve their prestige and image with the public by distributing specific messages or ideas to target audiences. Cause-related promotional activities are often supported by public relations and publicity campaigns. In addition, PR helps a firm establish awareness of goods and services and then builds a positive image of them.

<u>**Public relations**</u> refers to an organization's communications and relationships with its various public audiences, such as customers, vendors, news media, employees, stockholders, the government, and the general public. Many of these communication efforts serve marketing purposes. Public relations is an efficient, indirect communications channel for promoting products. It can publicize products and help create and maintain a positive image of the company.

The public relations department links a firm with the media. It provides the media with news releases and video and audio clips, as well as holding news conferences to announce new products, the formation of strategic alliances, management changes, financial results, and similar developments. Publications issued by the department include newsletters, brochures, and reports.

Publicity The type of public relations that is tied most closely to promoting a company's products is **publicity**—nonpersonal stimulation of demand for a good, service, place, idea, event, person, or organization by unpaid placement of information in print or broadcast media. Press releases generate publicity, as does news coverage. Ironically, sometimes even criticism can generate publicity. Spirit Airlines recently got a lot of negative publicity when it instituted new fees for carry-on luggage—but the airline's bookings increased 50 percent. This was because the airline also installed "pre-reclined" seats on its new planes, allowing it to add more seats and lower its airfares. Even though "pre-reclined" is a misnomer—the seats actually don't recline at all but stay permanently upright—some observers predict that consumers looking for the cheapest airfares will continue to book on Spirit.[41]

Not-for-profit organizations benefit from publicity when they receive coverage of events such as the Susan G. Komen Race for the Cure, which raises money for breast cancer research.[42] When a for-profit firm teams up with a not-for-profit firm in a fund-raising effort, the move usually generates good publicity for both organizations.

Assessment Check ✔

1. Why do retailers and manufacturers use sales promotions?

2. When does a firm use personal selling instead of nonpersonal selling?

3. How does public relations serve a marketing purpose?

Pushing and Pulling Strategies

Marketers can choose between two general promotional strategies: a pushing strategy or a pulling strategy. A **pushing strategy** relies on personal selling to market an item to wholesalers and retailers in a company's distribution channels. So companies promote the product to members of the marketing channel, not to end users. Sales personnel explain to marketing intermediaries why they should carry particular merchandise, usually supported by offers of special discounts and promotional materials. Marketers also provide **cooperative advertising** allowances, in which they share the cost of local advertising of their firm's product or line with channel partners. All of these strategies are designed to motivate wholesalers and retailers to push the good or service to their own customers.

A **pulling strategy** attempts to promote a product by generating consumer demand for it, primarily through advertising and sales promotion appeals. Potential buyers will then request that their suppliers—retailers or local distributors—carry the product, thereby pulling it through the distribution channel. Dove used this strategy when it launched its new Men + Care line of men's personal-care products during a recent Super Bowl. The 30-second commercial, with its tagline "Be comfortable in your own skin," generated significant online response, with consumers searching such terms as "Super Bowl," "ad," and "men" to find retailers that stocked the products.[43]

Most marketing situations require combinations of pushing and pulling strategies, although the primary emphasis can vary. Consumer products usually depend more heavily on pulling strategies than do B2B products, which favor pushing strategies.

Assessment Check ✔

1. Give an example of a pushing strategy.
2. Give an example of a pulling strategy.

Pricing Objectives in the Marketing Mix

Products offer utility, or want-satisfying power. However, we as consumers determine how much value we associate with each one. In the aftermath of a major storm, we may value electricity and food and water above everything else. If we commute a long distance or are planning a vacation, fuel may be of greater concern. But all consumers have limited amounts of money and a variety of possible uses for it. So the **price**—the exchange value of a good or service—becomes a major factor in consumer buying decisions.

Businesspeople attempt to accomplish certain objectives through their pricing decisions. Pricing objectives vary from firm to firm, and many companies pursue multiple pricing objectives. Some try to improve profits by setting high prices; others set low prices to attract new business. As Figure 13.5 shows, the four basic categories of pricing objectives are (1) profitability, (2) volume, (3) meeting competition, and (4) prestige.

At the makeup counter, salespeople provide a free makeup demonstration to reinforce the message of how their cosmetic products can enhance your look.

Robert Nystrom/iStockphoto

Profitability Objectives

Profitability objectives are the most common objectives included in the strategic plans of most firms. Marketers know that profits are the revenue the company brings in, minus its expenses. Usually a big difference exists between revenue and profit. Automakers try to produce at least one luxury vehicle for which they can charge $50,000 or more instead of relying entirely on the sale of $15,000 to $25,000 models.

Some firms maximize profits by reducing costs rather than through higher prices. Companies can maintain prices and increase profitability by operating more efficiently or by modifying the product to make it less costly to produce. One strategy is to maintain a steady price while reducing the size or amount of the product in the package—something that manufacturers of candy, coffee, and cereal have done over the years.

Volume Objectives

A second approach to pricing strategy—**volume objectives**—bases pricing decisions on market share, the percentage of a market controlled by a certain company or product. One firm may seek to achieve a 25 percent market share in a certain product category, and another may want to maintain or expand its market share for particular products. As a market becomes saturated—like the PC market—firms need to find ways to get consumers to upgrade or try new products. Setting a lower price can accomplish that objective, as long as the firm still makes a profit. Many PC makers—and retailers—have begun to offer their products at lower prices, particularly at the start of the school year. Although Microsoft's Windows 7 operating system sold well, giving that company and electronics retail giant BestBuy big profits, manufacturers of PCs such as Hewlett-Packard and Dell did not share in the success. They had hoped that consumers would be willing to pay more for their new PCs, loaded with Windows 7 and many other new features. Instead consumers resisted paying more, and retailers offered deep discounts during a recent holiday season.[44]

Pricing to Meet Competition

A third set of pricing objectives seeks simply to meet competitors' prices so that price essentially becomes a nonissue. In many lines of business, firms set their own prices to match those of established industry leaders. However, companies may not legally work together to agree on prices.

Because price is such a highly visible component of a firm's marketing mix, businesses may be tempted to use it to obtain an advantage over competitors. But sometimes the race to match competitors' prices results in a *price war*, which has happened periodically in the airline and fast-food industries. The ability of competitors to match a price cut leads many marketers to try to avoid price wars by favoring other strategies, such as adding value, improving quality, educating consumers, and establishing relationships.

Although price is a major component of the marketing mix, it is not the only one. Electronic readers such as the Kindle and the iPad are in a fierce pricing competition for digital books, as the "Solving an Ethical Controversy" feature explains.

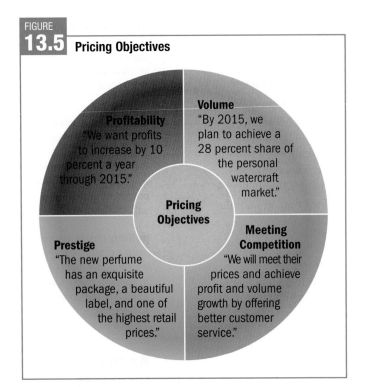

FIGURE 13.5 Pricing Objectives

Profitability
"We want profits to increase by 10 percent a year through 2015."

Volume
"By 2015, we plan to achieve a 28 percent share of the personal watercraft market."

Pricing Objectives

Prestige
"The new perfume has an exquisite package, a beautiful label, and one of the highest retail prices."

Meeting Competition
"We will meet their prices and achieve profit and volume growth by offering better customer service."

profitability objectives common objectives included in the strategic plans of most firms.

volume objectives bases pricing decisions on market share, the percentage of a market controlled by a certain company or product.

Solving an Ethical Controversy

Free E-Books: Good or Bad for Business?

When Amazon's Kindle electronic reader first became available, Amazon charged consumers $9.99 for each e-book they purchased. Publishers insisted that that price was too low to keep their business profitable. But Amazon actually gave some e-books away for free, including those of living authors who earn an income from their writing.

Amazon explained that the free e-books were a way to get consumers to check out unfamiliar writers. The hope was that they would then buy other works by those writers. But some publishers delay publication of electronic editions for several months after the hardcover books were issued, much as they delay paperback editions.

Should e-books be given away for free?

PRO

1. Some publishers regard free e-books as promotion to generate buzz about new or unknown authors.

2. Some publishers that give away e-books on a regular basis have noticed an increase in sales that's "all found money," as one executive says.

CON

1. "It is illogical to give books away for free," said David Young of Hachette Book Group, which publishes Stephanie Meyer's "Twilight" series.

2. The relatively low price of e-books may discourage consumers from buying actual books with suggested retail prices of $25 or more.

Summary

When Apple unveiled its iPad, it announced that it had negotiated with five of the six biggest publishers to charge anywhere from $12.99 to $14.99 for each e-book edition of adult fiction and nonfiction. But according to insiders, Apple required the publishers to agree to discounts on best-selling books, so that the publicized price range was actually a ceiling, and that some prices could be lower.

Sources: Stan Schroeder, "The E-Book Price War Isn't Over Yet," *Mashable*, February 18, 2010, http://mashable.com; Motoko Rich, "Apple's Prices for E-Books May Be Lower Than Expected," *The New York Times*, February 18, 2010, http://www.nytimes.com; Motoko Rich, "With Kindle, the Best Sellers Don't Need to Sell," *The New York Times*, January 23, 2010, http://www.nytimes.com; "The Kindle Pricing Strategy & the Kindle Pricing History," *askDeb.com*, January 20, 2010, http://www.askdeb.com.

Prestige Objectives

The final category of objectives encompasses the effect of prices on prestige. **Prestige pricing** establishes a relatively high price to develop and maintain an image of quality and exclusiveness. Marketers set such objectives because they recognize the role of price in communicating an overall image for the firm and its products. People expect to pay more for a Lexus, a Louis Vuitton purse, or a vacation on St. Kitts or Nevis in the Caribbean. Despite a recession, the British retailer Selfridges has had a 60 percent increase in sales of "must-have" handbags by the luxury brand Mulberry. Mulberry even has waiting lists for some of its styles.[45]

Scarcity can create prestige. Products that are limited in distribution or so popular that they become scarce generate their own prestige—allowing businesses to charge more for them. Unfortunately, scarcity can also invite crime. Recently, federal prosecutors charged four men with hacking into the computer systems of Ticketmaster, Major League Baseball, Telecharge, and Live Nation Entertainment to highjack 1.5 million tickets to concerts by Bruce Springsteen and Miley Cyrus, baseball playoff games at Yankee Stadium, and other events. The men or their agents posed as individual online buyers, electronically bypassed the vendors' security systems, and bought blocks of tickets that they resold at hugely inflated

prestige pricing establishes a relatively high price to develop and maintain an image of quality and exclusiveness.

Assessment Check ☑

1. Define *price*.
2. What is a second approach to pricing strategy?

Prestige pricing establishes a relatively high price to develop and maintain an image of quality and exclusiveness. People expect to pay more for a Louis Vuitton bag, just like the rock star in the ad.

prices. The scam had been in operation since 2002 and had generated almost $29 million in illegal profits.[46]

Pricing Strategies

People from different areas of a company contribute their expertise to set the most strategic price for a product. Accountants, financial managers, and marketers provide relevant sales and cost data, along with customer feedback. Designers, engineers, and systems analysts all contribute important data as well.

Prices are determined in two basic ways: by applying the concepts of supply and demand discussed in Chapter 3 and by completing cost-oriented analyses. Economic theory assumes that a market price will be set at the point at which the amount of a product desired at a given price equals the amount that suppliers will offer for sale at that price. In other words, this price occurs at the point at which the amount demanded and the amount supplied are equal. Online auctions, such as those conducted on eBay, are a popular application of the demand-and-supply approach.

Price Determination in Practice

Economic theory might lead to the best pricing decisions, but most businesses do not have all the information they need to make those decisions, so they adopt **cost-based pricing** formulas. These formulas calculate total costs per unit and then add markups to cover overhead costs and generate profits.

Cost-based pricing totals all costs associated with offering a product in the market, including research and development, production, transportation, and marketing expenses. An added amount, the markup, then covers any unexpected or overlooked expenses and provides a profit. The total becomes the price. Although the actual markup used varies by such factors as brand image and type of store, the typical markup for clothing is determined by doubling the wholesale price (the cost to the merchant) to arrive at the retail price for the item.

Breakeven Analysis

Businesses often conduct a **breakeven analysis** to determine the minimum sales volume a product must generate at a certain price level to cover all costs. This method involves a consideration of various costs and total revenues. *Total cost* is the sum of total variable costs and total fixed costs. *Variable costs* change with the level of production, as labor and raw materials do, while *fixed costs* such as insurance premiums and utility rates charged by water, natural gas, and electric power suppliers remain stable regardless of the production level. *Total revenue* is determined by multiplying price by the number of units sold.

Finding the Breakeven Point The level of sales that will generate enough revenue to cover all of the company's fixed and variable costs is called the *breakeven point*.

cost-based pricing formulas that calculate total costs per unit and then add markups to cover overhead costs and generate profits.

breakeven analysis pricing-related technique used to determine the minimum sales volume a product must generate at a certain price level to cover all costs.

It is the point at which total revenue just equals total costs. Sales beyond the breakeven point will generate profits; sales volume below the breakeven point will result in losses. The following formulas give the breakeven point in units and dollars:

$$\text{Breakeven Point (in units)} = \frac{\text{Total fixed costs}}{\text{Contribution to fixed costs per unit}}$$

$$\text{Breakeven Point (in dollars)} = \frac{\text{Total fixed costs}}{1 - \text{Variable cost per unit/Price}}$$

A product selling for $20 with a variable cost of $14 per unit produces a $6 per-unit contribution to fixed costs. If the firm has total fixed costs of $42,000, then it must sell 7,000 units to break even on the product. The calculation of the breakeven point in units and dollars is as follows:

$$\text{Breakeven Point (in units)} = \frac{\$42,000}{\$20 - \$14} = \frac{\$42,000}{\$6} = 7,000 \text{ units}$$

$$\text{Breakeven Point (in dollars)} = \frac{\$42,000}{1 - \$14/\$20} = \frac{\$42,000}{1 - 0.7} = \frac{\$42,000}{0.3} = \$140,000$$

Marketers use breakeven analysis to determine the profits or losses that would result from several different proposed prices. Because different prices produce different breakeven points, marketers could compare their calculations of required sales to break even with sales estimates from marketing research studies. This comparison can identify the best price—one that would attract enough customers to exceed the breakeven point and earn profits for the firm.

Most firms add consumer demand—determining whether enough customers will buy the number of units the firm must sell at a particular price to break even—by developing estimates through surveys of likely customers, interviews with retailers that would be handling the product, and assessments of prices charged by competitors. Then the breakeven points for several possible prices are calculated and compared with sales estimates for each price. This practice is referred to as *modified breakeven analysis.*

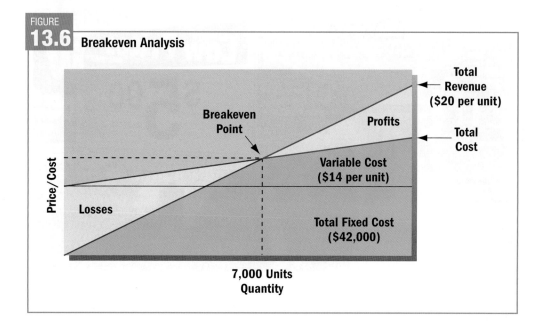

FIGURE 13.6 Breakeven Analysis

Alternative Pricing Strategies

The strategy a company uses to set its prices should grow out of the firm's overall marketing strategy. In general, firms can choose from four alternative pricing strategies: skimming, penetration, discount or everyday low pricing, and competitive pricing.

Skimming Pricing A **skimming pricing** strategy sets an intentionally high price relative to the prices of competing products. The term comes from the expression "skimming the cream." This pricing strategy often works for the introduction of a distinctive good or service with little or no competition, although it can be used at other stages of the product life cycle as well. A skimming strategy can help marketers set a price that distinguishes a firm's high-end product from those of competitors. It can also help a firm recover its product development costs before competitors enter the field. This is often the case with prescription drugs.

Penetration Pricing By contrast, a **penetration pricing** strategy sets a low price as a major marketing weapon. Businesses may price new products noticeably lower than competing offerings when they enter new industries characterized by dozens of competing brands. Once the new product achieves some market recognition through consumer trial purchases stimulated by its low price, marketers may increase the price to the level of competing products. However, stiff competition might prevent the price increase.

Everyday Low Pricing and Discount Pricing **Everyday low pricing (EDLP)** is a strategy devoted to maintaining continuous low prices rather than relying on short-term price-cutting tactics such as cents-off coupons, rebates, and special sales. This strategy has been used successfully by retailers such as Walmart and GNC to consistently offer low prices to consumers; manufacturers also use EDLP to set stable prices for retailers.

With *discount pricing*, businesses hope to attract customers by dropping prices for a set period of time. Automakers usually offer consumers special discounts on most or all of their

Stores such as Walmart use an everyday low pricing strategy, devoted to maintaining continuous low prices rather than relying on short-term price-cutting tactics such as cents-off coupons, rebates, and special sales.

Will Lower Prices Help Nokia Regain Its Edge?

For years the Finnish electronics giant Nokia owned an enormous share of the world's cell phone market, easily beating out early competitors such as Motorola and Sony Ericsson. Recently, however, it has found itself facing competition from Apple's iPhone, which has begun to lower its prices, and from Research in Motion's BlackBerry devices.

The company seems to be trying various strategies, but some observers think Nokia has lost its strategic focus. Nokia's chief executive, Olli-Pekka Kallasvuo, announced that the company would focus on software, citing a deal with Microsoft to create business-oriented mobile applications. Another executive declared that Nokia would become the "world's biggest entertainment media network." Indeed, it recently launched its "Comes with Music" downloading service, which was the first of its kind in the Middle East. But it has done poorly elsewhere due to stiff competition from Apple's iTunes. Yet another executive announced the debut of the Booklet 3G, a laptop computer that would make the "personal computer more social, more helpful, and more personal."

At a meeting in New Delhi, India, Tuula Rytilä-Uotila, Nokia's vice president of products, announced that the company planned to lower the prices of Nokia's smart phones. "We want to take smart phones to a wider audience by bringing down the prices of such phones. The strategy is to be present in all price ranges." The company hopes to stimulate demand for its low-end mobile phones and perhaps put some indirect pressure on Apple and Research in Motion, whose handsets are more sophisticated.

Questions for Critical Thinking

1. Do you think Nokia will regain lost ground with its new pricing strategy? Why or why not?
2. Will Nokia's low-end cell phones make good loss leaders (a product sold at a low price to stimulate other sales)? Why or why not?

Sources: Company Web site, www.nokia.com, accessed May 11, 2010; Arik Hesseldahl, "Nokia's Kallasvuo: We Must 'Move Even Faster,'" *BusinessWeek,* April 22, 2010, http://www.businessweek.com; Mark Ritson, "Nokia Brand Needs Firm Direction," *Branding Strategy Insider,* April 5, 2010, http://www.brandingstrategyinsider.com; Abbas Jaffar Ali, "Nokia Announces the X6 and 'Comes with Music' Service for the Middle East," *T-Break Tech,* February 11, 2010, http://tech.tbreak.com; John Paczkowski, "Nokia Agitating for a Handset Price War?" *All Things Digital,* February 1, 2010, http://digitaldaily.allthingsd.com.

---

vehicles during the holiday shopping season. After the holidays, prices usual rebound. But experts warn that discounting must be done carefully, or profits can disappear. Businesses should offer discounts only for a specified period of time and with a clear understanding of what they are trying to accomplish with the strategy. They should advertise the discount, so customers know it is a special deal. When the time period has elapsed, so should the discount.

Seeing its market share erode, Nokia is trying various ways to lure consumers back, including lowering prices on some of its cell phones; this strategy is discussed in the "Hit & Miss" feature.

Competitive Pricing Although many organizations rely heavily on price as a competitive weapon, even more implement **competitive pricing** strategies. They try to reduce the emphasis on price competition by matching other firms' prices and concentrating their own marketing efforts on the product, distribution, and promotional elements of the marketing mix. In fact, in industries with relatively homogeneous products, competitors must match one another's price reductions to maintain market share and remain competitive. By pricing their products at the levels of competing offerings, marketers largely negate the price variable in their marketing strategies.

Consumer Perceptions of Prices

How do you perceive prices for certain products? Marketers must consider this. If large numbers of potential buyers consider a price too high or too low, businesses must correct the situation. Price–quality relationships and the use of odd pricing are important considerations in setting prices.

competitive pricing strategy that tries to reduce the emphasis on price competition by matching other firms' prices and concentrating their own marketing efforts on the product, distribution, and promotional elements of the marketing mix.

Assessment Check ✔

1. What is a cost-based pricing formula?
2. Why do companies implement competitive pricing strategies?

Price–Quality Relationships

Research shows that a consumer's perception of product quality is closely related to an item's price. Most marketers believe that this perceived price–quality relationship remains steady over a relatively wide range of prices, although extremely high or low prices have less credibility. The price–quality relationship can critically affect a firm's pricing strategy.

Many consumers associate prestige, quality, and high price together—believing that paying a high price for an item such as an Infiniti car or a Chanel bag not only conveys prestige but also ensures quality. Others believe that eating at an expensive restaurant automatically means the food will be better than food served at a modestly priced eating establishment. Conversely, consumers may view an extremely low price as an indication that corners have been cut and quality will suffer. Interestingly, a recent study noted that California wines made from organically grown grapes are less expensive than those made from nonorganic grapes. But this actually seemed to be a disadvantage: labeling a wine as "made from organically grown grapes" actually drove the price down, whereas the same wine without the certification notice sold for more. A number of factors may be responsible for this paradox. In the 1970s and 1980s, when organic wines were first produced, the reds in particular gained a bad reputation for quickly turning to vinegar because they were made without preservatives, and this association still lingers in some consumers' minds. Also, although "green" consumers are well aware of the benefits of organically grown fruits and vegetables, the benefits of organically grown wines are not so well known. Growers will need to communicate to consumers that in this case at least, price and quality don't necessarily go together.[47]

Odd Pricing

Have you ever wondered why retailers set prices like $1.99 instead of $2 or $9.95 instead of $10? Before the age of cash registers and sales taxes, retailers reportedly followed this practice of **odd pricing**—pricing method using uneven amounts, which appear less than they really are to consumers—to force clerks to make correct change as part of their cash control efforts. But now **odd pricing** is commonly used because many retailers believe that consumers favor uneven amounts or amounts that sound less than they really are. However, some retailers also use this method to identify items that have been marked down. The odd price lets people know the item is on sale.

What's Ahead

The chapters in Part 4 have explained the main principles underlying marketing management and described how each fits a firm's overall business strategy. The next few chapters will help you understand how companies manage the technology and information that are available to businesses to create value for their customers and enhance their competitiveness in the marketplace. You'll also learn how firms manage their financial resources.

Assessment Check ☑

1. How does the price–quality relationship affect a firm's pricing strategy?
2. Why is odd pricing used?

⌐1¬ Discuss how integrated marketing communications (IMC) relates to a firm's overall promotional strategy, and explain the concept of a promotional mix along with outlining the objectives of promotion.

In practicing IMC, a firm coordinates promotional activities to produce a unified, customer-focused message. IMC identifies consumer needs and shows how a company's products meet them. Marketers select the promotional media that best target and reach customers. Teamwork and careful promotional planning to coordinate IMC strategy components are important elements of these programs.

A company's promotional mix integrates two components: personal selling and nonpersonal selling, which includes advertising, sales promotion, and public relations. By selecting the appropriate combination of promotional mix elements, marketers attempt to achieve the firm's five major promotional objectives: provide information, differentiate a product, increase demand, stabilize sales, and accentuate the product's value.

Assessment Check Answers ✔

1.1 What is the objective of an integrated marketing communications program? An IMC strategy focuses on customer needs to create a unified promotional message about a firm's goods or services.

1.2 Why do firms pursue multiple promotional objectives at the same time? Firms pursue multiple promotional objectives because they may need to convey different messages to different audiences.

1.3 What are product placement and guerrilla marketing? Product placement involves paying a fee to have a product showcased in certain media. Guerrilla marketing is innovative, low-cost marketing efforts designed to get consumers' attention in unusual ways.

⌐2¬ Summarize the different types of advertising and advertising media.

Advertising, the most visible form of nonpersonal promotion, is designed to inform, persuade, or remind. Product advertising promotes a good or service, while institutional advertising promotes a concept, idea, organization, or philosophy. Television, newspapers, and magazines are the largest advertising media categories. Others include direct mail, radio, and outdoor advertising. Interactive advertising directly involves the consumer, who controls the flow of information.

Assessment Check Answers ✔

2.1 What are the two basic types of advertising? Into what three categories do they fall? The two basic types are product and institutional. They fall into the categories of informative, persuasive, and reminder-oriented advertising.

2.2 What is the leading advertising medium in the U.S. According to the most recent statistics listed in Figure 13.2, television is the leading advertising medium in the U.S.

2.3 In what two major ways do firms benefit from sponsorship? Firms benefit from sponsorship in two ways: gain exposure to the event's audience, and association with the activity's image.

⌐3¬ Outline the roles of sales promotion, personal selling, and public relations in promotional strategy.

Sales promotion accounts for greater expenditures than advertising. Consumer-oriented sales promotions such as coupons, games, rebates, samples, premiums, contests, sweepstakes, and promotional products offer an extra incentive to buy a product. Point-of-purchase advertising displays and trade shows are sales promotions directed to the trade markets. Personal selling involves face-to-face interactions between seller and buyer. The primary sales tasks are order processing, creative selling, and missionary selling. Public relations is nonpaid promotion that seeks to enhance a company's public image.

Assessment Check Answers ✔

3.1 Why do retailers and manufacturers use sales promotions? Retailers and manufacturers use sales promotions to offer consumers extra incentives to buy their products.

3.2 When does a firm use personal selling instead of nonpersonal selling? Personal selling is generally used when customers are few and geographically concentrated, the product is technically complex or requires special handling, the price is high, or the product moves through direct-distribution channels.

3.3 How does public relations serve a marketing purpose? Public relations can be an efficient, indirect communications channel for promoting products. It can publicize products and help create and maintain a positive image of the company.

⌐4¬ Describe pushing and pulling promotional strategies.

A pushing strategy relies on personal selling to market a product to wholesalers and retailers in a company's distribution channels. A pulling strategy promotes the product by generating consumer demand for it, through advertising and sales promotion.

Assessment Check Answers ✔

4.1 Give an example of a pushing strategy. An example of a pushing strategy is that used by drug manufacturers, who used to market solely to physicians and hospitals. Today, they also use a pulling strategy by marketing directly to patients through advertising, which encourages patients to ask their doctors about medications.

4.2 Give an example of a pulling strategy. Pulling strategies are used by retailers and by manufacturers of consumer goods like cosmetics, automobiles, and clothing.

⌐5¬ Outline the different types of pricing objectives.

Pricing objectives can be classified as profitability, volume, meeting competition, and prestige. Profitability objectives are the most common. Volume objectives base pricing decisions on market share. Meeting competitors' prices makes price a nonissue in competition. Prestige pricing establishes a high price to develop and maintain an image of quality or exclusiveness.

Assessment Check Answers ✔

5.1 Define *price.* Price is the exchange value of a good or service.

5.2 What is a second approach to pricing strategy? A second approach to pricing strategy is **volume objectives**, which bases pricing decisions on market share.

⌐6⌐ Discuss how firms set prices in the marketplace, and describe the four alternative pricing strategies.

Although economic theory determines prices by the law of demand and supply, most firms use cost-based pricing, which adds a markup after costs. They usually conduct a breakeven analysis to determine the minimum sales volume a product must generate at a certain price to cover costs. The four alternative pricing strategies are skimming, penetration, everyday low pricing and discounting, and competitive pricing. A skimming strategy sets a high price initially to recover costs and then lowers it; a penetration strategy sets a lower price and then raises it later. Everyday low pricing and discounting offers a lower price for a period of time. Competitive pricing matches other firms' prices and emphasizes nonprice benefits of a product.

Assessment Check Answers ✔

6.1 What is a cost-based pricing formula? A cost-based pricing formula calculates the total costs per unit and then adds markups to cover overhead costs and generate profits.

6.2 Why do companies implement competitive pricing strategies? Companies use competitive pricing strategies to reduce the emphasis on price competition by matching other firms' prices and concentrating their own marketing efforts on the product, distribution, and promotional elements of the marketing mix.

⌐7⌐ Discuss consumer perceptions of price.

Marketers must consider how consumers perceive the price–quality relationship of their products. Consumers may be willing to pay a higher price if they perceive a product to be of superior quality. Marketers often use odd pricing to convey a message to consumers.

Assessment Check Answers ✔

7.1 How does the price–quality relationship affect a firm's pricing strategy? Consumers must believe that the price of an item reflects its quality, except in extreme cases. So a firm must try to set its prices accordingly.

7.2 Why is odd pricing used? Retailers believe that consumers favor uneven amounts or amounts that sound like less than they really are. Odd pricing may also be used to indicate a sale item.

▮ Business Terms You Need to Know

promotion 428	institutional advertising 434	missionary selling 446	cost-based
integrated marketing	cause advertising 434	telemarketing 446	pricing 452
communications (IMC) 429	sponsorship 440	public relations 448	breakeven analysis 452
promotional mix 430	infomercial 440	publicity 448	skimming
personal selling 430	sales promotion 441	pushing strategy 449	pricing 454
nonpersonal selling 430	specialty advertising 443	cooperative advertising 449	penetration pricing 454
positioning 431	trade promotion 443	pulling strategy 449	everyday low
product placement 432	point-of-purchase (POP)	price 449	pricing (EDLP) 454
guerrilla marketing 433	advertising 443	profitability objectives 450	competitive
advertising 434	order processing 445	volume objectives 450	pricing 455
product advertising 434	creative selling 445	prestige pricing 451	odd pricing 456

▮ Review Questions

1. What is the purpose of integrated marketing communications?
2. What are the five major objectives of a promotional strategy?
3. Identify and define each of the three categories of advertising based on their purpose. Which type of advertising might marketers use for the following products?
   a. deodorant   b. electronic reader
   c. organic produce   d. healthcare insurance
4. What are the benefits of online and interactive advertising? What might be some drawbacks?
5. For each of the following, describe potential benefits and drawbacks of a sponsorship relationship:
   a. LG and the Snowboard FIS World Cup
   b. ING Bank and the New York City Marathon

   c. Wrangler and the Wrangler Football Golf Classic (a golf tournament that raises money for high school football programs)
6. If you were a marketer for Rolex, what kind of sales promotion might you use for high-end watches?
7. Under what circumstances are firms likely to emphasize personal selling?
8. Describe the seven-step sales process.
9. Define the four basic categories of pricing objectives.
10. What are the four alternative pricing strategies used by marketers? Give an example of the circumstances under which each might be selected.

Projects and Teamwork Applications

1. Choose a product that you purchased recently. Identify the various media that were used to promote the product and analyze the promotional mix. Do you agree with the company's marketing strategy, or would you recommend changes to the mix? Why? Create your own print ad for the product you chose, using any business strategies or knowledge you have learned in this course so far.

2. Evaluate the price of the product you selected in the preceding exercise. What appears to be the pricing strategy used by its manufacturer? Do you think the price is fair? Why or why not? Choose a different strategy and develop a new price for the product based on the strategy. Poll your classmates to learn whether they would purchase the product at the new price—and why.

3. Some schools have received financial benefits by allowing companies to promote their goods and services to students.

Others have decided against the practice, and some states have laws banning this type of promotion. Find some examples of corporate sponsors in public elementary and high schools and on college campuses. With your class, discuss the pros and cons of promotion in public schools and on college campuses. In your view, is there a distinction between a public school and a college campus? Why or why not?

4. On your own or with a classmate, research a recent situation that has caused a business, a not-for-profit organization, or a government agency to suffer from bad publicity. Evaluate the situation and create a program outlining steps the organization might take to build better public relations.

5. You are the marketing manager that is introducing a new line of video games. What approach would you take for establishing prices?

Web Assignments

1. **Top advertisers.** *Advertising Age* compiles data annually on the top national advertisers. Visit the Web site listed here and access the most recent year. Answer the following questions:

   a. Who were the top ten advertisers in that year?

   b. How much did they spend on advertising?

   c. What was the most advertised brand that year?

   http://adage.com/datacenter/article?article_id=106348

2. **Online coupon fraud.** Go to the Web sites listed to learn about online coupon fraud. Prepare a brief report. Make sure to answer the following: How big a problem is online coupon fraud? What are some changes marketers have made in an attempt to reduce online coupon fraud?

   http://www.newser.com/story/35962/hackers-spread-coupon-scam.html

   http://online.wsj.com/article/SB124641121217977575.html

   http://multichannelmerchant.com/retail/news/0308-curtailing-online-coupon-fraud/

3. **Yield management.** Assume you're interested in flying between Seattle and Houston. Visit some travel sites. Search for fares, varying such factors as advance purchase, day, time of departure, and so forth. What did this exercise teach you about yield management?

   http://www.expedia.com

   http://www.kayak.com

   http://www.travelocity.com

   Note: Internet Web addresses change frequently. If you don't find the exact sites listed, you may need to access the organization's home page and search from there or use a search engine such as Bing or Google.

Dollar Stores Muscle In on the Big Discounters

CASE 13.1

Dollar stores, low-priced convenience retailers with limited assortments of basic goods, are spreading. Chains like Dollar General, Family Dollar, and 99¢ Only are among the fastest growing channels for food, drugs, and mass retailing in the United States. "Dollar stores combine pricing power, efficient operations, and small stores to make the model work," says one industry observer. But the chains will need to maintain their supplier relationships, manage their inventory, and keep operating expenses down by, for example, extending employees' hours instead of going to the expense of recruiting, hiring, and training extra workers during busy times.

Despite these challenges, dollar store chains are adding to their product offerings, increasing the number of food and household items they stock. Some might add national brands, if they can purchase them cheaply enough. That means suppliers that price and package their products for the dollar stores' needs will be able to take advantage of this new opportunity. At most dollar stores, prices are very low, but seldom just a dollar.

With consumer spending trending downward, dollar stores are likely to find plenty of room for expansion. "These low-priced, limited-assortment retailers are very entrenched among low-income households," said a senior vice president at ACNielsen.

In fact, although they can't compete on volume with chains like Kohl's, Target, and Wal-Mart—sales of the top three dollar chains combined are only about 6 percent of Wal-Mart's—they do seem able to attract customers away from the big chains, particularly shoppers who can't afford Wal-Mart. Dollar stores are also quick and easy to open. Unlike some of Wal-Mart's huge superstores, "You'll never hear them going up against the planning commission," said one retail consultant. They can close down just as quickly to cut their losses if a location isn't profitable.

Another advantage is their small size, which allows customers to get in and out quickly. To capitalize on this advantage, Dollar General and Family Dollar plan to carry less clothing and more food, health and beauty products, and household goods like laundry detergent that require more trips to the store.

Questions for Critical Thinking

1. If dollar stores carry low-end merchandise, are they really competing with stores like Wal-Mart and Target on price? Why or why not?

2. What are some of the ways dollar stores are able to keep their prices so low?

Sources: "Dollar Stores Outlook," About.com: Retail Industry, http://retailindustry.about.com, accessed March 26, 2009; Kelly Johnson, "Economic Woes Tighten Holiday Spending at Dollar Stores," *Sacramento Business Journal*, November 23, 2007, www.google.com; Steve Painter, "Bucking the Big Boys," *Arkansas Democrat-Gazette*, April 22, 2007, pp. 8–9.

CASE 13.2 — Marketing to the Teenage Crowd

Today's teenagers were born shortly before the turn of the 21st century. They represent billions of dollars in buying power, but the big question for marketers is how to reach them.

Unlike their parents, today's teens have grown up in this electronic age and take it for granted. Like those of earlier generations, today's teens like to communicate with each other. Unlike their predecessors, they now can do so almost constantly. One study estimates that teenagers spend more than seven hours a day using media of various kinds, mostly electronic. How do they log this astonishing amount of time? By sacrificing sleep and multitasking. Some older teens can perform seven activities at once. Parents often find their teens listening to music, watching TV program, doing homework, playing a videogame, and text messaging.

What media do teenagers neglect or ignore? They hardly ever read newspapers. Jeffrey Cole, the director of the Center for the Digital Future at the University of Southern California, predicts that printed newspapers will eventually become extinct as social media steadily increase in power. Teens want news, he explains, but only about the narrowly focused community of their peers.

Teenagers don't contact their peers through e-mail. One survey indicates that although 73 percent of teens visit social-networking sites, only about 8 percent use Twitter. They do like smart phones, especially those with apps for constant status updates, but don't make many phone calls. Instead, they text message sometimes sending up to ten messages an hour.

Marketers will need to learn how to reach teenagers by recognizing that teens like to be invited to get involved, rather than being told. This means asking for their input, listening to them with genuine respect, adopting their suggestions, and continuing to ask for feedback. Morgan Stewart of ExactTarget conducted a survey asking teens which brand they thought did the best job of communicating with them. To his surprise, Amazon got more write-in votes than any other brand, including Facebook. He says of Amazon, "Teens can read reviews, they can submit their own, and they can get recommendations based on what they like." Stewart believes that "managing your Amazon presence is more important than building out a Facebook strategy."

Of course, even Amazon is only one component of an integrated marketing plan. Teenagers are highly suspicious of anything that seems even remotely like advertising. When shopping, they depend heavily on the opinions of their peers. They also enjoy fun sites such as Sporcle.com, FunnyOrDie.com, and FailBlog.org. YouTube is another important tool for viral marketing, as well as being free.

Jeffrey Cole thinks that as today's teens move into adulthood, the allure of knowing everything about their friends will fade. What will endure will be something that every generation wants: they will still want to have "total control over their media" as a way of having "real control over their lives."

Questions for Critical Thinking

1. Do you think marketers can reach teens with specially tailored promotional campaigns for such goods and services as video games, smartphone apps, concert tickets, and so on? Why or why not?

2. How can marketers best target teens so as to appeal to them but without making them feel

talked down to? Suggest a marketing or promotional theme for one product that you think would appeal to a teen.

Sources: Steve Bauer, "Reaching the Elusive Teenager," *Word of Mouth,* April 13, 2010, http://wom.fleishmanhilliard.com; Carol Phillips, "Where Teens Hang Out Digitally," *Millennial Marketing,* March 12, 2010, http://millennialmarketing.com; Tim Loc, "Teens Love Social Media, Detest Newspapers," *iMedia Connection,* March 3, 2010, http://www.imediaconnection.com; Steve McClellan, "Teens Into Social Media, Not Newspapers," *Mediaweek,* March 2, 2010, http://www.mediaweek.com; Tamar Lewin, "If Your Kids Are Awake, They're Probably Online," *The New York Times,* January 20, 2010, http://www.nytimes.com; "Teen Marketing: A Look Ahead," (Pangea Media,) January 1, 2010, http://www.pangeamedia.com.

Pet Airways Handles Pets With Loving Care

CASE 13.3

Pet owners want the best for their dogs and cats, as evidenced by the $50 billion pet industry in the U.S., including everything from grooming services to squeaky toys. One area that has received little attention is travel. Although owners can find lodging that allows pets, and they can purchase travel carriers and gear, until recently there was little choice when it came to transport. If the animal had to travel long distance, it was relegated to the cargo hold of a plane. A couple of years ago, that changed when Dan Wiesel and Alysa Binder wanted to be able to transport their Jack Russell terrier safely and comfortably. So they started a pet transport business called Pet Airways.

"There are 80 million pets traveling around the U.S.," says Alysa Binder. "There's definitely a market for this. We're part of the pet community—we understand." Wiesel and Binder contracted with a firm that flies Beechcraft 1900 aircraft, selecting this plane for its versatility and safety record. They had the planes retrofitted to accommodate pet carriers in the main cabin. They launched their reservation system online and spread the word via social media. When traditional media heard of the new company, Wiesel and Binder appeared on such television shows as *Good Morning America* and *The Today Show,* as well as in magazines and newspapers. Because of this publicity, Pet Airways has spent nothing on advertising. Its greatest marketing challenge has been educating the public about their service. "Because we're the first to market, we have to tell people what we're all about," explains Binder.

Pet owners who want to book their animals on a Pet Airways flight make a reservation on the airline's Web site, http://www.petairways.com. One hour before departure, owners check in at the Pet Lounge. Pet passengers are boarded in their carriers, attended to by professional pet Attendants who accompany the animals on the flight, checking on them every 15 minutes to make sure they are secure and comfortable. Once the plane has landed, owners (or designated recipients) collect their pets in the Pet Lounge.

Pet Airways currently operates flights to nine cities around the U.S. Alysa Binder says the firm's goal is to reach 20 cities in the next 18 months. She notes that customers are willing and eager to pay for the service, considering it reasonable compared to traditional airlines.

Pet Airways fares start at $149. By comparison, American Airlines charges $100 for a pet to travel beneath a seat and $150 as baggage; Delta charges $150 and $275 respectively; and Northwest charges $150 and $225 respectively. Binder remarks that her customers don't usually consider price anyway because "we aren't the same as general carriers. It's a completely different service. People know that."

Pet Airways customers can register to receive the company's newsletter, which includes insider news on special flight deals and other promotions. They can join the MyPAWS Club, which offers a 40 percent discount on pet supplies at the Pet Airways online store, a 10 percent discount at pet-friendly hotels, 10 percent off at 1-800-PetMeds, 5 percent off on pet health insurance from Pets Best Insurance, and discounts and free samples from other Pet Airways partners.

Wiesel and Binder saw an opportunity in the marketplace and jumped at the chance to offer a safe, reliable solution for pet owners to transport their pets. "On Pet Airways, your pets aren't packages, they're passengers."

Questions for Critical Thinking

1. At this stage of Pet Airway's life cycle, what should be the company's primary promotional objectives? Why?

2. Pet Airways has not yet engaged in major advertising efforts. Which media would probably be most effective at reaching the firm's intended market? Why?

3. Pet Airways already offers some consumer-oriented promotions. Describe or outline an idea for a new promotion and explain your choice.

4. Outline Pet Airways' pricing objectives. How might these change over the next five years? Ten years? What do you think the best pricing strategy for Pet Airways should be? Why?

Sources: Pet Airways Web site, http://www.petairways.com, accessed August 25, 2010; "Pet Airways Combines with a Public Company Through Share Exchange with American Antiquities," *PR Newswire,* August 16, 2010, http://wwwprnewswire.com; "Doctors Call for Airline Pet Ban," *The Independent,* February 21, 2010, http://license.icopyright.net;" "Bone Voyage as Pets Get Airline," *BBC News,* April 17, 2009, http://news.bbc.co.uk.

PART 4

GREENSBURG, KS

Think Green, Go Green, Save Green

Not long ago, the phrase "hybrid SUV" would have seemed an oxymoron. But in just a few short years, fuel-efficient hybrids of all shapes and sizes have appeared in showrooms. This new generation of vehicles combines fuel-efficient gas engines, natural gas engines, and hydrogen fuel cells. As gas prices soar and concern over the environment grows, consumers will become more and more interested in them.

Enter Lee Lindquist, Alternative Fuels Specialist at Scholfield Honda in Wichita, Kansas. A passionate environmentalist, Lee was researching alternative-fuel vehicles when he learned that Honda had been selling a natural gas Civic GX in New York and California since 1998. Originally marketed to municipalities and corporations as a way of addressing air quality issues, the Civic GX seemed the perfect way for cost-conscious Kansans to combat rising fuel prices. It was also a way to promote local resources, since Kansas is a major producer of natural gas.

Lee took the idea of the Civic GX to his boss, owner Roger Scholfield, who was skeptical of it at first. Scholfield had long promoted the Honda as a fuel-efficient vehicle and didn't want to muddy the waters with this new vehicle. But eventually he warmed to the idea and began offering the car to his corporate customers.

When the tornado hit Greensburg, the idea of going green took on a whole new life at Scholfield Honda. One of the problems with offering the Civic GX had been the lack of natural gas fueling stations, as well as the high cost of

constructing one. Well aware of the media attention surrounding Greensburg, Scholfield decided to donate a natural gas Civic to the town, along with a fueling station.

Scholfield was up-front about the decision to donate the car. The investment was a costly one, and there were many less expensive ways of reaching his customers in Wichita. Scholfield admits he questioned his decision even as he drove into Greensburg for the presentation. But the bottom line was that it was the right thing to do. Today, when customers come into Scholfield's dealership, they are more interested in alternative-fuel and high-efficiency vehicles.

If you want to buy a Civic GX from Scholfield Honda today, get in line, because the staff can't keep them in stock. While you wait, enjoy a nice cup of coffee served in a compostable, corn-based disposable cup. Toss those old soda cans rattling around in your back seat into Scholfield's recycling bins. And on your way out, don't forget to take your complimentary Scholfield Honda reusable green shopping bag and water bottle.

Questions

After viewing the video, answer the following questions:

1. Do you think Scholfield's green marketing campaign will change consumers' opinions of hybrid and alternative-fuel cars?

2. Do you think Scholfield's donation of a natural gas Civic to the town of Greensburg will drive business to his dealership in Wichita? Why or why not?

LAUNCHING YOUR
[Marketing Career]

In Part 4, "Marketing Management," you learned about the goals and functions of marketing. The three chapters in this part emphasized the central role of customer satisfaction in defining value and developing a marketing strategy in traditional and nontraditional marketing settings. You learned about the part played by marketing research and the need for relationship marketing in today's competitive environment. You discovered how new products are developed and how they evolve through the four stages of the product life cycle, from introduction through growth and maturity to decline. You also learned about the role of different channels in creating effective distribution strategies. Finally, you saw the impact of integrated marketing communications on the firm's promotional strategy, the role of advertising, and the way pricing influences consumer behavior. Perhaps you came across some marketing tasks and functions that sounded especially appealing to you. Here are a few ideas about careers in marketing that you may want to pursue.

The first thing to remember is that, as the chapters in this part made clear, marketing is about a great deal more than personal selling and advertising. For instance, are you curious about why people behave the way they do? Are you good at spotting trends? *Marketing research analysts* seek answers to a wide range of questions about business competition, customer preferences, market trends, and past and future sales. They often design and conduct their own consumer surveys, using the telephone, mail, the Internet, or personal interviews and focus groups. After they analyze the data they've collected, their recommendations form input for managerial decisions about whether to introduce new products, revamp current ones, enter new markets, or abandon products or markets where profitability is low. As members of a new-product development team, marketing researchers often work directly with members of other business departments such as scientists, production and manufacturing personnel, and finance employees. Also, marketing researchers are increasingly asked to help clients implement their recommendations. With today's highly competitive economy, jobs in this area are expected to grow. Annual earnings for marketing research analysts average about $61,000.[1]

Another career path in marketing is sales. Do you work well with others and read their feelings accurately? Are you a self-starter? Being a *sales representative* might be for you. Selling jobs exist in every industry, and because many use a combination of salary and performance-based commissions, they can pay handsomely. Sales jobs are often a first step on the ladder to upper-management positions as well. Sales representatives work for wholesalers and manufacturing companies (and even for publishers such as the one that produces this book). They sell automobiles, computer systems and technology, pharmaceuticals, advertising, insurance, real estate, commodities and financial services, and all kinds of consumer goods and services.

If you're interested in mass communications, note that print and online magazines, newspapers, and broadcast companies such as ESPN and MTV generate most of their revenue from advertising, so sales representatives who sell space and time slots in the media contribute a great deal to the success of these firms.[2] And if you like to travel, consider that many sales jobs involve travel.

Advertising, marketing management, and *public relations* are other categories of marketing. In large companies, marketing managers, product managers, promotion managers, and public relations managers often work long hours under pressure; they may travel frequently or transfer between jobs at headquarters and positions in regional offices. Their responsibilities include directing promotional programs, overseeing advertising campaigns and budgets, and conducting communications such as press releases with the firm's publics. Thousands of new positions are expected to open up in the next several years; the field is expected to grow 14 percent over the next decade. Growth of the Internet and new media has especially increased demand for advertising and public relations specialists.[3]

Advertising and public relations firms employed about 458,000 people in a recent year.[4] About one in five U.S. advertising firms are located in New York or California, and more than a quarter of advertising industry workers live in those two states. Most advertising firms develop specialties; many of the largest are international in scope and earn a major proportion of their revenue abroad. Online advertising is just one area in which new jobs will be opening in the future, as more and more client firms expand their online sales operations.

Career Assessment Exercises in Marketing

1. Select a field that interests you. Use the Internet to research types of sales positions available in that field. Locate a few entry-level job openings and see what career steps that position can lead to. (You might wish to start with a popular job-posting site such as Monster.com.) Note the job requirements, the starting salary, and the form of compensation—straight salary? salary plus commission?—and write a one-page summary of your findings.

2. Use the Internet to identify and investigate two or three of the leading advertising agencies in the United States, such as Young & Rubicam or J. Walter Thompson. What are some of their recent ad campaigns, or who are their best-known clients? Where do the agencies have offices? What job openings do they currently list, and what qualifications should applicants for these positions have? Write a brief report comparing the agencies you selected, decide which one you would prefer to work for, and give your reasons.

3. Test your research skills. Choose an ordinary product, such as toothpaste or soft drinks, and conduct a survey to find out why people chose the brand they most recently purchased. For instance, suppose you wanted to find out how people choose their shampoo. List as many decision criteria as you can think of, such as availability, scent, price, packaging, benefits from use (conditioning, dandruff-reducing, and so on), brand name, and ad campaign. Ask eight to ten friends to rank these decision factors, and note some simple demographics about your research subjects such as their age, gender, and occupation. Tabulate your results. What did you find out about how your subjects made their purchase decision? Did any of your findings surprise you? Can you think of any ways in which you might have improved your survey?

PART 5

Using Technology, Information, and Accounting Tools

[Chapter 14]

Managing
Information
Technology

©Masterfile

Chapter 14

Learning Objectives

1 Distinguish between data and information, and explain the role of information systems in business.

2 List the components and different types of information systems.

3 Outline how computer hardware and software are used to manage information.

4 Describe networking and telecommunications technology and the types of computer networks.

5 Discuss the security and ethical issues involving computer information systems.

6 Explain the steps that companies go through in anticipating, planning for, and recovering from information systems disasters.

7 Review current trends in information systems.

Managing Information Technology

BlackBerry Storm Takes on the iPhone

Many technology experts predict that cell phones will soon rival PCs in computing capabilities. They already surpass them in compactness and convenience. Canada-based Research In Motion (RIM), the firm that brought us the BlackBerry, has been working feverishly to bring one more option to mobile computing—an innovative new smart phone to rival Apple's iPhone. After two years of development and a $100 million marketing campaign, RIM finally released the Storm, which immediately lived up to its name by generating a whirlwind of marketing buzz. The phone, which sold 500,000 units in its first month and soon reached 1 million units, was developed in conjunction with Verizon Wireless, one of the largest U.S. telecommunications providers and the sole U.S. carrier for the Storm. The first touch-screen BlackBerry, the Storm lacks a physical keyboard and comes packed with multiple communications features designed to help executives stay in touch with the office, suppliers, and customers. It also contains 128 megabytes of memory, so no matter how the user wants to communicate—via voice, text, or images—he or she has plenty of room to store applications, pictures, sound files, documents, and data. The SurePress "clickable" touch screen, which has earned a technology award, offers the physical sensation of a real keyboard, the first innovation in touch-screen technology in some time. Despite some early complaints from technophiles about software glitches, which RIM calls the "new reality" of releasing complex cell phones and which it rushed to correct, the Storm is winning praise for its user-friendly features. They include a high-resolution touch screen with navigation control keys, a programmable shortcut key, adjustable font type and size, powerful search capabilities, and the screen's ability to automatically rotate from portrait to landscape when the handset is turned sideways. The phone provides e-mail and Internet browsing, along with a satellite mapping system and a 3.2-megapixel digital camera with flash and video. The device also has a media player that can handle both music and video.

The Storm weighs less than 6 ounces and boasts simple finger controls to zoom, cut and paste, or scroll through e-mails and text. Users can instantly edit Word documents, Excel spreadsheets, and PowerPoint slides. A software upgrade is available to allow the creation of new documents. Preloaded instant message programs include those of Yahoo!, Windows Live, AOL, and ICQ. Networking applications include Facebook, MySpace, and Flickr; other options are available for downloading.

In fact, RIM is benchmarking not just Apple's iPhones but also its ground-breaking service for downloadable applications. Users of the BlackBerry Storm—and of other RIM devices including the Pearl, Curve, and Bold—now can enjoy the new applications center called BlackBerry App World, the equivalent of Apple's hugely popular App Store. RIM is offering games, networking and messaging applications, and a wide assortment of other software to improve personal productivity, check news headlines, schedule events, track stock tickers, and manage other communications tasks. Some applications are free; others are priced competitively but at rates starting a little higher than for the iPhone. That price differential signals RIM's intention to target the BlackBerry line to business users, who, at least in theory, are less interested in the simpler applications that many consumer cell phone users crave.

The Storm does offer a specific benefit in addition to all its communications options. Purchased applications from App World can be uploaded up to three separate times for one fee, a boon for users who upgrade their handsets regularly, as executives on the go tend to do. And for those whose business travels take them abroad, the Storm offers another breakthrough. The phone works with high-speed data services on both Verizon's and Vodafone's networks, giving it true built-in global capacity. Says one technology analyst, "For a lot of users, Verizon is the network of choice and a BlackBerry is the device of choice."

Building on its initial success with the Storm, RIM is manufacturing a million units a month in response to market demand. Selling for the same price as the iPhone after a mail-in rebate, the Storm is aiming to match or surpass the iPhone's 25 percent share of the still-expanding smart phone market in North America. RIM considers the Storm "an overwhelming success," and for those who still quibble over potential flaws, one financial consultant who is pleased with his new Storm has an answer: "No single device is going to be the end-all be-all for everyone."[1]

This chapter explores how businesses manage information as a resource, particularly how they use technology to do so. Today, virtually all business functions—from human resources to production to supply chain management—rely on information systems. The chapter begins by differentiating between information and data and then defines an information system. The components of information systems are presented, and two major types of information systems are described. Because of their importance to organizations, the chapter discusses databases, the heart of all information systems. Then the chapter looks at the computer hardware and software that drive information systems. Today, specialized networks make information access and transmission function smoothly, so the chapter examines different types of telecommunications and computer networks to see how businesses are applying them for competitive advantage. The chapter then turns to a discussion of the ethical and security issues affecting information systems, followed by a description of how organizations plan for, and recover from, information system disasters. A review of the current trends in information systems concludes the chapter.

Data, Information, and Information Systems

Every day, businesspeople ask themselves questions such as the following:

- How well is our product selling in Atlanta compared with Tampa? Have sales among consumers aged 25 to 45 increased or decreased within the past year?

- How will rising energy prices affect production and distribution costs?

- If employees can access the benefits system through our network, will this increase or decrease benefit costs?

- Can we communicate more efficiently and effectively with our increasingly dispersed workforce?

data raw facts and figures that may or may not be relevant to a business decision.

information knowledge gained from processing data.

An effective information system can help answer these and many other questions. **Data** consist of raw facts and figures that may or may not be relevant to a business decision. **Information** is knowledge gained from processing those facts and figures. So although businesspeople need to gather data about the demographics of a target market or the specifications of a certain product, the data are useless unless they are transformed into relevant information that can be used to make a competitive decision. For instance, data might be the sizes of various demographic groups. Information drawn from those data could be how many of those individuals are potential customers for a firm's products. Technology has advanced so quickly that all businesses, regardless of size or location, now have access to data and information that can make them competitive in a global arena.

An **information system** is an organized method for collecting, storing, and communicating past, present, and projected information on internal operations and external intelligence. Most information systems today use computer and telecommunications technology. A large organization typically assigns responsibility for directing its information systems and related operations to an executive called the **chief information officer (CIO)**. Often, the CIO reports directly to the firm's chief executive officer (CEO). An effective CIO can understand and harness technology so that the company can communicate internally and externally in one seamless operation. But small companies rely just as much on information systems as do large ones, even if they do not employ a manager assigned to this area on a full-time basis.

The role of the CIO is both expanding and changing as the technology to manage information continues to develop. Over the past ten years, the role of a CIO has changed from being a technical one to that of a business partner who often exerts strong influence over his or her company's strategy. CIOs will need to adapt their roles even further in the future. Moreover, CIOs and former CIOs are beginning to appear on company boards more often.[2]

Information systems can be tailored to assist many business functions and departments—from marketing and manufacturing to finance and accounting. They can manage the overwhelming flood of information by organizing data in a logical and accessible manner. Through the system, a company can monitor all components of its operations and business strategy, identifying problems and opportunities. Information systems gather data from inside and outside the organization; they then process the data to produce information that is relevant to all aspects of the organization. Processing steps could involve storing data for later use, classifying and analyzing it, and retrieving it easily when needed.

Many companies—and nations—combine high-tech and low-tech solutions to manage the flow of information. E-mail, wireless communications, and videoconferencing haven't totally replaced paper memos, phone conversations, and face-to-face meetings, but they are increasingly common. Information can make the difference between staying in business and going bankrupt. Keeping on top of changing consumer demands, competitors' actions, and the latest government regulations will help a firm fine-tune existing products, develop new winners, and maintain effective marketing.

Components and Types of Information Systems

The definition of *information system* in the previous section does not specifically mention the use of computers or technology. In fact, information systems have been around since the beginning of civilization and were, by today's standards, very low tech. Think about your college or university's library. At one time the library probably had card catalog files to help you find information. Those files were information systems because they stored data about books and periodicals in an organized manner on 3-by-5-inch index cards. Users could flip through the cards and locate library materials by author, title, or subject, although the process could be tedious and time consuming.

Today, however, when businesspeople think about information systems, they are most likely thinking about **computer-based information systems**. These systems rely on computer and related technologies to store information electronically in an organized, accessible manner. So, instead of card catalogs, your college library probably uses a computerized information system that allows users to search through library holdings much faster and easier.

information system
organized method for collecting, storing, and communicating past, present, and projected information on internal operations and external intelligence.

chief information officer (CIO) executive responsible for managing a firm's information system and related computer technologies.

Assessment Check ✓

1. Distinguish between data and information.
2. What is an information system?

computer-based information systems
information systems that rely on computer and related technologies to store information electronically in an organized, accessible manner.

Computer-based information systems consist of four components and technologies:

- computer hardware
- computer software
- telecommunications and computer networks
- data resource management.

Computer hardware consists of machines that range from supercomputers to smart phones. It also includes the input, output, and storage devices needed to support computing machines. Software includes operating systems, such as Microsoft's Windows 7 or Linux, and applications programs, such as Adobe Acrobat or Oracle's PeopleSoft Enterprise applications. Telecommunications and computer networks encompass the hardware and software needed to provide wired or wireless voice and data communications. This includes support for external networks such as the Internet and private internal networks. Data resource management involves developing and maintaining an organization's databases so that decision makers are able to access the information they need in a timely manner.

In the case of your college or university library, the computer-based information system is generally made up of computer hardware, such as monitors and keyboards, which are linked to the library's network and a database containing information on the library's holdings. Specialized software allows users to access the database. In addition, the library's network is likely also connected to a larger private network and the Internet. This connection gives users remote access to the library's database, as well as access to other computerized databases such as LexisNexis.

Databases

database centralized integrated collection of data resources.

The heart of any information system is its **database**, a centralized integrated collection of data resources. A company designs its databases to meet particular information processing and retrieval needs of its workforce. Businesses obtain databases in many ways. They can hire a staff person to build them on site, hire an outside source to do so, or buy packaged database programs from specialized vendors, such as Oracle. A database serves as an electronic filing cabinet, capable of storing massive amounts of data and retrieving it within seconds. A database should be continually updated; otherwise, a firm may find itself with data that are outdated and possibly useless. One problem with databases is that they can contribute to information overload—too much data for people to absorb or data that are not relevant to decision making. Because computer processing speed and storage capacity are both increasing rapidly, and because data have become more abundant, businesspeople need to be careful that their databases contain only the facts they need. If they don't, they can waste time wading through unnecessary data. Another challenge with databases is keeping them safe, as the "Hit & Miss" feature describes.

Masterfile

In the case of the *computer-based information system* in the library, it is generally made up of computer hardware linked to the library's network and a database containing information on the books in the library. Specialized software allows users to access the database.

Wyndham Hotels and Resorts Database Breached

In the third such incident in a year, Wyndham Hotels and Resorts—which owns Days Inn, Ramada, Super 8, and other hotel chains and restaurants—discovered that one of its secure databases had been compromised. From a single breach, a hacker gained access to customer information from several of the company's restaurants and other properties, then downloaded it to an off-site URL. The information included names and credit card numbers of guests, the cards' expiration dates, and other data from the magnetic strip on each card. Wyndham does not record customers' birth dates, Social Security numbers, addresses, or other identifying information, and those data were not included. The breach was discovered when a credit card processor and an issuer informed Wyndham that they had become concerned about "unusual fraud patterns" on the cards.

Wyndham took immediate steps to stop the break-in. In an open letter on its Web site, the company stated, "We deeply regret that this incident occurred," and detailed its investigation. The chain notified the U.S. Secret Service, which investigates counterfeiting, as well as the attorneys general of several states. It hired an outside investigator to appraise the damage and advise on improving security. It also hired a firm that specializes in credit card industry standards to look into each compromised property in order to improve compliance. In addition, Wyndham notified American Express, Visa, MasterCard, and Discover of card numbers that may have been involved.

Wyndham assured guests that identity theft was unlikely, but warned them to monitor their credit card statements and reports vigilantly and to report any suspicious activity to the cards' issuers. It offered affected guests free credit monitoring and set up a special toll-free line that all guests could call for more information.

Questions for Critical Thinking

1. What steps do you think Wyndham should take to prevent a future security breach?
2. What can Wyndham do to assure its guests that it will protect them from credit card fraud?

Sources: Company Web site, http://www.wyndhamworldwide.com/customer_care, accessed May 24, 2010; Angela Moscaritolo, "Wyndham Hotels Suffers Another Data Breach," *SC Magazine,* March 9, 2010, http://www.scmagazineus.com; Larry Barrett, "Wyndham Hotels' Networks Hacked—Again," *eSecurity Planet,* March 9, 2010; http://www.esecurityplanet.com; Robert McMillan, "Wyndham Hotels Hacked Again," *IDG News Service,* February 26, 2010, http://www.cio.com.

Decision makers can also look up online data. Online systems give access to enormous amounts of government data, such as economic data from the Bureau of Labor Statistics and the Department of Commerce. One of the largest online databases is that of the U.S. Census Bureau. The census of population, conducted every ten years, attempts to collect data on more than 120 million households across the United States. After attempting to count everyone in the country, the Census Bureau has selected participants fill out forms containing questions about marital status, place of birth, ethnic background, citizenship, workplaces, commuting time, income, occupation, type of housing, number of telephones and vehicles, even grandparents as caregivers. Households receiving the most recent questionnaire can respond in English as well as a variety of other languages including Spanish, Chinese, Vietnamese, and Korean. Not surprisingly, sifting through all the collected data takes time. Although certain restrictions limit how businesspeople can access and use specific census data, the general public may access the data via the American FactFinder on the Census Bureau's Web site (http://factfinder.census.gov), as well as at state data centers and public libraries.

Another source of free information is company Web sites. Interested parties can visit firms' home pages to look for information about customers, suppliers, and competitors. Trade associations and academic institutions also maintain Web sites with information on topics of interest.

Types of Information Systems

Many different types of information systems exist. In general, however, information systems fall into two broad categories: operational support systems or management support systems.

Operational Support Systems

Operational support systems are designed to produce a variety of information on an organization's activities for both internal and external users. Examples of operational support systems include transaction processing systems and process control systems. **Transaction processing systems** record and process data from business transactions. For example, major retailers use point-of-sale systems, which link electronic cash registers to the retailer's computer centers. Sales data are transmitted from cash registers to the computer center either immediately or at regular intervals. **Process control systems** monitor and control physical processes. A steel mill, for instance, may have electronic sensors linked to a computer system monitoring the entire production process. The system makes necessary changes and alerts operators to potential problems.

Commercial airplane manufacturer Airbus relies on a sophisticated information system based on RFID (radio-frequency identification) technology to track parts and tools used in the production and maintenance of its products, including its new A350 XWB planes. The information system follows parts, on which high-memory RFID tags have been placed, from warehouses to production facilities to the specific lines where they are attached to aircraft. The system also tracks how and where tools are used. Airbus expects the information system to improve overall supply chain management, reduce required inventory levels, and increase productivity.[3]

Clay Petway, American Airlines Aviation Maintenance Technician and TWU member

At American Airlines, the one thing we're not maintaining is the status quo.

In an aviation world where more maintenance work is being subcontracted overseas, American Airlines and the Transport Workers Union are bucking the trend with a groundbreaking business relationship to turn aircraft maintenance operations at our airports and maintenance bases into profit centers.

The big news is: it's working. We're keeping thousands of jobs in the U.S., thanks to innovative improvements in our business processes that are generating revenue from customer maintenance contracts and significantly reducing costs.

While our world-class mechanics and engineers are maintaining aircraft for American, the world's largest airline, we're also doing work for other airlines and aerospace companies in the U.S. and other parts of the world.

By working as a team and agreeing on a series of aggressive goals, American Airlines and the TWU are transforming aircraft maintenance into a whole new way of doing business.

AmericanAirlines®

For inquiries about American Airlines Maintenance Services, visit our web site at www.mroaa.com.

© American Airlines, Inc 2007

The complex process of airline maintenance is critical to passenger safety. To track parts, schedule inspections, and manage inventory levels, many airlines use an *operational support system*. In this ad, American Airlines reports that improved business processes have turned costly maintenance operations into a source of profit.

Management Support Systems

Information systems that are designed to provide support for effective decision making are classified as **management support systems**. Several different types of management support systems are available. A **management information system (MIS)** is designed to produce reports to managers and other professionals.

A **decision support system (DSS)** gives direct support to businesspeople during the decision-making process. For instance, a marketing manager might use a decision support system to analyze the impact on sales and profits of a product price change.

An **executive support system (ESS)** lets senior executives access the firm's primary databases, often by touching the computer screen, pointing and clicking a mouse, or using voice recognition. The typical ESS allows users to choose from many kinds of data, such as the firm's financial statements and sales figures, as well as stock market trends for the company and for the industry as a whole. If they wish, managers can start by looking at summaries and then access more detailed information when needed.

---

operational support systems information systems designed to produce a variety of information on an organization's activities for both internal and external users.

transaction processing systems operational support system to record and process data from business transactions.

process control systems operational support system to monitor and control physical processes.

management support systems information systems that are designed to provide support for effective decision making.

management information system (MIS) information system that is designed to produce reports to managers and other professionals.

decision support system (DSS) gives direct support to businesspeople during the decision-making process.

executive support system (ESS) lets senior executives access the firm's primary databases, often by touching the computer screen, pointing and clicking a mouse, or using voice recognition.

Finally, an **expert system** is a computer program that imitates human thinking through complicated sets of "if-then" rules. The system applies human knowledge in a specific subject area to solve a problem. Expert systems are used for a variety of business purposes: determining credit limits for credit card applicants, monitoring machinery in a plant to predict potential problems or breakdowns, making mortgage loans, and determining optimal plant layouts. They are typically developed by capturing the knowledge of recognized experts in a field whether within a business itself or outside it.

expert system computer program that imitates human thinking through complicated sets of "if-then" rules.

Computer Hardware and Software

It may be hard to believe, but only a few decades ago computers were considered exotic curiosities, used only for very specialized applications and understood by only a few people. The first commercial computer, UNIVAC I, was sold to the U.S. Census Bureau in the early 1950s. It cost $1 million, took up most of a room, and could perform about 2,000 calculations per second.[4] The invention of transistors and then integrated circuits (microchips) quickly led to smaller and more powerful devices. By the 1980s, computers could routinely perform several million calculations per second. Now, computers perform billions of calculations per second, and some fit in the palm of your hand.

When the first personal computers were introduced in the late 1970s and early 1980s, the idea of a computer on every desk, or in every home, seemed far-fetched. Today they have become indispensable to both businesses and households. Not only have computers become much more powerful and faster over the past 25 years, but they are less expensive as well. IBM's first personal computer (PC), introduced in 1981, cost well over $5,000 fully configured. Today, the typical PC sells for under $800.

Types of Computer Hardware

Hardware consists of all tangible elements of a computer system—the input devices, the components that store and process data and perform required calculations, and the output devices that present the results to information users. Input devices allow users to enter data and commands for processing, storage, and output. The most common input devices are the keyboard and mouse. Storage and processing components consist of the hard drive as well as various other storage components, including DVD drives and flash memory devices. Flash memory devices are becoming increasingly popular because they are small and can hold large amounts of data. Some, called thumb drives, can even fit on a keychain. To gain access to the data they hold, users just plug them into an unused USB (universal serial bus) port, standard on today's computers. Output devices, such as monitors and printers, are the hardware elements that transmit or display documents and other results of a computer system's work.

Different types of computers incorporate widely varying memory capacities and processing speeds. These differences define four broad classifications: mainframe computers, midrange systems, personal computers, and hand-held devices. A mainframe computer is the largest type of computer system with the most extensive storage capacity and the fastest processing speeds. Especially powerful mainframes called *supercomputers* can handle extremely rapid, complex calculations involving thousands of variables, such as weather modeling and forecasting. Today's supercomputers can perform a trillion or more calculations per second.

Midrange systems consist of high-end network servers and other types of computers that can handle large-scale processing needs. They are less powerful than mainframe computers

hardware all tangible elements of a computer system.

Assessment Check ✔

1. List the four components of a computer-based information system.
2. What is a database?
3. What are the two general types of information systems? Give examples of each.

server the heart of a midrange computer network

but more powerful than most personal computers. A **server** is the heart of a midrange computer network, supporting applications and allowing the sharing of output devices, software, and databases among networked users. Many Internet-related functions at organizations are handled by midrange systems. Midrange systems are also commonly employed in process control systems, computer-aided manufacturing (CAM), and computer-aided design (CAD).

Personal computers are everywhere today—in homes, businesses, schools, nonprofit organizations, and government agencies. Recent estimates of PC ownership say that more than two-thirds of American households have at least one personal computer. They have earned increasing popularity because of their ever-expanding capability to handle many of the functions that large mainframes performed only a few decades ago. Most desktop computers are linked to networks, such as the Internet.

Desktop computers used to be the standard PC seen in offices and homes. While millions of desktop computers remain on the job, notebook computers now account for more than half of all new PCs sold. The increasing popularity of notebooks can be explained by their lower prices, improved displays, faster processing speeds, larger storage capacities, and more durable designs. At the same time they are becoming more powerful, notebooks have never been lighter or thinner. For many users, the size, weight, and portability of notebooks offsets the fact that notebooks still cost more than comparable desktop computers.

One of the newest types of notebook computer is the *netbook*. These devices are very small and inexpensive; some cost less than $300. While they don't have the computing capability of the larger, more expensive notebooks, netbooks can still perform basic tasks (such as e-mail, word processing, and spreadsheet calculations) and can access the Internet through a wireless connection.

Hand-held devices—made by companies such as Apple, RIM, Nokia, Palm, and Samsung—are even smaller. Two kinds of hand-held devices are available to most business and consumer users. The original type is the personal digital assistant (PDA). PDAs keep schedules and contact information and have limited software applications such as word processing and spreadsheets. Most PDAs today allow users to access the Internet through wireless networks.

The other type of hand-held device is the *smart phone*. A smart phone is essentially a device that combines a cell phone with a PDA. Examples include Apple's iPhone, Google's Android, RIM's BlackBerry, and Samsung's BlackJack. In addition to making and receiving calls and text messages, smart phones allow users to surf the Internet, receive and send e-mail, check their schedules, and even open and edit documents. On short trips, many businesspeople find that they just rely on their smart phone. Given their added capability, it's not surprising that smart phone sales are growing much faster than sales of traditional PDAs. Moreover, most of the recent overall growth in the sale of cell phones can be attributed to smart phones.[5]

While smart phones can be terrific tools that boost productivity, some people overuse or even misuse them. The "Business Etiquette" feature describes some do's and don'ts of smart phone use in a business environment.

Jacob Wackerhausen/iStockphoto

While smart phones can boost productivity, some people overuse or even misuse them. Check out the "Business Etiquette" box for some helpful tips for courteous communication while using your hand-held device in a business environment.

In addition to PDAs and smart phones, specialized hand-held devices are used in a variety of businesses for different applications. Some restaurants, for example, have small wireless devices that allow servers to swipe a credit card and print out a receipt right at the customer's table. Drivers for UPS and FedEx use special hand-held devices to track package deliveries and accept delivery signatures. The driver scans each package as it is delivered, and the information is transmitted to the delivery firm's network. Within a few seconds, the sender, using an Internet connection, can obtain the delivery information and even see a facsimile of the recipient's signature.

Computer Software

Software includes all of the programs, routines, and computer languages that control a computer and tell it how to operate. The software that controls the basic workings of a computer system is its *operating system*. More than 90 percent of personal computers use a version of Microsoft's popular Windows operating system. Personal computers made by Apple use the Mac operating system. Most hand-held devices use either the Palm or Symbian operating system or a special version of Windows called Windows Mobile. But the Droid, iPhone, and BlackBerry models have their own operating systems. Other operating systems include Unix, which runs on many midrange computer systems, and Linux, which runs on both PCs and midrange systems.

A program that performs the specific tasks that the user wants to carry out—such as writing a letter or looking up data—is called *application software*. Examples of application software include Adobe Acrobat, Microsoft PowerPoint, and Quicken. Table 14.1 lists the major categories of application software. Most application programs are currently stored on individual computers. As the chapter's opening vignette discussed, the future of applications software is constantly changing. Some believe much of it will eventually become Web based, with the programs themselves stored in the "cloud," on Internet-connected servers. Others disagree, arguing that most computer users will not want to rely on an Internet connection to perform tasks such as preparing a spreadsheet using Microsoft Excel. The "Going Green" feature explains how some observers believe that cloud computing might help reduce greenhouse gases.

BusinessEtiquette

Courteous Communications via Wireless Devices

According to data from the U.S. Census Bureau and other sources, cell phone use in America has skyrocketed from about 3.5 million subscribers to about 285 million in a decade. With so many of us communicating instantly—and almost constantly—it is more important than ever to be courteous, whether speaking or e-mailing on a hand-held device.

1 *Be aware of your surroundings—and your neighbors.* If you're in a meeting or other place where a separate conversation would be disruptive, turn your ringtone off. If the call or e-mail simply can't wait, excuse yourself and leave the room before responding to it.

2 *Lower your voice when you're talking in public.* If the room you are in is quieter than your speaking voice, it's better to go somewhere else.

3 *When sending e-mail or texting, don't overabbreviate.* A business message can be concise without being cute or, worse, unintelligible. It is just as easy to say "See you at 3" as "cu@3."

4 *Before you send a text message or e-mail, read it over carefully.* Typos and grammatical errors don't look good, especially in a business message.

5 *Be careful about your Facebook profile photo.* Now that smart phones let users link all their contact information, your photo will appear on the other person's phone when you call. And people beyond those on your "friends" list will see it. Be sure your photo is appropriate for both friends and business callers.

Sources: Christopher Elliott, "E-Mail Etiquette for Wireless Devices: 7 Tips," Microsoft Small Business Center, http://www.microsoft.com, accessed May 24, 2010; Taya Flores, "Cell Phone Etiquette Is Important," *JC Online.com,* April 19, 2010, http://www.jconline.com; Mike Elgan, "Here Comes the New Cell Phone Etiquette," *IT World,* January 22, 2010, http://www.itworld.com.

software all the programs, routines, and computer languages that control a computer and tell it how to operate.

⌐14.1┐ Common Types of Applications Software

TYPE	DESCRIPTION	EXAMPLES
Word processing	Programs that input, store, retrieve, edit, and print various types of documents.	Microsoft Word, Pages (Apple)
Spreadsheets	Programs that prepare and analyze financial statements, sales forecasts, budgets, and similar numerical and statistical data.	Microsoft Excel, Numbers (Apple)
Presentation software	Programs that create presentations. Users can create bulleted lists, charts, graphs, pictures, audio, and even short video clips.	Microsoft PowerPoint, Keynote (Apple)
Desktop publishing	Software that combines high-quality type, graphics, and layout tools to create output that can look as attractive as documents produced by professional publishers and printers.	Adobe Acrobat, Microsoft Publisher
Financial software	Programs that compile accounting and financial data to create financial statements, reports, and budgets; they perform basic financial management tasks such as balancing a checkbook.	Quicken, QuickBooks
Database programs	Software that searches and retrieves data from a database; it can sort data based on various criteria.	Microsoft Access, Approach
Personal information managers	Specialized database programs that allow people to track communications with personal and business contacts; some combine e-mail capability.	Microsoft Outlook, Lotus Organizer
Enterprise resource planning	Integrated cross-functional software that controls many business activities, including distribution, finance, and human resources.	SAP Enterprise Resource Planning

Assessment Check ✔

1. List two input and output devices.

2. What accounts for the increasing popularity of notebook computers?

3. What is software? List the two categories of software.

Computer Networks

As mentioned earlier, virtually all computers today are linked to networks. In fact, if your PC has Internet access, you're linked to a network. Local area networks and wide area networks allow businesses to communicate, transmit and print documents, and share data. These networks, however, require businesses to install special equipment and connections between office sites. But Internet technology has also been applied to internal company communications and business tasks, tapping a ready-made network. Among these new Internet-based applications are intranets, virtual private networks (VPNs), and voice over Internet protocol (VoIP). Each has contributed to the effectiveness and speed of business processes, so we discuss them next.

Local Area Networks and Wide Area Networks

Most organizations connect their offices and buildings by creating **local area networks (LANs)**, computer networks that connect machines within limited areas, such as a building or several nearby buildings. LANs are useful because they link computers and allow them to share printers, documents, and information, as well as provide access to the Internet. Figure 14.1 shows what a small business computer network might look like.

Wide area networks (WANs) tie larger geographical regions together by using telephone lines and microwave and satellite transmission. One familiar WAN is long-distance

local area networks (LANs), computer networks that connect machines within limited areas, such as a building or several nearby buildings.

wide area networks (WANs) tie larger geographical regions together by using telephone lines and microwave and satellite transmission.

Can Cloud Computing Also Be "Green" Computing?

The rise in cloud computing has some observers hoping it will decrease the emission of greenhouse gases. However, others are increasingly concerned that it will cause emissions to increase because it will require larger and larger data storage centers that use more energy.

The environmental organization Greenpeace recently issued the "Cool IT Challenge" to the IT sector. Greenpeace urges these firms to reduce emissions by using renewable electricity to power their data centers and to pressure utility companies to improve access to renewable energy. In a recent report, Greenpeace declared that IT energy solutions can even encourage the growth of local, decentralized energy centers as opposed to large grids. These smaller, local networks could result in better energy choices for consumers as well as improved efficiency and more use of renewable energy.

Greenpeace has also published a chart that rates major data centers' use of power sources. Google's data center in Oregon was the leading user of renewable energy, with almost 51 percent of its energy coming from renewable sources as opposed to coal and nuclear power.

The Green Grid, a group of IT companies interested in improving energy efficiency, recently launched a downloadable tool that helps IT professionals lower overall energy use by using outside air and water to cool their data centers at little or no cost.

Even Greenpeace has come under fire for relying on coal and nuclear energy at some of its data centers, due to long-term agreements with local utilities. Gary Cook, one of the Cool IT Campaign's policy advisors, declared, "We're definitely trying to run the greenest operation we can. . . . We're in the process of reworking some of our IT infrastructure, and we'll clean that up."

Questions for Critical Thinking

1. Why do you think devices such as smart phones or the iPad, which rely on cloud computing, might contribute to increased greenhouse gas emissions?

2. Do you think that data centers' voluntary actions will be enough to lower greenhouse gas emissions? Why or why not?

Sources: Greenpeace Web site, http://www.greenpeace.org, accessed May 22, 2010; The Green Grid Web site, http://www.thegreengrid.org, accessed May 22, 2010; GreenerComputing Staff, "Green Grid Offers Tools for Free Data Center Cooling," *GreenBiz*, April 12, 2010, http://www.greenbiz.com; Rich Miller, "Greenpeace: Cloud Contributes to Climate Change," Data Center Knowledge, March 30, 2010, http://www.datacenter-knowledge.com; Matthew Wheeland, "Cloud Computing Is Efficient, But It's Not Green—Yet," *GreenBiz*, March 30, 2010, http://www.greenbiz.com; Rich Miller, "Greenpeace's Hosting: Not 'Truly Green,' " Data Center Knowledge, March 3, 2010.

---

telephone service. Companies such as AT&T and Verizon provide WAN services to businesses and consumers. Firms also use WANs to conduct their own operations. Typically, companies link their own network systems to outside communications equipment and services for transmission across long distances.

WiFi wireless network that connects various devices and allows them to communicate with one another through radio waves.

Wireless Local Networks

A wireless network allows computers, printers, and other devices to be connected without the hassle of stringing cables in traditional office settings. The current standard for wireless networks is called WiFi. **WiFi**—short for *wireless fidelity*—is a wireless network that connects various devices and allows them to communicate with one another through radio waves. Any PC with a WiFi receptor can connect with the Internet at so-called hot spots—locations with a wireless router and a high-speed Internet modem. There are almost hundreds of thousands of hot spots worldwide today. They are found in a variety of places, including airports, libraries, and coffee shops. Examples include Panera Bread's 1,300 bakery-cafes in the United States and Kansai International Airport in Osaka, Japan. Some locations provide free access, while others charge a fee.

WiFi connections are often called *hot spots*—locations with a wireless router and a high-speed Internet modem. There are almost hundreds of thousands of hot spots worldwide today found in a variety of places, including airports, libraries, and coffee shops.

FIGURE
14.1

A Local Area Network

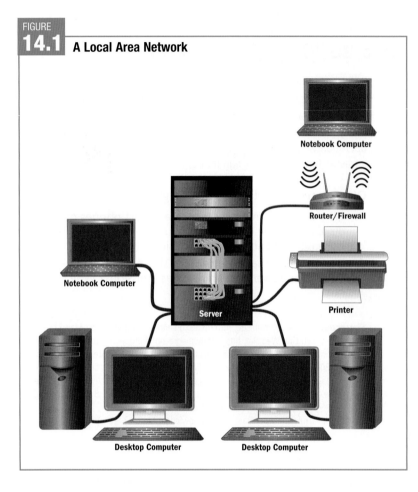

Many believe that the successor to WiFi will be *Wi-Max*. Unlike WiFi's relatively limited geographic coverage area—generally around 300 feet—a single Wi-Max access point can provide coverage over many miles. In addition, cell phone service providers, such as Sprint Nextel and AT&T, offer broadband network cards for notebook PCs. These devices allow users to access the provider's mobile broadband network from virtually any location where cell phone reception is available.

Intranets

A broad approach to sharing information in an organization is to establish a company network patterned after the Internet. Such a network is called an **intranet**. Intranets are similar to the Internet, but they limit access to employees or other authorized users. An intranet blocks outsiders without valid passwords from entering its network by incorporating both software and hardware known as a **firewall**. Firewalls limit data transfers to certain locations and log system use so that managers can identify attempts to log on with invalid passwords and other threats to a system's security. Highly sophisticated packages immediately alert system administrators about suspicious activities and permit authorized personnel to use smart cards to connect from remote terminals.

intranet computer network that is similar to the Internet but limits access to authorized users.

firewall limit data transfers to certain locations and log system use so that managers can identify attempts to log on with invalid passwords and other threats to a system's security.

virtual private networks (VPNs) secure connections between two points on the Internet.

Intranets solve the problem of linking different types of computers. Like the Internet, intranets can integrate computers running all kinds of operating systems. In addition, intranets are relatively easy and inexpensive to set up because most businesses already have some of the required hardware and software. For instance, a small business can simply purchase a DSL router and a few cables and create an intranet using phone jacks and internal phone lines. All the business's computers will be linked with each other and with the Internet.

Intranets also support teamwork among employees who travel or work from home. Any intranet member with the right identification, a PC, and some sort of Internet connection—either dial-up or broadband—can link to the intranet and gain access to group calendars, e-mail, documents, and other files. Intranets can also be used for videoconferencing and other forms of virtual meetings. Jetstar, an airline serving the Asian Pacific region, has more than 3,000 employees. But three-quarters of them—pilots, cabin crews, and airport staff, for example—will never go to the home office. Via the company's intranet, pilots can access constantly changing safety information, and home office employees can update the staff directory and transfer paper forms online. Corporate and staff communications, transmitted to all employees via Jetstar's intranet, help build a sense of community.[6]

Virtual Private Networks

To gain increased security for Internet communications, companies often turn to **virtual private networks (VPNs)**, secure connections between two points on the Internet.

These VPNs use firewalls and programs that encapsulate data to make them more secure during transit. Loosely defined, a VPN can include a range of networking technologies, from secure Internet connections to private networks from service providers like IBM. A VPN is cheaper for a company to use than leasing several of its own lines. It can also take months to install a leased line in some parts of the world, but a new user can be added to a VPN in a day. Because a VPN uses the Internet, it can be wired, wireless, or a combination of the two.

Colorado-based Advanced Systems Group (ASG) provides data storage and management services to other companies. As the company expanded and opened branch offices, its own security became a concern. ASG turned to Check Point, which created a secure VPN connecting ASG's home office and five branch offices. The VPN allows ASG to add new sites and new remote users automatically.[7]

VoIP

VoIP—which stands for *voice over Internet Protocol*—is an alternative to traditional telecommunication services provided by companies such as Verizon and Qwest. The VoIP telephone is not connected to a traditional phone jack but rather is connected to a personal computer with any type of broadband connection. Special software transmits phone conversations over the Internet, rather than through telephone lines. A VoIP user dials the phone as usual. The person can make and receive calls to and from those with traditional telephone connections (landline or wireless).

A growing number of consumers and businesses have embraced VoIP, mainly due to its cost savings and extra features. As technology continues to advance, demand for the service has increased. AT&T and Verizon Wireless recently announced that they would permit VoIP on some smartphones, and Google is developing its own VoIP service. The various VoIP providers are working together with the goal of creating a single VoIP standard that would permit seamless roaming worldwide.[8]

In spite of VoIP's apparent advantages, there are several potential drawbacks to replacing traditional telephony with Internet telephony. For one thing, your Internet phone service will be only as reliable as your broadband connection. If your broadband connection goes out, so will your phone service. Also, without extensive safeguards, VoIP can expose a phone system to the havoc that can affect the rest of the Internet, such as worms and viruses.

VoIP alternative to traditional telecommunication services provided by companies such as Verizon and Qwest.

Assessment Check ✔

1. What is a LAN?
2. What are the differences between an intranet and a VPN?
3. Briefly explain how VoIP works.

Security and Ethical Issues Affecting Information Systems

Numerous security and ethical issues affect information systems. As information systems become increasingly important business assets, they also become progressively harder and more expensive to replace. Damage to information systems or theft of data can have disastrous consequences. When computers are connected to a network, a problem at any individual computer can affect the entire network. Two of the major security threats are e-crime and so-called malware.

E-Crime

Computers provide efficient ways for employees to share information. But they may also allow people with more malicious intentions to access information. Or they may allow pranksters—who have no motive other than to see whether they can hack into a system—to gain access to private information. Common e-crimes involve stealing or altering data in several ways:

- Employees or outsiders may change or invent data to produce inaccurate or misleading information.

- Employees or outsiders may modify computer programs to create false information or illegal transactions or to insert viruses.

- Unauthorized people can access computer systems for their own benefit or knowledge or just to see if they can get in.

Individuals, businesses, and government agencies are all vulnerable to computer crime. Computer hackers—unauthorized users—sometimes work alone and sometimes work in groups. Hackers can break into computer systems just to show that they can do it; other times they have more sinister motives. A recent survey reported that although computer crime decreased slightly recently, the majority of such attacks may go undetected, because many firms have concentrated on foiling hackers and blocking pornography while leaving themselves open to cybercriminals who are developing increasingly sophisticated weapons. Even Apple computers, normally immune to cybercrime, are becoming vulnerable as more and more Mac users store data in the "cloud"—that is, on the Internet itself—rather than on hard drives. Until now there has been no single uniform system for reporting cyber crime, but the Internet Engineering Task Force (IETF) is working toward a common format that will have reliable time stamps, will be available in different languages, and will allow users to attach samples of malicious code. These automated tools will be able to analyze massive amounts of data much faster than human analysts can.[9]

Information system administrators implement two basic protections against computer crime: they try to prevent access to their systems by unauthorized users and the viewing of data by unauthorized system users. The simplest method of preventing access requires authorized users to enter passwords. The company may also install firewalls, described earlier. To prevent system users from reading sensitive information, the company may use encryption software, which encodes, or scrambles, messages. To read encrypted messages, users must use an electronic key to convert them to regular text. But as fast as software developers invent new and more elaborate protective measures, hackers seem to break through their defenses. Thus, security is an ongoing battle.

Another form of computer theft is as old as crime itself: theft of equipment. And because these machines may contain all kinds of important information for a business, employees need to be especially careful not to leave them unattended or within easy reach of others. Recently, someone stole 57 hard drives from a BlueCross BlueShield office in Chattanooga, Tennessee. Stored on the hard drives were 1 million customer support calls, about 50,000 hours of phone conversations. Although most of the customers did not reveal enough personal information for effective identity theft, Medicare subscribers had to give their Social Security numbers—which can be used in identity theft. The hard drives also contained about 300,000 screen shots of callers' information, which the BlueCross employees had brought up on screen while speaking with them. Many of the screen shots show callers' Social Security numbers. The only way for BlueCross BlueShield to identify customers whose information was compromised has been to review each of the audio and video files individually.[10]

As the size of computer hardware diminishes, it becomes increasingly vulnerable to theft. Hand-held devices, for instance, can easily vanish with a pickpocket or purse snatcher. Many notebook computers and hand-held devices contain special security software or passwords that makes it difficult for a thief or any unauthorized person to access the data stored in the computer's memory. If you have a notebook computer that contains sensitive personal information, you should consider having such safeguards.

Computer Viruses, Worms, Trojan Horses, and Spyware

Viruses, worms, Trojan horses, and spyware, collectively referred to as **malware**, are malicious software programs designed to infect computer systems. These programs can destroy data, steal sensitive information, and even render information systems inoperable. Recently, malware has been discovered in advertisements on major sites such as Yahoo, Fox, and Google as well as *The New York Times* and WhitePages.com. Malware attacks cost consumers and businesses billions of dollars annually. Although law enforcement has made progress against cybercrime, some observers predict that cybercriminals will target social-networking sites such as Facebook and Twitter.[11]

Computer **viruses** are programs that secretly attach themselves to other programs (called *hosts*) and change them or destroy data. According to the computer security company Symantec, there are currently almost 3 million active computer viruses worldwide.[12] Viruses can be programmed to become active immediately or to remain dormant for a period of time, after which the infections suddenly activate themselves and cause problems. A virus can reproduce by copying itself onto other programs stored in the same drive. It spreads as users install infected software on their systems or exchange files with others, usually by exchanging e-mail, accessing electronic bulletin boards, trading disks, or downloading programs or data from unknown sources on the Internet.

A **worm** is a small piece of software that exploits a security hole in a network to replicate itself. A copy of the worm scans the network for another machine that has a specific security hole. It copies itself to the new machine using the security hole and then starts replicating from there as well. Unlike viruses, worms don't need host programs to damage computer systems.

A **botnet** is a network of PCs that have been infected with one or more data-stealing viruses. Computer criminals tie the infected computers into a network, often without the owners being aware of it, and sell the botnet on the black market. They or others use the botnet to commit identity theft, send spam, buy blocks of concert tickets for scalping, and attack the Internet itself. About 4,000 to 6,000 botnets are active today. Spanish authorities recently brought down the Mariposa botnet, the world's largest to date, a network of 12.7 million infected computers. Some of the computers were inside *Fortune* 1,000 companies and major banks. Although the authorities made some arrests, the creator of the Mariposa botnet has not been caught.[13]

A **Trojan horse** is a program that claims to do one thing but in reality does something else, usually something malicious. For example, a Trojan horse might claim,

malware any malicious software program designed to infect computer systems.

viruses programs that secretly attach themselves to other programs (called *hosts*) and change them or destroy data.

worm small piece of software that exploits a security hole in a network to replicate itself.

botnet a network of PCs that have been infected with one or more data-stealing viruses.

Trojan horse program that claims to do one thing but in reality does something else, usually something malicious.

and even appear, to be a game. When an unsuspecting user clicks on the Trojan horse to launch it, the program might erase the hard drive or steal any personal data stored on the computer.

spyware software that secretly gathers user information through the user's Internet connection without his or her knowledge, usually for advertising purposes.

<u>Spyware</u> is software that secretly gathers user information through the user's Internet connection without his or her knowledge, usually for advertising purposes. Spyware applications are typically bundled with other programs downloaded from the Internet. Once installed, the spyware monitors user activity on the Internet and transmits that information in the background to someone else.

Attacks by malware are not limited to computers and computer networks; hand-held devices, including cell phones, have been affected as well. Smart phone users have reported a sharp increase in viruses, worms, and other forms of malware.[14]

Recently, a group of computer scientists cracked the security system that is used in 80 percent of the world's cell phones. The scientists said it was relatively easy and that they did it to encourage development of more sophisticated security.[15]

As viruses, worms, botnets, and Trojan horses become more complex, the technology to fight them must increase in sophistication as well. The simplest way to protect against computer viruses is to install one of the many available antivirus software programs, such as Norton AntiVirus and McAfee VirusScan. These programs, which also protect against worms and some Trojan horses, continuously monitor systems for viruses and automatically eliminate any they spot. Users should regularly update them by downloading the latest virus definitions. In addition, computer users should also install and regularly update antispyware programs because many Trojan horses are forms of spyware.

But management must begin to emphasize security at a deeper level: during software design, in corporate servers, at Web gateways, and through Internet service providers. Because more than 90 percent of the world's PCs run on Microsoft operating systems, a single virus, worm, or Trojan horse can spread among them quickly. Individual computer users should carefully choose the files they load onto their systems, scan their systems regularly, make sure their antivirus software is up to date, and install software only from known sources. They should also be very careful when opening attachments to e-mails because many viruses, worms, and Trojan horses are spread that way.

Information Systems and Ethics

The scope and power of today's information systems not surprisingly raise a number of ethical issues and concerns. These affect both employees and organizations. For instance, it is not uncommon for organizations to have specific ethical standards and policies regarding the use of information systems by employees and vendors. These standards include obligations to protect system security and the privacy and confidentiality of data. Policies also may cover the personal use of computers and related technologies, both hardware and software, by employees.

Assessment Check ☑

1. Explain computer hacking.
2. What is malware?
3. How does a computer virus work?

Ethical issues also involve organizational use of information systems. Organizations have an obligation to protect the privacy and confidentiality of data about employees and customers. Employment records contain sensitive personal information, such as bank account numbers, which, if not protected, could lead to identity theft. Another ethical issue is the use of computer technology to monitor employees while they are working. The "Solving an Ethical Controversy" feature debates the issue of employee monitoring further.

Solving an Ethical Controversy

Should Employers Monitor Employees' Internet Use?

According to an American Management Association/ePolicy Institute survey, two-thirds of employers monitor employees' use of the Internet. Technology now allows them to check Web sites their employees visit on company time, keystrokes on individual computers, and the amount of time spent online. Employers can even track employees with GPS-enabled phones.

On-the-job access to the Internet and e-mail is indispensable. A certain amount of Internet surfing for research purposes is necessary in some fields. A company's Facebook page can be either a powerful marketing tool or a liability if employees use their own social media sites to complain about the company.

Should employers monitor their employees' time online?

PRO

1. Surveys have estimated that employees spend between one and two hours every day online for personal use. Some employees perform innocent tasks such as banking, but others visit inappropriate Web sites. Either way, those hours mean lost productivity for the company.

2. Inappropriate use of office computers could leave a company vulnerable to hacking, viruses, or other security compromises.

CON

1. Some employers are concerned that monitoring employees could endanger an atmosphere of trust, commitment, and motivation.

2. Employees do have a legitimate concern about privacy, especially if they have not been informed beforehand that their online activities are being monitored.

Summary

Although federal law clearly gives employers the right to monitor computer activity, a case pending before the U.S. Supreme Court concerns the permissible range of monitoring a worker's use of a company-provided electronic device. Most analysts suggest that companies should establish clear policies on computer, Internet, and e-mail use; train employees and have them sign a document saying they understand those policies; and then trust their employees.

Sources: "How Do Employers Monitor Internet Usage at Work," *wiseGEEK,* http://www.wisegeek.com, accessed May 23, 2010; Susan M. Heathfield, "Electronic Surveillance of Employees," *About.com* Human Resources, http://humanresources.about.com, accessed May 23, 2010; Karen Codere, "Managing Social Media in the Workplace," *The Business Ledger,* April 28, 2010, http://www.thebusinessledger.com; Laura Petrecca, "More Employers Use Tech to Track Workers," *USA Today,* March 17, 2010, http://www.usatoday.com.

Disaster Recovery and Backup

Natural disasters, power failures, equipment malfunctions, software glitches, human error, and terrorist attacks can disrupt even the most sophisticated computer information systems. These disruptions can cost businesses and other organizations billions of dollars. Even more serious consequences can occur. For example, one recent study found that more than 93 percent of firms that lost their data centers for ten days or more went bankrupt within six months.[16]

Strand Associates, a multibranch civil engineering firm headquartered in Madison, Wisconsin, faced the challenge of ensuring reliable backups and data protection. Backups were in the form of magnetic tapes made weekly by local office personnel and sent to the home office. For data retrieval, branch offices had to request the home office to ship the physical magnetic tapes. The company's IT team spent many hours fixing hardware or

FalconStor is an IT firm that specializes in servicing engineering companies to set up a system of backups stored on remote servers before they are transferred to tape and stored off site.

tracking down lost tapes. Strand turned to FalconStor, an IT firm that specializes in servicing engineering companies. FalconStor met Strand's needs by setting up a system of double backups made hourly and stored on remote servers before being transferred to tape and stored off site. Data from local offices are duplicated to FalconStor hardware in Wisconsin, and data from the Wisconsin office are duplicated to a FalconStor appliance in Illinois. All files are also backed up weekly. Strand's network engineer, Justin Bell, explains, "This setup allows us to keep an offsite copy of everything, so that all of our data is protected."[17]

Disaster recovery planning—deciding how to prevent system failures and continue operations if computer systems fail—is a critical function of all organizations. Disaster prevention programs can avoid some of these costly problems. The most basic precaution is routinely backing up software and data—at the organizational and individual levels. However, the organization's data center cannot be the sole repository of critical data because a single location is vulnerable to threats from both natural and human-caused disasters. Consequently, off-site data backup is a necessity, whether in a separate physical location or online on the Internet itself. Companies that perform online backups store the encrypted data in secure facilities that in turn have their own backups. The initial backup may take a day or more, but subsequent ones take far less time because they involve only new or modified files.

According to security experts, there are five important tasks regarding off-site data storage. First is planning. The organization needs to decide what data need to be protected. Priority should be given to data having severe legal or business consequences should they be lost. Second, a backup schedule must be established and closely adhered to. Third, when data are transmitted off site, they must be protected by the highest level of security possible. Fourth, care should be taken in selecting the right security vendor. There are dozens of vendors offering different services and having different areas of expertise. Finally, the backup system should be continually tested and evaluated.

Assessment Check ✔

1. What are the types of disasters to which information systems are vulnerable?

2. List the tasks regarding off-site data storage.

Information System Trends

Computer information systems are constantly—and rapidly—evolving. To keep their information systems up-to-date, firms must continually keep abreast of changes in technology. Some of the most significant trends in information systems today include the growing demands of the so-called distributed workforce, the increased use of application service providers, on-demand computing, and cloud and grid computing.

The Distributed Workforce

As discussed in earlier chapters, many companies are relying more and more on a *distributed workforce*—employees who no longer work in traditional offices but rather in what are called *virtual offices*, including at home. Information technology makes a distributed workforce possible. Computers, networks, and other components of information systems allow many workers the ability to do their jobs effectively almost anywhere. For instance, none of JetBlue's reservations agents work in offices; they all work at home, connected to the airline's information system. JetBlue is hardly alone in its use of home-based workers. Boeing, Starbucks, Agilent Technologies, Sun Microsystems, and many other companies maintain "virtual" offices with thousands of workers. According to the Bureau of Labor Statistics (BLS), about 10 percent of full-time wage and salary workers work at home on any given day. Of the self-employed, more than one-third work at home on any given day.[18] The BLS statistics show that the vast majority of at-home workers use computers and related technologies. Virtual offices range from a mailing address, mail forwarding, and a phone answering service to a full office, usually leased by the month. The increasing demands of the distributed workforce will likely lead to more innovative and increasingly powerful information systems.

Application Service Providers

As with other business functions, many firms find that outsourcing at least some of their information technology function makes sense. Because of the increasing cost and complexity of obtaining and maintaining information systems, many firms hire an **application service provider (ASP)**, an outside supplier that provides both the computers and the application support for managing an information system. An ASP can simplify complex software for its customers so that it is easier for them to manage and use. When an ASP relationship is successful, the buyer can then devote more time and resources to its core businesses instead of struggling to manage its information systems. Other benefits include stretching the firm's technology dollar farther and giving smaller companies the kind of information power that in the past was available only to much larger organizations. Even large companies turn to ASPs to manage some or all of their information systems. Recently, Microsoft outsourced much of its internal information technology (IT) services to Infosys Technology to save money and streamline, simplify, and support its services.[19]

Companies that decide to use ASPs should check the backgrounds and references of these firms before hiring them to manage critical systems. In addition, customers should try to ensure that the service provider has strong security measures to block computer hackers or other unauthorized access to the data, that its data centers are running reliably, and that adequate data and applications backups are maintained.

On-Demand, Cloud, and Grid Computing

Another recent trend is **on-demand computing**, also called *utility computing*. Instead of purchasing and maintaining expensive software, firms essentially rent the software time from application providers and pay only for their usage of the software, similar to purchasing electricity from a utility. On-demand computing is particularly useful for firms that experience annual peaks in demand or seasonal spikes in customer usage of their applications. By renting the service they need only when they need it, they can avoid buying the software that is not routinely required. On-demand computing can also help companies remain current with the most efficient software on the market without purchasing huge upgrades.

Cloud computing uses powerful servers to store applications software and databases. Users access the software and databases via the Web using anything from a PC to a smart phone. The software as a service (SaaS) movement is an example of cloud computing.

application service provider (ASP) outside supplier that provides both the computers and the application support for managing an information system.

on-demand computing firms essentially rent the software time from application providers and pay only for their usage of the software

cloud computing powerful servers store applications software and databases for users to access the software and databases via the Web using anything from a PC to a smart phone.

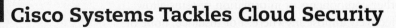
Cisco Systems Tackles Cloud Security

More and more businesses find themselves managing increasing amounts of e-mail and storing increasing amounts of data. Many save money and physical space by turning to cloud computing and storage, including software as a service (SaaS). Rather than installing software on site, with SaaS a business gains access to software over the Internet either by subscription or by a "pay as you go" plan. These businesses also need to protect their databanks from computer crime. In a traditional local area network, it is relatively easy to implement security applications at the network's borders. But in the borderless environment of cloud computing and with threats to security increasing, meeting this challenge is more difficult.

Cisco Systems has responded by developing security applications for cloud-based computing. One application directs a business's Web traffic to security towers located in 100 countries around the world. These locations use layers of antivirus and antimalware utilities to scan Web sites and quickly block access to them if they are compromised.

Another application offers both cloud-based and on-site e-mail security. The cloud-based application deletes spam and viruses. The on-site application provides data-loss prevention, e-mail encryption, and other services. Another e-mail encryption service provides cloud-based encryption for locally stored messages.

Other apps support security for off-site workers using desktops, laptops, tablets, and smart phones. One feature addresses the problem that occurs when an employee leaves a business. With one click of the mouse, an administrator can disable that person's access to every SaaS application he or she ever used. Also with one click, the administrator can enable access for a new employee.

As the vice president and general manager of Cisco's security technology unit states, "Securing the cloud is highly challenging. But it is one of the top challenges that the industry must rise to meet."

Questions for Critical Thinking

1. What are some advantages of storing data "in the cloud"? What are some disadvantages?
2. Why is it important to block a former employee's access to company data, e-mail, or applications?

Sources: Company Web site, *News@Cisco* press release, http://www.cisco.com, accessed June 4, 2010; James Urquhart, "Cloud Computing and the Economy," *CNET News,* April 13, 2010, http://news.cnet.com; Margaret Steen, "Cloud Services and SaaS: A Smarter Way to Do Business," *Cisco News,* March 29, 2010, http://newsroom.cisco.com; Stuart Young, Andy Taylor, and James Macaulay, "Small Businesses Ride the Cloud: SMB Cloud Watch—U.S. Survey Results," Cisco Internet Business Solutions Group, February 2010, http://www.cisco.com; Mike Kirkwood, "Rulers of the Cloud: Will Cloud Computing Be the Second Coming of Cisco?" *ReadWriteWeb,* February 19, 2010, http://www.readwriteweb.com.

---

grid computing consists of a network of smaller computers running special software.

Assessment Check ✔

1. What is an application service provider?
2. Explain on-demand computing.

The "Hit & Miss" feature describes how Cisco Systems provides security for cloud-based applications.

Small and medium-size companies occasionally find themselves with jobs that require more computing power than their current systems offer. A cost-effective solution for these firms may be something called **grid computing**, which consists of a network of smaller computers running special software. The software breaks down a large, complex job into smaller tasks and then distributes them to the networked computers. The software then reassembles the individual task results into the finished job. By combining multiple small computers, grid computing creates a virtual mainframe or even a supercomputer.

What's Ahead

This is the first of two chapters devoted to managing technology and information. The next chapter, "Using Accounting and Financial Information," focuses on accounting, financial information, and financing reporting. Accounting is the process of measuring, interpreting, and communicating financial information to enable people inside and outside the firm to make informed decisions. The chapter describes the functions of accounting and role of accountants; the steps in the accounting cycle; the types, functions, and components of financial statements; and the role of budgets in an organization.

⌐1¬ Distinguish between data and information, and explain the role of information systems in business.

It is important for businesspeople to know the difference between data and information. Data are raw facts and figures that may or may not be relevant to a business decision. Information is knowledge gained from processing those facts and figures. An information system is an organized method for collecting, storing, and communicating past, present, and projected information on internal operations and external intelligence. Most information systems today use computer and telecommunications technology.

Assessment Check Answers ✓

1.1 Distinguish between data and information. Data consist of raw facts and figures that may or may not be relevant to a decision. Information is the knowledge gained from processing data.

1.2 What is an information system? An information system is an organized method for collecting, storing, and communicating past, present, and projected information on internal operations and external intelligence.

⌐2¬ List the components and different types of information systems.

When people think about information systems today, they're generally thinking about computer-based systems, those that rely on computers and related technologies. Computer-based information systems rely on four components: computer hardware, software, telecommunications and computer networks, and data resource management. The heart of an information system is its database, a centralized integrated collection of data resources. Information systems fall into two broad categories: operational support systems and management support systems. Operational support systems are designed to produce a variety of information for users. Examples include transaction processing systems and process control systems. Management support systems are those designed to support effective decision making. They include management information systems, decision support systems, executive support systems, and expert systems.

Assessment Check Answers ✓

2.1 List the four components of a computer-based information system. The four components of a computer-based information system are computer hardware, software, telecommunications and computer networks, and data resource management.

2.2 What is a database? A database is a centralized, integrated collection of data resources.

2.3 What are the two general types of information systems? Give examples of each. The two categories of information systems are operational support systems (such as transactions processing and process control systems) and management support systems (such as management information, decision support, executive support, and expert systems).

⌐3¬ Outline how computer hardware and software are used to manage information.

Hardware consists of all tangible elements of a computer system, including input and output devices. Major categories of computers include mainframes, supercomputers, midrange systems, personal computers (PCs), and hand-held devices. Computer software provides the instructions that tell the hardware what to do. The software that controls the basic workings of the computer is its operating system. Other programs, called application software, perform specific tasks that users want to complete.

Assessment Check Answers ✓

3.1 List two input and output devices. Input devices include the keyboard and mouse. Output devices include the monitor and printer.

3.2 What accounts for the increasing popularity of notebook computers? Notebook computers account for more than half of all new personal computers sold. Their increased popularity is due to better displays, lower prices, more rugged designs, increasing computing power, and slimmer designs.

3.3 What is software? List the two categories of software. Computer software provides the instructions that tell the hardware what to do. The software that controls the basic workings of the computer is its operating system. Other programs, called application software, perform specific tasks that users want to complete.

⌐4¬ Describe networking and telecommunications technology and the types of computer networks.

Local area networks connect computers within a limited area. Wide area networks tie together larger geographical regions by using telephone lines, microwave, or satellite transmission. A wireless network allows computers to communicate through radio waves. Intranets allow employees to share information on a ready-made company network. Access to an intranet is restricted to authorized users and is protected by a firewall. Virtual private networks (VPNs) provide a secure Internet connection between two or more points. VoIP—voice over Internet protocol—uses a personal computer running special software and a broadband Internet connection to make and receive telephone calls over the Internet rather than over traditional telephone networks.

Assessment Check Answers ✓

4.1 What is a LAN? A local area network (LAN) is a computer network that connects machines within a limited area, such as a building or several nearby buildings.

4.2 What are the differences between an intranet and a VPN? An intranet is a computer network patterned after the Internet. Unlike the Internet, access to an intranet is limited to employees and other authorized users. A virtual private network (VPN) is a way of gaining increased security for Internet connections.

4.3 Briefly explain how VoIP works. The VoIP phone is connected to a personal computer with any type of broadband connection. Special software transmits phone conversations over the Internet. A VoIP user can make and receive calls to and from those with traditional telephone connections (either landline or wireless).

⌐5⌐ Discuss the security and ethical issues involving computer information systems.

Numerous security and ethical issues affect information systems. Two of the main security threats are e-crime and malware. E-crimes range from hacking—unauthorized penetration of an information system—to the theft of hardware. Malware is any malicious software program designed to infect computer systems. Examples include viruses, worms, botnets, Trojan horses, and spyware. Ethical issues affecting information systems include the proper use of the systems by authorized users. Organizations also have an obligation to employees, vendors, and customers to protect the security and confidentiality of the data stored in information systems.

Assessment Check Answers ✓

5.1 Explain computer hacking. Computer hacking is a breach of a computer system by unauthorized people. Sometimes the hackers' motive is just to see if they can get in. Other times, hackers have more sinister motives, including stealing or altering data.

5.2 What is malware? Malware is any malicious software program designed to infect computer systems.

5.3 How does a computer virus work? A virus is a program that secretly attaches itself to another program (called a host). The virus then changes the host, destroys data, or even makes the computer system inoperable.

⌐6⌐ Explain the steps that companies go through in anticipating, planning for, and recovering from information systems disasters.

Information system disasters, whether human caused or due to natural causes, can cost businesses billions of dollars. The consequences of a disaster can be minimized by routinely backing up software and data, both at an organizational level and at an individual level. Organizations should back up critical data at an off-site location. Some may also want to invest in extra hardware and software sites, which can be accessed during emergencies.

Assessment Check Answers ✓

6.1 What are the types of disasters to which information systems are vulnerable? Natural disasters, power failures, equipment malfunctions, software glitches, human error, and even terrorist attacks can disrupt even the most powerful, sophisticated computer information systems.

6.2 List the tasks regarding off-site data storage. The five tasks are planning and deciding which data to back up, establishing and following a backup schedule, protecting data when they are transmitted off site, choosing the right vendor, and continually testing and refining the backup system.

⌐7⌐ Review the current trends in information systems.

Information systems are continually and rapidly evolving. Some of the most significant trends are the increasing demands of the distributed workforce, the increased use of application service providers, on-demand computing, and grid computing. Many people now work in virtual offices, including at home. Information technology makes this possible. Application service providers allow organizations to outsource most of their IT functions. Rather than buying and maintaining expensive software, on-demand computing offers users the option of renting software time from outside vendors and paying only for their usage. Grid computing consists of a network of smaller computers running special software creating a virtual mainframe or even supercomputer.

Assessment Check Answers ✓

7.1 What is an application service provider? An application service provider (ASP) is an outside vendor that provides both the computers and application support for managing an information system. By using an ASP, the organization effectively outsources some, or all, of its IT function.

7.2 Explain on-demand computing. Instead of purchasing and maintaining expensive software, some organizations use on-demand computing. In this arrangement, software is rented from a vendor and the organization only pays for its actual usage.

▇ Business Terms you need to Know

data 468

information 468

information
  system 469

chief information
  officer (CIO) 469

computer-based
  information systems 469

database 470

operational
  support
  systems 472

transaction processing
  systems 472

process control
  systems 472

Review Questions

1. Distinguish between data and information. Why is the distinction important to businesspeople in their management of information?

2. What are the four components of an information system?

3. Describe the two different types of information systems, and give an example of how each might help a particular business.

4. Explain decision support systems, executive support systems, and expert systems.

5. What are the major categories of computers? What is a smart phone?

6. What is an intranet? Give specific examples of benefits for firms that set up their own intranets.

7. What steps can organizations and individuals take to prevent computer crime?

8. How does a computer virus work? What can individuals and organizational computer users do to reduce the likelihood of acquiring a computer virus?

9. Why is disaster recovery important for businesses? Relate your answer to a natural disaster such as a hurricane or fire.

10. Describe four information system trends.

Projects and Teamwork Applications

1. Suppose you've been hired to design an information system for a midsize retailer. Describe what that information system might look like, including the necessary components. Would the system be an operational support system, a management support system, or both?

2. Select a local company and contact the person in charge of its information system for a brief interview. Ask that individual to outline his or her company's information system. Also, ask the person what he or she likes most about the job. Did this interview make you more or less interested in a career in information systems?

3. Working with a partner, research the current status of Wi-Max. Prepare a short report on its growth, its current uses, and its future for business computing.

4. Your supervisor has asked your advice. She isn't sure the company's information system needs any elaborate safeguards because the company has little Web presence beyond a simple home page. However, employees use e-mail extensively to contact suppliers and customers. Make a list of the threats to which the company's information system is vulnerable. What types of safeguards would you suggest?

5. Has your computer ever been hacked or attacked by a virus? What steps did you take to recover lost files and data? How would you prevent something similar from happening again?

Web Assignments

1. **Operational support systems.** Go to the Web site listed below and click on "case studies." After reviewing the case study, prepare a brief report on what you learned about the advantages of operational support system software.

   https://h10078.www1.hp.com/cda/hpms/display/main/hpms content.jsp?zn=bto&cp=1-11-15-119^1195 4000 100

2. **Computer security.** Visit the Web site listed below. Review the material and answer the following questions:

   a. What are two current malware threats? How serious are they?

   b. What is a potentially unwanted program (PUP)? What are two recent PUPs?

   http://www.mcafee.com/us/threat center/default.asp

3. **Cloud computing.** IBM is one of the largest providers of so-called cloud computing. Visit the IBM Web site (http://www.ibm.com) and click on "solutions" and then "cloud computing." Print out the material and bring it to class to participate in a class discussion on the subject.

Note: Internet Web addresses change frequently. If you don't find the exact sites listed, you may need to access the organization's home page and search from there or use a search engine such as Bing or Google.

HP Rebounds Overseas

Just as the U.S. economy was tilting and some tech companies were sliding toward potential disaster, Hewlett-Packard (HP) surprised the experts by reporting substantial growth—in Brazil, China, India, Russia, and South Africa. In fact, the PC unit of the company reported sales growth of 24 percent during one quarter when other firms were posting flat growth or losses. Most of this revenue came from countries in which consumer markets are new and businesses are building their customer base. HP reported that 69 percent of its total revenue came from outside the United States, a significantly higher percentage than that of other high-tech firms. The four fastest-growing markets—Brazil, China, India, and Russia—accounted for a 35 percent jump in revenue.

But the African market has heads turning. HP Africa recently predicted growth of 25 percent per year for the next several years. Managing Director of HP Africa Rainer Koch explains the importance of that market, especially in light of a softer U.S. market and the amount of outsourcing occurring in India. "Because of outsourcing, salaries in India are skyrocketing, so I think you will see people recruiting in Africa," notes Koch. "Africa has a large English-speaking population and a large French-speaking population. I think it will really compete with India in 10 years." As global firms begin to hire qualified workers in Africa, they will need computers to conduct business. "In some places the market is exploding," he continues.

Despite some skepticism, Koch is optimistic about HP's future in Africa. "I was in Eastern Europe 15 years ago, and in some ways it is a similar picture. People thought things would never take off in Romania or Bulgaria, but they did." One important factor in the growth of technology and business throughout Africa is the introduction of cell phones, whose use has mushroomed over the last few years. Small businesses and average consumers now have an easier time with phone and Internet connections.

Africa's largest economy is South Africa, where the tech market is already well developed. But exciting opportunities are opening up in emerging, oil-rich countries such as Nigeria, Libya, Angola, and Ghana. All of these signs suggest a strong future for HP, which is making the most of its opportunities—and its own strengths—in overseas markets, where PCs and their accessories are newly in demand. "We like our position in many of the markets we are in," says CEO Mark Hurd. It's likely to get even stronger.

Questions for Critical Thinking

1. Visit the Hewlett-Packard Web site to learn more about its goods and services for a global market. In what ways do you think HP can serve small businesses in emerging countries in Africa, Asia, and South America? How might the company have to adapt to conditions in these countries?

2. How might HP have to adapt its products and business practices to succeed in countries like India, China, and South Africa? What about other nations?

Sources: "Hewlett-Packard Sees 'Exploding' Africa IT Growth," *Information Week,* April 22, 2008, www.google.com; Ryan Kim, "Chron 200: CEO of the Year," *San Francisco Chronicle,* April 20, 2008, www.google.com; Louise Lee, "HP's International Appeal," *BusinessWeek,* February 19, 2008, http://www.businessweek.com; Spencer Ante, "HP: A Steady Ship in Troubled Waters," *BusinessWeek,* November 20, 2007, http://www.businessweek.com.

Businesses both large and small, as well as most people with home computers or smart phones, have had unfortunate experiences with computer viruses. Once a virus has infiltrated a network or a device—a computer, tablet, PDA, or cell phone—it replicates and begins causing irritating slowdowns or worse, destroying data or stealing a user's identity.

Of the many software programs designed to catch and/or stop viruses and worms, those produced by Kaspersky Lab are among the most popular and the most effective. The company was founded by Russian-born Eugene Kaspersky. Kaspersky, an engineer, became interested in computer viruses when his own computer was attacked by the notorious Cascade virus in 1989. He developed a disinfection utility for it, then went on to compile a catalog of viruses and disinfection utilities. This database now includes 4 million entries. In 1997, he and several colleagues founded Kaspersky Lab.

With headquarters in Moscow and branches worldwide, the company has won many awards for its antivirus software packages. Only four years after establishing a presence in the Americas, Kaspersky Lab won an award for best e-mail security system. Today, Kaspersky Lab is the world's largest privately held antimalware company, with products for both corporate networks and home PC users in almost every country in the world. More than 300 million users rely on Kaspersky products for their security, and 150,000 new users join them every week.

One of Kaspersky Lab's success stories involves the Austrian National Tourist Office, the country's official tourist organization. It has 250 employees in 30 offices in Austria and in cities around the world, including New York, Sydney, Beijing, and Singapore. The tourist office's international Web site has pages in many languages and showcases Austria's many attractions for visitors. The office's travel services are Web based, and its employees rely constantly on the Internet for online research and e-mail from their colleagues in different branches. Well aware of the growing worldwide risk of viruses and other malware, the tourist office decided it needed a better security system.

The tourist office consulted the Austrian IT subsidiary Austrian Info Systems GmbH, which decided that the best solution would be to adopt the entire range of products in the Kaspersky Anti-Virus Business Optimal package. From the tourist bureau's home office in Vienna, the Kaspersky Administration Kit runs centralized monitoring and administration of all the office's servers and all of its antivirus protection. Other Kaspersky antivirus utilities protect all of the 250 workstations worldwide, the 25 file servers, and the 550 mailboxes making up the exchange infrastructure. A free administration kit helps Austrian Info Systems make regular searches of the tourist office's network for viruses.

For the home computer user, Kaspersky Lab offers programs that help prevent various forms of identity theft; offer protection against viruses, Trojan horses, spyware, and so on; and scan Web sites for malware. As more Mac users store data in the "cloud," on Internet servers, their computers can also become infected with viruses and other malware, so Kaspersky Lab also offers a Mac version of its antivirus software. And as smart phone users increasingly use their hand-held devices as PCs, they have a mobile security program as well.

As the company celebrated its 12th anniversary recently, its Web site declared that its "most valuable asset is the wealth of experience and knowledge it has gained in . . . combating viruses and other IT threats, enabling us to pre-empt trends in malware development. This helps us to remain one step ahead of the competition and provide our users with the most reliable protection from new types of attack."

Questions for Critical Thinking

1. Why is it so important for Kaspersky Lab—as a business—to stay ahead of new computer threats?

2. How do you protect your own computer or hand-held device from viruses and other malware? What steps would you take to improve your protection?

Sources: Company Web site, http://usa.kaspersky.com, accessed May 24, 2010; Austrian National Tourist Office Web site, http://www.austria.info, accessed May 24, 2010; Maxine Cheung, "Kaspersky CMO Outlines New Partner Initiatives and Resources," IT Business Canada, February 18, 2010, http://www.itbusiness.ca.

When you need a car, you want one. When you don't need a car, you don't want to be bothered with the hassle or the expense. That's what makes Zipcar so great. Zipcar is a car-sharing network based in Cambridge, Massachusetts that operates in urban and metropolitan areas and on university campuses around the U.S., Canada, and the United Kingdom. Currently, Zipcar serves more than 200 colleges and universities, and the number is growing steadily. "The service provides a new level of freedom for students, faculty, and staff," says Matthew Malloy, vice-president of international university operations for Zipcar. "Members can use Zipcars to run errands, attend meetings, or get away for the weekend on a pay-as-you-go basis. You no longer need to own to be free."

Once members sign up for the program, they receive a Zipcard that gives them access to any Zipcar parked around campus (or around town). The annual fee for the service is $35, and it includes fuel, insurance, and 180 travel miles per day. A member who wants to use a Zipcar simply goes online to reserve it, then picks up the designated car at the reserved time. "It's easy," says Erin Badger, a senior marketing student at the University of New Hampshire, where the Zipcar program is now in full swing. "You swipe your Zipcard [over a sensor] on the windshield and it unlocks the car. You get in, turn the key, and go." Each Zipcar comes equipped with an individually numbered Zipcard gas card that the driver uses to fill the tank with fuel. So members—especially budget-conscious students—don't need cash or their own credit cards when the gas gauge runs low. Members are asked to return each car with at least one-quarter of a tank of gas in it, so no one picks up a car with an empty tank.

Technology plays a huge role in the success of the Zipcar system. "When you think about the member experience, what makes it a seamless and enjoyable experience for the consumer is the technology infrastructure," observes Rob Weisberg, chief marketing officer at Zipcar. When marketing and setting up the system at colleges and universities,

Zipcar looks at how students use cars on campus, asking such questions as: Are there places on campus where use is more frequent, or do students want hybrids? "Any time you understand your consumers better, you are able to cater to them more effectively," says Weisberg. He notes that Zipcar puts a lot of effort into understanding demographic and psychographic (life style) trends on and around a campus.

Erin Badger likes the fact that she can use her iPhone app to reserve a Zipcar or extend the reservation if she is driving a car and isn't ready to return it. "The iPhone app relates to the student age group," she says. "They care about us." The Zipcar app was named to *Time* magazine's annual list of "Best Travel Gadgets" in one recent issue. "Beyond helping you manage reservations, find nearby pickup locations and browse car models available, the app offers clever capabilities like remote locking and unlocking and honking your car's horn from your phone when you inevitably forget what it looks like in a crowded lot," praises the *Time* review.

Zipcar is always looking toward the future and ways to better serve its customers. Rob Weisberg predicts that eventually Zipcar technology will allow for customized seat settings and even pre-set radio station settings that automatically click into place when a member reserves a car. Still, Weisberg emphasizes the importance of the personal touch. He recalls that when a student member posted a note on Twitter joking that he loved everything about Zipcar except the fact that there wasn't a package of Skittles waiting for him when he unlocked the car, a Zipcar employee left a package of Skittles on the dashboard the next time the student reserved a car.

"Technology will never replace human interaction," warns Weisberg. "You'd never take the recommendation of a computer over the recommendation of a friend or family member or colleague. So our laser focus on the customer experience and ensuring that it is second to none is really where we need to play. Technology enables that, but it's never going to replace the human touch."

Questions for Critical Thinking

1. Through member surveys and social media postings, Zipcar collects information about members and their lifestyles in order to design the best system for a community. Write ten questions that you think might elicit useful information for Zipcar about students at your own college or university.

2. What kind of data would Zipcar's operational support systems likely collect? What kind of information might they provide?

3. The Zipcar iPhone app already takes care of several tasks. If you were a Zipcar member, what new task would you add to the app?

4. Do you think your campus would be a good candidate for the Zipcar system? Why or why not? If your college or university already has Zipcar, are you a member? Why or why not?

Sources: Zipcar Web site, http://www.zipcar.com, accessed August 26, 2010; "Zipcar and SCVNGR, East Cambridge Neighbors, Partner on New Rewards Program," *Boston.com,* August 26, 2010, http://www.boston.com; "Zipcar, Inc.," *Bloomberg Business Week,* http://investing.businessweek.com, accessed August 24, 2010; University of New Hampshire Transportation Services, http://www.unh.edu/transportation, accessed August 24, 2010; PeterHa, "The Best Travel Gadgets of 2009," *Time,* November 2, 2009, http://www.time.com.

The Dog Ate My Laptop

The night of the tornado, Superintendent of Schools Darin Headrick heard the storm sirens go off on his way home from work. He stopped at the home of High School Principal Randy Fulton and the two men headed for the basement, just in case. The next thing they knew, the entire school system was gone. Textbooks were scattered everywhere, computers destroyed.

For the first three months after the storm, no one could live in town. People stayed in shelters or with friends and family outside of town. No one had a home phone anymore, but people were eager to connect with each other and find out what was happening. Although the Federal Emergency Management Agency (FEMA) was distributing information at checkpoints on the edges of town, people had to go to town to get it.

Like 95 percent of the town's 1,500 residents, Headrick himself was homeless. With just four months to rebuild an entire school system, all he had were his laptop and cell phone, so he got into his truck and began searching for a wireless signal. Taking a lesson from his students, he used text messaging to distribute information. Although very few people still had computers, almost everyone had a cell phone. Residents who subscribed to the text service could receive updates and instant messages over the phone, wherever they were.

Rebuilding the schools was a bigger task. Headrick secured temporary trailers for grades K–12 and received generous donations of desks and school supplies. By August 15, he had the basics needed to start the school year, but he still lacked textbooks. Technology would have to fill in the gaps, so the students didn't fall behind.

One of the school system's existing programs was ITV, for Interactive Distance Learning Network. ITV allowed Greensburg's rural schools to log in to classrooms around the state via Web cam. This type of real-time distance learning is referred to as *synchronous learning*, as opposed to the asynchronous online courses given on college campuses. After the tornado, all that was needed to get the program up and running again were a computer, an Internet connection, and a Web cam.

Early in the winter each of Greensburg High's students got an unexpected gift: a laptop computer containing e-books, handwriting recognition software, and a tablet screen for note taking. The new laptops replaced their tattered textbooks. Students would hand in their assignments via e-mail and receive feedback from their teachers via instant messaging.

Questions

After viewing the video, answer the following questions:

1. Was Greensburg Public Schools' investment in technology a smart move?
2. Would you consider enrolling in an asynchronous online course? What might be the benefits and drawbacks?
3. Do you think hand-held devices and text messaging improve productivity and communication or distract their users?

LAUNCHING YOUR
[Information Technology and Accounting Career]

Part 5, "Managing Technology and Information," includes Chapters 14 and 15, which discuss using computers and related technology to manage information and accounting and financial statements. In Chapter 14, we discussed well-known technology companies such as Google and Oracle, as well as a host of smaller organizations that use computer technology to manage information. In Chapter 15, you read about accounting firms such as Ernst & Young and a variety of public and private organizations, large and small, that generate and use accounting data. These examples illustrate that all organizations need to manage technology and information. And with the complexity and scope of technology and information likely to increase in the years ahead, the demand for accounting and information systems professionals is expected to grow.

According to the U.S. Department of Labor, employment in occupations such as accounting, auditing, computer software engineering and support specialists, and network systems administrators is expected to grow faster than the average for all occupations in the next decade. In fact, two of the top five occupations in which employment is expected to grow the fastest over the next few years are related to information systems.[1] In addition, recent graduates

with bachelor's degrees in accounting and information systems have among the highest average starting salaries of all business graduates. The median annual salary for accountants and auditors is almost $60,000, with the top 10 percent earning about $102,000.[2] Salaries in information systems vary widely based on education and experience. But starting salaries for computer science graduates average $61,000.[3] Those who are information systems managers earn about $112,000 per year.[4]

What types of jobs are available in information systems and accounting? What are the working conditions like? What are the career paths? Information systems and accounting are both fairly broad occupations and encompass a wide variety of jobs. In some cases you'll work in the accounting or information systems department of a business such as Procter & Gamble or Shell. In other cases, you'll work for a specialized accounting or information systems firm, such as PricewaterhouseCoopers or IBM, that provides these services to governments, not-for-profit organizations, and businesses.

Accounting and information systems are popular business majors, and many entry-level positions are available each year. For instance, many accounting graduates start their careers working for a public

accounting firm. Initially, their job duties involve auditing or tax services, usually working with more senior accountants. As their careers progress, accounting graduates take on more and more supervisory responsibilities. Some may move from public accounting firms to take accounting positions at other organizations. Many accounting and information systems graduates spend their entire careers in these fields, while others move into other areas. People who began their careers in accounting or information systems are well represented in the ranks of senior management today. Let's look briefly at some of the specific jobs you might find after earning a degree in accounting or information systems.

Public accountants perform a broad range of accounting, auditing, tax, and consulting services for their clients, which include businesses, governments, not-for-profit organizations, and individuals. Auditing is one of the most important services offered by public accountants, and many accounting graduates begin their careers in this field. Auditors examine a client's financial statements and accounting procedures to make sure they conform with all applicable laws and regulations. Public accountants either own their own businesses or work for public accounting firms. Many public accountants are certified public accountants (CPAs). To become a CPA, you have to meet educational and experience requirements and pass a comprehensive examination.

Management accountants work for an organization other than a public accounting firm. They record and analyze financial information and financial statements for their organizations. Management accountants are also involved in budgeting, tax preparation, cost management, and asset management. Internal auditors verify the accuracy of their organization's internal controls and check for irregularities, waste, and fraud.

Technical support specialists are troubleshooters who monitor the performance of computer systems; provide technical support and solve problems for computer users; install, modify, clean, and repair computer hardware and software; and write training manuals and train computer users.

Network administrators design, install, and support an organization's computer networks, including its local area network, wide area network, Internet, and intranet systems. They provide administrative support for software and hardware users and ensure that the design of an organization's computer networks and all of the components fit together efficiently and effectively.

Computer security specialists plan, coordinate, and implement an organization's information security. They educate users about how to protect computer systems, install antivirus and similar software, and monitor the networks for security breaches. In recent years, the role and importance of computer security specialists have increased in response to the growing number of attacks on networks and data.

Career Assessment Exercises in Information Systems and Accounting

1. The American Institute of Certified Public Accountants is a professional organization dedicated to the enhancement of the public accounting profession. Visit the organization's Web site (http://www.aicpa.org). Review the information on CPA standards and examinations. Write a brief summary on what you learned about how to become a CPA.

2. Assume you're interested in a career as a systems administrator. Go to the following Web site: http://www.sage.org. Prepare a brief report outlining the responsibilities of a systems administrator, who hires for these positions, and what kind of educational background you need to become one.

3. Identify a person working in your local area in the accounting field and arrange an interview with that person (your college career center may be able to help you). Ask that person about his or her job responsibilities, educational background, and the best and worst aspects of his or her job as an accountant.

PART [6]

Best Financial Practices

[Chapter 15]

Using Accounting and
Financial Information

[Chapter 16]

Today's Financial
Markets and
Institutions

[Chapter 17]

Managing the Firm's
Financial Resources

Learning Objectives

[1] Explain the functions of accounting, and identify the three basic activities involving accounting.

[2] Describe the roles played by public, management, government, and not-for-profit accountants.

[3] Identify the foundations of the accounting system, including GAAP and the role of the Financial Accounting Standards Board (FASB).

[4] Outline the steps in the accounting cycle, and define *double-entry bookkeeping* and the *accounting equation.*

[5] Explain the functions and major components of the four principal financial statements: the balance sheet, the income statement, the statement of owners' equity, and the statement of cash flows.

[6] Discuss how financial ratios are used to analyze a company's financial strengths and weaknesses.

[7] Describe the role of budgets in a business.

[8] Outline accounting issues facing global business and the move toward one set of worldwide accounting rules.

Using Accounting and Financial Information

Mark-to-Market Accounting: Who Takes the Hit?

Small business owners, everyday investors, and those with pension or retirement funds are rightfully worried about the value of their holdings these days. Certain accounting rules and practices receive extra scrutiny when markets nosedive. One of those rules, known as *mark-to-market accounting*, values the assets on a company's balance sheet based on their current, fair market value—if they were to be sold that day—not to the price that was paid for them. This accounting rule, formally known as Financial Accounting Standard No. 157, is overseen by the Financial Accounting Standards Board (FASB) and enforced by the Securities and Exchange Commission (SEC). The rule was adopted in the wake of the collapse of the savings-and-loan industry in the 1980s. Its goal was to create more accurate, reliable reporting by banks and financial institutions in particular, although it affects other organizations as well. But critics see problems with the mark-to-market rules, and banks are probably the hardest hit by what many experts believe are weak points in the regulations. When the value of an asset such as a home drops or a loan holder defaults, according to mark-to-market rules a bank must mark down the value of those assets, even though the value might increase later. Some industry experts believe that tying an asset to the market is not necessarily the best way to establish its value. Further complicating the situation is that not every type of investment instrument, such as those involving home mortgages, is traded every day. But they must be lumped in with those that are traded daily. So banks are forced to hold essentially worthless assets that they can't sell in the collapsed market. As a result, some argued that today's financial climate demanded that FAS 157 should be suspended or at least modified. "The current framework for accounting oversight, though well intentioned, has proved inadequate and must be fundamentally revised," noted Ed Yingling, president of the American Bankers Association. Even banks that were hardest hit by the credit crisis and the consequences of having to apply the mark-to-market rules to their balance sheets said that they could live with a revision instead of an outright abandonment of the accounting law. "Most of the banks that are hurting—if they were allowed to let these loans work themselves out over time as opposed to being forced to write them down and liquidate them—they would survive just fine," remarks Michael Chaffin, CEO and president of the First Choice Community Bank in Georgia. "It's just common sense," he argues. "We're throwing billions and even trillions of dollars into a hole that we could plug if we just adjusted accounting standards temporarily. I'm not saying give it to us forever." Chaffin pointed out that community banks like his were not the ones involved in making risky mortgage loans—yet his bank suffered because of the housing industry's downturn and the accounting rules apply to all.

Yet those on the other side of the debate believe that mark-to-market accounting practices are fair and valid. They argued that any temporary gains made by relaxing the rules would just delay the problem of valuing mortgage investments and create more doubt. Some maintained that the mark-to-market rules actually benefit investors. "I think that mark-to-market [accounting] does help the investor," said Conrad Hewitt, former chief accountant for the SEC. "Mark-to-market brought to focus the problems we have had in our financial institutions much faster." Despite requests to repeal the rule before he left office, Hewitt declined to do so.

To resolve the issue, legislation was proposed to create a new federal oversight agency that would make the ultimate decision about accounting practices. The proposed Federal Accounting Oversight Board (FAOB) would not replace the FASB but would approve the standards being set and decide how they would be applied. The new five-member board would include top officials from the Federal Reserve, the U.S. Treasury, the SEC, the Federal Deposit Insurance Corporation, and the Public Company Oversight Board. If you think this sounds like another layer of government bureaucracy, you are not alone. In addition, critics charged that creating a new board would dilute the authority of the SEC and FASB, undermining the government's efforts to stabilize the financial sector of the U.S. economy. Meanwhile, as bankers and lawmakers continued to press hard for changes in the mark-to market regulations, the FASB finally agreed to relax the rules—at least temporarily. Starting in the second quarter of 2009, bank managers were allowed to value their assets according to what they would go for in an "orderly" sale, not one forced in a distressed market. Still, some critics said the changes did not go far enough, while others said they only clouded the true picture of the banking industry. This issue will no doubt raise itself again.[1]

accounting process of measuring, interpreting, and communicating financial information to support internal and external business decision making.

Accounting professionals prepare the financial information that organizations present in their annual reports. Whether you begin your career by working for a company or by starting your own firm, you need to understand what accountants do and why their work is so important in contemporary business.

Accounting is the process of measuring, interpreting, and communicating financial information to enable people inside and outside the firm to make informed decisions. In many ways, accounting is the language of business. Accountants gather, record, report, and interpret financial information in a way that describes the status and operation of an organization and aids in decision making.

Millions of men and women throughout the world describe their occupation as accountant. In the United States alone more than 1.3 million people work as accountants. According to the Bureau of Labor Statistics, the number of accounting-related jobs is expected to increase by around 22 percent between now and 2018, a much faster rate of growth than the average for all occupations.[2]

The availability of jobs and relatively high starting salaries for talented graduates—starting salaries for accounting graduates average just under $50,000 per year—have made accounting one of the most in-demand majors on college campuses. After the recent financial downturn, hiring levels fell, but the most recent report estimates that firms will hire 5.3 percent more accounting graduates this year over last year.[3]

This chapter begins by describing who uses accounting information. It discusses business activities involving accounting statements: financing, investing, and operations. It explains the accounting process, defines double-entry bookkeeping, and presents the accounting equation. We then discuss the development of financial statements from information about financial transactions. The methods of interpreting these statements and the roles of budgeting in planning and controlling a business are described next. The chapter concludes with a discussion of the development and implementation schedule of a uniform set of accounting rules for global business.

Users of Accounting Information

People both inside and outside an organization rely on accounting information to help them make business decisions. Figure 15.1 lists the users of accounting information and the applications they find for that information.

Managers with a business, government agency, or not-for-profit organization are the major users of accounting information, because it helps them plan and control daily and long-range operations. Business owners and boards of directors of not-for-profit groups also rely on accounting data to determine how well managers are operating the organizations. Union officials use accounting data in contract negotiations, and employees refer to it as they monitor their firms' productivity and profitability performance.

To help employees understand how their work affects the bottom line, many companies share sensitive financial information with their employees and teach them how to understand and use financial statements. Proponents of what is often referred to as *open book management* believe that allowing employees to view financial information helps them better understand how their work contributes to the company's success, which, in turn, benefits them.

Outside a firm, potential investors evaluate accounting information to help them decide whether to buy a firm's stock. As we'll discuss in more detail later in the chapter, any company whose stock is traded publicly is required to report its financial results on a regular basis. So anyone, for example, can find out what Home Depot's sales were last year or how much money Research in Motion made during the last quarter. Bankers and other lenders use accounting information to evaluate a potential borrower's financial soundness. The Internal Revenue Service (IRS) and state tax officials use it to determine a company's tax liability. Citizens' groups and government agencies use such information in assessing the efficiency of operations such as Massachusetts General Hospital; the Topeka, Kansas, school system; Community College of Denver; and the Art Institute of Chicago.

Accountants play fundamental roles not only in business but also in other aspects of society. Their work influences each of the business environments discussed earlier in this book. They clearly contribute important information to help managers deal with the competitive and economic environments.

Less obvious contributions help others understand, predict, and react to the technological, regulatory, and social and cultural environments. For instance, thousands of people volunteer each year to help people with their taxes. One of the largest organized programs is Tax-Aide, sponsored by AARP (formally known as the American Association of Retired Persons). Its program has in excess of 34,000 IRS-trained volunteers helping low- and middle-income persons over 60 file their state and federal tax returns. More than 2.6 million clients used the free service in one recent year.[4]

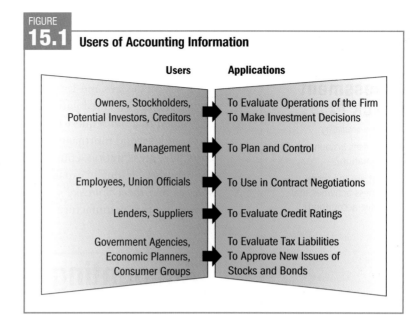

FIGURE 15.1 Users of Accounting Information

Users	Applications
Owners, Stockholders, Potential Investors, Creditors	To Evaluate Operations of the Firm To Make Investment Decisions
Management	To Plan and Control
Employees, Union Officials	To Use in Contract Negotiations
Lenders, Suppliers	To Evaluate Credit Ratings
Government Agencies, Economic Planners, Consumer Groups	To Evaluate Tax Liabilities To Approve New Issues of Stocks and Bonds

Accountants play a fundamental role in business and other areas of society by providing services to businesses, individuals, government agencies, and not-for-profit organizations.

Kathleen Finlay/Masterfile

Business Activities Involving Accounting

The natural progression of a business begins with financing. Subsequent steps, including investing, lead to operating the business. All organizations, profit oriented and not-for-profit, perform these three basic activities, and accounting plays a key role in each one:

1. Financing activities provide necessary funds to start a business and expand it after it begins operating.

2. Investing activities provide valuable assets required to run a business.

3. Operating activities focus on selling goods and services, but they also consider expenses as important elements of sound financial management.

Ken Solinsky, the president of New Hampshire-based Insight Technology Inc., performed all three activities during the start-up and growth of his specialized-imaging company. The accounting firm Ernst & Young recently named him Entrepreneur of the Year in Distribution and Manufacturing. Solinsky's company provides such products as night-vision devices and laser range-finding systems for the U.S. military, federal law enforcement, and allied nations. A year after Solinsky and his wife founded Insight, they responded to a bid request from the U.S. government for infrared equipment. Solinsky took out a second mortgage on his house and maxed out his credit cards to pay production costs. His presentation, conducted in rented office space, won Insight the contract, and the company has gradually expanded its range of products. To ensure the availability of supply sources that meet Solinsky's high standards, the company has purchased and formed several companies that manufacture the precision optical equipment its products require.[5]

Assessment Check ✔

1. Define *accounting*.

2. Who uses accounting information?

3. What are the three business activities that involve accounting?

Accounting Professionals

Accounting professionals work in a variety of areas in and for business firms, government agencies, and not-for-profit organizations. They can be classified as public, management, government, and not-for-profit accountants.

Public Accountants

A **public accountant** provides accounting services to individuals or business firms for a fee. Most public accounting firms provide three basic services to clients: (1) auditing, or examining, financial records; (2) tax preparation, planning, and related services; and (3) management consulting. Because public accountants are not employees of a client firm, they can provide unbiased advice about the firm's financial condition.

While there are hundreds of public accounting firms in the United States, a handful of firms dominate the industry. The four largest public accounting firms—Deloitte & Touche, Ernst & Young, KPMG, and PricewaterhouseCoopers (PwC)—collect almost $32 billion annually from U.S. clients alone. In contrast, the Minneapolis-based RSM McGladrey, the nation's fifth-largest accounting firm, has annual revenues of approximately $1.5 billion.[6]

Some years ago, public accounting firms came under sharp criticism for providing management consulting services to many of the same firms they audited. Critics argued that when a public accounting firm does both—auditing and management consulting—an inherent conflict of interest is created. In addition, this conflict of interest may undermine confidence in the quality of the financial statements accounting firms audit. The bankruptcies of some high-profile firms increased pressure on public accounting firms to end the practice. Legislation also established strict limits on the types of consulting services auditors can provide. For example, an accounting firm that audits a company's books cannot provide any other services to that company, including tax services. As a result, three of the four largest public accounting firms either sold large portions of their consulting practices or spun them off into separate companies, and they now concentrate on providing auditing and tax services. PwC, for instance, sold much of its consulting business to IBM.

As the "Hit & Miss" feature outlines, a growing number of public accountants are also certified as *forensic accountants*, and some smaller public accounting firms actually specialize in forensic accounting. These professionals, and the firms that employ them, focus on uncovering potential fraud in a variety of organizations.

public accountant
accountant who provides accounting services to other organizations.

Forensic Accountants: Fraud Busters

When most people think of accountants, the image that probably comes to mind is that of someone poring over stacks of ledgers or computer printouts, calculator in hand. Although a good deal of accounting does involve ledgers and printouts, forensic accountants don't simply accept a company's numbers at face value—they are crime fighters. People who work in this growing field investigate such white-collar crimes as business fraud, improper financial reporting, and illegal investment schemes.

Forensic accounting is accounting performed in preparation for legal review. Forensic accountants take the skeptical view, investigating below the surface of an organization's accounting system to find out what actually happened. They may also testify as expert witnesses if a case goes to trial. The job requires a bachelor's degree in accounting and CPA certification, with further training in investigative techniques for certification as a certified fraud examiner (CFE) or a certified forensic accountant (CrFA).

When the energy giant Enron Corporation collapsed, forensic accounting investigations revealed that for several years, company executives had issued false financial statements that exaggerated the company's earnings and thereby increased the firm's stock prices. The statements painted a rosy picture of steady profits that met earnings expectations. In reality, Enron's own investments were doing badly, and its profits were nonexistent. The company was actually losing money. Even after the truth began to leak out and the company's stock prices fell, the executives continued to issue false financial statements in the hope of slowing the fall. In a federal trial, two former executives were convicted of conspiracy, wire fraud, and securities fraud.

Tracy Coenen, a forensic accountant and the head of Milwaukee-based Sequence Inc., says, "Some people say I have a nose for fraud. . . . The more complicated the puzzle, the better I like it."

Questions for Critical Thinking

1. Describe how a shift in the economy has created a new career path for accounting students.

2. How might forensic accounting change the world of business?

Sources: "Forensic Accounting," PricewaterhouseCoopers New Zealand, http://www.pwc.com/nz, accessed June 1, 2010; Tracy L. Coenen, "Enron: The Good, the Bad, and the Ugly," Sequence Inc., http://www.sequence-inc.com, accessed June 1, 2010; James A. DiGabriele, "Applying Forensic Skepticism to Lost Profits Valuations," *Journal of Accountancy*, April 2010, http://www.journalofaccountancy.com; Bob Trompeter, "Why Do You Need a Forensic Accountant Hired Gun?" Hutson Resource Group, February 23, 2010, http://hutsonresourcegroup.com; Rick Romell, "Accountants Who Focus on Fraud," *Milwaukee Journal Sentinel*, January 24, 2010, http://www.jsonline.com.

Certified public accountants (CPAs) demonstrate their accounting knowledge by meeting state requirements for education and experience and successfully completing a number of rigorous tests in accounting theory and practice, auditing, law, and taxes. Other accountants who meet specified educational and experience requirements and pass certification exams carry the title *certified management accountant, certified fraud examiner*, or *certified internal auditor*.

Management Accountants

An accountant employed by a business other than a public accounting firm is called a *management accountant*. Such a person collects and records financial transactions and prepares financial statements used by the firm's managers in decision making. Management accountants provide timely, relevant, accurate, and concise information that executives can use to operate their firms more effectively and more profitably than they could without this input. In addition to preparing financial statements, a management accountant plays a major role in interpreting them. A management accountant should provide answers to many important questions:

- Where is the company going?

- What opportunities await it?

- Do certain situations expose the company to excessive risk?

- Does the firm's information system provide detailed and timely information to all levels of management?

Management accountants frequently specialize in different aspects of accounting. A cost accountant, for example, determines the cost of goods and services and helps set their prices.

An internal auditor examines the firm's financial practices to ensure that its records include accurate data and that its operations comply with federal, state, and local laws and regulations. A tax accountant works to minimize a firm's tax bill and assumes responsibility for its federal, state, county, and city tax returns. Some management accountants achieve a *certified management accountant (CMA)* designation through experience and passing a comprehensive examination.

Management accountants are usually involved in the development and enforcement of organizational policies on such items as employee travel. As part of their job, many employees travel and accumulate airline frequent flyer miles and hotel reward points. While some organizations have strict policies over the personal use of travel perks, many do not.

Changing federal regulations affecting accounting and public reporting have increased the demand for management accountants in recent years. As a result, salaries for these professionals are rising.

Government and Not-for-Profit Accountants

Federal, state, and local governments also require accounting services. Government accountants and those who work for not-for-profit organizations perform professional services similar to those of management accountants. Accountants in these sectors concern themselves primarily with determining how efficiently the organizations accomplish their objectives. Among the many government agencies that employ accountants are the National Aeronautics and Space Administration, the Federal Bureau of Investigation, the Internal Revenue Service, the Commonwealth of Pennsylvania, and the City of Fresno, California. The federal government alone employs thousands of accountants.

Not-for-profit organizations, such as churches, labor unions, charities, schools, hospitals, and universities, also hire accountants. In fact, the not-for-profit sector is one of the fastest growing segments of accounting practice. An increasing number of not-for-profits publish financial information because contributors want more accountability from these organizations and are interested in knowing how the groups spend the money that they raise.

The Foundation of the Accounting System

To provide reliable, consistent, and unbiased information to decision makers, accountants follow guidelines, or standards, known as <u>**generally accepted accounting principles (GAAP)**</u>. These principles encompass the conventions, rules, and procedures for determining acceptable accounting and financial reporting practices at a particular time.

All GAAP standards are based on four basic principles: consistency, relevance, reliability, and comparability. Consistency means that all data should be collected and presented in the same manner across all periods. Any change in the way in which specific data are collected or presented must be noted and explained. Relevance states that all information being reported should be appropriate and assist users in evaluating that information. Reliability implies that the accounting data presented in financial statements are reliable and can be verified by an independent party such as an outside auditor. Finally, comparability ensures that one firm's financial statements can be compared with those of similar businesses. In the United States, the <u>**Financial Accounting Standards Board (FASB)**</u> is primarily responsible for evaluating, setting, or modifying GAAP. The U.S. Securities and Exchange Commission (SEC), the chief federal regulator of the financial markets and accounting industry, actually has the

Assessment Check ✔

1. List the three services offered by public accounting firms.
2. What tasks do management accountants perform?

generally accepted accounting principles (GAAP) principles that encompass the conventions, rules, and procedures for determining acceptable accounting practices at a particular time.

Financial Accounting Standards Board (FASB) organization that interprets and modifies GAAP in the United States.

statutory authority to establish financial accounting and reporting standards for publicly held companies. (A publicly held company is one whose stock is publicly traded in a market such as the New York Stock Exchange.) However, the SEC's policy has been to rely on the accounting industry for this function, as long as the SEC believes the private sector is operating in the public interest. Consequently, the Financial Accounting Foundation—an organization made up of members of many different professional groups—actually appoints the members (currently five) of FASB, although the SEC does have some input. Board members are all experienced accounting professionals and serve five-year terms. They may be reappointed for a second five-year term. Board members must sever all connections with the firms they served prior to joining the board. The board is supported by a professional staff of more than 60 individuals.[7]

The FASB carefully monitors changing business conditions, enacting new rules and modifying existing rules when necessary. It also considers input and requests from all segments of its diverse constituency, including corporations and the SEC. One major change in accounting rules recently dealt with executive and employee stock options. Stock options give the holder the right to buy stock at a fixed price. The FASB now requires firms that give employees stock options to calculate the cost of the options and treat the cost as an expense, similar to salaries.

In response to well-known cases of accounting fraud, and questions about the independence of auditors, the Sarbanes-Oxley Act—commonly known as SOX—created the Public Accounting Oversight Board. The five-member board has the power to set audit standards and to investigate and sanction accounting firms that certify the books of publicly traded firms. Members of the Public Accounting Oversight Board are appointed by the SEC. No more than two of the five members of the board can be certified public accountants.

In addition to creating the Public Accounting Oversight Board, SOX also added to the reporting requirements for publicly traded companies. Senior executives including the CEO and chief financial officer (CFO), for example, must personally certify that the financial information reported by

BusinessEtiquette

Tips for Foreign Corrupt Practices Act Compliance

The Foreign Corrupt Practices Act is intended to prevent the bribery of foreign officials for the purpose of gaining or keeping business in another country. As more companies do business overseas, they are naturally concerned about becoming vulnerable to violations of this law. Federal enforcement of this act is at an all-time high and is expected to remain so. Penalties are severe and can include fines and imprisonment for anyone convicted. The Securities and Exchange Commission and the Department of Justice also expect strict compliance. The following are some ways that global firms can improve their compliance and mitigate risk:

1 Assess your firm's Foreign Corrupt Practices Act risk country by country. Does your firm do business with any state-owned foreign firms or foreign government officials? What risk is there of corruption and bribery?

2 Establish a Foreign Corrupt Practices Act compliance policy for your firm's employees in the United States and abroad. The policy should cover gifts and payments to foreign officials, charitable donations, accurate and complete records, and other areas vulnerable to risk.

3 Train your employees in the Foreign Corrupt Practices Act policy, and integrate it into your company's overall compliance. Have your HR department make it part of new-employee orientation.

4 Have a Foreign Corrupt Practices Act compliance team in place to monitor compliance and signal potential risks. The team should include company lawyers, accountants, and auditors and should be able to make both in-house and external investigations.

5 Plan any international investigations carefully. Many foreign countries do not recognize the attorney–client privilege as applying to company lawyers and employees.

Sources: "Foreign Corrupt Practices Act," Ernst & Young, http://www.ey.com, accessed June 1, 2010; U.S. Department of Justice, "Foreign Corrupt Practices Act: An Overview," http://www.justice.gov, accessed June 1, 2010; Gary Sturisky, "2010 Compliance Challenges: Three More Areas That Matter," *Corporate Compliance Insights*, March 4, 2010, http://www.corporatecomplianceinsights.com; Brian Loughman, Aaron Marcu, and Kerry Schalders, "Top Ten Tips for FCPA Compliance," Association of Corporate Counsel, March 1, 2010, http://www.acc.com; Nina Gross, "Foreign Corrupt Practices Act: Leading Practices to Consider," Deloitte, January 29, 2010, http://www.deloitte.com.

the company is correct. As we noted earlier, these requirements have increased the demand for accounting professionals, especially managerial accountants. One result of this increased demand has been higher salaries.

It is expensive for firms to adhere to GAAP standards and SOX requirements. Audits, for instance, can cost millions of dollars each year. These expenses can be especially burdensome for small businesses. Consequently, some have proposed modifications to GAAP and SOX for smaller firms, arguing that some accounting rules were really designed for larger companies. Others disagree.

The **Foreign Corrupt Practices Act** is a federal law that prohibits U.S. citizens and companies from bribing foreign officials in order to win or continue business. The law was later extended to make foreign officials subject to penalties if they in any way cause similar corrupt practices to occur within the United States or its territories. The "Business Etiquette" feature provides some tips on Foreign Corrupt Practices Act compliance.

The Accounting Cycle

Accounting deals with financial transactions between a firm and its employees, customers, suppliers, and owners; bankers; and various government agencies. For example, payroll checks result in a cash outflow to compensate employees. A payment to a vendor results in receipt of needed materials for the production process. Cash, check, and credit purchases by customers generate funds to cover the costs of operations and to earn a profit. Prompt payment of bills preserves the firm's credit rating and its future ability to earn a profit. The procedure by which accountants convert data about individual transactions to financial statements is called the **accounting cycle**.

Figure 15.2 illustrates the activities involved in the accounting cycle: recording, classifying, and summarizing transactions. Initially, any transaction that has a financial impact on the business, such as wages or payments to suppliers, should be documented. All of these transac-

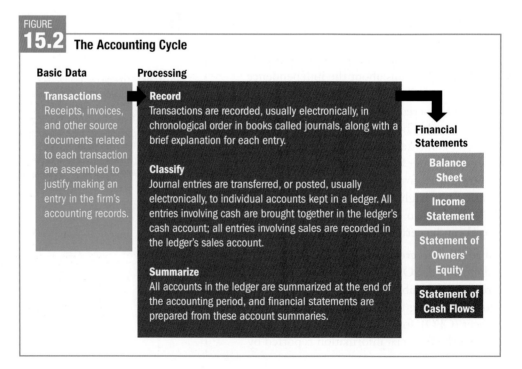

FIGURE 15.2 The Accounting Cycle

Basic Data

Transactions
Receipts, invoices, and other source documents related to each transaction are assembled to justify making an entry in the firm's accounting records.

Processing

Record
Transactions are recorded, usually electronically, in chronological order in books called journals, along with a brief explanation for each entry.

Classify
Journal entries are transferred, or posted, usually electronically, to individual accounts kept in a ledger. All entries involving cash are brought together in the ledger's cash account; all entries involving sales are recorded in the ledger's sales account.

Summarize
All accounts in the ledger are summarized at the end of the accounting period, and financial statements are prepared from these account summaries.

Financial Statements

Balance Sheet

Income Statement

Statement of Owners' Equity

Statement of Cash Flows

Assessment Check ✔

1. Define *GAAP*.

2. What are the four basic requirements to which all accounting rules must adhere?

3. What is the role played by the FASB?

accounting cycle set of activities involved in converting information and individual transactions into financial statements.

tions are recorded in journals, which list transactions in chronological order. Journal listings are then posted to ledgers. A ledger shows increases or decreases in specific accounts such as cash or wages. Ledgers are used to prepare the financial statements, which summarize financial transactions. Management and other interested parties use the resulting financial statements for a variety of purposes.

The Accounting Equation

Three fundamental terms appear in the accounting equation: assets, liabilities, and owners' equity. An **asset** is anything of value owned or leased by a business. Assets include land, buildings, supplies, cash, accounts receivable (amounts owed to the business as payment for credit sales), and marketable securities.

Although most assets are tangible assets, such as equipment, buildings, and inventories, intangible possessions such as patents and trademarks are often some of a firm's most important assets. This kind of asset is especially essential for many companies, including computer software firms, biotechnology companies, and pharmaceutical companies. For instance, Johnson & Johnson—which has both biotechnology and pharmaceutical operations—reported more than $31 billion in intangible assets (including goodwill) in one recent year, out of a total of almost $95 billion in assets.[8]

Two groups have claims against the assets of a firm: creditors and owners. A **liability** of a business is anything owed to creditors—that is, the claims of a firm's creditors. When a firm borrows money to purchase inventory, land, or machinery, the claims of creditors are shown as accounts payable, notes payable, or long-term debt. Wages and salaries owed to employees also are liabilities (known as *wages payable* or *accrued wages*).

Owners' equity is the owner's initial investment in the business plus profits that were not paid out to owners over time in the form of cash dividends. A strong owners' equity position often is used as evidence of a firm's financial strength and stability.

asset anything of value owned by a firm.

liability claims against assets by creditors.

owners' equity funds contributed by owners plus profits not distributed to owners in the form of cash dividends.

Nikada/iStockphoto

Although tangible assets like buildings, equipment, and inventories may look impressive, they are sometimes less important to a company than intangible assets, such as patents and trademarks.

accounting equation
relationship that states that
assets must always equal
the sum of liabilities and
owners' equity.

The **accounting equation** (also referred to as the *accounting identity*) states that assets must equal liabilities plus owners' equity. This equation reflects the financial position of a firm at any point in time:

$$\text{Assets} = \text{Liabilities} + \text{Owners' equity}$$

Because financing comes from either creditors or owners, the right side of the accounting equation also represents the business's financial structure.

double-entry book-
keeping process by which
accounting transactions are
entered; each individual
transaction always has an
offsetting transaction.

The accounting equation also illustrates **double-entry bookkeeping**—the process by which accounting transactions are recorded. Because assets must always equal liabilities plus equity, each transaction must have an offsetting transaction. For example, if a company increases an asset, either another asset must decrease, a liability must increase, or owners' equity must increase. So if a company uses cash to purchase inventory, one asset (inventory) is increased while another (cash) is decreased by the same amount. Similarly, a decrease in an asset must be offset by either an increase in another asset, a decrease in a liability, or a decrease in owners' equity. If a company uses cash to repay a bank loan, both an asset (cash) and a liability (bank loans) decrease, and by the same amount.

Two simple numerical examples will help illustrate the accounting equation and double-entry bookkeeping. First, assume the owner of a photo studio purchases a new camera system for $5,000 using her personal funds. The accounting transaction would look as follows:

Increase plant, property, and equipment (an asset) by $5,000
Increase owners' equity by $5,000

So, the left side of the accounting equation would increase by $5,000 and be offset by a $5,000 increase on the right side.

Second, assume a firm has a $100,000 loan from a bank and decides to pay it off using some of its cash. The transaction would be recorded as:

Decrease bank loan (liability) by $100,000
Decrease cash (asset) by $100,000

In this second example, the left side and right side of the accounting equation would both decrease by $100,000.

The relationship expressed by the accounting equation underlies development of the firm's financial statements. Three financial statements form the foundation: the balance sheet, the income statement, and the statement of owners' equity. The information found in these statements is calculated using the double-entry bookkeeping system and reflects the basic accounting equation. A fourth statement, the statement of cash flows, is also prepared to focus specifically on the sources and uses of cash for a firm from its operating, investing, and financing activities.

The Impact of Computers and the Internet on the Accounting Process

For hundreds of years, bookkeepers recorded, or posted, accounting transactions as manual entries in journals. They then transferred the information, or posted it, to individual accounts listed in ledgers. Computers have streamlined the process, making it both faster and easier. For instance, point-of-sale terminals in retail stores perform a number of

Going Green

Deloitte Educates Itself—and Others—on Sustainability

For many years, Deloitte has been one of the Big Four accounting and auditing firms. Recently the company decided not only to make its own internal operations greener but also to offer its clients training in green practices. It does seem logical for a firm that specializes in financial reporting to enter the realm of nonfinancial reporting as the business world changes course on green practices. Whereas firms once considered "going green" good public relations but financially unrewarding, many now see the importance of sustainability in an increasingly energy-limited environment.

Kathryn Pavlovsky, a co-leader of Deloitte's Enterprise Sustainability Group, says, "Nonfinancial reporting is evolving from voluntary communications to mandatory compliance, and the environmental regulatory and financial reporting worlds are converging." Activism by shareholders and changing consumer attitudes and behavior have also been heavily influential, as has the recent recession. Technological advances are making green practices increasingly feasible and affordable.

Deloitte's corporate responsibility policy declares that their U.S. firms will "advocate the sustainable use of natural resources and the environment." The company began its internal greening campaign by conducting a survey of its employees. Called "How green is your footprint?" the survey measured "greenness" on an individual basis, then made suggestions on how each employee could improve his or her performance. A second survey, "How green is your *other* footprint?" helps employees measure sustainability in their homes.

Deloitte also established a Green Leadership Council to maintain contact between the various company regions and management. The GLC educates employees about important green issues and promotes a unified message to all the company's offices. Deloitte employees now conduct virtual meetings and conferences whenever possible; when not, company travel offers green car-rental and hotel options. Deloitte has also adopted Leadership in Energy and Environmental Design (LEED) standards in building new offices and retrofitting existing ones. The company has focused on purchasing supplies that have a minimal impact on the environment, and worked with its suppliers for greater sustainability.

Deloitte's Center for Sustainability Performance (CSP) in Waltham, Massachusetts, is geared toward advising businesses on how to reduce their environmental impact and remain profitable. Among the areas covered are planning and strategy, revenue generation, tax incentives, and competitive branding. The CSP also explores sustainability opportunities for employees, offices, IT infrastructure, and communities. Among the center's activities are on-site training for client firms; research and development in sustainability measurement and reporting, publication of reports on these topics for corporate sustainability managers, and consulting and sales support.

One of the center's recent workshops for clients was "Sustainability Measurement and Reporting: Tools, Methods, and Metrics." The course was designed to help clients become acquainted with the current methods for measuring and reporting their own sustainability, as well as giving them a preview of new developments in these areas. According to Mark W. McElroy, the CSP's director, the course covered "tools, methods and metrics across all dimensions of corporate social responsibility and sustainability performance, including carbon, water, solid waste, social impacts, triple bottom line and nonfinancial measurement and reporting in general, both from an enterprise and product life cycle perspective."

In further developing its internal greening efforts, Deloitte recently introduced its Green Sync tool, which is intended to promote employee and stakeholder involvement. Thomas Dekar, the vice chairman of Deloitte LLP, says of Green Sync, "Because people are the most important asset of any organization, companies can benefit through increased recognition as an employer of choice—one that recruits and retains the best, most diverse talent, and has a collaborative culture that engages employees in achieving sustainability."

Questions for Critical Thinking

1. Why do you think Deloitte would find it relatively easy to expand from financial to nonfinancial reporting?
2. How would you go about answering the question, "How big is *your* carbon footprint?" What did you find that you could do to make your home and/or your workplace greener?

Sources: Deloitte Web site, http://www.deloitte.com, accessed June 1, 2010; Deborah Fleischer, "Deloitte: Best Practices for Going Green," *Triple Pundit*, February 1, 2010, http://www.triplepundit.com; Deborah Fleischer, "Deloitte: Green Training on Sustainability Measurement and Reporting," *Green Impact*, January 4, 2010, http://greenimpact.com; "Deloitte Launches Center for Sustainability Performance," press release, August 10, 2009, http://www.csrwire.com.

---

functions each time they record sales. These terminals not only recall prices from computer system memory and maintain constant inventory counts of individual items in stock but also automatically perform accounting data entry functions.

Accounting software programs are used widely in both large and small businesses today. They allow a do-it-once approach, in which a single input leads to automatic conversion of a sale into a journal entry, which then is stored until needed. Decision makers can then request up-to-date financial statements and financial ratios instantly. Improvements in accounting software continue to make the process even faster and easier. ABC Bus Companies Inc.—headquartered in Minnesota—sells, leases, customizes, and services motor coaches for companies and individuals. The company used a Sage Software product called SalesLogix Configuration Engine to replace its inefficient paper-based system and generate complex product bids for the hundreds of customizing options available. Jim Morrison, ABC's vice president of sales, immediately saw the advantage of using a computer-based system. "The quotes could be tied to the opportunities we already tracked in Sage SalesLogix. . . . That means we know what's happening with the customer all the way through the entire process."[9]

Because the accounting needs of entrepreneurs and small businesses differ from those of larger firms, accounting software makers have designed programs that meet specific user needs. Some examples of accounting software programs designed for entrepreneurs and small businesses, and designed to run on personal computers, include QuickBooks, Peachtree, and BusinessWorks. Software programs designed for larger firms, often requiring more sophisticated computer systems, include products from Oracle and SAP.

For firms that conduct business worldwide, software producers have introduced new accounting programs that handle all of a company's accounting information for every country in which it operates. The software handles different languages and currencies, as well as the financial, legal, and tax requirements of each nation in which the firm conducts business.

The Internet also influences the accounting process. Several software producers offer Web-based accounting products designed for small and medium-sized businesses. Among other benefits, these products allow users to access their complete accounting systems from anywhere using a standard Web browser. The "Going Green" feature explains how Deloitte is integrating sustainability into its infrastructure and its business services.

Assessment Check ✔

1. List the steps in the accounting cycle.

2. What is the accounting equation?

3. Briefly explain double-entry bookkeeping.

Financial Statements

Financial statements provide managers with essential information they need to evaluate the liquidity position of an organization—its ability to meet current obligations and needs by converting assets into cash; the firm's profitability; and its overall financial health. The balance sheet, income statement, statement of owners' equity, and statement of cash flows provide a foundation on which managers can base their decisions. By interpreting the data provided in these statements, managers can communicate the appropriate information to internal decision makers and to interested parties outside the organization.

Of the four financial statements, only the balance sheet is considered to be a permanent statement; its amounts are carried over from year to year. The income statement, statement of owners' equity, and statement of cash flows are considered temporary because they are closed out at the end of each year.

Public companies are required to report their financial statements at the end of each three-month period, as well as at the end of each fiscal year. Annual statements must be examined and verified by the firm's outside auditors. These financial statements

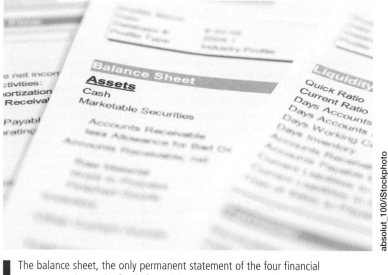

The balance sheet, the only permanent statement of the four financial statements, shows the firm's financial position on a particular date and its amounts are carried over from year to year.

absolut_100/iStockphoto

Solving an Ethical Controversy

Should Whistle-Blowers Be Rewarded?

The Sarbanes-Oxley Act of 2002 (SOX) was intended to reduce fraud, partly by requiring CEOs and CFOs to sign off on the accuracy of their companies' financial statements. However, the largest percentage of reported fraud is revealed by anonymous whistle-blowers or by journalists, auditors, or others.

The U.S. False Claims Act allows citizens to file lawsuits alleging fraud against the federal government. The biggest settlements have involved hospital chains and drug manufacturers; the largest fine was $1 billion. Some whistle-blowers have collected almost $47 million in rewards. Provisions of the Foreign Corrupt Practices Act (FCPA) can also potentially result in huge rewards. But whistle-blowers are not always successful; some have been fired, forced to quit, or demoted.

Should whistle-blowers be rewarded for reporting financial fraud?

PRO

1. A recent survey found that "a strong monetary incentive to blow the whistle does motivate people with information to come forward."

2. Despite strict penalties for fraud, such as those under SOX and the FCPA, one survey reported that 83 percent of fraud examiners believe that internal corporate controls over fraud will actually decline.

CON

1. Some observers feel that certain "whistle-blower-friendly" provisions of the FCPA may discourage accused firms from simply settling with the federal government and paying a fine to avoid costly legal procedures.

2. Not all whistle-blowers are innocent. A former UBS banker exposed tax evasion at the firm but was sentenced to prison because he did not reveal at first that he had participated in the fraud himself.

Summary

Legislation before Congress would require the Securities and Exchange Commission (SEC) to award whistle-blowers up to 30 percent of fines the government collects on the basis of "original information." Some observers worry that these changes could result in a "race to disclose" between companies that self-report and current or former employees. Currently, more than 1,000 whistle-blower cases are pending.

Sources: "Sarbanes-Oxley Can Help Curb Company Fraud," McGladrey, http://rsmmcgladrey.com, accessed June 1, 2010; Michael Connor, "Finance Reform Bill Could Increase Big Payouts to Whistleblowers," *Business Ethics*, May 2, 2010, http://business-ethics.com; "Whistle blowers Making Money Thanks to Law," *NewsChannel 8*, May 1, 2010, http://cfc.news.8.net; Deloitte Webcast Poll, "Poll: More Financial Statement Fraud Expected to Be Uncovered in 2010, 2011," *Corporate Compliance Insights*, April 28, 2010, http://www.corporate compliangeinsights.com; James Hyatt, "Who Detects Corporate Fraud? (Tip: It's Not Usually the SEC . . .)," *Business Ethics*, February 16, 2010, http://business-ethics.com; Michael Rubinkam, "UBS Tax Evasion Whistle-Blower Reports to Federal Prison," *USA Today*, January 8, 2010, http://www.usatoday.com.

---

are public information available to anyone. The "Solving an Ethical Controversy" feature discusses the problem of financial fraud.

A fiscal year does not have to coincide with the calendar year, and companies set different fiscal years. For instance, Starbucks's fiscal year runs from October 1 to September 30 of the following year. Nike's fiscal year consists of the 12 months between June 1 and May 31. By contrast, GE's fiscal year is the same as the calendar year, running from January 1 to December 31.

The Balance Sheet

A firm's **balance sheet** shows its financial position on a particular date. It is similar to a photograph of the firm's assets together with its liabilities and owners' equity at a specific moment in time. Balance sheets must be prepared at regular intervals, because a firm's

> **balance sheet** statement of a firm's financial position—what it owns and claims against its assets—at a particular point in time.

managers and other internal parties often request this information every day, every week, or at least every month. On the other hand, external users, such as stockholders or industry analysts, may use this information less frequently, perhaps every quarter or once a year.

The balance sheet follows the accounting equation. On the left side of the balance sheet are the firm's assets—what it owns. These assets, shown in descending order of liquidity (in other words, convertibility to cash), represent the uses that management has made of available funds. Cash is always listed first on the asset side of the balance sheet.

On the right side of the equation are the claims against the firm's assets. Liabilities and owners' equity indicate the sources of the firm's assets and are listed in the order in which they are due. Liabilities reflect the claims of creditors—financial institutions or bondholders that have loaned the firm money; suppliers that have provided goods and services on credit; and others to be paid, such as federal, state, and local tax authorities. Owners' equity represents the owners' claims (those of stockholders, in the case of a corporation) against the firm's assets. It also amounts to the excess of all assets over liabilities.

Figure 15.3 shows the balance sheet for Diane's Java, a small California-based coffee wholesaler. The accounting equation is illustrated by the three classifications of assets, liabilities, and owners' equity on the company's balance sheet. Remember, total assets must always equal the sum of liabilities and owners' equity. In other words, the balance sheet must always balance.

The Income Statement

income statement
financial record of a company's revenues and expenses, and profits over a period of time.

Whereas the balance sheet reflects a firm's financial situation at a specific point in time, the **income statement** represents the flow of resources that reveals the performance of the organization over a specific time period. Resembling a video rather than a photograph, the income statement is a financial record summarizing a firm's financial performance in terms of revenues, expenses, and profits over a given time period, say, a quarter or a year.

In addition to reporting the firm's profit or loss results, the income statement helps decision makers focus on overall revenues and the costs involved in generating these revenues. Managers of a not-for-profit organization use this statement to determine whether its revenues from contributions and other sources will cover its operating costs. Finally, the income statement provides much of the basic data needed to calculate the financial ratios managers use in planning and controlling activities. Figure 15.4 shows the income statement for Diane's Java.

An income statement (some times called *a profit-and-loss*, or *P&L, statement*) begins with total sales or revenues generated during a year, quarter, or month. Subsequent lines then deduct all of the costs related to producing the revenues. Typical categories of costs include those involved in producing the firm's goods or services, operating expenses, interest, and taxes. After all of them have been subtracted, the remaining net income may be distributed to the firm's owners (stockholders, proprietors, or partners) or reinvested in the company as retained earnings. The final figure on the income statement—net income after taxes—is the so-called *bottom line*.

Keeping costs under control is an important part of running a business. Too often, however, companies concentrate more on increasing revenue than on controlling costs. Regardless of how much money a company collects in revenues, it won't stay in business for long unless it eventually earns a profit.

FIGURE
15.3 Diane's Java Balance Sheet (Fiscal Year, Ending December 31)

1 Current Assets:
Cash and other liquid assets that can or will be converted to cash within one year.

2 Plant, Property, and Equipment (net):
Physical assets expected to last for more than one year; shown net of accumulated depreciation—the cumulative value that plant, property, and

3 **Value of assets such as patents and**

4 Current Liabilities:
Claims of creditors that are to be repaid within one year; accruals are expenses, such as wages, that have been incurred but not yet

5 Long-Term Debt:
Debts that come due one year or longer after the date on the balance sheet.

6 Owners' (or shareholders') Equity: **Claims of the owners against the assets of the firm; the difference between total assets and total liabilities.**

Diane's Java

Balance Sheet

($ thousands)	2012	2011
Assets		
1 Current Assets		
Cash	$ 800	$ 600
Short-term investments	1,250	940
Accounts receivable	990	775
Inventory	2,200	1,850
Total current assets	5,240	4,165
2 Plant, property, and equipment (net)	3,300	2,890
3 Goodwill and other intangible assets	250	250
Total Assets	8,790	7,305
Liabilities and Shareholders' Equity		
4 Current Liabilities		
Accruals	$ 350	$ 450
Accounts payable	980	900
Notes payable	700	500
Total current liabilities	2,030	1,850
5 Long-term debt	1,100	1,000
Total liabilities	3,130	2,850
6 Shareholders' equity	5,660	4,455
Total Liabilities and Equity	8,790	7,305

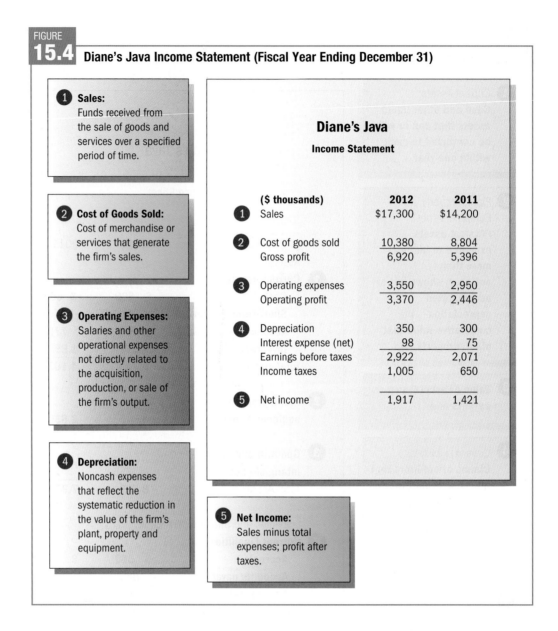

FIGURE 15.4 Diane's Java Income Statement (Fiscal Year Ending December 31)

① Sales:
Funds received from the sale of goods and services over a specified period of time.

② Cost of Goods Sold:
Cost of merchandise or services that generate the firm's sales.

③ Operating Expenses:
Salaries and other operational expenses not directly related to the acquisition, production, or sale of the firm's output.

④ Depreciation:
Noncash expenses that reflect the systematic reduction in the value of the firm's plant, property and equipment.

⑤ Net Income:
Sales minus total expenses; profit after taxes.

Diane's Java
Income Statement

($ thousands)	2012	2011
① Sales	$17,300	$14,200
② Cost of goods sold	10,380	8,804
Gross profit	6,920	5,396
③ Operating expenses	3,550	2,950
Operating profit	3,370	2,446
④ Depreciation	350	300
Interest expense (net)	98	75
Earnings before taxes	2,922	2,071
Income taxes	1,005	650
⑤ Net income	1,917	1,421

Statement of Owners' Equity

statement of owners' equity record of the change in owners' equity from the end of one fiscal period to the end of the next.

The **statement of owners'**, or shareholders', **equity** is designed to show the components of the change in equity from the end of one fiscal year to the end of the next. It uses information from both the balance sheet and income statement. A somewhat simplified example is shown in Figure 15.5 for Diane's Java.

Note that the statement begins with the amount of equity shown on the balance sheet at the end of the prior year. Net income is added, and cash dividends paid to owners are subtracted (both are found on the income statement for the current year). If owners contributed any additional capital, say, through the sale of new shares, this amount is added to equity. On the other hand, if owners withdrew capital, for example, through the repurchase of existing shares, equity declines. All of the additions and subtractions, taken together, equal the change in owners' equity from the end of the last fiscal year to the end of the current one. The new amount of owners' equity is then reported on the balance sheet for the current year.

FIGURE
15.5

Diane's Java Simplified Statement of Owners' Equity (Fiscal Year Ending December 31)

1 From the prior year's balance sheet.

2 From the current year's income statement.

3 Amount should equal the figure shown on the current year's balance sheet.

Diane's Java

Simplified Statement of Owners' Equity

($ thousands)	2012
1 Shareholders' equity (beginning of year)	$4,445
2 Add net income	1,917
Subtract cash dividends	(450)
Add sale of new shares	0
Subtract repurchase of existing shares	(262)
3 Equals shareholders' equity (end of year)	5,660

The Statement of Cash Flows

In addition to the statement of owners' equity, the income statement, and the balance sheet, most firms prepare a fourth accounting statement—the **statement of cash flows**. Public companies are required to prepare and publish a statement of cash flows. In addition, commercial lenders often require a borrower to submit a statement of cash flows. The statement of cash flows provides investors and creditors with relevant information about a firm's cash receipts and cash payments for its operations, investments, and financing during an accounting period. Figure 15.6 shows the statement of cash flows for Diane's Java.

Companies prepare a statement of cash flows due to the widespread use of accrual accounting. **Accrual accounting** recognizes revenues and costs when they occur, not when actual cash changes hands. As a result, there can be differences between what is reported as sales, expenses, and profits, and the amount of cash that actually flows into and out of the business during a period of time. An example is depreciation. Companies depreciate fixed assets—such as machinery and buildings—over a specified period of time, meaning that they systematically reduce the value of the asset. Depreciation is reported as an expense on the firm's income statement—see Figure 15.4—but does not involve any actual cash. The fact that depreciation is a noncash expense means that what a firm reports as net income (profits after tax) for a particular period actually understates the amount of cash the firm took in, less expenses, during that period of time. Consequently, depreciation is added back to net income when calculating cash flow.

The fact that *cash flow* is the lifeblood of every organization is evidenced by the business failure rate. Many former owners of failed firms blame inadequate cash flow for their company's demise. Those who value the statement of cash flow maintain that its preparation and scrutiny

statement of cash flows statement showing the sources and uses of cash during a period of time.

accrual accounting accounting method that records revenues and expenses when they occur, not necessarily when cash actually changes hands.

① **Operating Activities:**
The nuts and bolts of day-to-day activities of a company carrying out its regular business; Increases in accounts receivable and inventory are uses of cash, while increases in accruals and accounts payables are sources of cash; in financially healthy firms, net cash flow from operating activities should be positive.

② **Investing Activities:**
Transactions to accumulate or use cash in ways that affect operating activities in the future; often a use of cash.

③ **Financing Activities:**
Ways to transfer cash to or from creditors and to or from owners; can be either positive or negative.

④ **Net Cash Flow:**
The sum of cash flow from operating, investing, and financing activities, a reconcilement of cash from the beginning to the end of the accounting period (one year in this example).

Diane's Java

Statement of Cash Flows

($ thousands)	2012
Cash Flow from Operating Activities	
① Net income	$1,917
Depreciation	350
Change in accounts receivable	(215)
Change in inventory	(350)
Change in accruals	(100)
Change in accounts payable	80
Total cash flow from operating activities	1,682
② Cash Flow from Investing Activities	
Capital expenditures	(760)
Change in short-term investments	(310)
Total cash flow from investing activities	(1,070)
③ Cash Flow from Financing Activities	
Cash dividends	(450)
Sale/repurchase of shares	(262)
Change in notes payable	200
Change in long-term debt	100
Total cash flow from financing activities	(412)
④ Net Cash Flow	200
Cash (beginning of year)	600
Cash (end of year)	800

by various parties can prevent financial distress for otherwise profitable firms, too many of which are forced into bankruptcy due to a lack of cash needed to continue day-to-day operations.

Even for firms for which bankruptcy is not an issue, the statement of cash flows can provide investors and other interested parties with vital information. For instance, assume that a firm's income statement reports rising earnings. At the same time, however, the statement of cash flows shows that the firm's inventory is rising faster than sales—often a signal that demand for the firm's products is softening, which may in turn be a sign of impending financial trouble.

Financial Ratio Analysis

Accounting professionals fulfill important responsibilities beyond preparing financial statements. In a more critical role, they help managers interpret the statements by comparing data about the firm's current activities to those for previous periods and to results posted by other companies in the industry. *Ratio analysis* is one of the most commonly used tools for measuring a firm's liquidity, profitability, and reliance on debt financing, as well as the effectiveness of management's resource utilization. This analysis also allows comparisons with other firms and with the firm's own past performance.

Ratios assist managers by interpreting actual performance and making comparisons to what should have happened. Comparisons with ratios of similar companies help managers understand their firm's performance relative to competitors' results. These industry standards are important yardsticks and help pinpoint problem areas, as well as areas of excellence. Ratios for the current accounting period also may be compared with similar calculations for previous periods to spot developing trends. Ratios can be classified according to their specific purposes. The four major categories of financial ratios are summarized in Table 15.1. The ratios for Diane's Java for the 2011 and 2012 fiscal years are shown in Table 15.2.

Assessment Check ☑

1. List the four financial statements.
2. How is the balance sheet organized?
3. Define *accrual accounting*.

Table
15.1 Major Categories of Financial Ratios

CATEGORY	RATIO	DESCRIPTION
Liquidity ratios	Current ratio	Current assets divided by current liabilities
	Quick (acid-test) ratio	Current assets (minus inventory) divided by current liabilities
Efficiency ratios	Inventory turnover	Cost of goods sold divided by average inventory
	Receivables turnover	Credit sales divided by average accounts receivable
	Total asset turnover	Revenue or sales divided by average total assets
Leverage ratios	Debt ratio	Total liabilities divided by total assets
	Long term debt to equity	Long-term debt divided by owners' equity
Profitability ratios	Gross profit margin	Gross profit divided by revenue or sales
	Net profit margin	Net profit divided by revenue or sales
	Return on equity	Net profit divided by average owners' equity

[15.2] Financial Ratios for Diane's Java

FINANCIAL RATIO	2012 FISCAL YEAR	2011 FISCAL YEAR
Current ratio	2.58	2.25
Quick ratio	1.50	1.25
Inventory turnover	5.13	5.03
Receivables turnover	19.60	19.32
Total asset turnover	2.15	2.15
Debt ratio	35.6%	39.0%
Long-term debt to equity	19.4%	22.4%
Gross profit margin	40.0%	38.0%
Net profit margin	11.1%	10.0%
Return on equity	37.9%	36.6%

Liquidity Ratios

A firm's ability to meet its short-term obligations when they must be paid is measured by *liquidity ratios*. Increasing liquidity reduces the likelihood that a firm will face emergencies caused by the need to raise funds to repay loans. On the other hand, firms with low liquidity may be forced to choose between default or borrowing from high-cost lending sources to meet their maturing obligations.

Two commonly used liquidity ratios are the current ratio and the acid-test, or quick, ratio. The current ratio compares current assets to current liabilities, giving executives information about the firm's ability to pay its current debts as they mature. The current ratio of Diane's Java can be computed as follows (unless indicated, all amounts from the balance sheet or income statement are in thousands of dollars):

$$\text{Liquidity ratio} = \frac{\text{Current assets}}{\text{Current liabilities}} = \frac{5,240}{2,030} = 2.58$$

In other words, Diane's Java has $2.58 of current assets for every $1.00 of current liabilities. In general, a current ratio of 2:1 is considered satisfactory liquidity. This rule of thumb must be considered along with other factors, such as the nature of the business, the season, and the quality of the company's management team. Diane's Java's management and other interested parties are likely to evaluate this ratio of 2.58:1 by comparing it with ratios for previous operating periods and with industry averages.

The acid-test (or quick) ratio measures the ability of a firm to meet its debt payments on short notice. This ratio compares quick assets—the most liquid current assets—against current liabilities. Quick assets generally consist of cash and equivalents, short-term investments, and accounts receivable. So, generally quick assets equal total current assets minus inventory.

Diane's Java's current balance sheet lists total current assets of $5.24 million and inventory of $2.2 million. Therefore, its quick ratio is as follows:

$$\text{Acid-test ratio} = \frac{\text{Current assets} - \text{Inventory}}{\text{Current liabilities}} = \frac{(5,240 - 2,200)}{2,030} = 1.50$$

Because the traditional rule of thumb for an adequate acid-test ratio is around 1:1, Diane's Java appears to have a strong level of liquidity. However, the same cautions apply here as for the current ratio. The ratio should be compared with industry averages and data from previous operating periods to determine whether it is adequate for the firm.

Activity Ratios

Activity ratios measure the effectiveness of management's use of the firm's resources. One of the most frequently used activity ratios, the inventory turnover ratio, indicates the number of times merchandise moves through a business:

$$\text{Inventory turnover} = \frac{\text{Cost of goods sold}}{\text{Average inventory}} = \frac{10,380}{\left[(2,200 + 1,850)/2\right]} = 5.13$$

Average inventory for Diane's Java is determined by adding the inventory as of December 31, 2012 ($2.2 million) with the inventory as of December 31, 2011 ($1.85 million) and dividing it by 2. Comparing the 5.13 inventory turnover ratio with industry standards gives a measure of efficiency. It is important to note, however, that inventory turnover can vary substantially depending on the products a company sells and the industry in which it operates.

If a company makes a substantial portion of its sales on credit, measuring receivables turnover can provide useful information. Receivables turnover can be calculated as follows:

$$\text{Receivables turnover} = \frac{\text{Credit sales}}{\text{Average accounts receivable}}$$

Because Diane's Java is a wholesaler, let's assume that all of its sales are credit sales. Average receivables equals the simple average of 2012's receivables and 2011's receivables. The ratio for the company is:

$$\text{Receivables turnover} = \frac{17,300}{\left[(990 + 775)/2\right]} = 19.60$$

Dividing 365 by the figure for receivables turnover, 19.6, equals the average age of receivables, 18.62 days. Assume Diane's Java expects its retail customers to pay outstanding bills within 30 days of the date of purchase. Given that the average age of its receivables is less than 30 days, Diane's Java appears to be doing a good job collecting its credit sales.

Another measure of efficiency is total asset turnover. It measures how much in sales each dollar invested in assets generates:

$$\text{Total asset turnover} = \frac{\text{Sales}}{\text{Average total assets}}$$

$$= \frac{17,300}{\left[(8,790 + 7,305)/2\right]} = 2.15$$

Average total assets for Diane's Java equals total assets as of December 31, 2012 ($8.79 million) plus total assets as of December 31, 2011 ($7.305 million) divided by 2.

Diane's Java generates about $2.15 in sales for each dollar invested in assets. Although a higher ratio generally indicates that a firm is operating more efficiently, care must be taken when comparing firms that operate in different industries. Some industries simply require higher investment in assets than do other industries.

Profitability Ratios

Some ratios measure the organization's overall financial performance by evaluating its ability to generate revenues in excess of operating costs and other expenses. These measures are called *profitability ratios*. To compute these ratios, accountants compare the firm's earnings with total sales or investments. Over a period of time, profitability ratios may reveal the effectiveness of management in operating the business. Three important profitability ratios are gross profit margin, net profit margin, and return on equity:

$$\text{Gross profit margin} = \frac{\text{Gross profit}}{\text{Sales}} = \frac{6,920}{17,300} = 40.0\%$$

$$\text{Net profit margin} = \frac{\text{Net income}}{\text{Sales}} = \frac{1,917}{17,300} = 11.1\%$$

$$\text{Return on equity} = \frac{\text{Net income}}{\text{Average equity}} = \frac{1,1917}{\left[(5,660 + 4,455)/2\right]} = 37.9\%$$

This AFLAC advertisement, aimed at investors rather than insurance buyers, notes the firm's ten-year total return to shareholders of 18.3 percent. *Return on equity* is one measure of a company's profitability.

All of these ratios indicate positive evaluations of the current operations of Diane's Java. For example, the net profit margin indicates that the firm realizes a profit of slightly more than 11 cents on each dollar of merchandise it sells. Although this ratio varies widely among business firms, Diane's Java compares favorably with wholesalers in general, which have an average net profit margin of around 5 percent. However, this ratio, like the other profitability ratios, should be evaluated in relation to profit forecasts, past performance, or more specific industry averages to enhance the interpretation of results. Similarly, while the firm's return on equity of almost 38 percent appears outstanding, the degree of risk in the industry also must be considered.

Leverage Ratios

Leverage ratios measure the extent to which a firm relies on debt financing. They provide particularly interesting information to potential investors and lenders. If management has assumed too much debt in financing the firm's operations, problems may arise in meeting future interest payments and repaying outstanding loans. As we discuss in Chapter 17, borrowing money does have advantages. However, relying too heavily on debt financing may lead to bankruptcy. More generally, both investors and lenders may prefer to deal with firms whose owners have invested enough of their own money to avoid overreliance on borrowing. The debt ratio and long-term debt to equity ratio help interested parties evaluate a firm's leverage:

$$\text{Debt ratio} = \frac{\text{Total liabilities}}{\text{Total assets}} = \frac{3{,}130}{8{,}790} = 35.6\%$$

$$\text{Long-term debt to equity} = \frac{\text{Long-term debt}}{\text{Owners' equity}} = \frac{1{,}100}{5{,}660} = 19.64\%$$

A total liabilities to total assets ratio greater than 50 percent indicates that a firm is relying more on borrowed money than owners' equity. Because Diane's Java's total liabilities to total assets ratio is 35.6 percent, the firm's owners have invested considerably more than the total amount of liabilities shown on the firm's balance sheet. Moreover, the firm's long-term debt to equity ratio is only 19.64 percent, indicating that Diane's Java has only about 19.6 cents in long-term debt to every dollar in equity. The long-term debt to equity ratio also indicates that Diane's Java hasn't relied very heavily on borrowed money.

The four categories of financial ratios relate balance sheet and income statement data to one another, help management pinpoint a firm's strengths and weaknesses, and indicate areas in need of further investigation. Large, multiproduct firms that operate in diverse markets use their information systems to update their financial ratios every day or even every hour. Each company's management must decide on an appropriate review schedule to avoid the costly and time-consuming mistake of overmonitoring.

In addition to calculating financial ratios, managers, investors, and lenders should pay close attention to how accountants applied a number of accounting rules when preparing financial statements. GAAP gives accountants leeway in reporting certain revenues and expenses. Public companies are required to disclose, in footnotes to the financial statements, how the various accounting rules were applied.

Budgeting

Although the financial statements discussed in this chapter focus on past business activities, they also provide the basis for planning in the future. A **budget** is a planning and controlling tool that reflects the firm's expected sales revenues, operating expenses, and cash receipts and outlays. It quantifies the firm's plans for a specified future period. Because it reflects management estimates of expected sales, cash inflows and outflows, and costs, the budget is a financial blueprint and can be thought of as a short-term financial plan. It becomes the standard for comparison against actual performance.

Budget preparation is frequently a time-consuming task that involves many people from various departments within the organization. The complexity of the budgeting process varies with the size and complexity of the organization. Large corporations such as United Technologies, Paramount Pictures, and Verizon maintain complex and sophisticated budgeting systems. Their budgets help managers integrate their numerous divisions in addition to serving as planning and controlling tools. But budgeting in both large and small firms is similar to household budgeting in its purpose: to match income and expenses in a way that accomplishes objectives and correctly times cash inflows and outflows.

Because the accounting department is an organization's financial nerve center, it provides much of the data for budget development. The overall master, or operating, budget is

Assessment Check ☑

1. List the four categories of financial ratios.
2. Define the following ratios: *current ratio, inventory turnover, net profit margin,* and *debt ratio.*

budget organization's plans for how it will raise and spend money during a given period.

actually a composite of many individual budgets for separate units of the firm. These individual budgets typically include the production budget, cash budget, capital expenditures budget, advertising budget, and sales budget.

Technology has improved the efficiency of the budgeting process. The accounting software products discussed earlier—such as QuickBooks—all include budgeting features. Moreover, modules designed for specific businesses are often available from third parties. Many banks now offer their customers personal financial management tools (PFMs) developed by software companies. One such tool is FinanceWorks, an online finance program from Intuit's Digital Insight division. BBVA, a multinational Spanish banking group, offers Tu Cuentas ("you count"), based on a PFM program from Strands, a California software developer.[10]

One of the most important budgets prepared by firms is the *cash budget*. The cash budget, usually prepared monthly, tracks the firm's cash inflows and outflows. Figure 15.7 illustrates a sample cash budget for Birchwood Paper, a small Maine-based paper products company. The company has set a $150,000 target cash balance. The cash budget indicates months in which the firm will need temporary loans—May, June, and July—and how much it will need (close to $3 million). The document also indicates that Birchwood will generate

FIGURE **15.7** Four-Month Cash Budget for Birchwood Paper Company

Birchwood Paper Company
Four-Month Cash Budget

($ thousands)	May	June	July	August
Gross sales	$1,200.0	$3,200.0	$5,500.0	$4,500.0
Cash sales	300.0	800.0	1,375.0	1,125.0
One month prior	600.0	600.0	1,600.0	2,750.0
Two months prior	300.0	300.0	300.0	800.0
Total cash inflows	1,200.0	1,700.0	3,275.0	4,675.0
Purchases				
Cash purchases	1,040.0	1,787.5	1,462.5	390.0
One month prior	390.0	1,040.0	1,787.5	1,462.5
Wages and salaries	250.0	250.0	250.0	250.0
Office rent	75.0	75.0	75.0	75.0
Marketing and other expenses	150.0	150.0	150.0	150.0
Taxes		300.0		
Total cash outflows	1,905.0	3,602.5	3,725.0	2,327.5
Net cash flow				
(Inflows – Outflows)	(705.0)	(1,902.5)	(450.0)	2,347.5
Beginnning cash balance	250.0	150.0	150.0	150.0
Net cash flow	(705.0)	(1,902.5)	(450.0)	2,347.5
Ending cash balance	(455.0)	(1,752.5)	(300.0)	2,497.5
Target cash balance	150.0	150.0	150.0	150.0
Surplus (deficit)	(605.0)	(1,902.5)	(450.0)	2,347.5
Cumulative surplus (deficit)	(605.0)	(2,507.5)	(2,957.5)	610.0

Hit & Miss

Accounting Is Booming in Vietnam

Vietnam's economy is booming, thanks to the government's encouragement of connections with the global economy, and to foreign direct investment by overseas companies attracted by low labor costs and low overhead. Vietnam's state-of-the-art facilities include E-Town, a high-rise building reserved for high-tech firms and located a mile from the international airport in Ho Chi Minh City, the capital. Local entrepreneurs are thriving too, adding to the growing number of wealthy business owners.

What does all this activity and revenue add up to? Taxes. And that means Vietnam's fledging accounting industry is coming into its own. Begun in the 1990s, accounting in Vietnam has grown as rapidly as the manufacturing sector. The Big Four firms already book about $15 to $20 million worth of tax consulting business, a figure expected to grow as the government encourages increasing prosperity to widen the country's tax base among its 85 million citizens.

The industry is divided in several ways. At the top are PricewaterhouseCoopers, Ernst & Young, KPMG, and Deloitte & Touche, offering accounting, taxation, and corporate financial services, along with consulting, project management, and software engineering. Next are a handful of state-owned auditing firms that serve the country's remaining government-run businesses. One of these, Vietnam Auditing Company (VACO), was among the first to comply with new regulations that require accounting firms to be independent of the state, by becoming a full member of the Deloitte Global network. Midsize firms are next—some local and at least one foreign owned, Grant Thornton.

Another division is between north and south. The southern region, where the capital is located, is growing faster and will probably require more accounting services, at least in the near future.

Growth may create staffing and retention problems for Vietnamese accounting firms. At Grant Thornton, for instance, although salaries are rising, the biggest problem is how to motivate staff to stay. With the high demand for qualified auditors, the company pays its staff on par with international firms. But the firm is also looking at other factors that employees may value, such as "a sense of belonging, training, and salary, also the ability to balance home and work life. Several of our audit staff resigned in the past because of the hours," says the company's managing partner. "Managers are the key. . . . If you lose one [employee], a whole lot can go."

Questions for Critical Thinking

1. How might the mandate to privatize accounting firms in Vietnam affect those firms' operations and ethical standards?

2. What can Vietnamese accounting firms do to improve staffing and retention?

Sources: Company Web site, Grant Thornton Vietnam, http://www.gt.com.vn, accessed March 31, 2009; "Interview: Grant Thornton Vietnam: Opening the Doors," *International Accounting Bulletin*, June 22, 2007, http://o-www.lexisnexis.com; "Deloitte Global Admits Full Member Firm in Vietnam," *International Accounting Bulletin*, May 12, 2007, http://o-www.lexisnexis.com; David Hannon, "Business in Vietnam Defies Misconceptions," *Purchasing*, February 15, 2007, http://www.purchasing.com, accessed October 20, 2008.

---

a cash surplus in August and can begin repaying the short-term loan. Finally, the cash budget produces a tangible standard against which to compare actual cash inflows and outflows.

International Accounting

Today, accounting procedures and practices must be adapted to accommodate an international business environment. The Coca-Cola Company and McDonald's both generate more than half their annual revenues from sales outside the United States. Nestlé, the giant chocolate and food products firm, operates throughout the world. It derives 98 percent of its revenues from outside Switzerland, its home country. International accounting practices for global firms must reliably translate the financial statements of the firm's international affiliates, branches, and subsidiaries and convert data about foreign currency transactions to dollars. Also, foreign currencies and exchange rates influence the accounting and financial reporting processes of firms operating internationally.

As market economies in countries such as Poland and China have developed, the demand for accountants has increased. The "Hit & Miss" feature describes recent developments in the accounting profession in Vietnam.

Ilyas Dean/NewsCom

In Pakistan, a truck driver delivers Nestlé food products. Because the Swiss corporation operates around the world, its profits and its financial statements are affected by foreign exchange rates.

Exchange Rates

As defined in Chapter 4, an exchange rate is the ratio at which a country's currency can be exchanged for other currencies. Currencies can be treated as goods to be bought and sold. Like the price of any product, currency prices change daily according to supply and demand. So exchange rate fluctuations complicate accounting entries and accounting practices.

Accountants who deal with international transactions must appropriately record their firms' foreign sales and purchases. Today's sophisticated accounting software helps firms handle all of their international transactions within a single program. An international firm's consolidated financial statements must reflect any gains or losses due to changes in exchange rates during specific periods of time. Financial statements that cover operations in two or more countries also need to treat fluctuations consistently to allow for comparison.

In the United States, GAAP requires firms to make adjustments to their earnings that reflect changes in exchange rates. In general, a weakening dollar increases the earnings of a U.S. firm that has international operations because the same units of a foreign currency will translate into more U.S. dollars. By the same token, a strengthening dollar will have the opposite effect on earnings—the same number of units of a foreign currency will translate into fewer dollars. In one recent year, for example, currency fluctuations caused an $11 million drop in earnings from the same quarter of the previous year for PPG, the world's second largest paint manufacturer.[11]

International Accounting Standards

International Accounting Standards Board (IASB) established in 1973 to promote world-wide consistency in financial reporting practices.

International Financial Reporting Standards (IFRS) standards and interpretations adopted by the IASB.

The International Accounting Standards Committee (IASC) was established in 1973 to promote worldwide consistency in financial reporting practices. The IASC soon developed its first set of accounting standards and interpretations and, in 2001, became the **International Accounting Standards Board (IASB)**. **International Financial Reporting Standards (IFRS)** are the standards and interpretations adopted by the IASB. The IASB operates in much the same manner as the FASB does in the United States, interpreting and modifying IFRS.

Because of the boom in worldwide trade, there is a real need for comparability of and uniformity in international accounting rules. Trade agreements such as NAFTA and the expansion of the European Union have only heightened interest in creating a uniform set of global accounting rules. In addition, an increasing number of investors are buying shares in foreign multinational corporations, and they need a practical way to evaluate firms in other countries. To assist global investors, more and more firms are beginning to report their financial information according to international accounting standards. This practice helps investors make informed decisions.

Nearly 100 other countries currently require, permit the use of, or have a policy of convergence with IFRS. These nations include members of the European Union, India, Australia, Canada, and Hong Kong. At first, the United States was skeptical of IFRS, even though major American accounting organizations have been involved with the IASB since its inception. In fact, the SEC used to require all firms whose shares were publicly traded in the United States to report financial results using GAAP. This rule applied regardless of where firms were located.

This requirement started to change some years back, when the FASB and the IASB met and committed to the eventual convergence of IFRS with GAAP. This agreement was further clarified in 2005. Around the same time, the SEC began to loosen its rules on the use of IFRS by foreign firms whose shares trade in the United States. Today, many foreign companies can report results using IFRS as long as they reconcile these results to GAAP in a footnote. Some large U.S. companies were allowed to use international accounting standards beginning in 2009. By 2016, all U.S. firms will be required to do so. Almost half the companies polled in a recent survey said they wanted an option for early adoption of the standards.[12]

How does IFRS differ from GAAP? Although many similarities between IFRS and GAAP exist, there are some important differences. For example, under GAAP, plant, property, and equipment is reported on the balance sheet at the historical cost minus depreciation. Under IFRS, on the other hand, plant, property, and equipment is shown on the balance sheet at current market value. This gives a better picture of the real value of a firm's assets. Many accounting experts believe that IFRS is overall less complicated than GAAP and more transparent.[13]

Assessment Check ☑

1. How are financial statements adjusted for exchange rates?
2. What is the purpose of the IASB?

What's Ahead

This chapter describes the role of accounting in an organization. Accounting is the process of measuring, interpreting, and communicating financial information to interested parties both inside and outside the firm. The next two chapters discuss the finance function of an organization. Finance deals with planning, obtaining, and managing the organization's funds to accomplish its objectives in the most efficient and effective manner possible. Chapter 16 outlines the financial system, the system by which funds are transferred from savers to borrowers. Organizations rely on the financial system to raise funds for expansion or operations. The chapter includes a description of financial institutions, such as banks; financial markets, such as the New York Stock Exchange; financial instruments, such as stocks and bonds; and the role of the Federal Reserve System. Chapter 17 discusses the role of finance and the financial manager in an organization.

Summary of Learning Objectives

⌐1⌐ Explain the functions of accounting, and identify the three basic activities involving accounting.

Accountants measure, interpret, and communicate financial information to parties inside and outside the firm to support improved decision making. Accountants gather, record, and interpret financial information for management. They also provide financial information on the status and operations of the firm for evaluation by outside parties, such as government agencies, stockholders, potential investors, and lenders. Accounting plays key roles in financing activities, which help start and expand an organization; investing activities, which provide the assets it needs to continue operating; and operating activities, which focus on selling goods and services and paying expenses incurred in regular operations.

Assessment Check Answers ☑

1.1 Define *accounting*. Accounting is the process of measuring, interpreting, and communicating financial information in a way that describes the status and operation of an organization and aids in decision making.

1.2 Who uses accounting information? Managers of all types of organizations use accounting information to help them plan, assess performance, and control daily and long-term operations. Outside users of accounting information include government officials, investors, creditors, and donors.

1.3 What are the three business activities that involve accounting? The three activities involving accounting are financing, investing, and operating activities.

⌐2⌐ Describe the roles played by public, management, government, and not-for-profit accountants.

Public accountants provide accounting services to other firms or individuals for a fee. They are involved in such activities as auditing, tax return preparation, management consulting, and accounting system design. Management accountants collect and record financial transactions, prepare financial statements, and interpret them for managers in their own firms. Government and not-for-profit accountants perform many of the same functions as management accountants, but they analyze how effectively the organization or agency is operating, rather than its profits and losses.

Assessment Check Answers ☑

2.1 List the three services offered by public accounting firms. The three services offered by public accounting firms are auditing, management consulting, and tax services.

2.2 What tasks do management accountants perform? Management accountants work for the organization and are responsible for collecting and recording financial transactions, and preparing and interpreting financial statements.

⌈3⌋ Identify the foundations of the accounting system, including GAAP and the role of the Financial Accounting Standards Board (FASB).

The foundation of the accounting system in the United States is GAAP (generally accepted accounting principles), a set of guidelines or standards that accountants follow. There are four basic requirements to which all accounting rules should adhere: consistency, relevance, reliability, and comparability. The Financial Accounting Standards Board (FASB), an independent body made up of accounting professionals, is primarily responsible for evaluating, setting, and modifying GAAP. The U.S. Securities and Exchange Commission (SEC) also plays a role in establishing and modifying accounting standards for public companies, firms whose shares are traded in the financial markets.

Assessment Check Answers ☑

3.1 Define *GAAP*. GAAP stands for generally accepted accounting principles and is a set of standards or guidelines that accountants follow in recording and reporting financial transactions.

3.2 What are the four basic requirements to which all accounting rules must adhere? The four basic requirements to which all accounting rules must adhere are consistency, relevance, reliability, and comparability.

3.3 What is the role played by the FASB? The Financial Accounting Standards Board (FASB) is an independent body made up of accounting professionals and is primarily responsible for evaluating, setting, and modifying GAAP.

⌈4⌋ Outline the steps in the accounting cycle, and define *double-entry bookkeeping* and the *accounting equation*.

The accounting process involves recording, classifying, and summarizing data about transactions and then using this information to produce financial statements for the firm's managers and other interested parties. Transactions are recorded chronologically in journals, posted in ledgers, and then summarized in accounting statements. Today, much of this activity takes place electronically. The basic accounting equation states that assets (what a firm owns) must always equal liabilities (what a firm owes creditors) plus

owners' equity. This equation also illustrates double-entry bookkeeping, the process by which accounting transactions are recorded. Under double-entry bookkeeping, each individual transaction must have an offsetting transaction.

Assessment Check Answers ☑

4.1 List the steps in the accounting cycle. The accounting cycle involves the following steps: recording transactions, classifying these transactions, summarizing transactions, and using the summaries to produce financial statements.

4.2 What is the accounting equation? The accounting equation states that assets (what a firm owns) must always equal liabilities (what a firm owes) plus owners' equity. Therefore, if assets increase or decrease, there must be an offsetting increase or decrease in liabilities, owners' equity, or both.

4.3 Briefly explain double-entry bookkeeping. Double-entry bookkeeping means that every transaction must have an offsetting transaction.

⌈5⌋ Explain the functions and major components of the four principal financial statements: the balance sheet, the income statement, the statement of owners' equity, and the statement of cash flows.

The balance sheet shows the financial position of a company on a particular date. The three major classifications of balance sheet data are the components of the accounting equation: assets, liabilities, and owners' equity. The income statement shows the results of a firm's operations over a specific period. It focuses on the firm's activities—its revenues and expenditures—and the resulting profit or loss during the period. The major components of the income statement are revenues, cost of goods sold, expenses, and profit or loss. The statement of owners' equity shows the components of the change in owners' equity from the end of the prior year to the end of the current year. Finally, the statement of cash flows indicates a firm's cash receipts and cash payments during an accounting period. It outlines the sources and uses of cash in the basic business activities of operating, investing, and financing.

Assessment Check Answers ☑

5.1 List the four financial statements. The four financial statements are the balance sheet, the income statement, the statement of owners' equity, and the cash flow statement.

5.2 How is the balance sheet organized? Assets (what a firm owns) are shown on one side of the balance sheet and are listed in order of convertibility into cash. On the other side of the balance sheet are claims to assets, liabilities (what a firm owes), and owners' equity. Claims are listed in the order in which they are due, so liabilities are listed before owners' equity. Assets always equal liabilities plus owners' equity.

5.3 Define *accrual accounting*. Accrual accounting recognizes revenues and expenses when they occur, not when cash actually changes hands. Most companies use accrual accounting to prepare their financial statements.

6 Discuss how financial ratios are used to analyze a company's financial strengths and weaknesses.

Liquidity ratios measure a firm's ability to meet short-term obligations. Examples are the current ratio and the quick, or acid-test, ratio. Activity ratios, such as the inventory turnover ratio, accounts receivable turnover ratio, and the total asset turnover ratio, measure how effectively a firm uses its resources. Profitability ratios assess the overall financial performance of the business. The gross profit margin, net profit margin, and return on owners' equity are examples. Leverage ratios, such as the total liabilities to total assets ratio and the long-term debt to equity ratio, measure the extent to which the firm relies on debt to finance its operations. Financial ratios help managers and outside evaluators compare a firm's current financial information with that of previous years and with results for other firms in the same industry.

Assessment Check Answers ☑

6.1 List the four categories of financial ratios. The four categories of ratios are liquidity, activity, profitability, and leverage.

6.2 Define the following ratios: *current ratio, inventory turnover, net profit margin*, and *debt ratio*. The current ratio equals current assets divided by current liabilities; inventory turnover equals cost of goods sold divided by average inventory; net profit margin equals net income divided by sales; the debt ratio equals total liabilities divided by total assets.

7 Describe the role of budgets in a business.

Budgets are financial guidelines for future periods reflecting expected sales revenues, operating expenses, and cash receipts and outlays. They reflect management expectations for future occurrences and are based on plans that have been made. Budgets serve as important planning and controlling tools by providing standards against which actual performance can be measured. One important type of budget is the cash budget, which estimates cash inflows and outflows over a period of time.

Assessment Check Answers ☑

7.1 What is a budget? A budget is a planning and control tool that reflects the firm's expected sales revenues, operating expenses, cash receipts, and cash outlays.

7.2 How is a cash budget organized? Cash budgets are generally prepared monthly. Cash receipts are listed first. They include cash sales as well as the collection of past credit sales. Cash outlays are listed next. These include cash purchases, payment of past credit purchases, and operating expenses. The difference between cash receipts and cash outlays is net cash flow.

8 Outline accounting issues facing global business and the move toward one set of worldwide accounting rules.

One accounting issue that affects global business is exchange rates. An exchange rate is the ratio at which a country's currency can be exchanged for other currencies. Daily changes in exchange rates affect the accounting entries for sales and purchases of firms involved in international markets. These fluctuations create either losses or gains for particular companies. The International Accounting Standards Board (IASB) was established to provide worldwide consistency in financial reporting practices and comparability of and uniformity in international accounting standards. It has developed International Financial Reporting Standards (IFRS). Many countries have already adopted IFRS, and the United States is in the process of making the transition to it.

Assessment Check Answers ☑

8.1 How are financial statements adjusted for exchange rates? An exchange rate is the ratio at which a country's currency can be exchanged for other currencies. Fluctuations of exchange rates create either gains or losses for particular companies because data about international financial transactions must be translated into the currency of the country in which the parent company resides.

8.2 What is the purpose of the IASB? The International Accounting Standards Board (IASB) was established to provide worldwide consistency in financial reporting practices and comparability and uniformity of international accounting rules. The IASB has developed the International Financial Reporting Standards (IFRS).

▦ Business Terms You Need to Know

accounting 496	Foreign Corrupt Practices	double-entry	accrual accounting 511
public accountant 498	Act 502	bookkeeping 504	budget 517
generally accepted	accounting cycle 502	balance sheet 507	International Accounting
accounting principles	asset 503	income statement 508	Standards Board
(GAAP) 500	liability 503	statement of owners'	(IASB) 520
Financial Accounting	owners' equity 503	equity 510	International Financial
Standards Board	accounting	statement of cash	Reporting Standards
(FASB) 500	equation 504	flows 511	(IFRS) 520

Review Questions

1. Define *accounting*. Who are the major users of accounting information?

2. What are the three major business activities in which accountants play a major role? Give an example of each.

3. What does the term *GAAP* mean? Briefly explain the roles of the Financial Accounting Standards Board and the Securities and Exchange Commission.

4. What is double-entry bookkeeping? Give a brief example.

5. List the four major financial statements. Which financial statements are permanent and which are temporary?

6. What is the difference between a current asset and a long-term asset? Why is cash typically listed first on a balance sheet?

7. List and explain the major items found on an income statement.

8. What is accrual accounting? Give an example of how accrual accounting affects a firm's financial statement.

9. List the four categories of financial ratios and give an example of each. What is the purpose of ratio analysis?

10. What is a cash budget? Briefly outline what a simple cash budget might look like.

Projects and Teamwork Applications

1. Contact a local public accounting firm and set up an interview with one of the accountants. Ask the individual what his or her educational background is, what attracted the individual to the accounting profession, and what he or she does during a typical day. Prepare a brief report on your interview. Do you now want to learn more about the accounting profession? Are you more interested in possibly pursuing a career in accounting?

2. Suppose you work for a U.S. firm that has extensive European operations. You need to restate data from the various European currencies in U.S. dollars in order to prepare your firm's financial statements. Which financial statements and which components of these statements will be affected?

3. Identify two public companies operating in different industries. Collect at least three years' worth of financial statements for the firms. Calculate the financial ratios listed in Table 15.1. Prepare an oral report summarizing your findings.

4. You've been appointed treasurer of a local not-for-profit organization. You would like to improve the quality of the organization's financial reporting to existing and potential donors. Describe the kinds of financial statements you would like to see the organization's accountant prepare. Why do you think better quality financial statements might help reassure donors?

5. Adapting the format of Figure 15.7, prepare on a sheet of paper your personal cash budget for next month. Keep in mind the following suggestions as you prepare your budget:

    a. *Cash inflows.* Your sources of cash would include your payroll earnings, if any; gifts; scholarship monies; tax refunds; dividends and interest; and income from self-employment.

    b. *Cash outflows.* When estimating next month's cash outflows, include any of the following that may apply to your situation:

        i. Household expenses (rent or mortgage, utilities, maintenance, home furnishings, telephone/cell phone, cable TV, household supplies, groceries)

        ii. Education (tuition, fees, textbooks, supplies)

        iii. Work (transportation, clothing)

        iv. Clothing (purchases, cleaning, laundry)

        v. Automobile (auto payments, fuel, repairs) or other transportation (bus, train)

        vi. Insurance premiums
        - Renters (or homeowners)
        - Auto
        - Health
        - Life

        vii. Taxes (income, real estate, Social Security, Medicare)

        viii. Savings and investments

        ix. Entertainment/recreation (health club, vacation/travel, dining, movies)

        x. Debt (credit cards, installment loans)

        xi. Miscellaneous (charitable contributions, child care, gifts, medical expenses)

    c. *Beginning cash balance.* This amount could be based on a minimum cash balance you keep in your checking account and should include only the cash available for your use; therefore, money such as that invested in retirement plans should not be included.

Web Assignments

1. **International Accounting Standards Board (IASB).** The IASB is responsible for setting and modifying international accounting rules. Go to the IASB's Web site (http://www.iasb.org) and click on "about us." Print out the material and bring it to class to participate in a class discussion on the IASB.

2. **Certified management accountant (CMA).** As noted in the chapter, managerial accountants often seek CMA certifications. Visit the Web site of the Institute of Management Accountants (http://www.imanet.org). Click on "certification" and then "getting started." What are the educational and experiential requirements to obtain a CMA? How

many exams does a CMA candidate have to pass? What do these exams cover?

3. **Financial reporting requirements.** The chapter discussed the financial reporting requirements of public companies in the U.S. Public companies are those whose shares are traded on a stock exchange. Visit the Web site listed here. Type in the name of a public company and then click on "financials" to view the firm's current financial statements. Prepare a brief report comparing those statements to the ones shown in the chapter.

http://www.google.com/finance

Note: Internet Web addresses change frequently. If you don't find the exact sites listed, you may need to access the organization's home page and search from there or use a search engine such as Bing or Google.

Intacct Provides Accounting Software as a Service

CASE 15.1

As more businesses turn to cloud computing, they are making use of SaaS, or software as a service, instead of buying, installing, and maintaining software packages. With SaaS, a company subscribes to a Web site that leases software. The software remains on that provider's servers. Any approved company employee can access it from anywhere—an in-office computer; an off-site notebook; or even a BlackBerry, iPhone, or other hand-held device with Internet capability. All data are saved and stored on the Web site's servers. Smaller companies find SaaS offers many benefits. They don't have to buy expensive software packages, administer the software and on-site servers, or hire IT personnel.

Intacct, based in San José, California, was one of the first online SaaS providers of accounting software. More than 30,000 people across 3,000 companies use its products. Intacct provides two basic packages: Intacct Accounting Edition allows accounting firms and their clients to work on the same financial data simultaneously. It is used mostly by accounting firms whose clients have from five to 100 employees. The second package, called simply Intacct, is used by businesses that have grown too large to use QuickBooks or similar applications from Microsoft or Sage. These businesses generally have 25 to 1,000 employees. In this case, the business has the software and controls access to it; the accounting firm logs in as a user.

Daniel Druker, a senior vice president at Intacct, says, "Our research with the AICPA [American Institute of Certified Public Accountants] shows a 50 percent productivity improvement for accounting firms that switch to SaaS—plus roughly doubling in proactive consultation hours. And firms can serve around 10 percent more clients with the same staff, by reducing time for travel and error fixing."

One of Intacct's clients is ASP Global Services (ASPGS), a warehouse management solutions provider.

Intacct's software has enabled ASPGS to modernize and streamline its financial processes. The General Ledger program has improved ASPGS's ability to plan, budget, report, and analyze its business. The software also enables ASPGS to enter data faster and more efficiently without having to export those data into a program such as Microsoft Excel. Intacct allows ASPGS to see a real-time income statement at any given moment. As a result, ASPGS has more accurate financial reporting and has saved a great deal of time and resources.

Mike Mullane, the CEO of ASPGS, says, "Intacct is a huge time saver for us. With Intacct, there are a lot of processes you can set up once and then let them run automatically going forward. This allows us to be more effective in managing the company and enables us to spend more time looking forward instead of constantly looking at what has already happened."

Recently Intacct unveiled the latest edition of its financial management and accounting package. The program, called Winter 2010, enables GAAP and analysis without the need for additional software. It also includes modules for such options as accounting, purchasing, business intelligence, multicurrency support, and sales-tax management, among many others. Druker says about the new edition, "Our mindset is: If you're a small business, why run a system like this yourself. You don't have to install or configure a thing. We turn it on for you, and you use it as you would use Google or Amazon."

Questions for Critical Thinking

1. Do you see any potential disadvantages in using software to automate administrative processes such as accounting and financial reporting? If so, what are they?

2. Why is it important for users of financial accounting and other software packages to restrict access to certain kinds of information in the system?

Sources: Intacct Web site, http://us.intacct.com, accessed June 1, 2010; ASPGS Web site, http://unicode.com, accessed June 1, 2010; "Using Cloud Financial Applications from Intacct Cuts Monthly Close Process by More Than Two Weeks and Delivers $100,000 in Annual Salary Savings," *MarketWire,* March 29, 2010, http://www.marketwire.com; Daniel Dern, "Are You Being Served?" *Insight Magazine,* February–March 2010, http://www.icpas.org; "Intacct Launches Upgraded Online Accounting Program," *SmallBusinessComputing.com,* February 3, 2010, http://www.smallbusinesscomputing.com; "Intacct Winter 2010 Named One of the Top 10 Small Business Financial Applications by SmallBusinessComputing.com," press release, February 2, 2010, http://us.intacct.com.

CASE 15.2

BDO Seidman: Growing with the 20th Century and Beyond

In 1910, Maximillian Leonard Seidman (1888–1963), the son of Russian immigrants, founded the accounting firm of Seidman & Seidman in New York City. The profession of accounting was also brand new, but that situation soon changed.

When the income tax on individuals was established in 1913 by the Sixteenth Amendment to the U.S. Constitution, Seidman recognized the potential for growth as accountants took on a new role in tax planning for individuals. And when Congress enacted legislation in 1917 creating corporate income taxes, Seidman—now joined by two brothers—expanded the business to include corporations. The firm opened a second office in Michigan, just when the federal government converted furniture and woodworking factories to airplane manufacturing for WW I. Seidman & Seidman quickly became known for serving this industry when it developed a successful system for keeping track of furniture-plant costs.

Maximillian Seidman ran the firm for 45 years. He wrote many articles and served in many industry organizations. He advocated "Total Involvement" of his firm's employees in the business of their clients. In 1944 he declared, "It is the manner in which we serve our clients today that will determine whether we shall have them to serve as clients in the future."

Seidman & Seidman continued to expand, becoming a truly national firm by the 1960s. In 1963, it joined other accounting companies from Canada, Britain, the Netherlands and (then West) Germany in an international organization. In 1973, these firms formed a new group called BDO (Binder Dijker Otte & Co.). This group, now called BDO International, is the fifth largest accounting firm in the world, with 1,138 branches in 115 countries. The U.S. member, BDO Seidman LLP, has 17 branches and more than 400 independent locations.

Albert Lopez is the Southeast Regional Business Line Leader for Assurance Services at the Miami branch of BDO Seidman LLP. Its team-oriented approach and experience has enabled it to create and maintain long-term relationships as its many clients endure the recent ups and downs of the economy. Lopez says, "Success is about service. In this economy, it is especially important to be collaborative and to bring a variety of offerings, including tax, assurance and consulting to the table . . . we want our clients to know that senior team members are always available."

As BDO celebrates its 100th anniversary, it has received a number of industry honors. BDO recently announced that 39 of its U.S. offices (including Miami) had won the Alfred P. Sloan Award for Business Excellence in Workplace Flexibility. This award acknowledges the personal and workplace advantages of flexibility programs when a firm uses them to improve its effectiveness and to benefit its employees. *Accounting Today* magazine and Best Companies Group named BDO one of the "best accounting firms." The Best Accounting Firms program identifies the best employers in the accounting industry and their benefits to the U.S. economy, workforce, and businesses. And, the American Society of Women Accountants (ASWA) and the American Woman's Society of CPAs (AWSCPA) both named BDO one of the "best 2010 CPA firms for women."

Questions

1. What historic and economic factors do you think might have contributed to the growth and expansion of the accounting industry, and Seidman's firm, from the early 20th century to today?

2. What advantages does BDO Seidman LLP enjoy in belonging to a large, international group?

Sources: Company Web site, http://www.bdo.com, accessed June 1, 2010; "Business Profile: BDO Seidman, LLP," *Business Leader,* http://www.businessleader.com, accessed June 1, 2010; "BDO Named a Best CPA Firm for Women by American Society of Women Accountants and American Woman's Society of CPAs," press release, April 29, 2010, http://eon.businesswire.com; "BDO Wins Alfred P. Sloan Award for Business Excellence," press release, *Career-Journal,* February 1, 2010, http://www.career-journal.com.

It's great to love the business you're in, as do Alysa Binder and Dan Wiesel, co-founders of Pet Airways. They not only love their business, they also care for their customers, who happen to be furry and four-legged. But Pet Airways, the only service devoted entirely to transporting cats and dogs around the country by air, is also a business—which means that Binder and Wiesel must pay attention to the financial aspects of their company. "We're doing something that's a feel-good, do-good service and it's absolutely rewarding," says Dan Wiesel. But Wiesel knows that, without a thorough accounting of finances, any small business is likely to crash shortly after takeoff.

Binder and Wiesel started Pet Airways based on personal experience—they wanted a better, safer travel option for their Jack Russell terrier than being stashed in the cargo hold. With fluctuating temperatures and dark, cramped quarters, a trip aboard a commercial airline can be unsafe and traumatic for many animals. Binder and Wiesel, both of whom had backgrounds in business, decided they could do a better job than the passenger airlines by offering pet owners a choice.

As soon as they agreed on their business idea, Wiesel jumped into the financial questions. "I had to ask, 'Is this a viable financial enterprise? What would people pay for a service like this?'" recalls Wiesel. He researched such issues as how much it would cost to retrofit the climate-controlled cabin of a plane to carry animals; how much it would cost to fly a plane from one location to another; and how much it would cost to staff the company. He also researched how much demand there would really be for a pet airline, and how many pets would have to be booked on each flight in order for the trip to be profitable. He put all of these variables—and more—onto a spreadsheet so he could see what he and Binder would need to do for Pet Airways to take off.

Wiesel says that financial modeling, financial spreadsheets, and good research on costs and pricing can make or break the launch of any small business. "Accounting itself is an absolute full-time, big job," he admits. He wants to "know how much money is coming in, how much is going out, and what's the bottom line." In addition there are taxes, payroll, benefits, and other financial documentation. Wiesel advises that in many cases it's a good idea for small businesses to contract out their accounting to professionals. He prefers this because outsourcing actually contains the cost of accounting.

Running a business is a balancing act, observes Wiesel. "You have to be able to reconcile how much cash you have with how you are going to spend it." For

example, as Pet Airways looks to expand to more cities, the firm has to consider the cost of adding more flights and more staff as compared to how many more customers it might attract. Binder points out that, while it's exciting to think about growing, they have to factor in the expenditures of everything from additional hiring to developing a more sophisticated Web site and online reservation system.

All of this comes back to a sound financial plan, says Wiesel. "The financial plan is really the core of it because you can play the 'what if' game. You can look at the implications of certain decisions." For example, if Binder and Wiesel want to fly to a certain city, they can research which passenger airlines already serve that city. If it's United Airlines, they know that pet owners will be charged $175 for an animal to fly beneath a passenger's seat, or $250 to fly in the cargo hold. They can look at how many flights a day these airlines fly to the city, and probably learn how many pets are booked. And they can find out which terminal Pet Airways would use in addition to any airport taxes and fees. They can plug all this data into the financial plan and see if it works before making the final decision.

Binder and Wiesel usually agree on their company's goals and objectives. Wiesel says it all boils down to one question: "What's it going to cost you to achieve your plan?" Recently, Pet Airways announced its merger with the firm American Antiquities in a share-exchange agreement, a major step toward expansion. "We are delighted to complete this transaction . . . and believe this event represents a significant step in implementing our business plan and continued expansion," stated Wiesel.

Questions for Critical Thinking

1. In Pet Airways' accounting equation, what might be some of the firm's liabilities? What might be considered its assets?

2. Identify the types of costs that Pet Airways might list on its income statement.

3. Why is it important for a small company like Pet Airways to prepare a regular budget?

4. If Pet Airways decides to expand its operations overseas, what kinds of accounting issues would the firm have to take into consideration?

Sources: Pet Airways Web site, http://www.petairways.com, accessed August 25, 2010; "Pet Airways Combines with a Public Company Through Share Exchange with American Antiquities," *PR Newswire*, August 16, 2010, http://www.prnewswire.com; "Doctors Call for Airline Pet Ban," *The Independent*, February 21, 2010, http://license.icopyright.net.

Chapter 16

Learning Objectives

[1] Outline the structure and importance of the financial system.

[2] List the various types of securities.

[3] Define *financial market,* and distinguish between primary and secondary financial markets.

[4] Describe the characteristics of the major stock exchanges.

[5] Discuss the organization and functioning of financial institutions.

[6] Explain the functions of the Federal Reserve System and the tools it uses to control the supply of money and credit.

[7] Evaluate the major features of regulations and laws affecting the financial system.

[8] Describe the global financial system.

Today's Financial Markets and Institutions

Citigroup Closes Out the Financial Supermarket

©Mark Lennihan/AP/Wide World Photos

The merger seemed like a good idea at the time. The stock market was up, money was flowing freely, and huge acquisitions were commonplace. A little over a decade ago Travelers Group, a big insurance company, merged with Citibank's growing stable of banking and other financial businesses in a $76 billion deal.

Under the management of Sanford Weill, Travelers had already bought up brokerage firm Smith Barney, insurance firm Aetna, and Wall Street investment banking firm Salomon Brothers. The merger with Citibank, the nation's largest bank, made history by consolidating so many lines of financial business—banking, insurance, investments—into one huge conglomerate. Weill emerged as CEO of the new company, which some observers said offered one-stop shopping, calling it a financial supermarket. At its height Citigroup, as the new giant was called, had 374,000 employees in more than 100 countries. It seemed the only place it could go was up.

But the huge profits expected from the deal proved elusive, and executives at the top of the merged firm did not see eye-to-eye. Problems and infighting among the board members and the managers spread, costs ballooned, and the company's technology fell behind the times. Meanwhile, Citigroup's stock price plummeted—at one point sinking more than 75 percent to a 16-year low. Then the bottom dropped out in 2008 and 2009. Losses mounted into tens of billions of dollars as Citigroup was caught in the economic crisis that hit so many other financial players. The company had badly overextended itself by buying up highly risky mortgage-backed securities that even its own executives failed to understand.

"I cannot think of one positive that developed as a result of [merging] these two companies," said one industry observer. "The miracle of Citigroup is that it still is in the position it is in, given the massive mismanagement."

As economic conditions and losses worsened, Citigroup was at last forced to take some painful medicine to try to find its way back to financial health. It had to sell most of its business units—dismantling the financial supermarket. Sanford Weill had retired in 2006, leaving the company in the hands of Charles Prince III. Prince, a lawyer by training, had steered the company through some of the biggest corporate accounting and conflict-of-interest scandals of the late 1990s—the collapse of Enron and WorldCom—in both of which the titanic firm was said to be involved. However, not even Prince could save the company this time. As losses from mortgage investments climbed, Citigroup had to accept $45 billion under the U.S. government's Troubled Assets Relief Program. Prince was forced out, to be replaced by Vikram Pandit.

Prince had already sold the Travelers insurance business, so Pandit's first step was to streamline the remainder of the firm. Pandit sold the very businesses Weill had acquired. The first unit to go was brokerage firm Smith Barney. Morgan Stanley paid $2.7 billion for a 51 percent ownership stake and an option to complete the purchase in three years. Citigroup also announced plans to eliminate noncore businesses like consumer finance and a private-label credit card unit, to cut back its stock trading activities, and to sell its overseas brokerage and asset management firms. These changes came quickly, under pressure from federal regulators. Most observers applauded the breakup as the right solution, saying it had just come a few years too late.

Many factors likely contributed to the failure of the financial supermarket, including management mistakes, a scattered market focus, and bloated costs. Unchecked risk taking was another element, according to some experts. In addition, the growing ease of Internet banking with its favorable rates and terms helped undercut what Citigroup hoped would be major money makers among its operating units. Customers no longer needed to be physically present in a financial institution to purchase products. Some critics now question whether a financial supermarket was what banking customers really wanted after all.[1]

Businesses, governments, and individuals often need to raise capital. Assume a businessperson forecasts a sharp increase in sales for the coming year, and this expected increase requires additional inventory. If the business lacks sufficient cash to purchase the needed merchandise, it may turn to a bank for a short-term loan. On the other hand, some individuals and businesses have incomes that are greater than their current expenditures and wish to earn a rate of return on the excess funds. For instance, say your income this month is $3,000 but your expenditures are only $2,500. You can take the extra $500 and deposit it in your bank savings account, which pays you a rate of interest.

financial system process by which money flows from savers to users.

The two transactions just described are small parts of what is known as the **financial system**, the process by which money flows from savers to users. Virtually all businesses, governments, and individuals participate in the financial system, and a well-functioning one is vital to a nation's economic well-being. The financial system is the topic of this chapter.

We begin by describing the financial system and its components in more detail. Then, the major types of financial instruments, such as stocks and bonds, are outlined. Next we discuss financial markets, where financial instruments are bought and sold. We then describe the world's major stock markets, such as the New York Stock Exchange.

Next, banks and other financial institutions are described in depth. The structure and responsibilities of the U.S. Federal Reserve System, along with the tools the Fed uses to control the supply of money and credit, are detailed. The chapter concludes with an overview of the major laws and regulations affecting the financial system and a discussion of today's global financial system.

Understanding the Financial System

Households, businesses, government, financial institutions, and financial markets together form what is known as the financial system. A simple diagram of the financial system is shown in Figure 16.1.

On the left are savers—those with excess funds. For a variety of reasons, savers choose not to spend all of their current income, so they have a surplus of funds. Users are the opposite of savers; their spending needs exceed their current income, so they have a deficit. They need to obtain additional funds to make up the difference. Savings are provided by some households, businesses, and the government, but other households, businesses, and the government are also borrowers. Households may need money to buy automobiles or homes. Businesses may need money to purchase inventory or build new production facilities. Governments may need money to build highways and courthouses.

Generally, in the United States, households are net savers—meaning that as a whole they save more funds than they use—whereas businesses and governments are net

FIGURE
16.1
Overview of the Financial Systems and Its Components

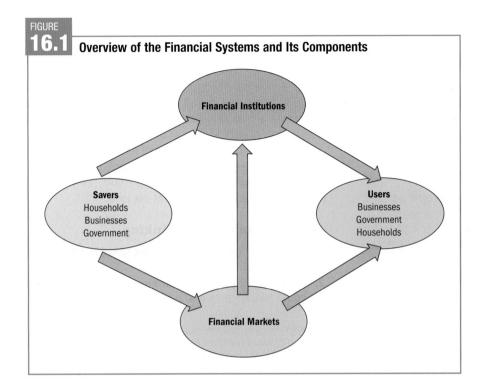

users—meaning that they use more funds than they save. The fact that most of the net savings in the U.S. financial system are provided by households may be a bit of a surprise initially, because Americans do not have a reputation for being thrifty. Yet even though the savings rate of American households is low compared with those of other countries, American households still save hundreds of billions of dollars each year.

How much an individual saves is a function of many variables. One of the most important is the person's age. People often transition from net borrowers to net savers as they get older. When you graduate from college and begin a career, you likely have little in the way of savings. In fact, you may be deeply in debt. In the early years of your career, you may spend more than you make as you acquire major assets, such as a home. So in these early years your *net worth*—the difference between what you own and what you owe—is very low and may even be negative. However, as your career progresses and your income rises, you will begin to build a financial nest egg to fund retirement and other needs. Your net worth will also increase. It will continue to increase until you retire and begin drawing on your retirement savings.

Funds can be transferred between savers and users in two ways: directly and indirectly. A direct transfer means that the user raises the needed funds directly from savers. While direct transfers occur, the vast majority of funds flow through either financial markets or financial institutions. For example, assume a local school district needs to build a new high school. The district doesn't have enough cash on hand to pay for the school construction costs, so it sells bonds to investors (savers) in the financial market. The district uses the proceeds from the sale to pay for the new school and in return pays bond investors interest each year for the use of their money.

The other way in which funds can be transferred indirectly is through financial institutions—for example, a commercial bank such as Cincinnati-based Fifth Third Bank or Alabama-based Regions Bank. The bank pools customer deposits and uses the funds to make

TD Bank: "As Green as Our Logo"

TD Bank's square, green logo is a familiar sight from Maine to Florida. TD Bank announced that it was the largest U.S. bank to go carbon neutral. The bank achieved carbon neutrality by reducing waste, using alternative sources of energy, and building environmentally friendly buildings from sustainable materials. With 1,000 branches, or "stores," TD has used its resources to pursue an aggressive "green" policy.

To demonstrate its goal of carbon neutrality, TD bank unveiled a new prototype store. The 3,800-square-foot design is designed to reduce energy use by 50 percent, compared with earlier models. Each new store will make up to 20 percent of its own electricity with solar panels on the roof. To keep interior temperatures comfortable, the windows will have specially coated glass that reflects or absorbs heat energy. Sensors will control lighting over the course of the day. The drive-through facility will also have a translucent solar canopy. Outside, the landscaping will feature drought-resistant plants and water-efficient plumbing.

Among other measures, TD Bank has bought a block of wind energy large enough to run its 2,300 ATMs. It plans to encourage its customers to save energy by emphasizing online banking and paperless statements. TD Bank has also located many of its branches near public transportation.

TD Bank's first fully green office opened in Queens Village, New York. This branch has applied for LEED (Leadership in Energy and Environmental Design) Platinum Certification, the highest level. The bank eventually plans to have all of its offices meet LEED standards.

Fred Graziano, TD Bank's head of retail banking, says, "We're taking the environment seriously and we strongly believe this is the right thing to do for our business, customers, employees and the community. We want TD Bank to be as green as our logo."

Questions for Critical Thinking

1. Why does "going green" make good business sense for TD Bank?

2. Think about your own banking practices. What steps could you take to make them greener?

Sources: Company Web site, http://www.tdbank.com, accessed June 21, 2010; James Comtois, "TD Bank's First Green Branch Sprouts in Queens," *Crain's New York Business.com,* March 23, 2010, http://www.crainsnewyork.com; Patrick Lo, "TD Bank Goes Carbon Neutral," *Green Street Journal,* March 16, 2010, http://www.gsjournal.com; "TD Bank Goes Carbon Neutral, Unveils 'Green Store' Prototype," *Environmental Leader,* February 22, 2010, http://www.environmentalleader.com; "TD Bank, America's Most Convenient Bank, Announces It's Now Carbon Neutral and Unveils New 'Green Store' Prototype Design," press release, February 18, 2010, http://multivu.prnewswire.com.

Assessment Check ✔

1. What is the financial system?

2. In the financial system, who are the borrowers and who are the savers?

3. List the two most common ways in which funds are transferred between borrowers and savers.

securities financial instruments that represent obligations on the part of the issuers to provide the purchasers with expected stated returns on the funds invested or loaned.

loans to businesses and households. These borrowers pay the bank interest, and it, in turn, pays depositors interest for the use of their money.

The accompanying "Going Green" feature describes how TD Bank has begun transforming all its branches so that they will be "carbon neutral."

Types of Securities

For the funds they borrow from savers, businesses and governments provide different types of guarantees for repayment. **Securities**, also called financial instruments, represent obligations on the part of the issuers—businesses and governments—to provide the purchasers with expected or stated returns on the funds invested or loaned. Securities can be grouped into three categories: money market instruments, bonds, and stock. Money market instruments and bonds are both debt securities. Stocks are units of ownership in corporations like General Electric, Best Buy, 3M, and PepsiCo.

Money Market Instruments

Money market instruments are short-term debt securities issued by governments, financial institutions, and corporations. All money market instruments mature within one year from the date of issue. The issuer pays interest to the investors for the use of their funds. Money market instruments are generally low-risk securities and are purchased by investors when they have surplus cash. Examples of money market instruments include U.S. Treasury bills, commercial paper, and bank certificates of deposit.

Treasury bills are short-term securities issued by the U.S. Treasury and backed by the full faith and credit of the U.S. government. Treasury bills are sold with a maturity of 30, 90, 180, or 360 days and have a minimum denomination of $1,000. They are considered virtually risk free and easy to resell. Commercial paper is securities sold by corporations, such as Raytheon, that mature in from 1 to 270 days from the date of issue. Although slightly riskier than Treasury bills, commercial paper is still generally considered a very low-risk security.

A certificate of deposit (CD) is a time deposit at a financial institution, such as a commercial bank, savings bank, or credit union. The sizes and maturity dates of CDs vary considerably and can often be tailored to meet the needs of purchasers. CDs in denominations of $250,000 or less per depositor are federally insured. CDs in larger denominations are not federally insured but can be sold more easily before they mature.

Bonds

Bondholders are creditors of a corporation or government body. By selling bonds, a firm obtains long-term debt capital. Federal, state, and local governments also acquire funds through bonds. Bonds are issued in various denominations, or face values, usually between $1,000 and $25,000. Each issue indicates a rate of interest to be paid to the bondholder— stated as a percentage of the bond's face value—as well as a maturity date on which the bondholder is paid the bond's full face value. Because bondholders are creditors, they have a claim on the firm's assets that must be satisfied before any claims of stockholders in the event of the firm's bankruptcy, reorganization, or liquidation.

Types of Bonds A prospective bond investor can choose among a variety of bonds. The major types of bonds are summarized in Table 16.1. *Government bonds* are bonds sold by the U.S. Department of the Treasury. Because government bonds are backed by the full faith and credit of the U.S. government, they are considered the least risky of all bonds. The Treasury sells bonds that mature in 2, 5, 10, and 30 years from the date of issue.

Municipal bonds are bonds issued by state or local governments. Two types of municipal bonds are available. A *revenue bond* is a bond issue whose proceeds will be used to pay for a project that will produce revenue, such as a toll road or bridge. The Oklahoma Turnpike Authority has issued such bonds. A *general obligation bond* is a bond whose proceeds are to be used to pay for a project that will not produce any revenue, such as a new Indiana State Police Post. General obligation bonds can be sold only by states or local governmental units—such as Grand Rapids, Michigan, or Bergen County, New Jersey—that have the power to levy taxes. An important feature of municipal bonds is that their interest payments are exempt from federal income tax. Because of this attractive feature, municipal bonds generally carry lower interest rates than either corporate or government bonds.

Corporate bonds are a diverse group and often vary based on the collateral—the property pledged by the borrower—that backs the bond. For example, a *secured bond* is backed by a specific pledge of company assets. These assets are collateral, just like a home is collateral for a mortgage. However, many firms also issue unsecured bonds, called *debentures*. These bonds are backed only by the financial reputation of the issuing corporation.

Another popular type of bond is the *mortgage pass-through security*. These securities are backed by a pool of mortgage loans purchased from lenders, such as savings banks.

16.1 Types of Bonds

ISSUER	TYPES OF SECURITIES	RISK	SPECIAL FEATURES
U.S. Treasury (government bonds)	Notes: Mature in 10 years or fewer from date of issue.	Treasury bonds and notes carry virtually no risk.	Interest is exempt from state income taxes.
	Bonds: Mature in 30 years from date of issue.		
State and local governments (municipal bonds)	General obligation: Issued by state or local governmental units with taxing authority; backed by the full faith and credit of the state where issued.	Risk varies, depending on the financial health of the issuer.	Interest is exempt from federal income taxes and may be exempt from state income taxes.
	Revenue: Issued to pay for projects that generate revenue, such as water systems or toll roads; revenue from project used to pay principal and interest.	Most large municipal bond issues are rated in terms of credit risk (AAA or Aaa is the highest rating).	
Corporations	Secured bonds: Bonds are backed by specific assets.	Risk varies depending on the financial health of the issuer.	A few corporate bonds are convertible into shares of common stock of the issuing company.
	Unsecured bonds (debentures): Backed by the financial health and reputation of the issuer.	Most corporate bond issues are rated in terms of credit risk (AAA or Aaa is the highest rating).	
Financial institutions	Mortgage pass-through securities.	Generally very low risk.	They pay monthly income consisting of both interest and principal.

As borrowers make their monthly mortgage payments, these payments are "passed through" to the holders of the securities. Most mortgage pass-through securities are relatively safe because all mortgages in the pool are insured. However, in recent years, mortgage pass-through securities consisting of pools of so-called *subprime mortgages*, loans made to borrowers with poor credit ratings, were issued. Many of these securities turned out to be quite risky and, in part, triggered what became known as the *credit crisis*. The extent of the crisis forced the federal government to undertake a massive bailout of the financial system. The Office of Financial Stability—part of the U.S. Treasury department—was created to purchase poor-quality mortgage-backed and other securities from financial institutions.

Quality Ratings for Bonds Two factors determine the price of a bond: its risk and its interest rate. Bonds vary considerably in terms of risk. One tool bond investors use to assess the risk of a bond is its *bond rating*. Several investment firms rate corporate and municipal bonds, the best known of which are Standard & Poor's (S&P), Moody's, and Fitch. Table 16.2 lists the S&P bond ratings. Moody's and Fitch use similar rating systems. Bonds with the lowest level of risk are rated AAA. As ratings descend, risk increases. Bonds with ratings of BBB and above are classified as *investment-grade bonds*. By contrast, bonds with ratings of BB and below are classified as *speculative* or *junk bonds*. Junk bonds attract investors by offering high interest rates in exchange for greater risk. Today, junk bonds pay about 50 percent

16.2 Standard & Poor's Bond Ratings

Highest	AAA	Investment grade
	AA	
	A	
	BBB	
	BB	Speculative grade
	B	
	CCC	
	CC	
Lowest	C	

Note: Standard & Poor's occasionally assigns a plus or minus following the letter rating. For instance, AA+ means that the bond is higher quality than most AA bonds but hasn't quite met AAA standards. Ratings below C indicate that the bond is currently not paying interest.

more in interest than do investment-grade corporate bonds. The credit crisis of recent years generated a great deal of criticism of the ratings companies.

The second factor affecting the price of a bond is its interest rate. Other things being equal, the higher the interest rate, the higher the price of a bond. However, everything else often is not equal; the bonds may not be equally risky, or one may have a longer maturity. Investors must evaluate the trade-offs involved.

Another important influence on bond prices is the *market interest rate*. Because bonds pay fixed rates of interest, as market interest rates rise, bond prices fall, and vice versa. For instance, the price of a ten-year bond, paying 5 percent per year, would fall by about 8 percent if market interest rates rose from 5 percent to 6 percent.

Most corporate and municipal bonds, and some government bonds, are callable. A *call provision* allows the issuer to redeem the bond before its maturity at a specified price. Not surprisingly, issuers tend to call bonds when market interest rates are declining. For example, if York County, Pennsylvania, had $50 million in bonds outstanding with a 5 percent annual interest rate, it would pay $2.5 million annually in interest. If interest rates decline to 3 percent, the county may decide to call the 5 percent bonds, repaying the principal from the proceeds of newly issued 3 percent bonds. Calling the 5 percent bonds and issuing 3 percent bonds will save the county $1 million a year in interest payments. The savings in annual interest expense should more than offset the cost of retiring the old bonds and issuing new ones.

Stock

The basic form of corporate ownership is embodied in **common stock**. Purchasers of common stock are the true owners of a corporation. Holders of common stock vote on major company decisions, such as purchasing another company or electing a board of directors. In return for the money they invest, they expect to receive some sort of return.

common stock basic form of corporate ownership.

This return can come in the form of cash dividend payments, expected price appreciation, or both. Dividends vary widely from firm to firm. As a general rule, faster-growing companies pay less in dividends because they need more funds to finance their growth. Consequently, investors expect stocks paying little or no cash dividends to show greater price appreciation compared with stocks paying more generous cash dividends.

Sometimes unforeseen events can have a profound effect on dividends. On April 20, 2010, the oil-drilling rig *Deepwater Horizon*, leased by the British oil firm BP, exploded and caught fire, killing 11 oil workers and injuring others. The oil well, off the southeast coast of Louisiana, began leaking millions of gallons of crude oil and methane, endangering countless fish, birds, and other marine animals in the Gulf of Mexico. This is the first oil rig disaster of this magnitude to occur in the United States. Fishermen and others who made their living on the gulf saw their livelihoods threatened. The oil reached land, polluting the wetlands and beaches of Louisiana, Mississippi, Alabama, and Florida, harming wildlife there as well as damaging the tourist industry. Local residents, the media, and government figures were severe in condemning BP for not preventing the explosion and spill in the first place, for not capping the leaking well quickly and efficiently, for underestimating the quantities of leaking oil and methane, and for assembling insufficient forces and equipment for the cleanup.

Amid intense public and political pressure, BP launched an advertising campaign in print and on television, featuring its CEO, Tony Hayward, promising to "make this right." In early June, more than 40 members of Congress called on BP to suspend its dividends, stop the ad campaign, and instead use that money to clean up the oil spill. BP's stock began to fall, and Standard & Poor's downgraded BP's debt rating from AA-minus to A, hinting that it might downgrade that rating further. BP's chairman, Carl-Henric Svanberg, announced that BP would cancel dividend payments to shareholders for the first quarter of the fiscal year and suspend dividend payments to shareholders for the second and third quarters.

Before the disaster, BP had been Britain's largest company, but in the following months its value fell by half. Although the dividend suspension is not likely to have a severe affect on American shareholders, many investors and retirees in Britain rely on those dividends for income. In fact, BP's stock is the source of roughly 12 percent of all dividends paid on the London Stock Exchange.

BP also agreed to create a fund to pay damages to fishermen, small-business owners, and others with financial losses caused by the oil spill. The fund, which will eventually total $20 billion and represents approximately one year's profit, will be administered by a neutral third party. Anyone whose claim is turned down will have the right of appeal. Scientists estimated the well was leaking more than 2.5 million gallons a day, making it the largest oil-related disaster in U.S. history.[2]

Common stockholders benefit from company success, and they risk the loss of their investments if the company fails. If a firm dissolves, claims of creditors must be satisfied before stockholders receive anything. Because creditors have the first (or senior) claim to assets, holders of common stock are said to have a residual claim on company assets.

The market value of a stock is the price at which the stock is currently selling. For example, Johnson & Johnson's stock price fluctuated between $59 and $69 per share during a recent year. What determines this market value is complicated; many variables cause stock prices to move up or down. However, in the long run stock prices tend to follow a company's profits.

Preferred Stock   In addition to common stock, a few companies also issue preferred stock—stock whose holders receive preference in the payment of dividends. General

Motors and Ford are examples of firms with preferred stock outstanding. Also, if a company is dissolved, holders of preferred stock have claims on the firm's assets that are ahead of the claims of common stockholders. On the other hand, preferred stockholders rarely have any voting rights, and the dividend they are paid is fixed, regardless of how profitable the firm becomes. Therefore, although preferred stock is legally classified as equity, many investors consider it to be more like a bond than common stock.

Convertible Securities Companies may issue bonds or preferred stock that contains a conversion feature. Such bonds or stock are called *convertible securities*. This feature gives the bondholder or preferred stockholder the right to exchange the bond or preferred stock for a fixed number of shares of common stock. Convertible bonds pay lower interest rates than those lacking conversion features, helping to reduce the interest expense of the issuing firms. Investors are willing to accept these lower interest rates because they value the potential for additional gains if the price of the firm's stock increases. For instance, at a price of $61 per share, Peabody Energy's convertible bond would have a common stock value of at least $1,043 ($61 × 17.1). Should the price of Peabody's common stock increase by $10 per share, the value of the convertible will increase by at least $171.

Financial Markets

Securities are issued and traded in **financial markets**. While there are many different types of financial markets, one of the most important distinctions is between primary and secondary markets. In the **primary markets**, firms and governments issue securities and sell them initially to the general public. When a company needs capital to purchase inventory, expand a plant, make major investments, acquire another firm, or pursue other business goals, it may sell a bond or stock issue to the investing public. For example, Russian

Richard Levine/Alamy

■ On the side of this building in Times Square, New York City, current stock prices and news updates are displayed.

Citigroup Spins Off Primerica Inc.

Not long ago, the banking giant Citigroup included not only banking but also insurance, among other interests. Following the recent financial crisis, Citigroup's CEO, Vikram Pandit, began to dispose of some of these holdings. He wanted to slim the company down to its original core banking business, focusing on large institutions and wealthy individuals.

Primerica Inc. was one of those holdings. Based in Duluth, Georgia, Primerica sells life insurance, mutual funds, and other financial products door-to-door. Its middle-class clients earn from $30,000 to $100,000 a year. The company never fit well with the rest of Citigroup, and its 100,000 fiercely independent salespeople liked it that way. As the financial crisis worsened, some of them called for cutting ties with the parent company.

Citigroup tried to sell Primerica but could not find a buyer willing to pay the asking price. So Citigroup announced that it would spin off Primerica instead. Primerica would issue an initial public offering (IPO), selling shares of stock for the first time. Primerica planned to sell 18 million shares at $12 to $14 a share. Under the terms of the IPO, Citigroup would take all the profits and keep Primerica's existing accounts. Primerica would emerge smaller but would keep any new policies. John Addison and Rick Williams, the co-CEOs of Primerica, said, "We're going to be a smaller, faster-growing company going forward."

The IPO exceeded expectations. Primerica sold more than 21 million shares at almost $20 each. Addison and Williams feel that the company's focus has contributed to its success. "No one else has our business model," Williams declared. "No one else focuses on the middle-income, middle market like we do." Analysts took the IPO's success as a sign that both the life insurance industry and the market were recovering from the recession.

Questions for Critical Thinking

1. Visit Citibank's and Primerica's Web sites. Why do you think these two companies did not mesh well together?

2. Although Citibank failed to find a buyer for Primerica, the IPO was very successful. Why do you think this was the case?

Sources: Primerica Web site, http://www.primerica.com, accessed June 21, 2010; Citigroup Web site, http://www.citigroup.com, accessed June 21, 2010; Kerri Shannon, "Citigroup Spin-Off Primerica Boasts Strong Stock Debut in Hot IPO Market," *Money Morning*, April 4, 2010, http://moneymorning.com; "Primerica IPO a Success as Shares Jump," *CNBC*, April 1, 2010, http://www.cnbc.com; Maria Aspan and Clare Baldwin, "Citi Spinoff Primerica Soars on Hopes for Economy," *Reuters*, April 1, 2010, http://www.reuters.com; David Enrich, "An IPO of Primerica Will End a Citi Era," *The Wall Street Journal*, November 6, 2009, http://www.online.wsj.com.

Nanotechnologies Corporation planned to sell $1.7 billion in bonds to pay for expansion and new projects. Similarly, with a massive budget deficit, California offered as much as $3.4 billion in Build America Bonds, which were part of the recent federal stimulus package.[3]

A stock offering gives investors the opportunity to purchase ownership shares in a firm such as the well-known drug maker Amgen and to participate in its future growth, in exchange for providing current capital. When a company offers stock for sale to the general public for the first time, it is called an *initial public offering (IPO)*. Many of these offerings were from Asian companies.[4] The "Hit & Miss" feature describes an American company's IPO.

Both profit-seeking corporations and government agencies also rely on primary markets to raise funds by issuing bonds. For example, the federal government sells Treasury bonds to finance part of federal outlays such as interest on outstanding federal debt. State and local governments sell bonds to finance capital projects such as the construction of sewer systems, streets, and fire stations.

Announcements of new stock and bond offerings appear daily in business publications such as *The Wall Street Journal*. These announcements are often in the form of a simple black-and-white ad called a *tombstone*.

Securities are sold to the investing public in two ways: in open auctions and through investment bankers. Virtually all securities sold through open auctions consist of U.S. Treasury securities. A week before an upcoming auction, the Department of the Treasury announces the type and number of securities it will be auctioning. Treasury bills are auctioned weekly, but longer-term Treasury securities are auctioned once a month or once a quarter. Sales of most corporate and municipal securities are made via financial institutions such as Morgan Stanley. These institutions purchase the issue from the firm or government and then resell the issue to investors. This process is known as *underwriting.*

Financial institutions underwrite stock and bond issues at a discount, meaning that they pay the issuing firm or government less than the price the financial institutions charge investors. This discount is compensation for services rendered, including the risk financial institutions incur whenever they underwrite a new security issue. Although the size of the discount is often negotiable, it usually averages around 5 percent for all types of securities. The size of the underwriting discount, however, is generally higher for stock issues than it is for bond issues. For instance, underwriting discounts for IPOs are generally between 7 and 10 percent.

Corporations and governments are willing to pay for the services provided by financial institutions because they are financial market experts. In addition to locating buyers for the issue, the underwriter typically advises the issuer on such details as the general characteristics of the issue, its pricing, and the timing of the offering. Several financial institutions commonly participate in the underwriting process. The issuer selects a lead, or primary, financial institution, which in turn forms a syndicate consisting of other financial institutions. Each member of the syndicate purchases a portion of the security issue, which it resells to investors.

Media reports of stock and bond trading are most likely to refer to trading in the **secondary market**, a collection of financial markets in which previously issued securities are traded among investors. The corporations or governments that originally issued the securities being traded are not directly involved in the secondary market. They make no payments when securities are sold nor receive any of the proceeds when securities are purchased. The New York Stock Exchange (NYSE), for example, is a secondary market. In terms of the dollar value of securities bought and sold, the secondary market is four to five times as large as the primary market. Each day, roughly 1.6 billion shares worth about $45 billion are traded on the NYSE.[5] The characteristics of the world's major stock exchanges are discussed in the next section.

Understanding Stock Markets

Stock markets, or **exchanges**, are probably the best-known of the world's financial markets. In these markets, shares of stock are bought and sold by investors. The two largest stock markets in the world, the New York Stock Exchange and the Nasdaq stock market, are located in the United States.

The New York Stock Exchange

The New York Stock Exchange—sometimes referred to as the Big Board—is the most famous and one of the oldest stock markets in the world, having been founded in 1792. Today, more than 3,000 common- and preferred-stock issues are listed on the NYSE. These stocks represent most of the largest, best-known companies in the United States and have a total market value exceeding $13 trillion. In terms of the total value of stock traded, the NYSE is the world's largest stock market.

secondary market
collection of financial markets in which previously issued securities are traded among investors.

Assessment Check ✔

1. What is a financial market?

2. Distinguish between a primary and a secondary financial market.

3. Briefly explain the role of financial institutions in the sale of securities.

stock markets (exchanges) market in which shares of stock are bought and sold by investors.

For a company's stock to be traded on the NYSE, the firm must apply to the exchange for listing and meet certain listing requirements. In addition, the firm must continue to meet requirements each year to remain listed on the NYSE. Corporate bonds are also traded on the NYSE, but bond trading makes up less than 1 percent of the total value of securities traded there during a typical year.

Trading on the NYSE takes place face-to-face on a trading floor. Buy and sell orders are transmitted to a specific post on the floor of the exchange. Buyers and sellers then bid against one another in an open auction. Only investment firms that are designated members of the NYSE and that own at least one trading license are allowed to trade on the floor of the exchange. The NYSE issues up to 1,366 trading licenses a year at a cost of about $40,000 each.[6]

Each NYSE stock is assigned to a specialist firm. Specialists are unique investment firms that maintain an orderly and liquid market in the stocks assigned to them. Specialists must be willing to buy when there are no other buyers and sell when there are no other sellers. Specialists also act as auctioneers and catalysts, bringing buyers and sellers together.

Some observers portray the NYSE and its trading practices as somewhat old fashioned, especially in this technological age. Most markets, they note, have abandoned their trading floors in favor of electronic trading. However, even though the NYSE still retains a trading floor, the exchange has become highly automated in recent years. Its computer systems automatically match and route most orders, which are typically filled within a few seconds.

The Nasdaq Stock Market

The world's second-largest stock market is the Nasdaq Stock Market. It is very different from the NYSE. Nasdaq—which stands for National Association of Securities Dealers Automated Quotation System—is actually a computerized communications network that links member investment firms. It is the world's largest intranet. All trading on Nasdaq takes place through its intranet, rather than on a trading floor. Buy and sell orders are entered into the network and executed electronically. All Nasdaq-listed stocks have two or more market makers—investment firms that perform essentially the same functions as NYSE specialists.

Around 5,000 companies have their stocks listed on Nasdaq. Compared with firms listed on the NYSE, Nasdaq-listed corporations tend to be smaller, less well-known firms. Some are relatively new businesses and cannot meet NYSE listing requirements. It is not uncommon for firms eventually to transfer the trading of their stocks from Nasdaq to the NYSE—16 did so in a recent year. However, dozens of major companies currently trade on Nasdaq—such as Amgen, Cisco Systems, Dell, Intel, and Microsoft—that would easily meet NYSE listing requirements. For a variety of reasons, these firms have decided to remain listed on Nasdaq.

Unlike the New York Stock Exchange, the Nasdaq does not have a trading floor; all transactions are done electronically. Firms listed on the Nasdaq tend to be smaller and younger than the large, established firms listed on the New York Stock Exchange.

UPI Photo/Landov

Other U.S. Stock Markets

In addition to the NYSE and Nasdaq, several other stock markets operate in the United States. The American Stock Exchange, or AMEX, focuses on the stocks of smaller firms, as well as other financial instruments such as options. In comparison with the NYSE and Nasdaq, the AMEX is tiny. Daily trading volume is generally less than 100 million shares compared with the +1 billion shares on each of the larger two exchanges.

Several regional stock exchanges also operate throughout the United States. They include the Chicago, Pacific (San Francisco), Boston, Cincinnati, and Philadelphia stock exchanges. Originally established to trade the shares of small, regional companies, the regional exchanges now list securities of many large corporations as well. In fact, more than half of the companies listed on the NYSE are also listed on one or more regional exchanges.

Foreign Stock Markets

Stock markets exist throughout the world. Virtually all developed countries and many developing countries have stock exchanges. Examples include Mumbai, Helsinki, Hong Kong, Mexico City, Paris, and Toronto. One of the largest stock exchanges outside the United States is the London Stock Exchange. Founded in the early 17th century, the London Stock Exchange lists approximately 3,000 stock and bond issues by companies from more than 70 countries around the world. Trading on the London Stock Exchange takes place using a Nasdaq-type computerized communications network.

The London Stock Exchange is the most international of all stock markets. Approximately two-thirds of all cross-border trading in the world—for example, the trading of stocks of American companies outside the United States—takes place in London. It is not uncommon for institutional investors in the United States to trade NYSE- or Nasdaq-listed stocks in London.

Because stock markets around the world are so closely interconnected, changes in one country's economy can affect other countries too, as the "Hit & Miss" feature explains.

ECNs and the Future of Stock Markets

For years a so-called *fourth market* has existed. The fourth market is the direct trading of exchange-listed stocks off the floor of the exchange, in the case of NYSE-listed stocks, or outside the network, in the case of Nasdaq-listed stocks. Until recently, trading in the fourth market was limited to institutional investors buying or selling large blocks of stock.

Now the fourth market has begun to open up to smaller, individual investors through markets called *electronic communications networks* (ECNs). In ECNs, buyers and sellers meet in a virtual stock market and trade directly with one another. No specialist or market maker is involved. ECNs have become a significant force in the stock market in recent years. Around half of all trades involving Nasdaq-listed stocks take place on INET or Archipelago—the two largest ECNs—rather than directly through the Nasdaq system. Some have suggested that ECNs represent the future for stock markets, given that INET and Archipelago were acquired within the last few years by Nasdaq and the NYSE, respectively.

How News Lifts—or Sinks—World Stocks

The growth of computerized trading has closely connected all the developed nations and many of the developing nations. A snapshot of the world markets at the end of a recent month illustrates how events in one country influence stock markets everywhere.

In the spring of 2010, Americans grew hopeful that the country was starting to climb out of the worst financial crisis since the Great Depression. The Federal Reserve announced that although American households were not spending as much as before the recession, the U.S. economy was slowly improving. Some companies were making a profit from rising consumer demand. Earlier in the recovery, companies had made money by cutting costs. Prices of stock in U.S. companies such as Apple saw some increases. The computer giant Hewlett-Packard announced that it was buying the smart phone maker Palm.

The credit crisis that America seemed to be emerging from struck Greece, which warned that it might not be able to pay off its debts. As a member of the European Union, Greece has adopted the euro as its currency. Other euro countries, like Spain and Portugal, faced financial troubles as well. Standard & Poor's reduced the bond rating of all three countries.

As it tried to recover, Greece adopted drastic measures, reducing government spending on social programs despite public protests. Prime Minister George Papandreou said that the public sector was "overly grown, overly expensive." He hoped the austerity program would "give us a cushion" that would "give us quite a bit of money."

Questions for Critical Thinking

1. Why would a financial crisis on the other side of the world affect the U.S. economy?

2. This "Hit & Miss" feature describes events at the end of April 2010. As you read this textbook, what has happened in Greece, Spain, and Portugal? Have they recovered from their economic crisis?

Sources: Mark Rohner, "Greece Ahead of Targets, Will Not Default, Papandreou Says," *Bloomberg Businessweek*, June 22, 2010, http://www.businessweek.com; European Union Web site, http://europa.eu, accessed June 21, 2010; Will Swarts, "Stocks Surge as Earnings Stay Robust," *SmartMoney*, April 29, 2010, http://www.smartmoney.com; Christine Hauser, "Stocks Higher as Earnings Lift Sentiment," *The New York Times*, April 28, 2010, http://www.nytimes.com; Reuters, "Earnings Lift World Stocks, Greece Stays in Focus," *Economic Times*, April 21, 2010, http://economictimes.indiatimes.com.

Investor Participation in the Stock Markets

Because most investors aren't members of the NYSE, or any other stock market, they need to use the services of a brokerage firm to buy or sell stocks. Examples of brokerage firms include Edward Jones and TD Ameritrade. Investors establish an account with the brokerage firm and then enter orders to trade stocks. The brokerage firm executes the trade on behalf of the investor, charging the investor a fee for the service. While some investors phone in orders or visit the brokerage firm in person, many today use their PCs and trade stocks online. The requirements for setting up an account vary from broker to broker. Selecting the right brokerage firm is one of the most important decisions investors make.

The most common type of order is called a *market order*. It instructs the broker to obtain the best possible price—the highest price when selling and the lowest price when buying. If the stock market is open, market orders are filled within seconds. Another popular type of order is called a *limit order*. It sets a price ceiling when buying or a price floor when selling. If the order cannot be executed when it is placed, the order is left with the exchange's market maker. It may be filed later if the price limits are met.

Financial Institutions

One of the most important components of the financial system is **financial institutions**. They are an intermediary between savers and borrowers, collecting funds from savers and then lending the funds to individuals, businesses, and governments. Financial institutions greatly increase the efficiency and effectiveness of the transfer of funds from savers to users.

Assessment Check ✓

1. What are the world's two largest stock markets?

2. Why is the London Stock Exchange unique?

3. Explain the difference between a market order and a limit order.

financial institutions
intermediary between savers and borrowers, collecting funds from savers and then lending the funds to individuals, businesses, and governments.

Because of financial institutions, savers earn more, and users pay less, than they would with-out them. In fact, it is difficult to imagine how any modern economy could function without well-developed financial institutions. Think about how difficult it would be for a business-person to obtain inventory financing or an individual to purchase a new home without finan-cial institutions. Prospective borrowers would have to identify and negotiate terms with each saver individually.

Traditionally, financial institutions have been classified into depository institutions—institutions that accept deposits that customers can withdraw on demand—and nondeposi-tory institutions. Examples of depository institutions include commercial banks, such as US Bancorp and Sun Trust; savings banks, such as Golden West Financial Corporation and Ohio Savings Bank; and credit unions, such as the State Employees Credit Union of North Carolina. Nondepository institutions include life insurance companies, such as Northwestern Mutual; pension funds, such as the Florida state employee pension fund; and mutual funds. In total, financial institutions have trillions of dollars in assets. Figure 16.2 illustrates the size of the most prominent financial institutions.

Commercial Banks

Commercial banks are the largest and probably most important financial institution in the United States, and in most other countries as well. In the United States, the approximately 6,800 commercial banks have total assets of more than $12 trillion. Commercial banks offer the most services of any financial institution. These services include a wide range of checking and savings deposit accounts, consumer loans, credit cards, home mortgage loans, business loans, and trust services. Commercial banks also sell other financial products, including securities and insurance.

Although 6,800 may sound like a lot of banks, the number of banks has actually declined dramatically in recent years; more than 25 years ago there were 14,000 commercial banks. At the same time, banks have grown larger: today, the typical commercial bank is about five times as large as it was ten years ago. Both changes can be explained by the fact that bank mergers are commonplace.

Although the overall trend in the banking industry has been toward fewer, larger banks, a countertrend has also emerged: the growth of small community banks. It is not uncommon for several dozen of these banks to begin operation in any one year. Community banks typically serve a single city or county and have millions, rather than billions, of dollars in assets and deposits. Many consumers and small-business owners prefer smaller banks because they believe they offer a higher level of personal service and often charge lower fees.

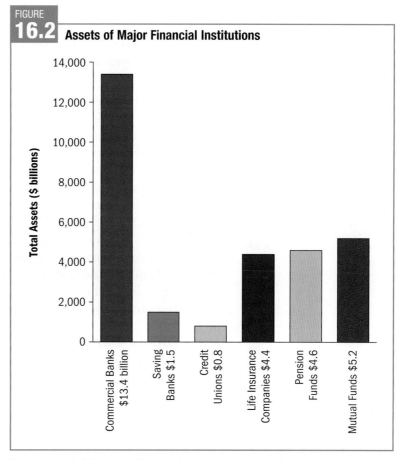

FIGURE 16.2 Assets of Major Financial Institutions

Source: Board of Governors of the Federal Reserve System, "Federal Reserve Statistical Release, Z.1, Flow of Funds Accounts of the United States," http://www.federalreserve.gov, accessed June 21, 2010.

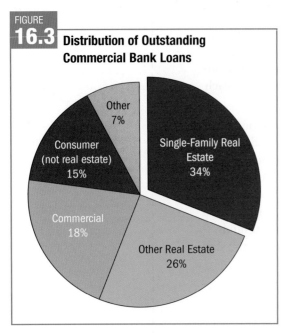

Source: Federal Deposit Insurance Corporation (FDIC), Statistics on Depository Institutions Report, http://www2.fdic.gov, accessed June 21, 2010.

FIGURE 16.3 Distribution of Outstanding Commercial Bank Loans

How Banks Operate Banks raise funds by offering a variety of checking and savings deposits to customers. The banks then pool these deposits and lend most of them out in the form of consumer and business loans. At the end of a recent year, banks held over $8.3 trillion in deposits and had almost $6.3 trillion in outstanding loans.[7] The distribution of outstanding loans is shown in Figure 16.3. As the figure shows, banks lend a great deal of money to both households and businesses for a variety of purposes. Commercial banks are an especially important source of funds for small businesses. When evaluating loan applications, banks consider the borrower's ability and willingness to repay the loan. Occasionally, banks reject applications.

Banks make money primarily because the interest rate they charge borrowers is higher than the rate of interest they pay depositors. Banks also make money from other sources, such as fees they charge customers for checking accounts and using automated teller machines.

In the aftermath of the recent credit crisis, many small business owners have suffered because banks have begun pulling their lines of credit. The "Business Etiquette" feature offers some suggestions if this happens to you.

Electronic Banking More and more funds each year move through electronic funds transfer systems (EFTSs), computerized systems for conducting financial transactions over electronic links. Millions of businesses and consumers now pay bills and receive payments electronically. Most employers, for example, directly deposit employee paychecks in their bank accounts, rather than issuing employees paper checks. Today nearly all Social Security checks and other federal payments made each year arrive as electronic data rather than paper documents.

One of the original forms of electronic banking, the automated teller machine (ATM) continues to grow in popularity. ATMs allow customers to make banking transactions at any time by inserting an electronic card into the machine and entering a personal identification number (PIN). Networked systems enable ATM users to access their bank accounts in distant states and even throughout the world. Most banks now offer customers debit cards—also called *check cards*—that allow customers to pay for purchases directly from their checking or savings account. A debit card looks like a credit card but acts like a check and replaces the customer's ATM card. Many large retailers—including Home Depot, Supervalu, Target, Walmart, and Walgreen's—have installed special terminals that allow customers to use their ATM or debit cards to make purchases. Customers are required to enter their personal identification numbers and can often get cash back. Consumers enjoy the convenience of this feature; at the same time, it eliminates the problem of bad checks for retailers. The number of annual ATM and debit card transactions is expected to exceed almost 41 billion within the next couple of years.[8]

Online Banking Today, many consumers do some or all of their banking on the Internet. According to one survey, more than one-half of American households use some online banking services regularly.[9] Two types of online banks exist: Internet-only banks, such as ING Direct, and traditional brick-and-mortar banks with Web sites, such as JPMorgan Chase and Citibank. A major reason people are attracted to online banking is convenience. Customers can transfer money, check account balances, and pay bills at any time.

Federal Deposit Insurance Most commercial bank deposits are insured by the <u>**Federal Deposit Insurance Corporation (FDIC)**</u>, a federal agency. Deposit insurance

Federal Deposit Insurance Corporation (FDIC) federal agency that insures deposits at commercial and savings banks.

means that, in the event the bank fails, insured depositors are paid in full by the FDIC, up to $250,000. Federal deposit insurance was enacted by the Banking Act of 1933 as one of the measures designed to restore public confidence in the banking system. Before deposit insurance, so-called *runs* were common as people rushed to withdraw their money from a bank, often just on a rumor that the bank was in precarious financial condition. With more and more withdrawals in a short period, the bank was eventually unable to meet customer demands and closed its doors. Remaining depositors often lost most of the money they had in the bank. Deposit insurance shifts the risk of bank failures from individual depositors to the FDIC. Although banks still fail today, no insured depositor has ever lost any money.

Savings Banks and Credit Unions

Commercial banks are by far the largest depository financial institution in the United States, but savings banks and credit unions also serve a significant segment of the financial community. Today savings banks and credit unions offer many of the same services as commercial banks.

Savings banks used to be called *savings and loan associations* or *thrift institutions*. They were originally established in the early 1800s to make home mortgage loans. Savings and loans originally raised funds by accepting only savings deposits and then lent these funds to consumers to buy homes. Today, there are around 1,170 savings banks with total assets of about $1.26 trillion.[10] Although savings banks offer many of the same services as commercial banks, including checking accounts, they are not major lenders to businesses. About 82.6 percent of their outstanding loans are real estate loans.[11] Deposits in savings banks are now FDIC insured.

Credit unions are cooperative financial institutions that are owned by their depositors, all of whom are members. Around 90 million Americans belong to one of the nation's approximately 8,000 credit unions. Combined, credit unions have more than $825 billion in assets.[12] By law, credit union members must share similar occupations, employers, or membership in certain organizations. This

BusinessEtiquette

What to Do When Your Credit Gets Pulled

For years, banks have issued business credit cards to small business owners. The cards come with a line of credit—usually several thousand dollars or more—that gives these businesses a safety net in case a client was late in paying or some other emergency. After the credit crisis hit, millions of small business owners found themselves working without a net as banks began either to call those loans in or to cap credit lines at the amount outstanding. The National Small Business Association reported that thousands of small business owners reported that their credit lines had been decreased or that extensions of their loans had been rejected. Marilyn Landis of the NSBA said, "A few years ago, losing a line of credit was a crisis—today it's the new normal." Here are some steps to consider if this happens to you.

1 Be careful not to max out whatever credit you have left; this could have a negative impact on your credit score.

2 Make your current monthly payment as quickly as possible, either online or by phone.

3 Apply for a new credit card as quickly as possible. It usually takes several weeks for any changes in your credit limit to appear in your credit report. If you act fast, you may get a new card before your credit score is lowered.

4 If possible, pay down your existing credit card debt. However, if you know you'll need money in the short run, weigh that need against your credit score before you write the check.

5 Keep careful track of your credit score. AnnualCreditReport.com is the only government-authorized source for the free annual credit report that you are legally entitled to.

Sources: Federal Trade Commission, "Credit and Your Consumer Rights," http://www.ftc.gov, accessed June 21, 2010; Sam Thacker, "Steps to Take When Your Credit Line Is Pulled," *All-Business,* http://www.allbusiness.com, accessed June 21, 2010; Jeffrey Weber, "What to Do When Your Credit Limit Is Decreased," *SmartBalanceTransfers.com,* March 4, 2010, http://www.smartbalancetransfers.com; Julie Bennett, "What to Do When the Bank Pulls Your Line of Credit," *Entrepreneur,* February 2010, http://www.entrepreneur.com.

With credit unions growing in popularity, the National Credit Union Administration is a good place to start when looking for a credit union in your area.

National Credit Union Administration

law effectively caps the size of credit unions. In fact, the nation's largest bank—Bank of America—holds more deposits than all the country's credit unions combined.

Credit unions are designed to serve consumers, not businesses. Credit unions raise funds by offering members a number of demand and saving deposits—checking accounts at credit unions are referred to as share draft accounts—and then, in turn, lend these funds to members. Because credit unions are not-for-profit institutions, they often pay savers higher rates of interest, charge lower rates of interest on loans, and have fewer fees than other financial institutions. Credit unions can have either state or federal charters, and deposits are insured by a federal agency, the National Credit Union Administration (NCUA), which functions essentially the same way that the FDIC does.

Nondepository Financial Institutions

Nondepository financial institutions accept funds from businesses and households, much of which they then invest. Generally, these institutions do not offer checking accounts (demand deposits). Three examples of nondepository financial institutions are insurance companies, pension funds, and finance companies.

Insurance Companies Households and businesses buy insurance to transfer risk from themselves to the insurance company. The insurance company accepts the risk in return for a series of payments, called *premiums*. Underwriting is the process insurance companies use to determine whom to insure and what to charge. During a typical year, insurance companies collect more in premiums than they pay in claims. After they pay operating expenses, they invest this difference. Insurance companies are a major source of short- and long-term financing for businesses. Life insurance companies alone have total assets of more than $4.5 trillion invested in everything from bonds and stocks to real estate.[13] Examples of life insurers include Prudential and New York Life.

Pension Funds Pension funds provide retirement benefits to workers and their families. They are set up by employers and are funded by regular contributions made by employers and employees. Because pension funds have predictable long-term cash inflows and very predictable cash outflows, they invest heavily in assets, such as common stocks and real estate. At one time, pension funds owned more than 25 percent of all common stocks. One study that compared U.S. pension funds and those in other countries found that even after the financial crisis, U.S. pension funds had more than 61 percent of their assets invested in stocks but only about 23 percent in less risky bonds; Germany, which was second, had only 34.5 percent in stocks and more than 61 percent in bonds. Recently, U.S. companies have begun quietly moving their pension assets out of stocks and have begun buying more long-term bonds. In contrast, some states and other government agencies, wanting to make up for funds lost in the crisis, have begun investing in higher-risk categories. In total, pension funds have more than $4.6 trillion in assets.[14]

Finance Companies Consumer and commercial finance companies, such as Ford Credit, John Deere Capital Corporation, and the Pennsylvania-based Dollar Financial, offer short-term loans to borrowers. A commercial finance company supplies short-term funds to businesses that pledge tangible assets such as inventory, accounts receivable, machinery, or property as collateral for the loan. A consumer finance company plays a similar role for consumers. Finance companies raise funds by selling securities or borrowing funds from commercial banks. Many finance companies, such as GMAC, are actually subsidiaries of a manufacturer. GMAC finances dealer inventories of new cars and trucks, as well as providing loans to consumers and other buyers of General Motors products.

Mutual Funds

One of the most significant types of financial institutions today is the mutual fund. *Mutual funds* are financial intermediaries that raise money from investors by selling shares. They then use the money to invest in securities that are consistent with the mutual fund's objectives. For example, a stock mutual fund invests mainly in shares of common stocks. Mutual funds have become extremely popular over the last few decades. The United States' more than 7,600 mutual funds have more than $11 trillion in assets and more than 270 million shareholder accounts; 20 years ago, there were just over 3,000 funds with a total of just over $1 trillion in assets. One reason for this growth is the increased popularity of 401(k) and similar types of retirement plans. It is estimated that about 47 percent of all 401(k) assets are invested in mutual fund shares.[15]

Mutual fund investors are indirect owners of a portfolio of securities. As the value of the securities owned by the mutual fund changes, so too will the value of the mutual fund's shares. Moreover, investment income, such as bond interest and stock dividends, is passed through to fund shareholders.

Slightly less than half of mutual fund assets, around $5.2 trillion, are invested in stock funds. Money market mutual funds—those that invest in money market instruments such as commercial paper—are also popular. These funds have total assets of just over 2.6 trillion.[16]

The Role of the Federal Reserve System

Created in 1913, the **Federal Reserve System**, or **Fed**, or is the central bank of the United States and is an important part of the nation's financial system. The Fed has four basic responsibilities: regulating commercial banks, performing banking-related activities for the U.S. Department of the Treasury, providing services for banks, and setting monetary policy. Not all banks belong to the Fed. Banks with federal charters are required to belong to the Fed, but membership is optional for state-chartered banks. Because the largest banks in the country are all federally chartered, the bulk of banking assets is controlled by Fed members. The Fed acts as the bankers' bank for members. It provides wire transfer facilities, clears checks, replaces worn-out currency, and lends banks money.

Organization of the Federal Reserve System

The nation is divided into 12 federal reserve districts, each with its own federal reserve bank. Each district bank supplies banks within its district with currency and facilitates the clearing of checks. District banks are run by a nine-member board of directors, headed by a president.

Assessment Check ☑

1. What are the two main types of financial institutions?

2. What are the primary differences between commercial banks and savings banks?

3. What is a mutual fund?

Federal Reserve System (Fed) central bank of the United States.

The governing body of the Fed is the board of governors. The board consists of seven members, including a chair and vice chair, appointed by the president and confirmed by the Senate. A full term for a Fed governor is 14 years. If a governor serves a full term, he or she cannot be reappointed. A governor can be reappointed if he or she was initially appointed to an unexpired term. The chair and vice chair serve in those capacities for four years and can be reappointed. The chair of the board of governors is a very important position. Some have commented, only half jokingly, that the Fed chair is the second most powerful person in the nation.

The Fed is designed to be politically independent. Terms for Fed governors are staggered in such a way that a president cannot appoint a majority of members, assuming that all members serve their entire terms. The Fed also has its own sources of revenue and does not depend on congressional appropriations.

An important part of the Fed is the *Federal Open Markets Committee (FOMC)*. The FOMC sets most policies concerning monetary policy and interest rates. It consists of 12 members—the 7 Fed board governors plus 5 representatives of the district banks, who serve on a rotating basis. The Fed chair is also chair of the FOMC.

Check Clearing and the Fed

As mentioned earlier, one of the Fed's responsibilities is to help facilitate the clearing of checks. Even in this age of electronic and online banking, Americans still write billions of paper checks each year. The clearing of a check is the process by which funds are transferred from the check writer to the recipient.

Assume the owner of Gulf View Townhouses of Tampa buys a $600 carpet cleaner from the local Home Depot and writes a check. If Home Depot has an account at the same bank as Gulf View, the bank will clear the check in house. It will decrease the balance in the owner's account by $600 and increase the balance in Home Depot's account by $600. If Home Depot has an account at another bank in Tampa, the two banks may still clear the check directly with one another. This process is cumbersome, however, so it is more likely that the banks will use the services of a local check clearinghouse.

But if Home Depot has its account with a bank in another state—perhaps in Atlanta, where Home Depot is based—the check will likely be cleared through the Federal Reserve System. Home Depot will deposit the check in its Atlanta bank account. That bank, in turn, will deposit the check in the Federal Reserve Bank of Atlanta. The Atlanta Federal Reserve bank will present the check to Gulf View's bank for payment, which pays the check by deducting $600 from Gulf View's account. Regardless of the method used, the Check Clearing for the 21st Century Act allows banks and the Fed to use electronic images of checks—rather than the paper documents themselves—during the clearing process. Because these images are transferred electronically, the time it takes to clear a check has been reduced substantially, often to less than 48 hours.

Monetary Policy

The Fed's most important function is controlling the supply of money and credit, or monetary policy. The Fed's job is to make sure that the money supply grows at an appropriate rate, allowing the economy to expand and inflation to remain in check. If the money supply grows too slowly, economic growth will slow, unemployment will increase, and the risk of a recession will increase. If the money supply grows too rapidly, inflationary pressures will build. The Fed uses its policy tools to push interest rates up or down. If the Fed pushes interest rates up, the growth rate in the money supply will slow, economic growth will slow, and inflationary pressures will ease. If the Fed pushes interest rates down, the growth rate in the money supply will increase, economic growth will pick up, and unemployment will fall.

The two common measures of the money supply are called M1 and M2. M1 consists of currency in circulation and balances in bank checking accounts. M2 equals M1 plus balances in some savings accounts and money market mutual funds. Figure 16.4 shows the approximate breakdowns of M1 and M2. The Fed has four major policy tools for controlling the growth in the supply of money and credit: reserve requirements, the discount rate, open market operations, and Term Auction Facility loans.

The Fed requires banks to maintain reserves—defined as cash in their vaults plus deposits at district Federal Reserve banks or other banks—equal to a certain percentage of what the banks hold in deposits. For example, if the Fed sets the reserve requirement at 5 percent, a bank that receives a $500 deposit must reserve $25, so it has only $475 to invest or lend to individuals or businesses. By changing the reserve requirement, the Fed can affect the amount of money available for making loans. The higher the reserve requirement, the less banks can lend out to consumers and businesses. The lower the reserve requirement, the more banks can lend out. Because any change in the reserve requirement can have a sudden and dramatic impact on the money supply, the Fed rarely uses this tool. Reserve requirements range from 0 to 10 percent, depending on the type of account.

Another policy tool is the so-called *discount rate*, the interest rate at which Federal Reserve banks make short-term loans to member banks. A bank might need a short-term loan if transactions leave it short of reserves. If the Fed wants to slow the growth rate in the money supply, it increases the discount rate. This increase makes it more expensive for banks to borrow funds. Banks, in turn, raise the interest rates they charge on loans to consumers and businesses. The end result is a slowdown in economic activity. Lowering the discount rate has the opposite effect.

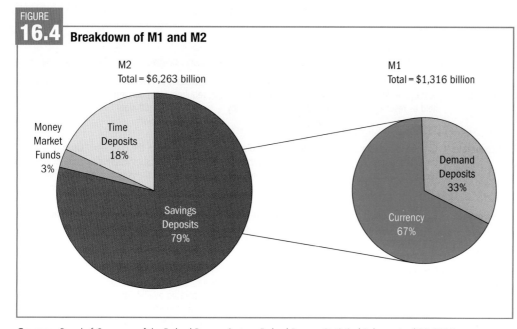

FIGURE 16.4 **Breakdown of M1 and M2**

M2
Total = $6,263 billion

M1
Total = $1,316 billion

Money Market Funds 3%

Time Deposits 18%

Savings Deposits 79%

Demand Deposits 33%

Currency 67%

Source: Board of Governors of the Federal Reserve System, Federal Reserve Statistical Release, April 29, 2010, http://www.federalreserve.gov, accessed June 21, 2010.

The third policy tool, and the one used most often, is *open market operations*, the technique of controlling the money supply growth rate by buying or selling U.S. Treasury securities. If the Fed buys Treasury securities, the money it pays enters circulation, increasing the money supply and lowering interest rates. When the Fed sells Treasury securities, money is taken out of circulation and interest rates rise. When the Fed uses open market operations it employs the so-called *federal funds rate*—the rate at which banks lend money to each other overnight—as its benchmark.

A relatively new monetary policy tool is the *term auction facility*. In these auctions, the Fed makes extra funds available to banks at low interest rates. A recent auction resulted in the Fed making $75 billion of 28-day loans to banks.[17] The more funds the Fed offers, and the lower the rate, the greater the impact on market interest rates, the supply of credit, and economic activity. Table 16.3 illustrates how the tools used by the Federal Reserve can stimulate or slow the economy.

The Federal Reserve has the authority to exercise selective credit controls when it thinks the economy is growing too rapidly or too slowly. These credit controls include the power to set margin requirements—the percentage of the purchase price of a security that an investor must pay in cash on credit purchases of stocks or bonds.

The Fed can also inject capital into the financial system in response to a financial crisis. During the recent credit crisis, the Fed pumped hundreds of billions of dollars into the financial system. The Fed even came to the rescue of AIG, a major insurance company, by purchasing some of the firm's stock.

Transactions in the foreign exchange markets also affect the U.S. money supply and interest rates. The Fed can lower the exchange value of the dollar by selling dollars and

Table 16.3 — Tools Used by the Federal Reserve to Regulate the Growth in the Money Supply

TOOL	BRIEF DESCRIPTION	IMPACT ON THE GROWTH RATE OF THE MONEY SUPPLY	IMPACT ON INTEREST RATES AND THE ECONOMY	FREQUENCY OF USE
1. Reserve requirements	Change in the percentage of deposits held as reserves.	Increases in reserve requirements slow the growth rate in the money supply.	Increases in reserve requirements push interest rates up and slow economic growth.	Rarely used.
2. Discount rate	Change in the rate the Fed charges banks for loans.	An increase in the discount rate slows the growth rate in the money supply.	An increase in the discount rate pushes interest rates up and slows economic growth.	Used only in conjunction with open market operations.
3. Open market operations	Buying and selling government securities to increase or decrease bank reserves.	Selling government securities reduces bank reserves and slows the growth rate in the money supply.	Selling government securities pushes interest rates up and slows economic growth.	Used frequently.
4. Term Auction Facility loans	Fed auctions 28-day loans to banks.	Auctions boost bank reserves, leading to increased availability of credit.	Increased availability of credit pushes interest rates lower and spurs economic activity.	Relatively new; used frequently when first introduced.

buying foreign currencies, and it can raise the dollar's exchange value by doing the opposite—buying dollars and selling foreign currencies. When the Fed buys foreign currencies, the effect is the same as buying securities because it increases the U.S. banking system's reserves. Selling foreign currencies, on the other hand, is like selling securities, in that it reduces bank reserves.

Regulation of the Financial System

Given the importance of the financial system, it is probably not surprising that many components are subject to government regulation and oversight. In addition, industry self-regulation is commonplace.

Bank Regulation

Banks are among the nation's most heavily regulated businesses. The main purpose of bank regulation is to ensure public confidence in the safety and security of the banking system. Banks are critical to the overall functioning of the economy, and a collapse of the banking system can have disastrous results. Many believe that one of the major causes of the Great Depression was the collapse of the banking system that started in the late 1920s.

All banks, whether commercial or savings, and credit unions have either state or federal charters. Most commercial banks are state chartered; however, federally chartered banks control more than half of all banking assets. State-chartered banks are regulated by the appropriate state banking authorities; federally chartered commercial banks are regulated by the Federal Reserve, the Federal Deposit Insurance Corporation, and the Comptroller of the Currency. Furthermore, state-chartered commercial banks that are federally insured—and virtually all are—are also subject to FDIC regulation.

At the federal level, savings banks are regulated by the Office of Thrift Supervision and the FDIC. Federal credit unions are subject to NCUA regulation. State-chartered savings banks and credit unions are also regulated by state authorities.

Banks and credit unions are subject to periodic examination by state or federal regulators. Examinations ensure that the institution is following sound banking practices and is complying with all applicable regulations. These examinations include the review of detailed reports on the bank's operating and financial condition, as well as on-site inspections. Regulators can impose various penalties on institutions deemed not in compliance with sound banking practices, including forcing the delinquent financial institution into a merger with a healthier one.

Government Regulation of the Financial Markets

Regulation of U.S. financial markets is primarily a function of the federal government, although states also regulate them. Federal regulation grew out of various trading abuses during the 1920s. To restore confidence and stability in the financial markets after the 1929 stock market crash, Congress passed a series of landmark legislative acts that have formed the basis of federal securities regulation ever since.

Assessment Check ✓

1. What is the Federal Reserve System?
2. How is the Fed organized?
3. List the four tools the Fed uses to control the supply of money and credit.

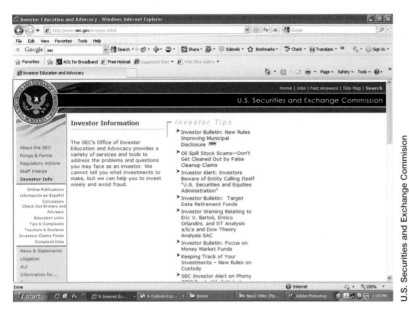

The Securities and Exchange Commission is a governmental agency charged with regulating financial markets. Its Web site featured here is a good source of information for would-be investors.

As noted in Chapter 15, the U.S. Securities and Exchange Commission, created in 1934, is the principal federal regulatory overseer of the securities markets. The SEC's mission is to administer securities laws and protect investors in public securities transactions. The SEC has broad enforcement power. It can pursue civil actions against individuals and corporations, but actions requiring criminal proceedings are referred to the U.S. Justice Department.

The SEC requires virtually all new public issues of corporate securities to be registered. As part of the registration process for a new security issue, the issuer must prepare a prospectus. The typical prospectus gives a detailed description of the company issuing the securities, including financial data, products, research and development projects, and pending litigation. It also describes the stock or bond issue and underwriting agreement in detail. The registration process seeks to guarantee full and fair disclosure. The SEC does not rule on the investment merits of a registered security. It is concerned only that an issuer gives investors enough information to make their own informed decisions.

Besides primary market registration requirements, SEC regulation extends to the secondary markets as well, keeping tabs on trading activity to make sure it is fair to all participants. Every securities exchange must by law follow a set of trading rules that have been approved by the SEC. In addition, the Market Reform Act of 1990 gave the SEC emergency authority to halt trading and restrict practices such as program trading—whereby computer systems are programmed to buy or sell securities if certain conditions arise—during periods of extreme volatility.

insider trading use of material nonpublic information about a company to make investment profits.

One area to which the SEC pays particular attention is insider trading. **Insider trading** is defined as the use of material nonpublic information about a company to make investment profits. Examples of material nonpublic information include a pending merger or a major oil discovery, which could affect the firm's stock price. The SEC's definition of insider trading goes beyond corporate insiders—people such as the company's officers and directors. It includes lawyers, accountants, investment bankers, and even reporters—anyone who uses nonpublic information to profit in the stock market at the expense of ordinary investors. Although some actions or communications are clearly insider trading, others are more ambiguous. Consequently, all employees of public companies have to be mindful of what is and isn't permitted.

Securities laws also require every public corporation to file several reports each year with the SEC; the contents of these reports become public information. The best known, of course, is the annual report. Public corporations prepare annual reports for their shareholders, and they file another report containing essentially the same information, Form 10-K, with the SEC. The SEC requires additional reports each time certain company officers and directors buy or sell a company's stock for their own accounts (Form 4) or anytime an investor accumulates more than 5 percent of a company's outstanding stock (Form 13-d). All of these reports are available for viewing and download at the Edgar Online Web site (http://www.freeedgar.com).

Industry Self-Regulation

The securities markets are also heavily self-regulated by professional associations and the major financial markets. The securities industry recognizes that rules and regulations designed to ensure fair and orderly markets promote investor confidence and benefit all participants. Two examples of self-regulation are the rules of conduct established by the various professional organizations and the market surveillance techniques used by the major securities markets.

Professional Rules of Conduct Prodded initially by federal legislation, the National Association of Securities Dealers (NASD) established and periodically updates rules of conduct for members—both individuals and firms. These rules are intended to ensure that brokers perform their basic functions honestly and fairly, under constant supervision. Failure to adhere to rules of conduct can result in disciplinary action. The NASD also established a formal arbitration procedure through which investors can attempt to resolve disputes with brokers without litigation.

Market Surveillance All securities markets use a variety of methods to spot possible violations of trading rules or securities laws. For example, the NYSE continuously monitors trading activity throughout the trading day. A key technical tool used by the NYSE is called Stock Watch, an electronic monitoring system that flags unusual price and volume activity. The NYSE then seeks explanations for unusual activity from the member firms and companies involved. In addition, all market participants must keep detailed records of every aspect of every trade (called an *audit trail*). The NYSE's enforcement division may impose a variety of penalties on members for rule violations. In addition, the exchange turns over evidence to the SEC for further action if it believes that violations of federal securities laws may have occurred.

Although self-regulation by the financial industry has been an important component of securities market regulation, some contend that the industry can never truly regulate itself effectively in today's market environment. The "Solving an Ethical Controversy" feature debates the pros and cons of industry self-regulation.

The Financial System: A Global Perspective

Not surprisingly, the global financial system is becoming more and more integrated each year. As we've noted, financial markets exist throughout the world. Shares of U.S. firms trade in other countries, and shares of international companies trade in the United States. In fact, investors in China and Japan own more U.S. Treasury securities than do domestic investors.

Financial institutions have also become a global industry. Major U.S. banks—such as JPMorgan Chase and Bank of America—have extensive international operations. They have offices, lend money, and accept deposits from customers throughout the world.

Assessment Check ✔

1. Who regulates banks?
2. Define *insider trading.*
3. List two ways in which the securities markets are self-regulated.

In Frankfurt, Germany, a sculpture of the euro—the symbol for the European Union's currency—stands outside the headquarters of Europe's central bank. The 12 gold stars represent all the peoples of Europe.

Solving an Ethical Controversy

Can Wall Street Regulate Itself?

"Those of us who have looked to the self-interest of lending institutions to protect shareholders' equity, myself included, are in a state of shocked disbelief."

So said Alan Greenspan, the former chairman of the Federal Reserve Board, in testimony before Congress after the credit crisis. He had long supported the idea that the market could always be trusted to regulate itself and should be left free to do so. But with these words, he rejected that policy. The crisis brought an end to a Wall Street bubble that had flourished partly due to unlimited, unregulated speculation. Stricter government regulation of the financial industry seems inevitable.

Can Wall Street be trusted to regulate itself?

PRO

1. Regulation of Wall Street would give the government too much power over a private industry.

2. The mere idea of regulation has made some institutions change their behavior voluntarily. For example, Bank of America recently announced it would eliminate overdraft fees for consumer accounts.

CON

1. Some analysts feel that existing government regulation was too lax. They believe that the Securities and Exchange Commission, which is supposed to regulate the financial industry, was too lenient with some large financial institutions.

2. Some observers feel that commercial banking was concentrated in too few big banks. The four biggest banks had almost 40 percent of all deposits and two-thirds of all credit card accounts. These observers would also like to see banking and investment management separated.

Summary

Public disapproval of Wall Street is bound to continue as long as the effects of the financial crisis unfold in people's everyday lives. Congress has considered new, stricter regulations on financial institutions. Some argue that those regulations are unnecessary and could even be harmful.

Sources: Bill Singer, "Analyzing a Troubling Wall Street Double Standard," *Corporate Compliance Insights,* May 4, 2010, http://www.corporatecomplianceinsights.com; Felix Salmon, "How the SEC Cracks Down on Unethical Behavior," *Reuters,* April 20, 2010, http://blogs.reuters.com; Peter Hamby, "DNC Ad: Wall Street Lobbyists Trying to Block Reform," *CNN,* April 20, 2010, http://politicalticker.blogs.cnn.com; Roger Lowenstein, "*The End of Wall Street* by Roger Lowenstein: Book Excerpt," *Bloomberg Businessweek,* April 8, 2010, http://www.businessweek.com; Andrew Ross Sorkin, "Extreme Makeover, Wall Street Edition," *The New York Times,* April 1, 2010, http://dealbook.blogs.nytimes.com; Charles H. Green, "Fixing What Ails Wall Street: Ethics, or Incentives?" Trusted Advisor Associates, September 21, 2009, http://trustedadvisor.com.

Assessment Check ✓

1. Where do U.S. banks rank compared with international banks?

2. Do other countries have organizations that play roles similar to those played by the Federal Reserve?

Although most Americans recognize large U.S. banks such as Citibank among the global financial giants, only 3 of the 30 largest banks in the world (measured by total assets) are U.S. institutions—JPMorgan Chase, Bank of America, and Citibank. The largest of the three, JPMorgan Chase, ranks only eighth. The other 27 are based in Belgium, China, France, Germany, Italy, Japan, the Netherlands, Switzerland, and the United Kingdom. The world's largest bank, BNP Paribas SA, based in Paris, has almost $3.5 trillion in assets. These international banks also operate worldwide, including in the United States.[18]

Virtually all nations have some sort of a central bank, similar to the U.S. Federal Reserve. Examples include the Banks of Canada, England, and Japan and the European Central Bank. These central banks play roles much like that of the Fed, such as controlling the money supply and regulating banks. Policymakers at other nations' central banks often respond to changes in the U.S. financial system by making similar changes in their own systems. For example, if the Fed pushes U.S. interest rates lower, central banks in Japan and Europe may also push their interest rates lower. These changes can influence events in countries around the world. Lower U.S. and European interest rates not only decrease the cost of borrowing for U.S. and European firms but also increase the amount of money available for loans to borrowers in other countries such as Chile and India.

What's Ahead

This chapter explored the financial system, a key component of the U.S. economy and something that affects many aspects of contemporary business. The financial system is the process by which funds are transferred between savers and borrowers and includes securities, financial markets, and financial institutions. The chapter also described the role of the Federal Reserve and discussed the global financial system. In the next chapter, we discuss the finance function of a business including the role of the financial managers, financial planning, asset management, and sources of short- and long-term funds.

Summary of Learning Goals

⌐1¬ Outline the structure and importance of the financial system.

The financial system is the process by which funds are transferred between those having excess funds (savers) and those needing additional funds (users). Savers and users are individuals, businesses, and governments. Savers expect to earn a rate of return in exchange for the use of their funds. Financial markets, financial institutions, and financial instruments (securities) make up the financial system. Although direct transfers are possible, most funds flow from savers to users through the financial markets or financial institutions, such as commercial banks. A well-functioning financial system is critical to the overall health of a nation's economy.

Assessment Check Answers ✓

1.1 What is the financial system? The financial system is the process by which funds are transferred between those having excess funds (savers) and those needing additional funds (users).

1.2 In the financial system, who are the borrowers and who are the savers? Savers and borrowers are individuals, businesses, and governments. Generally, individuals are net savers, meaning they spend less than they make, whereas businesses and governments are net borrowers.

1.3 List the two most common ways in which funds are transferred between borrowers and savers. The two most common ways funds are transferred are through the financial markets and through financial institutions.

⌐2¬ List the various types of securities.

Securities, also called *financial instruments*, represent obligations on the part of issuers—businesses and governments—to provide purchasers with expected or stated returns on the funds invested or loaned. Securities can be classified into three categories: money market instruments, bonds, and stock. Money market instruments and bonds are debt instruments. Money market instruments are short-term debt securities and tend to be low-risk securities. Bonds are longer-term debt securities and pay a fixed amount of interest each year. Bonds are sold by the U.S. Department of the Treasury (government bonds), state and local governments (municipal bonds), and corporations. Mortgage pass-through securities are bonds backed by a pool of mortgage loans. Most municipal and corporate bonds have risk ratings. Common stock represents ownership in corporations. Common stockholders have voting rights and a residual claim on the firm's assets.

Assessment Check Answers ✓

2.1 What are the major types of securities? The major types of securities are money market instruments, bonds, and stock.

2.2 What is a government bond? A municipal bond? A government bond is one issued by the U.S. Treasury. Municipal bonds are issued by state and local governments.

2.3 Why do investors purchase common stock? There are two primary motives for purchasing common stock. One is to receive dividends, cash payments to shareholders by the firm. The other is potential price appreciation of the shares.

3 Define *financial market,* and distinguish between primary and secondary financial markets.

A financial market is a market where securities are bought and sold. The primary market for securities serves businesses and governments that want to sell new security issues to raise funds. Securities are sold in the primary market either through an open auction or via a process called *underwriting*. The secondary market handles transactions of previously issued securities between investors. The New York Stock Exchange is a secondary market. The business or government that issued the security is not directly involved in secondary market transactions. In terms of the dollar value of trading volume, the secondary market is about four to five times larger than the primary market.

Assessment Check Answers ✔

3.1 What is a financial market? A financial market is a market in which securities are bought and sold.

3.2 Distinguish between a primary and a secondary financial market. The primary market for securities serves businesses and governments that want to sell new security issues to raise funds. The secondary market handles transactions of previously issued securities between investors.

3.3 Briefly explain the role of financial institutions in the sale of securities. Financial institutions purchase new securities issues from corporations or state and local governments and then resell the securities to investors. The institutions charge a fee for their services.

4 Describe the characteristics of the major stock exchanges.

The best-known financial markets are the stock exchanges. They exist throughout the world. The two largest—the New York Stock Exchange and Nasdaq—are located in the United States. The NYSE is bigger, measured in terms of the total value of stock traded. Larger and better-known companies dominate the NYSE. Buy and sell orders are transmitted to the trading floor for execution. The Nasdaq stock market is an electronic market in which buy and sell orders are entered into a computerized communication system for execution. Most of the world's major stock markets today use similar electronic trading systems. They may represent the future stock markets.

Assessment Check Answers ✔

4.1 What are the world's two largest stock markets? The world's two largest stock markets are the New York Stock Exchange and the Nasdaq Stock Market.

4.2 Why is the London Stock Exchange unique? The London Stock Exchange is probably the most international of the world's stock markets because a large percentage of the shares traded are not those of British firms.

4.3 Explain the difference between a market order and a limit order. A market order instructs the investor's

broker to obtain the best possible price when buying or selling securities. A limit order sets a maximum price (if the investor wants to buy) or a minimum price (if the investor wants to sell).

5 Discuss the organization and functioning of financial institutions.

Financial institutions act as intermediaries between savers and users of funds. Depository institutions—commercial banks, savings banks, and credit unions—accept deposits from customers that can be redeemed on demand. Commercial banks are the largest and most important of the depository institutions and offer the widest range of services. Savings banks are a major source of home mortgage loans. Credit unions are not-for-profit institutions offering financial services to consumers. Government agencies, most notably the Federal Deposit Insurance Corporation, insure deposits at these institutions. Nondepository institutions include pension funds and insurance companies. Nondepository institutions invest a large portion of their funds in stocks, bonds, and real estate. Mutual funds are another important financial institution. These companies sell shares to investors and, in turn, invest the proceeds in securities. Many individuals today invest a large portion of their retirement savings in mutual fund shares.

Assessment Check Answers ✔

5.1 What are the two main types of financial institutions? The two major types of financial institutions are depository institutions (those that accept checking and similar accounts) and nondepository institutions.

5.2 What are the primary differences between commercial banks and savings banks? Today commercial and savings banks offer many of the same services. However, commercial banks lend money to businesses as well as to individuals. Savings banks lend money primarily to individuals, principally in the form of home mortgage loans.

5.3 What is a mutual fund? A mutual fund is an intermediary that raises money by selling shares to investors. It then pools investor funds and purchases securities that are consistent with the fund's objectives.

6 Explain the functions of the Federal Reserve System and the tools it uses to control the supply of money and credit.

The Federal Reserve System is the central bank of the United States. The Federal Reserve regulates banks, performs banking functions for the U.S. Department of the Treasury, and acts as the bankers' bank (clearing checks, lending money to banks, and replacing worn-out currency). It controls the supply of credit and money in the economy to promote growth and control inflation. The Federal Reserve's tools include reserve requirements, the discount rate, open market operations, and term auction facility loans. Selective credit controls and purchases and sales of foreign currencies also help the Federal Reserve manage the economy.

Assessment Check Answers ✅

6.1 What is the Federal Reserve System? The Federal Reserve System is the U.S. central bank. It is responsible for regulating banks, providing banking-related services for the federal government, acting as the banker's bank, and setting monetary policy.

6.2 How is the Fed organized? The country is divided into 12 districts, each of which has a Federal Reserve Bank. The Fed is run by a seven-member board of governors headed by a chair and vice chair. An important part of the Fed is the Federal Open Markets Committee, which sets monetary and interest rate policy. The Fed is designed to be politically independent.

6.3 List the four tools the Fed uses to control the supply of money and credit. The four tools are reserve requirements, the discount rate, open market operations, and term auction facility loans.

⌐7⌐ Evaluate the major features of regulations and laws affecting the financial system.

Commercial banks, savings banks, and credit unions in the United States are heavily regulated by federal or state banking authorities. Banking regulators require institutions to follow sound banking practices and have the power to close noncompliant ones. In the United States, financial markets are regulated at both the federal and state levels. Markets are also heavily self-regulated by the financial markets and professional organizations. The chief regulatory body is the Securities and Exchange Commission. It sets the requirements for both primary and secondary market activity, prohibiting a number of practices, including insider trading. The SEC also requires public companies to disclose financial information regularly. Professional organizations and the securities markets also have rules and procedures that all members must follow.

Assessment Check Answers ✅

7.1 Who regulates banks? All banks have either state or federal charters. Federally chartered banks are regulated by the Federal Reserve, the FDIC, and the Comptroller of the Currency. State-chartered banks are regulated by state banking authorities and the FDIC.

7.2 Define *insider trading*. Insider trading is defined as the use of material nonpublic information to make an investment profit.

7.3 List two ways in which the securities markets are self-regulated. Professional organizations such as the National Association of Securities Dealers have codes of conduct that members are expected to follow. Major financial markets have trading rules and procedures to identify suspicious trading activity.

⌐8⌐ Describe the global financial system.

Financial markets exist throughout the world and are increasingly interconnected. Investors in other countries purchase U.S. securities, and U.S. investors purchase foreign securities. Large U.S. banks and other financial institutions have a global presence. They accept deposits, make loans, and have branches throughout the world. Foreign banks also operate worldwide. The average European or Japanese bank is much larger than the average American bank. Virtually all nations have central banks that perform the same roles as the U.S. Federal Reserve System. Central bankers often act together, raising and lowering interest rates as economic conditions warrant.

Assessment Check Answers ✅

8.1 Where do U.S. banks rank compared with international banks? Banks in Asia and Europe are generally much larger than U.S. banks. In fact, only 3 out of the world's 30 largest banks are based in the United States.

8.2 Do other countries have organizations that play roles similar to those played by the Federal Reserve? Yes, virtually all nations have central banks that perform many of the same functions that the U.S. Federal Reserve System does.

▦ Business Terms You Need to Know

financial system 534	primary markets 541	financial institutions 546	Federal Reserve
securities 536	secondary market 543	Federal Deposit	System (Fed) 551
common stock 539	stock markets	Insurance Corporation	insider trading 556
financial markets 541	(exchanges) 543	(FDIC) 548	

▦ Review Questions

1. What is the financial system? Why is the direct transfer of funds from savers to users rare?

2. What is a security? Give several examples.

3. List the major types of bonds. Explain a mortgage pass-through.

4. What are the differences between common stock and preferred stock?

5. Explain the difference between a primary financial market and a secondary financial market.

6. Why are commercial banks, savings banks, and credit unions classified as depository financial institutions? How do the three differ?

7. Why are life insurance companies, pension funds, and mutual funds considered financial institutions?

8. Briefly explain the role of the Federal Reserve and list the tools it uses to control the supply of money and credit.

9. What methods are used to regulate banks? Why are state-chartered banks also regulated by the FDIC?

10. Explain how the Federal Reserve, acting in conjunction with other central banks, could affect exchange rates.

Projects and Teamwork Applications

1. Collect current interest rates on the following types of bonds: U.S. Treasury bonds, AAA-rated municipal bonds, AAA-rated corporate bonds, and BBB-rated corporate bonds. Arrange the interest rates from lowest to highest. Explain the reasons for the ranking.

2. You've probably heard of U.S. savings bonds—you may even have received some bonds as a gift. What you may not know is that two different types of savings bonds exist. Do some research and compare and contrast the two types of savings bonds. What are their features? Their pros and cons? Assuming you were interested in buying savings bonds, which of the two do you find more attractive?

3. Working with a partner, assume you are considering buying shares of Lowe's or Home Depot. Describe how you would go about analyzing the two companies' stocks and deciding which, if either, you would buy.

4. Working in a small team, identify a large bank. Visit that bank's Web site and obtain its most recent financial statements.

Compare the bank's financial statements to those of a nonfinancial company, such as a manufacturer or retailer. Report on your findings.

5. Assume you're investing money for retirement. Specify several investment criteria you believe are most important. Go to the MSN Money Web Site (http://moneycentral .msn.com). Click "Fund Research" (under "Investing"), then choose either "Find top performers by category" or "Find using Easy Screener." Identify at least three mutual funds that most closely meet your criteria. Choose one of the funds and research it. Answer the following questions:

   a. What was the fund's average annual return for the past five years?

   b. How well did the fund perform relative to its peer group and relative to an index such as the Standard & Poor's 500?

   c. What are the fund's ten largest holdings?

Web Assignments

1. **Online stock trading.** Visit the Web site of a brokerage firm that offers online trading, such as E*Trade (www.etrade .com) or Charles Schwab (www.schwab.com), to learn more about online trading. Most electronic brokerage firms also offer a trading demonstration. Use the demonstration to see how you obtain price information, company news, place buy or sell orders, and check account balances. Make some notes about your experience and bring them to class to participate in a class discussion.

2. **Banking statistics.** Visit the Web site listed here. Access the most recent year you can find and answer the following questions:

   a. How many commercial banks were in operation at the end of the year? How many savings banks (institutions) were in operation?

   b. What were the total assets of commercial banks and savings banks at the end of the year?

   c. How many commercial banks had assets in excess of $5 billion at the end of the year? How many commercial banks had assets of less than $500 million at the end of the year?

   http://www2.fdic.gov/sdi/sob/

3. **Federal reserve system.** Go to the Web site of the Board of Governors of the Federal Reserve System (www.federalreserve.gov). Prepare a short report on the seven-member board. Who are the current members? What are their backgrounds? When were they appointed? When do their terms expire?

Note: Internet Web addresses change frequently. If you don't find the exact sites listed, you may need to access the organization's home page and search from there or use a search engine such as Bing or Google.

The Vanguard Group is the top seller of mutual funds in the United States, with more than $1 trillion in assets. Although it isn't the world's largest mutual fund company—American Funds earned that title—it is still the best seller among U.S. consumers. Many credit Vanguard's recent offering of ETFs (exchange traded funds), which took in a net of nearly $17 billion in one year, as a significant contributor to the firm's success. But Michael Miller, managing director for planning and development at Vanguard, points to the value the company creates for its customers. "We believe back to the basics made a difference with shareholders," he says. "[It's] low cost and high value."

Vanguard is well known for providing affordable investment opportunities to the average consumer. "Vanguard is the low-cost leader in the mutual fund realm, and their ETFs are often the lowest-cost option," observes Dan Colluton, an analyst with mutual fund rating firm Morningstar. This strategy is particularly effective when the economy appears uncertain or when consumers lack the confidence to spend more. "People focus on cost more when returns are low in the market," explains Dan Wiener, editor of *The Independent Advisor* for Vanguard investors.

But Vanguard has suffered somewhat in recent years from the perception that it is something of a maverick in the investment industry. In particular, some financial advisors complain that Vanguard doesn't reach out to them with phone calls, e-mails, and other communications to provide information about its products. "I've probably gotten mail from Vanguard, but their efforts are noticeably less intensive than those of rivals such as Barclays or State Street Global Advisors," says Rick Miller, a financial planner. Mark Balasa, another advisor, agrees with Miller,

remarking that Vanguard doesn't communicate much even when it launches new products. Unfortunately, this does not strengthen relationships with the advisors who could be offering Vanguard's products. "In some ways, we kind of dismissed them," concludes Balasa. While many agree that Vanguard falls short in this way, they are quick to agree on the value of Vanguard funds. "In the end, they have a great brand," admits Tom Lydon, president of Global Trends Investments.

"Are we perfect?" questions Vanguard chairman John J. Brennan. "No. Will we ask advisors if we can do better? Absolutely." In fact, Vanguard has launched a number of initiatives designed to help professionals, including the addition of new features to its advisor Web site to attract new clients, manage current clients, and even build their own careers. The firm holds financial symposiums for advisors and provides them with online services that allow them to earn education credits. If Vanguard handles this portion of its business well, it could create as much value for advisors as it does for their clients.

Questions for Critical Thinking

1. Do you think it is just as important for Vanguard to reach out to financial advisors as it is to reach out to investors who want to buy its funds? Why or why not?

2. How does Vanguard create value for its clients?

Sources: "The Vanguard Group," *BusinessWeek,* http://investing .businessweek.com, accessed March 2009; Sue Asci, "Vanguard Edges American as Top Mutual Funds Seller," *Investment News,* February 11, 2008, http://www.investmentnews.com; David Hoffman, "Vanguard Bolsters Efforts to Woo Financial Advisers," *Investment News,* http://www.investmentnews.com.

Credit Unions Find a Silver Lining in the Financial Crisis

Like the rest of the United States, mostly rural Meigs County, Tennessee, had suffered during the recent financial crisis and the recession that followed. As the three largest employers in the county heard many times, it was a bad year to try to start a credit union. But the Middle Tennessee Federal Credit Union, now worth $3 million, recently celebrated its first birthday.

The founders of the credit union, originally named the Mid East Tennessee Community Credit Union, had begun seeking a charter before the economic trouble. Their employees were resorting to predatory, high-interest payday loans to meet their financial needs, and the founders wanted to help them get small, short-term loans on more reasonable terms. The credit union opened for business in the midst of the recession. Jim Pitt, the chairman of the credit union's board and the CEO of Polyform Plastics, says, "Mostly I am proudest of our loans for the first year."

Whereas a bank is a for-profit institution beholden to its board members and shareholders, a credit union is a nonprofit cooperative owned by its members. Credit unions emphasize the basic finances of everyday life: savings and checking accounts, credit cards, and relatively small loans for homes or cars. Credit unions generally pay more interest on savings accounts and charge less interest on loans. Mark Wolff of the Credit Union National Association (CUNA) says, "The credit union channels any excess funds back to its members." Just as the FDIC does for banks, the federal government's National Credit Union Administration insures deposits of up to $250,000.

Credit unions are chartered to serve particular groups. Originally, most were affiliated with employers. For example, BECU (formerly the Boeing Employees' Credit Union) in Seattle once accepted only employees and their families. About ten years ago, credit unions began to ease their membership requirements. To join the Middle Tennessee Federal Credit Union, a person must simply either work, worship, live, or go to school in the local area.

With the big banks pulling or tightening consumer credit, consumers have had trouble getting even the most routine loans, for example, for a used car. Small-business owners have also suffered as banks have cut back. Credit unions have filled the gap. Around the country, credit unions now have 92 million members and have grown rapidly. In Michigan alone, they gained 59,000 new members in one year. Claudia York, the interim president and CEO of Chief Financial Federal Credit Union in Pontiac, Michigan, says, "We've been getting many more inquiries about [business loans]. We have not tightened up at all—we have money to loan. We're trying to be as generous as possible while still adhering to our [lending] guidelines."

Credit unions don't perform all the services of traditional banks, however. Only 59 percent of credit unions issue ATM cards. Those cards are usually part of a network of ATM machines at, for example, 7-Eleven, Walgreens, Costco, or even banks. Only 22 percent of credit unions have safe-deposit boxes. And most credit unions have only one branch, or even none.

Both the CUNA and NCUA Web sites have online tools to help you find a credit union near you. Allan McMorris, the president and CEO of Michigan's Oakland County Credit Union, said, "I'm very proud of the fact that in this tough economy, we are going to set a record in the number of loans disbursed. And of course, that's all local money on deposit and local loans. In our local economy, we think we're helping with the recovery."

Questions for Critical Thinking

1. Why is an organization such as the Credit Union National Association important to the credit union industry?
2. Use either the CUNA or the NCUA credit union locator tool to find a credit union near you. If you are eligible to join, compare the credit union with your current bank. What are the advantages to joining the credit union? What are the advantages to staying with your bank?

Sources: "Credit Union vs. Bank," Star Community Credit Union, http://www.starcreditunion.com, accessed June 21, 2010; Middle Tennessee Federal Credit Union Web site, http://www.midtenfcu.com, accessed June 21, 2010; National Credit Union Administration Web site, http://www.ncua.gov, accessed June 21, 2010; Credit Union National Association Web site, http://www.cuna.org, accessed June 21, 2010; David Morrison, "Year-Old Tenn. Credit Union Finds Success Despite Great Recession," *Credit Union Times,* April 28, 2010, http://www.cutimes.com; Bob Trebilcock, "Bye, Banks: Time to Join a Credit Union," *MoneyWatch/CBS News,* January 12, 2010, http://www.cbsnews.com; James Briggs, "Credit Unions Thrive as Big Banks Cut Back on Lending," *Oakland Press,* January 4, 2010, http://www.theoaklandpress.com.

"Fair Trade has always been part of my legacy in coffee," says RikKleinfeldt, president and co-founder of Rhode Island-based New Harvest Coffee Roasters. "That's where I started with New Harvest." But in less than a decade, New Harvest's business model has evolved beyond Fair Trade to something different.

New Harvest is a small-batch coffee roaster specializing in certified organic coffee that is grown and harvested by farms with sustainable practices. RikKleinfeldt notes that he built his company on two pillars: 1) the highest quality coffee, and 2) sustainable sourcing practices. "But these two weren't really gelling at first," he admits. At the beginning, Kleinfeldt tried to source from Fair Trade cooperatives, but this wasn't really fulfilling his objective. "Fair Trade is based on the commodity system," Kleinfeldt explains, "which creates a floor price at which coffee can't drop below. But it doesn't really address the issue of quality." The groups that work with Fair Trade are large cooperatives, sometimes encompassing several thousand small farms. All the coffee is blended together as a commodity, so it is impossible for a roaster like New Harvest to deal directly with each farm, selecting the specific harvest that it wants to buy.

Kleinfeldt is quick to point out that when Fair Trade began around a decade ago, it was a lifeline to small farmers because coffee prices were at an all-time low— these growers were selling their crops for less than it cost to produce them. Without Fair Trade, many of these farms would have gone out of business. With the coffee market somewhat stabilized though, commodity pricing brings its own set of problems. "The commodity pricing usually has nothing to do with the coffee itself," says Kleinfeldt. Prices are set at the New York Stock Exchange, not in the growing fields of Costa Rica or Colombia. He notes that roasters, retailers, and consumers may end up paying way too much or way too little for a particular year's crop.

So Kleinfeldt has become part of what he calls the Artisan Coffee movement—growers, roasters, and retailers who prefer to deal directly with each other as individual businesses. "We connect directly with our growers and determine price based on quality," he explains. Kleinfeldt and his staff, along with some of his retailers such as the owner of Blue State Coffee and the owner of Pejamajo Café, travel to the farms in Costa Rica and Colombia where they actually taste the coffee before purchasing a crop. Kleinfeldt believes this is the only way to get the best coffee on the market. These visits help develop strong relationships, find solutions to problems, and develop strategies for surviving and thriving as businesses. Through visiting, he says, "we can understand their challenges." One farm in particular is located in Colombia. The farmer

decided he didn't want to participate in a large Fair Trade cooperative—instead, he wanted to develop a market for his own coffee. So he approached New Harvest with the idea, and the match was ideal. He is now one of New Harvest's premier growers.

Sourcing the coffee beans directly from individual farms also helps New Harvest keep close track of organic and sustainability practices. GerraHarrigan, director of business development for New Harvest Coffee Roasters, notes that this is an important part of the firm's business. The owners of local coffee shops—and their customers— like the reassurance that New Harvest stands behind all of its claims. Harrigan takes the hands-on approach. "When we deal direct-trade coffee, the coffee has to be cared for a little more," she explains. Harrigan grades the coffee on several factors before pricing it for New Harvest.

Kleinfeldt wants consumers to know they are getting a great deal when they ask for New Harvest at their local shop. He points out that the price differentiation isn't as much as people might think. A visit to the supermarket reveals that Starbucks and Green Mountain sell for about $9 to $11 per pound, whereas most New Harvest coffee sells for about $11 to $13 a pound. Because of the richness of New Harvest, most customers actually get more cups of coffee from a pound of New Harvest than they do from the other premium brands.

Kleinfeldt hopes that the Artisan Coffee movement, as he refers to his company's practices, will flourish and grow. He believes that if you're going to drink a cup of coffee, it should be really fresh and of the highest quality—with beans preferably roasted by New Harvest.

Questions for Critical Thinking

1. What are the benefits and drawbacks of treating coffee as a commodity in the marketplace? What do you predict will be the future of Fair Trade?

2. Should the entire coffee market be regulated in any way? Why or why not? If so, how?

3. How would New Harvest change as a business if it made an initial public offering (IPO)?

4. What is your opinion of the so-called Artisan Coffee movement as a business model? Do you think it will be successful in the long run? Why or why not?

Sources: New Harvest Coffee Roasters Web site, http://www .newharvestcoffee.com, accessed August 18, 2010; "New Harvest Coffee Roasters," *GreenPeople,* http://www.greenpeople.org, accessed August 29, 2010; Richard Garcia, "Pejamajo Café & New Harvest Coffee Roasters," *Chefs Daily Food Bank,* May 4, 2010, http://www.chefsdailyfoodbank.com.

Chapter 17

Learning Objectives

[1] Define *finance,* and explain the role of financial managers.

[2] Describe the components of a financial plan and the financial planning process.

[3] Outline how organizations manage their assets.

[4] Compare the two major sources of funds for a business, and explain the concept of leverage.

[5] Identify sources of short-term financing for business operations.

[6] Discuss long-term financing options.

[7] Describe mergers, acquisitions, buyouts, and divestitures.

Managing the Firm's Financial Resources

Intel Places Its Chips on the Table—At Home

An old business saying advises, "It takes money to make money." Smart business owners know that they must invest a portion of their revenues for their firms to survive and grow. While this approach may be obvious in profitable times, you might question a company that sinks cash into new products and facilities when the economy is faltering and the future is far from certain. But that's exactly what Intel, the U.S. manufacturer of computer microprocessors, pledged to do. Just when thousands of companies were laying off workers, trimming operations, closing facilities, and removing products from their lines, Intel announced plans to expand existing manufacturing sites in Arizona, New Mexico, and Oregon, supporting about 7,000 jobs in those locations. In addition, the firm unveiled a strategy that included a new assembly test facility in Vietnam and a new factory in China. Why take such an aggressive stand as other firms retreated? "You never save your way out of recession," asserts Intel spokesman Chuck Mulloy. "You invest your way." The total price tag for Intel's strategy is a whopping $7 billion. Even more eye popping is that Intel is not raising capital in the financial markets to fund the expansion. Instead, the company is using internal cash to pay for what it is calling its largest-ever investment in a new manufacturing process. Although some experts might question the size of the investment during an economic downturn, no one argues with the necessity of continually moving ahead in the technology industry.

Intel's new product—its next-generation chip made with 32-nanometer technology—is critical to the firm's future growth. In the new chips, tiny transistors are squeezed together so tightly that one billion of them will fit on a chip the size of a dime. This innovation creates two forms of efficiency—less electricity is consumed, and the cost of producing each chip is lower. The 32-nanometer circuitry occupies only 71 percent of the space of current microchips. Intel outlined plans for producing the new chips long before the economy dropped, and executives believed that if the firm waited for a turnaround, it would lose the opportunity to be the first to bring the chips to market. At this time, Intel can launch the new microprocessors at a reasonable price. "One of the best ways to use this capacity [32-nanometer technology] is for what I call 'square-wave transition,' to bring massive amounts of new technology at a great price point," explains Intel CEO Paul Otellini. With lower costs, computer manufacturers can afford to use the new chips in such mainstream products as PCs, creating higher sales for Intel.

In this light, "it would be hard to argue that they shouldn't be making this investment," notes one observer. Even so, Intel must consider its commitment to retaining U.S. employees, whose wages are typically higher than those of workers in countries like China or India. "Our standard of living doesn't allow us to compete for low-wage jobs," states Otellini, who urges continued investment in education if the U.S. technology industry is to remain competitive. Although paying higher wages for U.S. workers may appear to be a luxury, Intel views it as a necessity for keeping a close eye on the manufacturing process, including quality and schedule. "One of Intel's tremendous strengths is process control [in manufacturing chips]," comments an industry expert. If highly technical manufacturing stays in the United States, the company can promote its quality and avoid the cost in dollars and time of setting up its technical manufacturing in foreign facilities. Otellini advocates keeping as much of Intel's manufacturing in the United States as possible to reap the advantage of getting new products to market quickly and monitoring quality more easily. Intel has closed some plants in Southeast Asia for financial and quality reasons. But the company does send certain processes overseas in specified plants in Vietnam and China. Aside from the value of keeping operations close to home, Otellini says Intel benefits from the "feel good" factor, particularly when bad economic news seems to be everywhere. "For a variety of reasons, the factories where we are in the best position to ramp this [32-nanometer] technology fast were the ones that happened to be in the United States," he says. "And there is a nice statement to be made by an American company to be investing in America right now."[1]

Previous chapters discuss two essential functions that a business must perform. First, the company must produce a good or service or contract with suppliers to produce it. Second, the firm must market its good or service to prospective customers. This chapter introduces a third, equally important, function: a company's managers must ensure that it has enough money to perform its other tasks successfully, in both the present and the future, and that these funds are invested properly. Adequate funds must be available to buy materials, equipment, and other assets; pay bills; and compensate employees. This third business function is **finance**—planning, obtaining, and managing the company's funds in order to accomplish its objectives as effectively and efficiently as possible.

An organization's financial objectives include not only meeting expenses and investing in assets but also maximizing its overall worth, often determined by the value of the firm's common stock. Financial managers are responsible for meeting expenses, investing in assets, and increasing profits to shareholders. Solid financial management is critical to the success of a business. A glance through the daily news provides examples of firms that, even though they offered good products to the marketplace, failed because funds were not managed properly.

This chapter focuses on the finance function of organizations. It begins by describing the role of financial managers, their place in the organizational hierarchy, and the increasing importance of finance. Next, the financial planning process and the components of a financial plan are outlined. Then the discussion focuses on how organizations manage assets as efficiently and effectively as possible. The two major sources of funds—debt and equity—are then compared, and the concept of leverage is introduced. The major sources of short-term and long-term funding are described in the following sections. A description of mergers, acquisitions, buyouts, and divestitures concludes the chapter.

finance planning, obtaining, and managing the company's funds to accomplish its objectives as effectively and efficiently as possible.

The Role of the Financial Manager

Because of the intense pressures they face today, organizations are increasingly measuring and reducing the costs of business operations, as well as maximizing revenues and profits. As a result, **financial managers**—executives who develop and implement their firm's financial plan and determine the most appropriate sources and uses of funds—are among the most vital people on the corporate payroll.

Figure 17.1 shows what the finance function of a typical company might look like. At the top is the chief financial officer (CFO). The CFO usually reports directly to the company's chief executive officer (CEO) or chief operating officer (COO). In some companies, the CFO is also a member of the board of directors. In the case of the software maker Oracle,

financial managers executive who develops and implements the firm's financial plan and determines the most appropriate sources and uses of funds.

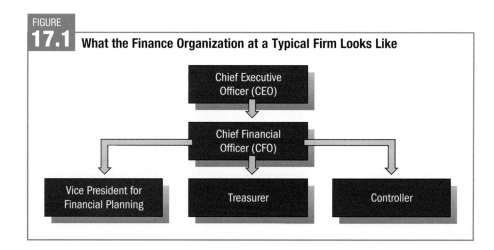

FIGURE
17.1 **What the Finance Organization at a Typical Firm Looks Like**

Chief Executive Officer (CEO)

Chief Financial Officer (CFO)

Vice President for Financial Planning

Treasurer

Controller

both the current CFO and the former CFO serve on that company's board, the latter as its chairman. Moreover, it's not uncommon for CFOs to serve as independent directors on other firms' boards, such as Hewlett-Packard, Microsoft, and Target. As noted in Chapter 15, the CFO, along with the firm's CEO, must certify the accuracy of the firm's financial statements.

Reporting directly to the CFO are often three senior managers. Although titles can vary, these three executives are commonly called the *vice president for financial management* (or *planning*), the *treasurer*, and the *controller*. The vice president for financial management or planning is responsible for preparing financial forecasts and analyzing major investment decisions, such as new products, new production facilities, and acquisitions. The treasurer is responsible for all of the company's financing activities, including cash management, tax planning and preparation, and shareholder relations. The treasurer also works on the sale of new security issues to investors. The controller is the chief accounting manager. The controller's functions include keeping the company's books, preparing financial statements, and conducting internal audits.

The growing importance of financial professionals is reflected in the growing number of CEOs who have been promoted from financial positions. Indra Nooyi, CEO of PepsiCo, and Jim Marsh, CEO of the British telecommunications company Cable and Wireless, both served as their firm's CFO prior to assuming the top job. The importance of finance professionals is also reflected in how much CFOs earn today. According to a survey by the executive compensation consulting firm Equilar, the median annual salary for CFOs of *Fortune* 500 companies is around $3.76 million.[2] The CFO of the investment firm Berkshire Hathaway is actually paid more than the company's famous chairman, Warren Buffett.[3]

In performing their jobs, financial professionals continually seek to balance risks with expected financial returns. Risk is the uncertainty of gain or loss; return is the gain or loss that results from an investment over a specified period of time. Financial managers strive to maximize the wealth of their firm's shareholders by striking the optimal balance between risk and return. This balance is called the **risk-return trade-off**. For example, relying heavily on borrowed funds may increase the return

risk-return trade-off
process of maximizing the wealth of the firm's shareholders by striking the optimal balance between risk and return.

Jin Lee/Bloomberg/Getty Images, Inc.

The growing importance of financial professionals is reflected in the growing number of CEOs who have been promoted from financial positions. Indra Nooyi, CEO of PepsiCo, served as CFO prior to assuming the top job.

Hit & Miss

UPS: Balancing Risks and Returns

Managing the risks and returns for a company as large as UPS is no easy task. UPS is the largest package delivery firm in the world and a leader in supply chain services for other businesses. But CFO Kurt Kuehn is happy to do the job. Kuehn has worked for Brown—the firm's nickname, from its huge brown delivery trucks—for more than 30 years. Most recently he served as senior vice president of global sales and marketing and was a member of the UPS management committee. Prior to that, he was vice president of investor relations. So he knows the company's finances from the inside out.

When Kuehn took over the CFO job, one of the first tasks he faced was a restructuring of the company's financial policy regarding its capital structure. The new structure is designed to create greater value for UPS's major stakeholders—its shareholders. Essentially, UPS plans to restructure its balance sheet in such a way that it increases its debt by reinvesting in the company, using a target debt ratio of up to 60 percent funds-from-operations to total debt. "We have been studying our capital structure options for some time," explained Kuehn when the plan was announced. "This change in policy will permit us to make increased investments in the business, pursue selective acquisitions, and undertake larger share repurchases."

In this case, debt is positive for the company, allowing it to plough more resources back into the business. CEO Scott Davis was quick to reassure shareholders and business customers of this fact. "UPS has had a long-standing commitment to a very strong balance sheet for decades, and that will not change," he insisted. "Indeed, we are putting the balance sheet strength to work more efficiently to deploy capital for the benefit of our shareholders. UPS's consistent, stable cash flows mean we can accept a higher degree of debt while continuing to strategically grow our business." A day after the new plan was announced, UPS stock rose more than 4 percent, indicating that investors approved of the strategy and felt secure in their investment.

Questions for Critical Thinking

1. Describe Kurt Kuehn's role as a financial manager at UPS.
2. Why is the idea of restructuring the firm's balance sheet to increase debt possibly a good business move for UPS?

Sources: UPS Adopts New Financial Policy to Enhance Shareholder Value," company press release, January 9, 2008, http://reuters.com; accessed April 2, 2009; Ruthie Ackerman, "UPS Manages Expectations," *Forbes*, April 23, 2008, http://www.forbes.com; Melanie Lindner, "Investors Impressed by UPS," *Forbes*, January 10, 2008, http://www.forbes.com; Roy Harris, "What Did Brown Do for Scott Davis? Made Him CEO," *CFO*, October 15, 2007, http://www.cfo.com.

(in the form of cash) to shareholders, but the more money a firm borrows, the greater the risks to shareholders. An increase in a firm's cash on hand reduces the risk of being unable to meet unexpected cash needs. However, because cash in and of itself does not earn much, if any, return, failure to invest surplus funds in an income-earning asset—such as in securities—reduces a firm's potential return or profitability. Many illustrations of the risk-return trade-off are provided throughout this chapter.

Every financial manager must perform this risk-return balancing act. For example, in the late 1990s, Airbus wrestled with a major decision: whether to begin development and production of the giant A380 jetliner. The development costs for the aircraft—the world's largest jetliner—were initially estimated at more than $10 billion. Before committing to such a huge investment, financial managers had to weigh the potential profits of the A380 with the risk that the profits would not materialize. With its future on the line, Airbus decided to go ahead with the development of the A380, spending more than $15 billion on research and development. The A380 entered commercial service a few years ago. Airbus currently has orders for approximately 200 jetliners at a list price of more than $359 million each.[4] At this time, however, it's still unclear whether the A380 investment will turn out to be a smart, and profitable, decision.

Financial managers must also learn to adapt to changes in the financial system. The recent credit crisis has made it more difficult for some companies to borrow money from traditional lenders such as banks. This, in turn, has forced firms to scale back expansion plans or seek funding from other sources such as commercial financing companies. In addition, financial managers must adapt to internal changes as well. The "Hit & Miss" feature discusses how financial policies at UPS have evolved since the company went public.

Assessment Check ✓

1. What is the structure of the finance function at the typical firm?
2. Explain the risk-return trade-off.

Financial Planning

Financial managers develop their organization's **financial plan**, a document that specifies the funds needed by a firm for a given period of time, the timing of inflows and outflows, and the most appropriate sources and uses of funds. Some financial plans, often called *operating plans*, are short-term in nature, focusing on projections no more than a year or two in the future. Other financial plans, sometimes referred to as *strategic plans*, have a much longer time horizon, perhaps up to five or ten years.

Regardless of the time period, a financial plan is based on forecasts of production costs, purchasing needs, plant and equipment expenditures, and expected sales activities for the period covered. Financial managers use forecasts to determine the specific amounts and timing of expenditures and receipts. They build a financial plan based on the answers to three questions:

1. What funds will the firm require during the planning period?

2. When will it need additional funds?

3. Where will it obtain the necessary funds?

Some funds flow into the firm when it sells its goods or services, but funding needs vary. The financial plan must reflect both the amounts and timing of inflows and outflows of funds. Even a profitable firm may face a financial squeeze as a result of its need for funds when sales lag, when the volume of its credit sales increases, or when customers are slow in making payments.

In general, preparing a financial plan consists of three steps. The first is a forecast of sales or revenue over some future time period. This projection is, in fact, the key variable in any financial plan because without an accurate sales forecast, the firm will have difficulty accurately estimating other variables, such as production costs and purchasing needs. The best method of forecasting sales depends on the nature of the business. For instance, a retailer's CFO might begin with the current sales-per-store figure. Then he or she would look toward the near future, factoring in expected same-store sales growth, along with any planned store openings or closings, to come up with a forecast of sales for the next period. If the company sells merchandise through other channels, such as online, the forecast is adjusted to reflect those additional channels.

Next, the CFO uses the sales forecast to determine the expected level of profits for future periods. This longer-term projection involves estimating expenses such as purchases, employee compensation, and taxes. Many expenses are themselves functions of sales. For instance, the more a firm sells, generally the greater its purchases. Along with estimating future profits, the CFO should also determine what portion of these profits will likely be paid to shareholders in the form of cash dividends.

After coming up with the sales and profit forecast, the CFO then needs to estimate how many additional assets the firm will need to support projected sales. Increased sales, for example, might mean the company needs additional inventory, stepped-up collections for accounts receivable, or even new plant and equipment. Depending on the nature of the industry, some businesses need more assets than do other companies to support the same amount of sales. The technical term for this requirement is *asset intensity*. For instance, the chemical manufacturer DuPont has approximately $0.68 in assets for every dollar in sales.

financial plan document that specifies the funds needed by a firm for a period of time, the timing of inflows and outflows, and the most appropriate sources and uses of funds.

Costco has a lower *asset intensity* than a typical manufacturing business might have.

So, for every $100 increase in sales, the firm would need about $68 of additional assets. The warehouse retailer Costco, by contrast, has only roughly $0.34 in assets for every dollar in sales. It would require an additional $34 of assets for every $100 of additional sales. This difference is not surprising; manufacturing is a more asset-intensive business than retailing.

A simplified financial plan illustrates these steps. Assume a growing company is forecasting that sales next year will increase by $40 million to $140 million. After estimating expenses, the CFO believes that after-tax profits next year will be $12 million and the firm will pay nothing in dividends. The projected increase in sales next year will require the firm to invest another $20 million in assets, and because increases in assets are uses of funds, the company will need an additional $20 million in funds. The company's after-tax earnings will contribute $12 million, meaning that the other $8 million must come from outside sources. So the financial plan tells the CFO how much money will be needed and when it will be needed. Armed with this knowledge, and given that the firm has decided to borrow the needed funds, the CFO can then begin negotiations with banks and other lenders.

The cash inflows and outflows of a business are similar to those of a household. The members of a household depend on weekly or monthly paychecks for funds, but their expenditures vary greatly from one pay period to the next. The financial plan should indicate when the flows of funds entering and leaving the organization will occur and in what amounts. One of the most significant business expenses is employee compensation.

A good financial plan also includes financial control, a process of comparing actual revenues, costs, and expenses with forecasts. This comparison may reveal significant differences between projected and actual figures, so it is important to discover them early to take quick action.

Bill Morrison is the CFO of Pittsburgh-based Genco Marketplace, which liquidates, or sells off, other companies' excess inventory. Genco buys inventory that is not selling well then resells it to wholesalers. In turn, the wholesalers sell the inventory to discount retailers. Always vigilant about the cost of freight, including fuel, Genco pays the transportation costs of taking the goods from their current location to where they will be liquidated. Some excess inventory is seasonal. When a retailer has winter coats left over in June, Genco will buy those coats, hold them in inventory, and sell them to a wholesaler in the fall, when demand rises again. But the longer a product remains unsold, the harder it will be to liquidate, even at a deep discount. In all cases, Morrison or members of his team have to prepare a financial plan that takes into account not only the benefits of buying the merchandise but the risks as well.[5]

Assessment Check ✔

1. What three questions does a financial plan address?

2. Explain the steps involved in preparing a financial plan.

Managing Assets

As we noted in Chapter 15, assets consist of what a firm owns. But assets also represent uses of funds. To grow and prosper, companies need to obtain additional assets. Sound financial management requires assets to be acquired and managed as effectively and efficiently as possible. The "Business Etiquette" feature offers tips for managing assets.

Short-Term Assets

Short-term, or current, assets consist of cash and assets that can be, or are expected to be, converted into cash within a year. The major current assets are cash, marketable securities, accounts receivable, and inventory.

Cash and Marketable Securities

The major purpose of cash is to pay day-to-day expenses, much as when individuals maintain balances in checking accounts to pay bills or buy food and clothing. In addition, most organizations strive to maintain a minimum cash balance in order to have funds available in the event of unexpected expenses. As noted earlier, because cash earns little, if any, return, most firms invest excess cash in so-called *marketable securities*—low-risk securities that either have short maturities or can be easily sold in secondary markets. Money market instruments—described in Chapter 16—are popular choices for firms with excess cash. The cash budget, which we discussed in Chapter 15, is one tool for managing cash and marketable securities because it shows expected cash inflows and outflows for a period of time. The cash budget indicates months when the firm will have surplus cash and can invest in marketable securities and months when it will need additional cash.

Critics of some companies' budgeting practices contend that occasionally firms hoard cash. Recently, Cisco Systems had more than $35 billion in cash and marketable securities. Yet firms may have good reasons for holding large amounts of cash and marketable securities. They may plan on using these funds shortly to make a large investment, pay dividends to shareholders, or repurchase outstanding bonds.

Accounts Receivable

Accounts receivable are uncollected credit sales and can be a significant asset. The financial manager's job is to collect the funds owed the firm as quickly as possible while still offering sufficient credit to customers to generate increased sales. In general, a more liberal credit policy means higher sales but also increased collection expenses, higher levels of bad debt, and a higher investment in accounts receivable.

Management of accounts receivable is composed of two functions: determining an overall

BusinessEtiquette

Tips for Managing Assets

These are challenging times for all businesses, whether one-person start-ups or large corporations. One of the most difficult problems is controlling costs. Here are some tips on managing assets—physical, financial, and human—while focusing on both short-term demands and long-term planning:

1 *Define your goals and objectives.* Be realistic in working out what resources you need to meet your immediate needs and what you will need to fulfill your long-term plans. If you need to borrow money, be aware that currently, credit is very tight.

2 *Examine your expenses.* You may find some areas—such as travel or discretionary spending—where you can reduce or eliminate unnecessary expenditures. Which makes more financial sense for your company, traditional hardware and storage or cloud computing?

3 *Communicate with all your associates.* Be sure that your employees, suppliers, and clients know what is happening with your business. Often when people hear nothing, especially during difficult times, they will assume the worst has happened.

4 *Cultivate your human assets.* Identify your valued employees and let them know that they are important. In difficult times, competing companies often try to lure away talented personnel. Constant communication is important here too. If your best employees hear nothing from you, they, too, will assume the worst has happened—and they will be more willing to leave for what seem to be better opportunities elsewhere.

5 *Have at least one backup plan.* Your goals and objectives may not work out the way you would like them to. You may plan for a certain amount of receivables, but what if they suddenly drop off? If possible, have sufficient financial reserves available to meet the unexpected. That way, you may be able to turn even disaster to your advantage.

Sources: "Managing Assets in Volatile Times: Nine Ways CFOs Can Adapt to Changing Financial Markets," Deloitte, http://www.deloitte.com, accessed June 24, 2010; Fred Jennings and R. W. Beck, "Leveraging Enterprise Value with Asset Management," *Utility Products*, January 14, 2010, http://www.elp.com; Daniel Solin, "Seven Shocking Tips to Boost Your Returns by 400% (or More)," *DailyFinance*, January 1, 2010, http://www.dailyfinance.com.

At Bed Bath & Beyond, inventory is the most valuable asset. Managing inventory can be a costly and highly complicated undertaking, especially for retailers.

Mark Peterson/Redux Pictures

credit policy and deciding which customers will be offered credit. Formulating a credit policy involves deciding whether the firm will offer credit and, if so, on what terms. Will a discount be offered to customers who pay in cash? Often, the overall credit policy is dictated by competitive pressures or general industry practices. If all your competitors offer customers credit, your firm will likely have to as well. The other aspect of a credit policy is deciding which customers will be offered credit. Managers must consider the importance of the customer as well as its financial health and repayment history.

One simple tool for assessing how well receivables are being managed is calculating accounts receivable turnover over successive time periods. We showed how this ratio is calculated in Chapter 15. If receivables turnover shows signs of slowing, it means that the average credit customer is paying later. This trend warrants further investigation.

Inventory Management For many firms, such as retailers, inventory represents the largest single asset. At the home furnishings retailer Bed Bath & Beyond, inventory makes up about 49 percent of total assets. Even for nonretailers, inventory is an important asset. At the heavy-equipment manufacturer Caterpillar, inventory is almost 12 percent of total assets. On the other hand, some types of firms, such as electric utilities and transportation companies, have no inventory. For the majority of firms, which do carry inventory, proper management of it is vital.

Managing inventory can be complicated. The cost of inventory includes more than just the acquisition cost. It also includes the cost of ordering, storing, insuring, and financing inventory, as well as the cost of stockouts, lost sales due to insufficient inventory. Financial managers try to minimize the cost of inventory. But production, marketing, and logistics also play important roles in determining proper inventory levels. The production considerations of inventory management were discussed in Chapter 10. In Chapter 12, we outlined the marketing and logistics issues surrounding inventory.

Trends in the inventory turnover ratio—described in Chapter 15—can be early warning signs of impending trouble. For instance, if inventory turnover has been slowing for several consecutive quarters, it indicates that inventory is rising faster than sales. In turn, this may suggest that customer demand is softening and the firm needs to take action, such as reducing production or increasing promotional efforts.

Capital Investment Analysis

In addition to current assets, firms also invest in long-lived assets. Unlike current assets, long-lived assets are expected to produce economic benefits for more than one year. These investments often involve substantial amounts of money. For example, as noted earlier in the chapter, Airbus invested more than $15 billion in development of the A380. In another example, in 2009 the auto manufacturer BMW recently spent $750 million on expanding its production facility in Spartanburg, South Carolina, bringing its total investment in the state to $4.6 billion.[6]

The process by which decisions are made regarding investments in long-lived assets is called *capital investment analysis*. Firms make two basic types of capital investment decisions: expansion and replacement. The A380 and the BMW South Carolina plant investments are examples of expansion decisions. Replacement decisions involve upgrading assets by substituting new ones. A retailer, such as Walmart, might decide to replace an old store with a new Supercenter, as it did in Oxford, Ohio.

Financial managers must estimate all of the costs and benefits of a proposed investment, which can be quite difficult, especially for very long-lived investments. Only those investments that offer an acceptable return—measured by the difference between benefits and costs—should be undertaken. BMW's financial managers believed that the benefits of expanding the South Carolina production facility outweighed the high cost. The expansion will allow BMW to produce three new models designed mainly for the North American market, so the expected profit from the sale of these models would be considered in the decision. Some other benefits cited by BMW include lower production costs and improved logistics. The Spartanburg facility recently produced its 1.5 millionth vehicle. In a ceremony marking that milestone, Josef Kerscher, president of BMW [U.S.] Manufacturing, noted, "Today's events represent a significant milestone for BMW, emphasizing both BMW's commitment to the U.S. market and its confidence in the future."[7]

Managing International Assets

Today, firms often have assets worldwide. Both McDonald's and The Coca-Cola Company generate more than half of their annual sales outside the United States. The vast majority of sales for Unilever and Nestlé occur outside their home countries (the Netherlands and Switzerland, respectively). Managing international assets creates several challenges for the financial manager, one of the most important of which is the problem of exchange rates.

As we discussed in several other chapters, an exchange rate is the rate at which one currency can be exchanged for another. Exchange rates can vary substantially from year to year, creating a problem for any company with international assets. As an example, assume a U.S. firm has a major subsidiary in the United Kingdom. Assume that the U.K. subsidiary earns an annual profit of £750 million (stated in British pounds). Over the past five years, the exchange rate between the U.S. dollar and the British pound has varied between 1.82 (dollars per pound) and 1.56.[8] This means the dollar value of the U.K. profits ranged from $1.37 billion to $1.17 billion.

Consequently, many global firms engage in activities that reduce the risks associated with exchange rate fluctuations. Some are quite complicated. However, one of the simplest and most widely used is called a *balance sheet hedge*. Essentially, a balance sheet hedge creates an offsetting liability to the non-dollar-denominated asset, one that is denominated in the same currency as the asset. In our example, the U.K. subsidiary is a pound-denominated asset. To create an offsetting liability, the firm could take out a loan, denominated in British pounds, creating a pound-denominated liability. If done correctly, this hedge will reduce or even eliminate the risk associated with changes in the value of the dollar relative to the pound. This will improve the financial performance of the firm, which can have a positive impact on its stock price.

Assessment Check ✔

1. Why do firms often choose to invest excess cash in marketable securities?

2. What are the two aspects of accounts receivable management?

3. Explain the difference between an expansion decision and a replacement decision.

Sources of Funds and Capital Structure

The use of debt for financing can increase the potential for return as well as increase loss potential. Recall the accounting equation introduced in Chapter 15:

$$\text{Assets} = \text{Liabilities} + \text{Owners' equity}$$

If you view this equation from a financial management perspective, it reveals that there are only two types of funding: debt and equity. *Debt capital* consists of funds obtained through borrowing. *Equity capital* consists of funds provided by the firm's owners when they reinvest earnings, make additional contributions, liquidate assets, issue stock to the general public, or raise capital from outside investors. The mix of a firm's debt and equity capital is known as its **capital structure**.

Companies often take very different approaches to choosing a capital structure. As more debt is used, the risk to the company increases since the firm is now obligated to make the interest payments on the money borrowed, regardless of the cash flows coming into the company. Choosing more debt increases the fixed costs a company must pay, which in turn makes a company more sensitive to changing sales revenues. Debt is frequently the least costly method of raising additional financing dollars, one of the reasons it is so frequently used.

Differing industries choose varying amounts of debt and equity to use when financing. Using the information provided by DataMonitor, the automotive industry has debt ratios (the ratio of liabilities to assets) of over 60 percent for both Toyota and Honda and over 90 percent for Ford. These companies are primarily using debt to finance their asset expenditures. Companies like the profit foodservice companies of McDonald's and Starbucks use only 49 percent debt and 27 percent debt, respectively. The mixture of debt and equity a company uses is a major management decision.

Leverage and Capital Structure Decisions

Raising needed cash by borrowing allows a firm to benefit from the principle of **leverage**, increasing the rate of return on funds invested by borrowing funds. The key to managing leverage is to ensure that a company's earnings remain larger than its interest payments, which increases the leverage on the rate of return on shareholders' investment. Of course, if the company earns less than its interest payments, shareholders lose money on their original investments.

Figure 17.2 shows the relationship between earnings and shareholder returns for two identical hypothetical firms that choose to raise funds in different ways. Leverage Company obtains 50 percent of its funds from lenders who purchase

capital structure mix of a firm's debt and equity capital.

leverage increasing the rate of return on funds invested by borrowing funds.

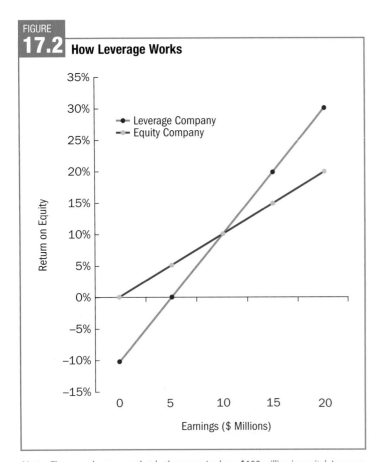

FIGURE 17.2 How Leverage Works

Note: The example assumes that both companies have $100 million in capital. Leverage company consists of $50 million in equity and $50 million in bonds (with an interest rate of 10 percent). Equity company consists of $100 million in equity and no bonds. This example also assumes no corporate taxes.

Solving an Ethical Controversy

Executive Pay: Should Shareholders Decide the Salaries of CEOs?

While the country was suffering through the financial crisis and its aftermath, the news media were filled with reports of astronomical salaries of CEOs and other top executives at large corporations.

At a recent Royal Dutch Shell annual meeting, shareholders voted down the proposed executive compensation package. In response to this reprimand, the company announced that it would freeze executive pay and base its bonuses on performance. The new CEO received a salary 20 percent lower than that of the previous CEO. The company said that the changes would "demonstrate appropriate restraint in the current economic environment. "Say-for-pay" voting by shareholders has become increasingly common—and controversial.

Should company shareholders help determine how much top executives are paid?

PRO

1. Publicly held corporations are owned by their shareholders, who should have the opportunity to vote on compensation for top executives. Robert E. Denham and Rajiv L. Gupta, co-chairs of The Conference Board Task Force on Executive Compensation, said, "Shareholders . . . and the public deserve to see executive compensation programs that serve shareholders' interests and are explained to shareholders. . . ."

2. Some analysts believe that lopsided pay structures had a part in the financial crisis. Federal Reserve Chairman Ben Bernanke said, "Compensation practices at some banking organizations have led to misaligned incentives and excessive risk-taking. . . ."

CON

1. Shareholders may not necessarily know what appropriate pay is. Many don't have the time or resources to do their own analysis and judge whether a pay program is suitable—or whether it promotes a risk-taking, get-rich-quick mentality in executives.

2. Shareholders recently turned down the chance to vote on executive pay at companies such as Johnson & Johnson and Dow Chemical. Many prefer to discuss pay structures with management and board members before voting.

Summary

A financial-regulation reform bill recently cleared a joint congressional committee and is schedule for a vote by the full Congress. One of its provisions gives shareholders the right to a nonbinding vote on executive pay.

Sources: Alix Stuart, "Reform Bill Mandates Say on Pay," *CFO.com*, June 29, 2010, http://www.cfo.com; Jim Kuhnhenn and Alan Fram, "Congress Agrees on Financial Oversight," *Philadelphia Inquirer*, June 26, 2010, http://www.philly.com; Ann Yerger, "Red Flags for Say-on-Pay Voting," Harvard Law School Forum on Corporate Governance and Financial Regulation, May 18, 2010, http://blogs.law.harvard.edu; A. G. Laffey, "Executive Pay: Time for CEOs to Take a Stand," *Harvard Business Review*, May 2010, http://hbr.org; Bryant Ruiz Switzky, "CEO Compensation Down in 2009," *Washington Business Journal*, May 7, 2010, http://washingtonbizjournals.com; "Shell Shareholder 'Rebellion' Leads to New Limits on Executive Pay, Bonuses," *Huffington Post*, February 26, 2010, http://www.huffingtonpost.com; Helen Coster, "The State of the CEO in 2010," *Forbes.com*, January 21, 2010, http://www.forbes.com; David R. Butcher, "Cracking Down on Excessive Executive Pay," IMT Industry Market Trends, October 29, 2009, http://news.thomasnet.com.

company bonds. Leverage Company pays 10 percent interest on its bonds. Equity Company raises all of its funds through sales of company stock.

Notice that if earnings double, from, say, $10 million to $20 million, returns to shareholders of Equity Company also double—from 10 percent to 20 percent. But returns to shareholders of Leverage Company more than double—from 10 percent to 30 percent. However, leverage works in the opposite direction as well. If earnings fall from $10 million to $5 million, a decline of 50 percent, returns to shareholders of Equity Company also fall by 50 percent—from 10 percent to 5 percent. By contrast, returns to shareholders of

Leverage Company fall from 10 percent to zero. Thus, leverage increases potential returns to shareholders but also increases risk.

Another problem with borrowing money is that an overreliance on borrowed funds may reduce management's flexibility in future financing decisions. If a company raises equity capital this year and needs to raise funds next year, it will probably be able to raise either debt or equity capital. But if it raises debt capital this year, it may be forced to raise equity capital next year.

Equity capital has drawbacks as well. Because shareholders are owners of the company, they usually have the right to vote on major company issues and elect the board of directors. Whenever new equity is sold, the control of existing shareholders is diluted, and the outcome of these votes could potentially change. One contentious subject today between companies and shareholders is whether shareholders should be able to vote on executive pay packages. The "Solving an Ethical Controversy" feature debates this issue.

Another disadvantage of equity capital is that it is more expensive than debt capital. First, creditors have a senior claim to the assets of a firm relative to shareholders. Because of this advantage, creditors are willing to accept a lower rate of return than shareholders are. Second, the firm can deduct interest payments on debt, reducing its taxable income and tax bill. Dividends paid to shareholders, on the other hand, are not tax deductible. A key component of the financial manager's job is to weigh the advantages and disadvantages of debt capital and equity capital, creating the most appropriate capital structure for his or her firm.

Mixing Short-Term and Long-Term Funds

Another decision financial managers face is determining the appropriate mix of short- and long-term funds. Short-term funds consist of current liabilities, and long-term funds consist of long-term debt and equity. Short-term funds are generally less expensive than long-term funds, but they also expose the firm to more risk. This is because short-term funds have to be renewed, or rolled over, frequently. Short-term interest rates can be volatile. During a recent 12-month period, for example, rates on commercial paper, a popular short-term financing option, ranged from a high of 6 percent to a low of less than 2 percent.[9]

Because short-term rates move up and down frequently, interest expense on short-term funds can change substantially from year to year. For instance, if a firm borrows $50 million for ten years at 5 percent interest, its annual interest expense is fixed at $2.5 million for the entire ten years. On the other hand, if it borrows $50 million for one year at a rate of 4 percent, its annual interest expense of $2 million is only fixed for that year. If interest rates increase the following year to 6 percent, $1 million will be added to the interest expense bill. Another potential risk of relying on short-term funds is availability. Even financially healthy firms can occasionally find it difficult to borrow money.

Because of the added risk of short-term funding, most firms choose to finance all of their long-term assets, and even a portion of their short-term assets, with long-term funds. Johnson & Johnson is typical of this choice. Figure 17.3 shows a recent balance sheet broken down between short- and long-term assets, and short- and long-term funds.

Dividend Policy

Along with decisions regarding capital structure and the mix of short- and long-term funds, financial managers also make decisions regarding a firm's

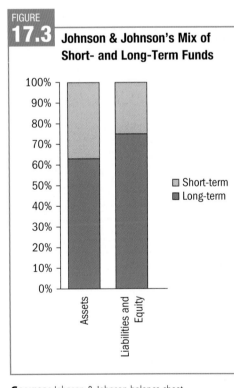

FIGURE 17.3 **Johnson & Johnson's Mix of Short- and Long-Term Funds**

■ Short-term
■ Long-term

Source: Johnson & Johnson balance sheet, Yahoo! Finance, http://finance.yahoo.com, accessed June 24, 2010.

dividend policy. *Dividends* are periodic cash payments to shareholders. The most common type of dividend is paid quarterly and is often labeled as a *regular dividend*. Occasionally, firms make one-time special or extra dividend payments, as Microsoft did some years ago. Earnings that are paid in dividends are not reinvested in the firm and don't contribute additional equity capital.

Firms are under no legal obligation to pay dividends to shareholders. Although some companies pay generous dividends, others pay nothing. Until 2010, Starbucks never paid a dividend to its shareholders. In contrast, 3M has paid dividends for 30-plus consecutive years, during which time the amount has more than quadrupled. Companies that pay dividends try to increase them or at the very least hold them steady from year to year. However, in rare cases firms must cut or eliminate dividends. As mentioned in Chapter 16, as a result of the oil spill in the Gulf of Mexico BP announced they were canceling dividend payments for the first quarter and suspending those payments to shareholders for the second and third quarters of their fiscal year.[10]

As a result of the oil spill in the Gulf of Mexico, BP announced they were canceling dividend payments for the first quarter and suspending them for the second and third quarters of their fiscal year.

Christopher Furlong/Getty Images, Inc.

Many factors determine a company's dividend policy, one of which is its investment opportunities. If a firm has numerous investment opportunities and wishes to finance some or all of them with equity funding, it will likely pay little, if any, of its earnings in dividends. Shareholders may actually want the company to retain earnings, because if they are reinvested, the firm's future profits, and the value of its shares, will increase faster. By contrast, a firm with more limited investment opportunities generally pays more of its earnings in dividends.

In addition to dividends, some firms buy back a portion of their outstanding stock. Home Depot, for instance, has repurchased more than $1 billion of stock over the past few years. Generally, shares are purchased on the secondary markets. The main purpose of share buy-backs is to raise the market value of the remaining shares, thus benefiting shareholders.

Short-Term Funding Options

Many times throughout a year, an organization may discover that its cash needs exceed its available funds. Retailers generate surplus cash for most of the year, but they need to build up inventory during the late summer and fall to get ready for the holiday shopping season. Consequently, they often need funds to pay for merchandise until holiday sales generate revenue. Then they use the incoming funds to repay the amount they borrowed. In these instances, financial managers evaluate short-term sources of funds. By definition, short-term sources of funds are repaid within one year. Three major sources of short-term funds exist: trade credit, short-term loans, and commercial paper. Large firms often rely on a combination of all three sources of short-term financing.

Trade Credit

Trade credit is extended by suppliers when a firm receives goods or services, agreeing to pay for them at a later date. Trade credit is common in many industries such as retailing and manufacturing. Suppliers routinely ship billions of dollars of merchandise to retailers

Assessment Check ✓

1. Explain the concept of leverage.

2. Why do firms generally rely more on long-term funds than short-term funds?

3. What is an important determinant of a firm's dividend policy?

each day and are paid at a later date. Without trade credit, the retailing sector would probably look much different—with fewer selections. Under this system, the supplier records the transactions as an account receivable, and the retailer records it as an account payable. Target alone currently has more than $6.5 billion of accounts payable on its books. The main advantage of trade credit is its easy availability because credit sales are common in many industries. The main drawback to trade credit is that the amount a company can borrow is limited to the amount it purchases.

What is the cost of trade credit? If suppliers do not offer a cash discount, trade credit is effectively free. For example, assume a supplier offers trade credit under the terms net 30—meaning that the buyer has 30 days to pay. This is similar to borrowing $100 and repaying $100 in 30 days. The effective rate of interest is zero. However, some suppliers offer a discount if they are paid in cash. If a discount is offered, trade credit can get quite expensive. Now assume that a 2 percent discount is offered to cash buyers. If they do not take the discount, they have 30 days to pay. Essentially, then, if the buyer doesn't pay cash, it is borrowing $98 today and repaying $100 30 days from today. The annual interest rate on such a loan exceeds 24 percent.

Short-Term Loans

Loans from commercial banks are a significant source of short-term financing for businesses. Often businesses use these loans to finance inventory and accounts receivable. For example, late fall and early winter is the period of highest sales for a small manufacturer of ski equipment. To meet this demand, it has to begin building inventory during the summer. The manufacturer also has to finance accounts receivable (credit sales to customers) during the fall and winter. So it takes out a bank loan during the summer. As the inventory is sold and accounts receivable collected, the firm repays the loan.

There are two types of short-term bank loans: lines of credit and revolving credit agreements. A line of credit specifies the maximum amount the firm can borrow over a period of time, usually a year. The bank is under no obligation to actually lend the money, however. It does so only if funds are available. Most lines of credit require the borrower to repay the original amount, plus interest, within one year. By contrast, a revolving credit agreement is essentially a guaranteed line of credit—the bank guarantees that the funds will be available when needed. Banks typically charge a fee, on top of interest, for revolving credit agreements.

The cash budget is an important tool for determining the size of a line of credit because it shows the months when additional financing will be needed or when borrowed funds can be repaid. For instance, assume the ski manufacturer's cash budget indicates that it will need $2.5 million for the June through November period. The financial manager might set up a line of credit with the bank for $2.8 million. The extra $300,000 is for any unexpected cash outflows.

In addition to commercial banks, commercial finance companies also make short-term loans to businesses. While most bank loans are unsecured, meaning that no specific assets are pledged as collateral, loans from commercial finance companies are often secured with accounts receivable or inventory.

Another form of short-term financing using accounts receivable is called *factoring*. The business sells its accounts receivable to either a bank or finance company—called a *factor*—at a discount. The size of the discount determines the cost of the transaction. Factoring allows the firm to convert its receivables into cash quickly without worrying about collections.

The cost of short-term loans depends not only on the interest rate but also on the fees charged by the lender. In addition to fees, some lenders require the borrower to keep so-called *compensating balances*—5 to 20 percent of the outstanding loan amount—in a checking account. Compensating balances increase the effective cost of a loan since the borrower doesn't have full use of the amount borrowed.

Say, for example, that a firm borrows $100,000 for one year at 5 percent interest. The borrower will pay $5,000 in interest (5 percent $\times$ $100,000). If the lender requires that 10 percent of the loan amount be kept as compensating balance, the firm has use of only $90,000. However, because it still will pay $5,000 in interest, the effective rate on the loan is actually 5.56 percent ($5,000 divided by $90,000).

Commercial Paper

Commercial paper is a short-term IOU sold by a company; this concept was briefly described in Chapter 16. Commercial paper is typically sold in multiples of $100,000 to $1 million and has a maturity that ranges from 1 to 270 days. Most commercial paper is unsecured. It is an attractive source of financing because large amounts of money can be raised at rates that are typically 1 to 2 percent less that those charged by banks. At the end of a recent year, almost $1.15 trillion in commercial paper was outstanding.[11] Although commercial paper is an attractive short-term financing alternative, only a small percentage of businesses can issue it. That is because access to the commercial paper market has traditionally been restricted to large, financially strong corporations.

Assessment Check ✓

1. What are the three sources of short-term funding?

2. Explain trade credit.

3. Why is commercial paper an attractive short-term financing option?

Sources of Long-Term Financing

Funds from short-term sources can help a firm meet current needs for cash or inventory. A larger project or plan, however, such as acquiring another company or making a major investment in real estate or equipment, usually requires funds for a much longer period of time. Unlike short-term sources, long-term sources are repaid over many years.

Organizations acquire long-term funds from three sources. One is long-term loans obtained from financial institutions such as commercial banks, life insurance companies, and pension funds. A second source is bonds—certificates of indebtedness—sold to investors. A third source is equity financing acquired by selling stock in the firm or reinvesting company profits.

Public Sale of Stocks and Bonds

Public sales of securities such as stocks and bonds are a major source of funds for corporations. Such sales provide cash inflows for the issuing firm and either a share in its ownership (for a stock purchaser) or a specified rate of interest and repayment at a stated time (for a bond purchaser). Because stock and bond issues of many corporations are traded in the secondary markets, stockholders and bondholders can easily sell these securities. Recently, when a European debt crisis seemed likely, it caused a massive slowdown in bond sales. But as fears of a crisis eased later in the year, bond sales reached their highest level since the same time the previous year. As of mid-2010, companies had sold about $307 billion of U.S. corporate bonds.[12] Public sales of securities, however, can vary substantially from year to year depending on conditions in the financial markets. Bond sales, for instance, tend to be higher when interest rates are lower.

In Chapter 16, we discussed the process by which most companies sell securities publicly—through investment bankers via a process called *underwriting*. Investment bankers purchase the securities from the issuer and then resell them to investors. The issuer pays a fee to the investment banker, called an *underwriting discount*.

Private Placements

Some new stock or bond issues are not sold publicly but instead to a small group of major investors such as pension funds and insurance companies. These sales are referred to as *private placements*. Most private placements involve corporate debt issues. More than $120 billion in corporate bonds were sold privately in a recent year in the United States.[13]

It is often cheaper for a company to sell a security privately than publicly, and there is less government regulation with which to contend because SEC registration is not required. Institutional investors such as insurance companies and pension funds buy private placements because they typically carry slightly higher interest rates than publicly issued bonds. In addition, the terms of the issue can be tailored to meet the specific needs of both the issuer and the institutional investors. Of course, the institutional investor gives up liquidity because privately placed securities do not trade in secondary markets.

Venture Capitalists

venture capitalists raise money from wealthy individuals and institutional investors and invest the funds in promising firms.

Venture capitalists are an important source of long-term financing, especially to new companies. **Venture capitalists** raise money from wealthy individuals and institutional investors and invest these funds in promising firms. Venture capitalists also provide management consulting advice as well as funds. In exchange for their investment, venture capitalists become part owners of the business. If the business succeeds, venture capitalists can earn substantial profits. The "Going Green" feature describes how Intel has joined with two dozen venture capitalist firms to create the "Invest in America" alliance to fund research into clean technology among other innovations.

One of the largest venture capital firms is Draper Fisher Jurvetson, based in Menlo Park, California. During the past 20 years, DFJ has invested in more than 300 small, start-up companies including Hotmail (acquired by Microsoft) and Skype (acquired by eBay). Currently the firm has more than $5.5 billion in capital commitments in companies throughout the world.[14]

Private Equity Funds

Similar to venture capitalists, *private equity funds* are investment companies that raise funds from wealthy individuals and institutional investors and use those funds to make large investments

Justin Sullivan/Getty Images, Inc.

Intel CEO, Paul Otellini, gives a speech in Washington, DC, announcing the creation of the Invest in America Alliance.

Intel Invests in U.S. Technology

Paul Otellini, the CEO of Intel Corporation, the world's largest chip manufacturer, noted that other countries, among them China, India, and Taiwan, have overtaken the United States as centers of innovation in the technology industry. Concerned that the United States faces fierce competition from other countries worldwide, Otellini recently announced a new initiative. The "Invest in America Alliance" teams Intel with 17 technology companies—including Google, Microsoft, Dell, and General Electric—and 24 leading venture capital firms. The alliance plans to invest $3.5 billion in start-up technology companies in the United States over two years. Intel Capital, Intel's own investment sector, plans to invest $200 million. The money will go to businesses in innovative fields such as information technology, clean technology, and biotechnology. But the fund will also invest in newer industries such as molecular diagnostics, electric vehicle ecosystems, and wireless infrastructure.

Among the venture capital firms that have signed on are Advanced Technology Ventures, Kleiner Perkins Caufield & Byars, and Draper Fisher Jurvetson. Arvind Sodhani, the president of Intel Capital and Intel's executive vice president, said, "Venture capital investments have played an important role in creating jobs at home and keeping America at the leading edge of technology globally."

The alliance is also seeking commitments from the technology industry to increase their hiring of recent college graduates. Among those who have made the pledge are Google, Microsoft, Yahoo!, Adobe, and Dell. The alliance's goal is to create a total of about 10,500 jobs, mostly in computer science and engineering. But jobs will also be available in financial planning, marketing, and sales. Intel has promised to hire more recent graduates as well. "It would be a long-term mistake to let our future scientists and engineers sit idle after graduation," Otellini said.

Questions for Critical Thinking

1. Why does "going green" make good business sense for venture capitalists?

2. How are jobs in financial planning, marketing, and sales important to the technology industry?

Sources: Company Web site, http://www.intel.com, accessed June 24, 2010; Claire Cain Miller, "A $3.5 Billion Effort Aims to Help Tech Start-Ups," *The New York Times*, February 24, 2010, http://www.nytimes.com; Blake Ellis, "Intel Plans $3.5 Billion Investment Fund," *CNNMoney.com*, February 23, 2010, http://money.cnn.com; Lance Whitney, "Intel Alliance to Invest $3.5 Billion in U.S. Tech," *CNET News*, February 23, 2010, http://news.cnet.com; Chloe Albanesius, "Intel, Tech Giants Pledge $3.5B in U.S. Investment," *PCMag.com*, February 23, 2010, http://www.pcmag.com.

---

in both public and privately held companies. Unlike venture capital funds, which tend to focus on small, start-up companies, private equity funds invest in all types of businesses, including mature ones. For example, Cerberus Capital Management, a private equity fund, recently bought the military contractor DynCorp International for about $1.5 billion.[15] Often, private equity funds invest in transactions that take public companies private, or leveraged buyouts (LBOs). In these transactions, discussed in more detail in the next section, a public company reverts to private status. The "Hit & Miss" feature profiles another large private equity fund, TPG Capital (formerly Texas Pacific Group).

A variation of the private equity fund is the so-called *sovereign wealth fund*. These companies are owned by governments and invest in a variety of financial and real assets, such as real estate. Although sovereign wealth funds generally make investments based on the best risk-return trade-off, political, social, and strategic considerations also play roles in their investment decisions.

Recently, several sovereign wealth funds made large investments in major U.S. financial firms, including Morgan Stanley and Citigroup. For instance, the Abu Dhabi Investment Authority (ADIA) invested in Citigroup, buying $7.5 billion in "equity shares" and becoming the giant bank's largest single shareholder in the process. However, ADIA has filed a claim against the bank, charging that Citigroup misled ADIA about its financial health. Citigroup called the charges "entirely without merit." ADIA may lose $4.8 billion when it must convert its equity units to shares.[16] The assets of the ten largest sovereign wealth funds are shown in Figure 17.4. Together, these ten funds have more than $2.3 trillion in assets.

Hit & Miss

TPG Hunts for the Hottest Deals

TPG is always hot on the trail of a good deal. The firm specializes in buyouts and investments in companies that are struggling, and it focuses on the United States, Europe, and Asia. TPG manages funds emphasizing private equity, venture capital, public equity, and debt investments. In general, TPG looks for companies that need an equity investment of anywhere between $100 million and $750 million in order to survive—companies that are established or even at the mature stage of their product offerings. Their goods and services may be suffering from obsolescence, or they may not be able to manage costs.

Some people might view TPG as a scavenger hunting for fallen prey, but founding partner David Bonderman views his firm in a more heroic light. Previously, he focused on investing in ailing corporations—those owned by shareholders—and taking them private in order to bring them back to life. If he succeeded, he and his company made a lot of money. "Private equity allows me to make long-term decisions and make investments in companies that are not valued by the market," Bonderman explained of this practice. But recently, Bonderman has taken the opposite approach: investing less in a company and keeping it public. One of these firms was Washington Mutual—the large mortgage lender. TPG invested $1.35 billion in Washington Mutual only to lose that investment several months later when the FDIC seized control of the bank.

Which approach is better business? The answer may depend on the state of the economy. When more credit is available, the public-to-private approach can result in enormous profits, although the risk is high.

TPG made several billion dollars taking wireless carrier Alltel private and then selling it a year later to Verizon. When less credit is available, investing private money in public companies is a necessity. Some good deals can be made, but even they carry some risk, as the Washington Mutual loss illustrates. Still, David Bonderman and his partners show no signs of slowing down. TPG has holdings in upscale Texas retail chain Neiman Marcus Group, Pennsylvania-based disaster recovery firm SunGard Data Systems, Italian motorcycle manufacturer Ducati, and others. Despite a business environment that sometimes resembles a bucking bronco, Bonderman isn't jumping from the saddle anytime soon.

Questions for Critical Thinking

1. Describe some of the risks encountered by a firm like TPG.
2. Why is it important for TPG to adjust its strategy to changes in the economic environment such as availability of credit? What other changes in the environment might require alternative strategies?

Sources: TPG," profile from *BusinessWeek*, http://investing.businessweek.com, accessed April 2, 2009; Amerendra Bhushan, "Texas Pacific Group Investor Letter—Humbled by WAMU Losses," *CEOWORLD Magazine*, September 27, 2008, http://ceoworld.biz; "TPG Capital," company profile, *Google Finance*, http://finance.google.com, accessed May 21, 2008; Andrew Ross Sorkin, "New Path for Kings of Buyouts," *The New York Times*, April 8, 2008, http://www.nytimes.com; Alistair Barr, "WaMu Gets $7 Billion from Group Led by Texas Pacific," *MarketWatch*, April 8, 2008, http://www.marketwatch.com.

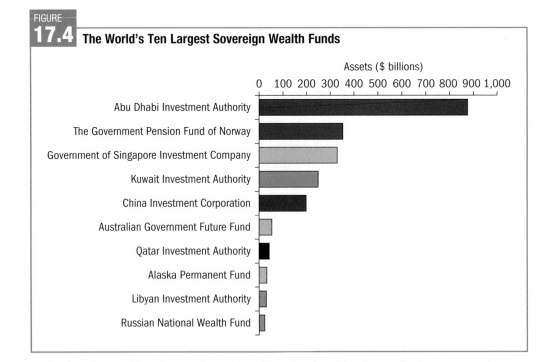

FIGURE 17.4 The World's Ten Largest Sovereign Wealth Funds

Source: Sovereign Wealth Fund Institute, "Sovereign Wealth Fund Rankings," http://www.swfinstitute.org, accessed June 24, 2010.

Hedge Funds

Hedge funds are private investment companies open only to qualified large investors. In recent years, hedge funds have become a significant presence in U.S. financial markets. Before the recent recession, some analysts estimated that hedge funds accounted for about 60 percent of all secondary bond market trading and around one-third of all activity on stock exchanges. More recently, hedge fund providers have begun selling these funds, in the form of mutual funds, to smaller investors for as little as $1,000.[17] They are also significant investors in noninvestment grade, or junk, bonds. Hedge funds are estimated to have total assets that exceed $1.82 trillion.[18] Unlike mutual funds, hedge funds are not regulated by the SEC.

Traditionally, hedge funds, unlike venture capitalists and private equity funds, did not make direct investments in companies, preferring instead to purchase existing stock and bond issues.

Mergers, Acquisitions, Buyouts, and Divestitures

Chapter 5 briefly described mergers and acquisitions. A merger is a transaction in which two or more firms combine into one company. In an acquisition, one firm buys the assets and assumes the obligations of another firm. Chapter 5 also listed the classifications of mergers and acquisitions—vertical, horizontal, and conglomerate—and noted that many of these transactions involve large sums of money. A recent example is Hewlett-Packard's acquisition of the smart phone maker Palm. In this section, we focus on the financial implications of not only mergers and acquisitions but also buyouts and divestitures.

Note that even in a merger, there is a buyer and seller. The seller is often referred to as the *target*. Financial managers evaluate a proposed merger or acquisition in much the same way they would evaluate any large investment—by comparing the costs and benefits. To acquire another company, the buying firm typically has to offer a premium for the target's shares—in other words, a higher price than the current market price. For instance, Hewlett-Packard offered $5.70 for each share of Palm, a premium of almost 20 percent over the existing price.[19]

When the buyer makes what is known as a **tender offer** for the target's shares, it specifies a price and the form of payment. The buyer can offer cash, securities, or a combination of the two. The Hewlett-Packard offer to Palm shareholders was all cash. The tender offer can be friendly, meaning it is endorsed by the target's board of directors, or unfriendly. Shareholders of both the buyer and target must vote to approve a merger.

Justifying such a premium requires the financial manager also to estimate the benefits of a proposed merger. These benefits could take the form of cost savings from economies of scale or reduced workforces or the buyer getting a bargain price for the target's assets. Sometimes, a buyer finds that the most cost-effective method of entering a new market is simply to buy an existing company that serves the market. Johnson & Johnson has a long history of making such acquisitions. When it decided to enter the contact lens market several years ago, Johnson & Johnson bought Vistakon, the firm that invented disposable contact lenses under the brand name Acuvue. Whatever the reasons, the term used to describe the benefits produced by a merger or acquisition is *synergy*—the notion that the combined firm is worth more than the buyer and target are individually.

tender offer offer made by a firm to the target firm's shareholders specifying a price and the form of payment.

leveraged buyouts (LBOs) transaction in which public shareholders are bought out and the firm reverts to private status.

<u>**Leveraged buyouts**</u>, or <u>**LBOs**</u>, were briefly introduced in the preceding section. In an LBO, public shareholders are bought out, and the firm reverts to private status. The term *leverage* comes from the fact that many of these transactions are financed with high degrees of debt—often in excess of 75 percent. Private equity companies and hedge funds provide equity and debt financing for many LBOs. The firm's incumbent senior management is often part of the buyout group. LBO activity decreased sharply with the recent economic downturn. As the economy began to recover, LBO activity increased again. According to Standard & Poor's, LBO financing recently grew to $13.6 billion, about 15 times the amount from the same time a year before. With more than $500 billion in funds, private equity companies and others were looking for acquisitions.[20]

Why do so many LBOs occur? One reason is that private companies enjoy benefits that public companies do not. Private companies are not required to publish financial results, are subject to less SEC oversight, and are not pressured to produce the short-term profits often demanded by Wall Street. Some argue that LBOs, because of the high degree of debt, enforce more discipline on management to control costs. Although LBOs do have advantages, history has shown that many companies that go private reemerge as public companies several years later.

divestiture sale of assets by a firm.

In a sense, a <u>**divestiture**</u> is the reverse of a merger. That is, a company sells assets such as subsidiaries, product lines, or production facilities. Two types of divestitures exist: sell-offs and spin-offs. In a *sell-off*, assets are sold by one firm to another. Verizon Wireless, an affiliate of Verizon Communications Inc., sold some of its wireless assets to AT&T. AT&T then announced plans to roll out its 3G wireless service to about 1.6 million former Verizon subscribers in rural areas across 18 states.

The other type of divestiture is a *spin-off*. In this transaction, the assets sold form a new firm. Shareholders of the divesting firm become shareholders of the new firm as well. For example, Motorola announced that it would split into two publicly traded firms. The parent company will handle its core business of mobile converged devices, digital home-entertainment devices, and video voice and data solutions. The spin-off firm will handle heavy-duty two-way radios, mobile computers, public security systems, wireless network infrastructure, and other business-oriented goods and services. Both entities will continue to use the Motorola brand name, with the parent company now named Motorola Mobile Devices and Home. Motorola shareholders will receive shares of the new company, Motorola Enterprise Mobility and Networks.

Firms divest assets for several reasons. Sometimes divestitures result from prior acquisitions that didn't work out as well as expected. In early 2001, America Online and Time Warner merged to create AOL Time Warner, Inc. Nine years later, Time Warner announced it would spin off AOL. The merger—now considered one of the worst mistakes in corporate history—failed to generate the much-heralded synergies between the two companies. Shortly after the merger, AOL had 27 million subscribers; more recently, that number had shrunk to about 6.3 million.

In other cases, a firm makes a strategic decision to concentrate on its core businesses and decides to divest anything that falls outside this core. That was the explanation that Motorola gave in response to criticism that the company had become too large and had seen its mobile-device business overtaken first by Nokia, then Samsung, and then Apple. Still another explanation relates to antitrust issues. Verizon originally wanted to buy Alltel. The U.S. Department of Justice required Verizon to divest itself of assets in markets where Alltel was already operating—mainly rural areas in many central states—before it would approve the purchase.

Assessment Check ✓

1. Define *synergy*.
2. What is an LBO?
3. What are the two types of divestitures?

What's Ahead

Contemporary Business concludes with five appendixes. Appendix A, "Business Law," outlines the main legal issues concerning business. It reviews the types of laws, the regulatory environment of business, and the core of business law, including discussions of contract law and property law. Appendix B examines risk management and insurance. It describes the concept of risk, alternative ways of dealing with risk, and the various kinds of insurance available to business and individuals. Appendix C discusses some of the important components of personal financial planning, such as budgeting, credit, and retirement planning. Appendix D describes how to write an effective business plan, and Appendix E discusses career searches and options to help you prepare for your future in business.

Summary of Learning Goals

1 Define *finance*, and explain the role of financial managers.

Finance deals with planning, obtaining, and managing a company's funds to accomplish its objectives efficiently and effectively. The major responsibilities of financial managers are to develop and implement financial plans and determine the most appropriate sources and uses of funds. The chief financial officer (CFO) heads a firm's finance organization. Three senior executives reporting to the CFO are the vice president for financial management, the treasurer, and the controller. When making decisions, financial professionals continually seek to balance risks with expected financial returns.

Assessment Check Answers ✓

1.1 What is the structure of the finance function at the typical firm? The head of the finance function of a firm has the title of chief financial officer (CFO) and generally reports directly to the firm's chief executive officer. Reporting to the CFO are the treasurer, the controller, and the vice president for financial management.

1.2 Explain the risk-return trade-off. Financial managers strive to maximize the wealth of their firm's shareholders by striking the optimal balance between risk and return. Often, decisions involving the highest potential returns expose the firm to the greatest risks.

2 Describe the components of a financial plan and the financial planning process.

A financial plan is a document that specifies the funds needed by a firm for a given period of time, the timing of inflows and outflows, and the most appropriate sources and uses of funds. The financial plan addresses three questions: What funds will

be required during the planning period? When will funds be needed? Where will funds be obtained? Three steps are involved in the financial planning process: forecasting sales over a future period of time, estimating the expected level of profits over the planning period, and determining the additional assets needed to support additional sales.

Assessment Check Answers ✓

2.1 What three questions does a financial plan address? The financial plan addresses three questions: What funds will be required during the planning period? When will funds be needed? Where will funds be obtained?

2.2 Explain the steps involved in preparing a financial plan. The first step is to forecast sales over a future period of time. Second, the financial manager must estimate the expected level of profits over the planning period. The final step is to determine the additional assets needed to support additional sales.

3 Outline how organizations manage their assets.

Assets consist of what a firm owns and also represent the uses of its funds. Sound financial management requires assets to be acquired and managed as effectively and efficiently as possible. The major current assets are cash, marketable securities, accounts receivable, and inventory. The goal of cash management is to have sufficient funds on hand to meet day-to-day transactions and pay any unexpected expenses. Excess cash should be invested in marketable securities, which are low-risk securities with short maturities. Managing accounts receivable, which are uncollected credit sales, involves collecting funds owed the firm as quickly as possible while also offering sufficient credit to customers to generate increased sales. The main goal of inventory management is to minimize the overall cost of inventory. Production, marketing, and logistics also play roles in determining proper inventory levels. Capital investment analysis is the process by which financial managers make decisions on long-lived assets. This involves comparing the benefits and costs of a proposed investment. Managing international assets poses additional challenges for the financial manager, including the problem of fluctuating exchange rates.

Assessment Check Answers ✔️

3.1 Why do firms often choose to invest excess cash in marketable securities? Cash earns no rate of return, which is why excess cash should be invested in marketable securities. These are low-risk securities that have short maturities and can be easily sold in the secondary markets. As a result, they are easily converted back into cash, when needed.

3.2 What are the two aspects of accounts receivable management? The two aspects of accounts receivable management are deciding on an overall credit policy (whether to offer credit and, if so, on what terms) and determining which customers will be offered credit.

3.3 Explain the difference between an expansion decision and a replacement decision. An expansion decision involves decisions about offering new products or building or acquiring new production facilities. A replacement decision is one that considers whether to replace an existing asset with a new one.

4 Compare the two major sources of funds for a business, and explain the concept of leverage.

Businesses have two sources of funds: debt capital and equity capital. Debt capital represents funds obtained through borrowing, and equity capital consists of funds provided by the firm's owners. The mix of debt and equity capital is known as the firm's capital structure, and the financial manager's job is to find the proper mix. Leverage is a technique of increasing the rate of return on funds invested by borrowing. However, leverage increases risk. Also, overreliance on borrowed funds may reduce management's flexibility in future financing decisions. Equity capital also has drawbacks. When additional equity capital is sold, the control of existing shareholders is diluted. In addition, equity capital is more expensive than debt capital. Financial managers are also faced with decisions concerning the appropriate mix of short- and long-term funds. Short-term funds are generally less expensive than long-term funds but expose firms to more risk. Another decision involving financial managers is determining the firm's dividend policy.

Assessment Check Answers ✔️

4.1 Explain the concept of leverage. Leverage is a technique of increasing the rate of return by borrowing funds. But leverage also increases risk.

4.2 Why do firms generally rely more on long-term funds rather than short-term funds? Although short-term funds are generally less expensive than long-term funds, short-term funds expose the firm to additional risks. The cost of short-term funds can vary substantially from year to year. In addition, at times short-term funds can be difficult to obtain.

4.3 What is an important determinant of a firm's dividend policy? The main determinant of a firm's dividend policy is its investment opportunities. Firms with more profitable investment opportunities often pay less in dividends than do firms with fewer such opportunities.

5 Identify sources of short-term financing for business operations.

The three major short-term funding options are trade credit, short-term loans from banks and other financial institutions, and commercial paper. Trade credit is extended by suppliers when a firm receives goods or services, agreeing to pay for them at a later date. Trade credit is relatively easy to obtain and costs nothing unless a supplier offers a cash discount. Loans from commercial banks are a significant source of short-term financing and are often used to finance accounts receivable and inventory. Loans can be either unsecured or secured, with accounts receivable or inventory pledged as collateral. Commercial paper is a short-term IOU sold by a company. Although large amounts of money can be raised through the sale of commercial paper, usually at rates below those charged by banks, access to the commercial paper market is limited to large, financially strong corporations.

Assessment Check Answers ✔️

5.1 What are the three sources of short-term funding? The three sources of short-term funding are trade credit, short-term loans from banks and other financial institutions, and commercial paper.

5.2 Explain trade credit. Trade credit is extended by suppliers when a buyer agrees to pay for goods and services at a later date. Trade credit is relatively easy to obtain and costs nothing unless a cash discount is offered.

5.3 Why is commercial paper an attractive short-term financing option? Commercial paper is an attractive financing option because large amounts can be raised by selling commercial paper at rates that are generally lower than those charged by banks.

6 Discuss long-term financing options.

Long-term funds are repaid over many years. There are three sources: long-term loans obtained from financial institutions, bonds sold to investors, and equity financing. Public sales of securities represent a major source of funds for corporations. These securities can generally be traded in secondary markets. Public sales can vary substantially from year to year depending on the conditions in the financial markets. Private placements are securities sold to a small number of institutional investors. Most private placements involve debt securities. Venture capitalists are an important source of financing for new companies. If the business succeeds, venture capitalists stand to earn large profits. Private equity funds are investment companies that raise funds from wealthy individuals and institutional investors and use the funds to make investments in both public and private companies. Unlike venture capitalists, private equity funds invest in all types of businesses. Sovereign wealth funds are investment companies owned by governments.

Assessment Check Answers ☑

6.1 What is the most common type of security sold privately? Corporate debt securities are the most common type of security sold privately.

6.2 Explain venture capital. Venture capitalists are important sources of funding, especially for new companies. Venture capitalists invest in these companies by taking an ownership position. If the business succeeds, venture capitalists can earn substantial profits.

6.3 What is a sovereign wealth fund? A sovereign wealth fund is a government-owned investment company. These companies make investments in a variety of financial and real assets, such as real estate. Although most investments are based on the best risk-return trade-off, political, social, and strategic considerations play roles as well.

┌─┐
│7│ **Describe mergers, acquisitions, buyouts, and divestitures.**
└─┘

A merger is a combination of two or more firms into one company. An acquisition is a transaction in which one company buys another. Even in a merger, there is a buyer and a seller (called the *target*). The buyer offers cash, securities, or a combination of the two in return for the target's shares. Mergers and acquisitions should be evaluated as any large investment is, by comparing the costs with the benefits. Synergy is the term used to describe the benefits a merger or acquisition is expected to produce. A leveraged buyout (LBO) is a transaction in which shares are purchased from public shareholders, and the company reverts to private status. Usually LBOs are financed with substantial amounts of borrowed funds. Private equity companies are often major financers of LBOs. Divestitures are the opposite of mergers, in which companies sell assets such as subsidiaries, product lines, or production facilities. A sell-off is a divestiture in which assets are sold to another firm. In a spin-off, a new firm is created from the assets divested. Shareholders of the divesting firm become shareholders of the new firm as well.

Assessment Check Answers ☑

7.1 Define *synergy*. Synergy is the term used to describe the benefits produced by a merger or acquisition. It is the notion that the combined firm is worth more than the buyer and the target are individually.

7.2 What is an LBO? An LBO—a leveraged buyout—is a transaction whereby public shareholders are bought out, and the firm reverts to private status. LBOs are usually financed with large amounts of borrowed money.

7.3 What are the two types of divestitures? A sell-off is a divestiture in which assets are sold to another firm. In a spin-off, a new firm is created from the assets divested. Shareholders of the divesting firm become shareholders of the new firm as well.

▓ Business Terms You Need to Know

finance 568	financial plan 571	venture	leveraged
financial managers 568	capital structure 576	capitalists 582	buyouts (LBOs) 586
risk-return trade-off 569	leverage 576	tender offer 585	divestiture 586

▓ Review Questions

1. Explain the risk-return trade-off and give two examples.

2. Describe the financial planning process. How does asset intensity affect a financial plan?

3. What are the principal considerations when determining an overall credit policy? How do the actions of competitors affect a firm's credit policy?

4. Why do exchange rates pose a challenge for financial managers of companies with international operations?

5. Discuss the concept of leverage. Use a numerical example to illustrate the effect of leverage.

6. What are the advantages and disadvantages of both debt and equity financing?

7. Compare and contrast the three sources of short-term financing.

8. Define *venture capitalist*, *private equity fund*, *sovereign wealth fund*, and *hedge fund*. Which of the four invests the most money in start-up companies?

9. Briefly describe the mechanics of a merger or acquisition.

10. Why do firms divest assets?

Projects and Teamwork Applications

1. Assume you would like to start a business. Put together a rough financial plan that addresses the three financial planning questions listed in the text.

2. Working with a partner, assume that a firm needs $10 million in additional long-term capital. It currently has no debt and $40 million in equity. The options are issuing a ten-year bond (with an interest rate of 7 percent) or selling $10 million in new equity. You expect next year's earnings before interest and taxes to be $5 million. (The firm's tax rate is 35 percent.) Prepare a memo outlining the advantages and disadvantages of debt and equity financing. Using the numbers provided, prepare a numerical illustration of leverage similar to the one shown in Figure 17.2.

3. Your new small business has really grown, but now it needs a substantial infusion of capital. A venture capital firm has agreed to invest the money you need. In return, the venture capital firm will own 75 percent of the business, and you will be replaced as CEO by someone chosen by the venture capitalist. You will retain the titles of founder and chairman of the board. Would you be willing to take the money but lose control over your business? Why or why not?

4. Working in a small team, select three publicly traded companies. Visit each firm's Web site. Most have a section devoted to information for investors. Review each firm's dividend policy. Does the company pay dividends? If so, when did it begin paying dividends? Have dividends increased each year, or have they fluctuated from year to year? Is the company currently repurchasing shares? Has it done so in the past? Prepare a report summarizing your findings.

5. As noted in the chapter, one of the most unfortunate mergers in corporate history involved Time Warner and America Online. Research this merger. Why did analysts expect it to be successful? Why did it fail? What has happened to AOL since then?

Web Assignments

1. **Jobs in financial management.** Visit the Web site listed here to explore careers in finance. How many people currently work as financial managers? What is the projected increase in employment over the next 10 to 20 years? What is the average level of compensation?

   http://www.bls.gov/oco/ocos010.htm

2. **Capital structure.** Go to the Web site listed here to access recent financial statements for the retailer Costco. Click on "balance sheet." What is the firm's current capital structure (the breakdown between debt and equity)? Has it changed significantly over the past five years? Why would a firm such as Costco choose to become more or less levered?

   http://moneycentral.msn.com/investor/invsub/results/statemnt.aspx?symbol=cost

3. **Mergers and acquisitions.** Using a news source, such as Google News (http://news.google.com) or Yahoo! News (http://news.yahoo.com), search for a recent merger or acquisition announcement. An example would be Hewlett-Packard's acquisition of Palm. (A link is shown here.) Print out the articles and bring them to class.

   http://www.hp.com/hpinfo/newsroom/press/2010/100428xa.html

   Note: Internet Web addresses change frequently. If you don't find the exact sites listed, you may need to access the organization's home page and search from there or use a search engine such as Bing or Google.

CASE 17.1

ConocoPhillips Divests to Return to Its Core

ConocoPhillips, with headquarters in Houston, Texas, is the third largest American oil company. It has nearly 30,000 employees in offices in 30 countries around the world. But for two years running, Conoco did poorly in the New York Stock Exchange, with its shares losing 40 percent of their value. Conoco more than doubled its debt when it bought Burlington Resources Inc., a natural-gas producer, for $36 billion. At the end of a recent year, Conoco's debt was three times that of the largest U.S. oil company, ExxonMobil, even though ExxonMobil was almost twice Conoco's size in terms of revenue. How could Conoco turn itself around?

At its annual analyst meeting, the company announced plans to enhance its value to its shareholders by increasing dividends by 10 percent and buying back some shares of its stock. Another goal is to raise $10 billion by 2012.

ConocoPhillips will raise these funds through divestiture, selling off some of its noncore assets. The company said that these assets did not fit well strategically with its core operations, they had high operation costs, and they were marketable. The company acknowledged that it would lose from 80,000 to 120,000 barrels of oil production per day and 400 to 600 million barrels of oil equivalent in reserve. But it hoped to emerge leaner and stronger, with a renewed focus on core projects that would bring in a higher return on investment.

Jim Mulva, the chairman and CEO, said, "We are focused on creating and delivering value to our shareholders. We are taking decisive action to sell assets, reduce debt, build on our record of shareholder distributions, and improve returns while growing production and reserves per share,"

Some analysts believed that Conoco's first priority was to sell its 9 percent stake in Syncrude, which one analyst referred to as one of Conoco's "crown jewels." Syncrude Canada Ltd. is located in the province of Alberta, just north of Montana, and is the world's largest producer of synthetic crude oil from oil sand deposits. Conoco recently announced that it sold its share in Syncrude to China's Sinopec for $4.65 billion, pending approval by the Chinese and Canadian governments. Mulva declared, "[W]e are pleased that [Sinopec] has recognized the value of this quality asset."

Another of Conoco's noncore assets was its 20 percent share in Lukoil, Russia's biggest oil producer. Conoco had invested heavily in Lukoil in hopes of large profits on some joint projects with Lukoil, but those profits had never materialized. This was in part because of strict Russian regulations concerning foreign companies in important industries. Lukoil's CEO, Vagit Alekperov, commented, "Initially, we were aiming for a large package of joint

projects, but it turned out to be rather narrow, which probably also disappointed [Conoco]." At first, Conoco hoped Lukoil would buy back half of its stake, but Lukoil turned that offer down. Conoco then offered those shares for sale on the open market, keeping a 10 percent share in Lukoil. Conoco hopes to earn about $5 billion from that sale and use those funds to repurchase some of its stock from shareholders.

Conoco's 25 percent share in the Rockies Express Pipeline is another of the company's "crown jewels." This high-speed, natural-gas pipeline runs almost 1,700 miles from northwestern Colorado to eastern Ohio. Conoco has offered its stake in the Rockies Express Pipeline for sale. Will ConocoPhillips achieve its goal of raising $10 billion by 2012? Time will tell.

Questions for Critical Thinking

1. Why is it important for ConocoPhillips to increase the value of its shares for its investors?
2. Research ConocoPhillips. How close has it come to raising the desired $10 billion?

Sources: Company Web site, ConocoPhillips, http://www.conocophillips.com, accessed July 1, 2010; Company Web site, Syncrude Canada Ltd., http://www.syncrude.ca, accessed July 1, 2010; Company Web site, China Petroleum and Chemical Corporation (Sinopec), http://english.sinopec.com, accessed July 1, 2010; Company Web site, Lukoil Oil Company, http://www.lukoil.com, accessed July 1, 2010; Company Web site, Rockies Express Pipeline, http://www.kindermorgan.com, accessed July 1, 2010; "ConocoPhillips Sells Syncrude Stake to Sinopec," press release, *Trading Markets.com,* June 30, 2010, http://www.tradingmarkets.com; Nastassia Astrasheuskaya, "LUKOIL CEO Sees Conoco Keeping 10 Pct Stake-Paper," *Reuters,* June 24, 2010, http://af.reuters.com; Steve Gelsi, "ConocoPhillips Sells Syncrude Stake for $4.65 Billion," *MarketWatch,* April 12, 2010, http://www.marketwatch.com; Eric Fox, "ConocoPhillips Aims to Boost Returns," *Investopedia,* March 26, 2010, http://stocks.investopedia.com; "Conoco Phillips Ups Ante for Shareholders," *Rigzone,* March 24, 2010, http://www.rigzone.com; Bloomberg News, "Lukoil Doesn't Plan to Buy Shares from ConocoPhillips," *Houston Chronicle,* March 23, 2010, http://www.chron.com; Edward Klump, "Conoco's Divestiture Plan Seen Hinging on Syncrude (Update 2)," *Bloomberg Businessweek,* February 25, 2010, http://www.businessweek.com.

Top Hedge Fund Managers Earn Record Paychecks

CASE 17.2

Along with the rest of the banking and investment industry, hedge fund managers experienced steep drops in income during the recent recession. But as the economy began to revive, the 25 top-earning hedge fund managers earned $25.3 billion. That figure shattered even the old record, set in the boom days before the crisis.

One of those managers was David Tepper of Appaloosa Management. Other investors feared that the banking sector would collapse again, but Tepper bet that the federal government would step in to prevent the biggest banks from failing. In late 2008 and early 2009, he invested heavily in preferred shares and bonds of the big banks, among other seemingly losing prospects. Tepper, formerly of Goldman Sachs, won big, earning $4 billion. "We bet on the country's revival," he said. "Those who keep their heads while others are panicking do well." The U.S. Treasury Department apparently agreed with him, because it also bought preferred stock in troubled banks to help shore them up. The Treasury has since sold many of those stocks at a handsome profit.

Hedge funds are elite, private investment companies that are open only to highly qualified, large investors. Unlike mutual funds, hedge funds are not regulated by the Securities and Exchange Commission. During the heady days before the financial crisis, hedge funds earned huge profits. Their managers did well, too, because they usually take a significant percentage of a hedge fund's annual earnings. When the crisis struck, even these funds experienced losses in the double digits, and their managers saw their income drop by as much as 50 percent. But when the market rallied, hedge funds resurged as well. Of the 25 top hedge fund managers, the lowest earner made $350 million.

As the United States and the rest of the world economies recovered, the news media reported the immense salaries of CEOs and other top corporate executives at banks and large brokerage houses. The stories stirred the critics, especially because ordinary people were losing their jobs, homes, and health insurance. But some analysts believe that hedge fund managers such as David Tepper earned their huge salaries because they dared to take big risks in the hope of big rewards.

Of course, not all hedge funds did well when the stock market revived. The gap between the highest-earning hedge funds and the losing ones grew wider. Nadia Papagiannis, a hedge fund analyst at Morningstar Inc., said, "The hedge funds that survived 2008 were able to capture the gains on the way up in 2009. This year is not going to be as lucrative as last year. There's not enough of room [*sic*] for another rally as big as we saw in '09."

Questions for Critical Thinking

1. Compare hedge funds with mutual funds.
2. Do you agree that the top hedge fund managers deserve their high salaries? Why or why not?

Sources: Jim Pavia, "Hedge Fund Manager Made $4B Last Year. And He Deserved It," *InvestmentNews,* April 8, 2010, http://www.investmentnews.com; Ben Rooney, "Hedge Fund Manager Paycheck: $4 Billion," *CNNMoney.com,* April 1, 2010, http://money.cnn.com; Jim Kim, "Hedge Fund Managers Earn Record Pay in 2009," *FierceFinance,* April 1, 2010, http://www.fiercefinance.com; Edward Helmore, "Hedge Fund Pay Soars—But 2010 Could be Tougher," *First Post,* April 1, 2010, http://www.thefirstpost.co.uk; Nelson D. Schwartz and Louise Story, "Pay of Hedge Fund Managers Roared Back Last Year," *The New York Times,* March 31, 2010, http://www.nytimes.com.

CASE 17.3 Comet Skateboards Rides the Triple Bottom Line

Jason Salfi, co-founder and president of Comet Skateboards, is the first to admit he can let the wheels get away from him. Since the inception of Comet Skateboards, he estimates that he has personally "tanked the company four times. I started the company with a friend and we would sacrifice everything for quality," Salfi admits. It's easy to see how this could happen. Salfi loves skateboarding and he's a fanatic about building the best skateboards on the market with the most sustainable materials available.

During the first years of production—when Comet moved from California to Ithaca, New York in order to source bio-composite materials—Salfi and his partner paid top dollar for all the materials they used in building the boards. "We weren't really watching how much money we were making," Salfi says sheepishly. They were so wrapped up in the excitement of developing and manufacturing an entirely new class of skateboard, they forgot to watch the bank account balance. Salfi recalls that they did all the stereotypical things that small start-ups do to obtain financing—maxed out their credit cards, got friends and family to co-sign for loans, found angel investors. But Comet Skateboards just seemed to roll through the money without enough return to ensure its survival.

Then the firm hired a manager to specialize in financial details. With a professional in place, Salfi began to understand the real and potential impacts certain buying decisions would have on the bottom line, and the way cash flow would affect getting products to the marketplace. Now, Comet can forecast better how a product release will affect cash flow, and how that in turn will affect the way they as a business can reach customers. "Ultimately we're trying to create a sustainable business platform to get our sustainable business vision out there in the marketplace," explains Salfi. But they couldn't do this without managing the company's financial resources.

Comet Skateboards is considered a triple bottom line company, carrying the B Corporation logo. This means that Comet strives to create benefit for the company owners (profit), the community (people), and the environment (planet). Currently there are more than two hundred B Corporations in thirty industries around the nation. Each company has submitted to rigorous evaluation and has put written standards in place addressing social and environmental responsibility. Everything that Comet does, from its closed-loop manufacturing process to its community involvement, refers to its triple bottom line commitment.

Jason Salfi insists that managing the finances for a triple bottom line company is pretty much the same as managing the finances for a traditional company. But there are some differences, particularly in the procurement of raw materials, energy use, and waste disposal. Also, triple bottom line companies are held accountable for the way they treat employees and how they are involved in the community. "The 'magic' is making sure we can afford all that," observes Salfi. "It's just a matter of prioritization. We're not going on $50,000 golf retreats. We're reinvesting the capital we have in the materials we use and the way we interact with people."

Despite the fact that he says he didn't pay attention to finances in the company's early days, Salfi has a good grasp on Comet's role in the larger economic picture. He likes the idea of projecting the impact Comet has on consumers' buying decisions, particularly young people. Teenagers who choose Comet skateboards are choosing products that are made by a triple bottom line firm. "If you look at the way a 14-year-old decides to buy things for the rest of his or her life, and you look at the number of decisions that young person is going to make over the span of 50 or 60 years, you could extrapolate that we have impacted 1,000 people in a certain way that could eventually transfer billions of dollars toward socially responsible businesses," explains Salfi. "We're influencing the buying decisions of youth."

Salfi believes that, decades ago, "commerce used to be about improving the quality of life, but somewhere along the line, profits skewed motivations." He likes the idea of the triple bottom line rebalancing the priorities of business. "We like to think that as a B Corporation, we are part of a group that wants to bring back the original motivation for business, which was all about creating an improved quality of life for everyone, not just a select few." It might actually be possible for a few well-engineered skateboards to change the world.

Questions for Critical Thinking

1. Hiring a financial manager was a major step for Comet Skateboards. Identify some of the factors the manager would have to consider when creating a plan for risk-return trade-off.

2. What might be some short-term funding options for Comet? Some long-term options? Which would be best for this company, and why?

3. Suppose a larger firm approached Comet with an offer of acquisition. Create a chart outlining the major pros and cons of such an offer.

4. How might Comet's designation as a B Corporation affect the way it answers the three essential questions for building a financial plan?

Sources: Comet Skateboards Web site, http://cometskateboards.com, accessed August 20, 2010; "GOOD Products," Halogen TV, http://www.halogentv.com, accessed August 20, 2010; Nadia Hosni, "Triple Bottom Line: Comet Skateboards," *Tonic*, April 27, 2010, http://www.tonic.com.

GREENSBURG, KS

So Much to Do, So Little Cash

When Dan Wallach started Greensburg GreenTown, he knew it wouldn't be easy. A self-proclaimed idea guy, he admits that the details of high finance elude him. What he is good at is rallying people around a cause and getting them to write a few big checks. This time, though, Wallach decided to involve the largest number of people possible. Greensburg GreenTown's One Million $5.00 Donations campaign was the result.

The money that is raised will be used to cover GreenTown's operating expenses, as well as to fund gaps in municipal projects, build model green homes, and educate residents about green building practices. Another aspect of GreenTown's work is to provide information and access to media organizations. Shortly after the tornado, the Planet Green cable channel began production on a television series that would chronicle the town's rebuilding. Wallach thought the exposure created by that show and others like it would be valuable in his fund-raising efforts.

As a not-for-profit organization, Greensburg GreenTown is heavily regulated by the IRS, because the donations it receives are fully tax deductible. It falls into the same category as religious organizations and educational institutions, which are exempt from federal income taxes but must pay other federal taxes, such as employment taxes. Because working through the red tape required to obtain this IRS status can take time, many organizations, GreenTown included, work through an approved intermediary while their applications are processed.

Although Greensburg GreenTown supports and educates Greensburg's residents, the town itself must rely on other sources of funding. All towns have budgets for repairs and improvements, but no one expected to have to rebuild the entire town. After the tornado, Greensburg had no roads, no hospital, no school system, no utilities, or any of the other services one might expect to find in a town. Money was tight even before the tornado, so rebuilding seemed an impossible task.

Luckily, various government and corporate organizations chipped in. The Federal Emergency Management Agency (FEMA) and the U.S. Department of Agriculture (USDA) provided aid in the form of grants. Corporations like Frito-Lay donated significant amounts of money to support the town's innovative business incubator. With millions of dollars at stake and hundreds of projects under way at once, Assistant Town Administrator and Recovery Coordinator Kim Alderfer says the hardest part is keeping track of it all.

Questions

After viewing the video, answer the following questions:

1. What are the key legal and financial distinctions of Greensburg GreenTown?
2. If you were in Kim Alderfer's shoes, what kind of financial contingency plan would you put in place for Greensburg's future?
3. Should not-for-profit organizations be required to open their books to donors? Why or why not?

LAUNCHING YOUR
[Finance Career]

Part 6, "Managing Financial Resources," describes the finance function in organizations. Finance deals with planning, obtaining, and managing an organization's funds to accomplish its objectives in the most effective way possible. In Chapter 16, we discussed the financial system, including the various types of securities, financial markets and institutions, the Federal Reserve System, financial regulators, and global financial markets. In Chapter 17, we examined the role financial managers play in an organization; financial planning; short- and long-term financing options; and mergers, acquisitions, buyouts, and divestitures. Throughout both chapters, we described the finance functions of a variety of businesses, governments, and not-for-profit organizations. As Part 6 illustrates, finance is a very diverse profession and encompasses many different occupations. According to the U.S. Department of Labor, over the next decade most finance-related occupations are expected to experience employment growth that is a little better than average for all occupations. However, employment in several finance occupations is expected to grow faster than average. Employment in the financial investment industry should be strong because of the number of Baby Boomers in their peak earning years with funds to invest and the globalization of securities markets.[1]

In most business schools, finance is one of the most popular majors among undergraduates. Combining finance with accounting is a common double major. Those with degrees in finance also enjoy relatively high starting salaries. A recent survey found that the average starting salary for a person with an undergraduate degree in finance was nearly $50,500 per year.[2]

All organizations need to obtain and manage funds, so they employ finance professionals. Financial institutions and other financial services firms employ a large percentage of finance graduates. These businesses provide important finance-related services to businesses, governments, and not-for-profit organizations. Some graduates with finance degrees take jobs with financial services firms such as Bank of America and JP Morgan Chase, while others begin their careers working in the finance departments of businesses in other industries such as 3M and Boeing, governments, or not-for-profit organizations. You may begin your career evaluating commercial loan applications for a bank, analyzing capital investments for a business, or helping a not-for-profit organization decide how to invest its endowment. Often finance professionals work as members of a team, advising top management. Some individuals spend their entire careers working in finance-related occupations; others use their finance experience to move into other areas of the firm. Today, the chief financial officer—the senior finance executive—holds one of the most critical jobs in any organization. In addition, the number of CEOs who began their careers in finance is growing.

Finance is a diverse, exciting profession. Here are a few of the specific occupations you might find after earning a degree in finance.

Financial managers prepare financial reports, direct investment activities, raise funds, and implement cash management strategies. Computer technology has significantly reduced the time needed to produce financial reports. Many financial managers spend less time preparing reports and more time analyzing financial data. All organizations employ financial managers, although roughly 30 percent of all financial managers work for financial services firms such as commercial banks and insurance companies.[3] Specific responsibilities vary with titles. For instance, credit managers oversee the firm's issuance of credit, establish standards, and monitor the collection of accounts. Cash managers control the flow of cash receipts and disbursements to meet the needs of the organization.

Most *loan officers* work for commercial banks and other financial institutions. They find potential clients and help them apply for loans. Loan officers typically specialize in commercial, consumer, or mortgage loans. In many cases, loan officers act in a sales capacity, contacting individuals and organizations about their need for funds and trying to persuade them to borrow the funds from the loan officer's institution. Thus, loan officers often need marketing as well as finance skills.

Security analysts generally work for financial services firms such as Fidelity or Raymond James & Associates. Security analysts review economic data, financial statements, and other information to determine the outlook for securities such as common stocks and bonds. They make investment recommendations to individual and institutional investors. Many senior security analysts hold a chartered financial analyst (CFA) designation. Obtaining a CFA requires a specific educational background, several years of related experience, and a passing grade on a comprehensive, three-stage examination.

Portfolio managers manage money for an individual or institutional client. Many portfolio managers work for pension funds or mutual funds for which they make investment decisions to benefit the funds' beneficiaries. Portfolio managers generally have extensive experience as financial managers or security analysts, and many are CFAs.

Personal financial planners help individuals make decisions in areas such as insurance, investments, and retirement planning. Personal financial planners meet with their clients, assess their needs and goals, and make recommendations. Approximately 30 percent of personal financial planners are self-employed, and many hold certified financial planner (CFP) designations. Like the CFA, obtaining a CFP requires a specific educational background, related experience, and passing a comprehensive examination.

Career Assessment Exercises in Finance

1. Assume you're interested in pursuing a career as a security analyst. You've heard that the CFA is an important designation and can help enhance your career. Visit the CFA's Web site (http://www.cfainstitute.org) to learn more about the CFA. Specifically, what are the requirements to obtain a CFA, and what are the professional benefits of having a CFA?

2. Arrange for an interview with a commercial loan officer at a local bank. Ask the loan officer about his or her educational background, what a typical day is like, and what the loan officer likes and doesn't like about his or her job.

3. Ameriprise Financial offers financial planning services to individuals and organizations. Visit the firm's careers Web site (http:///www.ameriprise.com/careers). Review the material and write a brief summary of what you learned about being a personal financial planner. Does such a career interest you? Why or why not?

GREENSBURG, KS

The Bumpy Road to Recovery

The road to recovery from any disaster is paved with bumps and potholes. Sometimes, as in the case of Greensburg, Kansas, there are no roads at all. After being slammed by an F5 tornado, the town—which was already ailing economically—was forced to recreate its entire infrastructure. But city administrator Steve Hewitt observes that total devastation was, in fact, a silver lining to the black tornado cloud. "After the storm, we had a blank canvas," he says. Hewitt observes that the destruction forced each resident and business owner to ask, "What do we need to change to become this thriving new community?" The city council passed a resolution that every facility would build at the greenest, most sustainable level possible.

Several years into the recovery, Hewitt says that while he knew the town faced great challenges, he wasn't prepared for the emotional roller coaster of the entire community. As city administrator, he admits that this has been difficult to manage. Karen Alderfer, former recovery coordinator for the city, agrees. Her job—until the funding ran dry—was to keep the town's financial matters organized, recording and allocating government grants, loans, and any other funds that arrived for the recovery effort. Both Hewitt and Alderfer note that they had hoped to be farther along than at 60 percent of infrastructure completion by now—but they are also proud of Greensburg and its accomplishments thus far. While many small firms and organizations around the country have held benefits to raise funds for Greensburg, a large corporation—preferably one involved with green technology—hasn't yet agreed to locate in Greensburg, which would give the town a significant boost in terms of jobs and other resources. Hewitt and Alderfer believe this has been due to a sluggish economy.

Still, there are concrete results. Recently the new $50-million Kiowa County Schools building opened to students. The building has such green features as windows placed strategically for natural light, cisterns that catch rainwater for landscaping, and a wind turbine for power. Other municipal buildings, including town hall and the hospital, have been or will be built to sustainable standards. And the Silo House, a project undertaken by Greensburg Green Town—the not-for-profit organization that is helping to raise money, build, and educate the public about sustainable practices—is a model for future projects. Built with a $50,000 grant from AT&T, the Silo House has a visitor and education center along with a suite for eco-tourists.

A visitor walking through the town of Greensburg would notice signs of both devastation and recovery. Piles of rubble and debris, empty lots, and treeless streets recall disaster. Yet Main Street is filled with residents and visitors who are determined to raise Greensburg from its ashes. Their optimism, along with the positive attitude of Steve Hewitt, is catching. "This is the best job in America to have," he claims, "to build from the ground up."

Questions for Critical Thinking

1. Building from the ground up has many challenges. Create a chart outlining what you believe to be the benefits and drawbacks to Greensburg's approach.
2. Discuss how a small business might get started on the new Main Street of Greensburg.
3. Greensburg relies on its relationship with the media to provide good publicity about its projects. Why is communication so important to Greensburg's rebuilding efforts?
4. Hewitt and Alderfer express the town's wish for a large, green-technology corporation to become part of the Greensburg community. In what ways would this benefit the town? What are the potential drawbacks?

Sources: Greensburg Web site, http://www.greensburgks.org, accessed September 12, 2010; Jenny Deam, "After the Tornado: Stronger, Better, Greener," *Los Angeles Times*, August 31, 2010, http://www.latimes.com; Al Letson, "Town Rebuilds Green After Devastating Tornado," *National Public Radio*, May 14, 2010, http://www.npr.org.

GREENSBURG, KS

What Lies Ahead?

Greensburg was an agricultural community before it was leveled by an F5 tornado, and its leaders believe that its cultural roots will never die. "Agriculture will always play a huge part in the economy," predicts Councilman Jeanette Siemens, economic development director for Kiowa County, "but maybe in new ways." As the population of rural towns like Greensburg declines, new economic opportunities must replace some of the old traditions.

"There's a great opportunity for some synergy between new green tech companies to work closely with the agricultural sector," says Matt Christenson, recovery project coordinator and member of the Greensburg city council. One example would be a manufacturing firm whose processes use the straw left over from a wheat harvest to fortify building panels.

As Greensburg tries to incorporate agriculture into its greener future, the community is witnessing another change—in demographics. "It's a younger community," observes city administrator Steve Hewitt. Growth recovery is coming from young business people who want to take a chance. One such entrepreneur is Kari Kyle, owner of the Green Bean Coffee Company in Greensburg. Kyle and her husband were both born and raised in the Greensburg area, but moved away for fourteen years. When they decided to return, Kyle applied for a business loan from the local bank, received it, and opened her shop in the business incubator space downtown. When a larger space became available across the street, she grabbed it and expanded her menu offerings to include ice cream malts and shakes, soda fountain drinks and smoothies, as well as food. She says that business has tripled and is optimistic about the future. "Heck yeah, I know I'm going to make it," she insists.

Joah Bussert and Stephanie Paterson are also part of Greensburg's future. With degrees in architecture, as project managers they are helping to manage the construction of new buildings with green technologies. One building project is the Chain of Eco-Homes—a group of twelve homes with names like Meadowlark House and Homestead House, all constructed using the latest technologies. Bussert describes these houses as "testing grounds" to see how the technologies will perform specifically in the Midwest. Features include natural gas fuelmakers, double-skin walls, rooftop gardens, household composters, driveways made with permeable pavers, and of course tornado shelters. Peterson loves her job. "It's like no other place in the world," she says.

Each person involved with the reconstruction of Greensburg is looking far beyond its pre-tornado status, to a more prosperous, sustainable future. Councilman Jeanette Siemens sees a community that supports the entrepreneurial spirit and will ultimately become an educational tourist destination. Steve Hewitt acknowledges that every step of recovery must "have the things that attract families and businesses. The community will grow from young, innovative people." He continues to be upbeat about Greensburg's prospects. "I love what we do," he concludes.

Questions for Critical Thinking

1. Give an example of how the factors of demand and supply are currently at work in Greensburg.
2. Why do Greensburg community leaders consider entrepreneurship such a key element in the recovery and growth of the city?
3. What steps can the city administrator, project managers, and others take to change pre-tornado views about Greensburg?
4. Create an advertisement for Greensburg, targeting either tourists or businesses.

Sources: Greensburg Web site, http://www.greensburgks.org, accessed September 12, 2010; Jenny Deam, "After the Tornado: Stronger, Better, Greener," *Los Angeles Times,* August 31, 2010; http://www.latimes.com; Al Letson, "Town Rebuilds Green After Devastating Tornado," *National Public Radio,* May 14, 2010, http://www.npr.org.

| Glossary |

360-degree performance review employee performance review that gathers feedback from co-workers, supervisors, managers, and sometimes customers.

401(k) plan retirement savings plan to which employees can make pretax contributions; employers often make additional contributions to the plan.

accounting process of measuring, interpreting, and communicating financial information to support internal and external business decision making.

accounting cycle set of activities involved in converting information and individual transactions into financial statements.

accounting equation relationship that states that assets must always equal the sum of liabilities and owners' equity.

accrual accounting accounting method that records revenues and expenses when they occur, not necessarily when cash actually changes hands.

acquisition agreement in which one firm purchases another.

activity ratios measures of how efficiently a firm utilizes its assets.

actuarial table probability of the number of events that are expected to occur within a given year.

advertising paid nonpersonal communication usually targeted at large numbers of potential buyers.

affective conflict disagreement that focuses on individuals or personal issues.

affinity program marketing effort sponsored by an organization that solicits involvement by individuals who share common interests and activities.

affirmative action programs programs designed by employers to increase job opportunities for women, minorities, disabled people, and other protected groups

agency legal relationship whereby one party, called a *principal,* appoints another party, called an *agent,* to enter into contracts with third parties on the principal's behalf.

alien corporation firm incorporated in one nation and operating in another nation.

angel investors wealthy individuals who invest directly in a new venture in exchange for an equity stake.

appellate courts courts that hear appeals of decisions made at the general trial court level; both the federal and state systems have appellate courts.

application service provider (ASP) outside supplier that provides both the computers and the application support for managing an information system.

arbitration bringing in an impartial third party called an arbitrator to render a binding decision in a dispute.

assembly line manufacturing technique that carries the product on a conveyor system past several workstations where workers perform specialized tasks.

asset anything of value owned by a firm.

asset intensity amount of assets needed to generate a given level of sales.

autocratic leadership management approach whereby leaders make decisions on their own without consulting employees.

balance of payments overall money flows into and out of a country.

balance of trade difference between a nation's exports and imports.

balance sheet statement of a firm's financial position—what it owns and claims against its assets—at a particular point in time.

balanced budget situation in which total revenues raised by taxes and fees equal total proposed government spending for the year.

bankruptcy legal nonpayment of financial obligations.

banner ad ad placed by an organization on another organization's Web site; interested parties click on the ad for more information.

benchmarking process of determining how well other companies perform business functions or tasks.

blog online journal written by a blogger.

board of directors governing body of a corporation.

bot short for *robot*—a program that allows online shoppers to compare prices for a specific product at several e-tailers.

botnet a network of PCs that have been infected with one or more data-stealing viruses.

boycott effort to prevent people from purchasing a firm's goods or services.

brand name, term, sign, symbol, design, or some combination that identifies the products of one firm and differentiates them from competitors' offerings.

brand equity added value that a respected and successful name gives to a product.

brand name part of a brand consisting of words or letters that form a name that identifies and distinguishes an offering from those of competitors.

brand name part of the brand consisting of words or letters included in a name used to identify and distinguish the firm's offerings from those of competitors.

branding process of creating an identity in consumers' minds for a good, service, or company; a major marketing tool in contemporary business.

breach of contract violation of a valid contract.

breakeven analysis pricing-related technique used to determine the minimum sales volume a product must generate at a certain price level to cover all costs.

budget organization's plan for how it will raise and spend money during a given period of time.

budget deficit situation in which the government spends more than the amount of money it raises through taxes.

budget surplus excess funding that occurs when government spends less than the amount of funds raised through taxes and fees.

business all profit-seeking activities and enterprises that provide goods and services necessary to an economic system.

business (B2B) product good or service purchased to be used, either directly or indirectly, in the production of other goods for resale.

business ethics standards of conduct and moral values regarding right and wrong actions in the work environment.

business incubator local programs designed to provide low-cost shared business facilities to small start-up ventures.

business intelligence activities and technologies for gathering, storing, and analyzing data to make better competitive decisions.

business interruption insurance type of insurance that protects firms from financial losses resulting from the suspension of business operations.

business law aspects of law that most directly influence and regulate the management of business activity.

business plan written document that provides an orderly statement of a company's goals, methods, and standards.

business-to-business (B2B) e-business electronic business transactions between organizations using the Internet.

business-to-consumer (B2C) e-business selling directly to consumers over the Internet.

call provision right of the issuer to buy a bond back from the investor before maturity at a specified price.

capital production inputs consisting of technology, tools, information, and physical facilities.

capital investment analysis process of comparing the costs and benefits of a long-term asset investment.

capital structure mix of a firm's debt and equity capital.

capitalism economic system that rewards firms for their ability to perceive and serve the needs and demands of consumers; also called the private enterprise system.

cash budget budget that shows cash inflows and outflows during a period of time.

cash flow sources of cash minus uses of cash during a specified period of time.

cash value policy type of life insurance that combines insurance protection with a savings feature.

category advisor vendor that is designated by the business customer as the major supplier to assume responsibility for dealing with all the other vendors for a project and presenting the entire package to the business buyer.

category manager person who oversees an entire group of products and assumes profit responsibility for the product group.

cause advertising form of institutional advertising that promotes a specific viewpoint on a public issue as a way to influence public opinion and the legislative process.

cause marketing marketing that promotes a cause or social issue, such as preventing child abuse, anti-littering efforts, and stop-smoking campaigns.

Central America–Dominican Republic Free Trade Agreement (CAFTA-DR) agreement among the United States, Costa Rica, the Dominican Republic, El Salvador, Guatemala, Honduras, and Nicaragua to reduce tariffs and trade restrictions.

centralization decision making based at the top of the management hierarchy.

certified management accountant (CMA) management accountant who meets specified educational and experience requirements and has passed an examination covering management accounting topics.

certified public accountant (CPA) public accountant who meets specified educational and experiential requirements and has passed a comprehensive examination on accounting theory and practice.

chain of command set of relationships that indicates who directs which activities and who reports to whom.

channel conflict conflict between two or more members of a supply chain, such as a manufacturer, wholesaler, or retailer.

chief information officer (CIO) executive responsible for managing a firm's information system and related computer technologies.

Class-Action Fairness Act of 2005 law that moves most large, multistate class-action lawsuits to federal courts, ensures judicial oversight of plaintiffs' compensation, bases lawyers' compensation on awards actually distributed or actual time spent, and ensures plaintiffs' interests are protected equally with their lawyers'.

classic entrepreneur person who identifies a business opportunity and allocates available resources to tap that market.

click-through rate number of visitors who click on a Web banner ad.

cloud computing powerful servers store applications software and databases for users to access the software and databases via the Web using anything from a PC to a smart phone.

cobranding cooperative arrangement in which two or more businesses team up to closely link their names on a single product.

code of conduct formal statement that defines how an organization expects its employees to resolve ethical issues.

cognitive ability tests tests that measure job candidates' abilities in perceptual speed, verbal comprehension, numerical aptitude, general reasoning, and spatial aptitude.

cognitive conflict disagreement that focuses on problem- and issue-related differences of opinion.

collective bargaining process of negotiation between management and union representatives.

comarketing cooperative arrangement in which two businesses jointly market each other's products.

committee organization organizational structure that places authority and responsibility jointly in the hands of a group of individuals rather than a single manager.

common law body of law arising out of judicial decisions, some of which can be traced back to early England.

common stock (Chap. 5, p. 173) shares that give owners voting rights but only residual claims to the firm's assets and income distributions.

communication meaningful exchange of information through messages.

communism economic system in which all property would be shared equally by the people of a community under the direction of a strong central government.

compensation amount employees are paid in money and benefits.

competition battle among businesses for consumer acceptance.

competitive differentiation unique combination of organizational abilities, products, and approaches that sets a company apart from competitors in the minds of customers.

competitive pricing strategy that tries to reduce the emphasis on price competition by matching other firms' prices and concentrating their own

marketing efforts on the product, distribution, and promotional elements of the marketing mix.

compressed workweek scheduling option that allows employees to work the regular number of hours per week in fewer than the typical five days.

computer-aided design (CAD) process that allows engineers to design components as well as entire products on computer screens faster and with fewer mistakes than they could achieve working with traditional drafting systems.

computer-aided manufacturing (CAM) computer tools to analyze CAD output and enable a manufacturer to analyze the steps that a machine must take to produce a needed product or part.

computer-based information systems information systems that rely on computer and related technologies to store information electronically in an organized, accessible manner.

computer-integrated manufacturing (CIM) production system in which computers help workers design products, control machines, handle materials, and control the production function in an integrated fashion.

conceptual skills ability to see the organization as a unified whole and to understand how each part interacts with others.

conflict when one person or group's needs do not match those of another, and attempts may be made to block the opposing side's intentions or goals.

conflict of interest situation in which an employee must choose between a business's welfare and personal gain.

conglomerate merger merger that combines unrelated firms, usually with the goal of diversification, spurring sales growth, or spending a cash surplus in order to avoid a takeover attempt.

consumer (B2C) product good or service that is purchased by end users.

consumer behavior actions of ultimate consumers directly involved in obtaining, consuming, and disposing of products and the decision processes that precede and follow these actions.

consumer orientation business philosophy that focuses first on determining unmet consumer wants and needs and then designing products to satisfy those needs.

Consumer Price Index (CPI) measurement of the monthly average change in prices of goods and services.

consumerism public demand that a business consider the wants and needs of its customers in making decisions.

contingency planning plans that allow a firm to resume operations as quickly and as smoothly as possible after a crisis while openly communicating with the public about what happened.

contract legally enforceable agreement between two or more parties regarding a specified act or thing.

controlling function of evaluating an organization's performance against its objectives.

convenience product item the consumer seeks to purchase frequently, immediately, and with little effort.

conversion rate percentage of visitors to a Web site who actually make a purchase.

convertible securities bonds or preferred stock issues that are convertible into a set number of shares of the issuing company's common stock.

cooperative organization whose owners join forces to collectively operate all or part of the functions in their business.

cooperative advertising allowances provided by marketers in which they share the cost of local advertising of their firm's product or product line with channel partners.

copyright protection of written material such as textbooks, designs, cartoon illustrations, photos, and computer software.

core inflation rate inflation rate of an economy after energy and food prices are removed.

corporate charter legal document that formally establishes a corporation.

corporate culture organization's system of principles, beliefs, and values.

corporate philanthropy effort of an organization to make a contribution to the communities in which it earns profits.

corporate Web site Web site designed to increase a firm's visibility, promote its offerings, and provide information to interested parties.

corporation legal organization with assets and liabilities separate from those of its owner(s).

cost-based pricing formulas that calculate total costs per unit and then add markups to cover overhead costs and generate profits.

countertrade barter agreement whereby trade between two or more nations involves payment made in the form of local products instead of currency.

creative selling persuasive type of promotional presentation.

creativity capacity to develop novel solutions to perceived organizational problems.

credit receiving money, goods, or services on the basis of an agreement between the lender and the borrower that the loan is for a specified period of time with a specified rate of interest.

critical path sequence of operations that requires the longest time for completion.

critical thinking ability to analyze and assess information to pinpoint problems or opportunities.

cross-functional team a team made up of members from different functions, such as production, marketing, and finance.

cyclical unemployment people who are out of work because of a cyclical contraction in the economy.

damages financial payments to compensate for a loss and related suffering.

data raw facts and figures that may or may not be relevant to a business decision.

data mining computer searches of customer data to detect patterns and relationships.

data warehouse customer database that allows managers to combine data from several different organizational functions.

database centralized integrated collection of data resources.

debenture unsecured corporate bond.

debt capital funds obtained from borrowing.

debt financing borrowed funds that entrepreneurs must repay.

decentralization decision makeup based at lower levels of the organization.

decision making process of recognizing a problem or opportunity, evaluating alternative solutions, selecting and implementing an alternative, and assessing the results.

decision support system (DSS) gives direct support to businesspeople during the decision-making process.

deflation opposite of inflation, occurs when prices continue to fall.

delegation managerial process of assigning work to employees.

demand willingness and ability of buyers to purchase goods and services.

demand curve graph of the amount of a product that buyers will purchase at different prices.

democratic leadership management approach whereby leaders delegate assignments, ask employees for suggestions, and encourage their participation.

demographic segmentation dividing markets on the basis of various demographic or socioeconomic characteristics such as gender, age, income, occupation, household size, stage in family life cycle, education, or ethnic group.

demographics statistical characteristics of the segment of the market that might purchase a product.

departmentalization process of dividing work activities into units within the organization.

deregulation regulatory trend toward elimination of legal restraints on competition in industries previously served by a single firm in an attempt to improve customer service and lower prices through increased competition.

devaluation reduction in a currency's value relative to other currencies or to a fixed standard.

direct distribution channel marketing channel that moves goods directly from producer to ultimate user.

directing guiding and motivating employees to accomplish organizational objectives.

disability income insurance type of insurance that pays benefits to those who cannot work due to some sort of disability.

discrimination biased treatment of a job candidate or employee.

dispatching phase of production control in which the manager instructs each department on what work to do and the time allowed for its completion.

display ad glossy-looking online ad often targeted at a specific user.

distribution channel path through which products—and legal ownership of them—flow from producer to consumers or business users.

distribution channels path that products – and legal ownership of them – follow from producer to consumers to business user.

diversity blending individuals of different genders, ethnic backgrounds, cultures, religions, ages, and physical and mental abilities to enhance a firm's chances of success.

divestiture sale of assets by a firm.

domestic corporation firm that operates in the state where it is incorporated.

double-entry bookkeeping process by which accounting transactions are entered; each individual transaction always has an offsetting transaction.

downsizing process of reducing the number of employees within a firm by eliminating jobs.

dumping selling products abroad at prices below production costs or below typical prices in the home market to capture market share from domestic competitors.

economics social science that analyzes the choices people and governments make in allocating scarce resources.

electronic bulletin board Internet chat room that allows users to post and read messages on a specific topic.

electronic business (e-business) conducting business via the Internet.

electronic data interchange (EDI) computer-to-computer exchanges of invoices, purchase orders, price quotations, and other information between buyers and sellers.

electronic exchange online marketplace that caters to an industry's specific needs.

electronic shopping cart file that holds items that the online shopper has chosen to buy.

electronic storefront company Web site that sells products to customers.

electronic wallet secure computer data file set up by an online shopper at an e-business site that contains credit card and personal identification information.

embargo total ban on importing specific products or a total halt to trading with a particular country.

employee benefits additional compensation such as vacation, retirement plans, profit-sharing, health insurance, gym membership, child and elder care, and tuition reimbursement, paid entirely or in part by the company.

employee ownership business ownership in which workers buy shares of stock in the company that employs them.

employee stock-ownership plan (ESOP) plan that benefits employees by giving them ownership stakes in the companies for which they work.

empowerment (Chap. 7, p. 235) giving employees shared authority, responsibility, and decision making with their managers.

employee separation broad term covering the loss of an employee for any reason, voluntary or involuntary.

encryption process of encoding data for security purposes, using software that encodes and scrambles messages.

end-use segmentation marketing strategy that focuses on the precise way a B2B purchaser will use a product.

enterprise zones specific geographic areas designated for economic revitalization.

entrepreneur person who seeks a profitable opportunity and takes the necessary risks to set up and operate a business.

entrepreneurship willingness to take risks to create and operate a business.

environmental impact study analyzes how a proposed plant would affect the quality of life in the surrounding area.

e-procurement use of the Internet by business and government agencies to solicit bids and purchase goods and services from suppliers.

Equal Employment Opportunity Commission (EEOC) this commission created to increase job opportunities for women and minorities and to help end discrimination based on race, color, religion, disability, gender, or national origin in any personnel action.

equilibrium price prevailing market price at which you can buy an item.

equity capital funds obtained from owners.

equity financing funds invested in new ventures in exchange for part ownership.

equity theory an individual's perception of fair and equitable treatment.

European Union (EU) 27-nation European economic alliance.

event marketing marketing or sponsoring short-term events such as athletic competitions and cultural and charitable performances.

everyday low pricing (EDLP) is a strategy devoted to maintaining continuous low prices rather than relying on short-term price cuts such as cents-off coupons, rebates, and special sales.

exchange control restriction on importation of certain products or against certain companies to reduce trade and expenditures of foreign currency.

exchange process activity in which two or more parties give something of value to each other to satisfy perceived needs.

exchange rate value of one nation's currency relative to the currencies of other countries.

exclusive distribution distribution strategy involving limited market coverage by a single retailer or wholesaler in a specific geographical territory.

executive summary one- to two-page snapshot of what the overall business plan explains in detail.

executive support system (ESS) lets senior executives access the firm's primary databases, often by touching the computer screen, pointing and clicking a mouse, or using voice recognition.

expansionary monetary policy increases the money supply in an effort to cut the cost of borrowing, which encourages business decision makers to make new investments, in turn stimulating employment and economic growth.

expectancy theory the process people use to evaluate the likelihood that their efforts will yield the results they want, along with the degree to which they want those results.

expert system computer program that imitates human thinking through complicated sets of "if-then" rules.

exports domestically produced goods and services sold in other countries.

external communication meaningful exchange of information through messages transmitted between an organization and its major audiences.

extranet secure network used for e-business and accessible through an organization's Web site; available to external customers, suppliers, and other authorized users.

factoring selling receivables to another party, called a factor, for cash.

factors of production four basic inputs for effective operation: natural resources, capital, human resources, and entrepreneurship.

fair trade a market-based approach to pay higher prices to producers on exports from developing countries to developed countries in order for the developing countries to obtain better trading conditions and promote sustainability.

family brand brand name used to identify several different, but related, products.

family leave the Family and Medical Leave Act of 1993 states that businesses with 50 or more employees must provide unpaid leave up to 12 weeks annually for any employee who wants time off for the birth or adoption of a child, to become

a foster parent, or to care for a seriously ill relative, spouse, or self if he or she has a serious health condition or injury.

Federal Deposit Insurance Corporation (FDIC) federal agency that insures deposits at commercial and savings banks.

Federal Open Markets Committee Fed body that has primary responsibility for money policy.

Federal Reserve System (Fed) central bank of the United States.

fee-for-service plan traditional form of health insurance in which the insured chooses his or her healthcare provider, pays for treatment, and is reimbursed by the insurance company; also called an indemnity plan.

finance planning, obtaining, and managing the company's funds to accomplish its objectives as effectively and efficiently as possible.

finance charge the difference between the amount borrowed and the amount repaid on a loan.

Financial Accounting Standards Board (FASB) organization that interprets and modifies GAAP in the United States.

financial institutions intermediary between savers and borrowers, collecting funds from savers and then lending the funds to individuals, businesses, and governments.

financial managers executive who develops and implements the firm's financial plan and determines the most appropriate sources and uses of funds.

financial markets market in which securities are bought and sold.

financial plan document that specifies the funds needed by a firm for a period of time, the timing of inflows and outflows, and the most appropriate sources and uses of funds.

financial system process by which money flows from savers to users.

financing section section of a business plan that demonstrates the cost of the product, operating expenses, expected sales revenue and profit, and the amount of the business owner's own funds that will be invested to get the business up and running.

firewall limit data transfers to certain locations and log system use so that managers can identify attempts to log on with invalid passwords and other threats to a system's security.

fiscal policy government spending and taxation decisions designed to control inflation, reduce unemployment, improve the general welfare of citizens, and encourage economic growth.

flexible benefit plan benefit system that offers employees a range of options from which they may choose the types of benefits they receive.

flexible manufacturing system (FMS) production facility that workers can quickly modify to manufacture different products.

flexible work plan employment that allows personnel to adjust their working hours and places of work to accommodate their personal needs.

flextime scheduling system that allows employees to set their own work hours within constraints specified by the firm.

follow-up phase of production control in which employees and their supervisors spot problems in the production process and determine needed adjustments.

foreign corporation firm that operates in states where it is not incorporated.

Foreign Corrupt Practices Act federal law that prohibits U.S. citizens and companies from bribing foreign officials to win or continue business.

foreign licensing agreement international agreement in which one firm allows another to produce or sell its product, or use its trademark, patent, or manufacturing processes, in a specific geographical area in return for royalties or other compensation.

formal communication channel messages that flow within the chain of command defined by an organization.

franchise contractual agreement in which a franchisee gains the right to produce and/or sell the franchisor's products under that company's brand name if they agree to certain operating requirements.

franchisee individual or business firm purchasing a franchise.

franchising contractual business arrangement between a manufacturer or other supplier, and a dealer such as a restaurant operator or retailer.

franchisor firm whose products are sold to customers by the franchisee.

free-rein leadership management style of leaders who believe in minimal supervision and leave most decisions to their subordinates.

frequency marketing marketing initiative that rewards frequent purchases with cash, rebates, merchandise, or other premiums.

frictional unemployment applies to members of the workforce who are temporarily not working but are looking for jobs.

General Agreement on Tariffs and Trade (GATT) international trade accord that substantially reduced worldwide tariffs and other trade barriers.

generally accepted accounting principles (GAAP) principles that encompass the conventions, rules, and procedures for determining acceptable accounting practices at a particular time.

geographical segmentation dividing an overall market into homogeneous groups on the basis of their locations.

global business strategy offering a standardized, worldwide product and selling it in essentially the same manner throughout a firm's domestic and foreign markets.

goal target, objective, or result that someone tries to accomplish.

goal-setting theory says that people will be motivated to the extent to which they accept specific, challenging goals and receive feedback that indicates their progress toward goal achievement.

government bonds bonds issued by the U.S. Department of the Treasury.

grapevine internal information channel that transmits information from unofficial sources.

green marketing a marketing strategy that promotes environmentally safe products and production methods.

grid computing consists of a network of smaller computers running special software.

grievance formal complaint filed by an employee or a union that management is violating some provision of a union contract.

gross domestic product (GDP) sum of all goods and services produced within a country's boundaries during a specific time period, such as a year.

guerrilla marketing innovative, low-cost marketing effort designed to get consumers' attention in unusual ways.

hardware all tangible elements of a computer system.

health insurance category of insurance that pays for losses due to illness or injury.

high-context culture society in which communication depends not only on the message itself but also on nonverbal cues, past and present experiences, and personal relationships between the parties.

home-based businesses firm operated from the residence of the business owner.

horizontal merger merger that joins firms in the same industry for the purpose of diversification, increasing customer bases, cutting costs, or expanding product lines.

human resource management function of attracting, developing, and retaining employees who can perform the activities necessary to accomplish organizational objectives.

human resources production inputs consisting of anyone who works, including both the physical labor and the intellectual inputs contributed by workers.

human skills interpersonal skills that enable a manager to work effectively with and through people; the ability to communicate with, motivate, and lead employees to accomplish assigned activities.

hygiene factors factors that if present are essential to job satisfaction, although they cannot motivate an employee.

hyperinflation economic situation characterized by soaring prices.

imports foreign goods and services purchased by domestic customers.

income statement financial record of a company's revenues, expenses, and profits over a period of time.

individual brand different brand names given to each product within a line.

inflation rising prices caused by a combination of excess consumer demand and increases in the costs of raw materials, component parts, human resources, and other factors of production.

infomercial form of broadcast direct marketing; 30-minute programs that resemble regular TV programs, but are devoted to selling goods or services.

informal communication channel messages outside formally authorized channels within an organization's hierarchy.

information knowledge gained from processing data.

information system organized method for collecting, storing, and communicating past, present, and projected information on internal operations and external intelligence.

infrastructure basic systems of communication, transportation, and energy facilities in a country.

initial public offering (IPO) sale of stock to the public for the first time.

insider trading use of material nonpublic information about a company to make investment profits.

institutional advertising involves messages that promote of concepts, ideas, philosophies, or goodwill for industries, companies, organizations, or government entities.

insurable interest demonstration that a direct financial loss will result if some event occurs.

insurable risk requirement that a pure risk must meet for an insurer to agree to provide coverage.

insurance contract by which the insurer for a fee agrees to reimburse the insured a sum of money if a loss occurs.

integrated marketing communications (IMC) coordination of all promotional activities—media advertising, direct mail, personal selling, sales promotion, and public relations—to produce a unified customer-focused message.

integrity adhering to deeply felt ethical principles in business situations.

intensive distribution distribution strategy that involves placing a firm's products in nearly every available outlet.

International Accounting Standards Board (IASB) established in 1973 to promote worldwide consistency in financial reporting practices.

International Financial Reporting Standards (IFRS) standards and interpretations adopted by the IASB.

international law regulations that govern international commerce.

International Monetary Fund (IMF) organization created to promote trade, eliminate barriers, and make short-term loans to member nations that are unable to meet their budgets.

International Organization for Standardization (ISO) organization whose mission is to develop and promote International Standards for business, government and society to facilitate global trade and cooperation.

intranet computer network that is similar to the Internet but limits access to authorized users.

intrapreneurship process of promoting innovation within the structure of an existing organization.

introduction section of a business plan that describes the company, the management team, and the product in detail.

inventory control function requiring production and operations managers to balance the need to keep stock on hand to meet demand against the costs of carrying inventory.

investment-grade bond bond with a rating of BBB or above.

job enlargement job design that expands an employee's responsibilities by increasing the number and variety of tasks assigned to the worker.

job enrichment change in job duties to increase employees' authority in planning their work, deciding how it should be done, and learning new skills.

job rotation systematically moving employees from one job to another.

job sharing program management decision that allows two or more employees to divide the tasks of one job.

joint venture partnership between companies formed for a specific undertaking.

judiciary court system, or branch of government that is responsible for settling disputes by applying laws.

just-in-time (JIT) system broad management philosophy that reaches beyond the narrow activity of inventory control to influence the entire system of production and operations management.

labor union group of workers who have banded together to achieve common goals in the areas of wages, hours, and working conditions.

law standards set by government and society in the form of either legislation or custom.

law of large numbers concept that seemingly random events will follow predictable patterns if enough events are observed.

leadership ability to direct or inspire people to attain certain goals.

leverage increasing the rate of return on funds invested by borrowing funds.

leverage ratios measures of the extent to which a company relies on borrowed funds.

leveraged buyouts (LBOs) transaction in which public shareholders are bought out and the firm reverts to private status.

LEED (Leadership in Energy and Environmental Design) voluntary certification program administered by the U.S. Green Building Council, aimed at promoting the most sustainable construction processes available.

liability claims against assets by creditors.

liability insurance a type of insurance that protects people against financial losses to others for acts for which the insured was responsible.

life insurance a type of insurance that protects people against the financial losses that occur with premature death.

lifestyle entrepreneur person who starts a business to reduce work hours and create a more relaxed lifestyle.

lifetime value of a customer revenues and intangible benefits (referrals and customer feedback) from a customer over the life of the relationship, minus the amount the company must spend to acquire and serve that customer.

limit order order that puts a ceiling or floor on a security purchase or sale.

limited-liability company (LLC) corporation that secures the corporate advantage of limited liability while avoiding the double taxation characteristic of corporations.

line manager executive involved with the functions of production, financing, or marketing.

line organization organizational structure that establishes a direct flow of authority from the chief executive to subordinates.

line-and-staff organization structure that combines the direct flow of authority of a line organization with staff departments that support the line departments.

liquidity ratios measures of a firm's ability to meet its short-term obligations.

listening receiving a message and interpreting its intended meaning by grasping the facts and feelings it conveys.

local area networks (LANs) computer networks that connect machines within limited areas, such as a building or several nearby buildings.

lockout management decision to put pressure on union members by closing the firm.

logistics process of coordinating flow of goods, services, and information among members of the supply chain.

low-context culture society in which communication tends to rely on explicit written and verbal messages.

macroeconomics study of a nation's overall economic issues, such as how an economy maintains and allocates resources and how a government's policies affect the standards of living of its citizens.

make, buy, or lease decision choosing whether to manufacture a needed product or component in house, purchase it from an outside supplier, or lease it.

malware any malicious software program designed to infect computer systems.

managed care plan healthcare plan in which most, if not all, of the insured's healthcare bills are paid by the insurance company; in exchange, the insured has much less say over his or her treatment.

management process of achieving organizational objectives through people and other resources.

management accountant accountant who works for a firm and provides accounting services to that firm.

management by objectives systematic approach that allows managers to focus on attainable goals and to achieve the best results based on the organization's resources.

management development program training designed to improve the skills and broaden the knowledge of current and potential executives.

management information system (MIS) information system designed to produce reports for managers and other professionals.

management support systems information systems that are designed to provide support for effective decision making.

manufacturer's (national) brand brand offered and promoted by a manufacturer or producer.

market order order that instructs the investor's broker to obtain the best possible price.

market penetration percentage of the market that has purchased your product.

market segmentation process of dividing a total market into several relatively homogeneous groups.

marketable securities low-risk securities with short maturities.

marketing organizational function and set of processes for creating, communicating, and delivering value to customers and for managing customer relationships in ways that benefit the organization and its stakeholders.

marketing concept companywide consumer orientation to promote long-run success.

marketing mix blending the four elements of marketing strategy—product, distribution, promotion, and pricing—to satisfy chosen customer segments.

marketing research collecting and evaluating information to support marketing decision making.

marketing strategy section of a business plan that presents information describing the market's need for a product and how the business will satisfy it.

marketing Web site Web site whose main purpose is to increase purchases by visitors.

Maslow's hierarchy of needs theory of motivation proposed by Abraham Maslow. According to the theory, people have five levels of needs that they seek to satisfy: physiological, safety, social, esteem, and self-actualization.

mass production system for manufacturing products in large quantities through effective combinations of employees with specialized skills, mechanization, and standardization.

materials requirement planning (MRP) computer-based production planning system that lets a firm ensure that it has all the parts and materials it needs to produce its output at the right time and place and in the right amounts.

matrix structure project management structure that links employees from different parts of the organization to work together on specific projects.

mediation dispute resolution process that uses a third party, called a mediator, to make recommendations for settling labor–management differences.

Medicare public health insurance program for those 65 or older.

merger agreement in which two or more firms combine to form one company.

microeconomics study of small economic units, such as individual consumers, families, and businesses.

microloans small-business loans often used to buy equipment or operate a business.

middle management second tier in the management pyramid that focuses on specific operations within the organizations.

mission statement written explanation of an organization's business intentions and aims.

missionary selling indirect form of selling in which the representative promotes goodwill for a company or provides technical or operational assistance to the customer.

mixed market economy economic system that draws from both types of economies, to different degrees.

monetary policy government actions to increase or decrease the money supply and change banking requirements and interest rates to influence bankers' willingness to make loans.

money market instruments short-term debt securities issued by financial institutions, companies, and governments.

monopolistic competition market structure in which large numbers of buyers and sellers exchange heterogeneous products so each participant has some control over price.

monopoly market situation in which a single seller dominates trade in a good or service for which buyers can find no close substitutes.

morale mental attitude of employees toward their employer and jobs.

motivator factors factors that can produce high levels of motivation when they are present.

multidomestic business strategy developing and marketing products to serve different needs and tastes of separate national markets.

multinational corporation (MNC) firm with significant operations and marketing activities outside its home country.

municipal bonds bonds issued by state and local governments.

mutual fund financial intermediary that pools funds from investors by selling shares of itself and uses the funds to purchase securities.

national debt money owed by government to individuals, businesses, and government agencies who purchase Treasury bills, Treasury notes, and Treasury bonds sold to cover expenditures.

natural resources all production inputs that are useful in their natural states, including agricultural land, building sites, forests, and mineral deposits.

nearshoring outsourcing production or services to locations near a firm's home base.

negotiable instrument commercial paper that is transferable among individuals and businesses.

net worth the difference between an individual or household's assets and liabilities.

newsgroup noncommercial online forum.

nonpersonal selling consists of advertising, sales promotion, direct marketing, and public relations.

nonprogrammed decision complex and unique problem or opportunity with important consequences for the organization.

nonverbal communication transmission of messages through actions and behaviors.

North American Free Trade Agreement (NAFTA) agreement among the United States, Canada, and Mexico to break down tariffs and trade restrictions.

not-for-profit corporation organization whose goals do not include pursuing a profit.

not-for-profit organizations organization that has primary objectives such as public service rather than returning a profit to its owners.

objectives guideposts by which managers define the organization's desired performance in such areas as new-product development, sales, customer service, growth, environmental and social responsibility, and employee satisfaction.

odd pricing pricing method using uneven amounts, which appear less than they really are to consumers.

offshoring relocation of business processes to lower-cost locations overseas.

oligopoly market structure in which relatively few sellers compete and high start-up costs form barriers to keep out new competitors.

on-demand computing firms essentially rent the software time from application providers and pay only for their usage of the software.

on-the-job training training method that teaches an employee to complete new tasks by performing them under the guidance of an experienced employee.

open book management practice of sharing financial information with employees and teaching them how to understand and use financial statements.

open market operations technique in which the Fed buys or sells government bonds to affect the supply of money and credit.

operational planning detailed standards that guide implementation of tactical plans.

operational support systems information systems designed to produce a variety of information on an organization's activities for both internal and external users.

order processing form of selling, mostly at the wholesale and retail levels, that involves identifying customer needs, pointing them out to customers, and completing orders.

organization structured group of people working together to achieve common goals.

organization chart visual representation of a firm's structure that illustrates job positions and functions.

organization marketing marketing strategy that influences consumers to accept the goals of, receive the services of, or contribute in some way to an organization.

organizing process of blending human and material resources through a formal structure of tasks and authority; arranging work, dividing tasks among employees, and coordinating them to ensure implementation of plans and accomplishment of objectives.

outsourcing (Chap. 1, p. 22) using outside vendors to produce goods or fulfill services and functions that were previously handled in-house or in-country.

owners' equity funds contributed by owners plus profits not distributed to owners in the form of cash dividends.

ownership utility orderly transfer of goods and services from the seller to the buyer; also called possession utility.

pacing program company-initiated and financed program to develop new products.

paid time off (PTO) bank of time that employees can use for holidays, vacation, and sick days.

partnership association of two or more persons who operate a business as co-owners by voluntary legal agreement.

patent guarantee to an inventor exclusive rights to an invention for 17 years.

penetration pricing strategy that sets a low price as a major marketing tactic.

performance appraisal evaluation of and feedback on an employee's job performance.

perpetual inventory system that continuously monitors the amount and location of a company's stocks.

person marketing use of efforts designed to attract the attention, interest, and preference of a target market toward a person.

personal financial management study of the economic factors and personal decisions that affect a person's financial well-being.

personal selling the most basic form of promotion: a direct person-to-person promotional presentation to a potential buyer.

PERT (Program Evaluation and Review Technique) chart that seeks to minimize delays by coordinating all aspects of the production process.

phishing high-tech scam that uses authentic looking e-mail or pop-up ads to get unsuspecting victims to reveal personal information.

physical distribution actual movement of products from producer to consumers or business users.

picketing workers marching at a plant entrance to protest some management practice.

place marketing attempt to attract people to a particular area, such as a city, state, or nation.

place utility availability of a product in a location convenient for customers.

planned economy government controls determine business ownership, profits, and resource allocation to accomplish government goals rather than those set by individual firms.

planning process of anticipating future events and conditions and determining courses of action for achieving organizational objectives.

podcast audio or video blog.

point-of-purchase (POP) advertising displays or demonstrations that promote products when and where consumers buy them, such as in retail stores.

pollution environmental damage caused by a company's products or operating processes.

pop-up ad Internet ad that pops-up in a new window; interested parties can click on the ad for more information.

positioning concept in which marketers attempt to establish their products in the minds of customers by communicating to buyers meaningful distinctions about the attributes, price, quality, or use of a good or service.

potential sales revenue amount of revenue the business would collect if its market penetration were 100 percent.

preferred stock shares that give owners limited voting rights, and the right to receive dividends or assets before owners of common stock.

premium amount paid by the insured to the insurer to exchange for insurance coverage.

pre-roll video ad a short advertising video clip that begins automatically whenever a user visits a particular Web site.

prestige pricing establishes a relatively high price to develop and maintain an image of quality and exclusiveness.

price exchange value of a good or service.

primary market financial market in which firms and governments issue securities and sell them initially to the general public.

private enterprise system economic system that rewards firms for their ability to identify and serve the needs and demands of customers.

private equity funds investment companies that raise funds from individuals and institutional investors and use the funds to take large stakes in a wide range of public and private companies.

private exchange secure Web site at which a company and its suppliers share all types of data related to e-business, from product design through order delivery.

private placements sale of securities to a small number of investors.

private property most basic freedom under the private enterprise system; the right to own, use, buy, sell, and bequeath land, buildings, machinery, equipment, patents, individual possessions, and various intangible kinds of property.

private (store) brand product that is not linked to the manufacturer, but instead carries the label of a retailer or wholesaler.

privatization conversion of government-owned and operated companies into privately held businesses.

problem-solving team temporary combination of workers who gather to solve a specific problem and then disband.

process control systems operational support system to monitor and control physical processes.

product bundle of physical, service, and symbolic attributes designed to satisfy buyers' wants.

product advertising consists of messages designed to sell a particular good or service.

product liability the responsibility of manufacturers for injuries and damages caused by their products.

product life cycle four basic stages—introduction, growth, maturity, and decline—through which a successful product progresses.

product line group of related products marked by physical similarities or intended for the same market.

product mix the assortment of product lines and individual goods and services that a firm offers to consumers and business users.

product placement form of promotion in which marketers pay fees to have their products showcased in various media, ranging from newspapers and magazines to television and movies.

production use of resources, such as people and machinery, to convert materials into finished goods and services.

production and operations management oversee the production process by managing people and machinery in converting materials and resources into finished goods and services.

production control creates a well-defined set of procedures for coordinating people, materials, and machinery to provide maximum production efficiency.

production planning phase of production control that determines the amount of resources (including raw materials and other components) a firm needs in order to produce a certain output.

productivity relationship between the number of units produced and the number of human and other production inputs necessary to produce them.

product-related segmentation dividing consumer markets into groups based on benefits sought by buyers, usage rates and loyalty levels.

profitability objectives common objectives included in the strategic plans of most firms.

profitability ratios measures of a company's overall financial performance by evaluating its ability to generate revenues in excess of expenses.

profits rewards for businesspeople who take the risks involved to offer goods and services to customers.

programmed decision simple, common, and frequently occurring problem for which a solution has already been determined.

promotion function of informing, persuading, and influencing a purchase decision.

promotional mix combination of personal and nonpersonal selling components designed to meet the needs of their firm's target customers and effectively and efficiently communicate its message to them.

property and liability insurance general category of insurance that protects against losses due to a number of perils.

psychographic segmentation dividing consumer markets into groups with similar attitudes, values, and lifestyles.

public accountant accountant who provides accounting services to other organizations.

public insurance agency public agency that provides certain types of insurance coverage.

public ownership organization owned and operated by a unit or agency of government.

public relations organization's communications and relationships with its various public audiences.

publicity nonpersonal stimulation of demand for a good, service, place, idea, event, person, or organization by unpaid placement of information in print or broadcast media.

pulling strategy promote a product by generating consumer demand for it, primarily through advertising and sales promotion appeals.

pure competition market structure, in which large numbers of buyers and sellers exchange homogeneous products and no single participant has a significant influence on price.

pure risk type of risk where there is only the possibility of loss.

pushing strategy personal selling to market an item to wholesalers and retailers in a company's distribution channels.

quality control measuring output against established quality standards.

quality good or service that is free of deficiencies.

quota limit set on the amounts of particular products that can be imported.

ratio analysis commonly used tool for measuring the financial strength of a firm.

recession cyclical economic contraction that lasts for six months or longer.

recycling reprocessing of used materials for reuse.

regulated monopolies local, state or federal government grants exclusive rights in a certain market to a single firm.

relationship era the business era in which firms seek ways to actively nurture customer loyalty by carefully managing every interaction.

relationship management collection of activities that build and maintain ongoing, mutually beneficial ties with customers and other parties.

relationship marketing developing and maintaining long-term, cost-effective exchange relationships with partners.

restrictive monetary policy reducing the money supply to curb rising prices, overexpansion, and concerns about overly rapid economic growth.

retailer distribution channel members that sell goods and services to individuals for their own use rather than for resale.

risk uncertainty about loss or injury.

risk-return trade-off process of maximizing the wealth of the firm's shareholders by striking the optimal balance between risk and return.

robot reprogrammable machine capable of performing numerous tasks that require manipulation of materials and tools.

routing phase of production control that determines the sequence of work throughout the facility and specifies who will perform each aspect of production at what location.

rule of indemnity requirement that the insured cannot collect more than the amount of the loss and cannot collect for the same loss more than once.

S corporation corporations that do not pay corporate taxes on profits; instead, profits are distributed to shareholders, who pay individual income taxes.

salary pay calculated on a periodic basis, such as weekly or monthly.

sales law law governing the sale of goods or services for money or on credit.

sales promotion consists of forms of promotion such as coupons, product samples, and rebates that support advertising and personal selling.

Sarbanes-Oxley Act federal legislation designed to deter and punish corporate and accounting fraud and corruption and to protect the interests of workers and shareholders through enhanced financial disclosures, criminal penalties on CEOs and CFOs who defraud investors, safeguards for whistle-blowers, and establishment of a new regulatory body for public accounting firms.

scheduling development of timetables that specify how long each operation in the production process takes and when workers should perform it.

search marketing paying search engines, such as Google, a fee to make sure that the company's listing appears toward the top of the search results.

seasonal unemployment joblessness of workers in a seasonal industry.

secondary market collection of financial markets in which previously issued securities are traded among investors.

Secure Sockets Layer (SSL) technology that secures a Web site by encrypting information and providing authentication.

securities financial instruments that represent obligations on the part of the issuers to provide the purchasers with expected stated returns in the funds invested or loaned.

seed capital initial funding needed to launch a new venture.

selective distribution distribution strategy in which a manufacturer selects only a limited number of retailers to distribute its product lines.

self-managed team work team that has the authority to decide how its members complete their daily tasks.

sell-off transaction in which assets are sold by one firm to another.

serial entrepreneur person who starts one business, runs it, and then starts and runs additional businesses in succession.

server the heart of a midrange computer network

set-aside program component of a government contract specifying that certain government contracts (or portions of those contracts) are restricted to small businesses and/or to women- or minority-owned companies.

sexism discrimination against members of either sex, but primarily affecting women.

sexual harassment unwelcome and inappropriate actions of a sexual nature in the workplace.

shopping product item typically purchased only after the buyer has compared competing products in competing stores.

skimming pricing strategy that sets an intentionally high price relative to the prices of competing products.

skunkworks project initiated by a company employee who conceives the idea, convinces top management of its potential, and then recruits human and other resources from within the firm to turn it into a commercial project.

small business independent business with fewer than 500 employees, not dominant in its market.

Small Business Administration (SBA) principal government agency concerned with helping small U.S. firms.

Small Business Investment Company (SBIC) business licensed by the Small Business Administration to provide loans to small businesses.

social audits formal procedure that identifies and evaluates all company activities that relate to social issues such as conservation, employment practices, environmental protection, and philanthropy.

social entrepreneur person who recognizes societal problems and uses business principles to develop innovative solutions.

social responsibility business's consideration of society's well-being and consumer satisfaction, in addition to profits.

socialism economic system characterized by government ownership and operation of major industries such as communications.

software all the programs, routines, and computer languages that control a computer and tell it how to operate.

sole proprietorship business ownership in which there is no legal distinction between the sole proprietor's status as an individual and his or her status as a business owner.

sovereign wealth funds government-owned investment companies

spam popular name for junk e-mail.

span of management number of subordinates a manager can supervise effectively.

specialty advertising promotional items that prominently display a firm's name, logo, or business slogan.

specialty product item that a purchaser is willing to make a special effort to obtain.

speculative (junk) bond a bond with a rating below BB.

speculative risk type of risk where the possibility of gain and loss both exist.

spin-off transaction in which divested assets form a new company.

sponsorship involves providing funds for a sporting or cultural event in exchange for a direct association with the event.

spyware software that secretly gathers user information through the user's Internet connections without his or her knowledge, usually for advertising purposes.

staff manager executive who provides information, advice, or technical assistance to aid line managers; does not have the authority to give orders outside his or her own department or to compel line managers to take action.

stakeholders customers, investors, employees, and public affected by or with an interest in a company.

standard of living necessities, comforts, and luxuries one seeks to obtain or to maintain.

statement of cash flows statement showing the sources and uses of cash during a period of time.

statement of owners' equity record of the change in owners' equity from the end of one fiscal period to the end of the next.

statutory law written law, including state and federal constitutions, legislative enactments, treaties of the federal government, and ordinances of local governments.

stock market (exchanges) market in which shares of stock are bought and sold by investors.

stock options rights to buy a specified amount of company stock at a given price within a given time period.

stockholders owners of a corporation due to their purchase of stock in the corporation.

strategic alliance partnership formed to create a competitive advantage for the businesses involved; in international business, a business strategy in which a company finds a partner in the country where it wants to do business.

strategic planning process of determining the primary objectives of an organization and then acting and allocating resources to achieve those objectives.

strike temporary work stoppage by employees until a dispute is settled or a contract signed.

structural unemployment people who remain unemployed for long periods of time, often with little hope of finding new jobs like their old ones.

subcontracting international agreement that involves hiring local companies to produce, distribute, or sell goods or services in a specific country or geographical region.

subprime mortgage loan made to a borrower with a poor credit rating.

supervisory management first-line management; includes positions such as supervisor, line manager, and group leader; responsible for assigning non-managerial employees to specific jobs and evaluating their performance every day.

supply willingness and ability of sellers to provide goods and services.

supply chain complete sequence of suppliers that contribute to creating a good or service and delivering it to business users and final consumers.

supply curve graph that shows the relationship between different prices and the quantities that sellers will offer for sale, regardless of demand.

sustainable the capacity to endure in ecology.

SWOT analysis SWOT is an acronym for *strengths, weaknesses, opportunities,* and *threats.* By systematically evaluating all four of these factors, a firm can then develop the best strategies for gaining a competitive advantage.

synergy notion that a combined firm is worth more than the two firms are individually.

tactical planning implementing the activities specified by strategic plans.

target market group of people toward whom an organization markets its goods, services, or ideas with a strategy designed to satisfy their specific needs and preferences.

tariff tax imposed on imported goods.

tax assessment by a governmental unit.

team group of people with certain skills who are committed to a common purpose, approach, and set of performance goals.

team cohesiveness extent to which team members feel attracted to the team and motivated to remain part of it.

team diversity variances or differences in ability, experience, personality, or any other factor on a team.

team level average level of ability, experience, personality, or any other factor on a team.

team norm standard of conduct shared by team members that guides their behavior.

technical skills manager's ability to understand and use techniques, knowledge, and tools and equipment of a specific discipline or department.

technology business application of knowledge based on scientific discoveries, inventions, and innovations.

telecommuter home-based employee.

telemarketing personal selling conducted entirely by telephone, which provides a firm's marketers with a high return on their expenditures, an immediate response, and an opportunity for personalized two-way conversation.

tender offer offer made by a firm to the target firm's shareholders specifying a price and the form of payment.

term policy pure type of life insurance policy providing only a death benefit.

test marketing introduction of a new product supported by a complete marketing campaign to a selected city or TV coverage area.

Theory X assumption that employees dislike work and will try to avoid it.

Theory Y assumption that employees enjoy work and seek social, esteem, and self-actualization fulfillment.

Theory Z assumption that employee involvement is key to productivity and quality of work life.

time utility availability of a good or service when customers want to purchase it.

top management managers at the highest level of the management pyramid who devote most of their time to developing long-range plans for their organizations.

tort civil wrong inflicted on another person or the person's property.

trade credit credit extended by suppliers in which the buyer agrees to pay for goods and services received now at a later date.

trade promotion sales promotion geared to marketing intermediaries rather than to final consumers.

trademark brand a legal protection that has been given.

transaction management building and promoting products in the hope that enough customers will buy them to cover costs and earn profits.

transaction processing systems operational support system to record and process data from business transactions.

trends consumer and business tendencies or patterns that firms can exploit to gain market share in an industry.

trial courts federal and state courts of general jurisdiction.

Trojan horse program that claims to do one thing but in reality does something else, usually something malicious.

underwriting process used by an insurance company to determine who, or what, to insure and how much to charge.

unemployment rate percentage of the total workforce actively seeking work but are currently unemployed.

Uniform Commercial Code The basis of U.S. business law; referred to as UCC.

utility power of a good or service to satisfy a want or need.

vendor-managed inventory process in which the producer and the retailer agree that the producer (or the wholesaler) will determine how much of a product a buyer needs and automatically ship new supplies when needed.

venture capital money invested in a business by another business firm or group of individuals in exchange for an ownership share.

venture capitalists business firms or groups of individuals that invest in new and growing firms in exchange for an ownership share.

vertical merger merger that combines firms operating at different levels in the production and marketing process.

virtual private networks (VPNs) secure connections between two points on the Internet.

virtual team group of geographically or organizationally dispersed coworkers who use a combination of telecommunications and information technologies to accomplish an organizational task.

viruses programs that secretly attach themselves to other programs (called *hosts*) and change them or destroy data.

vishing variation on phishing that involves a voice system in which the intended victim receives a voice message directing him or her to reveal personal financial information.

VoIP alternative to traditional telecommunication services provided by companies such as Verizon and Qwest.

volume objectives bases pricing decisions on market share, the percentage of a market controlled by a certain company or product.

wage pay based on an hourly rate or the amount of work accomplished.

Web-to-store use of the Web to aid shoppers at brick-and-mortar retailers.

wheel of retailing theory of retailing in which new retailers gain a competitive foothold by offering low prices and limited services and then add services and raise prices, creating opportunities for new low-price competitors.

whistle-blowing employee's disclosure to company officials, government authorities, or the media of illegal, immoral, or unethical practices committed by an organization.

wholesaler distribution channel member that sells primarily to retailers, other wholesalers, or business users.

wide area networks (WANs) tie larger geographical regions together by using telephone lines and microwave and satellite transmission.

WiFi wireless network that connects various devices and allows them to communicate with one another through radio waves.

wiki Web page that can be edited by users.

work team relatively permanent group of employees with complementary skills who perform the day-to-day work of organizations.

World Bank organization established by industrialized nations to lend money to less developed countries.

World Trade Organization (WTO) 153-member international institution that monitors GATT agreements and mediates international trade disputes.

worm small piece of software that exploits a security hole in a network to replicate itself.

Chapter 1

1. "Snuggie," *Consumer Reports,* February 2010, p. 18; "Local 540 News," January 19, 2010, http://www.fayettevilleflyer.com; Natalie Zmuda and Bryson York, "Marketers Make Most of Falling Mercury," Business and Company Resource Center, January 11, 2010, http://gatenet.gatenetgroup.com; David King, "Talking about Snuggies, Hogettes, and Robot Umpires," *Information Today,* December 2009, www.infotoday.com; Jack Neff, "Snuggie," *Advertising Age,* November 16, 2009.

2. http://nccs.urban.org/statistics/quickfacts.cfm, accessed February 9, 2010.

3. Ibid.

4. Organization Web site, http://www.stjude.org, accessed February 9, 2010.

5. Ginger Thompson, "As Haiti's Focus Turns to Shelter, Families Press Search for Missing, *The New York Times,* January 15, 2010., http://www.nytimes.com; Liz Robbins, "Haiti Relief Effort Faces 'Major Challenge,'" *The New York Times,* January 25, 2010, http://www.nytimes.com.

6. www.livestrong.org

7. Megan Barnett, "Inside the New Kindle," *Portfolio.com,* February 9, 2009, http://www.portfolio.com.

8. Company Web site, http://www.usps.com/onlinepostage/welcome.htm, accessed February 9, 2010; Anick Jesdanun, "Postal Agencies Respond to Mail Decline," *Associated Press,* February 4, 2008, http://news.yahoo.com.

9. "100 Best Companies to Work For: #1 SAS," *CNNMoney.com,* http://money.cnn.com, accessed February 4, 2010.

10. J. Jennings Moss, "It's a Small World," *Portfolio.com,* December 2, 2009, http://www.portfolio.com.

11. Google to Launch Google Docs App Store? *PCMag.com,* February 2, 2010, http://www.pcmag.com.

12. Jeffry Bartash, "FCC to Force Cable Operators to Share Sports Channels," January 20, 2010, http://www.marketwatch.com.

13. http://www.sba.gov/advo/stats/sbfaq.pdf

14. Eric Hansen, "That's Opportunity Knocking," *Portfolio.com,* December 10, 2009, http://www.portfolio.com.

15. Patrick May, "So Many Apps, So Little Time," *San Jose Mercury News,* February 7, 2010, www.mercurynews.com.

16. Company Web site, "History," http://www.graniterock.com, accessed February 9, 2010.

17. Company Web site, http://ir.homedepot.com, accessed February 4, 2010.

18. Mack Collier, "Examples of Great Company Blogs," http://www.searchengineguide.com, accessed February 4, 2010.

19. Company Web site, www.overstock.com, accessed February 9, 2010.

20. "R.C. Bigelow Company," Connecticut Clean Energy Fund, press release, http://www.ctcleanenergy.com, accessed February 4, 2010.

21. John Teresko, "Ford's Light Idea," *Industry Week,* November 1, 2007, http://www.industryweek.com.

22. Matt Richtel and John Markoff, "A Green Energy Industry Takes Root in California," *The New York Times,* February 1, 2008, http://www.nytimes.com.

23. "A Change in Climate," *The Economist,* January 17, 2008, http://www.economist.com.

24. "An Older and More Diverse Nation by Midcentury," press release, August 14, 2008, U.S. Census Bureau, http://www.census.gov.

25. "The Diversity Inc Top 50 Companies for Diversity," Diversity Inc, http://www.diversityinc.com, accessed February 4, 2010.

26. "Survey: Workplace Discrimination Still Prevalent," *Inc.com,* March 1, 2007, http://www.inc.com, accessed March 2, 2010.

27. Company Web site, http://phx.corporate-ir.net, accessed February 4, 2010; Amarendra Bhushan, "List of Top CEOs in the World to Watch for 2010," *CEOWorld Magazine,* January 14, 2010. http://ceoworld.biz.

28. Michael Wilson, "Flight 1549 Pilot Tells of Terror and Intense Focus," *The New York Times,* February 8, 2009, http://www.nytimes.com.

29. "America's Most Admired Companies 2008," *Fortune,* http://money.cnn.com, accessed February 9, 2010.

Chapter 2

1. Company Web site, http://www.entropysurfboards.com, accessed February 6, 2009; Evan Fontaine, "Interview: Jeremy Sherwin," *Surfline San Diego,* January 8, 2009, http://www.surfline.com; "Rey Banatao," *The Craftsman Chronicle,* October 11–12, 2008, http://www.ice-ninefoamworks.com; Andy Stone, "Green Wave," *Forbes,* September 1, 2008, pp. 58–60.

2. Dan Carney, "Chevy Volt to Hit the Roads (Quietly) Soon," MSNBC, February 1, 2010, http://www.msnbc.msn.com; California Cars Initiative, "All About Plug-In Hybrids," http://www.calcars.org/vehicles.html.

3. Company Web site, http://www.jnj.com, accessed February 2010.

4. Cliff Kuang, "Wal-Mart's Sustainability Push," *Good,* Fall 2009; Michael Garry, "Wal-Mart Cites Progress on Sustainability Index," *Supermarket News,* November 23, 2009.

5. Ethics Resource Center, "2009 National Business Ethics Survey," November 2009.

6. Daniel Franklin, "Just Good Business," *The Economist,* January 17, 2008, http://www.economist.com.

7. Ethics Resource Center, "National Business Ethics Survey," *November 2009.*

8. John Cox, "Radisson Hotels: Data Breach Affected 'Limited' Number of Sites, Guests," *ComputerWorld,* August 19, 2009, http://www.computerworld.com.

9. Jim Dwyer, "H & M Says It Will Stop Destroying Unworn Clothing," *The New York Times,* January 6, 2010; Jim Dwyer, "A Clothing Clearance Where More Than Just the Prices Have Been Slashed," *The New York Times,* January 5, 2010, http://www.nytimes.com.

10. "Obama Renews Ban on Ruby, Jade from Myanmar," *National Jeweler*, July 30, 2009, http://www.nationaljewelernetwork.com.

11. "Resigned: City Worker Who Lied On Resume Steps Down from Plush Post," 19 Action News, http://www.woio.com, January 20, 2010.

12. Heather Tooley, "Personal Internet Usage in the Workplace—A Serious Epidemic," Associated Content, January 17, 2010, http://www.associatedcontent.com; Jeffrey R. Smith, "No 'LOL' over Misuse of Email and Internet at Work," *Canadian HR Reporter*, September 28, 2009, http://chrremploymentlaw.wordpress.com.

13. U.S. Department of Commerce, Office of the Inspector General, "American Recovery and Reinvestment Act of 2009 Whistleblower Protection," http://www.nist.gov/recovery/whistleblower_factsheet.pdf, accessed February 4, 2010.

14. Jerry Seper, "Texas Whistleblower Fights Uphill Battle," *The Washington Times,* March 22, 2009, http://www.washingtontimes.com.

15. Company Web site, http://www.lockheedmartin.com/index.html, accessed February 4, 2010.

16. Company Web site, http://www.syrusglobal.com/sg/, accessed February 4, 2010.

17. Umaimah Mendhro and Abhinav Sinha, "Three Keys to Staying Ethical in the Age of Madoff," *Forbes.com*, February 6, 2009, http://www.forbes.com.

18. Company Web site, http://www.mercadien.com/index.html, accessed February 10, 2010; "Mercadien Donates Hundredes of Toys for Children in Need," http://www.mercadien.com/PDF/ToysforTots2009.pdf.

19. Company Web site, http://www.boxtops4education.com, accessed February 4, 2010.

20. Company Web site, http://www.subway.com/, accessed February 4, 2010; Jared Foundation, http://www.jaredfoundation.org, accessed February 4, 2010; "The Jared Foundation," North American Association of SUBWAY Franchises, http://www.naasf.org, accessed February 10, 2010; "SUBWAY's Jared Fogle Retires Famous Fat Pants," February 12, 2009, Bison Franchise, http://www.bison.com.

21. Tyler Kepner, "McGwire Admits That He Used Steroids," *The New York Times*, January 11, 2010, http://www.nytimes.com.

22. Roger Greenway, "Duke Energy Resolves Clean Air Act Violations," Environmental News Network, December 23, 2009, http://www.enn.com, accessed February 4, 2010.

23. "Where Can I Donate or Recycle My Old Computer and Other Electronic Products?" http://www.epa.gov, accessed February 4, 2010; "We Now Offer Electronics Recycling at All Best Buy Stores Nationwide," http://www.bestbuy.com, accessed February 4, 2010.

24. Tony Quiroga, "2011 Chevrolet Volt First Drive – Car News," *Car and Driver*, April 2009, http://www.caranddriver.com.

25. Institute of Scrap Recycling Industries, "Reducing Electronics Waste (E-waste): Electronics Recycling Facts & Electronics Recycling Statistics," http://www.isri.org, accessed February 4, 2010.

26. T. A. Boden, G. Marland, and R. J. Andres, "Global, Regional, and National Fossil-Fuel CO_2 Emissions," Carbon Dioxide Information Analysis Center, Oak Ridge National Laboratory, U.S. Department of Energy, Oak Ridge, Tennessee, http://cdiac.ornl.gov, accessed February 4, 2010; company Web site, http://www.cisco.com, accessed February 4, 2010; "Cisco Launches New 'Cultivated Innovation Model' to Accelerate Local Innovation in China," press release, April 17, 2009, http://newsroom .cisco.com/dlls/2009/prod_041709.html.

27. Martin LaMonica, "Bill Gates Investing in Vinod Khosla Green-Tech Fund," *CNET News*, January 25, 2010, http://news.cnet.com.

28. Company Web site, http://www.mars.com/global/index.aspx, accessed February 12, 2010.

29. U.S. Bureau of Labor Statistics, "Table 4. Quartiles and Selected Deciles of Usual Weekly Earnings of Full-Time Wage and Salary Workers by Selected Characteristics, Fourth Quarter 2009 Averages, Not Seasonally Adjusted," http://www.bls.gov, accessed February 12, 2010.

30. Cheerios Spoonfuls of Stories, http://promo.simonandschuster.com /spoonfulsofstories, accessed February 12, 2010.

31. "Diversity," Coca-Cola Web site, http://www.thecoca-colacompany.com, accessed February 12, 2010.

32. "Brand Partnerships," General Mills Web site, http://www.generalmills .com/corporate, accessed February 14, 2010.

33. "UPS Pilots Volunteer to Help Haiti Relief Effort," *Forbes.com*, January 14, 2010, http://www.forbes.com/.

34. David Liu, Ippolito Recalls Spinach in the U.S. and Canada," *Food Consumer*, September 20, 2009, http://www.foodconsumer.org; Food and Drug Administration, "Ippolito International, LP Voluntarily Recalls Bunch Spinach Because of Possible Health Risk Nationwide and Canada," September 18, 2009, http://www.fda.gov.

35. *Gemelas v. Dannon* Settlement Web site, http://www.dannonsettlement.com, accessed February 14, 2010; Nathan Olivarez-Giles, "Dannon Settles False Advertising Lawsuit over Activia, DanActive Yogurt," *Los Angeles Times*, September 19, 2009.

36. "FDA Warns Consumers about Counterfeit Alli," http://www.fda.gov, accessed February 13, 2010.

37. "eBay Rules and Policies Overview," eBay, http://pages.ebay.com/help/ policies/overview.html, accessed February 14, 2010.

38. "Teen Workers," U.S. Department of Labor, http://www.osha.gov/SLTC/ teenworkers/teenworkers.html, accessed February 14, 2010; Youth Rules!, http://youthrules.dol.gov, accessed February 14, 2010.

39. Annie Finnigan, Susan Goldberg, Patty Orsini, et al., "Working Mother 100 Best Companies 2009," *Working Mother*, http://www.workingmother.com, accessed March 17, 2010.

40. Robert Smithson, "Is Unlimited Vacation Time a Recipe for Business Success?" *Kelowna Capital News,* February 16, 2010, http://www.bclocalnews.com.

41. Web site http://www.eeoc.gov, accessed March 17, 2010.

42. Steven Greenhouse, "Democrats Working to Overturn Justices on Age Bias," *The New York Times*, October 6, 2009, http://www.nytimes.com; Warren Richey, "Supreme Court Sets High Bar For Age-Bias Suits," *Christian Science Monitor*, June 18, 2009, http://www.csmonitor.com.

43. Liz Wolgemuth, "20 Ways Older Workers Can Sell Themselves," *U.S. News & World Report*, November 26, 2008, http://www.usnews.com.

44. U.S. Department of Labor, *Occupational Outlook Handbook 2010–11,* http://www.bls.gov, accessed February 17, 2010.

45. U.S. Equal Employment Opportunity Commission, "Sexual Harassment," http://archive.eeoc.gov/types/sexual_harassment.html, accessed February 17, 2010.

46. S. 181: Lilly Ledbetter Fair Pay Act of 2009, http://www.govtrack.us/congress/bill.xpd?bill=s111-181&tab=summary, accessed February 14, 2010; Sheryl Gay Stolberg, "Obama Signs Equal-Pay Legislation," *The New York Times*, January 29, 2009; Linda Greenhouse, "Justices' Ruling Limits Lawsuits on Pay Disparity," *The New York Times*, May 30, 2007, http://www.newyorktimes.com.

47. Gail Zoppo, "Why Are Women Still Earning Less Than Men?" *Diversity Inc.*, April 28, 2009, http://www.diversityinc.com.

Chapter 3

1. Farhana Hossain, Amanda Cox, John McGrath, and Stephan Weitburg, "The Stimulus Plan: How to Spend $787 Billion," *The New York Times*, February 18, 2009, http://www.nytimes.com; James Oliphant, "Inside Stimulus Bill's Billions in Provisions, *Chicago Tribune*, February 15, 2009, section 1, p. 6; Jeremy Pelofsky and Richard Cowan, "House Approves Stimulus Plan; Senate Vote to Come," Reuters, February 13, 2009, http://news.yahoo.com; Annys Shin, "Economic Signs Turn from Grim to Worse," *The Washington Post*, January 30, 2009, http://www.washingtonpost.com; Jack Healy, "Steep Slide in U.S. Economy, but Not as Dire as Forecast," *The New York Times*, January 30, 2009, http://www.nytimes.com.

2. Nathan Eddy, "Video Game Sales Down 8 Percent in 2009," eWeek.com, http://www.eweek.com, accessed February 4, 2010.

3. Jeff Bercovici, "Soon, You'll Have to Pay for Hulu," *Daily Finance*, June 3, 2009, http://www.dailyfinance.com; Dawn C. Chmielewski and Alex Pham, "At Hulu, 'Free' May Turn to 'Fee,'" *Los Angeles Times*, January 21, 2010, http://articles.latimes.com.

4. Jad Mouawad, "Demand for Oil Set to Rise Anew," *The New York Times*, February 15, 2010, http://www.nytimes.com.

5. David P. Schulz, "Top 100 Retailers," *Stores*, NRF Stores, http://www.stores.org, accessed February 4, 2010.

6. Pascal Fletcher, "Freeze Mauls Florida Citrus, Significant Damage Seen," *Reuters*, January 11, 2010, http://www.reuters.com.

7. Beth Quimby, "Veggie Season Keeps Growing," *Portland Press Herald*, November 23, 2009, http://www.pressherald.com.

8. Bettina Wassener, "Fed's Move Prompts Drop in Asian Stocks, Oil and Gold, but Dollar Rises," *The New York Times*, February 20, 2010, http://www.nytimes.com; Lewa Pardomuan, "Gold Slips 1 Percent after Fed Raises Discount Rate," *Reuters*, February 19, 2010, http://www.reuters.com.

9. William Spain, "Fast-Food Outlook: Intense Competition, Margin Pressures," *MarketWatch*, January 14, 2010, http://www.marketwatch.com.

10. Michael Liedtke, "Yahoo-Microsoft Deal Set, Taking Aim at Google," *Associated Press*, February 18, 2010, http://hosted.ap.org; Hosting News, "Microsoft Exchange Server or Google Apps? A Comparison," September 5, 2009, http://www.thehostingnews.com; Sharon Gaudin, "Google vs. Microsoft: It's Going to Get Worse in 2010," *PC World*, December 23, 2009, http://www.pcworld.com.

11. Matthew Lasar, "Federal Court Upholds FCC Ban on Exclusive Cable Deals," *Ars Technica*, May 27, 2009, http://arstechnica.com.

12. Company Web site, http://www.aircanada.com, accessed February 4, 2010.

13. Central Intelligence Agency, *World Factbook*, https://www.cia.gov, accessed February 4, 2010.

14. Alexis Leondis, "U.S. Millionaires' Ranks Rose 16% in 2009, Study Says," *BusinessWeek*, March 9, 2010, http://www.businessweek.com.

15. Bureau of Labor Statistics, "Occupational Employment Statistics (OES) Highlights: An Occupational Analysis of Industries with Employment Gains," http://www.bls.gov, accessed February 4, 2010.

16. World Bank Web site, http://web.worldbank.org, accessed February 4, 2010; "Disaster Experts Share Lessons for Haiti," http://web.worldbank.org; Jack Ewing, "Emerging Economies Gain a Voice at Davos," *The New York Times*, January 26, 2010, http://www.nytimes.com.

17. U.S. and World Population Clocks, U.S. Census Bureau, http://www.census.gov, accessed February 4, 2010.

18. Justin Pritchard, "U.S. Agency Goes after Cadmium in Children's Jewelry," *ABC News*, January 11, 2010, http://abcnews.go.com.

19. "Coke vs. Pepsi: Battle of the Beverage Behemoths," *Seeking Alpha*, February 12, 2010, http://seekingalpha.com.

Chapter 4

1. "Lululemon Athletica Inc.," company profile, *BusinessWeek*, http://investing.businessweek.com, accessed February 13, 2009; company Web site, http://www.lululemon.com, accessed January 18, 2009; David Olive, "The Year of Living Dangerously," *The Star*, January 3, 2009, http://www.thestar.com; John Partridge, "Lululemon Pushing Expansion Despite Slowdown," *The Globe and Mail*, September 12, 2008, http://www.theglobeandmail.com; Karen Goldberg Goff, "Lifestyle for Sale at Lululemon," *The Washington Times*, September 3, 2008, http://www.washingtontimes.com; Melinda Peer, "Christine Day Breathes New Life into Lululemon," *Forbes*, April 3, 2008, http://forbes.com.

2. CIA *World FactBook*, "United States," www.cia.gov, accessed March 8, 2010.

3. U.S. Census Bureau, "International Data Base," www.census.gov, accessed March 8, 2010; "You Think! But Do You Know?" World Bank, http://youthink.worldbank.org, accessed March 8, 2010.

4. CIA, *World FactBook*, www.cia.gov, accessed March 8, 2010.

5. Matthew Boyle, "Wal-Mart's Painful Lessons," *BusinessWeek*, www.businessweek.com, October 13, 2009.

6. U.S. Census Bureau, "Top Ten Countries with Which the U.S. Trades, for the Month of December 2009," www.census.gov, accessed March 8, 2010.

7. U.S. Census Bureau, "State Exports for Texas," State Exports for California," *The 2010 Statistical Abstract: State Rankings*, www.census.gov, accessed March 8, 2010.

8. Company Web site, Sahar Saffron, http://safarsaffron.com, accessed March 8, 2010; http://www.spiceadvice.com, accessed March 8, 2010.

9. Steve Hamm, "Big Blue's Global Lab," *BusinessWeek*, www.businessweek.com, August 27, 2009.

10. U.S. Census Bureau, "Exhibit 1. U. International Trade in Goods and Services, January 2007 to December 2009," www.census.gov, accessed March 8, 2010.

11. Brooks Barnes, "China Approves Disney Theme Park in Shanghai," *The New York Times*, www.nytimes.com, November 4, 2009.

12. Bank for International Settlements, http://www.bis.org., accessed March 8, 2010.

13. Vivian Wai-yin Kwok, "How Kraft Won in China," *Forbes.com*, www.forbes.com, December 8, 2009.

14. Tanya Mohn, "Going Global, Stateside," *The New York Times*, www.nytimes.com, March 8, 2010.

15. "India Needs 400 Airports to Cater to People's Needs," *LiveMint*, www.livemint.com, posted March 3, 2010; Samar Halarnkar, "Delhi Airport's T3: Bags Packed, Ready to Go," *LiveMint*, www.livemint.com, posted February 28, 2010.

16. "China Tightens Internet Controls," *BBC News*, http://news.bbc.co.uk, February 23, 2010.

17. Transparency International, "Foreign Bribery and OECD Countries: A Hollow Commitment? Progress Report 2009," www.transparency.org, June 22, 2009.

18. "British Kids Swamped with Sexual Images," *ABC News*, www.abc.net.au, February 27, 2010.

19. Enterprise Europe Network, "SME Consultation on a Review of the WTO Information Technology Agreement (ITA) Related to ICT Products," www.een-ireland.ie, November 30, 2009.

20. "Administering Sugar Imports," The U.S. Department of Agriculture Foreign Agricultural Service, http://www.fas.usda.gov, accessed March 17, 2010.

21. Louis Uchitelle, "Glassmaking Thrives Offshore, But Is Declining in U.S.," *The New York Times*, www.nytimes.com, January 19, 2010.

22. World Trade Organization, "Lamy Calls for March Stocktaking to 'Inject Political Energy and Momentum' in the Negotiations," www.wto.org, February 22 and 23, 2010.

23. "G7 to Forgive Haiti Foreign Debt," *ABC News*, www.abc.net.au, February 7, 2010; press release, "World Bank Statement on Haiti Debt," The World Bank, www.worldbank.org, January 21, 2010.

24. CIA *World Factbook*, "United States," https://www.cia.gov, accessed March 17, 2010.

25. CIA *World Factbook*, "Canada," https://www.cia.gov, accessed March 17, 2010.

26. CIA *World Factbook*, "Mexico," https://www.cia.gov, accessed March 17, 2010.

27. CIA *World Factbook*, "European Union," https://www.cia.gov, accessed March 17, 2010.

28. Kerry A. Dolan, "Hycrete: Keeping the Water Out," *Forbes.com*, www.forbes.com, March 15, 2010; Raymund Flandez, "Looking Abroad for a Bigger Boost in Business," *The Wall Street Journal*, http://online.wsj.com, September 9, 2008.

29. Company Web site, Fuel Systems Solutions, www.fuelsystemssolutions.com, accessed March 9, 2010.

30. Company Web site, http://www.dominosbiz.com, accessed March 17, 2010.

31. Company Web site, Morinaga Co., www.morinagamilk.co.jp, accessed March 9, 2010.

32. Kate O'Sullivan, "Best Buys in Offshore Manufacturing," CFO.com, www.cfo.com, February 18, 2010.

33. "Polaris Acquires Engine Developer Swissauto," *Motorcycle-USA*, www.motorcycle-usa.com, February 3, 2010.

34. Company Web site, www.alcoa.com, accessed March 17, 2010.

End of Part 1: Launching Your Global Business and Economics Career

1. U.S. Department of Labor, "Tomorrow's Jobs," Occupational Outlook Handbook, 2010–2011 edition, U.S. Bureau of Labor Statistics, http://www.bls.gov.

2. U.S. Department of Labor, "Economists," Occupational Outlook Handbook, 2010–2011 edition, U.S. Bureau of Labor Statistics, http://www.bls.gov.

3. Adapted from Michael R. Czinkota, Ilkka A. Ronkainen, and Michael H. Moffett, "Criteria for Selecting Managers for Overseas Assignments," in International Business, 7th ed. (Mason, OH: SouthWestern, 2005), Table 19.2, p. 634.

4. "MBA Still Packs a Punch," January 28, 2008, Financial Times, http://www.ft.com.

5. Sattar Bawany, "Transition Coaching Helps Ensure Success for Global Assignments," Today's Manager, January 2008, accessed at Entrepreneur.com, March 17, 2010.

Chapter 5

1. Company Web site, http://www.nokia.com, accessed February 18, 2009; "Nokia Joins 8-Megapixel Phone Club with N86," *PC Magazine*, February 18, 2009, http://www.pcmag.com; Moon Ihlwan, "Samsung and LG Take Aim at Nokia," *BusinessWeek*, February 17, 2009, http://www.businessweek.com; Marin Perez, "Nokia Expands E Series of Smartphones," *InformationWeek*, February 17, 2009, http://www.informationweek.com; Marin Perez, "Nokia Jumps into Application Store Game," *InformationWeek*, February 17, 2009, http://www.informationweek.com; "Nokia Eyes Apple's Success in Mobile Downloads," *InternetNews*, February 16, 2009, http://www.internetnews.com.

2. "Advocacy Small Business Statistics and Research," U.S. Small Business Administration, http://web.sba.gov/faqs, accessed April 2, 2010.

3. Ibid.

4. Ibid.

5. John Tozzi, Stacy Perman, and Nick Lieber, "America's Best Young Entrepreneurs 2009," *BusinessWeek*, October 12, 2009, http://www.businessweek.com.

6. Ibid.

7. U.S. Department of Agriculture, *Agricultural Fact Book*, pp. 12–23, http://www.usda.gov/factobook, accessed April 2, 2010.

8. Cider Hill Farm Web site, http://www.ciderhill.com, accessed April 2, 2010.

9. "Advocacy Small Business Statistics and Research."

10. EBeanstalk Web site, http://www.ebeanstalk.com, accessed April 2, 2010; Jamie Roth, "Toy Testers to the Rescue," *ABC News*, http://abclocal.go.com, accessed April 2, 2010.

11. "Advocacy Small Business Statistics and Research."

12. "The Small Business Economy 2008," *Small Business Research Summary*, February 2009, http://www.sba.gov/advo.

13. "Advocacy Small Business Statistics and Research."

14. "The Small Business Economy 2008," *Small Business Research Summary,* no. 340, February 2009, http://www.sba.gov/advo.

15. Facebook Web site, http://www.facebook.com/press, accessed April 2, 2010.

16. Tozzi, Perman, and Leiber, "America's Best Young Entrepreneurs 2009."

17. Ibid.

18. "Advocacy Small Business Statistics and Research."

19. Ibid.

20. Carol Kopp, "The Tragedy of Krispy Kreme," *Yahoo! Finance,* October 13, 2009, http://finance.yahoo.news.

21. Patricia Schaefer, "The Seven Pitfalls of Business Failure and How to Avoid Them," *BusinessKnowHow.com,* http://www.businessknowhow.com/Startup/business-failure.htm, accessed April 2, 2010.

22. Ibid.

23. "Advocacy Small Business Statistics and Research."

24. Leona Liu, "Meet the Celebrity Gardener," *BusinessWeek,* October 13, 2009, http://www.businessweek.com/smallbiz.

25. "Advocacy Small Business Statistics and Research."

26. U.S. Department of Labor, "As an Employer, Are you Engaged in Commerce or in an Industry or Activity Affecting Commerce?", e-laws, Family and Medical Leave Act Advisor, http://www.dol.gov, accessed April 2, 2010.

27. "Business Tax Credits, IRS, http://www.irs.gov/business/small, updated November 3, 2009.

28. TOMs Shoes Web site, http://www.tomsshoes.com/Our-Movement, accessed April 2, 2010.

29. "Top 10 Tips for Writing Your Business Plan," *AllBusiness,* http://www.allbusiness.com/business-planning-structures, accessed April 2, 2010.

30. "Performance Stats for the SBA," *Inc.,* http://www.inc.com, accessed April 2, 2010.

31. "Programs and Services to Help You Start, Grow and Succeed," Small Business Administration, http://www.sba.gov/financialassistance, accessed April 2, 2010.

32. Ibid.

33. "Q&A For Small Business Owners," Small Business Administration, http://www.sba.gov, accessed April 2, 2010.

34. Ibid.

35. "Fact Sheet About U.S. Small Business Administration Disaster Loans," Small Business Administration, http://www.sba.gov, accessed April 2, 2010.

36. "Support Your Business with a Team of Experts," Small Business Administration, http://www.sba.gov/locaresources/index.html, accessed April 2, 2010.

37. "Mission," Thurston County Economic Development Council, http://www.thurstonedc.com, accessed April 2, 2010.

38. Thurston County EDC Web site, http://www.thurstonedc.com, accessed April 2, 2010.

39. National Business Incubator Association, http://www.nbia.org, accessed April 2, 2010.

40. John Tozzi, "Venture Capital's Favorite Startups," *BusinessWeek,* December 19, 2008, http://www.businessweek.com.

41. "Key Facts About Women-Owned Businesses," Center for Women's Business Research, http://www.womensbusinessresearchcenter.org, accessed April 2, 2010.

42. Tozzi, Perman, and Leiber, "America's Best Young Entrepreneurs 2009."

43. "Mentor-Protégé Program," Small Business Administration, http://www.sba.gov, accessed April 2, 2010.

44. Franchise Industries LLC, Statistics, http://www.franchisindustries.com, updated November 24, 2009.

45. Baskin-Robbins Web site, http://www.baskinrobbins.com/franchiseopportunities, accessed April 2, 2010; "2009 Franchise 500," *Entrepreneur,* http://www.entrepreneur.com, accessed April 2, 2010.

46. Subway Web site, http://www.subway.com, accessed April 2, 2010.

47. Edward N. Levitt, "What's So Great About Franchising?," *Franchise Trade,* http://www.franchisetrade.com, accessed April 2, 2010.

48. Ibid.

49. "Why People Are Drawn to Franchising," http://www.articles.directory.com, accessed April 2, 2010.

50. Levitt, "What's So Great About Franchising?"

51. "How Much Does a Franchise Cost?," *AllBusiness.com,* http://www.allbusiness.com, accessed April 2, 2010.

52. Levitt, "What's So Great About Franchising?"

53. Guard-a-Kid, http://www.entrepreneur.com/business-opportunities, accessed April 2, 2010.

54. Ashley M. Heher, "Food Fight: Burger King Franchisees Sue Chain," *Associated Press,* November 12, 2009, http://finance.yahoo.com.

55. Laura Northrup, "Recent Class Action Lawsuits: Are You Eligible?," *The Consumerist,* May 22, 2009, http://consumerist.com.

56. Internal Revenue Service, "IRS Launches Study of S Corporation Reporting Compliance," http://www.irs.gov, accessed April 2, 2010.

57. Corey Rosen, "The Employee Ownership Update," The National Center for Employee Ownership," December 1, 2009, http://www.nceo.org.

58. Michael J. Conway, JD, and Stephen J. Baumgartner, MSc, "The Family-Owned Business," *Graziado Business Report,* Pepperdine University, http://gbr.pepperdine.edu, accessed April 2, 2010.

59. Lara Bricker, "Soda Sparkles on West Coast," *Seacoast Sunday,* November 15, 2009, pp. A1, A11.

60. "About City Year," http://www.cityyear.org, accessed April 2, 2010.

61. "Company Directory by Business Classification," Hoover's, http://www.hoovers.com, accessed April 2, 2010.

62. "Amtrak," Federal Railroad Administration, http://www.fra.dot.gov, accessed April 2, 2010.

63. "Cabot's Cooperative Heritage," Cabot Creamery, http://www.cabotcheese.coop, accessed April 2, 2010.

64. Ibid.

65. Deborah Yao, "Comcast to Buy Controlling Stake in NBC Universal," *Associated Press,* December 3, 2009, http://tech.yahoo.com.

66. Christopher Null, "HP Jump-Starting Compaq Brand With Ultra-cheap Machines," *Yahoo! Tech,* October 13, 2009, http://tech.yahoo.com.

67. "About City Year," http://www.cityyear.org, accessed April 2, 2010; and "City Year on Morning Joe," November 9, 2009, http://www.cityyear.org.

68. Barbara Quinn, "Partnering on Sustainability," *Pollution Engineering,* January 2009, p. 17.

Chapter 6

1. Company Web site, http://www.revfoods.com, accessed February 25, 2009; "Meet Kristin Groos Richmond and KirstenTobey," *Net Impact,* http://www.netimpact.org, accessed February 18, 2009; Nicole Perlroth, "Revolution Foods, Inc.," *BusinessWeek,* http://investing.businessweek.com, accessed February 18, 2009; "Health Nuts," *Forbes,* February 2, 2009, p. 42; Sara Stroud, "Leading the Healthy Lunches Revolution," *San Jose Mercury News,* November 26, 2008, http://www.mercurynews.com; "Starting a Revolution," *Reuters,* March 11, 2008, http://www.reuters.com.

2. Walmart Web site, http://investors.walmartstores.com, accessed March 10, 2010.

3. Janet Steele Holloway, "Former Socialite Makes Horror Profitable," *Women Entrepreneur,* October 29, 2009, http://www.womenentrepreneur.com.

4. David Port, "Earn Your Bones with a Doggie Daycare," *Entrepreneur's StartUps,* March 2010, http://www.entrepreneur.com.

5. "Juha Christensen," *CrunchBase,* http://www.crunchbase.com, accessed March 10, 2010.

6. Navkirat Sodhi, "Meet India's Leading Ladies," *Women Entrepreneur,* September 22, 2009, http://www.womenentrpreneur.com.

7. "Kauffman Index of Entrepreneurial Activity, http://www.kauffman.org, accessed March 10, 2010.

8. Janet Steele Holloway, "Disabled Vet Designs the Perfect Tech Job," *Women Entrepreneur,* February 4, 2010, http://www.womenentrepreneur.com.

9. David Port, "Fitness Franchise Flexes Its Muscle," *Entrepreneur's StartUps,* March 2010, http://www.entrepreneur.com.

10. Laurie Burkitt, "Hint Thirsts for a Bigger Audience," *Forbes.com,* March 8, 2010, http://www.forbes.com.

11. Office of Advocacy, U.S. Small Business Administration, "The Facts About Small Businesses," http://www.sba.gov, accessed March 10, 2010.

12. Hannah Seligson, "Nine Young Chinese Entrepreneurs to Watch," *Forbes.com,* February 28, 2010, http://www.forbes.com.

13. Eve Gumpel, "Gypsy Tea Steeped in Health and Fun," *Women Entrepreneur,* January 24, 2010, http://www.womenentrepreneur.com.

14. "Kauffman Index of Entrepreneurial Activity."

15. Bhati Bead Web site, http://www.bhatibeads.com, accessed March 11, 2010.

16. Niels Bosma, Kent Jones, Erkko Autio and Jonathan Levie, "Global Entrepreneurial Monitor: Executive Report," http://www.gemconsortium.org, accessed March 11, 2010.

17. Sodhi, "Meet India's Leading Ladies."

18. "Entrepreneurship and Innovation Group," Northeastern University, http://www.cba.neu.edu, accessed March 11, 2010.

19. "Leadership and Career Connections," students in Free Enterprise, http://www.sife.org, accessed March 11, 2010.

20. Mark Henricks, "Honor Roll," *Entrepreneur,* http://www.entrepreneur.com, accessed March 11, 2010.

21. "Cool College Startups 2010," *Inc.com,* http://www.inc.com, accessed March 10, 2010.

22. Tamara Schweitzer, "Study: Inc. 500 CEOs Aggressively Use Social Media for Business," *Inc.,* November 25, 2009, http://www.inc.com.

23. "Kauffman Index of Entrepreneurial Activity."

24. "Cool College Start-ups 2010."

25. Ibid.

26. Pamela Canning, "Two Stores Open on Amesbury's Main Street," *Wicked Local Amesbury,* http://www.wickedlocal.com, accessed March 11, 2010.

27. Eve Gumpel, "The Accidental Inventor," *Women Entrepreneur,* August 18, 2009, http://www.womenentrepreneur.com.

28. "A Day in the Life of an Entrepreneur," *Princeton Review,* http://www.princetonreview.com, accessed March 14, 2010.

29. "Oprah Winfrey—About.com Readers' Most Admired Entrepreneur," http://www.entrepreneurs.about.com, accessed March 14, 2010.

30. Dan Moren, "Forget Oprah: Jobs Is Teens' Most Admired Entrepreneur," *About.com,* October 13, 2009, http://pcworld.about.com.

31. Sodhi, "Meet India's Leading Ladies."

32. Company Web site, http://www.bobbibrowncosmetics.com, accessed March 15, 2010; Bobbi Brown and Athena Schindelheim, "How I Did It," *Inc.,* http://www.inc.com, accessed March 15, 2010.

33. Amy S. Choi, "Entrepreneurs Who Thrive on Risky Business," *BusinessWeek,* December 4, 2009, http://www.businessweek.com.

34. Donna Fenn, "The Kid Behind a $170 Million Website," *Inc.com,* http://www.inc.com, accessed March 15, 2010.

35. "Cool College Start-ups 2010."

36. Choi, "Entrepreneurs Who Thrive on Risky Business."

37. Kasey Wehrum, "How I Did It: Ralph Braun of BraunAbility," *Inc.,* December 1, 2009, http://www.inc.com.

38. Jason Daley, "What, No Leotard?," *Entrepreneur,* March 2010, http://www.entrepreneur.com.

39. Tracy Stapp, "Young and Growing," *Entrepreneur,* March 2010, http://www.entrepreneur.com.

40. Robert Tuchman, "The Passion's Only as Good As the Plan," *Entrepreneur,* March 5, 2010, http://www.entrepreneur.com.

41. Nitasha Tiku, "Case Study: When Your Bank Stops Lending," *Inc.,* July 1, 2009, http://www.inc.com.

42. Ibid.

43. Helen Coster, "Offshore Odysseys Is No Typical Timeshare," *Forbes,* January 18, 2010, http://www.forbes.com.

44. Darren Dahl, "How to Read a Term Sheet," *Inc.,* March 1, 2010, http://www.inc.com.

45. Immigration Act of 1990 (IMMACT 90), http://www.labor.state.ny.us, accessed March 16, 2010.

46. Michael Goldman Inc., http://www.michaelgoldman.com, accessed March 16, 2010.

47. "A Culture of Innovation," 3M Web site, http://www.3M.com, accessed March 16, 2010; Michael Goldman Inc., http://www.michaelgoldman.com.

48. 3M Web site, http://www.3M.com.

End of Part 2: Launching Your Entrepreneurial Career

1. Michael Ames, cited in "Is Entrepreneurship for You?" Small Business Administration, http://www.sba.gov, accessed April 9, 2010.

2. U.S. Department of Labor, "Tomorrow's Jobs," *Occupational Outlook Handbook*, 2008–2009 edition, Bureau of Labor Statistics, http://www.bls.gov, accessed April 9, 2010.

3. Alex Salkever, "The Furniture Company Wanted to Sell Him Its Buildings—and Close Down. Should He Buy the Company, Too?" *Inc.*, November 2007, pp. 60–65.

4. U.S. Department of Labor, "Career Guide to Industries: Management, Scientific, and Technical Consulting Services," Bureau of Labor Statistics, http://www.bls.gov, accessed April 9, 2010.

5. U.S. Small Business Administration, "Protecting Your Ideas," http://www.sba.gov, accessed April 9, 2010.

Chapter 7

1. Emily Fredrix, "PepsiCo Will Cut Sodium, Sugar, Fat in Drinks, Chips," *USA Today*, March 29, 2010, http://www.usatoday.com; "Indra Nooyi on Global Growth, Future Plans of PepsiCo," *News Center*, March 25, 2010, http://www.moneycontrol.com; "India's 50 Most Powerful People 2009," *BusinessWeek*, http://images.businessweek.com, 2009; Bruce Einhorn, "Pepsi's Indra Nooyi Focuses on China," *BusinessWeek*, July 2, 2009, http://www.businessweek.com.

2. "The Stop and Shop Supermarket Company," *Hoovers.com*, http://www.hoovers.com, accessed march 28, 2010.

3. Victoria Barrett, "Taleo: Managing During Uncertainty," *Forbes.com*, January 28, 2010, http://www.forbes.com.

4. "*BusinessWeek* Names Customer Service Champs," *Customers 1st Blogspot*, February 23, 2010, http://www.customers1stblogspot.com.

5. Cold Stone Creamery Web site, http://www.coldstonecreamery.com, accessed March 28, 2010.

6. "Zappos.com Power by Service," http://about.zappos.com, accessed March 28, 2010.

7. Helen Coster, "The State of the CEO in 2010," *Forbes.com*, January 21, 2010, http://www.forbes.com.

8. "Fish Announces Retirement; Coffman Assumes CEO Position," *News Articles from St. Joseph's Hospital*, www.stjoeschipfalls.com, accessed April 30, 2010.

9. Christopher Steiner, "Go Green and Stay in the Black," *Forbes.com*, March 8, 2010, http://www.forbes.com.

10. Sarah E. Needleman, "Business Owners Try to Motivate Employees," *The Wall Street Journal*, January 14, 2010, http://online.wsj.com.

11. "America's Coolest College Start-ups 2010," *Inc.*, http://www.inc.com/college/2010/index.html, accessed March 16, 2010.

12. "About Us," Garmin Web site, http://www8.garmin.com, accessed March 29, 2010.

13. Coster, "The State of the CEO in 2010."

14. "Mattel Named One of the World's Most Ethical Companies Again in 2010," *Forbes.com*, March 22, 2010, http://www.forbes.com.

15. Reid Hoffman, as told to Mark Lacter, "How I Did It: Reid Hoffman of LinkedIn," *Inc.com*, May 1, 2009, http://www.inc.com.

16. Staples Announces Finalists of Global Search for the Next Green Office Product," *Boston.com*, March 24, 2010, http://finance.boston.com.

17. Ibid.

18. Sylvia Hui, "British Airways Cabin Crews Strike for 2nd Day," *Associated Press/Forbes.com*, March 21, 2010, http://www.forbes.com.

19. Company Web site, http://www.starbucks.com, accessed March 31, 2010; "Starbucks News! 2010," *Coffee Club Network*, January 22, 2010, http://www.cofeeclubnetwork.com.

20. "Starbucks news! 2010," *Coffee Club Network*.

21. Aaron Gold, "2010 Ford Taurus Drive," *About.com*, January 2010, http://www.about.com.

22. "Quiznos Helps Customers Eat Green," Quiznos Public Relations, February 25, 2010, http://pr.quiznos.com.

23. "2009 College Start-ups: Where Are They Now?," *Inc.com*, http://www2.inc.com, accessed March 16, 2010.

24. "How Companies Manage the Front Line Today," *McKinsey & Company*, pp 1–2.

25. Jena McGregor, Alli McConnon, and David Kiley, "Customer Service in a Shrinking Economy," *BusinessWeek*, March 9, 2010, http://www.businessweek.com.

26. Company Web site, http://www.apple.com, accessed April 1, 2010.

27. "CR's 100 Best Corporate Citizens 2010," *CR Magazine*, http://www.thecro.org, accessed March 16, 2010.

28. Bruce Horovitz, "CEO Profile: Campbell Exec Nears Extraordinary Goal," *USA Today*, January 26, 2009, http://www.usatoday.com.

29. Scott D. Anthony, "Google's Management Style Grows Up," *BusinessWeek*, March 9, 2010, http://www.businessweek.com.

30. Dean Foust, "US Airways: After the Miracle on the Hudson," *BusinessWeek*, March 9, 2010, http://www.businessweek.com.

31. "Corporate Information," Google Web site, http://www.google.com/corporate/culture.html, accessed March 30, 2010.

32. "Culture," Walt Disney Company Web site, http://corporate.disney.go.com/careers/culture.html, accessed March 30, 2010.

33. Ben Fritz, "Company Town," *Los Angeles Times*, March 30, 2010, http://latimesblogs.latimes.com.

34. "Enterprise Facts," Enterprise Rent-A-Car Web site, http://www.erac.com, accessed March 30, 2010.

35. "Products and Services," 3M Web site, http://www.3M.com, accessed April 5, 2010.

36. Brandon Gutman, "Zappos' Marketing Chief: 'Customer Service Is the New Marketing!' " *Fast Company*, March 15, 2010, www.fastcompany.com.

37. Mike Gordon, Chris Musso, Eric Rebentisch, and Nisheeth Gupta, "The Path to Successful New Products," *McKinsey Quarterly*, January 7, 2010, http://www.forbes.com.

38. Jason Del Rey, "How I Did It: Omniture's Josh James," *Inc.com*, March 1, 2010, http://www.inc.com.

Chapter 8

1. Company Web site, http://www.netapp.com, accessed February 25, 2009; "100 Best Companies to Work for, 2009," *Fortune*, http://money.cnn.com, accessed February 24, 2009; "NetApp: Culture-Values-Leadership—#1 on the 2009 List of the 100 Best Companies to Work for," Great Places to Work Institute, http://www.greatplacetowork.com, accessed February 24, 2009; Jim Finkle, "NetApp Revenue Misses Forecasts, Shares Fall," *Forbes*, http://www.forbes.com, February 11, 2009; Robert Levering and Milton Moskowitz, "And the Winners Are . . . ," *Fortune*, February 2, 2009, p. 67.

2. Jessica Dickler, "Great Job Openings, No Candidates," *CNNMoney.com*, November 7, 2009, http://cnn.money.com.

3. Alicia Chang, "Aerospace Companies Target Young Recruits Online," *Army Times*, http://www.armytimes.com, accessed April 13, 2010.

4. Jobs in Pods, http://www.jobsinpods.com, accessed April 13, 2010.

5. "Uniform Employee Selection Guidelines Interpretation and Clarification," *Uniform Guidelines.com*, http://www.uniformguidelines.com, accessed April 20, 2010.

6. Peter M. LaSorsa, "UPS Settles EEOC Lawsuit for $46,000," *Illinois Sexual Harassment Attorney Blog*, February 20, 2010, http://www.illinoissexualharassmentblog.com.

7. Hank Hayes, "Tennessee House Subcommittee Advances English-Only Bill," *Times News.net.* March 3, 2010, http://www.timesnews.net.

8. "Executive Recruiting Advice—Don't Underestimate the Cost of a Mis-Hire," *Fortune 100 Best Companies to Work For*, http://www.fortune100bestcompaniestoworkfor.com, accessed April 13, 2010.

9. "Verizon's Employee Training Programs Ranked Among the Top Four in the U.S.," Verizon Web site, February 2, 2010, http://newscenter.verizon.com.

10. "McDonald's Puts Apprenticeships on the Menu," http://www.aboutmcdonalds.com, accessed April 15, 2010.

11. "Welcome to EYU," http://www.ey.com, accessed April 15, 2010.

12. "Systems Integration Consulting Training," https://microsite.accenture.com, accessed April 13, 2010.

13. Glimmerglass Web site, http://www.glimmerglassgroup.com, accessed April 20, 2010.

14. Julia Werdigier, "Rothschilds Bring in an Outsider to Run the Show," *The New York Times*, March 29, 2010, http://www.nytimes.com.

15. Samuel A. Culbert, "Yes, Everyone Really Does Hate Performance Reviews," *The Wall Street Journal*, April 19, 2010, http://finance.yahoo.com.

16. "Turn Your Performance Review System into One That Works," *Quality Digest Magazine*, http://www.qualitydigest.com, accessed April 14, 2010.

17. "Gather and Analyze 360 Degree Feedback More Quickly and Easily," Halogen Software, http://www.halogensoftware.com, accessed April 13, 2010.

18. "25 Top-Paying Companies," *CNN Money.com*, http://money.cnn.com, accessed April 14, 2010.

19. "S.181 Lilly Ledbetter Fair Pay Act of 2009," *Open Congress*, http://www.opencongress.org, accessed April 28,2010.

20. "Employer Costs for Employee Compensation," Bureau of Labor Statistics, March 10, 2010, http://www.bls.gov.

21. "Paid Family Leave," Employment Development Department, http://www.edd.ca.gov, accessed April 14, 2010.

22. Lance Whitney, "SAS, Google Top Fortune's Best-Employer List," *CNET News*, January 25, 2010, http://news.cnet.com.

23. Christina Breda Antoniades, "Best Places to Work 2010," *Baltimore* magazine, http://www.baltimoremgazine.net, accessed April 14, 2010.

24. "Advantages and Disadvantages of Paid Time Off," *The Thriving Small Business*, March 19, 2010, http://www.thethrivingsmallbusiness.com.

25. Eugene Eteris, "European Social Market Economy: Flexibility Issues," *The Baltic Course*, March 16, 2010, http://www.baltic-course.com.

26. "Things You Should Know About BidShift," San Angelo Community Medical Center, http://www.sacmc.com, accessed April 14, 2010.

27. "Case Study: Macy's," *Commuter Challenge*, http://www.commuterchallenge.org, accessed April 14, 2010.

28. "Economists Push for Federal Job-Sharing Program," *Washington Independent*, February 24, 2010, http://washingtonindependent.com.

29. "Study: Remote-Work Programs Benefit Employers Too," *Microsoft News Center*, March 11, 2010, http://www.microsoft.com.

30. Anita Cooper, "Telecommuting," *Associated Content*, http://www.associatedcontent.com, accessed April 14, 2010.

31. Lisa Orrell, "5 Tips to Retain Gen Y Talent," *Women Entrepreneur*, April 12, 2010, http://www.womenentrepreneur.com.

32. Marshall Goldsmith, "How to Keep Good Employees in a Bad Economy," February 26, 2010, http://blogs.hbr.org.

33. Dustin Ensinger, "Why Layoffs Are Not Beneficial to Companies," *Economy in Crisis*, February 8, 2010, http://www.economyincrisis.org.

34. Ibid.

35. Christopher D. Zatzik, Mitchell L. Marks, Roderick D. Iverson, "Downsizing Case Studies," *MIT Sloan Management Review*, January 7, 2010, http://www.nationalpost.com.

36. Mike Rosenberg, "United Airlines Outsourcing Leads to Questions Over Aircraft Safety," *Inside Bay Area*, February 19, 2010, http://www.insidebayarea.com.

37. "Maslow's Hierarchy of Needs," *Accel-Team.com*, http://www.accel-team.com, accessed April 14, 2010.

38. Maggie Ginsberg-Schutz, "2010 Best Places to Work," *Madison Magazine*, http://www.madisonmagazine.com, accessed April 14, 2010.

39. Kenneth A. Dodge, "Make CEOs Help the Little Guy," *Post-Gazette*, February 7, 2010, http://www.post-gazette.com.

40. "Our Company," The Pampered Chef, http://www.pamperedchef.com, accessed April 14, 2010.

41. "Rotational Training Programs," http://www.emc.com, accessed April 14, 2010.

42. "Union Members Summary," Bureau of Labor Statistics, January 22, 2010, http://www.bls.gov.

43. "Major Work Stoppages (Annual) News Release," Bureau of Labor Statistics, February 10, 2010, http://www.bls.gov.

44. Jamie Doward, "BA Strike: Airline and Union Swap Barbs on Second Weekend of Walkouts," *Guardian*, March 27, 2010, http://www.guardian.co.uk.

45. Ibid.

46. James Sherk, "Majority of Union Members Now Work for the Government," *The Heritage Foundation*, January 22, 2010, no. 2773.

Chapter 9

1. Company Web site, http://www.ideo.com, accessed February 27, 2009; "IDEO Innovating Product Design Team," *Smithsonian National Museum of American History*, http://invention.smithsonian.org, accessed February 27, 2009; "Finding Innovation beyond Imagination," *CME Group Magazine*, Winter 2008, http://www.cmegroup.com; Bruce Nussbaum, "IDEO's Tim Brown on Innovation in the Harvard Business Review," *BusinessWeek*, June 25, 2008, http://www.businessweek.com.

2. Anderson & Associates Web site, http://www.andassoc.com, accessed April 19, 2010.

3. Becka Livesay, "The Culture Change Way: Empowering Direct Care Workers to Improve Care," *Direct Care Alliance*, March 2010, http://blog.directcarealliance.org.

4. "A Statistical Profile of Employee Ownership," The National Center for Employee Ownership, updated March 2010, http://www.nceo.org.

5. "Employee Stock Options and Ownership (ESOP)," http://www.referenceforbusiness.com, accessed April 19, 2010.

6. "A Statistical Profile of Employee Ownership," The National Center for Employee Ownership, updated March 2010, http://www.nceo.org.

7. "Employee Ownership as a Retirement Plan," The National Center for Employee Ownership, http://www.nceo.org, accessed April 19, 2010.

8. "Employee Stock Options Fact Sheet," The National Center for Employee Ownership, http://www.nceo.org, accessed April 19, 2010.

9. Ibid.

10. Toyota Web site, http://www.toyota.com/recall, accessed May 10, 2010.

11. "Our Core Values," Whole Foods Market Web site, http://www.wholefoodsmarket.com, accessed April 19, 2010.

12. "Harley-Davidson: The Sound of a Legend," http://www.lmsintl.com, accessed April 19, 2010.

13. BBC Web site, http://www.bbc.co.uk, accessed May 10, 2010; Lynda Gratton, Andreas Voigt, and Tamara Erickson, "Bridging Faultlines in Diverse Teams," *MIT Sloan Management Review*, Summer 2007, pp. 22-29.

14. Kate Rogers, "Commitment to Standards, Mission, Clients and Fun," *The Nonprofit Times*, April 1, 2010, http://nptimes.com.

15. Robert Grice, "How to Build a Unified Team," *Helium*, http://www.helium.com, accessed April 19, 2010.

16. "Alliance with Rock Valley Designed to Better Prepare Public School Graduates for College," District 205 Web Site, http://webs.rps.com, accessed April 19, 2010.

17. Nick Grabbe, "Experts: Don't Fear Workplace Conflict," *Gazettenet.com*, March 1, 2010, http://www.gazettenet.com.

18. Ken Thomas and Larry Margasak, "Toyota Waited Months to Tell U.S. About Sticking Accelerator Fixes It Gave to Dealers in Europe," *Associated Press*, April 6, 2010, http://blog.cleveland.com.

19. Ibid.

20. David Woods, "i-level Redesigns Its Employee reward Communication Strategy," *HR Magazine*, March 8, 2010, http://www.humanresourcesmagazine.co.uk.

21. Norma Chew, "Are You a Good Listener?" *Associated Content*, http://www.associatedcontent.com, accessed April 19, 2010.

22. "Why Outsource Email?" DakotaPro.biz Web site, http://www.dakotapro.biz, accessed April 19, 2010.

23. "Expand Trust in Your Organization," *Peter Stark.com*, http://www.peterstark.com, accessed April 19, 2010.

24. Joni F. Johnston, "How to Deal with Office Gossip," *Ezine Articles*, http://ezinearticles.com, accessed April 19, 2010.

25. John Boe, "How to Read Your Prospect Like a Book!," John Boe International, http://johnboe.com, accessed April 19, 2010.

26. Amar Toor, "Nestlé's Palm Oil PR Crisis Pervades Facebook," *Switched*, March 22, 2010, http://www.switched.com.

27. "Nestlé's Social Media PR Crisis: How Would You Handle It?" Pierce Mattie Public Relations, http://www.piercemattiepublicrelations.com, accessed April 19, 2010.

28. Emily Steel, "Nestlé Takes a Beating on Social-Media Sites," *The Wall Street Journal*, March 29, 2010, http://online.wsj.com.

Chapter 10

1. Tom Wright, "Pakistan Defends Its Soccer Industry," *The Wall Street Journal*, April 26, 2010, http://online.wsj.com; "Adidas Unveils World Cup Final Match Ball—Jo'bulani," *Shine2010*, April 20, 2010, http://www.shine2010.co.za; "Official 2010 FIFA World Cup Match Ball," *For Men Only*, March 1, 2010, http://toffsmen.com; Andrew Nusca, "The Science Behind the 2010 World Cup Soccer Ball, Adidas Jabulani," *SmartPlanet*, December 7, 2009, http://www.smartplanet.com; "Adidas Jabulani Official Match Ball of the 2010 FIFA World Cup," *Adidas Press Room*, December 4, 2009, http://www.press.adidas.com.

2. "William Levitt," *Entrepreneur*, http://www.entrepreneur.com, accessed April 26, 2010.

3. "Honda Builds Record 84% of 2009 U.S. Auto Sales in North America," *The Auto Channel*, http://www.theautochannel.com, accessed April 26, 2010.

4. Lydia Dishman, "Retire? Forget About It," *Entrepreneur*, January 11, 2010, http://www.entrepreneur.com.

5. Barbara Quinn, "Carving a Roadway to Sustainability," *Pollution Engineering*, May 2010, p. 17.

6. "LEED," U.S. Green Building Council Web site, http://www.usgbc.org, accessed May 27, 2010.

7. "Saks Will Use Kiva Robots," *The Boston Globe*, January 26, 2010, http://www.boston.com.

8. Brady Weber, "Machine Vision Protects Pharmaceutical Packaging," *Control Engineering*, February 1, 2010, http://www.controleng.com.

9. Clara Maria Cabrera, "CAD/CAM Dental Technology," *Associated Content*, http://www.associatedcontent.com, accessed April 26, 2010.

10. Roger Schreffler, "Nissan's Flexible Manufacturing Moves to India, Other JVs," *Wards Auto.com*, February 3, 2010, http://www.wardsauto.com.

11. Vince Lapinski, "We Are Print," Man Roland Web site, http://www.manroland.us.com.

12. Anupam Govil, "Shifting of the Global Sourcing Axis," *Near Shore Americas*, April 6, 2010, http;//www.nearshoreamericas.com.

13. Mike Pare, "VW Prototypes on Local Horizon," *Chattanooga Times Free Press*, January 11, 2010, http://www.timesfreepress.com.

14. "Holland Car's Assembly Line to Evolve," *Fortune,* April 18, 2010, http://www.addisfortune.com.

15. "Advantages and Disadvantages of Outsourcing," *The Thriving Small Business,* February 8, 2010, http://www.thethrivingsmallbusiness.com.

16. Marcia Pledger, "Outsourcing Tool Product Too Costly," *The Plain Dealer,* January 10, 2010, http://blog.cleveland.com.

17. "Supplier Mangement," Ariba Web site, http://www.ariba.com, accessed April 26, 2010.

18. Shruti Date Singh, "Deere Shortage Prompts Kansas Farmer to Buy Dragotec," *Bloomberg Businessweek,* April 26, 2010, http://www.businessweek.com.

19. "Roundy's Implements Inventory Management System," *Supermarket News,* January 6, 2010, http://www.supermarketnews.com.

20. "Oatey Company Selects Datalliance VMI," *News Blaze,* April 26, 2010, http://newsblaze.com.

21. "Seattle Children's Hospital Saves $2.5 Million in First Year with Streamlined Inventory Distribution," http://www.hfma.org, accessed April 26, 2010.

22. "Allan Candy Company," *Microsoft Case Studies,* April 19, 2010, http://www.microsoft.com.

23. Judy Miller, "Still Made in America: The Super Bowl Footballs from Ada, Ohio," *Encyclopedia Britannica Blog,* February 1, 2010, http://www.britannica.com.

24. JETCAM Web site, http://www.jetcam.com, accessed April 26, 2010.

25. "Success Stories: Sleepmaster, LTD," *User solutions.com,* http://www.usersolutions.com, accessed April 26, 2010.

26. "Contrite Facebook CEO Promises new Privacy Controls," *Yahoo! News,* May 24, 2010, http://news.yahoo.com.

27. Jamie Liddell, "Top Ten Tips for Better Benchmarking," *SSON Network,* http://www.ssonetwork.com, accessed April 26, 2010.

28. Vic Nanda, "Preempting Problems," *Six Sigma Forum Magazine,* February 2010, pp. 9–18.

29. "Maintaining the Benefits and Continual Improvement," International Organization for Standardization, http://www.iso.org, accessed April 26, 2010.

Part 3 Launching Your Management Career

1. U.S. Department of Labor, "Tomorrow's Jobs," *Occupational Outlook Handbook, 2010–2011 edition,* Bureau of Labor Statistics, accessed June 11, 2010, http://www.bls.gov.

2. U.S. Department of Labor, "Administrative Services Managers," *Occupational Outlook Handbook, 2010–2011 edition,* Bureau of Labor Statistics, accessed June 11, 2010, http://www.bls.gov.

3. U.S. Department of Labor, "Construction Managers," *Occupational Outlook Handbook, 2010–2011 edition,* Bureau of Labor Statistics, accessed June 11, 2010, http://www.bls.gov.

4. U.S. Department of Labor, "Food Service Managers," *Occupational Outlook Handbook, 2010–2011 edition,* Bureau of Labor Statistics, accessed June 11, 2010, http://www.bls.gov.

5. U.S. Department of Labor, "Human Resources, Training, and Labor Relations Managers and Specialists," *Occupational Outlook Handbook, 2010–2011 edition,* Bureau of Labor Statistics, accessed June 11, 2010, http://www.bls.gov.

6. U.S. Department of Labor, "Lodging Managers," *Occupational Outlook Handbook, 2010–2011 edition,* Bureau of Labor Statistics, accessed June 11, 2010, http://www.bls.gov.

7. U.S. Department of Labor, "Medical and Health Services Managers," *Occupational Outlook Handbook, 2010–2011 edition,* Bureau of Labor Statistics, accessed June 11, 2010, http://www.bls.gov.

8. U.S. Department of Labor, "Purchasing Managers, Buyers, and Purchasing Agents," *Occupational Outlook Handbook, 2010–2011 edition,* Bureau of Labor Statistics, accessed June 11, 2010, http://www.bls.gov.

9. U.S. Department of Labor, "Industrial Production Managers," *Occupational Outlook Handbook, 2010–2011 edition,* Bureau of Labor Statistics, accessed June 11, 2010, http://www.bls.gov.

Chapter 11

1. Company Web site, http://petshotel.com, accessed March 2, 2009; Carol Wolf, "Passion for Pets Makes PetSmart a Success," *The Seattle Times,* http://seattletimes.com, accessed March 2, 2009; Lawrence Rothman, "PetSmart: A Doggie Paradise," *Banking and Finance Crossing,* http://www.bankingandfinancecrossing.com, accessed March 2, 2009; "Hiring and Developing World Class Talent," *HR Strategy Forum,* February 11, 2009, http://www.hrstrategyforum.org; "Secret Shopper—Pet Product Reviews," *Dogtime.com,* September 23, 2008, http://blogs.dogtime.com.

2. American Marketing Association, "AMA Adopts New Definition of Marketing," *Marketing-Power,* www.danavan.net, accessed March 25, 2010.

3. Company Web site, http://www.target.com, accessed March 25, 2010; Brad Gilligan, "Target Starts Mobile Coupon Program," *All Tech Considered,* March 11, 2010, http://www.npr.org; Business Wire, "Target Launches First-Ever Scannable Mobile Coupon Program," *MarketWatch,* March 10, 2010, http://www.marketwatch.com; Marguerite Reardon, "Attention Shoppers: Target Offers Mobile Coupons," *CNET News,* March 10, 2010, http://news.cnet.com.

4. Company Web site, http://www.apple.com, accessed March 25, 2010; "Apple IPAD: Get to Know the Apple iPad," *NY Breaking News,* n.d., http://www.nybreakingnews.com; Arik Hesseldahl, "Apple's Hard iPad Sell," *BusinessWeek,* February 5, 2010, http://www.businessweek.com; Erica Ogg, "Who Will Buy the iPad?" *CNET News,* January 28, 2010, http://news.cnet.com.

5. "Facts and Figures about Charitable Organizations," *Independent Sector,* October 30, 2009, http://www.independentsector.org.

6. Lester M. Salamon, Megan A. Haddock, S. Wojciech Sokolowski, and Helen S. Tice, *Measuring Civil Society and Volunteering: Initial Findings from Implementation of the UN Handbook on Nonprofit Institutions,* Working Paper No. 23 (Baltimore: Johns Hopkins Center for Civil Society Studies, 2007), http://www.jhu.edu.

7. Join the Team Web site, https://www.jointheteam.com, accessed March 25, 2010; NFL and the United Way, http://www.unitedwaycapitalarea.org, accessed March 25, 2010.

8. Company Web site, http://www.avoncompany.com, accessed March 25, 2010; "Avon Foundation for Woman Grants $500,000 to the U.S. Department of State Secretary's Fund for Global Women's Leadership," press release, March 11, 2010, http://multivu.prnewswire.com.

9. "T-Mobile Brings Catherine Zeta-Jones Back," *The Wall Street Journal*, May 20, 2009, http://blogs.wsj.com.

10. "The Adventures of Quatchi, Miga, and Sumi Begin in Earnest," Vancouver 2010, http://www.vancouver2010.com, accessed March 25, 2010.

11. "Tour de Cure 2010," American Diabetes Association, http://tour.diabetes.org, accessed March 25, 2010.

12. Company Web site, http://www.deloitte.com, accessed March 25, 2010; "United Way Alternative Spring Break Sponsored by Deloitte," United Way, http://www.liveunited.org/asb.

13. Company Web site, http://www.seventhgeneration.com, accessed March 25, 2010.

14. Oprah's Angel Network Web site, http://oprahsangelnetwork.org, accessed March 25, 2010.

15. Take Care Clinic Web site, http://www.takecarehealth.com, accessed March 25, 2010; BusinessWire, "Take Care Clinics at Select Walgreens Offer Families Convenient and Affordable Option for Camp and Sports Physicals," press release, MarketWatch, March 10, 2010, http://www.marketwatch.com; Pamela Lewis Dolan, "Retail Clinics: Struggling to Find Their Place," *American Medical News,* March 1, 2010, http://www.ama-assn.org/amednews.

16. Marco Lui, "Subway Plans to Open 500 Stores across China in Next Five Years," *BusinessWeek*, March 11, 2010, http://www.businessweek.com; Farah Master, "Subway Eyes Matching McDonalds in China in 10 Years," *Reuters*, March 8, 2010, http://www.reuters.com.

17. Blank Label Web site, http://www.blank-label.com, accessed March 25, 2010; Spreadshirt Web site, http://www.spreadshirt.com, accessed March 25, 2010.

18. Chris Foreman, "iPhone Still Second-Place US Smartphone While Android Grows," *Ars Technica*, March 11, 2010, http://arstechnica.com; Philip Elmer-DeWitt, "ComScore: Android Gains on the iPhone," *Fortune Brainstorm Tech,* March 10, 2010, http://brainstormtech.blogs.fortune.cnn.com.

19. Christopher T. Heun, "Procter & Gamble Readies Online Market-Research Push," *InformationWeek,* http://www.informationweek.com, accessed March 29, 2010; Mark Clothier, "P&G's McDonald Pins Growth on Closer Shave than Mumbai Barber," *BusinessWeek*, March 11, 2010, http://www.businessweek.com.

20. Stephanie Rosenbloom, "In Bid to Sway Sales, Cameras Track Shoppers," *The New York Times*, March 20, 2010, http://www.nytimes.com.

21. Clothier, "P&G's McDonald Pins Growth on Closer Shave."

22. Pottery Barn Kids Web site, http://www.potterybarnkids.com, accessed March 25, 2010; "Unica Releases 'The State of Marketing 2010' Results," *CNNMoney.com*, March 10, 2010; http://money.cnn.com.

23. "About Idea Storm," Dell Web site, http://www.ideastorm.com, accessed March 25, 2010.

24. Declan McCullagh, "Why No One Cares about Privacy Anymore," *CNET News,* March 12, 2010, http://news.cnet.com; Leah Betancourt, "How Companies Are Using Your Social Media Data," *Mashable,* March 2, 2010, http://mashable.com; Jim Cooper, "Yahoo's Carol Bartz Touts Data," *Mediaweek,* March 1, 2010, http://www.mediaweek.com.

25. Company Web site, http://turiyamedia.com, accessed March 25, 2010; "Turiya Media Targets Game Publishers with Behavioral Data Mining," *GamesBeat,* March 10, 2010, http://games.venturebeat.com.

26. Amanda Lenhart, Kristen Purcell, Aaron Smith, and Kathryn Zickuhr, "Social Media and Young Adults," Pew Internet and American Life Project, February 3, 2010, http://www.pewinternet.org.

27. Andrea Chang, "Buyers at Toy Fair in New York Foresee Another Cutthroat Holiday Season," *Los Angeles Times,* February 15, 2010, http://articles.latimes.com; Stephanie Rosenbloom, "Toys 'R' Us Trims Losses by Making a Hamster Hot," *The New York Times*, December 19, 2009, http://www.nytimes.com.

28. Nelson Ireson, "2012 Ford Police Interceptor: Taurus Does Law and Order," *Motor Authority*, March 12, 2010, http://www.motorauthority.com; Brent Snavely, "Ford to Unveil Police Interceptor," *Frreep.com,* March 12, 2010, http://www.freep.com; "Ford Unveils Next-Generation, V-6-Only Taurus Police Car," *USA Today*, March 12, 2010, http://content.usatoday.com.

29. Emily Sohn, "Why (Most) Women Like to Shop," *DiscoveryNews*, December 11, 2009, http://news.discovery.com.

30. Marissa Miley and Ann Mack, "The New Female Consumer: The Rise of the Real Mom," *Advertising Age* White Paper, November 16, 2009, http://adage.com.

31. Constance Waschull, ed., "Women: The Fragile Financial Superpower," *Allianz Knowledge,* updated February 4, 2010, http://knowledge.allianz.com.

32. U.S. Census Bureau, "Resident Population Projections by Sex and Age: 2010 to 2050," *Statistical Abstract of the United States,* http://www.census.gov, accessed March 25, 2010.

33. Paul Briand, "Baby Boomers Shunning Usual Retirement Haunts," *Examiner.com,* March 26, 2010, http://www.examiner.com.

34. "Nielsen: Shopping Habits by Generation," *Convenience Store News,* March 29, 2010, http://www.csnews.com.

35. April MacIntyre, "TCA Tip Sheet: NBCU to Roll Out 'The mun2 Look' Coming Jan. 23," *Monsters and Critics,* January 7, 2010, http://www.monstersandcritics.com.

36. Judy Keen, "For Immigrants, Living the Dream Is Getting Tougher," *USA Today,* June 16, 2009, http://www.usatoday.com.

37. Company Web site, http://www.gmblogs.com, accessed March 25, 2010.

38. Ruth Mantell, "Despite Tough Times, Parents Spend Big on Kids," *MarketWatch,* May 4, 2010, www.marketwatch.com.

39. Company Web site, http://www.crateandbarrel.com, accessed March 25, 2010.

40. "Sodexho Marriott Services," *Claritas,* www.claritas.com, accessed March 29, 2010.

41. Katherine Glover, "More Bad News for Starbucks as McCafe Moves in For the Kill," *BNET,* April 20, 2009, http://industry.bnet.com.

42. Resources for Entrepreneurs staff, "Consumer Habits Could Be Permanently Changed by Recession," *Resources for Entrepreneurs,* March 25, 2010, http://www.gaebler.com.

43. Company Web site, http://www.timberland.com, accessed March 29, 2010.

44. Company Web site, http://www.marriott.com, accessed March 29, 2010.

45. Company Web site, http://www.apple.com/ipod/nike, accessed March 29, 2010.

46. Company Web site, http://www.netcall.com, accessed March 29, 2010.

Chapter 12

1. Company Web site, http://www.buckle.com, accessed March 2, 2009; "Brief: The Buckle January Same-Store Sales," *Forbes*, February 5, 2009, http://www.forbes.com; Christopher Palmeri, "Youth Will Be Served," *BusinessWeek*, January 26–February 2, 2009, p. 20; "The Buckle, Inc., Reports December 2008 Net Sales," *StreetInsider.com*, January 8, 2009, http://www.streetinsider.com; Kristin Graham, "A Retail Play for 2009," *The Motley Fool*, December 26, 2008, http://www.fool.com; Katherine Field, "Buckle Up," *Chain Store Age*, September 2008, http://www.chainstoreage.com.

2. Stan Schroeder, "Gartner: Most Kids Will Use PCs with Touchscreens by 2015," *Mashable*, April 7, 2010, http://mashable.com.

3. Associated Press, "Pepsi to Distribute New Line of Tampico Drinks," *msn.com*, April 9, 2010, http://news.moneycentral.msn.com.

4. General Mills, "Nourish Your Inner Goddess with the Goodness of New Yoplait Greek Yogurt," press release, March 4, 2010, http://www.generalmills.com; Company Web sites, http://www.generalmills.com, http://www.warnerbros.com, http://www.legendarypictures.com, accessed April 30, 2010.

5. Joachim Ebert, Shiv Shivaraman, and Paul Carrannanto, "Driving Growth through Ultra-Low-Cost Product Development," *Industry Week*, February 17, 2010, http://www.industryweek.com.

6. Tony Bradley, "Kindle Apps Blur the Line Between Gadgets," *PC World*, January 21, 2010, http://www.pcworld.com; Dan Frommer, "Amazon Rushes Kindle iPad App, Available in Time for iPad Launch," *SF Gate*, April 2, 2010, http://www.sfgate.com.

7. Alfred Poor, "HDTV Almanac—LED Backlight Prices Falling," *HDTV Magazine*, February 22, 2010, http://www.hdtvmagazine.com.

8. Elaine Wong, "Noxzema Tells Consumers to 'Come Clean,' " *Brandweek*, May 17, 2010, www.brandweek.com.

9. Matthew Moskovciak, "Blue-ray Quick Guide," *CNET Reviews*, February 25, 2010, http://reviews.cnet.com.

10. Adam Tschorn, "Old Spice Talks to the Ladies, Man," *Los Angeles Times*, March 6, 2010, http://articles.latimes.com; Drew Grant, "Old Spice's Spicy Ad Campaign," *Mediaite*, February 20, 2010, http://www.mediaite.com; Liz Shannon Miller, "The Viral Genius of Wieden+Kennedy's New Old Spice Campaign," *NewTeeVee*, February 19, 2010, http://newteevee.com.

11. Company Web site, http://www.mattel.com, accessed April 30, 2010; Amy Graff, "Are Today's Girls Abandoning Their Dolls Too Soon?" *SF Gate*, April 6, 2010, http://www.sfgate.com; Andrea Chang, "Toy Fair 2010: After Strong Holiday Sales, Barbie Flaunts New Jobs and Fashions," *Los Angeles Times*, February 14, 2010, http://latimesblogs.latimes.com; The White House Project, "Barbie Celebrates 125th Career with Global Initiative to Inspire Girls," press release, January 21, 2010, http://thewhitehouseproject.org.

12. Company Web site, http://www.febreze.com, accessed April 30, 2010; *PR Newswire*, "P&G Leads 2010 Edison Best New Product Award Finalists with Five Nods," press release, February 11, 2010, http://www.prnewswire.com.

13. Amy McCullough, "Plastic Helmets Fail Tests," *Army Times*, January 11, 2010, http://www.armytimes.com.

14. Company Web site, http://www.ea.com, accessed April 30, 2010; Ben Gilbert, "Report: EA Planning Premium, Pre-Launch DLC for Retail Games at $10–$15," *Joystiq*, March 22, 2010, http://www.joystiq.com.

15. Tom Merritt, "Top 10 Worst Products," *CNET*, www.cnet.com, accessed April 30, 2010; John Biggs, "Ten Years: The Biggest Product Flops of the Decade," *CrunchGear*, December 31, 2009, http://www.crunchgear.com.

16. CBS4, "Centennial IKEA Construction Begins May 4," April 20, 2010, http://cbs4denver.com; Paula Moore, "IKEA Tackles Tricky Terrain," *Denver Business Journal*, October 16, 2009, http://denverbizjournals.com.

17. J. Jennings Moss, "The Brand Stand," *Portfolio.com*, April 12, 2010, http://www.portfolio.com; "Survey: FedEx in Top 10 for Brand Awareness," *Memphis Business Journal*, April 12, 2010, http://memphis.bizjournals.com.

18. Company Web site, http://www.quiznos.com, accessed April 30, 2010; Quiznos, "Quiznos Rolls Out Green Packaging," press release, February 23, 2010, http://www.chainleader.com.

19. "FDA Issues Open Letter on Nutrition Labeling," *Packaging Digest*, March 4, 2010, http://www.packagingdigest.com; Robin Shreeves, "FDA Could Pull Foods over Labeling," *MNN Mother Nature Network*, March 4, 2010, http://www.mnn.com; U.S. Food and Drug Administration, "FDA Calls on Food Companies to Correct Labeling Violations; FDA Commissioner Issues an Open Letter to the Industry," March 3, 2010, http://www.fda.gov.

20. R. Kayne, "What Are Unlocked Cell Phones?" *wiseGeek*, April 26, 2010, http://www.wisegeek.com; Phil Goldstein, "Google's Nexus One Promises New Distribution Channel for Smartphones," *FierceWireless*, January 5, 2010, http://www.fiercewireless.com; Tom Krazit, "Google's Mobile Hopes Go Beyond Nexus One," *CNET News*, January 5, 2010, http://new.cnet.com.

21. Company Web site, http://www.fedex.com, accessed April 30, 2010.

22. U.S. Census Bureau, *"County Business Patterns,"* http://www.census.gov, accessed May 24, 2010; Bureau of Labor Statistics, "Occupational Outlook Handbook, 2010–11 Edition," http://www.bls.gov, accessed April 30, 2010.

23. Company Web site, http://retailadvantagegroup.com, accessed April 30, 2010.

24. U.S. Census Bureau, "Quarterly Retail E-Commerce Sales, 4th Quarter 2009," February 16, 2010, http://www.census.gov.

25. Company Web site, http://saksfifthavenue.com, accessed April 30, 2010; Kelly O'Reilly, "Saks' Special Delivery to 10022-SHOE," *NBC New York*, March 15, 2010, http://www.nbcnewyork.com; Jennifer Paull, "Saks Fifth Avenue Introduces Special Delivery: The Hottest Designer Shoes for Spring," *StyleList*, March 14, 2010, http://www.stylelist.com.

26. Company Web site, http://www.seventhgeneration.com, accessed April 30, 2010; Romy Ribitzky, "Talking about an Ad Generation," *Portfolio.com*, February 11, 2010, http://www.portfolio.com; Romy Ribitzky, "7 Facts about Seventh Generation," *Portfolio.com*, February 11, 2010, http://www.portfolio.com; Elaine Wong, "How Seventh Generation Is Going Mainstream," *Brandweek*, January 26, 2010, http://www.brandweek.com.

27. Company Web site, http://www.polaroid.com, accessed April 30, 2010; "Starlight to Expand Digital Entertainment Product Category under the Polaroid Brand," press release, March 24, 2010, http://www.foxbusiness.com.

28. Company Web site, http://www.traderjoes.com, accessed April 30, 2010.

29. Petco Web site, http://www.petco.com; PetSmart Web site, http://www.petsmart.com, both accessed April 30, 2010.

30. Company Web site, http://www.victoriagardensie.com, accessed April 30, 2010; Kristi Reedy, "Victoria Gardens Adds Sponsors to Offer Shoppers

a True Lifestyle Center," press release, March 23, 2010, http://www.free-press-release.com.

31. My Starbucks Idea Web site, http://mystarbucksidea.force.com, accessed April 30, 2010; Emily Bryson York, "Starbucks Gets Its Business Brewing Again with Social Media," *Advertising Age*, February 22, 2010, http://adage.com.

32. James Kanter, "Luxury Goods May Pick and Choose Venues for Sales," *The New York Times*, April 20, 2010, http://www.nytimes.com.

33. Company Web site, "About Us," http://www.easy.com, accessed April 30, 2010.

34. Samuel Axon, "How Small Businesses Are Using Social Media for Real Results," *Mashable,* March 22, 2010, http://mashable.com.

35. Brooke Crothers, "iPad Sold Out at Best Buy Nationwide," *CNET News,* April 7, 2010, http://news.cnet.com; Mary Ellen Lloyd, "Best Buy Shares Benefit from Apple iPad Launch," *Dow Jones Newswires,* April 5, 2010, http://www.foxbusiness.com; Michael Grothaus, "Best buy to Carry iPad on April 3 at ASC-stores Only," *TUAW,* March 26, 2010, http://www.tuaw.com.

36. Jessica Modawell, "Top Ten Outlet Malls in America," *Associated Content,* April 5, 2010, http://www.associatedcontent.com.

37. "Nano-Based RFID Tags Could Replace Bar Codes," *Science Daily,* March 19, 2010, http://www.sciencedaily.com; "Verayo Launches Next Generation of Unclonable RFID Chips," *BusinessWire,* March 2, 2010, http://www.businesswire.com.

38. "Trucking Statistics," *Truck Info,* http://www.truckinfo.net, accessed April 30, 2010.

39. Association of American Railroads, "Class I Railroad Statistics," April 12, 2010, http://www.aar.org; Vince Bond Jr., "Freight Trains Pull Their Weight in Energy Savings," *Great Lakes Echo,* January 12, 2010, http://greatlakesecho.org.

Chapter 13

1. Company Web site, http://www.etrade.com, accessed March 16, 2009; "E*Trade Super Bowl Commercial—the Cute Baby Hook," *Ad Savvy,* http://www.adsavvy.org, accessed March 4, 2009; Charles Leroux, "E*Trade Baby Ad Puts Shankopotamus in Play," *Chicago Tribune,* February 5, 2009, http://www.chicagotribune.com; "NBC Reportedly Struggling to Sell Out Super Bowl Pregame Ads," *Sports Business Daily,* January 26, 2009, http://www.sportsbusinessdaily.com; "E*Trade Announces Super Bowl XLIII Advertisement," Yahoo! Finance, January 23, 2009, http://biz.yahoo.com; Rafael Grillo, "The Online Brokerage Wars: E*Trade Offers Compelling Risk/Reward," *Seeking Alpha,* May 27, 2008, http://seekingalpha.com; "Talking and Trading Baby Blows Away Star-Studded Super Bowl Competition," *Reuters,* February 4, 2008, http://www.reuters.com.

2. "Monster.com Launches New Integrated Marketing Campaign to Help Job Seekers and Employers 'Get a Monster Advantage,' " press release, January 25, 2010, http://www.pr-inside.com.

3. Rebecca Ruiz, "Ten Misleading Drug Ads," *Forbes.com,* February 2, 2010, http://www.forbes.com.

4. Michelle Krebs, "For Upcoming Chevrolet Cruze, GM Bets Safety Will (Up) Sell," *Edmunds Auto Observer,* April 19, 2010, http://www.autoobserver.com.

5. "San Diego McDonald's to Promo Frappes with Taxi Tops," *QSR Web,* April 6, 2010, http://www.qsrweb.com; Mike Hughlett, "McDonald's Frappes Spreading in Chicago Area," *Chicago Breaking Business,* February 2, 2010, http://www.chicagobreakingbusiness.com.

6. Nielsen IAG PlaceViews Product-Placement Activity Report, *Advertising Age,* February 22, 2010, http://adage.com; Wayne Friedman, " 'Idol' Gives Coke Millions in Media Value," *MediaPost,* January 14, 2010, http://www.mediapost.com.

7. Christopher Wolf, "Let Me Entertain You," *QSR Magazine,* December 2009, http://www.qsrmagazine.com.

8. Mark Wyatt, "Guerilla [sic] Marketing Meets Social Media," *Articlesbase,* February 8, 2010, http://www.articlesbase.com.

9. David Griner, "To Hell and Back: EA's Guerrilla Marketing Campaign for 'Dante's Inferno,' " *AdFreak.com,* [Spring] 2010, http://adweek.blogs.com.

10. Jim Tierney, "Live from NEMOA: Why Your Brand Should Be Like Elvis," *Multichannel Merchant,* March 11, 2010, http://www.multichannelmerchant.com.

11. Laurel Wentz and Bradley Johnson, "Top 100 Global Advertisers Heap Their Spending Abroad," *Advertising Age,* November 30, 2009, http://adage.com; "Global Marketers 2009," *Advertising Age,* November 30, 2009, http://adage.com.

12. Ibid.

13. Avon company Web site, http://responsibility.avoncompany.com, accessed June 14, 2010.

14. "Foundation Fact Sheet," Bill and Melinda Gates Foundation, http://www.gatesfoundation.org, accessed May 14, 2010.

15. Nick Bilton, "Google and partners Seek TV Foothold," *The New York Times,* March 17, 2010, http://www.nytimes.com.

16. Jessica E. Vascellaro, "Google Tests TV Search Service," *The Wall Street Journal,* March 8, 2010, http://online.wsj.com.

17. Erick Schonfeld, "Estimate: 800,000 U.S. Households Abandoned Their TVs for the Web," *TechCrunch,* April 13, 2010, http://techcrunch.com; John Latchem, "More U.S. Homes Have Game Consoles than Cable Boxes," *Home Media Magazine,* March 3, 2010, http://www.homemediamagazine.com; Bill Carter, "DVR, Once TV's Mortal Enemy, Helps Ratings," *The New York Times,* November 2, 2009, http://www.nytimes.com.

18. "Super Bowl Ad Prices Dip, But Still Pricey," *CBS News,* January 11, 2010, http://www.cbsnews.com; Brian Steinberg, "'Sunday Night Football' Remains Costliest TV Show," *Advertising Age,* October 26, 2009, http://adage.com.

19. "Internet Radio—Traditional Radio's Future?" *Radio News,* April 7, 2010, http://www.radiostreamingnews.com.

20. "Google Audio Ads—The Future of Radio Advertising?" *Broadcast Advertising,* February 14, 2010, http://broadcastadvertising.doodig.com.

21. Federal Trade Commission, "Unsolicited Mail, Telemarketing and Email: Where to Go to 'Just Say No,' " FTC Consumer Alert, http://www.ftc.gov, accessed May 2010; James Limbach, "Credit Card Direct Mail Back on the Rise," *ConsumerAffairs.com,* January 29, 2010, http://www.consumeraffairs.com; Frank Washkuch, "Credit Card Direct Mail Up in Q4 2009: Mintel," *DMNews,* January 28, 2010, http://www.dmnews.com.

22. Outdoor Advertising Association of America, "Facts and Figures," n.d., http://www.oaaa.org.

23. Clear Channel Outdoor Advertising, "Reach the Mobile Consumer," http://www.clearchanneloutdoor.com, accessed May 11, 2010; Schaller Consulting, *The New York City Taxicab Factbook,* 2006, http://www.schallerconsult.com; Dave Bradley, "Taxi Top Digital Advertising—What Next?" *EzineArticles.com,* March 2, 2010, http://ezinearticles.com; North

Park University, "North Park Launches 2010 Outdoor Advertising Campaign," January 15, 2010, http://www.northpark.edu.

24. Natalie Zmuda, "Coca-Cola Gets Hands-on with Its Own Digital Billboards," *Advertising Age*, February 18, 2010, http://adage.com; "CBS Outdoor Brings 3D Outdoor Advertising to New York's Grand Central Station," press release, February 10, 2010, http://www.marketwatch.com.

25. Mike Sachoff, "Online Ad Spending to Outpace Print in 2010," *WebProNews*, March 8, 2010, http://www.webpronews.com.

26. Ford Motor Company Web site, http://www.fiestamovement2.com, accessed May 14, 2010; Jay Yarow, "YouTube Turning a Profit? Eric Schmidt 'Assumes' It Is," *Business Insider*, January 22, 2010, http://www.businessinsider.com; Grant McCracken, "How Ford Got Social Marketing Right," *Harvard Business Review*, January 7, 2010, http://blogs.hbr.org.

27. Jimm Fox, "The 5 Most Effective Viral Video Ads of 2009," *One Market Media*, January 4, 2010, http://www.onemarketmedia.com.

28. BzzAgent Web site, http://aboutbzzagent.com, accessed May 2010; Andrew M. Kaikati, "Let's Make a Deal," *The Wall Street Journal*, January 25, 2010, http://online.wsj.com.

29. Sporting News Wire Service, "Teams Struggle to Sustain Sponsorship Dollars," *NASCAR.com*, November 17, 2009, http://go.nascar.com.

30. "Effective Infomercials," Infomercial DRTV, http://www.infomercialdrtv.com, accessed May 14, 2010.

31. Edward C. Baig, "Target Puts Mobile Coupons on Customers' Cellphones," *USA Today*, March 11, 2010, http://www.usatoday.com; Phil Wahba, "Coupon Use Up 27 Pct Last Year—Inmar," *Shop Talk*, January 25, 2010, http://blogs.reuters.com.

32. Maisie Ramsay, "Verizon Drops Mail-In Rebate on Palm Pre, Pixi Plus," *Wireless Week*, March 5, 2010, http://www.wirelessweek.com; Rick Broida, "Take the Hassles Out of Mail-in Rebates," *The Washington Post*, February 9, 2010, http://www.washingtonpost.com.

33. Dan Fletcher, "How Facebook Is Redefining Privacy," *Time*, May 20, 2010, http://www.time.com; "Point of Purchase Marketing Turns to Digital Options," *POP Displays*, April 3, 2010, http://popdisplays.theproductjudge.com; Kunur Patel, "Forget Foursquare: Why Location Marketing Is New Point-of-Purchase," *Advertising Age*, March 22, 2010, http://adage.com.

34. U.S. Department of Labor, Economic News Release, Table 5. Employment by Major Occupational Group, 2008 and Projected 2018, December 11, 2009, http://data.bls.gov, accessed May 14, 2010.

35. Mark Huber, "Life of a Salesman," *Air Space Magazine*, February–March 2007, http://www.airspacemag.com.

36. Matthew Hathaway, "Recession-Weary Consumers Find Haggling Can Cut Costs," *Chicago Tribune*, March 14, 2010, http://articles.chicagotribune.com; Michael S. Rosenwald, "In Tough Economic Times, Shoppers Take Haggling to New Heights," *The Washington Post*, January 31, 2010, http://www.washingtonpost.com.

37. Lee Howard, "Pfizer Ups Its Commitment to E-Marketing, *The Day*, January 21, 2010, http://www.allbusiness.com.

38. Federal Trade Commission, "Q&A for Telemarketers and Sellers About the Do Not Call Provisions of the FTC's Telemarketing Sales Rule," *FTC Business Alert*, http://www.ftc.gov, accessed May 14, 2010.

39. Bruce Wilson, "Generating B2B Sales Leads Using Social Media," Many Doors Marketing, February 24, 2010, http://manydoors.net.

40. Nat Robinson, "SlideRocket Presentation Tip—4 Ways For Using MultiMedia Strategically," *SlideRocket*, April 1, 2010, http://www.sliderocket.com.

41. David Parker Brown, "Spirit Airlines Installs 'Pre-Reclined' Seats on New Airbus A320's," *Airline Reporter*, April 21, 2010, http://www.airlinereporter.com.

42. Susan G. Komen Race for the Cure Web site, http://ww5.komen.org, accessed May 2010.

43. Elaine Wong, "Dove Super Bowl Spot Scores Initial Points with Men," *Brandweek*, February 9, 2010, http://www.brandweek.com; Jack Neff and Rupal Parekh, "Dove Takes Its New Men's Line to the Super Bowl," *Advertising Age*, January 5, 2010, http://adage.com.

44. Justin Scheck, "Windows 7 Fails to Boost Profits of PC Makers," *WSJ.com*, January 31, 2010, http://online.wsj.com.

45. Sean Poulter, "The High Price of Fashion: Sales of Luxury It Bags Soar by 60%," *Mail Online*, March 12, 2010, http://www.dailymail.co.uk.

46. Richard Esposito, "'Wise Guys' Accused of Scalping $29 Million in Springsteen, Yankees, Miley Cyrus Tickets," *ABC News*, March 1, 2010, http://abcnews.go.com.

47. "For California Vintners, It's Not Easy Being Green," *Science Daily*, March 5, 2010, http://www.sciencedaily.com.

Part 4: Launching Your Marketing Career

1. U.S. Department of Labor, "Market and Survey Researchers," *Occupational Outlook Handbook*, 2010–2011, Bureau of Labor Statistics, accessed June 14, 2010, http://www.bls.gov.

2. U.S. Department of Labor, "Advertising Sales Agents," *Occupational Outlook Handbook*, 2010–2011, Bureau of Labor Statistics, accessed June 14, 2010, http://www.bls.gov.

3. U.S. Department of Labor, "Advertising and Public Relations Services," *Occupational Outlook Handbook*, 2010–2011, accessed June 14, 2010, http://www.bls.gov.

4. Ibid.

Chapter 14

1. Company Web site, http://www.rim.com, accessed March 6, 2009; "BlackBerry App World Poised to Bring App Goodness to BB Users," *San Francisco Chronicle*, March 5, 2009, http://www.sfgate.com; "Gartner Sees Unstable Handset Demand until 2010," *CNNMoney*, March 3, 2009, http://money.cnn.com; Al Sacco, "RIM Wins Mobile World Congress Award for BlackBerry Storm Screen," *CIO*, February 19, 2009, http://advice.cio.com; Priya Ganalati, "BlackBerry's Storm Rages On," *Portfolio.com*, January 29, 2009, http://www.portfolio.com; Amol Sharma and Sara Silver, "Bumpy Start for BlackBerry Storm," *The Wall Street Journal*, January 26, 2009, pp. B1, B5; Bonnie Cha, "RIM BlackBerry Storm (Verizon Wireless)," *CNET*, December 12, 2008, http://reviews.cnet.com; Stephen H. Wildstrom, "RIM's Impressive BlackBerry Storm," *BusinessWeek*, October 8, 2008, http://www.businessweek.com; Bonnie Cha, "Verizon Officially Debuts RIM BlackBerry Storm," *CNET News*, October 7, 2008, http://news.cnet.com.

2. Fred Cummins, "The Changing Focus of the CIO in 2010," hp Community Home, February 3, 2010, http://www.communities.hp.com;

Galen Gruman, "2010 CIO Priorities Shift to Lightweight Services, Virtualization," *InfoWorld*, January 19, 2010, http://www.infoworld.com; SearchCIO.com staff, "IT Salary Survey: How CIO, IT Salaries Vary by Industry," *SearchCIO.com*, January 7, 2010, http://searchcio.techtarget.com.

3. Rhea Wessel, "Airbus Signs Contract for High-Memory RFID Tags," *RFID Journal*, January 19, 2010, http://www.rfidjournal.com.

4. IEEE Computer Society, "History of Computing Timeline," http://www.computer.org; Computer History Museum Web site, http://www.computerhistory.org, accessed May 24, 2010; Roy Schestowitz, "Computer History Development Timeline: Microsoft Perspective," *Techrights*, February 4, 2010, http://techrights.org.

5. Gary C, "STATS: Android Popularity UP among Future Smart Phone Buyers, Market Share Nearly DOUBLED," *EuroDroid*, March 31, 2010, http://www.eurodroid.com; "Gartner Says Consumers Will Spend $6.2 Billion in Mobile Application Stores in 2010," press release, January 18, 2010, http://www.gartner.com; Lance Whitney, "Smartphones Continue to Surge," *CNET News*, January 5, 2010, http://news.cnet.com.

6. " 'Come Together'—Intranets Are Re-emerging as a Way to Connect Dislocated Employees," *HR Monthly*, April 12, 2010, http://www.intranetdashboard.com.

7. Company Web site, http://www.checkpoint.com, accessed May 24, 2010.

8. Elliott Drucker, "Tech Insights—The Future of Voice," *Wireless Week*, March 7, 2010, http://www.wirelessweek.com; "Future of VOIP in 2010, a New Beginning?" Cheapest VOIP Calls.net, January 2010, http://cheapestvoipcalls.net.

9. Diane Bartz, "Apple Users Lose Some Immunity to Cybercrime," *Reuters*, April 20, 2010, http://ca.news.yahoo.com; IDG News Service, "E-Crime Reporting Format Draws Closer to a Standard," *Reuters*, March 23, 2010, http://www.reuters.com; Sue Marquette Poremba, "Report: Dangers of Cyber Crime on the Rise," *IT Business Edge*, January 27, 2010, http://www.itbusinessedge.com.

10. Robert McMillan, "Data Theft Creates Notification Nightmare for BlueCross," *IDG News Service*, March 1, 2010, http://www.networkworld.com.

11. Elinor Mills, "Malware Delivered by Yahoo, Fox, Google Ads," *CNET News*, March 22, 2010, http://newsss.cnet.com; Joseph R. Perone, "Expect New, Evolving Computer Viruses in 2010," *Star-Ledger*, December 31, 2009, http://blog.nj.com.

12. Tony Bradley, "McAfee Debacle Shows Why Malware Defense Must Evolve," *TechWorld*, April 28, 2010, http://www.techworld.com.

13. Associated Press, "Mastermind of World's Worst Computer Virus Still at Large," *Fox News*, March 4, 2010, http://www.foxnews.com.

14. "New Security Threat Against 'Smart Phone' Users, Researchers Show," *Science Daily*, February 22, 2010, http://www.sciencedaily.com.

15. Erica Naone, "Experts Break Mobile Phone Security," *Technology Review*, December 29, 2009, http://www.technologyreview.com.

16. "Data Loss Statistics," Boston Computing Network, http://www.bostoncomputing.net, accessed May 24, 2010.

17. Company Web site, http://www.falconstor.com, accessed May 24, 2010.

18. "Bureau of Labor Statistics, "Work-at-Home Patterns by Occupation," *Issues in Labor Statistics*, March 2009, http://www.bls.gov.

19. "Infosys Technologies to Manage Microsoft's Internal IT Service," press release, April 13, 2010, http://www.infosys.com.

Chapter 15

1. Theo Francis, "New FASB Rules: Back to Square One?" *BusinessWeek*, April 2, 2009, http://www.businessweek.com; Karey Wutkowski, "U.S. Bill Would Revamp Accounting Oversight," *Reuters*, March 6, 2009, http://www.reuters.com; "House Panel Sets Hearing on Mark-to-Market Accounting," *The Washington Post*, March 5, 2009, http://voices.washingtonpost.com; Emily Chasan, "Ex-SEC Accounting Chief Refused to Nix Fair Value," *Reuters UK*, March 4, 2009, http://uk.reuters.com; Jeff Bishop, "Exec: Accounting Rule Hurting Local Banks," *Times-Herald*, February 16, 2009, http://www.times-herald.com; Allen Sloan, "Don't Blame Mark-to-Market Accounting," *The Washington Post*, October 28, 2008, http://www.washingtonpost.com; Elizabeth Williamson and Kara Scannell, "Momentum Gathers to Ease Mark-to-Market Accounting Rule," *The Wall Street Journal*, October 2, 2008, http://online.wsj.com; Alex Dumortier, "Mark-to-Market Accounting: What You Should Know," *The Motley Fool*, October 2, 2008, http://www.fool.com.

2. Bureau of Labor Statistics, *Occupational Outlook Handbook, 2010–2011* Edition, http://data.bls.gov.

3. "Spring Accounting Grads Fare Better in Hiring than Their Peers," *Accounting Web*, April 23, 2010, http://www.accountingweb.com.

4. AARP Foundation Web site, http://foundation.aarp.org, accessed June 1, 2010.

5. Ernst & Young, "The 2009 Entrepreneur of the Year Winners," press release, November 14, 2009, http://ey.com.

6. "The 2010 *Accounting Today* Top 100 Firms," March 15, 2010, http://www.webcpa.com.

7. FASB Web site, http://www.fasb.org, accessed June 1, 2010.

8. Johnson & Johnson financial statements, *MSN Investor*, http://moneycentral.msn.com, accessed June 1, 2010.

9. Sage Software, "Customer Success Story," http://www.sagesoftware.com, accessed June 1, 2010.

10. John Adams, "Success Story," *US Banker*, January 2010, http://www.americanbanker.com.

11. Thomas Black, "Weak Dollar Is "Welcome Change' for McDonald's, PPG Profits," *Bloomberg.com*, October 29, 2009, http://www.bloomberg.com.

12. "Despite Uncertainty, Initial Response to SEC's IFRS Announcement Finds Executives Won't Delay Their Own IFRS Planning," *PR Newswire*, March 9, 2010, http://www.prnewswire.com.

13. Ernst & Young, "SEC Reaffirms Its Commitment to IFRS," *Hot Topic*, February 24, 2010, http://www.ey.com; Ra'id Marie, "IFRS vs. GAAP—What Does This Have to Do with the Financial Crisis?" Meirc Training and Consulting, January 17, 2010, http://www.meirc.com.

Part 5: Launching Your Information Technology and Accounting Career

1. U.S. Department of Labor, "Tomorrow's Jobs," *Occupational Outlook Handbook, 2010–2011*, Bureau of Labor Statistics, accessed June 28, 2010, http://www.bls.gov.

2. U.S. Department of Labor, "Accountants and Auditors," *Occupational Outlook Handbook, 2010–2011*, Bureau of Labor Statistics, accessed June 28, 2010, http://www.bls.gov.

3. U.S. Department of Labor, "Computer Software Engineers," *Occupational Outlook Handbook, 2010–2011,* Bureau of Labor Statistics, accessed June 28, 2010, http://www.bls.gov.

4. U.S. Department of Labor, "Computer and Information Systems Managers," *Occupational Outlook Handbook, 2010–2011,* Bureau of Labor Statistics, accessed June 28, 2010, http://www.bls.gov.

Chapter 16

1. Thomas J. Slattery, "The Financial Supermarket Falls Apart, Again," *Risk & Insurance,* February 2, 2009, http://www.riskandinsurance.com; Andy Kessler, "The End of Citi's Financial Supermarket," *The Wall Street Journal,* January 16, 2009, http://online.wsj.com; Andrew Ross Sorkin, "Breaking Up a Must for Citi," *The New York Times,* January 15, 2009, http://www.dealbook.blogs.nytimes.com; Eric Dash, "Citigroup Plans to Split Itself Up, Taking Apart the Financial Supermarket," *The New York Times,* January 14, 2009, http://www.nytimes.com; "Long Live the Financial Supermarket," *The Wall Street Journal,* January 14, 2009, http://bw.dowjones.com; Eric Dash, "A Stormy Decade for Citi Since Travelers Merger," *The New York Times,* April 3, 2008, http://www.nytimes.com.

2. Andrew Ross Sorkin, ed., "S&P Cuts BP Ratings, Citing Liabilities and Politics," *The New York Times,* June 17, 2010, http:dealbook.blogs.nytimes.com; "BP Suspends Dividend after Deepwater Horizon Spill," *MarketWatch,* June 16, 2010, http://www.marketwatch.com; Peter Nicholas, "BP Will Create Fund to Pay Claims," *Los Angeles Times,* June 16, 2010, http://articles.latimes.com; AP/1010WINS, "Scientists: BP Oil Spill Leaking Up to 2.52M Gallons a Day," *1010WINS.com,* June 15, 2010, http://www.1010wins.com; Ben Baden, "The Case for (and against) BP Cutting Its Dividend," *U.S. News & World Report,* June 14, 2010, http://www.usnews.com; Jeff Plungis and Christopher Condon, "U.S. Lawmakers Say BP Should Suspend Dividends, Ads (Update 2)," *Bloomberg Businessweek,* June 9, 2010, http://www.businessweek.com; "Gulf of Mexico Oil Spill Worst in U.S. History," *MarketWatch,* May 27, 2010, http://www.marketwatch.com; Campbell Robertson, "Search Continues after Oil Rig Blast," *The New York Times,* April 21, 2010, http://www.nytimes.com.

3. Catarina Saraiva, William Selway, and Brendan A. McGrail, "California Markets Second-Biggest Taxable Bond Sale of 2010," *Bloomberg.com,* March 25, 2010, http://www.bloomberg.com; Katrina Nicholas, "Russian Nanotechnology Corporation Considers $1.7 Billion Bond Sale," *Nanowerk,* March 11, 2010, http://www.nanowerk.com.

4. "Strong Global IPO Market in Q1 Sets Tone for 2010," news release, Ernst & Young, April 8, 2010, http://www.ey.com; Eric Fox, "The Worst IPOs of 2009," *Investopedia,* December 16, 2009, http://stocks.investopedia.com.

5. "NYSE Euronext Announces First Quarter 2010 Financial Results," news release, May 4, 2010, http://www.nyse.com; "New York Stock Exchange," *Money-Zine,* http://www.money-zine.com, accessed June 21, 2010.

6. Rule 300. Trading Licenses, NYSE Euronext, 2010, http://www.nyse.com; Trading Licenses, NYSE Price List 2010, http://www.nyse.com, accessed June 21, 2010.

7. Federal Deposit Insurance Corporation, "Statistics on Depository Institutions Report," http://www2.fdic.gov, accessed June 21, 2010.

8. "Debit Cards—Holders, Number, Transactions, and Volume, 2000 and 2007, and Projections, 2010," U.S. Census Bureau, http://www.census.gov, accessed June 21, 2010.

9. Board of Governors, "Percentage of Households Using Selected Electronic Banking Technologies: 1995 to 2007," *Federal Reserve Bulletin,* http://www.census.gov, Table 1148, accessed June 21, 2010; Penny Crosman, "17% of U.S. Adults Use Mobile Banking, Survey Finds," *Bank Systems & Technology,* February 4, 2010, http://www.banktech.com.

10. Federal Deposit Insurance Corporation, "Table S112. Assets, FDIC-Insured Savings Institutions, United States and Other Areas," http://www2.fdic.gov, accessed June 21, 2010.

11. Federal Deposit Insurance Corporation, "Table S114. Federal Deposit Insurance Corporation, Loans and Leases, FDIC-Insured Savings Institutions, United States and Other Areas," http://www2.fdic.gov, accessed June 21, 2010.

12. "America's Largest Credit Unions," *Credit Union Access,* http://creditunionaccess.com, accessed June 21, 2010; Donna Fuscaldo, "Can You Join a Credit Union?" *Bankrate.com,* April 21, 2010, http://www.bankratecom.

13. "Life Insurance: The Life/Health Insurance Industry," Insurance Information Institute, http://www.iii.org, accessed June 21, 2010.

14. "Retirement Funds," Insurance Information Institute, http://www.iii.org, accessed June 21, 2010; Mary Williams Walsh, "Public Pension Funds Are Adding Risk to Raise Returns," *The New York Times,* March 8, 2010, http://www.nytimes.com; Joshua Brockman, "Stocks Weight Down U.S. Pension Funds," *NPR,* February 18, 2009, http://www.npr.org.

15. *2010 Investment Company Factbook,* Table 9, Number of Shareholder Accounts of the U.S. Mutual Fund Industry, and Table 1 Total Net Assets, Number of Funds, Number of Share Classes, and Number of Shareholder Accounts of the U.S. Mutual Fund Industry, http://www.icifactbook.org, accessed June 21, 2010; "Frequently Asked Questions about 401(k) Plans," Investment Company Institute, http://www.ici.org, accessed June 21, 2010; Investment Company Institute, "Trends in Mutual Fund Investing, March 2010," April 19, 2010, http://www.ici.org.

16. Investment Company Institute, "Trends in Mutual Fund Investing, March 2010."

17. Federal Reserve press release, January 12, 2010, http://www.federalreserve.gov, accessed June 21, 2010; Board of Governors of the Federal Reserve System, "Term Auction Facility Questions and Answers," http://www.federalreserve.gov, accessed June 21, 2010.

18. Bankers Almanac, "Top Banks in the World," http://www.bankersalmanac.com, accessed June 21, 2010.

Chapter 17

1. "Intel to Invest $7 Billion in U.S. Factory Upgrades," *Money News,* February 11, 2009, http://moneynews.newsmax.com; Franklin Paul and Janet Kornblum, "Intel to Invest $7 Billion in U.S. as Recession Deepens," *Reuters,* February 10, 2009, http://uk.reuters.com; Patrick Thibodeau, "Intel's $7 Billion 'Made in the USA' Investment," *ComputerWorld,* February 10, 2009, http://www.computerworld.com; Brian Caulfield, "Intel's Chief on His $7 Billion Bet," *Forbes,* February 10, 2009, http://www.forbes.com; Brian Forbes, "Stimulating Tech," *Forbes,* February 10, 2009, http://www.forbes.com.

2. "2010 CEO Pay Analysis & Strategies for Mid-Caps," *Equilar,* May 2010, http://www.equilar.com.

3. Josh Funk, "Warren Buffet Still Gets $100K Salary at Berkshire Hathaway, But Security Costs Grow to $345K," *Business News*, March 10, 2010, http://blog.taragana.com.

4. Aude Lagorce, "Emirates in Record Airbus A380 Order," *MarketWatch*, June 8, 2010, http://www.marketwatch.com; Andrea Rothman, "Airbus A380 Order Dearth Risks Double-Decker-Dud Fate (Update 1)," *Bloomberg Businessweek*, May 13, 2010, http://www.businessweek.com; David Kaminski-Morrow, "A380 to Remain a Financial Burden for Years: Airbus Chief," *Flightglobal*, January 12, 2010, http://www.flightglobal.com.

5. Sarah Johnson, "CFO: Stop Treating Your Inventories Like Fine Wine," *CFO.com*, September 10, 2009, http://cfo.com.

6. "South Carolina BMW Plant Expansion Nears Completion," *Auto Writer*, June 17, 2009, http://thearticlewriter.com.

7. Jonathon Ramsey, "BMW Plant in Spartanburg, SC Produces 1.5 Millionth Vehicle," *Autoblog*, September 10, 2009, http://www.autoblog.com.

8. Federal Reserve Bank of St. Louis, Series: AEXUSUK, U.S./U.K. Foreign Exchange Rate, May 11, 2010, http://research.stlouisfed.org.

9. Federal Reserve Board, "Commercial Paper," Federal Reserve Release, May 13, 2010, http://federalreserve.gov.

10. "BP Suspends Dividend after Deepwater Horizon Spill," *MarketWatch*, June 16, 2010, http://www.marketwatch.com; "The Case for (and against) BP Cutting Its Dividend," *U.S. News & World Report*, June 14, 2010, http://www.usnews.com; Jeff Plungis and Christopher Condon, "U.S. Lawmakers Say BP Should Suspend Dividends, Ads (Update 2)," *Bloomberg Businessweek*, June 9, 2010, http://www.businessweek.com; Whitney Kisling, "Dividend Slump Ending as Record Profits Lift Payouts for S&P 500," *China Post*, April 29, 2010, http://www.chinapost.com.tw.

11. Federal Reserve Board, Commercial Paper Outstanding, Federal Reserve Release, May 12, 2010, http://federalreserve.gov.

12. Dena Aubin, "CORRECTED—US Companies Sell Debt at Fastest Pace since March," *Reuters*, June 23, 2010, http://www.reuters.com; Michael Aneiro, "Credit Markets Pub on the Brakes," *The Wall Street Journal*, May 29, 2010, http://www.online.wsj.com.

13. Board of Governors of the Federal Reserve System, "Federal Reserve Statistical Release, Z.1, Flow of Funds Accounts of the United States," March 12, 2009, http://www.federalreserve.gov.

14. "About Draper Fisher Jurvetson," company Web site, http://dfj.com, accessed June 24, 2010; "SCI Secures $5 Million in Series A Funding with DFJ Ventures—Names Russ McMeekin, a Seasoned Senior Executive, as CEO," press release, March 29, 2010, http://www.scientificconservation.com.

15. "Moody's May Downgrade DynCorp's 'Ba3' Rating," *MarketWatch*, April 12, 2010, http://www.marketwatch.com.

16. Elena Logutenkova and Yalman Onaran, "Singapore, Abu Dhabi Face Losses on UBS, Citigroup (Update 2)," *Bloomberg Businessweek*, May 14, 2010, http://www.businessweek.com; Dakin Campbell and Andrew MacAskill, "Abu Dhabi Fund Seeks to End Citigroup Share purchase (Update 1)," *Bloomberg.com*, December 16, 2009, http://www.bloomberg.com.

17. Andrew Ross Sorkin, ed., "Hedge Fund Strategies, at Smaller Prices," *The New York Times.com*, January 11, 2010, http://dealbook.blogs.nytimes.com.

18. Margie Lindsay, "Global Hedge Fund AUM Hits $1.8 Trillion," *Hedge Funds Review*, March 8, 2010, http://www.hedgefundsreview.com.

19. Jon Swartz, "HP to Acquire Palm for about $1.2B," *USA Today*, April 29, 2010, http://www.usatoday.com; "HP to Acquire Palm for $1.2 Billion," press release, April 28, 2010, http://www.hp.com.

20. Emre Peker, "Cerberus Taps Banks for LBO as Leveraged Loan Rally Spurs M&As," *Bloomberg Businessweek*, May 14, 2010, http://www.businessweek.com; David Russell, "LBOs Loom as Credit Market Recovers," Nasdaq, March 19, 2010, http://www.nasdaq.com.

Part 6: Launching Your Finance Career

1. U.S. Department of Labor, "Tomorrow's Jobs," *Occupational Outlook Handbook, 2010–2011*, Bureau of Labor Statistics, accessed July 8, 2010, http://www.bls.gov.

2. National Association of Colleges and Employers, "Starting Salary Offers to College Class of 2010 Decline," accessed at http://www.career.vt.edu, accessed July 8, 2010.

3. U.S. Department of Labor, "Financial Managers," *Occupational Outlook Handbook, 2010–2011*, Bureau of Labor Statistics, accessed July 8, 2010, http://www.bls.gov.

Appendix A

1. Arik Hesseldahl, "Apple's Smartphone Battle Plan," *Bloomberg Businessweek*, April 26, 2010, http://wwwbusinssweek.com; Philip Elmer-DeWitt, "Apple Talks Tough to Handset Makers," *Fortune Technology*, March 9, 2010, http://tech.fortune.com; "Will Apple's Patents Banish HTC Phones?" *MIS Asia*, March 4, 2010, http://wwwmis-asia.com; Marguerite Reardon, "Apple Sues HTC Over iPhone Patents," *CNET News*, March 2, 2010, http://news.cnet.com; Brad Stone, "Apple Sues Nexus one Maker HTC," *The New York Times*, March 2, 2010, http://www.nytimes.com.

2. "Frivolous Lawsuits," *NFIB*, http://www.nfib.com, accessed May 7, 2010.

3. "All States Have Silly Laws," http://foodstamp.aphsa.org/olwkshps/AllSatesHaveSillyLaws.pdf, accessed May 7, 2010.

4. "United States Court of Appeals for the Fourth Circuit," http://www.ca4.uscourts.gov, accessed May 7, 2010.

5. "The Justices' Caseload," The Supreme Court of the United States, http://www.supremecourt.gov, accessed May 7, 2010.

6. Peter J. Brown, "US Lawsuit May Flood China Drywalls," *Asia Times*, April 10, 2010, http://www.atimes.com.

7. Beverly Blair Harzog, "New Credit Car Rules' Double Standard," *CNN Money.com*, February 22, 2010, http;//money.cnn.com.

8. Andrew Ramonas, "Senate Passes Short-Term Patriot Act Reauthorization," *Main Justice*, February 25, 2010, http://www.mainjustice.com.

9. RobPegoraro, "Court Cuts FCC's Net-Neutrality Power; Now What?" *The Washington Post*, April 7, 2010, http://voices.washingtonpost.com.

10. Jennifer Liberto, "No Senate Deal on Consumer Financial Protection," *CNN Money.com*, February 5, 2010, http://money.cnn.com.

11. "Food and Drug Administration Amendments Act (FDAAA) of 2007," U.S. Food and Drug Administration, http://www.fda.gov, accessed May 7, 2010.

12. Ameet Sachdev, "EEOC Sues Law Firm for Age Discrimination," *AARP Bulletin Today,* February 2, 2010, http://bulletin.aarp.org.

13. Miguel Helft, "Judge Sides With Google in Viacom Video Suit," *The New York Times,* June 23, 2010, http://www.nytimes.com; "Google's YouTube Secrets Exposed in Viacom Case," *Huffington Post,* April 15, 2010, http://www.huffingtonpost.com.

14. Kelly Kunsch, "Commercial Law and the Uniform Code," *Seattle University School of Law,* http://www.law.seattle.edu, accessed May 7, 2010.

15. Terry Pristin, "Lesson on Limits of Eminent Domain at Columbia," *The New York Times,* January 18, 2010, http://www.nytimes.com.

16. "Utah Eminent Domain Law: Governor Signs Bill Authorizing Eminent to Domain To Take Federal Land," *Huffington Post,* March 29, 2010, http://www.huffingtonpost.com.

17. Mark Sweney, "Google Wins Louis Vuitton Trademark Case," *The Guardian,* March 23, 2010, http://www.guardian.co.uk.

18. "Senate Judiciary Committee Unveils Details of Patent Reform Agreement," *Law Updates.com,* March 9, 2010, http://www.lawupdates.com.

19. B. Smith, "Google Digital Library Faces Major Public Outcry at NYC Hearing," *NY Daily News,* February 18, 2010, http://www.nydailynews.com.

20. "New Jersey Environmental Tort Lawsuit Filed by Pompton Lakes Residents," *About Lawsuits,* March 11, 2010, http://www.aboutlawsuits.com.

21. Duff Wilson, "Sharp Increase in March in Personal Bankruptcies," *The New York Times,* April 1, 2010, http://www.nytimes.com.

Appendix B

1. Michael Cass, "Nashville Property Damage Now At $1.9 Billion," *The Tennessean,* May 16, 2010, http://www.tennessean.com; Tom Weir, "In Nashville, a Way of Life Washed Away," *USA Today,* Mary 9, 2010, http://www.usatoday.com; Melinda Hudgins, "Few Take Advantage of Flood Insurance, *DNJ.com,* May 9, 2010, http://www.dnj.com; "Stories of Tragedy, Survival Surface as Tennessee Flood Waters Recede," *CNN.com,* May 9, 2010, http://www.cnn.com; Emily Holbrook, "Few in Tennessee Covered by Flood Insurance," *Risk Management Monitor,* May 6, 2010, http://www.riskmanagementmonitor.com; Geert de Lombaerde, "Less Than 4,000 Davidson Homes Insured Against Floods," *The City Paper,* May 4, 2010, http://nashvillecitypaper.com.

2. *ACLI Lilfe Insurance Fact Book 2009,* http://www.acli.com, accessed May 9, 2010.

3. "Lightning Sparks Concern for Insurance Industry; Homeowners Claims Rise Sharply Over Last Five Years," Insurance Information Institute, March 31, 2010, http://www.iii.org.

4. "Home Buyers Insurance Checklist," Insurance Information Institute, http://www.iii.org, accessed May 9, 2010.

5. "Insurance Requirements," Walmart Web site, http://walmartstores.com, accessed May 9, 2010.

6. "Healthcare Reform Legislation Update 2010," *JLBH Health,* March 22, 2010, http://www.jlbghealth.com.

Appendix C

1. Patrick Lohmann, "Campus Debtors," *Alibi,* May 6-12, 2010, http://alibi.com; David Ellis, "Credit Card Relief Is Here, But Watch Out for New Traps," *CNN Money.com,* February 22, 2010, http://money.cnn.com; Jennifer Liberto, "Under 21? Getting a Credit Card Just got Tougher," *CNN Money.com,* February 22, 2010, http://money.cnn.com; George Gombossy, "New Credit Card Rules go Into Effect Monday," *Connecticut Watchdog,* February 20, 2010, http://ctwatchdog.com; David K. Randall, "New Credit Card Choices for Students," *Forbes.com,* February 4, 2010, http://www.forbes.com.

2. "Income, Poverty, and Health Insurance Coverage in the United States," U.S. Census Bureau, http://www.census.gov, accessed May 9, 2010.

3. "Employee Tenure, 2008, and Retiree Health Benefit Trends Among the Medicare-Eligible Population," *Employee Benefit Research Institute,* 31, no. 1 January 2010, http://www.ebri.org.

4. Personal Bankruptcy Filings Rise Fast," *Money Central,* January 7, 2010, http://articles.moneycentral.msn.com.

5. "Consumer Credit," *Federal Reserve Statistical Release,* May 7, 2010, http://federalreserve.gov.

6. Keith Cronin, "Avoiding Credit Card Debt in College," *Campus Life,* May 8, 2010, http://campuslife.suite101.com.

Appendix D

1. Next Web site, http://nextrestaurant.com, accessed May 9, 2010; Pete Wells, "In Chicago, the Chef Grant Achatz Is Selling Tickets to His New Restaurant," *The New York Times,* May 5, 2010, http://www.nytimes.com; "US' Next Hot Restaurant Will Require Prepaid Tickets," *AOL News,* May 5, 2010, http://www.aolnews.com; Chuck Sudo, "Achatz's Next Two Projects: Time Travel, Cocktails," *Chicagoist,* May 4, 2010, http://chicagoist.com; Paul Frumkin, "Grant Achatz to Open New Restaurant and Bar," *Nation's Restaurant News Today,* May 4, 2010, http://www.nrn.com.

Appendix E

1. "Average Earnings of Year-Round, Full-Time Workers by Educational Attainment," *Current Population Reports,* U.S. Census Bureau, http://www.census.gov, accessed May 10, 2010.

2. Henry Devries, "How to Get a Job in Embedded Engineering," *San Diego News Network,* April 27, 2010, http://www.sdnn.com.

3. "College Grad Job Search Strategies," *JobDoc,* March 15, 2010, http://www.boston.com.

4. Lindsey Gerdes, "Best Places to Intern," *Bloomberg Businessweek,* December 10, 2009, http://www.businessweek.com.

5. "The Cooperative Education Model, National Commission for Cooperative Education," http://www.co-op.edu, accessed May 10, 2010.

6. "More Free Assessment Tests," *Career Explorer,* http://www.careerexplorer.net, accessed May 10, 2010; "Assessment Exercises," *Monster Careers,* http://www.monstercareeres.com, accessed May 10, 2010.

7. "Paula's Story," *Paula Deen.com,* http://www.pauladeen.com, accessed May 10, 2010.

8. Kim Isaacs, "Five Resume Tips for College Students," *Monster.com,* accessed May 10, 2010; "Top 10 Professional Resume Writing Tips for 2010," *An Elite Resume,* http://aneliteresume.com, accessed May 10, 2010; "Five Tips for Better Resume Writing," *Resume Writing for Dummies,* http://www.dummies.com, accessed May 10, 2010.

9. Kat Neville, "What Makes a Great Cover Letter, According to Companies?" *Smashing Magazine,* March 25, 2010, http://www.smashingmagazine.com.

10. "Tips for Submitting Your Online Resume," *An Elite Resume,* http://aneliteresume.com, accessed May 10, 2010.

11. Carole Martin, "Ten Tips to Boost Your Interview Skills," *Monster.com,* http://career-advice.monster.com, accessed May 10, 2010.

12. Jerome Young, "How to Answer the Hard Interview Questions," *Forbes.com,* April 9, 2010, http://www.forbes.com.

13. "Overview of the 2008–2018 Projections," U.S. Bureau of Labor Statistics, http://data.bls.gov, accessed May 10, 2010.

14. Ibid.

15. Ibid.

16. Ibid.

17. Anthony Balderama, "What Kind of Job Market Can the Class of 2010 Expect?" *The Work Buzz,* April 15, 2010, http://www.theworkbuzz.com.

Name Index

QuikTrip, 409
Quiznos, 213, 230, 400
QVC, 179
Qwest, 479

R
Rabin, Craig, 9
Radar, 310
Radisson Hotels, 40
Radius Images, 498
Raid, 145
Rail Maritime Transport Workers
    (RMT), 282
RailTronix, 193–194
Rainforest Alliance-certified farms,
    32, 53
Ralph Lauren, 409
Ralston, Mark, 183
Ramada, 471
Rao, Leena, 137
Rapid Response Swift Market
    Analysis Response Teams
    (SMART), 291
Rapleaf Inc., 365
Rappaport, Dave, 181
Rashid, Karim, 201
Rasulo, Jay, 67
Ratcliffe, Chris, 452
Ratiopharm, 567
Rawlings Sporting Goods, 79
Raymond James & Associates, 596
Raytheon Solipsys, 262
Reach Wondergrip, 139
Reader's Digest, 438
ReadWriteWeb, 486
Reckitt Benckiser, 434
Recreational Equipment Inc. (REI),
    171, A59
RecruitMilitary, 249
Red Cross, 6, 55
Red Cross/Red Crescent, 356
Redken, 399
Redux Pictures, 574
Reece, Daryl, 53
Reed, Jb, 170
Reed, Marc, 258
Reference for Business, 288
Refrigerated Transport, 403
Regency Energy Partners, 584
Regions Bank, 535
RE/MAX Int'l, 407
Research in Motion, 10, 363, 455,
    474, 501
Retail Advantage Group, 407
Retrofitness, 200
Reuters, 6, 104, 157, 217, 223,
    232, 428, 523, 542, 546,
    557, 558, 563, 591, A40
Revere, Paul, 533
Revlon, 179

Reynolds, Donna, 331
Rhodes, Troy, Jr., 222, 224
Rice, Larry, 310
Rich, Motoko, 451
Richards, Keith, 452
RIDGID, 15
Rigzone, 591
Ritson, Mark, 455
Ritz-Carlton Hotels, 220
Robitussin, 567
Rockefeller, John D., A5
Rockford Public Schools, 295
Rockies Express Pipeline, 591
Rock Valley College, 295
Rodriguez, Enrique, 424
Roeck, Jesse, 330
Rohner, Mark, 546
Rolex, 416, 432
Rolling Stones, A57
Romell, Rick, 503
Ronald McDonald House
    Charities, 67
Rooney, Ben, 592
Roosevelt, Theodore, A5
Roscoe Wind Complex, 7
Rose, Dan, 383
Rose, Lacey, 370
Rosenthal, Elisabeth, 68
Rossi, Bob, 211
de Rothschild, David, 258–259
Roundy's Supermarkets, 332
Rowe, John, 19
Royal Dutch Shell, 132, 577
Royle Systems Group, A14
RSM McGladrey, 502
Rubal, Steve, 383
Rubik's Cubes, 200
Rubin, Courtney, 383
Rubinfeld, Arthur, 48
Rubinkam, Michael, 511
Ruby Tuesday, 347
Ruíz, José, 387
Russian Nanotechnologies
    Corporation, 542
Russian National Wealth Fund, 584
Russo, Tina, 563
Rutland Herald, 442
Ryan, Eric, 200, 201
Ryan, Gary, 277
Rylaxer, 192
Rytilä-Uotila, Tuula, 455

S
SaaS, 529
Sacks, Danielle, 69, 181, 283
Safari, 356
Safeway, 409
Sagar, Chaitanya, 210
Sage.org, 496
Sage Software, 510, 529

St. John's University, 433
St. Joseph's Hospital, 221
St. Jude Children's Research
    Hospital, 6, 317
St. Luke's Health System, 570
Saks Fifth Avenue, 75, 321, 410
Salesforce.com, 259
Salesjobs.com, A59
SalesLogix Configuration
    Engine, 510
Salfi, Jason, 210–211, 592–593
Salmon, Felix, 558
Salter, Chuck, 119
Salvation Army, 238
Sam's Club, 409
Samsung, 71, 106, 139, 250,
    353, 467, 474, 585
San Angelo Community Medical
    Center, 264
Sanctis, Matt, 161
Sandler, Linda, 26
San Jose Mercury News, 163
The San Diego Union Tribune, 285
SAP, 476, 510
Saporito, Bill, 131
the Sartorialist, 423
SAS Institute, 8, 9, 30, 262
Sawhney, Robert, 523
S.C. Johnson & Son, 145,
    146, 173
Scelfo, Julie, 201
Schalders, Kerry, 505
Schenck, Barbara Findlay, A50
Schilling, Dianne, 301
Schmidt, Eric, 235, 439
Schmit, Julie, 19
Schmitt, Angie, 161
Scholfield, Roger, 462
Scholfield Honda, 462
Schuman, Scott, 423
Schwartz, Nelson D., 592
Schwarz, Tobias, 232
SC Magazine, 471
Scotch tape, 206
Seagate, 336
Sealand of the Pacific, 306
Search Engine Journal, 383
Sears, 337, 398, 408
Seattle Children's Hospital, 332
SeaWorld, 310
Secret Acres, 102–103, 425
Segar, Mike, 217
Segre, Alex, 454
Seidman, Maximillian Leonard, 530
Seidman & Seidman, 530
Seidner, Jennifer, 249
Selfish Giving, 67
Selfridges, 451
Selman, David, 216
Semcken, Kevin, 204
Senna, DeLynn, 153

Sephora, 179
Sequence Inc., 503
Serv-a-Palooza, 376
Service Employees International
    Union (SEIU), 274
ServiceMaster, 391
Servpro, 163
7-Eleven, 163, 409, 410, 564
Seventh Generation, 69, 181,
    282–283, 320, 360, 410, 411
Sevinsky, Mary, 266
Shaffer, Erica, 412
Shamu, the whale, 310
Shannon, Kerri, 542
Sharma, Amol, 137
Shell International, 258, 495
Shelton, Eric, 74
Sherk, James, 263
Shibui Designs, 319
Shiseido, 179–180
Shoemaker-Galloway, Jace, 68
Shout, 145
Shutterstock, 12, 37, 58, 156
Sieberg, Daniel, 138
Siegel, Larry, 249
Siemens, Jeanette, 598
The Sierra Club, 7, 196, 305
Silicon Valley, 325
Silo House, 597
Silpada, 408
Silverstein, Barry, 394
Simon, Bill, 249
Singer, Bill, 558
Singer, Natasha, 51, 384
Singh, Madhur, 116
Singletary, Michelle, 361
Sinopec, 591
Siranosian, Kathryn, 401
Sirius, 437
Sivaram, Siva, 326
Six Flags, 5
Skittles, 492
Skype, 335, 582
Sleeper, 425
Sleepmaster, 335
Sloan, Alfred P., 530
slo-business.com, 435
SmallBusinessComputing.com, 530
Small Business Investment
    Companies (SBIC), 159
Small Business Training
    Network, 159
SmartBalanceTransfers.com, 549
Smart Design, 138–139, 250
SmartDraw, 447
SmartGauge, 138
SmartMoney, 546
SMB Human Resources, 281
Smith, Adam, 9
Smith, Rick, 30
Smith, Sean, 344

Subject Index

A

Absolute advantage, 109–110
Accessory equipment, 390
Accident rate, motor vehicles, A23
Accountants
  government and
    not-for-profit, 504
  labor statistics for, 500
  management, 496, 503–504
  public, 495–496, 502–503
Accounting
  budgeting and, 521–523
  business activities involving,
    501–502
  careers in, 495–496
  financial ratio analysis and,
    517–521
  foundational system of, 504–506
  Hong Kong meets China, 523
  international standards for,
    524–525
  professionals, 502–504
  role of computers and Internet in,
    508–510
  software, 529–530
  users of, 500–502
Accounting cycle, 506
  accounting equation and,
    507–508
  role of computers and Internet in,
    508–510
Accounting equation, 507–508
Accounting information,
  users of, 501
Accounts receivable, 573–574
Accrual accounting, 515
Accrued wages, 507
Achievement need, 195
Acid rain, 51
Acquisitions, 174, 585–586
Action, ethical, 45
Active listening, 299
Activity ratios, 519–520
Actuarial tables, A23
Adaptation, 231, 363
Adaptation strategy, 132–133
ADEA. See Age Discrimination in
  Employment Act of 1967
Adidas, 315–316, 409
Adjourning, 294
Administrative agencies, A3–A4
Administrative services managers, 347
Advertising, 443, 449, 463. See
  also specific types of advertising
  campaigns for banks, 435
  for E-businesses, 31

explanation of, 434
on Facebook, 382–383
false or misleading, 56
media, 436–441
for prescription drugs, 51, 56
product life cycle and, 435–436
types of, 434–435
viral, 354, 433, 440
Advertising media, 441
  direct mail, 438
  Internet, 382–383, 439–440
  magazines, 438
  newspapers, 437
  outdoor, 438–439
  radio, 56, 436
  sponsorship, 430, 440
  television and, 3, 56, 429,
    436–437
Advertising specialties, 443
Advocacy advertising, 435
Affective conflict, 295–296
Affinity programs, **377–378**
**Affirmative action
  programs**, 256
Africa, 67, 82, 93, 115, 400–401
African Americans, 162
Age
  demographic segmentation and,
    369–370
  discrimination based on, 57,
    61–62, A7
  of U.S. population, 20–21,
    61–62
  world population and, 96
Age Discrimination in Employment
  Act of 1967 (ADEA), 60, 61
Agents, 407
Agreements
  contractual and foreign
    licensing, 129
  franchising, 163–164
  offset, 128
Agriculture
  in Colonial period, 13
  organic, 35–36
  pure competition and, 79–80
  sustainable, 35, 53, 105,
    190, 196
AIO statements, 372
Airline Deregulation Act, A6
Airline industry, 472, 478, 530,
    570, 574
  corporate culture of, 237
  deregulation in, A6
  distributed workforce in, 485
  Flight 1549 plane crash and, 235
  outsourcing in, 267
  pets and, 461, 531

private jets and, 353
Alien corporation, 172
Amazon.com, 7, 17, 71, 102,
    133, 148, 149, 150, 169,
    172, 221, 222, 344, 353,
    378, 393, 408, 410, 411,
    414, 424, 425, 438, 451,
    460, 529
Ambiguity, tolerance for, 198
American Jobs Creation Act, A8
American Management
  Association, 348
American Stock Exchange
  (AMEX), 545
Americans with Disabilities Act, 60,
    61, 256, A8
AMEX. See American Stock
  Exchange
Amish, 190
Analysts, 400
Android phones, 10, 71, 364, 467,
    475. See also Smart phones
Angel investors, 205
Anticybersquatting Consumer
  Protection Act, A9
Antitrust legislation, A5–A6
AOL, 266, 267, 585
Apparel. See Clothing retailers
Apparel manufacturing, 343
Appellate courts, A3
**Application service provider
  (ASP)**, 485
Application software, 475
Approaching, in sales process, 447
Apps, 9, 12, 101–102, 391
Apptio, 570
Arbitration, 275
Argentina, 105, 123, 137–138, 191
Articles of incorporation, 172
Artisan Coffee movement, 565
The Art of the Start (Kawasaki), A50
Asia, 83, 96, 107, 111, 129,
    139, 427
  as emerging market, 563
  as high-context culture, 297
Asian Americans, 162
Assembly lines, 14–15, 318
Asset intensity, 571, 572
Assets, 507, 572
  management of, 574–575
  short-term, 573–574
Associations, for business
  plans, A51
Atmosphere, store, 413
Audits, social, 49

Audit trail, 557
Australia, 83, 110, 112, 163,
    335, 524, 584
  trade barriers and, 113
  uranium and nuclear energy
    in, 100
Autocratic leadership, 234
Automatic merchandising, 408
Automobile industry, 14–15,
    575, 576
  benchmarking in, 336–337
  environmentally friendly cars and,
    37, 52, 93
  Ford Motor Company and, 248
  General Motors and, 289, 394
  location decisions for, 325
  OnStar and, 387
  product layout and, 329
  recalls, 131, 291
  strikes, 275
  synthetic rubber and, 330
  worst-made cars and, 397
Automobile insurance, A23, A26
Awards, customer-service, 17
Awareness, ethical, 44, 45

B

B2B products. See **Business-to-
  business (B2B) products**
B2C products. See **Business-to-
  consumer (B2C) products**
Baby Boom generation, 20, 22,
    96, 193, 241, 370, 595, A7
Balanced budget, 94
**Balance-of-payments
  deficit**, 110
**Balance-of-payments
  surplus**, 110
Balance of trade, 110
Balance sheet hedge, 575
Balance sheets, 511–512
Bank of America, 249, 378, 533,
    550, 557, 558, 595
Bankruptcy, 168, 483, 502,
    533, 584
  business, A16
  personal, A15–A16
  poor financial planning and, A36
Bankruptcy Abuse Prevention and
  Consumer Protection Act of
  2005, A15
Banks/banking. See also **Finan-
  cial system**; specific banks
  advertising campaigns for, 435
  carbon-neutral, 536

Pure competition, 79–80
Pure risk, A20
Pushing strategy, 449

Q

Qualifying, in sales process, 447
Quality
  explanation of, 336
  ISO standards for, 338–339
  of life for employees, 30, 58–59
  of life with entrepreneurship, 189, 190
  of workforce, 54
Quality control, 336–339
Quality-of-life issues, 281
  for employees, 30, 58–59
  entrepreneurship and, 189, 190
  for families, 58
Quotas, 121

R

Rack jobber, 406
Radio, 56, 436
Radio-frequency identification (RFID), 417
Railroad industry, 14, 171, 282
Raises, asking for, 266
Ratings, 538–539
Ratio analysis
  activity ratios for, 519–520
  leverage ratios for, 517, 520–521
  liquidity ratios for, 517, 518–519
  major categories of, 517
  profitability ratios for, 517, 520
Ratiopharm, 567
Raw materials, 390
Reasoning, ethical, 44, 45
Rebates, 442
Recalls, 131
Recession, 35, 67, 85–86, 101–102, 444. *See also* Economic downturn/crisis
  business ethics impacted by, 38–39
  executive-level misdeeds exposed by, 47
Recreation, 89
Recruitment
  finding qualified candidates, 255–256
  selection and hiring process as aspect of, 255–257
  steps in selection process and, 256
Recycling, 35, 36, 38, 48, 52
  biodiesel fuel and, 53
  electronics, 52, 71
  plastic shopping bags and, 442
Regional manager, 219
Regular dividend, 579

Regulated monopolies, 81
Regulation FD (Fair Disclosure), 63
Relationship era, 15–16, 355
Relationship management,
  technology and, 16
Relationship marketing, 375–378
Relief agencies, 6
Religious beliefs, as barriers to trade, 114–115
Reminder-oriented advertising, 436
Renewable Electricity Standard (RES), 85
Renewable energy sources, 19, 38. *See also* Energy
Repo, 499
RES. *See* Renewable Electricity Standard
Research. *See* **Marketing research**
Respondeat superior (let the master answer), A11
Responsibility. *See* **Social responsibility**
Restrictive monetary policy, 92
Results-oriented résumé, A61, A64
Résumés, 220
  building, A61–A65
  chronological, A62
  cover letters and, A64–A65
  creating strong, A61–A64
  embellishing, 43
  explanation of, A61
  finding qualified candidates and, 255
  functional, A63
  misrepresenting credentials on, 43
  organizing, A61
  results-oriented, A64
  submitting online, A65
Résumés of principals, 156, A49
Retail clinics, 362
Retailer-owned cooperatives, 407
Retailers, 404, 407
  clothing, 41–42
  competition among, 410–413
  nonstore, 408–409
  store, 409–410
Retirement savings plans, 262
Return on equity, 520
Revenue bonds, 537
Revolutionary War, 13
Rewards, 288–290, 511
Rights, in private enterprise system, 10–11
Risk management, 39, A20–A21
Risk-return trade-off, 569

Risks
  assessment of, 156
  avoiding, A20
  insurable, A22
  insurance companies and shifting, A21
  management of, 39, A20–A21
  reducing, A20–A21
  self-insuring against, A21
  of whistle-blowing, 44
Robinson-Patman Act, A6
Robots, 321–322, 336, 337
Routing, 334
Royal Dutch Shell, 577
Rubber, synthetic, 330
Rule of indemnity, A22–A23
Runs, 549
Russia, 87, 96, 108, 110, 117, 129, 163, 191, 234, 491, 530, 584
  as emerging market, 563
  global business strategies and, 132
  legal environment in, 118
  oil industry in, 591

S

Safety, 55–56, 58
Safety needs, 269
Salaries, 61, 260. *See also* **Compensation**; **Wages**
  computer-science graduates and starting, 495
  executive pay and, 577
  finance industry and starting, 595
  women/men and disparity between, 63
Sales. *See also* **Personal selling**
  creative selling and, 445–446
  increasing, 432
  Internet, 3
  missionary selling and, 446
  order processing and, 445
  process, 446–448
  stabilizing, 432
  telemarketing and, 446
Sales branches, 406
Sales era, 355
Sales law, A11
Sales office, 406
Sales promotion. *See also* **Promotion**
  consumer-oriented, 441–443
  personal selling and, 444–448
  trade-oriented, 443–444
Sales representative, 463
Samples, 442–443
Samsung, 71
Sandwich generation, 58
Sarbanes-Oxley Act, 39, 44, 63, 222, 223, 501, 505–506, 511, A8, A9

Satellite radio, 437
Savings and loan associations, 549
Savings banks, 549–550
SBIC. *See* Small Business Investment Companies
S.C. Johnson, 145
Scheduling, 334–335
Scooters, for disabled people, 198
S corporations, 168
Seasonal unemployment, 90–91
SeaWorld, 310
SEC. *See* Securities and Exchange Commission
Secondary data, 364
Secondary market, 543
Secret Acres, 425
Secured bonds, 537
Securities, 557
  bonds as, 537–539
  convertible, 541
  fraud, 26
  marketable, 573
  money market instruments as, 536–537
  public sale of, 581–582
  stocks as, 539–541
Securities and Exchange Commission (SEC), 26, 63
Securities Exchange Act, A8
Security analysts, 595–596
Security issues
  computers and, 198, 479–482
  credit cards and, 40, 471
  information systems and, 479–482
  job security and, 188–189
Seed capital, 203
Segmentation. *See* **Market segmentation**
Selective demand, 428
Selective distribution, 415
Self-actualization needs, 269
Self-confidence, 195–196
Self-financing, 203
Self-managed teams, 290, 291
Self-regulation, of securities markets, 557
Seller's market, 355
Sell-off, 586
Sender, in communication process, 297
Serial entrepreneur, 186
Server, 474
Services, classification of, 391
Sexism, 57, 63
Sexual harassment, 39, 57, 62–63
Shadow banking, 499
Sherman Act, 81, A6
Shipping, 68
Shopping malls, 412

International Index